THE BLUE BOOK

A History of
Western Province Cricket,
1890–2011

THE BLUE BOOK

A History of
Western Province Cricket,
1890–2011

André Odendaal, Krish Reddy and Andrew Samson

The authors and publishers would like to thank Nashua Mobile, team sponsor of the Cape Cobras, for helping to sponsor this book.

First published by Fanele, an imprint of Jacana Media (Pty) Ltd in 2012

10 Orange Street
Sunnyside
Auckland Park 2092
South Africa
(+27 11) 628-3200
www.jacana.co.za

© André Odendaal, Krish Reddy & Andrew Samson, 2012

All rights reserved

ISBN 978-1-920196-40-0

Cover design by publicide
Text design and layout by Jenny Young
Set in Melior and Frutiger
Printed by Ultra Litho
Job no. 001686

See a complete list of Jacana titles at www.jacana.co.za

Contents

About the authors
Abbreviations

Introduction

Understanding the history of Western Province cricket	1
Statistics and their meanings	7
'Saying yes to life itself'	13
Family tree of Western Province and South African cricket, 1890–2011	16

Part I: The colonial and apartheid eras, 1890–1991

1.	Western Province Cricket Union, 1890–1991	26
2.	Western Province Coloured Cricket Union, 1890s–1959	111
3.	Peninsula and Western Districts Cricket Board, 1923–1959	124
4.	Western Province Bantu (later African) Cricket Union, 1928–1977	134
5.	Western Province Indian Cricket Union, 1943–1959	145
6.	Hottentots Holland Cricket Union, 1945–1959	153
7.	Western Province Women's Cricket Union, 1951–1991	158
8.	Western Province Cricket Federation, 1952–1959	175
9.	Western Province Cricket Board, 1959–1991	183

Part II: The era of unity and democracy, 1991–2011

10.	Western Province Cricket Association, 1991–2011	216
11.	Western Province Women's Cricket Association, 1995–2011	268
12.	Cape Cobras, 2004–2011	283

Part III: Consolidated Western Province and Cape Cobras statistics, 1890–2011

13.	List of trophies won by Western Province and Cape Cobras, 1890–2011	308
14.	List of national players from Western Province and Cape Cobras, 1888–2011	312
15.	Western Province and Cape Cobras individual first-class career records, 1890–2011	320
16.	Western Province and Cape Cobras individual limited-overs career records, 1969–2011	362
17.	Biographical details of Western Province and Cape Cobras players, 1890–2011	379

On the making of this book	415
Endnotes	424

'I want to suggest that in the colonial situation
presence was the critical question, the crucial word.
Its denial was the keynote of colonialist ideology.'

– *Chinua Achebe, 'African Literature as a Celebration' (1992)*

About the Authors

André Odendaal is chief executive of the Western Province Cricket Association and Honorary Professor in History and Heritage Studies at the University of the Western Cape.

During his playing days, he captained Premier League winners in both the old Western Province Cricket Union (Stellenbosch University) and the old Western Province Cricket Board (United Cricket Club). He played first-class cricket for Boland (SACU), Transvaal (SACB), Western Province (SACB) and Cambridge University in England, where he was also selected for Combined Universities.

He was elected onto the last executive committee of the Western Province Cricket Board while still a player. After unity in June 1991, he became a member of the first executive of the Western Province Cricket Association, serving until 2004, when he was appointed chief executive. He chaired the Transformation Monitoring Committee of the United Cricket Board of South Africa between 1998 and 2002.

Odendaal is also a historian and writer. He graduated with a PhD in History from Cambridge University in 1984 and spent 13 years at the University of the Western Cape, where he founded the Mayibuye Centre for History and Culture in South Africa. He was also founding director of the Robben Island Museum, heading operations on the island from 1997 to 2002. His publications include *Cricket in Isolation* (1977),*Vukani Bantu!* (1984), *Beyond the Tryline* (1994, with Albert Grundlingh and Burridge Spies), and *The Story of an African Game* (2003).

Krish Reddy has been a keen follower of SACBOC and SACB cricket since the late 1950s. He has painstakingly recovered much of the lost statistical records of black and non-racial cricket in Natal and South Africa, details of which were published regularly in the *Mutual & Federal SA Cricket Annual* from 1996 to 2004. He was presented with a special scroll on behalf of the Annual for 'the accurate recording of the deeds of generations of cricketers' on the occasion of the publication of the 50th volume in 2003.

In 1986 he compiled a history of the Natal Cricket Board as part of their 25th anniversary celebrations. Subsequently, he wrote numerous articles on black cricket in national newspapers and magazines. He is the author of *The Other Side: A miscellany of black cricket in Natal*, published in 1999. He is also the co-author with Ashwin Desai, Vishnu Padayachee and Goolam Vahed of *Blacks in Whites: A century of cricket struggles in KwaZulu-Natal*, published in 2002. His detailed statistical record of Basil D'Oliveira in black cricket in South Africa was included as an appendix to Peter Oborne's book *Basil D'Oliveira: Cricket and conspiracy – The untold story* (2004).

After several years of close involvement with the non-racial Natal Cricket Board, Krish served a three-year term on the executive of the KwaZulu-Natal Cricket Union after unity in 1991. He was also a provincial selector for ten consecutive seasons from 1996/97 to 2005/06. The UK-based Association of Cricket Statisticians and Historians chose him as their Statistician of the Year in 2007 for his research on the scores of 233 first-class matches in non-racial cricket in South Africa during the period 1971–1991. In December 2009 he was awarded the ICC Volunteers' Medal 'in recognition of outstanding service to cricket'.

Andrew Samson is a statistician with a particular interest in cricket. He had a very moderate playing career as a strokeless opening batsman and enthusiastic leg-spinner who occasionally landed the ball on the pitch. He gave this up while still at school to follow the numbers of the game. He has been scoring and doing statistics for radio and TV since 1988 and was appointed official statistician to Cricket South Africa (then the United Cricket Board of South Africa) in 1994.

Andrew has contributed to the *Mutual & Federal SA Cricket Annual* and *Wisden Cricketers' Almanack* since 1994. He was official statistician for the ICC World Cup in 2003, ICC World T20 2007, ICC World Cup Qualifier 2009 and ICC Champions Trophy 2009. Between 2003 and 2007 he was on the committee of the Association of Cricket Statisticians and Historians.

He presents 'Go Figure', an insert on numbers on the David O'Sullivan Show on Radio 702. A keen baseball fan, he is a member of the Society for American Baseball Research. He also somehow finds the time to help his wife Carolien bring up their two young daughters, Charlotte and Hailey.

All the text in this book was written by André Odendaal. Chapter 9 was written with the help of Mogamad Allie and is based heavily on his book More than a Game *(2000). Michael Owen-Smith helped with the introduction to Chapter 1. The specific statistical contributions of each author in every chapter are noted and acknowledged in the footnotes.*

Abbreviations

CCSA	Cricket Council of South Africa
CSA	Cricket South Africa
HHCU	Hottentots Holland Cricket Union
PLCC	Peninsula Ladies' Cricket Club
PWDCB	Peninsula and Western Districts Cricket Board
SAACB	South African African Cricket Board
SABCB	South African Bantu Cricket Board
SACA	South African Cricket Association
SACB	South African Cricket Board
SACBOC	South African Cricket Board of Control
SACCA	South African Coloured Cricket Association
SACCB	South African Coloured Cricket Board
SACOS	South African Council on Sport
SACU	South African Cricket Union
SAICCB	South African Independent Coloured Cricket Board
SAICU	South African Indian Cricket Union
SAMCB	South African Malay Cricket Board
SARWCA	South Africa and Rhodesia Women's Cricket Association
UCBSA	United Cricket Board of South Africa
WCA	Women's Cricket Association
WCC	Western Cape Cricket (Pty) Ltd
WPBCU	Western Province Bantu (later African) Cricket Union
WPCA	Western Province Cricket Association
WPCB	Western Province Cricket Board
WPCCU	Western Province Coloured Cricket Union
WPCF	Western Province Cricket Federation
WPCU	Western Province Cricket Union
WPICU	Western Province Indian Cricket Union
WPWCA	Western Province Women's Cricket Association
WPWCU	Western Province Women's Cricket Union

Introduction

Understanding the history of Western Province cricket

The Blue Book provides the first consolidated statistical history for Western Province cricket and the Cape Cobras in the 121 years from 1890 to 2011. It goes beyond any similar sports history in South Africa to date, to lay bare the DNA sequence of cricket in a region with the longest tradition of cricket playing in the country and the continent. In the same way that recent advances in genetic research have enabled us to understand the distant origins of humankind (and each one of us), this book reveals a distant family history that is startlingly rich and hitherto either unknown or thought impossible to reconstruct. Based on decades of painstaking research, it comprehensively overturns old, exclusive, 'official' accounts of the past and introduces us to over 500 hitherto unrecognised Western Province players and 250 new Western Province matches.

The current Western Province Cricket Association (WPCA) and its related entities, such as the Cape Cobras team, were preceded by no less than nine different Western Province boards, which have each in their own way imprinted their character on our cricket today. Records from every one of them are provided here. With its 25,000 cricketers, part-owned Cape Cobras franchise and the famous 123-year-old Sahara Park Newlands Stadium, the WPCA has inherited a rich cricket legacy. The first recorded game in the country was played in Cape Town more than two hundred years ago on 5 January 1808. From here cricket spread to all parts of what we now call South Africa.

In the 1840s and 1850s, the first civilian cricket clubs and schools teams were started, taking the game beyond the camps of the colonising British army into communities. In the 1870s and 1880s the first leagues and inter-town competitions were started. These developments led to a level of organisation which enabled the first tour by an English team to southern Africa to take place in 1888/89. It was organised by Cape Town-based cricket officials, and the English tourists played the first-ever two games by an international team in South Africa at the newly opened Newlands ground in Cape Town on 21–23 December 1888 and 26–28 December 1888. A Western Province XXII (twenty-two) beat them by 17 runs in the first match. In the second, the English beat a Cape Colony XV (fifteen) by 11 runs. The Lancashire slow left-arm spin bowler and professional Johnny Briggs took 23 wickets for 136 runs in that first match, followed by 15 wickets for 28 runs in the test at Newlands later in the tour. His tally of 50 wickets in just three matches at the ground in that season is unlikely to be surpassed.[1]

This first international tour consolidated the game of cricket in South Africa by giving rise to the first national and regional cricket bodies and the first formalised competitions between different regions (later provinces). A South African Cricket Association was established in Kimberley in April 1890 and the local cricketers followed up to form a regional board, the Western Province Cricket Union, in September 1890. South African cricket was now organised on a modern footing. However, the new national and regional bodies were for whites only. Black and women cricketers were explicitly discriminated against. They were not permitted to join the 'official' clubs and unions or play in their competitions. Women were not allowed access to certain facilities – like the Long Room – at Newlands. So-called 'Non-Europeans' were not even permitted to sit in the stands. They were segregated instead into a fenced-off area, where the first formal seating was provided only in 1972.[2]

Down the years the whites-only Western Province Cricket Union was, in fact, at the forefront of implementing and institutionalising segregation and apartheid in sport. This was shown by the Union's actions in a defining moment in South African cricket history. In 1894 the talented local cricketer 'Krom' Hendricks was selected for the squad for the first South African tour to England. In the book *Cricket and Empire*, Jonty Winch has shown how the Western Province Cricket Union in the person of its president, William Milton, a close ally of the Prime Minister Cecil John Rhodes, successfully led a campaign to have Hendricks excluded on the basis that he was not white, even though influential figures from other regions supported his inclusion. The Union's leaders also kept Hendricks out of the Western Province team and the club leagues despite his obvious talent and persistent requests to participate.[3]

Again, in 1968, at the time the apartheid government cancelled an MCC tour to South Africa because the 'Non-White' Cape Town-born Basil D'Oliveira was selected, the Union's president Ernest McKay declared, 'I am disappointed but I support Mr Vorster on this.'[4] Cricket reflected society. For a hundred years the policy of the ruling classes in South Africa was that the so-called 'races' had to play separately.

Many cricketers opposed this system of racial segregation and discrimination over the years, particularly from the 1960s onwards. But by and large cricket was played in racial compartments during the colonial and apartheid period. The majority of South Africans were excluded from full citizenship rights, socially, politically and economically, and this applied in cricket as well.

Despite being sidelined because of institutionalised racism, players excluded from the mainstream grittily created their own cricket milieu and set out to emulate 'official' cricket. They started their own clubs and competitions and their own provincial and national organisations. As this book shows, Cape Town became a national stronghold of cricket. Nine different Western Provinces came into being between 1890 and 1990, and ten different 'national' boards all claiming the title 'South African'.

In 1991, as the country moved towards formal democracy after decades of struggle and the unbanning of organisations and the release from prison of Nelson Mandela, all cricketers in the country at last joined together for the first time to form the new United Cricket Board of South Africa (later, Cricket South Africa). All cricketers in the Western Province were similarly united for the first time under the new Western Province Cricket Association on 25 June 1991.[5] Cricket unity was based on the principles of inclusivity, non-racialism and equal rights. After 1991 the official culture of cricket changed fundamentally and became aligned with the ethos of South Africa's new democracy.

Today, South African cricketers have been united for just 20 years, a remarkable fact given that the history of the game spans two centuries in this country.

A rich twelve-part record

Below is a brief overview of the twelve Western Province-based provincial boards that have existed to date and their main achievements:

1. Western Province Cricket Union (1890–1991)
Winners of the Currie Cup for first-class cricket in 17 out of 63 tournaments held by the South African Cricket Association (SACA) and the South African Cricket Union (SACU) between 1889/90 and 1990/91. Winners of SACA's limited-overs Gillette Cup three out of eight times between 1969/70 and 1976/77. Winners of SACU's limited-overs Datsun/Nissan Shield twice out of 14 times between 1977/78 and 1990/91. Winners of SACU's limited-overs Benson & Hedges Series four out of ten times between 1981/82 and 1990/91.

2. Western Province Coloured Cricket Union (1898–1959)
Winners of the Barnato Memorial Trophy 12 out of 16 times under the South African Coloured (later Malay) Cricket Board between 1898/99 and 1959/60.

3. Peninsula and Western Districts Cricket Board (1923–1959)
Played as Western Province in the Sir David Harris Trophy tournaments. Winners 8 out of 12 times under the South African Independent Coloured Cricket Board (later the South African Coloured Cricket Association) between 1926/27 and 1957/58.

4. Western Province Bantu (later African) Cricket Union (1928–1977)
Winners of the NRC Trophy three out of 22 times under the South African Bantu (later African) Cricket Board between 1933/34 and 1975/76.

5. Western Province Indian Cricket Union (1943–1959)
Failed to win Christopher Trophy in the nine tournaments of the South African Indian Cricket Union in which it participated between 1946/47 and 1957/58 (because most people of Asian descent lived in Natal or Transvaal and were only thinly represented elsewhere). Runners-up in 1951 in Durban.

6. Hottentots Holland Cricket Union (1945–1959)
Failed to win Barnato Trophy in the two tournaments of the South African Coloured (later Malay) Cricket Board in which it participated between 1951/52 and 1954/55. Runners-up in 1951/52.

7. Western Province Women's Cricket Union (1951–1991)
Winners of the Simon Trophy five out of 26 times in the cricket weeks held by the South Africa and Rhodesia Women's Cricket Association between 1951/52 and 1985/86 (where the tournament winners are known). (Altogether there were 34 SARWCA cricket weeks in this time, the outcomes of some are still not known and on a few other occasions the Simon Trophy was not awarded.)

8. Western Province Cricket Federation (1952–1959)
An informal umbrella of existing Western Province unions and sub-unions who co-operated

with one another in the 1950s with the aim of promoting non-racial sport. Played friendlies against other provincial units and the South Africa Bantu team but did not participate in formal inter-provincial competitions or affiliate as an entity to a national federation.

9. Western Province Cricket Board (1959–1991)
Winners four out of five times in the centralised tournaments for the Dadabhay Trophy held by the South African Cricket Board of Control (SACBOC) between 1961/62 and 1969/70. Winners of the Dadabhay Trophy / SFW Trophy for first-class cricket three out of four times under SACBOC between 1971/72 and 1975/76. Winners of the Howa Bowl for first-class cricket 11 out of 14 times under the South African Cricket Board (SACB) between 1977/78 and 1990/91. Winners of SACBOC's limited-overs SFW Trophy one out of two times between 1973/74 and 1974/75. Winners of SACB's limited-overs Benson & Hedges Trophy three out of three times between 1982/83 and 1984/85.

10. Western Province Cricket Association, 1991 onwards
Winners four out of 13 times of the Castle Cup / SuperSport Series for first-class cricket under the United Cricket Board of South Africa (UCBSA) between 1991/92 and 2003/04. Winners two out of 16 times of the limited-overs Benson & Hedges Series / Standard Bank League / Standard Bank Cup during the same period.

11. Western Province Women's Cricket Association, 1995 onwards
Winners seven out of 16 times in the centralised inter-provincial tournaments and later decentralised inter-provincial competitions held by the South African Women's Cricket Association and, from 2006 onwards, Cricket South Africa.

12. Cape Cobras (falling under Western Cape Cricket (Pty) Ltd), 2004 onwards
Winner twice out of seven times of the SuperSport Series for first-class cricket under Cricket South Africa (CSA) from 2004/05 onwards. Winner once out of seven times of CSA's limited-overs Standard Bank Cup / MTN Domestic Championship / MTN 40. Winner twice out of eight times of CSA's Standard Bank Pro20 Trophy. Semi-finalists in the first Champions League T20 tournament held in India in October 2009 (described as the new World 'Club' Championships).

Structure

What these statistics show is that cricket has been popular for many years in many communities in Cape Town and its surrounds, and that our cricket foundations are much broader and stronger than we have imagined.

Each of the twelve provincial boards that have existed in the Western Province since 1890 are dealt with in separate chapters below. Each of the twelve chapters in turn contains the following: the name of the organisation, the period of its existence, the national bodies it was affiliated to and other basic information about its existence, including an overview history of the organisation; a list of national players produced by the organisation; a list of provincial players produced by the organisation; a list of the inter-provincial trophies won by the organisation over the years; and summarised scorecards of matches played by the provincial team.

The details in each chapter are given in as standardised a way as possible. Some chapters contain additional information, such as club winners or clubs to which provincial players belonged. In each chapter, those responsible for compiling the statistics of the organisation are acknowledged.

Where records are incomplete, this is indicated in the hope that future researchers will be able to fill the gaps. There are some tournaments that we know took place, but for which no match statistics have yet been found. For a number of other tournaments there are only partial details. In cases where information is missing, *[no details available]* will be indicated; and [x] is used to show a missing initial or missing bowling or batting figures, for example, [x] Buhlungu 8/[x].

The sources for the records in this book will be listed online or in the forthcoming *History of South African Cricket* so that the never-ending process of verification and recovery can continue independently of the authors.

After the introduction, which provides a historical and methodological background, the nine organisations that existed between 1890 and 1991 are dealt with in Part I. The period since cricket unity and democracy in South Africa is covered in Part II. Finally, in Part III the first ever effort is made to provide:

- a consolidated list of the Western Province and Cape Cobras teams that won inter-provincial competitions or trophies under the various national boards;
- a consolidated list of South African players produced for the various national boards by Western Province and the Cape Cobras;
- a consolidated list of cricketers who have played official ICC-recognised first-class and limited-overs cricket for Western Province and the Cape Cobras, together with their records;
- a consolidated list of more than a thousand players who have represented the different Western Provinces and the Cape Cobras since 1890, together with biographical details where these are available.

The publication of *The Blue Book* adds meaningfully to existing knowledge of Western Province cricket.

1. Summarised scorecards of more than 250 Western Province matches are added to what was previously perceived as being the 'official' history of Western Province cricket.
2. The research shows that the twelve Western Provinces and Western Province-related teams have so far won national, inter-provincial trophies in the country 123 times between them in 121 years.
3. For the first time ever, more than 500 new names are added to the list of cricketers who have represented 'Western Province'. While the list is still some way from being complete, it is now there to be built on in future.
4. A list of the national representatives of all the different Western Provinces that have existed to date is assembled here for the first time. Altogether 217 Western Province cricketers have so far gained national colours in the various South African boards that picked national teams at various times between 1889 and today. Intriguingly, the split is virtually 50/50 between black and white players during the apartheid years, even

though the SACA Springboks participating in test cricket for a century played much more often. Moreover, between 1991 and 2010 exactly half of all black players selected for South Africa – 15 out of 30 – were either produced in the Western Cape or played for the Cape Cobras, Western Province or Boland.

The single, contextualised narrative in this book, which moves beyond the old divisions of 'us' and 'them', helps us to understand our different pasts and explain the circumstances in which all the players listed in this book played. The myth that the story of Western Province cricket was just about the Owen-Smiths and other great players from the Western Province Cricket Union can now safely be buried. We can now also expand the list of role models to include those who overcame adversity beyond Basil D'Oliveira and his counterparts in the now famous 'SACBOC Springboks' of the 1950s or 'Lefty' Adams, Saait Magiet, Vincent Barnes, Faiek Davids and others who starred in the later non-racial 'board' era. A whole new set of flesh and blood cricketers who somehow survived despite cruel exclusion down the years can now be rightfully and meaningfully remembered. They have left enough of a footprint for us to reinsert them into the cricket records of the city, the province and the country.

While aspects of the past remain elusive and statistically incomplete, there is now a wholeness about this record which allows us to go forward into the future with real self-knowledge.

With the exception of KwaZulu-Natal (where a strong non-racial sport tradition exists and, therefore, also a strong sense of history) no other province has come close to a provincial cricket history with the same statistical depth and integrity revealed here.

The Blue Book takes the process of rewriting and redress to a new depth, getting closer to the grassroots than ever before.[6] The new insights here, based on solid evidence, will hopefully enable the Western Province Cricket Association to grow in self-knowledge and disseminate, imagine and celebrate its history in exciting new ways.

Statistics and their meanings

Statistics are integral to the culture and romance of cricket. Harold Pinter, the Nobel Prize-winning dramatist, summed it up nicely when he said, 'Sometimes when I feel a little exhausted with it all and the world's sitting heavy on my head, I pick up *Wisden* and read about Len Hutton's 37 in 24 minutes in Sydney in 1946'.[7]

How often haven't we heard cricket fans argue about who the best teams and players of different eras are? 'Look in the book,' one will say as he delves for comfort in the volumes of *Wisden Cricketers' Almanack* or other authoritative publications. 'Stats don't tell the whole story,' the other will answer. Little have people realised how true this latter saying has been in relation to South African cricket.

Cricket's statistics in South Africa have been shaped by a particular mindset and practice rooted in colonial and apartheid thinking. Thus the official record until relatively recently has been deeply racist and gendered and deliberately omitted the exploits of black cricketers and women cricketers. In official publications such as the respected *South African Cricket Annual* and *Wisden*, for example, virtually no trace can be found of cricket boards that functioned for decades, such as the Western Province Coloured Cricket Union, the Western Province Bantu Cricket Union, the Western Province Indian Cricket Union, the Western Province Women's Cricket Union, the Western Province Cricket Federation, and the Peninsula and Western Districts Cricket Board, as well as the nearly 100 inter-provincial tournaments they consistently organised and participated in over a 60-year period, although there were often newspaper and other contemporary records of these activities.

Only in volume 43 in 1996 did the *Mutual & Federal SA Cricket Annual* announce, 'this edition of the Annual takes a first step towards reflecting the outstanding deeds of those cricketers who played under the auspices of the South African Cricket Board of Control in the apartheid era.'[8]

The History of South African Cricket, a monumental, much-quoted, 850-page history of cricket's beginnings in this country, similarly ignored tournaments held by black cricketers; for example, the 'Malay Inter-Town Tournament' watched by thousands of spectators at Newlands in January 1890 and extensively covered by the *Cape Times* and the *Cape Argus*.[9] Similarly, the batting and bowling statistics of the 'England vs Malay XVIII' match at Newlands in March 1892 were 'not included in the averages' of the tour, even though the match scorecard itself was published.[10]

These so-called 'cricket bibles' were part of the colonial and apartheid establishments in Britain and South Africa. They helped construct whites-only narratives that reinforced the real-life exclusion of black people in sport and other spheres of life. They focused on only a segment of South African cricketers and ignored the activities of others on the basis of colour, giving legitimacy to the general marginalisation of people on racial grounds at that time. This exclusion also gave rise to the assumption that the others were not important and had no real history worth writing about. The argument is still often heard that as black and women cricketers are not present in the 'official' records, therefore they did not play.

This book exposes this fallacy and confirms that pre-1990 South African cricket statistics remain racist and incomplete. In addition, a study of the way the 'official' statistics of the past were compiled shows that this process was flawed and that the choices about which matches officially qualified as first-class were often random. The first 'official' Western Province first-class match in January 1890, for instance, happened several months *before* the Western Province Cricket Union was formed and was in later years declared first-class, despite its being a two-day game played by a Western Province Cricket Club side. Various other two-day matches and matches involving clubs and invitation teams were given first-class status, as were some matches in which substitutes batted and bowled as well as a match with an incomplete scorecard.[11]

Even at the international level, there have been doubts cast about the standard of some of the early international matches; some players almost certainly ended up playing in them on the basis of privilege rather than merit. In the days when the gentlemen and amateurs entered grounds through separate entrances and stayed at separate hotels on tour, several 'gentlemen' played 'international' cricket who certainly did not deserve to be there. One such example was the ex-Etonian JEP McMaster, who played his only first-class match (for England no less) in the first test held at Newlands in 1889. Despite a top score of 14 in club cricket, he was invited on the tour because he was 'such a damned good after-dinner speaker' and a member of the MCC. In the test, he scored a first-ball duck and dropped an easy catch at mid-wicket.[12]

As Tony Collins has demonstrated in his social history of rugby in England, the whole idea of the gentleman amateur in British sport was built on anti-competitive protocols and notions of class privilege – you belonged by not necessarily being the best but by 'playing the game' as was expected of you. A defining feature of the amateur was not to display too much seriousness about the result of the game.[13] It is ironic, therefore, that the 'merit' argument has been used so often against the official recognition of black cricketers. While McMaster sits there in *Wisden* sanctified as an international player, there have been hundreds of players from the unrecognised provincial boards described in this book who were better cricketers. How then do we properly recognise them – and Samsodien's fifty and Hendricks's four wickets against the English professionals in 1892?

'I want to suggest that in the colonial situation presence was the critical question, the crucial word,' the great African writer Chinua Achebe has written. And he concluded, 'Its denial was the keynote of colonialist ideology.'[14] South Africa's cricket statistics support his point. The people who drew up these statistical records were part of the establishment cricket system that excluded people on the basis of colour. Like Luckin in his *History*, they did not even think of including black cricketers. (Luckin also perpetuated the class snobbishness revealed in cricket scorecards of the British amateur age: the 'gentlemen' had their initials included, but the professionals only their surnames – if there were two or more professionals with the same name, their initials were inserted in brackets after their names, not in front of them like the 'gentlemen'.)

The most influential early South African statistician was NS Curnow, who in the 1920s drew up lists that had 'not found their way into the basic South African publications'. The governing SACA in those decades apparently 'made extremely few pronouncements on the matter' and rarely intervened. There was also a paucity of reliable statisticians, so Curnow in effect became the official arbiter of first-class statistics. 'He, apparently off his own bat and without consulting anybody, assumed them to be first-class. No one gainsaid his judgement at the time, or has done so since, except in one instance when he was clearly at fault (over a one-day game [which he gave first-class status]).'[15] It was only in 1947 that the criteria for first-class status were standardised and clear regulations drawn up. Definitions and decisions taken by the MCC since 1894 were formalised by the Imperial Cricket Conference and made applicable worldwide.[16]

The Association of Cricket Statisticians (ACS) in England, the world authority on first-class statistics, started publishing lists of first-class matches played in Britain and other countries from 1976 onwards 'so that statisticians in future may work from a common base'.[17] In 1981 the Association published *A Guide to Important Cricket Matches played in South Africa*. The records for South African cricket approved by the ACS in 1981 were drawn up by Denys Heesom, then editor of the *South African Cricket Annual*, based mainly on Curnow's work. In the final analysis, the ACS endorsed a partial (whites-only SACA) record as the whole statistical record for South Africa, taking the trouble to check up only on that organisation's details. Both the British and South African statisticians involved acted within the accepted paradigm of cricket at the time. None were qualified to make judgements on the history and statistics of the black cricketers whom we are now starting to recognise in this book. The ACS simply rubber-stamped a colonial narrative of the past.

Clearly there are white cricketers in the first-class lists who did not necessarily deserve to have first-class records, and black cricketers – from the time of 'Krom' Hendricks and the Malay teams in the 1890s through to Basil D'Oliveira and his contemporaries – who are not recognised as first-class but who were up to standard, if merit not race had been the criterion.

When the United Cricket Board of South Africa gave attention to this matter after unity in 1991 a convenient 'solution' offered itself to put an end to the embarrassment that the country's official statistics were glaringly racist. Krish Reddy had independently done a lone-ranger study of the three-day matches played by SACBOC and SACB from 1971 to 1991 and these were retrospectively declared first-class by the United Cricket Board and the ICC in 1996/97. Thus, an important part of the omission by the ACS and establishment white statisticians within South Africa was corrected. Reddy's statistics were quickly accorded an 'own affairs' status, published as abbreviated appendices in the back pages of thick annuals, and the mainline statisticians could carry on using their old data without questioning their own methodology or records.

Noting Curnow's individualistic approach, and the general shortage of quality statisticians in South Africa in the early years, the ACS said in 1981, 'There is no practical alternative now to accepting that position.' But is that still the case? What about other matches played by black cricketers between 1890 and 1970? And the limited-overs matches played by SACBOC and SACB in the 1970s and 1980s?[18] Despite the 1947 rulings standardising the criteria for first-class cricket, SACA still decided that a two-day game between North-Eastern Transvaal and the Australians in 1957/58 was first-class. Can this still be justified when SACBOC's Springboks captained by Basil D'Oliveira were playing both two and three-day games at the very same time, games that still have not been recognised as first-class? Another SACA and SACU anomaly in later years was the awarding of first-class status during the period of isolation to matches between the B teams of provinces.

We trust that this book and the comprehensive *History of South African Cricket* now in preparation for publication will provide sufficient evidence to move statisticians and cricket-governing bodies to reassess the body of cricket statistics. Certainly, old 'official' pre-unity and pre-democracy cricket records, first-class and otherwise, are not complete and cannot as a body be defended anymore.

The persistence of old mindsets

In 1998 the young United Cricket Board of South Africa adopted a Transformation Charter to bring cricket in line with the values of South Africa's new Constitution and the development of democracy. The Charter's main aim was to redress the inequalities of the past in order to create an inclusive national cricket dispensation. Its ten 'thrusts' specifically included the rewriting of South African cricket history to correct the distortions of the past.

As a result of these initiatives and the active participation of a number of historians, including academic historians, various important books and documentaries subsequently appeared, significantly enriching and adding to the story of cricket in South Africa. These included *Iqakamba (Hard ball)*, a four-part television documentary series produced by Junaid Ahmed and Primedia (1999); *The Other Side: A miscellany of cricket in Natal* by Krish Reddy (1999); *More than a Game: History of the Western Province Cricket Board, 1959–1991* by Mogamad Allie (2001); the path-breaking *Blacks in Whites: A century of cricket struggles in KwaZulu-Natal* (2002) by Ashwin Desai, Goolam Vahed, Vishnu Padayachee and Krish Reddy; Aslam Khota's edited volume, *Across the Divide: Transvaal cricket's joys, struggles and triumphs* (2003); and André Odendaal's *The Story of an African Game: Black cricketers and the unmasking of one of cricket's greatest myths, South Africa, 1850–2003* (2003). A whole line of complementary studies have recently bolstered these initial efforts from within South African cricket, most notably P Oborne, *Basil D'Oliveira: Cricket and conspiracy – The untold story* (2004) and B Murray and G Vahed (eds.), *Empire and Cricket: The South African experience, 1884–1914* (2009).[19]

The new histories have challenged and inverted old paradigms and understandings, giving shape to an emerging new institutional culture of cricket that is truly South African (in an African context). The present book is a by-product of this process. Its aim is not only to help correct the record of the past, but also to ensure that the hurts and discrimination that people suffered are not consciously or sub-consciously reproduced in future. This aim is easier said than done because official statistics, cricket organisations and those managing sites of cricket memory (including some top stadiums) today still perpetuate many of the inherently racist stereotypes of the past, even if unintentionally.

In case this statement is interpreted merely as tired, politically correct rhetoric, it is necessary to give some examples here. In a feature article in the *2009 Mutual & Federal SA Cricket Annual*, the arbiter of records which prides itself on its statistical reliability, it is noted that 'The Kimberley team took the Currie Cup way back in 1890/91 and aggressive wicketkeeper batsman Wendell Bossinger was there when the next domestic trophy was annexed at East London 108 years later in March 1999 when Griquas won the Standard Bank Cup'.[20] Clearly, in this analysis, the fact of Griquas annexing the Barnato Trophy in 1909/10 and the Sir David Harris Trophy in 1933/34 and 1946/47 did not qualify as 'domestic trophies'. The *Annual* draws a straight line from the whites-only competitions of the past to the supposedly unified, non-racial set-up of today (even ignoring the different formats), with not a thought given to the casual omission of whole chunks of history.

The South African Cricket Board's competitions and records were eventually officially awarded the same status as the old South African Cricket Association and South African Cricket Union by the UCBSA and ICC in the 1990s. But when a current provincial team wins a List A limited-overs competition it will wrongly be described as the *nth* time that province has won, adding the old white-establishment trophies to the ones since unity, but ignoring in the calculation the trophies that particular province captured under the old SFW and Benson & Hedges competitions of the non-racial Board.

The incorrect conflation of records of the old apartheid-establishment Board with those of today also happens at the level of individual statistics and partnership records. Faiek Davids played List A cricket before unity for the Board and afterwards for the Association. His official List A record includes only matches after unity in 1991. Alan Dawson played List A cricket before unity for the Union and afterwards for the Association. His official List A records include matches both before and after 1991. In this way our record-keepers, commentators and respected publications like the *Mutual & Federal SA Cricket Annual* perpetuate assumptions rooted in a privileged past that keep black cricketers 'invisible' – even now.

Similarly, the prejudices of the past are also built in a physical way into the very fabric of our modern cricket stadiums, president's suites and 'brand' identities. Honours boards, photographs and narratives often reinforce old hierarchies and understandings. The headquarters of the successful Nashua Titans franchise at SuperSport Park in Centurion, one of the main stadiums in the country, provides one example. As one walks into the offices and through them to the President's Suite and the press interview room, one is met by impressive displays of teams and players and memorabilia on the walls. But closer examination reveals that in this bulky family album there is virtually no trace of any black cricketers except for a few members of the current team. There is no sign, for example, of the old North-Eastern Transvaal Bantu Cricket Union, formed on 24 August 1947 with HH Zibi as president and Green Sulupha as secretary.[21] Or the Northern Transvaal women's cricket side in their 'duck-egg blue blazers' who hosted the annual South Africa and Rhodesia Women's Cricket Association inter-provincial tournament for the Simon Trophy in Pretoria from 9 to 14 April 1957 under the captaincy of the Oxbridge-educated Dr Pat Kessler.[22] Or the SACBOC-affiliated Eastern Transvaal Coloured and Indian Cricket

Association based in Benoni from the 1940s onwards.[23] After coming second in 1948/49, the North-Eastern Transvaal African team won the inter-provincial tournament and the NRC Trophy in 1954/55. The season before that, the side also won the Rev. BLE Sigamoney Trophy of the Transvaal Inter-Race Board, beating the Transvaal Coloured Cricket Union, the Witwatersrand Indian Cricket Union, their Transvaal African counterparts and various other teams. Eric Fihla and Julius Mahanjana, who captained the South African Bantu team, were the star batsmen. The opening bowlers, Gidi and Mashinqana, were regarded as the fastest seen at the inter-provincial tournaments since Majola and Masiza from Transvaal in 1935.[24]

The scrolls and framed photographs of captains, national representatives, presidents and other notables at SuperSport Park move effortlessly from the old whites-only system to unity, without a single sign of those sidelined by the apartheid system. The photo gallery of internationals includes those who played in the rebel tours, but not those who played in other unofficial South African teams. Black and women cricketers are still invisible here, where the brand is showcased, erased from the past and the present.

At other top stadiums and in many other pavilions, clubs and offices throughout the country you will find the same thing. This amounts to history as negation.[25]

The Blue Book hopefully shows the possibility that exists at provincial level to recognise all cricket communities in a way that has integrity and at the same time makes them feel they belong in a common space and culture. This includes the role of women in a game with a long history of patriarchy and open antagonism to the idea of women's participation. The notion of cricket being a 'gentleman's game', shaped in mid-Victorian times when opportunities for women in society were limited, lies at the heart of this attitude. Yet, as this book shows, women cricketers in the Western Province started a provincial association in 1951 and have competed regularly since then in 49 inter-provincial tournaments and competitions.

There is something immensely powerful in the simple act of paying respect and giving recognition. *The Blue Book* shows it is possible for all our provinces to explore and celebrate their pasts in ways thought impossible until now.

'Saying yes to life itself'

Only the actions of the just
Smell sweet and blossom in the dust

– James Shirley, *Death the Leveller*[26]

The generations who have gone before have left a remarkable legacy, which deserves respect. Since 1808 tens of thousands of people have played and supported the game and helped create a strong cricket culture in Cape Town. This book is dedicated to the memory of three of them, Nathaniel Umhalla, H 'Krom' Hendricks and Hassan Howa.

Umhalla, the son of a chief, took to cricket while studying at Zonnebloem College in the 1860s. He was one of the African pioneers of the game, as well as a leader in politics and journalism as Africans started 'shooting with the pen' to demand a place for themselves in the colonial order.[27]

'Krom' Hendricks was an outstanding bowler excluded from the South African, Western Province and club teams in the 1890s, for reasons other than merit, as cricket officials clustered around the arch-imperialist Cecil John Rhodes formalised a 'colour bar' in cricket that would have devastating long-term consequences for the game.[28] When it was suggested that he go along to England as the baggage boy, Hendricks replied, 'I would not think of going in that capacity.'[29]

Hassan Howa gave voice during the apartheid years to the feisty spirit amongst communities and sportsmen and women which harsh power could not subdue.[30]

These three people represent in various ways those cricketers in Cape Town forced for a hundred years to play the game in the margins under the most difficult circumstances. Through their skill, perseverance, knowledge and an irrepressible love for life, they moved beyond victimhood to lay the foundations of our modern cricket system. The writer André P Brink recognised something of these struggles and energies when he wrote, with reference to District Six: 'This … is what truly spells Cape Town for me: its indomitable, raucous, rebellious way of confirming a heretic otherness, of saying no – not only to apartheid, but to everything that tried to domesticate and inhibit the human spirit and its wild, affirmative freedom, its laughter, its compassion. And also its outrageous and jubilant way of saying yes to life itself.'[31]

'Non-whites' were left out of the official records of cricket, but far from being insignificant, the cricketers who played on the wrong side of the colour line in the old days inhabited deep cricket cultures. They were often the ones who really sowed the seeds for the future, and their inclusive goals and inherited legacies and imaginations will continue to influence and shape the way forward.

There were also a minority within the white cricket establishment that sought fairness in cricket whose contributions need to be recognised, starting with Harry Cadwallader, first secretary of the South African Cricket Association. He lost his position and the job of manager of the first South African tour to England in 1894 for supporting the selection of 'Krom' Hendricks. 'Old Caddy' was so airbrushed out of history that his name did not even appear in Luckin's *History of South African Cricket*, published 21 years afterwards.[32]

Let us also not forget remarkable local pioneers of the game like Wynnefred Jeffrey, Winifred Kingswell, Clarrie Peirce and Vicky Valentine-Brown. Kingswell, an early fighter for the right of women to vote, once knocked out a tooth of Springbok cricketer Percy Twentyman Jones with her bowling.[33] Jeffrey and Peirce played and administered cricket for over 50 years in Cape Town. Valentine-Brown, a quarter-finalist at Wimbledon and captain of Western Province during the 1950s, declared that, unlike tennis, cricket was not 'light-hearted and social'; 'cricket is an intelligent game and demands team work, enthusiasm, patience, knowledge and years of practising'. And, she added, 'it is my whole life.'[34] Women cricketers have always had to fight for their space in the game. Responding to the stock imputations that they were 'unfeminine' and not fulfilling their prescribed marriage and gender roles, one of Valentine-Brown's provincial opponents, Dr Muriel Ritchie from Southern Transvaal, explained simply: 'I have never had the time to get married - but have had it to play cricket ... It is the best game that a woman can play. It gives you excellent exercise, without over exerting one. It is a physically and emotionally healthy relaxation. It teaches you to concentrate, and it develops the co-ordination between brain and body ... it has no negative effects.'[35] Another Western Province stalwart, Christine Bald, also applied a simple logic in relation to the ideologically constructed 'gentleman's game' argument when she said, 'I see nothing unfeminine about cricket; it is no different from women playing tennis or golf.'[36]

During the freedom struggle in Mozambique, Samora Machel said, 'Our old people are our libraries.' By this he meant that the deep accounts of the history of that country were stored not so much in great libraries set up by strong colonial powers, but among the ordinary people resisting colonial oppression who kept alive and in circulation memories of a lived reality. *The Blue Book* could not have been imagined without old people with humble pasts sharing their lived experiences. More than the big cricket library at Newlands, which I so enjoyed as a young researcher, it was story-tellers who made Cape Town come alive for me when I set out in the 1970s to learn more about South Africa's cricket history.

In the years that followed, I was introduced to a world I did not know existed, by people like Uncle Matty Segers, Abubakar 'Carr' Hayward and 'Meneer' Effendi (aged 90, whose janaazah took place on the day I wrote this acknowledgement). Their narratives were like dreamtime stories. How could they have played games on the beach in Woodstock as young people when all we knew about the spot were the massive railway yards and the harbour that now stood there with a look of immovable permanence? How, when the jasmine-filled suburbs of Newlands and Claremont were so clearly lily-white and gentrified, could rowdy brown-skinned people wearing fezzes, rushing off to nearby mosques at lunchtime, have bowled and batted and owned market gardens in those green surroundings?

And did I know that there once had been cricket pitches on Rondebosch Common where today people of all shapes and sizes walk their dogs and struggle gamely to stay fit? (Eleven pitches in fact, as an aerial photo from 1946 has confirmed.) That every weekend cricketers pushed wheelbarrows loaded with matting wickets for miles so they could play there? That the fielders from different matches happening simultaneously stood, shoulder to shoulder, facing in opposite directions, as they waited to chase after balls in the knee-high grass, which they were not permitted to cut on this Council-owned land?

From these teachers, I began to understand how Cape Town had been ethnically cleansed under apartheid's Group Areas Act. Sixty thousand families were forced out of their homes in the fifties and sixties. In a disciplined way, applying the historical research skills I was busy acquiring as a student, I set out to see if this world of the imagination I had been introduced to could be translated from magical realism to sober details and statistics.

The contributions of the earliest journalists and community record-keepers were as massive as the players themselves. Starting with John Tengo Jabavu, the brilliant 23-year-old founding editor of *Imvo Zabantsundu* in 1884, who wrote about cricket in his first editorial (and broadened the Xhosa language by finding words to describe this new game), these record-keepers generated stories, produced brochures and sought to publicise what the cricket outcasts of the time were doing, as if this was as important as the matches played at Lord's. They left remarkable archives.

The South African Non-European Cricket Almanack in 1953/54 and 1954/55 and the successor *South African Cricket Almanack* in 1969, all three edited by Syd J Reddy and Damodar Damoo 'Bennie' Bansda, were especially important. The *Almanacks* were in effect the inside histories of black and non-racial cricket told from the perspective of those who were marginalised. For a quarter of a century, until the last decade or so, the few systematic attempts at writing about the history of black cricketers were based largely on these sources.

In the International Museum of Slavery in Liverpool, England, there is, amongst the exhibits, a quote by William Prestcott, a former slave, which laments the way in which enslaved people are rendered invisible: 'They will remember that we were sold, but not that we were strong. They will remember that we were bought, but not that we were brave.'[37] Like William Prestcott, the cricket people acknowledged here were not merely passive victims of an oppressive system. They were multi-dimensional characters who, through cricket, said yes in outrageous and jubilant ways to life itself.

Family tree of Western Province and South African cricket, 1890–2011

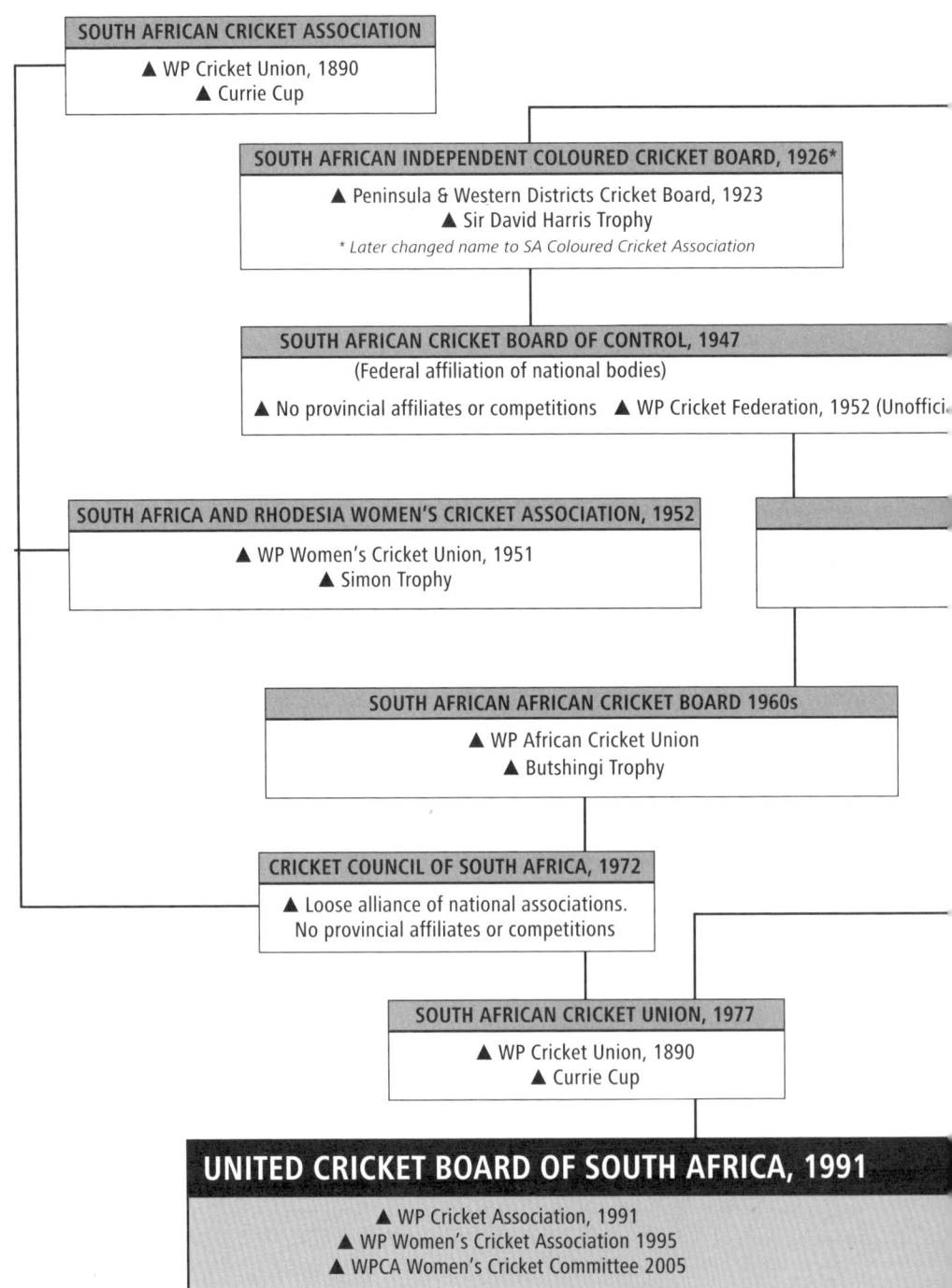

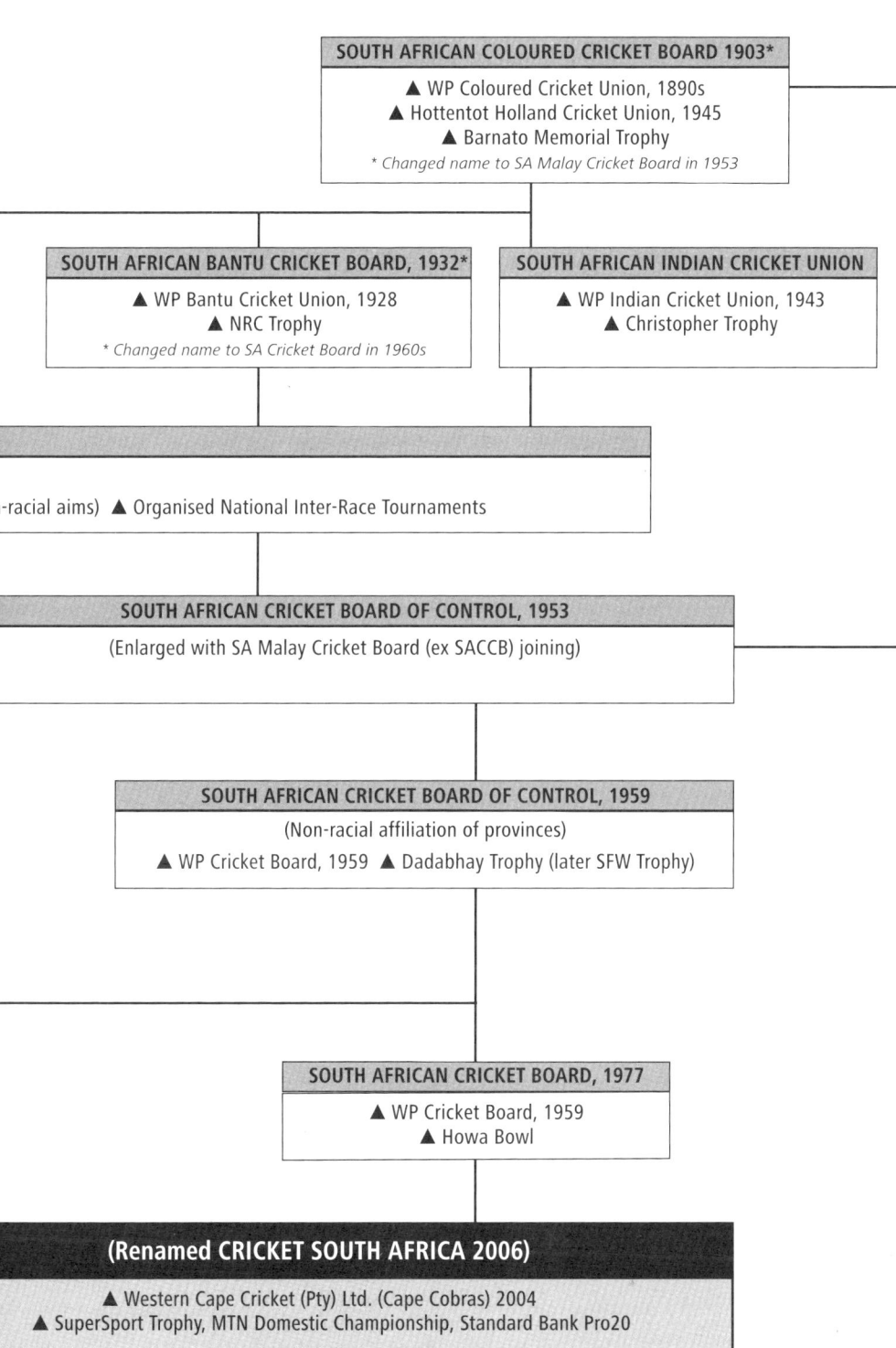

Family tree of Western Province and South African cricket, 1890–2011

In the same way that Western Province cricketers were for more than one hundred years segregated into separate racial bodies, no less than ten so-called 'national' associations were formed in South Africa between 1890 and 1991. At one stage six of these were operating at the same time, giving a whole new meaning to the words 'national' and 'South Africa'. To fully appreciate the chapters that follow, it is important to understand which of the various Western Provinces affiliated to which South African boards. This overview lays out the family tree so that we can better understand the history of each Western Province board and how it fitted into national cricket developments.[38]

Organised sport as we know it today in South Africa really got going in the years between 1875 and 1885, when the first rugby, football, athletics, cycling, jockey, golf and tennis clubs were formed, following a similar pattern in Britain after the industrial revolution. As people in England moved from the land to work in the new factories and industries, towns and cities grew rapidly and new forms of leisure appropriate to these crowded environments emerged. A similar process happened in South Africa after the discovery of diamonds and gold and the growth of new cities like Kimberley and Johannesburg. The establishment of the Union of South Africa in 1910, drawing together the Cape and Natal colonies and the former Boer republics of the Transvaal and Free State, also helped provide the context for the emergence of national cricket organisations and competitions.

South African Cricket Association (SACA), 1890–1977

The first major competition in South Africa was the Inter-Town Tournament for the Champion Bat started in 1876. Five of these tournaments were held up to 1890/91. In 1888/89 the first English touring team under Major Warton visited. This stimulated the formation of a South African Cricket Association in Kimberley in April 1890, and a new regional (later provincial) competition, the Currie Cup.

SACA was for whites-only. In keeping with the general practice in South African society, black cricketers, emerging in droves in Cape Town and the mission stations of the Eastern Cape, were excluded from its clubs, competitions and representative sides. Closely linked to the colonial and British establishments, SACA initiated regular contacts with other countries. Between March 1889 and March 1970 it organised 41 series involving 172 test matches. Only whites were eligible and the only opponents were the 'white' countries of empire, England, Australia and New Zealand. Until democracy in the 1990s, South Africa never once played against India, Pakistan, the West Indies and Sri Lanka. For more than 80 years, until 1977, no black players were allowed to participate in the Currie Cup either.

The SACA affiliate in our province was the Western Province Cricket Union (WPCU), which existed from 1890 to 1991.

South African Coloured Cricket Board (SACCB), 1903–1959

Although excluded from white organsiations, black sportspeople took to cricket from the start. Developments closely followed those of white cricket in many respects: from the introduction of cricket into schools (1857), to the formation of clubs (1869), the introduction of inter-town tournaments (1884), and of leagues and regional competitions (1890s), through to the formation of a national controlling body (1903).

As with the white cricket and rugby players, Kimberley administrators again took the lead in starting national competitions and associations. After forming Griqualand West boards for cricket (1892) and rugby (1894), the local sports leaders, headed by Isaiah Bud-Mbelle, brother-in-law of the famous writer Sol Plaatje, formed the South African Coloured Rugby Football Board in Kimberley in 1897. Starting in August 1898, the Rugby Board began organising regular tournaments along Currie Cup lines for the shiny new Rhodes Trophy, donated by the mining magnate and one-time Cape Prime Minister, Cecil John Rhodes. At the same time, Bud-Mbelle and his fellow administrators acquired the Barnato Memorial Trophy for cricket, named after another mining magnate. The first unofficial Barnato tournament was held in Port Elizabeth in December 1898.

Though the intention was to establish a new South African Coloured Cricket Board at the Port Elizabeth tournament, for some reason this did not happen. This meant a costly delay because the Anglo-Boer South African War broke out before the next cricket season and the formation of the SACCB had to wait until 1903. Remarkably, the SACCB was the second national cricket association in the world after SACA, pre-dating the Australian Cricket Board by a year or two and the formation of the Indian, West Indies and New Zealand Cricket Boards by more than two decades. (A private club, the MCC, ran English cricket.)

The SACCB organised 16 official Barnato tournaments before being disbanded in the late 1950s. It sought to represent all cricketers regardless of race and religion. Clause 25 of the SACCB constitution specifically stated that 'this Board does not recognise any distinction amongst the various sporting peoples of South Africa, whether by Creed, Nationality or otherwise'.[39]

The affiliate of the SACCB (which changed its name to the South African Malay Cricket Board in 1953 at the insistence of other national associations) in our province was the Western Province Coloured Cricket Union (WPCCU), which existed from the 1890s to 1959.

South African Independent Coloured Cricket Board (SAICCB), 1926–1959

Despite its inclusive goals, the SACCB, also known as the Barnato Board, started splintering after two decades. In 1926 a group of cricketers broke away to form the South African Independent Coloured Cricket Board. The SAICCB, headed by HJ Tobin, a member of a prominent Cape Town family, started organising its own inter-provincial tournaments for the Sir David Harris Trophy, named after another Cape parliamentarian involved in the mining industry. The breakaway was part of a broader pattern: from the 1920s onwards government policy increasingly encouraged segregation, and a similar split happened in rugby. The reasons were probably connected to religious tensions between Muslim and Christian cricketers and leadership struggles between Cape Town and Kimberley. The independent Board was for Christians only and Africans were not welcomed. Many clubs applied the 'pencil test', which disqualified people with hair that a pencil could not slide through.

The SAICCB affiliate in our province was the Peninsula and Western Districts Cricket Board (PWDCB), which existed from 1923 to 1959.

South African Bantu Cricket Board (SABCB), 1932–1977

The process of ethnic mobilisation among black cricketers went a step further when the South African Bantu Cricket Board (SABCB), led by HM Piliso, was formed in 1932 and once again was followed by a similar breakaway in rugby. The Bantu Board, in turn, started its own Chamber of Mines tournaments for the NRC Trophy; more than twenty were held up to 1974.

The reasons for African people organising separately from the 1930s were linked to the growth of urban segregation. The 1923 Native Urban Areas Act led to the stricter enforcement of segregation and soon people were forming area-based clubs in the new townships on the edges of the cities. Another reason was the gradual emergence of a more assertive African nationalism stressing African self-determination. Contemporary political developments were echoed in sport by complaints that African sportspeople were not getting a 'fair deal' under coloured leadership.

The Bantu Board functioned until 1977. In the 1960s it changed its name to the South African African Cricket Board as the term 'Bantu', used by an oppressive government, had by then assumed derogatory connotations.

The SABCB / SAACB affiliate in our province was the Western Province Bantu (later African) Cricket Union, which existed from 1928 to 1977.

South African Indian Cricket Union (SAICU), 1940–1959

In 1940 the South African Indian Cricket Union (SAICU) was formed. The first president was SL Singh, who was also a founder member of the South African Soccer Federation. Advocate Albert Christopher, who qualified at Lincoln's Inn in London and participated in passive resistance campaigns with Mahatma Gandhi, presented the Christopher Trophy for the Indian provincial tournaments. Perhaps because of their small numbers, Indian cricketers did not support the formation of different ethnic boards. However, they went ahead with forming an Indian Union after trying unsuccessfully in 1938 to revive the

1. Notice in the Cape Town Gazette and Advertiser of the first recorded cricket match in South Africa in Cape Town on 5 January 1808.
2. Zonnebloem College, established for the sons of African chiefs, and based first at Bishopscourt and then modern-day Walmer Estate in Cape Town, had two cricket teams in the early 1860s.

3–4. Newlands Cricket Ground, one of the oldest and most beautiful test grounds in the world, hosted the first match in South Africa involving an English touring team on 21–23 December 1888. Women were part of the game from the beginning.

5. WP XVIII v WW Read's English touring team in December 1891. Back row: G Cripps, VA van der Bijl, V van der Bijl, Lieut. Boyle, ES Steytler, GP Pemberton, CN Thomas (umpire). Middle row: H Calder, CH Mills, Captain Wright, WH Milton (captain), HH Castens, F Hearne, CS Hickley, TW Routledge. Front row: E Allen, M Bisset, Drummer Ellis, J Middleton.

6. Newspaper reports from the Cape Argus of the 'Malay' inter-town tournament held at Newlands in 1890.

CAPE TOWN UNION.

Batsman	Dismissal	Runs
M. Oxallic	c and b Ajoep	0
S. Salie	c E. Sakie, b Ajoep	5
L. Samsoedien	c Kariemdien, b Ajoep	29
M. Lamrah	b Fridericks	14
E. Ieshaak	c Baderdien, b Ajoep	0
R. Sxmsoddien	b Fridericks	1
A. Ijraan	st G. Fridericks, b Fridericks	0
M. Esmieh	c Baderien, b Fridericks	4
M. Samsoeden	b Ajoed	3
G. Jakoef	c Hendricks, b Ajoep	4
A. Jaijer	not out	9
Extras		14
Total		**83**

PORT ELIZABETH.

Batsman	Dismissal	Runs
E. Rasin	run out	0
G. Fredericks	c Gibier, b Ijerran	0
G. Kerindien	b Ijarran	14
L. Fredericks	c Lamme, b Jakoep	18
Ajoep	lbw, b Jakoep	0
H. Astril	b Jakoep	7
E. Sakiem	b Jakoep	3
G. Kasiem	st Esmiel, b L. Samsoedin	0
A. Samar	b Jakoep	1
J. Hendricks	b L. Samsoedien	2
A. Badierdien	not out	0
Extras		10

THE MALAYS.

THE Malays of Cape Town have not made such a show for several years as they have presented for us at the Cricket Tournament at Newlands this week. However we may have lamented the spread of Asiatic influence in Cape Town, we have always had a saving clause for the Malays. They have not come here to try for their own fortunes against the European; but their fathers were brought here against their own will as slaves for the convenience and comfort of our predecessors, and they have the same right that Europeans have to regard this country as their home. Of all the people benefited by emancipation, they have proved themselves most worthy. We have had no Hayti in Cape Town by reason of the presence of Malays in our midst. As far as men of alien race can amalgamate with a European community they have become an integral part of the population of Cape Town. We fancy that old inhabitants of Cape Town, although they may occasionally say unpleasant things of the Malays and regret that Cape Town should be exposed to the reproach of being a "Malay town," would feel a little sorry if they saw no more of the familiar figures in the streets—the trustworthy Malay mason, who knows exactly what kind of work we require; the Malay laundress, whose preparation of our shirt fronts is a fine wit; the steady Malay driver, who can complacently skirt a precipice; or the invaluable "old Malay man," who knows as much as an old English factotum, and perhaps a thing or two besides.

The Malays have been subject to some changes during the last few years, but such changes are not noted in our

SPORTING INTELLIGENCE.

TO-DAY'S CRICKET.

THE MALAY TOURNAMENT.

CAPE TOWN UNION CLUB vs. PORT ELIZABETH.

The cricket ground at Newlands presented a picturesque and a unusual appearance this morning when the Malay tournament was commenced, the field being fringed with Malays in their peculiar costumes, while the female portion of the onlookers lent plenty of colour to the scene. There was a large company composed wholly of Moslems, and judging by the numerous luncheon baskets they had determined evidently to make a day

7–8. The first provincial presidents: William Milton (WPCU) and Dr Abdullah Abdurahman (WPCCU).
9-10. The Currie Cup and Barnato Memorial Trophy were for decades the best-known trophies in South African domestic cricket. The WPCU won the Currie Cup (SACA) 17 out of 63 times. The WPCCU won the Barnato Trophy (SACCB) 12 out of 16 times.

11. Non-racialism in the making. Participating teams and officials from Western Province, Eastern Province, Griqualand West and Natal at the South African Coloured Cricket Board inter-provincial tournament for the Barnato Memorial Trophy, Kimberley, March–April 1913.

12. Western Province Cricket Union Currie Cup team, 1913/14. Back row: [x] Loxton (umpire), EA Budgen, RR Luyt, WH Mars, RHM Hands, WH Short, PAM Hands, [x] Adams (umpire). Front row: GAL Hearne, JM Blanckenberg, FD Conry (captain), JMM Commaille, PT Lewis.

Bye-Laws.

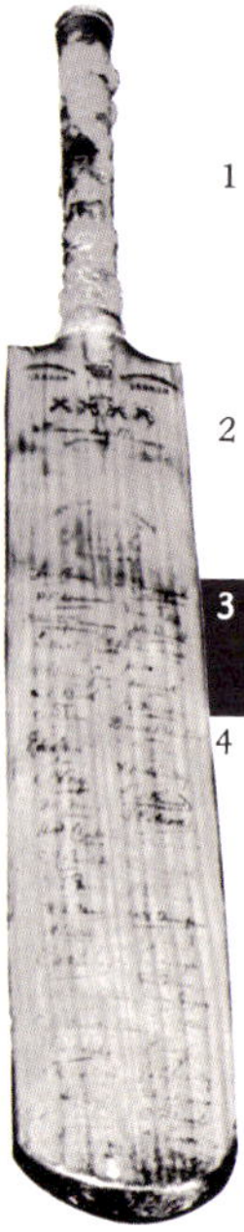

1. GENERAL. There shall be established the several divisions hereinafter provided for, the arrangement of the fixtures for which shall, subject to the Rules and Bye-Laws of the Union, be drawn up and approved before the commencement of the Season by the Committee.

2. No match shall be played on any date other than set down in the approved list of fixtures, unless the consent of the Committee has been obtained at least three days previous to the said date.

3. No coloured professionals or members shall be allowed to compete in any matches under the jurisdiction of the Union.

4. No player who is not a permanent resident in the Western Province shall be eligible to play for a club in any division unless he has been elected a bona-fide effective member of such club, and intends to reside in the Western Province for a period of 30 days immediately after the first day of the first such match in which he plays, and any club playing a member who shall fail to put in the 30 days' residence shall, in case of victory, be liable to forfeit the match.

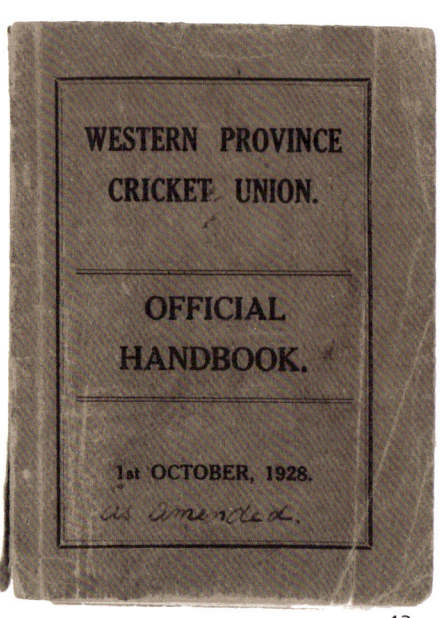

13–16. Black cricket fans were keen spectators and ran the scoreboard at Newlands, but they were not allowed to play for WPCU clubs, as the 1928 WPCU handbook emphasised.

17. Blazer belonging to 'Boon' Wallace.
18. The 1929/30 Western Province Cricket Union Currie Cup team. Back row: A Glantz, G Battison, FH Kossuth, IF Goulden, GL Napier, TR de Klerk, SSL Steyn, HGO Owen-Smith. Front row: AW Palm, LR Serrurier, JJ Kotze (manager), DPB Morkel (captain), AW 'Dave' Nourse, FC Martin, KCM Hands.

19. The Peninsula Ladies' Cricket Club, formed in 1930, was the precursor of the first provincial Board and affiliated to the Women's Cricket Association in England. The captain, Clarrie Peirce, and opening bowler, Wynnefred Jeffrey, remained active as players and administrators until the 1970s.

20. Girls' cricket had an early start in Cape Town. This Rustenburg School for Girls cricket team played an inter-schools match against Wynberg Girls' High in the 1909/10 season.

21. The 1931/32 Western Province Coloured Cricket Union, with the legendary Taliep Salie as captain and AJ 'Dol' Freeman ('the Malay Wally Hammond') as vice-captain, won the Barnato Memorial Trophy in Bloemfontein. Sitting next to Freeman (third from right in front) are Ismail 'Taliep' Behardien and Gamat 'Prop' Reinaard. 'Happie' Nordien is in the back row, far right.

22. The first-ever Western Province Bantu Cricket Union team, captained by P Walton Mama, were runners-up in the first Chamber of Mines tournament for the NRC Trophy, Johannesburg, December–January 1933/34. Back row: Don T Mtimkulu, MB Liphuko, A Matshikwe, S Bam, E Matshikwe, DN Mbali. Middle row: SM Fongqo, PK Petu, P Walton Mama, SM Ndlwana, CS Mbali. Front row: SS Msengana (scorekeeper).

23. Peninsula and Western Districts Cricket Board, winners of the Sir David Harris Trophy, Port Elizabeth, 1937/38. Back row: A February, E Lodewyk, G Fox, J Hermans, G Rutgers, A Sedgwick. Middle row: J Bessick (secretary), HC Abrahams (president), AW Adams (captain), A Arendse (treasurer), FJ Darius (vice-president). Front row: M Abrahams, C Adams, ED Adams, A Sassman.

24. The 1945/46 Western Province Coloured Cricket Union team, captained by Taliep Salie, winners of the Barnato Memorial Trophy.

25. The 1945/46 Western Province Cricket Union Currie Cup team, captained by 'Tuppy' Owen-Smith. From left are [M] Isaacs ('baggageman'), RE Middleton, S O'Linn, R Lofthouse (at back), G Georgeu, JE Cheetham, Miss Ray Hubner (scorer), S Kiel, LS Eckard, JB Plimsoll, DK Graham, Mr Mathews (manager), AS Carew, HGO 'Tuppy' Owen-Smith (captain) and AD Keen (vice-captain).

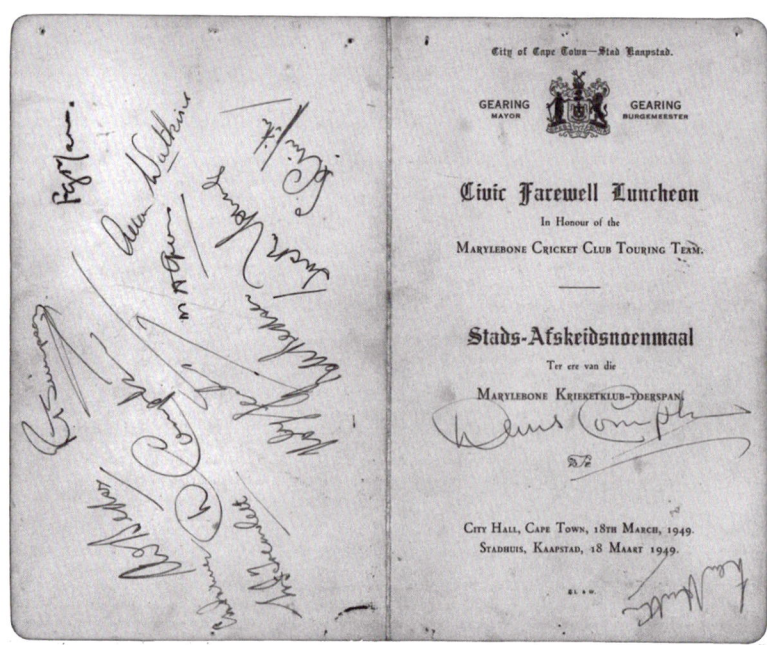

26. The Western Province Bantu Cricket Board team, which won the NRC Trophy of the SABCB for the first time in 1947/48. Back row: A Dunjwa (scorekeeper), TM Mgijima, SS Mafongosi, AM Mshumpela, JN Fassie (delegate). Middle row: SL Yengo, GB Kobi, T Mandla, BN Malamba, N Kawulela. Seated: MM Balfour, WB Lubelwana (delegate), SD Dyira (captain), MM Maxam (vice-captain), J Thema (manager), SM Ndlwana. In front: CM Scott, WW Kulathi.
27. Mayoral reception card for 1948/49 MCC team.

28–29. The 1958/59 SACBOC Springboks who toured East Africa and Rhodesia under Basil D'Oliveira. This was the first-ever team open to all South African cricketers. It included eleven Western Province players. Back: George Langa, Ben Malamba (WP) M Bulbulia, 'Laam' Raziet (WP), El Jeewa, Basil D'Oliveira (WP captain), 'Coetie' Neethling (WP), BD Pavadai (manager), 'Tiny' Abed (WP vice-captain), AI Deedat. Front: Owen Williams (WP), Cecil Abrahams (WP), Eric Petersen (WP), Sydney Solomon (WP) and 'Lobo' Abed (WP).

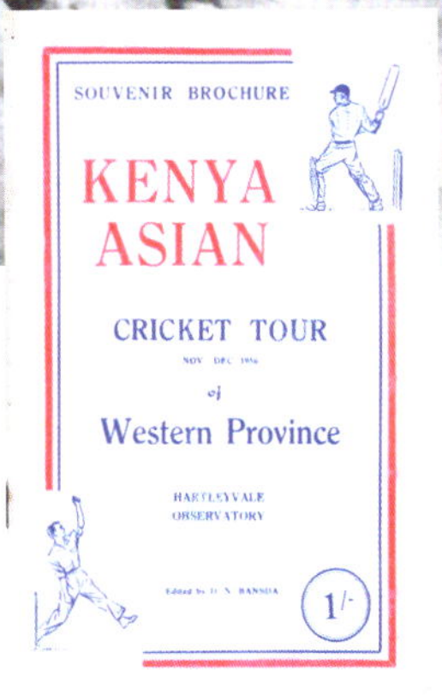

30. Capetonians enjoying the warm waters of the Indian Ocean. From left; 'Lobo' Abed, Cecil Abrahams, Ben Malamba, 'Coetie' Neethling, Basil D'Oliveira and 'Laam' Raziet.

31–32. 1956 captains of South Africa, Clive van Ryneveld (SACA) and Basil D'Oliveira (SACBOC), both from Western Province.

33. Ben Malamba (right), pictured here in his Springbok blazer with Al Seedat, was the best African cricketer of his generation.

34. The 1955/56 WPCU team, captained by Clive van Ryneveld, winners of the Currie Cup. Standing: JR Siedle, JBR Maile, DA Louw, HNP Roy, AJ Pithey, JE Pothecary, ERH Fuller. Seated: RJ Westcott, PGV van der Bijl (manager), CB van Ryneveld (captain), GE Crighton (manager), GAS Innes. In front: RR MacDonald, JH Ferrandi. Inset: JR Liddle.

35. The 1957/58 WPCCU team, captained by 'Tiny' Abed, winners of the Barnato Tournament. Back row: E Abrahams, C Ganief, A Adams, AA Osman, S 'Dik' Abed, GH Abed. Middle row: A George, G 'Tiny' Abed (captain), Sheikh Ganief Booley (manager), A Hattas. Front row: I 'Taliep' Behardien, T Hendricks.

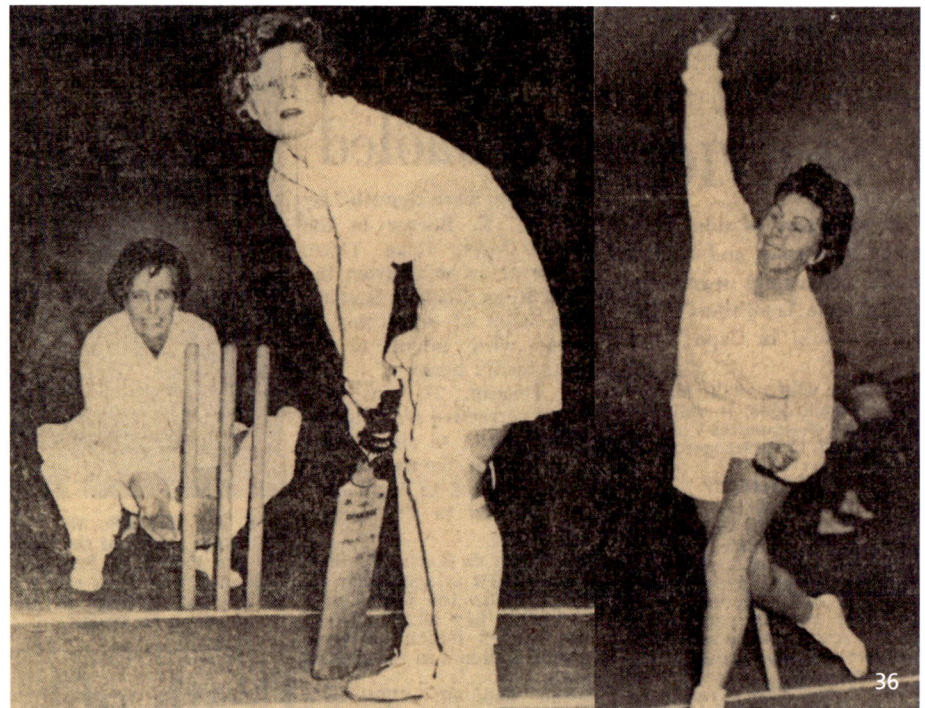

36. Some of Western Province's pioneering women's cricketers in the 1950s. From left: Clarrie Peirce, J Ruger and Beverley Lang.

37. The 1952/53 Western Province women's team, winners of the first official inter-provincial tournament for the Simon Trophy organised by the South Africa and Rhodesia Women's Cricket Association. Back row: J Saunders, A Johnson, J West, J Littlewort, G de Villiers, P Tremble. Front row: W Jeffrey, SN Charlton (vice-captain), V Valentine-Brown (captain), P Abernethy, M Chamberlain.

Barnato Board, which had fallen into decline in the 1930s, failing to organise any tournaments between 1932 and 1944. Natal and Transvaal were the strongest provinces of the new Indian Union by virtue of the fact that the majority of the Indian community lived in those areas. Each province won the trophy four times, and shared it once, between 1941 and 1958.

The SAICU affiliate in our province was the Western Province Indian Cricket Union (WPICU), which existed from 1943 to 1959.

South African Cricket Board of Control (SACBOC), 1947–1959

In January 1945 the South African Indian Cricket Union decided at a meeting in Durban that attempts should be made to reunite once again all black cricketers under a new South African Cricket Board of Control. After two years of negotiations, a body of that name was formed in July 1947. It was commonly known by its acronym, SACBOC.

The new SACBOC was a federal body of existing racial national associations. The various ethnic affiliates maintained their identities, but agreed to join forces to hold national 'inter-race' tournaments and promote the general interests of black cricketers. These inter-race tournaments were similar to the 'communal' triangular and quadrangular tournaments played in India before independence. All the existing black bodies joined SACBOC. Initially the old SACCB, or Barnato Board, was excluded but was later accepted when it agreed to give up its historic leading role and change its name to the South African Malay Cricket Board. The first president of the new federal structure was Bob Pavadai of the Indian Union.

SACBOC at first did not organise any provincial cricket or tournaments, but rather national inter-race tournaments from 1951 to 1958 between the best teams of the different racially based national associations. Between 1956 and 1958 a team of SACBOC 'Springboks', chosen from these inter-race tournaments, was selected to play opposition from Kenya, the Rhodesias, Tanganyika, Uganda and Zanzibar.

South Africa and Rhodesia Women's Cricket Association (SARWCA), 1952–1991

After World War Two, women cricketers began to form the first women's provincial associations. In 1952 the South Africa and Rhodesia Women's Cricket Association was established in Bloemfontein. From 1952 to the late 1980s SARWCA organised annual inter-provincial tournaments for the Simon Trophy. They also sought and gained affiliation to the International Women's Cricket Council, formed in 1958. Between 1960 and 1972 South Africa played three international series against England, the Netherlands and New Zealand before it was isolated internationally because of apartheid. Four rebel tours by the private Unicorns team from Britain were organised to make up for this.

The SARWCA affiliate in our province was the Western Province Women's Cricket Union (WPWCU), which existed from 1951 to 1991.

Apartheid and non-racial sport

The National Party won the whites-only general election in 1948 and the era of rigid, institutionalised apartheid arrived. Long-standing discrimination was extended and legalised in a way that eventually made South Africa an international pariah and caused immense suffering to the majority of its people. Deepening apartheid soon gave rise to its antithesis: a powerful national movement in favour of democracy and non-racialism in South Africa. In 1949, the ANC adopted a Programme of Action which rejected traditional moderate (and unsuccessful) methods of protest and embarked on direct action through boycotts, strikes and civil disobedience in a 'mass struggle for national freedom'. Pro-democracy Indian, coloured and white groups joined the ANC in the Congress Alliance, which in 1955 adopted the Freedom Charter emphasising that 'South Africa belongs to all who live in it, black and white'.

The application of apartheid and the intensification of resistance against it had a direct bearing on developments in sport. From the late 1940s onwards, racially compartmentalised black sports bodies, including those in cricket, rugby and soccer, sought to establish unity amongst themselves. They began to seek international contacts, and protest against discrimination much more forcefully than before, emulating in many ways the multi-racial co-operation happening at a political level.

South African Cricket Board of Control (SACBOC), 1959–1977

After organising four national inter-race tournaments for the Dadabhay Trophy and initiating sporting contacts for black cricketers by means of tours from Kenya and to Rhodesia and East Africa in the 1950s, SACBOC decided in 1959 to restructure itself into a unitary (rather than a federal) body. This meant that in direct opposition to apartheid, affiliation would be on the basis of non-racial provincial structures rather than racially based national ones. Moreover, the dominance of the white racial body was questioned and the goal of one controlling body and full citizenship rights for all cricketers in South Africa became the bottom line demand.

The restructured, non-racial SACBOC's affiliate in our province was the Western Province Cricket Board (WPCB), which existed from 1959 to 1991.

The South African Bantu Board agreed in principle with the new approach by SACBOC, but was the only black association not to go into the new non-racial arrangement. The main reason was apparently the way SACBOC demarcated its new provincial boundaries. At least three provincial affiliates of the old national bodies had to exist in an area for that area to achieve provincial status. This meant that, in areas where African cricket was strong but no other affiliates existed (for instance in the Orange Free State and parts of the Eastern Cape), African cricketers would be under-represented within SACBOC. They therefore proceeded on their own under the renamed South African African Board.

Cricket Council of South Africa (CCSA), 1972–1977

In the late 1960s, as opposition to apartheid increased both inside and outside South Africa, leading to the expulsion of racially exclusive South African teams from international sport, the government and white sports bodies started reaching out to black cricketers for the first time.

Desperate for black allies after the infamous D'Oliveira affair, the whites-only SACA started wooing SAACB and SACBOC with a view to some sort of co-operation. The African

Board responded positively to the overtures. It had few resources and argued that it needed to provide better facilities and opportunities for its players. The result was the Cricket Council of South Africa (CCSA) in 1972, an umbrella organisation based on federal lines.

Much like the old SACBOC model of the 1940s and 1950s, which had been rejected by this time, SACA and SAACB retained their own identities but worked together. SACBOC refused to participate, arguing that this was a false unity, which amounted to co-option and did nothing to change the status quo. Working closely with the National Party government and the private sector, SACA now more or less took over responsibility for African cricketers, who became increasingly compromised as political events unfolded.

The CCSA did not organise any provincial cricket or tournaments, leaving SACA to do so in the form of the Currie Cup.

South African Cricket Union (SACU), 1977–1991

As resistance to apartheid gained momentum in the 1970s, leading to the 1976 Soweto uprisings, the balance of power in South Africa started changing in favour of the majority. The government and white sports bodies were forced to make concessions through a new 'multi-national' sports policy, which allowed for limited mixing at 'international' level but maintained segregation at provincial, club and grassroots levels. The aim was to preserve long-standing international contacts without making any fundamental changes to 'traditional' apartheid policies.

Elements within SACBOC now saw an opportunity to achieve long-held goals of playing 'normal cricket' within one united cricket body. In 1976 the first efforts were made to play mixed cricket at club level. They proved chaotic because of government double-talk and the conservative attitudes of white administrators, who timidly followed the government line. Nevertheless, amidst great controversy, SACBOC president Rashid Varachia formally took the organisation and a minority of its players into the new unified South African Cricket Union on 18 September 1977. Varachia became president and the longstanding SACA, SAACB and SACBOC ceased to exist.

SACU's affiliate in our province was the already established, formerly whites-only Western Province Cricket Union (WPCU), which existed from 1890 to 1991.

South African Cricket Board (SACB), 1977–1991

Mr Varachia did not have the support of the majority in SACBOC when he went into the SACU. Dissatisfied SACBOC members regrouped to form the South African Cricket Board in November 1977, with the Howa Bowl as the main competition.

By this time the 1976 Soweto uprisings had forever changed the political landscape and the balance of power in South Africa. The demand by black cricketers was not to play together under certain conditions approved by the government, but for full citizenship rights for all South African cricketers. Under the leadership of the feisty Hassan Howa, SACB openly sided with the liberation movements and supported the sports boycott of apartheid South Africa. Non-racial sports organisations, grouped into the powerful South African Council on Sport (SACOS), coined the slogan 'No normal sport in an abnormal society'. The SACOS affiliates followed a strict policy of non-collaboration, aimed at isolating establishment sport and those black sportspeople seen as collaborators.

SACB's affiliate in our province was the already established Western Province Cricket Board (WPCB), which existed from 1959 to 1991.

United Cricket Board of South Africa (UCBSA), 1991 onwards (name changed to Cricket South Africa (CSA) on 3 August 2006)

In the 1980s, the final decade of the apartheid state, South Africa spiralled into repression and virtual civil war. Relations between SACB and SACU, situated on opposite sides of the fence, reflected this polarisation, particularly after SACU worked closely with the apartheid government to organise rebel tours with the use of taxpayers' money. Cricket entered the 1990s split by bitter antagonisms. These were mirrored by the mass demonstrations against the rebel cricket tour of Mike Gatting's English team in January–February 1990. Thousands of people took to the streets to vent their anger. Bombs exploded at cricket stadiums and the tour was called off. Apartheid sport had reached a dead end and South Africa's cricketers were polarised as never before. Yet just 18 months later, all cricketers in South Africa were united under a single cricket body for the first time after more than 100 years of division.

The turning point came in February 1990 when the apartheid government was forced to unban the ANC and other parties, release political prisoners and start negotiations. As part of its strategy to get South Africans to buy into this process of negotiation and national reconciliation, the ANC encouraged SACB and SACU to break old moulds and form a United Cricket Board of South Africa.

In record time, the UCBSA was established on 29 June 1991, South Africa became fully part of world cricket for the first time, the historic general elections of 1994 were held and Nelson Mandela became the first President of a democratic South Africa.

The old Western Province Cricket Board and Western Province Cricket Association formed the new united Western Province Cricket Association on 25 June 1991. The WPCA became a founding affiliate of the new UCBSA.

Later, in 2004 CSA launched the franchise system with the goal of strengthening domestic cricket. Six regions, rather than the eleven provinces, now competed for the premier honours. The WPCA and the Boland Cricket Board established Western Cape Cricket (Pty) Ltd and a combined team, the Cape Cobras, emerged to play in the new strength-vs-strength competitions.

Part I

The colonial and apartheid eras, 1890–1991

CHAPTER 1
Western Province Cricket Union, 1890–1991

Affiliated to the South African Cricket Association and South African Cricket Union

The Western Province Cricket Union (WPCU) was the first regional cricket body formed in the Western Province.[40] It was launched on 5 September 1890 at a meeting in the Thatched Tavern on Greenmarket Square. The founding clubs were Cape Town, Claremont, Sea Point and Western Province Cricket Club. The last club, described as the MCC of the Cape Colony, had built Newlands and organised the first tour by an English side in 1888. The other clubs now 'wished to wrest from the Western Province Cricket Club the apparent monopoly which they held in the administration of cricketing matters in the Western Province and obtain equal representation for all first-class local clubs on a duly constituted Board in whose hands the sole management should rest'.[41]

William Milton was elected as the first of the seventeen WPCU presidents to hold office in the hundred years of the organisation's existence. PH de Villiers became the first secretary/treasurer. Milton was a former England rugby player, who captained South Africa at cricket in one of the tests against the first English tourists in 1889. At the time, he was politically influential as private secretary to the Prime Minister of the Cape Colony, Cecil John Rhodes. He was also in charge of 'Native Affairs' and later became the first colonial Administrator of Rhodesia (Zimbabwe).[42]

AC Parker's official history notes that the following clubs were linked to WPCU at the time of its formation: Diocesan College, South African College, Wasps (later Mowbray), Woodstock, Garrison, Cape Times, United Services, Simon's Town, Letton, Barnett, Somerset, Caxton, Adderley, Wynberg Rovers, Central Telegraph, Zingari, Springfield, Reservoir, YMCA, Central, Alfred, Rosebud and Nil Desperandum. Cricket was also flourishing outside Cape Town in the rural towns of the colony.

In 1893/94 the WPCU started an 'official senior club championship' which much later, when the era of commercial sponsorship took off in the 1970s, was named the Markhams Premier League. Cape Town CC were the winners for the first eight times. Western Province CC won the most times – 20 as against 17 by Cape Town CC – during the 98 years of the league's existence. Green Point were strong between 1908/09 and 1946/47, winning 15 times, but thereafter never took the title again. Cape Technical College CC (later Techs Mutual) dominated with seven titles between 1965/66 and 1976/77.

The formation of the WPCU in September 1890 was stimulated by the formation of the new South African Cricket Association (SACA) earlier that year, and the beginnings of regional or provincial (as opposed to inter-town) cricket following the donation of the new Currie Cup. In fact, the first team bearing the name Western Province that is today recognised in the first-class record had already played its first game in January 1890 against Natal at Newlands.[43]

Western Province started participating in the new Currie Cup competition and won four out of five tournaments between 1892/93 and 1897/98. Thereafter Transvaal and Natal dominated the competition for many decades and Western Province won only six more times up to the 1960s. Indeed, after failing for ten years to win a trophy, the WPCU team was demoted to the B Section of the Currie Cup for three seasons from 1966/67 to 1968/69.

All in all, the WPCU produced over 70 players for the Springboks, as the SACA national team was called. Seven Western Province players captained SACA's South Africa team, namely William Milton (1889, 1892), Alf Richards (1896), Murray Bisset (1899), James 'Biddy' Anderson (1902), Jack Cheetham (1952–1955), Clive van Ryneveld (1956–1958) and Peter van der Merwe (1965–1967).

Michael Owen-Smith has observed that the WPCU's greatest contribution to South African cricket in the period from 1889 until the onset of isolation in 1970 was unquestionably the quality of captains it produced for the national team. When (Sir) Murray Bisset was appointed to lead the national team in two tests against England in 1898/99, he was only 22 years and 306 days old, and he remained South Africa's youngest ever captain until an even younger (22 years and 82 days) Graeme Smith, playing for the Western Province Cricket Association (WPCA), took the national reins in 2003.

But it was in the era after World War Two that national captains from the Western Province came to the fore within SACA. They were Jack Cheetham, Clive van Ryneveld and Peter van der Merwe. Van der Merwe became the second captain to lead South Africa to a test series victory in England and also was in charge of South Africa's first-ever test series win over Australia. Cheetham's team was part of a memorable test series in England in 1955 in which all five tests produced positive results. England led 2-0 before South Africa squared at 2-2 and then England won the decider on a treacherous pitch at The Oval, specially prepared for England off-spinner Jim Laker and his left-arm partner, Tony Lock.

Two other South African captains, Herby Taylor and Jock Cameron, represented Western Province but for only one season late in their careers, and another Western Province player, Denijs Morkel, was vice-captain of the national side in the early 1930s. 'Tuppy' Owen-Smith was invited to captain South Africa for the timeless test series against England, the last before World War Two, but had to decline for business reasons.

What made this list of captains even more remarkable was the fact that Western Province selections for the national side during this period were the exception rather than the rule. There were often as many as eight players from Transvaal in the side while Natal were also major contributors to the national cause. Apart from Bisset, the Western Province stars at the start of the 20th century were mainly bowlers. 'Kodgee' Kotze was the first of many outstanding fast bowlers to represent South Africa while 'Bonnor' Middleton and George Rowe were also part of this era. They were followed by the Hands brothers, Reggie and 'Pam', whose careers were cut short by World War One. Reggie was one of many cricketers to lose his life in that war.

Morkel, Owen-Smith (the national selectors still wanted to choose him against England in 1948/49 when he was almost 40 years old), Mick Commaille, Pieter van der Bijl and JM Blanckenberg were among those who represented South Africa between the two world wars while the 1950s produced fast bowler Eddie Fuller, off-spinner Martin Hanley and batsmen Gerald Innes, Jack Nel and Dick Westcott in addition to Cheetham and Van Ryneveld. 'Dave' Nourse, 'Tip' Snooke, 'Shunter' Coen and Michael Melle also represented Western Province but, like Cameron and Taylor, had very brief spells playing their cricket out of Newlands.

Spin bowling became Western Province's forte in the 1960s when both Harry Bromfield and 'Kelly' Seymour were called up for national duty along with seamer Jimmy Pothecary.

From 1969/70 (when the Eddie Barlow era started and Mike Procter was enticed to Cape Town) to 1990/91 Western Province once again became a champion team, winning five Currie Cup titles outright and sharing the trophy twice. They also did excellently with nine titles in the new format of one-day cricket after its introduction to South Africa in 1969/70. In this new limited-overs format, WPCU were winners of the Gillette Cup three out of eight times between 1969/70 and 1976/77 (runners-up twice); winners of the Datsun/Nissan Shield two out of fourteen times between 1977/78 and 1990/91 (runners-up five times); and winners of the Benson & Hedges Trophy for four out of ten times between 1981/82 and 1990/91 (runners-up twice).

The team that Barlow captained in 1976/77 was probably the strongest fielded by the WPCU. It consisted of Barlow, André Bruyns, Peter Kirsten, Kepler Wessels, Allan Lamb, Hylton Ackerman, Richard Morris, Peter Swart, Gavin Pfuhl, Garth le Roux, Stephen Jones and stand-out leg spinner Denys Hobson. The precocious talents of Kirsten, Lamb and Le Roux were followed in the late 1970s and 1980s by the arrival of stars such as Stephen Jefferies, Adrian Kuiper, Laurence Seeff, Kenny McEwan and Daryll Cullinan.

Throughout its existence, the WPCU, or 'Union', was responsible for hosting test matches at Newlands (which became famous in the cricket world for its beauty and setting) although the ground itself was owned by WPCC, or 'The Club'. The first test match was staged there in March 1889, only five years after the first test match at Lord's. In terms of results, however, the postcard-pretty ground became a graveyard for South Africa. The sorry picture was that in the hundred years before unity in 1991, when a whole new era of modern cricket dawned, South Africa won only three out of 24 tests played at Newlands. They won for the first time by the large margin of an innings and 16 runs against England in 1906, followed by another win in 1910, then had to wait another 60 years before the next victory in 1970 against Bill Lawry's Australia. The 24 tests at Newlands constituted 13.95 per cent of the total of 172 tests played by South Africa between 1889 and 1991. The overall statistics read as follows:[44]

Opponents	P	W	L	D
Australia	7	1	6	–
England	15	2	9	4
New Zealand	2	–	1	1
Total	**24**	**3**	**16**	**5**

In keeping with colonial and apartheid mentalities, only white cricketers were permitted to play for SACA's South Africa and they played against the *white* countries of the Empire only, namely England, Australia and New Zealand. This also applied at club and provincial level within the affiliated WPCU. Its constitution barred so-called 'Non-Europeans' from playing.[45] Black spectators were also limited to a segregated enclosure at Newlands, where temporary seating was provided for the first time only in 1972.[46]

As mentioned in the introduction to this book, the WPCU and WPCC in fact were probably more than anyone else responsible for officially introducing the colour bar, which sullied South African cricket for a century. William Milton (close ally of Cecil Rhodes) and local officials made sure H 'Krom' Hendricks was dropped from the first South African touring team to England in 1894 because of his colour.[47] In 1968, when the D'Oliveira affair erupted, the WPCU president Ernest McKay supported Prime Minister Vorster's decision to cancel the tour because it included the home-born Basil D'Oliveira, formerly from the Bo-Kaap in Cape Town.[48] These actions fixed the patterns of the game in Cape Town and forced black cricketers to form their own separate Western Province boards. Segregation and later rigid apartheid became the norm.

After the advent of 'normal cricket' in 1976, a variation of the government's multi-national policy, a few black clubs (most notably Avendale and Langa) joined the WPCU and a few black players were selected for its teams, starting with Rodney Malamba and Omar Henry, but the WPCU remained, in culture and in essence, an apartheid establishment institution.

The WPCU went out of existence in 1991 during its centenary year when cricket unity was finally achieved as the apartheid order crumbled and democracy approached. The Union now joined with the Western Province Cricket Board (WPCB) to form the new Western Province Cricket Association (WPCA), under which all cricketers in the province play today. At the time 41 clubs were affiliated.

The WPCU had 17 presidents in the hundred years of its existence. They were:

Milton, W	1890–1893
Steytler, ES	1893–1895
Smuts, LB	1895–1897
Reid, JA	1897–1902 and 1905–1907
Simkins, WV	1902–1905 and 1908–1911
Bisset, M	1907–1908 and 1911–1913
Fitzgerald, RP	1913–1914
Van der Byl, PV	1914–1927
Morris, GA	1927–1933
Pienaar, AJ	1933–1953
Bensimon, AS	1953–1957
Matthews, WJ	1957–1965
McKay, EL	1965–1970
Wallace, B	1970–1977
Myers, SB	1977–1981
Delport, RF	1981–1983
Bing, F	1983–1991

For a detailed history of the WPCU see, AC Parker, *Western Province Cricket 100 – Not Out* (WPCU, Cape Town, 1990). For a history of Newlands and the most prominent clubs affiliated to the WPCU, see also SEL West (compiler) and WJ Luker (ed.), *Century at Newlands, 1864–1964: A History of the Western Province Cricket Club* (WPCC, Cape Town, 1965).

1.1 Western Province Cricket Union, 1889/90–1990/91

1.1.1 Western Province Cricket Union National Players (SACA / SACU), 1889/90–1990/91[49]

South African Cricket Association Official Tests, 1889/90–1976/77

- This list includes all Western Province players who appeared for South Africa (SACA) in this period, including 1888/89, and not just official test players.
- Numbers of official test matches are shown.
- Dates are inclusive of all appearances for South Africa and not only official tests.
- An asterisk indicates that the player represented South Africa while playing for a province other than Western Province.

Name	*M*	*From*	*To*
Anderson, JH	1	1902/03	1902/03
Ashley, WH	1	1888/89	1888/89
Balaskas, XC	9	1930/31	1938/39
Barlow, EJ	30	1961/62	1969/70
Bell, AJ	16	1929	1935
Bisset, AVC	–	1901	1901
Bisset, M	3	1898/99	1909/10
Bissett, GF	4	1924	1927/28
Blanckenberg, JM	18	1913/14	1924
Bolton, JL	–	1924/25	1924/25
Bond, GE	1	1938/39	1938/39
Bromfield, HD	9	1961/62	1965
Budgen, EA	–	1919/20	1919/20
Buys, ID	1	1922/23	1924/25
Cameron, HB	26	1927/28	1935
Castens, HH	–	1894	1894
Cheetham, JE	24	1948/49	1955
Chevalier, GA	1	1969/70	1969/70
Coen, SK*	2	1927/28	1927/28
Commaille, JMM	12	1909/10	1927/28
Conyngham, DP*	1	1922/23	1924/25
Cripps, G	1	1891/92	1894
Crisp, RJ	9	1935	1935/36
Duminy, JP*	3	1927/28	1929
Francis, HH	2	1898/99	1898/99
Fuller, ERH	7	1952/53	1957/58
Graham, R	2	1898/99	1901
Hands, KCM	–	1924/25	1924/25
Hands, PAM	7	1913/14	1924
Hands, RHM	1	1913/14	1913/14
Hanley, MA	1	1948/49	1948/49
Hearne, F	4	1891/92	1895/96
Hearne, GAL	3	1919/20	1924

Name	M	From	To
Horwood, SE	–	1904	1904
Innes, GAS	–	1952/53	1952/53
Kotze, JJ	3	1901	1907
Kuys, F	1	1898/99	1898/99
Lewis, PT	1	1913/14	1913/14
Lundie, EB*	1	1913/14	1913/14
Macaulay, MJ*	1	1964/65	1965
Melle, MG*	7	1949/50	1952/53
Middleton, J	6	1894	1904
Mills, CH	1	1891/92	1894
Milton, WH	3	1888/89	1891/92
Morkel, DPB	16	1927/28	1931/32
Nel, JD	6	1949/50	1957/58
Norton, NO*	1	1909/10	1909/10
Nourse, AW*	45	1902/03	1924/25
O'Linn, S*	7	1960	1961/62
Ovenstone, DM	–	1947	1947
Owen-Smith, HGO	5	1929	1929
Palm, AW	1	1927/28	1927/28
Pithey, AJ	17	1956/57	1964/65
Pithey, DB*	8	1963/64	1966/67
Plimsoll, JB	1	1947	1947
Pothecary, JE	3	1960	1960
Prince, CFH*	1	1898/99	1901
Procter, MJ	7	1966/67	1969/70
Reid, A	–	1901	1901
Reid, N	1	1921/22	1921/22
Richards, AR	1	1895/96	1895/96
Richards, WHM	1	1888/89	1888/89
Robertson, JB	3	1935/36	1935/36
Routledge, TW	4	1891/92	1895/96
Rowe, GA	5	1894	1902/03
Seccull, AW*	1	1894	1895/96
Seymour, MA	7	1963/64	1969/70
Snooke, SD	1	1907	1907
Snooke, SJ	26	1906	1922/23
Steyn, SSL*	–	1931/32	1931/32
Taylor, HW*	42	1912	1931/32
Theunissen, NHCD	1	1888/89	1888/89
Twentyman Jones, PS	1	1902/03	1902/03
Van der Bijl, PGV	5	1938/39	1938/39
Van der Merwe, PL	15	1963/64	1966/67
Van Ryneveld, CB	19	1951	1957/58
Westcott, RJ	5	1953/54	1957/58
Wynne, OE	6	1948/49	1949/50

South African Cricket Union (Unofficial Matches), 1977/78–1990/91

An asterisk indicates that the player only represented South Africa (SACU) while playing for a province other than Western Province.

Name	From	To
Cullinan, DJ	1989/90	1989/90
Henry, O	1986/87	1986/87
Hobson, DL	1981/82	1983/84
Jefferies, ST	1981/82	1986/87
Kirsten, PN	1981/82	1989/90
Kuiper, AP	1981/82	1989/90
Le Roux, GS	1981/82	1986/87
Matthews, BA	1986/87	1986/87
McEwan, KS	1982/83	1986/87
McMillan, B	1986/87	1989/90
Pienaar, RF*	1985/86	1989/90
Procter, MJ*	1981/82	1983/84
Rundle, DB	1989/90	1989/90
Seeff, L	1982/83	1982/83
Simons, EO	1985/86	1985/86
Wessels, KC*[50]	1989/90	1989/90

1.1.2 Western Province Cricket Union First-Class Players, 1889/90–1990/91[51]

Name	M	From	To
Ackerman, HM	76	1970/71	1979/80
Allen, E	3	1893/94	1903/04
Allin, CR	2	1929/30	1930/31
Anderson, JH	13	1894/95	1907/08
Andrew, JC	1	1894/95	1894/95
Arnott, JG	3	1936/37	1936/37
Ashley, WH	3	1889/90	1890/91
Austen, MH	4	1987/88	1987/88
Bacchus, SFAF	9	1984/85	1984/85
Baguley, N	5	1953/54	1954/55
Bain, CA	6	1902/03	1908/09
Baker, EC	1	1956/57	1956/57
Balaskas, XC	5	1934/35	1935/36
Ballantyne, IR	2	1952/53	1952/53
Bam, I	2	1906/07	1907/08
Barlow, EJ	82	1968/69	1980/81
Barnes, IS	2	1988/89	1988/89
Battison, G	2	1929/30	1932/33
Bell, AJ	9	1925/26	1930/31
Bell, MA	1	1908/09	1908/09
Bennett, HW	2	1904/05	1909/10
Bensimon, Abel S	10	1912/13	1923/24
Bensimon, Alfred S	4	1931/32	1933/34

Name	M	From	To
Bing, F	8	1954/55	1960/61
Bisset, AVC	13	1902/03	1921/22
Bisset, EH	1	1889/90	1889/90
Bisset, M	21	1894/95	1909/10
Bissett, GF	1	1927/28	1927/28
Black, I	1	1937/38	1937/38
Blanckenberg, JM	18	1912/13	1922/23
Blanckenberg, N	11	1919/20	1926/27
Bleekers, LF	3	1989/90	1989/90
Bolton, JL	7	1921/22	1926/27
Bolus, GRM	10	1947/48	1951/52
Bond, FP	7	1910/11	1910/11
Bond, GE	25	1929/30	1938/39
Bowditch, MH	48	1964/65	1977/78
Bricknell, GA	3	1975/76	1976/77
Brinkhaus, JGB	8	1937/38	1939/40
Bromfield, HD	44	1956/57	1968/69
Brown, SV	4	1920/21	1920/21
Brown, TR	6	1963/64	1963/64
Bruce, SD	35	1971/72	1985/86
Bruyns, A	73	1965/66	1976/77
Budge, NR	27	1963/64	1972/73
Budgen, EA	11	1908/09	1919/20
Burmeister, IA	2	1947/48	1947/48
Burt, RJE	4	1934/35	1937/38
Butler, BCH	9	1966/67	1967/68
Butler, V	1	1949/50	1949/50
Buys, ID	9	1921/22	1923/24
Calder, H	3	1892/93	1894/95
Cameron, DP	2	1970/71	1973/74
Cameron, HB	1	1930/31	1930/31
Carew, AS	2	1945/46	1945/46
Carlsson, WE	4	1910/11	1910/11
Carolin, HW	9	1902/03	1907/08
Carstens, J	2	1912/13	1912/13
Castens, HH	3	1890/91	1893/94
Catt, AW	12	1965/66	1967/68
Cawood, JC	11	1970/71	1973/74
Challenor, EL	5	1895/96	1896/97
Chalmers, WR	1	1963/64	1963/64
Charnas, M	1	1958/59	1958/59
Cheetham, JE	36	1939/40	1954/55
Cheetham, JR	4	1972/73	1972/73
Chevalier, GA	41	1966/67	1973/74
Clark, RM	11	1972/73	1976/77
Clarke, TA	3	1981/82	1982/83

Name	M	From	To
Cloete, PHB	9	1936/37	1939/40
Coen, SK	9	1930/31	1931/32
Coggins, HC	2	1905/06	1905/06
Cole, JM	8	1965/66	1966/67
Colson, WWA	8	1910/11	1921/22
Commaille, JMM	31	1905/06	1923/24
Commins, JB	4	1989/90	1990/91
Commins, JE	10	1960/61	1968/69
Commins, KT	18	1951/52	1957/58
Conry, FD	23	1906/07	1923/24
Conyngham, DP	2	1930/31	1930/31
Cowper, SA	1	1907/08	1907/08
Cox, AE	2	1890/91	1890/91
Crawford, SNA	1	1930/31	1930/31
Crews, BH	4	1945/46	1947/48
Crighton, GE	3	1939/40	1939/40
Cripps, G	3	1892/93	1893/94
Crisp, RJ	18	1931/32	1935/36
Cullinan, DJ	45	1985/86	1990/91
Daniels, NP	1	1978/79	1978/79
Davidson, TM	2	1928/29	1928/29
Davies, DD	2	1903/04	1903/04
Davis, RP	4	1951/52	1952/53
Deane, J	3	1889/90	1890/91
De Klerk, TR	32	1925/26	1935/36
Delport, RF	14	1950/51	1963/64
Denne, PH	10	1971/72	1974/75
De Smidt, R	4	1912/13	1912/13
De Villiers, DI	1	1912/13	1912/13
De Villiers, PH	4	1889/90	1890/91
Difford, AN	11	1904/05	1907/08
Dimbleby, DE	5	1946/47	1947/48
Dimbleby, KG	11	1938/39	1947/48
Drummer, D	7	1960/61	1963/64
Drummer, FTM	26	1958/59	1967/68
Drummond, RA	14	1976/77	1978/79
Duff, BR	1	1889/90	1889/90
Dumbrill, JE	3	1956/57	1961/62
Duminy, JP	2	1919/20	1919/20
Du Plessis, M	4	1971/72	1973/74
During, J	9	1977/78	1982/83
During, JP	5	1907/08	1908/09
During, PB	1	1949/50	1949/50
Durr, JM	1	1921/22	1921/22
Du Toit, JD	10	1977/78	1982/83
Dyer, GD	9	1966/67	1967/68

Name	M	From	To
Eayrs, D	2	1939/40	1941/42
Eckard, LS	12	1936/37	1946/47
Elgar, AG	11	1984/85	1986/87
Emary, FE	2	1965/66	1965/66
Emburey, JE	15	1982/83	1983/84
Etlinger, TE	5	1895/96	1896/97
Evans, LLM	2	1939/40	1946/47
Fairclough, J	4	1964/65	1965/66
Farrell, JN	11	1974/75	1975/76
Farrell, RM	9	1952/53	1963/64
Fernley, DL	3	1957/58	1957/58
Ferrandi, JH	57	1949/50	1964/65
Fismer, KG	1	1941/42	1941/42
Fitzpatrick, GT	1	1890/91	1890/91
Fock, CAC	5	1902/03	1904/05
Foley, WBH	7	1937/38	1947/48
Foreman, DJ	3	1951/52	1951/52
Fouché, MR	1	1958/59	1958/59
Fox, JSM	8	1954/55	1960/61
Fox, LC	14	1921/22	1927/28
Francis, HH	3	1895/96	1902/03
Francis, MG	4	1934/35	1934/35
Frost, CE	1	1986/87	1986/87
Fuller, ERH	27	1950/51	1957/58
Fuller, HH	4	1920/21	1920/21
Gardiner, IB	9	1926/27	1928/29
Gentry, JD	5	1926/27	1926/27
Georgeu, G	40	1931/32	1949/50
Gibbs, HH	3	1990/91	1990/91
Gie, CA	11	1971/72	1973/74
Giles, MJ	9	1965/66	1971/72
Gill, RJ	4	1892/93	1896/97
Glantz, A	39	1929/30	1939/40
Godfrey, FA	4	1923/24	1926/27
Goldstein, FS	20	1971/72	1977/78
Gooch, GA	16	1982/83	1983/84
Gordon, ES	7	1978/79	1983/84
Goulden, IF	13	1925/26	1930/31
Graaff, D	2	1932/33	1932/33
Graham, DK	1	1945/46	1945/46
Graham, JM	1	1960/61	1960/61
Graham, MD	1	1889/90	1889/90
Graham, R	1	1897/98	1897/98
Graham, TL	2	1889/90	1889/90
Gronn, MJM	1	1951/52	1951/52
Groves, MGM	1	1960/61	1960/61

Name	M	From	To
Halvorsen, E	2	1980/81	1980/81
Hands, KCM	28	1921/22	1930/31
Hands, PAM	24	1906/07	1926/27
Hands, RHM	5	1912/13	1913/14
Hanley, MA	26	1946/47	1953/54
Hardy, JJE	10	1987/88	1990/91
Hearne, F	12	1889/90	1903/04
Hearne, GAL	23	1910/11	1926/27
Heldsinger, KMS	9	1956/57	1960/61
Henry, O	27	1978/79	1983/84
Hickley, CS	2	1890/91	1890/91
Hobson, AL	2	1990/91	1990/91
Hobson, DL	94	1971/72	1984/85
Hobson, TEC	2	1906/07	1906/07
Hodgson, AS	6	1967/68	1967/68
Hodgson, DGM	6	1961/62	1965/66
Holmes, TE	10	1906/07	1910/11
Hopley, FJV	1	1909/10	1909/10
Horwood, SE	12	1903/04	1909/10
Howell, HC	2	1949/50	1954/55
Hughes, E	1	1896/97	1896/97
Hughes, RJ	1	1897/98	1897/98
Hugo, SG	16	1967/68	1973/74
Hutchinson, CH	3	1931/32	1931/32
Impey, LLH	5	1946/47	1948/49
Innes, GAS	55	1950/51	1962/63
Jackman, RD	10	1971/72	1971/72
Jackson, DC	8	1908/09	1910/11
Jackson, KC	8	1990/91	1990/91
Jaffer, PD	10	1949/50	1953/54
Jefferies, ST	61	1978/79	1989/90
Johnson, AA	1	1989/90	1989/90
Jones, SA	29	1974/75	1980/81
Jordaan, HB	7	1934/35	1937/38
Keen, AD	13	1937/38	1949/50
Keith, GL	2	1968/69	1968/69
Kennedy, AC	6	1933/34	1934/35
Kerby, JC	12	1957/58	1963/64
Kiel, S	14	1939/40	1946/47
Kirsten, G	22	1988/89	1990/91
Kirsten, PN	133	1973/74	1989/90
Klette, JE	2	1967/68	1967/68
Kossuth, FH	3	1929/30	1929/30
Kotze, JJ	18	1903/04	1910/11
Kuiper, AP	87	1978/79	1990/91
Kuys, F	5	1896/97	1897/98

Name	M	From	To
Lamb, AJ[52]	61	1972/73	1981/82
Lange, T	1	1950/51	1950/51
Larkin, GM	3	1934/35	1937/38
Lawrenson, RR	2	1980/81	1981/82
Lazard, TN	22	1986/87	1989/90
Lazarus, RH	2	1925/26	1925/26
Lear, PN	7	1959/60	1965/66
Lee, JM	2	1957/58	1959/60
Le Roux, D	1	1965/66	1965/66
Le Roux, GS	83	1975/76	1988/89
Lewis, PT	6	1907/08	1913/14
Liddle, JR	8	1955/56	1956/57
Little, PA	8	1932/33	1935/36
Lofthouse, R	5	1941/42	1947/48
Lohmann, GA	5	1894/95	1896/97
Lotter, NB	3	1971/72	1975/76
Louw, DA	17	1955/56	1966/67
Lovegrove, AR	9	1923/24	1926/27
Lovell, GGS	3	1950/51	1952/53
Luck, AA	2	1947/48	1947/48
Lundie, EB	2	1909/10	1910/11
Luyt, FP	4	1908/09	1910/11
Luyt, RR	19	1906/07	1922/23
Macaulay, MJ	4	1960/61	1960/61
MacDonald, RR	8	1955/56	1957/58
MacRae, ASV	6	1923/24	1926/27
Mahoney, JE	1	1981/82	1981/82
Maile, JBR	23	1955/56	1960/61
Mainon, C	2	1893/94	1894/95
Manning, LM	28	1930/31	1939/40
Mars, WH	2	1912/13	1913/14
Marshall, AW	29	1941/42	1956/57
Martin, FC	18	1929/30	1932/33
Martin, PW	6	1989/90	1990/91
Matthews, BA	9	1984/85	1986/87
Matthews, CR	27	1987/88	1990/91
McAdam, SJ	4	1972/73	1973/74
McAdam, WJ	12	1966/67	1968/69
McCay, DLC	10	1966/67	1973/74
McClement, AJ	3	1989/90	1990/91
McCulloch, VT	21	1960/61	1966/67
McEwan, KS	37	1981/82	1986/87
McMeeking, DP	1	1965/66	1965/66
McMillan, BM	17	1989/90	1990/91
McMorrow, BA	1	1949/50	1949/50
Meeding, BK	1	1964/65	1964/65

Name	M	From	To
Melle, BGV	9	1908/09	1910/11
Melle, MG	2	1953/54	1953/54
Mentis, MJ	2	1975/76	1975/76
Middleton, IE	1	1960/61	1960/61
Middleton, J	13	1890/91	1903/04
Middleton, RE	3	1937/38	1945/46
Middleton, T	4	1924/25	1926/27
Millard, DES	4	1951/52	1954/55
Miller, HDS	5	1962/63	1962/63
Mills, CH	4	1892/93	1894/95
Milton, WH	3	1889/90	1890/91
Minnaar, CWR	1	1913/14	1913/14
Minnaar, MB	13	1985/86	1986/87
Moore, TE	1	1895/96	1895/96
Morby-Smith, L	16	1963/64	1966/67
Morgan, HW	13	1927/28	1933/34
Morkel, DPB	23	1924/25	1929/30
Morkel, RKB	5	1927/28	1930/31
Morris, JD	8	1961/62	1962/63
Morris, RET	61	1967/68	1978/79
Morris, SV	4	1958/59	1959/60
Muntingh, E	1	1981/82	1981/82
Muzzell, RK	17	1964/65	1967/68
Myles, HF	2	1930/31	1930/31
Napier, GL	3	1929/30	1935/36
Nel, JD	28	1947/48	1960/61
Nel, MJ	16	1974/75	1981/82
Newton-Thompson, JO	1	1948/49	1948/49
Nicholson, PS	7	1952/53	1953/54
Nieuwoudt, AB	27	1972/73	1978/79
Nolte, JE	3	1988/89	1989/90
Norman, D	10	1984/85	1985/86
Norton, NO	1	1902/03	1902/03
Nourse, AW	24	1927/28	1935/36
O'Grady, JM	1	1946/47	1946/47
O'Linn, S	2	1945/46	1946/47
Ovenstone, DM	9	1946/47	1947/48
Owen-Smith, HGO	14	1927/28	1949/50
Paine, AI	4	1896/97	1896/97
Palm, AW	37	1921/22	1933/34
Parker, AC	5	1970/71	1970/71
Pauling, NC	2	1892/93	1892/93
Paull, GB	5	1933/34	1939/40
Payne, DG	1	1989/90	1989/90
Payne, IA	4	1968/69	1974/75
Peters, AD	5	1931/32	1931/32

Name	M	From	To
Pfaff, BD	18	1952/53	1957/58
Pfaff, L	1	1926/27	1926/27
Pfister, CA	1	1928/29	1928/29
Pfuhl, GP	88	1967/68	1979/80
Pickup, J	6	1936/37	1937/38
Pienaar, RF	33	1981/82	1984/85
Pithey, AJ	12	1955/56	1957/58
Pithey, DB	1	1957/58	1957/58
Plimsoll, JB	18	1939/40	1947/48
Pothecary, JE	33	1954/55	1964/65
Price, D	14	1933/34	1939/40
Prince, CFH	8	1894/95	1904/05
Pringle, MW	15	1989/90	1990/91
Pritchard, JA	5	1902/03	1903/04
Procter, MJ	5	1969/70	1969/70
Rail, RA	1	1913/14	1913/14
Ralph, ARM	33	1931/32	1945/46
Rayner, PH	25	1982/83	1985/86
Reddick, TB	4	1950/51	1950/51
Rees, DW	1	1949/50	1949/50
Reid, A	20	1896/97	1908/09
Reid, ABJ	15	1939/40	1950/51
Reid, F	6	1910/11	1923/24
Reid, N	12	1920/21	1923/24
Reid-Ross, LJ	1	1975/76	1975/76
Richards, AR	8	1889/90	1895/96
Richards, J	2	1889/90	1889/90
Richardson, MHH	12	1958/59	1960/61
Richardson, RP	1	1984/85	1984/85
Robertson, JB	20	1931/32	1936/37
Rookledge, QJ	3	1971/72	1971/72
Roos, AC	1	1970/71	1970/71
Roscoe, BM-K	7	1937/38	1938/39
Ross, WC	3	1934/35	1939/40
Routledge, TW	1	1889/90	1889/90
Rowe, GA	15	1893/94	1906/07
Roy, HNP	14	1952/53	1956/57
Rundle, DB	34	1987/88	1990/91
Rush, EDB	1	1924/25	1924/25
Rush, WRG	4	1923/24	1923/24
Rushmere, CG	2	1957/58	1960/61
Rushmere, JW	8	1960/61	1962/63
Ryall, RJ	80	1980/81	1990/91
Seccull, AW	1	1893/94	1893/94
Seeff, L	94	1978/79	1990/91
Serrurier, LR	10	1927/28	1929/30

Name	M	From	To
Sewell, BW	1	1945/46	1945/46
Seymour, MA	19	1960/61	1969/70
Seymour, RA	1	1975/76	1975/76
Short, WH	12	1905/06	1913/14
Siedle, JR	5	1955/56	1956/57
Sierra, JP	1	1947/48	1947/48
Simons, EO	35	1983/84	1990/91
Smith, F	11	1912/13	1921/22
Snooke, SD	20	1904/05	1910/11
Snooke, SJ	11	1903/04	1907/08
Snyman, OJA	7	1972/73	1972/73
Spencer-Young, R	8	1962/63	1963/64
Steensma, S	5	1925/26	1932/33
Stephen, GW	4	1904/05	1910/11
Stephen, WM	9	1922/23	1926/27
Stephens, CG	21	1968/69	1971/72
Stephenson, EH	1	1903/04	1903/04
Stewart, JH	6	1902/03	1904/05
Steyn, GE	5	1957/58	1957/58
Steyn, RS	10	1965/66	1966/67
Steyn, SSL	30	1924/25	1937/38
Steytler, ES	4	1889/90	1892/93
Stoke, R	1	1930/31	1930/31
Swart, PD	94	1967/68	1980/81
Tasker, GJH	1	1953/54	1953/54
Tattersall, K	16	1965/66	1969/70
Taylor, GP	4	1912/13	1920/21
Taylor, HW	1	1935/36	1935/36
Taylor, WL	8	1958/59	1961/62
Theunissen, NHCD	2	1889/90	1889/90
Thomas, CH	5	1921/22	1922/23
Thwaits, SA	22	1949/50	1954/55
Touzel, FB	5	1990/91	1990/91
Touzel, FG	1	1968/69	1968/69
Treadaway, LG	5	1947/48	1957/58
Trickett, WS	1	1905/06	1905/06
Tucker, E	2	1936/37	1936/37
Tulleken, A	2	1960/61	1960/61
Turner, DR	2	1977/78	1977/78
Turner, GJ	4	1984/85	1986/87
Twentyman Jones, PS	8	1897/98	1905/06
Valentine, RC	2	1947/48	1947/48
Van der Bijl, PGV	27	1925/26	1939/40
Van der Bijl, V	2	1947/48	1947/48
Van der Bijl, VA	2	1892/93	1892/93
Van der Bijl, VAW	6	1890/91	1895/96

Name	M	From	To
Van der Merwe, PL	35	1958/59	1965/66
Van der Poel, CS	1	1923/24	1923/24
Van der Spuy, TMH	22	1935/36	1946/47
Van Niekerk, AP	15	1968/69	1974/75
Van Ryneveld, CB	31	1946/47	1962/63
Veal, VG	25	1920/21	1933/34
Viljoen, FDJ	4	1922/23	1923/24
Vincent, AJS	1	1957/58	1957/58
Virgin, RT	2	1972/73	1972/73
Voss, MF	3	1990/91	1990/91
Walker, PM	3	1962/63	1962/63
Wallace, B	14	1930/31	1937/38
Watson, VUT	4	1923/24	1924/25
Watt, HH	6	1933/34	1934/35
Weber, AC	2	1903/04	1904/05
Weeden, CC	1	1975/76	1975/76
Weinstein, LJ	17	1959/60	1965/66
Wells, CM	2	1984/85	1984/85
Wessels, KC	8	1976/77	1976/77
Westcott, RJ	46	1949/50	1961/62
White, JE	4	1962/63	1966/67
Whitefield, DWH	11	1960/61	1964/65
Whitehead, JG	26	1904/05	1920/21
Whiteing, LCG	3	1935/36	1946/47
Whitfield, AR	1	1960/61	1960/61
Whittingdale, R	1	1978/79	1978/79
Wightman, RW	1	1954/55	1954/55
Wiley, JWE	2	1947/48	1947/48
Wiley, WGA	4	1952/53	1953/54
Wilson, WD	4	1948/49	1950/51
Witte, EV	23	1946/47	1954/55
Wood, AF	2	1921/22	1925/26
Woolmer, RA	3	1980/81	1980/81
Wrentmore, CGC	4	1926/27	1934/35
Wrentmore, GM	5	1910/11	1910/11
Wynne, OE	12	1947/48	1958/59
Yeoman, WF	11	1908/09	1912/13
Young, S	1	1889/90	1889/90

Western Province' Players in Unofficial Matches against English Touring Teams, 1888/89–1895/96[53]

The history books record that the first three English touring teams to South Africa played matches against a Western Province XXII (22) in 1888/89, against a Western Province XVIII (18) and a Western Province XV (15) in 1891/92, and against a Western Province XV (15) in 1895/96. The first three of these matches lasted three days or more and the last one was a two-day match. They have not been declared first-class because the teams consisted of more than eleven players and, in the first instance, no provincial cricket union existed yet. The names of the cricketers who played in these unofficial games are listed below to show the continuity with the later WPCU and Currie Cup teams which were given first-class status (even though one of these games was by a club and others were only two-day matches). To ensure historical accuracy, '(Unofficial)' is added to these names and the scorecards listed below and they are not included in the consolidated list of the 12 boards in Part III below. Names with asterisks next to them also appear in the list of first-class players above.

Allen, E*	1891/92
Anderson, JH*	1895/96
Ashley, WH*	1888/89, 1891/92
Bathurst, Major [x]	1888/89
Bisset, EH*	1888/89
Bisset, M*	1891/92, 1895/96
Boyle, Lieutenant [x]	1891/92
Budler, E	1888/89
Calder, H*	1891/92
Castens, HH*	1891/92
Cox, AE*	1888/89
Cripps, G*	1891/92
Deane, J*	1888/89 (His surname appears as Dean in Luckin)
Ellis, Drummer [x]	1891/92
Forde, H	1888/89
Forde, J	1888/89
Francis, HH*	1895/96
Halkett, A	1888/89
Hearne, F*	1891/92, 1895/96
Hickley, CS*	1891/92
Middleton, J*	1891/92, 1895/96
Mills, CH*	1891/92
Milton, WH*	1888/89, 1891/92, 1895/96
Pemberton, GP	1891/92
Prince, CFH*	1895/96
Reid, A*	1895/96
Reid, WO	1888/89
Richards, AR*	1891/92, 1895/96
Richards, J*	1888/89
Richards, WHM	1888/89, 1891/92
Risk, Sergeant-Major [x]	1888/89
Robb, F	1888/89

Name		
Routledge, TW*	1891/92	
Rowe, GA*	1895/96	
Smith, Gunner [x]	1888/89	
Smith, [x]	1895/96	
Smuts, LB	1895/96	
Steyler, ES*	1888/89, 1891/92	
Stradling, EJ	1888/89	
Street, [x]	1895/96	
Theunissen, NHCD*	1888/89	
Van der Bijl, VA*	1891/92	
Van der Bijl, VAW*	1891/92, 1895/96	
Van Reenen, GB	1888/89	
Vaughan, CR	1888/89	
Vintcent, CH	1891/92	
Willoughby, J	1895/96	
Wright, Captain [x]	1891/92	
Young, S*	1888/89	

1.1.3 Western Province Cricket Union List A, Limited-Overs Players, 1969/70–1990/9[54]

Name	M	From	To
Ackerman, HM	20	1970/71	1979/80
Austen, MH	6	1987/88	1987/88
Bacchus, SFAF	8	1984/85	1984/85
Barlow, EJ	25	1969/70	1980/81
Bleekers, LF	15	1988/89	1989/90
Bowditch, MH	6	1970/71	1973/74
Bridgens, KJ	2	1986/87	1986/87
Bruce, J	1	1969/70	1969/70
Bruce, SD	20	1974/75	1985/86
Bruyns, A	16	1969/70	1976/77
Budge, NR	5	1969/70	1972/73
Cameron, DP	2	1970/71	1973/74
Cawood, JC	4	1970/71	1972/73
Cheetham, JR	1	1972/73	1972/73
Chevalier, GA	9	1969/70	1972/73
Clark, RM	5	1972/73	1982/83
Clarke, TA	5	1981/82	1984/85
Commins, JB	18	1987/88	1990/91
Cullinan, DJ	75	1984/85	1990/91
Daniels, NP	1	1977/78	1977/78
Denne, PH	2	1969/70	1969/70
Drummond, RA	2	1976/77	1978/79
Du Plessis, JH	2	1988/89	1988/89
Du Plessis, M	1	1973/74	1973/74
During, J	14	1979/80	1986/87
Du Toit, JD	10	1978/79	1982/83
Elgar, AG	18	1984/85	1986/87

Name	M	From	To
Emburey, JE	20	1982/83	1983/84
Fairclough, J	1	1971/72	1971/72
Farrell, JN	9	1975/76	1976/77
Fletcher, DAG	1	1984/85	1984/85
Gibbs, HH	1	1990/91	1990/91
Gie, CA	3	1972/73	1973/74
Giles, MJ	1	1971/72	1971/72
Goldstein, FS	10	1971/72	1975/76
Gooch, GA	21	1982/83	1983/84
Gordon, ES	2	1983/84	1983/84
Green, AD	1	1979/80	1979/80
Hardy, JJE	39	1987/88	1990/91
Henry, O	21	1978/79	1983/84
Hobson, DL	17	1974/75	1984/85
Hodgson, DGM	1	1970/71	1970/71
Hugo, SG	5	1969/70	1972/73
Igglesden, AP	4	1987/88	1988/89
Jackman, RD	1	1971/72	1971/72
Jackson, KC	11	1990/91	1990/91
Jefferies, ST	92	1980/81	1990/91
Johnson, AA	2	1989/90	1989/90
Jones, SA	7	1974/75	1979/80
Kirsten, G	26	1988/89	1990/91
Kirsten, PN	121	1973/74	1989/90
Klette, JE	2	1969/70	1969/70
Kuiper, AP	121	1979/80	1990/91
Lamb, AJ	20	1972/73	1981/82
Lawrenson, RR	1	1980/81	1980/81
Lazard, TN	28	1983/84	1989/90
Le Roux, GS	83	1975/76	1988/89
Louw, DA	1	1969/70	1969/70
Martin, PW	6	1989/90	1990/91
Matthews, BA	18	1985/86	1987/88
Matthews, CR	43	1987/88	1990/91
McAdam, SJ	1	1972/73	1972/73
McEwan, KS	42	1981/82	1986/87
McMillan, BM	31	1989/90	1990/91
Mentis, MJ	1	1975/76	1975/76
Minnaar, MB	3	1985/86	1985/86
Morris, RET	14	1972/73	1978/79
Muntingh, E	1	1981/82	1981/82
Nel, MJ	1	1981/82	1981/82
Nieuwoudt, AB	7	1972/73	1979/80
Nolte, JE	15	1988/89	1989/90
Norman, D	19	1984/85	1985/86

Name	M	From	To
Pfuhl, GP	21	1969/70	1979/80
Pienaar, RF	35	1981/82	1985/86
Pringle, MW	21	1989/90	1990/91
Procter, MJ	2	1969/70	1969/70
Rayment, PA	3	1990/91	1990/91
Rayner, PH	28	1982/83	1985/86
Richardson, RP	1	1988/89	1988/89
Rundle, DB	55	1984/85	1990/91
Ryall, RJ	99	1979/80	1990/91
Seeff, J	1	1981/82	1981/82
Seeff, L	106	1978/79	1990/91
Seymour, MA	1	1969/70	1969/70
Simons, EO	70	1983/84	1990/91
Snyman, OJA	1	1972/73	1972/73
Stephens, CG	7	1969/70	1971/72
Swart, PD	34	1969/70	1984/85
Thompson, PM	1	1980/81	1980/81
Tullis, GD	1	1988/89	1988/89
Turner, DR	1	1977/78	1977/78
Turner, GJ	3	1984/85	1986/87
Van der Merwe, WM	2	1985/86	1986/87
Van Niekerk, AP	7	1969/70	1972/73
Voss, MF	4	1990/91	1990/91
Wells, CM	1	1984/85	1984/85
Wessels, KC	2	1976/77	1976/77
Wingreen, IM	2	1984/85	1984/85

1.1.4 Western Province Cricket Union, Premier League Winners, 1895/96–1990/91[55]

Season	Winners
1893/94	Cape Town CC
1894/95	Unfinished
1895/96	Cape Town CC
1896/97	Cape Town CC
1897/98	Cape Town CC
1898/99	Cape Town CC
1899/1900	Cape Town CC
1900/01	Cape Town CC
1901/02	Cape Town CC
1902/03	Alma CC
1903/04	Cape Town CC
1904/05	Western Province CC
1905/06	Cape Town CC
1906/07	Cape Town CC
1907/08	Western Province CC
1908/09	Green Point CC

Season	Winners
1909/10	Green Point CC
1910/11	Green Point CC
1911/12	Cape Town CC
1912/13	Western Province CC
1913/14	Western Province CC
1914/15	Alma CC
1915/16	*War*
1916/17	*War*
1917/18	*War*
1918/19	*War*
1919/20	Green Point CC
1920/21	Claremont CC / Green Point CC
1921/22	Western Province CC
1922/23	Western Province CC
1923/24	Alma CC / Western Province CC
1924/25	Claremont CC
1925/26	Western Province CC
1926/27	Western Province CC
1927/28	Somerset West CC
1928/29	Western Province CC
1929/30	Somerset West CC
1930/31	Green Point CC
1931/32	Green Point CC
1932/33	Green Point CC
1933/34	Green Point CC A / Western Province CC
1934/35	Technical College CC
1935/36	Green Point A CC
1936/37	Green Point CC
1937/38	Western Province CC
1938/39	Green Point CC
1939/40	Western Province CC
1940/41	Green Point CC
1941/42	University of Cape Town CC
1942/43	Green Point CC
1943/44	Alma CC
1944/45	Western Province CC
1945/46	Western Province CC
1946/47	Green Point A CC
1947/48	University of Cape Town CC
1948/49	Western Province A CC
1949/50	Alma CC
1950/51	Western Province A CC
1951/52	Western Province A CC
1952/53	Cape Town CC
1953/54	Cape Town CC
1954/55	Western Province A CC

Season	Winners
1955/56	Alma CC
1956/57	Claremont CC
1957/58	Western Province A CC
1958/59	Alma CC
1959/60	University of Cape Town CC
1960/61	University of Cape Town CC
1961/62	Alma CC
1962/63	Pinelands CC
1963/64	Claremont CC
1964/65	University of Cape Town CC
1965/66	Cape Technical College CC
1966/67	Claremont CC
1967/68	Cape Technical College CC
1968/69	Cape Town CC
1969/70	University of Stellenbosch CC
1970/71	Cape Technical College CC
1971/72	Cape Technical College CC
1972/73	Claremont CC
1973/74	Cape Technical College CC
1974/75	Claremont CC
1975/76	Cape College for Advanced Technical Education CC
1976/77	Cape College for Advanced Technical Education CC
1977/78	University of Cape Town CC
1978/79	University of Stellenbosch CC
1979/80	Alma Marist CC
1980/81	Western Province CC
1981/82	Cape Town CC
1982/83	Claremont VOB
1983/84	Techs Mutual
1984/85	Cape Town CC
1985/86	Techs Mutual
1986/87	Cape Town CC
1987/88	Cape Town CC
1988/89	University of Cape Town CC
1989/90	University of Cape Town CC
1990/91	Claremont CC

1.1.5 Western Province Cricket Union Trophies[56]

Currie Cup, 1889/90–1990/91 (First-Class)

Season	Winners
1889/90	Transvaal
1890/91	Kimberley
1892/93	*Western Province*
1893/94	*Western Province*
1894/95	Transvaal
1896/97	*Western Province*
1897/98	*Western Province*
1902/03	Transvaal
1903/04	Transvaal
1904/05	Transvaal
1906/07	Transvaal
1908/09	*Western Province*
1910/11	Natal
1912/13	Natal
1920/21	*Western Province*
1921/22	Transvaal / Natal / *Western Province (tied)*
1923/24	Transvaal
1925/26	Transvaal
1926/27	Transvaal
1929/30	Transvaal
1931/32	*Western Province*
1933/34	Natal
1934/35	Transvaal
1936/37	Natal
1937/38	Natal / Transvaal (tied)
1946/47	Natal
1947/48	Natal
1950/51	Transvaal
1951/52	Natal
1952/53	*Western Province*
1954/55	Natal
1955/56	*Western Province*
1958/59	Transvaal
1959/60	Natal
1960/61	Natal
1962/63	Natal
1963/64	Natal
1965/66	Natal / Transvaal (tied)
1966/67	Natal (WP in Currie Cup B Section)
1967/68	Natal (WP in Currie Cup B Section)
1968/69	Transvaal (WP in Currie Cup B Section)
1969/70	Transvaal / *Western Province (tied)*
1970/71	Transvaal

Season	Winners
1971/72	Transvaal
1972/73	Transvaal
1973/74	Natal
1974/75	*Western Province*
1975/76	Natal
1976/77	Natal
1977/78	*Western Province*
1978/79	Transvaal
1979/80	Transvaal
1980/81	Natal
1981/82	*Western Province*
1982/83	Transvaal
1983/84	Transvaal
1984/85	Transvaal
1985/86	*Western Province*
1986/87	Transvaal
1987/88	Transvaal
1988/89	Eastern Province
1989/90	Eastern Province / *Western Province (tied)*
1990/91	*Western Province*

Currie Cup B Section (First-Class)

Season	Winners
1966/67	NE Transvaal
1967/68	Rhodesia
1968/69	*Western Province*

Gillette Cup (Limited Overs)

Season	Winners	Runners-up	Margin of victory
1969/70	*Western Province*	Natal	2 runs
1970/71	*Western Province*	Transvaal	3 wickets
1971/72	Eastern Province	Natal	31 runs
1972/73	*Western Province*	Eastern Province	7 wickets
1973/74	Transvaal	Natal	10 runs
1974/75	Natal	Western Province	31 runs
1975/76	Eastern Province	Western Province	128 runs
1976/77	Natal	Eastern Province	7 wickets

Datsun Shield (Limited Overs)

Season	Winners	Runners-up	Margin of victory
1977/78	Rhodesia	Eastern Province	runs/wkts ratio
1978/79	Transvaal	Natal	76 runs
1979/80	Transvaal	Western Province	7 wickets
1980/81	Transvaal	Eastern Province	7 wickets
1981/82	*Western Province*	Natal	2 runs
1982/83	Transvaal	Western Province	109 runs

Nissan Shield (Limited Overs)

Season	Winners	Runners-up	Margin of victory
1983/84	Transvaal	Western Province	89 runs
1984/85	Transvaal	Western Province	9 wickets
1985/86	Transvaal	Western Province	7 wickets
1986/87	Natal	Transvaal	faster scoring rate
1987/88	Eastern Province	Northern Transvaal	7 wickets
1988/89	*Western Province*	Transvaal	2–0 (best of three)
1989/90	Eastern Province	Northern Transvaal	2–0 (best of three)
1990/91	Transvaal	Eastern Province	7 wickets

Matches in the above competitions were contested over 60 overs per side from 1969/70 to 1980/81 and 55 overs per side from 1981/82 to 1990/91, except for 1986/87 when matches were contested over 50 overs per side.

Benson & Hedges Series (Limited Overs)

Season	Winners	Runners-up	Margin of victory
1981/82	Transvaal	Natal	3 wickets
1982/83	Transvaal	Western Province	6 wickets
1983/84	Natal	Eastern Province	7 wickets
1984/85	Transvaal	Northern Transvaal	7 wickets
1985/86	*Western Province*	Northern Transvaal	12 runs
1986/87	*Western Province*	Transvaal	41 runs
1987/88	*Western Province*	Transvaal	5 wickets
1988/89	Orange Free State	Western Province	61 runs
1989/90	Eastern Province	Natal	1 wicket
1990/91	*Western Province*	Natal	6 wickets

Matches were contested over 45 overs per side, except for 1981/82 when matches were contested over 50 overs per side.

1.1.6 Western Province Cricket Union Scores, 1889/90–1990/91 (First-Class)[57]

Western Province XXII beat England by 17 runs, 21–23 December 1888, Cape Town (Unofficial)[58]
WP 137 (WH Milton 36, CR Vaughan 22, WH Richards 16; J Briggs 9/52, [x] Fothergill 8/31) and 138 (WH Milton 40, A Halkett 13, WO Reid 13*; J Briggs 14/84)
Eng 135 ([x] Abel 38, [x] Wood 30*, JH Roberts 20, N Theunissen 5/46, WH Milton 2/16, WH Ashley 2/61) and 123 ([x] Read 44, [x] Abel 26; N Theunissen 6/55, WH Ashley 3/47)

Natal beat Western Province Cricket Club by 1 wicket, 6–7 January 1890, Cape Town (Later declared official WPCU first-class match)
WP 85 (GA Kempis 7/33) and 157 (F Hearne 58, NHCD Theunissen 49; PF Madden 6/56, GA Kempis 3/76)
Ntl 124 (DC Davey 33; PH de Villiers 4/47, NHCD Theunissen 5/55) and 119/9 (RP Spurway 34; NHCD Theunissen 6/53)

Cape Town Clubs beat Natal by 3 wickets, 8–9 January 1890, Cape Town (Later declared official WPCU first-class match)
Ntl 125 (CT Stuart 35*; WH Ashley 6/40) and 98 (CT Stuart 47; NHCD Theunissen 7/41)
WP 192 (F Hearne 53, TW Routledge 33, WH Milton 47; GA Kempis 3/73, SB Cheetham 3/10) and 33/7 (GA Kempis 5/20)

Western Province beat Eastern Province by an innings and 145 runs, 26–27 December 1890, Cape Town
EP 160 (BS Wimble 37, DC Parkin 63*; PH de Villiers 5/50) and 104 (BS Wimble 37; WH Ashley 4/21, PH de Villiers 4/29)
WP 409 (AE Cox 56, HH Castens 165, CS Hickley 45; DC Parkin 3/113, DG Proudfoot 3/64)

Western Province beat Griqualand West by 83 runs, 1–3 January 1891, Cape Town
WP 111 (AE Cooper 4/37, AWP Walshe 5/18) and 236 (AE Cox 48, J Deane 31, F Hearne 55, PH de Villiers 51; GK Glover 4/60, CE Finlason 3/50)
GW 139 (CE Finlason 46; VAW van der Bijl 6/56, J Middleton 3/43) and 125 (VAW van der Bijl 3/36, F Hearne 3/41)

Western Province XVIII drew with England, 19–22 December 1891, Cape Town (Unofficial)[59]
Eng 200 (W Chatterton 83, GG Hearne 34* WW Read 22; V van der Bijl 4/49, GP Pemberton 3/43, F Hearne 2/34) and 146/5 dec (W Chatterton 47, WL Murdoch 45*; M Bissett 4/60, F Hearne 1/6)
WP XVIII 145 (V van der Bijl 30, F Hearne 21, H Calder 18; [x] Ferris 6/19, [x] Martin 6/19, JT Hearne 3/48) and 127/6 (HH Castens 45*, T Routledge 26, H Calder 16; A Hearn 3/4, [x] Ferris 2/25)

England beat Western Province XV by nine wickets, 13–16 March 1892, Cape Town (Unofficial)[60]
WP XV 144 (G Cripps 32, F Hearne 23, WH Milton 18; JT Hearne 5/77, A Hearne 4/14, [x] Ferris 4/49) and 107 (A Richards 36, G Cripps 22, C Mills 17; AD Pougher 8/21, A Hearne 3/14)
Eng 204 (W Chatterton 77, WW Read 49, A Hearne 18; C Mills 6/60, WH Ashley 2/38, CH Vincent 2/64) and 48/1 (A Hearne 20*; WH Ashley 1/14)

Western Province beat Transvaal by 91 runs, 15–17 November 1892, Kimberley
WP 235 (F Hearne 102, RJ Gill 32; H Tudhope 3/65) and 221 (AR Richards 47, CH Mills 31, VAW van der Bijl 61; JH Sinclair 5/90, H Tudhope 3/68)
Tvl 230 (JH Sinclair 37, TW Routledge 66, FG Klinck 33, WO Reid 33; CH Mills 3/49, J Middleton 3/47) and 135 (EA Halliwell 36; CH Mills 5/50)

Western Province beat Griqualand West by 109 runs, 21–24 November 1892, Kimberley
WP 266 (F Hearne 96, G Cripps 31; GK Glover 3/82, D Lloyd 3/49) and 265 (G Cripps 102, VA van der Bijl 35*; GK Glover 5/94)
GW 292 (JM Powell 36, AWP Walshe 88, GK Glover 78; CH Mills 5/84) and 130 (CSE Rutherfoord 40; CH Mills 4/37, F Hearne 5/47)

Western Province beat Natal by an innings and 60 runs, 24–26 March 1894, Cape Town
WP 338 (AR Richards 108, AW Seccull 43, HH Castens 61; LG Robinson 5/95)
Ntl 154 (HM Taberer 35; CH Mills 4/57, GA Rowe 4/48) and 124 (LG Robinson 52; J Middleton 3/42, AW Seccull 6/48)

Transvaal beat Western Province by 58 runs, 18–22 April 1895, Durban
Tvl 134 (EA Halliwell 45; GA Lohmann 7/72) and 175 (AW Seccull 64, AE Ochse 41, EA Halliwell 36; GA Rowe 4/59, CH Mills 5/36)
WP 160 (H Calder 40*, J Middleton 32; JH Sinclair 3/52, JT Hings 3/47) and 91 (JH Sinclair 7/40)

Western Province XV beat England by 74 runs, 26–27 December 1895, Cape Town (Unofficial)[61]
WP XV 115 (F Hearne 19, [x] Smith 19, [x] Street 13; G Loughman 7/17, [x] Fry 5/31, HRB Davenport 2/23) and 130 (WH Milton 23, [x] Street 21, [x] Smith 20, HH Francis 17; G Loughman 7/43, [x] Fry 5/51)
Eng 79 (HRB Davenport 29, C Heseltine 16; J Middleton 7/50, G Rowe 2/23) and 92 (SJM Woods 45, [x] Hayward 17; [x] Willoughby 6/15, [x] Smith 3/22)

Match drawn between England and Western Province, 17–19 March 1896, Cape Town
Eng 224 (TW Hayward 83, CW Wright 68; J Middleton 7/85) and 168/9 (SMJ Woods 45; J Middleton 3/63, GA Rowe 3/56)
WP 122 (AR Richards 58; GA Lohmann 6/48, AJL Hill 3/29)

Western Province beat Eastern Province by an innings and 7 runs, 13–15 March 1897, Johannesburg
WP 315 (CFH Prince 55, TE Etlinger 85, EL Challenor 76, JH Anderson 38; E Tonks 3/46, H Calder 3/28)
EP 135 (GA Rowe 3/71, GA Lohmann 4/49) and 173 (DJ Daly 45; GA Lohmann 4/55)

Western Province beat Griqualand West by an innings and 338 runs, 16–17 March 1897, Johannesburg
GW 80 (AW Powell 31; GA Rowe 5/33, GA Lohmann 4/44) and 65 (GA Rowe 5/15, GA Lohmann 5/44)
WP 483 (AI Paine 220, TE Etlinger 111, M Bisset 58; C Glover 6/122)

Western Province beat Natal by 136 runs, 19–23 March 1897, Johannesburg
WP 185 (EL Challenor 46, JH Anderson 38*; PF Madden 4/60, CB Llewellyn 5/76) and 174 (PF Madden 3/58, CB Llewellyn 4/52, CFW Hime 3/28)
Ntl 94 (GA Rowe 6/43, GA Lohmann 3/42) and 129 (AH Hime 40; GA Rowe 4/60, GA Lohmann 4/26)

Western Province beat Transvaal by 72 runs, 24–27 March 1897, Johannesburg
WP 308 (F Kuys 31, M Bisset 124*, JH Anderson 61; AE Cooper 8/80) and 173 (EL Challenor 34, GA Lohmann 44; AE Cooper 3/56, AW Seccull 3/46, JH Sinclair 4/66)
Tvl 311 (AB Tancred 39, JH Sinclair 78, CJE Smith 70, LJ Tancred 40; GA Lohmann 5/96, GA Rowe 3/95) and 98 (G Beves 42; GA Lohmann 5/61, GA Rowe 3/12)

Western Province beat Transvaal by 8 wickets, 9–12 April 1898, Cape Town
Tvl 68 (GA Rowe 5/29, J Middleton 5/36) and 136 (GA Rowe 3/46, J Middleton 7/64)
WP 83 (PS Twentyman Jones 31; JH Sinclair 8/40) and 123/2 (M Bisset 60*, HH Francis 38)

Australians beat Western Province by 282 runs, 5–6 November 1902, Cape Town
Aus 172 (VT Trumper 49, C Hill 32; GA Rowe 5/86, J Middleton 5/50) and 274 (AJY Hopkins 39, J Darling 61, WP Howell 57*; GA Rowe 4/135, J Middleton 5/72)
WP 84 (PS Twentyman Jones 33; WP Howell 8/31) and 80 (PS Twentyman Jones 50; WP Howell 9/23)

Transvaal beat Western Province by 7 wickets, 14–16 April 1903, Port Elizabeth
WP 143 (F Hearne 63; JJ Kotze 4/36, GC White 3/21) and 140 (JA Pritchard 31, A Reid 52; JJ Kotze 5/53, JH Sinclair 4/42)
Tvl 243 (JH Sinclair 136, GH Shepstone 36; C Fock 5/72) and 43/3 (J Middleton 3/20)

Western Province beat Griqualand West by 48 runs, 26–28 November 1903, Kimberley
WP 185 (JA Pritchard 49, SE Horwood 30; GA Verheyen 4/71) and 169 (DD Davies 45; GA Verheyen 3/41, AEN Franklin 4/42)
GW 162 (EF Driver 37, AP Eland 39; J Middleton 5/46) and 144 (EF Driver 62; C Fock 3/47, J Middleton 5/28)

Western Province beat Border by an innings and 236 runs, 23–25 January 1904, Cape Town
WP 343 (JH Stewart 61, SJ Snooke 84, A Reid 47*, JH Anderson 109; AM Wilson 3/62, GPD Hartigan 3/62)
Bdr 55 (JJ Kotze 6/26, J Middleton 4/27) and 52 (C Fock 5/19, J Middleton 5/28)

Transvaal beat Western Province by 324 runs, 26–29 March 1904, Johannesburg
Tvl 254 (LJ Tancred 83, GC White 42, RO Schwarz 36; JJ Kotze 6/85, J Middleton 4/103) and 367 (LJ Tancred 102, CMH Hathorn 41, F Mitchell 37, GC White 30, GH Shepstone 49; JJ Kotze 5/135, J Middleton 3/99)
WP 139 (JA Pritchard 36; JH Sinclair 6/63) and 158 (JA Pritchard 53; JH Sinclair 7/61)

Western Province beat South Western Districts by an innings and 154 runs, 25–26 November 1904, Mossel Bay
SWD 60 (GA Rowe 8/25) and 45 (GA Rowe 3/25, C Fock 6/14)
WP 259 (JH Stewart 42, PS Twentyman Jones 37, CA Bain 40, HW Carolin 72; G Rodgers 3/60)

Western Province beat Eastern Province by 6 wickets, 26–28 December 1904, Cape Town
EP 148 (AT Lyons 37; HW Carolin 6/46) and 67 (JJ Kotze 7/18)
WP 133 (HW Carolin 42; AJ White 3/49, VD Mackay 4/22) and 83/4

Transvaal beat Western Province by 165 runs, 24–27 March 1905, Cape Town
Tvl 270 (PW Sherwell 57, RO Schwarz 63, JJ Slatem 41, GA Faulkner 35; HW Carolin 4/75, JG Whitehead 4/66) and 243 (LJ Tancred 50, WA Shalders 34, RO Schwarz 53; JJ Kotze 4/82, HW Carolin 4/60)
WP 192 (PS Twentyman Jones 53, SD Snooke 31, JG Whitehead 42; JH Sinclair 4/45) and 156 (AN Difford 37; JH Sinclair 6/51, RO Schwarz 3/46)

MCC beat Western Province by an innings and 127 runs, 2–5 December 1905, Cape Town
MCC 365 (PF Warner 56, D Denton 78, FL Fane 60, JN Crawford 46, AE Relf 61*; JG Whitehead 6/100)
WP 96 (S Haigh 5/29) and 142 (HC Coggins 43; JN Crawford 5/41)

MCC beat Western Province by 10 wickets, 9–12 December 1905, Cape Town
WP 81 (JN Crawford 4/27, WS Lees 3/22, S Haigh 3/10) and 233 (SJ Snooke 80, SE Horwood 74; JN Crawford 6/79)
MCC 272 (AE Relf 60, LJ Moon 57, S Haigh 61; WH Short 3/69, SJ Snooke 3/71) and 43/0

Western Province beat Orange Free State by 122 runs, 26–28 December 1906, Pretoria
WP 95 (HV Baumgartner 5/44, FJC Wyatt 5/18) and 233 (SJ Snooke 152; HV Baumgartner 5/89, FJC Wyatt 3/50)
OFS 109 (ML Clarke 31, JEV Isaac 34*; JJ Kotze 5/33) and 97 (JJ Kotze 8/57)

Western Province beat Eastern Province by an innings and 49 runs, 29–31 December 1906, Johannesburg
WP 227 (SD Snooke 57, TE Holmes 32; AEC Hewitt-Fox 5/39)
EP 71 (SJ Snooke 3/43, JJ Kotze 6/26) and 107 (MA Bell 32*, AEE Vogler 35; SJ Snooke 4/40, JJ Kotze 5/52)

Transvaal beat Western Province by an innings and 39 runs, 1–3 January 1907, Johannesburg
WP 141 (SD Snooke 35, M Bisset 40*; JH Sinclair 5/34) and 186 (SE Horwood 35, AN Difford 43; GA Faulkner 4/58)
Tvl 366 (PW Sherwell 30, EA Griffiths 37, GA Faulkner 95, RO Schwarz 45, LA Stricker 54; JJ Kotze 3/108, JG Whitehead 4/96)

Western Province beat Griqualand West by an innings and 359 runs, 3–4 January 1907, Johannesburg
WP 509 (SE Horwood 35, SD Snooke 31, AN Difford 103, SJ Snooke 121, A Reid 101*, GF Fletcher 5/99)
GW 77 (TA Eden 30*; I Bam 4/41, TEC Hobson 4/32) and 73 (JJ Kotze 5/6)

Natal beat Western Province by 165 runs, 7–9 January 1907, Johannesburg
Ntl 226 (J Budgen 31; JJ Kotze 6/57, JG Whitehead 3/78) and 339 (AW Nourse 112*, BC Cooley 113; SJ Snooke 5/105, JJ Kotze 5/121)
WP 158 (SE Horwood 36, M Bisset 45; J Budgen 3/21, AW Nourse 5/63) and 242 (SD Snooke 74, AN Difford 63; CP Carter 3/66, J Budgen 4/88)

Western Province beat Transvaal by 7 wickets, 6–8 April 1907, Cape Town
Tvl 98 (JJ Kotze 5/37, JG Whitehead 3/34) and 176 (AEE Vogler 40; JJ Kotze 6/88, JG Whitehead 3/35)
WP 145 (SJ Snooke 67; GA Faulkner 6/37) and 132/3 (SE Horwood 30, SJ Snooke 45*)

Western Province beat Natal by 3 wickets, 1–3 January 1908, Cape Town
Ntl 85 (JG Whitehead 3/25, HW Carolin 5/31) and 160 (AW Nourse 37, GL Dalton 32; JG Whitehead 7/58)
WP 154 (AW Nourse 5/52, CP Carter 3/57) and 94/7 (AW Nourse 6/37)

Match drawn between Western Province and Natal, 4–7 January 1908, Cape Town
WP 367 (PT Lewis 55, JP During 67, FD Conry 55, HW Carolin 80; AW Nourse 3/75, CP Carter 4/100) and 261/8 dec (AN Difford 82, M Bisset 35*, HW Carolin 58, RR Luyt 30*; CP Carter 5/100, TH O'Flaherty 3/58)
Ntl 231 (AW Nourse 98, WR Beningfield 48; JG Whitehead 3/62, CA Bain 3/54) and 301/5 (JJ Bisset 47, AW Nourse 200*)

Western Province beat Border by 2 wickets, 19–22 March 1909, Cape Town
Bdr 170 (GPD Hartigan 54, AE Cook 60; JJ Kotze 3/49, JG Whitehead 3/28, DC Jackson 3/12) and 171 (NO Norton 57, FW Porter 62; JG Whitehead 6/66)
WP 197 (JMM Commaille 74, WF Yeoman 65; NO Norton 3/47, SJ Snooke 4/54) and 148/8 (JP During 54*; NO Norton 4/35, SJ Snooke 3/56)

Western Province beat Eastern Province by an innings and 12 runs, 23–24 March 1909, Cape Town
EP 128 (AT Lyons 34*; DC Jackson 4/36) and 97 (AT Lyons 41*; RR Luyt 5/26)
WP 237 (WF Yeoman 60, RR Luyt 49; AT Lyons 3/68, EB Lundie 4/46, CK Allison 3/63)

Western Province beat Transvaal by 6 runs, 26–30 March 1909, Cape Town
WP 126 (JMM Commaille 34; GA Faulkner 6/72) and 232 (JMM Commaille 65, RR Luyt 34; AEE Vogler 3/54, GA Faulkner 4/94)
Tvl 170 (GA Faulkner 42, AEE Vogler 33; JJ Kotze 4/50, JG Whitehead 4/64) and 182 (JW Zulch 38, GA Faulkner 68*; JJ Kotze 6/60, JG Whitehead 3/75)

MCC beat Western Province by an innings and 133 runs, 4–6 December 1909, Cape Town
MCC 351 (JB Hobbs 114, FL Fane 40, MC Bird 76, HDG Leveson Gower 40; EB Lundie 3/83, JG Whitehead 3/106)
WP 67 (C Blythe 3/29, GJ Thompson 7/26) and 151 (CP Buckenham 4/26)

South Africans to Australia beat Western Province by an innings and 19 runs, 6–7 October 1910, Cape Town
WP 90 (SD Snooke 34; GA Faulkner 4/34, SJ Pegler 4/12) and 88 (AEE Vogler 3/7, SJ Pegler 3/30)
SA 197 (JW Zulch 31, COC Pearse 67; FP Bond 5/47)

Eastern Province beat Western Province by 5 wickets, 13–14 March 1911, Durban
WP 148 (SD Snooke 53; FL le Roux 3/27, WA Glisson 4/72) and 104 (FD Conry 46; FL le Roux 3/6, WA Glisson 4/48)
EP 109 (WA Glisson 35, C Barnes 30; JJ Kotze 3/17, FP Bond 3/43, DC Jackson 3/23) and 144/5 (CS Delbridge 48)

Western Province beat Border by 40 runs, 15–16 March 1911, Durban
WP 105 (WF Yeoman 39; NO Norton 3/21, GPD Hartigan 7/44) and 123 (FP Bond 46*; NO Norton 3/46, G Preston 4/23)
Bdr 118 (SD Snooke 4/16, DC Jackson 3/23) and 70 (SD Snooke 7/29)

Natal beat Western Province by 4 wickets, 17–18 March 1911, Durban
WP 162 (SD Snooke 41, BGV Melle 30, DC Jackson 36; SV Samuelson 5/79) and 132 (FD Conry 34; JL Cox 7/42)
Ntl 152 (HW Taylor 33, LD Dalton 47; JJ Kotze 7/47) and 143/6 (CD Saville 38, WK Thomson 31*; FP Bond 3/47)

Western Province beat Orange Free State by 10 wickets, 20–21 March 1911, Durban
OFS 137 (JE Jewell 64; JG Whitehead 5/31) and 155 (JE Jewell 88; JG Whitehead 3/36, EA Budgen 3/25)
WP 277 (DC Jackson 59, BGV Melle 79, FD Conry 76; HB Fawcus 3/64, HW Hill 4/79) and 16/0

Western Province beat Griqualand West by an innings and 116 runs, 24–25 March 1911, Durban
GW 69 (GL Tapscott 32*; JG Whitehead 4/7, EA Budgen 4/26) and 116 (NV Tapscott 37; EA Budgen 7/30)
WP 301 (WF Yeoman 64, BGV Melle 145, FD Conry 47; WGR Druce 4/67, WVS Ling 5/154)

Transvaal beat Western Province by 10 wickets, 27–28 March 1911, Durban
WP 182 (WF Yeoman 86, BGV Melle 30; CP Carter 4/42) and 210 (BGV Melle 78; JH Moulder 3/33)
Tvl 381 (LJ Tancred 160, NV Lindsay 64, BH Floquet 87; FP Bond 4/107, EA Budgen 5/76) and 12/0

Western Province beat Transvaal by 10 wickets, 26–27 December 1912, Cape Town
Tvl 228 (PJ Heather 53, DC Jackson 47*; WH Short 5/89, R de Smidt 4/65) and 131 (F Smith 3/35, R de Smidt 4/40)
WP 344 (GAL Hearne 53, PAM Hands 116, FD Conry 59; RO Saunders 4/109, HV Baumgartner 4/82) and 18/0

Western Province beat Orange Free State by 320 runs, 1–2 January 1913, Cape Town
WP 234 (JMM Commaille 55, R de Smidt 42*; FC Wille 3/60, JG van Schalkwyk 3/27) and 291/4 dec (JMM Commaille 103, GAL Hearne 39, PAM Hands 36, RHM Hands 79*)
OFS 120 (WH Mars 6/42, JM Blanckenberg 4/29) and 85 (WH Short 5/22)

Natal beat Western Province by 7 wickets, 22–24 March 1913, Durban
WP 159 (RHM Hands 34, FD Conry 39; JL Cox 3/50, AW Nourse 3/47) and 190 (JMM Commaille 48, RHM Hands 67*)
Ntl 263 (HW Taylor 48, JE Beningfield 39, COC Pearse 61*, CP Carter 46; JM Blanckenberg 4/61) and 89/3 (COC Pearse 33*, D Taylor jr 44*)

Western Province beat Eastern Province by an innings and 74 runs, 29–31 March 1913, Port Elizabeth
WP 238 (WF Yeoman 66, J Carstens 58, RHM Hands 32; HT Crouch 6/68, FW Porter 3/60)
EP 71 (EA Budgen 3/28, JM Blanckenberg 4/13) and 93 (WA Glisson 45; WH Short 4/20)

Match drawn between Western Province and MCC, 8–11 November 1913, Cape Town
WP 376 (JMM Commaille 30, PT Lewis 151, FD Conry 53; JW Hearne 4/108, AE Relf 5/67)
MCC 199 (JB Hobbs 72, MC Bird 32; EA Budgen 4/55) and 330 (JB Hobbs 80, JW Hearne 83, JWHT Douglas 61; EA Budgen 3/77, JM Blanckenberg 5/91)

Match drawn between Western Province and MCC, 7–10 March 1914, Cape Town
MCC 322 (JB Hobbs 40, JWHT Douglas 93, EJ Smith 34*; CWR Minnaar 4/95, JM Blanckenberg 4/102) and 177/4 dec (W Rhodes 35*, LH Tennyson 42, EJ Smith 35*)
WP 210 (JMM Commaille 52, PT Lewis 32; JW Hearne 7/78) and 178/9 (PT Lewis 59; W Rhodes 4/51)

Australian Imperial Forces beat Western Province by 2 wickets, 18–21 October 1919, Cape Town
WP 160 (GAL Hearne 41, PAM Hands 63; HL Collins 4/55, AW Lampard 5/29) and 179 (GAL Hearne 55, N Blanckenberg 48, JM Blanckenberg 33; AW Lampard 7/71)
AIF 141 (JM Gregory 36, AW Lampard 55; EA Budgen 7/70) and 200/8 (JM Gregory 43, WL Trenerry 55, JT Murray 41*; F Smith 6/67)

Match drawn between Australian Imperial Forces and Western Province, 6–9 December 1919, Cape Town
AIF 269 (HL Collins 33, WL Trenerry 52, CB Willis 94; EA Budgen 3/49) and 164/6 dec (HL Collins 44, CB Willis 33, WAS Oldfield 40*)
WP 153 (AW Lampard 3/40, CT Docker 5/37) and 141/7 (JMM Commaille 50, JP Duminy 38; WL Trenerry 3/28)

Western Province beat Border by an innings and 231 runs, 18–20 December 1920, Cape Town
WP 364/7 dec (GAL Hearne 46, JMM Commaille 156, PAM Hands 102, WWA Colson 30; HO Wood 4/84)
Bdr 47 (JG Whitehead 5/12, JM Blanckenberg 3/9) and 86 (GAL Hearne 3/9, JM Blanckenberg 4/39)

Match drawn between Western Province and Orange Free State, 27–28 December 1920, Bloemfontein
WP 276 (JMM Commaille 34, GAL Hearne 40, F Reid 43, HH Fuller 68; LR Tuckett 5/119, DI de Villiers 5/44) and 292/7 dec (JMM Commaille 45, GAL Hearne 30, HH Fuller 47*, JM Blanckenberg 87; DI de Villiers 3/59)
OFS 255 (KG Hill 44, R Johnson 45, CD Lincoln 36*, LG Storrier 31; Abel S Bensimon 3/53) and 275/6 (KG Hill 55, TE Holmes 64, JE Jewell 47, LR Tuckett 63*; Abel S Bensimon 4/75)

Match drawn between Transvaal and Western Province, 1–3 January 1921, Johannesburg
Tvl 159 (NV Lindsay 57, FL le Roux 30*; JM Blanckenberg 9/78) and 282/9 dec (AHC Cooper 83, FL le Roux 74, WT Gardner 35*; F Smith 3/94)
WP 264 (GAL Hearne 78, SV Brown 32*; FW Elworthy 3/57, EP Nupen 4/62) and 124/7 (JMM Commaille 63, F Reid 39; FL le Roux 3/19, AB Skottowe 3/20)

Western Province beat Griqualand West by 207 runs, 7–8 January 1921, Kimberley
WP 268 (GAL Hearne 51, WWA Colson 39, N Reid 47; CM Francois 3/58, GL Tapscott 4/74) and 305 (JMM Commaille 101*, JM Blanckenberg 63; CM Francois 3/74, GL Tapscott 3/56, LE Tapscott 3/34)
GW 242 (LE Tapscott 99, AE Raaff 36, CM Francois 30; JM Blanckenberg 3/77) and 124 (CWP Munn 31; F Smith 3/28, JM Blanckenberg 4/44)

Western Province beat Natal by 27 runs, 26–28 March 1921, Cape Town
WP 242 (GAL Hearne 30, JMM Commaille 35, PAM Hands 37, AVC Bisset 49, HH Fuller 53; JL Cox 3/58, AW Nourse 3/44) and 134 (RR Luyt 61; ME Billing 6/42)
Ntl 150 (DK Pearse 33, HW Chapman 62; VG Veal 3/29, JM Blanckenberg 6/54) and 199 (AW Nourse 83*; JM Blanckenberg 4/48, F Smith 3/84)

Australians beat Western Province by 8 wickets, 19–22 November 1921, Cape Town
WP 153 (GAL Hearne 76, CH Thomas 31; CG Macartney 5/40, AA Mailey 5/89) and 191 (GAL Hearne 33, JMM Commaille 62, PAM Hands 40; J Ryder 3/24, AA Mailey 6/88)
Aus 231 (HL Collins 32, W Bardsley 66, ER Mayne 43; VG Veal 3/45, N Reid 4/52) and 114/2 (ER Mayne 30, CG Macartney 62*)

Western Province beat Griqualand West by 6 wickets, 16–19 December 1921, Cape Town
GW 135 (WVS Ling 39; VG Veal 4/18, Abel S Bensimon 3/47) and 270 (LE Tapscott 39, WVS Ling 83, GL Tapscott 42)
WP 203 (GAL Hearne 30, PAM Hands 43, KCM Hands 36*, N Reid 33; CM Francois 4/65, GL Tapscott 5/47) and 204/4 (GAL Hearne 33, JMM Commaille 98*)

Western Province beat Transvaal by 177 runs, 2–4 January 1922, Cape Town
WP 198 (GAL Hearne 39, KCM Hands 39, JM Blanckenberg 40; AE Hall 7/73) and 273 (GAL Hearne 70, JM Blanckenberg 57, VG Veal 52; AE Hall 3/84)
Tvl 200 (RH Catterall 34, JB Perring 61; Abel S Bensimon 5/84) and 94 (GAL Hearne 3/52, JM Durr 4/22, Abel S Bensimon 3/6)

Western Province beat Orange Free State by 133 runs, 17–20 February 1922, Cape Town
WP 271 (GAL Hearne 33, JMM Commaille 46, PAM Hands 30, KCM Hands 34, JM Blanckenberg 39, N Reid 38*; EA Budgen 4/61, LR Tuckett 3/111) and 244 (GAL Hearne 50, N Reid 81*, RR Luyt 38; LR Tuckett 5/71)
OFS 182 (E Wille 48, CW Travers 50; JL Bolton 3/35) and 200 (DI de Villiers 48, BV Susskind 51; JL Bolton 5/76, N Reid 3/43)

Eastern Province beat Western Province by 6 wickets, 25–26 March 1922, Port Elizabeth
WP 162 (GAL Hearne 34, AW Palm 37, LC Fox 30*; W Boltman 6/51, C Munro 3/34) and 290 (GAL Hearne 36, AVC Bisset 35, JM Blanckenberg 85, LC Fox 30; C Munro 4/76)
EP 286 (CKA Gingell 35, WH Brann 97, CE Basson 50; JM Blanckenberg 5/17) and 170/4 (JE Brann 32, WH Brann 83*)

Natal beat Western Province by 8 wickets, 1–4 April 1922, Durban
WP 223 (GAL Hearne 106; AW Nourse 3/49, DP Conyngham 4/63) and 89 (ME Billing 5/37, DP Conyngham 4/21)
Ntl 252 (AW Nourse 77, HG Deane 46, RO Arbuckle 47*; VG Veal 3/67, ID Buys 5/65) and 61/2

MCC beat Western Province by 6 wickets, 10–13 November 1922, Cape Town
WP 145 (KCM Hands 49; PGH Fender 4/46) and 205 (JMM Commaille 40, PAM Hands 38, CH Thomas 44; VWC Jupp 4/49, FE Woolley 3/31)
MCC 311 (CP Mead 97, PGH Fender 96; ID Buys 5/121, Abel S Bensimon 3/50) and 40/4

MCC beat Western Province by 10 wickets, 3–6 March 1923, Cape Town
WP 118 (JMM Commaille 35; PGH Fender 3/24, VWC Jupp 4/31) and 181 (KCM Hands 33, PAM Hands 94; AS Kennedy 5/35)
MCC 236 (A Sandham 38, PGH Fender 33, FT Mann 47, AS Kennedy 39; ID Buys 3/48, VG Veal 3/33, JM Blanckenberg 3/54) and 64/0 (A Sandham 42*)

Western Province beat Orange Free State by 8 wickets, 17–18 October 1923, Cape Town
OFS 139 (FE Fuller 33, DI de Villiers 30; Abel S Bensimon 3/37, AR Lovegrove 4/37) and 173 (E Wille 33, FE Fuller 66; ID Buys 4/28)
WP 191 (AW Palm 43; F Buttner 4/56) and 123/2 (JMM Commaille 63)

Match drawn between Border and Western Province, 15–17 December 1923, Johannesburg
Bdr 172 (WE Roberts 46; ID Buys 6/49, AR Lovegrove 3/33) and 258 (HJC Kelly 60, AC Tarr 32, LE Miles 39, CEB Shearman 51; ID Buys 3/87, KCM Hands 4/25)
WP 278/7 dec (LC Fox 38, VUT Watson 88, PAM Hands 59) and 119/6 (VUT Watson 37; SH Francois 3/25)

Match drawn between Natal and Western Province, 19–20 December 1923, Johannesburg
Ntl 426/8 dec (AW Nourse 186, JM Blanckenberg 171; ID Buys 3/106)
WP 119 (CP Carter 3/43, JM Blanckenberg 5/24) and 297/5 (JMM Commaille 120*, PAM Hands 79, AR Lovegrove 36)

Match drawn between Western Province and Griqualand West, 22–24 December 1923, Johannesburg
WP 236 (VUT Watson 53, KCM Hands 31, F Reid 35*; JL Daly 4/56, WVS Ling 3/44) and 271/5 dec (JMM Commaille 132*, AW Palm 106*)
GW 309 (CD McKay 34, NV Tapscott 40, P Rigal 63, CM Francois 33, WA Dickens 68; WRG Rush 5/87, AR Lovegrove 3/92) and 158/7 (WVS Ling 51, LE Tapscott 42; AR Lovegrove 4/38)

Match drawn between Orange Free State and Western Province, 26–27 December 1923, Pretoria
OFS 216 (TE Holmes 36, DI de Villiers 34, KG Hill 38, E Wille 45, LR Tuckett 39; WRG Rush 5/53, WM Stephen 4/42) and 294/9 dec (KG Hill 126, JE Jewell 61; WM Stephen 4/65)
WP 343/8 dec (JMM Commaille 44, KCM Hands 34, PAM Hands 82, WRG Rush 79, AR Lovegrove 40*; EA Budgen 6/132) and 125/3 (KCM Hands 51*, FD Conry 58)

Transvaal beat Western Province by an innings and 54 runs, 28–29 December 1923, Johannesburg
WP 197 (JMM Commaille 52, KCM Hands 62, LC Fox 30; CD Dixon 6/74) and 192 (PAM Hands 119; EP Nupen 6/66)
Tvl 443/6 dec (JW Zulch 42, NV Lindsay 116, AHC Cooper 171*, MJ Susskind 55; WM Stephen 3/80)

Match drawn between SB Joel and Western Province, 14–15 November 1924, Cape Town
SBJ 252/9 dec (P Holmes 41, AS Kennedy 67*, CWL Parker 51*; JL Bolton 6/81)
WP 118 (AS Kennedy 5/42, CWL Parker 4/27) and 82/8 (EH Bowley 3/18)

Transvaal beat Western Province by an innings and 74 runs, 26–29 December 1925, Johannesburg
Tvl 491/7 dec (CN Frank 43, HW Taylor 120, MJ Susskind 41, JAJ Christy 107*, HB Cameron 41, HG Deane 51, WRG Rush 38; WM Stephen 4/63)
WP 240 (AW Palm 89, N Blanckenberg 55; CL Vincent 6/59) and 177 (PGV van der Bijl 45; AE Hall 3/40, CL Vincent 6/50)

Orange Free State beat Western Province by 46 runs, 31 December 1925 – 2 January 1926, Bloemfontein
OFS 303 (LG Cusworth 33, WJC Reid 37, LR Tuckett 30*, LG Fuller 84; VG Veal 4/68) and 250 (AEC Hewitt-Fox 60, LR Tuckett 70, F Caulfield 56*; IF Goulden 3/58)
WP 259 (DPB Morkel 43, TR de Klerk 79, IF Goulden 60; LR Tuckett 4/99) and 248 (DPB Morkel 39, AW Palm 75, VG Veal 33; F Caulfield 3/63)

Griqualand West beat Western Province by 6 wickets, 4–6 January 1926, Kimberley
WP 274 (PGV van der Bijl 48, DPB Morkel 40, VG Veal 58, IF Goulden 54; CM Francois 3/26, PE Stopforth 3/27) and 114 (WVS Ling 7/60)
GW 141 (PE Stopforth 49, WVS Ling 50; VG Veal 3/22, DPB Morkel 4/40) and 248/4 (FJ Farrelly 94, WVS Ling 72*; WM Stephen 3/43)

Western Province beat Eastern Province by 7 wickets, 30 January – 2 February 1926, Cape Town
EP 137 (AH Pattison 35, CKA Gingell 65; VG Veal 4/22, IF Goulden 4/54) and 286 (AH Pattison 51, HE Pagden 106, MG Cole 31; DPB Morkel 3/78, VG Veal 5/57)
WP 268 (GAL Hearne 65, KCM Hands 40, DPB Morkel 56*, N Blanckenberg 33; C Munro 4/79, JS Maguire 5/58) and 158/3 (AW Palm 59*, PAM Hands 33)

Western Province beat Natal by 83 runs, 3–6 April 1926, Cape Town
WP 239 (KCM Hands 42, PAM Hands 30, N Blanckenberg 37, T Middleton 31; L Lewin 3/63, HR Fawcett 3/67) and 317/8 dec (KCM Hands 171*, DPB Morkel 41, ASV MacRae 39*; HR Fawcett 3/73)
Ntl 216 (IJ Siedle 48, VC Robbins 30, AF Borland 31; VG Veal 3/62, IF Goulden 3/48) and 257 (VC Robbins 36, WJ Lee 82, HA Mackrory 47; DPB Morkel 3/40, VG Veal 3/45)

Western Province beat Griqualand West by 240 runs, 16–18 December 1926, Cape Town
WP 182 (DPB Morkel 31, AW Palm 65; JL Daly 3/37, AS Ward 3/22) and 415/7 dec (DPB Morkel 86, AW Palm 85, GAL Hearne 138, IB Gardiner 45; JL Daly 3/79)
GW 189 (FJ Farrelly 49, KG Viljoen 39, JP McNally 38; VG Veal 4/45) and 168 (FJ Farrelly 72; ASV MacRae 3/15, VG Veal 7/41)

Transvaal beat Western Province by an innings and 61 runs, 1–3 January 1927, Cape Town
WP 74 (GAL Hearne 34; EP Nupen 3/30, AE Hall 4/14) and 172 (DPB Morkel 68, GAL Hearne 35; EP Nupen 3/73, AE Hall 5/48)
Tvl 307 (AW Nourse 125, NV Lindsay 60; VG Veal 4/84)

Orange Free State beat Western Province by 24 runs, 29–31 January 1927, Cape Town
WP 393 (KCM Hands 114, FA Godfrey 36, DPB Morkel 58, AW Palm 71, JL Bolton 33; RKB Morkel 3/76) and 44 (RKB Morkel 3/13, AGC Reynolds 6/27)
OFS 163 (CW Travers 40; JL Bolton 5/40, DPB Morkel 4/42) and 298 (RTS Dick 55, JMM Commaille 60, RKB Morkel 41, LR Tuckett 44; JL Bolton 3/80, DPB Morkel 4/85)

Natal beat Western Province by an innings and 50 runs, 5–7 March 1927, Durban
Ntl 253 (IJ Siedle 85, JFW Nicolson 32, SH Martin 64*; DPB Morkel 5/52)
WP 55 (FJ Smith 6/16, AF Borland 3/24) and 148 (KCM Hands 43; ME Pennington 6/27)

Match drawn between Western Province and Border, 12–14 March 1927, King William's Town
WP 211 (AW Palm 65; RGA Bowen 3/60) and 135/5 (KCM Hands 67*)
Bdr 123 (HH Fuller 35; T Middleton 4/14)

Western Province beat Eastern Province by 9 wickets, 17–19 March 1927, Port Elizabeth
EP 207 (AH Pattison 82, CKA Gingell 64; VG Veal 7/40, DPB Morkel 3/83) and 138 (WHI Hards 30; VG Veal 4/38, DPB Morkel 5/54)
WP 317 (AW Palm 44, DPB Morkel 110, PGV van der Bijl 60*, T Middleton 55; AL Ochse 3/82, AH Pattison 3/26) and 29/1

Match drawn between MCC and Western Province, 12–15 November 1927, Cape Town
MCC 138 (P Holmes 40, GTS Stevens 44*; VG Veal 4/26, HGO Owen-Smith 4/53)
WP 67/6 (AP Freeman 5/15)

MCC beat Western Province by 8 wickets, 18–21 February 1928, Cape Town
MCC 415/8 dec (H Sutcliffe 62, GE Tyldesley 41, RES Wyatt 73, WE Astill 66, RT Stanyforth 71*, SJ Staples 35*; DPB Morkel 3/93, HW Morgan 3/41) and 87/2 (P Holmes 49)
WP 162 (LR Serrurier 74*; AP Freeman 5/49, WE Astill 3/54) and 339 (TR de Klerk 41, AW Nourse 42, AW Palm 71, SSL Steyn 51, HGO Owen-Smith 32; AP Freeman 5/102)

Western Province beat Orange Free State by 299 runs, 24–27 December 1928, Cape Town
WP 315 (LR Serrurier 59, DPB Morkel 41, AW Palm 30, HW Morgan 67, CA Pfister 35; AV Conlon 5/69) and 376/7 dec (LR Serrurier 51, DPB Morkel 145, AW Palm 76*; H Bishko 3/61)
OFS 289 (RTS Dick 100, C Munro 46, CW Travers 49; AJ Bell 5/53, TM Davidson 3/64) and 103 (TE Holmes 30; AJ Bell 3/13, IF Goulden 4/18)

Western Province beat Eastern Province by an innings and 316 runs, 28–29 December 1928, Cape Town
WP 441 (LR Serrurier 171, AW Nourse 66, VG Veal 58; AH Pattison 4/64)
EP 58 (AJ Bell 4/23, HGO Owen-Smith 4/11) and 67 (HGO Owen-Smith 5/11)

Match drawn between Transvaal and Western Province, 1–3 January 1929, Cape Town
Tvl 375 (AC Langebrink 48, MJ Susskind 41, HB Cameron 31, HG Deane 143, CD McKay 35) and 158/8 (Q McMillan 32, HB Cameron 34; AJ Bell 3/37, HGO Owen-Smith 4/42)
WP 143 (LR Serrurier 48; SW Brissenden 6/43) and 441 (IB Gardiner 76, LR Serrurier 30, AW Nourse 108, DPB Morkel 92, HGO Owen-Smith 45; SW Brissenden 4/110, FA Walsh 3/92)

Western Province beat Eastern Province by an innings and 218 runs, 14–16 December 1929, Cape Town
EP 128 (JH van den Berg 38, RA Mardon 53; AJ Bell 8/34) and 177 (JH van den Berg 47*, ON Flemmer 75; AJ Bell 5/27, TR de Klerk 3/21)
WP 523/4 dec (FC Martin 145, TR de Klerk 41, AW Nourse 163*, AW Palm 79*)

Western Province beat Border by an innings and 163 runs, 26–28 December 1929, Cape Town
Bdr 151 (SEP Farrer 33; HGO Owen-Smith 4/26, TR de Klerk 4/39) and 287 (CM Fraser-Grant 30, PS Hubbard 67, VC Schaefer 45, RS Cheshire 41, HD Bowley 30; HGO Owen-Smith 6/60)
WP 601 (LR Serrurier 30, SSL Steyn 261*, HGO Owen-Smith 50, AW Palm 40, DPB Morkel 114)

Match drawn between Western Province and Natal, 31 December 1929 – 2 January 1930, Cape Town
WP 538/6 dec (LR Serrurier 105, AW Nourse 41, DPB Morkel 208*, AW Palm 100*)
Ntl 177 (A Melville 66, AF Borland 51; AJ Bell 4/39, HGO Owen-Smith 6/61) and 458 (IJ Siedle 85, EL Dalton 31, HC Finlayson 30, AP Woods 93, AP Murray 58, AF Borland 62*; HGO Owen-Smith 5/124)

Griqualand West beat Western Province by an innings and 14 runs, 21–24 February 1930, Kimberley
GW 603 (CD McKay 34, F Nicholson 131, JMM Commaille 30, KG Viljoen 215, XC Balaskas 101, JPG Glover 31*; TR de Klerk 3/106)
WP 390 (AW Palm 173, DPB Morkel 62, HGO Owen-Smith 59; XC Balaskas 6/142, RH Henderson 3/40) and 199 (LR Serrurier 36, AW Nourse 59; XC Balaskas 6/93)

Western Province beat Orange Free State by 9 wickets, 26–27 February 1930, Bethlehem
OFS 238 (JC Newton 115, CW Travers 43; TR de Klerk 3/54, HGO Owen-Smith 3/53) and 93 (CW Travers 34*; FH Kossuth 3/11, TR de Klerk 3/20)
WP 209 (KCM Hands 51, TR de Klerk 40; CM Maritz 3/47, LE de Villiers 7/65) and 124/1 (LR Serrurier 53*, KCM Hands 34)

Transvaal beat Western Province by an innings and 16 runs, 1–3 March 1930, Johannesburg
WP 227 (AW Nourse 85, SSL Steyn 30; ES Newson 3/47, FA Walsh 4/47, EP Nupen 3/78) and 206 (AW Nourse 67, DPB Morkel 49; FA Walsh 4/50, EP Nupen 6/67)
Tvl 449 (HW Taylor 142, HG Deane 41, Q McMillan 75, FA Walsh 44; DPB Morkel 3/72, IF Goulden 3/136)

MCC beat Western Province by an innings and 177 runs, 8–11 November 1930, Cape Town
WP 113 (HF Myles 35; MW Tate 5/18) and 122 (FC Martin 31, AW Nourse 36; IAR Peebles 4/31, M Leyland 3/4, RES Wyatt 3/33)
MCC 412/7 dec (A Sandham 72, RES Wyatt 138, WR Hammond 100, EH Hendren 58*)

Western Province beat Griqualand West by 130 runs, 6–9 December 1930, Cape Town
WP 290 (AW Nourse 101, KCM Hands 102; NA Quinn 3/98, JAK Cochran 3/58) and 121 (GE Bond 39; NA Quinn 3/33, XC Balaskas 7/42)
GW 148 (XC Balaskas 59; AJ Bell 6/44, GE Bond 3/17) and 133 (F Nicholson 57; AJ Bell 3/44)

Match drawn between MCC and Western Province, 7–10 March 1931, Cape Town
MCC 254 (EH Hendren 61, MW Tate 115*) and 335/6 dec (MJL Turnbull 139, M Leyland 50, EH Hendren 50; R Stoke 3/58)
WP 316 (FC Martin 43, AW Palm 44, B Wallace 30, TR de Klerk 54, IF Goulden 75*; MJC Allom 6/42) and 141/2 (FC Martin 55, GE Bond 77*)

Match drawn between Western Province and Natal, 18–19 December 1931, Durban
WP 353/9 dec (FC Martin 84, SK Coen 67, GE Bond 47, ARM Ralph 71, JB Robertson 39; FJ Smith 4/67) and 67/2
Ntl 337 (HF Wade 130, LTH Trotter 56, AD Nourse 105; RJ Crisp 7/56)

Match drawn between Border and Western Province, 21–22 December 1931, Johannesburg
Bdr 178 (JG Phillips 57, CD White 32, ON Flemmer 34; TR de Klerk 5/46) and 212 (GWA Chubb 64, AL Wilkins 48*; TR de Klerk 5/76)
WP 236 (GE Bond 79, TR de Klerk 48, HW Morgan 32; C Closenberg 5/63) and 91/1 (SK Coen 54*)

Western Province beat Griqualand West by an innings and 80 runs, 23–24 December 1931, Johannesburg
WP 408 (FC Martin 57, SK Coen 56, GE Bond 97, AW Nourse 30, TR de Klerk 55, JB Robertson 45*; JP McNally 6/87, HLE Promnitz 3/86)
GW 114 (CD McKay 64; RJ Crisp 8/31) and 214 (F Nicholson 35, DG Helfrich 34, TH Boggan 39; TR de Klerk 7/48)

Match drawn between Eastern Province and Western Province, 26–28 December 1931, Pretoria
EP 260 (HD Freakes 59, SL White 125*; TR de Klerk 3/81, JB Robertson 5/64) and 262 (HD Freakes 111, RA Mardon 36, WA Cawood 40; CH Hutchinson 5/75)
WP 416 (FC Martin 127, SK Coen 124, ARM Ralph 42; AL Ochse 5/112) and 62/4 (AL Ochse 3/31)

Match drawn between Natal and Western Province, 29–30 December 1931, Johannesburg
Ntl 319 (HF Wade 64, LTH Trotter 102, AD Nourse 46; RJ Crisp 3/62, TR de Klerk 5/59)
WP 277/4 (FC Martin 35, GE Bond 70, ARM Ralph 80*, AW Nourse 39, AD Peters 35*)

Match drawn between Transvaal and Western Province, 1–2 January 1932, Johannesburg
Tvl 191 (AC Langebrink 48, TWT Baines 63, RH Catterall 41*; RJ Crisp 4/34, TR de Klerk 3/75) and 253/7 dec (AC Langebrink 53, TWT Baines 96, WBH Foley 35; RJ Crisp 3/56, TR de Klerk 3/97)
WP 349 (SK Coen 173, JB Robertson 40*, RJ Crisp 43; SW Brissenden 4/96, FA Walsh 3/49) and 28/3

Western Province beat Transvaal by 6 wickets, 26–29 March 1932, Cape Town
Tvl 217 (EAB Rowan 49, MJ Susskind 61, HM Kahn 35; AS Bensimon sr 4/72, TR de Klerk 3/72) and 295/7 dec (AC Langebrink 38, MJ Susskind 110, RE Somers Vine 61; TR de Klerk 3/77)
WP 391/6 dec (SK Coen 75, AW Nourse 160*, AW Palm 51, JB Robertson 40*) and 122/4 (SK Coen 33, HW Morgan 38*)

Transvaal beat Western Province by 6 wickets, 24–26 December 1932, Cape Town
WP 246 (FC Martin 41, ARM Ralph 30, LM Manning 52; AH Gyngell 5/110) and 220 (ARM Ralph 54, GE Bond 59; LS Brown 5/67)
Tvl 90 (RJ Crisp 5/25, VG Veal 4/16) and 377/4 (SH Curnow 192*, SK Coen 86, AW Briscoe 54*)

Match drawn between Natal and Western Province, 27–28 December 1932, Cape Town
Ntl 167 (LTH Trotter 72; RJ Crisp 7/43, TR de Klerk 3/42) and 210/4 (HF Wade 33, LTH Trotter 76, AD Nourse 54*)
WP 425/6 dec (AW Nourse 219*, SSL Steyn 104, G Georgeu 31; RE Davies 3/61)

Match drawn between Western Province and Rest of South Africa, 29–30 December 1932, Cape Town
WP 322 (FC Martin 58, D Graaff 67, G Georgeu 35, TR de Klerk 44; DS Tomlinson 6/127) and 193/7 (HW Morgan 78; DS Tomlinson 4/78)
RestSA 544/7 dec (RA Mardon 60, KG Viljoen 42, XC Balaskas 200*, ON Flemmer 105, JP McNally 74; TR de Klerk 3/117)

Transvaal beat Western Province by 10 wickets, 30 December 1933 – 2 January 1934, Cape Town
WP 256 (ARM Ralph 106, AW Nourse 45, SSL Steyn 32; NM McAlpine 3/50, ACB Langton 3/41, B Mitchell 3/64) and 212 (ARM Ralph 50, SSL Steyn 36, TR de Klerk 40; AH Gyngell 3/64, ACB Langton 3/22)
Tvl 385 (SH Curnow 34, B Mitchell 99, RH Catterall 50, HB Cameron 110; RJ Crisp 6/101, TR de Klerk 3/93) and 85/0 (SH Curnow 36*, EAB Rowan 46*)

Western Province beat Border by 2 wickets, 24–27 February 1934, East London
Bdr 114 (XC Balaskas 42; HH Watt 5/29, AS Bensimon sr 3/38) and 83 (XC Balaskas 37; RJ Crisp 4/21, AS Bensimon sr 5/30)
WP 135 (AW Palm 31, A Glantz 30*; JK Muzzell 4/36, XC Balaskas 5/56) and 64/8 (IB Gardiner 4/11, XC Balaskas 3/22)

Natal beat Western Province by 170 runs, 3–6 March 1934, Durban
Ntl 214 (IJ Siedle 77, EL Dalton 74*; RJ Crisp 9/64) and 324 (HF Wade 30, AD Nourse 63, EL Dalton 31, JH Hamilton 34, AP Woods 59, RJ Williams 50; RJ Crisp 3/99, JB Robertson 5/34)
WP 146 (ARM Ralph 51; RE Davies 4/43) and 222 (TR de Klerk 32, RJ Crisp 31; RE Davies 6/79, EL Dalton 4/37)

Western Province beat Eastern Province by an innings and 8 runs, 10–12 March 1934, Port Elizabeth
EP 83 (VG Veal 3/10, AS Bensimon sr 6/24) and 37 (RJ Crisp 4/24, VG Veal 3/6)
WP 128 (FG Rippon 3/27, CM Maritz 5/55)

Western Province beat Griqualand West by an innings and 113 runs, 31 March – 3 April 1934, Cape Town
WP 438 (ARM Ralph 75, HW Morgan 115, LM Manning 123; TMH van der Spuy 4/103)
GW 154 (TH Boggan 30, TA Harris 34; JB Robertson 6/22) and 171 (A Dunn 32, TH Boggan 50; GB Paull 6/61)

Western Province beat Eastern Province by an innings and 176 runs, 23–24 November 1934, Cape Town
WP 360 (ARM Ralph 49, PGV van der Bijl 80, XC Balaskas 61, MG Francis 49, GB Paull 31; DW Niland 3/75, RH Henderson 3/85)
EP 73 (XC Balaskas 6/24, JB Robertson 4/26) and 111 (HH Watt 3/14, XC Balaskas 5/33)

Western Province beat Border by an innings and 104 runs, 15–18 December 1934, Cape Town
Bdr 126 (RJ Crisp 4/32, XC Balaskas 3/38) and 213 (CRH Byron 35, FHB Spence 51, GV Wienand 30; JB Robertson 6/38)
WP 443/9 dec (ARM Ralph 142, LM Manning 53, MG Francis 94, JB Robertson 35; IB Gardiner 4/103)

Natal beat Western Province by 328 runs, 27–29 December 1934, Cape Town
Ntl 345 (LTH Trotter 53, AD Nourse 92, HW Taylor 30, EL Dalton 76; RJ Crisp 3/94, XC Balaskas 5/87) and 329/8 dec (HF Wade 31, HW Taylor 113, EL Dalton 123; XC Balaskas 5/96)
WP 188 (GE Bond 63; EL Dalton 3/48, RE Davies 3/46) and 158 (GE Bond 79*; IDE Anderson 3/28, RE Davies 5/42)

Transvaal beat Western Province by 81 runs, 1–3 January 1935, Cape Town
Tvl 259 (SH Curnow 49, RE Grieveson 32, B Mitchell 58, AW Briscoe 32; RJ Crisp 5/37) and 192 (B Mitchell 59, WBH Foley 39; XC Balaskas 4/63, JB Robertson 5/62)
WP 134 (GE Bond 33; B Mitchell 5/61, AH Gyngell 3/21) and 236 (GE Bond 38, LM Manning 65, ARM Ralph 62; RSK Rose 6/46)

Orange Free State beat Western Province by 4 wickets, 1–4 March 1935, Bloemfontein
WP 126 (RJE Burt 40; KG Viljoen 4/40, HLE Promnitz 5/41) and 245 (RJE Burt 36, LM Manning 30, PA Little 35, G Georgeu 60*, CGC Wrentmore 42; HLE Promnitz 4/78, CW Travers 3/30)
OFS 85 (HH Watt 3/21, WC Ross 4/27, D Price 3/37) and 288/6 (CJ Kaplan 37, EW Warner 70, JC Newton 33, CS Henchie 53)

Griqualand West beat Western Province by 7 wickets, 5–7 March 1935, Kimberley
WP 113 (SSL Steyn 31; JP McNally 7/46) and 405 (LM Manning 185, G Georgeu 65, CGC Wrentmore 58; EV Franz 3/68, DG Helfrich 3/87)
GW 312 (DG Helfrich 74, TA Harris 77, JP McNally 42; HH Watt 6/84, D Price 3/75) and 207/3 (F Nicholson 35, DG Helfrich 48, JP McNally 79*)

Australians beat Western Province by an innings and 44 runs, 30 November – 2 December 1935, Cape Town
WP 170 (G Georgeu 45; LO Fleetwood-Smith 7/71) and 104 (GE Bond 42; LO Fleetwood-Smith 5/32, CV Grimmett 3/36)
Aus 318 (WA Brown 58, JHW Fingleton 53, LS Darling 47, LPJ O'Brien 30; JB Robertson 8/96)

Australians beat Western Province by 8 wickets, 14–17 March 1936, Cape Town
WP 198 (ARM Ralph 30, AW Nourse 55; AG Chipperfield 3/84, WJ O'Reilly 6/35) and 262 (ARM Ralph 35, G Georgeu 84, SSL Steyn 49; EL McCormick 3/58, WJ O'Reilly 6/64)
Aus 398 (VY Richardson 49, LPJ O'Brien 46, MW Sievers 59, WA Brown 43, AG Chipperfield 107*, WAS Oldfield 34; XC Balaskas 3/119) and 63/2

Western Province beat Griqualand West by 10 wickets, 26–29 December 1936, Cape Town
WP 460/9 dec (PGV van der Bijl 195, ARM Ralph 75, LM Manning 31, B Wallace 41, TMH van der Spuy 45, G Georgeu 36*; A Dunn 3/51) and 5/0
GW 222 (FW Whelan 32, BA Helfrich 62, F Nicholson 58; PHB Cloete 4/58) and 241 (A Dunn 39, FW Whelan 32, TH Boggan 40, A Schultze 56, JP Gallagher 43; D Price 4/43, PHB Cloete 3/75)

Match drawn between Transvaal and Western Province, 1–4 January 1937, Cape Town
Tvl 455 (EAB Rowan 38, SH Curnow 161, KG Viljoen 53, WBH Foley 80, TA Harris 38; D Price 5/124, TMH van der Spuy 3/71) and 186/7 dec (CHK Jones 82, KG Viljoen 36; TMH van der Spuy 4/45)
WP 217 (ARM Ralph 96*; CB Gaydon 4/22) and 331/4 (PGV van der Bijl 55, LM Manning 50, B Wallace 81*, TMH van der Spuy 121*)

Western Province beat Orange Free State by an innings and 99 runs, 20–23 February 1937, Cape Town
WP 506/8 dec (PGV van der Bijl 73, GE Bond 30, ARM Ralph 74, SSL Steyn 162, G Georgeu 76*; L Tuckett 3/95)
OFS 161 (AI Barr 31; PHB Cloete 3/76, J Pickup 4/9) and 246 (CJ Kaplan 38, EW Warner 57, MG Francis 55; PHB Cloete 5/112, J Pickup 4/41)

Natal beat Western Province by an innings and 80 runs, 6–9 March 1937, Durban
WP 240 (ARM Ralph 99, SSL Steyn 46; EL Dalton 6/42) and 344 (ARM Ralph 49, GE Bond 170, SSL Steyn 30, LS Eckard 32; AJM Rennie 3/54, RL Harvey 5/70)
Ntl 664/6 dec (IJ Siedle 207, RL Harvey 50, AD Nourse 240, WW Wade 95; PHB Cloete 4/200)

Western Province beat Border by an innings and 106 runs, 13–15 March 1937, East London
WP 283 (GE Bond 75, LM Manning 70, TMH van der Spuy 32; PS Hubbard 7/107)
Bdr 91 (TMH van der Spuy 5/22, PHB Cloete 3/46) and 86 (GE Bond 4/17)

Match drawn between Eastern Province and Western Province, 18–20 March 1937, Port Elizabeth
EP 341 (KGM Dimbleby 104, RH Henderson 81, DE Dimbleby 54; TMH van der Spuy 6/95)
WP 287/6 (ARM Ralph 102*, LM Manning 122)

Match drawn between Griqualand West and Western Province, 11–14 December 1937, Kimberley
GW 265 (A Dunn 84, APC Steyn 36, FF Flanagan 32; BM-K Roscoe 6/75) and 294/8 dec (F Nicholson 62, TH Boggan 66, JP McNally 39)
WP 163 (PGV van der Bijl 59, SF Viljoen 3/37, AH Gyngell 3/50) and 138/4 (PGV van der Bijl 65*, TMH van der Spuy 44; SF Viljoen 3/25)

Transvaal beat Western Province by 9 wickets, 16–18 December 1937, Johannesburg
Tvl 379 (B Mitchell 114, RE Grieveson 36, AW Briscoe 127, ACB Langton 41) and 138/1 (B Mitchell 77*, ACB Langton 33*)
WP 165 (XC Balaskas 8/60) and 349 (PGV van der Bijl 138, TMH van der Spuy 43, LM Manning 42, SSL Steyn 40, B Wallace 40*; ACB Langton 3/49, XC Balaskas 3/124)

Western Province beat North-Eastern Transvaal by 3 wickets, 20–21 December 1937, Pretoria
NET 112 (RS Martin 34; D Price 3/46, BM-K Roscoe 3/20) and 183 (RC Hicks 32, RS Martin 35, LO Waller 39, LS Brown 42; BM-K Roscoe 4/51)
WP 122 (WP Lance 3/19, LS Brown 5/54) and 176/7 (SSL Steyn 56, A Glantz 53*; LS Brown 3/65)

Border beat Western Province by 7 wickets, 27–29 December 1937, Cape Town
WP 194 (GE Bond 71, B Wallace 33; RJ Evans 5/72) and 318 (ARM Ralph 110, GE Bond 62, WBH Foley 38; RJ Evans 4/92, PS Hubbard 3/57)
Bdr 399 (DF Dowling 84, HVL Whitfield 123, D Hayidakis 77; D Price 4/112) and 114/3 (IB Gardiner 43*, DF Dowling 40*; JGB Brinkhaus 3/35)

Match drawn between Western Province and Natal, 1–4 January 1938, Cape Town
WP 320 (PGV van der Bijl 86, GE Bond 38, TMH van der Spuy 114; AP Murray 4/86) and 328 (PGV van der Bijl 102, SSL Steyn 30, B Wallace 72*, BM-K Roscoe 36; AP Murray 4/77)
Ntl 325 (JKL Randles 71, RL Harvey 72, AD Nourse 120; BM-K Roscoe 3/96) and 261/4 (DR Fell 97, RL Harvey 79)

Western Province beat Eastern Province by 8 wickets, 19–22 February 1938, Cape Town
WP 474 (PGV van der Bijl 65, TMH van der Spuy 115, WBH Foley 54, GM Larkin 72, BM-K Roscoe 51; GA Upton 3/132, JM Buchanan 3/130) and 120/2 (HB Jordaan 43*, PGV van der Bijl 51*)
EP 221 (MB Ronaldson 94, LGF Randall 68; RE Middleton 4/38) and 369 (CS Smith 33, MB Ronaldson 37, RW Robson 73, BC Lynch 60, PL Holmes 52; TMH van der Spuy 3/63)

MCC beat Western Province by 8 wickets, 12–15 November 1938, Cape Town
WP 174 (WBH Foley 37, TMH van der Spuy 31*; K Farnes 3/32, WJ Edrich 4/10) and 169 (ARM Ralph 61*, TMH van der Spuy 31; K Farnes 7/38, DVP Wright 3/64)
MCC 276 (LEG Ames 45, HT Bartlett 91*; JGB Brinkhaus 3/69, BM-K Roscoe 3/41) and 69/2

Match drawn between Griqualand West and Western Province, 16-19 December 1939, Cape Town
GW 316 (TH Boggan 83, FF Flanagan 101, JP McNally 46; JB Plimsoll 3/61) and 242 (TH Boggan 75, LE McNamara 44, JP McNally 37*; JB Plimsoll 3/52, LLM Evans 4/59)
WP 267 (PGV van der Bijl 59, LM Manning 101, G Georgeu 52; JE Waddington 8/50) and 254/5 (S Kiel 36, LM Manning 46, G Georgeu 112)

Western Province beat North-Eastern Transvaal by 7 wickets, 26-28 December 1939, Cape Town
WP 339 (G Georgeu 154, ABJ Reid 81; LS Brown 4/57, EG Bock 4/67) and 235/3 (S Kiel 139*, ARM Ralph 53*)
NET 164 (DG Helfrich 59, RS Martin 36; D Price 4/40, LS Eckard 5/43) and 408 (DG Helfrich 59, RC Hicks 108, LO Waller 65, RS Martin 37, CG Bromham 32, LS Brown 38; JB Plimsoll 4/83, LS Eckard 4/107)

Transvaal beat Western Province by 12 runs, 30 December 1939 - 2 January 1940, Cape Town
Tvl 383 (SH Curnow 31, EAB Rowan 164, RE Somers Vine 39, OE Wynne 71, RNE Petersen 30*; GB Paull 3/79) and 225/7 dec (SH Curnow 31, JT Seccombe 35, AMB Rowan 71*, JHM Pickerill 44)
WP 242 (PGV van der Bijl 33, S Kiel 69, LM Manning 33, ARM Ralph 43*; N Gordon 5/87, AMB Rowan 3/53) and 354 (PGV van der Bijl 89, S Kiel 36, ARM Ralph 140, WC Ross 31; N Gordon 3/74, AMB Rowan 3/96)

Match drawn between Natal and Western Province, 2-5 March 1940, Durban
Ntl 553/7 dec (DS Turner 77, DV Dyer 185, RL Harvey 80, AD Nourse 87, WW Wade 57; JGB Brinkhaus 5/180)
WP 358 (S Kiel 43, GE Crighton 40, G Georgeu 50, ARM Ralph 119*, TMH van der Spuy 52; EL Dalton 5/113, NBF Mann 3/67) and 124/5 (TMH van der Spuy 38*)

Western Province beat Border by 6 wickets, 8-9 March 1940, East London
Bdr 189 (HVL Whitfield 37, GV Wienand 42; JGB Brinkhaus 7/60) and 162 (RP Richter 30; JB Plimsoll 5/60, PHB Cloete 4/58)
WP 206/9 dec (ARM Ralph 68*; RJ Evans 3/68) and 146/4 (S Kiel 54, G Georgeu 39*)

Match drawn between Western Province and Eastern Province, 13-15 March 1940, Port Elizabeth
WP 187 (TMH van der Spuy 74; JM Leibbrandt 5/55, SA Thwaits 3/30) and 318/9 dec (S Kiel 120, TMH van der Spuy 33, JE Cheetham 108*; AH Coy 6/94)
EP 195 (W Marais 42; JB Plimsoll 5/52, TMH van der Spuy 3/26) and 38/1

Transvaal beat Western Province by 8 wickets, 1-3 January 1942, Cape Town
WP 237 (KG Fismer 54, JE Cheetham 37, AD Keen 44) and 236/8 dec (S Kiel 128*, AD Keen 45; N Gordon 4/63)
Tvl 251/8 dec (JHM Pickerill 71, FB Warne 66, ACB Langton 50; R Lofthouse 4/63) and 166/6 (G Georgeu 68*, ACB Langton 39)

Match drawn between Western Province and Transvaal, 1-3 January 1946, Cape Town
WP 131 (N Gordon 4/32, XC Balaskas 3/38) and 348 (BW Sewell 34, G Georgeu 58, ARM Ralph 62, AD Keen 35, BH Crews 43; GWA Chubb 4/81, XC Balaskas 4/125)
Tvl 354 (TA Harris 111, KG Viljoen 116*, XC Balaskas 42; JB Plimsoll 6/101, LS Eckard 3/89) and 126/2 (RJ Gordon-Campbell 55*)

Natal beat Western Province by 9 wickets, 15-18 March 1946, Durban
Ntl 438/9 dec (AD Nourse 81, OC Dawson 126, EL Dalton 42, E Eaglestone 87*, VI Smith 31; R Lofthouse 3/63) and 38/1
WP 206 (KGM Dimbleby 56, G Georgeu 34, JE Cheetham 62*; VI Smith 3/56) and 269 (S Kiel 77, G Georgeu 64, JE Cheetham 48; EL Dalton 3/45)

Match drawn between North-Eastern Transvaal and Western Province, 20-21 March 1946, Brakpan
NET 180/9 dec (KR Gibson 60, TH Woolley 32, RS Martin 54*; JB Plimsoll 7/42)
WP 180/5 (KGM Dimbleby 56, JE Cheetham 84; WH Douglas 3/55)

Western Province beat Rhodesia by 4 wickets, 6-8 December 1946, Cape Town
Rhod 225 (C Harris 73, JHF Fuller 49; MA Hanley 8/55) and 222 (C Harris 47, JHF Fuller 35, PNF Mansell 57, F McDonald 45; JB Plimsoll 4/44, MA Hanley 3/57)
WP 136 (JE Cheetham 34, LS Eckard 31*; DS Tomlinson 6/56) and 313/6 (S Kiel 75, CB van Ryneveld 90*, AD Keen 63; DS Tomlinson 3/107)

Natal beat Western Province by 7 wickets, 16-18 December 1946, Durban
WP 196 (S Kiel 33, JE Cheetham 39; LW Payn 4/48, EL Dalton 3/29) and 147 (G Georgeu 31; VI Smith 5/42, HJ Tayfield 4/19)
Ntl 267 (DF Dowling 30, RR Yuill 45, OC Dawson 67; MA Hanley 3/59) and 77/3 (DV Dyer 37*; JB Plimsoll 3/30)

Western Province beat Griqualand West by 87 runs, 20–23 December 1946, Kimberley
WP 115 (TMH van der Spuy 36*; A Waddington 4/30, WEH Vincent 3/22) and 172 (DM Ovenstone 46; A Waddington 4/65, JE Waddington 4/63)
GW 136 (A Dunn 42*, JE Waddington 33; JB Plimsoll 3/53, EV Witte 6/53) and 64 (JB Plimsoll 7/35, EV Witte 3/19)

Western Province beat North-Eastern Transvaal by 9 wickets, 26–28 December 1946, Cape Town
NET 89 (HB Jordaan 40; MA Hanley 7/45) and 183 (HB Jordaan 83*; MA Hanley 5/79, AD Keen 3/16)
WP 261 (G Georgeu 68, EV Witte 51, JE Cheetham 66; HH Watt 3/75, RS Martin 3/34) and 12/1

Western Province beat Transvaal by 9 wickets, 1–3 January 1947, Cape Town
WP 361 (S Kiel 87, DM Ovenstone 52, G Georgeu 55, WBH Foley 87; N Gordon 3/56, DW Begbie 3/77) and 169/4 (S Kiel 54, G Georgeu 41)
Tvl 202 (EAB Rowan 38, KG Viljoen 36, TA Harris 31, DW Begbie 46*; EV Witte 3/24, MA Hanley 4/59) and 326/7 dec (KG Viljoen 53, B Mitchell 39, DW Begbie 110*, AMB Rowan 52*; JB Plimsoll 4/81, EV Witte 3/76)

Western Province beat Eastern Province by 6 wickets, 7–10 February 1947, Port Elizabeth
EP 159 (RG Draper 48; LLH Impey 3/44, MA Hanley 6/48) and 205 (RG Draper 108; LLM Evans 3/40, MA Hanley 5/60)
WP 300 (KGM Dimbleby 127, DE Dimbleby 66, LCG Whiteing 39; BC Lynch 3/30, NBF Mann 3/64) and 65/4 (JE Cheetham 37*)

Western Province beat Border by an innings and 71 runs, 5–6 December 1947, Cape Town
WP 357/7 dec (OE Wynne 134, DM Ovenstone 37, DE Dimbleby 114)
Bdr 80 (LLH Impey 3/31, MA Hanley 4/23) and 206 (DBH Hollard 32, RR Phillips 123; MA Hanley 6/72)

Match drawn between Western Province and Transvaal, 13–16 December 1947, Johannesburg
WP 115 (KGM Dimbleby 55; LJ Heaney 4/9) and 287/6 (OE Wynne 88, G Georgeu 76, JE Cheetham 55*; GWA Chubb 3/48)
Tvl 428/6 dec (EAB Rowan 68, B Mitchell 122, DW Begbie 55, KG Viljoen 97, TA Harris 36, AMB Rowan 30*)

Match drawn between Eastern Province and Western Province, 26–29 December 1947, Cape Town
EP 409 (RG Draper 37, HV Feltham 50, SF Hird 69, ARA Murray 133; JB Plimsoll 3/83, LLH Impey 3/88) and 70/4 (JB Plimsoll 4/19)
WP 205 (KGM Dimbleby 69, JE Cheetham 39; NBF Mann 8/59) and 325/9 dec (JE Cheetham 58, G Georgeu 104, JB Plimsoll 51; SA Thwaits 6/77)

Match drawn between Natal and Western Province, 1–3 January 1948, Cape Town
Ntl 420 (DR Fell 89, AD Nourse 124, WW Wade 37, DF Dowling 101*, HE Dalton 31; EV Witte 4/105, MA Hanley 4/146) and 180/4 dec (MH Lang 95, DBG King 60)
WP 375 (OE Wynne 70, DE Dimbleby 58, JE Cheetham 126*, AD Keen 77; LA Markham 7/106) and 134/3 (OE Wynne 78, DE Dimbleby 34*)

Western Province beat Rhodesia by 3 wickets, 5–7 March 1948, Salisbury
Rhod 173 (CJ Pretorius 72, KP Curran 52*; EV Witte 5/70, MA Hanley 4/45) and 187 (AP Singleton 36, KP Curran 35*; EV Witte 3/54, MA Hanley 4/58)
WP 165 (JWE Wiley 70, BH Crews 30; JM Leibbrandt 5/54) and 198/7 (BH Crews 33, AA Luck 34; ES Newson 3/46, JM Leibbrandt 4/78)

Orange Free State beat Western Province by 165 runs, 12–15 March 1948, Bloemfontein
OFS 237 (FB Lee 95; EV Witte 5/63) and 297/9 dec (JC Newton 74, WAM Howell 54; GRM Bolus 5/125)
WP 207 (JP Sierra 60, G Georgeu 38; L Tuckett 4/57, HF Wright 3/64) and 162 (EV Witte 47*; HF Wright 4/57)

MCC beat Western Province by 9 wickets, 29 October – 1 November 1948, Cape Town
WP 386/4 dec (OE Wynne 108, JO Newton-Thompson 78, G Georgeu 32, JE Cheetham 68*, HGO Owen-Smith 65*) and 88/4 dec (G Georgeu 41*; AV Bedser 4/30)
MCC 357/5 dec (JF Crapp 83, DCS Compton 34, FG Mann 112, RT Simpson 35*, TG Evans 52*; EV Witte 3/72) and 118/1 (L Hutton 38, C Washbrook 50*, DCS Compton 30*)

Match drawn between Australians and Western Province, 2–5 December 1949, Cape Town
Aus 235 (J Moroney 90, SJE Loxton 57, KA Archer 35; GRM Bolus 3/48, MA Hanley 3/100, SA Thwaits 4/45) and 216/6 dec (J Moroney 87, RN Harvey 42, CL McCool 34; SA Thwaits 3/84)
WP 189 (JD Nel 42, JE Cheetham 59; RR Lindwall 3/41, IWG Johnson 3/52) and 122/6 (PD Jaffer 41, GRM Bolus 35*; IWG Johnson 3/25)

Eastern Province beat Western Province by 61 runs, 23–26 December 1949, Port Elizabeth
EP 217 (KGM Dimbleby 43, RG Draper 41, AJ Curnick 62; EV Witte 4/70, MA Hanley 4/101) and 192/8 dec (RG Draper 110*; MA Hanley 5/101)
WP 248 (RJ Westcott 36, AW Marshall 77, HC Howell 32, DW Rees 32) and 100 (HB Birrell 5/33)

Match drawn between Western Province and Australians, 10–13 March 1950, Cape Town
WP 303 (JE Cheetham 98, OE Wynne 52, PD Jaffer 50; RR Lindwall 4/52) and 142/3 (JE Cheetham 55*, OE Wynne 38)
Aus 425/7 dec (AR Morris 103, J Moroney 46, KR Miller 58, RN Harvey 34, KA Archer 57, CL McCool 100*; MA Hanley 3/90)

Match drawn between Western Province and North-Eastern Transvaal, 3–6 November 1950, Cape Town
WP 358/9 dec (RJ Westcott 72, JE Cheetham 107, TB Reddick 56, PD Jaffer 31, SA Thwaits 37*; JW Blewett 4/90)
NET 202 (TH Woolley 84; CB van Ryneveld 4/92, AW Marshall 3/32) and 209/6 (H Ralphs 32, TH Woolley 86, HE Patterson 30*; CB van Ryneveld 3/75)

Western Province beat Border by 132 runs, 2–5 December 1950, East London
WP 308 (RJ Westcott 108, JD Nel 58, TB Reddick 42, CB van Ryneveld 56; IH Neuper 4/77, HVL Whitfield 3/76) and 268/5 dec (RJ Westcott 88, JE Cheetham 80*, MA Hanley 31*)
Bdr 273 (KN Kirton 95, RR Phillips 54; CB van Ryneveld 4/112, SA Thwaits 3/46) and 171 (KN Kirton 44, RR Phillips 49; MA Hanley 4/53, SA Thwaits 3/45)

Match drawn between Western Province and Orange Free State, 8–11 December 1950, Bloemfontein
WP 494/7 dec (RJ Westcott 30, JE Cheetham 271*, CB van Ryneveld 39, GAS Innes 35, AW Marshall 31, ABJ Reid 37*; HF Wright 3/112) and 38/0
OFS 187 (CB van Ryneveld 3/70, AW Marshall 4/34) and 479 (LB Koch 74, IEF Kirby 56, RC le Sueur 58, GFK Jackson 32, HF Wright 105*, DG Riemer 43, JR Liddle 57; CB van Ryneveld 3/115, AW Marshall 3/116)

Match drawn between Natal and Western Province, 15–18 December 1950, Durban
Ntl 329 (AD Nourse 114, RA McLean 49, HJ Tayfield 58*; SA Thwaits 5/92, CB van Ryneveld 4/98) and 51/1 dec (I de Gersigny 39)
WP 209 (JD Nel 49, SA Thwaits 32, TB Reddick 44; LA Markham 3/53) and 50/0

Western Province beat Rhodesia by 6 wickets, 22–26 December 1950, Cape Town
Rhod 235 (PNF Mansell 33, CJ Pretorius 54, JM Leibbrandt 50; RF Delport 7/54) and 161 (JMS Baldwin 34, JHA Wallace 31; SA Thwaits 6/29)
WP 221 (JD Nel 42, GAS Innes 31, SA Thwaits 71*; PNF Mansell 7/78) and 176/4 (JE Cheetham 63, CB van Ryneveld 44)

Transvaal beat Western Province by 148 runs, 30 December 1950 – 2 January 1951, Cape Town
Tvl 198 (GM Fullerton 112; SA Thwaits 5/56, CB van Ryneveld 4/95) and 353/9 dec (AI Taylor 52, GM Fullerton 94, WR Endean 99*; RF Delport 5/87)
WP 85 (GWA Chubb 5/34, A Tayfield 3/30) and 318 (CB van Ryneveld 138, PD Jaffer 59, GAS Innes 39, A Tayfield 4/94, DA Clark 3/65)

Western Province beat Transvaal by 5 wickets, 1–4 December 1951, Johannesburg
Tvl 156 (WR Endean 38; ERH Fuller 3/47) and 88/9 dec (ERH Fuller 7/54)
WP 113/9 dec (JE Cheetham 33; MG Melle 4/53, C Tayfield 4/27) and 133/5 (GAS Innes 43, JE Cheetham 58)

Match drawn between Natal and Western Province, 7–10 December 1951, Pietermaritzburg
Ntl 343 (DJ McGlew 186, HJ Tayfield 30; GRM Bolus 4/63, RF Delport 3/104) and 137/5 dec (DJ McGlew 64, I de Gersigny 42; SA Thwaits 3/24)
WP 249 (GAS Innes 34, JH Ferrandi 66, ERH Fuller 48; NE Markham 6/77) and 52/1

Match drawn between Eastern Province and Western Province, 14–17 December 1951, Port Elizabeth
EP 220 (ARA Murray 97, HG Emslie 54; CB van Ryneveld 5/68) and 253 (JHB Waite 44, ARA Murray 73, SD du Toit 37; ERH Fuller 3/100, SA Thwaits 4/41)
WP 292 (KT Commins 49, RJ Westcott 73, CB van Ryneveld 36, ERH Fuller 43, AW Marshall 39; JO Young 5/64, ARA Murray 3/69) and 156/8 (RJ Westcott 39, GAS Innes 75; AG Blenkinsop 5/49)

Match drawn between Eastern Province and Western Province, 24–27 December 1951, Cape Town
EP 326 (EB Norton 111, ARA Murray 77; ERH Fuller 3/85, SA Thwaits 3/83) and 183/4 (KGM Dimbleby 35, JHB Waite 56, EB Norton 31*)
WP 402 (JD Nel 59, RJ Westcott 32, GAS Innes 139, JE Cheetham 34, AW Marshall 58, JH Ferrandi 48; EJ Draper 6/114)

Natal beat Western Province by 3 wickets, 31 December 1951 – 2 January 1952, Cape Town
Ntl 253 (DJ McGlew 37, DF Dowling 63, RA McLean 74; GRM Bolus 5/50) and 80/7 (ERH Fuller 5/44)
WP 86 (HJ Tayfield 7/41) and 245 (GAS Innes 35, JE Cheetham 37, AW Marshall 78; HJ Tayfield 6/110)

Western Province beat Transvaal by an innings and 87 runs, 18–21 January 1952, Cape Town
WP 500/9 dec (JD Nel 139, JE Cheetham 41, CB van Ryneveld 130, ERH Fuller 53, JH Ferrandi 41*; LJ Heaney 3/82)
Tvl 163 (EAB Rowan 77, A Tayfield 33; AW Marshall 3/9) and 250 (EAB Rowan 32, SR Kimber 42, A Tayfield 72; CB van Ryneveld 5/50)

Orange Free State beat Western Province by 29 runs, 6–9 December 1952, Bloemfontein
OFS 361 (SL Hanson 36, LB Koch 63, RC le Sueur 112, ETE Hansen 56; EV Witte 3/87) and 153 (SL Hanson 66, KL Gibbs 40*; MA Hanley 6/40)
WP 230 (JD Nel 71, BD Pfaff 62; JR Liddle 4/70) and 255 (WGA Wiley 59, PS Nicholson 51, BD Pfaff 40, MA Hanley 38; KL Gibbs 4/56, HF Wright 3/63)

Natal beat Western Province by 5 wickets, 12–15 December 1952, Durban
WP 229 (RJ Westcott 106, AW Marshall 55; RMC Copland 3/67) and 156 (JD Nel 61; VI Smith 7/50)
Ntl 206 (I de Gersigny 63, RMC Copland 35*; EV Witte 5/68) and 180/5 (JL Lamb 87, I de Gersigny 32; MA Hanley 3/72)

Match drawn between Western Province and Eastern Province, 19–22 December 1952, Port Elizabeth
WP 156 (JD Nel 41; RL Forward 3/40) and 372/7 dec (JD Nel 217*, PS Nicholson 58, JH Ferrandi 58*; RL Forward 3/116, DES Millard 3/48)
EP 270 (KH Johnson 56, HG Emslie 81, DES Millard 41; EV Witte 4/48, MA Hanley 5/93) and 146/7 (R Gathorne 30, JO Young 51*; MA Hanley 4/42)

Western Province beat Orange Free State by an innings and 90 runs, 26–29 December 1952, Cape Town
OFS 235 (SL Hanson 50, RC le Sueur 48, AL Parker 42, ETE Hansen 38; MA Hanley 6/63) and 159 (LB Koch 55; MA Hanley 6/65, RP Davis 3/25)
WP 484/8 dec (PS Nicholson 100, JD Nel 36, AW Marshall 48, PD Jaffer 128, BD Pfaff 76; KL Gibbs 3/115)

Western Province beat Natal by 21 runs, 1–3 January 1953, Cape Town
WP 255 (AW Marshall 69, HNP Roy 50, BD Pfaff 62*; TL Goddard 3/51, VI Smith 3/60) and 279 (PS Nicholson 64, JD Nel 37, HNP Roy 42, BD Pfaff 74; VI Smith 7/108)
Ntl 169 (DBG King 33, DF Dowling 30, AL Upton 40; EV Witte 4/37, MA Hanley 4/54) and 344 (DF Dowling 84, AD Nourse 155, TL Goddard 48; EV Witte 3/71)

Western Province beat Eastern Province by 8 wickets, 6–9 February 1953, Cape Town
WP 383 (RJ Westcott 70, JD Nel 107, AW Marshall 41, PD Jaffer 65, HNP Roy 37) and 34/2
EP 152 (MA Hanley 4/40) and 264 (R Gathorne 60, HI Long 77, BB Bradfield 41*; MA Hanley 6/89)

Match drawn between Western Province and New Zealanders, 31 October – 3 November 1953, Cape Town
WP 314/8 dec (RJ Westcott 82, BD Pfaff 66, CB van Ryneveld 57; GWF Overton 4/51) and 229/8 dec (KT Commins 70, RJ Westcott 71, BD Pfaff 30; GO Rabone 6/99)
NZ 229 (B Sutcliffe 69, ME Chapple 71; MA Hanley 6/82) and 235/7 (JR Reid 111, FLH Mooney 52*)

Western Province beat Natal by 32 runs, 26–29 December 1953, Cape Town
WP 441 (KT Commins 92, GAS Innes 72, HNP Roy 37, LG Treadaway 50, MG Melle 59; VI Smith 3/100) and 194 (JD Nel 50, BD Pfaff 50; TL Goddard 5/73, VI Smith 5/91)
Ntl 426/8 dec (TL Goddard 174, DF Dowling 91, HJ Keith 86; MA Hanley 4/142) and 177 (CAR Duckworth 46, E Eaglestone 41, AL Upton 63*; MG Melle 3/28, MA Hanley 5/60)

Match drawn between Western Province and New Zealanders, 12–15 February 1954, Cape Town
WP 240 (RJ Westcott 40, JD Nel 48, GAS Innes 72; AR MacGibbon 4/71) and 241/9 dec (JD Nel 68, CB van Ryneveld 64; W Bell 3/69, B Sutcliffe 3/79)
NZ 324/8 dec (FLH Mooney 48, ME Chapple 33, JR Reid 75, B Sutcliffe 63, MB Poore 36; RF Delport 3/94) and 143/9 (AR MacGibbon 31; RF Delport 4/43)

Match drawn between Orange Free State and Western Province, 20–23 November 1954, Bloemfontein
OFS 417 (LB Koch 111, SL Hanson 58, EL Johnstone 42, RC le Sueur 162; ERH Fuller 4/126, JE Pothecary 3/86) and 242/7 dec (LB Koch 56, EL Johnstone 36, C Richardson 40; ERH Fuller 4/91)
WP 315 (RJ Westcott 51, GAS Innes 34, JE Cheetham 81, HC Howell 32, JE Pothecary 37; L Tuckett 4/70, JR Liddle 4/92) and 158/3 (KT Commins 64, RJ Westcott 37, BD Pfaff 39)

Match drawn between Natal and Western Province, 26–29 November 1954, Durban
Ntl 406/6 dec (DJ McGlew 91, TL Goddard 60, NE Markham 51, HJ Keith 111*, AL Upton 68*; JE Pothecary 4/100) and 95/0 (DJ McGlew 37*, TL Goddard 53*)
WP 297 (GAS Innes 50, BD Pfaff 43, JE Cheetham 42, AW Marshall 70, ERH Fuller 50*; VI Smith 4/122, HJ Tayfield 5/116)

Transvaal beat Western Province by an innings and 306 runs, 3–4 December 1954, Johannesburg
Tvl 511/8 dec (AI Taylor 180, JHB Waite 62, C Tayfield 34, WR Endean 127, PL Winslow 78; JE Pothecary 3/106)
WP 115 (JE Cheetham 42; NAT Adcock 4/29) and 90 (NAT Adcock 3/23, JC Kerby 3/19)

Western Province beat Orange Free State by 70 runs, 27–29 December 1954, Cape Town
WP 365 (RJ Westcott 98, GAS Innes 59, CB van Ryneveld 59, JE Cheetham 85*; ETE Hansen 3/86, JR Liddle 6/114) and 253 (RJ Westcott 68, BD Pfaff 78, ERH Fuller 45; JR Liddle 5/96)
OFS 349 (LB Koch 95, RC le Sueur 91, JHV Forbes 80, C Richardson 36; AW Marshall 5/36) and 199 (LB Koch 66, SL Hanson 33; CB van Ryneveld 8/48)

Match drawn between Western Province and Transvaal, 1–4 January 1955, Cape Town
WP 377 (RJ Westcott 93, CB van Ryneveld 44, BD Pfaff 34, AW Marshall 32, DES Millard 62, JSM Fox 31; AI Taylor 4/52) and 153/4 dec (GAS Innes 40, CB van Ryneveld 73)
Tvl 280 (KJ Funston 136*, A Tayfield 38; CB van Ryneveld 6/105) and 114/4 (A Tayfield 40*)

Natal beat Western Province by 107 runs, 7–10 January 1955, Cape Town
Ntl 364 (DJ McGlew 67, TL Goddard 64, HJ Keith 67, RA McLean 46, FC Bestall 52; SA Thwaits 5/57, CB van Ryneveld 3/120) and 228/8 dec (HJ Keith 64, RA McLean 85; ERH Fuller 4/93, SA Thwaits 4/67)
WP 232 (CB van Ryneveld 41, ERH Fuller 69, JH Ferrandi 30*; HJ Tayfield 8/129) and 253 (RJ Westcott 80, AW Marshall 40*, BD Pfaff 48; HJ Tayfield 5/115, VI Smith 4/108)

Western Province beat Transvaal by 61 runs, 17–20 December 1955, Cape Town
WP 277 (RJ Westcott 83, AJ Pithey 73, RR MacDonald 45, ERH Fuller 30; PS Heine 5/72) and 176 (CB van Ryneveld 80; PS Heine 5/78, DEJ Ironside 3/50)
Tvl 182 (A Tayfield 35, WR Endean 36; JR Liddle 7/72) and 210 (WR Endean 91*; JR Liddle 3/64, CB van Ryneveld 4/93)

Western Province beat Eastern Province by 41 runs, 24–27 December 1955, Port Elizabeth
WP 218 (RJ Westcott 40, GAS Innes 44, CB van Ryneveld 51; AH McKinnon 3/88) and 226 (AJ Pithey 65, HNP Roy 45; IF Anderson 3/46, GF Dakin 3/18)
EP 277 (GF Dakin 31, GD Varnals 30, EB Norton 30, HG Emslie 51, ARA Murray 43; JE Pothecary 3/70, JR Liddle 4/73) and 126 (ARA Murray 74; CB van Ryneveld 3/45)

Western Province beat Eastern Province by 4 wickets, 31 December 1955 – 3 January 1956, Cape Town
EP 309 (GF Dakin 68, HB Birrell 54, ARA Murray 89; JBR Maile 5/66) and 106 (AH McKinnon 31; ERH Fuller 3/30, JE Pothecary 3/31, JR Liddle 3/23)
WP 294 (GAS Innes 78, JR Siedle 127; ARA Murray 4/73, AH McKinnon 3/45) and 123/6 (RJ Westcott 67*)

Western Province beat Natal by 69 runs, 6–9 January 1956, Cape Town
WP 401 (AJ Pithey 101, CB van Ryneveld 49, HNP Roy 146, JE Pothecary 49*; TL Goddard 3/78, HJ Tayfield 5/170) and 203/9 dec (AJ Pithey 44, CB van Ryneveld 43; HJ Tayfield 5/101, VI Smith 3/79)
Ntl 327 (DJ McGlew 60, JC Watkins 38, LB Koch 99, HJ Tayfield 64; JR Liddle 5/132) and 208 (RA McLean 74, BP Armitage 36, HJ Tayfield 32; JR Liddle 6/60)

Natal beat Western Province by an innings and 39 runs, 10–13 February 1956, Pietermaritzburg
Ntl 404 (TL Goddard 92, CGD Burger 50, DJ McGlew 121*, NE Markham 78; ERH Fuller 5/53)
WP 101 (NE Markham 3/29, J Atkinson 3/24, TL Goddard 4/40) and 264 (CB van Ryneveld 46, JR Siedle 52, JH Ferrandi 89; NE Markham 3/43)

Western Province beat Transvaal by 2 wickets, 17–20 February 1956, Johannesburg
Tvl 81 (ERH Fuller 7/40, DA Louw 3/18) and 129 (ERH Fuller 4/30, DA Louw 3/33, JBR Maile 3/25)
WP 91 (CB van Ryneveld 39; DEJ Ironside 6/37) and 122/8 (PS Heine 4/33, NAT Adcock 3/35)

MCC beat Western Province by an innings and 76 runs, 26–29 October 1956, Cape Town
WP 129 (BD Pfaff 46; JB Statham 5/26) and 129 (AJ Pithey 34; JC Laker 6/47)
MCC 334 (ASM Oakman 63, PBH May 162; ERH Fuller 6/83)

Western Province beat Border by 1 wicket, 23–26 November 1956, East London
Bdr 212 (KN Kirton 57, RR Phillips 73; AW Marshall 4/53) and 276 (RI Geach 97, WD Wilson 84, RK Thorne 49; JE Pothecary 3/67, JR Liddle 3/64, AW Marshall 3/80)
WP 166 (HNP Roy 75; RK Thorne 6/60) and 324/9 (AJ Pithey 133, GAS Innes 72; S Knott 3/86)

Match drawn between Western Province and Natal, 30 November – 2 December 1956, Durban
WP 213 (AJ Pithey 33, JH Ferrandi 57, JBR Maile 36; TL Goddard 5/36) and 199/6 (AJ Pithey 50, GAS Innes 59, KMS Heldsinger 46)
Ntl 468 (RA Pearce 95, TL Goddard 135, CGD Burger 85, RA McLean 53, JC Watkins 35; JR Liddle 4/100, AW Marshall 3/95)

Match drawn between MCC and Western Province, 22–26 February 1957, Cape Town
MCC 335 (ASM Oakman 36, PBH May 116, DJ Insole 45, FH Tyson 30, GAR Lock 39; HD Bromfield 3/57, CB van Ryneveld 5/95) and 186/8 dec (PBH May 79, MC Cowdrey 48; ERH Fuller 5/26)
WP 257 (GAS Innes 75, CB van Ryneveld 50, JH Ferrandi 52*; JH Wardle 3/91, GAR Lock 5/69) and 176/8 (AJ Pithey 30, JH Ferrandi 60; GAR Lock 5/75)

Match drawn between Western Province and Natal, 8–11 November 1957, Cape Town
WP 304/9 dec (RJ Westcott 48, GAS Innes 35, JD Nel 110, BD Pfaff 45; BHP Jerome 4/74) and 138/1 (RJ Westcott 67*, GAS Innes 53)
Ntl 233 (DJ McGlew 65, HJ Keith 34, G Morby-Smith 58*; GE Steyn 4/67)

Australians beat Western Province by 10 wickets, 12–17 December 1957, Cape Town
WP 244 (AJ Pithey 52, JD Nel 30, GAS Innes 49, JH Ferrandi 32; I Meckiff 4/52) and 231 (AJ Pithey 40, RJ Westcott 60, JD Nel 33, CB van Ryneveld 53; R Benaud 3/68, LF Kline 6/65)
Aus 421 (JW Burke 72, RN Harvey 63, ID Craig 45, PJP Burge 41, R Benaud 38, AK Davidson 76; HD Bromfield 4/68) and 55/0 (R Benaud 32*)

Western Province beat Border by 219 runs, 26–28 December 1957, Cape Town
WP 194 (RJ Westcott 85; WR Chalmers 4/54) and 360/8 dec (KT Commins 88, RJ Westcott 101, JH Ferrandi 71, DL Fernley 36; EF Schreiber 3/114, WR Chalmers 3/41)
Bdr 162 (RI Geach 37, KH Johnson 36, BH Crews 30; GE Steyn 7/32) and 173 (D Fenner 65, RK Thorne 63; JC Kerby 6/33)

Western Province beat Eastern Province by 181 runs, 17–20 January 1958, Port Elizabeth
WP 182 (RJ Westcott 36, DL Fernley 61; JG Ferrant 3/49, AH McKinnon 6/62) and 258/5 dec (RJ Westcott 140, DL Fernley 44; IF Anderson 3/49)
EP 113 (GD Varnals 48, RA Grebe 34; ERH Fuller 6/41) and 146 (HI Long 37; GE Steyn 7/43)

Australians beat Western Province by an innings and 50 runs, 21–24 February 1958, Cape Town
WP 104 (RJ Westcott 51; I Meckiff 4/21, R Benaud 5/41) and 261 (AJ Pithey 47, GAS Innes 60, CB van Ryneveld 68; AK Davidson 5/38)
Aus 415 (LE Favell 40, KD Mackay 52, ID Craig 33, RB Simpson 33, AK Davidson 129, I Meckiff 48)

Match drawn between Western Province and Natal, 5–8 December 1958, Cape Town
WP 340 (GAS Innes 131, OE Wynne 75, JE Pothecary 31*; GM Griffin 4/54, PM Dodds 3/95) and 262 (RJ Westcott 92, JBR Maile 46, JH Ferrandi 30*; MK Elgie 3/16)
Ntl 310 (DJ McGlew 53, TL Goddard 137, L Morby-Smith 32, MS Smith 35; HD Bromfield 5/73)

Match drawn between Rhodesia and Western Province, 24–27 December 1958, Cape Town
Rhod 217 (LB Koch 32, KC Bland 62, RB Ullyett 35; JC Kerby 4/46) and 349/8 dec (AJ Pithey 138, LB Koch 63, PNF Mansell 37, KC Bland 38, DB Pithey 30; HD Bromfield 4/68)
WP 313 (OE Wynne 31, JBR Maile 92, MHH Richardson 132; HV Paton 3/17) and 151/7 (GAS Innes 50, JBR Maile 38; DB Pithey 4/45)

Western Province beat Transvaal by an innings and 52 runs, 1–3 January 1959, Cape Town
Tvl 179 (JHB Waite 61; PL van der Merwe 3/41, HD Bromfield 3/48) and 100 (PL van der Merwe 3/25, HD Bromfield 6/41)
WP 331 (RJ Westcott 34, GAS Innes 55, OE Wynne 140; GE Steyn 5/96)

Match drawn between Natal and Western Province, 6–9 February 1959, Pietermaritzburg
Ntl 358 (DJ McGlew 113, L Morby-Smith 49, RA McLean 57, C Wesley 35, AF Tillim 40; FTM Drummer 3/86, JE Pothecary 3/61) and 158/2 dec (MK Elgie 70, RA McLean 70*)
WP 254 (GAS Innes 31, JBR Maile 94; PM Dodds 5/60) and 134/2 (GAS Innes 62*, JBR Maile 42*)

Transvaal beat Western Province by 104 runs, 13–16 February 1959, Johannesburg
Tvl 156 (PH Kinsley 65; JE Pothecary 4/43, RJ Westcott 3/44) and 343 (GD Varnals 49, AI Taylor 55, PR Carlstein 31, GG Ritchie 59, JP Fellows-Smith 40, KL Gibbs 36; JBR Maile 4/67)
WP 122 (JH Ferrandi 35; KA Walter 4/36, KL Gibbs 3/34) and 273 (GAS Innes 106, JBR Maile 35, MHH Richardson 69; KA Walter 3/68, JP Fellows-Smith 4/50)

Rhodesia beat Western Province by 6 wickets, 21–22 February 1959, Salisbury
WP 69 (GB Lawrence 3/9, HV Paton 5/13) and 158 (JH Ferrandi 35; JT Partridge 6/40)
Rhod 133 (RB Ullyett 35; JBR Maile 4/40) and 95/4 (FTM Drummer 4/47)

Western Province beat Border by an innings and 52 runs, 27–30 November 1959, East London
WP 375 (RJ Westcott 59, GAS Innes 85, JBR Maile 108, JH Ferrandi 76*; EF Schreiber 3/95, WR Chalmers 3/117, AF Hagemann 3/56)
Bdr 127 (HD Bromfield 3/30, JBR Maile 3/27) and 196 (KT Commins 39, D Fenner 45, RK Thorne 45; JE Pothecary 5/42, HD Bromfield 3/53)

Natal beat Western Province by 123 runs, 4–7 December 1959, Durban
Ntl 151 (C Wesley 41; JE Pothecary 4/70, JBR Maile 4/21) and 190 (RA McLean 55, L Morby-Smith 55; JE Pothecary 4/48, PL van der Merwe 6/40)
WP 137 (MHH Richardson 64; GM Griffin 7/36, TL Goddard 3/54) and 81 (PL van der Merwe 30*; GM Griffin 4/22, TL Goddard 3/20, PM Dodds 3/24)

Transvaal beat Western Province by an innings and 49 runs, 11–14 December 1959, Johannesburg
Tvl 335 (AI Taylor 33, S O'Linn 73, JP Fellows-Smith 59, HJ Tayfield 34; JBR Maile 3/48)
WP 112 (JBR Maile 34; JP Fellows-Smith 4/19) and 174 (RJ Westcott 58, PL van der Merwe 32; GS Bunyard 3/26)

Western Province beat Border by 8 wickets, 26–28 December 1959, Cape Town
Bdr 163 (KT Commins 40; JM Lee 3/25, HD Bromfield 5/50) and 116 (AF Hagemann 31, KT Commins 39; JBR Maile 7/27)
WP 156 (MHH Richardson 34; S Knott 5/33, DN During 3/20) and 124/2 (RJ Westcott 54, GAS Innes 45*)

Transvaal beat Western Province by 79 runs, 1–4 January 1960, Cape Town
Tvl 281 (S O'Linn 83, JP Fellows-Smith 87; JBR Maile 4/91, HD Bromfield 5/69) and 241/8 dec (AI Taylor 39, PH Kinsley 57, JP Fellows-Smith 35*, HJ Tayfield 36; JBR Maile 5/106)
WP 312 (RJ Westcott 38, JH Ferrandi 67, KMS Heldsinger 63, PN Lear 45; HJ Tayfield 4/125, S Stanley 5/112) and 131 (RJ Westcott 45; HJ Tayfield 4/64, S Stanley 5/60)

Western Province beat Rhodesia by an innings and 19 runs, 15–18 January 1960, Cape Town
Rhod 189 (RA Gripper 30, DJ Lewis 33, RB Ullyett 31; JE Pothecary 3/30, HD Bromfield 5/52) and 170 (CAR Duckworth 67, RB Ullyett 31; JE Pothecary 5/29, HD Bromfield 3/35)
WP 378 (GAS Innes 99, PL van der Merwe 95, RJ Westcott 56; GB Lawrence 3/84, DC Napier 3/78, PD Oldham 3/93)

SA Universities beat Western Province by an innings and 98 runs, 3–6 December 1960, Cape Town
SAUniv 421 (GC Heath 32, EJ Brotherton 164*, KC Bland 124, RC White 34; JBR Maile 4/92, HD Bromfield 5/109)
WP 89 (JW Rushmere 6/32, GG Hall 4/24) and 234 (JSM Fox 63, JM Graham 30, F Bing 34, JH Ferrandi 30; GG Hall 9/122)

Western Province beat Transvaal B by 9 wickets, 9–12 December 1960, Cape Town
TvlB 240 (JH Baillie 44, RHM Corin 65, JC Kerby 42; JE Commins 4/65) and 127 (LR Harris 69*; JE Pothecary 3/15, JE Commins 4/17)
WP 320 (RJ Westcott 32, GAS Innes 76, JH Ferrandi 57, KMS Heldsinger 54; BD Thorp 3/74, Z Taliadoros 5/112) and 48/1

Natal beat Western Province by an innings and 86 runs, 26–27 December 1960, Durban
WP 90 (PL van der Merwe 40; NAT Adcock 3/23, CG Halse 3/21, JM Cole 3/35) and 99 (GAS Innes 31; TL Goddard 6/13)
Ntl 275 (RA McLean 102, MK Elgie 38, L Morby-Smith 41*, NAT Adcock 38; JE Commins 4/48)

Western Province beat Transvaal by 81 runs, 31 December 1960 – 3 January 1961, Cape Town
WP 251 (PL van der Merwe 96, VT McCulloch 60; KA Walter 3/53) and 243 (GAS Innes 104, PL van der Merwe 30, KMS Heldsinger 36; GS Bunyard 4/28, HJ Tayfield 4/78)
Tvl 252 (S O'Linn 61, LR Harris 70, HJ Tayfield 43; DA Louw 3/34) and 161 (HJ Tayfield 33*; HD Bromfield 7/60)

Eastern Province beat Western Province by 5 runs, 6–9 January 1961, Cape Town
EP 134 (RG Pollock 60; MJ Macaulay 4/41, JE Commins 5/32) and 307 (EJ Brotherton 76, RG Pollock 53, PH Copeland 58, ESW Pearce 31; HD Bromfield 3/60)
WP 127 (GAS Innes 66; JG Ferrant 3/36, AH McKinnon 5/28) and 309 (JD Nel 40, PL van der Merwe 113, VT McCulloch 57, MJ Macaulay 31; JG Ferrant 4/106, AH McKinnon 5/83)

Western Province beat Border by 237 runs, 21–24 January 1961, East London
WP 203 (VT McCulloch 53, DWH Whitefield 45, MJ Macaulay 40; AF Hagemann 3/39) and 273/8 dec (MGM Groves 45, F Bing 85, VT McCulloch 60, DWH Whitefield 55*; EC Baker 4/82)
Bdr 56 (MJ Macaulay 5/14, HD Bromfield 3/9) and 183 (WS Farrer 78; DA Louw 3/24, MJ Macaulay 5/54)

Orange Free State beat Western Province by 28 runs, 27–30 January 1961, Bloemfontein
OFS 180 (C Richardson 83, L Blou 46; PL van der Merwe 5/31, HD Bromfield 4/45) and 239 (C Richardson 40, SF Burke 65; PL van der Merwe 3/36, HD Bromfield 5/81)
WP 261 (F Bing 62, DA Louw 90; SF Burke 4/91, MHJ Moffett 3/70) and 130 (JSM Fox 34; WR Chalmers 3/16)

Match drawn between Western Province and New Zealanders, 24–27 November 1961, Cape Town
WP 315/9 dec (WL Taylor 56, PL van der Merwe 30, JH Ferrandi 81*) and 247 (WL Taylor 61, PL van der Merwe 47, DWH Whitefield 55; FJ Cameron 3/44, JC Alabaster 3/87)
NZ 523 (JT Sparling 37, GT Dowling 43, SN McGregor 51, JR Reid 203, ME Chapple 96, GA Bartlett 41; HD Bromfield 3/129)

Western Province beat Eastern Province by 8 wickets, 26–28 December 1961, Cape Town
EP 266 (RG Pollock 63, AL Wilmot 35, PH Copeland 77; JW Rushmere 3/75) and 110 (JSM Fox 31; GAS Innes 6/22)
WP 262 (JD Morris 77, JH Ferrandi 47; NN Wilmot 3/48, AH McKinnon 3/57, GG Hall 3/82) and 115/2 (JD Morris 58*)

Transvaal beat Western Province by an innings and 100 runs, 19–22 January 1962, Johannesburg
WP 57 (PS Heine 5/30, JR Lodwick 4/19) and 315 (PL van der Merwe 62, VT McCulloch 104, DGM Hodgson 52, JW Rushmere 36; PS Heine 3/81, KA Walter 4/77)
Tvl 472 (EJ Barlow 80, JHB Waite 45, S O'Linn 102, AS Wilson 94, HJ Tayfield 41, PS Heine 32; JW Rushmere 4/102)

Natal beat Western Province by 4 wickets, 7–10 December 1962, Cape Town
WP 215 (GAS Innes 30, VT McCulloch 33; NS Crookes 5/62) and 185 (JD Morris 30, JH Ferrandi 40, JW Rushmere 44)
Ntl 225 (D Gamsy 54, RA McLean 60, CGD Burger 40; PL van der Merwe 5/29) and 177/6 (CGD Burger 85, BJ Versfeld 34; HDS Miller 4/32)

Match drawn between Eastern Province and Western Province, 26–28 December 1962, Cape Town
EP 594/6 dec (GF Dakin 165, CG Rushmere 153, RG Pollock 137, PH Copeland 51; HDS Miller 3/127)
WP 309 (JD Morris 48, GAS Innes 104*, MA Seymour 33; AH McKinnon 5/124) and 266/7 (PL van der Merwe 95, CB van Ryneveld 73; PM Pollock 3/54)

Western Province beat Transvaal by 5 wickets, 1–3 January 1963, Cape Town
Tvl 297 (EJ Barlow 47, HR Lance 33, A Bacher 142, AF Tillim 32; HD Bromfield 5/100) and 178 (IR Fullerton 37; HDS Miller 3/35, HD Bromfield 5/64)
WP 223 (PL van der Merwe 83; MJ Macaulay 4/30) and 253/5 (LJ Weinstein 91, PL van der Merwe 88)

Eastern Province beat Western Province by 63 runs, 26–29 January 1963, Port Elizabeth
EP 173 (RG Pollock 37, PM Pollock 33*; HDS Miller 3/54, PL van der Merwe 3/12) and 212 (CG Rushmere 56, AL Wilmot 48, PM Pollock 31; HDS Miller 3/52, HD Bromfield 3/46)
WP 95 (LJ Weinstein 42; PM Pollock 7/19) and 227 (JW Rushmere 49, HD Bromfield 44; PM Pollock 3/29, JG Ferrant 3/40)

Western Province beat Natal by 1 wicket, 2–5 February 1963, Pietermaritzburg
Ntl 190 (GD Varnals 67; FTM Drummer 3/40, MA Seymour 3/40) and 225 (RA McLean 47, D Gamsy 36, NS Crookes 35; FTM Drummer 3/58, MA Seymour 3/51)
WP 135 (PL van der Merwe 36, VT McCulloch 33; TL Goddard 3/30, CG Halse 3/22) and 285/9 (JD Morris 32, LJ Weinstein 35, PL van der Merwe 61, R Spencer-Young 61, VT McCulloch 51; CG Halse 3/60)

Transvaal beat Western Province by an innings and 66 runs, 8–11 February 1963, Johannesburg
Tvl 431/7 dec (IR Fullerton 145, PR Carlstein 203, HR Lance 47; JW Rushmere 4/87)
WP 233 (LJ Weinstein 49, PM Walker 60, JW Rushmere 46*; KA Walter 5/73, MJ Macaulay 3/43) and 132 (JH Ferrandi 52*; KA Walter 5/40, JR Lodwick 3/23)

Match drawn between Western Province and Eastern Province, 26–28 December 1963, Cape Town
WP 346 (L Morby-Smith 99, VT McCulloch 61, DWH Whitefield 45, RM Farrell 72*; JE Dumbrill 4/79, GG Hall 3/98) and 291/7 dec (TR Brown 36, L Morby-Smith 41, R Spencer-Young 51, VT McCulloch 37*, RM Farrell 85; JG Ferrant 3/87)
EP 306 (CG Rushmere 44, LJ Nel 124, NW Mallett 90; JC Kerby 4/62, D Drummer 4/68) and 167/5 (CG Rushmere 50, LJ Nel 33)

Transvaal beat Western Province by 6 wickets, 31 December 1963 – 2 January 1964, Cape Town
WP 171 (NR Budge 36, L Morby-Smith 60, JE Pothecary 49; D Mackay-Coghill 3/44, AH McKinnon 5/61) and 329 (L Morby-Smith 101, R Spencer-Young 65, DWH Whitefield 31, JC Kerby 31, JE Pothecary 34; AH McKinnon 3/109, AF Tillim 5/78)
Tvl 312 (AC Rex 53, A Bacher 97, S O'Linn 39, M Henning 33; JC Kerby 3/69, WR Chalmers 3/68) and 192/4 (AC Rex 43, A Bacher 53, HR Lance 50*)

Natal beat Western Province by 6 wickets, 4–7 January 1964, Cape Town
Ntl 418 (DJ McGlew 121, RA McLean 54, CGD Burger 50, R Dumbrill 91, NS Crookes 33; HD Bromfield 7/148) and 108/4 (DS Murdoch 42*, RA McLean 58*; JE Pothecary 3/33)
WP 215 (L Morby-Smith 77, JC Kerby 35*; JM Cole 3/33) and 308 (L Morby-Smith 31, R Spencer-Young 39, JE Pothecary 32, VT McCulloch 47, JC Kerby 34, DWH Whitefield 59*; PHJ Trimborn 3/44, R Dumbrill 3/56)

Natal beat Western Province by 9 wickets, 24–27 January 1964, Durban
WP 145 (LJ Weinstein 59, VT McCulloch 37; PW Schultz 3/49, PHJ Trimborn 5/18) and 191 (NR Budge 36, R Spencer-Young 94; JM Cole 6/16)
Ntl 247 (DJ McGlew 43, D Gamsy 31, RA McLean 36, CGD Burger 44; FTM Drummer 3/63, HD Bromfield 4/101) and 90/1 (DJ McGlew 45*)

Transvaal beat Western Province by 153 runs, 31 January – 2 February 1964, Johannesburg
Tvl 272 (IR Fullerton 30, A Bacher 36, HR Lance 102, KA Walter 30*; FTM Drummer 4/64, HD Bromfield 3/76) and 321/7 dec (IR Fullerton 116, A Bacher 38, HR Lance 92)
WP 255 (NR Budge 30, VT McCulloch 35, TR Brown 31, DA Louw 61, FTM Drummer 32; AH McKinnon 5/70) and 185 (LJ Weinstein 38, VT McCulloch 38, DA Louw 63*; KA Walter 3/54)

Match drawn between Western Province and Eastern Province, 6–9 March 1964, Port Elizabeth
WP 317 (NR Budge 92, RF Delport 46, L Morby-Smith 35, VT McCulloch 33, DA Louw 56; GG Hall 4/99, JE Dumbrill 4/84) and 246/6 dec (DA Louw 50*, JE Pothecary 81*; JB Brodie 3/65)
EP 250 (LJ Nel 31, AL Wilmot 126; JE Pothecary 3/49, NR Budge 3/35) and 188/8 (CGM Archibald 57, AL Wilmot 54*; FTM Drummer 6/57)

Border beat Western Province by 5 wickets, 30 October – 2 November 1964, East London
WP 96 (RK Thorne 7/33) and 256 (NR Budge 46, L Morby-Smith 56, DA Louw 63; S Knott 3/49, RK Thorne 3/53)
Bdr 181 (RK Thorne 42, CP Wilkins 31; J Fairclough 4/35, JE Pothecary 3/48) and 175/5 (WS Farrer 43, P Fenix 42; MA Seymour 3/44)

Match drawn between Eastern Province and Western Province, 6–9 November 1964, Port Elizabeth
EP 192 (EJ Barlow 43, RG Pollock 30; MA Seymour 3/77)
WP 215/3 (L Morby-Smith 127, PL van der Merwe 53*)

Match drawn between MCC and Western Province, 27 November – 1 December 1964, Cape Town
MCC 441 (G Boycott 106, ER Dexter 43, KF Barrington 169*, PH Parfitt 44; HD Bromfield 3/67) and 228/6 dec (JM Brearley 64, KF Barrington 82)
WP 357 (LJ Weinstein 53, L Morby-Smith 33, PL van der Merwe 121, PN Lear 37; NI Thomson 3/52) and 158/8 (LJ Weinstein 42, PL van der Merwe 34; FJ Titmus 3/32, RNS Hobbs 3/33)

SA Universities beat Western Province by 40 runs, 11–14 December 1965, Cape Town
SAUniv 383/8 dec (K Tattersall 39, BJ Versfeld 141, FE Emary 45, RS Steyn 32*; HD Bromfield 3/65, DP McMeeking 3/95) and 187/6 dec (BJ Versfeld 63*, FE Emary 34)
WP 208 (NR Budge 34, L Morby-Smith 64, AW Catt 31; RK Muzzell 4/60, PD de Vaal 3/13) and 322 (MJ Giles 73, PL van der Merwe 91; FE Emary 5/71)

Match drawn between Eastern Province and Western Province, 17–20 December 1965, Port Elizabeth
EP 224 (EJ Barlow 87, AL Wilmot 30; HD Bromfield 3/59, RS Steyn 4/56) and 167/3 dec (EJ Barlow 64, NW Mallett 46, RG Pollock 39*)
WP 163 (RS Steyn 44, FTM Drummer 44*; PM Pollock 3/30, EJ Barlow 3/21) and 145/3 (LJ Weinstein 30, A Bruyns 50*)

Rhodesia beat Western Province by 6 wickets, 27–29 December 1965, Cape Town
WP 194 (LJ Weinstein 32, PL van der Merwe 61; JT Partridge 5/85, GB Lawrence 3/56) and 99 (LJ Weinstein 36; GB Lawrence 8/42)
Rhod 172 (AJ Pithey 38, JH du Preez 38, GB Lawrence 32*; JM Cole 5/45) and 122/4 (RA Gripper 51)

Match drawn between Transvaal and Western Province, 1–4 January 1966, Cape Town
Tvl 349 (BJ Clark 73, HR Lance 147, D Mackay-Coghill 38; FTM Drummer 4/51) and 229 (HR Lance 62, D Mackay-Coghill 30; RS Steyn 4/64)
WP 318 (A Bruyns 56, L Morby-Smith 65, PL van der Merwe 34, FE Emary 66, AW Catt 44; HR Lance 3/47, AH McKinnon 6/107) and 227/9 (A Bruyns 49, L Morby-Smith 50, PL van der Merwe 77; HR Lance 3/48, AH McKinnon 5/66)

Natal beat Western Province by 233 runs, 21–24 January 1966, Cape Town
Ntl 144 (MH Bowditch 9/52) and 257 (BJ Versfeld 45, MJ Procter 67, C Wesley 41, CGD Burger 45; MH Bowditch 3/68, HD Bromfield 3/60)
WP 83 (L Morby-Smith 30; PHJ Trimborn 5/38, MJ Procter 4/19) and 85 (A Bruyns 33; PHJ Trimborn 3/19, NS Crookes 4/14)

Transvaal beat Western Province by 8 wickets, 18–21 February 1966, Johannesburg
WP 285 (NR Budge 37, PL van der Merwe 62, RK Muzzell 101*; AH McKinnon 5/82) and 233 (D le Roux 33, PL van der Merwe 60, DA Louw 41; R Dumbrill 4/44)
Tvl 465/9 dec (BJ Clark 52, A Bacher 32, HR Lance 96, RC White 117, R Dumbrill 51; NR Budge 3/67, MH Bowditch 3/83) and 56/2 (HR Lance 34*)

Western Province beat Orange Free State by 8 wickets, 5–8 November 1966, Bloemfontein
OFS 87 (N Rosendorff 48; FTM Drummer 4/32, JM Cole 5/25) and 352 (R van der Poll 84, EP Hardiman 71, N Rosendorff 89; RS Steyn 6/68)
WP 267 (BCH Butler 50, RK Muzzell 64, DA Louw 39, RS Steyn 49; DF Kuter 3/54) and 175/2 (JE White 46, L Morby-Smith 75*, VT McCulloch 30*)

Western Province beat Border by an innings and 55 runs, 10–11 November 1966, East London
Bdr 175 (CP Wilkins 39, PJ Muzzell 63, WS Farrer 53; FTM Drummer 3/41, GA Chevalier 4/29) and 68 (FTM Drummer 8/28)
WP 298 (RK Muzzell 150, AW Catt 54, FTM Drummer 58*; AF Hagemann 3/68, TC Overton 5/62)

Australians beat Western Province by an innings and 108 runs, 18–21 November 1966, Cape Town
Aus 504/9 dec (IR Redpath 154, RM Cowper 78, G Thomas 36, KR Stackpole 138*, GD McKenzie 35; RS Steyn 3/85)
WP 191 (RK Muzzell 35, DLC McCay 82; GD McKenzie 3/36, RM Cowper 4/8) and 205 (RS Steyn 44, AW Catt 41, FTM Drummer 48; GD Watson 3/28)

Match drawn between North-Eastern Transvaal and Western Province, 9–12 December 1966, Cape Town
NET 524/6 dec (TL Goddard 222, HM Ackerman 200*, CI Dey 33; FTM Drummer 3/140) and 82/2 (NCM Holmes 32)
WP 431 (A Bruyns 103, MJ Giles 146, RK Muzzell 78*, L Morby-Smith 52; TL Goddard 4/131, JS Pressdee 3/92)

Western Province beat Natal B by 9 wickets, 27–30 January 1967, Cape Town
NtlB 222 (GC Heath 53, NS Crookes 63, RM Nicholson 32; DLC McCay 6/78) and 193 (PR Carlstein 83; DLC McCay 8/76)
WP 397 (A Bruyns 197, MJ Giles 41, GD Dyer 52, L Morby-Smith 36; GC Heath 3/57) and 20/1

Match drawn between Western Province and SA Universities, 8–11 December 1967, Cape Town
WP 249 (MJ Giles 42, BCH Butler 78, FTM Drummer 41; SG Hugo 4/56, RK Muzzell 3/58) and 275/8 dec (MJ Giles 61, GD Dyer 104, JE Klette 41; SG Hugo 4/33)
SAUniv 359 (AM Short 31, RK Muzzell 67, AL Biggs 156, DD Dyer 45; FTM Drummer 4/65, RET Morris 4/107) and 161/6 (AM Short 66, DLC McCay 40)

Western Province beat Orange Free State by 210 runs, 21–23 December 1967, Cape Town
WP 218 (GD Dyer 54, FTM Drummer 45; NM Riley 3/60) and 323/6 dec (A Bruyns 72, RK Muzzell 96, WJ McAdam 45; NM Riley 3/72)
OFS 121 (FTM Drummer 4/41, SG Hugo 3/31) and 210 (N Rosendorff 47, NM Riley 59; FTM Drummer 3/47, SG Hugo 4/31)

Match drawn between Western Province and Rhodesia, 26–28 December 1967, Cape Town
WP 505/8 dec (A Bruyns 160, RK Muzzell 161, GP Pfuhl 65; EF Parker 4/110)
Rhod 272 (RB Ullyett 37, PR Carlstein 89, EF Parker 31, DW Townshend 35; AS Hodgson 4/50, RET Morris 3/38) and 243/7 (JK Clarke 112*, RB Ullyett 42, PR Carlstein 37; SG Hugo 4/37)

Match drawn between Transvaal B and Western Province, 1–3 January 1968, Cape Town
TvlB 325 (BF Bath 64, VS Greve 76, GG Ritchie 50, LW Vorster 47, SJ Katz 41; FTM Drummer 4/47) and 164/6 (GG Ritchie 30, LW Vorster 51*; RET Morris 3/48)
WP 345/9 dec (GD Dyer 37, RK Muzzell 51, FTM Drummer 62, DLC McCay 30, SG Hugo 54, RET Morris 50*; VS Greve 3/77)

Match drawn between Western Province and Griqualand West, 12–15 January 1968, Kimberley
WP 357/6 dec (K Tattersall 112, BCH Butler 39, RK Muzzell 40, GD Dyer 50*, FTM Drummer 52*) and 193 (A Bruyns 45, WJ McAdam 74; G Fleeton 5/62, DJ Schonegevel 4/47)
GW 322 (DJ Schonegevel 43, EJ Draper 51, KTM Saggers 70, P Morris 31, WJ Wilson 39; FTM Drummer 3/43) and 180/6 (DJ Schonegevel 49, KTM Saggers 37; RK Muzzell 3/61)

Match drawn between Western Province and Natal B, 18–20 January 1968, Durban
WP 202 (GD Dyer 46, GP Pfuhl 57*; AG Pistorius 3/71, NA McDonald 5/27) and 86/6 (A Bruyns 32; AG Pistorius 3/31, NA McDonald 3/20)
NtlB 154 (BS Groves 52, RM Nicholson 37; SG Hugo 4/52, DLC McCay 4/30)

Western Province beat Border by 86 runs, 23–26 February 1968, East London
WP 361 (RK Muzzell 54, MJ Giles 132, PD Swart 36; NA Wrede 3/76, TD Ziemann 3/74) and 90/7 dec (GW Nelson 6/34)
Bdr 244 (GW Nelson 43, KG Marshall 48, WS Farrer 42, GA Minkley 33*; SG Hugo 3/31) and 121 (CP Wilkins 45, RTD Kemp 32; FTM Drummer 4/33, GA Chevalier 3/23)

Western Province beat Orange Free State by an innings and 13 runs, 22–25 November 1968, Bloemfontein
OFS 172 (N Rosendorff 57; PD Swart 4/36) and 188 (N Rosendorff 89; MA Seymour 5/44)
WP 373/9 dec (K Tattersall 39, GP Pfuhl 74, PD Swart 109, SG Hugo 68*; WT Strydom 3/69, RA le Roux 4/77)

Western Province beat Natal B by 9 wickets, 29–30 November 1968, Durban
NtlB 128 (GC Heath 30, HM Ackerman 32; PD Swart 3/24, GA Chevalier 5/38) and 72 (PD Swart 3/38, EJ Barlow 7/26)
WP 179 (K Tattersall 41, A Bruyns 32; RF de Villiers 3/44, MJ Smithyman 4/25) and 23/1

Match drawn between Western Province and Border, 26–28 December 1968, Cape Town
WP 430 (EJ Barlow 100, K Tattersall 51, A Bruyns 50, MH Bowditch 89, SG Hugo 64; MWL Scott 3/90, AW Greig 3/118, GW Nelson 3/82)
Bdr 127 (MA Seymour 4/40, SG Hugo 3/26) and 136/9 (PJ Muzzell 77; EJ Barlow 7/40)

Western Province beat North-Eastern Transvaal by an innings and 205 runs, 31 December 1968 – 2 January 1969, Cape Town
WP 503/6 dec (K Tattersall 38, CG Stephens 153, WJ McAdam 129, PD Swart 106*)
NET 173 (NCM Holmes 46, CI Dey 37, NV Alistoun 38*; EJ Barlow 3/45, MA Seymour 3/25) and 125 (CI Dey 57; MA Seymour 3/40, GA Chevalier 4/41)

Match drawn between Transvaal and Western Province, 4–7 January 1969, Cape Town
Tvl 349 (BF Bath 65, DR Lindsay-Smith 108, D Mackay-Coghill 33, HR Lance 58; EJ Barlow 5/44) and 206/4 dec (BF Bath 46, D Mackay-Coghill 35*, AA During 75; GA Chevalier 4/52)
WP 249 (A Bruyns 113, CG Stephens 40; D Mackay-Coghill 4/65) and 191/3 (K Tattersall 39, CG Stephens 53*, WJ McAdam 37*, SG Hugo 41)

Natal beat Western Province by 10 wickets, 17–20 January 1969, Cape Town
WP 164 (CG Stephens 54, MH Bowditch 36; TL Goddard 3/32, NS Crookes 3/45) and 175 (GP Pfuhl 58)
Ntl 215 (BA Richards 82, MJ Procter 42; MA Seymour 5/82) and 125/0 (BA Richards 81*, TL Goddard 42*)

Western Province beat Transvaal B by an innings and 76 runs, 14–17 February 1969, Cape Town
TvlB 158 (AA During 32, JR Cheetham 77; EJ Barlow 5/36) and 156 (JR Cheetham 42, JPD Flanagan 36; GA Chevalier 3/52, AP van Niekerk 4/16)
WP 390 (K Tattersall 34, CG Stephens 165, MH Bowditch 58, GP Pfuhl 58; PD de Vaal 4/76)

Western Province beat Griqualand West by an innings and 9 runs, 28 February – 3 March 1969, Kimberley
WP 290/9 dec (EJ Barlow 45, K Tattersall 82, MH Bowditch 73, GP Pfuhl 33)
GW 99 (GA Chevalier 5/29) and 182 (CA Perring 31, LA McNamara 48, A Kellerman 36*; FG Touzel 7/86)

Western Province beat Rhodesia by an innings and 76 runs, 8–11 November 1969, Bulawayo
WP 371/9 dec (K Tattersall 42, A Bruyns 149, CG Stephens 88; AJ Traicos 4/103, JH du Preez 4/121)
Rhod 139 (MJ Procter 3/35) and 156 (RA Gripper 37, SD Robertson 41; MJ Procter 4/18)

Western Province beat Natal by 9 wickets, 14–17 November 1969, Durban
Ntl 157 (TL Goddard 85*; MJ Procter 3/39) and 232 (BA Richards 100, BJ Versfeld 60; MA Seymour 5/70, GA Chevalier 4/47)
WP 374/6 dec (EJ Barlow 62, K Tattersall 40, CG Stephens 118*, MH Bowditch 120) and 19/1

Match drawn between Western Province and Eastern Province, 28 November – 1 December 1969, Cape Town
WP 327 (EJ Barlow 68, MJ Procter 124, GP Pfuhl 37, MA Seymour 33; GM Den 3/104, RV Taylor 3/71) and 226/5 dec (EJ Barlow 51*, A Bruyns 46, CG Stephens 64*, MH Bowditch 32; GM Den 3/71)
EP 269 (LML Barnwell 30, KJ Bond 70, AL Wilmot 61, PM Pollock 43*, NW Mallett 37; MJ Procter 3/44, GA Chevalier 4/76) and 153/7 (AL Biggs 64, RG Pollock 52; MA Seymour 3/62)

Match drawn between Transvaal and Western Province, 1–3 January 1970, Cape Town
Tvl 302 (A Bacher 68, BF Bath 40, BL Irvine 107; MJ Procter 3/57, EJ Barlow 4/74) and 190/6 dec (BF Bath 34, AA During 54, BL Irvine 34)
WP 227 (A Bruyns 71, MH Bowditch 39, GP Pfuhl 50*; GLG Watson 3/61) and 110/6 (PD de Vaal 5/45)

Match drawn between Australians and Western Province, 13–16 March 1970, Cape Town
Aus 354/4 dec (KR Stackpole 79, IR Redpath 84, JT Irvine 33, KD Walters 44, AP Sheahan 76*; EJ Barlow 3/46) and 262/5 dec (KD Walters 109, AP Sheahan 84*)
WP 343/9 dec (CG Stephens 32, MJ Procter 155, MH Bowditch 58; LC Mayne 3/57, AN Connolly 4/56) and 211/5 (EJ Barlow 133; AA Mallett 3/57)

Match drawn between Western Province and Natal, 27–30 November 1970, Durban
WP 232 (HM Ackerman 31, CG Stephens 68, GP Pfuhl 48, AC Parker 31) and 18/2
Ntl 282/6 dec (DD Dyer 31, AA Hipkin 111, D Gamsy 35*)

Match drawn between Western Province and Eastern Province, 26–29 December 1970, Durban
WP 462/9 dec (EJ Barlow 141, A Bruyns 41, CG Stephens 51, HM Ackerman 120*, PD Swart 32; AW Greig 4/132)
EP 131 (P Fenix 41; EJ Barlow 3/29, GA Chevalier 3/32) and 476/9 (AL Biggs 145, LML Barnwell 40, P Fenix 35, RG Pollock 76, AL Wilmot 95)

Match drawn between Western Province and Transvaal, 1–4 January 1971, Cape Town
WP 326 (EJ Barlow 76, A Bruyns 58, HM Ackerman 30, MH Bowditch 65, GP Pfuhl 39; BF Bath 6/94) and 165/7 dec (CG Stephens 41, MH Bowditch 52)
Tvl 197 (BF Bath 56, PR Carlstein 51; GA Chevalier 7/57) and 191/8 (PR Carlstein 75, BL Irvine 43, AA During 34*; PD Swart 3/28)

Western Province beat Eastern Province by 9 wickets, 8–11 January 1971, Cape Town
EP 197 (SJ Bezuidenhout 35, P Fenix 33, PM Pollock 37*; MH Bowditch 4/37, GA Chevalier 4/73) and 268 (AL Biggs 45, AL Wilmot 49, KP Reid 36, KJ Bond 71*; EJ Barlow 3/65, MH Bowditch 3/40, PD Swart 3/53)
WP 340 (EJ Barlow 52, A Bruyns 37, CG Stephens 33, HM Ackerman 82, MH Bowditch 47, GP Pfuhl 40; KP Reid 3/68, AL Biggs 5/135) and 128/1 (EJ Barlow 53, AC Parker 47*)

Western Province beat Natal by 152 runs, 22–25 January 1971, Cape Town
WP 452/4 dec (EJ Barlow 129, A Bruyns 134, CG Stephens 104*, HM Ackerman 37) and 75/5 dec
Ntl 280 (DD Dyer 33, AA Hipkin 79, DL Orchard 55; GA Chevalier 4/119) and 95 (AM Short 55; GA Chevalier 6/23, RET Morris 4/23)

Match drawn between Western Province and Transvaal, 12–15 February 1971, Johannesburg
Tvl 252 (A Bacher 33, PR Carlstein 36, BL Irvine 47, CEB Rice 31; PD Swart 4/64) and 201/7 dec (RC White 61, A Bacher 58)
WP 223 (NR Budge 36, HM Ackerman 62; CEB Rice 4/26, PD de Vaal 3/33)

Rhodesia beat Western Province by 7 wickets, 5–7 March 1971, Salisbury
Rhod 383 (MJ Procter 254, HAB Gardiner 69; GA Chevalier 4/108) and 142/3 (RA Gripper 49, JD McPhun 71*)
WP 189 (NR Budge 34, MH Bowditch 39; RH Kaschula 5/72) and 334 (HM Ackerman 35, MH Bowditch 31, GP Pfuhl 117, PD Swart 33; DAG Fletcher 3/57, JH du Preez 3/89)

Match drawn between Western Province and Natal, 26–29 November 1971, Cape Town
WP 256/9 dec (NR Budge 53, A Bruyns 68, GP Pfuhl 78; PP Henwood 3/72, IR Tayfield 4/76) and 263/3 dec (FS Goldstein 59, NR Budge 64, A Bruyns 103*)
Ntl 420 (BA Richards 169, AM Short 33, DD Dyer 61, IR Tayfield 55, VAP van der Bijl 35; RD Jackman 3/57, GA Chevalier 4/131)

Western Province beat SA Universities by 214 runs, 10–13 December 1971, Cape Town
WP 289/9 dec (NR Budge 65, GP Pfuhl 40, PD Swart 50, RET Morris 58*; M du Plessis 4/71) and 146/4 dec (A Bruyns 74, GP Pfuhl 30*)
SAUniv 94 (MH Bowditch 3/29, GA Chevalier 3/27) and 127 (RR Collins 30; GA Chevalier 4/38, RET Morris 5/45)

Western Province beat Transvaal by 4 wickets, 1–4 January 1972, Cape Town
Tvl 273 (A Bacher 42, BF Bath 86, PD de Vaal 41; GA Chevalier 4/64) and 238/8 dec (BF Bath 52, PR Carlstein 45, BL Irvine 37, KA McKenzie 30; RD Jackman 3/53, GA Chevalier 3/80)
WP 313 (QJ Rookledge 80, A Bruyns 67, PH Denne 55, GP Pfuhl 43, MH Bowditch 31; WR Kerr 3/54) and 199/6 (A Bruyns 108*)

Rhodesia beat Western Province by 2 wickets, 7–10 January 1972, Cape Town
WP 263/9 dec (A Bruyns 108, MH Bowditch 85; BF Davison 3/26) and 180 (NR Budge 36, RET Morris 75; MJ Procter 3/52, RH Kaschula 3/30, JH du Preez 3/32)
Rhod 326 (BH Oldrieve 36, JC Mitchell 58, MJ Procter 62, BF Davison 35, JD McPhun 48, HAB Gardiner 51*; RD Jackman 3/67, PD Swart 3/52) and 118/8 (MJ Procter 31)

Natal beat Western Province by 158 runs, 14–17 January 1972, Pietermaritzburg
Ntl 76 (RD Jackman 4/34, PD Swart 5/24) and 263 (BA Richards 73, AM Short 64, MB Madsen 33, GD Dyer 30; PD Swart 6/85)
WP 121 (VAP van der Bijl 8/35) and 60 (VAP van der Bijl 5/18, PP Henwood 4/13)

Match drawn between Western Province and Eastern Province, 4–7 February 1972, Cape Town
WP 237 (HM Ackerman 82, MH Bowditch 56, RET Morris 44*; AW Greig 5/39) and 252/6 dec (EJ Barlow 118, NR Budge 48, MH Bowditch 32*; HC Pittaway 4/38)
EP 259 (B Wood 34, RG Pollock 37, AL Wilmot 95; RD Jackman 5/37, GA Chevalier 3/85) and 155/7 (GA Chevalier 3/52, RET Morris 4/32)

Match drawn between Rhodesia and Western Province, 19–21 February 1972, Salisbury
Rhod 261 (SD Robertson 50, BF Davison 66, JC Mitchell 45*; EJ Barlow 4/74) and 250/6 dec (BD Barbour 57, SD Robertson 59, MJ Procter 46, JH du Preez 47*; RD Jackman 3/98)
WP 283 (EJ Barlow 101, NR Budge 32, A Bruyns 39, HM Ackerman 44; MJ Procter 5/70) and 68/2 (EJ Barlow 35)

Match drawn between Transvaal and Western Province, 25–28 February 1972, Johannesburg
Tvl 311 (BF Bath 64, KA McKenzie 37, VS Greve 38, WR Kerr 57; RD Jackman 3/89, EJ Barlow 3/122, M du Plessis 3/60) and 147/2 dec (KA McKenzie 61*, VS Greve 40*)
WP 200/7 dec (EJ Barlow 56, NR Budge 37, A Bruyns 51; D Mackay-Coghill 6/74) and 166/4 (A Bruyns 61, MH Bowditch 34*)

Rhodesia beat Western Province by 7 wickets, 10–13 March 1972, Cape Town
WP 272 (FS Goldstein 34, A Bruyns 71, PD Swart 51; MJ Procter 4/33, PB Clift 3/71) and 118 (RET Morris 54, PD Swart 34; MJ Procter 5/9)
Rhod 322/8 dec (SD Robertson 118, MJ Procter 86, JH du Preez 57; RET Morris 3/100, GA Chevalier 3/78) and 69/3

Western Province beat Eastern Province by an innings and 96 runs, 24–25 March 1972, Port Elizabeth
WP 68/9 dec (AW Greig 5/20, PM Pollock 3/15) and 92 (A Bruyns 40; AW Greig 5/23)
EP 256/9 dec (RG Pollock 130*, HC Pittaway 45; RD Jackman 4/61)

Western Province beat Natal by 115 runs, 24–27 November 1972, Cape Town
WP 251/9 dec (NR Budge 35, HM Ackerman 70, MH Bowditch 38, GP Pfuhl 30; BD Gessner 3/63, PHJ Trimborn 5/34) and 205/9 dec (EJ Barlow 45, HM Ackerman 69; PHJ Trimborn 4/41)
Ntl 108 (A Bruyns 35, AJS Smith 34; AB Nieuwoudt 4/13, PD Swart 3/41, RET Morris 3/17) and 233 (BA Richards 99, AM Short 37, DL Orchard 44; AB Nieuwoudt 4/47)

Western Province beat Rhodesia by 45 runs, 21–23 December 1972, Cape Town
WP 214 (MH Bowditch 53, GP Pfuhl 33; MJ Procter 6/67) and 281 (EJ Barlow 106, PD Swart 63, MH Bowditch 44; MJ Procter 4/64, JH du Preez 3/55)
Rhod 286 (JC Mitchell 61, MJ Procter 32, BF Davison 74, JH du Preez 43; AB Nieuwoudt 3/43, PD Swart 3/76) and 164 (JC Mitchell 41, PR Carlstein 69; EJ Barlow 7/53)

Match drawn between Transvaal and Western Province, 30 December 1972 – 2 January 1973, Cape Town
Tvl 250/9 dec (RK Muzzell 40, RC White 101; EJ Barlow 3/61, PD Swart 3/49) and 244/8 (A Bacher 65, RK Muzzell 30, RC White 43, SJ Cook 34; AB Nieuwoudt 3/42)
WP 326/9 dec (EJ Barlow 62, JR Cheetham 124, HM Ackerman 33; BF Bath 3/55)

Western Province beat DH Robins by 121 runs, 5–8 January 1973, Cape Town
WP 371/2 dec (EJ Barlow 147, OJA Snyman 133*, JR Cheetham 54, HM Ackerman 35*) and 175/2 dec (OJA Snyman 70, HM Ackerman 36, CA Gie 62*)
DHR 234 (CT Radley 40, JH Hampshire 65, FC Hayes 50; MH Bowditch 5/31) and 191 (FC Hayes 59; AB Nieuwoudt 4/47)

Western Province beat Eastern Province by 5 wickets, 12–15 January 1973, Cape Town
EP 200/9 dec (AL Wilmot 42, KS McEwan 85; EJ Barlow 5/46) and 184 (SJ Bezuidenhout 30, CP Wilkins 34, AL Wilmot 34; EJ Barlow 3/26, PD Swart 3/25)
WP 299 (OJA Snyman 85, AJ Lamb 58, MH Bowditch 43, PD Swart 32, GP Pfuhl 39; E Schmidt 3/39, KP Reid 4/58) and 88/5 (AJ Lamb 32; CP Wilkins 3/25)

Western Province beat Natal by an innings and 9 runs, 9–10 February 1973, Durban
Ntl 76 (SJ McAdam 3/30, EJ Barlow 7/24) and 172 (BA Richards 82; EJ Barlow 3/27)
WP 257 (EJ Barlow 64, HM Ackerman 68, CA Gie 40; VAP van der Bijl 5/55)

Rhodesia beat Western Province by an innings and 27 runs, 24–26 February 1973, Salisbury
WP 158 (EJ Barlow 42; MJ Procter 4/43) and 159 (HM Ackerman 57*, RM Clark 45; MJ Procter 3/23, PB Clift 3/45, JC Mitchell 3/12)
Rhod 344 (SD Robertson 115, JC Mitchell 41, MJ Procter 44, BF Davison 66; EJ Barlow 3/53, GA Chevalier 4/53)

Transvaal beat Western Province by an innings and 27 runs, 2–5 March 1973, Johannesburg
WP 129/9 dec (HM Ackerman 53; DF Becker 3/28, DR Neilson 3/36) and 90 (D Mackay-Coghill 7/40, CEB Rice 3/13)
Tvl 239 (A Bacher 57, BL Irvine 53; PD Swart 4/38, EJ Barlow 3/77)

Eastern Province beat Western Province by 8 wickets, 16–19 March 1973, Port Elizabeth
WP 271/8 dec (EJ Barlow 35, OJA Snyman 33, HM Ackerman 47, CA Gie 53; DJ Brickett 3/54) and 175/5 dec (FS Goldstein 38, CA Gie 55, SG Hugo 44*)
EP 276/7 dec (AL Biggs 70, KP Reid 31, CP Wilkins 118*) and 174/2 (SJ Bezuidenhout 88, AL Biggs 42)

Match drawn between Western Province and DH Robins, 26–29 October 1973, Cape Town
WP 286/4 dec (FS Goldstein 54, HM Ackerman 179*, CA Gie 39) and 149/5 (EJ Barlow 33*, PD Swart 31*; JW Gleeson 3/25)
DHR 375/4 dec (MJ Smith 44, BC Francis 194, JH Edrich 118)

Western Province beat Natal by 9 wickets, 10–12 November 1973, Pietermaritzburg
Ntl 278/4 dec (BA Richards 186*, AJS Smith 38) and 130 (AB Nieuwoudt 4/43, EJ Barlow 3/37)
WP 368/7 dec (FS Goldstein 104, HM Ackerman 107, RM Clark 66*, PHJ Trimborn 3/77) and 41/1

Match drawn between Western Province and Eastern Province, 15–18 December 1973, Cape Town
WP 172 (RM Clark 49, GP Pfuhl 33*; RW Hanley 3/51, DJ Brickett 3/56) and 308 (EJ Barlow 33, A Bruyns 35, PN Kirsten 68, PD Swart 46, GP Pfuhl 41; RW Hanley 4/63)
EP 151/9 dec (RG Pollock 66) and 296/6 (SJ Bezuidenhout 32, AL Biggs 62, RG Pollock 78, CP Wilkins 41, DJ Brickett 48*)

Match drawn between Western Province and Eastern Province, 26–28 December 1973, Port Elizabeth
WP 130 (EJ Barlow 51; DJ Brickett 8/49) and 355/7 (EJ Barlow 42, FS Goldstein 53, A Bruyns 38, PN Kirsten 74, PD Swart 40*, RET Morris 32; E Schmidt 3/41)
EP 338 (SJ Bezuidenhout 37, AM Short 50, RG Pollock 54, AL Wilmot 128; RM Clark 5/70)

Match drawn between Transvaal and Western Province, 31 December 1973 – 2 January 1974, Cape Town
Tvl 302 (A Bacher 42, RK Muzzell 35, BL Irvine 64, NG Featherstone 79; MH Bowditch 5/21) and 269/8 dec (A Bacher 35*, BL Irvine 132)
WP 249 (HM Ackerman 82, RM Clark 58; D Mackay-Coghill 4/66, CEB Rice 3/47) and 238/5 (FS Goldstein 61, CA Gie 63*, MH Bowditch 53)

Western Province beat Rhodesia by 125 runs, 4–7 January 1974, Cape Town
WP 252/9 dec (A Bruyns 76; RD Jackman 5/58) and 170 (A Bruyns 44, HM Ackerman 32; MJ Procter 4/43, RD Jackman 3/58)
Rhod 110 (SD Robertson 46; EJ Barlow 4/28, AB Nieuwoudt 5/19) and 187 (MJ Procter 53, PB Clift 35*; DL Hobson 3/48, AB Nieuwoudt 6/45)

Natal beat Western Province by 221 runs, 15–18 February 1974, Cape Town
Ntl 224 (BA Richards 61, HR Fotheringham 50, AJS Smith 32; EJ Barlow 3/29, M du Plessis 3/47) and 303/5 dec (BA Richards 80, DD Dyer 36, BS Groves 42, HR Fotheringham 32, RA Woolmer 61)
WP 132/9 dec (A Bruyns 37; VAP van der Bijl 5/40, PHJ Trimborn 4/51) and 174 (EJ Barlow 39, GP Pfuhl 70*; VAP van der Bijl 7/45)

Transvaal beat Western Province by 82 runs, 22–25 February 1974, Johannesburg
Tvl 299/9 dec (A Bacher 37, RK Muzzell 38, BL Irvine 71, PD de Vaal 50) and 240/2 dec (BF Bath 108*, BL Irvine 108*)
WP 237 (EJ Barlow 44, PN Kirsten 40, GP Pfuhl 54; D Mackay-Coghill 7/102) and 220 (EJ Barlow 84, FS Goldstein 36; DR Neilson 3/33, JPD Flanagan 4/56)

Western Province beat Rhodesia by 148 runs, 2–4 March 1974, Bulawayo
WP 162 (PN Kirsten 40; MJ Procter 3/19, AJ Traicos 3/36) and 274 (EJ Barlow 37, FS Goldstein 63, HM Ackerman 80; RD Jackman 3/33)
Rhod 81 (BF Davison 30; DL Hobson 6/28) and 207 (JH du Preez 34, DAG Fletcher 52; DLC McCay 3/27, DL Hobson 4/101)

Rhodesia beat Western Province by 113 runs, 2–4 November 1974, Salisbury
Rhod 246 (BF Davison 81, HAB Gardiner 31*; PD Swart 4/50) and 267/9 dec (PB Clift 74*, HAB Gardiner 99; JN Farrell 4/40)
WP 114 (HM Ackerman 35*; RD Jackman 6/51, PB Clift 3/16) and 286 (FS Goldstein 66, PN Kirsten 42, GP Pfuhl 34, DL Hobson 32*; JH du Preez 6/102)

Match drawn between Transvaal and Western Province, 8–11 November 1974, Johannesburg
Tvl 354/7 dec (PD de Vaal 45, CEB Rice 56, BL Irvine 127, KA McKenzie 51, NG Featherstone 57; JN Farrell 3/46) and 46/1
WP 251 (EJ Barlow 44, PD Swart 38, DL Hobson 34*; GLG Watson 3/62)

Western Province beat Eastern Province by 52 runs, 29 November – 2 December 1974, Cape Town
WP 272 (MJ Nel 46, HM Ackerman 83, PN Kirsten 34; JW Gleeson 7/73) and 131 (PD Swart 63; RW Hanley 4/29, DJ Brickett 4/55)
EP 242 (AM Short 37, AL Wilmot 78; JN Farrell 4/47) and 109 (DL Hobson 5/30, PD Swart 5/27)

Eastern Province beat Western Province by 161 runs, 26–28 December 1974, Port Elizabeth
EP 342/8 dec (SJ Bezuidenhout 64, CP Wilkins 54, RG Pollock 121, KS McEwan 36; RET Morris 4/83) and 183/7 dec (KS McEwan 74*; SA Jones 4/56)
WP 262 (PD Swart 79, RET Morris 39*, DL Hobson 31; RW Hanley 5/82) and 102 (RW Hanley 5/50)

Western Province beat Transvaal by 108 runs, 1–3 January 1975, Cape Town
WP 331/8 dec (EJ Barlow 163, MJ Nel 46, GP Pfuhl 37*, DL Hobson 54*; DR Neilson 4/53, CEB Rice 3/54) and 207/6 dec (EJ Barlow 42, HM Ackerman 76, AP van Niekerk 33*; PD de Vaal 3/46)
Tvl 325/9 dec (PD de Vaal 95, CEB Rice 36, KA McKenzie 47, NG Featherstone 34; HM Ackerman 3/39) and 105 (EJ Barlow 5/45, DL Hobson 5/27)

Western Province beat Rhodesia by 85 runs, 17–20 January 1975, Cape Town
WP 317/8 dec (EJ Barlow 152, A Bruyns 58, PN Kirsten 48*; AJ Traicos 3/78) and 174/7 dec (EJ Barlow 40, HM Ackerman 45; DAG Fletcher 3/30)
Rhod 245 (K Tattersall 70, MJ Procter 64, BF Davison 42; SA Jones 3/35, DL Hobson 4/68) and 161 (JH du Preez 33, PB Clift 32*; JN Farrell 4/35)

Western Province beat Natal by 85 runs, 24–27 January 1975, Cape Town
WP 181 (HM Ackerman 52, AP van Niekerk 48; PHJ Trimborn 3/38, MJ Smithyman 3/30) and 248/7 dec (MJ Nel 37, A Bruyns 82, PD Swart 61*; VAP van der Bijl 3/52, PP Henwood 3/75)
Ntl 231 (HR Fotheringham 72, VAP van der Bijl 30; EJ Barlow 5/52) and 80/3 (DD Dyer 39*)

Match drawn between Natal and Western Province, 15–17 February 1975, Durban
Ntl 235/9 dec (BA Richards 55, D Bestall 45, RA Woolmer 40; SA Jones 3/44, EJ Barlow 4/49) and 169/6 dec (AJS Smith 31, HR Fotheringham 51; JN Farrell 3/25)
WP 171 (GP Pfuhl 45; VAP van der Bijl 4/21, PHJ Trimborn 3/34, PP Henwood 3/39) and 64/6

Match drawn between Western Province and DH Robins, 21–24 March 1975, Cape Town
WP 231 (EJ Barlow 69, FS Goldstein 73, RET Morris 36; MHN Walker 4/59) and 206 (EJ Barlow 47, RET Morris 69, DL Hobson 45)
DHR 295/6 dec (RW Tolchard 55, FC Hayes 66, AW Greig 38*, TJ Jenner 33*; DL Hobson 3/52) and 99/5 (EJ Barlow 3/35)

Match drawn between Eastern Province and Western Province, 7–10 November 1975, Port Elizabeth
EP 207 (AL Wilmot 44, KS McEwan 57, DJ Brickett 37) and 302/5 dec (CP Wilkins 39, RG Pollock 140*, KS McEwan 50*)
WP 229 (PN Kirsten 47, RET Morris 38, DL Hobson 37; E Schmidt 4/39) and 209/6 (EJ Barlow 74, PN Kirsten 66; CF Ahlfeldt 3/43)

Western Province beat Rhodesia by an innings and 57 runs, 5–8 December 1975, Cape Town
Rhod 146/9 dec (JG Heron 47, JH du Preez 30; DL Hobson 4/28) and 149 (DAG Fletcher 43, HAB Gardiner 38; JN Farrell 4/43)
WP 352/4 dec (AJ Lamb 37, PN Kirsten 128*, A Bruyns 93, HM Ackerman 60)

Natal beat Western Province by 10 wickets, 26–28 December 1975, Durban
Ntl 338/6 dec (BA Richards 140, A Barrow 54, KM Hosken 73*, GA Katz 30; NB Lotter 3/84) and 57/0 (BA Richards 35*)
WP 133/9 dec (EJ Barlow 54; VAP van der Bijl 3/37, PP Henwood 3/27) and 259 (HM Ackerman 36, RET Morris 135; VAP van der Bijl 4/68, PP Henwood 3/74)

Match drawn between Western Province and Transvaal, 1–3 January 1976, Cape Town
WP 340/4 dec (EJ Barlow 41, PN Kirsten 33, A Bruyns 155, HM Ackerman 100*) and 231/7 (A Bruyns 39, HM Ackerman 43*, GP Pfuhl 35; DS van der Knaap 3/71)
Tvl 472 (DD Dyer 111, WJ van der Linden 94, CEB Rice 52, BL Irvine 56, NG Featherstone 38, AJ Kourie 49; RET Morris 3/67, PD Swart 3/60)

Western Province beat Eastern Province by 5 wickets, 16–19 January 1976, Cape Town
EP 227 (RG Pollock 38, D Bestall 51, JW Stephenson 51; GS le Roux 3/42) and 211 (SJ Bezuidenhout 40, CP Wilkins 33, RG Pollock 74*; DL Hobson 4/57)
WP 168 (EJ Barlow 48, PN Kirsten 34; PH Edmonds 5/50) and 271/5 (EJ Barlow 99, RA Seymour 32*)

Western Province beat DH Robins by 78 runs, 23–26 January 1976, Cape Town
WP 262/8 dec (EJ Barlow 31, PN Kirsten 55, HM Ackerman 38, AJ Lamb 59*; P Carrick 3/62) and 151/7 dec (AJ Lamb 34; GA Cope 3/45)
DHR 144 (P Carrick 31, TM Chappell 46; GS le Roux 5/30, DL Hobson 3/37) and 191 (DS Steele 110*; DL Hobson 5/63)

Match drawn between Rhodesia and Western Province, 7–9 February 1976, Salisbury
Rhod 410/9 dec (BD Barbour 44, DBE Bawden 36, MJ Procter 41, BF Davison 74, DAG Fletcher 43, JH du Preez 41, JN Shepherd 65; AB Nieuwoudt 4/87) and 120/7 (BD Barbour 32, JN Shepherd 33; DL Hobson 3/28, PD Swart 3/46)
WP 170/9 dec (EJ Barlow 31, HM Ackerman 52, PN Kirsten 37; JH du Preez 3/56, JN Shepherd 3/34) and 374 (EJ Barlow 104, A Bruyns 30, PN Kirsten 123, AJ Lamb 31, PD Swart 37; JH du Preez 4/116, MJ Procter 4/109)

Transvaal beat Western Province by 5 wickets, 13–16 February 1976, Johannesburg
WP 244 (EJ Barlow 31, AJ Lamb 33, RET Morris 73*; CEB Rice 7/62) and 217 (EJ Barlow 59, A Bruyns 31, AJ Lamb 51; DR Neilson 3/68, CEB Rice 4/50)
Tvl 334/6 dec (DD Dyer 45, SJ Cook 55*, CEB Rice 90, BL Irvine 88; GS le Roux 3/58) and 128/5 (BL Irvine 40*, PD de Vaal 37*; GS le Roux 4/56)

Western Province beat Natal by 74 runs, 5–8 March 1976, Cape Town
WP 265 (AJ Lamb 83, RM Clark 50, RET Morris 68; PHJ Trimborn 3/22, PP Henwood 4/55) and 106/4 dec (EJ Barlow 32, HM Ackerman 39*)
Ntl 149 (BA Richards 43; DL Hobson 7/52) and 148 (HR Fotheringham 54; DL Hobson 7/61)

Western Province beat Rhodesia by 10 wickets, 6–8 November 1976, Bulawayo
Rhod 136 (PB Clift 40*, AWR Fletcher 33; GS le Roux 3/36, SA Jones 3/40, DL Hobson 3/30) and 237 (BF Davison 44, SD Robertson 79; DL Hobson 3/82)
WP 361 (EJ Barlow 30, PN Kirsten 30, A Bruyns 35, HM Ackerman 94, AJ Lamb 109; RD Jackman 4/66, B Horton 4/72) and 13/0

Match drawn between Western Province and Eastern Province, 3–6 December 1976, Cape Town
WP 399/5 dec (KC Wessels 38, PN Kirsten 173*, HM Ackerman 114, AJ Lamb 40) and 203/7 (KC Wessels 43, PN Kirsten 103)
EP 225 (SJ Bezuidenhout 59, CP Wilkins 64, DJ Brickett 49; GS le Roux 3/67, SA Jones 4/40) and 469/8 dec (SJ Bezuidenhout 97, CP Wilkins 69, KS McEwan 49, RG Pollock 180*, P Carrick 33)

Match drawn between Transvaal and Western Province, 17–20 December 1976, Johannesburg
Tvl 285/9 dec (DD Dyer 75, CEB Rice 47, PD de Vaal 36, KA Barlow 32*; GS le Roux 5/58) and 260 (RK Muzzell 39, BL Irvine 74, KA McKenzie 41, PD de Vaal 39*; GS le Roux 3/99, EJ Barlow 4/43, RET Morris 3/42)
WP 325 (PN Kirsten 165, AJ Lamb 66; DR Neilson 5/92) and 181/7 (EJ Barlow 43, AJ Lamb 52; DR Neilson 4/58)

Match drawn between Natal and Western Province, 26–28 December 1976, Durban
Ntl 361/9 dec (A Jones 47, BS Groves 49, HR Fotheringham 108, AJS Smith 30, MB Madsen 64*; RET Morris 4/76, DL Hobson 3/94) and 155/3 (BS Groves 39, HR Fotheringham 78*)
WP 431 (PN Kirsten 111, AJ Lamb 105, RET Morris 87; MJ Procter 3/121, VAP van der Bijl 4/109)

Transvaal beat Western Province by 4 runs, 1–4 January 1977, Cape Town
Tvl 334/7 dec (DD Dyer 53, RK Muzzell 30, KA McKenzie 42, LJ Barnard 43, PD de Vaal 54*, DR Neilson 47*; EJ Barlow 3/46) and 283/7 dec (DD Dyer 46, RK Muzzell 78, CEB Rice 41, SJ Cook 49*, DR Neilson 48*; DL Hobson 5/79)
WP 366/8 dec (A Bruyns 60, PN Kirsten 128, HM Ackerman 36, RA Drummond 31; DS van der Knaap 4/65) and 247 (A Bruyns 95, KC Wessels 71; DR Neilson 3/70, CEB Rice 3/6)

Western Province beat Rhodesia by 4 wickets, 7–10 January 1977, Cape Town
WP 387/7 dec (A Bruyns 49, PN Kirsten 44, KC Wessels 136, AJ Lamb 60, RET Morris 39; DAG Fletcher 3/73) and 166/6 (KC Wessels 71; AJ Traicos 4/48)
Rhod 202/9 dec (JG Heron 39, AJ Traicos 38, B Dudleston 49; DL Hobson 7/99) and 347 (JC Mitchell 66, B Dudleston 142, DAG Fletcher 64, BF Davison 37; DL Hobson 3/129, EJ Barlow 3/46)

Eastern Province beat Western Province by 6 wickets, 21–24 January 1977, Port Elizabeth
WP 248 (EJ Barlow 63, A Bruyns 30, HM Ackerman 35, RET Morris 30; AL Biggs 3/102, P Carrick 4/73) and 206 (A Bruyns 43, PN Kirsten 39, HM Ackerman 34; AL Biggs 3/62, P Carrick 4/63)
EP 281 (KS McEwan 46, RG Pollock 138, JW Stephenson 34; GS le Roux 4/63, GA Bricknell 3/42) and 174/4 (RG Pollock 82*, P Carrick 30*)

Western Province beat Natal by 70 runs, 25–28 February 1977, Cape Town
WP 158/9 dec (PN Kirsten 63, AJ Lamb 52; MJ Procter 6/28) and 252 (A Bruyns 32, PN Kirsten 43, KC Wessels 33, AJ Lamb 69*; MJ Procter 3/87, VAP van der Bijl 4/54, AR Lilley 3/47)
Ntl 240 (A Jones 47, HR Fotheringham 54, MJ Procter 56; DL Hobson 3/78, RET Morris 3/35) and 100 (EJ Barlow 3/19, DL Hobson 4/37)

Match drawn between Rhodesia and Western Province, 11–13 November 1977, Salisbury
Rhod 160 (B Dudleston 36, BF Davison 33, JH du Preez 37*; GS le Roux 5/29) and 335/8 dec (JG Heron 35, B Dudleston 98, SD Robertson 49, BF Davison 100*)
WP 266 (PN Kirsten 37, HM Ackerman 83, PD Swart 38, SA Jones 36; RH Kaschula 3/71) and 28/0

Western Province beat Eastern Province by 7 wickets, 18–20 November 1977, Cape Town
EP 294/9 dec (SJ Bezuidenhout 61, CP Wilkins 110, KP Reid 46; GS le Roux 4/73, AB Nieuwoudt 4/61) and 115 (DJ Brickett 36*; GS le Roux 6/48)
WP 293 (RET Morris 62, PD Swart 97, FS Goldstein 37, GP Pfuhl 35; DJ Brickett 4/65) and 117/3 (RET Morris 54*, AJ Lamb 32)

Transvaal beat Western Province by 7 wickets, 17–20 December 1977, Johannesburg
WP 178 (MJ Nel 62; DR Neilson 3/63, RC Ontong 3/56) and 167 (PD Swart 60; DR Neilson 3/53, RW Hanley 4/20)
Tvl 243 (WJ van der Linden 30, KA McKenzie 42, NG Featherstone 59, RC Ontong 54; GS le Roux 3/50, PD Swart 3/70) and 106/3 (LJ Barnard 38; GS le Roux 3/47)

Match drawn between Western Province and Transvaal, 31 December 1977 – 3 January 1978, Cape Town
WP 337/8 dec (PN Kirsten 106, PD Swart 71, GS le Roux 47*; RW Hanley 3/49, DS van der Knaap 3/86)
Tvl 122 (GS le Roux 5/30, DL Hobson 3/57) and 314/8 (PD de Vaal 43, NG Featherstone 37, NT Day 68*; AB Nieuwoudt 3/39)

Match drawn between Western Province and Natal, 7–9 January 1978, Durban
WP 250 (MJ Nel 65, HM Ackerman 32, AJ Lamb 109; VAP van der Bijl 4/61, JF Steele 3/41) and 173/8 dec (PN Kirsten 50, AJ Lamb 36; VAP van der Bijl 3/46, DK Pearse 3/61)
Ntl 184 (D Bestall 37, MB Madsen 45; GS le Roux 3/48, DL Hobson 5/65) and 192/8 (A Barrow 31, BS Groves 77; RET Morris 4/29)

Western Province beat Rhodesia by 8 wickets, 27–30 January 1978, Cape Town
Rhod 202 (SD Robertson 37, BF Davison 36; DL Hobson 6/49) and 259 (JC Mitchell 35, TW Dunk 78, SD Robertson 74; GS le Roux 3/68, RET Morris 5/44)
WP 372 (MJ Nel 86, RA Drummond 76, PN Kirsten 40, HM Ackerman 37, JD du Toit 41; B Horton 3/61, RH Kaschula 6/124) and 92/2 (RA Drummond 30*, HM Ackerman 38*)

Western Province beat Eastern Province by an innings and 189 runs, 10–11 February 1978, Port Elizabeth
WP 361/9 dec (MJ Nel 39, HM Ackerman 47, AJ Lamb 66, PD Swart 55, JD du Toit 43, RET Morris 44; DJ Brickett 3/66, CP Wilkins 3/60)
EP 80 (PD Swart 5/17) and 92 (GS le Roux 7/40, PD Swart 3/40)

Western Province beat Natal by 5 wickets, 3–6 March 1978, Cape Town
Ntl 385/8 dec (A Barrow 61, BS Groves 36, HR Fotheringham 87, MB Madsen 92*, AJS Smith 41; GS le Roux 4/79, PD Swart 3/57) and 174/9 dec (A Barrow 43; RET Morris 5/58)
WP 322/8 dec (MJ Nel 31, PN Kirsten 48, AJ Lamb 72, PD Swart 46, GS le Roux 38; KR Cooper 3/73) and 238/5 (RA Drummond 69, PN Kirsten 106; KR Cooper 4/62)

Western Province beat Eastern Province by 7 wickets, 24–27 November 1978, Cape Town
EP 267 (SJ Bezuidenhout 37, G Cook 73, RA Seymour 42; AB Nieuwoudt 4/69, DL Hobson 3/62) and 219 (SJ Bezuidenhout 60, G Cook 36, DJ Brickett 77; DL Hobson 9/64)
WP 332/7 dec (PD Swart 44, JD du Toit 97, RET Morris 116*) and 156/3 (L Seeff 38, RA Drummond 58, PN Kirsten 40)

SA Universities beat Western Province by 3 wickets, 5–7 December 1978, Stellenbosch
WP 460/9 dec (HM Ackerman 31, PN Kirsten 197, AJ Lamb 51, PD Swart 56, SD Bruce 53; AP Kuiper 6/96) and 219/3 dec (L Seeff 52, NP Daniels 100*, SD Bruce 35)
SAUniv 181 (NT Day 63, JD du Toit 42; ES Gordon 6/47) and 500/7 (LJ Barnard 74, NE Wright 97, E Muntingh 51, NT Day 55, AP Kuiper 110*, JD du Toit 37; PD Swart 3/91)

Western Province beat Eastern Province by an innings and 10 runs, 26–27 December 1978, Port Elizabeth
EP 200 (SJ Bezuidenhout 30, RJD Whyte 33; DL Hobson 5/35) and 74 (AB Nieuwoudt 6/25)
WP 284 (HM Ackerman 32, PD Swart 87, RET Morris 39; W Els 3/57, DJ Brickett 5/71)

Match drawn between Western Province and Transvaal, 30 December 1978 – 2 January 1979, Cape Town
WP 357/9 dec (HM Ackerman 65, RA Drummond 58, PN Kirsten 105; DR Neilson 5/84) and 128/3 (AJ Lamb 56*; AJ Kourie 3/46)
Tvl 466/8 dec (RG Pollock 233, LJ Barnard 55, AJ Kourie 42, PD de Vaal 32, DR Neilson 32*; PD Swart 3/77)

Match drawn between Western Province and Rhodesia, 6–9 January 1979, Cape Town
WP 249 (PN Kirsten 35, AJ Lamb 39, SD Bruce 109*; CB Jonker 3/43, PB Clift 3/48) and 254/7 dec (PN Kirsten 65, AJ Lamb 107, AP Kuiper 30*)
Rhod 241 (JC Mitchell 47*, DL Houghton 33; DL Hobson 4/93, PD Swart 3/27) and 215/7 (JG Heron 122*, PB Clift 33)

Natal beat Western Province by 3 wickets, 27–29 January 1979, Durban
WP 268/9 dec (PN Kirsten 33, AP Kuiper 46*, DL Hobson 61; VAP van der Bijl 5/74) and 110 (AJ Lamb 31; VAP van der Bijl 5/32, KR Cooper 3/46)
Ntl 169 (A Barrow 60; SA Jones 5/34) and 210/7 (AA Hipkin 40, MB Madsen 86, VAP van der Bijl 39*; SA Jones 3/32)

Natal beat Western Province by 127 runs, 9–12 February 1979, Cape Town
Ntl 186 (AJS Smith 57, D Bestall 36, VAP van der Bijl 33; GS le Roux 4/45, SA Jones 4/50) and 245 (CP Wilkins 51, AJS Smith 52, VAP van der Bijl 61, KR Cooper 30; GS le Roux 3/80, DL Hobson 4/87)
WP 77 (MJ Procter 6/25, KR Cooper 3/27) and 227 (RA Drummond 38, HM Ackerman 39, AJ Lamb 36, DL Hobson 45; MJ Procter 5/65)

Western Province beat Rhodesia by 194 runs, 3–5 March 1979, Salisbury
WP 204 (PN Kirsten 52, HM Ackerman 44, SD Bruce 36; PB Clift 3/48, B Dudleston 3/14) and 169/5 dec (SD Bruce 51*; PB Clift 3/52)
Rhod 115 (B Dudleston 35; GS le Roux 3/48, SA Jones 3/25) and 64 (GS le Roux 3/25, SA Jones 3/12)

Transvaal beat Western Province by 127 runs, 9–12 March 1979, Johannesburg
Tvl 291/9 dec (DD Dyer 44, SJ Cook 46, HR Fotheringham 72, RG Pollock 50, AJ Kourie 33; PD Swart 5/43) and 228/3 dec (DD Dyer 36, RG Pollock 103*, CEB Rice 64*)
WP 136 (PN Kirsten 51; RW Hanley 4/41, GE McMillan 3/16) and 256 (L Seeff 33, PN Kirsten 44, SD Bruce 62, AP Kuiper 30; CEB Rice 3/28, AJ Kourie 4/60)

Natal beat Western Province by 4 wickets 24–26 November 1979, Durban
WP 163 (L Seeff 46; MJ Procter 3/60, VAP van der Bijl 3/36, KR Cooper 4/46) and 223 (PN Kirsten 49, AJ Lamb 40, SD Bruce 60; VAP van der Bijl 5/44, KR Cooper 4/56)
Ntl 197 (CP Wilkins 50; EJ Barlow 5/51, PD Swart 4/46) and 191/6 (A Barrow 111*; EJ Barlow 4/32)

Western Province beat Eastern Province by 7 wickets, 15–18 December 1979, Cape Town
EP 217 (RLS Armitage 40, KW Gradwell 48, I Foulkes 34; GS le Roux 3/32, PD Swart 4/43) and 269 (AL Wilmot 86, DJ Brickett 72; GS le Roux 3/71, DL Hobson 3/114)
WP 307/9 dec (EJ Barlow 136, AJ Lamb 75; WK Watson 3/112, DJ Brickett 3/48) and 184/3 (EJ Barlow 31, L Seeff 94)

Western Province beat Northern Transvaal by an innings and 84 runs, 26–28 December 1979, Cape Town
WP 352/8 dec (PN Kirsten 93, AJ Lamb 51, SD Bruce 49, GS le Roux 70*; PD de Vaal 3/114)
NT 152 (RC Ontong 37, E Muntingh 30, PD de Vaal 31*; PD Swart 4/8) and 116 (GS le Roux 5/32)

Match drawn between Western Province and Transvaal, 31 December 1979 – 2 January 1980, Cape Town
WP 378/8 dec (L Seeff 114, AJ Lamb 95, SD Bruce 38, GS le Roux 56*; N Minnaar 4/71) and 198/2 (L Seeff 37, PN Kirsten 83*, AJ Lamb 50*)
Tvl 451 (HR Fotheringham 166, KA McKenzie 57, AJ Kourie 127*, DR Neilson 34; DL Hobson 4/129)

Western Province beat Zimbabwe-Rhodesia by 9 wickets, 26–28 January 1980, Salisbury
ZimRho 186 (GS Clinton 38, RM Bentley 60; GS le Roux 4/49, DL Hobson 3/52) and 177 (RM Bentley 34; DL Hobson 3/68, EJ Barlow 4/25)
WP 330 (L Seeff 71, PN Kirsten 35, AJ Lamb 54, PD Swart 52) and 34/1

Match drawn between Transvaal and Western Province, 1–4 February 1980, Johannesburg
Tvl 314/6 dec (CEB Rice 121*, KA McKenzie 60, AJ Kourie 46; EJ Barlow 3/68) and 231/5 dec (SJ Cook 68, RG Pollock 39, RV Jennings 42; EJ Barlow 3/53)
WP 246 (PN Kirsten 69, PD Swart 61; AJ Kourie 3/18) and 167/9 (AJ Lamb 64; CEB Rice 4/29, AJ Kourie 3/40)

Western Province beat Eastern Province by 6 wickets, 22–25 February 1980, Port Elizabeth
EP 285 (G Cook 47, I Foulkes 67, AL Wilmot 89*; GS le Roux 3/52) and 144 (DH Howell 38; GS le Roux 6/33)
WP 219/5 dec (PN Kirsten 57, PD Swart 68*, HM Ackerman 51*; MK van Vuuren 3/56) and 211/4 (EJ Barlow 30, PN Kirsten 39, AJ Lamb 99, SD Bruce 33*; MK van Vuuren 3/59)

Match drawn between Natal and Western Province, 7–10 March 1980, Cape Town
Ntl 146 (CP Wilkins 37; DL Hobson 4/37) and 235/6 dec (CP Wilkins 150)
WP 227 (EJ Barlow 51, PN Kirsten 41, PD Swart 31, JD du Toit 36; MJ Procter 3/39)

Western Province beat Eastern Province by 10 wickets, 21–24 November 1980, Port Elizabeth
EP 225 (G Cook 61, DJ Brickett 58; GS le Roux 3/29, PD Swart 4/58) and 235 (G Cook 42, SJ Bezuidenhout 53, I Foulkes 31, DJ Richardson 39; GS le Roux 3/53)
WP 362 (L Seeff 58, PN Kirsten 35, AJ Lamb 52, PD Swart 68, SD Bruce 50, O Henry 44; WK Watson 4/87) and 99/0 (EJ Barlow 58*, L Seeff 33*)

Western Province beat Northern Transvaal by 5 wickets, 29 November – 2 December 1980, Cape Town
NT 323 (VF du Preez 100, CS Stirk 32, AM Ferreira 39, KG Motley 36, B McBride 42; GS le Roux 3/69, PD Swart 4/46) and 117 (A Barrow 45; ST Jefferies 3/27, DL Hobson 4/31)
WP 251/6 dec (PN Kirsten 73, PD Swart 37, GS le Roux 31*, O Henry 36*) and 191/5 (EJ Barlow 37, L Seeff 65, AJ Lamb 54*)

Transvaal beat Western Province by an innings and 22 runs, 26–29 December 1980, Johannesburg
Tvl 322/8 dec (SJ Cook 32, RG Pollock 166*; ST Jefferies 3/84)
WP 128 (AJ Kourie 3/12) and 172 (EJ Barlow 38*, PN Kirsten 68; RW Hanley 3/31, CEB Rice 5/47)

Natal beat Western Province by 10 wickets, 1–3 January 1981, Cape Town
WP 132 (AJ Lamb 54; VAP van der Bijl 4/35, KR Cooper 3/40) and 216 (L Seeff 36, AJ Lamb 50, GS le Roux 50; PB Clift 5/36)
Ntl 287 (CP Wilkins 109, NP Daniels 56*; GS le Roux 3/66, DL Hobson 5/88) and 62/0 (CP Wilkins 45*)

Match drawn between Western Province and Eastern Province, 16–19 January 1981, Cape Town
WP 234 (EJ Barlow 99, AJ Lamb 38, O Henry 35; WK Watson 4/43) and 285/3 dec (EJ Barlow 36, L Seeff 81, AJ Lamb 95*, PD Swart 63*)
EP 317/6 dec (SJ Bezuidenhout 76, RLS Armitage 39, DH Howell 30, JM Winstanley 48*, DJ Richardson 77*) and 166/5 (G Cook 63, RLS Armitage 41)

Match drawn between Transvaal and Western Province, 6–9 February 1981, Cape Town
Tvl 310/6 dec (DD Dyer 131, SJ Cook 69, CEB Rice 50; DL Hobson 3/84) and 225/4 dec (SJ Cook 78, RG Pollock 50*, RV Jennings 31; DL Hobson 3/70)
WP 375 (L Seeff 71, PN Kirsten 62, AJ Lamb 130; AJ Kourie 8/113) and 145/7 (PN Kirsten 43; AJ Kourie 5/44)

Natal beat Western Province by 141 runs, 21–23 February 1981, Durban
Ntl 176 (BJ Whitfield 50, CP Wilkins 63; EJ Barlow 5/29, PD Swart 4/42) and 165/8 dec (RM Bentley 35, NP Daniels 73)
WP 106 (L Seeff 41; VAP van der Bijl 5/43, KR Cooper 3/23) and 94 (VAP van der Bijl 6/30)

Western Province beat Northern Transvaal by 45 runs, 27 February – 2 March 1981, Pretoria
WP 237 (EJ Barlow 31, L Seeff 36, MJ Nel 36, AJ Lamb 43; HW Raath 4/49) and 119 (EJ Barlow 53; FE Joubert 4/31, AM Ferreira 3/38)
NT 191 (A Barrow 57, B McBride 37, DN Edwards 32; PD Swart 4/40, DL Hobson 3/43) and 120 (KG Motley 41*; PD Swart 3/23, DL Hobson 7/49)

Western Province beat Eastern Province by 10 wickets, 6–9 November 1981, Cape Town
EP 172 (DJ Brickett 55, WK Watson 36; GS le Roux 5/30) and 158 (RLS Armitage 37; ST Jefferies 4/51, DL Hobson 4/65)
WP 284 (L Seeff 47, PN Kirsten 114, AJ Lamb 32; WK Watson 4/52) and 50/0

Western Province beat Northern Transvaal by an innings and 31 runs, 27–30 November 1981, Pretoria
NT 129 (VF du Preez 48; GS le Roux 3/22, ST Jefferies 5/46) and 208 (BJ Whitfield 70, A Barrow 45, RC Ontong 36*; DL Hobson 5/82)
WP 368/9 dec (L Seeff 37, PN Kirsten 86, AJ Lamb 38, KS McEwan 53, ST Jefferies 63; AM Ferreira 3/81)

Match drawn between Western Province and Transvaal, 5–7 December 1981, Johannesburg
WP 269 (AJ Lamb 62, AP Kuiper 63, GS le Roux 34; J Fairclough 5/44) and 118/2 (L Seeff 57*, PN Kirsten 38)
Tvl 397/6 dec (SJ Cook 48, AI Kallicharran 129, RG Pollock 70, CEB Rice 70; J During 4/114)

Western Province beat SA Universities by 84 runs, 14–17 December 1981, Cape Town
WP 130 (O Henry 36; JD du Toit 3/40, J During 3/31) and 309 (L Seeff 56, AJ Lamb 69, KS McEwan 37; JD du Toit 5/59)
SAUniv 249 (RJ East 63, RG Fensham 37, DJ Richardson 32; RR Lawrenson 3/54, RF Pienaar 4/64) and 106 (IL Howell 32*; RF Pienaar 3/34, O Henry 7/22)

Natal beat Western Province by 5 wickets, 26–28 December 1981, Durban
WP 157 (AP Kuiper 89; VAP van der Bijl 7/31) and 144 (KS McEwan 34; LB Taylor 4/47, VAP van der Bijl 4/33)
Ntl 143 (RM Bentley 39; RF Pienaar 5/24) and 160/5 (RM Bentley 48, D Bestall 57; ST Jefferies 4/50)

Match drawn between Western Province and Transvaal, 1–4 January 1982, Cape Town
WP 353/9 dec (L Seeff 44, AP Kuiper 72, SD Bruce 89, GS le Roux 43, O Henry 53; AJ Kourie 6/88) and 186/7 dec (L Seeff 31, KS McEwan 42, O Henry 30*; AJ Kourie 5/102)
Tvl 251 (SJ Cook 72, KA McKenzie 78, CEB Rice 35; ST Jefferies 3/73, GS le Roux 5/63) and 118/3 (RG Pollock 41*)

Western Province beat Northern Transvaal by an innings and 96 runs, 29 January – 1 February 1982, Cape Town
NT 251 (BJ Whitfield 53, NG Featherstone 99; GS le Roux 6/44) and 75 (GS le Roux 3/23, ST Jefferies 4/25)
WP 422/9 dec (L Seeff 50, PN Kirsten 130, KS McEwan 61, O Henry 31, GS le Roux 42, ST Jefferies 35*; CM Old 3/75)

Western Province beat Natal by 7 wickets, 12–15 February 1982, Cape Town
Ntl 169 (BA Richards 38, D Bestall 43; ST Jefferies 3/40, O Henry 4/22) and 243 (BA Richards 34, D Bestall 37, MJ Procter 63, NP Daniels 32; GS le Roux 3/64, ST Jefferies 4/65, DL Hobson 3/53)
WP 363 (AJ Lamb 89, KS McEwan 117, AP Kuiper 50; MJ Procter 3/61, NP Daniels 3/78) and 51/3

Match drawn between Western Province and SAB English XI, 8–10 March 1982, Cape Town
WP 263/8 dec (AP Kuiper 90, SD Bruce 42, TA Clarke 41, O Henry 33*; JE Emburey 4/88) and 204/7 dec (L Seeff 48, PN Kirsten 67*, ST Jefferies 45)
SABEng 219 (DL Amiss 52, GA Gooch 58; ST Jefferies 3/47, DL Hobson 4/57) and 225/8 (G Boycott 95, DL Amiss 30)

Western Province beat Eastern Province by 10 wickets, 31 March – 2 April 1982, Port Elizabeth
EP 120 (RG Fensham 38*; GS le Roux 5/28, ST Jefferies 4/48) and 307 (SJ Bezuidenhout 110, RLS Armitage 34, DJ Richardson 34, RJD Whyte 46, RG Fensham 39; GS le Roux 5/51, ST Jefferies 3/88)
WP 384/3 dec (L Seeff 79, PN Kirsten 151, AJ Lamb 106*) and 46/0

Match drawn between Arosa Sri Lanka and Western Province, 30 October – 1 November 1982, Cape Town
AROSA 275 (NDP Hettiaratchy 37, JBN Perera 69, LWS Kaluperuma 67; GS le Roux 4/31) and 307 (GJAF Aponso 92, AN Ranasinghe 52, JBN Perera 47, JF Woutersz 42*; AP Kuiper 5/60)
WP 400/7 dec (KS McEwan 149, L Seeff 105, PN Kirsten 70*; AN Ranasinghe 3/115) and 106/6 (RF Pienaar 37; ARM Opatha 4/49)

Match drawn between Natal and Western Province, 4–6 December 1982, Durban
Ntl 324 (RM Bentley 47, D Bestall 69, RA Smith 39, NP Daniels 49; GS le Roux 5/88) and 124 (RA Smith 33; JE Emburey 6/36)
WP 121 (LB Taylor 3/35, KR Cooper 5/25) and 247/4 (GA Gooch 87, L Seeff 47, PN Kirsten 44, KS McEwan 35)

Western Province beat Eastern Province by 9 wickets, 26–28 December 1982, Port Elizabeth
WP 444/6 dec (PN Kirsten 81, KS McEwan 106, AP Kuiper 71, SD Bruce 74*, GS le Roux 51*) and 8/1
EP 218 (W Larkins 40, RG Fensham 35, GS Cowley 64*) and 233 (RG Fensham 58, P Willey 46, RJD Whyte 34; ST Jefferies 5/56)

Transvaal beat Western Province by 122 runs, 31 December 1982 – 3 January 1983, Cape Town
Tvl 196 (HR Fotheringham 61, CEB Rice 43, KA McKenzie 43; JE Emburey 5/53) and 328/6 dec (HR Fotheringham 61, CEB Rice 62, KA McKenzie 70)
WP 202 (PN Kirsten 65; AI Kallicharran 5/45) and 200 (JE Emburey 42, DL Hobson 35*; AJ Kourie 7/79)

Western Province beat Eastern Province by 10 wickets, 26–28 February 1983, Cape Town
EP 170 (DJ Richardson 40, P Willey 35; JE Emburey 6/33) and 223 (DJ Richardson 68, DH Howell 37; JE Emburey 3/62, DL Hobson 6/73)
WP 377 (GA Gooch 38, L Seeff 32, PN Kirsten 69, KS McEwan 33, RF Pienaar 112, AP Kuiper 66; WK Watson 6/87) and 20/0

Match drawn between Western Province and Transvaal, 4–6 March 1983, Johannesburg
WP 349/9 dec (PN Kirsten 55, RF Pienaar 61, PH Rayner 121*, ST Jefferies 39, J During 31; VAP van der Bijl 3/45) and 260/7 dec (GA Gooch 104, L Seeff 42, AP Kuiper 39, ST Jefferies 31; NV Radford 5/116)
Tvl 286 (HR Fotheringham 45, RG Pollock 41, KA McKenzie 38, AJ Kourie 72*, VAP van der Bijl 30; ST Jefferies 6/91) and 101/0 (SJ Cook 51*, HR Fotheringham 43*)

Western Province beat Northern Transvaal by 9 wickets, 11–14 March 1983, Cape Town
NT 237 (KD Verdoorn 50, PJA Visagie 72; ST Jefferies 5/85) and 117 (LJ Barnard 46*; ST Jefferies 3/38, JE Emburey 3/28)
WP 295 (GA Gooch 126, ST Jefferies 60; AM Ferreira 3/89) and 60/1

Western Province beat Natal by 9 wickets, 20–22 March 1983, Cape Town
Ntl 134 (BA Richards 46; GS le Roux 5/34) and 189 (RM Bentley 41, AJS Smith 37*; ST Jefferies 3/51, DL Hobson 3/57)
WP 256 (GA Gooch 41, L Seeff 63, PN Kirsten 70; LB Taylor 4/59, JK Lever 3/105, KR Cooper 3/65) and 68/1 (GA Gooch 31*)

Western Province beat Northern Transvaal by 4 wickets, 25–28 March 1983, Pretoria
NT 284/8 dec (VF du Preez 78, LJ Barnard 39, AM Ferreira 32, GE McMillan 50; AP Kuiper 3/55) and 191 (VF du Preez 37, LJ Barnard 33; ST Jefferies 3/64, GA Gooch 4/15)
WP 304 (RJ Ryall 42, KS McEwan 100, ST Jefferies 49; GE McMillan 3/64, AM Ferreira 4/63) and 175/6 (GA Gooch 34, RF Pienaar 67*, PH Rayner 47; AM Ferreira 3/62)

Match drawn between Transvaal and Western Province, 2–5 April 1983, Johannesburg
Tvl 475 (SJ Cook 49, HR Fotheringham 89, AI Kallicharran 151, KA McKenzie 92; ST Jefferies 3/161, O Henry 4/48) and 97/1 (HR Fotheringham 44*)
WP 228 (RF Pienaar 51, ST Jefferies 38, O Henry 50; VAP van der Bijl 3/23, NV Radford 3/68) and 490/7 dec (GA Gooch 36, L Seeff 71, PN Kirsten 168, KS McEwan 130*; VAP van der Bijl 4/109)

Match drawn between Natal and Western Province, 29–31 October 1983, Durban
Ntl 367/4 dec (BJ Whitfield 116, MB Logan 63, RM Bentley 53, RA Smith 75)
WP 205 (GA Gooch 43, AP Kuiper 61, GS le Roux 40; MJ Procter 5/63, G Miller 4/71) and 420/5 (GA Gooch 47, PN Kirsten 62, RF Pienaar 151*, AP Kuiper 104; G Miller 3/107)

Western Province beat Eastern Province by an innings and 5 runs, 5–7 November 1983, Cape Town
EP 373 (W Larkins 35, RLS Armitage 70, P Willey 111, DH Howell 74*; JE Emburey 3/62) and 209 (W Larkins 110, DJ Brickett 30; GS le Roux 4/53, DL Hobson 5/75)
WP 587/7 dec (GA Gooch 163, L Seeff 128, PN Kirsten 58, O Henry 79*, JE Emburey 52*; P Willey 4/145)

Match drawn between Western Province and Transvaal, 19–21 November 1983, Cape Town
WP 244 (PN Kirsten 100, RF Pienaar 42; RW Hanley 3/43, AJ Kourie 3/79) and 316/6 dec (GA Gooch 42, PN Kirsten 80, PH Rayner 30, KS McEwan 30, AP Kuiper 35*, ST Jefferies 40*)
Tvl 279 (RG Pollock 154, RV Jennings 34; DL Hobson 5/43) and 176/2 (SJ Cook 58, CEB Rice 85*)

Match drawn between West Indies XI and Western Province, 25–28 November 1983, Cape Town
WIXI 291 (SFAF Bacchus 61, MA Lynch 105; DL Hobson 5/92, JE Emburey 4/63) and 300 (SFAF Bacchus 40, MA Lynch 39, CL King 75, FD Stephenson 73; DL Hobson 7/129)
WP 322/8 dec (PN Kirsten 71, PH Rayner 54, KS McEwan 54, AP Kuiper 30, GS le Roux 46, JE Emburey 31*; ST Clarke 3/87) and 57/1

Western Province beat Northern Transvaal by 8 wickets, 2–3 December 1983, Pretoria
NT 230 (NT Day 50, PJA Visagie 56; AP Kuiper 6/55) and 128 (EO Simons 4/30, AP Kuiper 3/32)
WP 282 (PH Rayner 46, KS McEwan 67, AP Kuiper 67; AM Ferreira 5/76) and 79/2 (KS McEwan 36*)

Western Province beat Eastern Province by 67 runs, 10–13 February 1984, Port Elizabeth
WP 293 (GA Gooch 67, L Seeff 42, PH Rayner 54, RJ Ryall 32; P Willey 3/78, TG Shaw 5/127) and 353/6 dec (GA Gooch 171, PN Kirsten 36, AP Kuiper 64*)
EP 334 (P Willey 38, TB Reid 34, GS Cowley 98, TG Shaw 66; ST Jefferies 4/86, DL Hobson 3/63) and 245 (DH Howell 40, P Willey 88, DG Emslie 48; ST Jefferies 6/45)

Transvaal beat Western Province by 141 runs, 24–27 February 1984, Cape Town
Tvl 425/7 dec (SJ Cook 93, AI Kallicharran 73, RG Pollock 94, CEB Rice 41, KA McKenzie 45) and 179 (KA McKenzie 61*; ST Jefferies 7/105)
WP 327 (L Seeff 41, PN Kirsten 57, PH Rayner 36, RF Pienaar 51, AP Kuiper 37, O Henry 44; ST Clarke 3/59, RW Hanley 4/85) and 136 (RF Pienaar 38*; AJ Kourie 6/57)

Western Province beat Eastern Province by 5 wickets, 16–17 November 1984, Cape Town
WP 313/9 dec (L Seeff 30, PH Rayner 64, RF Pienaar 32, AP Kuiper 87, ST Jefferies 31; EA Moseley 4/33, DJ Brickett 3/63) and 45/5 (EA Moseley 4/13)
EP 133 (DJ Richardson 37; GS le Roux 3/30, ST Jefferies 3/25, DL Hobson 3/39) and 221 (GS Cowley 56; GS le Roux 4/49)

Eastern Province beat Western Province by an innings and 3 runs, 26–28 December 1984, Port Elizabeth
WP 167 (RF Pienaar 61; EA Moseley 4/48, TG Shaw 3/44) and 250 (PH Rayner 69, RF Pienaar 34, AP Kuiper 55, ST Jefferies 71; EA Moseley 5/48, KG Bauermeister 4/66)
EP 420/5 dec (IK Daniell 95, PG Amm 74, RLS Armitage 100*, DJ Richardson 63)

Transvaal beat Western Province by 15 runs, 1–3 January 1985, Cape Town
Tvl 227 (CR Norris 55, CEB Rice 62; D Norman 4/53, DL Hobson 3/44) and 275/8 dec (RG Pollock 38, CEB Rice 57, KA McKenzie 55, AJ Kourie 31*; ST Jefferies 3/84)
WP 232 (SFAF Bacchus 59, PH Rayner 40, PN Kirsten 43; ST Clarke 5/41) and 255 (PH Rayner 38, L Seeff 30, PN Kirsten 80, AP Kuiper 68; ST Clarke 4/106, AJ Kourie 4/62)

Match drawn between Western Province and Natal, 12–14 January 1985, Cape Town
WP 295 (SFAF Bacchus 36, PH Rayner 37, PN Kirsten 52, GS le Roux 48*; HL Alleyne 5/103) and 198/2 (SFAF Bacchus 65, PH Rayner 69*)
Ntl 392 (BJ Whitfield 57, RM Bentley 50, D Bestall 134*, CL King 94; GS le Roux 3/79, DL Hobson 5/92)

Western Province beat Northern Transvaal by an innings and 20 runs, 18–21 January 1985, Cape Town
NT 169 (LJ Barnard 54; ST Jefferies 4/39, DL Hobson 3/44) and 219 (M Yachad 37, LJ Barnard 44, A Geringer 30, AM Ferreira 42*; ST Jefferies 4/61, DL Hobson 3/62)
WP 408/8 dec (PH Rayner 37, L Seeff 71, PN Kirsten 126*, AP Kuiper 64; WF Morris 4/97)

Match drawn between Natal and Western Province, 26–28 January 1985, Durban
Ntl 228 (MB Logan 37, D Bestall 35, TR Madsen 54; GS le Roux 4/46, DL Hobson 4/54) and 245/6 dec (BJ Whitfield 96*, MB Logan 48; DL Hobson 3/70)
WP 280 (PN Kirsten 133, RF Pienaar 42, AP Kuiper 45; HL Alleyne 4/83, TJ Packer 4/75) and 46/1

Match drawn between Northern Transvaal and Western Province, 8–11 February 1985, Pretoria
NT 140 (NT Day 51; D Norman 5/38, RP Richardson 3/23) and 205/7 dec (LJ Barnard 65, CPL de Lange 36; AP Kuiper 4/55)
WP 104 (EO Simons 4/26, AM Ferreira 4/32) and 93/6 (L Seeff 52; EO Simons 3/20)

Transvaal beat Western Province by an innings and 71 runs, 15–17 February 1985, Johannesburg
WP 150 (L Seeff 73; ST Clarke 3/14, NV Radford 3/32, HA Page 3/58) and 148 (L Seeff 40; HA Page 4/56, AJ Kourie 4/40)
Tvl 369/6 dec (SJ Cook 37, HR Fotheringham 80, MS Venter 37, RG Pollock 52, CEB Rice 67, AJ Kourie 41*, RV Jennings 41*)

Northern Transvaal beat Western Province by 8 wickets, 22–26 February 1985, Pretoria
WP 325 (SFAF Bacchus 58, L Seeff 76, AP Kuiper 86, GJ Turner 36; EO Simons 4/62) and 160 (GJ Turner 40; EO Simons 3/31, AM Ferreira 3/26)
NT 371 (M Yachad 120, W Kirsh 31, LJ Barnard 51, A Geringer 56, EO Simons 58; GS le Roux 3/104) and 120/2 (M Yachad 62, LJ Barnard 33*)

Western Province beat Orange Free State by an innings and 24 runs, 25–28 October 1985, Bloemfontein
WP 402/8 dec (L Seeff 51, KS McEwan 142, DJ Cullinan 43, ST Jefferies 51*)
OFS 196 (JJ Strydom 53; ST Jefferies 4/38) and 182 (RA le Roux 41, JJ Strydom 39*; GS le Roux 3/27, PN Kirsten 6/48)

Match drawn between Northern Transvaal and Western Province, 15–18 November 1985, Pretoria
NT 299 (VF du Preez 43, RF Pienaar 40, AM Ferreira 105, CD Mitchley 36; EO Simons 5/52) and 242/5 dec (RF Pienaar 79, KD Verdoorn 30, A Geringer 67*)
WP 272 (AG Elgar 66, PN Kirsten 41, KS McEwan 36, GS le Roux 30; CD Mitchley 3/41) and 99/1 (L Seeff 44*, PN Kirsten 38*)

Western Province beat Natal by 107 runs, 23–25 November 1985, Durban
WP 314/7 dec (KS McEwan 101, DJ Cullinan 46, AP Kuiper 36, GS le Roux 57*; GR Dilley 4/73) and 235/4 dec (PN Kirsten 52, KS McEwan 82*, AP Kuiper 55*; EJ Hodkinson 3/31)
Ntl 260 (MB Logan 39, RM Bentley 45, CL King 69, GS Cowley 40*; GS le Roux 4/45, MB Minnaar 3/65) and 182 (MB Logan 33, GS Cowley 35; GS le Roux 5/54)

Western Province beat Eastern Province by an innings and 19 runs, 29–30 November 1985, Cape Town
WP 266 (AG Elgar 30, L Seeff 40, PN Kirsten 51, AP Kuiper 33; WK Watson 6/47)
EP 91 (GS le Roux 3/17, ST Jefferies 5/30) and 156 (GS le Roux 3/41, D Norman 3/17)

Western Province beat Border by an innings and 21 runs, 10–11 January 1986, Cape Town
WP 388/7 dec (PH Rayner 34, AG Elgar 81, PN Kirsten 83, DJ Cullinan 30, SD Bruce 36, GS le Roux 86; EN Trotman 4/94)
Bdr 115 (NP Minnaar 33; GS le Roux 4/42, ST Jefferies 3/39) and 252 (VG Cresswell 51, GCG Fraser 39, IL Howell 34*; MB Minnaar 4/61)

Match drawn between Transvaal and Western Province, 8–10 February 1986, Cape Town
Tvl 364 (SJ Cook 124, HR Fotheringham 42, BM McMillan 85, HA Page 51; GS le Roux 4/52) and 188/4 dec (MS Venter 49, HR Fotheringham 44, B Roberts 43*)
WP 223 (KS McEwan 56, DJ Cullinan 49, AP Kuiper 33; HA Page 3/39, AJ Kourie 3/68) and 153/4 (AG Elgar 48, KS McEwan 47*)

Match drawn between Western Province and Transvaal, 7–10 March 1986, Cape Town
WP 368/6 dec (AG Elgar 65, L Seeff 44, PN Kirsten 66, DJ Cullinan 56, AP Kuiper 48; NV Radford 3/96) and 80/8 (HA Page 3/18)
Tvl 212 (HR Fotheringham 59, RG Pollock 32, AJ Kourie 46; ST Jefferies 5/50) and 298 (SJ Cook 102, BM McMillan 34, AJ Kourie 82; GS le Roux 3/67, ST Jefferies 4/90, BA Matthews 3/66)

Match drawn between Natal and Western Province, 25–27 October 1986, Cape Town
Ntl 348 (D Bestall 113, CM Lister-James 98, TR Madsen 60; BA Matthews 3/54, MB Minnaar 4/92) and 193/5 (BJ Whitfield 77*, RM Bentley 57)
WP 528/7 dec (AG Elgar 65, L Seeff 141, PN Kirsten 204*, GS le Roux 39; HL Alleyne 4/105)

Western Province beat Northern Transvaal by 75 runs, 22–24 November 1986, Cape Town
WP 260 (AG Elgar 33, KS McEwan 52, DJ Cullinan 50, GS le Roux 59, ST Jefferies 33; CD Mitchley 4/56, RC Ontong 3/67) and 256/4 dec (L Seeff 46, KS McEwan 104*, AP Kuiper 42*)
NT 218 (VF du Preez 41, LJ Barnard 46, MJR Rindel 43, RC Ontong 37*; ST Jefferies 4/62) and 223 (LJ Barnard 77, AM Ferreira 31; GS le Roux 4/44, ST Jefferies 3/36, BA Matthews 3/49)

Eastern Province beat Western Province by an innings and 35 runs, 28–30 November 1986, Port Elizabeth
WP 190 (L Seeff 32, KS McEwan 102; WK Watson 3/43, TG Shaw 4/53) and 111 (EO Simons 57; DJ Capel 3/14, RLS Armitage 4/18)
EP 336 (KC Wessels 40, M Michau 47, DJ Capel 134; GS le Roux 4/41)

Western Province beat Orange Free State by 10 wickets, 12–15 December 1986, Bloemfontein
WP 406/7 dec (TN Lazard 166, KS McEwan 125, DJ Cullinan 53) and 27/0
OFS 115 (BT Player 51*; EO Simons 3/16, AP Kuiper 4/20) and 317 (DP le Roux 50, JJ Strydom 107, LJ Wilkinson 36, RJ East 32; ST Jefferies 3/66, MB Minnaar 4/73)

Transvaal beat Western Province by 7 wickets, 19–21 December 1986, Johannesburg
WP 252 (PN Kirsten 69, EO Simons 47; NV Radford 3/89, HA Page 4/68) and 82 (NV Radford 3/21, HA Page 3/30)
Tvl 178 (M Yachad 36, LP Vorster 34, AJ Kourie 42*, RV Jennings 37; GS le Roux 4/42) and 159/3 (M Yachad 33, LP Vorster 69*)

Western Province beat Border by 8 wickets, 24–26 January 1987, Cape Town
Bdr 192 (AL Wilmot 52, GM Gower 30; GS le Roux 3/32) and 300 (BW Lones 68, AL Wilmot 95*, EN Trotman 47; GS le Roux 3/57, ST Jefferies 3/74, MB Minnaar 3/56)
WP 439/6 dec (TN Lazard 129, L Seeff 114, PN Kirsten 50, AP Kuiper 57*, ST Jefferies 41*; EN Trotman 4/128) and 54/2

Western Province beat Eastern Province by 47 runs, 6–9 March 1987, Port Elizabeth
WP 288/7 dec (TN Lazard 62, KS McEwan 79, DJ Cullinan 51*, GS le Roux 39; RJ McCurdy 5/65) and 256 (TN Lazard 43, PN Kirsten 54, DJ Cullinan 60, AP Kuiper 37; RJ McCurdy 4/61, TG Shaw 4/110)
EP 331/7 dec (PG Amm 30, KC Wessels 129, MW Rushmere 74) and 166 (PG Amm 40, KC Wessels 83; GS le Roux 6/53, MB Minnaar 3/26)

Match drawn between Western Province and Transvaal, 13–16 March 1987, Johannesburg
WP 280/7 dec (PN Kirsten 54, AP Kuiper 50, GS le Roux 71*) and 274/3 dec (L Seeff 122*, PN Kirsten 30, KS McEwan 37*, DJ Cullinan 55)
Tvl 340/7 dec (SJ Cook 110, RV Jennings 99, CEB Rice 34, AJ Kourie 31*) and 176/2 (HR Fotheringham 72*, RG Pollock 63*)

Match drawn between Natal and Western Province, 19–21 December 1987, Durban
Ntl 266 (AC Hudson 72, NP Daniels 41, RK McGlashan 30*; DB Rundle 5/59) and 208 (MB Logan 47, TR Madsen 50; DB Rundle 6/37)
WP 396/8 dec (TN Lazard 90, L Seeff 125, GS le Roux 47*; CM Lister-James 3/65) and 71/5 (TJ Packer 4/40)

Western Province beat Orange Free State by an innings and 76 runs, 26–28 December 1987, Cape Town
OFS 134 (DB Rundle 5/33) and 113 (AJ Lamb 30*; ST Jefferies 10/59)
WP 323 (TN Lazard 69, L Seeff 50, PN Kirsten 51, AP Kuiper 50, GS le Roux 30; ST Clarke 3/82, CJPG van Zyl 3/45)

Transvaal beat Western Province by 8 wickets, 1–3 January 1988, Cape Town
WP 157 (JJE Hardy 43, AP Kuiper 40; NV Radford 3/38, RO Estwick 3/28, GE McMillan 3/38) and 246 (TN Lazard 40, PN Kirsten 57, DJ Cullinan 50; NV Radford 4/68)
Tvl 370/6 dec (LP Vorster 174, B Roberts 104, CEB Rice 44*; GS le Roux 3/58) and 37/2

Match drawn between Orange Free State and Western Province, 8–11 January 1988, Bloemfontein
OFS 248 (LJ Wilkinson 33, AJ Lamb 39, JW Lloyds 38, CJPG van Zyl 37*; GS le Roux 4/60) and 226/9 dec (AJ Lamb 101, RJ East 58*; ST Jefferies 3/66, EO Simons 3/33)
WP 130 (ST Clarke 4/49, AA Donald 3/46, CJPG van Zyl 3/27) and 205/4 (PN Kirsten 82, DJ Cullinan 95*)

Western Province beat Northern Transvaal by 6 wickets, 15–16 January 1988, Cape Town
NT 195 (NT Day 60, GR Grobler 42; GS le Roux 3/43, ST Jefferies 4/55) and 96 (AM Ferreira 34; ST Jefferies 5/48, AP Kuiper 4/12)
WP 120 (ST Jefferies 30; PS de Villiers 4/29, T Bosch 4/38) and 173/4 (MH Austen 83, PN Kirsten 48*)

Eastern Province beat Western Province by an innings and 27 runs, 22–24 January 1988, Port Elizabeth
WP 274 (TN Lazard 66, L Seeff 48, PN Kirsten 42, AP Kuiper 51; TG Shaw 6/112) and 91 (TN Lazard 38; TG Shaw 3/17, AL Hobson 3/19)
EP 392/9 dec (PG Amm 61, MW Rushmere 136, KS McEwan 88; ST Jefferies 3/91, DB Rundle 4/96)

Match drawn between Western Province and Eastern Province, 29–31 January 1988, Cape Town
WP 454/9 dec (TN Lazard 76, MH Austen 202*, PN Kirsten 43; JG Thomas 4/122)
EP 292 (MW Rushmere 37, KC Wessels 41, KS McEwan 97; GS le Roux 4/72, CR Matthews 3/56) and 217/4 (MW Rushmere 43, KC Wessels 34, KS McEwan 53*, DJ Callaghan 72)

Western Province beat Natal by 7 wickets, 17–19 December 1988, Durban
Ntl 239 (KM Curran 36, JN Rhodes 108; GS le Roux 4/26, DB Rundle 3/75) and 212 (AC Hudson 34, CM Lister-James 30*, RJ Varner 32; ST Jefferies 3/74, EO Simons 3/18, DB Rundle 4/77)
WP 255/4 dec (TN Lazard 85, PN Kirsten 53, DJ Cullinan 30, AP Kuiper 80*) and 199/3 (L Seeff 41, PN Kirsten 44, DJ Cullinan 55*, AP Kuiper 31*)

Match drawn between Western Province and Northern Transvaal, 26–28 December 1988, Cape Town
WP 235 (DJ Cullinan 39, PN Kirsten 66, EO Simons 40*; PS de Villiers 6/47, GR Grobler 3/47) and 276/4 dec (TN Lazard 99*, L Seeff 82, AP Kuiper 65)
NT 250 (M Yachad 56, LJ Barnard 79, MJR Rindel 55; ST Jefferies 3/55, EO Simons 4/34) and 259/9 (M Yachad 34, MJR Rindel 109)

Match drawn between Western Province and Transvaal, 31 December 1988 – 2 January 1989, Cape Town
WP 144 (RO Estwick 3/34, CEB Rice 4/21) and 358/3 (TN Lazard 122*, L Seeff 59, DJ Cullinan 140)
Tvl 389 (SJ Cook 76, HR Fotheringham 33, RF Pienaar 112, B Roberts 33, BM McMillan 36; EO Simons 3/94, DB Rundle 3/51)

Northern Transvaal beat Western Province by 1 wicket, 6–8 January 1989, Verwoerdburg
WP 258 (L Seeff 74, AP Kuiper 31, G Kirsten 81*; AM Ferreira 4/46) and 211 (EO Simons 57, PN Kirsten 44; PS de Villiers 3/67, GR Grobler 5/56)
NT 295/6 dec (M Yachad 42, GR Grobler 80, MJR Rindel 110*) and 177/9 (VF du Preez 49; EO Simons 4/42)

Match drawn between Eastern Province and Western Province, 13–15 January 1989, Cape Town
EP 440/8 dec (MW Rushmere 140, AV Birrell 105, KC Wessels 108, KS McEwan 40; EO Simons 4/99, DB Rundle 3/91)
WP 175 (TN Lazard 33, PN Kirsten 32, DB Rundle 39; JG Thomas 5/45, TG Shaw 3/40) and 213/9 (PN Kirsten 55; JG Thomas 3/59)

Match drawn between Western Province and Orange Free State, 20–22 January 1989, Cape Town
WP 301/7 dec (DJ Cullinan 100*, AP Kuiper 67, G Kirsten 35) and 196/6 (TN Lazard 51, L Seeff 32, G Kirsten 41*; CJPG van Zyl 3/37)
OFS 449 (PJR Steyn 178, AA Metcalfe 64, LJ Wilkinson 53, CJPG van Zyl 37*; EO Simons 3/110, AP Kuiper 3/71)

Transvaal beat Western Province by 9 wickets, 27–29 January 1989, Johannesburg
WP 103 (PN Kirsten 34; NV Radford 5/22) and 130 (PN Kirsten 61; RO Estwick 3/42)
Tvl 224 (SJ Cook 110; EO Simons 4/66, DB Rundle 4/29) and 12/1

Match drawn between Western Province and Border, 22–24 September 1989, East London
WP 341/5 dec (TN Lazard 36, G Kirsten 96, DJ Cullinan 105, AP Kuiper 42; FD Toppin 3/70) and 184/3 (L Seeff 50, JB Commins 44*, LF Bleekers 35)
Bdr 215/7 dec (BM Osborne 46, EN Trotman 75, GL Long 44; EO Simons 3/35)

Match drawn between Western Province and Natal, 13–15 October 1989, Durban
WP 142 (AP Kuiper 34, BM McMillan 44; TJ Packer 3/31, RK McGlashan 4/54) and 338/6 dec (AP Kuiper 161*, BM McMillan 41, LF Bleekers 34, EO Simons 51; PWE Rawson 4/83)
Ntl 171 (JN Rhodes 43, PWE Rawson 47; AP Kuiper 4/29) and 192/4 (BJ Whitfield 46*, TR Madsen 45*, PWE Rawson 60*)

Western Province beat Northern Transvaal by 8 wickets, 20–22 October 1989, Cape Town
NT 154 (AM Ferreira 33, WF Morris 34; BM McMillan 3/31) and 203 (VF du Preez 37, MD Haysman 63; ST Jefferies 3/49, CR Matthews 3/35)
WP 255 (DJ Cullinan 137; PS de Villiers 3/52, S Elworthy 3/78) and 105/2 (PN Kirsten 31, AP Kuiper 35*)

Match drawn between Western Province and Orange Free State, 26–28 December 1989, Cape Town
WP 328/8 dec (L Seeff 55, PN Kirsten 185, BM McMillan 38; CJPG van Zyl 3/71) and 181 (PN Kirsten 44, JJE Hardy 36; AA Donald 4/39)
OFS 290/9 dec (JJ Strydom 80, LJ Wilkinson 94; MW Pringle 3/60) and 134/8 (DB Rundle 3/45)

Match drawn between Western Province and Transvaal, 30 December 1989 – 2 January 1990, Cape Town
WP 387 (PW Martin 41, L Seeff 55, PN Kirsten 60, BM McMillan 89, CR Matthews 34, DB Rundle 32*; CE Eksteen 6/169) and 13/0
Tvl 331 (SB Smith 55, SJ Cook 44, CEB Rice 45, DR Laing 59, HA Page 58; BM McMillan 3/54)

Match drawn between Western Province and Transvaal, 6–8 January 1990, Johannesburg
WP 355 (L Seeff 35, AP Kuiper 40, JJE Hardy 119, BM McMillan 38; RP Snell 5/84) and 137/3 dec (L Seeff 50, AP Kuiper 38*)
Tvl 207/8 dec (RF Pienaar 70, CEB Rice 78) and 237/7 (SJ Cook 72, RF Pienaar 65, CEB Rice 30; CR Matthews 4/52)

Western Province beat Natal by 234 runs, 12–14 January 1990, Cape Town
WP 317/8 dec (L Seeff 79, AP Kuiper 104*, JJE Hardy 40; D Norman 3/35) and 211/6 dec (G Kirsten 80, AP Kuiper 56; D Norman 3/70)
Ntl 184 (HR Fotheringham 50, RM Bentley 51, KJ Hughes 34; MW Pringle 7/60, DB Rundle 3/54) and 110 (TR Madsen 30; MW Pringle 3/36, DB Rundle 4/15)

Western Province beat Eastern Province by 201 runs, 19–21 January 1990, Port Elizabeth
WP 264 (G Kirsten 45, DJ Cullinan 113; RJ McCurdy 3/90, JN Maguire 3/59) and 217/4 dec (DJ Cullinan 40, AP Kuiper 103*, JJE Hardy 54*; RJ McCurdy 3/46)
EP 155 (MW Rushmere 31, TG Shaw 32*; MW Pringle 3/64, BM McMillan 4/28) and 125 (KS McEwan 78; DB Rundle 5/32)

Match drawn between Western Province and Eastern Province, 26–31 January 1990, Port Elizabeth
WP 507/9 dec (L Seeff 65, G Kirsten 175, PN Kirsten 128, DJ Cullinan 41; RJ McCurdy 4/129, JN Maguire 5/137) and 166/6 dec (PN Kirsten 42, AP Kuiper 31, JJE Hardy 36; TG Shaw 3/35)
EP 404 (MW Rushmere 81, KC Wessels 33, KS McEwan 101, TG Shaw 36; DB Rundle 3/96) and 18/2

Match drawn between Western Province and Boland, 5–7 October 1990, Worcester
WP 332/8 dec (G Kirsten 189, DJ Cullinan 42, RJ Ryall 40*; PA Koen 3/72) and 176/3 dec (L Seeff 30, DJ Cullinan 36, BM McMillan 69*, EO Simons 33*)
Bol 211 (M Erasmus 47; CR Matthews 3/20, EO Simons 4/19) and 244/6 (WS Truter 56, R Marais 32*, PA Koen 41*; AL Hobson 3/84)

Match drawn between Western Province and Orange Free State, 13–15 October 1990, Bloemfontein
WP 324/6 dec (L Seeff 53, G Kirsten 57, DJ Cullinan 102*, EO Simons 45; CJPG van Zyl 3/50) and 84/2 (L Seeff 38*)
OFS 471 (WJ Cronje 61, LJ Wilkinson 167, CJ van Heerden 36, O Henry 88, GJ Parsons 52*)

Western Province beat Natal by 4 runs, 19–21 October 1990, Durban
WP 91/2 dec (L Seeff 36*, DJ Cullinan 35) and 207/6 dec (BM McMillan 80*, DB Rundle 48*; TJ Packer 3/35)
Ntl 91/3 dec (AC Hudson 35, KD Robinson 35) and 203 (KJ Hughes 65, JN Rhodes 57; BM McMillan 5/45, DB Rundle 3/58)

Match drawn between Northern Transvaal and Western Province, 26–28 December 1990, Cape Town
NT 235 (MD Haysman 72, LJ Barnard 33, S Elworthy 45; MW Pringle 4/55, CR Matthews 3/15) and 269/6 dec (MD Haysman 135*)
WP 276 (G Kirsten 113, BM McMillan 45, CR Matthews 43*; PS de Villiers 4/40, WF Morris 3/57) and 218/9 (G Kirsten 31, DJ Cullinan 52, BM McMillan 44; WF Morris 3/51)

Match drawn between Western Province and Transvaal, 31 December 1990 – 2 January 1991, Cape Town
WP 352/7 dec (KC Jackson 113, BM McMillan 127, EO Simons 38, DB Rundle 35*; RP Snell 3/71) and 148 (BM McMillan 41; RP Snell 4/45)
Tvl 295/6 dec (RF Pienaar 102, CEB Rice 99*; MW Pringle 3/70, CR Matthews 3/76) and 126/5 (RF Pienaar 53*)

Northern Transvaal beat Western Province by 8 wickets, 5–7 January 1991, Verwoerdburg
WP 142 (EO Simons 44*, CR Matthews 30; T Bosch 3/37, PS de Villiers 3/30) and 365 (KC Jackson 39, HH Gibbs 35, EO Simons 83, CR Matthews 105; T Bosch 4/62)
NT 238 (M Yachad 52, LJ Barnard 79; MW Pringle 4/67, CR Matthews 6/58) and 273/2 (M Yachad 115, MJR Rindel 115*)

Match drawn between Eastern Province and Western Province, 11–13 January 1991, Cape Town
EP 171 (DJ Callaghan 48, DJ Richardson 40*; BM McMillan 3/25, CR Matthews 5/30) and 289/7 dec (PG Amm 39, MW Rushmere 79, DJ Richardson 39; EO Simons 3/77)
WP 220 (AP Kuiper 58; BN Schultz 3/51, JN Maguire 5/56) and 113/7 (DJ Cullinan 58; BN Schultz 4/22)

Match drawn between Western Province and Eastern Province, 18–20 January 1991, Port Elizabeth
WP 246/8 dec (G Kirsten 58, KC Jackson 53, DJ Cullinan 38, BM McMillan 32; JN Maguire 3/43) and 233/7 dec (KC Jackson 50, DJ Cullinan 74, EO Simons 35; TG Shaw 3/49)
EP 251/2 dec (PG Amm 104, KC Wessels 107) and 177/6 (PG Amm 90, DJ Richardson 34)

Western Province beat Transvaal by 5 runs, 22–24 February 1991, Johannesburg
WP 148 (S Jacobs 6/35) and 140 (SD Jack 4/46, RP Snell 5/43)
Tvl 151 (CR Matthews 4/19) and 132 (BM McMillan 4/28, CR Matthews 4/25)

Western Province beat Natal by 9 wickets, 1–3 March 1991, Cape Town
Ntl 147 (RM Bentley 39; CR Matthews 3/22) and 121 (JN Rhodes 40; EO Simons 4/16)
WP 183 (G Kirsten 46, MF Voss 30, BM McMillan 56*; SJS Kimber 4/51) and 86/1 (G Kirsten 38*, KC Jackson 36*)

Western Province beat Orange Free State by 15 runs, 8–10 March 1991, Cape Town
WP 199 (G Kirsten 50, DJ Cullinan 32; AA Donald 3/51, CJ van Heerden 5/41) and 199/8 dec (G Kirsten 35, EO Simons 30*, DB Rundle 39; NW Pretorius 5/60)
OFS 115 (O Henry 36; CR Matthews 4/30) and 268 (PJR Steyn 30, JM Arthur 35, CJ van Heerden 57, O Henry 31, AA Donald 46*; CR Matthews 5/48, DB Rundle 3/60)

1.1.7 Western Province Cricket Union List A, Limited-Overs Scores, 1969/70–1990/91[62]

Western Province beat Griqualand West by 150 runs, 30 March 1970, Cape Town
WP 333/6 (EJ Barlow 62, NR Budge 84, A Bruyns 53, AP van Niekerk 52; MJD Doherty 3/61)
GW 183/8 (MJD Doherty 39, LA McNamara 32, DJ Schonegevel 41; MA Seymour 3/15)

Western Province beat Eastern Province by 13 runs, 4 April 1970, Johannesburg
WP 355/7 (EJ Barlow 186, CG Stephens 55)
EP 342 (AL Biggs 41, RG Pollock 169)

Western Province beat Natal by 2 runs, 6 April 1970, Johannesburg
WP 132 (PD Swart 34; DL Orchard 3/47)
Ntl 130 (BJ Versfeld 31; EJ Barlow 3/30, PD Swart 3/21)

Western Province beat Border by 245 runs, 21 November 1970, East London
WP 360/4 (EJ Barlow 148, HM Ackerman 127, MH Bowditch 51*)
Bdr 115 (MH Bowditch 3/23, GA Chevalier 6/32)

Western Province beat Eastern Province by 116 runs, 6 February 1971, Cape Town
WP 289/9 (A Bruyns 113, CG Stephens 104; PM Pollock 5/51)
EP 173 (SJ Bezuidenhout 62, RG Pollock 47; MH Bowditch 3/41, GA Chevalier 5/22)

Western Province beat Transvaal by 3 wickets, 13 March 1971, Johannesburg
Tvl 287/9 (FS Goldstein 82, RC White 48, PD de Vaal 54*; GA Chevalier 4/45)
WP 288/7 (A Bruyns 91, MH Bowditch 66, GP Pfuhl 31, PD Swart 32*)

Natal beat Western Province by faster scoring rate, 20 November 1971, Durban
WP 155/9 (GP Pfuhl 47, RD Jackman 31; PP Henwood 4/18)
Ntl 80/2 (BA Richards 43*)

Western Province beat Orange Free State by 7 wickets, 21 October 1972, Bloemfontein
OFS 175 (N Rosendorff 32, KC Bland 36; RET Morris 4/31)
WP 178/3 (EJ Barlow 61, HM Ackerman 68*)

Western Province beat Northern Transvaal by 8 wickets, 17 February 1973, Cape Town
NT 145 (DT Lindsay 57, CI Dey 33; AB Nieuwoudt 3/16)
WP 146/2 (EJ Barlow 86*)

Western Province beat Eastern Province by 7 wickets, 10 March 1973, Johannesburg
EP 232/8 (SJ Bezuidenhout 35, AL Biggs 32, AL Wilmot 66; PD Swart 3/40)
WP 235/3 (EJ Barlow 58, FS Goldstein 77, HM Ackerman 46*, CA Gie 38*)

Western Province beat Eastern Province by 3 wickets, 3 November 1973, Port Elizabeth
EP 253/5 (SJ Bezuidenhout 41, AL Wilmot 101*, CP Wilkins 31)
WP 257/7 (EJ Barlow 93, HM Ackerman 52; KP Reid 3/65)

Transvaal beat Western Province by 66 runs, 9 February 1974, Cape Town
Tvl 223/9 (BL Irvine 59, CEB Rice 48*)
WP 157 (EJ Barlow 40; JPD Flanagan 4/49)

Western Province beat Northern Transvaal by 191 runs, 19 October 1974, Pretoria
WP 304/5 (EJ Barlow 140, FS Goldstein 45, A Bruyns 59)
NT 113 (DL Hobson 7/27)

Western Province beat Eastern Province by 22 runs, 8 February 1975, Port Elizabeth
WP 229 (EJ Barlow 72, FS Goldstein 91; CP Wilkins 5/40)
EP 207 (SJ Bezuidenhout 36, RG Pollock 34, AL Wilmot 44; SA Jones 4/34)

Natal beat Western Province by 31 runs, 8 March 1975, Johannesburg
Ntl 215 (DD Dyer 53, HR Fotheringham 32; EJ Barlow 3/43, HM Ackerman 3/29)
WP 184 (RET Morris 42)

Western Province beat Griqualand West by 4 wickets, 25 October 1975, Kimberley
GW 85 (SA Jones 5/31)
WP 89/6 (EJ Barlow 37; TE Jesty 3/22)

Western Province beat Natal by 44 runs, 31 January 1976, Cape Town
WP 248 (EJ Barlow 58, A Bruyns 62, HM Ackerman 59; VAP van der Bijl 5/25)
Ntl 204 (BA Richards 71, A Barrow 55, AJS Smith 46; EJ Barlow 3/16)

Eastern Province beat Western Province by 128 runs, 28 February 1976, Johannesburg
EP 276/6 (SJ Bezuidenhout 41, CP Wilkins 32, RG Pollock 63, AL Wilmot 46, D Bestall 33*, PH Edmonds 30)
WP 148 (HM Ackerman 55, PN Kirsten 41; GS Cowley 6/32, CP Wilkins 3/33)

Western Province beat Griqualand West by 7 wickets, 16 October 1976, Kimberley
GW 124 (NL Heale 33, MJD Doherty 31; GS le Roux 3/31)
WP 125/3 (KC Wessels 41)

Eastern Province beat Western Province by 58 runs, 29 January 1977, Cape Town
EP 217/7 (KS McEwan 32, AL Biggs 67*, DJ Brickett 61; EJ Barlow 3/38)
WP 159 (KC Wessels 30; P Carrick 3/39, AL Biggs 3/14)

Transvaal beat Western Province by 1 wicket, 28 November 1977, Johannesburg
WP 98 (DR Neilson 3/14, RC Ontong 4/20)
Tvl 102/9 (GS le Roux 4/19, SA Jones 3/28)

Orange Free State beat Western Province by 8 wickets, 21 October 1978, Bloemfontein
WP 144 (RA Drummond 32, PD Swart 35; JRT Barclay 3/30)
OFS 145/2 (JRT Barclay 93*)

Western Province beat Griqualand West by 70 runs, 13 October 1979, Kimberley
WP 234/9 (PN Kirsten 60, SD Bruce 43; RD Engelbrecht 3/53)
GW 164/7 (SN Turner 37*, MJD Doherty 51)

Western Province beat Eastern Province by 5 wickets, 12 January 1980, Cape Town
EP 183 (I Foulkes 36, AL Wilmot 43, RG Fensham 38; SA Jones 4/36)
WP 185/5 (SD Bruce 62*, PD Swart 30)

Transvaal beat Western Province by 7 wickets, 16 February 1980, Johannesburg
WP 224/9 (AJ Lamb 56, SD Bruce 33; CEB Rice 3/31)
Tvl 228/3 (SJ Cook 113*, RG Pollock 58, CEB Rice 33*)

Western Province beat Orange Free State by 7 wickets, 25 October 1980, Bloemfontein
OFS 131 (LW Griessel 40; ST Jefferies 4/14)
WP 135/3 (AJ Lamb 64*)

Western Province beat Eastern Province by 6 wickets, 22 December 1980, Cape Town
EP 101 (JD du Toit 5/36)
WP 102/4 (AJ Lamb 46*; WK Watson 3/15)

Eastern Province beat Western Province by 1 wicket, 10 January 1981, Port Elizabeth
WP 201/8 (AJ Lamb 63, PD Swart 31, GS le Roux 41*; WK Watson 3/23)
EP 202/9 (RLS Armitage 71, RJD Whyte 52; GS le Roux 3/12, ST Jefferies 3/41, EJ Barlow 3/42)

Eastern Province beat Western Province by 7 wickets, 13 January 1981, Port Elizabeth
WP 116 (MK van Vuuren 3/19)
EP 117/3 (SJ Bezuidenhout 35, RLS Armitage 33*)

Western Province beat Northern Transvaal by 8 wickets, 21 November 1981, Cape Town
NT 98 (ST Jefferies 3/17)
WP 101/2 (L Seeff 42*, PN Kirsten 32)

Western Province beat Boland by 74 runs, 19 December 1981, Cape Town
WP 258/4 (RF Pienaar 67, AJ Lamb 90, PN Kirsten 57*)
Bol 184/9 (EJ Barlow 43, C van der Merwe 42, PD Swart 51; AP Kuiper 3/16, RF Pienaar 3/32)

Western Province beat Boland by 118 runs, 9 January 1982, Stellenbosch
WP 236/9 (RF Pienaar 42, KS McEwan 32, SD Bruce 47, GS le Roux 42*, JD du Toit 42; SA Jones 4/52)
Bol 118 (SA Jones 40; ST Jefferies 4/34, J During 3/20)

Western Province beat Natal by 2 runs, 20 February 1982, Johannesburg
WP 178/8 (PN Kirsten 35, AP Kuiper 38; LB Taylor 4/26)
Ntl 176/8 (D Bestall 47; ST Jefferies 3/17)

Western Province beat Eastern Province by 16 runs, 3 April 1982, Cape Town
WP 188 (AJ Lamb 56; GS Cowley 4/29)
EP 172 (RLS Armitage 30, JW Stephenson 51*; ST Jefferies 4/26)

Transvaal beat Western Province by 4 wickets, 5 April 1982, Johannesburg
WP 268/8 (AJ Lamb 67, RF Pienaar 50, ST Jefferies 74*; IFN Weideman 3/66)
Tvl 269/6 (RV Jennings 81, RG Pollock 120)

Western Province beat Boland by 8 wickets, 23 October 1982, Stellenbosch
Bol 130/9 (SA Jones 45; JD du Toit 3/28)
WP 134/2 (L Seeff 46, PN Kirsten 52*)

Western Province beat Northern Transvaal by 26 runs, 10 November 1982, Cape Town
WP 156 (L Seeff 55, ST Jefferies 30; SP Hughes 3/25, AM Ferreira 3/35)
NT 130/9 (CS Stirk 42; GS le Roux 3/13)

There was no result between Western Province and Natal, 2 December 1982, Pietermaritzburg
WP 214/6 (GA Gooch 34, PN Kirsten 94, RF Pienaar 51)
Ntl 9/1

Western Province beat Natal by 29 runs, 18 December 1982, Durban
WP 263/9 (GA Gooch 43, PN Kirsten 119, KS McEwan 36; JK Lever 3/46, MD Clare 3/60)
Ntl 234 (BA Richards 54, RM Bentley 55, D Bestall 40, RA Smith 45)

Western Province beat Transvaal by 6 wickets, 29 December 1982, Cape Town
Tvl 212 (HR Fotheringham 68, AI Kallicharran 41, KA McKenzie 31; GS le Roux 5/17)
WP 215/4 (GA Gooch 92, PN Kirsten 36, AP Kuiper 37*; KA McKenzie 3/39)

Western Province beat Natal by 72 runs, 8 January 1983, Cape Town
WP 252/8 GA Gooch 51, PN Kirsten 82, KS McEwan 45; JK Lever 3/38, KR Cooper 3/49)
Ntl 180 (RM Bentley 50*, TR Madsen 30)

Western Province beat Eastern Province by 3 wickets, 12 January 1983, Cape Town
EP 299/9 (W Larkins 117, P Willey 79; GS le Roux 3/39)
WP 300/7 (GA Gooch 41, PN Kirsten 51, KS McEwan 81, RF Pienaar 58, O Henry 40*; JA Carse 3/47)

West Indies XI beat Western Province by 21 runs, 15 January 1983, Cape Town
WIXI 204/9 (LG Rowe 66, CL King 79*; ST Jefferies 4/31)
WP 183 (GA Gooch 64, KS McEwan 37; EA Moseley 4/23)

Transvaal beat Western Province by 109 runs, 19 February 1983, Johannesburg
Tvl 303/5 (SJ Cook 70, HR Fotheringham 67, AI Kallicharran 74, RG Pollock 55)
WP 194 (KS McEwan 57, RF Pienaar 36; NV Radford 3/40)

Western Province beat Eastern Province by 4 runs, 2 March 1983, Johannesburg
WP 226/9 (GA Gooch 65, PN Kirsten 44; JA Carse 3/37, DJ Brickett 3/37)
EP 222/6 (DJ Richardson 94, P Willey 50; ST Jefferies 3/32)

Transvaal beat Western Province by 6 wickets, 18 March 1983, Johannesburg
WP 275/8 (GA Gooch 85, RF Pienaar 61, ST Jefferies 67, PH Rayner 33*; VAP van der Bijl 3/52)
Tvl 277/4 (SJ Cook 34, HR Fotheringham 77, AI Kallicharran 31, RG Pollock 45, CEB Rice 44*, KA McKenzie 37*)

Western Province beat Natal by 33 runs, 12 October 1983, Cape Town
WP 230/8 (L Seeff 49, O Henry 73*, GS le Roux 30; LB Taylor 3/84, DJ Thomas 3/43)
Ntl 197 (RM Bentley 39, D Bestall 32; GS le Roux 4/33, GA Gooch 3/31)

Western Province beat Northern Transvaal by 67 runs, 22 October 1983, Pretoria
WP 216/9 (GA Gooch 55, PH Rayner 52; PA Robinson 4/56)
NT 149 (M Yachad 62; AP Kuiper 3/28, GA Gooch 3/24)

Western Province beat Eastern Province by 58 runs, 26 October 1983, Cape Town
WP 284/4 (GA Gooch 46, L Seeff 68, PN Kirsten 58, RF Pienaar 46*, PH Rayner 53)
EP 226 (MB Billson 33, RLS Armitage 41, P Willey 48, JD Ogilvie 48, WK Watson 31; PN Kirsten 3/7)

Western Province beat Northern Transvaal by 50 runs, 16 November 1983, Cape Town
WP 241/9 (PH Rayner 67, PN Kirsten 40; PA Robinson 3/50)
NT 191 (M Yachad 45, KD Verdoorn 72, NT Day 34; PN Kirsten 6/17)

Western Province beat Natal by 6 wickets, 10 December 1983, Cape Town
Ntl 190/9 (TR Madsen 37; JE Emburey 3/17)
WP 195/4 (GA Gooch 38, PH Rayner 45, KS McEwan 48*)

Western Province beat Natal by 27 runs, 4 February 1984, Durban
WP 246 (GA Gooch 60, RF Pienaar 45, AP Kuiper 46)
Ntl 219 (BJ Whitfield 50, MB Logan 32, RM Bentley 32, PB Clift 30; AP Kuiper 3/36)

Transvaal beat Western Province by 89 runs, 3 March 1984, Johannesburg
Tvl 305/5 (SJ Cook 51, AI Kallicharran 107, RG Pollock 49, CEB Rice 45*)
WP 216 (RF Pienaar 84; ST Clarke 3/22, CD Mitchley 3/54)

Western Province beat Northern Transvaal by faster scoring rate, 7 March 1984, Pretoria
WP 251/8 (GA Gooch 106, PN Kirsten 70; GL Ackermann 4/51)
NT 64/5 (JE Emburey 3/6)

Transvaal beat Western Province by 1 wicket, 14 March 1984, Cape Town
WP 136 (O Henry 33*; CD Mitchley 3/28, CEB Rice 3/27)
Tvl 137/9 (KA McKenzie 69; ST Jefferies 5/10)

Natal beat Western Province by 6 wickets, 21 March 1984, Cape Town
WP 164 (GA Gooch 36, PN Kirsten 62, ST Jefferies 36*; CL King 3/33, PB Clift 3/29)
Ntl 165/4 (BJ Whitfield 33*, MB Logan 52, RM Bentley 44)

Western Province beat Northern Transvaal by 10 runs, 31 October 1984, Pretoria
WP 224/9 (SFAF Bacchus 41, DB Rundle 39, TA Clarke 35, GS le Roux 39*; GL Ackermann 4/36)
NT 214 (AM Ferreira 31; D Norman 3/43)

Western Province beat Western Province B by 7 wickets, 3 November 1984, Cape Town
WPB 138 (AG Elgar 37, IM Wingreen 38; AP Kuiper 4/14)
WP 139/3 (L Seeff 49, SFAF Bacchus 32, PH Rayner 33*)

Eastern Province beat Western Province by 60 runs, 14 November 1984, Cape Town
EP 212/6 (DH Howell 30, P Willey 109*; D Norman 3/72)
WP 152 (CM Wells 47, AP Kuiper 37; EA Moseley 3/17, GS Cowley 3/22)

Western Province beat Natal by 151 runs, 28 November 1984, Durban
WP 275/5 (SFAF Bacchus 132, IM Wingreen 31, PN Kirsten 52; RM Bentley 3/54)
Ntl 124 (TR Madsen 31; GS le Roux 4/18)

Western Province beat Northern Transvaal by 69 runs, 1 December 1984, Pretoria
WP 246/7 (PN Kirsten 105, PH Rayner 46, RF Pienaar 50)
NT 177 (NT Day 43, A Geringer 32; D Norman 3/33)

Transvaal beat Western Province by 6 wickets, 21 December 1984, Cape Town
WP 175/9 (SFAF Bacchus 36, ST Jefferies 30; HA Page 3/35, CR Norris 3/42)
Tvl 176/4 (SJ Cook 60, CEB Rice 35, RG Pollock 52*; AP Kuiper 3/40)

Western Province beat Northern Transvaal by 7 runs, 5 January 1985, Cape Town
WP 218 (SFAF Bacchus 42, PH Rayner 45, L Seeff 52; A Geringer 5/38)
NT 211 (A Geringer 67, WF Morris 44; ST Jefferies 4/26)

Western Province beat Impalas by 54 runs, 30 January 1985, Cape Town
WP 166 (SFAF Bacchus 53, PN Kirsten 50; CJ van Heerden 5/18)
Imp 112 (PN Kirsten 3/8)

Transvaal beat Western Province by 9 wickets, 2 February 1985, Johannesburg
WP 200/8 (L Seeff 67; HA Page 3/42)
Tvl 202/1 (SJ Cook 85, HR Fotheringham 103*)

Transvaal beat Western Province by 22 runs, 22 March 1985, Johannesburg
Tvl 158 (RF Pienaar 4/37)
WP 136 (AP Kuiper 37; CD Mitchley 3/41)

Western Province beat Border by 58 runs, 12 October 1985, East London
WP 222/9 (PH Rayner 86, PN Kirsten 72; GM Gower 4/24, SFAF Bacchus 3/44)
Bdr 164/9 (GCG Fraser 36*; MB Minnaar 5/23)

Western Province beat Northern Transvaal by 3 wickets, 16 October 1985, Pretoria
NT 218/9 (LJ Barnard 37, A Geringer 41, KD Verdoorn 37; RF Pienaar 3/38)
WP 219/7 (PH Rayner 34, PN Kirsten 52)

Natal beat Western Province by 9 runs, 3 November 1985, Durban
Ntl 240/7 (MB Logan 87, RM Bentley 42, CL King 50)
WP 231 (PN Kirsten 52, KS McEwan 33, DJ Cullinan 39, AP Kuiper 50; GR Dilley 4/47, TJ Packer 5/32)

Western Province beat Natal by 4 wickets, 7 December 1985, Cape Town
Ntl 235/6 (MB Logan 31, RM Bentley 65, D Bestall 57*, NP Daniels 34; EO Simons 5/45)
WP 236/6 (AG Elgar 84, PN Kirsten 38, KS McEwan 76; GR Dilley 3/28)

Western Province beat Natal by 24 runs, 11 December 1985, Cape Town
WP 243/8 (PH Rayner 65, AG Elgar 59, KS McEwan 54)
Ntl 219 (MB Logan 74, D Bestall 46; GS le Roux 3/28, D Norman 4/56)

Australian XI beat Western Province by 48 runs, 21 December 1985, Cape Town
AusXI 260/4 (J Dyson 126*, KJ Hughes 61)
WP 212/9 (PN Kirsten 96, DJ Cullinan 41; RM Hogg 4/36)

Western Province beat Natal by 6 wickets, 14 January 1986, Durban
Ntl 204/8 (RM Bentley 73)
WP 207/4 (AG Elgar 45, DJ Cullinan 57*)

Transvaal beat Western Province by 7 wickets, 22 February 1986, Johannesburg
WP 230/6 (PN Kirsten 44, KS McEwan 66, AP Kuiper 47*)
Tvl 234/3 (SJ Cook 39, HR Fotheringham 71, BM McMillan 39*, CEB Rice 59*)

Western Province beat Eastern Province by 5 wickets, 28 February 1986, Cape Town
EP 211/7 (DJ Richardson 68, DJ Capel 34; AP Kuiper 4/33)
WP 216/5 (PN Kirsten 33, KS McEwan 101, AP Kuiper 60*; PA Rayment 3/30)

No result between Western Province and Transvaal, 14 March 1986, Johannesburg
WP 158/2 (AG Elgar 63, L Seeff 54)
Tvl 46/1

Western Province beat Eastern Province by 5 wickets, 19 March 1986, Port Elizabeth
EP 159 (GS le Roux 4/22, AP Kuiper 3/23)
WP 161/5 (KS McEwan 45, AP Kuiper 34*)

Western Province beat Northern Transvaal by 12 runs, 26 March 1986, Johannesburg
WP 265/4 (PN Kirsten 39, KS McEwan 102*, DJ Cullinan 33)
NT 253/9 (RF Pienaar 35, NT Day 47, RC Ontong 62; GS le Roux 3/32, BA Matthews 3/26)

Eastern Province beat Western Province by 37 runs, 22 October 1986, Port Elizabeth
EP 220/9 (KC Wessels 78; PN Kirsten 3/26)
WP 183 (PN Kirsten 54, GS le Roux 43; WK Watson 3/43)

Western Province beat Eastern Province by 2 runs, 1 November 1986, Cape Town
WP 236/4 (PN Kirsten 117*, DJ Cullinan 44)
EP 234/8 (KC Wessels 49, MW Rushmere 99)

Western Province beat Border by 25 runs, 8 November 1986, Cape Town
WP 242/9 (L Seeff 66, AP Kuiper 104; BM Osborne 5/35)
Bdr 217/9 (BW Lones 34, EN Trotman 31, JG Thomas 49*; GS le Roux 4/55)

Western Province beat Northern Transvaal by faster scoring rate, 15 November 1986, Verwoerdburg
NT 202/8 (AM Ferreira 57, MJR Rindel 53; GS le Roux 3/33)
WP 194/5 (L Seeff 60, KS McEwan 68*)

Western Province beat Impalas by 134 runs, 19 November 1986, Virginia
WP 239/6 (L Seeff 60, KS McEwan 63)
Imp 105 (O Henry 32; ST Jefferies 4/26)

Transvaal beat Western Province by 3 wickets, 3 December 1986, Cape Town
WP 190/7 (L Seeff 57, KS McEwan 46; NV Radford 3/52)
Tvl 191/7 (BM McMillan 43*)

Natal beat Western Province by 2 wickets, 9 January 1987, Cape Town
WP 161 (L Seeff 78; D Norman 3/33, HL Alleyne 3/29)
Ntl 164/8 (TR Madsen 35, NP Daniels 51*; AP Kuiper 3/25)

Western Province beat Northern Transvaal by 16 runs, 14 January 1987, Cape Town
WP 208/6 (TN Lazard 67, GS le Roux 36*; AM Ferreira 3/34)
NT 192 (VF du Preez 40, LJ Barnard 31, PJA Visagie 36, NT Day 35; EO Simons 4/21)

Transvaal beat Western Province by 20 runs, 18 February 1987, Johannesburg
Tvl 252 (SJ Cook 59, RG Pollock 100; GS le Roux 3/49, BA Matthews 4/46)
WP 232/7 (TN Lazard 50*, PN Kirsten 44, EO Simons 30)

Transvaal beat Western Province by 2 wickets, 21 February 1987, Cape Town
WP 172 (PN Kirsten 38, GS le Roux 37; HA Page 4/25)
Tvl 176/8 (RG Pollock 57)

Western Province beat Natal by 5 wickets, 20 March 1987, Cape Town
Ntl 208/8 (RM Bentley 72*, NP Daniels 57; GS le Roux 4/44)
WP 210/5 (TN Lazard 96*, PN Kirsten 49)

Western Province beat Transvaal by 41 runs, 27 March 1987, Cape Town
WP 205/6 (L Seeff 84, DJ Cullinan 49; NV Radford 3/39)
Tvl 164 (CEB Rice 35; BA Matthews 4/22)

Northern Transvaal beat Western Province by 9 runs, 16 October 1987, Verwoerdburg
NT 229/5 (RF Pienaar 83, LJ Barnard 86)
WP 220 (PN Kirsten 65; AM Ferreira 5/44)

Orange Free State beat Western Province by 2 wickets, 24 October 1987, Bloemfontein
WP 211/9 (PN Kirsten 52, ST Jefferies 46*; AI Kallicharran 3/43)
OFS 212/8 (PJR Steyn 57, LJ Wilkinson 65; CR Matthews 3/38)

Western Province beat Border by 168 runs, 14 November 1987, Cape Town
WP 282/6 (L Seeff 100, PN Kirsten 62, DJ Cullinan 33)
Bdr 114 (GL Hayes 33; ST Jefferies 4/15)

Western Province beat Impalas by 71 runs, 18 November 1987, Stellenbosch
WP 272/7 (TN Lazard 40, L Seeff 50, DJ Cullinan 74, JJE Hardy 40)
Imp 201 (EN Trotman 66; CR Matthews 4/65)

Western Province beat Natal by 7 wickets, 25 November 1987, Cape Town
Ntl 209/7 (MB Logan 110, NP Daniels 36; CR Matthews 3/29)
WP 210/3 (TN Lazard 88*, PN Kirsten 55, DJ Cullinan 41)

Western Province beat Transvaal by 5 wickets, 28 November 1987, Johannesburg
Tvl 176 (LP Vorster 32, BM McMillan 43, B McBride 32; AP Kuiper 3/32)
WP 177/5 (L Seeff 41, PN Kirsten 72, DJ Cullinan 43)

Western Province beat Eastern Province by 11 runs, 12 December 1987, Port Elizabeth
WP 145/8 (GS le Roux 33; RJ McCurdy 4/13)
EP 134 (MW Rushmere 35)

Transvaal beat Western Province by 101 runs, 15 December 1987, Cape Town
Tvl 224/8 (SJ Cook 38, M Yachad 72, LP Vorster 32, BM McMillan 36; GS le Roux 4/25)
WP 123/9 (GS le Roux 39; NV Radford 3/15, KJ Kerr 3/41)

Eastern Province beat Western Province by 1 wicket, 20 February 1988, Cape Town
WP 174 (JJE Hardy 31, ST Jefferies 30; JG Thomas 3/32, DJ Callaghan 3/23)
EP 178/9 (KC Wessels 38, DJ Richardson 49, TG Shaw 30; GS le Roux 3/22, CR Matthews 3/19)

Western Province beat Orange Free State by 91 runs, 24 February 1988, Cape Town
WP 244/4 (MH Austen 54, L Seeff 82, AP Kuiper 48*)
OFS 153/9 (JJ Strydom 55*; EO Simons 3/25)

Eastern Province beat Western Province by 4 wickets, 27 February 1988, Port Elizabeth
WP 244/5 (L Seeff 35, DJ Cullinan 57, AP Kuiper 37*, EO Simons 51*; TG Shaw 3/21)
EP 248/6 (PG Amm 80, MW Rushmere 81, KC Wessels 44)

Western Province beat Impalas by 143 runs, 16 March 1988, Stellenbosch
WP 257/6 (PN Kirsten 93, JJE Hardy 75*; SJ Base 3/45)
Imp 114 (KG Bauermeister 48; GS le Roux 3/28, ST Jefferies 3/13)

Western Province beat Impalas by 48 runs, 18 March 1988, Cape Town
WP 185/9 (AP Kuiper 76; SJ Base 4/37)
Imp 137 (MS Nackerdien 47, SA Jones 37; EO Simons 3/34)

Western Province beat Transvaal by 5 wickets, 25 March 1988, Johannesburg
Tvl 189 (LP Vorster 41, B Roberts 31; AP Kuiper 4/28)
WP 190/5 (L Seeff 42, PN Kirsten 64)

Western Province beat Northern Transvaal by 60 runs, 15 October 1988, Cape Town
WP 276/4 (TN Lazard 34, L Seeff 88, PN Kirsten 58, AP Kuiper 62)
NT 216/9 (M Yachad 93, VF du Preez 44; AP Kuiper 4/44)

Western Province beat Northern Transvaal by 18 runs, 22 October 1988, Verwoerdburg
WP 242/7 (PN Kirsten 94, DJ Cullinan 83; ST Clarke 3/30)
NT 224 (M Yachad 40, MD Haysman 34, MJR Rindel 75, WF Morris 38; GS le Roux 3/40, CR Matthews 3/45)

Orange Free State beat Western Province by 5 wickets, 11 November 1988, Virginia
WP 190/8 (AP Kuiper 64; GJ Parsons 3/29)
OFS 191/5 (PJR Steyn 48, WJ Cronje 36, AA Metcalfe 38)

Western Province beat Eastern Province by 4 wickets, 25 November 1988, Port Elizabeth
EP 162/8 (MW Rushmere 58; AP Kuiper 4/33)
WP 163/6 (PN Kirsten 61, JJE Hardy 42; RJ McCurdy 3/28)

Western Province beat Northern Transvaal by 61 runs, 30 November 1988, Cape Town
WP 186/8 (G Kirsten 37, DB Rundle 30*)
NT 125 (M Yachad 34; ST Jefferies 3/23)

Transvaal beat Western Province by 7 wickets, 2 December 1988, Johannesburg
WP 173/8 (AP Kuiper 47; CEB Rice 3/30)
Tvl 177/3 (SJ Cook 36, HR Fotheringham 37, RF Pienaar 53, LP Vorster 31*)

Western Province beat Natal by 58 runs, 15 December 1988, Cape Town
WP 168/8 (L Seeff 46; RJ Varner 4/34)
Ntl 110 (EO Simons 4/31)

Western Province beat Eastern Province by 90 runs, 11 February 1989, Cape Town
WP 221/5 (L Seeff 40, PN Kirsten 108, DJ Cullinan 30)
EP 131/7

Western Province beat Eastern Province by 78 runs, 18 February 1989, Port Elizabeth
WP 248/6 (JJE Hardy 41, L Seeff 88, DJ Cullinan 79; RJ McCurdy 3/41)
EP 170 (MW Rushmere 73; ST Jefferies 3/45)

Western Province beat Transvaal by 4 wickets, 25 February 1989, Cape Town
Tvl 216/6 (HR Fotheringham 58, MS Venter 31)
WP 217/6 (L Seeff 49, DJ Cullinan 75*)

Western Province beat Impalas by 97 runs, 1 March 1989, Cape Town
WP 178 (PN Kirsten 55, AP Kuiper 59; P McLaren 4/21, EN Trotman 3/25)
Imp 81 (O Henry 35; JE Nolte 3/17, AP Kuiper 3/10)

Western Province beat Transvaal by 6 runs, 4 March 1989, Johannesburg
WP 241/5 (JJE Hardy 80, PN Kirsten 73, AP Kuiper 42*; RO Estwick 3/49)
Tvl 235 (SJ Cook 79, CEB Rice 53; EO Simons 4/44, AP Kuiper 5/47)

Western Province beat Transvaal by 3 wickets, 7 March 1989, Johannesburg
Tvl 134 (EO Simons 4/21, DB Rundle 3/27)
WP 137/7 (L Seeff 71; NV Radford 3/33)

Western Province beat Transvaal by 32 runs, 16 March 1989, Cape Town
WP 195/5 (L Seeff 41, PN Kirsten 86)
Tvl 163 (SJ Cook 75, CEB Rice 35)

Orange Free State beat Western Province by 61 runs, 22 March 1989, Cape Town
OFS 213/8 (WJ Cronje 73, AA Metcalfe 71; AP Kuiper 3/41)
WP 152 (PN Kirsten 72; AA Donald 4/18)

Western Province beat Natal CD by 100 runs, 25 October 1989, Empangeni
WP 258/6 (PW Martin 78, PN Kirsten 63, DJ Cullinan 60*; CF Craven 3/43)
NtlCD 158/9 (AD Faure 43; CR Matthews 3/21)

Transvaal beat Western Province by 159 runs, 29 October 1989, Johannesburg
Tvl 270/7 (SJ Cook 45, RF Pienaar 95, CEB Rice 50; AP Kuiper 3/53)
WP 111 (DJ Cullinan 37; S Jacobs 3/23, PJ Botha 3/31)

Western Province beat Transvaal by 3 wickets, 4 November 1989, Cape Town
Tvl 199 (SB Smith 32, CEB Rice 30; EO Simons 3/53, CR Matthews 3/28)
WP 201/7 (PN Kirsten 77)

Western Province beat Transvaal by 63 runs, 5 November 1989, Cape Town
WP 277/8 (L Seeff 54, PN Kirsten 126, DJ Cullinan 74; CEB Rice 3/38)
Tvl 214 (SB Smith 33, SJ Cook 77; PN Kirsten 3/39)

Eastern Province beat Western Province by 10 wickets, 11 November 1989, Cape Town
WP 209/8 (PN Kirsten 52, DJ Cullinan 39, AP Kuiper 45; JN Maguire 3/40)
EP 211/0 (KC Wessels 101*, PG Amm 102*)

Eastern Province beat Western Province by 113 runs, 18 November 1989, Port Elizabeth
EP 230/6 (KC Wessels 31, PG Amm 39, MW Rushmere 49, DJ Callaghan 39)
WP 117 (DJ Cullinan 65; BD Robey 3/17)

Natal beat Western Province by 26 runs, 22 November 1989, Cape Town
Ntl 203/9 (HR Fotheringham 70, TR Madsen 50; EO Simons 3/42)
WP 177/8 (PW Martin 60, PN Kirsten 49; KM Curran 3/27)
MoM: HR Fotheringham

Eastern Province beat Western Province by 67 runs, 29 November 1989, Cape Town
EP 195/5 (PG Amm 136, DJ Richardson 34*)
WP 128 (PN Kirsten 39)
MoM: PG Amm

Western Province beat Northern Transvaal by faster scoring rate, 13 December 1989, Verwoerdburg
WP 159/8 (RJ Ryall 41*)
NT 118/6 (LJ Barnard 45; MW Pringle 3/26)

Western Province beat Transvaal by faster scoring rate, 21 December 1989, Cape Town
Tvl 162/7 (SJ Cook 41, S Jacobs 47*)
WP 116/5 (L Seeff 42, TN Lazard 43)
MoM: DB Rundle

Western Province beat Border by faster scoring rate, 22 December 1989, East London
WP 194/5 (PN Kirsten 104*, JJE Hardy 46)
Bdr 128 (DH Howell 32, IL Howell 32; MW Pringle 6/30, CR Matthews 3/34)
MoM: PN Kirsten

Western Province beat Orange Free State by 19 runs, 2 March 1990, Bloemfontein
WP 165/8 (PN Kirsten 32)
OFS 146 (JJ Strydom 32; MW Pringle 3/19, CR Matthews 3/22)
MoM: CR Matthews and MW Pringle

Western Province beat Impalas by 7 wickets, 6 March 1990, Cape Town
Imp 154 (KJ Bridgens 38, GM Charlesworth 30; MW Pringle 3/34, PN Kirsten 3/32)
WP 160/3 (DJ Cullinan 35*, PN Kirsten 69)
MoM: PN Kirsten

Eastern Province beat Western Province by 9 wickets, 21 March 1990, Port Elizabeth
WP 182/6 (AP Kuiper 42, BM McMillan 54*, EO Simons 32; RJ McCurdy 3/42)
EP 183/1 (KC Wessels 54, PG Amm 89*)
MoM: PG Amm

Eastern Province beat Western Province by losing fewer wickets, 23 March 1990, Cape Town
WP 160/8 (BM McMillan 63, DB Rundle 34*; RJ McCurdy 3/49, JN Maguire 3/37)
EP 160/6 (KS McEwan 36)
MoM: BM McMillan

Western Province beat Eastern Province CD by 167 runs, 27 October 1990, Cradock
WP 240/7 (G Kirsten 54, DJ Cullinan 68; CD Handley 3/48)
EPCD 73 (EO Simons 6/8)
MoM: EO Simons

Eastern Province beat Western Province by 77 runs, 31 October 1990, Port Elizabeth
EP 168/7 (PG Amm 55, MW Rushmere 46; MW Pringle 4/23)
WP 91 (EO Simons 30; TG Shaw 3/8)
MoM: TG Shaw

Western Province beat Boland by 6 wickets, 3 November 1990, Cape Town
Bol 125 (EO Simons 5/20)
WP 129/4 (JB Commins 56*, AP Kuiper 40)
MoM: EO Simons

Western Province beat Natal by 4 wickets, 7 November 1990, Durban
Ntl 120/9 (D Norman 31*)
WP 121/6 (L Seeff 48)
MoM: RJ Ryall

Western Province beat Boland by 172 runs, 10 November 1990, Stellenbosch
WP 235/6 (G Kirsten 41, JB Commins 36, BM McMillan 40)
Bol 63 (MW Pringle 3/22, CR Matthews 5/11)
MoM: CR Matthews

Western Province beat Northern Transvaal by 58 runs, 21 November 1990, Cape Town
WP 149/8 (BM McMillan 56; PS de Villiers 3/37)
NT 91 (MW Pringle 3/24)
MoM: BM McMillan

Western Province beat Eastern Province by faster scoring rate, 28 November 1990, Port Elizabeth
EP 234/8 (KC Wessels 47, PG Amm 89, MW Rushmere 38; EO Simons 4/44)
WP 172/6 (AP Kuiper 43*)

Eastern Province beat Western Province by 5 wickets, 1 December 1990, Cape Town
WP 206/9 (L Seeff 36, DJ Cullinan 61; BN Schultz 3/41)
EP 207/5 (PG Amm 101, DJ Richardson 49*)
MoM: PG Amm

Eastern Province beat Western Province by 5 wickets, 2 December 1990, Cape Town
WP 204/9 (AP Kuiper 36, JJE Hardy 32, EO Simons 45; TG Shaw 3/31)
EP 206/5 (MW Rushmere 79*, DJ Richardson 47*)
MoM: MW Rushmere

Transvaal beat Western Province by faster scoring rate, 12 December 1990, Johannesburg
WP 244/6 (L Seeff 48, DJ Cullinan 35, KC Jackson 41, AP Kuiper 39)
Tvl 215/7 (RF Pienaar 37, CEB Rice 68, S Jacobs 33, RP Snell 32*; BM McMillan 3/27)
MoM: BM McMillan

Orange Free State beat Western Province by 2 wickets, 19 December 1990, Cape Town
WP 194/8 (AP Kuiper 58)
OFS 195/8 (PJR Steyn 33, JM Arthur 73; PA Rayment 4/25)
MoM: JM Arthur

Western Province beat Border by 6 wickets, 6 February 1991, Cape Town
Bdr 194/4 (BM Osborne 30, EN Trotman 50*, CS Stirk 43*)
WP 195/4 (G Kirsten 49, DJ Cullinan 47, AP Kuiper 48)
MoM: AP Kuiper

Western Province beat Impalas by 9 wickets, 14 February 1991, Cape Town
Imp 86 (BM McMillan 3/18)
WP 87/1 (G Kirsten 41*)
MoM: BM McMillan

Eastern Province beat Western Province by faster scoring rate, 20 March 1991, Cape Town
EP 167/8 (KC Wessels 40, DJ Callaghan 38; AP Kuiper 3/18)
WP 152 (AP Kuiper 79; TG Shaw 3/20)
MoM: AP Kuiper

Western Province beat Eastern Province by 6 runs, Port Elizabeth, 22 March 1991
WP 215/6 (KC Jackson 36, DJ Cullinan 77, AP Kuiper 32)
EP 209/7 (KC Wessels 79, PG Amm 49)
MoM: DJ Cullinan

Western Province beat Eastern Province by 16 runs, 23 March 1991, Port Elizabeth
WP 193/8 (KC Jackson 36, DJ Cullinan 32, MF Voss 33; RJ McCurdy 4/48)
EP 177 (MW Rushmere 72; EO Simons 4/32)

Western Province beat Natal by 6 wickets, 27 March 1991, Cape Town
Ntl 164/8 (ELR Stewart 49; EO Simons 3/27)
WP 168/4 (KC Jackson 58, AP Kuiper 43*)
MoM: EO Simons

1.2 Western Province Cricket Union B, 1975/76–1990/91

After the resurgence of Western Province cricket in the Barlow era, SACA and its successor, SACU, entered a WPCU B team in the Currie Cup B Section competition from the 1975/76 season through to 1990/91. (This followed the introduction of B teams from the other two major provinces, namely Transvaal B in 1959/60 and Natal B in 1965/66). From 1977/78 to 1979/80 the competition was renamed the Castle Bowl, from 1980/81 to 1982/83 the SAB Bowl, from 1983/84 to 1987/88 the Castle Bowl, and between 1988/89 and 1990/91 the Bowl.[63] For these seasons, WPCU had two first-class teams playing in domestic competitions. The following sections deal with this WPCU B team, which also played in a handful of limited-overs List A games.

1.2.1 Western Province Cricket Union B, First-Class Players, 1975/76–1990/91[64]

Name	M	From	To
Ackerman, HM	15	1979/80	1981/82
Ackermann, GL	1	1977/78	1977/78
Ackermann, JP	11	1979/80	1982/83
Austen, MH	10	1982/83	1988/89
Barnes, IS	8	1979/80	1989/90
Base, SJ	2	1981/82	1983/84
Bing, GJ	1	1987/88	1987/88
Bleekers, LF	16	1988/89	1990/91
Bowditch, MH	14	1975/76	1978/79
Bowley, RJ	4	1980/81	1981/82
Bricknell, GA	11	1975/76	1976/77
Bridgens, KJ	11	1986/87	1987/88
Bristow, JW	3	1980/81	1980/81
Bruce, SD	27	1975/76	1986/87
Burns, ND	3	1985/86	1985/86
Carse, JA	1	1980/81	1980/81
Clark, RM	7	1975/76	1977/78
Clarke, TA	30	1975/76	1984/85
Commins, JB	25	1985/86	1990/91
Daniels, NP	3	1977/78	1978/79
Drummond, RA	12	1975/76	1979/80
Du Plessis, JH	5	1988/89	1988/89
During, J	42	1977/78	1988/89
Du Toit, JD	27	1975/76	1983/84
Elgar, AG	15	1983/84	1990/91
Fairweather, L	2	1980/81	1982/83
Farrell, JN	4	1976/77	1977/78
Finnan, OMP	1	1979/80	1979/80
Fletcher, DAG	1	1984/85	1984/85
Frost, CE	3	1985/86	1985/86
Gibbs, HH	3	1990/91	1990/91
Goldstein, FS	2	1975/76	1975/76

Name	M	From	To
Gordon, ES	10	1978/79	1983/84
Grant, DAC	4	1975/76	1975/76
Green, AD	4	1979/80	1980/81
Griffiths, AV	1	1988/89	1988/89
Halvorsen, E	5	1979/80	1982/83
Hardy, JJE	6	1987/88	1990/91
Hawtrey, PT	4	1983/84	1983/84
Henry, O	22	1977/78	1982/83
Hilterman, C	1	1976/77	1976/77
Hobson, AL	6	1990/91	1990/91
Hobson, DL	2	1980/81	1983/84
Holdstock, AT	2	1989/90	1989/90
Hooper, JJ	1	1979/80	1979/80
Howell, DH	1	1976/77	1976/77
Hugo, SG	3	1975/76	1977/78
Igglesden, AP	5	1987/88	1987/88
Jackson, KC	3	1988/89	1990/91
Jefferies, ST	11	1978/79	1990/91
Johnson, AA	1	1989/90	1989/90
Jones, SA	7	1976/77	1980/81
Kirsten, AM	11	1986/87	1989/90
Kirsten, G	13	1987/88	1989/90
Knowles, P	2	1979/80	1979/80
Knowles, RJ	3	1978/79	1984/85
Koen, LJ	9	1987/88	1989/90
Koen, PA	4	1984/85	1986/87
Kohler, DL	1	1976/77	1976/77
Kruger, WG	12	1982/83	1985/86
Kuiper, AP	8	1977/78	1980/81
Lawrenson, RR	20	1980/81	1984/85
Lazard, TN	14	1983/84	1990/91
Le Roux, DP	1	1983/84	1983/84
Le Roux, GS	3	1975/76	1975/76
Lillie, CC	5	1988/89	1988/89
Lloyd, SM	2	1975/76	1975/76
Lotter, NB	8	1975/76	1981/82
Louw, JL	3	1981/82	1981/82
Mahoney, JE	7	1976/77	1981/82
Malan, DJ	3	1978/79	1979/80
Martin, BP	7	1980/81	1985/86
Martin, GG	4	1985/86	1986/87
Martin, PW	19	1978/79	1990/91
Matthews, BA	17	1984/85	1987/88
Matthews, CR	4	1986/87	1988/89
McClement, AJ	15	1986/87	1990/91
Mellor, MD	8	1981/82	1983/84

Name	M	From	To
Mentis, MJ	9	1975/76	1976/77
Minnaar, MB	35	1977/78	1989/90
Mitchell, TJ	8	1989/90	1990/91
Muntingh, E	9	1978/79	1981/82
Nel, MJ	8	1975/76	1981/82
Nieuwoudt, AB	1	1978/79	1978/79
Nolte, JE	8	1986/87	1989/90
Norman, D	10	1983/84	1985/86
Parker, AC	1	1975/76	1975/76
Parker, DC	4	1976/77	1976/77
Passmore, AG	2	1980/81	1980/81
Payne, DG	10	1988/89	1990/91
Payne, IA	15	1975/76	1977/78
Pfuhl, GP	4	1976/77	1978/79
Pienaar, RF	3	1981/82	1984/85
Place, DW	1	1975/76	1975/76
Plantema, AP	11	1987/88	1989/90
Pringle, MW	1	1990/91	1990/91
Procter, AC	2	1979/80	1979/80
Pycroft, AJ	8	1975/76	1978/79
Rayment, PA	8	1984/85	1990/91
Rayner, PH	7	1981/82	1982/83
Richardson, RP	7	1984/85	1988/89
Roberts, TM	1	1986/87	1986/87
Ross, CK	2	1975/76	1975/76
Rundle, DB	12	1984/85	1986/87
Ryall, RJ	6	1981/82	1982/83
Ryan, LJ	8	1988/89	1990/91
Seeff, J	18	1980/81	1984/85
Seeff, L	7	1977/78	1985/86
Seymour, RA	4	1975/76	1975/76
Simons, EO	17	1982/83	1989/90
Snyman, NM	2	1982/83	1982/83
Snyman, OJA	3	1975/76	1976/77
Solomon, IR	1	1989/90	1989/90
Spilhaus, CF	4	1990/91	1990/91
Stonier, MP	6	1988/89	1990/91
Swart, PD	9	1983/84	1984/85
Taljaard, M	7	1979/80	1981/82
Thompson, PM	23	1977/78	1981/82
Tolson, DJH	3	1976/77	1976/77
Touzel, FB	22	1984/85	1990/91
Tullis, GD	13	1983/84	1988/89
Turner, GJ	12	1984/85	1986/87
Upton, PAH	1	1990/91	1990/91
Van der Merwe, WM	9	1985/86	1986/87

Name	M	From	To
Van Niekerk, AP	1	1975/76	1975/76
Vercueil, S	4	1981/82	1981/82
Voss, MF	4	1984/85	1990/91
Weeden, CC	15	1975/76	1978/79
Whittingdale, R	4	1977/78	1980/81
Wingreen, IM	22	1983/84	1986/87

1.2.2 Western Province Cricket Union B, Currie Cup B Section / Bowl Trophies (First-Class)[65]

Season	Winners
1975/76	Orange Free State
1976/77	Transvaal B
1977/78	Northern Transvaal
1978/79	Northern Transvaal
1979/80	Natal B
1980/81	*Western Province B*
1981/82	Boland
1982/83	*Western Province B*
1983/84	*Western Province B*
1984/85	Transvaal B
1985/86	Boland
1986/87	Transvaal B
1987/88	Boland
1988/89	Border
1989/90	Border / *W Province B (shared)*
1990/91	Border / *W Province B (shared)*

1.2.3 Western Province Cricket Union B, First-Class Scores, 1975/76–1990/91[66]

Western Province B beat Griqualand West by an innings and 62 runs, 7–8 November 1975, Cape Town
WPB 330 (SD Bruce 135, RA Seymour 48; TE Jesty 4/55, FW Swarbrook 3/57)
GW 99 (CW Symcox 46*; DAC Grant 3/34) and 169 (NL Heale 47, MJD Doherty 37; GA Bricknell 4/59, CC Weeden 5/20)

Western Province B beat Northern Transvaal by 5 wickets, 26–29 December 1975, Cape Town
NT 193 (A Jones 62, N Rynners 34*; GS le Roux 3/21, GA Bricknell 3/51) and 221 (FJ le Roux 32, KD Verdoorn 58, N Rynners 53; RA Seymour 4/57, GA Bricknell 4/55)
WPB 240 (RM Clark 37, RA Seymour 41; B Stead 3/43, AH Jordaan 4/80) and 176/5 (SD Bruce 57*)

Natal B beat Western Province B by an innings and 29 runs, 3–5 January 1976, Pinetown
WPB 245 (MJ Mentis 47, SD Bruce 47, AJ Pycroft 33) and 162 (SD Bruce 47, AJ Pycroft 35; BD Gessner 3/22, NH Harvey 4/62)
NtlB 436/8 dec (MG Mathews 75, KN Hosken 85, BS Groves 47, AA Hipkin 75, NP Daniels 103; GS le Roux 3/106, RA Seymour 3/57)

Transvaal B beat Western Province B by an innings and 8 runs, 9–12 January 1976, Johannesburg
WPB 133/9 (DR Neilson 3/33) and 121 (IA Payne 45; GE Field 5/16, RK Muzzell 3/48)
TvlB 262 (DW Dunlop 38, SJ Cook 48, PD de Vaal 51, NT Day 75*; RA Seymour 4/68)

Match drawn between Orange Free State and Western Province B, 16–18 January 1976, Bloemfontein
OFS 155 (RA le Roux 74; TA Clarke 4/39, JD du Toit 4/39) and 173 (LH Coetzee 37, KC Wessels 30, RJ East 43; JD du Toit 4/44, DW Place 3/19)
WPB 225 (MJ Mentis 92, IA Payne 43; FJ Titmus 3/57, RA le Roux 3/52)

Western Province B beat Border by an innings and 39 runs, 6–7 February 1976, Cape Town
Bdr 200/9 dec (RC Ontong 86, DC McKenna 41; GA Bricknell 3/52, CC Weeden 3/5) and 82 (NB Lotter 5/36, GA Bricknell 4/10)
WPB 321 (IA Payne 132, CC Weeden 47, TA Clarke 40; MR Ballantyne 3/74, SJ Schmidt 4/68)

Match drawn between Western Province B and Orange Free State, 5–8 November 1976, Cape Town
WPB 310 (IA Payne 52, RM Clark 75, MH Bowditch 40; TG Botha 3/75) and 179/2 dec (IA Payne 77*, SD Bruce 62*)
OFS 236 (RA le Roux 50, IC Gericke 48, TG Botha 32*; NB Lotter 3/70, GA Bricknell 4/58) and 130/8 (GR Botha 41*; NB Lotter 4/44, GA Bricknell 3/44)

Match drawn between Western Province B and Northern Transvaal, 3–6 December 1976, Pretoria
WPB 404/8 dec (IA Payne 97, MJ Mentis 81, SD Bruce 83, DJH Tolson 39, CC Weeden 47; HW Raath 3/91) and 308/8 dec (IA Payne 65, MJ Mentis 102, OJA Snyman 39; HW Raath 4/55)
NT 415/6 (FJ le Roux 110, AH Jordaan 78, K Burrow 110, HW Raath 62*) and 65 (FJ le Roux 30*, P Tudge 30*)

Transvaal B beat Western Province B by an innings and 167 runs, 27–28 December 1976, Cape Town
WPB 137 (RA Drummond 53; AJ Kourie 4/27, VS Greve 3/22) and 150 (CC Weeden 33, GA Bricknell 34; KA Barlow 3/20, DS van der Knaap 3/46)
TvlB 454/9 dec (LJ Barnard 138, NT Day 41, NG Featherstone 45, AJ Kourie 115, KA Barlow 41; JD du Toit 4/86, GA Bricknell 3/136)

Western Province B beat Griqualand West by 278 runs, 29 January – 1 February 1977, Kimberley
WPB 297/9 dec (MJ Mentis 42, SD Bruce 33, SA Jones 31, JD du Toit 101*; GK Funston 3/50) and 192/6 dec (IA Payne 105*, DC Parker 34; K McLaren 3/79)
GW 156 (AP Beukes 72; GA Bricknell 6/55) and 55 (JD du Toit 5/19)

Western Province B beat Border by 40 runs, 3–5 February 1977, East London
WPB 386/7 dec (DC Parker 174*, CC Weeden 118, JD du Toit 32; GM Gower 3/68) and 105/8 dec (IA Payne 30; GD Boucher 4/61, GM Gower 3/41)
Bdr 269 (GW Nelson 43, DC McKenna 56, I Foulkes 52, RTD Kemp 39; SA Jones 3/58, JE Mahoney 4/41) and 182 (ID Harty 39; SA Jones 3/29, GA Bricknell 3/63)

Western Province B beat Natal B by 8 wickets, 11–14 March 1977, Cape Town
NtlB 147 (TR Madsen 30; JE Mahoney 3/34) and 201 (FB Hill 86, KN Hosken 43; JN Farrell 4/29, GA Bricknell 5/69)
WPB 246 (IA Payne 40, RA Drummond 51, DJH Tolson 38, DL Kohler 32; KR Cooper 3/64, BD Gessner 4/64) and 103/2 (IA Payne 43*, SD Bruce 31*)

Match drawn between Western Province B and Northern Transvaal, 18–21 November 1977, Pretoria
WPB 197 (MJ Nel 88; JP le Roux 3/54) and 416/9 (NP Daniels 69, SD Bruce 37, MH Bowditch 147, CC Weeden 75; CA Gie 3/98)
NT 405 (FJ le Roux 104, KD Verdoorn 97, CA Gie 58, AM Ferreira 60*, T Quirk 30; J During 3/94, NP Daniels 3/13)

Match drawn between Griqualand West and Western Province B, 17–20 December 1977, Cape Town
GW 310/7 dec (MD Tramontino 55, MJD Doherty 42, JR Gray 57, DL Bairstow 74, AP Beukes 31; J During 3/39) and 150/6 dec (MD Tramontino 67*, MJD Doherty 41; MB Minnaar 3/58)
WPB 200/5 dec (IA Payne 63, SD Bruce 36, MH Bowditch 51; K McLaren 3/76) and 210/6 (SD Bruce 89, MH Bowditch 61; K McLaren 4/54)

Match drawn between Western Province B and Northern Transvaal, 26–28 December 1977, Cape Town
WPB 346/8 dec (RA Drummond 96, MH Bowditch 80, CC Weeden 65; AM Ferreira 5/101) and 300/4 dec (IA Payne 81, RA Drummond 50, SD Bruce 74, MH Bowditch 52*, CC Weeden 31*)
NT 403/7 dec (KC Wessels 146, KD Verdoorn 46, AM Ferreira 76, T Quirk 43*) and 65/2 (FJ le Roux 51)

Western Province B beat Griqualand West by 9 wickets, 27–30 January 1978, Kimberley
GW 153 (MD Tramontino 33, MJD Doherty 35; O Henry 6/31) and 119 (K McLaren 38; NB Lotter 5/34, SA Jones 3/28)
WPB 206 (IA Payne 32, AP Kuiper 32, SD Bruce 45; JD Ogilvie 3/26) and 68/1 (PM Thompson 31*)

Western Province B beat Rhodesia B by 151 runs, 24–26 November 1978, Bulawayo
WPB 284 (NP Daniels 73, AP Kuiper 95, O Henry 33*; CB Jonker 4/84, RM Bentley 4/80) and 267/5 dec (PM Thompson 39, E Muntingh 40, NP Daniels 45, SD Bruce 83; CB Jonker 3/81)
RhodB 146 (RD Brown 41; ES Gordon 5/42) and 254 (DL Houghton 72, WJ Houghton 65; ES Gordon 4/31, O Henry 3/56)

Match drawn between Western Province B and Natal B, 26–28 December 1978, Cape Town
WPB 390 (L Seeff 156, AJ Pycroft 77; IR Tayfield 4/91) and 293/9 dec (NP Daniels 87, SA Jones 70, ST Jefferies 55; JS Muil 3/62)
NtlB 452/9 dec (FB Hill 32, DR Turner 142, AA Hipkin 195, IR Tayfield 44; O Henry 5/104) and 36/1

Western Province B beat Transvaal B by 109 runs, 25–27 January 1979, Cape Town
WPB 272 (L Seeff 112, JD du Toit 33, CC Weeden 32; KA Barlow 4/34)
TvlB 157 (KA Barlow 53; J During 3/52, O Henry 3/15) and 262 (WJ van der Linden 52, DN Edwards 43, RW Adair 75, JR Argyle 34; JD du Toit 5/62, O Henry 3/89)

Match drawn between Western Province B and Eastern Province B, 22–24 February 1979, Port Elizabeth
WPB 159 (L Seeff 61; JS Timm 3/22) and 322/7 dec (L Seeff 101, RJ Knowles 46, GP Pfuhl 32*, O Henry 44*; MR Searle 3/81)
EPB 225 (KW Gradwell 68, GS Cowley 50; J During 3/47) and 209/6 (JM Winstanley 38, GS Cowley 34*; O Henry 4/53)

Natal B beat Western Province B by 85 runs, 17–20 November 1979, Cape Town
NtlB 226 (BJ Whitfield 61, FB Hill 39, KD Verdoorn 74; ES Gordon 4/55, M Taljaard 3/45) and 114 (J During 4/21, M Taljaard 3/7)
WPB 94 (EJ Hodkinson 4/35, MK Thompson 5/36) and 161 (MK Thompson 4/48, I Ebrahim 3/37)

Western Province B beat Border by 153 runs, 22–24 November 1979, Cape Town
WPB 164 (JD du Toit 52; IA Greig 5/60) and 254 (AD Green 47, PM Thompson 38, AP Kuiper 46; GL Hayes 3/24)
Bdr 116 (DC McKenna 33; O Henry 3/22, AP Kuiper 4/7) and 149 (DC McKenna 37, GL Hayes 37; O Henry 4/35, JP Ackermann 3/3)

Western Province B beat Eastern Province B by 6 wickets, 15–18 December 1979, Port Elizabeth
EPB 275/9 dec (KP Reid 109, RJD Whyte 36, RG Fensham 33; SA Jones 5/47, JP Ackermann 4/33) and 194 (RG Fensham 65, DG Emslie 36; J During 4/48, O Henry 3/29)
WPB 262 (PM Thompson 44, RA Drummond 99, ST Jefferies 38*, ME Collins 4/71) and 210/4 (AD Green 49, JP Ackermann 63, PM Thompson 33, RA Drummond 35; MK van Vuuren 3/42)

Western Province B beat Transvaal B by 15 runs, 19–22 January 1980, Johannesburg
WPB 217 (RA Drummond 71; NV Radford 3/43, KJ Kerr 4/38) and 113 (NV Radford 5/47)
TvlB 157 (NE Wright 43, LJ Barnard 32; ES Gordon 3/38, J During 3/39) and 158 (NT Day 67; ES Gordon 6/56)

Western Province B beat Griqualand West by 138 runs, 24–26 January 1980, Kimberley
WPB 223 (HM Ackerman 114; AP Beukes 4/44) and 202/7 dec (PM Thompson 35, HM Ackerman 36, TA Clarke 43; AP Beukes 3/27)
GW 178 (AP Beukes 45, JJ Reyneke 46; O Henry 3/38, JP Ackermann 3/36) and 109 (MJD Doherty 30; ES Gordon 4/35, O Henry 3/2)

Western Province B beat Orange Free State by 9 wickets, 2–5 February 1980, Cape Town
OFS 92 (TA Lloyd 35, LH Coetzee 44; J During 5/29) and 150 (E Halvorsen 44, HM Ackerman 69, ST Jefferies 37; E Schmidt 5/33)
WPB 196 (ES Gordon 3/36, JD du Toit 6/37) and 49/1

Western Province B beat Border by 7 wickets, 22–25 November 1980, Cape Town
Bdr 111 (RA Stretch 31, GL Hayes 33, ET Laughlin 76*; ES Gordon 6/49) and 205 (HM Ackerman 36, JD du Toit 40; GD Boucher 4/46, SJ Ker-Fox 3/33)
WPB 171 (E Halvorsen 52*, J Seeff 57) and 146/3

Match drawn between Western Province B and Boland, 12–15 December 1980, Stellenbosch
WPB 326/5 dec (PM Thompson 59, E Halvorsen 95, SD Bruce 45, AP Kuiper 66*) and 189/8 dec (HM Ackerman 55; AH Potgieter 3/34)
Bol 268 (C van der Merwe 37, J Kennedy 31, LL Roberts 50, D Traut 36, C Viljoen 30; RJ Bowley 3/54) and 195/7 (HN Basson 49, A du Toit 58)

Western Province B beat Boland by an innings and 78 runs, 26–29 December 1980, Cape Town
Bol 110 (LL Roberts 35; RR Lawrenson 6/24) and 125 (C van der Merwe 32; ES Gordon 3/46, DL Hobson 4/22)
WPB 313/7 dec (PM Thompson 67, J Seeff 43, TA Clarke 54, ES Gordon 47, BP Martin 35*)

Western Province B beat Border by an innings and 40 runs, 1–3 January 1981, East London
Bdr 193 (RA Stretch 31, JP Hosking 36; RR Lawrenson 4/58, JE Mahoney 3/39) and 128 (RE Frisch 32; RR Lawrenson 6/42)
WPB 361 (TA Clarke 100, O Henry 105*; GM Gower 4/89, BM Osborne 3/78)

Match drawn between Eastern Province B and Western Province B, 15–17 January 1981, Port Elizabeth
EPB 349 (TB Reid 47, RG Fensham 145, DG Emslie 39, VG Cresswell 32; RJ Bowley 4/64) and 226/7 dec (JW Furstenburg 36, RG Fensham 58, GCG Fraser 34*; BP Martin 3/86)
WPB 240 (HM Ackerman 47, AG Passmore 73, BP Martin 51; C Wulfsohn 4/74, GL Long 6/60) and 60/1

Western Province B beat Eastern Province B by 7 wickets, 19–21 February 1981, Cape Town
EPB 128 (TG Shaw 41*; M Taljaard 4/37) and 207 (TB Reid 78, JW Stephenson 33; RR Lawrenson 6/72, M Taljaard 3/62)
WPB 241 (MJ Nel 73, J Seeff 50, M Taljaard 36; C Wulfsohn 6/46, N Mandy 4/99) and 96/3 (MJ Nel 43)

Western Province B beat Transvaal B by 133 runs, 13–17 March 1981, Johannesburg
WPB 203 (TA Clarke 96, AP Kuiper 38; IFN Weideman 4/50) and 299 (MJ Nel 48, SD Bruce 35, AP Kuiper 81; NV Radford 4/50)
TvlB 284 (NT Day 71, RF Pienaar 57, NV Radford 45; RR Lawrenson 5/81, JD du Toit 3/74) and 85 (RR Lawrenson 4/23, M Taljaard 5/18)

Orange Free State beat Western Province B by 2 wickets, 6–9 November 1981, Bloemfontein
WPB 129 (RR Lawrenson 39, MB Minnaar 30*; CJPG van Zyl 6/50, A Sidebottom 4/32) and 278 (E Muntingh 36, TA Clarke 82, HM Ackerman 86*; A Sidebottom 5/50)
OFS 218 (DP le Roux 37, LW Griessel 43, RJ East 54; RR Lawrenson 3/40, JD du Toit 5/46) and 190/8 (LW Griessel 47; JD du Toit 3/66, MB Minnaar 3/58)

Match drawn between Western Province B and Griqualand West, 12–14 November 1981, Kimberley
WPB 282/8 dec (PM Thompson 90, E Muntingh 69; EF Parker 3/46) and 166/5 (PM Thompson 52, PW Martin 44; HJ Liebenberg 3/71)
GW 288 (K Sharp 44, MJD Doherty 55, AD Methven 68, AP Beukes 49; TA Clarke 5/30)

Western Province B beat Griqualand West by 5 wickets, 27–30 November 1981, Cape Town
GW 108 (MJD Doherty 34; JE Mahoney 3/33, JD du Toit 6/26) and 203 (K Sharp 40, MJD Doherty 82, PL Symcox 46; RR Lawrenson 3/59, JD du Toit 4/41)
WPB 210 (E Muntingh 46, TA Clarke 54; R Canny 3/34, MC Smit 5/68) and 104/5 (J Seeff 43*; HJ Liebenberg 3/40)

Western Province B beat Orange Free State by 243 runs, 4–7 December 1981, Cape Town
WPB 252 (MJ Nel 38, HM Ackerman 31, JD du Toit 43; WM van der Merwe 4/38, A Sidebottom 4/36) and 215/8 dec (MJ Nel 36, J Seeff 32, O Henry 43*; WM van der Merwe 4/37, CJPG van Zyl 3/37)
OFS 92 (S Regenstein 31; O Henry 5/34) and 132 (O Henry 4/48, JD du Toit 4/24)

Western Province B beat Natal B by 10 wickets, 26–29 December 1981, Cape Town
WPB 349/5 dec (PM Thompson 55, MJ Nel 38, J Seeff 113*, TA Clarke 31, SD Bruce 100*) and 14/0
NtlB 99 (RR Lawrenson 5/50) and 260 (MD Tramontino 69, CL Smith 40, SM Hedley 53; JL Louw 4/52, O Henry 3/59)

Match drawn between Western Province B and Natal B, 13–15 February 1982, Pietermaritzburg
WPB 212 (TA Clarke 63; EJ Hodkinson 4/31, DK Pearse 3/34) and 281/9 dec (J Seeff 38, E Muntingh 35, RF Pienaar 34, RR Lawrenson 87, RJ Ryall 39*; EJ Hodkinson 6/68)
NtlB 238 (CL Smith 65, KD Verdoorn 61; RR Lawrenson 3/85, JL Louw 3/30) and 177/8 (MD Tramontino 33, KD Verdoorn 47, PJ Allan 41; JD du Toit 3/43, HM Ackerman 4/61)

Boland beat Western Province B by 149 runs, 24–27 March 1982, Stellenbosch
Bol 237 (PD Swart 30, J de Villiers 46, SS Barnard 40; RR Lawrenson 3/53, JD du Toit 3/42, TA Clarke 4/35) and 291 (EJ Barlow 48, A du Toit 30, A Odendaal 31, PD Swart 89, J de Villiers 33; JL Louw 7/57)
WPB 115 (J Seeff 32; CJ Coetzee 3/35, P Anker 3/40, EJ Barlow 3/4) and 264 (PM Thompson 36, MD Mellor 60, J Seeff 30, E Muntingh 67; P Anker 5/73)

Western Province B beat Orange Free State by 10 wickets, 4–6 November 1982, Bloemfontein
OFS 346/7 dec (RA le Roux 144, DP le Roux 39, SN Hartley 61, RJ East 52; JD du Toit 3/72) and 70 (JD du Toit 4/21, O Henry 6/19)
WPB 416 (J Seeff 68, WG Kruger 80, RF Pienaar 109, O Henry 49) and 1/0

Western Province B beat Natal B by 8 wickets, 12–14 November 1982, Cape Town
NtlB 200 (MD Tramontino 45, TR Madsen 68; EO Simons 3/41, O Henry 3/72) and 181 (MD Tramontino 32, CP Wilkins 40, TR Madsen 36; RR Lawrenson 4/45, O Henry 3/63)
WPB 248 (MD Mellor 50, WG Kruger 51, PH Rayner 32; MD Clare 5/61) and 134/2 (JP Ackermann 70*, MD Mellor 50)

Western Province B beat Boland by 77 runs, 27–29 December 1982, Stellenbosch
WPB 227 (J Seeff 53, WG Kruger 58, PH Rayner 64; SA Jones 4/22, J Hendricks 3/27) and 150 (J Seeff 30; SA Jones 3/30, P Anker 4/48)
Bol 199 (KJ Barnett 91, PD Swart 34; O Henry 5/58) and 101 (O Henry 6/32)

Western Province B beat Eastern Province B by 5 wickets, 1–3 January 1983, Uitenhage
EPB 245 (DH Howell 59, DG Emslie 48, TG Shaw 57; RR Lawrenson 3/32, J During 3/55) and 265 (IK Daniell 96, GL Long 31, C Wulfsohn 30*)
WPB 385 (J Seeff 34, PH Rayner 162, O Henry 39, RJ Ryall 51; GL Long 4/94, TG Shaw 4/86) and 127/5 (J Seeff 33, PH Rayner 32; IL Howell 3/39)

Western Province B beat Transvaal B by an innings and 81 runs, 4–6 February 1983, Cape Town
WPB 434/8 dec (MD Mellor 53, NM Snyman 37, SD Bruce 176, O Henry 34, JD du Toit 63; KJ Kerr 4/125)
TvlB 166 (B Roberts 37, CR Norris 33; O Henry 5/63) and 187 (A Barrow 31, W Kirsh 32; J During 3/35, O Henry 4/50)

Match drawn between Western Province B and Border, 5–7 March 1983, Cape Town
WPB 242 (MH Austen 34, J Seeff 33, TA Clarke 68, BP Martin 30; GL Hayes 3/81) and 258 (MD Mellor 37, SD Bruce 43, O Henry 54; GM Gower 4/64)
Bdr 191 (LM Pearson 48, W du Plessis 52, GD Pfuhl 31*; RR Lawrenson 3/64, EO Simons 4/56, JD du Toit 3/34) and 1/0

Western Province B beat Natal B by 6 wickets, 29–31 October 1983, Cape Town
NtlB 209 (PH Williams 58, DK Pearse 41; D Norman 4/41, DL Hobson 4/75) and 189 (PH Williams 38, GN Lister-James 61, PJ Allan 37; D Norman 4/47)
WPB 235 (PD Swart 49, PT Hawtrey 48, J During 32; EJ Hodkinson 6/70) and 169/4 (IM Wingreen 46, WG Kruger 33, TA Clarke 40*; BW Proctor 3/73)

Match drawn between Boland and Western Province B, 10–12 November 1983, Stellenbosch
Bol 280 (A du Toit 117, NM Lambrechts 34, HWH Bergins 38; ST Jefferies 3/42) and 241/9 dec (IS Anderson 43, A du Toit 35, NM Lambrechts 30, SA Jones 32; MB Minnaar 3/71)
WPB 255 (MH Austen 38, IM Wingreen 72, PD Swart 42, ST Jefferies 36; SA Jones 4/28) and 147/5 (WG Kruger 32, TA Clarke 35, ST Jefferies 55*)

Western Province B beat Eastern Province B by 6 wickets, 21–23 December 1983, Port Elizabeth
EPB 379/9 dec (RG Fensham 97, AP Nell 82, IL Howell 109, C Wulfsohn 38; J During 3/70) and 228/9 dec (VG Cresswell 45, RG Fensham 64, TG Shaw 38; D Norman 4/72, MB Minnaar 3/74)
WPB 342 (IM Wingreen 37, PD Swart 81, JD du Toit 128; BD Robey 7/88) and 270/4 (IM Wingreen 97, TA Clarke 79*, PT Hawtrey 35*; TG Shaw 3/94)

Match drawn between Western Province B and Orange Free State, 5–7 January 1984, Bloemfontein
WPB 312/9 dec (TN Lazard 117, PT Hawtrey 40, D Norman 33, MB Minnaar 34*; CJPG van Zyl 5/57) and 149/6 dec (TA Clarke 41, PD Swart 52; WM van der Merwe 4/31)
OFS 220 (RA le Roux 78, CJ Richards 73) and 100/6 (A Sidebottom 42; MB Minnaar 4/29)

Western Province B beat Transvaal B by 10 wickets, 21–23 January 1984, Cape Town
WPB 374/5 dec (L Seeff 70, TN Lazard 121, TA Clarke 81) and 1/0
TvlB 161 (MS Venter 30, CR Norris 33*; D Norman 3/43, MB Minnaar 5/59) and 213 (PL Selsick 60, HA Page 35, CR Norris 47; J During 4/43)

Western Province B beat Border by 252 runs, 10–12 March 1984, Cape Town
WPB 191 (IM Wingreen 38, TN Lazard 39, GD Tullis 30; GM Gower 3/37, I Foulkes 3/41) and 313/9 dec (TA Clarke 138*, GD Tullis 46; RC Ontong 4/109)
Bdr 113 (MD Tramontino 33; RR Lawrenson 4/35, MB Minnaar 4/42) and 139 (NP Minnaar 55; AG Elgar 6/24)

Western Province B beat Boland by 95 runs, 22–24 November 1984, Cape Town
WPB 175 (AG Elgar 38, DB Rundle 41; GJ Parsons 4/65, JS Justus 3/39) and 297 (IM Wingreen 72, TA Clarke 82, PD Swart 61; GJ Parsons 5/106, O Henry 4/71)
Bol 173 (KJ Barnett 36, HJ Joubert 45; BA Matthews 3/46, J During 4/37) and 204 (KJ Barnett 46, NM Lambrechts 30, GJ Parsons 76; BA Matthews 3/38, PD Swart 3/42)

Border beat Western Province B by 7 wickets, 26–28 December 1984, East London
WPB 176 (GJ Turner 51, J During 34; EN Trotman 5/30, I Foulkes 3/20) and 237 (AG Elgar 49, GD Tullis 56; JG Thomas 5/68)
Bdr 305 (EN Trotman 59, RC Ontong 32, I Foulkes 45, IL Howell 64, GCG Fraser 32; MB Minnaar 5/92, AG Elgar 3/54) and 109/3 (I Foulkes 42*; AG Elgar 3/48)

Transvaal B beat Western Province B by 10 wickets, 18–20 January 1985, Johannesburg
TvlB 374/7 dec (PL Selsick 41, GW Johnson 50, B Roberts 90, KJ Rule 68, NR Boonzaaier 52*; BA Matthews 4/58, RR Lawrenson 3/91) and 53/0 (AG Elgar 41, IM Wingreen 62, WG Kruger 34; CD Mitchley 4/40, JJ Hooper 4/65)
WPB 222 (AG Elgar 62, IM Wingreen 83; JJ Hooper 3/32, KJ Kerr 5/36) and 203

Eastern Province B beat Western Province B by 6 wickets, 25–27 January 1985, Cape Town
WPB 335 (AG Elgar 97, IM Wingreen 42, DB Rundle 110; J Havenga 5/88) and 263/9 dec (WG Kruger 39, DB Rundle 40, GJ Turner 41, RP Richardson 30; AV Birrell 3/57)
EPB 275/4 dec (AV Birrell 82, DH Howell 33, TB Reid 120*; DB Rundle 3/55) and 326/4 (DH Howell 42, TB Reid 111, MW Rushmere 119*)

Northern Transvaal B beat Western Province B by 8 runs, 14–16 February 1985, Pretoria
NTB 156 (PL Symcox 63; RR Lawrenson 4/32, PA Koen 4/31) and 163 (S Vercueil 32, PL Symcox 43; BA Matthews 3/29, RR Lawrenson 3/30, DB Rundle 4/37)
WPB 131 (GJ Turner 35; GL Ackermann 5/42, JC van Duyker 3/42) and 180 (GJ Turner 36, RJ Knowles 44; GL Ackermann 7/69)

Match drawn between Orange Free State and Western Province B, 28 February – 2 March 1985, Cape Town
OFS 471 (AM Green 84, AI Kallicharran 79, RJ East 163*, WM van der Merwe 48; BA Matthews 4/109) and 54/4 (BM Osborne 32)
WPB 280 (AG Elgar 94, RF Pienaar 39, DB Rundle 35, GD Tullis 37; CJPG van Zyl 4/62, WM van der Merwe 4/41) and 310 (AG Elgar 36, IM Wingreen 62, FB Touzel 34, DB Rundle 39, RP Richardson 52*; CJPG van Zyl 5/82)

Western Province B beat Natal B by 3 wickets, 21–23 November 1985, Cape Town
NtlB 253 (AC Hudson 44, KD Dawson 53, DA Scott 31; D Norman 3/75, BP Martin 3/43) and 151 (CM Lister-James 54*; D Norman 6/56)
WPB 201/8 dec (AG Elgar 43, GJ Turner 69*; MR Hobson 5/56) and 207/7 (AG Elgar 41, IM Wingreen 37, SD Bruce 44)

Eastern Province B beat Western Province B by 4 wickets, 28–30 November 1985, Uitenhage
WPB 241 (IM Wingreen 103, DB Rundle 49; CB Hutchings 3/51) and 163/7 dec (DB Rundle 39; BD Robey 4/73)
EPB 148 (IK Daniell 43; BA Matthews 4/50, BP Martin 4/40) and 259/6 (DJ Callaghan 33, DG Emslie 111*, PA Tullis 64*; BA Matthews 3/48)

Western Province B beat Boland by 41 runs, 12–14 December 1985, Cape Town
WPB 137 (MB Minnaar 35; EE van Rooyen 4/50, A Watts 3/32) and 174 (TN Lazard 43, IM Wingreen 32; O Henry 5/67)
Bol 148 (SA Jones 65, A Watts 33; WM van der Merwe 3/32) and 122 (WM van der Merwe 5/35, J During 3/17)

Western Province B beat Griqualand West by 3 runs, 10–12 January 1986, Kimberley
WPB 252/9 dec (GJ Turner 58, J During 37*, D Norman 56; GJ Parsons 3/56) and 177 (TN Lazard 40; GJ Parsons 3/20, GW Symmonds 4/57)
GW 251 (PJR Steyn 53, L Potter 41, LM Phillips 47, GJ Parsons 52; BA Matthews 4/47) and 175 (L Potter 57, LM Phillips 43; BA Matthews 4/32, D Norman 3/44)

Western Province B beat Northern Transvaal B by 119 runs, 1–3 February 1986, Cape Town
WPB 186 (IM Wingreen 36, GJ Turner 38, WM van der Merwe 30; PS de Villiers 3/38) and 138 (TN Lazard 40; GL Ackermann 3/24, JC van Duyker 4/31)
NTB 136 (MW Pfaff 48; WM van der Merwe 3/22, BA Matthews 3/29, J During 3/33) and 69 (J During 5/20)

Match drawn between Transvaal B and Western Province B, 7–9 February 1986, Johannesburg
TvlB 248 (GB Tucker 31, GE McMillan 59, KJ Kerr 74; BA Matthews 5/32) and 193/3 dec (CR Norris 101*, KJ Rule 61*; J During 3/24)
WPB 126/7 dec (GJ Turner 42*; GE McMillan 3/40) and 3/1

Natal B beat Western Province B by 8 wickets, 25–27 October 1986, Pietermaritzburg
WPB 286 (FB Touzel 47, SD Bruce 41, WM van der Merwe 33, J During 47*; MR Hobson 5/72) and 120/7 dec (WM van der Merwe 51*; EJ Hodkinson 3/71, MR Hobson 3/36)
NtlB 220 (MD Mellor 30, AC Hudson 37, KD Dawson 42; WM van der Merwe 4/48, J During 3/46) and 187/2 (MD Mellor 63, LM Fuhri 81*)

Western Province B beat Griqualand West by 57 runs, 13–15 December 1986, Cape Town
WPB 302 (KJ Bridgens 79, RP Richardson 42, PA Koen 30, J During 44*; GJ Parsons 4/78, GW Symmonds 3/44) and 276/9 dec (FB Touzel 60, JB Commins 49, WM van der Merwe 79*, PA Koen 32)
GW 351 (AJ Moles 142, WE Schonegevel 40, BE van der Vyver 57, AP Beukes 42; J During 6/53) and 170 (AP Beukes 61; WM van der Merwe 4/50)

Transvaal B beat Western Province B by an innings and 15 runs, 19–21 December 1986, Cape Town
TvlB 404/6 dec (W Kirsh 90, MJ Mitchley 116*, RW Adair 39, GE McMillan 104*; WM van der Merwe 3/93)
WPB 146 (KJ Bridgens 78*; JJ Hooper 7/29) and 243 (AG Elgar 39, FB Touzel 64, KJ Bridgens 34; KJ Kerr 5/63)

Northern Transvaal B beat Western Province B by 3 wickets, 30 January – 1 February 1987, Verwoerdburg
WPB 257 (MH Austen 36, J During 66*, AJ McClement 72; MD Clare 4/53, JC van Duyker 3/55) and 196/5 dec (MH Austen 54, JB Commins 42, AM Kirsten 45*)
NTB 183 (CPL de Lange 32, CE Eksteen 44; WM van der Merwe 4/49, AJ McClement 3/21) and 271/7 (MS Venter 61, KD Verdoorn 91, CPL de Lange 42; BA Matthews 4/57)

Western Province B beat Eastern Province B by 6 wickets, 11–13 February 1987, Cape Town
EPB 314/8 dec (PG Amm 42, IK Daniell 94, DG Emslie 57, DJ Callaghan 93; J During 6/59) and 101 (PA Rayment 42; AJ McClement 6/47)
WPB 291 (JB Commins 89, KJ Bridgens 50, J During 32*; PA Rayment 4/65) and 128/4 (FB Touzel 42*)

Western Province B beat Boland by 9 wickets, 6–9 March 1987, Stellenbosch
WPB 281/9 dec (AM Kirsten 50, DB Rundle 87, J During 37; RA Brown 5/64, P Anker 3/69) and 27/1
Bol 110 (JE Nolte 4/18) and 197 (SA Jones 52; IS Barnes 4/65)

Boland beat Western Province B by 44 runs, 13–16 November 1987, Stellenbosch
Bol 195 (SA Jones 79; AP Igglesden 5/52) and 198 (KJ Barnett 45, SA Jones 41; AP Igglesden 5/61)
WPB 199 (JB Commins 51, MB Minnaar 40*; SJ Base 3/44, PJ Newport 4/32, O Henry 3/67) and 150 (MH Austen 38; SJ Base 3/23, P Anker 3/42, O Henry 3/57)

Match drawn between Western Province B and Border, 26–28 November 1987, Cape Town
WPB 353/8 dec (G Kirsten 163*, EO Simons 68, MB Minnaar 31) and 195/4 dec (KJ Bridgens 40, FB Touzel 75*)
Bdr 278/7 dec (BM Osborne 68, AL Wilmot 31, IL Howell 55*, KG Bauermeister 74; EO Simons 3/70) and 221/7 (IL Howell 49, KG Bauermeister 72*)

Match drawn between Eastern Province B and Western Province B, 11–13 December 1987, Cape Town
EPB 179 (AV Snyman 58; AP Igglesden 3/46, EO Simons 3/55) and 242 (AV Snyman 43, BE van der Vyver 54, C Wulfsohn 36; AP Igglesden 3/84, EO Simons 3/49, MB Minnaar 3/66)
WPB 227/6 dec (MH Austen 35, AP Plantema 37, G Kirsten 80*) and 131/6 (MH Austen 33; MW Pringle 6/33)

Match drawn between Border and Western Province B, 26–28 December 1987, East London
Bdr 325/9 dec (MJP Ford 67, EN Trotman 54, AL Wilmot 105; AJ McClement 4/77) and 246/5 (MJP Ford 41, BW Lones 57, BM Osborne 41, EN Trotman 101*)
WPB 400 (MH Austen 121, FB Touzel 38, G Kirsten 56, KJ Bridgens 79, J During 41*; HC Lindenberg 3/100, IL Howell 6/89)

Western Province B beat Boland by 68 runs, 8–11 January 1988, Cape Town
WPB 289/6 dec (AP Plantema 66, JJE Hardy 75, JB Commins 63, G Kirsten 38*; PJ Newport 3/81) and 186/9 dec (AJ McClement 33*; SJ Base 3/84, PJ Newport 3/36, JD du Toit 3/42)
Bol 273 (KJ Barnett 44, GP Thomas 47, MS Nackerdien 60, JD du Toit 36, PJ Newport 32; AP Igglesden 4/73) and 134 (KJ Barnett 33; AP Igglesden 4/57, J During 3/30)

Western Province B beat Eastern Province B by 60 runs, 29–31 January 1988, Port Elizabeth
WPB 150 (AP Plantema 69; MK van Vuuren 3/47, GA Katz 3/23) and 263 (AP Plantema 49, JJE Hardy 71, MB Minnaar 36*; RLS Armitage 6/64, DJ Ferrant 3/62)
EPB 268 (PI Barclay 82, PA Amm 40, MK van Vuuren 38*; AP Igglesden 4/60) and 85 (EO Simons 4/35, AJ McClement 3/14)

Western Province B beat Boland by 120 runs, 25–27 November 1988, Stellenbosch
WPB 305/6 dec (JB Commins 78, G Kirsten 73, LF Bleekers 71*; O Henry 3/56) and 178/6 dec (MH Austen 33, JB Commins 50, LF Bleekers 31; O Henry 3/56)
Bol 177 (JP Stephenson 63*; JE Nolte 3/47, IS Barnes 3/58) and 186 (J Hendricks 41; JE Nolte 3/65, IS Barnes 4/71)

Match drawn between Natal B and Western Province B, 21–23 December 1988, Cape Town
NtlB 303 (IB Hobson 46, ELR Stewart 78, PH Williams 40, RK Illingworth 42; JE Nolte 3/80, IS Barnes 4/105) and 256/5 (KD Robinson 40, IB Hobson 105*, ELR Stewart 35, PH Williams 31; IS Barnes 3/55)
WPB 305 (JB Commins 58, LF Bleekers 67, JH du Plessis 96*, JE Nolte 39; RK Illingworth 5/87)

Border beat Western Province B by 157 runs, 17–19 January 1989, Cape Town
Bdr 154 (BW Lones 61*; JE Nolte 6/57) and 333/9 dec (BM Osborne 76, EN Trotman 111, AL Wilmot 39; LJ Ryan 3/86)
WPB 223 (MP Stonier 34, CR Matthews 43*; WK Watson 3/37) and 107 (PW Martin 38; WK Watson 3/37, HC Lindenberg 7/31)

Western Province B beat Boland by 5 wickets, 27–29 January 1989, Cape Town
Bol 300 (JP Stephenson 118, O Henry 47, R Marais 33; CC Lillie 4/59) and 140 (R Marais 42*; LJ Ryan 4/64, IS Barnes 5/39)
WPB 212 (JJE Hardy 49, LJ Koen 55, JH du Plessis 33; SJ Base 3/55, O Henry 3/56) and 229/5 (PW Martin 45, JJE Hardy 44, LJ Koen 54*, JH du Plessis 37*; O Henry 4/100)

Border beat Western Province B by 7 wickets, 17–19 February 1989, East London
WPB 312 (PW Martin 119, JB Commins 78, LJ Koen 44; FD Toppin 3/38) and 111 (FD Toppin 3/24, HC Lindenberg 6/34)
Bdr 254/5 dec (EN Trotman 106*, IL Howell 101*) and 170/3 (BW Lones 45*, EN Trotman 91)

Match drawn between Western Province B and Natal B, 21–23 February 1989, Durban
WPB 427/6 dec (KC Jackson 46, G Kirsten 159, JB Commins 138, LJ Koen 33; RA Lyle 3/46)
NtlB 179 (AC Hudson 61, IB Hobson 30; MB Minnaar 5/57) and 94/5 (IB Hobson 37)

Western Province B beat Griqualand West by 118 runs, 13–15 December 1989, Kimberley
WPB 348/6 dec (LF Bleekers 72, G Kirsten 56, JJE Hardy 102*, EO Simons 46, TJ Mitchell 32) and 191/2 dec (LF Bleekers 102*, JJE Hardy 64*)
GW 287/6 dec (JM Arthur 34, GFJ Liebenberg 84, GM Charlesworth 70, GC Abbott 45*) and 134 (HF Wilson 57; AJ McClement 7/25)

Orange Free State B beat Western Province B by 4 wickets, 17–19 December 1989, Bloemfontein
WPB 197 (G Kirsten 32, AM Kirsten 39; NW Pretorius 3/43) and 230 (G Kirsten 57, TJ Mitchell 86, AJ McClement 30*; NW Pretorius 4/103, PW Henning 3/18)
OFSB 261 (JM Truter 71, D Ferreira 64, PJL Radley 30; EO Simons 5/61, DG Payne 3/38) and 168/6 (K Craigen 35, JM Truter 38)

Western Province B beat Orange Free State B by 10 wickets, 6–8 January 1990, Cape Town
OFSB 136 (ST Jefferies 5/77, JE Nolte 4/47) and 283 (MJ Cann 120, RE Cullinan 60; ST Jefferies 5/63, AJ McClement 4/75)
WPB 406/5 dec (LJ Koen 40, AG Elgar 66, G Kirsten 153*, LF Bleekers 65, AM Kirsten 38) and 14/0

Griqualand West beat Western Province B by 43 runs, 19–21 January 1990, Cape Town
GW 236 (GC Abbott 38, HF Wilson 39, P McLaren 48*; AA Johnson 5/75, IR Solomon 5/56) and 234 (JM Arthur 69, GC Abbott 35, DG Mills 30, GP van Rensburg 31; LJ Ryan 5/79, AG Elgar 3/39)
WPB 251 (EO Simons 95, AA Johnson 42; HF Wilson 3/38) and 176 (TN Lazard 63, AP Plantema 45*; IM Kidson 3/33)

Match drawn between Western Province B and Transvaal B, 9–12 February 1990, Verwoerdburg
WPB 325/7 dec (PW Martin 78, JB Commins 100*, AT Holdstock 45) and 192 (TN Lazard 65, AM Kirsten 62; PE Smith 3/49, DR Laing 3/35)
TvlB 189 (B McBride 31, KJ Kerr 31; AJ McClement 5/63) and 224/9 (MS Venter 43, B McBride 50, GE McMillan 40*; AJ McClement 6/52)

Match drawn between Border and Western Province B, 23–26 February 1990, East London
Bdr 506/9 dec (GC Holmes 182, GL Long 156, EN Trotman 78; MB Minnaar 5/143)
WPB 273 (TN Lazard 54, FB Touzel 46, PW Martin 68, EO Simons 32; HC Lindenberg 3/78, NR Boonzaaier 3/37) and 179/9 (FB Touzel 38, EO Simons 51*; HC Lindenberg 5/70)

Western Province B beat Natal B by 10 wickets, 23–25 November 1990, Durban
NtlB 204 (IB Hobson 32, ELR Stewart 40; ST Jefferies 6/42) and 158 (J Payn 35; AL Hobson 5/61)
WPB 334/8 dec (PW Martin 40, FB Touzel 85, KC Jackson 150; DN Crookes 5/117) and 29/0

Match drawn between Western Province B and Transvaal B, 10–12 December 1990, Cape Town
WPB 339/4 dec (FB Touzel 49, HH Gibbs 77, JB Commins 110*, TJ Mitchell 30*) and 175/9 dec (LF Bleekers 75, TJ Mitchell 39; NE Wright 3/58)
TvlB 278/6 dec (BM White 92, JJ Strydom 97; DG Payne 3/36) and 140/5 (JJ Strydom 55*, VG Cresswell 44*)

Match drawn between Eastern Province B and Western Province B, 20–22 December 1990, Cape Town
EPB 234 (GC Victor 97, SJ Palframan 33; ST Jefferies 3/59) and 258/7 dec (MC Venter 36, DJ Ferrant 44, CB Rhodes 68*; PA Rayment 3/33)
WPB 296 (FB Touzel 92, MF Voss 68; JR Meyer 3/48, C Roelofse 3/80, RE Veenstra 3/56) and 193/7 (FB Touzel 62, JB Commins 35)

Western Province B beat Northern Transvaal B by 7 wickets, 5–7 January 1991, Cape Town
WPB 289/7 dec (PW Martin 44, MP Stonier 31, PAH Upton 100, TJ Mitchell 57) and 108/3 (LF Bleekers 46, MP Stonier 34*)
NTB 129 (BJ Sommerville 33; AJ McClement 7/51) and 264 (MB Mare 88, IA Hoffmann 30, PA Tullis 37*; AJ McClement 6/86)

Western Province B beat Orange Free State B by 11 runs, 8–10 February 1991, Bloemfontein
WPB 169 (MF Voss 70; CF Craven 6/25) and 261/8 dec (FB Touzel 47, LF Bleekers 66, HH Gibbs 54; MI Gidley 3/51, MJ Karsten 3/60)
OFSB 136 (JM Truter 41; MW Pringle 4/44, AL Hobson 3/44) and 283 (RA Brown 55, GFJ Liebenberg 61, MI Gidley 57*, NW Pretorius 33; PA Rayment 3/44)

Match drawn between Western Province B and Border, 8–11 March 1991, East London
WPB 327 (TN Lazard 58, PW Martin 48, LF Bleekers 31, HH Gibbs 56; SJ Base 4/84, BC Fourie 3/80) and 237/8 dec (JB Commins 104*, HH Gibbs 51; BC Fourie 4/75)
Bdr 200 (PN Kirsten 41, EN Trotman 44, DH Howell 55; DG Payne 7/63) and 53/2

1.2.4 Western Province Cricket Union B, List A, Limited-Overs Players, 1981/82–1990/91

Name	M	From	To
Ackerman, HM	1	1981/82	1981/82
Ackermann, JP	1	1983/84	1983/84
Austen, MH	1	1983/84	1983/84
Base, SJ	1	1983/84	1983/84
Clarke, TA	3	1981/82	1984/85
During, J	1	1984/85	1984/85
Du Toit, JD	1	1984/85	1984/85
Elgar, AG	1	1984/85	1984/85
Kruger, WG	1	1983/84	1983/84
Lawrenson, RR	1	1983/84	1983/84
Mahoney, JE	1	1981/82	1981/82
Martin, BP	1	1983/84	1983/84
Matthews, BA	1	1984/85	1984/85
Mellor, MD	1	1983/84	1983/84
Minnaar, MB	1	1984/85	1984/85
Muntingh, E	1	1981/82	1981/82
Nieuwoudt, AB	1	1981/82	1981/82
Norman, D	2	1983/84	1984/85
Pagden, ND	1	1981/82	1981/82
Rayner, PH	1	1981/82	1981/82
Rundle, DB	1	1984/85	1984/85
Seeff, J	2	1981/82	1984/85
Snyman, NM	1	1983/84	1983/84
Taljaard, M	1	1981/82	1981/82
Thompson, PM	1	1981/82	1981/82
Tullis, GD	2	1983/84	1984/85
Van Niekerk, AP	1	1981/82	1981/82
Wingreen, IM	1	1984/85	1984/85

1.2.5 Western Province Cricket Union B, List A, Limited-Overs Scores, 1981/82–1990/91

Orange Free State beat Western Province B by 20 runs, 24 October 1981, Cape Town
OFS 253/6 (SN Hartley 39, GW Humpage 99, WM van der Merwe 44*)
WPB 233 (PH Rayner 143; WM van der Merwe 4/49)

Transvaal beat Western Province B by 9 wickets, 15 October 1983, Cape Town
WPB 93 (ST Clarke 5/10, AJ Kourie 3/25)
Tvl 95/1 (HR Fotheringham 41*)

Western Province beat Western Province B by 7 wickets, 3 November 1984, Cape Town
WPB 138 (AG Elgar 37, IM Wingreen 38; AP Kuiper 4/14)
WP 139/3 (L Seeff 49, SFAF Bacchus 32, PH Rayner 33*)

CHAPTER 2

Western Province Coloured Cricket Union, 1890s–1959

Affiliated to South African Coloured (later Malay) Cricket Board

The Western Province Coloured Cricket Union (WPCCU) was formed sometime in the 1890s as a home for the cricketers in Cape Town who were excluded from the whites-only Western Province Cricket Union (WPCU).[67] The exact founding date is not known, but an official Western Province team was in action by 1898 and the WPCCU soon had a solid base, given the active cricket-playing tradition in Cape Town.

Ottomans Cricket Club, based in the Bo-Kaap, was established as early as 1882.[68] Named after the Ottoman Empire, it was for cricketers in the Muslim communities of Cape Town. Another early club was St Augustine's Cricket Club, established in 1899 by the Rev. Warren Sydney Lavis to cater for Christian cricketers. Lavis, who went on to become a bishop (one of the suburbs of Cape Town is named after him), was then the minister at St Paul's Church in the city centre and started 'Saints' as 'a community-based cricket club and primarily to offer alternatives to the "idle youth" of the time'.[69] Both Ottomans and St Augustine's are still in existence today.

In January 1890, the same month that the first white Western Province team was selected, local black cricketers hired Newlands for what was described as a 'Malay' inter-town tournament. Claremont and Cape Town Union played as separate teams against Kimberley and Port Elizabeth in front of large crowds of several thousand people.[70] In the final game of the tournament, a combined Cape Town and Claremont team played a combined Port Elizabeth and Johannesburg team. This was in effect the first Western Province side outside the whites-only Union.[71]

The next year, during Easter, a Cape Town team was selected for a follow-up inter-town tournament in Kimberley for the Glover Cup.[72] After the tournament, a South African Malay side was picked to play against a white Kimberley Invitation team captained by the donor of the cup, F Glover, a prominent local cricketer who played for Griqualand West against the 1891/92 English tourists. Four Cape Town cricketers – C Abrams, E Ariefdien, K du Toit and L Samsodien – were selected for that first South African team.

Then on 22–23 March 1892, at the end of the second English cricket tour to South Africa, a Cape Town team took on the professionals in WW Read's side. This was after South Africa was annihilated by an innings and 189 runs in the only test of the tour at Newlands. With time left before the tourists' boat departed for England, the locals challenged the English and an 'extra match, for the benefit of the professionals' was played at Newlands. England beat this 'Malay XVIII' by 10 wickets, but they performed creditably, doing better than most sides against the visitors.[73] L Samsodien scored one of only two fifties against the English and the visitors were hugely impressed by H 'Krom' Hendricks, comparing him with the famous Australian bowler Frederick 'The Demon' Spofforth. Hendricks so impressed the white colonial cricket establishment that he was actually selected for the first South African team to play in England in 1894 but was later left out.

It was on these foundations that the WPCCU was built. The union was geographically separated into a Town Section, covering the District Six, Bo-Kaap and City areas, playing mostly at Green Point Common, and a Suburban Section, based in Claremont and Newlands, and playing on Rondebosch Common. In 1900 the important Cape District Cricket Union was formed.[74]

By 1910 'the championship of the Western Province between the different Unions' included four teams. They were Woodstock and Metropolitan, the City League, Cape District, and Claremont and District.[75] The formation of the Maitland and Districts Cricket Union followed in 1912. The WPCCU represented Western Province at the Barnato Board and at the inter-provincial tournaments, but whether all the above-mentioned unions in Cape Town affiliated to it is not clear. The *APO* newspaper reported in 1912 that 'the Board is making a serious effort this year to bring all the existing Unions in the Peninsula into one Union'.[76]

Cape Town and its suburbs were racially mixed areas in those days. This only changed with the forced removal of tens of thousands of families under the Group Areas Act from the late 1950s onwards. For example, half the population of Claremont in 1902 was made up of so-called Non-Europeans. Palmboom Road in Newlands, one of the venues for meetings of the WPCCU and today a gentrified area with little trace of this history, was 'particularly mixed, with a high proportion of coloured residents at the top end'. Flourishing cricket cultures developed amongst these Muslim and Christian communities in the city, who were often lumped incorrectly together as 'Malays' at the time. 'Krom' Hendricks, for example, asked, 'My father was born of Dutch parents in Cape Town and my mother hails from St Helena – then why am I termed a Malay?'[77]

The first known WPCCU team was selected in 1898 for the first inter-provincial tournament for the Barnato Memorial Trophy in Port Elizabeth.[78] Western Province won this tournament and thereafter made a habit of keeping the trophy, winning 13 out of 15 of the tournaments they played in. There were altogether 17 Barnato tournaments, but Western Province did not participate in 1909/10, seemingly because of disunity relating to religion, and in 1959/60, in opposition to the continuation of racially based tournaments.

The Barnato tournaments were organised by the South African Coloured Cricket Board (SACCB), formed in 1903. The WPCCU was a founder member of the board, together with Eastern Province and Griqualand West. This new national board of black cricketers excluded from the mainstream white body had the distinct achievement of preceding the national cricket boards of Australia, India, New Zealand, West Indies and other countries. Its goal, as specifically stated in the constitution, was to be a non-discriminatory organisation open to all cricketers regardless of race, class or religion. The famous Dr Abdullah Abdurahman, the first black medical doctor in South Africa and a Cape Town city councillor for 40 years, was the first president of the affiliated WPCCU.

After the five Barnato tournaments up to 1913, World War One badly disrupted sport across South Africa and led to a break of nine seasons before the next tournament in 1922. There were five more Barnato tournaments between 1922 and 1932. We have not been able to find records for any of these because the long-running *APO* newspaper serving the coloured community had collapsed. We do know that Western Province won all five tournaments under the captaincy for 12 consecutive seasons of the great all-rounder Taliep Salie. Salie scored 224 against Natal in one of the Barnato tournaments and he was the long-standing captain of the famous District Six-based Roslyns Club. Salie so impressed English touring teams that he was invited to play in England but he turned down the invitation owing to 'social pressure'.

From the late 1920s, the WPCCU's parent body, the SACCB, went into decline. As racial segregation deepened in South African society, first the 'coloured' (1926), then the African (1932) and finally the Indian cricketers (1940) broke away to form separate national organisations. This fracture happened at provincial level too. New coloured (1923), African (1928) and Indian (1943) provincial bodies emerged after breakaways from the long-standing WPCCU, as the chapters that follow show.

The national body became dormant in the 1930s and the Barnato tournaments stopped being held. Despite this, the WPCCU continued to operate and its leagues and standard of play remained strong. Newspaper reports in 1935/36 mentioned that matches between Ottomans and Roslyns, perhaps the most famous, always generated great excitement and 'spectators included many old-time Moslem players'. Other important WPCCU clubs at the time were Primrose, Violets, Arabian College, Hamediahs, Good Hope, Glider, Red Roses, Rocklands and Pirates. Second division clubs mentioned were Squares, Good Hope, Protea and junior sides of the senior clubs mentioned.[79]

Ten years later, in 1945/46, the standard in the WPCCU was arguably the highest in the country outside the white cricket boards. In that season the WPCCU had 37 teams participating in its first and second divisions. Each division was divided into a Town Section and a Suburban Section, as we have mentioned. The main town clubs at this stage were Ottomans, Roslyns, Good Hope, Rocklands, Hamediahs, Red Roses, Arabian College, Young Ideas, Warwickshires, Walmer Estate and Melbournes. The main suburban clubs were Vineyards, Violets, Pirates, Alphenians, Primrose and Green Roses.[80] Besides playing in leagues, clubs regularly went on tours to other parts of the country, and also hosted reciprocal tours.[81]

After World War Two, the WPCCU and its provincial counterparts in Transvaal and Griqualand West revived both the pioneering Barnato inter-provincial tournaments and the SACCB[82] (although the latter had to change its name to the South African Malay Cricket Board in 1953 at the insistence of the other racially based affiliates before being allowed to join the umbrella South African Cricket Board of Control). The new post-war series of Barnato tournaments kicked off at the Mowbray Sports Grounds in Cape Town in December 1945. The fields were situated where St George's Grammar School now stands in Mowbray. Western Province, led by Taliep Salie, continued on its winning ways in this tournament. Transvaal took the remaining two tournaments in the 1940s, but then Western Province came back and won all three tournaments it participated in in the 1950s.

The WPCCU was not only the strongest Barnato affiliate, it also won the Moslem Progressive Trophy in both 1952/53 and 1953/54 when those cricketers seeking closer co-operation across the racial divides played inter-union games in Cape Town. Dol Freeman's team beat the provincial Indian and 'Bantu' sides, as well as Hottentots Holland and some of the Peninsula and Western Districts affiliates who ignored their parent body's opposition.

As the 1950s wore on, the WPCCU became unhappy about the racially based nature of cricket. It helped launch the Western Province Cricket Federation to work across colour lines in 1952 (see Chapter 8), boycotted the final Barnato tournament in 1959/60 in protest and then, finally, joined together with other black cricketers to launch the united, non-racial Western Province Cricket Board in 1959. The pioneering Barnato tournaments, started in 1898 – 17 in total – came to an end and today the Barnato Trophy stands proudly in the President's Suite at Newlands.

2.1 Western Province Coloured Cricket Union National Players (SACCB / SAMCB / SACBOC), 1889/90–1959/60

South African Malay Team, 1891[83]

(Selected after inter-town tournament in Kimberley, precursor to South African Coloured Cricket Board tournaments)

Abrams, C	1890/91
Ariefdien, E	1890/91
Du Toit, K	1890/91
Samsodien, L	1890/91

South African Malay Cricket Board*, 1953–1959[84]

Name	Season
Abed, G 'Tiny'	1954/55 vice-captain, 1957/58 captain
Abed, GH	1957/58
Abed, S 'Lobo'	1952/53, 1954/55, 1957/58
Bardien, S	1952/53
Behardien, I 'Taliep'	1957/58
Du Toit, M	1957/58
Freeman, AJ 'Dol'	1952/53
George, A	1957/58
Hendricks, A	1954/55
Lakay, Y 'Timmy'	1954/55
Nackerdien, S	1954/55 captain
Osman, AA 'Bakar'	1952/53
Petersen, E	1952/53, 1954/55, 1957/58

Known as South African Coloured Cricket Board from 1903 to 1953

South African Cricket Board of Control, 1956/57–1958/59

Name	Season
Abed, G 'Tiny'	1958/59
Abed, S 'Lobo'	1956/57, 1958/59
George, A	1956/57
Petersen, E	1958/59

2.2 Western Province Coloured Cricket Union Players, 1889/90–1959/60[85]

The list below also includes the names of those cricketers who played for selected teams in the Malay inter-town tournaments in 1889/90 and 1890/91 and in the Malay XVIII against England in 1891/92. By doing this, and showing the clear continuity with the Barnato tournaments from 1898/99 onwards, we in effect list the first Western Province sides outside the whites-only WPCU, and name, detail and recognise for the first time the first generation of elite cricketers from the excluded communities. To ensure historical accuracy, '(Unofficial)' is added to these names and they are not included in the consolidated list of the 12 boards in Part III below.

Abdol, [x] (Claremont Union)	1889/90 (Unofficial), 1898/99
Abed, G (Roslyns)	1957/58
Abed, GH 'Tiny' (Roslyns)	1951/52, 1953/54, 1954/55, 1957/58
Abed, S 'Lobo' (Roslyns/Hamediahs)	1949/50, 1951/52, 1953/54, 1954/55, 1957/58
Abrahams, A* (Primrose)	1951/52
Abrahams, A 'Karrie'* (Pirates)	1951/52, 1954/55
Abrahams, E* (Good Hope)	1947/48, 1957/58
Abrahams, H[86] (Claremont Union/Combined XI)	1889/90 (Unofficial), 1890/91 (Unofficial)
Abrahams, W[87] (Claremont Union/Combined XI)	1889/90 (Unofficial)
Adams, A* (Violets)	1957/58
Adams, E (Claremont Union/Combined XI)	1889/90 (Unofficial), Malay XVIII 1891/92 (Unofficial)
Adams, I	1903/04
Addrjance, H[88] (Claremont Union)	1889/90 (Unofficial)
Addrjance, W[89] (Claremont Union)	1889/90 (Unofficial)
Alexander, K (Roslyns)	1945/46
Alexander, M* (Arabian College)	1947/48
Allie, [x][90] (Claremont Union)	1889/90 (Unofficial)
Allie, [x][91]	1898/99
Allie, A	1912/13
Allie, KB* (Vineyards)	1945/46, 1947/48
Amerein, [x]	Malay XVIII 1891/92 (Unofficial)
Ariefdien, A[92] (Cape Town Union)	1889/90 (Unofficial)
Ariefdien, E[93] (Cape Town Union/Combined XI)	1889/90 (Unofficial), 1890/91 (Unofficial), Malay XVIII 1891/92 (Unofficial)
Armar, T (Cape Town Union)	1889/90 (Unofficial)
Baderoon, [x]	Malay XVIII 1891/92 (Unofficial)

Badin, O	1912/13
Bardien, S* (Squares)	1949/50, 1951/52, 1953/54
Barnett, J* (Roslyns)	1945/46
Behardien, I 'Taliep' (Vineyards)	1931/2, 1945/46, 1947/48 captain, 1949/50
Behardien, I 'Taliep' (Vineyards)	1957/58
Bohardien, I 'Fatty' (Good Hope)	1954/55
Charles, B	1898/99, 1903/04
Christian, M	1912/13
Conrad, HG 'Karriem'[94] (Vineyards)	1945/46
Danter, D	Malay XVIII 1891/92 (Unofficial)
Davids, A* (Squares)	1951/52
Davids, AL	1912/13
Davids, H* (Pirates)	1949/50
Dollie, A* (Ottomans)	1949/50
Dollie, E* (Victorians)	1951/52
Du Toit, K[95]	1890/91 (Unofficial), Malay XXII 1891/92 (Unofficial)
Du Toit, M (Ottomans)	1945/46, 1947/48, 1957/58
Esmieh, M (Cape Town Union)	1889/90 (Unofficial)
Eshaak, L (Cape Town Union)	1889/90 (Unofficial)
Fakie, [x]	1898/99
Fakier, M 'Baby' (Muslims)	1954/55
Fataar, Mogamad Ganief 'Taatjie' (Ottomans)	1921/22
Fredricks, F	1898/99
Fredricks, L	1898/99
Fredricks, [x]	1903/04
Freeman, AJ 'Dol' (Roslyns)	1931/32, 1945/46, 1947/48, 1949/50 captain, 1951/52
Ganief, C* (Violets)	1949/50, 1954/55, 1957/58
George, A* (Ottomans)	1947/48, 1954/55
Gertzen, A	1912/13 captain
Gertzen, E	1912/13
Gertzen, G	1903/04, 1912/13
Gihier, A (Cape Town Union)	1889/90 (Unofficial)
Goder, M* (Hamediahs)	1957/58
Grant, [x]	Malay XVIII 1891/92 (Unofficial)
Haroun, MY* (Vineyards)	1949/50, 1951/52
Hartley, MA (Red Roses)	1947/48
Hattas, A 'Bakar' (Violets)	1957/58
Hendricks, [x]	1898/99
Hendricks, A	Malay XVIII 1891/92 (Unofficial), 1898/99, 1903/04, 1912/13
Hendricks, H	Malay XVIII 1891/92 (Unofficial)
Hendricks, O	1912/13
Hendricks, S (Cape Town and Claremont)	1889/90 (Unofficial), Malay XVIII 1891/92 (Unofficial)
Hendricks, T	Malay XVIII 1891/92 (Unofficial), 1898/99

Hendricks, Toyer (Primrose)	1957/58
Hendricks, [x]	1898/99
Hendrikse, H* (Primrose)	1949/50
Hermans, J* (Roslyns)	1947/48
Holmes, G 'Tape' (Good Hope)	1951/52, 1954/55
Ijraan, A (Cape Town Union)	1889/90 (Unofficial)
Isaacs, A* (Vineyards)	1947/48
Isaacs, C	1912/13
Isaacs, M	1912/13
Isaacs Mogammadien	[1920s–1930s]
Ishaak, D (Cape Town Union)	1889/90 (Unofficial)
Ismael, M[96] (Cape Town Union/Combined XI)	1889/90 (Unofficial)
Jacobs, J	Malay XVIII 1891/92 (Unofficial)
Jaijer, A (Cape Town Union)	1889/90 (Unofficial)
Jakoef, G[97] (Cape Town Union)	1889/90 (Unofficial)
Jammie, I	1912/13
Johnson, [x]	Malay XVIII 1891/92 (Unofficial)
Joseph, [x]	1898/99
Kenny, A	1898/99, 1903/04
Khan, M* (Primrose)	1945/46
Laban, D (Claremont Union)	1889/90 (Unofficial)
Laban, H (Claremont Union)	1889/90 (Unofficial)
Lakay, Y 'Timmy' (Squares)	1954/55
Lamrah, M (Cape Town Union/Combined XI)	1889/90 (Unofficial)
Leich, C	Malay XVIII 1891/92 (Unofficial)
Le Roux, A[98]	1890/91 (Unofficial), Malay XVIII 1891/92 (Unofficial)
Magied, [x]	1903/04
Magmoet, J (Roslyns)	1945/46
Manoor, S[99] (Claremont Union/Combined XI)	1889/90 (Unofficial), Malay XVIII 1891/92 (Unofficial)
Meyer, CA 'Tim'* (Squares)	1949/50, 1951/52
Mufti, Abdullah 'Hadji' (Ottomans)	1921/22 captain
Nackerdien, S 'Sharkey' (Vineyards)	1945/46, 1951/52 captain, 1954/55 captain
Nordien, AG 'Happie'* (Squares)	1931/32, 1949/50
Osman, AA 'Bakar'* (Squares)	1949/50, 1951/52, 1953/54, 1957/58
Oxallie, M[100] (Cape Town Union)	1889/90 (Unofficial)
Petersen, E (Pirates/Warwickshire)	1951/52, 1954/55, 1957/58
Rasdien, G* (Vineyards)	1951/52
Reinaard, Gamat 'Prop' (Hamediahs)	1931/32
Salam, H (Claremont Union)	1889/90 (Unofficial)
Salie, F (Cape Town Union)	1889/90 (Unofficial)
Salie, S (Cape Town Union)	1889/90 (Unofficial)
Salie, S (Ottomans)	1945/46, 1949/50
Salie, T* (Roslyns)	1922-1932 captain, 1945/46 captain
Samaai, R (Squares)	1954/55
Samsodien, K (Squares)	1954/55

Samsodien, L [101] (Cape Town Union/Combined XI)	1889/90 (Unofficial), 1890/91 (Unofficial), Malay XVIII 1891/92 (Unofficial)
Samsodien, M[102] (Cape Town Union)	1889/90 (Unofficial)
Samsodien, R[103] (Cape Town Union)	1889/90 (Unofficial)
Saardian, [x] (Cape Town and Claremont)	1889/90 (Unofficial)
Satarien, A* (Vineyards)	1949/50
Sheldon, A	1903/04
Solomon, A	1912/13
Solomon, AB	1912/13
Solomons, G (Hamediahs)	1945/46, 1947/48
Stemmet, [x] (Claremont Union)	1889/90 (Unofficial)
Taliep, [x][104]	1898/99
Toefie, [x][105]	1898/99
Van der Schyff, B[106] (Claremont Union/Combined XI)	1889/90 (Unofficial)
Van der Schyff, H	Malay XVIII 1891/92 (Unofficial)
Van Haaght, S 'Hudson' (Ottomans)	1945/46, 1947/48

2.3 Western Province Coloured Cricket Union Winners in the Barnato Memorial Trophy Tournaments, 1898/99–1959/60[107]

Season	Winners
1898/99	Western Province (Unofficial)
1903/04	Western Province
1907/08	Western Province
1909/10	Griqualand West [Western Province did not participate]
1912/13	Western Province
1921/22	Western Province
1924/25	Western Province
1927/28	Western Province
1929/30	Western Province
1931/32	Western Province
1945/46	Western Province
1947/48	Transvaal
1949/50	Transvaal
1951/52	Western Province
1954/55	Western Province
1957/58	Western Province
1959/60	Eastern Province [Western Province did not participate]

No tournaments were held between 1933 and 1944 because the SACCB was dormant.

2.4 Western Province Coloured Cricket Union Scores, 1898/99–1959/60[108]

BARNATO MEMORIAL TROPHY TOURNAMENT, 28 DECEMBER 1898 – 5 JANUARY 1899, PORT ELIZABETH (UNOFFICIAL – PRESACCB)[109]
Participating teams Western Province, Griqualand West, Port Elizabeth (Eastern Province), Queenstown, Southern Border (East London/King William's Town).
Winners: Western Province

Western Province beat Southern Border by 37 runs
WP 27 ([x] Taliep 16; [x] Buhlungu 8[?]) and 219 (A Hendricks 65, A Kenny 62, [x] Joseph 23; [x] Kunene 6/[x], [x] Buhlungu 2/[x])
S Bdr 145 ([x] Bopi 40*, W Ntshona 34, [x] Buhlungu 24; [x] Abdol 5/[x], [x] Hendricks 2/[x]) and 64 ([x] Rashe 20; [x] Abdol 4/[x], T Hendricks 3/[x], T Fredericks 3/[x])

Western Province beat Griqualand West by 6 wickets, 2 January 1899
GW 72 and 198 (Mondel 63, Abrams 43)
WP 145 and 127/4

Western Province vs Port Elizabeth
[no details available]

1ST SACCB BARNATO MEMORIAL TROPHY TOURNAMENT, 30 MARCH – 5 APRIL 1904, KIMBERLEY[110]
Participants: Western Province, Eastern Province and Griqualand West. Matches played to conclusion, including 3-day period.
Winners: Western Province

Western Province beat Griqualand West by 23 runs, 30–31 March 1904, Eclectic CC Grounds
WP 130 (Magied 32, Fredericks 23; Jabaar 5/13, Jacobs 5/31) and 79 (Jabaar 9/40, Jacobs 1/26)
GW 86 (A Sheldon 8/45, G Gertzen 2/33) and 100 (Hendricks 41, M Schroder 21, [x] 4/[x], [x] 4/[x])

Western Province beat Eastern Province by [x], 2, 4 and 5 April 1904, Eclectic CC Grounds
WP 139 (A Kennie 46, B Charles 22, A Hendricks 21, [x] 4/45) and [x]
EP 197 (G Abrahams 123, E Sakiem 20; A Sheldon 6/46, G Gertzen 2/37) and [x]

2ND SACCB BARNATO MEMORIAL TROPHY TOURNAMENT, DECEMBER/JANUARY 1907/08 OR MARCH/APRIL 1908, CAPE TOWN
Winners: Western Province
[no details available]

3RD SACCB BARNATO MEMORIAL TROPHY TOURNAMENT, MARCH/APRIL 1910, PORT ELIZABETH
Winners: Griqualand West.
[Western Province did not participate[111]]

4TH SACCB BARNATO MEMORIAL TROPHY TOURNAMENT, MARCH/APRIL 1913, KIMBERLEY
Participants: Western Province, Eastern Province, Griqualand West and Natal.
Winners: Western Province

Western Province beat Eastern Province by an innings and 213 runs[112]
WP 290 (G Christian 91, L Davids 73*, AB Solomon 56)
EP 33 (M Isaacs 5/[x], I Jammie 4/[x]) and 44 (M Isaacs 8/[x], I Jammie 2/[x])

Western Province beat Natal by an innings and 66 runs[113]
WP 296 (M Isaacs 55, G Christian 54, A Solomon 50, I Jammie 30; SA Kudos 4/60, D Kaisval 2/29)
Ntl 119 (B Subban 28, R Bughwan 22; A Allie 3/16, G Christian 3/30, M Isaacs 3/33) and 111 (MB Lazarus 24, B Subban 20; G Christian 5/23, M Isaacs 3/30, O Hendricks 2/2)

Western Province beat Griqualand West by 183 runs[114]
WP 190 (L Davids 31, M Isaacs 29, AB Solomon 40*; E Jacobs 6/66, A Jabaar 4/74) and 155 (AB Solomon 74, O Hendricks 25*; E Jacobs 6/57, A Jabaar 2/52)
GW 73 (J Kokazela 22; B Badin 5/30, G Christian 3/9) and 89 (A Jabaar 30; B Badin 5/40, G Christian 5/42)

5TH SACCB BARNATO MEMORIAL TROPHY TOURNAMENT, DECEMBER/JANUARY 1921/22 OR MARCH/APRIL 1922, CAPE TOWN
Winners: Western Province
[no details available]

6TH SACCB BARNATO TROPHY TOURNAMENT, DECEMBER/JANUARY 1924/25 OR MARCH/APRIL 1925, JOHANNESBURG
Winners: Western Province
[no details available]

7TH SACCB BARNATO TROPHY TOURNAMENT, DECEMBER/JANUARY 1927/28 OR MARCH/APRIL 1928, KIMBERLEY
Winners: Western Province
[no details available]

8TH SACCB BARNATO TROPHY TOURNAMENT, DECEMBER/JANUARY 1929/30 OR MARCH/APRIL 1930, JOHANNESBURG
Winners: Western Province
[no details available]

9TH SACCB BARNATO MEMORIAL TROPHY TOURNAMENT, DECEMBER/JANUARY 1931/32 OR MARCH/APRIL 1932, BLOEMFONTEIN
Winners: Western Province
[no details available]

No Barnato Trophy Tournaments took place between 1933 and 1944.

10TH SACCB BARNATO MEMORIAL TROPHY TOURNAMENT, DECEMBER/JANUARY 1945/46, CAPE TOWN
Participants: Western Province, Transvaal and Griqualand West.
Winners: Western Province

Western Province beat Griqualand West by an innings and 167 runs
GW 68 (E Barnes 20; S van Haaght 4/15, Conrad 3/17, T Salie 2/14) and 68 (C Amsterdam 11, M Barnes 10; AJ Freeman 4/20)
WP 303 (M du Toit 72, J Salie 70, S Salie 38*, S van Haaght 24; A Hassan 6/90, G Adams 2/30, N Adams 2/60)

Western Province beat Transvaal by an innings and 52 runs
WP 288 (S Salie 101*)
Tvl 107 (D Hassen 28, A Kirsten 34; Alexander 6/21) and 129

Western Province beat Transvaal and Griqualand West by an innings and 17 runs
Tvl/GW 159 (A Kirsten 72, S Bagus 36; T Salie 5/41, M du Toit 3/27) and 66 (H Salie 14, D Hassen 11, C Jacobs 11; S van Haaght 4/13, Alexander 3/26, M du Toit 2/20)
WP 242 (T Salie 71, AJ Freeman 37, M du Toit 36, J Magmoet 23; A Rubidge 4/45, Adams 4/67)

11TH SACCB BARNATO MEMORIAL TROPHY TOURNAMENT, DECEMBER/JANUARY 1947/48, JOHANNESBURG
Participants: Transvaal, Western Province, and Griqualand West.
Winners: Transvaal

Western Province beat Griqualand West by 10 wickets
WP 165 (G Solomon 48*, AJ Freeman 38; J Barnes 5/43) and 3/0
GW 59 and 108 (J Barnes 29; MA Harley 4/12)

Transvaal beat Western Province by 39 runs
Tvl 140 (AB Davids 50) and 46/5 dec
WP 69 (A Rubidge 6/17, Adams 3/8) and 78

12TH SACCB BARNATO MEMORIAL TROPHY TOURNAMENT, DECEMBER/JANUARY 1949/50, KIMBERLEY
Participants: Transvaal, Western Province, Griqualand West and Eastern Transvaal.
Winners: Transvaal

13TH SACCB BARNATO MEMORIAL TROPHY TOURNAMENT, DECEMBER/JANUARY 1951/52, CAPE TOWN[115]
Participants: Western Province, Transvaal, Eastern Province, Griqualand West, Eastern Transvaal and Hottentots Holland.
Winners: Western Province

Western Province beat Eastern Transvaal by 207 runs
WP 162 (AA Osman 44, S Nackerdien 33, S Bardien 30*; Moosa 6/43, Kanjee 3/28) and 182 (G Abed 38, S Nackerdien 37; Ally 4/68, Kanjee 3/46, Moosa 3/67)
ET 66 (AJ Freeman 3/9, S Bardien 3/15) and 71 (S Bardien 8/26)

Western Province beat Eastern Province by an innings and 19 runs
EP 83 (E Petersen 5/22, S Bardien 3/19) and 95 (S Bardien 3/9, CA Meyer 3/22)
WP 197 (AA Osman 36, G Abed 34*; G de Monk 3/36, A Hendricks 3/48)

Western Province beat Griqualand West by an innings and 364 runs
GW 45 (CA Meyer 5/18, E Petersen 4/12) and 110 (AJ Freeman 3/13, E Petersen 3/35)
WP 519/8 dec (AA Osman 133, G Abed 114, AJ Freeman 100, Holmes 93)

Western Province beat Transvaal by 7 wickets
Tvl 133 (A Kirsten 29*, O Abrahams 23; S Bardien 5/49, AJ Freeman 2/2) and 164 (A Rubidge 50, A Kirsten 48*, M Docrat 35; S Bardien 6/51, E Petersen 2/29, AJ Freeman 2/42)
WP 61 (S Abed 26; G Martin 5/23, A Rubidge 4/33) and 240/3 (S Nackerdien 102, AJ Freeman 90*)

WESTERN PROVINCE CRICKET FEDERATION INTER-UNION MATCHES, 1952/53–1953/54[116]
Western Province Coloured Cricket Union beat Stellenbosch and District Cricket Union by an innings and 18 runs, 26–27 December 1952
Stellenbosch 91 (E Rhoode 23*; H Noordien 6/30, E Petersen 2/18) and 68 (S Raziet 27; AJ Freeman 6/34, H Noordien 2/21)
WPCCU 177 (A Abrahams 27, M du Toit 22, G Abed 28, GT Holmes 31, H Noordien 31; A Manuel 3/39, E Davidson 3/51, S Raziet 2/34)

Western Province Coloured Cricket Union beat Western Province Indian Cricket Union by 10 wickets, 14–15 February 1953
WPICU 58 (J Magmoet 24; E Petersen 5/5, I Bohardien 3/28) and 162 (N Fakier 72, M Abrahams 40; I Bohardien 5/45, E Petersen 4/23)
WPCCU 185 (O Fataar 47, E Dollie 30, G Abed 29; J Gheewala 4/26, I Pangarkar 2/38, A Desai 2/10) and 38/0 (L Less 22*)

Western Province Coloured Cricket Union beat Western Province Bantu Cricket Union by 8 wickets, 28 February – 1 March 1953
WPBCU 59 (E Petersen 8/27) and 73 (I Bohardien 6/29, E Petersen 3/21, A Freeman 1/2)
WPCCU 83 (AK Abrahams 20; AM Mshumpela 3/19, B Cossie 3/17, N Kawulela 1/5) and 55/2 (AA Osman 18*)

Western Province Coloured Cricket Union beat Wynberg and District Cricket Union by 8 wickets, 7–8 March 1953
Wynberg 78 (G Abed 4/24, E Petersen 5/46) and 160 (C Ravens 20, A Eckles 27, O Kafaar 56; E Petersen 4/47, G Abed 2/21)
WPCCU 166 (AJ Freeman 20, GT Holmes 27, S Abed 27, E Abrahams 25, E Petersen 23; J da Rocha 4/47, J Francis 3/64) and 74/2

Western Province Coloured Cricket Union beat Hottentots Holland Cricket Union by 10 wickets, 11–12 April 1953
HH 60 (A Bagus 18; E Petersen 3/15, AJ Freeman 3/23, S Bardien 4/15) and 110 (S Abels 20; E Petersen 6/29, H Noordien 2/52, G Abed 1/9)
WPCCU 153 (G Abed 36, H Noordien 33, AJ Freeman 23; G Baderoen 5/52, N Daniels 1/10, S Arendse 1/12) and 22/0 (A Davids 19*)

Central Cricket League beat Western Province Coloured Cricket Union on the first innings, [x]
Centrals 288 (P Thomas 149, M Coetzee 27, A Sabotker 26*; G Abed 6/87, S Bardien 4/65)
WPCCU 106 (G Abed 37, AA Osman 23; L Robertson 6/44, M Coetzee 2/9, C Felix 2/11) and 231/9 (GT Holmes 54, G Abed 51, E Dollie 32; M Coetzee 4/52)

Western Province Coloured Cricket Union beat Central Cricket League on the first innings, 21–22 November 1953
Centrals 110 (S Viret 22, S Solomons 36, P Thomas 31; E Petersen 3/37, H Noordien 4/25) and 151/7 dec (D Koks 37*, P Thomas 14, J Truter 15, A Sabotker 49*; A Davids 2/25, H Noordien 2/32)
WPCCU 128 (L Less 31, G Abed 13, T Hendricks 13, H Noordien 19, E Petersen 13, M Coetzee 4/33, A Sabotker 4/82, H Moody 2/8) and 95/4 (T Hendricks 40*, AJ Freeman 19, L Less 15; P Thomas 3/37)

Western Province Coloured Cricket Union beat Western Province Indian Cricket Union by an innings and 30 runs, 13 December 1953
WPICU 72 (M Rahbeeni 28, S Abrahams 12; G Abed 3/15, AJ Freeman 3/12, E Petersen 2/24) and 80 (H Hendricks 16, A Desai 42, S van Haaght 11; AJ Freeman 4/25, E Abrahams 4/45)
WPCCU 182 (AJ Freeman 33, G Abed 41, AA Osman 27, GT Holmes 21, L Less 14, S Abed 14*; S Abrahams 4/50, M Naidoo 2/21)

Western Province Coloured Cricket Union beat Hottentots Holland Cricket Union (match forfeited), 17 and 31 January 1954
WPCCU 152 (T Hendricks 52, A Satarien 18, S Abed 21*, G Adams 15; G Baderoon 4/46, G Adams 5/57) and 185/4 (L Less 46, A Satarien 64, K Samsodien 44, G Abed 13*; A Bagus 3/43)
HH 58 (I Latief 18; E Petersen 8/22, G Abed 2/13)

Western Province Coloured Cricket Union beat Western Province Bantu Cricket Union by an innings and 16 runs, 21 February 1954
WPCCU 259 (E Abrahams 40, J Solomons 43, AJ Freeman 51, L Less 21, A Abrahams 19, A Latief 30, AM Mshumpela 4/52, B Cossie 2/37, J Nyamakazi 2/64)
WPBCU 103 (CM Scott 20, J Nyamakazi 27*, B Mabuto 18, S Hoho 15, E Petersen 3/26, E Abrahams 4/39, AJ Freeman 2/8) and 140 (J Nyamakazi 50, AM Mshumpela 32*, B Cossie 16, E Petersen 5/29, J Solomons 2/15)

Western Province Coloured Cricket Union beat Stellenbosch and District Cricket Union on the first innings, 20–26 March 1954
Stellenbosch 116 (S Rasiet 50, T King 24, KT Poole 13; E Petersen 4/22, G Bohardien 2/14, E Abrahams 2/21, AJ Freeman 2/38) and 43/2 (E Rhoode 15*)
WPCCU 208 (AJ Freeman 52, G Abed 45, T Hendricks 19, E Petersen 17, S Abed 12*, G Bohardien 21; HO Rasiet 3/27, A Manuel 2/54)

14TH SAMCB BARNATO MEMORIAL TROPHY TOURNAMENT, DECEMBER/JANUARY 1954/55, JOHANNESBURG
Winners: Western Province

Western Province beat Hottentots Holland by 308 runs on first innings, 26–27 December 1954, Natalspruit Grounds
HH 88 (R Ingham 21, I Latief 17, A Gafieldien 11; A George 5/23, G Abed 2/15, E Petersen 2/41)
WP 396/8 (G Abed 66*, K Samsodien 60, K Abrahams 58, R Samaai 36)

Western Province beat Transvaal by 10 runs, [x], [x]
WP 116 (Y Lakay 24, G Holmes 23; G Martin 4/34, A Rubidge 4/49) and 207 (S Abed 55, Y Lakay 42, S Nackerdien 40, M du Toit 28; S Patel 2/13, P Henry 2/30, AB Davids 2/32, G Martin 2/49)
Tvl 93 (S Patel 21; A George 6/32, E Petersen 3/26) and 220 (AB Davids 78, A Rubidge 64, J Barnes 33; C Ganief 3/44, G Abed 2/31, E Petersen 2/83)

15TH SAMCB BARNATO MEMORIAL TROPHY TOURNAMENT, DECEMBER/JANUARY 1957/58, KIMBERLEY
Participants: Western Province, Eastern Province, Transvaal, Griqualand West and Eastern Transvaal
Winners: Western Province

Western Province beat Eastern Province by 8 wickets
EP 107 (MA Abrahamse 42, E Abrahamse 25; E Petersen 5/39, A George 4/29) and 102 (A Hendricks 23; A George 5/27)
WP 181/9 dec (A Hattas 70, T Behardien 69; G Connelly 7/59) and 29/2

Western Province beat Eastern Transvaal by an innings and 6 runs
WP 273 (T Behardien 73, T Hendriks 61)
ET 68 (GH Abed 6/20) and 199 (E Petersen 5/46)

Western Province beat Griqualand West by 10 wickets
GW 127 (M Richards 25, G Richards 24; A George 4/30) and 128
WP 251/5 dec (GH Abed 100, M du Toit 77, E Abrahams 36) and 5/0

Transvaal beat Western Province on first innings
WP 125 (G Abed 33; M Davids 6/37) and 269/8 dec (G Abed 70, A Hattas 55*; M Davids 5/88)
Tvl 231 (G Gallie 67) and 55/0

16TH SAMCB BARNATO MEMORIAL TROPHY TOURNAMENT, DECEMBER/JANUARY 1959/60, PORT ELIZABETH
Participants: Eastern Province, Eastern Transvaal, Griqualand West and Natal. [WP did not participate because of its opposition to continuing racial tournaments.]
Winners: Eastern Province

CHAPTER 3

Peninsula and Western Districts Cricket Board, 1923–1959

Played as Western Province under South African Independent Coloured Cricket Board
(later South African Coloured Cricket Association)

The Peninsula and Western Districts Cricket Board (PWDCB) was formed in 1923 when a section of cricketers in the Western Province decided to split from the multi-ethnic Western Province Coloured Cricket Union, which had been in existence since the 1890s.[117] They formed a separate board 'to promote and foster the Cricket of the Coloureds in the Peninsula and surrounding districts'.[118] Led by HC Abrahams of the Metropolitan and Suburban Cricket Union, the new board was clearly meant to be for Christian 'coloureds' as opposed to the Muslim (or so-called Malay) 'coloureds' and Africans.

The PWDCB had a number of regionally based unions affiliated to it. These unions in turn organised their own leagues and picked representative sides to play inter-union matches. The PWDCB's premier competitions were for the Richardson & Luyt Trophy and the Abrahams Trophy. Later there was also a knock-out competition between the champion clubs of the different unions for the Fester Trophy.

The seven unions (and their representatives) at the inception of the PWDCB were the City Cricket League (C Carew and F Netta), Metropolitan and Suburban Cricket Union (DN Adams and J Ashbury), Maitland and District Cricket Union, started in 1912 (SJ Fester and C Fortuin), Claremont and District Cricket Union, started in 1900 (C Roodt and HC Sassman), Somerset West and District Cricket Union (FJ Darius and F Paulse), Paarl Prolific and District Cricket Union (Messrs Kearns and Cupido), and Stellenbosch and District Cricket Union (Messrs Van Dyk and Scheepers).[119]

This provincial breakaway was to have important consequences. According to those on the inside of the organisation, the Cape Town grouping 'was later instrumental in forming' a separate coloureds-only national body as well.[120] In 1926, representatives from the PWDCB, Messrs Abrahams, HW Herman and W van Vrede, met in Kimberley together with like-minded people from that city and Durban to form the new South African Independent Coloured Cricket Board (SAICCB). It set itself up in opposition to the existing South African Coloured Cricket Board (SACCB), also commonly called the Barnato Board, which had been in existence since 1903. The three founding provinces were later joined by a Transvaal affiliate. Splits in cricket that had occurred on the local level in Kimberley in the 1890s, in Johannesburg in 1913 and in Cape Town in 1923, as a result of cultural and religious differences, now became institutionalised nationally as well.[121]

Having broken away from the old SACCB, the new SAICCB started its own provincial tournaments. The headquarters were in Kimberley and HJ Tobin was elected first president of the South African Independent Coloured Cricket Board.[122] Tobin was a member of a prominent Cape Town political family involved in the political mobilisation of the coloured communities in the city. John Tobin was one of the founders of the APO, for many years the most prominent coloured political organisation. In 1905 Tobin and the APO president, W Collins, were expelled for dividing the membership by pushing (white) party political agendas, and Dr Abdullah Abdurahman took over the reins, starting his 35-year term as APO president. For two decades Tobin and Abdurahman were political adversaries. These different political traditions, overlaid by religious and ethnic differences, seemingly also spilled over into sport and had at least some influence on the formation of the SAICCB.[123]

The provincial leadership of the PWDCB remained very consistent. HC Abrahams was still president after 15 years in 1938. AA Arendse was treasurer from the board's inception until his death 30 years later in 1953.[124] The rest of the first executive consisted of G Fox (vice-president), F Seale (secretary), and JJ Marinus (assistant secretary).

The PWDCB combined team played as Western Province in the new SAICCB's provincial tournaments for the Sir David Harris Trophy and was always the team to beat. Initially, however, it did not dominate the inter-provincial tournaments like its Barnato counterpart. Of the five tournaments organised in the 13 seasons before the outbreak of World War Two, the first four all produced different winners. Natal won first time round in 1926/27; Western Province took the trophy in 1928/29, Eastern Province in 1930/31 and Griqualand West in 1933/34. We have been unable to find details for these tournaments but the very first tournament was apparently decentralised with matches played on a home and away basis, while the other three were centralised. The matches in 1933/34 were played over two days, which seems to have been the norm in these tournaments, if reports from later years are anything to go by.

The fifth Sir David Harris tournament was not held until the 1937/38 season in Port Elizabeth, and by then six provinces participated in the 15-match cricket week. The newcomers were South Western Districts and Eastern Province.[125] Western Province needed to win the last match against Transvaal to take the trophy and it turned out to be a thrilling affair. 'Seven runs were required [chasing 187] when the last Transvaler strode to the crease. Archie Sassman sent down the first ball of the new over. It flashed past the wicketkeeper, A.W. Adams, on the leg side for three byes. The atmosphere was charged. The crowd held their breath. One boundary hit would suffice. Archie ran up to the wicket, sent down a straight one to J. Jordaan, who snicked the ball, which was deflected off the wicketkeeper's glove into the safe hand of Jimmy Herman and the match was over ... Province had beaten Transvaal and won the Tournament Championship by the narrow margin of three runs. The crowd cheered wildly and rushed onto the field to congratulate the victorious Province players.'[126]

The star of the 1938 team was C Adams, the number three batsman from Heatherdale CC. He topped the batting averages, scored the highest score in the tournament (120), and also took the most wickets, opening the bowling.[127] The victorious team was given a reception befitting their achievement on their return to Cape Town. It was reported that 'The executive of the Union will entertain the teams at a breakfast which will be partaken of at Gool's Hostel, Leeuven Street, at 9.30 a.m. Mr H.C. Abrahams, president of the Union will preside.'[128]

In 1938, the SAICCB mandated Abrahams and the Cape Town-based PWDCB officials to approach the white SACA with a view to organising a match for a SAICCB side against the MCC during the 1938/39 tour (when the timeless test was played).[129] Nothing came of this, but clearly there was confidence within SAICCB ranks.[130]

World War Two badly affected the SAICCB's functioning, as it did most other national sporting associations. It took another nine seasons before the next Sir David Harris competition was held in 1946/47. Western Province now started dominating, winning seven out of the eight post-war trophies of the SAICCB, which changed its name to the South African Coloured Cricket Association (SACCA) in 1948.

This first post-war competition in 1946/47 was decentralised, with two-day matches ('limited to 16 hours per match') in Cape Town, Wellington, Port Elizabeth and Kimberley. During the season's finale over the Easter weekend, a record crowd 'thronged' the Kimberley Athletic Club grounds to see Griquas achieve an unexpected victory by two wickets to force a three-way tie for the Sir David Harris Trophy. The loyal Cape Town press reported that the visitors were at a disadvantage because they had to start the match shortly after disembarking from a 33-hour train journey.[131]

The only survivor from the 1937/38 tournament in the 1946/47 PWDCB Western Province team was the ever-reliable D Hurling, who took nine wickets against Griquas, bowling unchanged from one end in the second innings for figures of 16.5-5-39-5. The team was captained by Wally Hendricks, with the upcoming star Basil Waterwich as his deputy.[132] Waterwich hit two half-centuries in the match, including a six which 'landed in the midst of a circus arena'. A reporter, surely employing poetic licence, noted that 'one ball was actually caught by an elephant, and there was great fun as the Griqua fielder tried to recover the ball'.[133] Basil Waterwich's father, JCG Waterwich, had started playing in the City and Suburban leagues in 1898, and Basil himself became provincial and national captain and a prominent administrator, exemplifying how steeped in cricket tradition Cape Town was.[134]

In 1948/49 Western Province won, exacting revenge on Griquas by giving them a 216-run thumping. A promising youngster called Basil D'Oliveira made his debut for the champions, scoring 48 not out against Griquas. D'Oliveira went on to become the outstanding SACBOC player of his generation. Starting senior league at 14, 'Dolly' scored 82 club and representative hundreds between 1947 and 1960. His achievements included:

- 155 not out and two other hundreds in the Sir David Harris Trophy tournaments of SACCA;
- Highest individual innings (153), run-scorer (572 at 57.20) and best tournament average of 91.00 in the SACBOC inter-race tournaments;
- Average of 55.87 in SACBOC 'test' matches in 1956 and 1958 and an average of 46.28 on the East Africa tour;
- In the 1970s, he also hit the second highest score – 182 after Rohan Kanhai (188*) – and averaged 95.33 in SACBOC three-day first-class cricket in 1972–1974.[135]

Basil D'Oliveira, of course, went on to achieve cricketing immortality as an England player involved in one of international cricket's greatest dramas in the 1960s.[136]

After the 1950/51 Christmas tournament in Johannesburg, the first-ever SACCA side was selected to play in SACBOC's first inter-race tournament. The veteran D Hurling, the only centurion, was elected captain. Four other Western Province players received national honours as well, namely AJ Bell, D Joshua, L Maclons and B Waterwich.

The SACCA team won two of the four inter-race tournaments in the 1950s. It was probably the strongest of the four bodies for black cricketers in that decade. This was also demonstrated by the fact that most players picked for the combined SACBOC Springboks from 1956 to 1958 under the captaincy of Basil D'Oliveira were from SACCA and particularly its Western Province affiliate. The last two provincial tournaments in 1956/57 and 1957/58 underlined Western Province's dominance. Boasting players of the calibre of Basil D'Oliveira, Cecil Abrahams, 'Coetie' Neethling, Owen Williams, Sidney Solomon, Basil Witten and Adam Sabotker, they secured nine victories by an innings and one by the margin of nine wickets in ten matches.

On the local level in Cape Town, Peninsula and Western Districts held inter-union matches for the Richardson & Luyt and Abrahams trophies. These also served as trials for the regular Sir David Harris tournaments. There were altogether 50 'teams' in the PWDCB in the early 1950s and the champion clubs in each of the unions also played a knock-out tournament against one another for the Fester Trophy. The champions in 1952/53 were Avenirs CC from the Maitland-Parow Union; Oaks CC from the Somerset West Union; and Hand and Heart CC from the Cape and District Cricket Union in Claremont (in existence since 1900); St Augustine's CC from Metropolitan and District Cricket Union in Athlone, and Green Roses CC from Paarl Prolific and District Cricket Union. (The City League Cricket Union champions were not listed.)[137]

The PWDCB went out of existence after the formation in 1959 of the non-racial Western Province Cricket Board, which united the different bodies amongst disenfranchised cricketers in Cape Town.[138]

3.1 Peninsula and Western Districts Cricket Board National Players (SAICCB / SACCA), 1926/27–1958/59[139]

South African Coloured Cricket Association, 1950/51–1957/58

Abrahams, CJ	1952/53
Bell, AJ	1950/51, 1952/53
D'Oliveira, BL	1952/53, 1954/55 captain, 1957/58 captain
Erickson, B	1957/58
Hinrichsen, D	1957/58
Hurling, D	1950/51 captain
January, P	1957/58
Joshua, D	1950/51
Lakay, H 'Tim'	1954/55
Lakay, N	1957/58

Maclons, L	1950/51
Neethling, JJ 'Coetie'	1954/55, 1957/58
Poole, C	1957/58
Raziet, S 'Laam'	1957/58
Sabotker, A	1957/58 vice-captain
Solomon, SN	1957/58
Southgate, I	1957/58
Sylvester, D	1952/53
Waterwich, B	1950/51, 1952/53 captain
Williams, OL	1957/58
Witten, B	1954/55, 1957/58

South African Cricket Board of Control, 1956/57–1958/59

Abrahams, CJ	1956/57, 1958/59
Bell, AJ	1956/57
D'Oliveira, BL	1956/57 captain, 1958/59 captain
Neethling, JJ 'Coetie'	1958/59
Raziet, S 'Laam'	1956/57, 1958/59
Solomon, SN	1958/59
Williams, OL	1956/57, 1958/59

3.2 Peninsula and Western Districts Cricket Board Players, 1926/27–1958/59[140]

Abrahams, CJ	1952/53, 1956/57, 1957/58
Abrahams, M	1937/38
Adams, AW	1937/38 captain
Adams, C	1937/38
Adams, ED	1937/38
Anthony, A	1957/58
Bell, AJ	1950/51, 1952/53
Bell, W	1954/55
Botha, M	1937/38
Carelse, H	1957/58
Daniels, E	1952/53
Darius, FJ	1937/38
Davids, J	1946/47
Davids, [x]	1948/49
D'Oliveira, BL	1948/49, 1952/53, 1954/55, 1956/57, 1957/58
Erickson, B	1957/58
Fairbairn, W	1952/53, 1954/55
February, A	1937/38
February, V	1946/47
Harlet, P	1956/57
Hector, C	1946/47
Heeger, A	1957/58

Hendricks, B	1946/47
Hendricks, W	1946/47 captain
Herman, D	1956/57
Hermans, J	1937/38
Hinrichsen, D	1957/58
Hurling, D	1937/38, 1946/47
January, P	1957/58
Joshua, D	1950/51
Joshua, R	1946/47, 1948/49
Lakay, H	1952/53, 1954/55
Lakay, N	1957/58
Latief, I	1956/57
Lodewyk, E	1937/38
Maclons, L	1946/47, 1948/49, 1950/51, 1952/53, 1954/55
Maclons, R	1956/57
Miller, W	1946/47, 1954/55
Neethling, JJ	1952/53, 1954/55, 1956/57, 1957/58
Petersen, C	1937/38
Poole, C	1957/58
Ravens, C	1946/47
Ravens, N	1946/47
Raziet, C	1957/58
Raziet, O	1946/47
Raziet, S	1956/57, 1957/58
Rutgers, G	1937/38
Sabotker, A	1952/53, 1954/55, 1956/57, 1957/58
Sassman, A	1937/38
Sedgwick, A	1937/38
Siljeur, C	1946/47
Solomon, SN	1956/57, 1957/58
Southgate, I	1957/58
Sylvester, D	1952/53
Thomas, A	1950/51
Thomas, P	1957/58
Tobin, R	1946/47
Truter, J	1952/53, 1954/55
Van Graan, C	1948/49
Waterwich, B	1946/47, 1948/49, 1950/51, 1952/53, 1954/55
Williams, OL	1956/57, 1957/58
Witten, B	1952/53, 1954/55, 1956/57, 1957/58
Yon, W	1957/58

3.3 Peninsula and Western Districts Cricket Board Trophies in the Sir David Harris Tournaments, 1926/27–1957/58[141]

Season	Winners
1926/27	Natal
1928/29	Western Province
1930/31	Eastern Province
1933/34	Griqualand West
1937/38	Western Province
1946/47	Western Province/Eastern Province/Griqualand West
1948/49	Western Province
1950/51	Western Province/Transvaal (shared)
1952/53	Eastern Province
1954/55	Western Province
1956/57	Western Province
1957/58	Western Province

The South African Coloured Cricket Association was formed by cricketers who broke away from the Barnato group in 1926. Until 1948 it was known as the South African Independent Coloured Cricket Board.

3.4 Peninsula and Western Districts Cricket Board Scores, 1926/27–1957/58[142]

1ST SAICCB SIR DAVID HARRIS TROPHY TOURNAMENT (DECENTRALISED) (REPORTED TO HAVE BEEN PLAYED ON A HOME AND AWAY BASIS, 1926/27)
Participants: Natal, Western Province, Transvaal and Griqualand West.
Winners: Natal
[no details available]

2ND SAICCB SIR DAVID HARRIS TROPHY TOURNAMENT, DECEMBER/JANUARY 1928/29, KIMBERLEY
Winners: Western Province
[no details available]

3RD SAICCB SIR DAVID HARRIS TROPHY TOURNAMENT, DECEMBER/JANUARY 1930/31, CAPE TOWN OR JOHANNESBURG
Winners: Eastern Province
[no details available]

4TH SAICCB SIR DAVID HARRIS TROPHY TOURNAMENT, DECEMBER/JANUARY 1933/34, CAPE TOWN OR JOHANNESBURG
Winners: Griqualand West
[no details available]

5TH SAICCB SIR DAVID HARRIS TROPHY TOURNAMENT, DECEMBER/JANUARY 1937/38, PORT ELIZABETH[143]
Participants: Western Province, Eastern Province, Transvaal, Natal, Griqualand West and South Western Districts.
Winners: Western Province

Western Province beat Natal by an innings and 41 runs, 27-28 December 1937, Pirates Ground, PE
WP 175 (J Herman 73, C Peterson, 27, A Sedgwick 25; I Jacobs 6/30)
Ntl 57 (J Mentjies 13, M Botha 3/10; C Adams 3/18, D Hurling 3/20) and 77 (E Montgomery 30; M Abrahams 7/28)

Western Province beat Griqualand West by 223 runs
WP 156 (AW Adams 67; H Jampies, 4/42, L Crowie 3/18) and 351/8 dec (AW Adams 120*, M Botha 64, J Herman 60)
GW 99 (A Crowie 27; D Hurling 4/37, C Adams 3/26) and 185 (no scores available)

Western Province beat Eastern Province by 81 runs
WP 104 (H Abrahams 23, A February 21; EB Meyer 5/28) and 156 (C Adams 46, D Hurling 38, E Adams 25; EW Meyer 3/31)
EP 50 (J Noordien 15; D Hurling 6/26) and 129 (C Adams 5/35)

Western Province beat South Western Districts by 10 wickets
SWD 91 (J Carelse 39, W Williams 28; G Rutgers 5/23) and 123 (J Carelse 48, J Koert 30; E Adams 4/69, A Sassman 3/15, D Hurling 3/17)
WP 201 (C Adams 51, C Petersen 31, AW Adams 31; J Koert 5/46) and 14/0

Western Province beat Transvaal by 3 runs
WP 171 (M Abrahams 27, C Petersen 24; G Carr 6/53) and 161 (A Sassman 40, C Petersen 36; F Greybe 3/34, M Rose 3/46)
Tvl 146 (J Cornelius 42, C Jousten 21; C Adams 5/26) and 183 (M Rose 60, E Peters 38*; D Hurling 5/47, A Sassman 3/51)

6TH SAICCB COMPETITION FOR THE SIR DAVID HARRIS TROPHY, 1946/47 (DECENTRALISED)
Participants: Western Province, Eastern Province, Griqualand West, Transvaal and Boland.
Winners: Western Province/Eastern Province/Griqualand West

Western Province beat Boland by an innings and 113 runs, 14 and 16 December 1946, Wellington[144]
WP 213 (D Hurling 49, W Hendricks 36, B Waterwich 33)
Bol 45 (L Maclons 6/16, D Hurling 4/29) and 55 (John Adonis 23; N Ravens 5/12, L Maclons 3/11, G Hector 2/28)

Western Province beat Eastern Province by an innings and 48 runs, 18-19 December 1946, Rosmead, Cape Town[145]
WP 255 (R Tobin 76, C Ravens 47, G Hendricks 21; A Ryan 5/70, S Finnis 2/11)
EP 54 (J Nordien 32*; D Hurling 7/21, L Maclons 3/30) and 153 (J Noordien 87, S Finnis 34; B Waterwich 4/18, L Maclons 2/35)

Western Province beat Transvaal by 314 runs, 20-21 December 1946, Rosmead, Cape Town[146]
WP 261 (R Tobin 62, L Maclons 52, O Raziet 50, D Hurling 30) and 245 (W Hendricks 65, L Maclons 62; AV Hoskins 4/52)
Tvl 105 (AV Hoskins 26; L Maclons 3/39, W Hendricks 2/8, D Hurling 2/20) and 87 (C September 26)

Griqualand West beat Western Province by 2 wickets, 12 and 14 April 1947, Kimberley Athletic Club[147]
WP 175 (B Waterwich 59, D Hurling 32; AG Sexaine 3/10, A Reed 2/20) and 191 (B Waterwich 50*, R Joshua 44; AG Sexaine 3/39, A Reed 3/54)
GW [no details available]

7TH SACCA SIR DAVID HARRIS TROPHY TOURNAMENT, DECEMBER/JANUARY 1948/49, CAPE TOWN
Winners: Western Province

Western Province beat Griqualand West by 216 runs
WP 261 (L Maclons 59, BL D'Oliveira 48*, C van Graan 46, R Joshua 45; A Sexaine 4/47, N Kester 3/42) and 194/7 dec (B Waterwich 86, Davids 38, L Maclons 21; N Kester 2/31, Jampies 2/56)
GW 183 (L Crowie 83, A Barron 25; A Scheepers 3/37, L Maclons 2/34, D Hurling 2/46) and 56 (Ravens 3/12, A Scheepers 3/12, D Hurling 2/13)

Western Province beat Eastern Province by an innings and 9 runs
EP 137 and 60
WP 206 (L Maclons 82)

8TH SACCA SIR DAVID HARRIS TROPHY TOURNAMENT, DECEMBER/JANUARY 1950/51, JOHANNESBURG
Participants: Western Province, Transvaal, Eastern Province and Griqualand West.
Winners: Western Province and Transvaal

Transvaal beat Western Province on first innings
Tvl 189 (P Sampson 51*; A Thomas 3/42) and 124/5
WP 151 (D Joshua 77; CA Meyer 4/26, AV Hoskins 4/42)

Western Province beat Griqualand West on first innings
GW 55 (B Waterwich 5/25) and 161 (L Maclons 6/30)
WP 155

Western Province beat Eastern Province by an innings and 5 runs
EP 54 (J Clarke 22*; B Waterwich 7/21, L Maclons 3/33) and 162 (L Rowan 54, J Clarke 35; L Maclons 4/10)
WP 221/8 dec (D Joshua 43*, AJ Bell 40, B Waterwich 37; L Rowan 3/31, J France 3/45)

9TH SACCA SIR DAVID HARRIS TROPHY TOURNAMENT, DECEMBER/JANUARY 1952/53, PORT ELIZABETH
Participants: Eastern Province, Western Province, Transvaal, Natal and Griqualand West.
Winners: Eastern Province

Western Province beat Griqualand West by 134 runs
WP 97 (B Waterwich 54; J Niekerk 6/36) and 299 (C Siljeur 77, BL D'Oliveira 40, B Waterwich 35*, E Daniels 31; A Sexaine 7/64)
GW 150 (J McAnda 98; L Maclons 3/26, B Waterwich 3/36) and 112 (J McAnda 39; CJ Abrahams 7/29)

Western Province beat Transvaal by 9 wickets
WP 199 (C Siljeur 64, W Miller 47, B Waterwich 46; W Amsterdam 5/32) and 38/1
Tvl 140 (E Rosenberg 70; CJ Abrahams 3/18, D Sylvester 3/22) and 95 (D Sylvester 3/34)

Western Province beat Natal by an innings and 90 runs
WP 307/9 dec (CJ Abrahams 53, AJ Bell 52, E Daniels 47, B Waterwich 39, J Gordon 33*; D Davis 4/103, R Montgomery 3/88)
Ntl 153 (S Kirsten 70, R Richards 50; D Sylvester 3/21) and 64 (CJ Abrahams 4/35, D Sylvester 3/21)

Eastern Province beat Western Province by 31 runs
EP 113 (E Clarke 36*, L Rowan 28; L Maclons 4/38, CJ Abrahams 2/11) and 210 (A Philander 45, J Finnis 36, R Simon 29, G Hendricks 27; B Waterwich 6/47)
WP 93 (AJ Bell 31, L Maclons 25; R Simon 5/27, A Philander 3/33, E Clarke 2/10) and 199 (L Maclons 60, B Waterwich 25, E Daniels 22, I Bowles 3/26, A Philander 3/74, R Simon 2/36)

10TH SACCA SIR DAVID HARRIS TROPHY TOURNAMENT, DECEMBER/JANUARY 1954/55, DURBAN
Participants: Western Province, Eastern Province, Transvaal, Griqualand West and Natal.
Winners: Western Province

Western Province beat Griqualand West on first innings
GW 168 (L Herman 48, E September 29, J McAnda 23, J Niekerk 21, C Jacobs 21; H Lakay 5/23) and 178 (L Herman 54, R Crowie 22*)
WP 187 (L Maclons 67, W Fairbairn 44, BL D'Oliveira 31; J Niekerk 6/71) and 119/8 (W Fairbairn 59, L Maclons 25; R Crowie 3/11)

Western Province beat Transvaal by 107 runs
WP 129 (B Waterwich 26, JJ Neethling 24*; AJ Bell 6/44, C September 4/45) and 238 (BL D'Oliveira 155*, W Fairbairn 25; CA Meyer 4/47, AJ Bell 3/58)
Tvl 110 (CA Meyer 37; L Maclons 3/18, H Lakay 3/24, A Sabotker 2/31) and 150 (E Rosenberg 56, CA Meyer 26; JJ Neethling 6/49, W Bell 2/29)

Western Province beat Natal by an innings and 67 runs
Ntl 168 (S Kirsten 69; B Waterwich 4/33) and 81 (W Bell 5/51, H Lakay 4/21)
WP 316 (B Witten 127*, BL D'Oliveira 112, B Waterwich 48; J Jaffar 4/38, C Dutlow 4/49)

Western Province beat Eastern Province by an innings and 53 runs
EP 91 (H Clarke 33; JJ Neethling 4/20) and 96 (J Finnis 37*; H Lakay 6/26)
WP 240 (J Truter 74, JJ Neethling 66; R Simon 5/71)

11TH SACCA SIR DAVID HARRIS TROPHY TOURNAMENT, DECEMBER/JANUARY 1956/57, KIMBERLEY
Participants: Western Province, Transvaal, Eastern Province, Natal, Griqualand West and Orange Free State.
Winners: Western Province

Western Province beat Transvaal by an innings and 102 runs
WP 237 (SN Solomon 70*, R Maclons 40, S Raziet 40, JJ Neethling 32; D Amsterdam 5/89, R May 3/45)
Tvl 75 (P Irwin 23; JJ Neethling 4/18, A Sabotker 3/24, OL Williams 2/9) and 60 (SN Solomon 7/21, JJ Neethling 2/14)

Western Province beat Griqualand West by an innings and 203 runs
GW 65 (OL Williams 5/21, A Sabotker 2/17, JJ Neethling 2/22) and 51 (JJ Neethling 5/11)
WP 319 (BL D'Oliveira 112*, CJ Abrahams 70, B Witten 25; J Niekerk 4/78, R Williams 2/48)

Western Province beat Natal by 9 wickets
Ntl 241 (J Jaffar 54, R Montgomery 35, D Davis 26, N Williamson 24, N Jacobs 21, A Abrahams 20; JJ Neethling 6/76, A Sabotker 3/73) and 162 (S Kirsten 41, R Montgomery 30, A Rose 27, A Abrahams 25; SN Solomon 4/44, R Maclons 2/18, A Sabotker 2/53)
WP 342 (JJ Neethling 109, D Herman 102, P Harley 53, R Maclons 38; A Rose 4/64, D Davis 2/72) and 66/1 (SN Solomon 28*, D Herman 28*)

Western Province beat Eastern Province by an innings and 188 runs
EP 100 (E Clarke 28; OL Williams 4/31, A Sabotker 4/36) and 105 (G Potgieter 39; I Latief 5/38)
WP 393 (CJ Abrahams 113, SN Solomon 82, BL D'Oliveira 71, OL Williams 36*; R Simon 4/66, P van Vuuren 3/45, A Philander 3/156)

Western Province beat Orange Free State by an innings and 195 runs
WP 282/9 dec (B Witten 70, P Harley 61, SN Solomon 51, I Latief 45; G Murison 4/89, De Koeker 2/49)
OFS 26 (A Sabotker 8/14, CJ Abrahams 2/4) and 61 (OL Williams 4/14, SN Solomon 4/20)

12TH SACCA SIR DAVID HARRIS TROPHY TOURNAMENT, DECEMBER/JANUARY 1957/58, CAPE TOWN
Participants: Western Province, Eastern Province, Transvaal, Griqualand West, Natal, and South Western Districts.
Winners: Western Province

Western Province beat Transvaal by an innings and 220 runs
WP 355/6 dec (S Raziet 108, CJ Abrahams 70, P Thomas 63*, C Pool 44, H Carelse 32, B Witten 23; R May 4/128)
Tvl 70 (E Rosenberg 24; OL Williams 6/19, W Yon 3/17) and 65 (P Sampson 14; A Sabotker 4/3, OL Williams 2/33)

Western Province beat Natal by an innings and 111 runs
WP 205 (JJ Neethling 63, A Anthony 34, W Yon 29, CJ Abrahams 26; A Rose 5/52, M Boomgaard 2/8, D Davis 2/60)
Ntl 37 (OL Williams 6/16, JJ Neethling 4/2) and 57 (R Easthorpe 15; CJ Abrahams 6/8, JJ Neethling 2/5)

Western Province beat South Western Districts by an innings and 133 runs
WP 202/8 dec (A Heeger 76, A Anthony 40, C Poole 30, BL D'Oliveira 25; C du Plessis 3/44, H Carelse 2/13, J van Wyk 2/36)
SWD 44 (A Sabotker 5/19, CJ Abrahams 2/6, A Heeger 2/17) and 25 (OL Williams 5/13, A Sabotker 4/10)

Western Province beat Eastern Province by an innings and 67 runs
WP 227 (CJ Abrahams 110, BL D'Oliveira 51, A Sabotker 27; A Philander 5/102, D Sinjanie 3/67)
EP 63 (OL Williams 5/21, JJ Neethling 3/18) and 97 (G Hendricks 44, P Snyman 21; W Yon 5/19, A Sabotker 3/38)

Western Province beat Griqualand West by an innings and 282 runs
GW 46 (C Jacobs 16, L Herman 15; CJ Abrahams 5/5, OL Williams 3/6) and 56 (OL Williams 5/24, A Sabotker 4/27)
WP 384 (H Carelse 129, CJ Abrahams 67, JJ Neethling 60*, BL D'Oliveira 48, S Raziet 44, P September 5/102, C Abrahams 2/81)

CHAPTER 4

Western Province Bantu (later African) Cricket Union, 1928–1977

Affiliated to the South African Bantu (later African) Cricket Board[148]

Though African cricketers have always been pushed to the margins in Cape Town, they have been present from the beginnings. Sons of chiefs first played the game at Zonnebloem College in the 1860s,[149] and by the 1890s there were eight clubs in Cape Town.[150] After the formation of a 'native location' at Ndabeni in 1902, 'Malay' teams came to play, but this was not looked on favourably by the authorities, who were intent on enforcing the segregation of Africans in the city.[151]

Until the 1920s African clubs were members of the Metropolitan Cricket Union. But, in 1923 the government passed the Urban Areas Act which deepened segregation in the cities and led to the creation of Langa township in 1925. As a result of the momentum towards segregation and the unhappiness amongst African cricketers who felt 'they were not getting a fair deal both on the field of play and in administrative matters' in the 'coloured' leagues, the Western Province Bantu Cricket Union (WPBCU) was formed in 1928. BM Cebindevu was the first president and Mr Nyangiwe was the first chairman. There were five affiliated clubs, namely Home Bachelors, Oriental, Far East, Wanderers and Great Powers.[152]

The WPBCU was also one of the founder members of the South African Bantu Cricket Board (SABCB) in 1932. African cricketers followed the 'coloureds' in breaking away from the old multi-ethnic South African Coloured Cricket Board with its Barnato tournaments. The new SABCB started the Chamber of Mines inter-provincial tournaments, playing for the Native Recruiting Corporation (NRC) Trophy. Between 1933 and 1975, some 23 of these tournaments were held.

Western Province, captained and managed by P Walton Mama, were runners-up in the first Chamber of Mines tournament in 1933. They achieved the highest team and individual scores in their match against Griquas, with 368 for 6 declared, including centuries by SM Fongqo (121) and SM Ndlwana (105).[153] The standards were said to be high because they had 'graduated at the Coloured Union'. Western Province won the NRC Trophy for the first time in East London in the 1947/48 season under the captaincy of SD Dyira. A 'very young team' captained by 'Pat' Cossie repeated this achievement in the 1952/53 tournament held at home in Cape Town and again in 1954/55.

The Cape Town tournament involved 'ten days of continuous cricket without a break' at the City and Suburban Grounds in Mowbray, generally reserved for 'non-white' sportsmen. In 1952 the South African Bantu Cricket Board headquarters were moved to Cape Town on a rotational basis. The Western Province president, ID Mkize, principal of Langa High School (after whom the ID Mkize High School is named) became president of the SABCB, with 'Pat' Cossie as the secretary. The provincial headquarters were Langa High School. The WPBCU executive, which organised the tournament, consisted of ID Mkize (president), JZ Fuku (vice-president), WB Lubulwana (chairman), J Mazula (vice-chairman), BPB 'Pat' Cossie (secretary and match secretary), BT Bhuda (assistant secretary), SG Magodla (treasurer), Alex M Mashumpela (auditor) and VI Magodla and AI Bhuttie (trustees).[154]

In the late 1950s, Western Province went into something of a slump. The province lost the top all-rounder, Ben Malamba, the star African player in the country, and missed both the 1956/57 and 1958/59 inter-provincial tournaments. *Imvo Zabantsundu* reported that there was 'deadlock within the officials' and dissatisfaction was so high that Malamba (after his return from a temporary sojourn in Natal) and others left to play in one of the other boards in the province. It was suggested that Hlubi Mvinjelwa and his executive 'will have to pull up their socks'.[155]

From 1959 to 1961 all the old racially based national cricket bodies from the disenfranchised population united under the South African Cricket Board of Control (SACBOC) to start a new era of non-racial cricket. The plan was for the different racial bodies to dissolve and play under one national board and for the different provincial units in each area to form one provincial board. The SABCB initially supported these moves and, therefore, no Chamber of Mines tournaments took place between 1958/59 and 1964/65. Some African players from the Eastern Cape and Transvaal participated in the first non-racial inter-provincial tournaments organised by SACBOC in 1961/62 and 1963/64. In line with these new moves, the WPBCB also initiated plans to dissolve and play as Langa Cricket Union in the new, non-racial Western Province Cricket Board.

However, from 1964/65 a section of the old Bantu Board withdrew from SACBOC and reconstituted itself as a separate racial body. The board, now called the South African African (rather than Bantu) Cricket Board, continued with its separate inter-provincial tournaments and started rebuilding itself. The Western Province African Cricket Board aligned itself with the separatist moves of the mother body and gave up on the idea of joining the Western Province Cricket Board (WPCB). The WPCB's historian claims the African players did not join because they felt their administration was inadequate to meet the WPCB's standards.[156] Another version is that the Africans were unhappy with how the new unity was being implemented. For example, many migrant workers who had to work on Saturdays preferred to play on Sundays, but the WPCB did not play Sunday games.[157] Whatever the reason, African cricketers in the Western Province, like their reconstituted mother body, remained aloof from the new WPCB and once again participated in Africans-only inter-provincial tournaments. About ten of these tournaments took place between the mid-1960s and mid-1970s, but unfortunately we have found no records for them.

Concomitant with the withdrawal of African cricketers from the non-racial alliance of disenfranchised cricketers under SACBOC and the WPCB was their increasing co-operation with and reliance on the mining houses, the government and the whites-only South African Cricket Association (SACA) for resources and opportunities. Particularly after the D'Oliveira affair in 1968, the apartheid establishment made serious efforts to find black allies in order to avoid international isolation and a policy of 'multi-national' sport was announced – a much trumpeted 'new way' aimed at window-dressing the apartheid idea of segregation and separate 'groups'.[158]

The poorly resourced South African African Cricket Board now entered into an alliance with the whites-only body. The local state and white cricket bodies started providing help with coaching courses and facilities. One of the results of this new partnership was the beginning of annual inter-provincial John Passmore tournaments for schools from 1971 onwards. In 1973 a national African team toured Rhodesia (Zimbabwe) with the help of the white SACA and started playing in SACA-organised fixtures against invitation touring teams from England.[159]

A survey conducted by SAACB in 1967 showed Western Province had nine clubs and 500 players.[160] The champion club in 1966, Home Boy CC, had 12 Western Province players in its ranks, including William Magitshima and 'Cannon' Ziba (both were picked for the national team), Ashton Dunjwa, Ben Malamba and Hlubi Mvinjelwa. Following the national trend, local African cricketers in the late 1960s approached the white Western Province Cricket Club for help. This led to a relationship with the club and, in particular, one of its officials, John Passmore, who made it his life's work to support local African communities through cricket. Through his business, cricket and political connections he raised funds, helped upgrade facilities and, eventually, set up the John Passmore Trust. This co-operation led in turn to the first John Passmore Schools tournament, held in Cape Town in January 1971. Here a South African Schools team was selected to play against the Western Province senior team. Local player Stanford Somyo won the award for the best batsman in the tournament. By 1974 the Langa ground had been upgraded and became the venue for a match between the Derrick Robins touring team from England and the South African African team.[161] Langa CC became the centre of cricket in the local townships.

During the 1970s Ashton Dunjwa of Western Province, who was heavily involved in the discredited 'homeland' and local government structures, became president of the South African African Cricket Board. Under his leadership, this board (and thus the affiliated Western Province African Cricket Union) went out of existence in 1977 when it merged with the whites-only SACA to form the new South African Cricket Union (SACU).

Most African players with a base in Langa Cricket Club now joined the formerly all-white Western Province Cricket Union (WPCU) and played in its lower leagues and youth competitions, such as the Passmore and Nuffield weeks. Langa CC played its first well-publicised league match at home against the neighbouring white Pinelands CC in October 1976. The mainstay and 'father' of the club was Mathemba Ndlumbini. Together with such people as HH Zibi (grandfather of Thami Tsolekile) and 'Swift' Mama (son of P Walton Mama, first WPBCU captain in 1932), Mr Ndlumbini was one of the few Langa 'old-timers' who stayed involved in the 1970s and 1980s. He worked tirelessly to keep the club going. Stanford Somyo and 'Killer' Mshumpela were among the top players entering 'normal' cricket. Solomon Fassie (half-brother of the famous singer Brenda Fassie) scored the first century for Langa in the WPCU leagues. Other players to emerge in the late 1970s and 1980s included the sons of the legendary Ben Malamba – competitive and talented Ben junior, Rodney and Basil – as well as Junior Tengo Sokanyile, Ezra Cagwe, Victor Tyutyu, wicketkeeper Mtunzi Fezi and Edward Cuba. By 1983 the standard of the young Langa cricketers was such that the Passmore team beat the Western Province Nuffield team with Gary Kirsten in its ranks.

Solomon Makosana, a school principal and inspector, became the most prominent new-generation Langa administrator in the 1980s – he learned his cricket as a youngster while selling meat at the migrant workers' hostels in Makaza. Supported by the Passmore Trust and white cricketers, Langa became a key development area for the Western Province Cricket Union. The former England cricketer Bob Woolmer also helped establish a strong hockey club in the township. Top young cricketers who emerged later from Langa included all-rounder Morgan Mfobo, the first African player to make the South African schools team after unity in 1992 (together with Lulama Masikizana of Eastern Province), opening bowler Freeman Simelela, Ronald Masinda and, of course, the double cricket and hockey international, Thami Tsolekile. (For a history of Langa Cricket Club, see J Young, *Langa Cricket Club: 21 Years* (Langa CC, 1997).)

Veteran cricketer Ezra Cagwe explains that while the Langa and Nyanga clubs that joined the formerly white WPCU included some members supporting the banned ANC and PAC during those politically tumultuous years, '*labelandela nje isport*' – 'they just followed sport', also watching multi-racial boxing and other competitions.[162]

A minority of African players in Cape Town chose not to go the same route. Some activists from Luyolo Community Centre in Section 3, Gugulethu, formed the Luyolo Cricket Club in 1977 and subsequently linked up with the 'non-racial', non-collaborationist Western Province Cricket Board (WPCB) instead. In 1979, they were joined by non-racial rugby players from the SARU- and SACOS-affiliated Western Province Rugby Board, who 'played cricket as a summer code' for Luyolo. The club also went on a tour to the Eastern Cape, which was the heartland of non-racial sport. The new club drew its support mainly from Gugulethu, which was known for its militancy in the struggle years. Some Langa CC players who lived in Gugulethu were 'politically converted' and joined Luyolo. The club actively supported 'the struggle' and the principle of 'no normal sport in an abnormal society'. Luyolo CC leaders included Gerald Mxolisi Njengele, a school principal and son of the leading black rugby 'Springbok', Henry Ngxatha Njengele. After going into decline Luyolo CC was resuscitated again in 1989 at a meeting at the Community Centre in Section C in Gugulethu called by Ngconde Balfour, who became Minister of Sport after democracy.[163] He was on the run from the police in the Eastern Cape and had moved to Cape Town. The club was used as a 'political cover' by Balfour and other cadres such as Albert Tyulu, Vuyani Ngcuka, his brother Bulelani Ngcuka (the constitutional lawyer who later became head of the National Prosecuting Authority) and Ben Tengimfene, a school headmaster, former Border Cricket president and Robben Island prisoner, whose five children were all in exile. After unity, Luyolo CC became Gugulethu CC.[164]

4.1 Western Province Bantu (later African) Cricket Union National Players (SABCB / SACBOC / SAACB), 1933/34–1974/75[165]

South African Bantu (later African) Cricket Board

Magitshima, WV	1966/67, 1974/75
Magodla, TH	1966/67
Malamba, BN	1950/51, 1952/53, 1954/55
Mawu, H	1952/53, 1954/55
Mshumpela, AM	1952/53, 1957/58
Mvinjelwa, H	1954/55[166]
Scott, CM	1950/51
Sihawu, GG	1966/67
Somyo, S	1974/75, 1975/76
Zibi, GM 'Cannon'	1966/67 vice-captain

South African Cricket Board of Control, 1956/57–1958/59

Malamba, BN	1956/57, 1958/59

4.2 Western Province Bantu (later African) Cricket Union Provincial Players, 1933/34–1974/75[167]

Adam, A	1965/66, 1967/68
Balfour, A 'Don'	1952/53, 1965/66
Balfour, MM	1947/48
Bam, S	1933/34
Buka, [x]	1935/36, 1936/37
Cakwebe, H	1971/72
Cossie, BPB 'Pat'	1952/53 captain
Davids, [x]	1936/37
Dikweni, T[168]	1950/51, 1952/53
Dlanga, D	1952/53
Dlokweni, C	1950/51, 1952/53
Dyira, SD	1947/48 captain
Dyira, [x][169]	1936/37
Fesi, M	1965/66
Fongqo, SM	1933/34
Fuku, [x]	1936/37
Fuzani, [x]	1936/37
Gwarube, S	1965/66
Hlahleni, H	1965/66
Hobongwana, L	1950/51, 1952/53
Hoho, F	1952/53
Kawulela, N[170]	1947/48, 1952/53
Kewana, D	1965/66
Kobi, GB	1947/48
Kulathi, WW	1947/48

Landani, K	1965/66
Liphuko, MB	1933/34
Mabeqe, [x]	1967/68
Mabuto, B	1952/53
Mafongosi, SS	1947/48
Magitshima, WV	1965/66, 1966/67, 1967/68, 1971/72, 1974/75
Magodla, [x][171]	1966/67, 1967/68
Malamba, BN 'Ben'	1935/36, 1936/37, 1947/48, 1950/51, 1952/53, 1967/68, 1971/72
Malamba T	1952/53
Malamba, [x]	1936/37
Mama, P 'Walton'	1933/34 captain
Mandla, T	1947/48
Mapila, G	1971/72
Mapila, H	1965/66
Matshikwe, A[172]	1933/34
Matshikwe, E	1933/34, 1935/36
Mawu, H	1965/66 captain, 1967/68
Maxam, MM[173]	1947/48
Maxama, [x]	1936/37
Mbali, CS[174]	1933/34, 1935/36
Mbali, DN	1933/34
Mbolo, [x]	1935/36
Mgijima, TM	1947/48, 1950/51, 1952/53, 1967/68
Mlumbi, O	1952/53
Mpilwana, [x]	1936/37
Mshumpela, AM	1947/48, 1950/51, 1952/53
Mtimkulu, DT 'Don'	1933/34
Mvinjelwa, H	1952/53
Mxotwa, S	1965/66
Ndlumbini, MS	1965/66, 1971/72
Ndlwana, G	1935/36
Ndlwana, SM 'Mac'[175]	1933/34, 1935/36, 1947/48, 1952/53
Ngwevela, K	1965/66
Nkolombe, M	1952/53
Nqoko, W	1950/51
Ntshona, A	1952/53
Nyamakazi, J	1952/53
Petu, PK	1933/34, 1935/36, 1936/37
Scott, CM	1947/48, 1952/53
Shanyela, [x]	1936/37
Sihawu, GG	1966/67
Siyaya, G 'Shanks'	1952/53
Siyaya, H	1952/53
Sokanyile, H	1952/53
Somyo, S	1974/75, 1975/76
Yengo, SL	1947/48, 1952/53 (also spelt Vengo)
Zibi, GM 'Cannon'	1965/66, 1966/67, 1967/68

4.3 Western Province Bantu (later African) Cricket Union Trophies in the Native Recruiting Corporation (NRC) Tournaments, 1933/34–1958/59[176]

Season	Winners	Season	Winners
1933/34	Transvaal	1956/57	Eastern Province
1934/35	Transvaal	1958/59	Eastern Province
1935/36	Border	1964/65	[no details available]
1936/37	Border	1965/66	[no details available]
1938/39	Transvaal	1967/68	Eastern Province
1940/41	Transvaal	1968/69	[no details available]
1946/47	Transvaal	1969/70	Border
1947/48	Western Province	1970/71 or 1971/72*	[no details available]
1950/51	Transvaal	1972/73	[no details available]
1952/53	Western Province	1973/74	[no details available]
1954/55	Western Province	1974/75	Transvaal

* The tournament took place in 1971, but it is not clear in which season.

No Chamber of Mines tournaments took place between 1958/59 and 1964/65 because the South African African Cricket Board had decided to affiliate to SACBOC, which held its first non-racial provincial tournament in 1961/62, and the second in 1963/64. However, from 1964/65 a section of SAACB reconstituted itself as a racial body and the African inter-provincial tournaments were resumed.

4.4 Western Province Bantu (later African) Cricket Union Scores, 1933/34–1974/75[177]

1ST SABCB NRC TROPHY TOURNAMENT, DECEMBER/JANUARY 1933/34, JOHANNESBURG[178]
Participants: Transvaal (15 points), Western Province (12), Eastern Province (11), Griqualand West (6) and Border (0).
Winners: Transvaal

Transvaal beat Western Province by 3 wickets, 23 December 1933, Bantu Sports Club grounds
WP 127 and 102
Tvl 188 and 42/7

Western Province beat Border by 183 runs, xx, xx
WP 165 and 74/7
Bdr 76 and [?]

Eastern Province beat Western Province on the first innings, 29 December 1933, Duma Oval, Crown Mines
WP 206 (SM Fongqo 49, DT Mtimkulu 43, SS Msengana 30, PK Petu 22*) and 224 (DN Mbali 65, SM Ndlwana 50, DT Mtimkulu 39, [x] Matshikwe 20)
EP 276 (R Dlepu 80, W Ntshekisa 56, Nakani 47, JB Marwanqa 32) and 20/0

Western Province beat Griqualand West by an innings and 189 runs
WP 368/6 dec (SM Fongqo 121, SM Ndlwana 105, DT Mtimkulu 43, S Bam 33)
GW 89 (J Mzondeki 31, [x] Sibenya 19, MB Liphuko 11*) and 90

2ND SABCB NRC TROPHY TOURNAMENT, DECEMBER/JANUARY 1934/35, PORT ELIZABETH[179]
Winners: Transvaal
[no details available]

3RD SABCB NRC TROPHY TOURNAMENT, DECEMBER/JANUARY 1935/36, EAST LONDON
Participants: Border, Western Province, Eastern Province, Transvaal, Griqualand West and Natal.
Winners: Border

Western Province beat Eastern Province by 57 runs
WP 116 and 125
EP 57 and 127

Western Province beat Natal by 20 runs
WP 63 ([x] Malamba 25, SM Ndlwana 22, E Matshikwe 15) and 96 (PK Petu 35*)
Ntl 88 ([x] Palmer 21, [x] Gqwabaza 16) and 51 ([x] Ntwasa 18, [x] Senaoana 14)

Western Province beat Transvaal by 34 runs, 30–31 December 1934
Tvl 122 (F Roro 23, PSA Gwele 19, E Masiza 17) and 33
WP 64 (SM Ndlwana 18, [x] Buka 12) and 125 (G Ndlwana 28, [x] Malamba 25, CS Mbali 17)

Border beat Western Province by 37 runs, 2–3 January 1935
Bdr 197 ([x] De Wet 47, [x] Sozi 30, [x] Maho 30) and 114
WP 132 9[x] Malamba 40, CS Mbali 30, SM Ndlwana 20, E Matshikwe 19, PK Petu 11) and 142

Western Province drew against Griqualand West
[Match cut short because of time – no further details]

4TH SABCB NRC TROPHY TOURNAMENT, DECEMBER/JANUARY 1936/37, CAPE TOWN
Winners: Border

Western Province beat Eastern Province by an innings and 91 runs
WP 157 ([x] Buka 34, SM Ndlwana 33)
EP 37 (Nangu 18) and 29

Border beat Western Province by an innings and 34 runs
WP 33 (Kompi 6/16, Chiepe 3/16) and 22 (Kotobe 9/9)
Bdr 89 (Kotobe 20, Maho 15*; [x] Dyira 3/7, [x] Malamba 3/17, SM Ndlwana 3/31)

Western Province beat Transvaal by 70 runs
WP 116 ([x] Matshikwe 35; [x] Mahlanyana 6/28, [x] Mpiliso 2/33) and [x]
Tvl 47 ([x] Mpilwana 5/17 [x] Buka 3/7, [x] Dyira 2/15) and [x]

5TH SABCB NRC TROPHY TOURNAMENT, DECEMBER/JANUARY 1938/39, DURBAN
Participants: Transvaal, Border, Eastern Province, Natal, Griqualand West, Orange Free State and North-East Cape.
[Western Province did not participate]
Winners: Transvaal

6TH SABCB NRC TROPHY TOURNAMENT, DECEMBER/JANUARY 1940/41, PORT ELIZABETH
Winners: Transvaal
[no details available]

7TH SABCB NRC TROPHY TOURNAMENT, DECEMBER/JANUARY 1946/47, JOHANNESBURG
Winners: Transvaal
[no details available]

8TH SABCB NRC TROPHY TOURNAMENT, DECEMBER/JANUARY 1947/48, EAST LONDON
Participants: Western Province, Transvaal, Eastern Province, Orange Free State, North-Eastern Transvaal, Border and Natal.
Winners: Western Province

Western Province beat Transvaal on the first innings
WP 125 (BN Malamba 37, MM Maxam 26) and 76
Tvl 65 and [x]/[x] (F Roro 33)

Western Province beat Eastern Province by an innings and 57 runs
WP 152 (BN Malamba 48, MM Maxam 28)
EP 58 ([x] Kom 16) and 37 ([x] Kom 15)

9TH SABCB NRC TROPHY TOURNAMENT, DECEMBER/JANUARY 1950/51, KIMBERLEY

Participants: Transvaal, Western Province, North-Eastern Transvaal, Orange Free State, Eastern Province, Griqualand West and Natal.

Winners: Transvaal

Western Province beat Natal on the first innings
Ntl 78 (3 batsmen absent)
WP 138 (T Dikweni 39)

Western Province vs North-Eastern Transvaal: Match abandoned without a ball bowled because of rain

Western Province beat Eastern Province by an innings and 37 runs
WP 202 (L Hobongwana 60)
EP 80 (L Hobongwana 3/2) and 85 (W Nqoko 3/2)

Western Province beat Orange Free State on the first innings
WP 315 (C Dlokweni 121)
OFS 78 (AM Mshumpela 4/11, W Nqoko 3/7) and 55/1

Western Province beat Griqualand West by an innings and 154 runs
WP 303/5 dec (C Dlokweni 123, TM Mgijima 46)
GW 105 and 44 (BN Malamba 4/6, C Dlokweni 4/9)

Transvaal beat Western Province by 5 wickets
WP 68 and 106
Tvl 113 (F Roro 50) and 62/5

10TH SABCB NRC TROPHY TOURNAMENT, DECEMBER 1952, CAPE TOWN

Participants: Western Province, Natal, Orange Free State, Griqualand West, Eastern Province, Border, Transvaal, and North-Eastern Transvaal.[180]

Winners: Western Province

Western Province beat Orange Free State by 9 runs
WP 118 (PB Cossie 40*, S Vengo 26, SM Ndlwana 22; I Thoka 5/26, B Burgess 2/11) and 95 (PB Cossie 28, TM Mgijima 25, N Kawulela 17; I Thoka 5/27)
OFS 138 (E Murrison 49, B Burgess 21, W Ledimo 19, F Arnold 18; PB Cossie 4/35, AM Mshumpela 3/23) and 66 (B Burgess 26; J Nyamakazi 6/30, AM Mshumpela 3/27)

Western Province beat Griqualand West by 214 runs
WP 152 (A Ntshona 58*, TM Mgijima 23, SM Ndlwana 20; L Ngobeza 5/54, G Dondolo 4/61) and 261 (TM Mgijima 71, N Kawulela 46, A Ntshona 39, SM Ndlwana 25, J Nyamakazi 22; S Sebego 4/52)
GW 77 (L Ngobeza 22, S Sebego 18; A Balfour 7/19, AM Mshumpela 3/22) and 122 (L Dondolo 57, P Masiza 26, J Nyamakazi 2/14, PB Cossie 2/25, N Kawulela 2/38)

Final: Western Province beat Natal by 117 runs
WP 230 (N Kawulela 60, A Balfour 42*, S Vengo 20; Japtha Mahanjana 6/65, W Zantsi 3/41) and 157 (A Ntshona 45, S Vengo 27, SM Ndlwana 26, N Kawulela 23; BN Malamba 4/33, Japtha Mahanjana 4/69)
Ntl 188 (S Qangule 52, B Gqabasa 35, S Mayekiso 35; N Kawulela 2/25, AM Mshumpela 2/33, PB Cossie 2/40, A Balfour 2/51) and 82 (G Gqabasa 26; A Balfour 7/37, AM Mshumpela 3/36)

WESTERN PROVINCE CRICKET FEDERATION INTER-UNION MATCHES, 1952/53–1953/54[181]

Western Province Bantu Cricket Union beat Western Province Indian Cricket Union on the first innings, 1–2 November 1952
WPBCU 171 (B Cossie 60, A Ntshona 25, S Vengo 32; J Gheewala 6/40 and A Desai 3/25) and 111 (S Vengo 71; J Gheewala 6/36, A Desai 3/30)
WPICU 141 (O Magmoet 34, M Abrahams 54; B Cossie 4/43, N Kawulela 4/60, AM Mshumpela 1/10) and 53/4 (O Magmoet 29*; A Balfour 2/8, B Cossie 1/4)

Hottentots Holland Cricket Union beat Western Province Bantu Cricket Union by 8 wickets, 6–7 December 1952
WPBCU 68 (B Cossie 32) and 234 (B Cossie 61, TM Mgijima 35, N Kawulela 28, AM Mshumpela 26, T Diweni 30; H Siyaya 21)
Hottentots Holland 248 (M Dlanga 3/40, A Balfour 3/48, AM Mshumpela 2/48) and 55/2

Wynberg and District Cricket Union beat Western Province Bantu Cricket Union by 47 runs, 13–14 December 1952
Wynberg and District 45 (J da Rocha 22; AM Mshumpela 5/16, A Balfour 3/26) and 74 (A Balfour 7/46, AM Mshumpela 3/16)
WPBCU 22 (T Francis 6/14, J da Rocha 4/6) and 50 (O Kafaar 8/10)

Stellenbosch and District Cricket Union beat Western Province Bantu Cricket Union by an innings and 89 runs, 2–3 January 1953
WPBCU 116 (B Cossie 30, J Nyamakazi 30, AM Mshumpela 22*; A Manuel 3/15, W Anthony 4/47) and 118 (BN Malamba 30, F Hoho 34*; G Gabriel 2/28, D Hendricks 4/24, W Anthony 2/22)
Stellenbosch 323/9 dec (E Rhoode 54, A Manuel 96, A Poole 64, D Hendricks 52*)

Central Cricket League beat Western Province Bantu Cricket Union by 24 runs, 31 January – 1 February 1953
Central 100 (P Thomas 33, A Sabotker 27*; AM Mshumpela 3/30, BN Malamba 2/16, J Nyamakazi 2/13) and 147/7 dec (P Thomas 38, J Truter 32*, A Sabotker 34*; A Balfour 3/52, J Nyamakazi 2/21)
WPBCU 120 (B Cossie 45*, BN Malamba 34; A Sabotker 5/40, H Moody 2/21, P Thomas 2/5) and 103 (C Dlokweni 20, B Cossie 20; A Sabotker 4/32, P Thomas 6/23)

Western Province Coloured Cricket Union beat Western Province Bantu Cricket Union by 8 wickets, 28 February – 1 March 1953
WPBCU 59 (E Petersen 8/27) and 73 (I Bohardien 6/29, E Petersen 3/21, A Freeman 1/2)
WPCCU 83 (AK Abrahams 20; AM Mshumpela 3/19, B Cossie 3/17, N Kawulela 1/5) and 55/2 (AA Osman 18*)

Western Province Bantu Cricket Union beat Western Province Indian Cricket Union on the first innings, 21–22 November 1953
WPBCU 99 (B Cossie 33, W Nqoko 22, CM Scott 17; S van Haaght 3/28, J Gheewala 3/26) and 136 (B Cossie 20, H Mvinjelwa 33, J Nyamakazi 25, CM Scott 18; J Gheewala 3/28)
WPICU 84 (I Shaik 24, A Desai 14, F du Preez 11; J Nyamakazi 3/20, O Mlumbi 3/15, W Nqoko 3/9) and 74/8 (O Magmoet 22, S van Haaght 14, A Desai 13; W Nqoko 4/14)

Central League beat Western Province Bantus by 10 wickets, [x]
WPBCU 38 (A Sabotker 5/10, C Viret 5/12) and 147 (B Mabuto 61*, S Hoho 19, CM Scott 17, AM Mshumpela 16; M Coetzee 4/40, A Sabotker 4/75)
Central 151 (S Solomons 37*, J Truter 32, S Viret 34, D Koks 16; B Cossie 3/40, AM Mshumpela 3/27) and 35/0 (S Solomons 18*, P Liederman 17*)

Western Province Coloured Cricket Union beat Western Province Bantu Cricket Union by an innings and 16 runs, 21 February 1954
WPCCU 259 (E Abrahams 40, J Solomons 43, AJ Freeman 51, L Less 21, A Abrahams 19, A Latief 30; AM Mshumpela 4/52, B Cossie 2/37, J Nyamakazi 2/64)
WPBCU 103 (CM Scott 20, J Nyamakazi 27*, B Mabuto 18, S Hoho 15; E Petersen 3/26, E Abrahams 4/39, AJ Freeman 2/8) and 140 (J Nyamakazi 50, AM Mshumpela 32*, B Cossie 16; E Petersen 5/29, J Solomons 2/15)

11TH SABCB NRC TROPHY TOURNAMENT, DECEMBER/JANUARY 1954/55, DURBAN
Participants: North-Eastern Transvaal, Natal, Midlands/Cape, Transvaal, Orange Free State, Western Province and Eastern Province.
Winners: North-Eastern Transvaal
[no details available]

12TH SABCB NRC TROPHY TOURNAMENT, DECEMBER/JANUARY 1956/57, PORT ELIZABETH
Participants: Eastern Province, North-Eastern Transvaal, Natal, Midlands/Cape, Orange Free State and Transvaal. [Western Province did not participate]
Winners: Eastern Province

13TH SABCB NRC TROPHY TOURNAMENT, DECEMBER/JANUARY 1958/59, JOHANNESBURG
Participants: Eastern Province, North-Eastern Transvaal, Transvaal, Midlands/Cape, Border, Natal, Orange Free State and Transkei. [Western Province did not participate]
Winners: Eastern Province

No Chamber of Mines tournaments took place between 1958/59 and 1964/65 because the South African African Cricket Board had decided to affiliate to SACBOC, which held its first non-racial provincial tournament in 1961/62, and the second in 1963/64. However, from 1964/65 a section of SAACB reconstituted itself as a racial body and the old Chamber of Mines tournaments were resumed.

14TH SAACB CHAMBER OF MINES TOURNAMENT, 1964/65, UMTATA
[no details available]

15TH SAACB CHAMBER OF MINES TOURNAMENT, 1965/66, JOHANNESBURG
Participants: Transvaal, Eastern Province, Western Province, [x][182]
[no details available]

16TH SAACB CHAMBER OF MINES TOURNAMENT, 26 DECEMBER 1967 – 5 JANUARY 1968, NEW BRIGHTON, PORT ELIZABETH[183]
Participants: Border, Eastern Province, Orange Free State, Transkei, Transvaal, Western Province.
Winners: Eastern Province

Western Province vs Orange Free State, 26–27 December 1967, Wolfson Stadium, New Brighton
[no details available]

Eastern Province vs Western Province, 30–31 December 1967
[no details available]

Western Province beat Transkei by an innings and 76 runs, [x], Wolfson Stadium, New Brighton
Tra 94 (S Nqana 25, S Mgudlwa 24; TM Mgijima 6/33, [x] Magodlwa 3/22) and 67 (A Adam 4/16)
WP 237 (TM Mgijima 70, H Mawu 57, [x] Magodlwa 52*)

17TH SAACB TOURNAMENT, 26 DECEMBER 1968 – EARLY JANUARY 1969, QUEENSTOWN ('SPECIAL REVIVAL' TOURNAMENT – UNOFFICIAL. HM BUTSHINGI TROPHY PRESENTED FOR THE FIRST TIME)[184]
Participants: Border, Eastern Province, Midlands, North-Eastern Districts, North-Eastern Transvaal, Transkei, Transvaal, Western Province.
Winners: Eastern Province
[no details available]

18TH SAACB TOURNAMENT, DECEMBER/JANUARY 1969/70, TEMBISA, GERMISTON[185]
Participants: Border, Eastern Province, North-Eastern Districts, North-Eastern Transvaal, Orange Free State, Western Province.
Winners NRC Trophy Border and H.M. Butshingi Trophy Eastern Province

Border beat Western Province by an innings and 83 runs
Bdr 153 (Z Mbatani 49)
WP 43 and 27
[no other details available]

19TH SAACB TOURNAMENT, 1970/71 OR 1971/72, WELKOM[186]
Participants: Border, Eastern Province, Goldfields, Midlands, Orange Free State, North-Eastern Districts, North-Eastern Transvaal, Transkei, Transvaal, Western Province.

Western Province beat Midlands on the first innings
WP 159 (H Cakwebe 51, W Magitshima 17; P Nyati 5/34, P Sonwabe 4/33) and 78 (B Malamba 23, B Ndayi 13; S Nqabeni 4/25, M Stofile 4/19, [x] Sonwabe 2/11)
Midlands 93 (S Hoko 44; G Mapila 6/14, MS Ndlumbini 2/34) and 14/1

20TH SAACB TOURNAMENT, SOWETO, 1972/73, JOHANNESBURG
Participants: Border, Eastern Province, North-Eastern Transvaal, Goldfields, Midlands, North-Eastern Districts, Transkei, Transvaal, Western Province.
[no details available]

21ST SAACB TOURNAMENT, SOWETO, 26 DECEMBER 1973 – 6 JANUARY 1974, JOHANNESBURG
[Tournament cancelled at the last moment]

22ND SAACB TOURNAMENT, MOROKA, SOWETO, DECEMBER 1974 – JANUARY 1975, JOHANNESBURG
Participants: Eastern Province, Transvaal, Transkei, [others unknown]. Played on four grounds.
Winners: Transvaal
[no details available]

CHAPTER 5
Western Province Indian Cricket Union, 1943–1959

Affiliated to South African Indian Cricket Union

The Western Province Indian Cricket Union (WPICU), perhaps the smallest of the Western Province boards, came into existence almost by default in the 1940s.[189] Its mother body, the South African Indian Cricket Union (SAICU), was established in 1940 as part of the racial splintering from the original multi-ethnic South African Coloured Cricket Board (1903). First a national 'coloured' board broke away (1926) and then a national 'Bantu' board (1932). The SAICU, apparently a reluctant participant in this trend of separate racial bodies, then launched its own provincial affiliates and tournaments, like the other national boards: this was no easy task, given the patterns of settlement by immigrants from India. Natal and Transvaal were the only provinces with substantial populations of Asian origin where settled cricket cultures could develop. Asians were regarded as 'aliens' in apartheid South Africa and were not even allowed to sleep overnight in the Orange Free State. They experienced deep-seated hostility and discrimination because of their perceived cultural strangeness, which is today often conveniently forgotten.[190]

The criterion for provincial recognition and participation was set at three clubs. Only one other province, Eastern Province, was able to join Natal and Transvaal from the start in competing for the Christopher Trophy. Western Province managed to become the fourth affiliate to the SAICU in 1943 and started participating in the inter-provincial tournaments only in the fourth tournament in 1947.

According to Syd Reddy and Bennie Bansda's pioneering *South African Non-European Cricket Almanack,* 'Cricket was first started by the Indians in Cape Town from the year 1930, by a small group known as the Cape Hindoos. Later the Muslim C.C. followed by the Kismet C.C. eventually led to the formation of the Western Province Cricket Union. To the following, credit must go for the formation of this body, namely, Messrs. L.C. Cheewala, P.C. Chavda, C.C. Palsania, C.B. Patel, Dr. A. Safeda, I. Moosa Essa, and others.'[191] The *Almanack* notes that Western Province's 'debut was not impressive', but from 1947/48 the 'progressive era of this Union' took off 'when Adv. H.E. Mall, then a student at the Cape Town University, took over the cudgels'. Hassan Mall, father of the top first-class cricketer and administrator Enver Mall, went on to become a distinguished judge after the advent of democracy. He was 'ably assisted by Messrs. H.E. Parker, D.N. Bansda, A. Desai, N. Anter, A.B. Allie, E.S. Moosa and others' in building the WPICU.

145

The outstanding cricketers to emerge from the WPICU system were the famous Abed brothers. The Abed family, originally from Durban, lived in Muir Street in District Six, the area around the mosque and market where many members of the Indian community lived. Salie 'Lobo' Abed made his debut for the WPICU as a batsman and off-spinner in the 1946/47 tournament in Johannesburg. When the wicketkeeper Sheikh Moosa Goder was injured, 'Lobo' took the gloves and the rest is history – he is remembered as a legend behind the stumps, standing up to the fastest bowlers. The Cape Town-born England cricketer Basil D'Oliveira noted that 'Abed at his peak was the best wicketkeeper in the world'. The 6 ft 5 in 'Tiny' Abed made his debut for the WPICU in the 1949 tournament in Port Elizabeth and won the 'best all-rounder' prize. 'Lobo', 'Tiny' and younger brothers Goolam and 'Dik' all went on to achieve higher honours in sport, with three of them eventually plying their trade abroad.[192]

The best-known club to emerge from the Indian community was Montrose CC, formed in 1950. At first a modest second division outfit, it grew into the most powerful club in Cape Town in the 'Board' (WPCB) era and is still in existence today. (In the 1980s it captured either the premier league and limited-overs trophies twelve times.) The president for several decades was Hamza Ebrahim and he was succeeded by his son Mohamed Ebrahim, who also became president of the Western Province Cricket Association in 2006. The Allie family, prominent in local banana distribution, were long-time sponsors of Montrose.

The WPICU leadership in 1953/54, as recorded by the *Almanack*, was as follows: president: Mr G Munsook; vice-presidents: HE Parker, DN Bansda, A Peerbhai, AS Randaree, A Hayat, OM Adhikari and A Vallie; hon. secretary: LJ Alexander (succeeded by GM Khan); assistant secretary: K Desai; hon. treasurer: ES Moosa; hon. match secretary: Y Rasool; captain: AH Khan; vice-captain: S van Haaght.

Western Province's best achievement in six tournaments for the Christopher Trophy was second place in the 1951 tournament in Durban. In January the next year, the South African Indian Cricket Union headquarters moved to Cape Town, ahead of the city's hosting the seventh inter-provincial tournament there between 5 and 17 January 1953. The Cape Town-based officials who took over as the SAICU office-bearers were HE Parker (president), DN Bansda (secretary) and I Begg (treasurer), the father of Yaseen Begg, a top-class Transvaal wicketkeeper of the 1980s. The vice-presidents representing the different provinces were AH Rawat, G Munsook, GR Padayachee, MR Varachia, S Reddy and PK Patel.

The 1953 tournament took place at the popular Mowbray Sports Ground, where St George's Grammar School stands today. Six teams participated as Griqualand West and Southern Rhodesia had in the meantime affiliated. Western Province came third at home after a narrow loss in a tight match to eventual winners Transvaal. Ismail Shaikh broke the tournament record with 137 not out against Griqualand West. For this he received the 'Mr Barclay – Lion Beers Bat' for the highest score and the 'Mr Bo Wintle Bat' for the best batting average. His team-mate Saait van Haaght won the 'Bagus Allie Bros Bat' for the best all-rounder in the tournament. Abdullah Abass, who went on to become long-standing president of the non-racial South African Rugby Union, won the bat for the most runs and Dawood Asmal of Natal was adjudged the best fielder. Asmal was the brother of Professor Kader Asmal, an internationally recognised human rights campaigner who played a prominent part in drafting the constitution of South Africa and became a minister in Nelson Mandela's first Cabinet.

Shaikh and Van Haaght were two of seven Western Province players who were selected for the national South African Indian team for the inter-race tournaments in the 1950s. Among the others were two of the famous Abed brothers, 'Tiny' and Goolam. Van Haaght captained the South African Indian team in 1955, making a mockery of the racial classifications in cricket at the time as he was officially designated a 'Malay'. The WPICU was hamstrung by these classifications and successfully proposed a motion that the mother body allow 'the three Cape centres – Western Province, Eastern Province and Griqualand West – to play four cricketers of non-Indian descent, whereas previously they were allowed only four players of Malay descent'. The purpose was both practical (because these were provinces where numbers were few) and political. Bobby Harrypersadh, sports editor of *The Leader* newspaper, described it as 'a fundamental contribution to race relations in this country'.[193]

The WPICU went out of existence in 1959, after less than 20 years, when it became a founding member of the new, non-racial Western Province Cricket Board, together with the Western Province Coloured Cricket Union and the Peninsula and Western Districts Cricket Board.

Valuable early sources on the WPICU and its parent body are SJ Reddy and DN Bansda (eds.), *The South African Non-European Cricket Almanack 1953/54* and *1954/55* (The South African Non-European Cricket Publications, Cape Town, [1954 and 1955]).

5.1 Western Province Indian Cricket Union National Players (SAICU), 1940/41–1958/59[194]

Abed, G 'Tiny'	1950/51, 1954/55
Abed, GH	1954/55
Osmany, MS	1957/58
Pangarkar, SI	1952/53, 1957/58
Shaikh, IE	1952/53
Thomas, P	1954/55
Van Haaght, S	1952/53, 1954/55 captain

5.2 Western Province Indian Cricket Union Provincial Players, 1940/41–1958/59[195]

Abed, G 'Tiny'	1949/50, 1951/52
Abed, GH	1955/56
Abed, S 'Lobo'	1947/48
Abrahams, M	1953/54
Abrahams, S	1955/56
Allie, H	–
Allie, M	–
Allie, O	1955/56
Banoo, A	1947/48
Bansda, DN	1949/50
Basier, A	–
Bawasa, I	1947/48 (Bavasah, I?)
Begg, A	–
Begg, I	–
Begg, [x]	1957/58
Clarke, A	–
Desai, A	1953/54
Ebrahim, N	1949/50
Fredericks, E	–
Fredericks, G	1955/56
Frieslaar, N	–
Gafaar, GO	1955/56
Gardee, A	1955/56
Gheewala, IT	–
Gheewala, J	1953/54
Gheewala, S	–
Goder, ME	1955/56
Hayat, I	–
Hayat, M	1947/48, 1949/50
Hector, E	1957/58
Hoosain, G	–
Jamal, EM	1953/54
Jamal, Y	–
Kafaar, O	1957/58
Kajee, I	1949/50, 1951/52
Kamaldien, M	–
Katieb, C	–
Katieb, K	–
Khan, AH	1951/52
Khan, R	–
Magan, B	–
Magmoet, J	1951/52, 1953/54
Magmoet, O	1951/52, 1953/54
Mall, H	1947/48
Moosa, E	1947/48

Naidoo, M	1951/52
Osmany, MS	1957/58
Pangarkar, SI	1953/54, 1957/58
Pangarkar, T	1957/58
Parker, A	–
Rasool, Y	–
Rahbeeni, M	1953/54 (also spelt Rahbreni)
Shaikh, IE	1953/54
Thomas, P	1955/56
Van Haaght, S	1953/54, 1955/56
Woodman, [x]	1957/58

5.3 Western Province Indian Cricket Union Trophies in the Christopher Trophy Tournaments (SAICU), 1940/41–1957/58[196]

The Western Province Indian Cricket Union did not win any of the nine Christopher Trophy tournaments held by the South African Indian Cricket Union.

Season	*Winners*
1940/41	Natal
1941/42	Natal
1944/45	Natal
1946/47	Transvaal
1948/49	Transvaal
1950/51	Natal
1952/53	Transvaal
1954/55	Transvaal
1957/58	Transvaal / Natal (shared)

5.4 Western Province Indian Cricket Union Scores, 1940/41–1957/58[197]

1ST SAICU CHRISTOPHER TROPHY TOURNAMENT, APRIL 1941, DURBAN
Participants: Natal, Transvaal and Eastern Province. [Western Province did not participate]
Winners: Natal

2ND SAICU CHRISTOPHER TROPHY TOURNAMENT, APRIL 1942, JOHANNESBURG
Participants: Natal, Transvaal and Eastern Province. [Western Province did not participate]
Winners: Natal

3RD SAICU CHRISTOPHER TROPHY TOURNAMENT, APRIL 1945, DURBAN
Participants: Natal, Transvaal and Eastern Province. [Western Province did not participate]
Winners: Natal

4TH SAICU CHRISTOPHER TROPHY TOURNAMENT, APRIL 1947, JOHANNESBURG
Participants: Transvaal, Natal, Eastern Province and Western Province.
Winners: Transvaal

Natal drew with Western Province
Ntl 153/6 dec (H Mall 2/21, M Hayat 2/58)
WP 56/6 (AHE Coovadia 3/11)

Transvaal beat Western Province by 8 wickets
WP 72 (A Dinath 6/18, M Anthony 3/29) and 133 (S Abed 44, I Bawasa 35; A Dinath 5/41, M Anthony 3/34)
Tvl 162/5 dec (A Dinath 69, E Saloojee 40*; M Hayat 2/41, H Mall 2/48) and 49/2

Eastern Province beat Western Province by 13 runs
EP 135 (NV Coopoo 36, EB Meyer 33*; H Mall 3/16, M Hayat 3/32, E Moosa 2/29) and 73 (H Mall 6/40, M Hayat 3/14)
WP 153 (A Banoo 44, M Hayat 32; M Safedien 4/53, T Morgan 3/27) and 42 (A Safedien 6/23, M Safedien 3/7)

5TH SAICU CHRISTOPHER TROPHY TOURNAMENT, FEBRUARY 1949, PORT ELIZABETH
Participants: Transvaal, Natal, Eastern Province and Western Province.
Winners: Transvaal

Transvaal beat Western Province by an innings and 78 runs
WP 34 (M Hayat 11; S Bhagalia 3/7, M Anthony 3/8, A Dinath 3/11) and 33 (S Bhagalia 5/10, A Dinath 3/5)
Tvl 145/3 dec (D Chota 46, M Rama 44*, H Salie 25*)

Eastern Province beat Western Province by 9 wickets
EP 185/9 dec (NV Coopoo 42, A Meyer 40, T Verrie 26; G Abed 3/44, I Kajee 3/48, N Ebrahim 2/30) and 51/1 (M Abrahams 36*)
WP 85 (DN Bansda 22; T Morgan 3/35, M Abrahams 2/15) and 145 (G Abed 44, I Kajee 40; T Verrie 4/30, NV Coopoo 3/33, W Sandan 2/16)

Natal beat Western Province by an innings and 11 runs
WP 80 (I Kajee 34; EI Jeewa 5/21, AKA Kajee 2/0, T Chetty 2/20) and 59 (EI Jeewa 7/31, AS Randeree 2/4)
Ntl 150/9 dec (DJ Chellan 28, S Danabalan 22; G Abed 3/50, I Kajee 2/19)

6TH SAICU CHRISTOPHER TROPHY TOURNAMENT, JANUARY 1951, DURBAN
Participants: Natal, Transvaal, Eastern Province and Western Province.
Winners: Natal

Transvaal beat Western Province on first innings
Tvl 203 (E Cassim 55, M Garda 42, M Rama 31, R Patel 20; H Mall 4/88, AH Khan 3/18, G Abed 3/36) and 43/5 (I Kajee 3/25, AH Khan 2/9)
WP 39 (S Bhagalia 5/9, M Anthony 5/20) and 256 (G Abed 111, J Magmoet 62; A Dinath 5/112, S Bhagalia 3/55)

Natal beat Western Province by an innings and 66 runs
Ntl 255 (RV Bhana 65, W Stephens 45, EI Bhorat 44, DJ Chellan 37, GHM Docrat 28; AH Khan 6/63, G Abed 2/25, I Kajee 2/46)
WP 120 (G Abed 31, O Magmoet 20; EI Bhorat 3/6, EI Jeewa 3/26, IA Timol 2/33) and 69 (I Kajee 27, J Magmoet 21; RV Bhana 5/33, EI Jeewa 3/20)

Western Province beat Eastern Province by 4 wickets
EP 81 (G Vasuthevan 34; G Abed 5/26, M Naidoo 2/15, AH Khan 2/23) and 100 (GK Nulliah 48; G Abed 3/13, AH Khan 3/14, I Kajee 2/15)
WP 123 (G Abed 33, O Magmoet 24, AH Khan 24; EB Meyer 7/28) and 60/6 (G Abed 60*; T Morgan 3/14, EB Meyer 2/24)

7TH SAICU CHRISTOPHER TROPHY TOURNAMENT, JANUARY 1953, CAPE TOWN
Participants: Transvaal, Natal, Eastern Province, Western Province, Griqualand West and Southern Rhodesia.
Winners: Transvaal

Western Province beat Southern Rhodesia by an innings and 19 runs
SR 119 (S Vithal 31, P Gulab 26; SI Pangarkar 4/10, M Abrahams 4/37) and 105 (JD Naik 34, C Gulab 33; J Gheewala 6/50, O Magmoet 3/7)
WP 243 (S van Haaght 69, J Magmoet 45, IE Shaikh 42, M Rahbeeni 33; C Gulab 6/103, G Rodrigues 2/35)

Transvaal beat Western Province by 3 wickets
WP 160 (S van Haaght 54, J Magmoet 27; E Wadvalla 3/31, S Bhagalia 2/20, D Naran 2/32, M Anthony 2/55) and 186 (IE Shaikh 46, S van Haaght 31, M Abrahams 30, J Magmoet 24; M Anthony 6/51, M Garda 2/27)
Tvl 161 (A Dinath 76, A Dadabhai 35; S van Haaght 4/48, M Abrahams 2/24, SI Pangarkar 2/41) and 188/7 (AS Bulbulia 84*, A Dadabhai 27; M Abrahams 3/31, J Gheewala 2/30)

Western Province beat Griqualand West by an innings and 135 runs
GW 132 (E Jinnah 35, A Bhayat 34; A Desai 4/4, S van Haaght 4/16) and 80 (M Rahbeeni 3/15, A Desai 3/27, SI Pangarkar 2/22)
WP 347/7 dec (IE Shaikh 137*, J Magmoet 58, EM Jamal 44, A Desai 41, M Abrahams 25, S van Haaght 23; I Ackerdien 4/117)

Western Province beat Eastern Province on the double innings
[no details available]

WESTERN PROVINCE CRICKET FEDERATION INTER-UNION MATCHES, 1952/53–1953/54[198]

Western Province Bantu Cricket Union beat Western Province Indian Cricket Union on the first innings, 1–2 November 1952
WPBCU 171 (B Cossie 60, A Ntshona 25, S Vengo 32; J Gheewala 6/40 and A Desai 3/25) and 111 (S Vengo 71; J Gheewala 6/36, A Desai 3/30)
WPICU 141 (O Magmoet 34, M Abrahams 54; B Cossie 4/43, N Kawulela 4/60, AM Mshumpela 1/10) and 53/4 (O Magmoet 29*; A Balfour 2/8, B Cossie 1/4)

Western Province Coloured Cricket Union beat Western Province Indian Cricket Union by 10 wickets, 14–15 February 1953
WPICU 58 (J Magmoet 24; E Petersen 5/5, I Bohardien 3/28) and 162 (N Fakier 72, M Abrahams 40; I Bohardien 5/45, E Petersen 4/23)
WPCCU 185 (O Fataar 47, E Dollie 30, G Abed 29, J Gheewala 4/26, I Pangarkar 2/38, A Desai 2/10) and 38/0 (L Less 22*)

Central Cricket League beat Western Province Indian Cricket Union by an innings and 85 runs, 7–8 March 1953
WPICU 55 (M Rahbeeni 20; L Robertson 4/21, H Moody 3/4, S Solomon 3/2) and 186 (A Desai 35, O Magmoet 38, S van Haaght 39, A Gardee 21; L Robertson 5/42, A Sabotker 2/32)
Central 326 (S Solomon 107, I Dantu 40, H Moody 30, A Sabotker 35, D Hermans 26, P Liederman 23; M Abrahams 3/53, A Gardee 2/38)

Match between Western Province Indian Cricket Union and Hottentots Holland Cricket Union forfeited

Western Province Bantu Cricket Union beat Western Province Indian Cricket Union on the first innings, 21–22 November 1953
WPBCU 99 (B Cossie 33, W Nqoko 22, CM Scott 17; S van Haaght 3/28, J Gheewala 3/26) and 136 (B Cossie 20, H Mvinjelwa 33, J Nyamakazi 25, CM Scott 18; J Gheewala 3/28)
WPICU 84 (I Shaik 24, A Desai 14, F du Preez 11; J Nyamakazi 3/20, O Mlumbi 3/15, W Nqoko 3/9) and 74/8 (O Magmoet 22, S van Haaght 14, A Desai 13; W Nqoko 4/14)

Stellenbosch and District CU beat Western Province Indian Cricket Union on the first innings, 5 and 12 December 1953
Stellenbosch 214 (S Rasiet 29, HO Rasiet 53, A Manuel 27, T King 34, AA Poole 34, E Davidse 20; M Naidoo 3/33, F Abrahams 2/30, M Rahbeeni 2/25) and 154/9 (HO Rasiet 51*, AA Poole 38, E Davidse 33; F Abrahams 3/17, H Hendricks 3/28)
WPICU 161 (A Gardee 46, M Rahbeeni 44, H Hendricks 23, EM Jamal 12; A Manuel 3/22, AA Poole 2/33)

Western Province Coloured Cricket Union beat Western Province Indian Cricket Union by an innings and 30 runs, 13 December 1953
WPICU 72 (M Rahbeeni 28, S Abrahams 12; G Abed 3/15, AJ Freeman 3/12, E Petersen 2/24) and 80 (H Hendricks 16, A Desai 42, S van Haaght 11; AJ Freeman 4/25, E Abrahams 4/45)
WPCCU 182 (AJ Freeman 33, G Abed 41, AA Osman 27, GT Holmes 21, L Less 14, S Abed 14*; S Abrahams 4/50, M Naidoo 2/21)

Central Cricket League beat Western Province Indian Cricket Union by 28 runs, 26–27 December 1953
Central 226 (S Viret 44, D Koks 32, F Smith 41, D Hermans 29, R Felton 22*; A Desai 4/32, M Rahbeeni 2/35, BN Malamba 2/50) and 127 (D Koks 25, D Hermans 31, W Adonis 18; B Malamba 7/54, M Naidoo 3/44)
WPICU 226 (S van Haaght 85, A Desai 61, BN Malamba 41; L Robertson 5/101, R Felton 4/29) and 99 (A Desai 56, F du Preez 12; L Robertson 6/38, W Adonis 3/26)

8TH SAICU CHRISTOPHER TROPHY TOURNAMENT, JANUARY 1955, JOHANNESBURG
Participants: Transvaal, Natal, Eastern Province, Western Province and Griqualand West.
Winners: Transvaal

Natal beat Western Province on the first innings
WP 107 (GH Abed 36, P Thomas 36; CM Seedat 4/33, IA Timol 3/19) and 244/4 (S van Haaght 106*, A Gardee 42, G Fredericks 20*)
Ntl 189 (IE Seedat 40, AE Asmal 39*, DM Seedat 29, IA Timol 28, AKC Asmal 27; GH Abed 3/38, S Abrahams 2/1, S van Haaght 2/47, GO Gafaar 2/66)

Transvaal beat Western Province on the first innings
WP 246 (GH Abed 87, ME Goder 35, S van Haaght 32; A Kazi 6/43, M Garda 2/66) and 293 (P Thomas 97, A Gardee 76, GH Abed 53, GO Gafaar 36; D Naran 5/62, M Garda 3/80)
Tvl 364/5 dec (M Docrat 109*, A Kazi 67*, S Bata 48, AS Bulbulia 46, R Khota 31)

Western Province beat Eastern Province by 5 wickets
EP 165 (H Ayoob 86; S Abrahams 5/58, P Thomas 2/12) and 185 (NP Umley 47*, NV Coopoo 43, P Pillay 41; GO Gafaar 4/26, S van Haaght 2/35)
WP 177 (O Allie 35, P Thomas 34; SD Raga 9/77) and 180/5 (S van Haaght 43, A Gardee 36*, P Thomas 31*)

Western Province beat Griqualand West on the first innings
GW 113 (E Fredericks 3/32, GO Gafaar 2/20, S Abrahams 2/29) and 83/2 (A Bhayat 37)
WP 333/4 dec (ME Goder 131, P Thomas 100*, O Allie 41)

9TH SAICU CHRISTOPHER TROPHY TOURNAMENT, JANUARY 1958, PORT ELIZABETH
Participants: Natal, Transvaal, Western Province, Eastern Province and Griqualand West.
Winners: Natal and Transvaal

Natal beat Western Province on the first innings
Ntl 186 (O Rambaran 35, AI Deedat 29, EI Jeewa 25, T Parsuramen 23; E Hector 3/29, O Kafaar 2/23) and 15/5
WP 77 (T Parsuramen 7/19) and 158 (Woodman 43, T Pangarkar 28, SI Pangarkar 23; T Parsuramen 3/25, EI Jeewa 3/52)

Western Province beat Griqualand West by 109 runs
WP 98 (Abrahams 25, T Pangarkar 21, MS Osmany 17; B Bhayat 4/6, O Ghoor 3/30, Y Bhayat 2/10) and 179/9 dec (Woodman 57, Begg 36; A Patel 6/60)
GW 108 (Abbas 50, Daya 26; SI Pangarkar 5/29, [x] Woodman 3/23) and 60

Transvaal beat Western Province by 150 runs
Tvl 170 (Mossom 52) and 193/9 dec (Bulbulia 63*)
WP 102 (Pangarkar 33) and 111

Western Province beat Eastern Province by 6 wickets
EP 83 (R Doraswami 33, Appoo 23; SI Pangarkar 5/36, MS Osmany 3/20) and 148 (Davids 47*; SI Pangarkar 7/55)
WP 176 and 61/4

CHAPTER 6

Hottentots Holland Cricket Union, 1945–1959

Affiliated to South African Coloured Cricket (later Malay) Cricket Board

The Hottentots Holland Cricket Union was formed in 1945 with headquarters in the Strand near Somerset West.[199] Its establishment was part of the revival of the South African Coloured Cricket Board (SACCB), known as the Barnato Board, after World War Two. As the SACCB (which changed its name to the South African Malay Cricket Board in 1953) started organising regular biennial tournaments for the Barnato Memorial Trophy from 1945/46, new provincial affiliates were created to join the original big three of Western Province (founded 1890), Griqualand West (1894) and Transvaal (1904). Hottentots Holland CU was the first of the newcomers in 1945, followed by the Benoni-based Eastern Transvaal Coloured and Indian Cricket Association, formed in July 1948, the Eastern Province Coloured Cricket League in Port Elizabeth (1950) and the Border Coloured Cricket Union with headquarters in East London (October 1951).[200]

The Hottentots Holland CU played in only two of the Barnato tournaments organised between its formation in 1945 and the seventeenth and last tournament in 1959/60. It made its debut at the tournament played in Cape Town in 1951/52 and took part again in the next one in Johannesburg in 1954/55. The Hottentots Holland CU also participated over the years in the inter-union matches that took place regularly in Greater Cape Town. These matches between units of different provincial bodies were formalised under the short-lived Western Province Cricket Federation in the early 1950s (see chapter 8 below). Hottentots Holland more or less held its own, except against the strong Western Province 'Barnato' side led by 'Dol' Freeman and the Central Cricket League team from Peninsula and Western Districts Cricket Board, which boasted players of the calibre of Cecil Abrahams, Sydney Solomon and Adam Sabotker.

This sub-union status matched more closely the Hottentots Holland CU's true stature than one would assume from its elevation to provincial level in order to beef up the 'Barnato Board' nationally. Nevertheless, the record of the Somerset West–Strand cricketers was five wins out of seven games in the two Barnato tournaments in which they played, an achievement underlining the relative strength of cricket in the Western Province compared with the rest of the country. Hottentots Holland beat Griqualand West, Eastern Transvaal (twice), Eastern Province and Border, losing only to Transvaal, in a close contest, and Western Province. Hottentots Holland's best result in these Barnato tournaments was a joint second place in Cape Town in 1951/52. Ronnie Ingham (125) scored the only century, with fifties from Rashaad Salie, Solly Arendse, Dennis Josephs, Haroen Gafieldien and Ismail Latief. The side's strength was its bowling as Latief's seven hauls of five wickets show. His best figures were 7/50, 6/30 and 5/11. Latief was well backed up by Allie Bagus, captain in Johannesburg, who had a string of good tournament figures: 4/4, 4/16, 4/18, 4/36, 3/14 and 3/35. Allie Bagus was the son of an immigrant from India who became a successful businessman. Allie and his brother were sent to the best available schools in Cape Town before they joined their father in the family greengrocer business, which operated out of 'double-storey buildings' in the CBDs of both Strand and Somerset West. This world came tumbling down after the Group Areas Act 'removed them from the CBD'.[201]

Ismail Latief, who played for the Summer Roses CC, was the only player from Hottentots Holland to be picked for the South African Malay team. He played in the 1953 SACBOC Inter-Race Tournament at the age of 21. His best figures were 12-1-47-5 against the strong South African Coloured side led by Basil D'Oliveira. According to the community historian Ebrahim Rhoda, he was a player *'van formaat'*, a 'great spinner, excellent fielder and good batsman, a real master'. 'He was our Shane Warne.' Like Allie Bagus, Latief came from a family that made a mark in the local community. His father, Abdurakiep Latief, was Imam at the Nurul Islam congregation or *Jama'ah* in Strand. Initially educated at the Strand Moslem Primary School set up by the community and then mentored by his father, Ismail followed him as Imam at the young age of 23, occupying the position for 50 years from 1955 until his death in 2005. As a religious leader, Latief courted controversy by replacing Arabic with Afrikaans in his sermons and at weddings and funerals.[202]

The Muslim community in Somerset West–Strand, which was the feeder for the Hottentots Holland CU, has deep roots. The first Imam, who was active as early as 1822, was one of the freed Robben Island prisoners from modern-day Indonesia who helped establish Islam at the Cape. The earliest known cricket club in this community was the Arabian Stars CC, formed in 1906. Rugby also became popular. During the era of non-racial sport in the 1970s and 1980s, the Somerset West Rugby Board played as a province in the competitions of the South African Rugby Union (SARU) in much the same way as the Hottentots Holland CU did under the SACCB/SAMCB.[203]

After the decision by the various ethnically based national cricket associations to unite and play 'non-racial' cricket in 1959, the Hottentots Holland CU – acting in tandem with other affiliates of the 'Barnato Board' – joined the new, non-racial Western Province Cricket Board (WPCB). The Somerset West and District Cricket Union, formerly affiliated to the rival 'coloured' Peninsula and Western Districts Cricket Board, likewise joined the new board. The two former rivals played as separate sub-unions in the WPCB inter-union competitions, with the Somerset West Union contributing players such as Des February, Mornay 'Kulu' Maclons, Allan Maclons and Jamie Sylvester to the Western Province team.

After 1976, when the WPCB did away with its inter-union competitions and replaced them with club-based leagues, the old Hottentots Holland CU players reconstituted themselves as the Hottentots Holland Cricket Club and the old Somerset West and District players formed the Helderberg Cricket Club. Hottentots Holland CC won the WPCB's Golden Yolk limited-overs competition in 1978/79 and three of its players, Sheraat Arnold, Ebrahim Gafieldien (son of the 1950s Hottentots Holland CU player Haroen) and the strapping all-rounder Yunus Thomas, represented Western Province.

In the 1990s, after cricket unity and the formation of a single United Cricket Board of South Africa in 1991, these two clubs became part of the Western Province Cricket Association (WPCA). The late Mohamed Bagus, son of former Hottentots Holland CU captain Allie Bagus, became chairman of the WPCA Umpires Association and a member of the executive committee in this new dispensation.

6.1 Hottenots Holland Cricket Union National Players (SAMCB), 1951/52–1958/59

Latief, I	1952/53

6.2 Hottentots Holland Cricket Union Provincial Players, 1951/52–1958/59[204]

Barnato Tournaments, 1951/52 & 1954/55

Abel, S	1951/52 captain
Adams, G	1951/52
Adonis, B	1951/52
Arendse, Solly*	1954/55
Arendse, Stanley*	1954/55
Baderoen, G	1954/55
Bagus, A	1951/52, 1954/55 captain
Crombie B	1951/52
Crombie, T	1951/52
Daniels, A	1954/55
Danies, N	1954/55
Gafieldien, H[205]	1951/52, 1954/55
Garder, E	1954/55
Ingham, R	1951/52, 1954/55
Josephs, D	1954/55
Karan, Y	1954/55
Latief, I	1951/52, 1954/55
Railoun, I	1951/52
Railoun, S	1951/52
Rhoda, MK	1954/55
Salie, R	1951/52
Thomas, R 'Tienie'	1954/55
Waggie, W	1954/55

Non-Tournament Games, 1954/55

Arendse, Neville*	1954/55
Arnold, E	1954/55
Bekkers, J	1954/55
Khan, A	1954/55
Khan, E	1954/55
Khan, K	1954/55

Maclons, T	1954/55
Petersen, S	1954/55
Railoun, K	1954/55

*Three Arendses appear in the list, Solly, Stanley and Neville. An Arendse also played in the 1951/52 tournament but his initials are unknown, making it impossible to verify who he was.

6.3 Trophies and Competitions (Barnato Memorial Trophy)

Season	Winners
1951/52	Western Province
1954/55	Western Province

6.4 Hottenots Holland Cricket Union Scores, 1951/52–1954/55[206]

13TH SACCB BARNATO MEMORIAL TROPHY TOURNAMENT, DECEMBER/JANUARY 1951/52, CAPE TOWN
Participants: Western Province, Transvaal, Eastern Province, Griqualand West, Eastern Transvaal and Hottentots Holland.
Winners: Western Province.

Hottentots Holland beat Griqualand West by 1 run
HH 112 (I Latief 36*; L Hermans 4/29; N Gamaldien 3/20) and 133 ([x] Salie 45; [x] Mallett 4/24; L Hermans 4/43)
GW 120 (A Gamaldien 44; I Latief 5/36) and 124 (L Hermans 50*; I Latief 7/50)

Hottentots Holland beat Eastern Transvaal by an innings and 186 runs
HH 263 ([x] Ingham 125; T Crombie 33, Solly Arendse 31; [x] Moosa 3/54)
ET 44 (I Latief 4/7; [x] Adams 3/10) and 33 (I Latief 5/11; [x] Bagus 4/16)

Transvaal beat Hottentots Holland by 5 wickets
HH 86 (A Rubidge 7/30; G Martin 3/51) and 137 ([x] Salie 66; [x] Gafieldien 32; A Rubidge 8/56)
Tvl 125 (M Docrat 32; [x] Bagus 4/4) and 101/5 (J Barnes 30, [x] Bagus 3/64)

Hottentots Holland beat Eastern Province by 138 runs
HH 162 (A Hendricks 3/50) and 185 (Solly Arendse 57; I Agherdien 3/30; G de Monk 3/32)
EP 124 (I Latief 5/23; [x] Bagus 3/14) and 85 (S Baderoon 50; [x] Bagus 4/18; [x] Adonis 3/8)

14TH SAMCB BARNATO MEMORIAL TROPHY TOURNAMENT, DECEMBER/JANUARY 1954/55, JOHANNESBURG
Winners: Western Province
[no details available]

WESTERN PROVINCE CRICKET FEDERATION INTER-UNION MATCHES, 1952/53–1953/54[207]

Wynberg and District Cricket Union beat Hottentots Holland Cricket Union on the first innings, 29–30 November 1952
HH 95 (H Gafieldien 35; G Ravens 5/30, O Kafaar 3/18, J da Rocha 2/27) and 264/9 dec (I Latief 75, H Gafieldien 36*, R Thomas 30, S Abels 62, E Railoun 20; G Ravens 3/73, M Fakier 2/45, J da Rocha 2/60)
W&D 122 (C Ravens 25, G Campbell 29*; I Latief 4/37, G Baderoen 2/31, E Railoun 1/0) and 182/9 (C Ravens 78, O Kafaar 22, J da Rocha 35; I Latief 4/53, A Khan 3/32)

Hottentots Holland Cricket Union beat Western Province Bantu Cricket Union by 8 wickets, 6–7 December 1952
WPBantu 68 (B Cossie 32) and 234 (B Cossie 61, TM Mgijima 35, N Kawulela 28, AM Mshumpela 26, T Dikweni 30, H Siyaya 21)
HH 248 (M Dlanga 3/40, A Balfour 3/48, AM Mshumpela 2/48) and 55/2

Central Cricket League beat Hottentots Holland Cricket Union by 73 runs, 7-8 February 1953
Central 110 (D Hermans 22, S Solomons 34, A Hendricks 24; G Baderoen 7/26, I Latief 2/19) and 93 (R Wilsnach 27, G Baderoen 5/26)
HH 42 (L Robertson 7/7, A Sabotker 3/28) and 88 (N Daniels 24, R Ingham 20; A Sabotker 6/32, L Robertson 4/37)

Western Province Coloured Cricket Union beat Hottentots Holland Cricket Union by 10 wickets, 11-12 April 1953
HH 60 (A Bagus 18; E Petersen 3/15, AJ Freeman 3/23, S Bardien 4/15) and 110 (S Abels 20; E Petersen 6/29, H Noordien 2/52, G Abed 1/9)
WPCCU 153 (G Abed 36, H Noordien 33, AJ Freeman 23; G Baderoen 5/52, N Daniels 1/10, S Arendse 1/12) and 23/0 (A Davids 19*)

Hottentots Holland Cricket Union beat Stellenbosch Cricket Union on the first innings, 7 and 14 March 1953
Stel 176 (S Raziet 52, T King 23, AA Pool 27*; S Arendse 3/19, G Baderoen 3/27, H Arendse 2/26) and 199/8 (S Raziet 75*, T King 34, E Davidse 23*, A Bagus 2/35, S Arendse 2/43)
HH 241 (R Ingham 47, S Arendse 47, R Sadie 45; W Anthony 3/49, E Davidse 2/22, AA Pool 2/39)

Match between Western Province Indian Cricket Union and Hottentots Holland Cricket Union forfeited

Stellenbosch and District Cricket Union beat Hottentots Holland Cricket Union by 21 runs, 21 and 28 November 1953
Stel 205 (E Rhoode 64, G Gabriels 27, A Manuel 16, AA Poole 36; A Bagus 5/36) and 59 (AA Poole 18; G Adams 5/24, B Crombie 2/21, H Gafieldien 2/5)
HH 141 (G Adams 15, C Railoun 14, A Bagus 16, I Latief 20, R Salie 39; AA Poole 4/42, S Rasiet 3/26) and 102 (B Crombie 21, R Ingham 26, I Latief 15, R Salie 12; S Rasiet 4/44, A Manuel 4/33)

Central Cricket League beat Hottentots Holland Cricket Union by an innings and 39 runs, 19-20 December 1953
Central 326 (J Truter 106*, P Liederman 47, D Koks 38, R Felton 46, A Sabotker 30, F Smith 25, S Viret 13, S Solomons 19; G Adams 5/104, A Bagus 3/61)
HH 89 (R Salie 34, I Latief 20; L Robertson 7/43, M Coetzee 3/27) and 198 (R Salie 86, H Gafieldien 41, S Abel 15, B Crombie 15; A Sabotker 3/40, P Thomas 3/42)

Western Province Coloured Cricket Union beat Hottentots Holland Cricket Union (match forfeited), 17 and 31 January 1954
WPCCU 152 (T Hendricks 52, A Satarien 18, S Abed 21*, G Adams 15; G Baderoen 4/46, G Adams 5/57) and 185/4 (L Less 46, A Satarien 64, K Samsodien 44, G Abed 13*; A Bagus 3/43)
HH 58 (I Latief 18; E Petersen 8/22, G Abed 2/13)

15TH SACCB BARNATO MEMORIAL TROPHY TOURNAMENT, JOHANNESBURG, DECEMBER/JANUARY 1954/55
Participants: Western Province, Transvaal, Eastern Province, Griqualand West, Eastern Transvaal and Hottentots Holland.
Winners: Western Province

Western Province beat Hottentots Holland by 308 runs on the first innings, Natalspruit Grounds, 26-27 December 1954
HH 88 (R Ingham 21, I Latief 17, A Gafieldien 11; A George 5/23, G Abed 2/15, E Petersen 2/41)
WP 396/8 (G Abed 66*, K Samsodien 60, K Abrahams 58, R Samaai 36)

Hottentots Holland beat Eastern Transvaal by an innings and 68 runs, Natalspruit Grounds, 28-29 December 1954
E Tvl 89 (N Vally 24, B Singh 21, H Sattar 16, I Latief 5/24, A Bagus 3/35) and 101 (A Laily 15*, M Ally 15, N Vally 13, I Latief 5/45, A Bagus 4/36)
HH 258/5 dec (D Josephs 87, I Latief 60, R Ingham 46, A Daniels 35)

Hottentots Holland beat Border on the first innings by 124 runs, Natalspruit Grounds, 1-2 January 1955
HH 258 (I Latief 88, H Gafieldien 52, A Daniels 41; A Meyer 5/54, EB Meyer 3/61)
Bdr 134 (K le Grange 59, EB Meyer 19; I Latief 6/30) and 56/2 rain stopped play (EB Meyer 35*; A Bagus 2/25)

CHAPTER 7
Western Province Women's Cricket Union, 1951–1991

Affiliated to the South Africa and Rhodesia Women's Cricket Association (SARWCA)

In the past, it was assumed that women did not play cricket, but recent research has shown that they have been involved in the game from the very beginning in this country.[208] The first record of women playing cricket on a social level in Cape Town dates from 1889.[209] In 1894 there was an unsuccessful proposal to allow women to become members of the Western Province Cricket Club.[210] Girls' cricket was introduced into schools by the early 1900s and in 1909, for example, Wynberg Girls' High beat Rustenburg. Both schools subsequently appointed physical education teachers trained at institutions in Britain which were starting to popularise the previously taboo notion that sport was good for girls. In 1915, the Peninsula Girls' Games Union was formed to organise inter-schools sport, including cricket.[211]

The first serious effort to organise women's cricket in South Africa on a formal basis was the Peninsula Ladies' Cricket Club (PLCC), formed in Cape Town in 1930, at the same time that international women's cricket was starting with contests between England and Australia. The PLCC, which played friendlies against men's teams, affiliated to the eight-year-old Women's Cricket Association (WCA) in England in 1934. The WCA was to all intents and purposes the international governing body or women's MCC. The PLCC's aim was to build on this by sending teams to play the Ramblers' Club in Bloemfontein and the Wanderers' Club in Johannesburg and, thereafter, to form a South African Women's Cricket Association, 'after which international games in England, Scotland and Australia will be possible'.[212] However, for various reasons, including the outbreak of World War Two, it took another two decades before a national controlling body, the South Africa and Rhodesia Women's Cricket Association (SARWCA), was finally established in 1952.

As part of the post-war recovery, women players in Cape Town became active again in 1949, and in September 1951 the new Western Province Women's Cricket Union (WPWCU) was started. It had three affiliated clubs, namely Alma, Liesbeek Park and Tresdecim, with a membership of 55. Two men, W 'Boggels' Matthews and Major Cilliers, were elected WPWCU president and chairman. Four women completed the executive committee, including Clarrie Peirce, captain of the PLCC in the early 1930s.[213]

Between 1952 and the 1980s around 30 national women's tournaments for the Simon Trophy were held. Western Province won the first three. The captain in 32 consecutive matches through to 1960 was Vicky Valentine-Brown. Educated at Cheltenham Ladies' College in England, she had also played tennis at Wimbledon, reaching the last 16 in the ladies' doubles.[214]

In 1960 South Africa got its first taste of international women's cricket when the England team toured. The fourth test was played at Newlands and several Western Province players were chosen, with Sheilagh Nefdt (née Charlton) as captain. Nefdt stood out at the early inter-provincial tournaments, stacking up a century and two record-breaking hat-tricks with her leg-breaks. The daughter of a school principal at Bishops, she grew up grounded in cricket. But instead of lifting Western Province women's cricket to a new level, the England tour exacerbated a decline that became evident when Western Province failed to send a side to the 1959/60 inter-provincial tournament. Having been champions three times in a row at the outset and having hosted the previous tournament in Cape Town, Western Province players now participated in the week in East London in the B Section as members of the composite South Westerns and Combined Provinces sides.

The costs associated with the 1960 England tour seemed to take the sails out of Western Province completely. By 1962 there were fewer than 20 registered players and, therefore, according to the SARWCA constitution, WP had to be deregistered.[215] Joy Littlewort now headed a 'caretaker committee' to look after cricket in the province.

Despite there being no longer an official Western Province team, enthusiasts pulled together scratch sides of Bellville and Alma players to ensure the region at least remained represented at the national tournaments[216] (albeit in the B section). For example, at the tournament in Durban in January 1964, eight Bellville Cricket Club members with three guest players from Border (which also could not field a team) played as Combined Western Province / Border under the captaincy of Maureen Payne. Despite attempts to revive organised cricket in Cape Town again in 1965 and 1969, according to newspaper reports,[217] Alma was still participating as a club in the 1970 national tournament, this time bolstered by three Natal players. The decline was felt in other provinces as well. The regular SARWCA tournaments held since 1952 were downgraded in the mid-1960s from an inter-provincial tournament to a cricket week involving also clubs and invitation teams because of the irregular attendance of official provincial teams.

The decline in domestic cricket went hand in hand with an end to South Africa's short-lived international status. After the England series in 1960, two further series followed against the Netherlands and New Zealand in 1969 and 1972 (when Western Province again provided the captain, Maureen Payne). Thereafter, the all-white SARWCA was also isolated internationally. While South African officials continued to attend meetings of the International Women's Cricket Association, the country was excluded from the World Cup from its inception in 1972 and given no further official international games.

The annual cricket week reached a nadir in Johannesburg in 1973/74. The situation had deteriorated so much that for the first time in twenty years the Simon Trophy was not awarded. The organisers, Southern Transvaal, the one truly viable province in the country, announced: 'It is with regret that the STWCA note that due to the withdrawal of Natal and Border, and the unofficial nature of the Western Province team, the tournament cannot be considered an inter-provincial competition. The Simon Trophy will therefore not be contested and the competition will be known as Cricket Week.'[218]

However, the Western Province Women's Cricket Union began slowly to re-establish itself in the 1970s, with Christine Bald and Janet Burger playing important roles. Western Province once again affiliated to SARWCA, and between 1976/77 and 1985/86 it hosted four of the nine known cricket weeks in Cape Town. From the 1974/75 week Western Province and Southern Transvaal were the only provinces with official teams participating. Two exceptions were a Border team playing in 1975/76 and a Natal team listed in 1978/79, when East London and Durban respectively hosted the tournaments. The contest for the Simon Trophy was by now more or less reduced to the winner of one match in the tournament: Southern Transvaal versus Western Province.[219]

In view of this sparse diet of formal inter-provincial matches, the annual weeks were spiced up with the introduction of girls' teams, double-wicket competitions and matches between Composite XIs made up of individuals from the different provinces, especially Southern Transvaal. Western Province players maintained a steady, even if small, presence. Anchored by the strong Southern Transvaal, where there were club and school leagues, the annual cricket weeks in effect became the one event where the shrinking family of South African women cricketers could meet as individuals and where the struggling national body could hold its AGM and strategise on how to survive.

The participation of a British invitation team, the Unicorns, in four tournaments in 1974/75, 1975/76, 1978/79 and 1985/86, provided a lifeline that kept things going. The Unicorns were the women's equivalent of the Derrick Robins tours for men. As the noose of isolation tightened on apartheid sport, conservative friends in Britain rallied in support by organising private tours. The Unicorns generally participated in the annual cricket week and also stopped over for friendlies in Johannesburg and in Cape Town. In the last three tours they also played so-called tests against SARWCA's national team, which was awarded Springbok colours. When the Unicorns' tours were stopped because of international anti-apartheid protests in the mid-1980s, the whole enterprise ground to a halt. The cricket weeks came to an end after 33 tournaments, and the national and provincial bodies went into hibernation. It would only be after the advent of democracy that women's cricket in both the Western Province and the country was revived.

7.1 Western Province Women's Cricket Union National Players (SARWCA), 1951/52–1985/86

Official International Cricket

Lang, B	1960/61 England
Nefdt, SN	1960/61 England captain
Payne, M	1960/61 England, 1971/72 New Zealand captain
Van Zyl, J	1971/72 New Zealand
Weyers, D	1971/72 New Zealand

South African Teams for Unofficial Matches vs Unicorns (English Invitation XI)

Austen, Y	1985
Burger, J	1978/79
Hannah, J	1978/79, 1985
McLeod, M	1978/79, 1985 captain
Price, K	1985
Van der Merwe, M	1985

7.2 Western Province Women's Cricket Union Provincial Players, 1951/52–1985/86[220]

The list of Western Province players below was drawn up from newspaper and official reports, programmes and scoresheets of the 33 inter-provincial tournaments held by the South Africa and Rhodesia Women's Cricket Association between 1951 and 1986. (For specific sources for each tournament, see footnote 220 below.) The seasons behind the players' names indicate the tournaments in which they participated. For caps against international touring sides, the year only and the teams are given, for example, 1960 England, 1969 Netherlands, 1972 NZ (for New Zealand) and 1973 Unicorns (from England).

From the 1960s, as Western Province and other associations battled to select official teams, the inter-provincial tournament became designated simply as 'cricket week'. At times Alma or Bellville players played as Western Province or combined with others – three Border players in 1963/64 and three Natal players in 1969/70, for example – to form composite teams. From 1970 onwards Western Province and Southern Transvaal were the only provinces to consistently send official teams. A few times when this did not happen (1979/80), Western Province players played as individuals in composite teams together with individuals from other provinces. When Western Province players participated in unofficial teams in the inter-provincial tournaments, this is indicated by putting the names of the particular unofficial teams in brackets behind the year or season; for example, 1963/64 (Bellville), 1965/66 (Alma), 1979/80 (Composite XIs).

Abernethy, P	1951/52, 1953/54
Alcobia, L	1985/86
Alexander, C	1958/59, 1959/60
Appleton, E	1956/57
Ashton, N	1954/55, 1957/58, 1958/59
Austen, Y	1971/72, 1972 NZ, 1972/73, 1973/74, 1974/75, 1978/79 captain, 1979/80 (Composite XIs), 1983/84, 1984/85, 1985/86
Bailey, P	1978/79
Bald, C	1962/63, 1965/66 (Alma), 1967/68 (Alma), 1969 Netherlands, 1969/70 (Alma), 1970/71, 1971/72, 1972 NZ, 1972/73, 1973/74, 1974/75
Blankenberg, M	1958/59
Botha, T	1983/84, 1984/85, 1985/86
Bridger, S	1971/72, 1972 NZ, 1972/73, 1973/74, 1974/75, 1978/79, 1979/80 (Composite XIs)
Brookes, R	1957/58, 1958/59
Burger, J	1962/63, 1963/64 (Bellville), 1965/66 (Alma), 1967/68 (Alma), 1969 Netherlands, 1969/70 captain (Alma), 1970/71 captain, 1971/72, 1972 NZ, 1972/73, 1973/74, 1974/75, 1978/79, 1979/80 (Composite XIs)
Burgess, M	1970/71
Chamberlain, M	1951/52, 1952/53
Chamberland, M	1953/54
Charlton, SN	See Nefdt, SN
Clark, A	1962/63, 1965/66 (Alma)
Conradie, G	1952/53
Copping, L	1969 Netherlands, 1972/73

Crosier, J	1969/70 (Alma), 1970/71, 1971/72, 1972 NZ, 1978/79, 1979/80 (Composite XIs)
Dale, J	1962/63
Davey, E	1984/85, 1985/86
Davies, HA	1984/85, 1985/86
De Beer, K	1962/63
De Villiers, G	1951/52, 1952/53
Dowling, N	1953/54, 1954/55, 1956/57, 1957/58, 1958/59, 1959/60
Du Plessis, D.	1954/55
Eaton, P	1965/66 (Alma), 1967/68 (Alma)
Eberhardt, N	1953/54
Fernandes, D	1979/80 (Composite XIs)
Fortune, E	1984/85, 1985/86
Genower, J	1953/54
Genower, P	1953/54
Gerrans, M	1972/73, 1973/74, 1974/75
Gordon, J	1969/70 (Alma)
Hannah, J	1969 Netherlands, 1970/71, 1971/72, 1972 NZ, 1972/73, 1973/74, 1974/75, 1983/84, 1984/85, 1985/86
Hardcastle, S	1953/54
Harran, P	1957/58, 1958/59
Harris, K	1983/84
Hefer, A	1984/85, 1985/86
Hendrikse, A	1979/80 (Composite XIs)
Herbert, J	1969/70 (Alma)
Hodges, C	1962/63, 1963/64 (Bellville)
Hodges, Y	1963/64 (Bellville)
Honeyman, E	1965/66 (Alma)
Howe, H	1973/74, 1974/75, 1978/79
Jeffrey, W	1951/52, 1952/53, 1953/54, 1956/57, 1957/58, 1959/60
Johnson, A	1951/52, 1952/53, 1953/54, 1957/58
Kerr, E	1972/73, 1973/74, 1974/75
Killian, B	1984/85, 1985/86
Kingswell, E	1953/54
Lancaster, L	1983/84
Lang, B	1952/53, 1953/54, 1954/55, 1959/60
Lawrence, J	1979/80 (Composite XIs)
Ledingham, J	1953/54, 1954/55
Leviton, A	1969 Netherlands
Lewis, G	1967/68 (Alma), 1969 Netherlands, 1979/80 (Composite XIs)
Littlewort, J	1951/52, 1952/53, 1953/54, 1954/55, 1956/57, 1957/58, 1958/59, 1959/60, 1962/63 captain, 1963/64 (Bellville)
Lock, J	1953/54
Lotter, T	1962/63, 1963/64 (Bellville) 1965/66 (Alma)
Manefeldt, D	1983/84
Marais, A	1971/72, 1972 NZ, 1972/73, 1973/74, 1974/75
Marneveld, D	1979/80 (Composite XIs)

McLeod, M	1978/79, 1979/80 (Composite XIs), 1983/84, 1984/85, 1985/86
Moolenschot, S	1952/53, 1953/54, 1954/55
Müller, Elize	1965/66 (Alma), 1967/68 (Alma), 1971/72, 1972 NZ
Nefdt, SN (née Charlton)	1951/52, 1952/53, 1953/54, 1954/55, 1956/57
Nel, D	1985/86
Nortier, M	1969/70 (Alma)
Owen, S	1984/85
Paine, P	1967/68 (Alma)
Patersen, A	1974/75
Payne, M	1956/57, 1957/58, 1958/59, 1959/60, 1962/63, 1963/64 captain (Bellville), 1965/66 (Alma), 1967/68 captain (Alma), 1971/72 captain, 1972 captain NZ, 1972/73 captain, 1973/74 captain, 1974/75
Peirce, C	1952/53, 1953/54, 1954/55, 1956/57, 197/58, 1958/59, 1959/60
Pickering, J	1958/59
Piggot, M	1969/70 (Alma), 1970/71, 1972/73, 1973/74, 1974/75
Pistorius, A	1978/79
Poole, W	1979/80 (Composite XIs)
Price, K	1978/79, 1979/80 (Composite XIs), 1983/84, 1984/85, 1985/86
Rayfield, S	1984/85
Rowles, M	1953/54, 1954/55
Rousseau, J	1983/84
Sacks, R	1978/79, 1979/80 (Composite XIs), 1983/84
Saunders, J	1951/52, 1952/53, 1953/54
Scott, B-J	1967/68 (Alma)
Skog, WH	1962/63, 1963/64 (Bellville), 1965/66 (Alma), 1967/68 (Alma), 1969 Netherlands
Smart, D	1956/57, 1959/60
Smart, E	1953/54
Tremble, P	1951/52, 1952/53, 1953/54
Valentine-Brown, V	1951/52 captain, 1952/53 captain, 1953/54 captain, 1954/55 captain, 1956/57 captain, 1957/58 captain, 1958/59 captain, 1960 captain England
Van der Merwe, M	1974/75, 1978/79, 1979/80 (Composite XIs), 1983/84, 1984/85, 1985/86
Van Zyl, J	1969 Netherlands, 1969/70 (Alma), 1970/71, 1971/72, 1972 NZ, 1972/73, 1973/74, 1974/75, 1979/80 (Composite XIs)
Vincent, I	1957/58, 1959/60, 1963/64 (Bellville), 1965/66 (Alma), 1967/68 (Alma), 1969 Netherlands, 1972/73
Ward, L	1969 Netherlands
Waugh, C	1979/80 (Composite XIs)
West, J	1951/52
Weyers, D	1962/63, 1965/66 (Alma), 1967/68 (Alma), 1969 captain Netherlands, 1970/71, 1971/72, 1972 NZ, 1972/73, 1973/74, 1974/75, 1978/79, 1979/80 (Composite XIs)
Williamson, G	1969 Netherlands
Wright, K	1953/54, 1956/57, 1957/58
Young, D	1956/57, 1957/58, 1958/59, 1959/60, 1962/63
Young, J	1953/54, 1954/55

7.3 Western Province Women's Cricket Union Winners in Annual SARWCA Inter-Provincial Tournaments for Simon Trophy, 1951/52–1985/86[221]

Season	Winners	Venue	Dates
1951/52	*Western Province*	Johannesburg	12–14 April 1952
1952/53	*Western Province*	Bloemfontein	1–4 January 1953
1953/54	*Western Province*	Cape Town	1–6 February 1954
1954/55	Southern Transvaal	Durban	5–11 January 1955
1955/56	Natal	Pretoria	9–14 January 1956
1956/57	Eastern Province	Port Elizabeth	7–12 January 1957
1957/58	Southern Transvaal	Johannesburg	6–11 January 1958
1958/59	Southern Transvaal	Cape Town	12–17 January 1959
1959/60	Natal	East London	11–16 January 1960
1960/61	[No tournament because of English tour][222]		
1961/62	Natal	Bloemfontein	[Dates not available]
1962/63	Eastern Province	Port Elizabeth	14–19 January 1963
1963/64	Natal	Durban	2–8 January 1964
1964/65	Natal	Johannesburg	[x–x] January 1965
1965/66	Southern Transvaal A	Bloemfontein	3–8 January 1966
1966/67	Natal	[Details not available]	1967
1967/68	Southern Transvaal	Cape Town	1–5 January 1968
1968/69	Southern Transvaal	Johannesburg	4–10 January 1969
1969/70	Southern Transvaal	East London	5–10 January 1970
1970/71	Southern Transvaal	Bloemfontein	4–8 January 1971
1971/72	Southern Transvaal	Pietermaritzburg	3–8 January 1972
1972/73	Southern Transvaal	Cape Town	29 Dec 1972 – 4 Jan 1973
1973/74*	Southern Transvaal	Johannesburg	30 Dec 1973 – 4 Jan 1974
1974/75	Southern Transvaal A	Bloemfontein	28 Dec 1974 – 4 Jan 1975
1975/76	*Western Province*	East London	24 Dec 1975 – 1 Jan 1976
1976/77	Southern Transvaal	Cape Town	27 Dec 1976 – 1 Jan 1977
1977/78	Southern Transvaal	Johannesburg	2–8 January 1978
1978/79	*Western Province*	Durban	1–6 January 1979
1979/80	*Western Province* or Southern Transvaal	Cape Town	31 Dec 1979 – 5 Jan 1980
1980/81	*Western Province* or Southern Transvaal	Johannesburg	28 Dec 1980 – 3 Jan 1981
1981/82	[Details not available]	[Details not available]	
1982/83	*No winner*	Cape Town	3–8 January 1983
1983/84	[Details not available]	Johannesburg	28 Dec 1983 – 3 Jan 1984
1984/85	*Western Province* or Southern Transvaal A or B	Durban	31 Dec 1984 – 5 Jan 1985
1985/86	*Western Province* or Southern Transvaal	Cape Town	28 Dec 1985 – 7 Jan 1986

*Simon Trophy not presented because only one province was officially represented.

7.4 Western Province Women's Cricket Union Scores, 1951/52–1985/86[223]

1ST INTER-PROVINCIAL TOURNAMENT FOR THE SIMON TROPHY, 12–14 APRIL 1952, JOHANNESBURG (UNOFFICIAL BECAUSE SARWCA NOT YET FORMED)[224]
Participating teams: Border, Griqualand West, Southern Transvaal, Western Province.
Winners Simon Trophy: Western Province

Western Province beat Griqualand West by an innings and 71 runs, 12 April 1952
GW 33 (SN Charlton 6/8) and 34 (W Jeffrey 3/6, SN Charlton 3/9)
WP 138/4 dec (V Valentine-Brown 55, SN Charlton 56*; [x] Oberholtzer 3/55)

Western Province beat Border by an innings and 10 runs, 13 April 1952
WP 102/5 dec (V Valentine-Brown 34, A Johnson 23*; M Chalmers 2/9)
Bdr 41 (SN Charlton 4/17) and 51 (SN Charlton 7/15)

Western Province beat Southern Transvaal on the first innings, 14 April 1952
S Tvl 155 ([x] Lilford 55, W Jeffrey 4/25)
WP 159/5 (SN Charlton 62)

1ST OFFICIAL SARWCA INTER-PROVINCIAL TOURNAMENT, 1–4 JANUARY 1953, BLOEMFONTEIN[225]
Participating teams: Border, Eastern Province, Griqualand West, Orange Free State, Rhodesia, Southern Transvaal, Natal, Northern Transvaal, Western Province.
Winners Simon Trophy (A Section): Western Province. Winners B Section: Orange Free State

Western Province beat Griqualand West by an innings and 16 runs, 1 January 1953
GW 56 (V Fountain 21, SN Charlton 6/24) and 63 (W Jeffrey 2/3, J Littlewort 3/7)
WP 135/1 dec (C Peirce 85*, J Littlewort 40)

Western Province beat Natal on the first innings, 2 January 1953
Ntl 66 (G Conradie 5/10) and 88 ([x] Harrison 26, [x] Scholtz 25; B Lang 6/7, SN Charlton 3/29)
WP 137 (W Jeffery 26; [x] Harrison 5/42, [x] Gradwell 4/38)

Western Province beat Southern Transvaal on the first innings, 3 January 1953
S Tvl 140 ([x] Mortimer 35, [x] Jordaan 25; A Johnson 3/16, W Jeffrey 3/26, G Conradie 2/11)
WP 157/7 (C Peirce 62 retd, W Jeffery 28*, SN Charlton 20; [x] Dyer 2/32, [x] Zuidmeer 2/43)

Western Province beat Orange Free State by an innings and 21 runs, 4 January 1953
OFS 83 ([x] Du Plessis 41*; W Jeffery 5/24, SN Charlton 2/11, G Conradie 2/31) and 72 (V Creighton 20*; G Conradie 2/16, S Moolenschot 2/15, SN Charlton 3/26, A Johnson 2/8)
WP 176

2ND SARWCA INTER-PROVINCIAL TOURNAMENT, 1–6 FEBRUARY 1954, CAPE TOWN[226]
Participating teams: Border (4), Natal (9), Port Elizabeth and Districts (4), Southern Transvaal (12), Western Province A (24), Western Province B (14).
Winners Simon Trophy: Western Province A

Western Province beat Southern Transvaal by an innings and 36 runs, 1 February 1954, Liesbeek Park
S Tvl 54 (E Hurly 37, SN Nefdt 6/27 including hat-trick) and 32 (D, Wood 10; SN Nefdt 6/21 including hat-trick)
WP 122 (SN Nefdt 37, J Young 16*; F Zuidmeer 5/31, R Jordaan 2/17, E Hurly 2/10)

Western Province beat Border by an innings and 57 runs, 2 February 1954, Rhodes Rec
Bdr 77 (D Wright 41*; J Moolenschot 4/5) and 32 (N Dowling 5/12, SN Nefdt 5/12)
WP 166/3 dec (V Valentine-Brown 54, C Peirce 28, B Lang 25; SN Nefdt 16*)

Western Province beat Western Province A by an innings and 51 runs, 3 February 1954, [x]
WP 128/8 dec (SN Nefdt 50*, W Jeffrey 20; J Genower 3/22, M Rowles 2/14)
WP A 50 (B Kingswell 16; N Dowling 4/7, W Jeffrey 4/11) and 27 (J Littlewort 5/6, N Dowling 2/2)

Western Province beat Eastern Province by an innings and 90 runs, 4 February 1954, Rhodes Rec
WP 151/0 dec (C Peirce 64*, V Valentine-Brown 76*)
EP 26 (D Mather-Pyke 19; J Young 4/3, J Littlewort 3/8, B Lang 3/8) and 35 (B Lang 4/3, SN Nefdt 3/23)

Western Province beat Natal on the first innings, 5 February 1954, Rhodes Rec
WP 171/6 dec (SN Nefdt 70, N Dowling 35*; [x] Harrison 3/55)
Ntl 36 (SN Nefdt 3/9, J Littlewort 3/9) and 34/1 (A Johnson 1/3)

Western Province beat The Rest on the first innings, 6 February 1954, Liesbeek Park A
WP 203/6 dec (SN Nefdt 100*, B Lang 48; F Zuidmeer 4/29, D Evenden 2/53)
The Rest 52 (F Zuidmeer 16, I Ellis 9; B Lang 2/8, SN Nefdt 4/5, J Littlewort 3/12)

Western Province A beat Eastern Province by an innings and 6 runs, 1 February 1954, Rhodes Rec
EP 62 (D Mather-Pyke 17; J Genower 6/12) and 30 (P Sapsford 14, D Mather-Pyke 10; M Rowles 6/9)
WP A 98 (M Rowles 24, J Genower 20; P Sapsford 6/15)

Western Province A beat Southern Transvaal on the first innings, 2 February 1954, Liesbeek Park B
S Tvl 62 (L Blake 13, B Cairncross 12, R Jordaan 10*; D Smart 3/18, P Abernethy 3/18, [J or P] Genower 2/8) and 65/3 (E Hurly 43*)
WP A 95 (E Kingswell 20; R Jordaan 3/16)

Western Province A beat Natal on the first innings, 4 February 1954, Liesbeek Park A
WP A 81 (B Kingswell 23, J Genower 20; Harrison 5/30, N Froude 3/19)
Ntl 40 (J Irwin 25*, M Rowles 6/12, E Smart 4/25)

Western Province A beat Border on the first innings, 5 February 1954, [x]
WP A 67 (J Saunders 19, [J or P] Genower 16; S Gersowsky 4/19) and 65/0 dec (E Kingswell 28*, [J or P] Genower 32*)
Bdr 41 (A Thomas 14; M Rowles 5/12, P Abernethy 5/14) and 60/5 (D Wright 24; [J or P] Genower 3/20)

3RD SARWCA INTER-PROVINCIAL TOURNAMENT, 5–11 JANUARY 1955, DURBAN[227]
Participating teams: Eastern Province, Natal, Northern Transvaal, Southern Transvaal, Southern Transvaal B, Western Province, Western Province B.
Winners Simon Trophy (A Section): Southern Transvaal. (B Section): Eastern Province

SECTION A
Western Province beat Northern Transvaal by 110 runs, 5–6 January 1955, Kingsmead No 2
WP 104 (V Valentine-Brown 52; S Grimbeek 9/34) and 104 (J Moolenschot 34*, C Peirce 22; SN Nefdt 3/4)
N Tvl 58 (L Kilfoil 13; M Rowles 5/13, SN Nefdt 3/4) and 40 (P Kessler 12; SN Nefdt 3/11)

Western Province beat Natal by 98 runs, 7–8 January 1955, Kingsmead No 1
WP 159 (SN Nefdt 57, C Peirce 35; J Irwin 4/50, J Harrison 3/46, O Gradwell 3/24) and 104/3 dec (V Valentine-Brown 33; J Irwin 1/41, J Harrison 1/30)
Ntl 80 (J Harrison 33, N Motyer 17; SN Nefdt 3/22, M Rowles 3/32) and 85 (T Wilson 21, J Irwin 20; SN Nefdt 6/41)

Southern Transvaal beat Western Province by 8 wickets, 10–11 January 1955, Kingsmead No 2
WP 57 (J Moolenschot 18; F Zuidmeer 5/20, I Ellis 3/19, J McNaughton 2/19) and 98 (C Peirce 33, B Lang 31; D Evenden 4/11, I Ellis 3/18, F Zuidmeer 3/25)
S Tvl 55 (S McCarthy 15, D Wood 13; N Dowling 3/12, SN Nefdt 3/13) and 103/2 (S McCarthy 37*, F Zuidmeer 23*; SN Nefdt 2/20)

SECTION B
Southern Transvaal B beat Western Province B on the first innings, 6 January 1955, [x]
S Tvl B 92 (N Blignault 22, R Campbell 17; E Dreyer 4/29) and 2/1 dec
WP B 24 (J Hardie 5/10) and 12/2

Eastern Province beat Western Province B on the first innings, 8 January 1955, [x]
EP 38 (M Potgieter 13; M Payne 3/3) and 42 (B O'Grady 11, [x] Dickie 11; M Payne 4/12, E Dreyer 4/15)
WP B 32 (J Law 8; E Moseley 5/14) and 45/8 (J Law 13; C Mennie 4/27)

Western Province B beat Southern Transvaal B by 9 wickets, 10 January 1955, [x]
S Tvl B 23 (D Smart 9/8) and 18 (D Smart 3/8, E Dreyer 4/9)
WP B 37 (D Smart 10; J Hardie 4/17) and 6/1

Eastern Province beat Western Province B on the first innings, 11 January 1955, [x]
WP B 33 (C Bald 13; C Mennie 5/13, E Moseley 3/4) and 27 (C Mennie 5/9)
EP 39 (M Main 11; D Smart 4/11, E Dreyer 4/13) and 20/1

4TH SARWCA INTER-PROVINCIAL TOURNAMENT, 9–14 JANUARY 1956, PRETORIA[228]
Participating teams: Eastern Province, Natal, Northern Transvaal, Southern Transvaal B, Western Province.
Winners Simon Trophy: Natal

SECTION A
Natal beat Western Province by 10 wickets, 11–12 January 1956
WP 83 (C Peirce 36, SN Nefdt 29; B Lang 4/20, R Kelly 4/21) and 153 (C Peirce 47, V Valentine-Brown 32, A Johnson 27; R Kelly 8/48)
Ntl 229/5 dec (B Lang 61*, E Lambert 60, J Harrison 57; J Littlewort 3/41) and 9/0

Southern Transvaal beat Western Province by 2 wickets, 13–14 January 1956
WP 84 (D Evenden 5/24) and 67 (I Ellis 5/10)
S Tvl 74 (S McCarthy 24; SN Nefdt 6/28) and 78/8 (B Cairncross 24; SN Nefdt 5/25)

5TH SARWCA INTER-PROVINCIAL TOURNAMENT, 7–12 JANUARY 1957, PORT ELIZABETH[229]
Participating teams: Eastern Province A, Eastern Province B, Natal, Northern Transvaal, Southern Transvaal, Southern Transvaal A, Southern Transvaal B, Western Province.
Winners Simon Trophy: Eastern Province

Western Province beat Eastern Province B by 8 wickets, 7-8 January 1957, General Motors
WP 78/7 dec and 30/2
EP B 28 (A Johnson 6/7) and 79 (C Mennie 30)

Western Province beat Northern Transvaal by an innings and 35 runs, 9 January 1957, xx
N Tvl 87 and 33 (SN Nefdt 5/10)
WP 155 (SN Nefdt 72*, N Dowling 53)

Western Province beat Natal on the first innings, 9–10 January 1957, Algoa
Ntl 94 ([x] Harrison 30, [x] Lambert 29) and 51/5
WP 140/9 (N Dowling 53, [x] Brown 39)

Western Province beat Southern Transvaal A on the first innings, 9–10 January 1957, Walmer
WP 199 (SN Nefdt 95, [x] Brown 37, N Dowling 30; [x] Brown 4/45, [x] Van Mentz 6/54)
S Tvl A 141 (B Cairncross 35, [x] Harvey 35; SN Nefdt 4/35, A Johnson 3/32)

Eastern Province A beat Western Province on the first innings, 11–12 January 1957, [x]
EP A 152 (M Hartnell 44, H Pyott 21, A Jackson 21; SN Nefdt 4/51)
WP 141 (C Peirce 48; A Jackson 4/35, L Daniels 3/18)

6TH SARWCA INTER-PROVINCIAL TOURNAMENT, 6–11 JANUARY 1958, JOHANNESBURG
Participating teams: Section A: Eastern Province, Natal, Southern Transvaal, Western Province. Section B: Border, Northern Transvaal, Northern Rhodesia, Southern Transvaal B.
Winners Simon Trophy (A Section): Southern Transvaal

Natal vs Western Province, 8–9 January, Wanderers B
[no details available]

Southern Transvaal vs Western Province, 10–11 January, Wanderers A
[no details available]

7TH SARWCA INTER-PROVINCIAL TOURNAMENT, 12–17 JANUARY 1959, CAPE TOWN[230]
Participating teams: Natal, Southern Transvaal, Western Province, Northern Rhodesia, North Westerns, Eastern Province, Border, Southern Transvaal B, Combined XI.
Winners Simon Trophy: Southern Transvaal

Western Province beat Northern Rhodesia by an innings and 104 runs, 12–13 January, Liesbeek Park B
WP 189/5 dec (N Dowling 105, V Valentine-Brown 24; SN Nefdt 3/80)
N Rhod 35 (N Dowling 5/4, C Alexander 3/3) and 50 (W Jeffrey 5/28, N Ashton 3/4)

Natal beat Western Province on the first innings, 14–15 January, Liesbeek Park A
WP 90 (N Dowling 31; Kelly 5/36, L Ward 3/41) and 195 (N Ashton 108*, C Peirce 20; Kelly 4/105)
Ntl 200/9 dec (Irwin 89, N Dowling 4/48)

Southern Transvaal beat Western Province by 10 wickets, 12–13 January, Liesbeek Park A
WP 75 (V Valentine-Brown 22; [x] Van Mentz 8/27) and 121 (May 3/45, [x] Van Mentz 3/26, [x] Hollett 2/0)
S Tvl 170 (Hurley 66, [x] Van Mentz 43; N Ashton 3/41, D Young 3/34) and 30/0

8TH SARWCA INTER-PROVINCIAL TOURNAMENT, 11–16 JANUARY 1960, EAST LONDON[231]
Participating teams: Border, Combined Provinces, Eastern Province, Natal, Northerns, Southern Transvaal A, Southern Transvaal B, South Westerns. [Western Province did not officially participate, but individual players from Western Province played in the B Section matches for South Westerns and Combined Provinces.]
Winners Simon Trophy: Natal

No SARWCA Inter-Provincial Tournament held in 1960/61 season because of international tour by England women's team

ENGLISH WOMEN'S CRICKETERS TOUR OF SOUTH AFRICA, NOVEMBER 1960 – JANUARY 1961[232]

England beat Western Province Composite XI by 10 wickets, Paarl, 12 November 1960
WP 59 (C Bald 17, M Robison 14; E Irwin 3/10, A Sanders 3/14, A Jago 2/7) and [x] (J Littlewort 25*, D Young 17) [75/4 at one stage]
Eng 193/3 dec (H Sharpe 88, K Smith 69; G Ronaldson 1/21) and [x/x]

England beat Western Province by 103 runs, Cape Town, 14–15 November 1960, Newlands[233]
Eng 172 (K Smith 24, OM Marshall 76*; M Payne 8/38) and 106/4 dec (AB Ratcliffe 33*, OM Marshall 27; N Dowling 1/21, SN Nefdt 1/16, [x] Gove 2/34)
WP 143 (N Dowling 34, B Lang 30, D Young, 19; OM Marshall 1/39, ME Hunt 6/27) and 32 (N Dowling 21; OM Marshall 1/13, ME Hunt 7/12)

9TH SARWCA INTER-PROVINCIAL TOURNAMENT, 1961/62, BLOEMFONTEIN, [X][234]
Participating teams: Alma (representing Western Province), Natal A, Natal B, Nomads, Southern Transvaal A, Southern Transvaal B.
Winners Simon Trophy: Natal A

Southern Transvaal A beat Alma by an innings and 61 runs, 20–21? January 1961, [x]
S Tvl A 161
Alma 30 and 70 (I Vincent 24, W Skog 19; L Ward 3/14, A Johnson 3/7)

Southern Transvaal B beat Alma
S Tvl B [no details available]
Alma 117 (I Vincent 32, C Bald 26, D Weyers 20)

10TH SARWCA INTER-PROVINCIAL TOURNAMENT, 14–19 JANUARY 1963, PORT ELIZABETH[235]
Participating teams: Eastern Province, Eastern Province/Border, Natal, Southern Transvaal A, Southern Transvaal B, Western Province.
Winners Simon Trophy: Eastern Province

SECTION B
Southern Transvaal B vs Western Province
[no details available]

Western Province vs Eastern Province/Border
[no details available]

11TH SARWCA INTER-PROVINCIAL TOURNAMENT, 2–8 JANUARY 1964, DURBAN[236]
Participating teams: Eastern Province, Natal, Southern Transvaal A, Combined Western Province/Border.[237]
Winners Simon Trophy: Natal

Combined Western Province/Border beat Southern Transvaal B on first innings
WP/Bdr 115 (Hodges 45; S Carroll 6/22) and 157/7 dec (J Littlewort 36)
S Tvl B 107 (P Lander 52; M Payne 6/24) and 153/6 (Katz 96)

Combined Western Province/Border beat Combined XI by 83 runs
WP/Bdr 128 (C Bald 28; D Ten-Cate 4/27) and 165 ([x] Bald 51; [x] Price-Williams 4/36)
Combined XI 112 (D Ten-Cate 48; [x] Lewis 3/20) and 98 ([x] Clark 4/27)

Natal A beat Combined Western Province/Border by an innings and 147 runs
Ntl A 227/6 dec
WP/Bdr 43 (L Ward 8/8) and 37 (N Motyer 5/1, J Gove 4/7)

12TH SARWCA INTER-PROVINCIAL TOURNAMENT, JANUARY 1965, JOHANNESBURG[238]
Participating teams: Natal A, Southern Transvaal B, Western Province, Southern Transvaal A, Combined XI, Natal B
Winners Simon Trophy: Natal

Western Province vs Southern Transvaal A
S Tvl A 183/9 dec (D Ten Cate 49, S Beech 39*, G Williamson 34)
WP 35 (L Egan 4/7, B Campbell 2/11) and [x] (C Hodges 20, M Minny [x], B Campbell [x], G Williams [x])

Southern Transvaal A beat Western Province by an innings and 50 runs
WP 35 (Egan 4/7, Campbell 2/4) and 98 (Campbell 3/23)
S Tvl A 183/9 dec (D Ten-Cate 49, F Beech 39)

Western Province beat Natal B by an innings and 75 runs, 14 January 1965, Greenside
Ntl B 79 (M Minny 3/2, M Payne 3/25) and 49 (M Payne 9/6)
WP 203/6 dec (C Bald 103*)

Western Province beat Combined XI by 83 runs
[no details available]

13TH SARWCA INTER-PROVINCIAL TOURNAMENT, 3–8 JANUARY 1966, BLOEMFONTEIN[239]
Participating teams: Alma, Natal A, Natal B, Nomads, Southern Transvaal A, Southern Transvaal B.
Winners Simon Trophy: Southern Transvaal A

Southern Transvaal A beat Alma by [x], 3–4 January 1966, CBC
S Tvl 161 (C Gildenhuys 43, S Johnson 35, S Edwards 31; D Weyers 3/21, M Payne 3/33)
Alma 30 (Ward 3/14, Johnson 3/4?) and [x] (I Vincent 24, W Skog 19; [x] Johnson 3/7, [x] Ward 3/14) [68/9 at one stage]

Alma beat Southern Transvaal B by [x], 5–6 January 1966, Ramblers A
Alma 117 (I Vincent 32, C Bald 26, D Weyers 20; G Webb 5/11, V Mennell 3/18) and [x] (M Payne 30, D Weyers 29, P Eaton 24)
S Tvl B 136 (P Nielson 45, P Ladner 23; M Payne 5/38, Clark 2/18) and [x]

Alma beat Nomads by an innings and 71 runs, 7–8 January 1966, Ramblers B
Alma 190
Nomads 66 and 53 (J Herselman 24, G Lewis 13; J Burger 7/1, E Muller 1/8, D Weyers 1/9)

14TH SARWCA INTER-PROVINCIAL TOURNAMENT, 1966/67, [X][240]
Winners Simon Trophy: Natal
[no details available]

15TH SARWCA INTER-PROVINCIAL TOURNAMENT, 1–5 JANUARY 1968, CAPE TOWN[241]
Winners Simon Trophy: Southern Transvaal

Southern Transvaal Schools vs Alma, 1 January 1968, 2A
[no details available]

Alma vs Sandpipers, 2 January 1968, 2B
[no details available]

Alma vs Swallows, 3 January 1968, Oval
[no details available]

Alma vs Seagulls, 4 January 1968, 2A
[no details available]

Alma vs Natalians, 5 January 1968
[no details available]

NEDERLANDSE DAMES CRICKET BOND TOUR OF SOUTH AFRICA, DECEMBER 1968 – JANUARY 1969[242]

Western Province drew with NDCB, 7 January 1969, Green Point Oval, Cape Town
Netherlands 23 (D Weyers 5/5) and 101/8 (C van der Flier 34, M Keizer 23*; G Lewis 3/10)
WP 102/4 dec (G Lewis 40*; L Schnitger 3/8)

16TH SARWCA INTER-PROVINCIAL TOURNAMENT, 6–10 JANUARY 1969, JOHANNESBURG[243]
Participating teams: Southern Transvaal Invitation XI, Southern Transvaal Girls A and B, Netherlands and five composite teams, namely Kingfishers, Natalians, Kookaburras, Woodpeckers and Tulips. [Western Province did not participate]
Winners Simon Trophy: Southern Transvaal

17TH SARWCA INTER-PROVINCIAL TOURNAMENT, 5–10 JANUARY 1970, EAST LONDON[244]
Winners Simon Trophy: Southern Transvaal

Natal beat Alma by an innings and 32 runs, 6 January 1970
Alma 23 (M Nortier 7, J Crosier 6; [x] Coetzee 7/8, [x] Iversen 3/9) and 64 (J Gordon 26, C Bald 19; [x] Moe 8/34, [x] Coetzee 1/5)
Ntl 119/2 dec ([x] Moe 44*, [x] Jones 40, [x] Grove 16*; J Burger 1/33)

Southern Transvaal Schools beat Alma by an innings and 41 runs, 7 January 1970
Alma 57 (C Bald 14, G Lewis 10, [x] Bailey 9; [x] Hatherall 4/6, [x] McLeod 3/13, [x] Moran 2/15) and 40 (C Bald 15, M Piggot 5*; [x] McLeod 5/9, [x] Botha 2/2)
S Tvl 138/2 dec ([x] Botha 67, [x] McLeod 27*, [x] Hatherall 23; J Crosier 1/30)

Southern Transvaal A beat Alma by an innings and 39 runs, 8 January 1970
Alma 41 (G Lewis 10, M Nortier 9; [x] Webb 4/9, [x] Skog 2/2, [x] Lankenau 2/15) and 58 (C Bald 17, J Gordon 12, [x] Varty 12*; [x] Neilson 3/25, [x] Mennell 2/1, [x] Webb 2/6)
S Tvl 138/5 dec ([x] Mennell 52*, [x] Van der Maas 28, [x] Lankenau 28; J Burger 4/38, J Gordon 1/54)

Alma beat Buffaloes by an innings and 1 run, 9 January 1970
Buffaloes 45 ([x] Burgess 13, [x] Sheard 11, [x] De Klerk 11; J Crosier 3/5, J Gordon 3/17, [x] Human 2/4) and 72 ([x] Sheard 41*, [x] McTavish 10, J Crosier 2/42, J Gordon 3/20, J Burger 5/21)
Alma 118 ([x] Human 40*, M Nortier 18, J Crosier 15; [x] Burgess 8/43, [x] Sheard 2/50)

18TH SARWCA INTER-PROVINCIAL TOURNAMENT, 4–8 JANUARY 1971, BLOEMFONTEIN[245]
Participating teams: Natal, Southern Transvaal A, Southern Transvaal B, Southern Transvaal C, Southern Transvaal Schools, Western Province.
Winners Simon Trophy: Southern Transvaal

Southern Transvaal C vs Western Province, 4 January, Schoeman Park
[no details available]

Western Province vs Southern Transvaal A, 5 January, Ramblers
[no details available]

Natal vs Western Province, 6 January, Schoeman Park
[no details available]

Southern Transvaal B vs Western Province, 7 January, Ramblers
[no details available]

Western Province vs Southern Transvaal Schools, 8 January, Schoeman Park
[no details available]

19TH SARWCA INTER-PROVINCIAL TOURNAMENT, 3–8 JANUARY 1972, PIETERMARITZBURG[246]
Participating teams: Border, Natal, Southern Transvaal, Southern Transvaal 1, Western Province.
Winners Simon Trophy: Southern Transvaal

Western Province beat Southern Transvaal on the first innings, [x] January 1972, Pietermaritzburg
S Tvl 64 (M Payne 5/18) and 11/4 (D Weyers 3/6)
WP 148/8 dec

Western Province vs Natal, [x] January 1972, Pietermaritzburg
WP [x]
Ntl [x] (D Weyers 6/9)

Western Province beat Border by 129 runs, [x] January 1972, Sax Young Ground, Pietermaritzburg
WP 138/2 dec (D Weyers 60, C Bald 30) and 71/2 dec (J Crosier 39, J Hannah 30*)
Bdr 70 (A Slogrove 24*) and 10/5 (J Burger 3/0)

New Zealanders drew with Western Province, 24 February 1972, Coetzenburg, Stellenbosch[247]
WP 48 (Weyers 10, Payne 7; Allan 3/10, Carrick 5/17) and 110/8 dec (Weyers 56, Payne 16, Burger 16*; Allan 3/32, Carrick 2/36, Lord 2/33)
NZ 121/5 dec (White 35, McKelvey 27, Cowles 26; Weyers 2/15, Muller 2/19) and 8/2

20TH SARWCA INTER-PROVINCIAL TOURNAMENT, 29 DECEMBER 1972 – 4 JANUARY 1973, CAPE TOWN[248]
Participating teams: Southern Transvaal (24), Southern Transvaal '1' (16), Southern Transvaal A (19), Western Province (22).
Winners Simon Trophy: Southern Transvaal

Western Province beat Southern Transvaal on the first innings, 30 December 1972, C Field
WP 114 (J Burger 40*, A Marais 31; C Hatherall 6/30, P Nellson 2/20)
S Tvl 37 (C Orsmond 16*; D Weyers 3/15, J van Zyl 3/19) and 41/5 (W Skog 13, P Nellson 10*; D Weyers 3/19)

Western Province beat Southern Transvaal '1' by 67 runs, 2 January 1973, C Field
WP 153/9 (J van Zyl 47, L Copping 24, D Weyers 22, Y Austin 22; M Ogston 2/14, L Killfoil 2/37)
S Tvl '1' 86 (M Ogston 45; J van Zyl 3/28, D Weyers 2/13, J Burger 2/14, M Payne 2/17)

Southern Transvaal vs Western Province, 3 January 1973, Stephan Oval
[no details available]

Western Province beat Southern Transvaal A on the first innings, 4 January 1973, Stephan Oval
WP 132 (L Copping 37, D Weyers 20, M Payne 18; D Ten-Cate 3/6, B Botha 3/25, J Webb 2/21)
S Tvl A 67 (B Williams 18; Y Austen 4/13, M Payne 4/17, J van Zyl 2/8)

21ST SARWCA CRICKET WEEK, 30 DECEMBER 1973 – 4 JANUARY 1974, JOHANNESBURG[249]
Participating teams: Southern Transvaal 20, Southern Transvaal A (Witwatersrand) 27, Southern Transvaal '1' (Highveld) 15, Western Province 20.
Winners: Southern Transvaal A (Witwatersrand) but no Simon Trophy awarded – unofficial tournament because only one official provincial team.

Southern Transvaal 1 (Highveld) vs Western Province [result not known], 31 December 1973, Marks Park
Highveld 106 (G Williamson 32) and [x] (D Ten-Cate 106, J Burley 68)
WP [x] and 133/8

Southern Transvaal A (Witwatersrand) drew with Western Province, 2 January 1974, Marks Park
Wits 'over' 200 (J Nel 57, P Nielson 41, S Moran 37)
WP did not bat – rain

Southern Transvaal beat Western Province on the first innings, 3 January 1974, Marks Park
S Tvl 225/5 dec (B Williams 108, C Hatherall 43, B Botha 42) and 91/4 dec (V Skog 46, Brentnall 32; M Gerrans 2/4)
WP 141 (J Hannah 46, A Marais 43; B Botha 5/35, V Skog 2/31) and 125/8 (A Marais 65, M Payne 36; B Botha 4/41)

22ND SARWCA CRICKET WEEK, 28 DECEMBER 1974 – 4 JANUARY 1975, BLOEMFONTEIN[250]
Participating teams: Combined XI (23), Southern Transvaal A (54), Southern Transvaal B (22), Unicorns (British Invitation XI) (61), Western Province (34). 60 overs per innings/every team to bat full 60 overs. Tournament ended with double-wicket tournament between 16 sides and Unicorns versus SA Invitation XI.
Winners: Unicorns (English Invitation XI). Winners: Simon Trophy: Southern Transvaal A

Unicorns beat Western Province, 28 December 1974
WP 145/9 (J van Zyl 81)
Unicorns 177/9 (C Whatmough 78)

Southern Transvaal A beat Western Province, 29 December 1974
S Tvl A 212/6 (D Ten-Cate 94, S Moran 43, B Botha 31)
WP 51 (V Skog 4/11)

Western Province vs Combined XI, Municipals, 31 December 1974
[no details available]

Western Province beat Southern Transvaal B, 2 January 1975
WP 124 (J Hannah 43, J van Zyl 31; A Kenny-Wade 5/44)
S Tvl B 90 (V Halbisch 25; D Weyers 4/16, M Gerrans, 3/17)

TOUR MATCH: UNICORNS (ENGLISH INVITATION XI) BEAT WESTERN PROVINCE BY NINE WICKETS, 8 JANUARY 1975, WELLINGTON[251]
60-over match
WP 72 (J Burger 15*, J Court 4/14)
Unicorns 75/1 (A Disbury 41*, D Weyers 1/12)

'20 overs resumed'
WP 96/2 (J van Zyl 42*)
Unicorns 74/9 (M Payne 2/13, Y Austen 2/6)

23RD SARWCA CRICKET WEEK, 24 DECEMBER 1975 – 1 JANUARY 1976, EAST LONDON[252]
Winners: Unicorns (English Invitation XI) (Cricket Week Trophy) and Western Province (Simon Trophy)

Unicorns (English Invitation XI) beat Western Province by 44 runs, 29 December 1975, East London
Unicorns 144 (J Court 28, K Brown 32, L Judd 38; J Burger 4/34, Y Austen 3/14)
WP 100 (J Hannah 26, D Weyers 23; I Crocker 4/34, J Lloyd 1/1)

[No details of other provincial games available]

TOUR MATCH: UNICORNS (ENGLISH INVITATION XI) BEAT WESTERN PROVINCE BY 62 RUNS, 4 JANUARY 1976, CAPE TOWN
Unicorns 203/5 dec (A Disbury 70, J Court 33, K Brown 24*; D Weyers 2/45)
WP 141 (J Hannah 34, J van Zyl 31; M Pilling 3/14)

24TH SARWCA CRICKET WEEK, 27 DECEMBER 1976 – 1 JANUARY 1977, CAPE TOWN[253]
Two official provinces only participating: Southern Transvaal, Western Province. Plus six composite teams (The Penguins, The Duikers, The Seagulls, The Sharks, The Harders and The Sardines) playing 15 matches, three per day.
Winners Simon Trophy: Southern Transvaal

Western Province vs Southern Transvaal, 1 January 1977, Alma Marist CC (Only official Inter-Provincial fixture)
[no details available]

25TH SARWCA CRICKET WEEK, 2–8 JANUARY 1978 (SILVER JUBILEE CRICKET WEEK), JOHANNESBURG[254]
Two official provinces only participating: Southern Transvaal, Western Province. Plus six composite teams (Botha XI, Neilson XI, Ten-Cate XI, Toms XI, Weyers XI and Williams XI, playing 15 matches, three per day.
Winners Simon Trophy: Southern Transvaal

Southern Transvaal beat Western Province by [x], 7 January 1978 (Only Inter-Provincial fixture)
S Tvl [x]
WP [x]

26TH SARWCA CRICKET WEEK, 1–6 JANUARY 1979, DURBAN[255]
Participating teams: Combined Provinces, Natal, Southern Transvaal A, Southern Transvaal B', Unicorns (British Invitation XI), Western Province.
Winners Simon Trophy: Western Province

Unicorns beat Western Province by 8 wickets, 1 January 1979, University of Natal A Field, Durban
WP 68 (Y Austen 20*; J Court 4/11, G McConway 4/15)
Unicorns 69/2 (M Taylor 25, M Botha 20)

Western Province drew with Southern Transvaal 'A', 2 January 1979, University of Natal A Field, Durban
[no details available]

Western Province beat Southern Transvaal B on the first innings, 3 January 1979, University of Natal A Field, Durban
WP [x] (M McLeod 55)
S Tvl B [x] (D Weyers 5/30, M McLeod [x]/[x])
[no details available]

Western Province beat Natal by an innings and 37 runs, 4 January 1979, University of Natal B Field, Durban
Ntl 47 (S Everitt 17, D Moe 14; Y Austen 4/1 J Burger 3/5, D Weyers 3/14) and 31 (M McLeod 6/11)
WP 115/7 dec (M McLeod 53*; S Everitt 4/41)

TOUR MATCH: UNICORNS DREW WITH WESTERN PROVINCE, 9 JANUARY 1979, ALMA MARIST CC, CAPE TOWN[256]
Unicorns 180/5 (J Pritchard 54, M Botha 46; D Weyers 3/53)
WP 153/2 (M McLeod 61*, Y Austen 32*; Norman 1/21)

27TH SARWCA CRICKET WEEK, 31 DECEMBER 1979 – 5 JANUARY 1980, RONDEBOSCH BOYS HIGH SCHOOL, CAPE TOWN[257]
Participating teams: Western Province, Southern Transvaal. Plus six composite teams (A, B, C, D, E, F), playing 15 matches, three per day.
Winners Simon Trophy: Western Province or Southern Transvaal

Southern Transvaal vs Western Province, 5 January 1980, Rondebosch Boys High School
[no details available]

Southern Transvaal Juniors vs Western Province Juniors, 5 January 1980, Rondebosch Boys High School
[no details available]

28TH SARWCA CRICKET WEEK, MARKS PARK, 28 DECEMBER 1980–3 JANUARY 1981, JOHANNESBURG[258]
Participating teams: Western Province, Southern Transvaal.
Winners Simon Trophy: Western Province or Southern Transvaal

Southern Transvaal 'A' vs Western Province, 3 January 1984, Top Field, Marks Park
[no details available]

Southern Transvaal Juniors vs Western Province Juniors, 3 January 1984, Middle Field, Marks Park
[no details available]

29TH SARWCA CRICKET WEEK, 1981/82, [X], [X]
Participating teams: Western Province.
Winners Simon Trophy: [no details available]
[no details available]

30TH SARWCA CRICKET WEEK, 3–8 JANUARY 1983, CAPE TOWN[259]
Participating teams: Southern Transvaal only official team. Four composite teams (A, B, C, D) play 8 games, two per day at Impala, Keurboom and Bishops. Select XI chosen to play Southern Transvaal. Western Province and Southern Transvaal schoolgirls also played. Unicorns were scheduled to participate but tour called off.
Winners Simon Trophy: none [no official provincial games]

31ST SARWCA CRICKET WEEK, 28 DECEMBER 1983 – 3 JANUARY 1984, MARKS PARK, JOHANNESBURG[260]
Participating teams: Western Province, Southern Transvaal, Unicorns. Plus six composite teams (1, 2, 3, 4, 5, 6) play 15 games, three per day.
Winners Simon Trophy: [no details available]

Southern Transvaal A vs Western Province, 31 December 1983, Top Field, Marks Park
[no details available]

32ND SARWCA CRICKET WEEK, 31 DECEMBER 1984 – 5 JANUARY 1985, DURBAN[261]
Participating teams: Western Province, Southern Transvaal A, Southern Transvaal B. Plus five composite teams (Marlins, Dolphins, Seals, Otters, Porpoises) playing 8 games, two per day.
Winners Simon Trophy: Western Province or Southern Transvaal A or Southern Transvaal B

Southern Transvaal B vs Western Province, 2 January 1985
[no details available]

Southern Transvaal A vs Western Province, 5 January 1985
[no details available]

33RD SARWCA CRICKET WEEK, 28 DECEMBER 1985 – 7 JANUARY 1986, CAPE TOWN[262]
Participating teams: Western Province, Southern Transvaal, Unicorns. Plus six composite teams (Disas, Ericas, Roses, Nerinas, Flame Lilies, Barberton Daisies) play 12 games, three per day at Impala, Ohlssons and YMCA fields.
Winners Simon Trophy: Western Province or Southern Transvaal

Unicorns vs Western Province, 28 December 1985, Impala
[no details available]

Southern Transvaal vs Western Province, 3 January 1986, Impala
[no details available]

CHAPTER 8
Western Province Cricket Federation, 1952–1959

Combined team of different Western Province racial affiliates of the South African Cricket Board of Control

By the 1950s there were five different cricket control bodies in the Western Province. The Western Province Cricket Federation (WPCF), started on 10 September 1952 'after numerous negotiations', was an attempt by socially aware cricketers from various of these organisations to work across ethnic lines.[263] It was formed at exactly the time in the early apartheid years that the National Party government was trying to disenfranchise 'coloured' voters and remove them from the common voters' roll. For the Federation's initiators, it did not make sense from the point of view of numbers and playing strength that so-called 'non-white' cricketers in Cape Town played in a host of separate bodies. Moreover, the notion of playing cricket along ethnic lines was increasingly becoming discredited politically.

According to the pioneering *South African Non-European Cricket Almanack*, 'the administrators responsible for the formation of this body' were the elegant cricketer and rugby star AJ 'Dol' Freeman, the city councillor Hoosain E Parker, the journalist DN Bansda and the African administrators 'Pat' Cossie and WB Lubulwana (whose daughter Peggy married Ray Mali, who went on to become president of Cricket South Africa and the International Cricket Council in 2007). The administrators in the new Federation brought together the Western Province Coloured Cricket Union, Western Province Bantu Cricket Union, Western Province Indian Cricket Union, Central Cricket League and Hottentots Holland Cricket Union. The powerful Peninsula and Western Districts Cricket Board (PWDCB) was reluctant to participate in the WPCF. Officials claimed in later years that part of the reason for not co-operating was that the PWDCB was the best-resourced organisation and was not prepared to subsidise the others, but there were racial and religious undertones as well. The PWDCB and its mother body pushed openly segregationist positions at this time.[264] Muslims and dark-skinned cricketers were turned away by some affiliates.[265] However, two notable exceptions were the Wynberg and District Cricket Union under Clifford Ravens (based in Ottery Road, Wynberg) and the Stellenbosch and District Cricket Union, led by Archie Pool and the young Matt Segers, who became a stalwart of the non-racial sports struggle in the next few decades. These sub-unions of the PWDCB in due course decided to join with other 'race' groups, despite the disapproval of their mother bodies at provincial and national level.

The first elected executive of the WPCF consisted of AJ Freeman (president), EC Hodges and WB Lubulwana (vice-presidents), DN Bansda (hon. secretary), J Wilcox (assistant secretary), HE Parker (hon. treasurer), G Baderoen and C Ravens (hon. auditors). The Moslem Progressive Society and Mr E Schroeder presented a trophy, which the Western Province Coloured Cricket Union won in the first season. Central Cricket League came second. The *Almanack* reports that 'the Inaugural Year turned out to be very, very successful. The standard of cricket was of the highest order. Every match was played in the best of spirit.' The Federation 'is something more, and something better, than an Inter-Race body', it concluded.[266]

In December 1952, the new WPCF organised a match against the South African Bantu Cricket Board's national team, following the tenth inter-provincial tournament of the Africans in Cape Town. The match, played on the Mowbray Sports Ground, reflected the intentions of the new Federation to build unity amongst black cricketers. The Federation won by ten wickets. The team was captained by its president, the legendary 'Dol' Freeman. One of the players in the African side was Eric Majola, father of the current chief executive of Cricket South Africa, Gerald Majola. The *Non-European Cricket Almanack* reported that a feature of the match was 'the spirit in which it was played'. 'The playing of this match has been a milestone in the short history of the Federation, for certain Unions, affiliated for the first time, had a taste of representative cricket, higher than Inter-Union matches.'

The next big step for the Federation was to arrange a goodwill tour to Port Elizabeth and Durban in December 1953, joining up with like-minded people in the Eastern Province and Natal to promote the idea of inter-provincial cricket that ignored racial boundaries. It also organised a match against a team of top local white cricketers captained by the provincial player Alan Marshall in the same season.

The tour manager, Matt Segers, recalled in later years how important the goodwill tour had been in building unity. Travelling together in a tarpaulin-covered truck, the team covered two thousand miles and played ten matches, including three two-day games, in 15 days. The team won nine out of the ten matches. It was captained by 'Happie' Nordien and consisted of players from six different unions and sub-unions in the Western Province.[267] Commenting on the tour, the *Sun* newspaper said it gave credence to the views of those in cricket who 'stressed the need for running the South African Non-European Cricket Tournament on provincial lines and not a tribal system as at present'. It added that the tour had shown that the time had arrived to play provincial cricket on an integrated basis. 'It would be a good idea if tours of this nature could be undertaken by the other provinces. This one was very successful from both the players' and spectators' point of view. I have had talks with cricket personalities in Port Elizabeth and Durban and all agreed that Non-European cricket would definitely be on the upgrade if Inter-Provincial rather than Inter-Racial games were played ... Let us, therefore, sink whatever petty differences we may have, dismiss this racial business from our minds and build a strong "United Cricket Federation".'

However, the initiators of the Federation were ahead of their time and the inter-union games of that season were to be the last. The Federation folded after this because of a lack of funds and, especially, a lack of support from 'coloured' cricketers in the strong Peninsula and Western Districts Board. Nevertheless, the seed sown by the Federation grew. In 1956, a combined Western Province team was selected to play against the Kenya Asians during the first international tour organised by SACBOC. Those involved belonged to the old Federation network. They were prominent again in 1959 when the non-racial Western Province Cricket Board was formed, inaugurating a new era in the history of Western Province cricket.

8.1 Western Province Cricket Federation National Players

None. Players picked for combined SACBOC Springboks in 1950s were selected as members of separate national associations, although some played for the provincial Federation as well.

8.2 Western Province Cricket Federation Provincial Players, 1952/53–1956/57[268]

Abed, G 'Tiny'	WP Coloured Cricket Union	1952/53, 1953/54, 1956/57
Abed, S 'Lobo'	WP Coloured Cricket Union	1953/54, 1956/57
Abrahams, CJ	PWDCB	1956/57
Bagus, A	Holland Coloured Cricket Union	1952/53
Bardien, S	WP Coloured Cricket Union	1952/53, 1956/57
Bhayat, MA	[x]	1956/57
Coetzee, M	Central Cricket League	1952/53, 1953/54
Desai, A	WP Indian Cricket Union	1952/53
D'Oliveira, BL	PWDCB	1956/57
Freeman, AJ 'Dol'	WP Coloured Cricket Union	1952/53, 1953/54
Hendricks, T	WP Coloured Cricket Union	1953/54
Holmes, G	WP Coloured Cricket Union	1953/54
Lakay, Y 'Timmy'	[x]	1956/57
Latief, I	Hottentots Holland Coloured Cricket Union	1952/53, 1953/54
Nordien, H	WP Coloured Cricket Union	1953/54
Malamba, BN	[x]	1956/57
Osman, AA 'Bakar'	WP Coloured Cricket Union	1952/53
Osmany, MS	[x]	1956/57
Petersen, E	WP Coloured Cricket Union	1953/54
Ravens, C	Wynberg and District Cricket Union	1953/54
Raziet, S 'Laam'	Stellenbosch and District Cricket Union	1952/53, 1956/57
Rhoode, E	Stellenbosch and District Cricket Union	1953/54
Sabotker, A	Central Cricket League	1953/54
Shaikh, IE	WP Coloured Cricket Union	1953/54
Solomon, SN	Central Cricket League	1953/54
Thomas, P	Central Cricket League	1952/53, 1953/54
Truter, J	Central Cricket League	1953/54
Wilsnach, R	Central Cricket League	1952/53
Witten, B	PWDCB	1956/57

8.3 Trophies and Competitions

None. Inter-union league in Cape Town and friendlies only.

8.4 Western Province Cricket Federation Scores, 1952/53–1956/57[269]

8.4.1 Western Province Cricket Federation Inter-Provincial and Friendly Matches, 1952/53-1956/57

Western Province Cricket Federation beat South African Bantu Cricket Board XI by 10 wickets, December 1952, Mowbray Sports Grounds, Cape Town
SABCB 154 (E Fihla 49, G Voss 25; S Bardien 4/29, I Latief 3/21) and 103 (W Ximiya 18, E Fihla 15; S Raziet 5/47, A Bagus 2/12)
WP 124 (G Abed 66, I Latief 38, M Coetzee 35*; G Langa 4/64, BN Malamba 4/75) and 17/0[270] (S Raziet 8*, A Desai 7*)

Western Province Cricket Federation beat combined Eastern Province by an innings and 33 runs, December 1953, Port Elizabeth
EP 20 (G Abed 5/11, A Sabotker 5/8) and 88 (H Ayoob 40; E Petersen 5/21)
WP 141 (G Abed 54*, I Latief 21, E Petersen 20; SV Coopoo 5/30)

Eastern Province Coloured Cricket League beat WP Cricket Federation on the first innings, December 1953, Port Elizabeth
EP Coloureds 86 (S Hendricks 20; A Sabotker 9/31) and 92/6 (S Baderoon 34, E Baderoon 22)
WP 52 (G Connelly 5/3, S Baderoon 3/28)

Western Province Cricket Federation beat Eastern Province Bantu Cricket Union by an innings and 101 runs, December 1953, Port Elizabeth
EP Bantus 61 (I Latief 6/9, G Abed 3/15) and 74 (L Maqoma 25; I Latief 8/49)
WP 236/7 dec (M Coetzee 50, T Hendricks 48, E Rhoode 36, P Thomas 35, G Holmes 26*; E Majola 3/59)

Western Province Cricket Federation beat Eastern Province Indian Cricket Union on the first innings, December 1953, Port Elizabeth
EP Indians 56 (G Abed 4/20, M Coetzee 3/17) and 104/8 (H Ayoob 36, P Pillay 26, NV Coopoo 22*; G Abed 4/20)
WP 182 (E Rhoode 36, M Coetzee 33, T Hendricks 27, I Latief 26, G Abed 20; T Morgan 6/21)

Western Province Cricket Federation beat Eastern Province Cricket Federation by an innings and 108 runs, December 1953, Port Elizabeth
WP 235 (J Truter 65, E Rhoode 41, E Petersen 37, T Hendricks 34; E Majola 5/52, T Morgan 3/68)
EP 89 (G Masiza 24*; I Latief 4/10, G Abed 3/28, E Petersen 3/39) and 38 (M Coetzee 6/9)

Durban A beat Western Province Cricket Federation on the first innings, December 1953, Durban
WP 114 (G Abed 41; El Jeewa 6/49)
Dbn A 152 (S Pather 42, IA Timol 34, MI Yusuf 35, IS Osman 29; A Sabotker 3/36, AJ Freeman 4/29)

Western Province Cricket Federation beat Durban B by an innings and 12 runs, December 1953, Durban
Dbn B 58 (E Petersen 6/18) and 100 (W Stephens 41; E Petersen 4/15, H Nordien 3/24)
WP 170 (S Solomon 38, G Abed 39, S Abed 20, A Sabotker 24*)

Western Province Cricket Federation beat Durban Liquor & Caterers Cricket Union by an innings and 113 runs, December 1953, Durban
DLCCU 35 (M Coetzee 3/10, A Sabotker 7/24) and 39 (M Coetzee 4/13, A Sabotker 5/26)
WP 187/7 dec (T Hendricks 20, P Thomas 36, IE Shaikh 50*, C Ravens 26, J Truter 43; V Bobby 3/36)

Western Province Cricket Federation beat Natal Schools XI by an innings and 131 runs, December 1953, Durban
Ntl Schools XI 12 (M Coetzee 8/4) and 84 (D Ackojee 27*; AJ Freeman 6/25)
WP 227 (AJ Freeman 29, G Abed 102*, I Latief 40; O Rambaran 3/75, H Harrilal 3/27)

Western Province Cricket Federation beat Natal Indian XI by eight wickets, December 1953, Durban
Ntl Indian XI 77 (IE Jeewa 21*) and 111 (IE Seedat 37, MI Yusuf 24; AJ Freeman 4/25, P Thomas 6/32)
WP 105 (J Truter 30; AI Timol 3/36) and 89/2 (S Solomon 38, AJ Freeman 29*)

Alan Marshall XI beat Western Province Cricket Federation by 34 runs, January 1954, Vineyard grounds, Claremont
Marshall XI 93 (B Killian 33, F Bing 11; E Petersen 5/30, M Coetzee 4/10) and 113/4 dec (F Bing 45, B Phaf 25)
WP 38 (L Less 15; B Peacock, 8/15) and 134 (L Abed 38, G 'Tiny' Abed 23, P Thomas 23; A Marshall 4/30)

Kenyan Asians beat Western Province (Combined) by 155 runs, 1–3 December 1956, Hartleyvale, Cape Town[271]
Kenyan Asians 174 (Ramanbhai Patel 55, GB Jhalla 48; BN Malamba 5/64, CJ Abrahams 3/40) and 261 (Arvind Patel 70, G Ahmed 58, Chandrakant Patel 42; C Abrahams 4/53, S Bardien 4/65)
WP 183 (C Abrahams 54, S Raziet 35, G Abed 22, BL D'Oliveira 20; Rasik Patel 4/46) and 97 (BL D'Oliveira 39; JR Jabbar 4/17, GB Jhalla 2/25, B D'Cunha 2/34)

Kenyan Asians beat Paarl–Stellenbosch (the latter previously a participant in the WPCF) by 10 wickets, 5 December 1956, Paarl
Paarl–Stellenbosch 183 (D Cupido 62, R Salie 49, Lawrence 22; MH Hirani 5/40, B D'Cunha 4/47) and 109/9 dec (A Manuel 63*, Poole 21; Rasik Patel 4/34, B D'Cunha 3/29)
Kenyan Asians 185/8 dec (Arvind Patel 52*, S Ahmed 27, Mehboob Ali 24, Mubarak Ali 22, B D'Cunha 21*; G Roux 5/57) and 110/0 (S Ahmed 50*, Mubarak Ali 55*)

8.4.2 Western Province Cricket Federation Inter-Union Matches, 1952/53–1953/54

Western Province Bantu Cricket Union beat Western Province Indian Cricket Union on the first innings, 1–2 November 1952
WPBCU 171 (B Cossie 60, A Ntshona 25, S Vengo 32; J Gheewala 6/40 and A Desai 3/25) and 111 (S Vengo 71; J Gheewala 6/36, A Desai 3/30)
WPICU 141 (O Magmoet 34, M Abrahams 54; B Cossie 4/43, N Kawulela 4/60, AM Mshumpela 1/10) and 53/4 (O Magmoet 29*; A Balfour 2/8, B Cossie 1/4)

Wynberg and District Cricket Union beat Hottentots Holland Cricket Union on the first innings, 29–30 November 1952
HH 95 (H Gafieldien 35, G Ravens 5/30, O Kafaar 3/18, J da Rocha 2/27) and 264/9 dec (I Latief 75, H Gafieldien 36*, R Thomas 30, S Abels 62, E Railoun 20, G Ravens 37; M Fakier 2/45, J da Rocha 2/60)
WDCU 122 (C Ravens 25, G Campbell 29*; I Latief 4/37, G Baderoen 2/31, E Railoun 1/0) and 182/9 (C Ravens 78, O Kafaar 22, J da Rocha 35; I Latief 4/53, A Khan 3/32)

Hottentots Holland Cricket Union beat Western Province Bantu Cricket Union by 8 wickets, 6–7 December 1952
WPBCU 68 (B Cossie 32) and 234 (B Cossie 61, TM Mgijima 35, N Kawulela 28, AM Mshumpela 26, T Dikweni 30, H Siyaya 21)
HH 248 (M Dlanga 3/40, A Balfour 3/48, AM Mshumpela 2/48) and 55/2

Wynberg and District Cricket Union beat Western Province Bantu Cricket Union by 47 runs, 13–14 December 1952
WDCU 45 (J da Rocha 22; AM Mshumpela 5/16, A Balfour 3/26) and 74 (A Balfour 7/46, AM Mshumpela 3/16)
WPBCU 22 (T Francis 6/14, J da Rocha 4/6) and 50 (O Kafaar 8/10)

Central Cricket League beat Wynberg and District Cricket Union by an innings and 51 runs, 20 and 27 December 1952
WDCU 84 (B Bennet 43, M Coetzee 3/21, A Sabotker 3/48, S Solomon 3/5) and 135 (G van Schalkwyk 67, L Robertson 332, M Coetzee 3/37, H Moody 214)
CCL 270 (R Wilsnach 107, D Koks 62, P Thomas 54, G van Schalkwyk 5/51, O Kafaar 1/17, N Ravens 2/105)

Western Province Coloured Cricket Union beat Stellenbosch and District Cricket Union by an innings and 18 runs, 26–27 December 1952
Stel 91 (E Rhoode 23*; H Noordien 6/30, E Petersen 2/18) and 68 (S Raziet 27; AJ Freeman 6/34, H Noordien 2/21)
WPCCU 177 (A Abrahams 27, M du Toit 22, G Abed 28, GT Holmes 31, H Noordien 31; A Manuel 3/39, E Davidson 3/51, S Raziet 2/34)

Stellenbosch and District Cricket Union beat Western Province Bantu Cricket Union by an innings and 89 runs, 2–3 January 1953
WPBC 116 (B Cossie 30, J Nyamakazi 30, AM Mshumpela 22*; A Manuel 3/15, W Anthony 4/47) and 118 (BN Malamba 30, F Hoho 34*; G Gabriel 2/28, D Hendricks 4/24, W Anthony 2/22)
Stel 323/9 dec (E Rhoode 54, A Manuel 96, A Poole 64, D Hendricks 52*; A Balfour 2/72)

Wynberg and District Cricket Union beat Stellenbosch and District Cricket Union by 5 wickets, 17 and 24 January 1953
Stel 133 (S Raziet 62*, W Anthony 25; G van Schalkwyk 4/37, J Seegers 4/26) and 158/8 dec (S Raziet 59, W Anthony 31, A Manuel 24, E Sylvester 20; J Seegers 4/30)
WDCU 188 (C Ravens 75, T Francis 33, A Manuel 3/39, E Davidse 2/33, S Raziet 3/9) and 104/5 (B Bennet 27, C Ravens 34*; A Manuel 3/33)

Central Cricket League beat Western Province Bantu Cricket Union by 24 runs, 31 January – 1 February 1953
CCL 100 (P Thomas 33, A Sabotker 27*; AM Mshumpela 3/30, BN Malamba 2/16, J Nyamakazi 2/13) and 147/7 dec (P Thomas 38, J Truter 32*, A Sabotker 34*; A Balfour 3/52, J Nyamakazi 2/21)
WPBCU 120 (B Cossie 45*, BN Malamba 34; A Sabotker 5/40, H Moody 2/21, P Thomas 2/5) and 103 (C Dokweni 20, B Cossie 20; A Sabotker 4/32, P Thomas 6/23)

Central Cricket League beat Hottentots Holland Cricket Union by 73 runs, 7–8 February 1953
CCL 110 (D Hermans 22, S Solomons 34, A Hendricks 24; G Baderoen 7/26, I Latief 2/19) and 93 (R Wilsnach 27, G Baderoen 5/26)
HH 42 (L Robertson 7/7, A Sabotker 3/28) and 88 (N Daniels 24, R Ingham 20; A Sabotker 6/32, L Robertson 4/37)

Western Province Coloured Cricket Union beat Western Province Indian Cricket Union by 10 wickets, 14–15 February 1953
WPICU 58 (J Magmoet 24; E Petersen 5/5, I Bohardien 3/28) and 162 (N Fakier 72, M Abrahams 40; I Bohardien 5/45, E Petersen 4/23)
WPCCU 185 (O Fataar 47, E Dollie 30, G Abed 29; J Gheewala 4/26, I Pangarkar 2/38, A Desai 2/10) and 38/0 (L Less 22*)

Central Cricket League tied with Stellenbosch and District Cricket Union, 14 and 21 February 1953
CCL 186 (H Moody 49, J Truter 57, I Dantu 32, D Hermans 21, O Raziet 3/11, E Rhoode 3/10) and 152/5 dec (D Hermans 49, I Dantu 23, A Hendricks 41, D Hendricks 2/39)
Stel 119 (E Rhoode 70, T King 53, A Poole 21, A Sabotker 5/57, L Robertson 3/64) and 219

Western Province Coloured Cricket Union beat Western Province Bantu Cricket Union by 8 wickets, 28 February – 1 March 1953
WPBCU 59 (E Petersen 8/27) and 73 (I Bohardien 6/29, E Petersen 3/21, A Freeman 1/2)
WPCCU 83 (AK Abrahams 20; AM Mshumpela 3/19, B Cossie 3/17, N Kawulela 1/5) and 55/2 (AA Osman 18*)

Central Cricket League beat Western Province Indian Cricket Union by an innings and 85 runs, 7–8 March 1953
WPICU 55 (MH Rahbeeni 20; L Robertson 4/21, H Moody 3/4, S Solomon 3/2) and 186 (A Desai 35, O Magmoet 38, S van Haaght 39, A Gardee 21; L Robertson 5/42, A Sabotker 2/32)
CCL 326 (S Solomon 107, I Dantu 40, H Moody 30, A Sabotker 35, D Hermans 26, P Liederman 23; M Abrahams 3/53, A Gardee 2/38)

Western Province Coloured Cricket Union beat Wynberg and District Cricket Union by 8 wickets, 7–8 March 1953
WDCU 78 (G Abed 4/24, E Petersen 5/46) and 160 (C Ravens 20, A Eckles 27, O Kafaar 56; E Petersen 4/47, G Abed 2/21)
WPCCU 166 (AJ Freeman 20, GT Holmes 27, S Abed 27, E Abrahams 25, E Petersen 23; J da Rocha 4/47, J Francis 3/64) and 74/2

Western Province Coloured Cricket Union beat Hottentots Holland Cricket Union by 10 wickets, 11–12 April 1953
HH 60 (A Bagus 18; E Petersen 3/15, AJ Freeman 3/23, S Bardien 4/15) and 110 (S Abels 20, E Petersen 6/29, H Noordien 2/52, G Abed 1/9)
WPCCU 153 (G Abed 36, H Noordien 33, AJ Freeman 23; G Baderoen 5/52, N Daniels 1/10, S Arendse 1/12) and 22/0 (A Davids 19*)

Hottentots Holland Cricket Union beat Stellenbosch Cricket Union on the first innings, 7 and 14 March 1953
Stel 176 (S Raziet 52, T King 23, AA Pool 27*; S Arendse 3/19, G Baderoen 3/27, H Arendse 2/26) and 199/8 (S Raziet 75*, T King 34, E Davidse 23*; A Bagus 2/35, S Arendse 2/43)
HH 241 (R Ingham 47, S Arendse 47, R Sadie 45; W Anthony 3/49, E Davidse 2/22, AA Poole 2/39)

Matches between Western Province Indian Cricket Union vs Hottentots Holland Cricket Union and Wynberg and District Cricket Union vs Stellenbosch and District Cricket Union forfeited

Central Cricket League beat Western Province Coloured Cricket Union on the first innings, [x]
CCL 288 (P Thomas 149, M Coetzee 27, A Sabotker 26*; G Abed 6/87, S Bardien 4/65)
WPCCU 106 (G Abed 37, AA Osman 23; L Robertson 6/44, M Coetzee 2/9, C Felix 2/11) and 231/9 (GT Holmes 54, G Abed 51, E Dollie 32; M Coetzee 4/52)

Western Province Bantu Cricket Union beat Western Province Indian Cricket Union on the first innings, 21–22 November 1953
WPBCU 99 (B Cossie 33, W Nqoko 22, CM Scott 17; S van Haaght 3/28, J Gheewala 3/26) and 136 (B Cossie 20, H Mvinjelwa 33, J Nyamakazi 25, CM Scott 18; J Gheewala 3/28)
WPICU 84 (I Shaik 24, A Desai 14, F du Preez 11, J Nyamakazi 3/20, O Mlumbi 3/15, W Nqoko 3/9) and 74/8 (O Magmoet 22, S van Haaght 14, A Desai 13; W Nqoko 4/14)

Western Province Coloured Cricket Union beat Central Cricket League on the first innings, 21–22 November 1953
CCL 110 (S Viret 22, S Solomons 36, P Thomas 31; E Petersen 3/37, H Noordien 4/25) and 151/7 dec (D Koks 37*, P Thomas 14, J Truter 15, A Sabotker 49*; A Davids 2/25, H Noordien 2/32)
WPCCU 128 (L Less 31, G Abed 13, T Hendricks 13, H Noordien 19, E Petersen 13; M Coetzee 4/33, A Sabotker 4/82, H Moody 2/8) and 95/4 (T Hendricks 40*, AJ Freeman 19, L Less 15; P Thomas 3/37)

Stellenbosch and District Cricket Union beat Hottentots Holland Cricket Union by 21 runs, 21 and 28 November 1953
Stel 205 (E Rhoode 64, G Gabriels 27, A Manuel 16, AA Poole 36; A Bagus 5/36) and 59 (AA Poole 18; G Adams 5/24, B Crombie 2/21, H Gafieldien 2/5)
HH 141 (G Adams 15, C Railoun 14, A Bagus 16, I Latief 20, R Salie 39; AA Poole 4/42, S Rasiet 3/26) and 102 (B Crombie 21, R Ingham 26, I Latief 15, R Salie 12; S Raziet 4/44, A Manuel 4/33)

Stellenbosch and District CU beat Western Province Indian Cricket Union on the first innings, 5 and 12 December 1953
Stel 214 (S Raziet 29, HO Raziet 53, A Manuel 27, T King 34, AA Poole 34, E Davidse 20; M Naidoo 3/33, F Abrahams 2/30, M Rahbeeni 2/25) and 154/9 (HO Raziet 51*, AA Poole 38, E Davidse 33; F Abrahams 3/17, H Hendricks 3/28)
WPICU 161 (A Gardee 46, M Rahbeeni 44, H Hendricks 23, EM Jamal 12; A Manuel 3/22, AA Poole 2/33)

Western Province Coloured Cricket Union beat Western Province Indian Cricket Union by an innings and 30 runs, 13 December 1953
WPICU 72 (M Rahbeeni 28, S Abrahams 12; G Abed 3/15, AJ Freeman 3/12, E Petersen 2/24) and 80 (H Hendricks 16, A Desai 42, S van Haaght 11; AJ Freeman 4/25, E Abrahams 4/45)
WPCCU 182 (AJ Freeman 33, G Abed 41, AA Osman 27, GT Holmes 21, L Less 14, S Abed 14*; S Abrahams 4/50, M Naidoo 2/21)

Central Cricket League beat Western Province Indian Cricket Union by 28 runs, 26–27 December 1953
CCL 226 (S Viret 44, D Koks 32, F Smith 41, D Hermans 29, R Felton 22*; A Desai 4/32, M Rahbeeni 2/35, B Malamba 2/50) and 127 (D Koks 25, D Hermans 31, W Adonis 18; BN Malamba 7/54, M Naidoo 3/44)
WPICU 226 (S van Haaght 85, A Desai 61, BN Malamba 41; L Robertson 5/101, R Felton 4/29) and 99 (A Desai 56, F du Preez 12; L Robertson 6/38, W Adonis 3/26)

Central Cricket League beat Hottentots Holland Cricket Union by an innings and 39 runs, 19–20 December 1953
CCL 326 (J Truter 106*, P Liederman 47, D Koks 38, R Felton 46, A Sabotker 30, F Smith 25, S Viret 13, S Solomon 19; G Adams 5/104, A Bagus 3/61)
HH 89 (R Salie 34, I Latief 20; L Robertson 7/43, M Coetzee 3/27) and 198 (R Salie 86, H Gafieldien 41, S Abel 15, B Crombie 15; A Sabotker 3/40, P Thomas 3/42)

Western Province Coloured Cricket Union beat Hottentots Holland Cricket Union (match forfeited), 17 and 31 January 1954
WPCCU 152 (T Hendricks 52, A Satarien 18, S Abed 21*, G Adams 15; G Baderoen 4/46, G Adams 5/57) and 185/4 (L Less 46, A Satarien 64, K Samsodien 44, G Abed 13*; A Bagus 3/43)
HH 58 (I Latief 18; E Petersen 8/22, G Abed 2/13)

Central League beat Western Province Bantus by 10 wickets, [x]
WPBCU 38 (A Sabotker 5/10, C Viret 5/12) and 147 (B Mabuto 61*, S Hoho 19, C Scott 17, AM Mshumpela 16; M Coetzee 4/40, A Sabotker 4/75)
CCL 151 (S Solomons 37*, J Truter 32, S Viret 34, D Koks 16; B Cossie 3/40, AM Mshumpela 3/27) and 35/0 (S Solomons 18*, P Liederman 17*)

Western Province Coloured Cricket Union beat Western Province Bantu Cricket Union by an innings and 16 runs, 21 and 28 February 1954
WPCCU 259 (E Abrahams 40, J Solomons 43, AJ Freeman 51, L Less 21, A Abrahams 19, A Latief 30; AM Mshumpela 4/52, B Cossie 2/37, J Nyamakazi 2/64)
WPBCU 103 (CM Scott 20, J Nyamakazi 27*, B Mabuto 18, S Hoho 15; E Petersen 3/26, E Abrahams 4/39, AJ Freeman 2/8) and 140 (J Nyamakazi 50, AM Mshumpela 32*, B Cossie 16; E Petersen 5/29, J Solomons 2/15)

Stellenbosch and District Cricket Union beat Central League on the first innings (bad light stopped play), 6 and 13 March 1954
Stel 75 (G Gabriel 18; M Coetzee 4/29, A Sabotker 5/34) and 200/6 dec (HO Raziet 42, A Manuel 53*, S Raziet 33; A Sabotker 3/48)
CCL 60 (S Viret 28; AA Poole 3/33, J Jacobs 3/9) and 153/8 (J Truter 67, A Sabotker 45; AA Poole 4/63, A Manuel 4/54)

Western Province Coloured Cricket Union beat Stellenbosch and District Cricket Union on the first innings, 20 and 26 March 1954
Stel 116 (S Raziet 50, T King 24, KT Poole 13; E Petersen 4/22, G Bohardien 2/14, E Abrahams 2/21, AJ Freeman 2/38) and 43/2 (E Rhoode 15*)
WPCCU 208 (AJ Freeman 52, G Abed 45, T Hendricks 19, E Petersen 17, S Abed 12*, G Bohardien 21; HO Raziet 3/27, A Manuel 2/54)

CHAPTER 9
Western Province Cricket Board, 1959–1991

Affiliated to the South African Cricket Board of Control (SACBOC) and South African Cricket Board (SACB)

The Western Province Cricket Board (WPCB) was formed at a meeting at the Immaculata Girls' High School in Wynberg on 1 February 1959.[272] Building on the work of the short-lived Western Province Cricket Federation, 'the Board', as it was commonly known, was led by a generation of administrators 'determined to remove all mention of race from its activities'.[273] The first president was John van Harte, a school principal. His executive consisted of city councillor Hoosain Parker (vice-president), the later head of the Hewat Teachers' Training College Abu Desai (secretary), AW le Roux (assistant secretary), Hassan Howa (treasurer) and Alec Anthony (match and registration secretary).

The formation of the WPCB took place only a few days after the different national bodies for 'coloureds', 'Malays', 'Bantus' and 'Indians', operating under the umbrella of the South African Cricket Board of Control (SACBOC), decided to change SACBOC from a federal body, where racial affiliates retained their identity, into a single, merged, non-racial national body with single, merged provincial affiliates. The different racial boards were given three years to disband and ensure their affiliates in the provinces united with their various counterparts. This was a sign of the determination of black cricketers to oppose apartheid in sport.[274]

In the process, old racially based Western Province provincial bodies removed their ethnic labels and became sub-unions of the new WPCB. For example, the old Western Province Indian Union became the United Cricket Union, the Western Province Coloured Cricket Union became, somewhat confusingly, the Western Province Cricket Association. The Peninsula and Western Districts Cricket Board dissolved and its affiliated unions participated under their own names, namely Cape District, Central, Cosmopolitan, Metropolitan, Maitland–Parow, Paarl Prolific, Stellenbosch and District, and Somerset West. The old 'Barnato' groupings outside Cape Town – Hottentots Holland Cricket Union and Paarl Cricket Union (ex-WPCA and Country) – were also absorbed into the WPCB. The Western Province Bantu Cricket Board planned to play as Langa Cricket Union but eventually did not join because they felt their administration was inadequate to meet the WPCB's standards.[275]

From 1966/67 a super league contested by the best combined teams selected from the clubs in each sub-union was introduced. It was played on a round-robin basis, over two Saturdays. The super league was evenly contested, with five teams winning or sharing the title in the first ten years. In addition to this, there was also a two-day competition in which the unions competed on a knockout basis for the Fester Trophy. In 1972/73, the Fester Trophy switched to a one-day knock-out format. Rosmead-based Cape District won the Fester Trophy four out of nine times.

The WPCB played its first friendly game against Eastern Province at Green Point Common in February 1961. The national body, SACBOC, was finally reconstituted in August that year. SACBOC now moved from playing inter-race cricket on a national level to 'non-racial' provincial cricket.[276] The first of five centralised SACBOC biennial inter-provincial tournaments was held in Johannesburg in December 1961. The hosts won the Dadabhay Trophy, but Western Province were champions in the next four tournaments held in Port Elizabeth (1963/64), Durban (1965/66), Cape Town (1967/68) and Kimberley (1969/70), where the trophy was shared with Transvaal.[277] 'Gertjie' Williams produced the best bowling figures for Western Province in an innings with 8/11 against Border in Port Elizabeth, while 'Dickie' Conrad's 194 not out against Griqualand West in Durban was the top score in these tournaments.

After a decade, SACBOC's centralised tournaments were followed by an experimental season of two-day matches played at different venues in 1970/71. Thereafter, SACBOC introduced a home-and-away three-day competition in 1971/72. The initiative to start formal first-class matches was part of the drive by SACBOC to win international recognition and challenge the whites-only South African Cricket Association as the official body in South Africa.[278]

Another way in which the Board cocked a snook at discrimination and 'official' white cricket was for top local players to follow in the footsteps of Basil D'Oliveira, playing as professionals in the leagues in England. In the 1960s and early 1970s, 'Coetie' Neethling, Cecil Abrahams, Owen Williams, the Abed brothers Goolam and 'Dik', Rushdi Magiet, Des February and 'Dickie' Conrad, all went abroad to get further experience, thanks to the initiative of Damoo Bansda, a barman and part-time journalist. Abrahams settled in England and his son John went on to play first-class cricket for Lancashire, and later became the England junior coach. 'Dik' Abed ended up playing for and living in Holland. The brilliant Owen Williams emigrated to Adelaide, Australia, while 'Dik' Abed also had a spell in Perth on the recommendation of Dennis Lillee.[279] No fewer than six members of the SACBOC Springbok team of the 1950s eventually were to live abroad permanently. This exodus of cricketers was part of a broader flight of thousands of professional and middle-class 'coloured' people from South Africa following the devastation of the Group Areas Act, and it led to a loss of skills the country could ill afford.

The Dadabhay Trophy remained the premier trophy when the switch to three-day cricket happened in the 1971/72 season. It was replaced by the SFW Trophy in 1975/76 when SACBOC entered the era of commercial sponsorship. But this experiment lasted only one season. An important reason for this was the objection of Muslim players to liquor sponsorship – top players like Rushdi and Saait Magiet, 'Lefty' Adams and 'Braima' Isaacs all refused to play that season. In any case, SACBOC went out of existence in 1976/77. A realignment of cricket followed and two new rival national bodies, the South African Cricket Union (SACU) and the South African Cricket Board (SACB), emerged.

In January 1976, a so-called 'normal cricket' agreement was signed by the different national bodies, which envisaged cricket unity in South Africa. However, in the end this did not happen. The WPCB considered joining with the rival Western Province Cricket Union but, unimpressed by the commitment of white cricketers and the government to change, it instead helped form the South African Cricket Board (SACB) in 1977 in opposition to the white-dominated SACU. A small number of players and clubs (most notably Avendale) left the WPCB to join the WPCU at this time, but the overwhelming majority remained loyal to the Board.

The Howa Bowl (named after the president) now became SACB's major trophy. Western Province was one of four teams that competed in the premier first-class competitions of SACBOC and its successor, SACB, in the twenty years between 1971 and 1991. The others were Eastern Province, Natal and Transvaal. The 'big four' played altogether 216 inter-provincial three-day games in that time. Each province thus took part in just over 100 first-class games. Following the example of their predecessors in the Barnato and Sir David Harris tournaments, Western Province completely dominated the provincial first-class competitions, being champions or joint champions 14 out of 18 times.

Western Province players consequently featured prominently in the national first-class records of SACBOC/SACB. Opening bowler Vincent Barnes was the highest wicket taker in the country, with 277 scalps in 55 matches. Next in line were leg-spinners Seraj Gabriels (245) and Armien Jabaar (234), seamer Saait Magiet (175) and left-arm spinner 'Lefty' Adams (115). Barnes also had the best match analysis of 12/82. He took ten wickets in a match five times. Together with Mustapha Khan of Natal and Khaya Majola, Gabriels was one of only three players to score 2000 runs and take 200 wickets in first-class cricket. The leading run-scorers were Saait Magiet (2296), Seraj Gabriels (2040), Munsoor Abdullah (2198) and Faiek Davids (1610). There were 24 centuries scored by Western Province batsmen. 'Dickie' Conrad's 166 against Transvaal in 1972/73 was the highest score.[280]

Vincent Barnes's bowling figures and the fact that Faiek Davids was the only Western Province batsman to reach an average of over 30 runs per innings (36.59) showed the unequal contest between bat and ball that existed in SACBOC/SACB cricket. The poor pitches were 'the biggest single factor affecting standards and the nature of SACB games', one top player recalled. Vincent Barnes concurs. 'Most of the wickets we played on were underprepared. For me, as a bowler, it was great. But, for the batsmen, it was always a struggle. We never played at a set provincial venue where a groundsman could work on the wickets.'[281]

Most critics and cricketers agree that Saait Magiet, the most capped player with 63 appearances, was probably *the* player of the Board era. 'In my mind he was always our version of Clive Rice and Ian Botham,' says Mogamad Allie, 'although probably not in the same league.'[282] Playing greats like Khaya Majola agree. Besides those already mentioned above, other top talents of the Board era included 'Lobo' Abed (rated by Basil D'Oliveira as the best wicketkeeper in the world in his time), Eric Petersen (interestingly, saluted by all across the spectrum in the WPCB as the best bowler in the 1950s and 1960s), 'Braima' Isaacs, Archie Sonn, 'Gertjie' Williams, Viccie Moodie, Neville Lakay, 'Taliep' Behardien and Jumannah Khan (a 'prodigiously talented spin bowler and fly-half, who gave up sport while in his prime').

The WPCB had 15 captains in its 32-year existence, namely Gesant 'Tiny' Abed, Owen Williams, Salie 'Lobo' Abed, 'Coetie' Neethling, 'Gertjie' Williams, 'Lefty' Adams, 'Dickie' Conrad, Brian O'Connell, Rushdi Magiet, Charles van Schalkwyk, Armien Jabaar, Saait Magiet, Goolam Allie, Vincent Barnes and Seraj Gabriels.[283]

After limited-overs domestic cricket was introduced by the establishment white body from 1969/70 onwards (copying innovations in county cricket in England), SACBOC / SACB tried to follow suit with its own one-day competitions alongside the three-day first-class matches. However, due to a lack of sponsorship, the non-racial Board managed to run official one-day provincial fixtures (today called List A games) in only five seasons: for the SFW Trophy in 1973/74 and 1974/75 and for the Benson & Hedges Trophy from 1982/83 to 1984/85. Western Province won the trophy in four out of the five seasons, sharing it with Eastern Province in 1983/84.

During the realignments of the mid-1970s, the WPCB also restructured its local leagues from the 1976/77 season onwards. This move was partly so that the Board would be ready to participate with white teams if joint leagues eventuated. It was also in response to the devastation wrought by the Group Areas Act. Sixty thousand families in Cape Town were forced to leave their homes in areas now designated 'white' and settle on the barren Cape Flats, far away from long-established schools, churches, mosques and other facilities. Cricket communities and infrastructures, generations old, came undone in the face of this human tragedy. For example, the old Western Province Cricket Association, based mainly in the city centre and Claremont, which had 50 teams playing under it in the 1950s, virtually disintegrated under the pressure. It broke up into three clubs: United CC, an amalgam of many old, broken inner-city clubs, Montrose CC and Ottomans CC. St Augustine's CC, formed in 1899, a survivor from the Metropolitan sub-union, was forced from the city centre to facilities in Athlone and later, in 1975, to the Elfindale Ground in Princess Vlei, Diep River, 15 kilometres away.[284] Primrose (initially a Claremont-based affiliate of the WPCA) moved to Rosmead and the Wynberg Cricket Union, which later merged with Cape District. Victoria CC became the strongest team from the old Cape District Union and Tygerberg CC emerged strongest from the old Maitland and Parow Union.

In the 15 seasons of club cricket from 1976/77 onwards, three clubs – Primrose, Montrose and United – dominated, winning 28 out of 31 times. Primrose, based at the Rosmead ground in Wynberg, won the league six times and the one-day competition or grand challenge seven times. Montrose, coming to the fore for the first time only in 1981/82, won the league six times and the grand challenge six times. United won the grand challenge three times and the league twice. The only other clubs to come into the picture in those 15 years were Hottentots Holland (limited-overs Golden Yolk winners in 1978/79), Victoria (league winners in 1980/81) and Stellenbosch (grand challenge winners in 1990/91).[285]

The strongly anti-apartheid WPCB had five presidents between 1959 and 1991, namely John van Harte, Hassan Howa, Sadick Emeran, Abe Adams and Percy Sonn. The fiery Hassan Howa became a national icon of the non-racial sports struggle in the 1970s and 1980s. Charismatic and outspoken, he tackled apartheid sport head-on, emphasising the fact that until all cricketers were given equal treatment, whites could forget about international competition. His condemnation of paternalistic white administrators and white hypocrisy made him the person the government and the establishment press and sports bodies loved to hate. He was routinely described as 'intransigent', 'hardline' and 'hotheaded' by the establishment, but he became the champion of the underdog and effectively used the platform he had to promote the Board's non-collaboration approach, summed up in the phrase 'no normal sport in an abnormal society'. The non-racial sports movement now demanded full equality for all South Africans, nothing less.[286]

After many years of principled struggle for non-racial cricket, the unbanning of political organisations and the release of Nelson Mandela from prison in the early 1990s paved the way for cricket unity. On 25 June 1991, the WPCB and the rival Western Province Cricket Union finally joined together to form the Western Province Cricket Association.[287] At last, 101 years after the first Western Province provincial body was formed, a single unified structure for all cricketers in the province finally came into being.

For an in-depth history of the WPCB, see the labour of love by Mogamad Allie, *More than a Game: History of the Western Province Cricket Board 1959–1991* (Cape Argus and WPCA, Cape Town, 2000), on which this chapter is largely based.

9.1 Western Province Cricket Board, 1959–1991

9.1.1 Western Province Cricket Board National Players (SACBOC/SACB), 1961/62–1990/91[288]

Abdullah, M	1982/83, 1987/88
Barnes, VA	1982/83, 1986/87, 1987/88, 1990/91
Behardien, I 'Miley'	1987/88, 1990/91
Cupido, R 'Joey'	1987/88
Davids, F	1987/88, 1990/91
Fortune, N	1982/83
Gabriels, S	1986/87, 1987/88
Hendricks, S	1987/88
Isaacs, E 'Braima'	1982/83
Jabaar, A	1982/83
Magiet, S	1982/83, 1986/87 captain, 1987/88, 1990/91 captain
Van Schalkwyk, C	1982/83 captain
White, N	1990/91

9.1.2 Western Province Cricket Board Players, 1961/62–1990/91[289]

9.1.2.1 Western Province Cricket Board Provincial Players, 1961/62–1969/70

(Centralised tournaments and first decentralised competition: non-first-class)

Abed, G 'Tiny'	(WP Cricket Association) 1961/62 captain
Abed, S 'Lobo'	(WP Cricket Association) 1963/64, 1965/66 captain, 1967/68-1969/70
Abed, S 'Dik'	(WP Cricket Association) 1963/64-1969/70
Adams, A 'Lefty'	(WP Cricket Association) 1965/66-1969/70
Abrahams, N	(Central) 1963/64
Alexander, R	(WP Cricket Association) 1965/66
Anthony, F	(Wynberg) 1963/64
Behardien, T	(Stellenbosch/Vineyards) 1961/62, 1965/66, 1969/70
Blaauw, K	(Wynberg) 1969/70
Carelse, H	(Wynberg) 1963/64, 1965/66
Conrad, S 'Dickie'	(WP Cricket Association) 1963/64-1969/70
Dagnin, I	(Wynberg) 1967/6-1969/70
D'Oliveira, I	(Metropolitan) 1961/62
Dollie, MS 'Pettie'	(Wynberg) 1967/68
February, D	(Somerset West) 1963/64-1967/68
Fester, D	(Maitland-Parow) 1969/70
Finnan, M	(Metropolitan) 1967/68-1969/70
Isaacs, E 'Braima'	(Metropolitan) 1967/68
Jardine, G	(Cape District) 1961/62
Joshua, C	(WP Cricket Association) 1963/64, 1965/66
Kleintjies, B	(Wynberg) 1961/62
Lakay, N	(Cape District) 1961/62-1969/70
Lakay, Y 'Timmy'	(WP Cricket Association) 1963/64
Lambert, J	(WP Cricket Association) 1965/66
Le Roux, J	(Metropolitan), 1967/68
Maclons, A	(Somerset West) 1961/62-1963/64
Maclons, M 'Kulu'	(Maitland-Parow) 1967/68-1969/70
Magiet, MR	(Wynberg), 1969/70
Martin, L	(Metropolitan) 1965/66
Minnies, P	(Stellenbosch) 1968/69
Moodie, DV	(Maitland-Parow) 1968/69-1969/70
Mulder, D	(Cape District) 1961/62
Neethling, JJ 'Coetie'	(Maitland-Parow) 1961/62-1965/66, 1967/68-1969/70 captain
Petersen, E	(WP Cricket Association) 1961/62
Pick, M	(Maitland-Parow) 1967/68
Raziet, S 'Laam'	(Stellenbosch) 1961/62
Rodrigues, K	(Metropolitan) 1968/69
Sylvester, J	(Somerset West) 1961/62
Tromp, I	(Worcester) 1967/68
Van Stavel, J	(Cape District) 1961/62
Williams, G	(Maitland-Parow) 1963/64-1969/70
Williams, OL	(Cape District) 1961/62, 1963/64 (captain), 1969/70

9.1.2.2 First-Class Three-Day Matches in Dadabhay Trophy, SFW Trophy and Howa Bowl, 1971/72–1990/91

- Players whose names are followed by an asterisk also played in the Dadabhay tournaments prior to the start of the three-day competition.
- Prior to the 1976/77 season, players represented unions playing in a super league rather than clubs.

Name	Club(s)	Matches	Debut
Abdullah, M	United, Montrose	39	21–23 January 1978
Abrahams, CJ	Overseas professional	5	23–25 November 1974
Adams, A 'Lefty'	Pirates, Primrose, WPCA, Metropolitan CA	24 (10 as capt)	26–28 December 1971
Adams, Y 'Gogs'	Blue Bells, Primrose	7	17–19 November 1979
Ahmed, MH	Kenston, Montrose	4	28–30 December 1985
Allie, G	Primrose	16 (3 as capt)	26–28 November 1977
Allie, MZ 'Muis'	Primrose, Montrose	4	26–28 December 1978
Antulay, N	Montrose	18	26–28 December 1982
Arendse, NM	Metropolitan, Victoria	2	26–28 November 1977
Arenz, H	St Augustine's, Metropolitan CA	1	16–18 March 1974
Arnold, S	Hottentots Holland, Primrose	3	4–6 March 1978
Barnes, VA	Victoria, Montrose	53	18–20 November 1978
Behardien, I 'Miley'	Blue Bells, United	25	15–17 March 1986
Benjamin, F	Primrose	14	1–3 January 1983
Bergins, HWH	Bellville, UWC, Maitland–Parow CA	6	22–24 November 1975
Booysen, N	Tigers	5	16–18 March 1985
Brache, N	Ashtondale, Avendale, Metropolitan CA	2	18–20 January 1975
Burns, A 'Astie'	United	1	15–17 March 1986
Carelse, WF 'Pinky'	Wynberg, Cape District CA	6	22–24 November 1975
Coericius, A	UWC, Tigers	1	16–18 November 1985
Conrad*, S 'Dickie'	Vineyards, Primrose, WPCA, Wynberg CA	8 (5 as capt)	26–28 December 1971
Conrad, S	United, Montrose	9	28–30 December 1985
Cupido, R 'Joey'	St Augustine's, Metropolitan	19	17–19 March 1984
Dagnin*, I	Silver Crowns, Wynberg CA, Peninsula	4	26–28 December 1971
Dammert, B	Bellville	4	[x] November 1989
Damon, E 'Baby'	United	14	26–28 December 1977
Davids, F	Primrose, United	32	18–20 February 1984
Davids, Z	United, Primrose	5	15–17 March 1980
Dawson, H	Ashtondale, Metropolitan CA, Westridge	9	22–24 November 1975
Doman, ME	Victoria	12	11–13 February 1978
Dyason, C	Rivertonians	3	21–23 January 1989
Ebrahim, F	Elsies River, United, Primrose	12	16–18 November 1985

Name	Club(s)	Matches	Debut
Ebrahim, M	Elsies River, United	1	11–13 February 1978
Ebrahim, Y	Elsies River, United, Primrose	1	17–19 January 1979
February, R 'Koela'	Stellenbosch, Montrose	12	15–17 March 1986
Felix, C	Rivertonians	1	17–19 March 1984
Finnan*, M	Victoria	4	26–28 November 1977
Fortune, N	Metropolitan, Victoria	25	17–19 February 1979
Gabriels, S	United, Primrose	48	21–22 November 1981
Gafieldien, E	Hottentots Holland, Primrose	7	20–22 January 1990
Galant, M	United	2	27–29 December 1988
Galant, S	United, Primrose	1	4–6 January 1980
Green, S	United	1	27–29 December 1988
Harris, E	Victoria	10	1–3 January 1983
Haupt, M	Metropolitan, Victoria	1	19–21 January 1985
Hendricks, I	Primrose	1	20–22 November 1982
Hendricks, S	Montrose	35	30 December 1980–1 January 1981
Hendricks, WD	Victoria, Wynberg CA	18	16–18 November 1973
Hendrikse, C	Stellenbosch	7	18–20 February 1989
Henry, O	Excelsior, Stellenbosch CA	8	16–18 March 1974
Holder, JW	Overseas professsional	1	23–25 November 1974
Isaacs*, E 'Braima'	Pirates, Primrose, Metropolitan CA, Wynberg CA	51	26–28 December 1971
Isaacs, M	Primrose	1	16–18 February 1991
Jabaar, A	Arabian College, WPCA, United, Montrose	44	14–16 December 1974
Jacobs, LP	Newtons, Elma, Stellenbosch CA, Maitland–Parow CA	15	16–18 February 1974
Jakoet, A 'Manie'	United	3	18–20 November 1978
Jassiem, S	Ottomans	6	21–23 January 1978
Katts, A	All Saints, Somerset West CA, Helderberg CC	6	1–3 January 1976
Kemp, D	Crusaders, St Augustine's, Montrose	18	21–23 November 1987
Kemp, N	Blue Bells, United	1	16–18 November 1979
Khan, G	Ottomans	2	18–20 January 1986
Khan, J	Silvertree, WPCA	6	27–29 January 1973
Kleinveldt, J	Metropolitan, Victoria, Montrose	10	16–18 November 1979
Kolbe, C	St Augustine's, Metropolitan CA	4	8–10 January 1972
Lakay*, N[290]	Oakdale, Cape District CA	1	1–4 January 1972
Lambert*, J	Young Ideas, Primrose, St Augustine's, WPCA, Wynberg CA	7	26–28 December 1971
Loggenstein, QF	Rivertonians	2	8–10 December 1990

Name	Club(s)	Matches	Debut
Maclons, M 'Kulu'*	Elsies River, Somerset West CA, Maitland–Parow CA	17	8–10 January 1972
Magiet*, MR	Combine, Primrose, Wynberg CA	34	26–28 December 1971
Magiet, S	Primrose, Wynberg CA	64	1–4 January 1972
Mahoney, JE 'Jock'	St Augustine's, UWC, Metropolitan CA	19	27–29 January 1973
Manack, AA 'Jack'	Ottomans	5	25–27 November 1989
Martin, C	Primrose	13	26–28 November 1977
Martin, N	Ottomans	5	26–28 December 1978
Martin, S	Primrose	1	28–30 December 1982
Meyer, MA	Blue Bells, Montrose	6	17–19 November 1990
Miller, C	Hands and Heart, Cape District CA	1	[x] March 1976
Miller, G	St Augustine's	4	17–19 November 1984
Mohamed, E 'Barney'	Primrose, Ottomans	7	17–19 November 1984
Moodie*, DV	Elsies River, Maitland–Parow CA	17	26–28 December 1971
Muller, N	Stellenbosch, Montrose	8	29–31 December 1987
Musson, R	Victoria, United	18	15–17 November 1980
Neethling*, JJ 'Coetie'	Elma, Elsies River, Maitland–Parow CA	12	26–28 December 1971
O'Connell, B	Melbourne, Cape District CA	8 (7 as capt)	16–18 March 1974
Odendaal, A	United	1	17–19 November 1985
Petersen, B	Ashtondale, St Augustine's, Metropolitan CA	3	1–4 January 1972
Petersen, G	Primrose	2	18–20 February 1984
Price, H	Blue Bells	1	1–3 January 1983
Rasmus, M	Stellenbosch, Montrose	3	21–23 January 1989
Ravens, C 'Kosie'	Blue Bells, Montrose	2	18–20 January 1986
Richards, T	Metropolitan, Victoria	3	16–18 November 1979
Roberts, LL	Stellenbosch, Montrose	2	28–30 December 1985
Salie, R	Ottomans	5	26–28 November 1978
Seconds, T	Rivertonians, Primrose	3	21–23 January 1989
September, M	St Augustine's, Metropolitan CA	1	1–3 January 1973
Simpson, R	Victoria, Wynberg CA	2	1–3 January 1973
Smith, V	Peninsula, Primrose	4	11–13 February 1978
Solomons, F	Ottomans, Primrose	21	21–23 January 1978
Sonn, A	Bellville, Maitland–Parow CA	10	1–3 January 1973
Theron, M	Montrose	8	13–15 March 1981
Thomas, K	St Augustine's, Primrose	2	18–20 November 1978
Thomas, Y	Hottentots Holland, Primrose	38	28–30 December 1982
Timol, I	Primrose, Wynberg CA	2	13–15 March 1976
Van Graan, K 'Kitty'	St Athens, Metropolitan CA	9	1–3 January 1975
Van Graan, R 'Jacko'	Victoria, Westridge, Montrose	2	23–25 January 1982
Van Graan, R 'Robbie'	St Athens, Metropolitan CA	15	1–3 January 1973

Name	Club(s)	Matches	Debut
Van Oordt, G	Tigers, Maitland–Parow CA, Metropolitan CA	22	[x] March 1976
Van Schalkwyk, C	Victoria, Wynberg CA	26 (14 as WP capt)	[x] March 1976
Viljoen, A	St Augustine's	3	5–7 January 1991
Wadvalla, A	Primrose	2	26–28 December 1977
White, N	St Augustine's, Montrose	25	28–30 December 1982
Williams*, G 'Gertjie'	Valiants, Elsies River, Maitland–Parow CA	16 (8 as capt)	26–28 December 1971
Williams, HS 'Bollie'	Stellenbosch	1	17–19 November 1990
Williams, J 'Kosie'	Valiants, Elsies River, Maitland–Parow CA	5	26–28 December 1971
Williams*, OL	Oakdale, Cape District CA	2	26–28 December 1971
Witbooi, R	Primrose	2	26–28 December 1978

9.1.2.3 Western Province Cricket Board, List A, Limited-Overs Provincial Caps, 1974/75–1990/91[291]

Abdullah, M	1982/83, 1983/84, 1984/85
Abrahams, CJ	1975/76
Allie, G	1983/84, 1984/85
Antulay, N	1983/84, 1984/85
Arendse, NM	1982/83
Barnes, VA	1982/83, 1983/84, 1984/85
Booysen, N	1984/85
Cupido, R 'Joey'	1984/85
Dagnin, I	1974/75
Damon, E 'Baby'	1982/83, 1983/84
Felix, C	1983/84
Fortune, N	1982/83, 1983/84
Gabriels, S	1984/85
Harris, E	1983/84, 1984/85
Hendricks, S	1984/85
Hendricks, WD	1974/75, 1975/76
Holder, JW	1975/76
Isaacs, E 'Braima'	1982/83, 1983/84
Jabaar, A	1982/83, 1983/84, 1984/85
Jacobs, LP	1974/75, 1975/76
Katts, A	1975/76
Kolbe, C	1975/76
Lambert, J	1974/75
Maclons, M 'Kulu'	1974/75, 1975/76
Magiet, S	1982/83, 1983/84, 1984/85
Mahoney, JE 'Jock'	1974/75, 1975/76
Martin, A	1982/83
Martin, S	1982/83

Miller, C	1983/84
Mohamed, E 'Barney'	1984/85
Moodie, DV	1974/75
Musson, R	1982/83
Neethling, JJ 'Coetie'	1974/75
Petersen, B	1974/75, 1975/76
Solomons, F	1983/84, 1984/85
Sonn, A	1974/75
Theron, M	1982/83
Thomas, Y	1982/83, 1983/84, 1984/85
Van Graan, K 'Kitty'	1974/75, 1975/76
Van Graan, R 'Jacko'	1974/75
Van Schalkwyk, C	1982/83
Williams, G 'Gertjie'	1974/75
Witbooi, R	1975/76

9.1.3 Western Province Cricket Board League and One-Day Competitions, 1959–1991[292]

Prior to 1967/68 club champions in the different sub-unions played against each other for the Fester Trophy in a limited-overs format. From 1966/67 a Super League contested by the best combined teams from the clubs in the different sub-unions was introduced. Sub-unions rather than their champion clubs also now competed for the limited-overs Fester Trophy. In 1976/77, the WPCB dissolved the old sub-unions and started club-based league and limited-overs competitions.

Season	Super League	Fester Trophy
1966/67	Maitland-Parow	Maitland-Parow
1967/68	Cape District	–
1968/69	Western Province Cricket Association	Stellenbosch
1969/70	Western Province Cricket Association/ Maitland-Parow	Western Province Cricket Association
1970/71	Western Province Cricket Association	Metropolitan
1971/72	Metropolitan	Cape District
1972/73	Metropolitan	Wynberg
1973/74	Metropolitan	Cape District
1974/75	Cape District	Cape District
1975/76	Cape District	Cape District

Season	League Champions	Grand Challenge
1976/77	Primrose	Primrose
1977/78	United	Primrose
1978/79	Primrose	Primrose
1979/80	Primrose	United
1980/81	Victoria	Primrose and Montrose
1981/82	Montrose	United
1982/83	Montrose	Montrose
1983/84	Primrose	Primrose
1984/85	Montrose	Montrose

Season	Super League	Fester Trophy
1985/86	Montrose	United
1986/87	Primrose	Montrose
1987/88	Montrose	Primrose
1988/89	Primrose	Montrose
1989/90	United	United
1990/91	Montrose	Stellenbosch

9.1.4 Western Province Cricket Board Trophies in Tournaments of the South African Cricket Board of Control / South African Cricket Board, 1961/62–1990/91[293]

Dadabhay Trophy (Centralised Tournaments)

Season	Venue	Winners
1961/62	Johannesburg	Transvaal
1963/64	Port Elizabeth	*Western Province*
1965/66	Durban	*Western Province*
1967/68	Cape Town	*Western Province*
1969/70	Kimberley	*Western Province* / Transvaal (shared)

The above tournaments were centralised with two-day matches being played on an inter-provincial non-racial basis. Thereafter matches were decentralised.

1970/71	*Western Province* and Transvaal (shared)

This competition was contested over a single round of two-day matches.

Dadabhay Trophy (First-Class)

Season	Winners
1971/72 – 1972/73	*Western Province* and Natal (shared) (three-day matches, home-and-away round robin played over two seasons)
1973/74	*Western Province* (three-day matches, home-and-away round robin played in one season)
1974/75	Transvaal

SFW Trophy (First-Class)

Season	Winners
1975/76	*Western Province*
1976/77	No competition

Howa Bowl (First-Class)

Season	Winners
1977/78	*Western Province*
1978/79	Eastern Province
1979/80	*Western Province*
1980/81	*Western Province*
1981/82	*Western Province*
1982/83	*Western Province*

1983/84	*Western Province*
1984/85	Eastern Province
1985/86	Eastern Province
1986/87	*Western Province*
1987/88	*Western Province*
1988/89	*Western Province*
1989/90	*Western Province*
1990/91	*Western Province*

SFW Trophy (Limited Overs)

Season	*Winners*
1973/74	*Western Province*
1974/75	Natal

Benson & Hedges Trophy (Limited Overs)

Season	*Winners*
1982/83	*Western Province*
1983/84	*Western Province* / Eastern Province (shared)
1984/85	*Western Province*

9.1.5 Western Province Cricket Board Scores, 1961/62–1990/91[294]

9.1.5.1 Dadabhay Trophy Tournaments, 1961/62–1970/71

**1ST SACBOC DADABHAY INTER-PROVINCIAL NON-RACIAL TOURNAMENT,
27 DECEMBER 1961 – 7 JANUARY 1962, JOHANNESBURG**
Participants: Transvaal, Western Province, Eastern Province, Natal and Griqualand West.
Winners: Transvaal

Western Province beat Eastern Province by 147 runs
WP 78 (I D'Oliveira 27; G Connelly 6/13) and 304 (S Raziet 93, I D'Oliveira 76, G Abed 56*; G Connelly 3/50, P Smith 3/58)
EP 134 (G Connelly 35*, F Abrahams 34; A Maclons 4/39, JJ Neethling 4/43) and 101 (P Smith 38; B Kleintjies 6/22)

Natal beat Western Province by 18 runs
Ntl 195 (El Laher 44, S Kirsten 33, YI Laher 33, M Boomgaard 32; A Maclons 4/27) and 116 (El Laher 39; OL Williams 3/14)
WP 131 (G Jardine 27, I D'Oliveira 26; OFE Sader 5/37, T Parsuramen 4/43) and 162 (I D'Oliveira 60, OL Williams 44; OFE Sader 4/59, T Parsuramen 3/39)

Western Province beat Griqualand West by an innings and 150 runs
GW 77 (R Cader 23; N Lakay 3/15, MS Dollie 3/29) and 155 (R Cader 72*; N Lakay 6/44, OL Williams 3/51)
WP 382/3 dec (I D'Oliveira 145, G Jardine 132, H Carelse 55*)

Western Province beat Transvaal on the first innings
Tvl 147 (OL Williams 5/37, G Abed 3/29) and 253/5 dec (R Khota 83*, H Abrahams 71)
WP 263/9 dec (G Abed 100*, OL Williams 34, S Raziet 32; A Barnes 3/46, A Rubidge 3/65) and 42/1

**2ND SACBOC DADABHAY INTER-PROVINCIAL NON-RACIAL TOURNAMENT,
26 DECEMBER 1963 – 10 JANUARY 1964, PORT ELIZABETH**
Participants: Western Province, Transvaal, Natal, Eastern Province, Griqualand West, South Western Districts and Border.
Winners: Western Province

Western Province beat South Western Districts by an innings and 86 runs
SWD 22 (OL Williams 7/6) and 94 (MB Maclons 43; OL Williams 4/22, N Abrahams 3/18)
WP 202 (S Conrad 58, F Anthony 45, H Carelse 36; A Maclons 5/27, C Petersen 5/80)

Western Province beat Border by an innings and 312 runs
WP 388/7 dec (D February 110, Y Lakay 103*, JJ Neethling 55, S Abed 37, H Carelse 34; M Jacobs 4/140)
Bdr 29 (G Williams 8/11) and 47 (Y Lakay 3/10)

Western Province beat Eastern Province by 85 runs
WP 154 (D February 53, SD Abed 26, JJ Neethling 23; P Snyman 4/29) and 114 (SD Abed 23, JJ Neethling 20; P Snyman 5/33, N Francis 3/22)
EP 104 (M Wilson 35, A Douglas 22; OL Williams 5/25, JJ Neethling 4/31) and 79 (N Francis 35; C Joshua 4/6)

Western Province beat Griqualand West by 10 wickets
GW 94 (K Saloojee 40; OL Williams 3/14) and 57 (I Kajee 23; OL Williams 5/18, SD Abed 4/16)
WP 143 (D February 54; AL Adams 5/60, Y Bhayat 4/34) and 9/0

Western Province beat Transvaal by 9 wickets
Tvl 81 (N Lakay 5/19, OL Williams 3/25) and 59 (OL Williams 4/14, N Lakay 3/6)
WP 80 (S Conrad 24, JJ Neethling 24; H Ayob 5/30, A Barnes 4/20) and 61/1 (S Conrad 43*)

3RD SACBOC DADABHAY INTER-PROVINCIAL NON-RACIAL TOURNAMENT, 5–11 APRIL 1966, DURBAN
Participants: Natal, Western Province, Transvaal and Griqualand West.
Winners: Western Province.

Western Province beat Griqualand West on the first innings
GW 76 (D Richards 26; R Alexander 6/39) and 288 (S Saloojee 104, D Richards 48; G Williams 4/59, J Lambert 3/32, AL Adams 3/66)
WP 337/4 dec (S Conrad 194*, N Lakay 83) and 0/0

Western Province beat Natal by 8 wickets
Ntl 62 (D February 6/40, R Alexander 3/19) and 251 (J Govender 90, O Vawda 41, MA Patricks 38; JJ Neethling 5/32)
WP 220 (N Lakay 64, L Martin 48, SD Abed 29, JJ Neethling 26*; I Ebrahim 4/48, H Samuel 4/75) and 95/2 (J Lambert 50*, L Martin 30)

Western Province beat Transvaal on the first innings
Tvl 167 (A Barnes 61, M Saleh 28, A Bhamjee 25; N Lakay 4/33, JJ Neethling 3/57) and 138/8 dec (A Kirsten 40, A Moola 32, A Barnes 28; JJ Neethling 7/58)
WP 189 (J Lambert 37, G Williams 33, T Behardien 32; A Moola 3/35, A Barnes 3/49, H Ayob 3/58) and 6/0

4TH SACBOC DADABHAY INTER-PROVINCIAL NON-RACIAL TOURNAMENT, 9–19 JANUARY 1968, CAPE TOWN
Participants: Western Province, Transvaal, Natal, Eastern Province, Griqualand West and South Western Districts.
Winners: Western Province.

Western Province beat South Western Districts by an innings and 167 runs
SWD 55 (AL Adams 6/21, MS Dollie 3/10) and 39 (JJ Neethling 4/11)
WP 261 (N Lakay 62, G Williams 46, MB Maclons 43, MS Dollie 40)

Western Province beat Griqualand West by an innings and 108 runs
GW 47 (AL Adams 4/10, I Tromp 4/13) and 72 (AL Adams 6/25)
WP 227 (G Williams 68*, JJ Neethling 40; AL Cader 3/11)

Transvaal beat Griqualand West by 6 wickets
GW 61 (S Chothia 6/12) and 109 (A Moola 3/21, S Chothia 3/48)
Tvl 85 (AL Cader 4/24, K Johnson 3/10) and 86/4 (A Barnes 37)

Western Province beat Natal by 10 wickets
Ntl 121 (MA Patricks 32; I Tromp 4/36, AL Adams 3/13) and 139 (MSI Randeree 44, O Vawda 40; AL Adams 4/37)
WP 235 (N Lakay 44, DV Moodie 39, D February 32; G Manicum 5/62) and 28/0

Western Province beat Eastern Province by an innings and 127 runs
EP 165 (A Douglas 56, N Francis 36; D February 7/40) and 97 (AL Adams 5/16)
WP 389 (J Le Roux 104*, JJ Neethling 70, MB Maclons 59, D February 47; M Wilson 3/49)

Transvaal beat Western Province on the first innings
Tvl 262 (A Barnes 86, E Cajee 57, S Chothia 55, H Ayob 40; AL Adams 4/81, I Tromp 3/40)
WP 132 (MB Maclons 49; H Ayob 4/40, H Jairam 3/16) and 325/7 (N Lakay 119, MB Maclons 93, DV Moodie 41; H Ayob 4/70)

5TH SACBOC DADABHAY INTER-PROVINCIAL NON-RACIAL TOURNAMENT, 27 DECEMBER 1969 – 7 JANUARY 1970, KIMBERLEY
Participants: Western Province, Transvaal, Natal, Eastern Province, Griqualand West and South Western Districts.
Winners: Western Province/Transvaal.

Western Province beat Griqualand West by 9 wickets
GW 90 (C Jacobs 41; SD Abed 4/28) and 97 (G Peerbhai 42; AL Adams 5/25, SD Abed 3/29)
WP 115 (I Dagnin 26; RD Engelbrecht 6/59, S Saloojee 4/56) and 75/1 (I Dagnin 36*, S Conrad 34)

Western Province beat Eastern Province by 128 runs
WP 212 (JJ Neethling 91*; E Clarke 4/74) and 201/4 dec (I Dagnin 82, AL Adams 50*, M Finnan 35)
EP 159 (D Govindjee 41*, N Francis 36; AL Adams 6/45) and 126 (N Francis 42; JJ Neethling 4/28, SD Abed 4/42)

Western Province beat Natal on the first innings
Ntl 135 (MA Patricks 48, O Vawda 33; D Fester 3/25, AL Adams 3/37) and 221/8 (J Govender 126; JJ Neethling 5/58)
WP 335/6 dec (S Conrad 104, MB Maclons 72, K Rodrigues 56, SD Abed 35, I Dagnin 30)

Western Province beat Transvaal on the first innings
WP 424 (SD Abed 145*, S Conrad 93, JJ Neethling 52*, N Lakay 48, I Dagnin 30; H Ayob 3/59, A Barnes 3/115)
Tvl 122 (I Garda 47; OL Williams 6/22) and 152/8 (A Gabru 54, A Barnes 39; OL Williams 4/40, AL Adams 3/42)

Western Province beat South Western Districts by an innings and 34 runs
SWD 93 (E Walburgh 40; OL Williams 5/27) and 77 (E Walburgh 40; AL Adams 7/27)
WP 204/3 dec (I Dagnin 100*, MB Maclons 64)

6TH SACBOC DADABHAY INTER-PROVINCIAL NON-RACIAL TOURNAMENT (DECENTRALISED), 26 DECEMBER 1970 – 13 MARCH 1971
Participants: Western Province, Transvaal and Natal.
Winners: Western Province/Transvaal.

Western Province beat Transvaal on the first innings, 1-2 January 1971, Cape Town
Tvl 211 (I Garda 55, A Bhamjee 54; SD Abed 4/37, OL Williams 3/43) and 42/1
WP 336 (G Williams 77*, S Conrad 71, AL Adams 55, R Magiet 38; S Chothia 5/141)

Western Province beat Natal on the first innings, 12-13 March 1971, Durban
WP 230 (AL Adams 52, SD Abed 48; Y Omar 3/27) and 140/8 (R Magiet 29, S Conrad 26; J Govender 3/36)
Ntl 152 (Y Omar 36, El Laher 30; OL Williams 4/20, G Williams 3/38)

9.1.5.2 WESTERN PROVINCE CRICKET BOARD FIRST-CLASS SCORES, 1971/72–1990/91

Match drawn between Transvaal and Western Province, 26–28 December 1971, Johannesburg
Tvl 369 (I Garda 68, A Bhamjee 75, A Barnes 88, S Rubidge 42, Moosa Mangera 36; G Williams 3/61)
WP 332 (S Conrad 139, E Isaacs 50, JJ Neethling 35, G Williams 31; H Ayob 3/63, H Jairam 3/84)

Natal beat Western Province by 8 wickets, 1–4 January 1972, Cape Town
WP 108 (E Isaacs 31; G Manicum 5/32, I Ebrahim 3/25) and 164 (G Williams 67; M Govender 3/35, I Ebrahim 3/60, Y Omar 3/13)
Ntl 222 (I Timol 44, MA Patricks 51) and 52/2

Match drawn between Western Province and Eastern Province, 8–10 January 1972, Port Elizabeth
WP 320 (DV Moodie 45, M Maclons 31, G Williams 80, S Magiet 89) and 104 (C Langson 5/20)
EP 300 (K Barry 58, M Wilson 64, N Francis 38, C Houlie 58*, P Snyman 40; G Williams 4/99, A Adams 3/75) and 63/4 (A Snyman 30) and 63/4

Western Province beat Transvaal by an innings and 229 runs, 30 December 1972 – 2 January 1973, Cape Town
Tvl 109 (A Sonn 3/19) and 86 (A Adams 4/14)
WP 424/8 dec (S Conrad 166, DV Moodie 100, Robbie van Graan 57; S Chothia 3/151, H Jairam 4/129)

Western Province beat Eastern Province by 5 wickets, 27–29 January 1973, Cape Town
EP 180 (A Douglas 69*; JE Mahoney 3/33, A Sonn 4/57) and 137 (D Jacobs 42; A Adams 3/22, G Williams 4/25)
WP 208 (DV Moodie 56, JJ Neethling 53; A Snyman 7/47) and 113/5

Western Province beat Natal by 6 wickets, 17–19 February 1973, Durban
Ntl 167 (Y Omar 52, KH Barker 31; A Adams 6/54) and 189 (J Govender 33, MA Patricks 81; A Adams 5/83, G Williams 3/14)
WP 289/9 dec (S Conrad 99, E Isaacs 54; I Ebrahim 4/81) and 59/4 (I Ebrahim 3/25)

Match drawn between Rest and Western Province, 3–5 March 1973, Cape Town
Rest 199 (I Garda 34, S Chothia 34, Y Omar 40; MR Magiet 5/29) and 314/7 dec (I Garda 106, BL D'Oliveira 100*; MR Magiet 3/65)
WP 221 (Robbie van Graan 31, JJ Neethling 37, MR Magiet 48; A Snyman 3/44) and 200/9 (S Magiet 50; I Ebrahim 3/34)

Match drawn between Eastern Province and Western Province, 16–18 November 1973, Cape Town
EP 181 (A Douglas 58, BL D'Oliveira 81*; A Adams 5/53) and 302 (M Wilson 40, BL D'Oliveira 99, I Hendricks 51; A Adams 3/59)
WP 253 (J Lambert 137; I Hendricks 5/45, T Williams 3/52) and 27/0

Match drawn between Western Province and Transvaal, 26–28 December 1973, Lenasia
WP 154 (MR Magiet 64; S Chothia 3/28) and 148/7 (Robbie van Graan 35, M Maclons 49)
Tvl 314/9 dec (A Bhamjee 36, A Barnes 104, S Chothia 44; MR Magiet 3/44, G Williams 3/88)

Western Province beat Natal by 120 runs, 31 December 1973 – 2 January 1974, Cape Town
WP 174 (R Simpson 43, J Lambert 34, S Magiet 44; KH Barker 5/39, LS Naidoo 4/42) and 156/8 dec (Robbie van Graan 31; I Ebrahim 3/39)
Ntl 85 (JJ Neethling 5/51, S Magiet 4/21) and 125 (Y Omar 36, KH Barker 33; JJ Neethling 3/24, J Lambert 4/18)

Western Province beat Eastern Province by 4 wickets, 18–20 January 1974, Port Elizabeth
EP 89 (JE Mahoney 5/39, A Adams 3/4) and 138 (N Francis 31, D Govindjee 33; A Adams 6/50, G Williams 4/53)
WP 152 (Robbie van Graan 35, JE Mahoney 30; D Carter 5/53) and 76/6

Western Province beat Transvaal by 3 wickets, 16–18 February 1974, Cape Town
Tvl 169 (A Manack 43; MR Magiet 3/47) and 195 (Y Snyders 31; A Adams 3/35, MR Magiet 3/27, C Kolbe 4/52)
WP 265 (LP Jacobs 33, C Kolbe 50, Robbie van Graan 67; A Manack 3/45, G Johannessie 4/63) and 105/7

Match drawn between Natal and Western Province, 16–18 March 1974, Durban
Ntl 208 (MA Patricks 81; JE Mahoney 3/33, G Williams 5/43) and 158 (KH Barker 56, V Ellery 32)
WP 136 (M Maclons 75*; KH Barker 4/27, I Ebrahim 4/29) and 51/2

Match drawn between Eastern Province and Western Province, 23–25 November 1974, Cape Town
EP 184 (J Vaghmaria 37, I Hendricks 30, D Govindjee 32; S Magiet 3/27) and 79 (WD Hendricks 5/9)
WP 163 (WD Hendricks 50; M Wilson 3/27) and 73/7 (T Williams 4/23)

Natal beat Western Province by 3 wickets, 14–16 December 1974, Durban
WP 154 (A Jabaar 48, S Magiet 52; LS Naidoo 6/50, MA Patricks 3/35) and 88 (I Ebrahim 3/28)
Ntl 113 (Y Randeree 57*; S Magiet 4/24, MR Magiet 4/24) and 130/7 (J Govender 65*; S Magiet 3/40, MR Magiet 3/28)

Transvaal beat Western Province by 27 runs, 31 December 1974 – 2 January 1975, Cape Town
Tvl 214 (A Gabru 34, RB Kanhai 104; A Adams 3/52, G Williams 3/30) and 160 (A Bhabha 35, S Chothia 46; A Adams 4/36)
WP 165 (WD Hendricks 44, CJ Abrahams 40; H Ayob 5/41, A Manack 3/29) and 182 (JE Mahoney 68*, MR Magiet 38; H Ayob 4/53, I Kara 3/56)

Western Province beat Eastern Province by 10 wickets, 18–20 January 1975, Port Elizabeth
WP 254 (LP Jacobs 33, CJ Abrahams 35, S Magiet 32, MR Magiet 76, JE Mahoney 32; JH Frans 3/37, D Govindjee 3/65, M Wilson 3/71) and 23/0
EP 92 (S Magiet 5/25) and 184 (D Jacobs 43, J Vaghmaria 39, Glen Cuddumbey 47; S Magiet 3/39)

Western Province beat Natal by 3 wickets, 15–17 February 1975, Cape Town
Ntl 131 (J Govender 36; MR Magiet 3/13) and 137 (S Magiet 6/24, J Khan 3/25)
WP 143 (WD Hendricks 35, S Magiet 32; I Ebrahim 6/70, MA Patricks 3/11) and 127/7 (I Ebrahim 5/54)

Match drawn between Transvaal and Western Province, 15–17 March 1975, Lenasia
Tvl 219 (A Gabru 45, Moosa Mangera 34; MR Magiet 4/52) and 254/7 (I Garda 32, A Gabru 44, A Barnes 104, S Chothia 39; CJ Abrahams 3/18)
WP 90 (S Chothia 4/30, A Barnes 4/44)

Western Province beat Eastern Province 11 runs, 22–24 November 1975, Port Elizabeth
WP 181 (LP Jacobs 48, B O'Connell 46*; Z Davids 4/48) and 178 (DV Moodie 65; T Pono 3/47)
EP 143 (J Sandan 57; JE Mahoney 6/42, HWH Bergins 3/49) and 205 (K Barry 37, J Sandan 33, D Govindjee 31; O Henry 3/47, WD Hendricks 4/57)

Western Province beat Transvaal by 10 wickets, 26–28 December 1975, Lenasia
Tvl 95 (HWH Bergins 6/27) and 70 (HWH Bergins 5/24, WD Hendricks 3/16)
WP 133 (DV Moodie 48; S Chothia 3/57, A Barnes 5/26) and 34/0

Western Province beat Natal by 10 wickets, 3–5 January 1976, Cape Town
Ntl 111 (JE Mahoney 5/37) and 130 (Y Omar 56; WF Carelse 5/15)
WP 212 (WD Hendricks 60, M Maclons 37, WF Carelse 30; G Allie 3/44) and 31/0

Match drawn between Western Province and Eastern Province, 24–26 January 1976, Cape Town
WP 190 (LP Jacobs 23, K van Graan 17, WF Carelse 36, B O'Connell 43; D Govindjee 3/22) and 287 (DV Moodie 42, K van Graan 44, WF Carelse 61*, B O'Connell 79; M Wilson 3/39)
EP 145 (D Jacobs 33, Z Davids 33; HWH Bergins 3/41, WF Carelse 3/27) and 142/4 (D Jacobs 36, J Sandan 38)

Match drawn between Western Province and Transvaal, 21–23 February 1976, Cape Town
WP 67 (S Rubidge 4/6) and 303 (B O'Connell 77, WF Carelse 40, O Henry 62*; Moosa Mangera 4/92) and 303
Tvl 177 (A Barnes 40, E Bhamjee 41; HWH Bergins 4/41, WF Carelse 5/37) and 81/7 (WF Carelse 4/9)

Match drawn between Natal and Western Province, 13–15 March 1976, Durban
Ntl 158 (F Timol 57; G van Oordt 3/32) and 92/8 (S Geldenhuys 33*; WD Hendricks 3/21)
WP 169 (WF Carelse 38, G van Oordt 37; G Allie 4/56, M Govender 5/35)

Rest of SACBOC beat Western Province by 9 wickets, 27–29 March 1976, Stellenbosch
WP 151 (LP Jacobs 50; A Barnes 4/23, I Ebrahim 4/51) and 167 (DV Moodie 55; A Barnes 6/44)
Rest 312 (I Garda 112, F Timol 34, Y Omar 33, S Chothia 52; WD Hendricks 4/50) and 8/1

Western Province beat Eastern Province by 6 wickets, 26–28 November 1977, Cape Town
EP 134 (S Magiet 4/53) and 60 (G van Oordt 3/11, MR Magiet 4/14)
WP 144 (C Martin 56; T Pono 3/26, W Fischer 3/14) and 51/4 (M Finnan 31)

Western Province beat Transvaal by an innings and 28 runs, 26–28 December 1977, Johannesburg
Tvl 53 (S Magiet 4/19, E Damon 4/21) and 43 (S Magiet 4/13, MR Magiet 3/9)
WP 124 (Derek Jacobs 3/32, E Amod 3/36)

Western Province beat Natal by an innings and 68 runs, 31 December 1977 – 2 January 1978, Cape Town
Ntl 56 (G van Oordt 3/18, A Jabaar 6/9) and 117 (T Roberts 37; A Jabaar 5/36)
WP 241 (S Magiet 54, A Jabaar 48, C van Schalkwyk 49*, G van Oordt 36; R Rogers 5/55)

Eastern Province beat Western Province by 34 runs, 21–23 January 1978, Port Elizabeth
EP 209 (KE Majola 41, Faghme Abrahams 83; A Jabaar 5/33) and 208 (H Lorgat 48, Faghme Abrahams 41, T Pono 46*; S Magiet 3/49, G van Oordt 5/30)
WP 176 (A Jabaar 35, S Jassiem 43*; T Pono 3/57, M Kara 3/30) and 207 (M Abdullah 45, E Isaacs 62, S Magiet 48; M Kara 4/41)

Western Province beat Transvaal by 5 wickets, 11–13 February 1978, Cape Town
Tvl 130 (O Visser 55; MR Magiet 5/23) and 140 (O Visser 32, D Stamper 42; MR Magiet 5/33)
WP 226 (F Solomons 40, S Magiet 62; S Gabriels 6/80) and 46/5

Match drawn between Natal and Western Province, 4–6 March 1978, Durban
Ntl 209 (T Roberts 30, J Govender 34, R Rogers 32; S Arnold 4/50) and 80/4 (Y Omar 33; J Williams 3/21)
WP 145 (A Jabaar 30; M Govender 3/45) and 20/2

Western Province beat Eastern Province by 5 wickets, 18–20 November 1978, Cape Town
EP 178 (Faghme Abrahams 60, D Govindjee 42) and 132 (A Frans 31; A Jabaar 5/28, MR Magiet 4/19)
WP 207 (R Salie 31, S Magiet 45, A Jabaar 34; D Jacobs 6/52) and 104/5 (K Thomas 31, A Jabaar 32*)

Natal beat Western Province by an innings and 25 runs, 26–28 December 1978, Durban
Ntl 334 (Y Omar 149, F Timol 85; MR Magiet 3/58)
WP 177 (MR Magiet 33; M Govender 5/48) and 132 (N Martin 37, E Isaacs 36; C Nicholson 5/41, Y Omar 3/26)

Western Province beat Transvaal by 6 wickets, 30 December 1978 – 1 January 1979, Cape Town
Tvl 153 (S Gabriels 43; JE Mahoney 3/24, S Jassiem 4/27) and 107 (MR Magiet 7/35)
WP 176/9 dec (N Martin 43; N Abrahams 4/40, S Gabriels 4/54) and 85/4 (N Martin 40)

Eastern Province beat Western Province by an innings and 53 runs, 20–22 January 1979, Zwide
EP 294/8 dec (J Sandan 59, D Jacobs 81, W Fischer 33*; A Adams 3/74)
WP 67 (D Jacobs 4/7) and 174 (N Fortune 33, JE Mahoney 43; KE Majola 6/69)

Western Province beat Natal by 64 runs, Cape Town, 17–19 February 1979, Cape Town
WP 262/8 dec (N Fortune 38, E Isaacs 32, C Martin 60, S Magiet 46; RCD Compton 3/42) and 94/7 (S Magiet 38)
Ntl 116 (F Timol 51; MR Magiet 4/24, S Magiet 3/20) and 176 (C Nicholson 40, J Govender 39; A Adams 4/86, S Magiet 3/25)

Western Province beat Transvaal by an innings and 1 run, 17–19 March 1979, Potchefstroom
WP 225 (A Jakoet 64, E Isaacs 38; N Abrahams 3/51, S Gabriels 4/54)
Tvl 75 (MR Magiet 4/9) and 149 (O Latha 34, S Nana 34; A Sonn 3/12, A Adams 3/39, C van Schalkwyk 3/7)

Eastern Province beat Western Province by 123 runs, 16–18 November 1979, Port Elizabeth
EP 150 (V Malgas 42; S Magiet 3/23, A Adams 3/13) and 234/9 (D Jacobs 40, KE Majola 37, W Fischer 63)
WP 147 (Y Adams 55, MR Magiet 40; JH Frans 3/36, S Draai 4/19, KE Majola 3/29) and 114 (S Magiet 37, MR Magiet 39; S Draai 5/40)

Western Province beat Natal by 4 runs, 31 December 1979–2 January 1980, Durban
WP 223 (E Isaacs 103, N Fortune 71; MM Khan 4/74) and 119 (S Magiet 54; L Barnard 4/55, MM Khan 4/39)
Ntl 161 (R Rogers 42; J Kleinveldt 3/40) and 177 (J Govender 41, MM Khan 37; J Kleinveldt 4/35, A Adams 5/38)

Match drawn between Western Province and Transvaal, 4–6 January 1980, Johannesburg
WP 228 (C Martin 66, MR Magiet 39, G van Oordt 32; F Kimmie 3/43, Derek Jacobs 3/37) and 19/2
Tvl 229 (C Vergie 34, S Gabriels 41, F Kimmie 44; A Adams 6/54)

Western Province beat Transvaal by 222 runs, 19–21 January 1980, Cape Town
WP 207 (N Fortune 32, ME Doman 64; F Kimmie 6/47) and 242 (N Fortune 59, C Martin 30, ME Doman 62*, MR Magiet 32)
Tvl 120 (R Cassim 40; VA Barnes 6/32) and 107 (F Kimmie 45; A Adams 4/31)

Western Province beat Natal by 149 runs, 16–18 February 1980, Cape Town
WP 249 (VA Barnes 41*, A Adams 39; A Sathar 6/70) and 194/7 dec (E Isaacs 31, S Magiet 63, G van Oordt 34, K van Graan 31*; F Timol 4/63)
Ntl 153 (A Adams 6/24) and 141 (F Timol 53; MR Magiet 6/23)

Western Province beat Eastern Province by 19 runs, 15–17 March 1980, Cape Town
WP 70/6 dec and 79 (JH Frans 3/33, I Hendricks 3/14, S Draai 3/21)
EP 88 (Z Hendricks 40; S Magiet 5/25, A Adams 4/8) and 42 (S Magiet 4/18, A Adams 6/7)

Western Province beat Transvaal by 7 wickets, 15–17 November 1980, Johannesburg
Tvl 172 (A Manack 50, I Bhagalia 33; J Kleinveldt 4/37, A Jabaar 3/38) and 237 (A Manack 36, S Gabriels 70, N Edwards 36; A Jabaar 3/80)
WP 276/8 dec (E Isaacs 34, R Musson 98, MR Magiet 57*, Z Davids 32*; F Kimmie 3/50, S Gabriels 4/71) and 136/3 (R Musson 64*)

Western Province beat Natal by 53 runs, 26–28 December 1980, Cape Town
WP 209 (R Musson 90*; RCD Compton 3/72, MM Khan 6/55) and 145/4 dec (E Isaacs 73)
Ntl 109 (MA Vahed 39, MM Khan 34; Z Davids 4/29) and 192 (Y Moorad 55*, F Hassim 32; VA Barnes 4/30, A Jabaar 3/72)

Western Province beat Transvaal by an innings and 5 runs, 30 December 1980 – 1 January 1981, Cape Town
WP 263/9 dec (R Musson 108, A Jabaar 66; I Bhagalia 3/51, A Manack 3/28)
Tvl 102 (A Jabaar 3/14, J Kleinveldt 3/24) and 156 (M Jajbhay 31; A Jabaar 4/43)

Western Province beat Eastern Province by 174 runs, 16–18 January 1981, Cape Town
WP 256 (M Abdullah 81, A Katts 40, J Kleinveldt 43; E Frans 3/56, D Govindjee 3/63) and 158 (E Frans 6/35)
EP 153 (KE Majola 48; VA Barnes 3/32, A Jabaar 3/19) and 87 (VA Barnes 6/31, S Magiet 3/19)

Natal beat Western Province by 2 wickets, 20–22 February 1981, Chatsworth
WP 137 (N Fortune 46; M Govender 3/38, C Pentiah 4/44) and 136 (M Abdullah 31; E Govender 6/30)
Ntl 170 (F Timol 40; VA Barnes 3/27, G van Oordt 4/32) and 105/8 (F Timol 44; G van Oordt 4/25)

Eastern Province beat Western Province by 9 runs, 13–15 March 1981, Port Elizabeth
EP 85 (E Damon 3/36, S Magiet 5/22) and 150 (J Sandan 31, KE Majola 41; S Magiet 3/27, M Theron 4/52)
WP 143 (ME Doman 53, C van Schalkwyk 50; S Draai 5/44) and 83 (A Katts 32; E Frans 7/37)

Western Province beat Eastern Province by 77 runs, 21–23 November 1981, Cape Town
WP 175 (E Isaacs 47, M Abdullah 52; S Draai 3/16, KE Majola 3/47) and 164/9 (N Fortune 44, E Isaacs 56*; S Draai 3/23)
EP 136 (GB Cuddumbey 34, H Lorgat 36; S Gabriels 3/31, A Jabaar 3/34) and 126 (Z Hendricks 30; S Gabriels 3/45, A Jabaar 3/30, C van Schalkwyk 4/15)

Western Province beat Transvaal by 178 runs, 26–28 December 1981, Lenasia
WP 175 (S Gabriels 30, C van Schalkwyk 56; A Manack 5/43) and 306/9 dec (S Hendricks 45, N Fortune 70, S Gabriels 45, C van Schalkwyk 51*, A Jabaar 33; M Gokal 3/43)
Tvl 162 (D Nagin 55; VA Barnes 3/26, A Jabaar 4/32) and 141 (A Manack 34; A Jabaar 3/51, M Theron 4/35)

Natal beat Western Province by 1 wicket, 1–3 January 1982, Chatsworth
WP 201 (N Fortune 53, G van Oordt 51; E Govender 3/49, MM Khan 5/62) and 115 (M Abdullah 68; E Govender 4/21, MM Khan 3/38)
Ntl 176 (S Gabriels 3/26) and 141/9 (Stanley Govender 47; VA Barnes 5/61)

Western Province beat Eastern Province by 3 wickets, 23–25 January 1982, Port Elizabeth
EP 191 (V Malgas 58, Faghme Abrahams 32; S Magiet 5/37) and 107 (S Magiet 4/24, VA Barnes 3/37, A Jabaar 3/35)
WP 234 (M Abdullah 41, C van Schalkwyk 46, A Jabaar 44*; T Kadi 3/64) and 65/7 (S Draai 6/29)

Western Province beat Transvaal by 142 runs, 20–22 February 1982, Cape Town
WP 138 (S Hendricks 41; M Gokal 5/34, A Manack 5/29) and 225/4 dec (N Fortune 65, M Abdullah 58)
Tvl 38 (S Gabriels 4/9) and 183 (A Manack 102*, Ashraf Kolia 30; S Gabriels 6/59)

Western Province beat Natal by an innings and 122 runs, 21–22 March 1982, Cape Town
WP 263/9 dec (N Fortune 143, S Magiet 37; S Munsoor 4/48, E Govender 3/62)
Ntl 39 (S Magiet 4/23, M Theron 3/5) and 102 (E Govender 41; A Jabaar 7/38, M Theron 3/21)

Eastern Province beat Western Province by 8 wickets, 20–22 November 1982, Zwide
EP 210 (Z Hendricks 52, D Govindjee 42; M Theron 4/62) and 21/2
WP 41 (S Draai 4/8) and 188 (E Isaacs 35, M Abdullah 65; S Draai 6/59, H Lorgat 3/30)

Western Province beat Natal by 87 runs, 28–30 December 1982, Cape Town
WP 110 (Y Thomas 42; S Mansoor 3/29, E Govender 5/47) and 208 (N Fortune 59, N Antulay 64; E Govender 3/49, MM Khan 4/79)
Ntl 129 (EH Mall 35, Stanley Govender 36; VA Barnes 5/30, A Jabaar 3/31) and 102 (M Moodley 59; VA Barnes 3/35, E Damon 4/36, A Jabaar 3/20)

Western Province beat Transvaal by 2 wickets, 1–3 January 1983, Cape Town
Tvl 115 (VA Barnes 5/26) and 120 (O Visser 36; Y Thomas 5/6)
WP 131 (E Harris 43, N Antulay 35; A Variawa 3/30, N Edwards 4/12) and 105/8 (E Isaacs 42*; J Kleinveldt 3/17, A Variawa 4/26)

Western Province beat Natal by an innings and 83 runs, 22–24 January 1983, Durban
WP 244 (S Hendricks 40, R Musson 31, M Abdullah 49, Y Thomas 44; MM Khan 5/85)
Ntl 61 (VA Barnes 8/29) and 100 (VA Barnes 3/23)

Western Province beat Eastern Province by 8 wickets, 19–21 February 1983, Cape Town
EP 83 (GB Cuddumbey 34*; VA Barnes 7/19) and 123 (A Jabaar 3/20)
WP 159 (S Hendricks 35, E Harris 50; S Draai 3/30) and 49/2

Western Province beat Transvaal by 190 runs, 12–14 March 1983, Lenasia
WP 192 (R Musson 52, M Abdullah 40; A Variawa 3/54, J Kleinveldt 3/33, F Kimmie 4/31) and 275 (M Abdullah 79, Y Thomas 59; F Kimmie 3/55, N Edwards 3/45)
Tvl 164 (S Mohammed 30, O Visser 42, F Kimmie 31; VA Barnes 5/57) and 113 (S Mohammed 33; A Jabaar 5/60, M Theron 3/26)

Match tied between Eastern Province and Western Province, 19–21 November 1983, Port Elizabeth
EP 171 (GB Cuddumbey 52; VA Barnes 3/26, A Jabaar 3/48) and 46/2
WP 171 (A Jabaar 70; JH Frans 4/27, KE Majola 4/47)

Western Province beat Transvaal by an innings and 16 runs, 27–29 December 1983, Lenasia
Tvl 233 (A Rajah 83, N Edwards 58; A Jabaar 4/58, S Gabriels 3/71) and 182 (A Rajah 32, A Wadvalla 30, N Edwards 34; A Jabaar 5/49, S Gabriels 5/78)
WP 431 (N Antulay 48, F Solomons 67, M Abdullah 107, Y Thomas 85, A Jabaar 43*; A Variawa 4/67, N Edwards 3/75)

Western Province beat Natal by 4 wickets, 31 December 1983 – 2 January 1984, Ladysmith
Ntl 211 (Stanley Govender 40, MM Khan 38; VA Barnes 3/36, E Damon 3/51) and 156 (EH Mall 49; VA Barnes 9/46)
WP 222 (N Antulay 43, A Jabaar 39, S Gabriels 56; M Rampersad 3/39) and 146/6 (A Jabaar 35*; MM Khan 3/41)

Western Province beat Eastern Province by 10 wickets, 21–23 January 1984, Cape Town
EP 93 (S Magiet 5/29, A Jabaar 4/18) and 142 (A Jabaar 7/40)
WP 205 (M Abdullah 102; E Frans 4/29, A Frans 3/57) and 34/0

Western Province beat Transvaal by an innings and 128 runs, 18–20 February 1984, Cape Town
WP 343/9 dec (E Harris 58, F Solomons 68, Y Thomas 100*, A Jabaar 61; A Ganchi 3/73, N Edwards 3/69)
Tvl 121 (E Amod 32; S Gabriels 6/40) and 94 (A Jabaar 5/25)

Western Province beat Natal by an innings and 121 runs, 17–18 March 1984, Cape Town
WP 302/9 dec (F Solomons 52, S Gabriels 50, R Cupido 62, Z Davids 55*; MM Khan 3/105)
Ntl 67 (S Gabriels 5/27) and 114 (S Gabriels 7/56)

Match tied between Eastern Province and Western Province, 17–19 November 1984, Cape Town
EP 109 (AD Peters 37; Ebrahim Mohamed 5/33) and 109 (J Sandan 39*; Ebrahim Mohamed 4/23, G Allie 6/45)
WP 97 (N Antulay 42; S Draai 5/20) and 121 (F Solomons 34, M Abdullah 36; JH Frans 3/23, H Lorgat 4/21)

Western Province beat Transvaal by an innings and 25 runs, 26–28 December 1984, Cape Town
Tvl 85 (VA Barnes 3/13, A Jabaar 4/13) and 90 (A Jabaar 3/24, Ebrahim Mohamed 3/25)
WP 200/9 dec (S Magiet 61; F Kimmie 4/38)

Western Province beat Natal by 10 wickets, 1–3 January 1985, Cape Town
Ntl 94 (VA Barnes 3/14, G Allie 3/18, A Jabaar 3/32) and 117 (VA Barnes 3/19, A Jabaar 5/29)
WP 206 (Y Thomas 35, A Jabaar 49; M Rampersad 4/39, Y Omar 4/36) and 9/0

Eastern Province beat Western Province by 5 wickets, 19–21 January 1985, Port Elizabeth
EP 280/8 dec (GB Cuddumbey 47, MG Majola 69, H Lorgat 63, KE Majola 38; A Jabaar 4/69) and 78/5 (GB Cuddumbey 32*)
WP 103 (S Magiet 33; H Lorgat 5/36, S Draai 4/26) and 253 (S Hendricks 56, H Ahmed 39, M Haupt 36, A Jabaar 30; KE Majola 8/96)

Western Province beat Transvaal by 7 wickets, 16–18 February 1985, Lenasia
Tvl 57 (VA Barnes 5/17, S Magiet 4/24) and 158 (VA Barnes 3/28, S Gabriels 4/45)
WP 134 (S Magiet 75; AA Manack 7/61) and 86/3 (M Abdullah 34*)

Western Province beat Natal by 208 runs, 16–18 March 1985, Tongaat
WP 269 (S Gabriels 58, F Solomons 35, M Abdullah 38, N Booysen 37; E Govender 4/65, T le Roux 3/69) and 245/5 dec (S Hendricks 54, S Gabriels 101*, M Abdullah 41; P Singaram 3/49)
Ntl 176 (R Ramsaroop 33; Ebrahim Mohamed 3/34, S Magiet 4/11) and 130 (A Jabaar 4/40)

Eastern Province beat Western Province by 1 wicket, 16–18 November 1985, Port Elizabeth
WP 120 (N Antulay 34; JH Frans 3/13, E Frans 3/32, H Lorgat 3/31) and 138 (F Ebrahim 70; JH Frans 4/26, H Lorgat 5/43)
EP 107 (H Lorgat 41; F Davids 5/57, G Allie 5/30) and 152/9 (K Miller 61; A Jabaar 3/38)

Match drawn between Western Province and Natal, 28–30 December 1985, Chatsworth
WP 328/9 dec (S Hendricks 49, N Antulay 69, M Abdullah 86; MM Khan 3/73)
Natal 145 (S Gabriels 8/53) and 216/9 (G Hoosen 41*; S Gabriels 3/68)

Transvaal beat Western Province by 4 wickets, 1–3 January 1986, Lenasia
Tvl 245 (A Rajah 63, A Dinath 45, N Dindar 38; F Davids 3/36) and 170/6 (N Edwards 49)
WP 60 (VA Barnes 8/29) and 351 (S Gabriels 31, F Ebrahim 42, M Abdullah 36, F Davids 58, Y Thomas 116; VA Barnes 4/70)

Eastern Province beat Western Province by 19 runs, 18–20 January 1986, Cape Town
EP 177 (Y Thomas 3/30) and 280 (H Lorgat 121, A Frans 83; F Davids 5/50, S Gabriels 3/60)
WP 147 (S Hendricks 38; H Lorgat 5/57) and 291 (G Khan 52, N Antulay 41, F Davids 81, S Magiet 61, C Ravens 30; H Lorgat 4/76)

Match drawn between Western Province and Natal, 22–24 February 1986, Cape Town
WP 177 (S Hendricks 34, S Conrad 54; N Ramnarain 5/61, Y Omar 3/36) and 150/7 dec (Y Thomas 37, S Conrad 49; T le Roux 4/43)
Ntl 195 (EH Mall 60, N Moodley 36; S Gabriels 8/64) and 44/2

Western Province beat Transvaal by 8 wickets, 15–17 March 1986, Cape Town
Tvl 53 (R February 3/12, G Allie 4/18) and 199 (M Saleh 31, F Kimmie 44, Y Begg 42*; A Jabaar 5/48)
WP 223 (I Behardien 32, S Conrad 44, R February 30; AA Manack 4/68) and 31/2

Western Province beat Eastern Province by 10 wickets, 22–24 November 1986, Cape Town
EP 224 (S Kruger 54, KE Majola 43*, JH Frans 41; VA Barnes 4/48, S Gabriels 3/9) and 92 (VA Barnes 7/41, N Booysen 3/35)
WP 214 (I Behardien 33, S Magiet 60, N White 39; S Draai 5/50) and 103/0 (S Hendricks 51*, S Gabriels 42*)

Western Province beat Natal by an innings and 102 runs, 27–29 December 1986, Cape Town
WP 436/6 dec (I Behardien 72, M Abdullah 109, F Davids 31, S Magiet 100*, Y Thomas 43)
Ntl 110 (N Booysen 3/29, S Gabriels 3/22) and 224 (Y Omar 107; VA Barnes 4/40, N Booysen 3/61)

Western Province beat Transvaal by 10 wickets, 31 December 1986 – 2 January 1987, Cape Town
Tvl 111 (E Amod 36; VA Barnes 6/45) and 73 (VA Barnes 3/21, S Magiet 5/16)
WP 151 (N Booysen 38; AA Manack 4/34) and 35/0

Eastern Province beat Western Province by 2 wickets, 24–26 January 1987, Port Elizabeth
WP 99 (S Magiet 32; V Frans 3/19, S Draai 3/41) and 102 (M Abdullah 34; JH Frans 3/25, RB Dolley 3/20, KE Majola 3/22)
EP 95 (AD Peters 31; VA Barnes 3/37, G Allie 4/33) and 112/8 (AD Peters 40; VA Barnes 3/51, G Allie 5/33)

Match drawn between Western Province and Natal, 21–23 February 1987, Pietermaritzburg
WP 175 (I Behardien 35, M Abdullah 40; N Ramnarain 3/25, T le Roux 3/30, MM Khan 3/37) and 209/7 dec (S Magiet 100*)
Ntl 165 (JM Chellan 74; G Allie 3/30) and 74/4 (RL Naidoo 30*; VA Barnes 3/25)

Western Province beat Transvaal by an innings and 64 runs, 14–16 March 1987, Lenasia
Tvl 119 (S Gabriels 6/27) and 159 (H Lorgat 40, Moosa Mangera 66; VA Barnes 5/30, S Gabriels 4/37)
WP 342/9 dec (S Hendricks 137, S Gabriels 50, M Abdullah 61, S Magiet 30; H Lorgat 3/97, Moosa Mangera 4/61)

Western Province beat Eastern Province by 3 wickets, 21–23 November 1987, Port Elizabeth
EP 236 (AD Peters 73; VA Barnes 3/55, F Benjamin 4/69) and 173 (GB Cuddumbey 47, RB Dolley 44; R February 3/34, S Gabriels 3/52)
WP 272 (S Gabriels 62, S Conrad 31, I Behardien 31, F Davids 51; KE Majola 4/89) and 138/7 (S Gabriels 56*; S Abrahams 4/48)

Match drawn between Natal and Western Province, 29–31 December 1987, Pietermaritzburg
Ntl 148 (MM Khan 39; R February 4/28, N Muller 3/14) and 326/8 (Stanley Govender 38, MM Khan 99*, RL Naidoo 58; N Muller 3/31)
WP 272 (R Cupido 38, I Behardien 50, D Kemp 33, N Muller 35, R February 37; M Rampersad 3/60, MM Khan 4/67)

Match drawn between Western Province and Transvaal, 2–4 January 1988, Lenasia
WP 350/8 dec (S Gabriels 58, R Cupido 52, M Abdullah 51, D Kemp 57) and 257/7 dec (D Kemp 30, M Abdullah 37, F Davids 107*; AA Manack 3/39)
Tvl 298 (A Dinath 32, M Jajbhay 61*, N Dindar 61; VA Barnes 3/50) and 150/7 (I Khan 37; S Gabriels 4/45)

Western Province beat Eastern Province by 10 wickets, 23–25 January 1988, Cape Town
WP 367/5 dec (S Gabriels 40, S Hendricks 70, M Abdullah 78*, F Davids 146; KE Majola 3/106) and 29/0
EP 98 (KE Majola 33; VA Barnes 3/19, R February 3/10, S Gabriels 4/31) and 297 (GB Cuddumbey 30, AC Jordaan 56, KE Majola 42, A Coetzee 35; R February 3/65, S Gabriels 4/82)

Western Province beat Natal by an innings and 271 runs, 20–22 February 1988, Cape Town
Ntl 78 (VA Barnes 6/28) and 69 (S Gabriels 6/17)
WP 418 (I Behardien 40, M Abdullah 94, D Kemp 54, S Magiet 32, R Cupido 37*, R February 31; MM Khan 5/71)

Western Province beat Transvaal by 7 wickets, 19–21 March 1988, Cape Town
Tvl 190 (A Dinath 41, M Jajbhay 58; R February 6/73) and 156 (M Desai 32; VA Barnes 4/26, F Davids 3/8)
WP 254 (D Kemp 34, F Davids 85, S Magiet 85; AA Manack 6/82, H Lorgat 3/50) and 95/3 (S Hendricks 36, R Cupido 41)

Match drawn between Western Province and Eastern Province, 26–28 November 1988, Port Elizabeth
WP 285 (S Gabriels 60, I Behardien 40, F Davids 89; KE Majola 6/92) and 162/5 dec (S Hendricks 63, F Davids 47)
EP 163 (AD Peters 62; VA Barnes 6/32) and 139/5 (KE Majola 47)

Western Province beat Natal by an innings and 182 runs, 27–29 December 1988, Cape Town
Ntl 49 (VA Barnes 5/11) and 65 (M Patel 33; VA Barnes 5/22, S Green 3/26)
WP 296/7 dec (S Hendricks 35, S Gabriels 35, D Kemp 148*; MM Khan 5/92)

Match drawn between Western Province and Transvaal, 31 December 1988 – 2 January 1989, Cape Town
WP 234 (S Gabriels 53, Y Thomas 56; AA Manack 6/34) and 192/5 dec (I Behardien 44, F Davids 50*, D Kemp 51)
Tvl 233 (H Lorgat 61, N Dindar 54, AA Manack 32; VA Barnes 6/53) and 34/1

Western Province beat Eastern Province by 5 wickets, 21–23 January 1989, Cape Town
EP 120 (Ebrahim Mohamed 5/30) and 333 (Glenton Miller 32, R Yearwood 96, A Frans 45, P Hufkie 43; S Gabriels 6/47)
WP 321 (C Dyason 30, D Kemp 66, F Davids 64, Y Thomas 43; M Mali 4/96) and 134/5 (F Davids 63*; M Mali 3/47)

Western Province beat Natal by 7 wickets, 18–20 February 1989, Durban
Ntl 163 (F Suleman 44, Sagren Moodley 32*; R February 3/30, C Hendrikse 3/16) and 171 (EH Mall 57, LD Naidoo 51; C Hendrikse 6/20)
WP 226/8 dec (C Dyason 40, M Rasmus 31, C Hendrikse 31*; MM Khan 4/57) and 110/3 (S Gabriels 38*, D Kemp 31)

Match drawn between Western Province and Transvaal, 11–13 March 1989, Lenasia
WP 194 (Y Adams 31, F Davids 46; H Lorgat 6/53) and 124/5 (F Davids 62*)
Tvl 318 (N Dindar 132*, H Lorgat 43, A Jabaar 31; R February 4/63)

Match drawn between Eastern Province and Western Province, 25–27 November 1989, Cape Town
EP 190 (AD Peters 70; N Booysen 3/36, AA Manack 5/39) and 192 (P Hufkie 38, A Coetzee 38; S Gabriels 3/33)
WP 121 (M Mali 3/28, G Koen 3/33, RB Dolley 3/43) and 191/9 (F Davids 91; M Mali 4/81)

Western Province beat Transvaal by an innings and 66 runs, 27–29 December 1989, Lenasia
WP 305/6 dec (F Davids 106, B Dammert 57, Y Thomas 59*; N Dindar 3/29)
Tvl 134 (I Munshi 30; AA Manack 3/27, F Davids 4/11) and 105 (AA Manack 5/48, F Davids 4/29)

Western Province beat Natal by 8 wickets, 1–3 January 1990, Durban
Ntl 180 (E Govender 41, Stanley Govender 46; VA Barnes 3/31, F Benjamin 3/48) and 115 (M Patel 39; F Benjamin 6/35)
WP 272 (I Behardien 108, N White 76; LD Naidoo 3/45) and 24/2

Western Province beat Natal by an innings and 22 runs, 20–22 January 1990, Cape Town
Ntl 142 (Stanley Govender 57*; VA Barnes 5/23) and 162 (JM Chellan 32, F Suleman 30; F Davids 3/27)
WP 326 (E Gafieldien 48, S Gabriels 52, Y Thomas 30, N Muller 74; P Moodley 6/139)

Transvaal beat Western Province by 7 wickets, 3–5 March 1990, Cape Town
WP 240 (I Behardien 38, F Davids 48, D Kemp 31, Y Thomas 41; M Sarang 3/47, HA Manack 4/77) and 113 (I Behardien 33, Y Thomas 52; M Sarang 3/27, H Lorgat 3/29, A Jabaar 3/44)
Tvl 297 (I Khan 73, HA Manack 72, A Jabaar 38; VA Barnes 4/56, S Gabriels 3/51) and 58/3

Western Province beat Eastern Province by 3 wickets, 17–19 March 1990, Port Elizabeth
EP 50 (AA Manack 7/17) and 155 (KE Majola 40, MG Majola 30*; T Seconds 6/47)
WP 1/0 dec and 207/7 (E Gafieldien 86, S Gabriels 33*; S Abrahams 4/64)

Western Province beat Natal by an innings and 128 runs, 17–19 November 1990, Bellville
Ntl 117 (MA Meyer 5/22) and 104 (LD Naidoo 30; HS Williams 3/23, S Gabriels 5/57)
WP 349/6 dec (I Behardien 142, N White 125*)

Western Province beat Eastern Province by 8 wickets, 8–10 December 1990, Bellville
EP 141 (AD Peters 77*; S Conrad 4/35) and 240 (R Yearwood 58, P Hufkie 33)
WP 240 (Y Thomas 70, S Magiet 69, MA Meyer 36; M Mali 3/53, KE Majola 5/81) and 143/2 (S Conrad 63, S Magiet 36*)

Match drawn between Western Province and Trasnvaal, 5–7 January 1991, Lenasia
WP 168 (A Viljoen 48, N White 57; AA Manack 4/49, HA Manack 3/22) and 209/5 (I Behardien 48, N White 64*, Y Thomas 75*)
Tvl 189 (M Jajbhay 42, I Khan 30; MA Meyer 3/53, F Davids 4/28)

Western Province beat Transvaal by 77 runs, 26–28 January 1991, Bellville
WP 94 (MA Meyer 33*; AA Manack 5/26) and 282/9 dec (A Viljoen 81, N White 109, Y Thomas 42; HA Manack 3/18, H Lorgat 3/68)
Tvl 105 (MA Meyer 3/34, VA Barnes 3/13) and 194 (M Jajbhay 67, HA Manack 32; MA Meyer 4/30, VA Barnes 3/47)

Eastern Province beat Western Province by 6 runs, 16–18 February 1991, Port Elizabeth
EP 170 (E van Heerden 72; VA Barnes 5/37, S Gabriels 3/19) and 93 (R Yearwood 33; MA Meyer 4/29, VA Barnes 3/21)
WP 161 (N White 36, S Magiet 97; BS Forbes 3/47) and 96 (BS Forbes 3/33, F Sarrahwitz 5/40)

Match drawn between Natal and Western Province, 9–11 March 1991, Durban
Ntl 92 (MA Meyer 3/27, F Benjamin 3/20) and 162/5 (JM Chellan 37, Stanley Govender 35*)
WP 179 (F Davids 62, S Magiet 37; Sagren Moodley 3/39, G Moses 4/47)

9.1.5.3 Western Province Cricket Board, List A Matches, 1973/74–1984/85[295]

SFW KNOCKOUT COMPETITION, 1973/74

Western Province beat Griqualand West by 115 runs (Quarter-final)
WP 250 (M Maclons 59, W Hendricks 49, R van Graan 41, J Lambert 30)
Gri 135 (S Saloojee 38, K Connor 31; J Mahoney 1/21, J Neethling 2/13, G Williams 2/24)

Western Province beat Eastern Province by 35 runs (Semi-final)
WP 111 (K van Graan 28, J Lambert 27, L Jacobs 19; T Williams 1/20, B D'Oliviera 4/14, S Draai 2/16)
EP 76 (A Douglas 20, M Wilson 11; A Sonn 1/20, J Neethling 1/17, G Williams 1/10, K van Graan 1/6, B Petersen 5/17)

Natal beat Western Province B by 67 runs
Ntl 125 (J Govender 35, I Ebrahim 26, G Montgomery 25*; C van Schalkwyk 4/20, A Kallis 2/9, HWH Bergins 2/15)
WP B 58 (H Arenz 21, Y Omar 3/12; K Barker 2/9, MA Patricks 2/11, LS Naidoo 2/17)

Eastern Province beat Western Province C by 37 runs
EP 174 (D Govindjee 93, D Jacobs 31; I Tromp 4/31, T le Cordeur 3/36)
WP C 137 (C Kolbe 58, A Katts 23, S Snyders 21; T Williams 4/27, D Govindjee 2/24)

Western Province beat Transvaal by 36 runs (Final)
WP 179 (K van Graan 46, L Jacobs 24, G Williams 15*; S Chothia 2/14, A Barnes 2/32, S Rubidge 2/26)
Tvl 143 (A Gabru 60, M Mangera 24; J Mahoney 3/17, A Sonn 2/15, G Williams 5/32)

SFW KNOCKOUT COMPETITION, 1974/75

Natal beat Western Province B by 60 runs (Quarter-final)
Ntl 175/8 (G Francois 36, G Govender 26, Y Omar 22; J Mahoney 1/30, R Witbooi 3/53, B Petersen 2/32)
WP B 115 (L Jacobs 34, A Katts 24, C Abrahams 17; K Barker 2/13, I Ebrahim 2/17, MA Patricks 3/21)

BENSON & HEDGES TROPHY, 1982/83

Western Province beat Natal by 56 runs (Quarter-final)
WP 141/7 (M Abdullah 43, A Jabaar 24, N Arendse 14; E Govender 2/20)
Ntl 85 (S Govender 28, E Mall 21, N Moodley 12; E Damon 1/21, Y Thomas 2/12, A Jabaar 5/11, C van Schalkwyk 1/12)

Western Province beat Transvaal B by 7 wickets (Semi-final)
Tvl B 184 (A Manack 77, Y Begg 32, D George 29; V Barnes 2/28, S Magiet 2/31, Y Thomas 2/45)
WP 185/3 (E Isaacs 89, N Fortune 36, M Abdullah 26*; R Khan 1/30, E Amod 2/38)

Western Province beat Eastern Province by 96 runs (Final)
WP 155/8 (N Fortune 46, M Abdullah 28, M Theron 13; M Abrahams 2/16, H Lorgat 1/19, G Harrison 3/23)
EP 59 (G Abrahams 22, H Lorgat 10, F Abrahams 10; [x] Damon 1/15, A Jabaar 3/7, M Theron 5/16)

BENSON & HEDGES TROPHY, 1983/84

Western Province beat Transvaal B by 9 wickets (Quarter-final)
Tvl B 137 ([x] Jajbhai 55, [x] Desai 28; V Barnes 2/22, S Magiet 3/13, Y Thomas 2/12)
WP 141/1 (E Harris 48*, N Fortune 47*, N Antulay 33; [x] Dinath 1/26)

Western Province beat Natal by 79 runs (Semi-final)
WP 212/8 (M Abdullah 76, N Antulay 37, E Isaacs 22; [x] Gangat 2/23, Y Omar 3/31)
Ntl 133 (Y Omar 40, M Khan 31, P Maharaj 11; V Barnes 3/15, A Jabaar 1/19, N Antulay 2/12)

Rain stopped play between Western Province and Eastern Province (Final), trophy shared
EP 136 (KE Majola 39*, J Frans 28; [x] Damon 2/13, S Magiet 3/10, M Allie 2/26)
WP [did not bat]

BENSON & HEDGES TROPHY, 1984/85

Western Province beat Natal B by 137 runs (Quarter-final)
WP 206/4 (S Gabriels 56, M Abdullah 34, F Solomons 31; [x] Ramsaroop 2/32)
Ntl B 69 ([x] Patel 29, [x] Moodley 12; V Barnes 3/5, A Jabaar 2/29, M Allie 3/16)

Western Province beat Eastern Province by 45 runs (Semi-final)
WP 173 (N Antulay 58, S Hendricks 56; E Frans 1/25, A Frans 3/33)
EP 128 (KE Majola 28, A Frans 21, D Reid 16; V Barnes 1/10, S Magiet 2/21, S Gabriels 5/32)

Western Province beat Transvaal by 80 runs (Final)
WP 225/7 (S Magiet 73, S Gabriels 57, S Hendricks 25, A Jabaar 23; N Edwards 2/28, M Mangera 2/22)
Tvl 145/6 (M Moosagie 44, N Edwards 27, A Odendaal 16; V Barnes 2/18, N Booysen 2/24, S Gabriels 1/21)

9.2 Western Province Cricket Board B and U-21

The Western Province Cricket Board also entered B and U-21 teams in the SACBOC and SACB B Division, which was played regularly for 19 seasons from 1970/71 to 1990/91 (the only exceptions being 1972/73 and 1976/77).[296]

The nature of the B Division competition varied. It was either centralised or decentralised. For several seasons the teams were divided into zones, and at times there were two, three or four sections, with ensuing semi-finals or finals as necessary.

B division cricket was first played in the season 1970/71 on a decentralised basis. The Eastern Province senior team, Border, competed with Griqualand West and South Western Districts. Eastern Province were unbeaten and so won promotion to join Western Province, Transvaal and Natal in the new senior three-day inter-provincial competition held from 1971/72 up to unity in 1991.[297] In 1975/76 Rashid Varachia, president of SACBOC, presented the MR Varachia Trophy, to be competed for in the B division. Under SACB, from 1977/78 until unity in 1991, B division teams played for the Booley Bowl.

Western Province won the B Division Trophy at least four times and shared it once. WP U-21 played B Division cricket for ten seasons from 1981/82 to 1990/91 and won the trophy twice. It is likely Western Province B won on other occasions too, but the winners are for several seasons unknown and still to be researched; for example, the centralised tournament in Kimberley in 1977/78 and the finals in 1978/79, 1979/80 and 1983/84, in which Western Province played. In 1986/87 Western Province B won Section II of this competition and qualified to play the possible winners of Section I in the final, but this was shelved because fixtures in Section I were not completed.

9.2.1 Western Province Cricket Board B and U-21 Trophies

Season	Winners
1970/71	Eastern Province [WPCB B did not participate]
1971/72	Transvaal B
1973/74	*Western Province B*
1974/75	*Western Province B*
1975/76	*Western Province B*
1977/78	Centralised
1978/79	[winner unknown – Final Western Province B vs SASSSA]
1979/80	[winner unknown – Final Western Province B vs SASSSA]
1980/81	Natal B/Eastern Province B
1981/82	*Western Province B*
1982/83	Eastern Province B
1983/84	[winner unknown – Final Western Province B vs Transvaal B]
1984/85	Eastern Province B
1985/86	*Western Province U-21*
1986/87	No winner [final shelved]
1987/88	Griqualand West
1988/89	*Western Province B*/Transvaal U-21
1989/90	Eastern Province B
1990/91	*Western Province U-21*

9.2.2 Western Province Cricket Board B, First-Class Scores

CENTRALISED TOURNAMENT, DECEMBER/JANUARY 1971/72, KIMBERLEY[298]

Western Province B beat Griqualand West on the first innings
GW 102 (C Jacobs 25; J Lewis 5/35) and 287/8 dec (C Jacobs 140*)
WPB 129 (O Henry 34, A Benjamin 25, L Crotz 22; R Engelbrecht 4/47, Y Bhayat 3/23) and 156/1 (A Nackerdien 73*, L Jacobs 44 ret. hurt)

Transvaal B beat Western Province B on the first innings
TvlB 394 (E Amod 134, A Wadvalla 85, H Naik 51; T Le Cordeur 6/85, J Lewis 4/110)
WPB 286 (L Jacobs 100, L Crotz 46, H Daniels 32, O Arnolds 29*; Z Mohammed 3/65)

SOUTH ZONE CENTRALISED TOURNAMENT, DECEMBER 1973, MOSSEL BAY[299]

Western Province B beat South Western Districts by 5 wickets, 26–27 December 1973
SWD 173 (R Africa 48, G Malgas 42, E Walburgh 27; E Damon 4/36, HWH Bergins 3/33) and 96 (R Africa 21; O Henry 4/34)
WPB 185 (S Galant 51, R Simpson 37, O Henry 35*, A Jabaar 22; D Malgas 4/63, C Peterson 3/50) and 91/5 (L Jacobs 35)

Western Province B beat Eastern Province B by an innings and 86 runs, 28–29 December 1973
WPB 237 (O Henry 52*, S Galant 45, W Hendricks 42, R Simpson 21; W Fisher 5/86)
EPB 76 (A Frans 20, E Damon 4/24) and 75 (J Sandan 31; O Henry 5/22, C van Schalkwyk 3/22)

Western Province B beat Natal B by 191 runs, 23-25 February 1975, Currie's Fountain, Durban (Final)
WPB 93 (G Govender 5/17) and 294 (A Jabaar 61, B O'Connell 58, W Hendricks 41, C van Schalkwyk 40, O Henry 39; S Pentiah 3/34, B David 3/35)
NtlB 83 (HWH Bergins 6/39, E Damon 3/29) and 113 (H Naik 52, M Ebrahim 22; O Henry 4/28, HWH Bergins 3/32)

ZONE A CENTRALISED TOURNAMENT, 26–31 DECEMBER 1974, KIMBERLEY[300]

Western Province B beat Transvaal B on the first innings, 28–29 December 1974
TvlB 188 (S Nana 72, R Cajee 41, A Wadvalla 26; S Jassiem 4/34, E Damon 3/63) and 107/7 (A Wadvalla 35*, G Feerbhai 23*; O Henry 3/34)
WPB 230 (N Brache 66, R February 39, H Dawson 30, S Jassiem 29; F Omar 3/51)

Griqualand West beat Western Province B on the first innings, 30–31 December 1974
GW 212 (Y Snyders 62, D Appollis 44, R Engelbrecht 43, D Visser 21) and 164/8 dec (I Hendricks 44, D Appollis 43, A Williams 32, Y Snyders 22; HWH Bergins 3/33)
WPB 141/5 dec (R Allen 56, R February 31*, N Brache 24, H Dawson 23; R Engelbrecht 3/57) and 96/2 (R Allen 47*, H Dawson 33*)

Western Province B beat Eastern Province B by an innings and 120 runs, 1–3 March 1975
WPB 298/9 dec (M Abdullah 104, I Timol 85, S Gabriels 42; D Jordaan 3/45, A Frans 3/49)
EPB 115 (D Jacobs 60; A Sonn 4/27) and 63 (S Hendricks 17; O Henry 4/11, A Sonn 3/12)

CENTRALISED TOURNAMENT, 27 DECEMBER 1975 – 9 JANUARY 1976[301]

Western Province B beat Eastern Province B on the first innings, 27–28 December 1975
WPB 186 (M Abdullah 50, I Timol 36, C Miller 23; K le Roux 3/54) and 30/1
EPB 130 (I Ajam 32, A Frans 21)

Western Province B beat Griqualand West on the first innings, 29-30 December 1975
WPB 263/9 dec (I Timol 145*, P Hendricks 21, S Jassiem 20; A Williams 3/46)
GW 119 (K Connor 38, Y Snyders 27; S Jassiem 3/7, S Gabriels 3/21) and 203/7 (P Cader 55, D Appollis 37, Y Snyders 29; C Miller 4/28)

Western Province B beat South Western Districts on the first innings, 30 December 1975 – 1 January 1976
WPB 233 (I Timol 56*, N Brache 52, A Jabaar 41, G van Oordt 33; W Matthews 5/47) and 132/5 dec (A Jabaar 42*, N Brache 26, M Abdullah 22, G van Oordt 21*)
SWD 174 (D Malgas 60, A Coericius 25, G Malgas 20; G van Oordt 4/26, R February 3/48, A Jabaar 3/67) and 67/6 (S Green 3/16)

Western Province B beat Natal B on the first innings, 2–3 January 1976
Ntl B 189 (Y Pillay 49, S Geldenhuys 40; A Jabaar 3/27) and 51/1 (M Vahed 24*)
WPB 205 (N Brache 44, C Miller 43, C February 32, A Jabaar 28, S Gabriels 23; H Moonilal 6/65)

Western Province B beat Transvaal B on the first innings, 8–9 January 1976
WPB 208 (S Gabriels 52, G van Oordt 45*, P Hendricks 44; R Rubidge 6/75)
TvlB 142 (A Francis 27*, S Mohammed 24, Y Rubidge 23; G van Oordt 3/13, S Gabriels 3/43, A Jabaar 3/50)

CENTRALISED TOURNAMENT, 27 DECEMBER 1977 – 1 JANUARY 1978, KIMBERLEY[302]

Western Province B beat Transvaal B by 10 wickets, 27–28 December 1977
TvlB 142 (A Sujee 36, R Davy 23; S Jassiem 4/58, S Arnold 3/30) and 145 (S Jassat 36, A Abrahams 36; R Witbooi 5/27)
WPB 267 (S Jassiem 62*, V Smith 53, M Abdullah 52, M Ebrahim 43; F Gangat 3/59) and 24/0

Western Province B vs Griqualand West
[no details available]

Western Province B vs South Western Districts
[no details available]

CENTRALISED SOUTHERN SECTION, 26 DECEMBER 1978 – 1 JANUARY 1979, CAPE TOWN[303]

Western Province B beat South Western Districts by an innings and 45 runs, 26–27 December 1978, Pacaltsdorp
SWD 83 (R Africa 21; V Barnes 5/16, J Kleinveldt 4/26) and 54 (J Conradie 19; J Kleinveldt 7/42, V Barnes 3/12)
WPB 182 (M Najaar 104, N Fortune 27; R Jardine 4/38)

Western Province B beat Border by 3 wickets, 28–29 December 1978, Pacaltsdorp
Bdr 96 (X Pilisani 29, X Nkwinti 26, A Mali 24; J Kleinveldt 4/17, V Barnes 4/32) and 80 (M Nkwinti 30*; V Barnes 5/33, J Kleinveldt 4/41)
WP [x] and 74/7 (M Najaar 25; T Pond 4/26)

Western Province B beat Eastern Province B by 70 runs, 30 December 1978 – 1 January 1978, Pacaltsdorp
WPB 112 (M Najaar 40, J Martin 25; G Koen 4/8) and 159/9 dec (V Smith 65, M Ebrahim 32; G Koen 4/65)
EPB 69 (S Kruger 25; V Barnes 6/30, J Kleinveldt 3/296) and 132 (A Kader 44, V Malgas 27, D Reid 25; V Barnes 4/30, J Kleinveldt 3/60)

Western Province B vs SASSSA, [x], [x] (Final)
[no details available]

CENTRALISED SOUTH SECTION TOURNAMENT, 2–7 JANUARY 1980, MDANTSANE, EAST LONDON[304]

Western Province B beat South Western Districts by 2 wickets, 2–3 January 1980, Mdantsane, East London
SWD 55 (V Barnes 4/10) and 150 (C de Waal 29, R Africa 27*, B Deal 23, A du Plessis 21, R da Silva 20; V Barnes 4/28)
WPB 84 (M Doman 19, J Hansen 19; M Nicholas 6/38) and 122/8 (M Doman 46, P Wyngaard 22; M Davids 4/32)

Western Province B beat Border by an innings and 3 runs, 4–5 January 1980
WPB 219 (M Doman 61, P Wyngaard 37, E Harris 43; A Mali 4/42, G Fredericks 4/88)
Bdr 91 (M Nkwinti 20; V Barnes 6/19, R van Graan 4/33) and 125 (G Gamiet 41, A Mali 23; V Barnes 4/28)

Western Province B beat Eastern Province B by 5 wickets, 6–7 January 1980
EPB 156 (E Frans 70, G Koen 36*, T le Roux 4/46, V Barnes 3/49) and 110 (E Frans 36, M Philander 31, T le Roux 4/33, V Barnes 3/19)
WPB 128 (R van Graan 29*, T le Roux 26, M Doman 20, A Frans 4/31) and 141/5 (M Doman 38, S Salie 23*)

Western Province B vs SASSSA (Final)
[no details available]

CENTRALISED SOUTH SECTION TOURNAMENT, 2-9 JANUARY 1981, CAPE TOWN[305]

South Western Districts beat Western Province B on the first innings, 2–3 January 1981, Avonwood
SWD 115 (W Jeffrey 36, N Jeffrey 29, T le Roux 7/46) and 185 (W Jeffrey 39, G Moodien 38, J Daniels 27, B Deal 20, A Kahaar 3/29)
WPB 77 (M Davids 6/35) and 164/8 (N Leendertz 31, R Salie, 30, B Deal 3/16)

Western Province B beat Border by 8 wickets, 6–7 January 1981, Cloetesville
Bdr 143 (A Mali 52, T Pono 38*, G Allie 5/27, S Arnold 3/26) and 141 (T Pono 45*, Z Nkwinti 33, T le Roux 5/48)
WPB 243 (Y Ebrahim 108, K Kahaar 66*, M Abdullah 23, T Pono 3/64) and 42/2 (K Kahaar 20*, T Pono 2/21)

Eastern Province B beat Western Province B on the first innings, 8–9 January 1981, Avonwood
WPB 93/6 dec (M Abdullah 30*, F Patel 25, D Jordaan 3/35) and 125/8 (K Kahaar 38*, M Abdullah 22, T le Roux 22, D Jordaan 5/33)
EPB 226 (A Jordaan 51, A Kader 44, A Frans 44, M Majola 22*, T le Roux 4/26, M Abdullah 3/37)

1981/82, CAPE TOWN[306]

A preliminary round was played in four sections before the centralised tournament proper took place in Cape Town. Sectional winners: A – Griqualand West, B – Western Province U-21, C – Western Province B, D – SASSSA. Western Province U-21 would have played at least 2 matches in the preliminary round and then at least three matches (against Griqualand West, Western Province B and SASSSA). Western Province B would have played at least two matches in the preliminary round and then at least three matches (against Griqualand West, Western Province U-21 and SASSSA) to win the Booley Bowl in this season. Only the scorecard below has been found.

Western Province U-21 beat Eastern Province B by 79 runs, [x] November 1981, Avonwood
WP U-21 73 (B Dammert 19; H Bergins 4/6, GA Abrahams 3/35) and 135 (A Carolissen 25, B Dammert 23; H Bergins 3/36)
EPB 85 (V Malgas 41; Y Abed 5/27) and 44 (S Kader 22; F Benjamin 5/8, A Carolissen 3/4)

ZONE C TOURNAMENT, 1982/83, [DATES AND VENUES UNKNOWN][307]

Western Province Beat Boland by an innings and 48 runs
WPB 105 (G Majiet 33, L Wehr 27, M Nicholas 20; Y Abed 2/10) and 103 (D Vermeulen 36; R van Graan 5/38, U Booysen 3/8)
Bol 254 (E Harris 65, H Price 62, Y Abed 38, S Jakoet 32; B Ontong 3/37, J Opperman 3/48)

Western Province B beat Western Province U-21 by 8 wickets
WP U-21 87 (D Roelf 27*; R February 3/9) and 154 (R Poggenpoel 33, D Roelf 31; S Gabriels 4/48)
WPB 192 (H Price 64, R van Graan 31, C Ravens 22; R Poggenpoel 4/32) and 51/2 (S Jakoet 22*)

Western Province U-21 beat Boland by 10 wickets
WP U-21 186 (S Thomas 44, R Tobin 33, W Smith 30*, R Cupido 21; B Damon 3/21) and 5/0
Bol 103 (M Haupt 3/17) and 84 (B Damon 29; F Benjamin 5/22)

Western Province B vs SASSSA (Semi-final)
[details unknown]

Eastern Province B beat Western Province B on the first innings, [x] March 1983 (Final)
EPB 240 ([x] Sandan 34, [x] Frans 29, [x] Peters 28, [x] Tobias 24, [x] Koen 23*, [x] Dolley 22, [x] Nongango 2; S Gabriels 5/62) and 133/5 ([x] Majola 53*, [x] Frans 34; [x] February 3/21)
WPB 169 (C Ravens 47, [x] Jakoet 23, S Gabriels 20; [x] Frans 6/44)

DECENTRALISED SECTION C TOURNAMENT, 1983/84[308]

Western Province B beat Boland by an innings and 41 runs, 30 November – 1 December 1983
Bol 59 (L Saayman 14; R February 2/11, S Gabriels 2/12) and 141 (F Manuel 31, J Africa 28; R February 5/30)
WPB 241/6 dec (R van Graan 85, S Gabriels 71, F Solomons 37, R Salie 21)

Western Province U-21 vs Boland, 17–18 December 1983
[no details available]

Western Province B beat South Western Districts on the first innings, 18–19 December 1983, Oudtshoorn
SWD 117 (G Makok 34, W Matthews 32*, M Theron 7/32) and 164/6 (N Jeffrey 76*, E Erasmus 26, G van Oordt 3/13)
WPB 232 (T Richards 80, R Salie 36, N Kemp 33, R February 29, M Davids 4/47)

Western Province B vs Western Province U-21, 21–22 December 1983, Rocklands, Cape Town
[no details available]

Western Province U-21 beat South Western Districts by 8 wickets, 27–28 December 1983, Rocklands, Cape Town
SWD 129 (J van Wyk 34, W Matthews 31, W Jeffreys 22, R Strydom 3/24) and 179 (W Jeffreys 70, G Coericius 52, B Deal 23, M Haupt 5/60, M Julius 3/18)
WP U-21 278 (M Haupt 68, N Muller 28*, B Deal 3/49) and 31/2

Western Province B beat SASSSA by 7 wickets, 18–19 February 1984, Rocklands, Cape Town (Semi-final)
SASSSA 202 (G de Wet 46, R Isaacs 38, R Hannie 37, I Behardien 30, I Khan 29, G Allie 4/55) and 118 (N White 27, R van Graan 3/32, M Theron 3/40)
WPB 215 (A Katts 76, [x] Richards 52, R van Graan 44, I Khan 5/62, [x] Isaacs 4/27) and 106/3 (MZ Allie 31*, [x] Ebrahim 27, [x] Richards 26*)

Western Province B vs Transvaal B, 10–11 March 1984, Lenasia (Final)
[no details available]

DECENTRALISED SECTION C TOURNAMENT, 1984/85[309]

Western Province U-21 beat Western Province B by 189 runs, 15–16 December 1984, Cape Town
WPU-21 116 (F Davids 28, G Petersen 23, G Miller 4/6) and 213/9 dec (D Kemp 35, R Strydom 35, B Kriel 27, R van Graan 3/44, P Strauss 3/48)
WPB 71 (G van Schalkwyk 26, N Miller 4/22, R Petersen 4/29) and 69 (N Fortune 16, F Davids 5/26, R Petersen 4/27)

Western Province U-21 beat Boland by 1 wicket
Bol 98 (I Tromp 18, P Hurling 17, F Manuel 17, F Davids 5/20, S Christiansen 3/30) and 166 (F Manuel 43, J Africa 39*, M Nicholas 36, F Davids 4/54)
WPU-21 89 (D Kemp 27, F Manuel 5/22, M Nicholas 3/15) and 179/9 (G Petersen 67*, W Hendricks, D Kemp 22, B Kriel 22, S Christiansen 20, M Nicholas 3/34)

Western Province B beat Boland by 9 wickets, 29–30 December 1984, Atlantis
Bol 107 (P Hurling 28, M Nicholas 22*, R Allie 5/11, Y Abed 3/38) and 97 (J Ontong 28, [x] Cravens 5/30)
WPB 196 (R Musson 49, M Haupt 46, E Harris 36, F Manuel 4/62, M Nicholas 3/31) and 9/1

Western Province U-21 beat Border by an innings and 46 runs, 26–27 January 1985 (Semi-final)
WPU-21 250/9 dec (G Petersen 110, S Taliep 43, K Haupt 27, T Pono 5/51)
Bdr 87 (N Selani 26, G Fredericks 22, F Davids 5/18, K Humdulay 3/12) and 117 (M Fredericks 22*, L Fortuin 4/49, D Katts 3/15)

Eastern Province beat Western Province U-21 by [x], 23-24 February 1985 (Final)
[no details available]

DECENTRALISED SECTION C TOURNAMENT, 1985/86[310]

Western Province B beat Boland on the first innings, 23 and 30 November 1985, Worcester
Bol 101 (N Arendse 37*, Y Thomas 5/15, F Benjamin 4/27)
WPB 123 (Y Thomas 34, L Roberts 28*, I Tromp 4/38, M Nicholas 3/36)

Western Province U-21 beat Western Province B by 4 wickets, 14–15 December 1985, Cape Town
WPB 171 (R Musson 96, S Hendricks 30, S Conrad 3/50, L Fortuin 3/59) and 129 (E Harris 28, H Dawson 24, S Green 21, S Conrad 3/35, I Behardien 3/47)
WPU-21 93 (K Haupt 23, I Behardien 22, N White 21, F Benjamin 7/30) and 209/6 (S Conrad 81, I Behardien 34, M Rasmus 28, G Peterson 21*, S Green 2/16)

Western Province U-21 beat Boland by an innings and 21 runs, 11 and 18 January 1986, Worcester
Bol 94 (R Engeldoe 29, N Arendse 25, S Isaacs 5/39, I Behardien 3/13) and 79 (P Hurling 32, R Petersen 4/18, L Arendse 3/9)
WPU-21 194 (N White 65*, I Behardien 55, A Newman 3/38, G Jacobs 3/41)

Western Province U-21 beat Victoria East by an innings and 104 runs, 15–16 February 1986, Alice (Semi-final)
Vic 115 (S Pango 31, R Makapela 26, S Conrad 4/22, G Petersen 3/40) and 108 (P Mgijima 35, L Nontshinga 25, I Behardien 4/30, G Petersen 3/0)
WPU-21 327/9 dec (N White 102, S Ahmed 89, G Petersen 63, N Maxham 3/51, G Somyo 3/52)

Western Province U-21 beat Griqualand West by 10 wickets, 1–2 March 1986, Green Point Track, Cape Town (Final)
GW 50 (Y Snyders 13, S Conrad 5/11, S Isaacs 3/9) and 86 (B Williams 35, S Isaacs 3/43)
WPU-21 104 (S Ahmed 24, S Conrad 22, A Williams 3/22, B Bennett 3/28, B Williams 3/29) and 33/0 (K Haupt 21*)

SECTION II: DECENTRALISED TOURNAMENT, 1986/87[311]

Western Province B beat Eastern Province B by 102 runs, 15–16 November 1986, Adcock, Port Elizabeth
WPB 125 (S Ahmed 51, G Petersen 26, A Jallil 4/14) and 153 (I Behardien 47, G Miller 41, E van Vuuren 3/15, K Miller 3/21)
EPB 116 (E van Vuuren 36*, G Coericius 22, F Benjamin 6/58, G Miller 3/17) and 60 (E van Vuuren 17, F Benjamin 5/33)

Western Province U-21 beat South Western Districts by an innings and 37 runs [x], [x]
SWD 136 (H Abrahams 25, N Jeffrey 24, S Conrad 6/60) and 116 (R Avontuur 23, S Conrad 4/53)
WPU-21 289/7 dec (D Kemp 57, O Martinsen 51, M Rasmus 49, L van Graan 51*, N Jeffrey 4/68)

Western Province B beat Western Province U-21 on the first innings, 13–14 December 1986, Cape Town
WPU-21 173 (R Petersen 36, D Azer 33, D Malander 26, D Kemp 24, S Isaacs 20)
WPB [x]

Western Province U-21 beat Eastern Province B on the first innings, 27–28 December 1986, Cape Town
EPB 155 (R Isaacs 31, P Hufkie 27, I Abrahams 21, S Conrad 3/20, Q Loggenstein 3/23) and 190 (P Hufkie 62, S George 25, C Malgas 25, L Jackson 23, S Conrad 6/82)
WP U-21 238 (D Kemp 100, N van Schalkwyk 34*, S Conrad 30, O Martinsen 25, R Isaacs 3/43) and 90/7 (R Isaacs 5/43)

Western Province B beat South Western Districts by an innings and 260 runs, 31 December 1986 – 1 January 1987, Cape Town
SWD 86 (W Matthews 23*, G Miller 6/22, F Benjamin 4/45) and 66
WPB 412/6 dec (G Miller 204, C Martin 82*, J Kleinveldt 55, F Ebrahim 28, P Witbooi 5/125)

Final shelved because fixtures were not completed.

DECENTRALISED SECTION A TOURNAMENT, 1987/88[312]

Western Province B beat Boland by 128 runs, 28–29 November 1987, Ceres
WPB 121 (R Cupido 30, R Musson 27, J Robinson 5/24, C le Roux 3/31) and 146/8 dec (R Cupido 45, N Miller 32, M Nicholas 4/38, G Jacobs 3/48)
Bol 85 (N Arendse 28) and 54 (S Green 5/23)

South Western Districts beat Western Province U-21 by 5 wickets, 28–29 November 1987, Florida Park, Cape Town
WPU-21 83 (A Viljoen 17, G Everts 3/14, H Ellis 3/18) and 123 (M Solomons 42*, W Matthews 5/26)
SWD 86 (C Stalmeester 20, A Meyer 5/10, C Dyson 3/25) and 122/5 (R Avontuur 24*, R Coeries 21*, A Meyer 2/17)

Western Province B beat Western Province U-21 by 104 runs, 12–13 December 1987, Florida Park, Cape Town
WPB 296 (Y Thomas 104, S Conrad 68, T Seconds 31, L Fortuin 4/72) and 79/2 dec (R Musson 34, B Williams 24*)
WPU-21 154 (A Viljoen 23, M Isaacs 22, R Africa 22, B Minnis 20*, S Conrad 6/44) and 117 (M Isaacs 26, N Luddy 21*, A Viljoen 21, T Seconds 4/17)

Western Province B beat South Western Districts by 23 runs, 16–17 January 1988, Pacaltsdorp
WPB 125 (M Slamang 35, R Musson 23, G Everts 6/28) and 155 (N White 57, S Conrad 26, Y Thomas 20, W Matthews 5/42, R Smith 3/8)
SWD 111 (G Coericius 32, S Conrad 5/24, F Benjamin 3/37) and 146 (A Du Plessis 45, S Conrad 4/32, F Benjamin 6/66)

Boland beat Western Province U-21 on the first innings, 16–17 January 1988
WPU-21 125 (R Africa 26, Q Loggenstein 24, C Dyson 22, A Viljoen 22, M Isaacs 23, G Jacobs 5/17, F Manuel 4/25) and 164/6 (C Dyson 44*, R Africa 30, M Solomons 25, A Viljoen 23, C le Roux 4/58)
Bol 164 (R Engeldoe 36, N Arendse 28, F Manuel 34, L Fortuin 5/43, A Meyer 3/26)

Griqualand West beat Western Province B, 13–14 February 1988, Diamond Park, Kimberley (Semi-final)
GW 209 (G Erlank 40, A Hannie 37, N Moodley 37)
WPB 151 (C Martin 41, T Seconds 26, N Antulay 24, R Hannie 3/28)

DECENTRALISED SECTION A, 1988/89[313]

Western Province B beat Western Province U-21 by 60 runs, 26–27 November 1988, Green Point Track, Cape Town
WPB 147 (N Antulay 26, F Ebrahim 26, C Dyason 6/33) and 196/6 dec (C Martin 42*, F Ebrahim 37, C Ravens 37, R Musson 34)
WPU-21 152/9 dec (A Viljoen 36, M Solomons 21*, A Meyer 21, R Abrahams 5/48) and 131 (R Africa 56, M Solomons 24, A Viljoen 20, F Ebrahim 4/16)

Western Province B beat Boland by 76 runs, 28–29 December 1988, Atlantis
WPB 247 (E Gafieldien 125, T Seconds 36*, C Martin 31, Y Adams 28, E Newman 4/44, C Savahl 4/62) and 173/4 dec (B Williams 56, C Ravens 37*, Y Adams 25, S Zimsi 23, S Jacobs 2/48)
Bol 169 (E Newman 71*, A Alexander 33, S Jacobs 22, R Abrahams 5/38, T Seconds 3/23) and 175 (E Newman 77, S Jacobs 26, R Abrahams 6/47)

Western Province beat South Western Districts by 7 wickets, 21–22 January 1989
SWD 125 (A Spies 24, R Koeries 20, F Benjamin 5/56) and 240/6 dec (A Spies 104*, R Avontuur 55, J Philander 24, C Hendricks 4/58)
WPB 194 (F Ebrahim 68, I Behardien 39, I Spies 4/27) and 174/3 (E Gafieldien 59, F Ebrahim 34, I Behardien 30, N Fortune 26*)

Boland beat Western Province U-21 by 2 wickets, 21–22 January 1989
WPU-21 108 (N van Schalkwyk 48, M Williams 41, E Newman 7/31) and 176/9 dec (A Viljoen 32, N van Schalkwyk 29, N Luddy 25, D Miller 3/40)
Bol 117 (A Alexander 38, N van Schalkwyk 6/23, Z Fredericks 3/24) and 168/8 (E Williams 37, A Alexander 32, A Newman 32, F Vermeulen 21*, N van Schalkwyk 4/29)

Western Province Cricket Board

SECRETARY'S ANNUAL REPORT

REPORT OF
MATCH & REGISTRATION SECRETARY

TREAS. AUDITED FINANCIAL STATEMENT
SEASON 1959/60

FOR SUBMISSION TO
THE ANNUAL GENERAL MEETING OF THE BOARD
TO BE HELD IN CAPE TOWN ON 11TH SEPTEMBER 1960

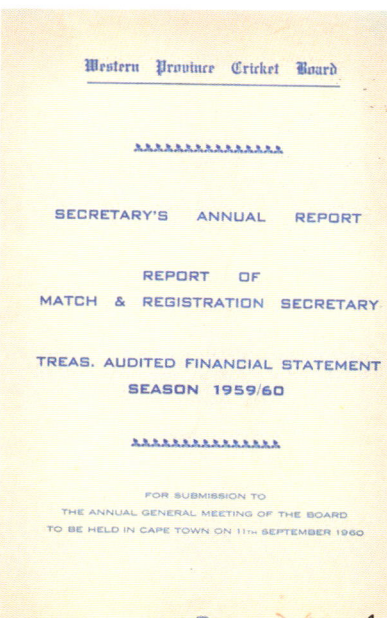

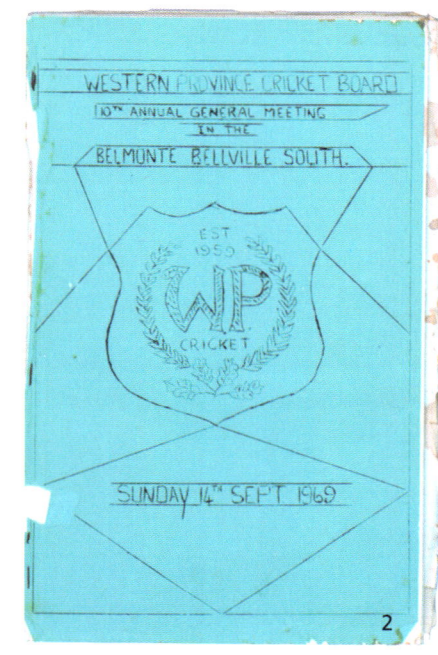

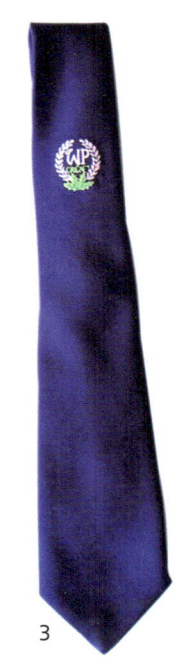

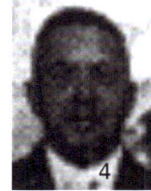

1–4. Formation of the non-racial Western Province Cricket Board (WPCB) under John van Harte in 1959.

5. The first WPCB team to win SACBOC's new inter-provincial competition for the Dadabhay Trophy in 1963/64. Back row: 'Timmy' Lakay, Colin Joshua, Gert Williams, Norman Abrahams, 'Dik' Abed, Des February, Frank Anthony, 'Dickie' Conrad. Front row: Howie Carelse, Neville Lakay, Owen Williams (captain), Sheikh Ganief Booley (manager), 'Coetie' Neethling, 'Lobo' Abed, Alan Maclons.

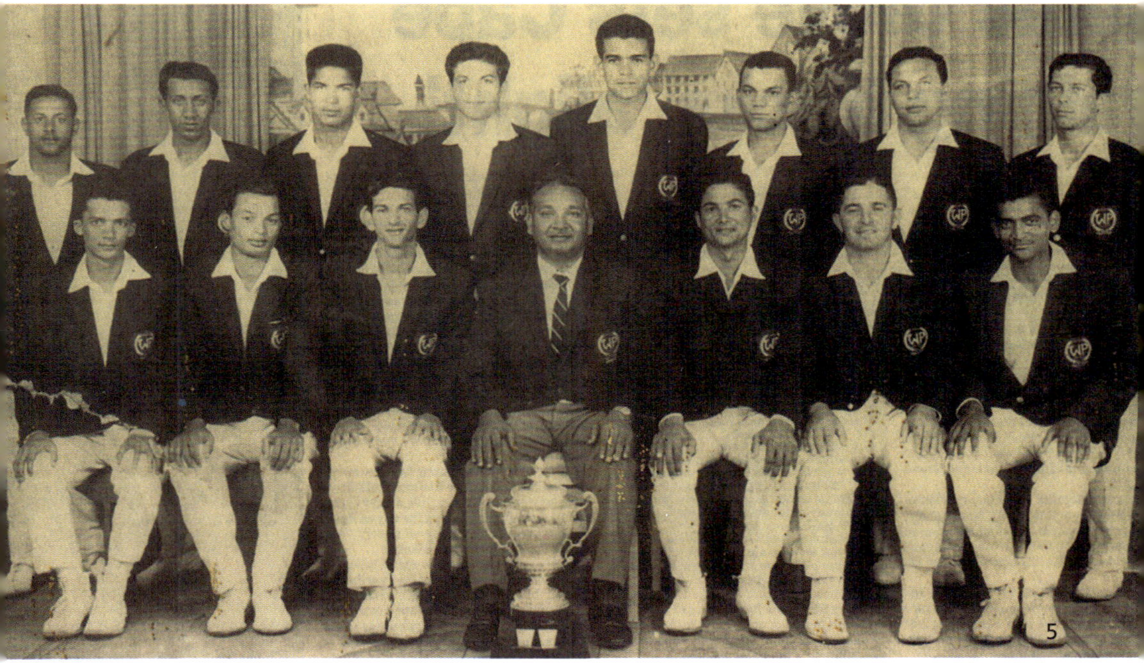

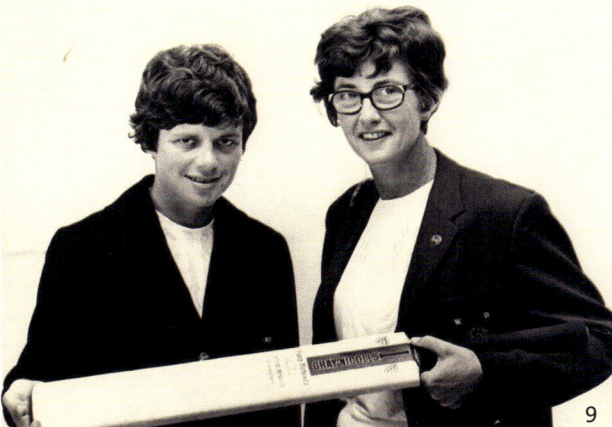

6–9. The first women's test series was held in the 1960/61 season. South Africa (SARWCA) played England at Newlands in the fourth test, with the WPWCU's Sheilagh Nefdt as captain. Maureen Payne similarly captained South Africa against New Zealand in 1972; she is pictured here with her New Zealand counterpart, Patricia McKelvey.

10. The English women playing a against a Western Province composite XI in Paarl in November 1960.

11. Dr Verwoerd, the Prime Minister, was guest of honour at the 75th anniversary celebrations of Newlands in 1964/65, with the South Africa (SACA) and MCC captains, Trevor Goddard and Mike Smith.

12. One of the ubiquitous apartheid signs found at Newlands and other public places until the 1980s.

13–14. Frustrated by apartheid, WPCB's Basil D'Oliveira pursued his cricket career abroad and was picked for England in 1966.

15. The 1969/70 WPCU side, joint winners of the Currie Cup. Back row: Neville Budge, Peter Swart, Chris Stephens, Keith Tattersall, 'Attie' van Niekerk, Mike Bowditch, Gavin Pfuhl, 'Deon' Hugo. Front row: Mike Procter, 'Kelly' Seymour, Ernie McKay (president), Eddie Barlow (captain), Fritz Bing (manager), André Bruyns, Grahame Chevalier.
16. Eddie Barlow, seen here with new WP recruit Mike Procter, took the WPCU team to a new level with an attacking, winning brand of cricket.

17

W.P.
Tvl.
Natal
E.P.
G.W.
SWD

SOUTH AFRICAN CRICKET
BOARD OF CONTROL

FOURTH
INTER-PROVINCIAL
CRICKET TOURNAMENT

SOUVENIR
PROGRAMME

CAPE TOWN
9th to 19th
JAN. 1968

Go for the Man's Brand!!...

CARLING
Black Label
BEER

America's Lusty Lively Beer

18

INTER-PROVINCIAL CRICKET

WESTERN PROVINCE

VS.

TRANSVAAL

AT

WILLIAM HERBERT SPORTSGROUND

ON

FRIDAY 1st, SATURDAY 2nd JAN., 1971

HOURS OF PLAY:
FRIDAY: 9.45 a.m. – 12 Noon; 2 – 4 p.m.; 4.15 – 7 p.m.
SATURDAY: 10.30 a.m. – 1.15 p.m.; 1.45 – 3.45 p.m.; 4 – 6.15 p.m.

ENJOY EXCELLENT SERVICE AND PERSONAL ATTENTION AT...
LANDDROST HOTEL
CATERERS FOR
WEDDINGS, BIRTHDAYS and SPORTS FUNCTIONS
LANSDOWNE ROAD, LANSDOWNE — Phone 77-1115

PRICE 5c

19

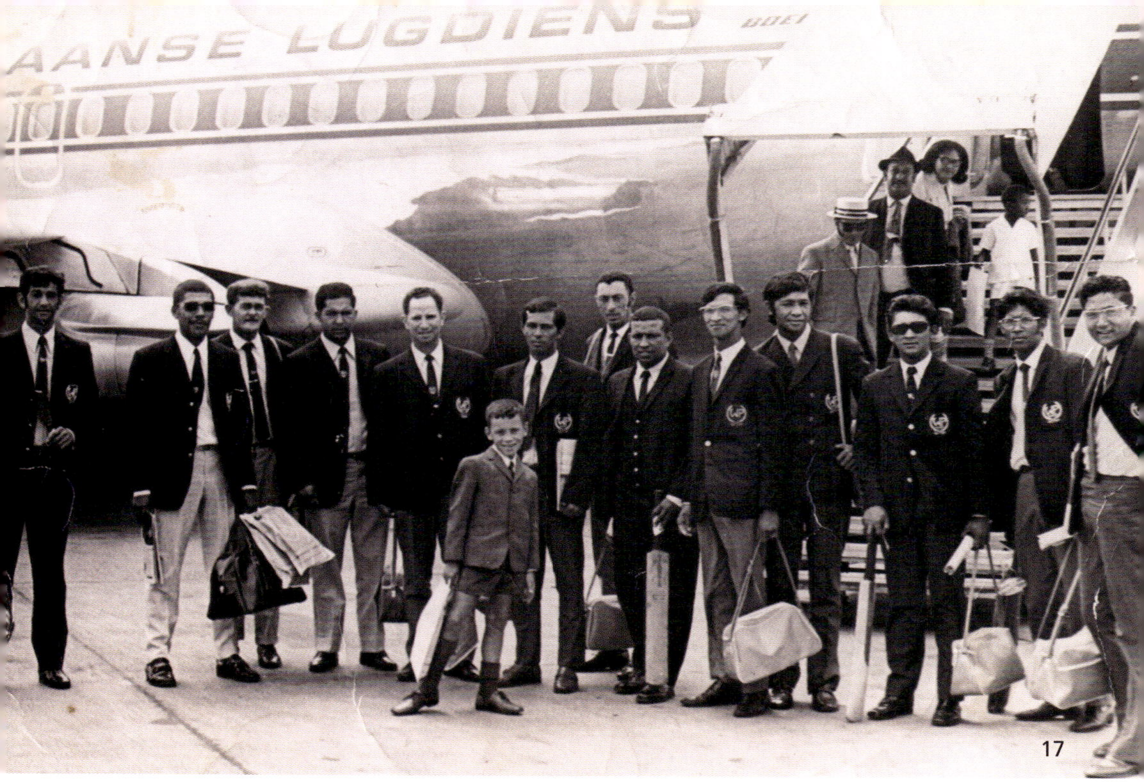

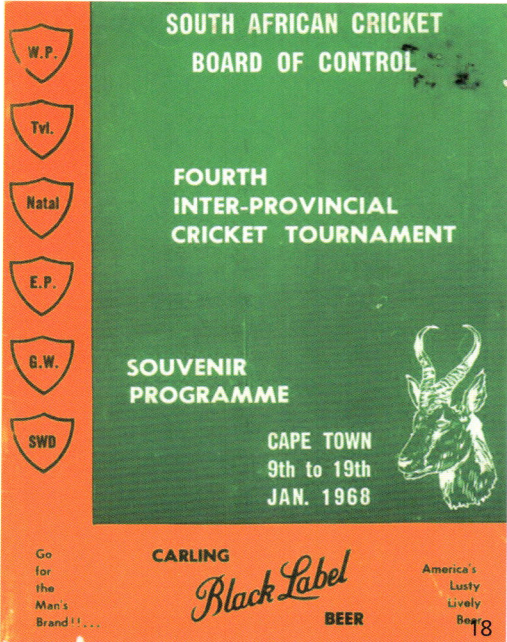

17–19. In 1967/68 WPCB hosted (and won) the centralised inter-provincial tournament, and the 1969/70 team pictured here shared the trophy with Transvaal in Kimberley. From left are Owen Williams, Basil Petersen, 'Lefty' Adams, Gert Williams, Barney Leendertz (manager), 'Dickie' Conrad, Ivan Dagnin, Armien Jabaar, Viccie Moodie, Rushdie Magiet, 'Braima' Isaacs, Kosie Williams, 'Coetie' Neethling.

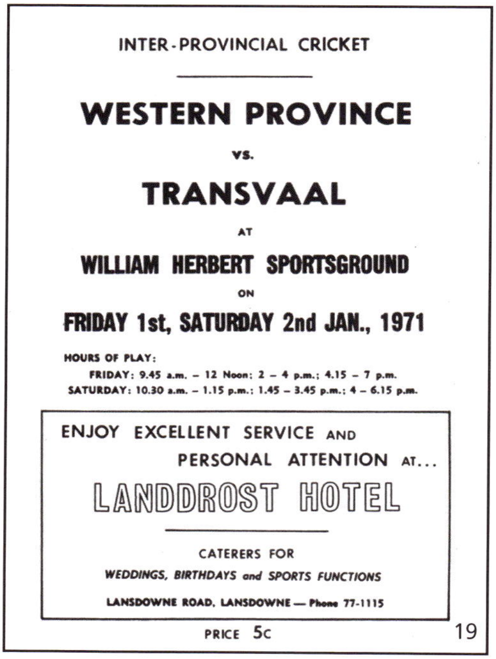

20. The WPACU's Ashton Dunjwa, president of the South African African Cricket Board, and the WPCU's 'Boon' Wallace, president of the South African Cricket Association, worked together in the 1970s under the government's multi-national sports policies to play 'normal cricket'. Wallace's predecessor as both WPCU and SACA president was the former SACA national captain Jack Cheetham.

21. The SAACB team that toured Rhodesia (Zimbabwe) in 1975 was the first black touring side to have left South Africa since SACBOC's tour to East Africa and Rhodesia in 1958. Back row: Bridgeman Mokuena, Peter Bacela, Philip Carrick, Phil Njokweni, Sam Sonwabe, Gus Toyana, Edward Habane. Front row: Edmund Ntikinca, Zimasa Mbatani (vice-captain), Don Wilson (captain), Eric Ellerine (sponsor), Ashton Dunjwa (manager), William Magitshima (WP), Lennox Mlonzi.

22. The WPCB's Hassan Howa, president of the South African Cricket Board of Control and later of the South African Cricket Board, became an icon of the struggle against apartheid in the 1970s and 1980s.

23. Langa Cricket Club took to the field in its first match against Pinelands in the second division of the previously whites-only WPCU in October 1976. Mathemba Ndlumbini, 'father' of the club, and Solomon Makosana, stalwart president in the 1980s, can be seen second from left and second from right in front, respectively.

24. The WPCB stayed out of 'normal cricket', seeing it as insincere window-dressing, and demanded full citizenship rights for all South Africans before sport could be normalised. Pictured here is the 1976 team captained by Brian O'Connell.

25. Newlands, historic home of the WPCU, saw many great performances by WPCU teams in the 1970s and 1980s.
26. The 1979/80 WPCU team for the Datsun Shield final versus Transvaal at the Wanderers Stadium. Back row: Denys Hobson, Allan Lamb, Stephen Bruce, Garth le Roux, John During, André 'Houtie' Nieuwoudt, Hylton Ackerman, Ken Funston (manager). Front row: Peter Kirsten, Lawrence Seeff, Eddie Barlow (captain), Gavin Pfuhl, Peter Swart.

27–28. As the struggle against apartheid intensified in the 1980s, SACOS held its own 'Olympics of the Oppressed' and began selecting national teams. Seven WPCB players were selected for the SACB South African team (called the SACOS XI) in the 1982/83 season. Back row: Morgan Naidoo, Charlie van Schalkwyk (captain), Enver Mall, Eddie Harris (WPCB), Abe Adams (SACOS president), MN Pather, Saait Magiet (WPCB), Neil Fortune (WPCB), Munsoor Abdullah (WPCB), Hassan Howa (SACB president). Front row: Armien Jabaar (WPCB), Ebrahim Isaacs (WPCB), Jeff Frans, Khaya Majola, Mustapha Khan, Vincent Barnes (WPCB).

29–30. The rebel tours initially gave the establishment WPCU sustenance during the 1980s, but as the struggle against apartheid intensified opposition to them became stronger. Seven WPCU players were also selected for the SACU South African team to play against the rebel Sri Lankan XI in 1982/83. Back row: Adrian Kuiper (WPCU), Stephen Jefferies (WPCU), Ray Jennings, Alan Kourie, Jimmy Cook, Denys Hobson (WPCU), Lawrence Seeff (WPCU), Omar Henry (WPCU). Front row: Clive Rice, Peter Kirsten (WPCU captain), E Eriksen (manager), Graeme Pollock, Garth le Roux (WPCU).

The WPCB and WPCU were frequent champions in the 1970s and 1980s, winning over 40 national trophies between them, including B section and other competitions.
31. Celebrations in the dressing room for captain Adrian Kuiper and the 1990/91 WPCU Currie Cup winning team.
32. The WPCB captain, Armien Jabaar (left), and all-rounder Saait Magiet celebrate with the team manager, Paul Saville, at the Athlone Civic Centre after yet another Howa Bowl triumph during the 1980s.

33. WPCB, winners of the Howa Bowl in 1989/90. Back row: Ebrahim Gafieldien, Rashaad Musson, Vincent Barnes, Trevor Seconds, Faizel Ebrahim, Nazeem White, Quinton Logenstein. Middle row: Yunus Thomas, Abe Adams (president), Seraj Gabriels (captain), Rushdie Magiet (manager), Faiek Davids. Front row: Abdulhack 'Jack' Manack, Deon Kemp.

34. WPCU, winners of the Nissan Shield in 1988/89. Back row: Peter Swart (coaching staff), Gary Kirsten, Dave Rundle, Jon Hardy, John Commins, Craig Matthews, Terence Lazard, Willem van der Merwe, Daryll Cullinan, Lance Bleekers. Front row: Eric Simons, Lawrence Seeff, Richard Morris (manager), Adrian Kuiper (captain), Fritz Bing (president), Peter Kirsten, Richie Ryall.

MDM/NSC

PROTEST RALLY

STOP THE REBEL CRICKET TOUR

REV ARNOLD STOFILE -	NSC
TERROR LEKOTA -	UDF
TREVOR MANUEL -	UDF
JOHN ERNTZEN -	COSATU
KRISH MACKERDHUJ -	SA Cricket Board
FAIK DAVIDS -	WP Cricket Board
ANDRE ODENDAAL -	WP Cricket Board

CITY HALL
TUE 16 JAN 7.30p.m.

35

BAN RACIST TOURS - ISOLATE APARTHEID SPORT!

Mike Gatting and his mercenaries must go home now! We demand an immediate end to the racist tour of Ali Bacher and the South African Cricket Union (SACU). They must bear full responsibility for the brutal attacks on our people by the SAP.

15 Million rands could be used for:

- Housing
- Education
- Sports facilities for all
- A living wage

PROTEST
At the Wanderers Cricket ground:
Thursday 9:30 am
Friday 9:30 am
Saturday 10:00 am (march)
Join in the peaceful, legal protest

STOP THE TOUR!!!
issued by: anti-tour committee

36

35–39. *Amid growing civil unrest in the country, protests against SACU's rebel tours to South Africa shook cricket to the core.*

Mayor to snub rebel cricketers?

37

SACU committed to rebel tour

38

UDF UNITES — APARTHEID DIVIDES

UDF

UNITED DEMOCRATIC FRONT

39

TOUR PROTEST ... Protesters hold up placards outside the De Beers Stadium on Saturday demanding the end of the rebel England cricket tour.

Tour demo ends in township riot

40. In 1990 the WPCU celebrated its centenary as mass demonstrations against the rebel tours took place.
41. WPCU presidents Fritz Bing (back left) and 'Boon' Wallace (centre back) with Executive Committee members and staff.

DECENTRALISED SECTION A, 1989/90[314]

Match drawn between Western Province B and Boland, [x] November 1989, Cape Town
[no details available]

Match drawn between Western Province U-21 and South Western Districts, [x] November 1989, Oudtshoorn
[no details available]

Match drawn between Western Province U-21 and Boland, [x] December 1989, Worcester
[no details available]

Western Province B beat South Western Districts by 9 wickets, [x] December 1989, Cape Town
[no details available]

Western Province B beat Western Province U-21 by 9 wickets, [x] January 1990, Cape Town
[no details available]

DECENTRALISED SECTION A TOURNAMENT, 1990/91[315]

Western Province U-21 beat Boland by 105 runs, [x] November 1990
[no details available]

Western Province B beat South Western Districts by an innings and 6 runs, [x] November 1990, Oudtshoorn
[no details available]

Western Province U-21 beat Western Province B by 27 runs, [x] December 1990, Cape Town
WPU-21 203 ([x] Haupt 57, [x] Daniels 34, [x] Karriem 34; [x] Williams 4/60, [x] Karriem 3/86) and 117 (Z Muller 30, [x] Haupt 21; S Christiansen 4/32)
WPB 160 (R Cupido 33, A Viljoen 25, S Christiansen 25, [x] Dammert 22; [x] Appollis 3/16, [x] Abrahams 3/34, Z Muller 3/44) and 133 (R Cupido 35, N van Schalkwyk 23; [x] Appollis 3/16)

Western Province U-21 beat South Western Districts by 88 runs, [x] January 1991, Cape Town
[no details available]

Boland beat Western Province B by 131 runs, [x] January 1991, Cape Town
[no details available]

Eastern Province B beat Western Province U-21 by [x], [date and venue unknown] (Semi-final)
[no details available]

Western Province U-21 beat Northern Natal by 10 wickets, 9–10 March 1991 (Final)
NNtl 88 (M Pillay 22, D McHelm 4/19, Z Muller 4/23) and 184 (M Badat 67, R Omar 30*; D McHelm and Z Miller took 3 wickets each)
WPU-21 187 (C Haupt 43, Z Muller 22, B October 20; Shane Moodley 7/64) and 86/0 (C Haupt 55*, B October 28*)

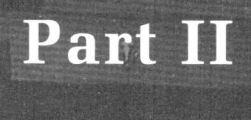

Part II

The era of unity and democracy, 1991–2011

CHAPTER 10

Western Province Cricket Association, 1991–2011

Affiliated to the United Cricket Board of South Africa
and (after name change on 3 August 2006) Cricket South Africa

Cape Town has a legacy of cricket going back more than 200 years, but it was only on 25 June 1991 that all the cricketers in the province united for the first time to form the Western Province Cricket Association (WPCA), the first single controlling body for cricket in the region.[316] Unity was made possible by the dramatic political changes in the early 1990s. On 11 February 1990 Nelson Mandela walked through the prison doors to freedom and negotiations for a new political dispensation commenced. On 27 April 1994 the first democratic elections were held. Two weeks later Mandela became President. In a relatively short time, a remarkable turnabout had occurred in the political history of South Africa.

Developments in cricket mirrored the broader changes taking place. By the end of the 1980s cricketers were deeply polarised. But, coinciding with the political turnabout, the rebel tours which were propping up apartheid sport were brought to an end and the South African Cricket union (SACU) sought to negotiate with the South African Cricket Board (SACB) through the offices of the newly unbanned ANC.

On 4 August 1990 the non-racial SACB agreed to enter into discussions with the SACU. The first formal meeting between the two organisations took place on 8 September in Durban. At a follow-up meeting in Port Elizabeth on 16 December 1990, SACU and SACB announced their intention to form 'one non-racial democratic controlling body under a single constitution' and to 'contribute through cricket to a just society in South Africa'.[317] The two bodies set up a national steering committee to drive the unification process. This committee instructed the provinces to prepare the foundations for unity by May 1991 so that formal national unity and a new organisation could be established by mid-June. While there were reservations within the Western Province Cricket Board about the intentions of white cricketers and the speed of the unity process being driven from above, the Board decided on 20 February 1991 to go ahead with unity talks with the rival Western Province Cricket Union. The two executive committees met for the first time at Newlands on 4 March 1991 and set up committees to negotiate the terms of unity. These dealt with constitutional matters, schools and junior cricket, competitions and demarcation, coaching, facilities, selection and umpires. The new WPCA was formed on 25 June 1991. The launch of the United Cricket Board of South Africa followed a few days afterwards on 29 June 1991 at a ceremony in Johannesburg.[318]

Given the strong and long-standing tradition of non-racial cricket in Cape Town, the ex-Board administrators were from the start insistent on entering unity as equals, rather than being towed behind in the slipstream as junior partners by the old establishment Union. From the outset, non-racial principles were asserted and implemented as the fundamental philosophy of the new organisation, thanks to the leadership of administrators like Percy Sonn and Sadick Emeran. This enabled a relatively smooth transition to happen, unlike in Gauteng, for example, where deep racial divisions and unhappiness with control by the old establishment still sour unity 20 years later.

For the first two years of unity, the old Union and old Board were guaranteed equal representation on the new executive committee. The position of president was also rotated between two lawyers, Clem Druker and Percy Sonn, who gave the Association a good start with their consensus-building leadership. Open elections were held from 1993/94, with a respectful balance being maintained by the new cricket partners.

Newlands was declared the headquarters of the new WPCA. The first staff members were those inherited from the Union, as the Board had had no permanent employees. Kevin Commins was the first chief executive and Rushdi Magiet was the first new appointment from the old Board.[319] The new, integrated club leagues started in October 1991. Cricketers who had for long been excluded had their first taste of playing at grounds such as Newlands, Claremont/Constantia, the Vineyard Oval, University of Cape Town, Plumstead and Green Point CC.

Montrose CC, the strongest team in the Board during the 1980s, were joint winners of the one-day club competition in the first season, but the old Union clubs dominated the leagues throughout the 1990s. This can be seen by the fact that up to 2011 Claremont CC (which at one stage briefly changed name to Constantia) and the University of Cape Town each won the league four times and the one-day competition five times. This trend has now been reversed. In the eleven seasons from 2000/01 to 2010/11, clubs with ex-Board biases won the league, limited-overs and 'Ama20/20' competitions 16 times out of 27. First, Victoria CC, led by veteran administrator Patrick Wyngaard, and then the University of the Western Cape (UWC) emerged as strong nurseries for provincial cricket. UWC announced its arrival by winning the double in 2007/08. Reaping the rewards of the innovative 'Sport Skills for Life Skills' bursary and mentoring programme started by Advocate Nic Kock and Dr Johann Graaff, 'Bush' (as it was known in the apartheid years) produced 15 provincial players and 63 cricket-playing graduates in a decade and also started beating both UCT and Stellenbosch – an achievement that would have been thought inconceivable at the time of unity. Unfortunately, UCT proceeded on a downward curve and were relegated from the first league in 2010/11 for the first time in the club's history. Cricket South Africa statistics in 2011 showed that around 70 per cent of club cricketers and cricket-playing schools in the WPCA were from previously disenfranchised communities and that Western Province and neighbouring Boland are the only provinces in the country where there is not a mismatch between the overall provincial demographics and those in cricket.[320]

At the first-class and provincial levels, the same pattern was initially evident. Players, coaches and selectors from the old Union initially dominated and ex-Board and township players had difficulty entering the professional team. In the six seasons up to 1996/97, only seven ex-Board players were included in the senior team and only two of them, Faiek

Davids and Dean MacHelm, played more than two games. Compensation came in the form of new talents – Herschelle Gibbs and Paul Adams – emerging from the new integrated schools set-up. Morgan Mfobo, the only member of the 1992 South African Schools team not called up straightaway into senior squads, recalls the frustration of spending three years with the B team as the perpetual twelfth man without ever getting a game. The Transformation Charter adopted by the United Cricket Board of South Africa in 1998 introduced targets at all levels and helped speed up integration at the elite level. Players like Ashwell Prince, Mulligan George, Hassan Pangarker, Rashaad Magiet, Thami Tsolekile and Roger Telemachus started appearing more regularly from 1997/98 onwards as the glass ceilings were broken. Today the majority of Western Province and Cape Cobras players are from previously excluded communities.

Western Province provided the first three black players to play for South Africa in official international cricket. They were Omar Henry (who debuted at the 1991/92 World Cup while playing for Orange Free State), the spin freak with the 'X' factor Paul Adams, who came from nowhere in 1995/96 to take 134 test wickets in 45 tests with his unorthodox 'frog-in-a-blender' action, and the batting and fielding genius Herschelle Gibbs, who played his first match for the Proteas in 1996/97.

Between unity in 1991/92 and the 2003/04 season, when the franchise system was introduced (and Western Province was absorbed into the Cape Cobras regional team for professional domestic cricket), the province contributed 23 players to the South African test and limited-overs teams. They included such greats of the international game as Gary Kirsten, Jacques Kallis, Gibbs and Graeme Smith. Master batsman Peter Kirsten and powerful all-rounder Adrian Kuiper were unfortunately past their peak when international cricket proper arrived, but they and Western Province stars like Brian McMillan, Craig Matthews, Meyrick Pringle, Brett Schultz and Alan Dawson all donned the new Proteas shirts. Desmond Haynes, the famous West Indian opening batsman, was another pillar of experience in the team in the 1990s. Eric Simons, Western Province's 'Mr Cricket' in that decade, was a dependable all-rounder and captain, but he played for South Africa only in one-day internationals. Today Jacques Kallis can lay claim to being perhaps the greatest all-rounder in the history of cricket. His record (as of July 2011) of 11,947 test runs, including 40 centuries, and 270 test wickets, and an equally impressive 11,227 runs and 264 wickets in limited-overs cricket, puts him in a league of his own.

In the thirteen seasons between 1991/92 and 2003/04, Western Province won six trophies. After going trophyless for the first four seasons after unity, the team secured the Castle Cup in 1995/96 under CEO Arthur Turner and coach Duncan Fletcher. Fletcher, a former Zimbabwean international, turned Western Province into a strong team with a professional ethos and top-class players. However, the six trophies in all formats in the 1990s and early 2000s – four first-class and two limited-overs – meant the Association after unity was not as successful in terms of winning trophies as either the old Board or Union had been in the 1970s and 1980s (see chapter 13).

The WPCA had seven presidents between 1991 and 2011. They were Clem Druker, Percy Sonn (who rose up the ladder to become president of Cricket South Africa and the International Cricket Council), Arnold Bloch, Solomon Makosana, Norman Arendse (also CSA president), Mohamed Ebrahim and Beresford Williams, who took over the reins in

July 2011. There were three CEOs – Kevin Commins, Arthur Turner and André Odendaal. Until the advent of the franchise system in 2004/05, Hylton Ackerman, Duncan Fletcher, Vincent Barnes, Eric Simons and Peter Kirsten were the coaches of the Western Province professional side. Following in the footsteps of fellow Capetonian Bob Woolmer, who coached South Africa and later Pakistan, Fletcher (England and India), Simons (South Africa) and Gary Kirsten (India and South Africa) also went on to become national coaches, while Vincent Barnes became a long-serving assistant coach to the Proteas.

One of the key tasks of the WPCA after cricket unity was to redevelop and buy Newlands, one of the oldest test grounds in the world, for a new era of international cricket. With the collapse of apartheid and the change to democracy in the 1990s, South Africa truly became part of world cricket for the first time. A whole new world opened up for local fans as India (with its little magician, Tendulkar), Pakistan, West Indies, Sri Lanka and other countries made their debuts at Newlands. The Newlands faithful were introduced, too, to the new format of one-day international cricket, which South Africa had until then not experienced because of two decades of isolation caused by apartheid in sport. To add icing to the cake, in the 1990s South Africa started on a winning streak at Newlands in both formats of international cricket, completely turning around the dismal set of results of the preceding century when only three tests out of 24 were won.

In the 2000s, Twenty20 cricket arrived as well and the stadium (renamed Sahara Park Newlands for commercial reasons in 2004) hosted three major international tournaments, the 2003 ICC World Cup, the 2007 ICC World T20 championship and the 2009 Indian Premier League. This included the opening ceremonies for the World Cup and the IPL.[321]

South Africa had a high win rate at Sahara Park Newlands in the two decades after unity. The statistics for tests and ODIs from 1991 to mid-2011 are as follows:[322]

Opponents 1991-2011	Tests				One-Day Internationals[323]			
	P	W	L	D	P	W	L	NR
Australia	4	1	3	–	6	4	2	–
England	4	3	–	1	4	4	–	–
India	4	2	–	2	3	2	1	–
Kenya	–	–	–	–	1	1	–	–
New Zealand	2	1	–	1	4	4	–	–
Pakistan	2	2	–	–	4	4	–	–
Sri Lanka	2	2	–	–	1	1	–	–
West Indies	3	2	–	1	5	4	1	–
Zimbabwe	1	1	–	–	1	1	–	–
Total	22	14	3	5	29	25	4	–

On 25 June 2011, the WPCA celebrated its twentieth birthday. It was a very different creature from that which took its first small steps at unity. Radical changes for the better had taken place after 1991. Firstly, the number of cricketers in the WPCA increased from around 11,000 at unity to roughly 26,000 (including soft-ball mini-cricket) by 2011. The feeders were the clubs and 522 schools (192 of them high schools). Secondly, the WPCA hosted more international cricket games at Newlands in two decades than in the century before. Moreover, the WPCA invested more than R120 million in building new stands

and buying the stadium, putting cricket's headquarters in the hands of the council of 66 clubs, rather than a single, exclusive club as in the past. When the old Union and Board first got together their cash reserves stood at R720,000 and R15,000 respectively.[324] Starting with R1.8 million in 1991/92, WPCA income exceeded R10 million for the first time in 2000 and grew to R19.967 million in 2004 and R49.789 million in 2010/11.[325] This growth led to a far more professional administrative set-up than before and the official ethos of Western Province cricket, actively promoting the values of equality, access and redress enshrined in the new Constitution of South Africa, is a far cry from the apartheid past. Cricket in the Western Province and South Africa has indeed come a long way since the first provincial Board was established in 1890.

10.1 Western Province Cricket Association Statistics, 1991/92–2003/04

10.1.1 Western Province Cricket Association National Players (UCBSA), 1991/92–2003/04[326]

An asterisk indicates Western Province players who represented South Africa while playing for other provinces.

NAME	TEST			ODI			T20		
	M	From	To	M	From	To	M	From	To
Ackerman, HD	4	1997/8	1997/8	–	–	–	–	–	–
Adams, PR	45	1995/6	2003/4	24	1995/6	2003	–	–	–
Commins, JB*	3	1994/5	1994/5	–	–	–	–	–	–
Cullinan, DJ*	70	1992/3	2000/1	138	1992/3	2000/01	–	–	–
Dawson, AC	2	2002/3	2002/3	19	1998/9	2004	–	–	–
Gibbs, HH	90	1996/7	2007/8	248	1996/7	2009/10	23	2005/6	2010
Harris, PL*	37	2006/7	2010/11	3	2007/8	2007/8	–	–	–
Henderson, CW	7	2001/2	2002/3	4	2001/2	2001/2	–	–	–
Henry, O*	3	1992/3	1992/3	3	1991/2	1991/2[327]	–	–	–
Kallis, JH	144	1995/6	2010/11	309	1995/6	2010/11	16	2005/6	2010
Kirsten, G	101	1993/4	2003/4	185	1993/4	2002/3	–	–	–
Kirsten, PN*	12	1991/2	1994	40	1991/2	1994	–	–	–
Koen, LJ*	–	–	–	5	1996/7	1999/00[328]	–	–	–
Kuiper, AP	1	1991/2	1991/2	25	1991/2	1995/6	–	–	–
Matthews, CR	18	1992/3	1995/6	56	1991/2	1996/7	–	–	–
McMillan, BM	38	1992/3	1998	78	1991/2	1997/8	–	–	–
Prince, AG	62	2001/2	2010/11	49	2002/3	2006/7	1	2005/6	2005/6
Pringle, MW	4	1991/2	1995/6	17	1991/2	1994/5	–	–	–
Rundle, DB	–	–	–	2	1993/4	1993/4	–	–	–
Schultz, BN	9	1992/3	1997/8	1	1992/3	1992/3	–	–	–
Simons, EO	–	–	–	23	1993/4	1994/5	–	–	–
Smith, GC	90	2001/2	2010/1	171	2001/2	2010/11	31	2005/6	2010/1
Telemachus, R	–	–	–	37	1997/8	2006/7	3	2005/6	2006/7
Tsolekile, TL	3	2004/5	2004/5	–	–	–	–	–	–
Wessels, KC*	16	1991/2	1994	55	1991/2	1994/5[329]	–	–	–
Willoughby, CM	2	2002/3	2003	3	1999/0	2002/3	–	–	–

10.1.2 Western Province Cricket Association Players, 1991/92–2003/04[330]

NAME	FIRST–CLASS			LIMITED OVERS		
	M	From	To	M	From	To
Abderouf, F	1	1995/96	1995/96	–	–	–
Ackerman, HD	74	1993/94	2002/03	92	1993/94	2002/03
Ackermann, S	1	1999/00	1999/00	2	1999/00	1999/00
Adams, PR	34	1995/96	2003/04	21	1995/96	2001/02
Baguley, BC	1	1991/92	1991/92	–	–	–
Barnes, VA	1	1991/92	1991/92	5	1991/92	1991/92
Bassage, DJ	4	2003/04	2003/04	–	–	–
Benjamin, F	2	1993/94	1993/94	–	–	–
Best, CA	7	1993/94	1993/94	11	1993/94	1993/94
Bleekers, LF	6	1991/92	1993/94	10	1992/93	1993/94
Cilliers, A	3	1995/96	1995/96	1	1995/96	1995/96
Commins, JB	31	1991/92	1999/00	43	1991/92	1999/00
Davids, F	17	1991/92	1997/98	26	1991/92	1997/98
Dawson, AC	73	1992/93	2003/04	99	1993/94	2003/04
De Nobrega, JJ	4	1997/98	1997/98	–	–	–
De Stadler, M	–	–	–	9	1999/2000	2003/04
De Villiers, MC	1	1996/97	1996/97	3	1996/97	1996/97
Donachie, HH	–	–	–	4	1994/95	1994/95
Duminy, J–P	10	2001/02	2003/04	10	2002/03	2003/04
English, CV	3	1993/94	1994/95	4	1993/94	1994/95
Ferreira, LD	38	1997/98	2003/04	45	1997/98	2003/04
Friend, Q	8	2002/03	2003/04	10	2001/02	2003/04
George, MF	6	1997/98	1998/99	4	1997/98	1999/00
Gibbs, HH	41	1991/92	2003/04	77	1991/92	2003/04
Harris, PL	2	1999/2000	2001/02	–	–	–
Haynes, DL	21	1994/95	1996/97	26	1994/95	1996/97
Henderson, CW	38	1998/99	2003/04	50	1998/99	2003/04
Holdstock, AT	2	1992/93	1992/93	–	–	–
Jackson, KC	9	1991/92	1993/94	21	1991/92	1992/93
Jefferies, ST	1	1991/92	1991/92	3	1991/92	1991/92
Joffe, R	5	1998/99	1999/00	–	–	–
Johnson, NC	26	1999/2000	2003/04	33	1999/2000	2003/04
Jordaan, D	10	1993/94	1994/95	12	1993/94	1994/95
Kallis, JH	31	1994/95	2003/04	47	1994/95	2003/04
Kirsten, G	51	1991/92	2003/04	67	1991/92	2003/04
Kirsten, P	37	1995/96	1999/00	49	1995/96	1998/99
Kleinveldt, RK	2	2002/03	2003/04	6	2002/03	2003/04
Koch, DM	–	–	–	1	1997/98	1997/98
Koenig, SG	29	1993/94	1996/97	14	1994/95	1996/97
Koster, RA	2	1992/93	1993/94	6	1992/93	1993/94
Kuiper, AP	20	1991/92	1993/94	31	1991/92	1994/95
Lamb, AJ	5	1992/93	1992/93	12	1992/93	1992/93
Lazard, TN	15	1991/92	1992/93	16	1991/92	1992/93

NAME	FIRST-CLASS			LIMITED OVERS		
	M	From	To	M	From	To
MacHelm, DQ	12	1992/93	1996/97	1	1992/93	1992/93
Magiet, R	11	1999/00	2002/03	–	–	–
Maron, R	5	1996/97	1997/98	–	–	–
Martyn, A	22	1992/93	1996/97	28	1993/94	1996/97
Matthews, CR	45	1991/92	1999/00	76	1991/92	1999/00
McClement, AJ	2	1991/92	1991/92	–	–	–
McLean, JJ	5	2001/02	2003/04	2	2002/03	2002/03
McMillan, BM	35	1991/92	1999/00	53	1991/92	1999/00
Meyer, MA	2	1991/92	1993/94	3	1993/94	1994/95
Mitchell, TJ	5	1991/92	1994/95	7	1994/95	1995/96
Moleon, EO	–	–	–	1	1997/98	1997/98
Munnik, R	17	1998/99	2002/03	25	1998/99	2003/04
Murphy, BA	5	1997/98	1997/98	–	–	–
Oosthuizen, RC	1	1999/00	1999/00	–	–	–
Pangarker, H	7	1997/98	1999/00	5	1997/98	1997/98
Payne, DG	10	1991/92	1997/98	10	1991/92	1998/99
Philander, VD	1	2003/04	2003/04	–	–	–
Plantema, AP	1	1992/93	1992/93	4	1992/93	1992/93
Player, BT	8	1997/98	1998/99	15	1997/98	1998/99
Prince, AG	38	1997/98	2003/04	53	1998/99	2003/04
Pringle, MW	39	1991/92	1996/97	61	1991/92	1996/97
Puttick, AG	26	1999/2000	2003/04	36	1999/00	2003/04
Rundle, DB	35	1991/92	1996/97	68	1991/92	1997/98
Ryall, RJ	34	1991/92	1994/95	45	1991/92	1994/95
Schultz, BN	10	1996/97	1997/98	11	1996/97	1997/98
Seeff, L	2	1991/92	1991/92	–	–	–
Simons, EO	53	1991/92	1998/99	86	1991/92	1998/99
Smith, GC	17	1999/2000	2003/04	31	1999/2000	2003/04
Solomon, IR	–	–	–	1	1994/95	1994/95
Solomons, MT	2	1996/97	1998/99	2	1998/99	1998/99
Stelling, WF	1	1991/92	1991/92	2	1991/92	1991/92
Telemachus, R	24	1999/00	2003/04	37	1999/00	2003/04
Touzel, FB	6	1992/93	1993/94	6	1992/93	1993/94
Trott, IJL	8	2001/02	2001/02	10	2001/02	2001/02
Tsolekile, TL	33	1999/00	2003/04	39	1998/99	2003/04
Van Reenen, A	1	1995/96	1995/96	–	–	–
Voss, MF	7	1991/92	1992/93	4	1991/92	1991/92
Willoughby, CM	30	1999/2000	2003/04	36	1999/2000	2003/04

10.1.3 Western Province Cricket Association League and One–Day Club Competition Winners, 1991/92–2010/11[331]

YEAR	LEAGUE	ONE–DAY	'AMA20/20'
1991/92	Claremont	Montrose and Claremont	–
1992/93	Claremont	UCT	–
1993/94	Bellville	Constantia (Claremont)	–
1994/95	Bellville	UCT	–
1995/96	Constantia (Claremont)	Constantia (Claremont)	–
1996/97	Constantia (Claremont)	Constantia (Claremont) and WPCC	–
1997/98	Cape–Tech Green Point	Bellville	–
1998/99	UCT & Pinelands	UCT	–
1999/2000	UCT	Techs	–
2000/01	Victoria	Victoria	–
2001/02	UCT	UCT	–
2002/03	UCT	Victoria	–
2003/04	Almar	Almar	–
2004/05	Primrose	UCT	–
2005/06	Victoria	Claremont	–
2006/07	WPCC	Primrose	UWC[332]
2007/08	UWC	UWC	UWC
2008/09	United	Glamorgan	Durbanville
2009/10	Police	Police	United
2010/11	WPCC	UWC	Pinelands

10.1.4 Western Province Cricket Association Trophy Winners (UCBSA), 1991/92–2003/04[333]

CASTLE CUP / SUPERSPORT SERIES (FIRST-CLASS)

Castle Cup

Season	Winners
1991/92	Eastern Province
1992/93	Orange Free State
1993/94	Orange Free State
1994/95	Natal
1995/96	*Western Province*

SuperSport Series

Season	Winners
1996/97	Natal
1997/98	Free State
1998/99	*Western Province*
1999/2000	Gauteng
2000/01	*Western Province*
2001/02	KwaZulu-Natal
2002/03	Easterns
2003/04	*Western Province*

Nissan Shield/Total Power Series (Limited Overs)

NISSAN SHIELD

Season   *Winners*
1991/92   Orange Free State

TOTAL POWER SERIES

Season   *Winners*
1992/93   Orange Free State

Matches in above competitions were contested over 55 overs per side.

Benson & Hedges Series (Limited Overs)

Season   *Winners*
1991/92   Eastern Province
1992/93   Transvaal
1993/94   Orange Free State
1994/95   Orange Free State
1995/96   Free State

Matches were contested over 45 overs per side except for 1993/94 when matches were contested over 50 overs per side.

Standard Bank League (Limited Overs)

Season   *Winners*
1996/97   Northern Transvaal
1997/98   *Western Province*
1998/99   Northerns

From 1999/2000, the Standard Bank competition was played as a single tournament.

Standard Bank Cup / MTN Domestic Championship (Limited Overs)

Season   *Winners*
1996/97   Natal
1997/98   Gauteng
1998/99   Griqualand West
1999/2000   Boland
2000/01   KwaZulu-Natal
2001/02   KwaZulu-Natal
2002/03   *Western Province*
2003/04   Gauteng

10.1.5 Western Province Cricket Association First-Class Scores, 1991/92–2003/04[334]

Western Province beat Northern Transvaal by 6 wickets, 12–14 September 1991, Verwoerdburg
N Tvl 269/2 dec (M Yachad 102, VF du Preez 111*) and 272/6 dec (LP Vorster 83, MJR Rindel 59, AM Ferreira 63*)
WP 261/6 dec (TN Lazard 150*, L Seeff 54) and 284/4 (JB Commins 85, G Kirsten 49, AP Kuiper 66, F Davids 35)

Northern Transvaal beat Western Province by 21 runs, 28 November – 1 December 1991, Verwoerdburg
N Tvl 220 (MD Haysman 93, MJR Rindel 40; MW Pringle 3/51) and 210 (M Yachad 66, LP Vorster 75; MW Pringle 6/37)
WP 220 (TN Lazard 108*; T Bosch 6/54) and 189 (TN Lazard 56, G Kirsten 39; EA Moseley 4/43, T Bosch 5/50)

Western Province beat Natal by 3 wickets, 26–29 December 1991, Durban
Ntl 272 (AC Hudson 45, MB Logan 44, JN Rhodes 64, ELR Stewart 57; MW Pringle 4/60, BM McMillan 5/60) and 206 (AC Hudson 52, PWE Rawson 32, TJ Packer 32; MW Pringle 3/59)
WP 320 (TN Lazard 130, KC Jackson 36, AP Kuiper 32; RJ McCurdy 3/67, PWE Rawson 3/52) and 162/7 (MF Voss 30, G Kirsten 56)

Western Province beat Transvaal by 4 wickets, 1–4 January 1992, Cape Town
Tvl 223 (DJ Cullinan 73, CEB Rice 35; MW Pringle 5/57) and 266/8 dec (NE Wright 49, RF Pienaar 46, DJ Cullinan 32, CEB Rice 80*; MW Pringle 3/69, AJ McClement 5/86)
WP 221 (BM McMillan 40, DB Rundle 35; DR Laing 3/34) and 272/6 (KC Jackson 61, AP Kuiper 89, BM McMillan 32; CE Eksteen 4/87)

Western Province beat Border by 7 wickets, 24–26 January 1992, Cape Town
WP 335 (G Kirsten 31, AP Kuiper 122, BM McMillan 88, MW Pringle 30; WK Watson 4/83, SJ Base 4/80) and 32/3 (SJ Base 3/11)
Bdr 155 (SJ Palframan 36, IL Howell 36, WK Watson 37*; MW Pringle 6/42) and 209 (KS McEwan 54; BM McMillan 3/35, CR Matthews 3/26)

Match drawn between Western Province and Eastern Province, 7–10 February 1992, Port Elizabeth
WP 263 (G Kirsten 91, EO Simons 50; BN Schultz 4/66, EAE Baptiste 5/30) and 235 (HH Gibbs 41, G Kirsten 52, EO Simons 51; PA Rayment 5/41)
EP 328 (LJ Koen 72, GC Victor 83, EAE Baptiste 32; DG Payne 3/86, EO Simons 5/93) and 151/8 (PG Amm 36)

Match drawn between Orange Free State and Western Province, 21–24 February 1992, Cape Town
OFS 372/7 dec (PJR Steyn 30, GFJ Liebenberg 104, LJ Wilkinson 67, JF Venter 63*; CR Matthews 3/69, EO Simons 3/99) and 167 (CJ van Heerden 40, JF Venter 82; CR Matthews 4/41, EO Simons 4/45)
WP 197 (MF Voss 36, HH Gibbs 44, EO Simons 40; FD Stephenson 5/39, BT Player 3/37) and 155/4 (MF Voss 56, G Kirsten 43*)

Western Province beat Yorkshire by 126 runs, 17–19 March 1992, Cape Town
WP 188 (TN Lazard 48, LF Bleekers 50; P Carrick 6/70) and 243/9 dec (TN Lazard 100, G Kirsten 38, DB Rundle 42; PJ Hartley 3/56, JD Batty 3/76)
York 123 (CR Matthews 6/22) and 182 (AA Metcalfe 50, RJ Blakey 64; DB Rundle 5/56)

Match drawn between Western Province and Natal, 14–16 September 1992, Durban
WP 249 (TN Lazard 57, G Kirsten 35, F Davids 33; PWE Rawson 4/57, DJ Pryke 3/45) and 106/3 (MF Voss 45*)
Ntl 333 (NE Wright 69, JN Rhodes 77, ELR Stewart 42, PWE Rawson 43; CR Matthews 3/54)

Western Province beat Northern Transvaal by 183 runs, 30 October – 2 November 1992, Cape Town
WP 248 (BM McMillan 34, AP Kuiper 35, EO Simons 55*, MW Pringle 43; PS de Villiers 5/83, PJ Newport 3/54) and 341/5 dec (AJ Lamb 206*, AP Kuiper 79, PS de Villiers 4/64)
N Tvl 133 (MD Haysman 36, MJR Rindel 38; MW Pringle 3/36) and 273 (MD Haysman 46, BJ Sommerville 47, MJR Rindel 79; MW Pringle 3/44, DB Rundle 3/83)

Match drawn between Western Province and Transvaal, 6–9 November 1992, Johannesburg
WP 410/8 dec (G Kirsten 109, AJ Lamb 134, AP Kuiper 33, EO Simons 50; S Jacobs 3/48) and 46/3 (RP Snell 3/25)
Tvl 333 (SJ Cook 123, M Yachad 42, DJ Cullinan 72, RP Snell 44; CR Matthews 6/50)

Western Province beat Natal by 5 wickets, 20–23 November 1992, Cape Town
Ntl 102 (BM McMillan 5/35, A Martyn 3/22) and 294 (CEB Rice 46, MD Marshall 35, PL Symcox 33, TJ Packer 44, RA Lyle 35*; MW Pringle 5/92, A Martyn 3/83)
WP 219 (G Kirsten 32, AJ Lamb 87, MD Marshall 3/56, PWE Rawson 5/43) and 178/5 (G Kirsten 66, AJ Lamb 30, BM McMillan 43)

Eastern Province beat Western Province by 8 wickets, 19–22 December 1992, Cape Town
WP 278 (G Kirsten 65, AJ Lamb 121; RE Bryson 5/66) and 202 (G Kirsten 36, AT Holdstock 37, EO Simons 57; RE Bryson 5/55, BN Schultz 3/45)
EP 350 (MW Rushmere 36, LJ Koen 54, M Michau 86, EAE Baptiste 40, PA Tullis 33*, BN Schultz 31; EO Simons 3/83, DQ MacHelm 3/58) and 134/2 (PG Amm 52, MW Rushmere 50*)

Border beat Western Province by 1 wicket, 1–4 January 1993, East London
WP 171 (TN Lazard 32, AP Kuiper 55; OD Gibson 3/47, BC Fourie 3/25) and 328 (AJ Lamb 38, AP Kuiper 33, EO Simons 93, DB Rundle 47, RJ Ryall 45*; OD Gibson 7/104)
Bdr 245 (SJ Palframan 45, IL Howell 40*; DB Rundle 5/70) and 257/9 (GC Victor 62, IL Howell 34*; DB Rundle 6/74)

Orange Free State beat Western Province by 114 runs, 9–12 January 1993, Bloemfontein
OFS 266 (LJ Wilkinson 41, O Henry 104*; MW Pringle 6/60) and 303/1 dec (WJ Cronje 161*, JM Arthur 71, PJR Steyn 56*)
WP 165 (EO Simons 40) and 290 (KC Jackson 34, G Kirsten 105, EO Simons 50; O Henry 5/68)

Match drawn between Western Province and Yorkshire, 26–28 March 1993, Cape Town
WP 258/5 dec (FB Touzel 37, HH Gibbs 34, TN Lazard 63*, RA Koster 45) and 131/6 dec (F Davids 35; JD Batty 4/54)
York 110 (MW Pringle 5/31) and 172/5 (MD Moxon 97; A Martyn 3/54)

Match drawn between Western Province and Boland, 17–19 September 1993, Worcester
WP 345/5 dec (FB Touzel 44, D Jordaan 63, AP Kuiper 129*, EO Simons 32, RA Koster 31*) and 152/4 (D Jordaan 76*, AP Kuiper 34)
Bol 575/5 dec (TN Lazard 307*, JB Commins 165)

Western Province beat Mashonaland by 91 runs, 12–14 October 1993, Harare
WP 310/6 dec (FB Touzel 57, G Kirsten 75, DB Rundle 59*, CR Matthews 36*) and 143/4 dec (FB Touzel 40, D Jordaan 39, AP Kuiper 36*; SG Peall 3/26)
Mash 116 (A Flower 43; DB Rundle 4/14) and 246 (GW Flower 71, ADR Campbell 64; AC Dawson 4/49, G Kirsten 3/26)

Western Province beat Boland by 10 wickets, 22–25 October 1993, Stellenbosch
WP 366 (G Kirsten 58, AP Kuiper 47, BM McMillan 116, DB Rundle 81; PAJ DeFreitas 5/80, M Erasmus 3/59) and 73/0 (FB Touzel 33*, D Jordaan 39*)
Bol 139 (TN Lazard 44; BM McMillan 3/32, DB Rundle 3/36) and 296 (WN van As 44, O Henry 39, CSN Marais 38, PAJ DeFreitas 54; A Martyn 3/78, DQ MacHelm 4/74)

Western Province beat Northern Transvaal by 7 wickets, 29 October – 1 November 1993, Verwoerdburg
WP 510/7 dec (G Kirsten 192, CA Best 71, AP Kuiper 90, BM McMillan 34) and 67/3 (FB Touzel 36*)
N Tvl 210 (PS de Villiers 39; A Martyn 3/36) and 366 (CB Lambert 137, RF Pienaar 42, KJ Rule 122; MW Pringle 4/43, G Kirsten 6/68)

Western Province beat Eastern Province by 65 runs, 25–28 November 1993, Port Elizabeth
WP 188 (EO Simons 31; RE Veenstra 4/32) and 294 (G Kirsten 116, AP Kuiper 53, EO Simons 40; EAE Baptiste 4/43, TG Shaw 3/51)
EP 231 (PG Amm 64, M Michau 32, EAE Baptiste 58; A Martyn 4/60) and 186 (PG Amm 36, M Michau 32; MW Pringle 3/37, AC Dawson 3/20)

Match drawn between Western Province and Natal, 10–13 December 1993, Pietermaritzburg
WP 300 (CA Best 63, EO Simons 96, AC Dawson 56; MD Marshall 3/62, PWE Rawson 4/29) and 173/6 (CA Best 44, AP Kuiper 49*)
Ntl 429 (CRB Armstrong 39, NE Wright 89, DM Benkenstein 50, MD Marshall 120*, DN Crookes 46; A Martyn 3/91)

England A beat Western Province by 10 wickets, 26–28 December 1993, Cape Town
WP 177 (D Jordaan 65; MC Ilott 3/42, D Gough 3/47, DG Cork 3/52) and 178 (SG Koenig 33, HH Gibbs 43; MC Ilott 3/26, D Gough 4/57)
EngA 321 (JP Crawley 51, MB Loye 68, A Dale 64; AC Dawson 5/42) and 35/0

Transvaal beat Western Province by 180 runs, 1–4 January 1994, Cape Town
Tvl 255 (BM White 108, MD Haysman 42; MW Pringle 3/34, EO Simons 4/41) and 282/7 dec (M Yachad 51, MD Haysman 37, MW Rushmere 37, SJ Cook 85, N Pothas 32; MW Pringle 3/47)
WP 131 (CA Best 33; CE Eksteen 7/29) and 226 (AP Kuiper 76, RJ Ryall 58; CE Eksteen 5/66)

Match drawn between Western Province and Orange Free State, 21–24 January 1994, Cape Town
WP 318 (SG Koenig 64, HH Gibbs 31, LF Bleekers 87; CJPG van Zyl 3/21, N Boje 4/96) and 220/9 dec (SG Koenig 52, CA Best 33, EO Simons 54*, MW Pringle 33; FD Stephenson 3/43, BT Player 3/35)
OFS 273 (PJR Steyn 46, LJ Wilkinson 105; MW Pringle 4/55, A Martyn 4/65) and 49/1

Border beat Western Province by 1 wicket, 26 February – 1 March 1994, Cape Town
WP 210 (BM McMillan 61, CR Matthews 34; A Badenhorst 4/37, PJ Botha 4/45) and 327/7 dec (SG Koenig 121*, G Kirsten 78, EO Simons 47; BC Fourie 3/85, IL Howell 3/86)
Bdr 231 (MP Stonier 30, BM Osborne 39, PJ Botha 35, IL Howell 52*; BM McMillan 3/48) and 309/9 (MP Stonier 59, AG Lawson 38, PN Kirsten 51, PC Strydom 31, IL Howell 30*, SJ Base 32; BM McMillan 3/48)

Orange Free State beat Western Province by 4 wickets, 11–14 November 1994, Cape Town
WP 105 (NW Pretorius 3/31, BT Player 4/34) and 386 (DL Haynes 96, G Kirsten 50, HD Ackerman 58, BM McMillan 37, RJ Ryall 39, EO Simons 36*, MW Pringle 32; FD Stephenson 5/60, NW Pretorius 3/89)
OFS 215 (LJ Wilkinson 74, JF Venter 36; CR Matthews 5/35) and 278/6 (PJR Steyn 84, WJ Cronje 111, GFJ Liebenberg 50; DB Rundle 3/77)

Match drawn between Border and Western Province, 18–21 November 1994, East London
Bdr 268 (MP Stonier 30, FJC Cronje 42, DJ Cullinan 42, PC Strydom 60; CR Matthews 3/51, DB Rundle 3/47) and 314/7 (DJ Cullinan 150*, PC Strydom 55)
WP 471/9 dec (SG Koenig 64, HD Ackerman 93, JH Kallis 46, EO Simons 73, MW Pringle 51*; PAN Emslie 3/90)

Match drawn between Natal and Western Province, 10–13 December 1994, Cape Town
Ntl 390 (DJ Watson 60, NC Johnson 53, L Klusener 50, PL Symcox 74*, SM Pollock 44; MW Pringle 3/100, DB Rundle 3/97) and 246/5 dec (NE Wright 61, ML Bruyns 84)
WP 303 (SG Koenig 89, DL Haynes 42, JH Kallis 39, RJ Ryall 30*; MD Marshall 3/58, L Klusener 4/62) and 193/6 (SG Koenig 73, DL Haynes 70)

Western Province beat Boland by an innings and 23 runs, 16–19 December 1994, Cape Town
WP 500/8 dec (DL Haynes 54, HH Gibbs 102, HD Ackerman 45, BM McMillan 140, MW Pringle 54*; CW Henderson 3/93)
Bol 206 (MS Nackerdien 49, JB Commins 83, M Erasmus 38*; BM McMillan 3/28, AC Dawson 4/51) and 271 (LD Ferreira 52, MS Nackerdien 54, KM Curran 73; DB Rundle 5/76)

Western Province beat Pakistanis by 192 runs, 26–29 December 1994, Cape Town
WP 436 (DL Haynes 44, HD Ackerman 118, JH Kallis 53, EO Simons 102*, DB Rundle 50; Ata-ur-Rehman 3/101, Manzoor Elahi 3/81) and 270/8 dec (HH Gibbs 35, HD Ackerman 32, JH Kallis 74, AC Dawson 51; Kabir Khan 4/45)
Pak 308 (Saeed Anwar 51, Shakeel Ahmed 43, Asif Mujtaba 55, Basit Ali 53; DG Payne 3/62, CV English 3/70) and 206 (Asif Mujtaba 65, Inzamam-ul-Haq 57; DB Rundle 6/51)

Eastern Province beat Western Province by 5 wickets, 13–16 January 1995, Port Elizabeth
WP 326/5 dec (SG Koenig 149*, JH Kallis 77, RJ Ryall 42*) and forfeit
EP 0/0*and 327/5 (KC Wessels 107, LJ Koen 138*; DG Payne 3/64)

Match drawn between Western Province and Transvaal, 27–30 January 1995, Johannesburg
Tvl 376 (MW Rushmere 134, GA Pollock 74, C Grainger 54, SJ Cook 37; AC Dawson 6/86) and 223/5 (DR Laing 42, GA Pollock 38, SJ Cook 55*, N Pothas 30*; DG Payne 3/42)
WP 442 (G Kirsten 150, BM McMillan 91, JH Kallis 52, AC Dawson 52; TC Webster 3/58, CE Eksteen 5/128)

Western Province beat Northern Transvaal by 5 wickets, 3–6 February 1995, Cape Town
NT 272 (RF Pienaar 42, KJ Rule 102, LP Vorster 56; DG Payne 4/50, EO Simons 3/30) and 216 (MJR Rindel 48, JJ Strydom 46; DG Payne 4/56, DB Rundle 4/91)
WP 286 (HH Gibbs 79, HD Ackerman 44, JH Kallis 38, TJ Mitchell 33; PS de Villiers 6/47) and 203/5 (G Kirsten 85, HD Ackerman 62)

Orange Free State beat Western Province by 5 wickets, 17–20 February 1995, Bloemfontein
WP 186 (HD Ackerman 55; NW Pretorius 3/72, FD Stephenson 5/61) and 287 (D Jordaan 97, TJ Mitchell 32, DB Rundle 33, MW Pringle 60*; FD Stephenson 3/37, NW Pretorius 4/93)
OFS 308 (JM Arthur 49, GFJ Liebenberg 81, CF Craven 46; DG Payne 3/91) and 168/5 (GFJ Liebenberg 42, FD Stephenson 37*, CF Craven 31*; MW Pringle 3/45)

Queensland beat Western Province by 6 wickets, 26–28 September 1995, Brisbane
WP 112 (JH Kallis 58; MS Kasprowicz 6/17) and 478/3 dec (G Kirsten 130, JH Kallis 186*, JB Commins 120)
Qld 275 (TJ Barsby 65, IA Healy 41, MS Kasprowicz 33; EO Simons 3/21) and 316/4 (TJ Dixon 122, ML Love 60, SG Law 73, A Symonds 31*)

New South Wales beat Western Province by 126 runs, 3–5 October 1995, Sydney
NSW 244/6 dec (MG Bevan 45, SR Waugh 47, S Lee 84, PA Emery 36*; CR Matthews 4/46) and 202/3 dec (MG Bevan 119*, S Lee 67*)
WP 128 (P Kirsten 32; AM Stuart 3/31) and 192 (SG Koenig 57, HD Ackerman 48; DA Freedman 5/75)

Transvaal beat Western Province by 79 runs, 27–30 October 1995, Cape Town
Tvl 375 (KR Rutherford 134, DR Laing 72, ND McKenzie 67, S Jacobs 35; CR Matthews 4/72) and 266 (N Pothas 66, MW Rushmere 83, GA Pollock 52; CR Matthews 5/43)
WP 304 (G Kirsten 53, JH Kallis 146; SD Jack 3/53, CE Eksteen 3/94) and 258 (DL Haynes 52, JH Kallis 49, JB Commins 37, BM McMillan 60; SD Jack 4/55, S Jacobs 3/44)

Western Province beat Northern Transvaal by 8 wickets, 4–7 November 1995, Centurion
N Tvl 344 (AJ Seymore 124, MJR Rindel 42, GJ Smith 68; CR Matthews 3/55) and 231 (RF Pienaar 38, S Elworthy 32; PR Adams 6/101)
WP 451 (DL Haynes 71, JB Commins 94, BM McMillan 116, HD Ackerman 30, EO Simons 54, DB Rundle 30; MJG Davis 3/86) and 126/2 (DL Haynes 46*, JH Kallis 55)

Western Province beat Eastern Province by 7 wickets, 10–12 November 1995, Cape Town
EP 234 (GC Victor 39, LJ Koen 37, DJ Callaghan 58, TG Shaw 31*; A Martyn 4/68, EO Simons 4/38) and 109 (MW Pringle 6/32)
WP 121 (SG Koenig 32, DL Haynes 37; A Badenhorst 5/49, DJ Callaghan 4/17) and 224/3 (SG Koenig 47, G Kirsten 104*, HD Ackerman 50*)

Western Province beat Border by an innings and 21 runs, 8–11 December 1995, East London
Bdr 173 (SO Tikolo 37; MW Pringle 4/30, CR Matthews 4/46) and 306 (PN Kirsten 104, DJ Cullinan 56, SO Tikolo 55; AC Dawson 4/25, PR Adams 5/128)
WP 500/5 dec (DL Haynes 52, G Kirsten 244, JH Kallis 53, HD Ackerman 83*; IL Howell 3/114)

Match drawn between Western Province and Free State, 15–18 December 1995, Cape Town
FS 247 (D Jordaan 33, HH Dippenaar 46, LJ Wilkinson 48, HC Bakkes 43; MW Pringle 5/89) and 252 (D Jordaan 41, FD Stephenson 104, N Boje 31; MW Pringle 4/76)
WP 257 (SG Koenig 65, HH Gibbs 35, JB Commins 55; NW Pretorius 5/79, JF Venter 4/52) and 162/4 (SG Koenig 47, HD Ackerman 34, JB Commins 36*; N Boje 4/39)

Western Province beat Boland by an innings and 68 runs, 26–29 December 1995, Paarl
Bol 231 (KC Jackson 56; MW Pringle 5/67, A Martyn 3/80) and 123 (TN Lazard 44, KC Jackson 35; MW Pringle 6/41, A Martyn 3/32)
WP 422/9 dec (DL Haynes 38, SG Koenig 35, HH Gibbs 112, HD Ackerman 84, JB Commins 57, DB Rundle 50; CW Henderson 4/147, M Erasmus 5/87)

Match drawn between Western Province and Natal, 26–29 January 1996, Durban
Ntl 277 (NC Johnson 33, DM Benkenstein 34, DN Crookes 111*; BM McMillan 3/46, PR Adams 3/65)
WP 85 (L Klusener 8/34) and 273/7 (G Kirsten 76*, JH Kallis 31, BM McMillan 32, HD Ackerman 50)

Western Province beat Border by 92 runs, 9–12 February 1996, Cape Town
WP 266 (JB Commins 31, HD Ackerman 106*, EO Simons 71; PC Strydom 3/22) and 230 (SG Koenig 56, P Kirsten 46, MW Pringle 43; BP Horan 4/43, IL Howell 3/52)
Bdr 206 (FJC Cronje 35, W Wiblin 32, MV Boucher 37, IL Howell 43; MW Pringle 4/73, A Martyn 5/63) and 198 (PC Strydom 69, FJC Cronje 48; MW Pringle 5/67)

Match drawn between Western Province and Mashonaland, 26–28 September 1996, Harare
WP 303 (MC de Villiers 84, SG Koenig 67, AC Dawson 30*; PA Strang 4/111) and 237/9 dec (SG Koenig 49, JB Commins 104, DB Rundle 41; PA Strang 4/110, GJ Rennie 3/15)
Mash 276/8 dec (BC Strang 68, CB Wishart 53, ADR Campbell 32; A Martyn 4/46) and 74/4 (CB Wishart 30*)

Western Province beat Northern Transvaal by 38 runs, 1–4 November 1996, Cape Town
WP 220 (HD Ackerman 51, JB Commins 81*; S Elworthy 3/77, RE Bryson 4/64) and 399 (R Maron 35, SG Koenig 97, DL Haynes 71, JB Commins 38, EO Simons 61, P Kirsten 43; RE Bryson 3/83)
N Tvl 355 (RF Pienaar 95, RB Richardson 56, DJ van Zyl 35, S Elworthy 40; A Martyn 3/73) and 226 (RF Pienaar 43, S Elworthy 34, I Pistorius 32*; MW Pringle 3/82)

Western Province beat Boland by an innings and 65 runs, 14–17 November 1996, Cape Town
Bol 239 (LD Ferreira 39, DJ Millns 44; PR Adams 4/68) and 205 (AP Kuiper 33; A Martyn 3/32, AC Dawson 5/30)
WP 509/7 dec (DL Haynes 33, SG Koenig 119, HD Ackerman 65, JB Commins 148*, EO Simons 38, AC Dawson 64; CW Henderson 3/163)

Match drawn between Western Province and Free State, 29 November – 2 December 1996, Bloemfontein
WP 446 (SG Koenig 52, JH Kallis 143, DB Rundle 81*, AC Dawson 59; JF Venter 3/94)
FS 280 (GFJ Liebenberg 90, JF Venter 41, PJL Radley 44; MW Pringle 4/61, A Martyn 4/76) and 483/2 (D Jordaan 80, GFJ Liebenberg 91, HH Dippenaar 151*, LJ Wilkinson 139*)

Western Province beat Border by 8 wickets, 13–15 December 1996, Cape Town
Bdr 210 (PJ Botha 34, MV Boucher 71; BN Schultz 3/61, AC Dawson 3/31) and 185 (MV Boucher 68*; MW Pringle 4/26, BN Schultz 5/69)
WP 290 (DL Haynes 99, CR Matthews 96; M Ntini 6/49) and 106/2 (SG Koenig 42)

Eastern Province beat Western Province by 5 wickets, 3–6 January 1997, Port Elizabeth
WP 401/2 dec (DL Haynes 202*, JH Kallis 94, HD Ackerman 45*) and 228/6 dec (JH Kallis 79, HD Ackerman 102*; EAE Baptiste 3/48)
EP 300/9 dec (LJ Koen 128, MW Rushmere 74, TG Shaw 37*; MW Pringle 4/79) and 331/5 (KC Wessels 179, DJ Callaghan 88; MW Pringle 3/75)

Western Province beat Griqualand West by an innings and 5 runs, 17–19 January 1997, Kimberley
GW 298 (MI Gidley 117, WM Dry 31, CV English 51; CR Matthews 4/44) and 167 (JM Arthur 46; BN Schultz 5/49, CR Matthews 3/34)
WP 470/5 dec (DL Haynes 91, JH Kallis 40*, HH Gibbs 49, JB Commins 200*, HD Ackerman 47)

Match drawn between Transvaal and Western Province, 8–11 February 1997, Johannesburg
Tvl 371 (ND McKenzie 139, S Jacobs 85; BN Schultz 5/64) and 263/8 dec (MR Benfield 33, CE Eksteen 32, KR Rutherford 126*)
WP 227 (HH Gibbs 47, EO Simons 80, P Kirsten 50; EW Kidwell 3/34, CE Eksteen 4/65) and 352/7 (HH Gibbs 103, HD Ackerman 122, EO Simons 58*; RA Lyle 3/40)

Australians beat Western Province by 32 runs, 15–17 February 1997, Cape Town
Aus 439/4 dec (ML Hayden 112, MA Taylor 85, MTG Elliott 74, SR Waugh 69, GS Blewett 48*, JL Langer 31*) and 175/6 dec (GS Blewett 86, MTG Elliott 36; JH Kallis 4/46)
WP 261/5 dec (G Kirsten 37, SG Koenig 45, JH Kallis 31, JB Commins 59*) and 321 (SG Koenig 38, HH Gibbs 80, JB Commins 51, HD Ackerman 37; AJ Bichel 5/62, MG Bevan 3/113)

Match drawn between Western Province and Natal, 7–10 March 1997, Cape Town
WP 433/3 dec (DL Haynes 83, JH Kallis 138, HH Gibbs 163*) and 222 (BM McMillan 63, CR Matthews 64; DN Crookes 3/72)
Ntl 359 (AC Hudson 32, NC Johnson 52, DM Benkenstein 46, DN Crookes 96, ELR Stewart 44; BN Schultz 3/95) and 55/1 (AC Hudson 35*)

Free State beat Western Province by 6 wickets, 14–17 November 1997, Cape Town
FS 387 (GFJ Liebenberg 72, LJ Wilkinson 81, JF Venter 86, N Boje 76; CR Matthews 4/71) and 61/4
WP 193 (JH Kallis 52, JB Commins 44, BM McMillan 37; CJ Vorster 3/49) and 253 (HD Ackerman 82, JB Commins 30, BT Player 30, P Kirsten 31; SA Cilliers 3/54)

Match drawn between Western Province and Gauteng, 21–24 November 1997, Cape Town
WP 267/7 (JB Commins 40, P Kirsten 91*, CR Matthews 41*)
Gau did not bat

West Indies A beat Western Province by 23 runs, 28 November – 1 December 1997, Cape Town
WIA 290 (JC Adams 52, LR Williams 110, NB Francis 46; MF George 4/79) and 174 (LV Garrick 35, JC Adams 53, WW Hinds 32; BN Schultz 8/36)
WP 199 (HD Ackerman 47, P Kirsten 63; OD Gibson 4/36, D Ramnarine 3/25) and 242 (H Pangarker 53, HD Ackerman 72; OD Gibson 5/85, D Ramnarine 3/55)

Boland beat Western Province by 67 runs, 12–15 December 1997, Paarl
Bol 165 (AP Kuiper 36; BN Schultz 4/42, AC Dawson 4/42) and 265 (JB Mackey 45, AP Kuiper 30, KM Curran 67, SJ Palframan 40; AC Dawson 4/51)
WP 121 (R Telemachus 4/36, CW Henderson 3/39) and 242 (LD Ferreira 69, EO Simons 48, CR Matthews 40*; R Telemachus 5/52, CW Henderson 3/88)

Match drawn between Western Province and Border, 16–19 January 1998, East London
Bdr 375 (W Wiblin 177, SC Pope 100; AC Dawson 5/80) and 270/8 dec (W Wiblin 119*, PC Strydom 33, CC van der Merwe 34; BT Player 4/96)
WP 395 (HD Ackerman 114, F Davids 61, P Kirsten 37; D Taljard 3/50, PAN Emslie 3/94) and 106/3 (LD Ferreira 56*)

Natal beat Western Province by 7 wickets, 23–26 January 1998, Durban
Ntl 500/5 dec (ML Bruyns 135, DJ Watson 145, ELR Stewart 51, AC Hudson 119*) and 25/3 (DG Payne 3/10)
WP 205 (LD Ferreira 41, EO Simons 41, P Kirsten 47; GM Gilder 4/54, CR Tatton 4/60) and 319 (JJ de Nobrega 30, HD Ackerman 131, BA Murphy 41, P Kirsten 32; RB MacQueen 5/125, CR Tatton 3/84)

Western Province beat Eastern Province by 123 runs, 6–9 February 1998, Cape Town
WP 145 (LD Ferreira 34; M Hayward 3/20, JM Kemp 4/12) and 427/8 dec (HH Gibbs 152, HD Ackerman 100, BT Player 53*, PR Adams 38*)
EP 204 (MW Rushmere 31, CC Bradfield 34, JM Kemp 30; MF George 3/33, EO Simons 3/39) and 245 (LJ Koen 52, KC Wessels 40, DJ Callaghan 37, JM Kemp 38; PR Adams 6/90, BT Player 3/84)

Western Province beat Griqualand West by an innings and 45 runs, 13–16 February 1998, Cape Town
GW 239 (JM Arthur 31, W Bossenger 85, M Strydom 43; MF George 6/61, AC Dawson 3/65) and 216 (MI Gidley 88; PR Adams 7/69)
WP 500/6 dec (AG Prince 60, HD Ackerman 174, EO Simons 157*)

Match drawn between Western Province and Northerns, 13–16 March 1998, Centurion
Nor 483/8 dec (PJR Steyn 141, G Dros 38, M van Jaarsveld 139*, P de Bruyn 50; AC Dawson 3/80) and 120/5
WP 153 (P Kirsten 47; GJ Smith 6/35) and 581/7 dec (G Kirsten 32, JH Kallis 111, HH Gibbs 63, HD Ackerman 202*, BM McMillan 64, AG Prince 42; DJJ de Vos 3/117)

Match drawn between Western Province and Gauteng, 30 October – 2 November 1998, Johannesburg
Gau 452/7 dec (SG Koenig 95, AM Bacher 135, KR Rutherford 51, ND McKenzie 74, N Pothas 37*; CW Henderson 3/96, PR Adams 3/135) and 277/4 dec (AM Bacher 69, SG Koenig 44, ND McKenzie 51*, KR Rutherford 86; PR Adams 3/93)
WP 503/9 dec (LD Ferreira 116, HH Gibbs 35, BM McMillan 31, AG Prince 86, EO Simons 41, R Munnik 64, CR Matthews 76; CE Eksteen 4/106)

Western Province beat Free State by 22 runs, 13–16 November 1998, Bloemfontein
WP 223 (JH Kallis 63, HH Gibbs 35, CW Henderson 33; PV Mpitsang 4/37) and 414 (G Kirsten 194, JH Kallis 66, BM McMillan 65; N Boje 3/42)
FS 269 (JF Venter 67, N Boje 116; AC Dawson 6/79) and 346 (JF Venter 36, GFJ Liebenberg 40, HH Dippenaar 54, N Boje 97*, D Pretorius 43; CW Henderson 3/140, CR Matthews 4/70)

Western Province beat Boland by an innings and 47 runs, 19–21 November 1998, Cape Town
Bol 59 (AC Dawson 4/19, EO Simons 5/14) and 219 (JM Henderson 35, EJ Ferreira 31, S Ackermann 30, SJ Palframan 70; JH Kallis 4/36, EO Simons 3/19)
WP 325 (G Kirsten 40, JH Kallis 32, HD Ackerman 61, AG Prince 35, AC Dawson 33; CM Willoughby 3/63, HS Williams 3/87)

Northerns beat Western Province by 9 wickets, 11–12 December 1998, Cape Town
WP 129 (AG Prince 54, R Munnik 39; S Elworthy 3/31, DH Townsend 3/31, Q Ferreira 3/50) and 75 (DH Townsend 3/9, Q Ferreira 3/19)
Nor 129 (G Dros 33, M van Jaarsveld 43; EO Simons 5/35) and 79/1 (G Dros 48*)

Western Province beat Eastern Province by 7 wickets, 8–11 January 1999, Port Elizabeth
EP 220 (CC Bradfield 61, DJ Callaghan 54, MW Rushmere 35; EO Simons 5/43, PR Adams 4/72) and 159 (LJ Koen 41, JM Kemp 31; EO Simons 5/43, R Munnik 3/30)
WP 239 (G Kirsten 94, P Kirsten 38; MW Pringle 4/51) and 144/3 (G Kirsten 79*)

Western Province beat KwaZulu-Natal by 4 wickets, 12–15 February 1999, Cape Town
KZN 210 (ML Bruyns 72, ELR Stewart 45; CW Henderson 4/53, CR Matthews 4/15) and 336/7 dec (ML Bruyns 109, AC Hudson 46, JC Kent 40, A Mall 72; AC Dawson 4/66)
WP 257 (LD Ferreira 33, BM McMillan 62, JB Commins 50; RB MacQueen 4/60) and 292/6 (LD Ferreira 30, BM McMillan 64, AG Prince 38, JB Commins 70, R Munnik 31; RB MacQueen 4/54)

Western Province beat Griqualand West by 134 runs, 19–22 February 1999, Kimberley
WP 334 (AG Prince 133, HD Ackerman 33, R Munnik 43; GJ Kruis 6/84) and 240/5 dec (LD Ferreira 77, BM McMillan 75, AG Prince 52*; OD Gibson 4/56)
GW 191 (JM Arthur 43, MI Gidley 51; AC Dawson 3/41) and 249 (JM Arthur 56, FC Brooker 78, WM Dry 36, OD Gibson 32; EO Simons 3/38, CW Henderson 5/57)

Match drawn between Western Province and Border, 25–28 February 1999, Cape Town
Bdr 428/9 dec (PJ Botha 65, PC Strydom 42, SC Pope 54, I Mitchell 96, GT Love 85*; R Joffe 3/85, BT Player 3/141) and 181/6 dec (BM White 63, PJ Botha 41; BT Player 3/58, CW Henderson 3/63)
WP 246 (LD Ferreira 51, BM McMillan 49, JB Commins 35; GT Love 5/72, PC Strydom 4/73) and 107/3 (BM McMillan 58*)

Western Province beat Border by 163 runs, 4–8 March 1999, East London
WP 302 (EO Simons 75, AC Dawson 143; T Henderson 4/82) and 249 (LD Ferreira 36, AG Prince 41, HD Ackerman 98*; VC Drakes 5/48, D Taljard 3/61)
Bdr 191 (CB Sugden 44, SC Pope 61; EO Simons 3/48) and 197 (CB Sugden 41, BM White 33; R Joffe 3/51, EO Simons 3/46)

Match drawn between Western Province and Free State, 14–17 October 1999, Bloemfontein
WP 284 (JH Kallis 40, HD Ackerman 64, JB Commins 60; AA Donald 5/47, PV Mpitsang 4/61) and 278 (JH Kallis 44, HD Ackerman 91, AG Prince 41; PV Mpitsang 4/42)
FS 444/9 dec (AI Gait 59, HH Dippenaar 128, WJ Cronje 124, N Boje 37, GL Brophy 40; AC Dawson 4/77, PR Adams 5/143) and 117/6 (GFJ Liebenberg 34, WJ Cronje 39; R Telemachus 3/30)

Match drawn between Western Province and Boland, 21–24 October 1999, Paarl
Bol 247 (LJ Koen 113, JL Ontong 50; AC Dawson 3/54, JH Kallis 6/60) and 255/9 dec (JM Henderson 70, LJ Koen 60, JL Ontong 40, SJ Palframan 50; CW Henderson 4/101, PR Adams 3/88)
WP 137 (JH Kallis 58; HS Williams 3/24, CM Willoughby 4/29) and 178/3 (TL Tsolekile 33, BM McMillan 104*)

KwaZulu-Natal beat Western Province by 10 wickets, 28–31 October 1999, Cape Town
WP 222 (R Magiet 46, AG Prince 73; RB MacQueen 4/65) and 260 (JB Commins 56, BM McMillan 95*, R Telemachus 46; GM Gilder 6/61)
KZN 451/6 dec (ML Bruyns 30, DJ Watson 62, DM Benkenstein 71, ELR Stewart 151*, EAE Baptiste 75*; R Telemachus 3/77) and 34/0

Western Province beat North West by 9 wickets, 18–20 November 1999, Cape Town
NW 148 (GM Hewitt 40, MJ Lavine 59; R Telemachus 3/24, CR Matthews 3/21) and 200 (AG Lawson 30, C Light 91, CT Enslin 36; R Telemachus 3/41, PR Adams 6/78)
WP 284 (G Kirsten 59, LD Ferreira 50, JB Commins 95*; JN Dreyer 5/97) and 66/1 (G Kirsten 48*)

Match drawn between Western Province and Eastern Province, 3–6 December 1999, Cape Town
EP 338 (MR Benfield 55, JDC Bryant 131, MW Rushmere 60; R Telemachus 4/56, PR Adams 5/110) and 270/4 (JDC Bryant 129, DJ Callaghan 48, MW Rushmere 38*)
WP 473/7 dec (G Kirsten 63, HH Gibbs 119, HD Ackerman 86, AG Prince 117, AC Dawson 33*)

Match drawn between Western Province and Northerns, 10–13 December 1999, Centurion
WP 287/8 dec (BM McMillan 47, AG Prince 77*, AC Dawson 48; GJ Smith 5/81)
Nor 132/3 (PJR Steyn 58, M van Jaarsveld 34*)

Gauteng beat Western Province by 93 runs, 14–17 January 2000, Cape Town
Gau 411/6 dec (AM Bacher 128, SG Koenig 104, G Toyana 46, Z de Bruyn 50*, MR Street 33*; R Telemachus 3/84) and 164/6 dec (SG Koenig 43, G Toyana 62; CW Henderson 4/72)
WP 240 (HD Ackerman 119, AC Dawson 54; DJ Terbrugge 3/52, AJ Hall 3/71) and 242 (BM McMillan 54, AG Prince 50, AC Dawson 57*; CE Eksteen 3/70, WB Masimula 3/37)

Border beat Western Province by an innings and 74 runs, 21–23 January 2000, East London
WP 111 (R Magiet 35; VC Drakes 5/37, T Henderson 3/14) and 155 (AG Prince 51, S Ackermann 31; M Ntini 3/42)
Bdr 340 (BM White 44, GT Love 52, SC Pope 39, LL Gamiet 44; AC Dawson 6/51, CW Henderson 3/97)

Western Province beat Eastern Province by 127 runs, 27–30 October 2000, Port Elizabeth
WP 362 (HH Gibbs 61, GC Smith 35, HD Ackerman 128, NC Johnson 30, AG Prince 47; M Ngam 4/78) and 212/8 dec (GC Smith 80, AC Dawson 53*; M Ngam 3/59)
EP 282 (DJ Callaghan 129, JM Kemp 44) and 165 (JDC Bryant 40; CW Henderson 5/40)

Western Province beat Border by 77 runs, 3–6 November 2000, East London
WP 350/9 dec (HH Gibbs 91, AG Puttick 66, HD Ackerman 42, NC Johnson 31, AG Prince 46*; L Graham 3/69) and 222/4 dec (HH Gibbs 46, AG Puttick 30, HD Ackerman 68, NC Johnson 53*)
Bdr 252 (W Wiblin 51, PC Strydom 30, I Mitchell 61, GT Love 30; CM Willoughby 3/52, CW Henderson 3/79, PR Adams 3/33) and 243 (LL Gamiet 30, I Mitchell 46*; CM Willoughby 3/57)

Match drawn between Western Province and KwaZulu-Natal, 10–13 November 2000, Cape Town
WP 352 (HH Gibbs 43, G Kirsten 38, JH Kallis 99, PR Adams 42*; L Klusener 4/111, JC Kent 3/70) and 221/5 dec (G Kirsten 54, JH Kallis 84, HD Ackerman 33, NC Johnson 36*)
KZN 293 (AC Hudson 38, DM Benkenstein 37, JC Kent 74*; AC Dawson 4/69) and 134/5 (DJ Watson 60*)

Western Province beat Easterns by 194 runs, 24–27 November 2000, Cape Town
WP 332/8 dec (GC Smith 57, AG Puttick 153*, HD Ackerman 50; KCG Benjamin 3/59) and 285/6 dec (TL Tsolekile 95, AG Puttick 39, NC Johnson 50, AG Prince 40*)
Eas 228 (MJR Rindel 91, DN Crookes 79; AC Dawson 5/51, PR Adams 3/61) and 195 (D Jennings 53, DN Crookes 87*; R Telemachus 3/20, AC Dawson 3/32)

Match drawn between Western Province and Boland, 1–4 February 2001, Cape Town
Bol 398 (JM Henderson 42, JG Strydom 34, JL Ontong 84, IJL Trott 93, H Davids 42; JH Kallis 3/77) and 255 (JG Strydom 73, LJ Koen 46, SJ Palframan 30; R Telemachus 6/54)
WP 394 (GC Smith 126, JH Kallis 69, NC Johnson 75; NM Carter 6/122) and 205/5 (GC Smith 52, JH Kallis 40, PR Adams 61*)

Western Province beat North West by an innings and 7 runs, 1–3 March 2001, Potchefstroom
NW 330 (MJ Lavine 39, M Strydom 124, AC Thomas 95*; CM Willoughby 3/64, AC Dawson 4/11) and 126 (BC de Wett 30, M Strydom 33*; CM Willoughby 3/34, CW Henderson 3/25)
WP 463 (LD Ferreira 201, AG Prince 39, NC Johnson 76, TL Tsolekile 78; MJ Lavine 4/144, GA Roe 5/79)

Western Province beat Free State by 127 runs, 8–11 March 2001, Cape Town
WP 265 (GC Smith 41, AG Prince 43, NC Johnson 38, R Munnik 45, TL Tsolekile 31; JJ van der Wath 3/46, D Pretorius 4/78) and 299/8 dec (AG Puttick 60, LD Ferreira 34, HD Ackerman 100*, R Munnik 35; JF Venter 5/103)
FS 291 (AI Gait 34, JF Venter 86, JJ van der Wath 49, GL Brophy 36; CW Henderson 4/71) and 146 (JF Venter 42; CM Willoughby 5/26, PL Harris 3/56)

Western Province beat Northerns by 298 runs, 15–18 March 2001, Centurion
WP 316/9 dec (LD Ferreira 62, AG Prince 79, NC Johnson 84, TL Tsolekile 49; RE Bryson 4/65) and 314/3 dec (AG Puttick 31, HD Ackerman 109*, AG Prince 120*)
Nor 267/9 dec (JA Rudolph 71, AN Petersen 30, PJR Steyn 35, P Joubert 35*; R Munnik 4/58) and 65 (CW Henderson 5/6)

Western Province beat Border by an innings and 26 runs, 21–24 March 2001, Cape Town
Bdr 252 (SC Pope 58, DL Makalima 42*, VC Drakes 46; R Telemachus 4/47) and 191 (LL Gamiet 80; CW Henderson 5/62)
WP 469 (GC Smith 183, LD Ferreira 81, AG Prince 53, TL Tsolekile 53; VC Drakes 3/127, GT Love 7/116)

Western Province beat Easterns by 10 wickets, 5–8 October 2001, Cape Town
Eas 236 (JA Morkel 87*, BL Reddy 41; CM Willoughby 3/56) and 141 (CM Willoughby 3/15, PR Adams 4/54)
WP 336 (AG Puttick 45, HD Ackerman 31, IJL Trott 93, TL Tsolekile 43, AC Dawson 51, R Telemachus 31; RE Bryson 4/74, AJ Hall 3/86) and 42/0 (GC Smith 30*)

Western Province beat Gauteng by an innings and 81 runs, 12–14 October 2001, Johannesburg
Gau 230 (AM Bacher 50, SC Cook 52, JM Otto 37, CE Eksteen 30; CM Willoughby 4/44) and 136 (MR Street 40, FA Rose 39; CM Willoughby 3/45, AC Dawson 4/27)
WP 447 (R Magiet 32, GC Smith 156, AG Puttick 51, NC Johnson 74, AC Dawson 32; JT Mafa 3/88)

Match drawn between Western Province and North West, 19–22 October 2001, Potchefstroom
NW 297 (M Strydom 36, MC Venter 85, CT Enslin 32, EO Moleon 30; CM Willoughby 5/46, CW Henderson 3/80) and 293/9 dec (DJ Jacobs 67, DJJ de Vos 47, AC Thomas 54*; CM Willoughby 3/57)
WP 180 (IJL Trott 45, NC Johnson 86; AC Thomas 6/20) and 268/4 (R Magiet 50, AG Puttick 30, HD Ackerman 85*, NC Johnson 57*)

Western Province beat Griqualand West by 8 wickets, 25–28 October 2001, Cape Town
GW 326 (BH Tucker 110, MJ Powell 44, LL Bosman 89; CM Willoughby 3/68, PR Adams 4/78) and 178 (MI Gidley 46, GJ Kruis 36; CM Willoughby 3/44, PR Adams 3/42)
WP 368 (GC Smith 40, IJL Trott 62, NC Johnson 62, TL Tsolekile 84; ZA Abrahim 5/67) and 141/2 (GC Smith 38, IJL Trott 73*)

Match drawn between Western Province and Boland, 2–5 November 2001, Paarl
WP 492/4 dec (GC Smith 122, AG Puttick 229*, HD Ackerman 87) and 136/3 dec (GC Smith 72, IJL Trott 37)
Bol 374 (AW Cyster 52, JM Henderson 53, LJ Koen 86, WJ Smit 44, CK Langeveldt 33*, HS Williams 35; CW Henderson 5/129) and 163/5 (JG Strydom 34, H Davids 60*)

Western Province beat Eastern Province by 90 runs, 15–18 February 2002, Cape Town
WP 504/8 dec (HH Gibbs 53, G Kirsten 244, HD Ackerman 59, R Munnik 30; JM Kemp 3/104) and 189/4 dec (G Kirsten 72, IJL Trott 63)
EP 404/9 dec (CC Bradfield 50, JDC Bryant 90, DJ Callaghan 72, Z Homani 40, JM Kemp 52*; PL Harris 3/131) and 199 (CC Bradfield 79, JDC Bryant 50; CM Willoughby 6/44)

Match drawn between Western Province and Northerns, 8–11 March 2002, Centurion
Nor 394/9 dec (JA Rudolph 39, M van Jaarsveld 49, JG Myburgh 51, G Dros 50, P Joubert 112*, CFK van Wyk 30; R Telemachus 3/69, CM Willoughby 3/110, CW Henderson 3/92) and 205/7 dec (M van Jaarsveld 45, G Dros 50, AC Dawson 3/60)
WP 178 (LD Ferreira 56, JJ McLean 38; S Elworthy 6/50) and 337/7 (AG Puttick 107, HD Ackerman 140*; MF George 3/73)

KwaZulu-Natal beat Western Province by 159 runs, 16–19 March 2002, Cape Town
KZN 374 (DM Benkenstein 145, JC Kent 92, L Klusener 68; CM Willoughby 3/95, CW Henderson 4/97) and 272 (HM Amla 32, JC Kent 48, L Klusener 59, DL Brown 34, GH Bodi 50; R Telemachus 3/62, CW Henderson 3/105)
WP 275 (R Magiet 54, AG Puttick 58, HD Ackerman 81; L Klusener 3/53) and 212 (AG Puttick 86, JJ McLean 33, AC Dawson 48; L Klusener 3/55)

Western Province beat Free State by an innings and 14 runs, 20–23 September 2002, Bloemfontein
FS 164 (GFJ Liebenberg 39, JJ van der Wath 56; CM Willoughby 5/49) and 198 (JA Beukes 31, JC Adams 67*, HC Bakkes 32; CM Willoughby 5/54)
WP 376/9 dec (G Prince 98, JJ McLean 57, R Munnik 87, TL Tsolekile 35; D Pretorius 3/74, PV Mpitsang 3/66)

Match drawn between Western Province and Griqualand West, 27–30 September 2002, Kimberley
GW 330 (LL Bosman 140, W Bossenger 64; R Telemachus 4/72, CM Willoughby 4/74) and 345 (BH Tucker 67, MI Gidley 54, W Bossenger 82, ZA Abrahim 45*; CW Henderson 7/99)
WP 351 (LD Ferreira 124, AG Prince 64, R Munnik 67, R Telemachus 37; GJ Kruis 5/66) and 108/2 (G Kirsten 56*)

Western Province beat Boland by an innings and 20 runs, 4–6 October 2002, Bellville
WP 411/4 dec (G Kirsten 121, AG Prince 133, HD Ackerman 59*, NC Johnson 43)
Bol 191 (VG Kambli 68, SJ Palframan 42; PR Adams 4/25) and 200 (CD de Lange 61*, CK Langeveldt 38; AC Dawson 3/15, CM Willoughby 3/60, CW Henderson 4/53)

Western Province beat KwaZulu-Natal by an innings and 4 runs, 11–14 October 2002, Durban
KZN 354 (JN Rhodes 37, HM Amla 75, L Klusener 56, JC Kent 59; AC Dawson 3/90) and 236 (AM Amla 31, A Mall 51, JN Rhodes 49, L Klusener 37; AC Dawson 3/56)
WP 594/8 dec (GC Smith 56, HH Gibbs 203, G Kirsten 35, AG Prince 143, NC Johnson 69, TL Tsolekile 43; JC Kent 3/108)

Match drawn between Western Province and Border, 18–21 October 2002, Bellville
Bdr 348 (CB Sugden 121, PC Strydom 32, I Mitchell 59, T Henderson 47*; CM Willoughby 3/63, Q Friend 4/59) and 335/9 dec (CB Sugden 42, ML Bruyns 32, SC Pope 101, PC Strydom 37, I Mitchell 35; J-P Duminy 4/89)
WP 255/8 dec (NC Johnson 119, R Munnik 43) and 258/8 (AG Puttick 44, LD Ferreira 33, J-P Duminy 33, AC Dawson 32, Q Friend 36*)

Easterns beat Western Province by 273 runs, 1–5 November 2002, Benoni
Eas 238 (DN Crookes 34, P de Bruyn 120, G Toyana 41; AC Dawson 3/50, CM Willoughby 5/55) and 472 (AJ Seymore 147, Z de Bruyn 169, D Jennings 47; CM Willoughby 5/106, CW Henderson 3/156)
WP 309 (GC Smith 62, AG Prince 79, NC Johnson 30, R Munnik 54; AJ Hall 6/77) and 128 (HH Gibbs 33; AJ Hall 5/22, AG Botha 3/40)

Match drawn between Western Province and Northerns, 17–20 October 2003, Centurion
Nor 198 (AN Petersen 95, AB de Villiers 58; CM Willoughby 7/56) and 259/7 dec (AB de Villiers 61, M van Jaarsveld 90; CM Willoughby 4/67)
WP 173 (AG Prince 38, CW Henderson 40; NE Mbhalati 4/37, AC Thomas 3/38) and 11/0

Western Province beat North West by 10 wickets, 31 October – 3 November 2003, Cape Town
WP 480/5 dec (AG Puttick 101, DJ Bassage 69, AG Prince 50, NC Johnson 135, J-P Duminy 80*) and 16/0
NW 266 (GV Grace 39, DJJ de Vos 42, M Strydom 43, TA Bula 60*; CM Willoughby 3/69, R Telemachus 3/62, CW Henderson 3/74) and 229 (JM Henderson 32, RT Bailey 82; CW Henderson 4/61, J-P Duminy 3/49)

Western Province beat Border by 176 runs, 7–10 November 2003, East London
WP 239 (AG Puttick 64, HH Gibbs 45, G Kirsten 36; T Henderson 4/74, CK Langeveldt 4/61) and 304 (AG Puttick 35, G Kirsten 78, J-P Duminy 70, TL Tsolekile 33; T Henderson 4/62)
Bdr 217 (ML Bruyns 101, JP Kreusch 59; CM Willoughby 3/50, R Telemachus 4/59, CW Henderson 3/59) and 150 (T Henderson 43; R Telemachus 3/50, CW Henderson 4/59)

Match drawn between Western Province and Gauteng, 14–17 November 2003, Cape Town
WP 520/6 dec (AG Puttick 46, AG Prince 84, JH Kallis 105, G Kirsten 125, J-P Duminy 105*)
Gau 225 (JM Otto 91; PR Adams 4/50) and 505/7 (SC Cook 135, AM Bacher 65, HD Ackerman 54, JM Otto 34, U Abrahams 134*; CM Willoughby 3/101)

Western Province beat Griqualand West by an innings and 186 runs, 4–7 March 2004, Cape Town
GW 185 (LL Bosman 34, W Bossenger 68; AC Dawson 6/55) and 183 (MI Gidley 48, B Hector 70, LL Bosman 32; AC Dawson 4/37, Q Friend 5/34)
WP 554/2 dec (AG Puttick 250*, DJ Bassage 48, LD Ferreira 130, J-P Duminy 100*)

Western Province beat KwaZulu-Natal by 154 runs, 11–14 March 2004, Cape Town
WP 311 (NC Johnson 58, TL Tsolekile 63, CW Henderson 71; NAM McLean 4/53, L Klusener 3/100) and 371/4 dec (DJ Bassage 61, LD Ferreira 100, AG Prince 110*, NC Johnson 46*)
KZN 332 (DJ Watson 58, HM Amla 50, AM Amla 75, DM Benkenstein 75; AC Dawson 3/84) and 196 (L Klusener 80*, ANW Tweedie 30; AC Dawson 3/38, CM Willoughby 3/54, CW Henderson 3/46)

Western Province beat Free State by 8 wickets, 19–21 March 2004, Bloemfontein
FS 322 (GFJ Liebenberg 45, HH Dippenaar 69, JF Venter 47, JJ van der Wath 30, WA Deacon 59; CW Henderson 5/71) and 78 (CM Willoughby 3/15, Q Friend 3/20, CW Henderson 3/20)
WP 202 (AG Puttick 35, TL Tsolekile 56, CW Henderson 42; WA Deacon 3/60, JJ van der Wath 4/35) and 199/2 (AG Puttick 45, DJ Bassage 79, LD Ferreira 43*)

Western Province beat KwaZulu-Natal by 108 runs, 31 March – 4 April 2004, Cape Town
WP 217 (AG Puttick 70, AC Dawson 56; L Klusener 7/70) and 315 (TL Tsolekile 36, J-P Duminy 89, CW Henderson 53, Q Friend 38*; L Klusener 5/90)
KZN 187 (I Khan 35, HM Amla 79*; CW Henderson 3/27) and 237 (I Khan 62, HM Amla 72, JC Kent 32; AC Dawson 4/51, CM Willoughby 4/71)

10.1.6 Western Province Cricket Association, List A, Limited-Overs Scores, 1991/92–2003/04[335]

Impalas beat Western Province by 8 wickets, 23 October 1991, Cape Town
WP 203/6 (AP Kuiper 37, BM McMillan 44, JB Commins 43, DB Rundle 36*)
Imp 204/2 (MJ Cann 60, NM Snyman 54, WS Truter 32*, LJ Koen 45*)

Western Province beat Border by 8 wickets, 1 November 1991, East London
Bdr 47 (BM McMillan 3/8, EO Simons 4/3)
WP 51/2

Western Province beat Northern Transvaal by 6 wickets, 6 November 1991, Verwoerdburg
N Tvl 187/5 (M Yachad 42, MD Haysman 96)
WP 190/4 (TN Lazard 77*, KC Jackson 31, JB Commins 50)

Western Province beat Western Transvaal by 8 wickets, 23 November 1991, Potchefstroom
W Tvl 162 (JJ Scholtz 48, HG Prinsloo 32, AJ van Deventer 35; CR Matthews 3/29)
WP 164/2 (TN Lazard 65, KC Jackson 51*)

Western Province beat Orange Free State by 27 runs, 9 December 1991, Bloemfontein
WP 209/9 (KC Jackson 40, BM McMillan 57; AA Donald 4/32)
OFS 182/8 (JM Arthur 126*; EO Simons 3/35)

Eastern Province beat Western Province by 6 wickets, 15 December 1991, Port Elizabeth
WP 261/8 (TN Lazard 105, KC Jackson 58, AP Kuiper 42; EAE Baptiste 3/52)
EP 263/4 (KC Wessels 57, MW Rushmere 108*, MC Venter 47)

Western Province beat Transvaal by 7 wickets, 18 December 1991, Cape Town
Tvl 178 (RF Pienaar 62, CEB Rice 58; MW Pringle 5/36, EO Simons 4/54)
WP 181/3 (TN Lazard 76*, BM McMillan 31*)

Eastern Province beat Western Province by 12 runs, 21 December 1991, Cape Town
EP 215/5 (M Michau 94, DJ Richardson 51*; CR Matthews 3/30)
WP 203 (KC Jackson 59, BM McMillan 44, F Davids 30; RE Bryson 3/35, BN Schultz 3/36, PA Rayment 3/33)

Western Province beat Natal by 5 runs, 12 February 1992, Cape Town
WP 181/7 (KC Jackson 45, EO Simons 38*, DB Rundle 75)
Ntl 176/8 (IB Hobson 55; CR Matthews 3/41)

Western Province beat Eastern Province by 65 runs, 5 March 1992, Cape Town
WP 213/6 (KC Jackson 37, G Kirsten 56)
EP 148 (GC Victor 56)

Western Province beat Transvaal by 3 wickets, 11 March 1992, Johannesburg
Tvl 198/9 (DJ Cullinan 104*; VA Barnes 3/39)
WP 201/7 (TN Lazard 88, KC Jackson 47)

Western Province beat Transvaal by 4 wickets, 13 March 1992, Cape Town
Tvl 140 (HA Page 44; VA Barnes 3/18)
WP 141/6 (G Kirsten 39, MF Voss 41; HA Page 4/25)

Eastern Province beat Western Province by 6 wickets, 1 April 1992, Johannesburg
WP 244/2 (TN Lazard 108*, AP Kuiper 107*)
EP 246/4 (KC Wessels 103, PG Amm 33, MW Rushmere 64)

Western Province beat Border CD by 127 runs, 3 October 1992, Queenstown
WP 277/4 (G Kirsten 103, BM McMillan 58*, F Davids 35*)
BdrCD 150 (MW Pringle 3/33, DQ MacHelm 4/41)

Western Province beat Impalas by 56 runs, 8 October 1992, Springs
WP 173/3 (TN Lazard 41, G Kirsten 42)
Imp 117/9 (NM Snyman 41, SE Mitchley 32*; CR Matthews 4/24)

Natal beat Western Province by 4 wickets, 21 October 1992, Durban
WP 186/5 (AP Kuiper 62*, EO Simons 43)
Ntl 188/6 (MB Logan 38, CEB Rice 46*)

Western Province beat Border by 66 runs, 16 January 1993, East London
WP 228/5 (AP Plantema 32, G Kirsten 88, BM McMillan 46)
Bdr 162 (BM Osborne 30, GC Victor 31; EO Simons 4/22)

Western Province beat Orange Free State by 5 wickets, 23 January 1993, Cape Town
OFS 153/7 (GFJ Liebenberg 37*, O Henry 34)
WP 154/5 (G Kirsten 33)

Orange Free State beat Western Province by 1 run, 30 January 1993, Bloemfontein
OFS 224/9 (GFJ Liebenberg 37, LJ Wilkinson 52, O Henry 48)
WP 223/8 (AJ Lamb 42, BM McMillan 56, EO Simons 36*; BT Player 3/35)

Orange Free State beat Western Province by 7 wickets, 31 January 1993, Bloemfontein
WP 224/8 (KC Jackson 45, G Kirsten 41, AJ Lamb 53)
OFS 225/3 (JM Arthur 56, GFJ Liebenberg 35, WJ Cronje 72, LJ Wilkinson 57*)

Western Province beat Northern Transvaal by 3 wickets, 3 March 1993, Cape Town
N Tvl 187/8 (PH Barnard 32, BC Lara 36, JJ Strydom 38; DB Rundle 3/44)
WP 191/7 (EO Simons 59*; T Bosch 3/36)

Western Province beat Border by 5 wickets, 10 March 1993, Cape Town
Bdr 149 (GC Victor 30, PC Strydom 37; EO Simons 3/39)
WP 151/5 (AJ Lamb 51)

Transvaal beat Western Province by 4 runs, 17 March 1993, Johannesburg
Tvl 188/5 (M Yachad 47, SJ Cook 53, RP Snell 39*)
WP 184/6 (FB Touzel 66, AJ Lamb 35, BM McMillan 32)

Eastern Province beat Western Province by 6 wickets, 19 March 1993, Port Elizabeth
WP 207/7 (FB Touzel 40, AJ Lamb 62, BM McMillan 44)
EP 211/4 (DJ Callaghan 82*, MC Venter 65*)

Western Province beat Orange Free State by 20 runs, 24 March 1993, Cape Town
WP 107 (FD Stephenson 5/10)
OFS 87 (EO Simons 3/16, DB Rundle 3/10)

Natal beat Western Province by 39 runs, 30 March 1993, Cape Town
Ntl 173/5 (AC Hudson 38, MB Logan 37, JN Rhodes 47*)
WP 134 (AJ Lamb 34, DB Rundle 34; MD Marshall 4/15)

Natal beat Western Province by 4 wickets, 2 April 1993, Durban
WP 164/9 (G Kirsten 38; DN Crookes 4/37)
Ntl 165/6 (MB Logan 40)

No result between Transvaal and Western Province, 5 November 1993, Johannesburg
Tvl 166/5 (M Yachad 56, SJ Cook 52, DR Laing 38*; DB Rundle 3/63)
WP did not bat

Western Province beat Border by 21 runs, 12 November 1993, East London
WP 252/4 (D Jordaan 91, G Kirsten 68, AP Kuiper 56*)
Bdr 231 (PJ Botha 73, OD Gibson 36, IL Howell 50; A Martyn 4/52)

Orange Free State beat Western Province by 61 runs, 19 November 1993, Bloemfontein
OFS 271/8 (JM Arthur 38, JF Venter 55, CJPG van Zyl 59*; AC Dawson 3/45)
WP 210 (G Kirsten 31, AP Kuiper 66, AC Dawson 31; FD Stephenson 3/19)

Western Province beat Impalas by 30 runs, 15 December 1993, Cape Town
WP 257/5 (D Jordaan 116, AP Kuiper 75)
Imp 227/8 (JE Morris 68, WE Schonegevel 46, AJ van Deventer 47; AC Dawson 4/45)

Western Province beat Boland by 95 runs, 17 December 1993, Cape Town
WP 217/8 (AP Kuiper 52, EO Simons 67; PAJ DeFreitas 3/22, HS Williams 3/43)
Bol 122 (EO Simons 4/14)

Western Province beat Northern Transvaal by 5 wickets, 22 December 1993, Cape Town
N Tvl 161 (MJR Rindel 82; MW Pringle 4/36, EO Simons 3/20, AC Dawson 3/33)
WP 162/5 (D Jordaan 40, HH Gibbs 53*)

Western Province beat Eastern Province by 11 runs, 7 January 1994, Cape Town
WP 206/7 (CA Best 57, AP Kuiper 30, AC Dawson 44*; TG Shaw 3/22)
EP 195/7 (TG Shaw 56*, PA Rayment 45*; AC Dawson 3/39, AP Kuiper 3/26)

Natal beat Western Province by 102 runs, 12 January 1994, Durban
Ntl 249/7 (NE Wright 40, ML Bruyns 38, DM Benkenstein 33, MD Marshall 63, DN Crookes 37*)
WP 147 (EO Simons 31; MD Marshall 3/19, L Klusener 3/24)

Western Province beat Orange Free State by 74 runs, 2 February 1994, Cape Town
WP 192/9 (MW Pringle 31, EO Simons 55*; BT Player 4/41)
OFS 118 (MA Meyer 4/26, EO Simons 4/19)

Orange Free State beat Western Province by 63 runs, 4 February 1994, Bloemfontein
OFS 237/7 (JM Arthur 44, WJ Cronje 120)
WP 174 (AP Kuiper 52; N Boje 3/38)

Orange Free State beat Western Province by 5 runs, 6 February 1994, Bloemfontein
OFS 145 (FD Stephenson 44, N Boje 34*; DB Rundle 3/33)
WP 140 (DB Rundle 44, CR Matthews 31*; FD Stephenson 3/12)

Northern Transvaal beat Western Province by 4 wickets, 21 October 1994, Verwoerdburg
WP 248/7 (SG Koenig 43, DL Haynes 104, D Jordaan 41)
N Tvl 251/6 (MJR Rindel 108*, JJ Strydom 47)

Griqualand West beat Western Province by 4 wickets, 28 October 1994, Kimberley
WP 182/8 (DL Haynes 50, DB Rundle 47*)
GW 183/6 (WE Schonegevel 46, RA Koster 53; DB Rundle 3/34)

Western Province beat Eastern Province by 5 wickets, 23 November 1994, Cape Town
E Tvl 161 (IA Hoffmann 33, SM Skeete 31; DB Rundle 3/23, EO Simons 3/29)
WP 162/5 (HH Gibbs 32, JH Kallis 31*, EO Simons 34)

Western Province beat Natal by 25 runs, 1 February 1995, Durban
WP 197/9 (G Kirsten 52, SG Koenig 38; SM Pollock 3/35)
Ntl 172 (ML Bruyns 49, NC Johnson 36; EO Simons 3/23)

Western Province beat Boland by 3 wickets, 10 February 1995, Paarl
Bol 171/9 (LD Ferreira 68; F Davids 3/23)
WP 174/7 (HD Ackerman 34)

Western Province beat Border by 4 wickets, 24 February 1995, Cape Town
Bdr 176 (SJ Palframan 56, FJC Cronje 39; DG Payne 5/40)
WP 179/6 (HD Ackerman 77, AP Kuiper 38*)

Eastern Province beat Western Province by 1 wicket, 3 March 1995, Port Elizabeth
WP 215/4 (HD Ackerman 40, JH Kallis 116*)
EP 218/9 (PG Amm 68, LJ Koen 45, EAE Baptiste 48*)

Western Province beat Orange Free State by 48 runs, 15 March 1995, Cape Town
WP 201/8 (HD Ackerman 68; AA Donald 3/37)
OFS 153 (PJR Steyn 64; AC Dawson 5/39)

Western Province beat Western Transvaal by 4 wickets, 24 March 1995, Cape Town
W Tvl 124/9 (CP Dettmer 41)
WP 128/6 (G Kirsten 31, AP Kuiper 41)

Orange Free State beat Western Province by 24 runs, 31 March 1995, Cape Town
OFS 253/8 (PJR Steyn 63, WJ Cronje 101)
WP 229 (DL Haynes 92; FD Stephenson 3/41, AA Donald 3/35)

Western Province beat Free State by 6 wickets, 13 October 1995, Bloemfontein
FS 216/6 (PJL Radley 39, LJ Wilkinson 72, HH Dippenaar 37*)
WP 217/4 (JH Kallis 101, HD Ackerman 78*)

Western Province beat Easterns by 99 runs, 1 November 1995, Springs
WP 256/6 (DL Haynes 37, JB Commins 37, BM McMillan 69*; SM Skeete 3/59)
Eas 157 (CR Norris 34, GP Cooke 50; MW Pringle 3/27, CR Matthews 3/23)

Western Province beat Eastern Province by 8 wickets, 22 November 1995, Port Elizabeth
EP 171/5 (KC Wessels 82, LJ Koen 31)
WP 172/2 (G Kirsten 104*)

Western Province beat Griqualand West by faster scoring rate, 29 November 1995, Cape Town
WP 164/8 (EO Simons 74*, P Kirsten 40; CV English 3/24)
GW 66/5

Western Province beat Northern Transvaal by 7 wickets, 22 December 1995, Cape Town
NT 185 (RF Pienaar 31, MJR Rindel 41; MW Pringle 3/44)
WP 186/3 (DL Haynes 102, JH Kallis 63*)

Western Province beat England XI by 3 wickets, 6 January 1996, Cape Town
Eng 196 (NH Fairbrother 46, C White 46; MW Pringle 4/34)
WP 200/7 (F Davids 55*, P Kirsten 32*)

Western Province beat Border by 59 runs, 20 January 1996, Cape Town
WP 249/6 (DL Haynes 106, HH Gibbs 45, HD Ackerman 30)
Bdr 190/9 (SJ Palframan 68, SC Pope 42*)

Western Province beat Boland by 13 runs, 2 February 1996, Cape Town
WP 245/3 (HH Gibbs 57, HD Ackerman 81, JB Commins 67*)
Bol 232 (TN Lazard 89, KC Jackson 81; A Martyn 3/47)

Western Province beat Western Transvaal by 9 wickets, 14 February 1996, Fochville
WT 134 (AJ van Deventer 39, BD Esterhuysen 41; MW Pringle 3/16, DB Rundle 4/19)
WP 135/1 (SG Koenig 42, HH Gibbs 73*)

Western Province beat Transvaal by faster scoring rate, 19 February 1996, Johannesburg
Tvl 188 (KR Rutherford 45; EO Simons 3/28)
WP 185/3 (HH Gibbs 89*, JB Commins 56)

Western Province beat Natal by 54 runs, 1 March 1996, Cape Town
WP 226/4 (HH Gibbs 101, HD Ackerman 55, F Davids 32*)
Ntl 172 (KA Forde 32, DN Crookes 34; A Martyn 3/16)

Free State beat Western Province by 5 wickets, 15 March 1996, Bloemfontein
WP 204 (G Kirsten 48, BM McMillan 37, P Kirsten 37; AA Donald 3/44)
FS 205/5 (FD Stephenson 36, CF Craven 59*; BM McMillan 4/36)

Free State beat Western Province by 4 wickets, 22 March 1996, Cape Town
WP 160/9 (BM McMillan 50; FD Stephenson 4/16, AA Donald 3/20)
FS 162/6 (FD Stephenson 40, WJ Cronje 59*)

Western Province beat Natal by 51 runs, 11 October 1996, Durban
WP 206/8 (G Kirsten 60; T Bosch 3/39)
Ntl 155 (KA Forde 33*)

Northern Transvaal beat Western Province by 1 wicket, 18 October 1996, Centurion
WP 182/8 (DL Haynes 45, JB Commins 50*)
N Tvl 186/9 (MJR Rindel 43, DJ van Zyl 44*; JH Kallis 3/42)

Western Province beat Easterns by faster scoring rate, 23 October 1996, Cape Town
Eas 113/7
WP 129/5 (JB Commins 53, EO Simons 49*; JR Meyer 3/21)

Western Province beat Boland by 6 wickets, 25 October 1996, Paarl
Bol 135 (LD Ferreira 37, AR Wylie 35*; EO Simons 4/17)
WP 136/4 (HD Ackerman 38, EO Simons 36*)

Western Province beat North West by 3 wickets, 9 November 1996, Fochville
NW 243/5 (M Strydom 92, GM Hewitt 31, MC Venter 77*; EO Simons 3/43)
WP 244/7 (DL Haynes 34, JB Commins 84*, EO Simons 42, DB Rundle 34)

Western Province beat Griqualand West by 5 wickets, 20 November 1996, Cape Town
GW 163/8 (WM Dry 55)
WP 164/5 (DL Haynes 48, JH Kallis 31, JB Commins 37*; VA Walsh 3/41)

Western Province beat Border by 72 runs, 23 November 1996, East London
WP 174/6 (HD Ackerman 62*, DB Rundle 73; VC Drakes 3/38)
Bdr 102 (SC Pope 31; BN Schultz 4/19, EO Simons 3/5)

Eastern Province beat Western Province by 9 runs, 27 November 1996, Cape Town
EP 217/9 (GC Victor 72, MW Rushmere 34*; EO Simons 3/40)
WP 208 (JH Kallis 78, DB Rundle 39; M Hayward 4/26)

Western Province beat Free State by 110 runs, 7 December 1996, Cape Town
WP 291/3 (DL Haynes 94, JH Kallis 72, HD Ackerman 61*)
FS 181 (JF Venter 37; EO Simons 4/39)

Western Province beat Transvaal by 15 runs, 20 December 1996, Cape Town
WP 229/7 (JH Kallis 72, HH Gibbs 53)
Tvl 214/9 (AM Bacher 86; MW Pringle 3/32)

Western Province beat Transvaal by 8 runs, 19 February 1997, Cape Town
WP 188 (JH Kallis 50, JB Commins 30; S Jacobs 3/28)
Tvl 180/8 (N Pothas 44, AJ Hall 57*)

No result between Western Province and Northern Transvaal, 20 April 1997, Centurion
WP 230/7 (HH Gibbs 39, JH Kallis 86, HD Ackerman 32, EO Simons 30; PS de Villiers 3/41)
N Tvl 30/0

Western Province beat Northern Transvaal by 73 runs, 21 April 1997, Centurion
WP 215/7 (HD Ackerman 57, BM McMillan 33, EO Simons 59*; S Elworthy 3/28)
N Tvl 142 (M van Jaarsveld 41, AJ Seymore 34; AC Dawson 3/30)

Western Province beat Natal by 6 wickets, 25 April 1997, Cape Town
Ntl 174 (L Klusener 34, NC Johnson 49, DM Benkenstein 30; EO Simons 3/24)
WP 175/4 (G Kirsten 62, HH Gibbs 30, JH Kallis 43)

Natal beat Western Province by 3 wickets, 27 April 1997, Durban
WP 238/7 (G Kirsten 63, HH Gibbs 40, HD Ackerman 42, BM McMillan 31)
Ntl 239/7 (AC Hudson 37, DJ Watson 60, JN Rhodes 46*)

Natal beat Western Province by 2 wickets, 28 April 1997, Durban
WP 228/8 (G Kirsten 33, JH Kallis 56, HD Ackerman 40, EO Simons 35)
Ntl 232/8 (DJ Watson 53, PL Symcox 40, JN Rhodes 31, DM Benkenstein 37*)

Western Province beat Griqualand West by 4 wickets, 3 October 1997, Kimberley
GW 227/9 (JM Arthur 38, MI Gidley 40, WM Dry 53)
WP 228/6 (JB Commins 78, AC Dawson 31*)

Western Province beat Free State by 6 wickets, 22 October 1997, Bloemfontein
FS 211 (GFJ Liebenberg 101)
WP 212/4 (HH Gibbs 110*, JB Commins 42)

Western Province beat Gauteng by 3 runs, 31 October 1997, Johannesburg
WP 243/9 (LD Ferreira 76, EO Simons 54)
Gau 240/6 (KR Rutherford 60, DR Laing 57, N Pothas 39*)

Western Province beat Easterns by 8 wickets, 1 November 1997, Benoni
Eas 70 (DG Payne 3/16)
WP 71/2

Western Province beat North West by 9 wickets, 7 November 1997, Cape Town
NW 145/8 (EG Poole 36*, JN Dreyer 45*; BM McMillan 3/18)
WP 147/1 (HH Gibbs 94)

Western Province beat Eastern Province by 12 runs, 9 November 1997, Port Elizabeth
WP 224/9 (BT Player 34, HD Ackerman 41, P Kirsten 67; MW Pringle 3/48, M Hayward 3/49)
EP 212 (KC Wessels 80, MW Rushmere 72; AC Dawson 3/32)

Border beat Western Province by 1 run, 10 December 1997, Cape Town
Bdr 220/9 (CC van der Merwe 94, PC Strydom 58; CR Matthews 4/24)
WP 219/7 (LD Ferreira 46, BT Player 39, JB Commins 36; BM White 4/31)

Western Province beat Boland by faster scoring rate, 17 December 1997, Cape Town
WP 179/8 (P Kirsten 40*; R Telemachus 3/24)
Bol 84 (AC Dawson 4/13, EO Simons 3/14)

Western Province beat Natal by 3 wickets, 23 December 1997, Cape Town
Ntl 206 (NC Johnson 46, AC Hudson 38, DM Benkenstein 59; AC Dawson 3/19, EO Simons 3/50)
WP 208/7 (DB Rundle 32, P Kirsten 38)

Western Province beat Northerns by 33 runs, 1 January 1998, Cape Town
WP 221/5 (LD Ferreira 55, H Pangarker 68, HD Ackerman 35*)
Nor 188 (MJR Rindel 35, S Elworthy 67; EO Simons 4/30)

Free State beat Western Province by 74 runs, 9-10 January 1998, Cape Town
FS 204/9 (JF Venter 40, GFJ Liebenberg 31, WJ Smit 43*; AC Dawson 3/26)
WP 130 (HD Ackerman 38, EO Simons 31; HC Bakkes 5/7)

North West beat Western Province by 103 runs, 2 October 1998, Fochville
NW 273/6 (M Strydom 93, LP Vorster 34, MJ Lavine 42, A Jacobs 31, CT Enslin 32*)
WP 170 (BM McMillan 62, HH Gibbs 31, HD Ackerman 32; D Rossouw 3/43, M Strydom 4/16)

No result between Northerns and Western Province, 9 October 1998, Centurion
Nor 35/0
WP did not bat

Western Province beat Griqualand West by faster scoring rate, 4 December 1998, Cape Town
GW 166/9 (KC Wessels 44, PH Barnard 34)
WP 116/3 (G Kirsten 42*, HH Gibbs 53; AJ Swanepoel 3/24)

Eastern Province beat Western Province by 58 runs, 16 December 1998, Cape Town
EP 207/8 (GV Grace 62, JDC Bryant 32, MW Rushmere 39; R Munnik 3/24)
WP 149 (JH Kallis 47; EAE Baptiste 4/22)

Western Province beat Gauteng by 16 runs, 23 December 1998, Cape Town
WP 225/5 (G Kirsten 58, HH Gibbs 74, JH Kallis 58)
Gau 209 (N Pothas 35, AJ Hall 32, RE Veenstra 40)

Western Province beat by 78 runs, 23 January 1999, Cape Town
WP 270/5 (LD Ferreira 56, BM McMillan 100, HD Ackerman 59)
FS 192 (JF Venter 39, JA Beukes 35, LJ Wilkinson 31; R Munnik 3/47, PR Adams 3/37)

Easterns beat Western Province by 43 runs, 29 January 1999, Cape Town
Eas 126/7 (D Brand 35, CR Norris 37*; EO Simons 3/24)
WP 83 (LD Botha 3/26)

Western Province beat KwaZulu-Natal by 110 runs, 31 January 1999, Durban
WP 217/4 (BM McMillan 32, HD Ackerman 85*)
KZN 107 (AC Hudson 47; PR Adams 3/12)

Western Province beat Boland by 139 runs, 6 February 1999, Paarl
WP 203/9 (BM McMillan 39, JB Commins 76; CK Langeveldt 3/27)
Bol 64 (R Munnik 3/14)

Border beat Western Province by 7 wickets, 10 February 1999, East London
WP 56 (M Ntini 3/18, T Henderson 5/5)
Bdr 57/3 (PC Strydom 31*)

Western Province beat Boland by 5 wickets, 10 March 1999, Cape Town
Bol 154/9 (KC Jackson 33; CR Matthews 4/35)
WP 155/5 (BM McMillan 63*; DM Koch 3/25)

Griqualand West beat Western Province by 19 runs, 14 March 1999, Kimberley
GW 207/6 (KC Wessels 42, FC Brooker 40, OD Gibson 42, PL Symcox 37*; BT Player 3/50)
WP 188 (JB Commins 53; GA Roe 4/33)

Western Province beat Gauteng by 4 wickets, 15 December 1999, Cape Town
Gau 195/6 (SG Koenig 45, AJ Hall 46, G Toyana 41; R Telemachus 3/37, CR Matthews 3/39)
WP 196/6 (AG Prince 39, BM McMillan 44*, TL Tsolekile 37*)

KwaZulu-Natal beat Western Province by 29 runs, 22 December 1999, Cape Town
KZN 214/5 (DJ Watson 57, DM Benkenstein 78*, L Klusener 48*; AC Dawson 3/24)
WP 185 (JH Kallis 46, HD Ackerman 58; EAE Baptiste 3/33)

Northerns beat Western Province by 6 wickets, 18 February 2000, Cape Town
WP 174 (LD Ferreira 43)
Nor 177/4 (M van Jaarsveld 73*, G Dros 33*)

Eastern Province beat Western Province by 84 runs, 20 February 2000, Port Elizabeth
EP 186/8 (MR Benfield 38, DJ Callaghan 50, JM Kemp 57*)
WP 102 (MW Pringle 4/15)

Western Province beat Free State by 24 runs, 23 February 2000, Bloemfontein
WP 144 (HD Ackerman 42, AC Dawson 31; PV Mpitsang 3/26, JF Venter 3/23)
FS 120 (R Telemachus 3/28, CR Matthews 3/13)

North West beat Western Province by 3 wickets, 25 February 2000, Cape Town
WP 126 (DJ Pryke 4/16)
NW 130/7 (M Strydom 35)

Boland beat Western Province by 19 runs, 1 March 2000, Paarl
Bol 161 (IJL Trott 37, PK Amre 38, KC Jackson 54; BM McMillan 4/23)
WP 142 (CM Willoughby 3/26, CK Langeveldt 5/35)

Griqualand West beat Western Province by 22 runs, 5 March 2000, Cape Town
GW 222/5 (MI Gidley 60, GD Elliott 44, LL Bosman 44*)
WP 200/6 (TL Tsolekile 44, HD Ackerman 78*, AG Prince 34)

Northerns beat Western Province by 3 wickets, 6 October 2000, Centurion
WP 229/6 (HD Ackerman 92, AG Puttick 75*; S Elworthy 3/34, P Joubert 3/51)
Nor 232/7 (PJR Steyn 111*, G Dros 36; AC Dawson 3/38)

North West beat Western Province by 4 wickets, 13 October 2000, Potchefstroom
WP 258/5 (GC Smith 106, NC Johnson 58, LD Ferreira 38; GA Roe 3/55)
NW 261/6 (GM Hewitt 42, HM de Vos 82*, C Light 33, MJ Lavine 44; GC Smith 3/46)

Western Province beat Griqualand West by 144 runs, 18 October 2000, Kimberley
WP 229/7 (HH Gibbs 71, G Kirsten 51)
GW 85 (AC Dawson 5/13)

KwaZulu-Natal beat Western Province by 28 runs, 17 November 2000, Durban
KZN 216/9 (A Mall 40, JN Rhodes 42, ELR Stewart 45*)
WP 188/9 (NC Johnson 48, AG Prince 76*; EAE Baptiste 3/17)

Border beat Western Province by 4 wickets, 1 December 2000, Cape Town
WP 220/7 (NC Johnson 94)
Bdr 222/6 (LL Gamiet 45, SC Pope 55, CB Sugden 33)

Western Province beat Easterns by 7 runs, 8 December 2000, Cape Town
WP 248/4 (NC Johnson 111, GC Smith 47, HD Ackerman 41*)
Eas 241/4 (MJR Rindel 82, DN Crookes 73, GA Pollock 34*)

Gauteng beat Western Province by 21 runs, 16 December 2000, Johannesburg
Gau 226/7 (AM Bacher 73, JM Otto 47*; R Munnik 4/50)
WP 205 (HH Gibbs 105; DJ Terbrugge 4/31)

Western Province beat Eastern Province by 9 wickets, 22 December 2000, Cape Town
EP 198/6 (CC Bradfield 34, JDC Bryant 105*, DJ Callaghan 35; JH Kallis 5/47)
WP 200/1 (G Kirsten 85*, HH Gibbs 90)

Western Province beat Free State by 50 runs, 27 December 2000, Cape Town
WP 244/5 (NC Johnson 91, AG Prince 67*)
FS 194 (JF Venter 80, WJ Smit 35; AC Dawson 4/29, R Telemachus 3/33, CW Henderson 3/46)

Western Province beat Boland by 5 runs, 19 January 2001, Cape Town
WP 191/9 (NC Johnson 43, AG Prince 61; CK Langeveldt 3/42)
Bol 186 (JL Ontong 66; R Telemachus 3/37)

Western Province beat Easterns by 8 wickets, 18 November 2001, Benoni
Eas 200/9 (AJ Seymore 55, AJ Hall 55)
WP 201/2 (GC Smith 60, NC Johnson 41, AG Puttick 37*, HD Ackerman 45*)

Western Province beat Gauteng by 73 runs, 23 November 2001, Cape Town
WP 227/7 (GC Smith 83, AG Puttick 34, AG Prince 41*; JT Mafa 4/49)
Gau 154 (NJ Trainor 56; CW Henderson 4/33)

Western Province beat North West by 7 runs, 7 December 2001, Cape Town
WP 224/7 (GC Smith 97, IJL Trott 50)
NW 217/9 (GV Grace 35, MC Venter 59; R Telemachus 3/37, PR Adams 3/46)

Western Province beat Free State by 47 runs, 19 December 2001, Bloemfontein
WP 227/6 (GC Smith 87, HD Ackerman 32, AG Prince 30)
FS 180 (JA Beukes 33, HC Bakkes 52; GC Smith 3/35)

Northerns beat Western Province by 2 wickets, 26 December 2001, Cape Town
WP 185/9 (LD Ferreira 65)
Nor 186/8 (G Dros 35; AC Dawson 3/40)

Boland beat Western Province by 4 wickets, 28 December 2001, Paarl
WP 262/5 (GC Smith 91, LD Ferreira 46, NC Johnson 56)
Bol 263/6 (JG Strydom 135*, LJ Koen 40)

Border beat Western Province by 99 runs, 9 January 2002, East London
Bdr 235/7 (ML Bruyns 41, BC de Wett 47, PC Strydom 55; AC Dawson 3/34)
WP 136 (NC Johnson 33, HD Ackerman 39; PC Strydom 6/17)

Western Province beat Griqualand West by 24 runs, 18 January 2002, Cape Town
WP 195/9 (GC Smith 70; GJ Kruis 3/52)
GW 171 (LL Bosman 37, MI Gidley 32, BH Tucker 32; CW Henderson 4/29, GC Smith 3/36)

Western Province beat Eastern Province by faster scoring rate, 25 January 2002, Port Elizabeth
EP 185/7 (RJ Peterson 47, MR Benfield 39, BR Friderichs 30*, MW Pringle 39*)
WP 203/2 (GC Smith 73, LD Ferreira 62, AG Prince 32*)

Western Province beat North West by 3 wickets, 30 January 2002, Potchefstroom
NW 235 (A Jacobs 73, MC Venter 67; R Telemachus 3/25, GC Smith 3/51)
WP 238/7 (LD Ferreira 134; R Niewoudt 3/39)

Western Province beat North West by 89 runs, 1 February 2002, Cape Town
WP 229/4 (GC Smith 117*, LD Ferreira 46, IJL Trott 30*)
NW 140

KwaZulu-Natal beat Western Province by 28 runs, 8 February 2002, Durban
KZN 223/6 (DM Benkenstein 77*, ELR Stewart 53; Q Friend 3/52)
WP 195/9 (AG Puttick 51, AC Dawson 52*; NAM McLean 3/35, ANW Tweedie 4/33)

Western Province beat Namibia by 62 runs, 13 November 2002, Cape Town
WP 186/5 (J-P Duminy 78, R Munnik 57*)
Nam 124 (D Keulder 44, AJ Burger 33; AC Dawson 5/14)

Western Province beat Eastern Province by 18 runs, 20 November 2002, Cape Town
WP 231/2 (AG Puttick 113*, HD Ackerman 74)
EP 213/8 (ML Price 34, JDC Bryant 58*; R Munnik 3/37)

Western Province beat Gauteng by 44 runs, 22 November 2002, Johannesburg
WP 243/4 (NC Johnson 98, HD Ackerman 66, AG Prince 42)
Gau 199 (JM Otto 37, VB van Jaarsveld 57; AC Dawson 3/31, M de Stadler 3/20)

Western Province beat Free State by 6 wickets (D/L method), target revised to 124 in 32 overs, 21 December 2002, Cape Town
FS 125/7 (HH Dippenaar 44; CM Willoughby 3/29)
WP 124/4 (G Kirsten 53*)

Boland beat Western Province by 4 wickets, 29 December 2002, Paarl
WP 194/8 (AG Prince 42, J-P Duminy 69, AC Dawson 33; HS Williams 3/34, CK Langeveldt 3/45)
Bol 198/6 (C Baxter 32, VG Kambli 63, SJ Palframan 31*)

Western Province beat Border by 23 runs, 10 January 2003, East London
WP 228/7 (JH Kallis 88, G Kirsten 103)
Bdr 205 (T Henderson 39, CB Sugden 50, LL Gamiet 33, L Graham 32*; AC Dawson 3/42, JH Kallis 3/44)

Western Province beat Griqualand West by 9 wickets, 15 January 2003, Cape Town
GW 125 (MI Gidley 59; AC Dawson 3/15, CW Henderson 4/26)
WP 129/1 (HH Gibbs 67*, G Kirsten 46*)

Western Province beat Border by 6 wickets, 21 November 2003, Cape Town
Bdr 218/9 (SC Pope 34, MV Boucher 70, LL Gamiet 37)
WP 222/4 (GC Smith 67, HH Gibbs 59, NC Johnson 40*, JH Kallis 32)

Western Province beat Free State by 6 wickets, 28 November 2003, Bloemfontein
FS 234/8 (MN van Wyk 51, JA Beukes 43, HH Dippenaar 76)
WP 237/4 (GC Smith 114*, NC Johnson 42, AG Prince 40*; WA Deacon 4/39)

Western Province beat Griqualand West by 10 runs, 30 November 2003, Kimberley
WP 243/3 (NC Johnson 81, JH Kallis 109*)
GW 233/6 (B Hector 62, MI Gidley 58, W Bossenger 34*)

Western Province beat Boland by 138 runs, 5 December 2003, Cape Town
WP 272/3 (GC Smith 71, HH Gibbs 98, NC Johnson 61*, AG Prince 35*)
Bol 134 (JG Strydom 45; CM Willoughby 3/29, CW Henderson 3/27)

Western Province beat Eastern Province by 7 wickets, 7 December 2003, Port Elizabeth
EP 193/8 (RJ Peterson 32, WR Wingfield 39, I Mitchell 39; JH Kallis 3/42, M de Stadler 4/35)
WP 194/3 (GC Smith 51, HH Gibbs 47, JH Kallis 30*)

Western Province beat KwaZulu-Natal by 6 wickets, 20 December 2003, Cape Town
KZN 154 (JC Kent 40*; CW Henderson 3/29)
WP 155/4 (JH Kallis 74*, AG Puttick 39*)

Gauteng beat by 4 runs (D/L method), target revised to 118 in 22 overs, 9 January 2004, Johannesburg
Gau 185/7 (SC Cook 34, JM Otto 36, DN Crookes 45; AC Dawson 3/33)
WP 113/7

Western Province beat North West by 9 wickets, 11 January 2004, Potchefstroom
NW 173/8 (DJJ de Vos 52*, GA Roe 34*; RK Kleinveldt 3/26)
WP 177/1 (AG Puttick 59, NC Johnson 104*)

No result between Western Province and Northerns, 14 January 2004, Cape Town
WP 45/2
Nor did not bat

Western Province beat Easterns by 9 runs, 8 February 2004, Cape Town
WP 244/6 (LD Ferreira 56, J-P Duminy 88; GE Flusk 3/54)
Eas 235/5 (SG Koenig 49, AJ Seymore 41, Z de Bruyn 68, P de Bruyn 30, DJ Cullinan 39*)

Easterns beat Western Province by 4 wickets, 20 February 2004, Cape Town
WP 197/8 (J-P Duminy 51, R Munnik 33; Z de Bruyn 5/44)
Eas 198/6 (SG Koenig 95*, DJ Cullinan 31; AC Dawson 3/30)

10.2 Western Province Cricket Association B, 1991/92–2003/04

For eight years after cricket unity, the United Cricket Board of South Africa continued with the so-called B Section competitions of its predecessors, the South African Cricket Union and the South African Cricket Board, as a means of developing younger talent. In this case, the B team played only first-class cricket, no official limited-overs games. WPCA B won the UCB Bowl once (shared with Transvaal B in 1993/94) in six seasons. Western Province B did not play any games in the UCB Bowl in 1991/92 (playing in the President's Competition instead) and in 1992/93 no B teams played in the UCB Bowl. Western Province B won the UCB Bowl (limited overs) two times out of six from 1993/94 to 1998/99. It also won the Bowl three-day competition five times out of five and the Bowl limited-overs competition two times out of five from 1999/2000 to 2003/04, but the scores and players' details are not included here as these matches were not given first-class status. By the turn of the century this competition was no longer serving its purpose – there were now a plethora of opportunities for young cricketers which made it redundant. Listed below are the WPCA B caps, trophy winners and scorecards between 1991/92 and 1998/99.

10.2.1 Western Province Cricket Association B First-Class Players, 1991/92–1998/99[336]

Name	M	From	To
Ackerman, HD	5	1993/94	1993/94
Adams, N	3	1997/98	1997/98
Adams, PR	1	1995/96	1995/96
Baguley, BC	5	1994/95	1994/95
Barnes, VA	6	1991/92	1994/95
Benjamin, F	3	1993/94	1993/94
Bleekers, LF	9	1991/92	1993/94
Bramwell, G	4	1994/95	1994/95
Bulbring, SL	1	1993/94	1993/94
Cilliers, A	4	1995/96	1995/96
Commins, JB	1	1991/92	1991/92
Conrad, Shukri	5	1994/95	1994/95
Conrad, Siraaj	2	1998/99	1998/99
Copeland, CA	2	1998/99	1998/99
Crosoer, MJ	7	1996/97	1998/99
Damon, I	1	1998/99	1998/99
Davids, F	21	1991/92	1998/99
Dawson, AC	9	1993/94	1996/97
De Kock, GA	6	1995/96	1996/97
De Nobrega, JJ	5	1997/98	1998/99
De Villiers, MC	7	1993/94	1996/97
Donachie, HH	2	1994/95	1994/95
English, CV	7	1993/94	1994/95
Ferreira, LD	4	1997/98	1998/99
George, MF	4	1997/98	1997/98
Gibbs, HH	13	1991/92	1995/96
Gillett, GF	3	1995/96	1995/96
Harris, PL	1	1998/99	1998/99

Name	M	From	To
Henderson, CW	1	1998/99	1998/99
Henry, D	1	1997/98	1997/98
Hofmeyr, S	8	1996/97	1997/98
Jackson, KC	2	1991/92	1991/92
Joffe, R	2	1998/99	1998/99
Jordaan, D	7	1993/94	1994/95
Kalis, AD	3	1997/98	1998/99
Kallis, JH	3	1993/94	1993/94
Kirsten, P	5	1994/95	1994/95
Koch, DM	4	1997/98	1997/98
Koenig, SG	4	1993/94	1995/96
Koster, RA	5	1993/94	1993/94
Lewis, MR	1	1998/99	1998/99
Logenstein, QF	3	1993/94	1993/94
Loon, GI	1	1996/97	1996/97
MacHelm, DQ	19	1993/94	1997/98
Magiet, R	3	1998/99	1998/99
Maron, R	11	1995/96	1998/99
Martyn, A	4	1993/94	1995/96
McClement, AJ	6	1991/92	1993/94
Meyer, MA	6	1993/94	1995/96
Mitchell, TJ	16	1991/92	1996/97
Moleon, EO	8	1996/97	1998/99
Mullins, AK	1	1998/99	1998/99
Munnik, R	8	1997/98	1998/99
Paleker, A	2	1997/98	1997/98
Pangarker, H	19	1991/92	1998/99
Payne, DG	19	1991/92	1998/99
Player, BT	7	1997/98	1998/99
Robertson, T	4	1995/96	1995/96
Rundle, DB	9	1991/92	1996/97
Ryall, RJ	2	1993/94	1993/94
Ryan, LJ	1	1991/92	1991/92
Schultz, BN	1	1996/97	1996/97
Solomon, IR	4	1995/96	1995/96
Solomons, MT	14	1995/96	1997/98
Spilhaus, CF	5	1991/92	1991/92
Stelling, WF	2	1991/92	1993/94
Taliep, MS	2	1998/99	1998/99
Thomas, AC	3	1998/99	1998/99
Touzel, FB	24	1991/92	1996/97
Upton, PAH	1	1993/94	1993/94
Van Beuge, BW	6	1998/99	1998/99
Van Olst, M	2	1997/98	1997/98
Van Reenen, A	3	1995/96	1996/97
Voss, MF	5	1991/92	1991/92

10.2.2 Western Province B Trophy Winners, 1991/92–2003/04

President's Cup (First-Class)

Season	Winners
1992/93	Western Province

UCB Bowl (First-Class)

Season	Winners
1991/92	Eastern Transvaal [Western Province did not participate]
1992/93	Boland [Western Province did not participate]
1993/94	Transvaal B / *Western Province B (shared)*
1994/95	Natal B
1995/96	Griqualand West / Natal B (shared)
1996/97	Eastern Province B
1997/98	North West
1998/99	North West

UCB Bowl (Not First-Class)

Season	Winners
1999/2000	*Western Province B*
2000/01	*Western Province B*
2001/02	*Western Province B*
2002/03	*Western Province B*
2003/04	*Western Province B*

UCB Bowl (Limited Overs)

Season	Winners
1993/94	Orange Free State B
1994/95	Natal B
1995/96	*Western Province B*
1996/97	Eastern Province B
1997/98	Northerns B
1998/99	*Western Province B*
1999/2000	Free State B
2000/01	Zimbabwe Board XI
2001/02	*Western Province B*
2002/03	Free State B
2003/04	*Western Province B*

10.2.3 Western Province Cricket Association B First-Class Scores, 1991/92–1998/99[337]

Western Province B beat Orange Free State B by 42 runs, 18–20 October 1991, Cape Town
WPB 82/5 dec (MJ Karsten 3/29) and 235/7 dec (KC Jackson 39, LF Bleekers 43, F Davids 51, TJ Mitchell 38; CA van Ee 4/66)
OFSB 82/1 dec (D Jordaan 54*) and 193 (JM Truter 56, LJ Wenzler 31, FJC Cronje 33; DG Payne 3/33, AJ McClement 4/72)

Western Province B beat Northern Transvaal B by an innings and 74 runs, 29 November – 1 December 1991, Cape Town
NTB 180 (MB Mare 38, JD du Toit 37; DG Payne 3/51, TJ Mitchell 3/30) and 159 (IA Hoffmann 58; DG Payne 3/68)
WPB 413/8 dec (FB Touzel 69, MF Voss 115, F Davids 63, HH Gibbs 31, TJ Mitchell 59*; C van Noordwyk 3/89, DW McCosh 3/101)

Western Province B beat Transvaal B by 3 wickets, 13–15 December 1991, Johannesburg
TvlB 209 (PJ Botha 30, JJ Strydom 59, JP van der Westhuizen 46; AJ McClement 5/65) and 310/6 dec (PJ Botha 95, WV Rippon 65, JJ Strydom 58; AJ McClement 3/91)
WPB 279/6 dec (MF Voss 37, HH Gibbs 81, LF Bleekers 68) and 242/7 (FB Touzel 48, MF Voss 65, LF Bleekers 36*; AA Manack 3/59)

Match drawn between Western Province B and Eastern Province B, 10–12 January 1992, Cape Town
WPB 338/8 dec (HH Gibbs 90, F Davids 146, TJ Mitchell 30; KG Bauermeister 3/33) and 281/9 dec (FB Touzel 132, H Pangarker 36, F Davids 66; NC Johnson 4/86, BS Forbes 4/41)
EPB 193/9 dec (CB Rhodes 30, GC Victor 30, PC Strydom 46, KG Bauermeister 39; DG Payne 3/56, VA Barnes 3/60) and 194/2 (MP Stonier 73*, GC Victor 79*)

Match drawn between Natal B and Western Province B, 24–26 January 1992, Pietermaritzburg
NtlB 256 (MR Woodburn 31, AJ Forde 41, GW Bashford 79*; VA Barnes 3/44) and 210/7 dec (J Payn 36, BA Nash 36, RJ Varner 41; WF Stelling 3/52)
WPB 204 (TJ Mitchell 61, DB Rundle 31, WF Stelling 53; RJ Varner 4/42) and 167/5 (MF Voss 64*, HH Gibbs 36; DN Crookes 3/69)

Match drawn between Western Province B and Eastern Transvaal, 7–9 October 1993, Springs
WPB 244/6 dec (SG Koenig 57, HD Ackerman 30, LF Bleekers 33, TJ Mitchell 53*, CV English 35*; LCR Jordaan 4/59) and 224/5 dec (SG Koenig 33, HD Ackerman 57, TJ Mitchell 32*, PAH Upton 37*)
ET 207 (WR Radford 68, CR Norris 73*; A Martyn 6/60) and 174/9 (CR Norris 68; F Benjamin 4/40)

Match drawn between Eastern Province B and Western Province B, 29–31 October 1993, Cape Town
EPB 403/9 dec (MG Beamish 62, SC Pope 65, M Michau 35, CC Wait 103, PA Tullis 76, PA Rayment 32; MA Meyer 3/65, TJ Mitchell 3/61)
WPB 244 (HH Gibbs 43, RA Koster 43, TJ Mitchell 39, MA Meyer 34*; GA Roe 4/42, AV Birrell 3/45) and 322/3 (HH Gibbs 152*, LF Bleekers 55, RA Koster 68*)

Western Province B beat Boland B by 169 runs, 10–13 December 1993, Cape Town
WPB 299/8 dec (FB Touzel 35, HD Ackerman 42, MC de Villiers 50*, TJ Mitchell 68, MA Meyer 42; ST Jefferies 4/93) and 185/5 dec (FB Touzel 36, HD Ackerman 54, RA Koster 32; AG Elgar 3/34)
BolB 207 (WN van As 62, L-M Germishuys 68; MA Meyer 7/67) and 108 (WN van As 33; F Benjamin 4/41, TJ Mitchell 3/0)

Match drawn between Western Province B and Western Transvaal, 21–23 January 1994, Potchefstroom
WPB 384/8 dec (FB Touzel 47, JH Kallis 30, TJ Mitchell 90, RJ Ryall 61, MA Meyer 89; AH Gray 3/45)
WT 169 (AJ van Deventer 61; DQ MacHelm 6/31) and 116/3 (HM Smith 37*, HG Prinsloo 30*)

Western Province B beat Griqualand West by 43 runs, 10–12 February 1994, Kimberley
WPB 284/4 dec (HD Ackerman 154, JH Kallis 54*) and 259/1 dec (D Jordaan 105*, FB Touzel 128*)
GW 285/9 dec (WE Schonegevel 59, BE van der Vyver 127; DQ MacHelm 7/85) and 215 (JE Morris 41, KC Dugmore 66; DQ MacHelm 4/82, SL Bulbring 3/73)

Match drawn between Western Province B and Transvaal B, 12–14 March 1994, Johannesburg
WPB 171 (HH Gibbs 35, RA Koster 54, AC Dawson 37; AG Pollock 3/20) and 313/6 (D Jordaan 58, JH Kallis 69, HH Gibbs 57*, RA Koster 95)
TvlB 382/6 dec (NR Rhodes 37, WV Rippon 92, PM Boa 63, C Grainger 70, S Jacobs 41*, JP van der Westhuizen 33*)

Western Province B beat Western Transvaal by 9 wickets, 11–13 November 1994, Cape Town
WT 242 (HM de Vos 35, HG Prinsloo 82, L Botes 64; MA Meyer 3/41, DQ MacHelm 4/93) and 127 (LCW van Wyk 33; TJ Mitchell 3/15)
WPB 300/8 dec (BC Baguley 133*, HH Gibbs 60; L Botes 3/67, HG Prinsloo 3/68) and 70/1 (BC Baguley 39*)

Natal B beat Western Province B by an innings and 62 runs, 17–19 November 1994, Durban
WPB 157 (HH Gibbs 59; L Klusener 5/46, RE Veenstra 4/40) and 246 (BC Baguley 72, D Jordaan 31, FB Touzel 37, HH Gibbs 35; RK McGlashan 6/100)
NtlB 465/8 dec (DJ Watson 45, DM Benkenstein 69, DN Crookes 74, RE Veenstra 75, L Klusener 105, UH Goedeke 44*)

Western Province B beat Griqualand West by an innings and 2 runs, 2–4 December 1994, Cape Town
GW 208 (HA Page 89; G Bramwell 5/74, TJ Mitchell 3/23) and 176 (RA Koster 64, P McLaren 33*; CV English 4/30, DQ MacHelm 4/38)
WPB 386 (HH Gibbs 101, S Conrad 32, TJ Mitchell 85, AC Dawson 42; AP van Troost 3/81, P McLaren 3/66)

Match drawn between Western Province B and Northern Transvaal B, 17–19 December 1994, Verwoerdburg
WPB 278/9 dec (FB Touzel 44, S Conrad 61, HH Donachie 35, F Davids 46; GJ Kruis 3/57, N Martin 3/63) and 181 (D Jordaan 39, HH Donachie 66; DJJ de Vos 3/58, MC Krug 3/38)
NTB 241/7 dec (PH Barnard 59, WM Dry 41, C van Noordwyk 35*; DQ MacHelm 3/32) and 178/9 (I Pistorius 32, G Dros 31; DQ MacHelm 3/70, G Bramwell 3/49)

Match drawn between Western Province B and Zimbabwe Board XI, 26–28 January 1995, Cape Town
WPB 284/8 dec (FB Touzel 77, CV English 108, G Bramwell 30*; BC Strang 4/73) and 257 (BC Baguley 76, F Davids 33; PA Strang 5/88, U Ranchod 3/54)
ZimBrd 260 (SV Carlisle 47, DN Erasmus 81; F Davids 3/28, DQ MacHelm 5/57) and 86/4 (GK Bruk-Jackson 33*; F Davids 3/20)

Match drawn between Easterns and Western Province B, 27–29 October 1995, Springs
Eas 391/9 dec (MJ Mitchley 92, CR Norris 59, C Grainger 119, T Jamal 36; PR Adams 3/48) and 207/6 (B Randall 43, MJ Mitchley 58*; IR Solomon 3/53)
WPB 360/6 dec (SG Koenig 89, FB Touzel 102, F Davids 46)

Match drawn between Natal B and Western Province B, 16–18 November 1995, Cape Town
NtlB 243 (DM Benkenstein 98, RK McGlashan 64; A Martyn 6/67) and 417 (SW Broughton 31, KA Forde 40, MS Dada 34, UH Goedeke 137, AG Small 72; DB Rundle 3/49)
WPB 350 (DB Rundle 103, MT Solomons 67; KG Storey 4/78, DJ Pryke 5/92) and 7/0

Western Province B beat Free State B by 9 wickets, 25–27 November 1995, Cape Town
FSB 206 (HLM Wessels 31, IG van Aswegen 46, C Light 44, BT Player 44; A Cilliers 3/53, F Davids 4/24) and 124 (IG van Aswegen 32; AC Dawson 6/18)
WPB 289 (F Davids 52, GF Gillett 65, AC Dawson 55; SA Cilliers 3/77, H Botha 3/77) and 43/1

Match drawn between Western Transvaal and Western Province B, 25–27 January 1996, Potchefstroom
WT 97 (A Martyn 6/22, DB Rundle 3/26)
WPB 229/9 (FB Touzel 90, T Robertson 32, HH Gibbs 47; G Radford 6/70)

Western Province B beat Border B by 6 wickets, 8–10 February 1996, East London
BdrB 242 (SC Pope 44, PB du Plessis 101; A van Reenen 5/47) and 285/5 dec (CR Wilson 47, SC Pope 71, PB du Plessis 104*; DB Rundle 3/37)
WPB 275/6 dec (FB Touzel 40, MC de Villiers 88, TJ Mitchell 40, DB Rundle 69*) and 256/4 (FB Touzel 75, MC de Villiers 86, TJ Mitchell 50*; PB du Plessis 3/49)

Match drawn between Natal B and Western Province B, 14–16 November 1996, Durban
NtlB 251/6 dec (J Buxton-Forman 70, NJ Parsons 84, AG Botha 41*) and 178/5 (CB Sugden 85*, UH Goedeke 42*; BN Schultz 3/43)
WPB 277 (R Maron 41, S Hofmeyr 30, F Davids 65, GA de Kock 36; GM Gilder 4/66, KG Storey 3/82)

Easterns beat Western Province B by 28 runs, 29 November – 1 December 1996, Cape Town
Eas 304/9 dec (MJ Mitchley 201*, CR Norris 50; DG Payne 3/68, DQ MacHelm 3/90) and 96 (CR Norris 31; DG Payne 5/26)
WPB 191 (H Pangarker 34, GA de Kock 50; JR Meyer 6/43) and 181 (H Pangarker 44; CR Norris 4/47)

Western Province B beat Eastern Province B by 10 wickets, 12–14 December 1996, Port Elizabeth
EPB 241 (MG Beamish 108, CN du Plessis 30, AV Birrell 34; DB Rundle 3/57) and 178 (AG Prince 78, P Botha 40; DB Rundle 3/42, GA de Kock 3/8)
WPB 298 (F Davids 52*, H Pangarker 92, S Hofmeyr 51; A Badenhorst 3/81, P Botha 3/43, S Abrahams 3/81) and 123/0 (R Maron 65*, FB Touzel 52*)

North West beat Western Province B by 27 runs, 17–18 January 1997, Cape Town
NW 116 (LP Vorster 33; DG Payne 5/20) and 221 (M Strydom 91, D Rossouw 49, M van Schalkwyk 31*; DG Payne 3/57)
WPB 193 (H Pangarker 31, F Davids 33, MT Solomons 32, DG Payne 41*; MJ Lavine 3/57, M van Schalkwyk 4/17) and 117 (R Maron 34; F Baird 4/33, D Rossouw 4/30)

Match drawn between Transvaal B and Western Province B, 5–7 February 1997, Cape Town
TvlB 385/7 dec (HA Manack 173, DR Gain 42, RP Snell 46, NA Fusedale 44*; DQ MacHelm 3/76) and 256 (DR Gain 47, Z de Bruyn 34, RP Snell 52, GH Bodi 33; GA de Kock 3/29)
WPB 350/8 dec (H Pangarker 144, F Davids 38, GA de Kock 67, DG Payne 33*; Z de Bruyn 6/120)

Western Province B beat Natal B by 4 wickets, 30 October – 1 November 1997, Cape Town
NtlB 324 (KD Donaldson 50, UH Goedeke 124, JL Cooke 37; R Munnik 4/63) and 212 (J Buxton-Forman 43, WR Wingfield 39, AM Amla 57; MF George 3/37, DM Koch 4/35)
WPB 296/2 dec (R Maron 65, JJ de Nobrega 64, H Pangarker 128*) and 241/6 (R Maron 40, DM Koch 46*, MT Solomons 59*; RM Nienaber 3/58)

Match drawn between Northerns B and Western Province B, 13–15 November 1997, Centurion
NorB 322/9 dec (P de Bruyn 103, E de Bruyn 41, JA Rudolph 56; R Munnik 3/58, F Davids 3/47) and 217/9 dec (LL Gamiet 39, DJ Smith 59, JA Rudolph 55; MF George 4/39)
WPB 245 (R Maron 59, S Hofmeyr 31, F Davids 36, N Adams 36; RT Coetzee 7/74) and 181/6 (S Hofmeyr 35, N Adams 81*)

Eastern Province B beat Western Province B by 5 wickets, 11–13 December 1997, Bellville
WPB 290 (F Davids 109*, BT Player 79; W Walker 4/70, S Abrahams 5/71) and 305/9 dec (S Hofmeyr 31, BT Player 56, DM Koch 54, MF George 42*; S Abrahams 6/93)
EPB 339/8 dec (CC Bradfield 34, GC Victor 36, DW Murray 103*, Q Ferreira 38; BT Player 4/8) and 257/5 (GC Victor 85, JDC Bryant 63, CC Bradfield 40*, S Abrahams 33*)

Western Province B beat Easterns by 23 runs, 6–8 February 1998, Benoni
WPB 308 (MJ Crosoer 38, H Pangarker 55, R Munnik 32, MT Solomons 35, M van Olst 54; A Nel 3/63, C Kruger 4/50, J Uys 3/77) and 244/8 dec (MJ Crosoer 64, S Hofmeyr 41, A Paleker 46; J Uys 5/87)
Eas 303 (JS Lerm 112, NA Fusedale 34, CR Norris 53; DG Payne 3/65, R Munnik 3/55) and 226 (MJ Mitchley 37, JS Lerm 41, G White 32)

North West beat Western Province B by 9 wickets, 5–7 March 1998, Potchefstroom
WPB 284 (R Maron 75, R Munnik 57; DJ Pryke 5/38, EFJ Wyma 3/44) and 151 (H Pangarker 78, M van Olst 41; DJ Pryke 6/43)
NW 373/9 dec (S Nicolson 42, HM de Vos 101, A Jacobs 112, MJ Lavine 43, D Rossouw 37*; DG Payne 4/93) and 64/1 (HM de Vos 30*)

Northerns B beat Western Province B by 10 wickets, 22–24 October 1998, Cape Town
WPB 101 (EO Moleon 41; DH Townsend 6/44) and 310 (BW van Beuge 61, H Pangarker 101, AD Kalis 41, R Munnik 35; DH Townsend 3/75, MA Conyers 3/67)
NorB 318 (QR Still 56, P de Bruyn 60, G Morgan 58, JA Rudolph 35; R Munnik 3/86, F Davids 3/48) and 94/0 (JG Myburgh 75*)

Western Province B beat Griqualand West B by an innings and 22 runs, 6–7 November 1998, Kimberley
GWB 202 (AC Botha 64; BT Player 5/28) and 128 (AP McLaren 34; BT Player 3/9)
WPB 352 (H Pangarker 41, R Munnik 138, BT Player 105; ZA Abrahim 3/80, AC Botha 4/52)

Eastern Province B beat Western Province B by 19 runs, 13–15 November 1998, Port Elizabeth
EPB 242 (JDC Bryant 39, NG Brouwers 52, AD Peters 65; DG Payne 3/25, BT Player 3/44) and 230/6 dec (NG Brouwers 38, AD Peters 98, JP Smith 36)
WPB 157 (LD Ferreira 44, F Davids 37; A Badenhorst 3/36, GJ-P Kruger 4/23) and 296 (JJ de Nobrega 32, LD Ferreira 121, R Munnik 67; A Badenhorst 4/59, JW Shutte 3/21)

Match drawn between North West and Western Province B, 6–8 February 1999, Cape Town
NW 270 (AG Lawson 36, HM de Vos 37, MC Venter 73, C Light 50; DG Payne 3/53, CW Henderson 4/48) and 153/7 (MJ Lavine 41*; CW Henderson 4/39)
WPB 113 (F Davids 35; LCR Jordaan 6/30) and 319 (R Maron 31, H Pangarker 50, AC Thomas 35, BT Player 104; DJ Pryke 3/43)

Western Province B beat Easterns by 10 wickets, 19–21 February 1999, Cape Town
WPB 385/6 dec (R Magiet 79, MJ Crosoer 115, MS Taliep 44, BT Player 70*, AC Thomas 35) and 17/0
Eas 164 (Shakeel Ahmed 46, CB Crew 39; R Joffe 4/40, CA Copeland 3/50) and 235 (D Brand 33, J Uys 57; CA Copeland 5/111, BT Player 3/42)

Western Province B beat KwaZulu-Natal B by 131 runs, 25–27 February 1999, Durban
WPB 265 (R Magiet 122, MJ Crosoer 72; RA de Vry 4/19, ANW Tweedie 3/66) and 224/8 dec (MS Taliep 37, H Pangarker 122*; KP Pietersen 3/40)
KZNB 190 (MD Sanders 83, KS Bender 34; AK Mullins 3/23, CA Copeland 6/77) and 168 (RA de Vry 43; EO Moleon 3/28)

WESTERN PROVINCE CRICKET ASSOCIATION B: UCB BOWL THREE-DAY (NOT FIRST-CLASS), 1999/00–2003/04

Western Province B beat Eastern Province B by 7 wickets, 14-16 October 1999, Cape Town
EPB 178 (AD Peters 27, MW Creed 42, RJ Peterson 47; R Joffe 2/53, JW Shutte 2/32, PL Harris 5/24) and 303 (D Moffat 41, KD Duckworth 140, MW Creed 30; R Joffe 3/67, JW Shutte 5/56)
WPB 306/6 dec (AG Puttick 154*, R Magiet 49, H Pangarker 45, MR Lewis 25*; MW Creed 2/60, D Willemse 2/67) and 177/3 (R Magiet 55, AG Puttick 40, H Pangarker 47*; M Marele 2/43)

Match drawn between Western Province B and Free State B, 21-23 October 1999, Bloemfontein
WPB 339 (AG Puttick 66, R Magiet 25, LD Ferreira 84, AC Thomas 51, MR Lewis 39, RC Oosthuizen 32; JJ van der Wath 4/78, G Fourie 2/51, AP Abrahams 3/56)
FSB 353/9 (WJ Smit 26, JA Beukes 34, MN van Wyk 184*, CJ Vorster 30; MR Lewis 3/51, A Nkomo 3/72)

Western Province B beat Namibia by an innings and 61 runs, 4–5 November 1999, Windhoek
Nam 78 (R Joffe 2/29, R Munnik 2/11, AC Thomas 2/8, LD Ferreira 3/5) and 121 (R Joffe 3/23, R Munnik 3/23, AC Thomas 2/20)
WPB 260 (M Adams 43, AC Thomas 52, RC Oosthuizen 41; BL Kotze 3/62, I van Schoor 2/21, JL Louw 2/11)

Western Province B beat Griqualand West B by 6 wickets, 16–18 December 1999, Cape Town
GWB 272/7 (MC Arthur 33, BH Tucker 108, WM Dry 32, AP McLaren 39*; AK Mullins 3/43, R Munnik 2/43) and 221/6 dec (MA Alexander 30, MC Arthur 55, WM Dry 73*; R Munnik 2/33, MR Lewis 2/34)
WPB 270 (MJ Crosoer 36, LD Ferreira 26, R Munnik 49, AC Thomas 48, RC Oosthuizen 28*; GA Roe 4/60, AC Botha 2/57) and 224/4 (R Magiet 45, H Pangarker 101, R Munnik 29*; GA Roe 3/46)

Western Province B beat Boland B by 5 wickets, 11–13 January 2000, Bellville
BolB 368/7 (JG Strydom 60, DR Gain 35, H Davids 74, MM Brink 122; MF George 2/67, AK Mullins 2/73) and 168 (CV English 69, GN Myers 34; MF George 3/55, AK Mullins 2/32, R Munnik 2/26, PL Harris 2/18)
WPB 301/5 dec (BC Baguley 59, H Pangarker 138*, R Munnik 29, S Ackermann 29; CV English 2/53) and 237/5 (BC Baguley 37, MJ Crosoer 57, H Pangarker 33, R Munnik 57*, S Ackermann 37; N Vermeulen 3/109)

Western Province B beat KwaZulu-Natal B by 10 wickets, 4–6 February 2000, Cape Town
KZNB 106 (KG Storey 33*; R Joffe 3/20, MR Lewis 3/26) and 217 (A Mall 49, KS Bender 54, GH Bodi 31; R Joffe 4/32, MF George 2/49, PL Harris 4/66)
WPB 316 (R Magiet 45, LD Ferreira 54, R Munnik 44, S Ackermann 79, MR Lewis 25; KG Storey 2/51, CR Tatton 2/43, RB MacQueen 2/54, KS Bender 2/52) and 8/0

Western Province B beat Free State B by 117 runs, 26–28 October 2000, Cape Town
WPB 269 (LD Ferreira 80, H Pangarker 43, R Munnik 26, M de Stadler 34; C Bothma 2/22, MR Lewis 2/51, CE Feris 3/26, AP Abrahams 2/58) and 233/9 dec (R Magiet 71, JJ McLean 44, LD Ferreira 42; C Bothma 2/63, MR Lewis 3/45, CE Feris 4/26)
FSB 224 (G Fourie 64, WJ Smit 40, CE Feris 26; JW Shutte 3/54, M de Stadler 5/53) and 161 (WJ Smit 30, JA Beukes 43, MD Mokopanele 31; PL Harris 6/72, S Ackermann 2/32)

Western Province B beat Griqualand West B by 9 wickets, 2–4 November 2000, Kimberley
GWB 138 (AK Kruger 26, APT Mabuya 41; M de Stadler 4/19, R Munnik 2/17, PL Harris 2/34) and 154 (JL Aspeling 43, BH Tucker 53; PL Harris 6/55, M de Stadler 3/22)
WPB 213 (S Ahmed 54, S Ackermann 46, R Munnik 43; EW Kidwell 6/58, AJ Swanepoel 2/35, DK Dobson 2/35) and 83/1 (R Magiet 35*, LD Ferreira 40*)

Match drawn between Boland B and Western Province B, 16–18 November 2000, Cape Town
BolB 257 (AW Cyster 42, MS de Kock 34, JG Strydom 39, H Davids 38, B Hector 33; GA de Kock 2/32, M de Stadler 2/42, R Munnik 3/43, PL Harris 2/68)
WPB 354/7 (R Magiet 87, S Ahmed 64, LD Ferreira 111, R Munnik 29; WJ du Toit 2/66, CD de Lange 2/92)

Match drawn between Eastern Province B and Western Province B, 25–27 January 2001, Port Elizabeth
EPB 228 (U Abrahams 46, KD Duckworth 62, BR Friderichs 30, D Willemse 27*; M de Stadler 2/35, PL Harris 2/70, PR Adams 4/49) and 244 (KD Duckworth 44, GI Loon 32, GV Grace 44, MW Creed 52; PL Harris 6/97)
WPB 241 (R Magiet 42, GC Smith 103, TL Tsolekile 62; GS Hayward 6/72, D Willemse 3/58) and 169/7 (AG Puttick 39, LD Ferreira 47; GS Hayward 2/50, D Willemse 3/39)

Western Province B beat Namibia by 1 run, 15–17 February 2001, Cape Town
WPB 271 (R Magiet 26, AG Puttick 31, JJ McLean 51, W Euley 38, M de Stadler 42, PL Harris 31; BL Kotze 5/67) and 223/3 dec (R Magiet 26, AG Puttick 75, LD Ferreira 100*; BL Kotze 2/47)
Nam 162 (GB Murgatroyd 51; PL Harris 8/57) and 331 (D Seager 57, AJ Burger 29, GB Murgatroyd 121, DB Kotze 26, RJ Kirtley 27*; R Joffe 2/56, PL Harris 4/96, R Munnik 2/50)

Western Province B beat Zimbabwe Board XI by 6 wickets, 15–17 March 2001, Cape Town
ZimBrd 194 (GJ Rennie 29, AM Blignaut 72, T Taibu 35; R Joffe 2/47, Q Friend 3/59, PL Harris 4/42) and 214 (GJ Rennie 37, H Masakadza 42, DD Ebrahim 64; R Joffe 3/44, PL Harris 4/77)
WPB 323 (J-P Duminy 39, JJ McLean 72, H Pangarker 50, W Euley 60, Q Friend 27; BT Watambwa 2/72, AM Blignaut 2/57, PA Strang 2/57, RW Price 2/59) and 90/4 (J-P Duminy 31*, W Euley 36; CN Evans 2/10)

Western Province B beat Namibia by 4 wickets, 11–13 October 2001, Windhoek
Nam 230 (JM van der Merwe 65, D Keulder 38, GB Murgatroyd 42; Q Friend 2/38, M de Stadler 2/25, GA de Kock 2/39, PL Harris 3/58) and 200 (R Walters 29, D Keulder 31, DB Kotze 39, BO van Rooi 42; Q Friend 2/30, PL Harris 6/60)
WPB 223 (W Wyngaard 26, R Cotterell 30, R Munnik 29, S Ackermann 34; BL Kotze 2/41, RJ van Vuuren 2/41, DB Kotze 2/53, LJ Burger 2/11) and 208/6 (R Cotterell 49, R Maron 72, S Ackermann 46*; LJ Burger 3/70, BO van Rooi 2/54)

Match drawn between KwaZulu-Natal Inland and Western Province B, 9–11 November 2001, Cape Town
KI 273/9 dec (MB Hampson 27, T Essack 33, M Badat 60, J Anderson 74; Q Friend 2/41, AK Mullins 2/43, PL Harris 2/79) and 350 (P Landman 60, M Badat 30, MB Hampson 57, A van Vuuren 90, J Anderson 30; AK Mullins 2/75, PL Harris 4/130, S Ackermann 2/40, M de Stadler 2/38)
WPB 387/9 (W Wyngaard 120, R Maron 74, AG Prince 104, JJ McLean 28; A van Vuuren 2/104, J Anderson 4/102) and 6/1

Match drawn between Free State B and Western Province B, 23–25 November 2001, Bloemfontein
FSB 169 (JJ van der Wath 35, J Vorster 50*; M de Stadler 2/14, PR Adams 2/36, PL Harris 2/16) and 115 (JJ van der Wath 33; GK Berg 2/18, M de Stadler 3/35, PL Harris 3/43, PR Adams 2/4)
WPB 215 (JJ McLean 52, PR Adams 40*; JJ van der Wath 2/33, J Vorster 3/43) and 64/4 (JJ van der Wath 2/23)

Western Province B beat Eastern Province B by an innings and 87 runs, 19–21 January 2002, Cape Town
EPB 227 (KD Duckworth 158; M de Stadler 3/52, PL Harris 4/63, PR Adams 2/35) and 207 (KD Duckworth 38, CN du Plessis 82*; R Munnik 2/47, GK Berg 2/42, M de Stadler 4/42)
WPB 521/5 dec (J-P Duminy 58, JJ McLean 250*, R Munnik 30, W Euley 131*; D Bergins 5/72)

Boland B beat Western Province B by 1 wicket, 1–3 February 2002, Paarl
WPB 142 (R Maron 43, M de Stadler 26; JM van Wyk 3/50, DM Koch 2/33, WA Albertyn 4/46) and 254 (R Magiet 35, J-P Duminy 70, R Munnik 36, W Euley 26; JM van Wyk 3/70, DM Koch 3/35, WA Albertyn 3/36)
BolB 214 (B Hector 105, DM Koch 36; R Munnik 2/58, GK Berg 5/39, PL Harris 3/32) and 183/9 (AW Cyster 68, KC Jackson 28; PL Harris 2/63, PR Adams 5/60)

Western Province B beat Griqualand West B by an innings and 46 runs, 21–22 February 2002, Cape Town
GWB 83 (J Louw 38; Q Friend 3/3, M de Stadler 6/28) and 138 (AP McLaren 31, J Louw 36; R Munnik 2/22, M de Stadler 7/41)
WPB 267 (R Magiet 30, W Wyngaard 46, W Euley 62, PR Adams 44*; AK Kruger 2/71, C Pietersen 3/46)

Western Province B beat Northerns B by 68 runs, 22–25 March 2002, Cape Town
WPB 165 (R Maron 34, W Euley 51, M de Stadler 26*; F de Wet 4/35, CJ Karemaker 2/38, GM Hampson 2/40) and 351 (R Magiet 52, JJ McLean 152, W Wyngaard 49, R Munnik 33, W Euley 28; GM Hampson 2/75, JG Myburgh 6/61)
NorB 274 (MA Aronstam 33, F de Wet 25, JA Jordaan 56, GM Hampson 26; GK Berg 2/50, RN ten Doeschate 2/45, and 174 (A Paleker 62, CJ Karemaker 26; PL Harris 8/53)

Western Province B beat Griqualand West B by an innings and 14 runs, 4–6 October 2002, Kimberley
GWB 147 (AP McLaren 28, HK Moreeng 27, BW Lemmetjies 32; Q Friend 2/30, RK Kleinveldt 4/27, M de Stadler 2/33, MR Masinda 2/39) and 150 (AK Kruger 29, BW Lemmetjies 31; RK Kleinveldt 7/62)
WPB 311 (DJ Bassage 64, J-P Duminy 107, Q Friend 25, RK Kleinveldt 66; AJ Swanepoel 2/70, ES Tsamaisi 2/49, DK Dobson 4/52)

Western Province B beat Border B by 170 runs, 25–27 October 2002, Cape Town
WPB 325/6 dec (DJ Bassage 100, JJ McLean 138*, W Euley 26; GT Love 3/100) and 192/9 dec (W Euley 35, WC Hantam 32, RK Kleinveldt 27*; WR Hinkel 2/60, GT Love 4/57)
BdrB 253 (MM Matika 78, AM Sodumo 104; RK Kleinveldt 4/66, WC Hantam 3/46, RT Bailey 2/30) and 94 (JP Kreusch 45; RK Kleinveldt 6/22, M de Stadler 2/31, J-P Duminy 2/22)

Western Province B beat Gauteng B by 10 wickets, 8–10 November 2002, Bellville
GauB 72 (WC Hantam 4/15, M de Stadler 4/14) and 215 (SC Cook 34, GM Smith 49, SL Letshela 34, MJ Harris 39; RK Kleinveldt 2/56, M de Stadler 6/63, SC Nyulu 2/32)
WPB 280 (AG Puttick 68, JJ McLean 58, J-P Duminy 34, RT Bailey 41; JT Mafa 3/73, S Burger 3/43) and 8/0

Western Province B beat Eastern Province B by 8 wickets, 15–17 November 2002, Port Elizabeth
WPB 316/6 dec (AG Puttick 76, J-P Duminy 125, JJ McLean 38, N Kruger 25, RT Bailey 26; L Meyer 2/77, CN du Plessis 2/33) and 110/2 (DJ Bassage 33, AG Puttick 32, J-P Duminy 38*; D Willemse 2/38)
EPB 136 (DL Makalima 35, U Abrahams 42, RR Jeggels 41; SC Nyulu 3/30, M de Stadler 4/30) and 286 (ML Price 27, DL Makalima 48, RR Jeggels 97, CN du Plessis 27, Z Homani 49; RK Kleinveldt 3/61, M de Stadler 3/77, WC Hantam 2/28, SC Nyulu 2/68)

KwaZulu-Natal B beat Western Province B by 129 runs, 22–24 November 2002, Cape Town
KZNB 233 (DJ Watson 41, MD Sanders 102; RK Kleinveldt 2/62, WC Hantam 2/26, SC Nyulu 2/42, VD Philander 3/14) and 270 (MD Sanders 105, FB Lazarus 58, S Govender 29; Q Friend 5/53)
WPB 225 (DJ Bassage 48, R Magiet 27, JJ McLean 63, WC Hantam 27; RP Symcox 2/44, ASS Ndovela 2/33, RB MacQueen 5/83) and 149 (JJ McLean 26, RT Bailey 34, WC Hantam 35; RP Symcox 2/37, ASS Ndovela 2/19, GH Bodi 5/51)

Western Province B beat Northerns B by 99 runs, 7–10 December 2002, Cape Town
WPB 246 (R Magiet 55, AG Puttick 41, JJ McLean 40, M de Stadler 31; H Millard 2/40, MA Aronstam 3/47) and 276 (J-P Duminy 55, M de Stadler 88*, WC Hantam 40; CJ Karemaker 3/50, MA Aronstam 2/48)
NorB 130 (AN Smith 37, JG Myburgh 35, A Paleker 28; Q Friend 6/60, M de Stadler 3/32) and 293 (N van Woerkom 96, A Paleker 84, DR Nation 44; Q Friend 2/53, RK Kleinveldt 4/86, M de Stadler 4/79)

Match drawn between Western Province B and KwaZulu-Natal B, 17–19 October 2003, Cape Town
WPB 359/8 dec (DJ Bassage 48, R Maron 49, W Wyngaard 44, VD Philander 78, RCC Canning 94; RP Symcox 2/65, Y Singh 2/74) and 257/7 dec (W Wyngaard 92, RK Kleinveldt 66*; RP Symcox 3/48, GH Bodi 3/79)
KZNB 330/8 dec (R Gobind 70, A Mall 26, GH Bodi 66, D Smit 122*; MW Olivier 2/57, SC Nyulu 2/85) and 175/5 (A Mall 63*, R Gobind 44; MW Olivier 3/39)

Western Province B beat KwaZulu-Natal B by 8 wickets, 31 October – 2 November 2003, Durban
KZNB 159 (D Smit 45, RB MacQueen 26; Q Friend 3/45, RK Kleinveldt 3/39, M de Stadler 2/30, F Behardien 2/13) and 121 (T Essack 58*; Q Friend 6/39)
WPB 195 (W Wyngaard 97; U Govender 2/48, ND Hewer 7/86) and 86/2 (R Maron 47*)

Western Province B beat KwaZulu-Natal Inland by 201 runs, 6–8 November 2003, Pietermaritzburg
WPB 258 (R Maron 47, RCC Canning 34, F Behardien 38, Q Friend 77; L Adendorff 4/45, PS Jensen 2/56) and 230/5 dec (AJA Gray 101*, R Maron 39, W Wyngaard 46, R Munnik 33; TD Groenewald 3/56)
KI 118 (MB Hampson 62; Q Friend 2/30, RK Kleinveldt 7/25) and 169 (S Dorasamy 33, M Badat 45; RK Kleinveldt 4/31, SC Nyulu 3/61)

Western Province B beat Boland B by 4 wickets, 13–15 November 2003, Brackenfell
BolB 260 (EJ Hendrikse 45, J Clark 105, W Euley 43; Q Friend 4/30, RK Kleinveldt 3/52, SC Nyulu 2/68) and 243 (AW Cyster 39, EJ Hendrikse 49, J Clark 30, W Euley 36, R Jephta 54*; Q Friend 2/47, M de Stadler 5/35)
WPB 305 (R Maron 49, W Wyngaard 122, R Munnik 39; PJ Swanepoel 2/71, R Botha 2/41, R Jephta 2/8) and 199/6 (R Maron 94, W Wyngaard 51; BC Adams 4/50)

Western Province B beat Boland B by an innings and 118 runs, 30 January – 1 February 2004, Bellville
BolB 171 (MJ Friedlander 50*; RK Kleinveldt 3/23, R Munnik 2/22, PR Adams 3/68) and 177 (AW Cyster 26, PA Stuurman 29; F Behardien 3/31, PR Adams 5/59)
WPB 466/7 dec (DJ Bassage 42, R Maron 80, W Wyngaard 83, R Munnik 100*, RCC Canning 37, RK Kleinveldt 55; MJ Friedlander 2/80, SN Phillips 2/67)

Western Province B beat KwaZulu-Natal Inland by 52 runs, 13–15 February 2004, Cape Town
WPB 221 (R Maron 39, W Wyngaard 29, R Munnik 73; TD Groenewald 4/76, PS Jensen 3/35, S Dorasamy 2/19) and 146 (W Wyngaard 27, R Munnik 40; TD Groenewald 5/67, PS Jensen 3/41, P Landman 2/18)
KI 165 (D Sharp 43, MB Hampson 81; Q Friend 4/87, WC Hantam 6/43) and 150 (MB Hampson 40, M Badat 63; Q Friend 3/29, WC Hantam 2/53, PR Adams 4/28)

Western Province B beat Free State B by 5 wickets, 19–21 March 2004, Cape Town
FSB 288 (G Botha 36, MS van Vuuren 99, SP Summers 58; CJ Alexander 3/46, F Behardien 3/56, SC Nyulu 2/33) and 276 (HG de Kock 108, JR Schorn 41, R McLaren 43; CJ Alexander 4/46, WC Hantam 3/49)
WPB 252 (W Wyngaard 28, WC Hantam 47, F Behardien 26, R Telemachus 26; R McLaren 3/49, D du Preez 2/56, QG Samson 3/54) and 316/5 (R Maron 108, A Magiet 59, VD Philander 38, RCC Canning 37*; R McLaren 2/85, QG Samson 2/88)

Western Province B beat Gauteng B by 93 runs, 26–28 March 2004, Paarl
WPB 184 (JJ McLean 53, VD Philander 37, RCC Canning 29; S Burger 3/19, JT Mafa 3/59, S Conrad 3/34) and 147 (R Maron 36, RCC Canning 38, WC Hantam 29; S Burger 4/37, MJ Oosthuyzen 2/46, JT Mafa 3/41)
GauB 153 (WA Dugmore 33, MR Street 29; CJ Alexander 2/40, WC Hantam 2/25, F Behardien 2/32, SC Nyulu 2/19) and 85 (CJ Alexander 2/32, WC Hantam 3/19, SC Nyulu 2/13, VD Philander 2/6)

10.2.4 Western Province Cricket Association B, UCB Bowl One-Day (Not List A) Scores, 1999/2000–2003/04 (Unofficial)

Eastern Province B beat Western Province B by 7 wickets, 17 October 1999, Cape Town
WPB 215/4 (R Magiet 33, MJ Crosoer 35, H Pangarker 57*, AC Thomas 47*; RJ Peterson 2/21)
EPB 219/3 (D Moffat 43, KD Duckworth 100, MW Creed 36*; R Joffe 2/31)

Western Province B beat Free State B by 59 runs, 24 October 1999, Bloemfontein
WPB 253/6 (LD Ferreira 114*, H Pangarker 34, R Munnik 33, RC Oosthuizen 27*; CE Feris 2/28)
FSB 194 (JJ van der Wath 126; MR Lewis 5/40)

Western Province B beat Namibia by 26 runs, 7 November 1999, Windhoek
WPB 283/5 (LD Ferreira 154, RI Dalrymple 28, R Munnik 26*; JL Louw 2/19)
Nam 257/9 (D Keulder 53, GB Murgatroyd 111; AC Thomas 4/41, LD Ferreira 2/32)

Western Province B beat Griqualand West B by 10 runs, 19 December 1999, Cape Town
WPB 211/4 (H Pangarker 45, S Ackermann 75*, R Munnik 50*; AJ Swanepoel 3/31)
GWB 201/9 (FC Brooker 59, BH Tucker 62; R Joffe 2/17, MF George 2/24, R Munnik 3/35)

Boland B beat Western Province B by 47 runs, 16 January 2000, Bellville
BolB 212/9 (DR Gain 33, JG Strydom 26, H Davids 51; MF George 3/27, PL Harris 2/34)
WPB 165/8 (AC Thomas 39, MR Lewis 42*; NM Carter 2/31, JM van Wyk 3/33)

Western Province B beat Free State B by 8 wickets, 29 October 2000, Cape Town
FSB 156 (WJ Smit 54, JA Beukes 25, EE Meyer 29; M de Stadler 4/37, PL Harris 3/33)
WPB 157/2 (R Magiet 49*, LD Ferreira 79)

Western Province B beat Griqualand West B by 2 runs, 5 November 2000, Kimberley
WPB 230/8 (LD Ferreira 43, H Pangarker 44, R Munnik 43, GA de Kock 52*; AK Kruger 2/63, ES Tsamaisi 3/39)
GWB 228/4 (DK Dobson 100*, AK Kruger 69; GA de Kock 2/46)

Western Province B beat Boland B by 13 runs, 19 November 2000, Cape Town
WPB 223/8 (R Magiet 48, AG Puttick 34, R Munnik 45; JM van Wyk 3/57)
BolB 210/8 (AW Cyster 74, B Hector 28, CD de Lange 33*; GA de Kock 2/41, M de Stadler 2/43, PL Harris 2/39)

Western Province B beat Eastern Province B by 130 runs, 28 January 2001, Port Elizabeth
WPB 239/9 (R Magiet 56, GC Smith 46, JJ McLean 62; GS Hayward 4/47, D Willemse 2/23, GV Grace 2/4)
EPB 109/9 (GV Grace 32, R Domingo 40*; S Ackermann 2/16, AK Mullins 2/18, PL Harris 3/26)

Western Province B beat Namibia by 46 runs, 18 February 2001, Cape Town
WPB 240/6 (AG Puttick 97, S Ackermann 79; BL Kotze 2/46)
Nam 194/9 (SJ Swanepoel 30, DB Kotze 25, W Rademeyer 30, JL Louw 27; M de Stadler 3/24, PL Harris 4/45)

Zimbabwe Board XI beat Western Province B by 3 wickets, 13 March 2001, Cape Town
WPB 215/5 (R Magiet 49, H Pangarker 106; DT Mutendera 2/35)
ZimBrd 216/7 (AM Blignaut 90, CB Wishart 49; R Joffe 2/41)

Western Province B beat Namibia by 8 wickets, 14 October 2001, Windhoek
Nam 206/8 (GB Murgatroyd 77, LJ Burger 31*; AK Mullins 2/43, Q Friend 2/33, PL Harris 2/27)
WPB 210/2 (W Wyngaard 66, R Cotterell 29, R Maron 73*, R Munnik 32*)

Western Province B beat KwaZulu-Natal Inland by 4 wickets, 12 November 2001, Cape Town
KI 188 (T Essack 36, M Badat 48; GK Berg 2/24, M de Stadler 3/25)
WPB 189/6 (W Wyngaard 27, LD Ferreira 50, JJ McLean 26, R Munnik 28; A van Vuuren 2/32)

Western Province B beat Eastern Province B by 35 runs, 22 January 2002, Cape Town
WPB 189/9 (W Euley 29, IJL Trott 27, RN ten Doeschate 33; MP Nienaber 2/32, MW Creed 2/42, D Willemse 2/26)
EPB 154 (ML Price 39, CN du Plessis 41; M de Stadler 2/23, RN ten Doeschate 2/27, WC Hantam 4/20)

Western Province B beat Boland B by 1 wicket, 4 February 2002, Stellenbosch
BolB 186/8 (AW Cyster 30, EJ Hendrikse 37, GC Marais 42, B Ess 26; RN ten Doeschate 3/35, WC Hantam 2/30)
WPB 187/9 (R Munnik 77, RN ten Doeschate 26; JM van Wyk 2/27, WA Albertyn 4/26)

Western Province B beat Griqualand West B by 5 wickets, 23 February 2002, Cape Town
GWB 259 (MA Alexander 58, EE Meyer 70, AP McLaren 32; R Munnik 4/59, M de Stadler 2/58, PL Harris 2/34)
WPB 261/5 (R Magiet 87, R Maron 33, R Munnik 92*; EW Kidwell 3/30)

Western Province B beat Border B by 5 wickets, 27 March 2002, Cape Town
BdrB 192/6 (LL Gamiet 27, BC de Wett 34, W Wiblin 31; GK Berg 2/33)
WPB 193/5 (R Maron 60, J-P Duminy 39, JJ McLean 40*; L Graham 2/44)

Western Province B beat Griqualand West B by 20 runs, (D/L method), target revised to 185 in 35 overs, 7 October 2002, Kimberley
WPB 250/5 (DJ Bassage 83, N Kruger 60, JJ McLean 58*; APT Mabuya 2/41)
GWB 164/8 (C de Swardt 28, HK Moreeng 38, AP McLaren 33; RK Kleinveldt 3/21, M de Stadler 2/25, JJ McLean 2/40)

Border B beat Western Province B by 9 runs, 28 October 2002, Cape Town
BdrB 202/9 (MM Matika 30, JP Kreusch 40, AM Sodumo 39; L Ntantela 3/42, M de Stadler 3/19)
WPB 193 (AG Puttick 34, JJ McLean 64, W Euley 29, WC Hantam 30; AAW Pringle 5/37, M Maketa 2/23)

Western Province B beat Gauteng B by 50 runs, 11 November 2002, Bellville
WPB 282/3 (AG Puttick 82, LD Ferreira 92, J-P Duminy 44*, HD Ackerman 49; S Burger 2/57)
GauB 232/8 (SC Cook 60, GM Smith 27, J Buxton-Forman 45, MJ Harris 25; L Ntantela 2/67, WC Hantam 2/57, RT Bailey 2/39)

Western Province B beat Eastern Province B by 114 runs, 18 November 2002, Port Elizabeth
WPB 223/8 (DJ Bassage 52, R Magiet 25, W Euley 55; L Dipha 2/31, CN du Plessis 2/50)
EPB 109 (U Abrahams 36; GK Berg 3/25, SC Nyulu 2/15)

Western Province B beat KwaZulu-Natal B by 98 runs, 25 November 2002, Cape Town
WPB 245/9 (N Kruger 51, W Euley 43, RN ten Doeschate 28, Q Friend 41; RP Symcox 3/42, N Dladla 2/53, RB MacQueen 2/17)
KZNB 147 (GH Bodi 52, RP Symcox 25; GK Berg 2/21, RK Kleinveldt 3/16, L Ntantela 2/25)

Free State B beat Western Province B by 8 wickets, 14 December 2002, Bloemfontein
WPB 153 (AG Puttick 75; R McLaren 2/21, TS Motsamai 3/25, G Botha 2/26, CE Feris 2/32)
FSB 156/2 (JR Schorn 31, WA Deacon 47*, GFJ Liebenberg 43*)

Match tied between Western Province B and KwaZulu-Natal B, 20 October 2003, Cape Town
WPB 220/7 (DJ Bassage 39, R Maron 78*, RK Kleinveldt 33; RP Symcox 2/46, Y Singh 2/38)
KZNB 220/8 (R Gobind 68, A Mall 27, GH Bodi 47*; RK Kleinveldt 2/51, SC Nyulu 3/23)

KwaZulu-Natal B beat Western Province B by 30 runs, 3 November 2003, Durban
KZNB 224/9 (T Essack 80, GH Bodi 60; RK Kleinveldt 3/39, M de Stadler 3/26, F Behardien 2/26)
WPB 194 (W Wyngaard 35, RCC Canning 41; RB MacQueen 4/39, T Essack 2/28)

Western Province B beat KwaZulu-Natal Inland by 104 runs, 9 November 2003, Pietermaritzburg
WPB 299/6 (R Maron 66, WC Hantam 78, R Munnik 49*, RCC Canning 42; TD Groenewald 2/44, A van Vuuren 2/36)
KI 195 (MB Hampson 84, J Anderson 26; M de Stadler 3/27, WC Hantam 2/32, SC Nyulu 3/40)

Western Province B beat Boland B by 5 wickets, 16 November 2003, Paarl
BolB 193/7 (AW Cyster 25, EJ Hendrikse 54, W Euley 37, J Krynauw 29*; M de Stadler 2/40, SC Nyulu 2/28)
WPB 196/5 (DJ Bassage 58, JJ McLean 66, R Munnik 34*; SN Phillips 2/38, QK Kannemeyer 2/39)

Boland B beat by Western Province B by 6 wickets, 2 February 2004, Bellville
WPB 176 (WC Hantam 47, JJ McLean 33; PSE Sandri 3/34)
BolB 177/4 (MD Sanders 74, WJ Louw 72; WC Hantam 2/32)

Western Province B beat KwaZulu-Natal Inland by 8 wickets, 16 February 2004, Bellville
KI 108 (Q Friend 2/32, R Munnik 3/13, F Behardien 2/14)
WPB 110/2 (DJ Bassage 43*, TL Tsolekile 30)

Western Province B beat Free State B by 23 runs, 6 March 2004, Bloemfontein
WPB 235/5 (W Wyngaard 48, VD Philander 70*, RCC Canning 34; WA Deacon 2/47, MS van Vuuren 2/36)
FSB 212/7 (HG de Kock 28, WA Deacon 100*; F Behardien 3/51, VD Philander 2/33, SC Nyulu 2/48)

Western Province B beat Northerns B by 2 wickets, 14 March 2004, Centurion
NorB 214/9 (AN Smith 32, H Malan 48, MJ Mokonyama 39; R Telemachus 3/43, WC Hantam 3/24)
WPB 217/8 (JJ McLean 52, VD Philander 40, WC Hantam 33, RCC Canning 25*; GM Hampson 2/54, AM Phangiso 2/23)

10.3 Western Province Cricket Association, 2004/05–2010/11 (Amateur Team)

The introduction of the strength-versus-strength regional franchise system in 2004/05 reduced the number of teams playing in the premier competition of the United Cricket Board of South Africa (UCBSA) from 11 to 6. The top 100 or so players were creamed off into the professional elite system and, to provide for the next layer of players, the UCBSA started an amateur provincial competition for the 11 provinces and 3 associate provinces. These provincial teams still enjoyed first-class status, but the old traditional inter-provincial system now became a secondary product, supplemented as the premier system by the franchise competitions of the six professional regional teams.

From October 2004, with the inauguration of the new regional franchise system, a Western Province Cricket Association amateur team started participating as Western Province and the former Western Province professionals were absorbed into the Western Cape Cricket (Pty) Ltd franchise team.

10.3.1 Western Province Cricket Association First-Class And List A Players in Cricket South Africa Amateur Competition, 2004/05–2010/11[338]

NAME	FIRST-CLASS			LIMITED OVERS		
	M	From	To	M	From	To
Abbas, M	10	2008/09	2009/10	9	2008/09	2009/10
Abrahams, S	–	–	–	1	2005/06	2005/06
Adams, MQ	4	2007/08	2010/11	20	2005/06	2010/11
Adams, PR	15	2004/05	2007/08	12	2005/06	2007/08
Alexander, CJ	5	2004/05	2006/07	3	2004/05	2006/07
Allie, Z	3	2009/10	2009/10	7	2009/10	2009/10
Arkell, CJF	2	2008/09	2008/09	1	2008/09	2008/09
Bassage, DJ	10	2004/05	2006/07	7	2004/05	2006/07
Behardien, F	3	2004/05	2004/05	6	2004/05	2005/06
Behardien, M	6	2010/11	2010/11	4	2010/11	2010/11
Bennett, BL	3	2007/08	2008/09	8	2007/08	2009/10
Birch, CWS	12	2006/07	2007/08	7	2006/07	2007/08
Bothma, JP	7	2010/11	2010/11	6	2010/11	2010/11
Brand, D	–	–	–	2	2009/10	2009/10
Canning, RCC	34	2004/05	2010/11	31	2004/05	2010/11
Carolus, D	3	2010/11	2010/11	–	–	–
Conrad, S	6	2004/05	2005/06	2	2005/06	2005/06
Cooke, CB	6	2009/10	2009/10	14	2008/09	2009/10
De Stadler, M	26	2004/05	2007/08	22	2004/05	2007/08
Engelbrecht, SA	9	2009/10	2010/11	14	2008/09	2010/11
Euley, W	2	2006/07	2006/07	6	2005/06	2007/08
Fearon, GG	1	2007/08	2007/08	1	2006/07	2006/07
Fernandez, AR	–	–	–	1	2005/06	2005/06
Friend, Q	12	2004/05	2006/07	7	2004/05	2006/07
Geoghegan, JP	3	2005/06	2007/08	12	2005/06	2007/08
George, SG	1	2005/06	2005/06	6	2005/06	2005/06
Gomes, SP	–	–	–	2	2010/11	2010/11
Gray, AJA	39	2004/05	2010/11	34	2004/05	2010/11
Hantam, WC	9	2004/05	2007/08	14	2004/05	2007/08
Haupt, DL	1	2005/06	2005/06	5	2005/06	2005/06
Hendricks, BE	13	2009/10	2010/11	7	2009/10	2010/11
Holmes, M	1	2009/10	2009/10	1	2009/10	2009/10
Homani, Z	9	2005/06	2006/07	7	2005/06	2006/07
Jappie, R	–	–	–	1	2006/07	2006/07
Jardine, F	2	2005/06	2006/07	2	2004/05	2005/06
Khan, S	–	–	–	3	2010/11	2010/11
Kleinveldt, MC	11	2010/11	2010/11	4	2010/11	2010/11
Kleinveldt, RK	3	2005/06	2005/06	5	2005/06	2010/11
Kohn, J	–	–	–	2	2008/09	2008/09
Kuiper, JM	15	2005/06	2008/09	21	2005/06	2008/09
Laing, PC	6	2008/09	2009/10	7	2008/09	2009/10
Levi, RE	17	2006/07	2010/11	18	2004/05	2010/11

NAME	FIRST-CLASS			LIMITED OVERS		
	M	From	To	M	From	To
Lotter, RB	1	2008/09	2008/09	1	2008/09	2008/09
Magiet, A	2	2004/05	2005/06	5	2004/05	2005/06
Magiet, R	1	2004/05	2004/05	1	2004/05	2004/05
Mahlombe, M	23	2005/06	2010/11	37	2005/06	2010/11
Masinda, MR	1	2005/06	2005/06	1	2005/06	2005/06
Mdodana, TJ	6	2006/07	2007/08	1	2006/07	2006/07
Mgijima, A	13	2009/10	2010/11	12	2009/10	2010/11
Mjekula, S	4	2006/07	2006/07	1	2006/07	2006/07
Moleon, EO	–	–	–	3	2007/08	2007/08
Munnik, R	8	2004/05	2005/06	5	2004/05	2005/06
Northcote, AM	2	2008/09	2008/09	2	2008/09	2008/09
Nyulu, SC	4	2004/05	2004/05	2	2004/05	2004/05
Olivier, MW	7	2009/10	2009/10	7	2009/10	2009/10
Paterson, D	17	2009/10	2010/11	12	2008/09	2010/11
Philander, VD	5	2004/05	2009/10	4	2004/05	2009/10
Piedt, DL-R	13	2009/10	2010/11	20	2008/09	2010/11
Plaatjies, FC	3	2006/07	2008/09	8	2006/07	2009/10
Puttick AG	–	–	–	1	2010/11	2010/11
Qomoyi, A	–	–	–	1	2007/08	2007/08
Rabie, GR	15	2008/09	2010/11	15	2008/09	2010/11
Ramoo, RJ	13	2008/09	2009/10	16	2008/09	2009/10
Richards, RR	14	2009/10	2010/11	12	2009/10	2010/11
Rippon, MJ	–	–	–	1	2010/11	2010/11
Samsodien, W	1	2004/05	2004/05	2	2004/05	2004/05
Simetu, S	3	2009/10	2010/11	10	2010/11	2010/11
Simpson, AR	3	2004/05	2004/05	2	2004/05	2004/05
Simpson, LF	16	2005/06	2008/09	3	2005/06	2008/09
Sodumo, AM	6	2007/08	2008/09	4	2007/08	2008/09
Telo, FD	23	2005/06	2010/11	21	2005/06	2010/11
Temoor, A-A	16	2007/08	2009/10	5	2007/08	2009/10
Townsend, TKM	6	2009/10	2009/10	6	2008/09	2010/11
Tsolekile, TL	7	2007/08	2008/09	7	2007/08	2008/09
Vallie, MY	22	2009/10	2010/11	22	2008/09	2010/11
Van Schalkwyk, SC	–	–	–	4	2007/08	2008/09
Van Wyk, EP	13	2007/08	2009/10	21	2006/07	2009/10
Vilas, DJ	3	2010/11	2010/11	3	2010/11	2010/11
Walters, MD	29	2005/06	2010/11	25	2005/06	2010/11
Wernars, KO	2	2009/10	2010/11	11	2009/10	2010/11
Williams, CD	7	2007/08	2008/09	–	–	–
Williamson, M	19	2005/06	2009/10	29	2005/06	2010/11
Worth, D	4	2004/05	2004/05	3	2004/05	2004/05
Wyngaard, W	17	2004/05	2006/07	12	2004/05	2006/07
Xongo, L	1	2004/05	2004/05	1	2004/05	2004/05
Zondeki, M	3	2009/10	2010/11	5	2005/06	2010/11

10.3.2 Western Province Cricket Association Trophy Winners, 2004/05–2010/11

UCB PROVINCIAL CUP / SAA THREE-DAY CHALLENGE / CSA THREE-DAY CHALLENGE (FIRST-CLASS)

UCB Provincial Cup

Season	Winners
2004/05	Griqualand West
2005/06	Northerns

SAA Three-Day Challenge

Season	Winners
2006/07	Gauteng
2007/08	Griqualand West
2008/09	Griqualand West

CSA Three-Day Challenge

Season	Winners
2009/10	Eastern Province
2010/11	*Western Province*

Note: At the Annual General Meeting of the United Cricket Board of South Africa on 3 August 2006 it was decided to change the name of the governing body to Cricket South Africa.

UCB PROVINCIAL SHIELD / SAA ONE-DAY CHALLENGE / CSA ONE-DAY CHALLENGE (LIMITED OVERS)

UCB Provincial Shield

Season	Winners
2004/05	Free State
2005/06	Northerns

SAA One-Day Challenge

Season	Winners
2006/07	KwaZulu-Natal
2007/08	Gauteng
2008/09	Boland

CSA One-Day Challenge

Season	Winners
2009/10	Northern
2010/11	*Western Province*

10.3.3 Western Province Cricket Association First-Class Scores in the Amateur Competitions for the UCB Provincial Cup (2004/05 and 2005/06), SAA Three-Day Challenge (2006/07–2008/09) and CSA Three-Day Challenge (2009/10 and 2010/11)[339]

Match drawn between Western Province and Eastern Province, 21–23 October 2004, Port Elizabeth
EP 178 (L Meyer 38, M Slwana 37; R Munnik 3/23) and 300 (Z Homani 83, RR Jeggels 43, R Nel 59, GE Howell 55; CJ Alexander 3/48, F Behardien 3/48, M de Stadler 3/58)
WP 228 (DJ Bassage 30, RCC Canning 51, F Behardien 60; L Meyer 4/52) and 142/6 (R Munnik 55*; D Willemse 4/61)

Western Province beat North West by an innings and 80 runs, 28–30 October 2004, Cape Town
WP 276/7 (AR Simpson 48, D Worth 71, R Munnik 65*, F Behardien 34; EO Moleon 3/35)
NW 98 (WL Coetsee 50; Q Friend 3/37, M de Stadler 5/18) and 98 (Q Friend 3/28, M de Stadler 3/18, A Magiet 3/0)

Griqualand West beat Western Province by 6 wickets, 4–6 November 2004, Kimberley
WP 173 (VD Philander 66, RCC Canning 40; J Coetzee 7/42) and 283 (VD Philander 168, RCC Canning 32; AK Kruger 4/50, AJ Swanepoel 4/48)
GW 311 (PJ Koortzen 43, W Bossenger 45, M Bosman 106; VD Philander 3/61) and 146/4 (AP McLaren 47*, W Bossenger 44)

Boland beat Western Province by 58 runs, 20–22 January 2005, Cape Town
Bol 106 (L-R Walters 30*; WC Hantam 3/16, VD Philander 4/15) and 316 (R Bailey 42, J Clark 58, H Davids 99, H Fourie 45; M de Stadler 5/61)
WP 101 (AJA Gray 32; WA Albertyn 3/24, H Fourie 3/16) and 263 (AJA Gray 48, W Wyngaard 37, VD Philander 39, R Munnik 35, WC Hantam 36; HH Paulse 3/44, WA Albertyn 4/29)

Western Province beat KwaZulu-Natal by 10 wickets, 13–15 October 2005, Chatsworth
KZN 164 (MD Sanders 31, K Smit 34; LF Simpson 3/22) and 150 (R Frylinck 31; Q Friend 7/31)
WP 244 (R Munnik 75, RK Kleinveldt 115*; ZA Abrahim 3/93, R Frylinck 6/94) and 71/0 (AJA Gray 41*)

Western Province beat Eastern Province by 6 wickets, 20–21 October 2005, Cape Town
EP 59/9 dec (M de Stadler 4/17, M Mahlombe 3/11) and 168 (RR Jeggels 41, E Potgieter 30, L Meyer 33; RK Kleinveldt 6/57, M de Stadler 3/48)
WP 121 (R Munnik 59*; L Meyer 5/38) and 107/4 (M Williamson 35, W Wyngaard 37*)

Match drawn between Western Province and Boland, 3–5 November 2005, Paarl
WP 278 (FD Telo 61, RCC Canning 57, PR Adams 47; HH Paulse 5/65) and 263/5 dec (AJA Gray 112*, W Wyngaard 31, FD Telo 44, RCC Canning 33)
Bol 234 (JG Strydom 44, WA Albertyn 67; RK Kleinveldt 4/73, M de Stadler 3/45) and 252/8 (JG Strydom 40, WC Swan 50, WE September 63*; RK Kleinveldt 3/71, M de Stadler 4/48)

Western Province beat Zimbabwe U-23 by 233 runs, 10–12 November 2005, Cape Town
WP 207 (Z Homani 74, WC Hantam 38; C de Grandhomme 3/26) and 228/6 dec (AJA Gray 51, W Wyngaard 70, FD Telo 50)
ZimU23 77 (WC Hantam 6/39) and 125 (GM Strydom 54)

Western Province beat Border by 56 runs, 17–19 November 2005, Cape Town
WP 364/4 dec (M Williamson 44, Z Homani 118, W Wyngaard 132*) and 265/4 dec (AJA Gray 77, W Wyngaard 101*, FD Telo 46)
Bdr 256 (GE von Hoesslin 36, LL Gamiet 39, AZM Dyili 47, L Mbane 45; S Conrad 5/64, M Mahlombe 3/62) and 317 (BL Bennett 150, AZM Dyili 65; S Conrad 5/111)

KwaZulu-Natal beat Western Province by 10 wickets, 2–3 February 2006, Cape Town
WP 114 (RCC Canning 30; U Govender 3/43, ND Hewer 4/31, S Mlongo 3/27) and 158 (AJA Gray 41, RCC Canning 32; U Govender 4/50, S Mlongo 5/25)
KZN 175 (WR Wingfield 49; M de Stadler 3/42, WC Hantam 4/57) and 100/0 (DR Miller 64*, R Gobind 31*)

Western Province beat Eastern Province by 9 wickets, 9–11 February 2006, Port Elizabeth
EP 309/4 dec (CA Ingram 169, U Abrahams 100*) and 122 (CA Ingram 39; M de Stadler 3/21, S Conrad 6/45)
WP 260 (AJA Gray 85, DJ Bassage 42, WC Hantam 30*, Q Friend 36; LL Tsotsobe 3/67, J Theron 3/40) and 172/1 (AJA Gray 31, DJ Bassage 108*)

Western Province beat Boland by 398 runs, 16–18 February 2006, Cape Town
WP 297 (AJA Gray 108, Z Homani 42, JM Kuiper 81*; PSE Sandri 3/67) and 298/6 dec (DJ Bassage 32, W Wyngaard 104*, RCC Canning 72)
Bol 123 (WC Swan 33; WC Hantam 3/29, M de Stadler 5/42) and 74 (PC Laing 46; Q Friend 3/32, M de Stadler 3/6)

Western Province beat Border by 10 wickets, 2–4 March 2006, East London
Bdr 129/9 dec (LL Gamiet 34; Q Friend 4/65) and 249 (LL Gamiet 93, AZM Dyili 60, S de Kock 30; F Jardine 5/118)
WP 377 (AJA Gray 45, FD Telo 72, R Munnik 52, RCC Canning 64*; DL Brown 3/83) and 4/0

Northerns beat Western Province by 100 runs, 6–9 April 2006, Cape Town
Nor 267 (MA Aronstam 69, A Paleker 48, G Dros 59; VD Philander 3/57, M de Stadler 3/74, S Conrad 3/79) and 333/6 dec (MA Aronstam 40, JG Myburgh 64, CFK van Wyk 104, G Dros 62)
WP 317 (FD Telo 43, VD Philander 66, RCC Canning 68, M de Stadler 37; MA Aronstam 5/82) and 183 (R Munnik 32, RCC Canning 56; P Joubert 3/10)

Western Province beat Kei by an innings and 133 runs, 5–6 October 2006, Cape Town
Kei 198 (KM Moerane 37, TT Kraai 57; Q Friend 4/15, CWS Birch 3/25) and 78 (LF Simpson 5/7)
WP 409/8 dec (AJA Gray 46, W Wyngaard 33, PR Adams 70, RCC Canning 103*, CWS Birch 51)

Western Province beat Border by an innings and 114 runs, 26–28 October 2006, East London
Bdr 84/9 dec (Q Friend 4/33, M de Stadler 4/19) and 223 (BL Bennett 42, V Makhaphela 31, GE von Hoesslin 50; M de Stadler 3/82, PR Adams 4/53)
WP 421/6 dec (AJA Gray 96, M Williamson 121, RE Levi 82*, CWS Birch 61; DL Brown 3/105)

Western Province beat South Western Districts by 9 wickets, 9–10 November 2006, Cape Town
SWD 103/9 dec (M de Stadler 5/22) and 107 (M de Stadler 3/27)
WP 126 (M Williamson 60; N Nobebe 4/40, NM Murray 4/30) and 85/1 (AJA Gray 33*, M Williamson 31)

Match drawn between Western Province and KwaZulu-Natal Inland, 18–20 January 2007, Cape Town
WP 326 (RE Levi 104, JM Kuiper 113, M de Stadler 43*; LL Lwana 4/42, GM Hampson 3/65) and 297/7 dec (DJ Bassage 37, M Williamson 72, RE Levi 76; GM Hampson 3/69)
KI 299 (CS Bowyer 43, MB Hampson 34, L Brown 54, GM Hampson 44, M Gqadushe 54*, LL Lwana 38; CJ Alexander 3/50, S Mjekula 3/63) and 147/9 (CS Bowyer 34, A van Vuuren 57; S Mjekula 4/28, M de Stadler 3/18)

Match drawn between Western Province and KwaZulu-Natal, 1–3 February 2007, Chatsworth
KZN 268 (WL Madsen 86; CWS Birch 5/47) and 319/4 (R Gobind 118*, WL Madsen 132, M Bekker 30)
WP 315 (M Williamson 51, W Euley 93, CWS Birch 87; NM Serame 3/82, M Bekker 3/12)

Western Province beat Boland by 7 wickets, 15–17 February 2007, Cape Town
Bol 248 (B Hector 46, CD de Lange 39, JP Bothma 31*; S Mjekula 4/56, PR Adams 3/43) and 185 (BC Adams 37, TJ Botes 37; CWS Birch 3/41, M de Stadler 3/38, PR Adams 3/37)
WP 178 (JM Kuiper 44, CWS Birch 51; JP Bothma 4/36, CD de Lange 5/36) and 256/3 (RE Levi 103*, JM Kuiper 38, W Euley 71*)

Match drawn between Western Province and Eastern Province, 1–3 March 2007, Cape Town
EP 322/7 dec (CA Ingram 102, RR Jeggels 151*, WE Bell 30; S Mjekula 3/60) and 114/0 (CA Ingram 68*, C Baxter 40*)
WP 273 (DJ Bassage 36, RE Levi 150*; J Theron 3/44, WD Parnell 3/48, CA Ingram 4/101)

Western Province beat KwaZulu-Natal by 91 runs, 18–20 October 2007, Cape Town
WP 304/6 (CD Williams 66, JM Kuiper 49, FD Telo 35, RCC Canning 53*, WC Hantam 36; KC Africa 3/55) and 333 (JM Kuiper 102, CWS Birch 82, PR Adams 35; TD Pillay 3/56, KC Africa 3/69)
KZN 273 (K Smit 62, M Bekker 56, CA Flowers 31, R Frylinck 52; LF Simpson 6/58) and 273 (W Hauptfleisch 62, M Bekker 114; M de Stadler 4/78, PR Adams 3/72)

Eastern Province beat Western Province by 214 runs, 25–27 October 2007, Port Elizabeth
EP 224 (MBA Smith 70, ACR Birch 41; M de Stadler 3/67, EP van Wyk 3/29) and 259/7 dec (J-JT Smuts 45, U Abrahams 115*, L Meyer 30)
WP 173 (M Williamson 43; B-D Walters 3/31, ACR Birch 3/44) and 96 (J Theron 6/22)

Western Province beat South Western Districts by 8 wickets, 1–3 November 2007, Oudtshoorn
SWD 132 (JA Beukes 71; EP van Wyk 5/20) and 205 (S-JE Avontuur 80, NM Murray 51; WC Hantam 3/58, EP van Wyk 4/47, PR Adams 3/38)
WP 251 (CD Williams 69, FD Telo 34, RCC Canning 42, EP van Wyk 41; BL Fransman 5/36) and 87/2 (BL Bennett 44*)

Boland beat Western Province by 9 wickets, 15–17 November 2007, Paarl
WP 210 (FD Telo 134*; PSE Sandri 3/26, T Henderson 7/67) and 337 (GG Fearon 42, CD Williams 31, RE Levi 63, FD Telo 132, RCC Canning 36; T Henderson 3/48, SF Grobler 5/113)
Bol 499/8 dec (B Hector 183, BC Adams 42, PC Laing 154, L-R Walters 32; A-A Temoor 3/143) and 49/1

Western Province beat KwaZulu-Natal Inland by 225 runs, 31 January – 2 February 2008, Cape Town
WP 284/7 (AJA Gray 68, M Williamson 30, EP van Wyk 99*, CWS Birch 35; RD McMillan 4/57) and 236/4 dec (AJA Gray 56, RE Levi 37, TL Tsolekile 50*, AM Sodumo 56*)
KI 140 (G Penford 36, A van Vuuren 41; EP van Wyk 5/44) and 155 (A van Vuuren 41, B Moses 40; LF Simpson 5/59, PR Adams 4/26)

Western Province beat Border by an innings and 5 runs, 14–15 February 2008, Cape Town
Bdr 83 (LF Simpson 3/17, CWS Birch 3/17, M de Stadler 3/17) and 182 (AZM Dyili 30, DL Brown 69; M de Stadler 4/42, A-A Temoor 4/58)
WP 270 (AJA Gray 60, TL Tsolekile 55, CWS Birch 36; Y Pangabantu 3/60, DL Brown 3/62)

Griqualand West beat Western Province by 42 runs, 13–15 March 2008, Kimberley
GW 144 (PJ Koortzen 36; LF Simpson 5/27, CWS Birch 3/41) and 227 (W Bossenger 38, AR Swanepoel 59; CWS Birch 3/65)
WP 155 (RE Levi 49; C Pietersen 4/41, J Coetzee 4/8) and 174 (FD Telo 99*; C Pietersen 4/64, J Coetzee 3/29)

Match drawn between Western Province and KwaZulu-Natal Inland, 2–4 October 2008, Bellville
WP 197 (AJA Gray 41, CD Williams 43; A van Vuuren 3/39, MS van Vuuren 3/14) and 73/1 (RE Levi 40*)
KI 244/9 (MS van Vuuren 43, DJ Watson 84, M Gqadushe 33; LF Simpson 4/25)

Namibia beat Western Province by 301 runs, 16–18 October 2008, Windhoek
Nam 328/9 (G Snyman 84, LJ Burger 125, C Williams 35; GR Rabie 6/48) and 287/8 dec (AJ Burger 79, SF Burger 33, C Williams 37, T Verwey 72; GR Rabie 3/26)
WP 168 (JM Kuiper 34, RE Levi 51, EP van Wyk 31; KB Burger 5/69, SF Burger 4/22) and 146 (MD Walters 75; KB Burger 5/47)

Match drawn between Northerns and Western Province, 15–17 January 2009, Pretoria
Nor 295/6 (PJ Malan 60, HE van der Dussen 87, AJ Seymore 62, PM Selowa 48*)and 252/9 dec (HE van der Dussen 35, AJ Seymore 56, JR Jumat 58*; M Mahlombe 3/48)
WP 287/8 (MD Walters 49, RJ Ramoo 43, PC Laing 32, TL Tsolekile 47*, A-A Temoor 30; LMG Masekela 6/46) and 135/4 (AJA Gray 36, PC Laing 41*)

Match drawn between Western Province and Free State, 29–31 January 2009, Bloemfontein
WP 337/3 (AJA Gray 188*, MD Walters 106) and 19/1
FS 398/7 (DJ van Wyk 69, LLL Sesele 41, JA Beukes 117, HO von Rauenstein 63, GN Nieuwoudt 30, SC van Schalkwyk 31*; M Mahlombe 3/78)

Border beat Western Province by 113 runs, 12–14 February 2009, Cape Town
Bdr 218 (MF Richardson 70, KD Bennett 56; M Mahlombe 3/43, AJA Gray 5/31) and 278 (S de Kock 43, KD Bennett 47, DL Brown 38, AZM Dyili 58, L Mbane 37; LF Simpson 3/40, AJA Gray 3/101)
WP 228 (AJA Gray 45, AM Northcote 30, EP van Wyk 86*; L Mbane 4/73, DL Brown 4/65) and 155 (M Mahlombe 32; Y Pangabantu 3/45, S de Kock 4/44)

North West beat Western Province by 8 wickets, 5–7 March 2009, Cape Town
WP 157 (RJ Ramoo 65, M Mahlombe 36; HH Paulse 3/31, MP Siboto 3/28) and 238 (BL Bennett 59, M Abbas 50, EP van Wyk 79*, TL Tsolekile 30; MP Siboto 5/56)
NW 244 (JF Mostert 105*, C Jonker 51) and 157/2 (JF Mostert 68*, WL Coetsee 63)

Match drawn between KwaZulu-Natal Inland and Western Province, 1–3 October 2009, Pietermaritzburg
KZN 250 (GN Addicott 104, DJ Watson 53*, OE Humphries 31, A-A Temoor 2/70, 1/31 GR Rabie) and 124 (M Olivier 44, B Moses 40, GN Addicott 22*, A-A Temoor 1/18, AJA Gray 1/18)
WP 266 (A-A Temoor 57, M Abbas 50, AJA Gray 46, K Nipper 4/97, B Moses 2/7)

Western Province beat South Western Districts by 5 wickets, 15–17 October 2009, Cape Town
SWD 280/8 dec (SE Avontuur 123, JG Strydom 52, RP Hugo 36, W Olivier 2/64, GR Rabie 1/23, AJA Gray 1/41) and 228 (BC de Wett 83, PA Stuurman 37, WC Hantam 32, A-A Temoor 5/31, AJA Gray 2/33)
WP 236 (RJ Ramoo 76, AJA Gray 64, EP van Wyk 20, NG Brouwers 5/83, W Hartslief 2/54) and 274/5 (AJA Gray 123, Abbas 64, Z Allie 38, WC Hantam 1/68, NG Brouwers 1/74)

Western Province beat Border by 4 wickets, 29–31 October 2009, East London
Bor 258 (L Mbane 59, D Randall 46, KD Bennett 42, VD Philander 4/45, A-A Temoor 3/41, SA Engelbrecht 2/74) and 279 (KD Bennett 112*, BJ Thomas 42, LL Mnyanda 26, VD Philander 4/35, AJA Gray 2/75)
WP 359/9 dec (AJA Gray 85, MY Vallie 84, VD Philander 46, S de Kock 5/87, LL Mnyanda 1/46, LL Lwana 1/54) and 179/6 (RCC Canning 51*, AJA Gray 42, VD Philander 17*, S de Kock 3/84, LL Mnyanda 2/63, L Mbane 1/32)

Match drawn between Western Province and North West, 5–7 November 2009, Potchefstroom
NW 273 (C Jonker 67, WC April 50, JF Mostert 49, VD Philander 5/16, AJA Gray 2/33) and 291/8 (JF Mostert 163*, BJ Pelser 66, C Jonker 22, A-A Temoor 3/89, AJA Gray 2/70, VD Philander 1/6)
WP 287 (MY Vallie 107, VD Philander 102, MD Walters 34, E Gerber 4/73, VCM Mazibuko 2/47, MP Siboto 2/41)

Griqualand West beat Western Province by 107 runs, 19–21 November 2009, Kimberley
GW 210 (AP McLaren 70, J Coetzee 31, GR de Wee 26, RR Richards 4/41, D Paterson 3/31, MW Olivier 2/42) and 307 (C Pietersen 140, AP McLaren 76, W Bossenger 34, MW Olivier 6/97, RR Richards 4/66)
WP 270 (MD Walters 88, MY Vallie 79, Z Allie 29, J Coetzee 4/54, R Pietersen 3/60, APT Mabuya 2/53) and 140 (MY Vallie 42*, M Williamson 22, A Mgijima 21, R Pietersen 7/41, APT Mabuya 2/37)

Western Province beat KwaZulu-Natal by an innings and 95 runs, 14–16 January 2010, Chatsworth
KZN 131 (KW Eccles 59, C Delport 27, GR Rabie 5/29, M Zondeki 2/24) and 180 (K Zondo 49, KA Maharaj 22, C Delport 21, A-A Temoor 4/64, M Zondeki 4/69)
WP 406 (MY Vallie 113, RJ Ramoo 93, PC Laing 56*, V Gobind 3/99)

Gauteng beat Western Province by 146 runs, 21–23 January 2010, Cape Town
Gau 324 (DJ Vilas 95, T Bavuma 61, D Conway 46*, M Zondeki 3/65) and 216 (J Symes 110, T Bavuma 60*, GR Rabie 1/31, A-A Temoor 1/33)
WP 114 (CB Cooke 33, A-A Temoor 21, S Burger 3/21, P Matshikwe 3/22) and 280 (AJA Gray 92, A-A Temoor 39, RJ Ramoo 34, T Shamsi 6/89)

Match drawn between Western Province and Northerns, 11–13 February 2010, Cape Town
Nor 316 (CF Schoeman 100, MJ Mokonyama 58, ER Links 44*, BE Hendricks 3/47, AJA Gray 2/33) and 190 (CF Schoeman 63, MJ Mokonyama 46, PJ Malan 40, RR Richards 3/55, A-A Temoor 3/37)
WP 272 (RCC Canning 116, AJA Gray 36, RJ Ramoo 32, MA Mashimbyi 5/81, LG Nel 1/34) and 131/5 (TKM Townsend 50*, A Mgijima 54*, MA Mashimbyi 3/29)

Western Province beat Free State by 8 wickets, 18–20 February 2010, Cape Town
FS 356 (W Lategan 87, RK Terblanche 62, DJ van Wyk 49, RR Richards 3/71) and 164 (DJ van Wyk 63, GN Nieuwoudt 29, AJ Pienaar 23, A Mgijima 5/24)
WP 394 dec (MY Vallie 119, TKM Townsend 53, RR Richards 45, AJ Pienaar 3/54, PV Mpitsang 2/77) and 129/2 (TKM Townsend 39, AJA Gray 35, MY Vallie 32*)

Namibia beat Western Province by 8 wickets, 25–27 February 2010, Cape Town
WP 70 (RJ Ramoo 18, M Abbas 12, L Klazinga 4/19, C Williams 4/30) and 286 (MD Walters 110, M Abbas 545, CB Cooke 32, L Klazinga 5/50)
Nam 327 (E Steenkamp 91, NRP Scholtz 62, C Williams 36, BE Hendricks 5/52) and 32/2

Western Province beat Eastern Province by 1 wicket, 4–6 March 2010, Cape Town
EP 305 (MBA Smith 66, SR Harmer 54*, RR Jeggels 50, MW Olivier 3/41, D Paterson 3/43) and 241 (ML Price 83, MBA Smith 79, D Paterson 3/59)
WP 166 (CB Cooke 44*, M Abbas 26, A Mgijima 22, L Meyer 5/38, ACR Birch 4/65) and 384/9 (AJA Gray 127, M Abbas 52, MY Vallie 40, ACR Birch 4/115)

Easterns beat Western Province by 7 wickets, 11–13 March 2010, Benoni
WP 197 (RCC Canning 74*, MY Vallie 34, RJ Ramoo 21, I Tahir 4/66, GC Viljoen 3/34) and 102 (TKM Townsend 33, MY Vallie 25, I Tahir 3/9, JJ Pienaar 3/15)
Eas 235 (I Tahir 55*, J Booysen 49, TM Bodibe 49, DL-R Piedt 3/65) and 66/3 (JJ Pienaar 46*, RR Richards 3/20)

Boland beat Western Province by 6 wickets, 25–27 March 2010, Cape Town
WP (MY Vallie 92*, M Abbas 28, M Holmes 27, CJ August 4/69) and 119 (MW Olivier 48, TKM Townsend 24, KO Wernars 22*, CJ August 9/37)
Bol 232 (EC Kriek 69, OJ Erasmus 67, OA Ramela 45, DL-R Piedt 3/63, S Simetu 2/28) and 93/4

Match drawn between Eastern Province and Western Province, 21–23 October 2010, Cape Town
EP 284/4 (ML Price 119, DJ White 33, MBA Smith 50*) and 177/9 dec (KR Smuts 62; BE Hendricks 3/25, SA Engelbrecht 3/66)
WP 244/8 (MC Kleinveldt 41, MD Walters 85, M Behardien 47*; CR Dolley 4/70) and 74/2 (MD Walters 47)

Western Province beat KwaZulu-Natal Inland by 145 runs, 28–30 October 2010, Cape Town
WP 367/4 (MD Walters 180*, FD Telo 96, MC Kleinveldt 36) and 238/8 dec (AJA Gray 31, FD Telo 32, M Behardien 52, DL-R Piedt 60*; BL Barends 4/67)
KI 304/9 (B Moses 65, M Gqadushe 74, CAH Barron 48, OE Humphries 39) and 156 (B Moses 43, RE Hillermann 58*; AJA Gray 5/62)

Western Province beat Free State by 9 wickets, 18–20 November 2010, Bloemfontein
FS 133 (GR Rabie 5/45) and 188 (LN Mosena 31, GN Nieuwoudt 35, AJ Pienaar 48; D Carolus 4/75, D Paterson 5/30)
WP 178 (FD Telo 44; DF Haasbroek 5/31, WJ van Zyl 3/53) and 145/1 (AJA Gray 89*)

Western Province beat Griqualand West by 5 wickets, 16–18 December 2010, Cape Town
GW 139 (AR Swanepoel 37, J Brooker 42; BE Hendricks 5/43, D Paterson 3/26) and 341 (AP McLaren 146, AR Swanepoel 49, J Brooker 43; D Paterson 6/76)
WP 364 (MD Walters 31, MY Vallie 62, RE Levi 67, SA Engelbrecht 81, M Behardien 52; C Pietersen 3/59, DD Carolus 4/73) and 119/5 (MY Vallie 44*, SA Engelbrecht 34; RG Modise 4/32)

Match drawn between Gauteng and Western Province, 6–8 January 2011, Johannesburg
Gau 158 (TG Mokoena 31, R Cameron 41; RR Richards 4/17, DL-R Piedt 3/36) and 188/5 (DA Hendricks 42, TG Mokoena 90)
WP 400/9 dec (MY Vallie 49, RE Levi 95, DJ Vilas 123*, A Mgijima 40; E O'Reilly 5/82)

Western Province beat Namibia by an innings and 71 runs, 13–15 January 2011, Windhoek
WP 293 (MC Kleinveldt 55, MD Walters 41, MY Vallie 77, FD Telo 33, DL-R Piedt 31; BM Scholtz 6/89, Z Groenewald 3/14)
Nam 107 (L Klazinga 38; DL-R Piedt 3/16) and 115 (R van Schoor 35; D Paterson 4/26)

Match drawn between North West and Western Province, 27–29 January 2011, Cape Town
NW 213 (AP Agathangelou 78, DR Deeb 39; D Paterson 3/31, DL-R Piedt 3/63) and 292 (BJ Pelser 108, PM Selowa 49, CJ Alexander 37*; D Paterson 6/66)
WP 252 (RCC Canning 40, SA Engelbrecht 114; LC Terblanche 3/49, DR Deeb 4/58) and 209/6 (MD Walters 46, MY Vallie 77*, RCC Canning 37; DR Deeb 4/69)

Western Province beat Northerns by an innings and 39 runs, 3–5 February 2011, Pretoria
Nor 215 (DKC Bunn 42, CF Schoeman 60, S Naidoo 45; RR Richards 5/26, D Paterson 3/46) and 187 (GJJ van der Merwe 35, S Naidoo 57; RR Richards 4/34)
WP 441/4 (MC Kleinveldt 115, MY Vallie 151*, FD Telo 106, M Behardien 36*)

South Western Districts beat Western Province by 2 runs, 10–12 February 2011, Oudtshoorn
SWD 254 (RD McMillan 34, S-JE Avontuur 57, BI Louw 78; SA Engelbrecht 5/74) and 204/5 dec (RD McMillan 93, N Bredenkamp 73)
WP 192 (MD Walters 34, AJA Gray 65; RD McMillan 3/19) and 264 (SA Engelbrecht 31, RCC Canning 111, M Mahlombe 54; GR Rabie 3/50, RD McMillan 3/36)

Western Province beat Easterns by an innings and 127 runs, 24–25 February 2011, Cape Town
WP 368 (AJA Gray 74, MC Kleinveldt 60, MY Vallie 106, SA Engelbrecht 52, DL-R Piedt 39; IC Hlengani 4/99)
Eas 156 (IC Hlengani 35, SP O'Connor 46; RR Richards 3/13, DL-R Piedt 5/49) and 85 (DL-R Piedt 5/38, D Paterson 4/16)

Western Province beat Border by 10 wickets, 10–11 March 2011, Cape Town
Bdr 105 (DL Brown 48; RR Richards 3/24, D Paterson 4/19) and 110 (D Paterson 3/41, DL-R Piedt 3/30)
WP 200 (MC Kleinveldt 30, MQ Adams 94*; L Rodolo 5/51) and 16/0

Western Province beat KwaZulu-Natal by 2 wickets, 17–19 March 2011, Durban
KZN 291 (DJ van Wyk 98, I Khan 37, CS Delport 89; JP Bothma 4/83, DL-R Piedt 5/95) and 194/5 dec (I Khan 36, N Govender 45; DL-R Piedt 3/67)
WP 202 (MC Kleinveldt 47, AJA Gray 43, RCC Canning 74; BL Whatmore 5/29, AH Razak 3/46) and 289/8 (MY Vallie 49, MQ Adams 40, RCC Canning 87, KO Wernars 39*; BJ Young 3/68)

Western Province beat Boland by 10 wickets, 24–25 March 2011, Paarl
WP 328/8 (MC Kleinveldt 160, RE Levi 40, SA Engelbrecht 38, M Mahlombe 44*) and 22/0
Bol 173 (JN Frylinck 50*; BE Hendricks 4/51, S Simetu 4/41) and 173 (W van Vuuren 37, UKJ Birkenstock 56, L van Wyk 35; JP Bothma 6/44)

10.3.4 Western Province Cricket Association List A Scores in the Amateur Competitions for the UCB Provincial Shield (2004/05 and 2005/06), SAA One-Day Challenge (2006/07–2008/09) and CSA One-Day Challenge (2009/10 and 2010/11)[340]

Eastern Province beat Western Province by 7 runs, 24 October 2004, Port Elizabeth
EP 219/9 (L Meyer 33, R Nel 32, Z Homani 36, GE Howell 61; WC Hantam 4/53, M de Stadler 3/31)
WP 212/8 (A Magiet 41, W Wyngaard 73; ML Price 3/25)

North West beat Western Province by 52 runs, 31 October 2004, Cape Town
NW 210/9 (EO Moleon 43*; F Behardien 3/41, W Samsodien 4/34)
WP 158 (D Worth 52, W Wyngaard 42; WL Coetsee 4/20, MC Rosenberg 3/17)

Western Province beat Griqualand West by 17 runs, 7 November 2004, Kimberley
WP 261/5 (D Worth 64, AR Simpson 44, W Wyngaard 71*, RCC Canning 37*; M Bosman 3/31)
GW 244 (MC Arthur 63, BW Lemmetjies 31, ES Tsamaisi 43*; VD Philander 3/49, W Samsodien 3/44)

Boland beat Western Province by 53 runs, 23 January 2005, Cape Town
Bol 252/5 (H Davids 60, C Prinsloo 100, WJ Louw 30)
WP 199/9 (RCC Canning 65, CJ Alexander 31*; MW Olivier 5/40)

Western Province beat KwaZulu-Natal by 2 runs, 16 October 2005, Chatsworth
WP 265/6 (M Williamson 94, R Munnik 109)
KZN 263 (K Smit 73, M Bekker 66*, R Frylinck 47)

Western Province beat Eastern Province by 77 runs, 22 October 2005, Cape Town
WP 246/7 (M Williamson 35, FD Telo 67; S Mjekula 4/50)
EP 169/9 (C Baxter 58; M Mahlombe 3/34, SG George 3/35)

Boland beat Western Province by 5 wickets, 6 November 2005, Paarl
WP 200 (WC Hantam 53, RCC Canning 65; BL Fransman 6/40, WA Albertyn 3/26)
Bol 201/5 (C Prinsloo 88, WC Swan 49*)

Western Province beat Zimbabwe U-23 by 9 wickets, 13 November 2005, Cape Town
ZimU23 162 (B Mlambo 43, GM Strydom 42; DL Haupt 4/21, MQ Adams 3/53)
WP 163/1 (M Williamson 68*, AJA Gray 48)

Border beat Western Province by 5 wickets, 20 November 2005, Cape Town
WP 121 (RR Richards 3/13, Y Pangabantu 3/33)
Bdr 122/5 (BL Bennett 42)

KwaZulu-Natal beat Western Province by 63 runs, 4 February 2006, Cape Town
KZN 148 (MD Sanders 30; WC Hantam 5/31, JP Geoghegan 3/47)
WP 85 (S Mlongo 5/29, KC Africa 3/23)

Western Province beat Eastern Province by 4 wickets, 12 February 2006, Port Elizabeth
EP 228/9 (C Baxter 41, CA Ingram 39, E Potgieter 31, L Meyer 37; M de Stadler 4/42)
WP 232/6 (AJA Gray 46, DJ Bassage 65, W Wyngaard 30*)

Western Province beat Boland by 6 wickets, 19 February 2006, Cape Town
Bol 242/8 (JG Strydom 49, WC Swan 96*, GC Stevens 43; WC Hantam 3/51)
WP 243/4 (AJA Gray 70, JP Geoghegan 77, Z Homani 44)

Western Province beat Border by 4 runs, 5 March 2006, East London
WP 271/8 (FD Telo 90, RCC Canning 31, F Behardien 37; M Ngam 4/49)
Bdr 267/4 (MF Richardson 69, LL Gamiet 134*)

Western Province beat Kei by 10 wickets, 7 October 2006, Cape Town
Kei 118 (T Ngqolo 40*; WC Hantam 5/22, EP van Wyk 3/26)
WP 121/0 (AJA Gray 66*, M Williamson 48*)

Western Province beat Border by 52 runs (D/L method), target revised to 167 in 32 overs, 29 October 2006, East London
WP 189/9 (M Williamson 37; DL Brown 3/32)
Bdr 114/8 (MF Richardson 38; WC Hantam 3/27)

Western Province beat South Western Districts by 6 wickets, 11 November 2006, Cape Town
SWD 175/7 (NG Brouwers 38, W Hartslief 30*; CWS Birch 3/50)
WP 176/4 (JP Geoghegan 88*, M de Stadler 39*)

Western Province beat KwaZulu-Natal Inland by 8 wickets, 21 January 2007, Cape Town
KI 189/8 (MB Hampson 36, B Moses 48, GM Hampson 45; JP Geoghegan 3/8)
WP 191/2 (M Williamson 101*, RE Levi 30, JM Kuiper 44*)

Western Province beat KwaZulu-Natal by 5 runs (D/L method), target revised to 165 in 33 overs, 4 February 2007, Chatsworth
KZN 221/8 (R Gobind 41, DL Brown 33, KC Africa 33*; EP van Wyk 3/39, M de Stadler 3/34)
WP 169/4 (M Williamson 32, RE Levi 64*, JP Geoghegan 52)

Western Province beat Boland by 38 runs, 18 February 2007, Cape Town
WP 259/6 (JM Kuiper 88*, W Euley 70; CS Abrahams 3/61)
Bol 221 (BC Adams 69, WD Hayward 34, SP Summers 39; EP van Wyk 3/50, M de Stadler 3/36)

Western Province beat Eastern Province by 9 runs, 4 March 2007, Cape Town
WP 222/8 (RCC Canning 46; ACR Birch 3/31)
EP 213 (CA Ingram 65, MBA Smith 30; M de Stadler 3/39)

Northerns beat Northerns by 5 wickets, 17 March 2007, Bellville
WP 164 (JM Kuiper 30)
Nor 165/5 (MA Aronstam 50, P de Bruyn 39*)

Western Province beat KwaZulu-Natal by 5 wickets, 21 October 2007, Cape Town
KZN 246/8 (M Bekker 42, KC Africa 48, DR Miller 71; M Mahlombe 3/39, EP van Wyk 3/47)
WP 250/5 (M Williamson 83, FD Telo 83, JM Kuiper 30)

Western Province beat Eastern Province by 4 wickets, 28 October 2007, Port Elizabeth
EP 244/7 (U Abrahams 34, MBA Smith 55, ACR Birch 37*)
WP 245/6 (M Williamson 70, BL Bennett 42, MQ Adams 44, EP van Wyk 43*)

Western Province beat South Western Districts by 86 runs, 4 November 2007, Oudtshoorn
WP 180 (FD Telo 41, RCC Canning 67, EP van Wyk 32; BL Fransman 3/30)
SWD 94 (JA Beukes 50*; WC Hantam 3/15, EP van Wyk 3/20)

Boland beat Western Province by 4 wickets, 18 November 2007, Paarl
WP 221 (JP Geoghegan 83, AM Sodumo 58; JP Bothma 5/37)
Bol 222/6 (JG Strydom 46, B Hector 55*)

Western Province beat KwaZulu-Natal Inland by 162 runs, 3 February 2008, Cape Town
WP 270/7 (RE Levi 102, JP Geoghegan 107)
KI 108 (FC Plaatjies 4/24)

Border beat Western Province by 8 runs, 16 February 2008, Cape Town
Bdr 263/6 (S de Kock 94*, AZM Dyili 80)
WP 255 (M Williamson 87, JP Geoghegan 32, MQ Adams 35; DL Brown 3/35)

Western Province beat KwaZulu-Natal Inland by 46 runs, 5 October 2008, Bellville
WP 195/9 (AJA Gray 57, SC van Schalkwyk 33*; GM Hampson 4/31, MS van Vuuren 3/38)
KI 149 (MS van Vuuren 57, GM Hampson 32; GR Rabie 3/28, EP van Wyk 2/17, SC van Schalkwyk 2/22, AJA Gray 2/13)

Western Province beat Namibia by 7 wickets, 19 October 2008, Windhoek
Nam 145 (SF Burger 63; GR Rabie 3/22, SC van Schalkwyk 5/30)
WP 146/3 (JM Kuiper 38, RJ Ramoo 46*; L Klazinga 2/28)

Northerns beat Western Province by 4 wickets, 18 January 2009, Pretoria
WP 254/7 (AJA Gray 29, JM Kuiper 97, MD Walters 40, PC Laing 35; LMG Masekela 3/52)
Nor 257/6 (PJ Malan 169*; AJA Gray 2/54)

Western Province beat Free State by 3 wickets, 1 February 2009, Bloemfontein
FS 256/9 (DJ van Wyk 28, LLL Sesele 34, JA Beukes 29, HO von Rauenstein 87; LF Simpson 3/72, AJA Gray 3/31)
WP 260/7 (AJA Gray 86, JM Kuiper 33, AM Northcote 30, TL Tsolekile 30*, CJF Arkell 25; WJ van Zyl 4/34)

Western Province beat Border by 1 run, 15 February 2009, Cape Town
WP 260/5 (AJA Gray 123, CB Cooke 35, RJ Ramoo 74*; DL Brown 2/58)
Bdr 259/9 (MF Richardson 60, BJ Thomas 34, DL Brown 73, AZM Dyili 45*; EP van Wyk 4/42, SA Engelbrecht 3/35)

Western Province beat North West by 5 wickets, 8 March 2009, Cape Town
NW 145 (VCM Mazibuko 36*; EP van Wyk 2/34, J Kohn 2/31, M Mahlombe 2/29, DL-R Piedt 2/30)
WP 146/5 (JM Kuiper 48, MD Walters 52*; MP Siboto 2/33, AN Joubert 2/37)

KwaZulu-Natal beat Western Province by 6 wickets, 28 March 2009, Cape Town
WP 187/9 (EP van Wyk 48, CB Cooke 26; U Govender 2/31, M Shezi 2/44, M Bekker 2/40)
KZN 188/4 (R Gobind 51, P de Bruyn 30*, C Chetty 51*)

Western Province beat KwaZulu-Natal Inland by 6 wickets, 4 October 2009, Pietermaritzburg
KI 199/8 (MS van Vuuren 51, K Nipper 39*, B Moses 33, MW Olivier 5/37, GR Rabie 2/29)
WP 203/4 (MD Walters 56*, AJA Gray 49, Y Vallie 44*, MS van Vuuren 2/33)

South Western Districts beat Western Province by 2 runs, 18 October 2009, Cape Town
SWD 247/6 (BC de Wett 74, JG Strydom 66, RP Hugo 54*, AJA Gray 2/32)
WP 245/7 (AJA Gray 49, Z Allie 39, RJ Ramoo 68)

Western Province beat Border by 128 runs, 1 November 2009, East London
WP 239/7 (Z Allie 29, CB Cooke 31, M Abbas 111*)
Bdr 111 (DL Brown 33, RR Richards 3/35, EP van Wyk 5/33, A-A Temoor 2/18)

North West beat Western Province by 3 wickets (D/L method), target revised to 178 in 31 overs, 8 November 2009, Potchefstroom
WP 199 (M Abbas 37, MY Valllie 38, RCC Canning 41, E Gerber 2/46, VCM Mazibuko 2/38, WL Coetsee 3/41)
NW 178/7 (R Bhayat 79*, BJ Pelser 51, GR Rabie 3/33, EP van Wyk 2/26)

Griqualand West beat Western Province by 5 wickets, 22 November 2009, Kimberley
WP 216/8 (M Williamson 34, SA Engelbrecht 69*, FS Hotszhausen 3/33)
GW 217/5 (AR Swanepoel 60, W Bossenger 55*, C Pietersen 45, MW Olivier 2/53)

Western Province beat KwaZulu-Natal by 32 runs, 17 January 2010, Chatsworth
WP 174/9 (RJ Ramoo 27, PC Laing 31, Q Friend 2/38, V Gobind 2/22, KA Maharaj 3/30)
KZN 142 (KG Buckthorp 51, M Zondeki 3/22, GR Rabie 3/31, MW Olivier 2/14)

Gauteng beat Western Province by 4 wickets, 24 January 2010, Cape Town
WP 248/8 (MD Walters 98, M Abbas 30, RCC Canning 35, P Matshikwe 2/36, R Cameron 2/53)
Gau 249/6 (TG Mokoena 27, DJ Vilas 111, T Bavuma 45, GR Rabie 2/57)

Northerns beat Western Province by 14 runs, 14 February 2010, Cape Town
Nor 213/6 (PJ Malan 40, HE van der Dussen 46, SJ Myburgh 53, FC Plaatjies 3/40, DL-R Piedt 2/37)
WP 199 (MD Walters 77, RJ Ramoo 56, MA Mashimbyi 5/35, LMG Masekela 2/22)

Western Province beat Free State by 43 runs, 21 February 2010, Cape Town
WP 235 (MY Vallie 63, MD Walters 75, PV Mpitsang 5/44, MN Erland 2/33)
FS 192 (DJ van Wyk 59, J van Wyk 31, AJ Pienaar 29, PC Laing 3/46, AJA Gray 4/30, DL-R Piedt 2/28)

Western Province beat Namibia by 99 runs, 28 February 2010, Cape Town
WP 237/8 (MY Vallie 43, M Abbas 49, CB Cooke 58*, L Klazinga 2/45, C Williams 2/43, C Viljoen 2/37)
Nam 138 (E Steenkamp 43, GJ Rudolph 32, A Mgijima 2/14, AJA Gray 4/30, DL-R Piedt 2/28)

Eastern Province beat Western Province by 5 wickets, 7 March 2010, Cape Town
WP 201 (TKM Townsend 37, MY Vallie 36, CB Cooke 27, CR Dolley 3/29, VB Viret 2/28)
EP 203/5 (MBA Smith 26, ML Pirce 30, U Abrahams 75*, D Paterson 2/28)

Easterns beat Western Province by 4 runs, 14 March 2010, Benoni
Eas 270/7 (TM Bodibe 55, J Booysen 82, D Wiese 73, BE Hendricks 2/26, A Mgijima 2/9)
WP 266/7 (MY Vallie 89, RE Levi 29, RJ Ramoo 51, BD Walters 2/58, IC Hlengani 2/39)

No result between Western Province and Boland, 28 March 2010, Cape Town
WP 220/9 (CB Cooke 109*, CJ August 3/26, JP Bothma 3/33, GC Stevens 2/45)
Bol 43/2

Western Province beat Eastern Province by 6 wickets (D/L method), target revised to 123 in 28 overs, 24 October 2010, Cape Town
EP 148 (CN Ackermann 65; D Paterson 3/37)
WP 127/4 (MQ Adams 30*; DJ White 4/21)

Western Province beat KwaZulu-Natal Inland by 5 wickets, 31 October 2010, Cape Town
KI 145/9 (M Olivier 33, K Nipper 39; DL-R Piedt 3/15)
WP 150/5 (AJA Gray 52)

Western Province beat Free State by 3 wickets, 21 November 2010, Bloemfontein
FS 193 (AJ Pienaar 87, RK Terblanche 40; M Mahlombe 4/21)
WP 195/7 (M Williamson 51, MY Vallie 53, RCC Canning 54*; GA Vries 4/28)

Western Province beat Griqualand West by 30 runs, 19 December 2010, Cape Town
WP 208/6 (MD Walters 39, RE Levi 116; AR Swanepoel 3/38)
GW 178/9 (AP McLaren 94; GR Rabie 4/52, BE Hendricks 3/28)

Western Province beat Gauteng by 4 runs (D/L method), target revised to 104 in 25.3 overs, 9 January 2011, Johannesburg
Gau 177 (TG Mokoena 36, DM van Wyk 43, S Burger 41*; KO Wernars 6/27)
WP 107/4

Western Province beat Namibia by 8 runs, 16 January 2011, Windhoek
WP 250/5 (DJ Vilas 120, MY Vallie 50, KO Wernars 37*)
Nam 242 (R van Schoor 46, G Snyman 67, AJ Burger 67; D Paterson 3/30)

Western Province beat North West by 32 runs, 30 January 2011, Cape Town
WP 221/7 (MY Vallie 53, SA Engelbrecht 47, RCC Canning 47, MQ Adams 37*)
NW 189 (AP Agathangelou 63, BJ Pelser 35; M Mahlombe 4/21, DL-R Piedt 3/44)

Northerns beat Western Province by 91 runs, 6 February 2011, Pretoria
Nor 208/6 (JR Richards 54, DKC Bunn 61, CF Schoeman 30)
WP 117 (ER Links 3/26)

Western Province beat South Western Districts by 113 runs, 13 February 2011, Oudtshoorn
WP 203/9 (MD Walters 36, AJA Gray 38, MQ Adams 41; ED Ewerts 3/30)
SWD 90 (RD McMillan 36; DL-R Piedt 4/9, S Simetu 4/5)

Western Province beat Easterns by 8 wickets, 26 February 2011, Cape Town
Eas 195/6 (RA du Plessis 32, G Toyana 62, R Jappie 30)
WP 196/2 (M Williamson 38, MQ Adams 121*)

Western Province beat Border by 7 wickets, 12 March 2011, Cape Town
Bdr 197/9 (BL Bennett 54, CC Young 52; RK Kleinveldt 3/14)
WP 200/3 (MQ Adams 50, AJA Gray 87*, SA Engelbrecht 47*)

Western Province beat KwaZulu-Natal by 149 runs, 20 March 2011, Durban
WP 317/6 (MC Kleinveldt 36, MQ Adams 84, AJA Gray 73, MY Vallie 40*, RK Kleinveldt 55; KW Eccles 3/63)
KZN 168 (C Chetty 35*; DL-R Piedt 4/46)

Boland beat Western Province by 20 runs, 26 March 2011, Paarl
Bol 232/6 (EC Kriek 52, L-R Walters 54*, TWR Cloete 38*; AJA Gray 3/31)
WP 212 (AJA Gray 95*, SA Engelbrecht 51)

CHAPTER 11
Western Province Women's Cricket Association, 1995–2011

Affiliated to the South African Women's Cricket Association and United Cricket Board of South Africa and (after name change on 3 August 2006) Cricket South Africa

The transition to democracy in South Africa, cricket unity and the full admission of South Africa to international cricket for the first time in the 1990s also stimulated the revival of women's cricket in this country after the old South African Women's Cricket Association had fallen into disorganisation in the 1980s.[341]

In June 1991 the United Cricket Board of South Africa (UCBSA) was formed, bringing together all cricketers in the country for the first time. Its entry into world cricket, including the World Cup, gave the game a huge boost. The Development Programme and later the Transformation Charter became key programmes to broaden the base among constituencies that were previously sidelined. The UCBSA came to recognise women cricketers as part of the high-priority 'targeted groups' earmarked for 'accelerated advancement because of historical imbalances', together with black African and disabled cricketers.

Women's cricket not only started growing again, but it also became racially integrated. The principles of redress and equality, including gender equality, became enshrined in the constitution of the new democracy. The issue of women's rights in society, including participation in sport, gained emphasis and helped break down the old view of cricket as strictly a males-only 'gentleman's game'.

The impetus for the reorganisation of women's cricket came from the UCBSA via Conrad Hunte, the legendary West Indian batting star, who was working for the UCBSA on development projects. He called a meeting with Colleen Roberts, vice-president of the then dominant South African Women's Cricket Association (SAWCA), and other stalwarts in October 1995 in Durban, where they decided to 'revive' SAWCA and restart the inter-provincial tournaments that had come to an end in 1986.

What was described as the 'inaugural women and under-19 girls inter-provincial cricket week' took place at Marks Park in Johannesburg on 11–17 December 1995. At a meeting during the tournament, SAWCA was revived 'under a new constitution'. First among the governing principles was 'No limit of gender, race or religion on the committee'. Conrad Hunte was elected president and the four founding provinces – Western Province, KwaZulu-Natal, Northern Transvaal and Transvaal – committed themselves to building the new SAWCA in their areas.[342]

The provincial tournaments became regular annual events. SAWCA expanded, absorbing more provincial affiliates. For the first time an official South African team toured England in 1997 and later that year participated in the World Cup in India. The UCBSA sponsored these first steps by women's cricket to the amount of R650,000 and SAWCA formally became an associate member of the UCBSA at the AGM on 17 June 1997.[343]

Western Province, one of the four founding members, played an important part in the new SAWCA. Rodney Austen was one of four people elected on to the executive. Kim Price, a veteran called out of retirement to play, was made captain of the national team for its first tour abroad. Provincial team-mates Helen Davies, Denise Reid and Aluis Kuylaars were included as well. In addition, Peter Snowball was one of the national selectors and former cricketer Marie van der Merwe went along as the physiotherapist.

Alison Hodgkinson (2000) and Shandré Fritz (2007) were subsequently selected to captain South Africa, but the latter unfortunately injured herself in a diving accident and missed the opportunity. All in all, 16 Western Province players have represented South Africa since the country became part of world cricket in 1997. Internationals Alison Hodgkinson, Cri-Zelda Brits and Suné van Zyl were core players for the province in the 2000s and all-rounders Ashlyn Kilowan and Shandré Fritz, wicketkeeper-batsman Olivia Anderson and fast-bowler Shabnim Ismail provided the main firepower later in the decade. Kilowan became the first Western Province women's cricketer to be listed in the top 20 of the ICC rankings when these were started in 2008/09. In 2010/11, Shandré Fritz hit the fastest Pro20 century in international cricket history, when she scored 116 not out off 71 balls against the Netherlands during the ICC Women's Challenge Twenty20 held in Potchefstroom.

The SAWCA held eight inter-provincial weeks between December 1995 and April 2003 – each of them in a different city. Western Province were the hosts in March 2002 when the tournament was held in Cape Town. The provinces were divided into two groups and the two top teams in both competed against each other in the semi-finals and finals.

From the 2003/04 season, a decentralised inter-provincial league system involving home-and-away games was introduced. This was a sign that women's cricket was coming into its own. UCBSA provided a small annual grant for teams to travel, sometimes by air, and the matches received coverage from official statisticians for the first time.

In 2002, the ICC and the women's IWCC decided to amalgamate, bringing men and women cricketers under one global co-ordinating body. South Africa followed suit, and in September 2005 SAWCA was dissolved and women were fully incorporated into Cricket South Africa (CSA). They now operate under the Amateur Cricket department and a Women's Cricket Committee, headed by former national player Kerri Laing. The Western Province Women's Cricket Association was similarly phased out and the Western Province Women's Committee was incorporated into the Western Province Cricket Association (WPCA) in 2008/09.

This integration of women into mainstream cricket will one day be seen in future as an important step forward. Unfortunately, the current situation of women's cricket in South Africa leaves much to be desired. Standards remain low and only a few provinces have functioning leagues. South Africa is someway behind the top countries in the world, namely Australia, New Zealand, India and England (where women cricketers now play on a professional basis). In 2010, CSA disbanded the Women's Committee because of its lack of representivity and its inability to hold annual general meetings. Greater resources, and support from generally uninterested male cricket establishments, are urgently needed to ensure the future health of the women's game.

Western Province have been provincial champions 7 out of 16 times since the beginning of the new era in cricket. Between 2005/06 and 2008/09, Western Province captured the title three times in four years. Gauteng and Northerns are the next most successful provinces with three titles each. The keenest competition in the 2000s was with neighbours Boland, who were twice champions. Several top former Western Province national players joined Boland, adding needle to these contests.

Just under 100 women's cricketers have represented Western Province since the start of the modern era in 1995. There have been six captains: Avril Kenney-Wade (1995/96), Kim Price (1996/97–1999/2000), Alison Hodgkinson (2000/01–2006/07), Claire Cowan (2003/04), Shandré Fritz (2004/05–2006/07) and Olivia Anderson (2008/09–2010/11). Anderson led the team to three national titles. She played on a semi-pro basis, going over for several winters to Ireland and England, where she turned out for men's club sides and played with success for Surrey.[344]

The president of the WPCA Women's Committee in 2010/11 was Raymond Esterhuizen. Administrators from 1995 onwards included Rodney and Robyn Austen, Kim Price, Rodney Willenberg, Amy Connolly, Shaheed Khan, Isla Manus, Ruby Fritz, Eddie Anderson, Cobus Roodt and Fatima and Labeeb Fortuin.

Eight women's teams were registered to play in the WPCA league in the 2010/11 season, namely Atlantis CC, Bellville A, Bellville B, Langa CC, Old Mutual CC, Tygerberg CC, Somerset West CC and University of the Western Cape. Bellville and Old Mutual have been the two dominant clubs, regularly sharing the league titles between them. The Western Province girls' team plays in the under-19 national tournaments, and in 2009/10 promising women cricketers were taken up in the Western Cape Cricket Academy for the first time.

The WPCA belatedly made women's cricket a strategic priority in the second half of the 2000s. The Association allocated more resources and technical support to the women and involved them in WPCA events and functions.[345] However, women's cricket remains marginal and it will take considerable all-round effort before it becomes fully part of the cricket mainstream. The introduction of cricket in schools is especially important for future sustainability.

11.1 Western Province Women's Cricket Association (later WPCA Women's Cricket Committee) National Players (SAWCA / UCBSA / CSA), 1997/98–2010/11[346]

NAME	TEST			ODI			T20		
	M	From	To	M	From	To	M	From	To
Anderson, OV	–	–	–	5	2007/8	2008	2	2008	2008
Brits, C-Z	4	2001/2	2007	51	2001/2	2010/11	15	2007	2010/11
Cowan, CS	2	2003	2003	–	–	–	–	–	–
Davies, HA	–	–	–	25	1997	2000/1	–	–	–
Dermota, B	–	–	–	3	1997/8	1997/8	–	–	–
Fritz, SA	–	–	–	35	2003	2010/11	13	2008	2010/11
Hodgkinson, AL	3	2001/2	2003	32	2000	2004/5	–	–	–
Ismail, S	1	2007	2007	20	2006/7	2010/11	11	2007	2010/11
Jacobs, LZ	2	2003	2003	–	–	–	–	–	–
Kilowan, APC	1	2007	2007	32	2003	2009/10	11	2007	2009/10
Kuylaars, A	–	–	–	23	1997	2000/1	–	–	–
Lewis, LP	–	–	–	9	1998/9	2000/1	–	–	–
Price, K	–	–	–	26	1997	2000/1	–	–	–
Reid, DJ	1	2001/2	2001/2	17	1997	2001/2	–	–	–
Van der Westhuizen, Y*	–	–	–	2	2008/9	2008/09	–	–	–
Van Zyl, SD	2	2001/2	2003	18	1998/9	2003/04	–	–	–

11.2 Western Province Women's Cricket Association (later WPCA Women's Cricket Committee) Players, 1995/96–2010/11[347]

- Players marked with an asterisk have appeared for South Africa
- 'T' indicates players who played in the centralised inter-provincial tournaments between 1995/96 and 2002/03
- Number shows matches played since the beginning of the decentralised inter-provincial league system in 2003/04

Name	Appearances	Seasons
Abrahams, M	1	2006/07
Adams, G	T	1995/96, 2000/01
Anderson, OV*	61	2004/05, 2005/06, 2006/07, 2007/08, 2008/09 captain, 2009/10, 2010/11
Appels, R	18	2008/09, 2009/10, 2010/11
Auret, E	T/9	2000/01 WP B, 2005/06, 2006/07
Austen, R	T	1995/96, 1996/97, 1997/98, 2000/01 WP B
Austen, W	T	1996/97, 1997/98, 1998/99, 2000/01 WP B
Barnard, J	T	1998/99, 1999/2000, 2000/01, 2001/02, 2002/03
Bester, L	1	2007/08

Name	Appearances	Seasons
Blackshaw, D	T	1995/96
Boome, S	T	1995/96, 1997/98, 1998/99, 1999/2000, 2000/01, 2001/02
Bright, C	T	2000/01 WP B, 2001/02 WP B
Brits, C-Z*	T/5	2002/03, 2003/04
Cartledge, B	T	2000/01 WP B, 2001/02 WP B
Clarke, G	T	1995/96, 1996/97
Cohen, S	T	1995/96, 2000/01 WP B, 2001/02 WP B
Cowan, CS*	T/12	1999/2000, 2000/2001, 2001/02, 2002/03, 2003/04 captain, 2004/05
Cronje, I	T	2001/02 WP B
Crossman, B	6	2007/08, 2008/09
Daniels, A	1	2010/11
Davies, HA*	T	1996/97, 1997/98, 1999/2000, 2001/02
De Koker, S	2	2007/08
De Kuiler, S		
Dermota, B*	T	1995/96, 1996/97, 1997/98, 1998/99, 1999/2000, 2000/01, 2001/02
Edeam, W	T	2000/01 WP B
Enright, P	19	2003/04, 2004/05, 2005/06, 2006/07
Esterhuizen, C	59	2003/04, 2004/05, 2005/06, 2006/07, 2007/08, 2008/09, 2009/10, 2010/11
Fondling, R	29	2005/06, 2006/07, 2007/08, 2008/09, 2009/10, 2010/11
Fourie, Y	26	2007/08, 2007/08, 2008/09, 2009/10, 2010/11
Freeman, A	15	2004/05, 2005/06
Fritz, C	T	2001/02, 2002/03
Fritz, G	T/2	2001/02 WP B, 2002/03, 2003/04
Fritz, L	T	2002/03
Fritz, SA*	66	2003/04, 2004/05 captain, 2005/06, 2006/07, 2008/09, 2009/10, 2010/11
Gilbert, M	T/3	2002/03, 2003/04
Godfrey, L	T	1999/2000
Goliath, C	17	2006/07, 2007/08
Gregg, S	T	1995/96, 1997/98, 1998/99
Hattingh, M	1	2005/06
Heldsinger, A	6	2009/10, 2010/11
Hendricks, N	6	2010/11
Herandien, S	6	2008/09, 2009/10, 2010/11
Hercules, S	43	2003/04, 2004/05, 2005/06, 2006/07, 2007/08
Hodgkinson, AL*	T/30	1999/2000, 2000/01 captain, 2001/02, 2002/03, 2003/04, 2006/07 captain
Ismail, S*	60	2005/06, 2006/07, 2007/08, 2008/09, 2009/10, 2010/11
Jacobs, LZ*	T/30	2001/02 WP B, 2003/04, 2004/05, 2005/06, 2006/07, 2007/08, 2008/09, 2009/10, 2010/11
Jacobs, M	T	2000/01 WP B
Kenney-Wade, A	T	1995/96 captain

Name	Appearances	Seasons
Kilowan, APC*	68	2004/05, 2005/06, 2006/07, 2007/08, 2008/09, 2009/10, 2010/11
Koopman, N	5	2006/07
Kuylaars, A*	T	1995/96, 1996/97, 1997/98, 1998/99, 1999/2000, 2000/01
Le Breton, A	T/72	2001/02 WP B, 2002/03, 2003/04, 2004/05, 2005/06, 2006/07, 2007/08, 2008/09, 2009/10, 2010/11
Lewis, LP*	T	1997/98, 1998/99, 1999/2000
Lotter, MM	T	1998/99, 1999/2000, 2000/01, 2001/02, 2002/03
Marks, E	T	2000/01
Masiba, N	3	2003/04, 2004/05, 2005/06
Meyer, N	T	2000/01 WP B
Moodley, N	5	2010/11
O'Connell, T	T/13	2000/01 WP B, 2001/02 WP B, 2003/04, 2004/05, 2005/06, 2006/07, 2007/08, 2008/09, 2009/10
Parry, H	T/5	2000/01, 2001/02, 2003/04
Penny, L	T/12	2001/02 WP B, 2002/03, 2003/04, 2004/05
Phillips, L	T	1996/97
Pipers, N	38	2006/07, 2007/08, 2008/09, 2009/10, 2010/11
Presens, L	T	2002/03
Price, K*	T	1996/97 captain, 1997/98 captain, 1998/99 captain, 1999/2000 captain
Reid, DJ*	T	1995/96, 1996/97, 1997/98, 1998/99, 1999/2000, 2000/01, 2001/0
Scholtz, P	T	2001/02 WP B
Sewsunker, C	4	2005/06, 2006/07, 2007/08
Shaw, M	10	2006/07, 2007/08
Shopz, P	T	2000/01 WP B
Siljeur, H	T	1996/97
Snowball, S	T	2000/01 WP B
Stofberg, L	T	1995/96, 1996/97, 1997/98, 1998/99
Store, M	T	2000/01 WP B
Town, B	T/6	2001/02 WP B, 2004/05
Van der Heever, T	T	1999/2000
Van der Westhuizen, Y*	16	2005/06, 2006/07
Van Eck, R	17	2008/09, 2009/10, 2010/11
Van Rensburg, Adri	T/2	1995/96
Van Rensburg, Annelize		2001/02 WP B, 2005/06, 2006/07
Van Rensburg, R	T	1995/96, 1996/97
Van Rensburg, T	T	1995/96
Van Zyl, SD*	T/6	1995/96, 1997/98, 1998/99, 1999/2000, 2000/01, 2001/02, 2002/03, 2003/04
Weyers, G	T	2001/02 WP B
Willemse, M	1	2007/08
Williams, K	2	2008/09
Williams, N	T	2000/01, 2001/02
Windsor, J	T	1997/98

11.3 Western Province Women's Cricket Association (later WPCA Women's Cricket Committee) Trophy Winners, 1995/96–2010/11

SAWCA organised eight inter-provincial tournaments from 1995/96 to 2002/03. From 2003/04 new regional provincial leagues replaced annual tournaments, with play-offs between the top teams in two groups at the semi-final stage.

1995/96	Transvaal, 11–17 December 1995, Johannesburg
1996/97	Transvaal, 9–14 December 1996, Durban
1997/98	*Western Province*, 5–17 April 1998, Bloemfontein
1998/99	Northerns, 4–9 April 1999, Pretoria
1999/2000	*Western Province*, 3–7 April 2000, Klerksdorp
2000/01	Northerns, 1–6 April 2001, Stellenbosch
2001/02	*Western Province*, 25–30 March 2002, Cape Town
2002/03	*Western Province*, 31 March – 4 April 2003, East London
2003/04	Boland
2004/05	Gauteng
2005/06	*Western Province*
2006/07	*Western Province*
2007/08	Boland
2008/09	*Western Province*
2009/10	KwaZulu-Natal
2010/11	Northerns

11.4 Western Province Women's Cricket Association / WPCA Women's Cricket Committee Scores, 1995/96–2010/11

FIRST SAWCA INTER-PROVINCIAL TOURNAMENT, 11–17 DECEMBER 1995, JOHANNESBURG[348]
Participating teams: Natal, Northerns, Transvaal, Western Province.
Winners: Transvaal

Transvaal vs Western Province, 11 December 1995, Jeppe Quondam
[no details available]

Western Province vs Natal, 12 December 1995, Athlone Boys High
[no details available]

Western Province vs Northerns, 14 December 1995, Marks Park A
[no details available]

Transvaal vs Western Province, 15–16 December 1995, Marks Park A
[no details available]

SECOND SAWCA INTER-PROVINCIAL TOURNAMENT, 9–14 DECEMBER 1996, DURBAN[349]
Participating teams: Eastern Province, Free State, KwaZulu-Natal, Northern Transvaal, North West, Transvaal, Western Province.
Winners: Transvaal

Western Province vs Northern Transvaal, 9 December 1996, University Field 2
[no details available]

Eastern Province vs Western Province, 10 December 1996, Siripat Road Field 1
[no details available]

Western Province vs Free State, 11 December 1996, University Field 1
[no details available]

Transvaal vs Western Province, 12 December 1996, Siripat Road Field 1
[no details available]

Western Province vs Natal, 13 December 1996, University Field 3
[no details available]

THIRD SAWCA CALTRATE INTER-PROVINCIAL TOURNAMENT, 5–17 APRIL 1998, BLOEMFONTEIN[350]
Participating teams in alphabetical order (per group): Group A – Easterns, England U-21, Gauteng, Kimberley Development, KwaZulu-Natal, Northerns; Group B – Boland, Border, Eastern Province, Free State, North West, Western Province.
Winners: Western Province

Western Province vs North West, 5 April 1998, St Andrew's A
[no details available]

Boland vs Western Province, 6 April 1998, Municipals
[no details available]

Free State vs Western Province, 7 April 1998, St Andrew's A
[no details available]

Western Province vs Eastern Province, 8 April 1998, Schoeman Park A
[no details available]

Border vs Western Province, 9 April 1998, Grey A
[no details available]

Western Province beat [x], 11 April 1998, St Andrew's A (Semi-final)
[no details available]

Western Province beat [x], 13 April 1998, Springbok Park (Final)
[no details available]

FOURTH SAWCA INTER-PROVINCIAL TOURNAMENT, 4–9 APRIL 1999, PRETORIA[351]
Participating teams in alphabetical order (per group): Platinum Group – Boland, Combined XI, Easterns, Free State, North West, Western Province; Gold Group – Border, Eastern Province, Gauteng, Invitation XI, KwaZulu-Natal, Northerns.
Winners: Northerns

Western Province vs Boland, 4 April 1999, Telkom A
[no details available]

Easterns vs Western Province, 5 April 1999, Kentron
[no details available]

Combined XI vs Western Province, 6 April 1999, Weermag Oval
[no details available]

Free State vs Western Province, 7 April 1999, Tukkies Oval
[no details available]

Western Province vs North West, 8 April 1999, Tukkies 1
[no details available]

Semi-finals and Final
[no details available]

FIFTH SAWCA INTER-PROVINCIAL TOURNAMENT, 3–7 APRIL 2000, KLERKSDORP[352]
Participating teams in alphabetical order (per group): Platinum Group – Eastern Province, Free State, Gauteng, Northerns, North West, Western Province; Gold Group – Boland, Border, Conrad Hunte XI, Easterns, Griqualand West, KwaZulu-Natal.
Winners: Western Province

North West vs Western Province, 3 April 2000, Milner High A
[no details available]

Free State vs Western Province, 4 April 2000, Victory Park A
[no details available]

Western Province vs Eastern Province, 5 April 2000, Markotter
[no details available]

Western Province vs Northerns, 6 April 2000, Markotter
[no details available]

Western Province vs Gauteng, 7 April 2000, Milner High A
[no details available]

Western Province beat [x], (Semi-final)
[no details available]

Western Province beat [x], (Final)
[no details available]

SIXTH SAWCA INTER-PROVINCIAL TOURNAMENT, 1–6 APRIL 2001, STELLENBOSCH[353]
Participating teams in alphabetical order (per group): Platinum Group – Easterns, Free State, Gauteng, Northerns, North West, Western Province A; Gold Group – Boland, Border, Eastern Province, Griqualand West, KwaZulu-Natal, Western Province B.
Winners: Northerns

Western Province vs Free State, 2 April 2001, Van der Stel A
[no details available]

Griqualand West vs Western Province B, 2 April 2001, Van der Stel B
[no details available]

Western Province vs Easterns, 3 April 2001, Idas Valley A
[no details available]

KwaZulu-Natal vs Western Province B, 3 April 2001, Idas Valley B
[no details available]

Western Province vs Gauteng, 4 April 2001, Boland PKS
[no details available]

Boland vs Western Province B, 4 April 2001, Idas Valley A
[no details available]

Western Province vs Northerns, 5 April 2001, Idas Valley A
[no details available]

Eastern Province vs Western Province B, 5 April 2001, Idas Valley B
[no details available]

Western Province vs North West, 6 April 2001, Van der Stel A
[no details available]

Border vs Western Province B, 6 April 2001, Cloetesville
[no details available]

SEVENTH SAWCA INTER-PROVINCIAL TOURNAMENT, 25–30 MARCH 2002, CAPE TOWN[354]
Participating teams in alphabetical order (per group): A Division – Eastern Province, Eastern Transvaal (Easterns), Gauteng, Northern Transvaal, North West, Western Province; B Division – Boland, Border, Free State, Griqualand West, Natal, Western Province Strikers (WP B).
Winners: Western Province

Western Province vs Eastern Province, 25 March 2002, Durbanville A
[no details available]

1. Unity at last. The Western Province Cricket Association was formed on 25 June 1991, bringing all cricketers in the province under one umbrella for the first time in more than a hundred years.

2. Kevin Commins, Percy Sonn, Eric van Vlaanderen and Clem Druker (all WPCA) with Krish Mackerdhuj and Geoff Dakin (the first vice-president and president of UCBSA), Clive Lloyd (West Indies) and Ali Bacher (CSA CEO).
3. The Executive Committee of the first united Western Province Cricket Association, 1991/92. Back row: Abubakar Taliep, Mickey Giles, Gavin Pfuhl, Richard Morris, Eric Saxon, Dave Martin, Rushdie Magiet, Steve Anderson, Peter Heeger, Yunus Adams. Front row: Ray Bharoochi, Frank Brache, Kevin Commins (CEO), Clem Druker (president), Percy Sonn, Eric van Vlaanderen, Sadick Emeran, Chris Schutte. Insets: Shafiek Mowzer, André Odendaal, Cyril O'Connor, Donovan Jurgens.

4–7. A key goal of cricket unity was to create opportunities for young people across boundaries of race, class and gender. Top: First unified Western Province schools team, 1991. Back row: GH Taliep, AI Finlayson, AG Corbellari, PG Bester. Middle row: MM Mfobo, GH Hudson, RG Krige, T Robertson, GH Mulholland. Front row: FB Simelela, MS Bredell (captain), KC Richardson (manager), HH Gibbs, M Liebrecht.

8. Cricket unity and democracy led to South Africa becoming truly part of world cricket, and countries such as India, Pakistan, Sri Lanka and West Indies played at Newlands for the first time. Cricket legend Sachin Tendulkar of India (second left) met Nelson Mandela at Newlands in January 1993.

Newlands underwent a complete change of face as the post-unity surge in international cricket led to the building of several new pavilions.
9. Newlands as it looked for the Millennium Test in 2000.
10. Part of a historic precinct including Kelvin Grove Club, the Newlands rugby stadium and the Brewery.

11. First trophy after unity: Castle Cup champions, 1995/96. Back row: Paul Adams, Sven Koenig, Alan Dawson, Herschelle Gibbs, Hylton Ackerman, Aubrey Martyn, Meyrick Pringle, Jacques Kallis, Dave Rundle, Alex Cilliers, Dean MacHelm, Faiek Davids, Paul Kirsten. Front row: Brian McMillan, Mike Minnaar (convener of selectors), John Commins, Clem Druker (president), Eric Simons (captain), Arthur Turner (CEO), Craig Matthews, Duncan Fletcher (manager), Gary Kirsten.

12. SuperSport Series champions, 1998/99. Back row: Ashwell Prince, Renier Munnik, Mulligan George, Ryan Joffe, Claude Henderson, Bradley Player, Lloyd Ferreira, Hassan Pangarker. Front row: HD Ackerman, Goolam Allie (convener of selectors), John Commins, Percy Sonn (president), Craig Matthews (captain), Arthur Turner (CEO), Eric Simons, Duncan Fletcher (manager), Alan Dawson.

13. Democracy brought more opportunities for women's cricketers. 13. The South African touring team to England in 2003. Back row: Shayamal Vallabhjee (trainer), Leighshé Jacobs (WP), Shandré Fritz (WP), Ashlyn Kilowan (WP), Claire Cowan (WP), Cri-Zelda Brits (WP), Alicia Smith, Johmari Logtenberg, Charlize van der Westhuizen, Raymond Booi (coach), Amy Connolly (manager, WP). Front row: Claire Terblanche, Josie Barnard (WP), Nolubabalo Ndzundzu, Alison Hodgkinson (captain, WP), Yulandi van der Merwe (vice-captain), Daleen Terblanche, Suné van Zyl (WP). Kilowan was the first WP player to reach the ICC top twenty player rankings.

14. The 2000/01 Western Province team that won the SuperSport Series Trophy. Back row: Vincent Barnes (coach), Andrew Puttick, Charl Willoughby, Lloyd Ferreira, Renier Munnik, Neil Johnson, Eric Simons, Alan Dawson. Front row: Claude Henderson, Thami Tsolekile, Roger Telemachus, HD Ackerman (captain), Graeme Smith, Ashwell Prince.

15

16

17

19

18

15. Desmond Haynes, Brian McMillan, Gary Kirsten, Eric Simons, Craig Matthews and Meyrick Pringle became part of the cellphone revolution that hit South Africa in the 1990s.
16. New crop: Jacques Kallis, Alan Dawson, Herschelle Gibbs (front) and HD Ackerman.
17. Thami Tsolekile, Roger Telemachus, HD Ackerman and Alan Dawson.
18. Coaches and senior players: Eric Simons, Duncan Fletcher and Gary Kirsten.
19. Peter Kirsten (right) with groundsman James Sebezo.
20. Paul 'Gogga' Adams took 134 test wickets with his unorthodox spin.

20

21. The opening ceremony of the ICC World Cup at Newlands in March 2003. In the same year the WPCA bought the stadium from the Western Province Cricket Club, which had owned it since 1888. Newlands also hosted the first ICC World T20 in 2007 and the opening of the IPL in 2009, as well as high-profile concerts involving Elton John, Lionel Richie and Rod Stewart.
22. President Thabo Mbeki officially opened the World Cup 2003.

23–25. New brand. In 2004/05 Cricket South Africa inaugurated a new era of franchise cricket. Six new regional teams were formed, including the Cape Cobras (initially called Nashua Western Province Boland), replacing the traditional provincial teams at the professional level. This innovation coincided with the emergence of the new 20/20 format, which revolutionised cricket globally.

26. Graeme Smith, most capped SA captain.
27. Jacques Kallis, statistically the greatest all-rounder in the history of cricket.
28. Herschelle Gibbs, hero of the 438 ODI, represented WP and the Cape Cobras for 21 seasons.
29. Thami Tsolekile, captain when the Cape Cobras won their first silverware in 2006/07.
30. Charl Langeveldt, regarded in his prime as the best 'death' bowler in the world.
31. J-P Duminy, an exquisite talent, who played some memorable innings for the Cape Cobras.
32. Andrew Puttick, the leading run-scorer for the Cape Cobras up to 2011.
33. Vernon Philander, the leading wicket-taker for the Cape Cobras up to 2011.
34. Dale Steyn, ranked number one bowler in the world by the ICC, joined the Cape Cobras in the 2010/11 season.
35. Omar Henry, convener of selectors, 2008–11.
36. Ashwell Prince, the first black cricketer to captain South Africa.
37. Double champions, 2010/11: Justin Kemp, most appearances for the Cape Cobras as captain, with coach Richard Pybus.

38. The first four WPCA presidents meet Nelson Mandela: Norman Arendse, Arnold Bloch, Percy Sonn (also CSA and ICC president) and Clem Druker (right) with Peter Heeger (centre).
39. Fifth president, Solomon Makosana (left), with Nabeal Dien and Rushdie Magiet.
40. Haroon Lorgat, former WPCA treasurer, became chief executive of the International Cricket Council in 2008.
41. Peter Cyster, president of Boland Cricket Board and chairman of Western Cape Cricket.
42. Archbishop Desmond Tutu rededicated Newlands stadium on its 120th anniversary, 2 January 2008. Roshan Mahanama (ICC match referee and former Sri Lankan cricketer), Mickey Arthur (SA coach), Mohamed Ebrahim (president WPCA), Logan Naidoo and Norman Arendse (vice-president and president of CSA), Archbishop Desmond Tutu, Shandré Fritz (SA Women) and André Odendaal (CEO).
43. The WPCA Executive Committee in 2009/10. Back row: Ameena Smith, Desmond Barnes, Fezile Mguqulwa, Ashraf Burns, Barry Saunders, David Shandler, Trevor Blake. Front row: Beresford Williams, John Bester (treasurer), Nic Kock (vice-president), Mohamed Ebrahim (president), André Odendaal (CEO), Patrick Wyngaard.

From 2005 onwards, the WPCA made women's cricket a strategic priority.
44. Star Indian all-rounder Anjum Chopra with Madelein Lotter (WP and SA) at Newlands in 2002.
45. WP captain Olivia Anderson receives the inter-provincial trophy for 2008/09 from CSA president Dr Mtutuzeli Nyoka. Raymond Estherhuizen, chairperson of the WP Women's Committee, looks on.
46. Fast-bowler Shabnim Ismail and all-rounders Ashlyn Kilowan and Shandré Fritz were regular members of the national side in the 2000s.

47. First trophy for the Cape Cobras: winners of the MTN Domestic Championship in 2006/07. Back row: Monde Zondeki, Andrew Puttick, Shukri Conrad (coach), Benji Hector. Middle row: Paul Adams, Dominic Telo, Rory Kleinveldt, Vernon Philander. Front row: J-P Duminy, Thami Tsolekile (captain), Adam Bacher, Alan Dawson, Ashwell Prince, Con de Lange.

48. 2008/09 winners of the Standard Bank Pro20 Trophy celebrate. From left are Justin Ontong, Graeme Smith, Andrew Puttick, Herschelle Gibbs, Claude Henderson (obscured) Sybrand Engelbrecht, Charl Langeveldt, Henry Davids, Francois Plaatjies, J-P Duminy, Rob Peters and Leila Steyn (team management).

49. 2009/10 winners of the SuperSport Trophy. Back row: Leila Steyn (administrator), Ryan Canning, Henry Davids, Alastair Gray, Stiaan van Zyl, Shukri Conrad (coach), Johann Louw, Andrew Puttick (captain), Rory Kleinveldt, André Odendaal (CEO), Vernon Philander. Seated: Richard Levi, Terry-Jill Malherbe (physio), Justin Kemp, Jason Douglas (video analyst), Robin Peterson, Johan Pretorius (trainer), Monde Zondeki.

50. Double champions: winners of the SuperSport Series and Standard Bank Pro20 Trophy, 2010/11. Back row: Mohammed Yaseen Vallie, Dane Piedt, Richard Levi, Stiaan van Zyl, Beuran Hendricks, Vernon Philander, Johann Louw, Alistair Gray, Ryan Canning. Front row: Owais Shah, Charl Langeveldt, Justin Ontong, Justin Kemp (captain), Richard Pybus (coach), Andrew Puttick, Rory Kleinveldt.

51. Remembering where we have come from. Mr Jamiel Magmoet, last surviving member of the 1945/46 Barnato Memorial-winning team, received the trophy on behalf of the WPCA from donor San Reddy in 2004. With them were joint franchise captains Ashwell Prince and Graeme Smith.

52. Facing the future. The Cape Cobras beat Australian champions New South Wales convincingly at the Champions League tournament in India in September 2011. From left: Robin Peterson, Richard Levi, J-P Duminy and Dale Steyn.

Western Province B vs Griqualand West, 25 March 2002, Durbanville B
[no details available]

Western Province vs North West, 26 March 2002, Vineyard Oval
[no details available]

Western Province B vs Natal, 26 March 2002, Rhodes Rec
[no details available]

Western Province vs Gauteng, 27 March 2002, Rhodes Rec
[no details available]

Western Province B vs Border, 28 March 2002, Rhodes Rec
[no details available]

Western Province vs Easterns, 29 March 2002, [x]
[no details available]

Western Province B vs Free State, 29 March 2002, Vineyard Oval
[no details available]

Western Province vs Northern Transvaal, 30 March 2002, Newlands
[no details available]

Western Province B vs Free State, 30 March 2002, Alma Marist
[no details available]

Western Province beat [x], (Semi-final)
[no details available]

Western Province beat [x], (Final)
[no details available]

EIGHTH SAWCA INTER-PROVINCIAL TOURNAMENT, 31 MARCH – 4 APRIL 2003, EAST LONDON[355]
Participating teams in alphabetical order (per group): Platinum – Border, Easterns, Eastern Province, North West, Northerns, Western Province; Gold – Boland, Free State, Gauteng, Griqualand West, KwaZulu-Natal, SAWCA Invitation 12.
Winners: Western Province

Western Province vs Eastern Province, 31 March 2003, United
[no details available]

Western Province vs Border, 1 April 2003, Buffalo Park
[no details available]

Western Province vs North West, 2 April 2003, Old Boys
[no details available]

Western Province vs Easterns, 3 April 2003, Buffalo Park
[no details available]

Western Province vs Northerns, 4 April 2003, Bohemians
[no details available]

Western Province beat [x], (Semi-final)
[no details available]

Western Province beat [x], (Final)
[no details available]

2003/04 ONWARDS: NEW DECENTRALISED REGIONAL PROVINCIAL LEAGUES, WITH PLAY-OFFS BETWEEN TOP TEAMS IN TWO GROUPS AT SEMI-FINAL STAGE[356]
Winners: Boland

Boland beat Western Province by 5 wickets, 11 October 2003, Cape Town
WP 153/9 (CS Cowan 69*)
Bol 154/5 (J Barnard 54; SD van Zyl 3/19)

Eastern Province beat Western Province by 2 runs, 18 October 2003, Cape Town
EP 179/7 (CS Terblanche 72*)
WP 177/6 (T O'Connell 46; D van As 3/29)

Match between Western Province and Border abandoned without a ball bowled, 25 October 2003, Cape Town

Western Province beat Free State by 143 runs, 26 October 2003, Cape Town
WP 238/6 (C-Z Brits 53, T O'Connell 32, SD van Zyl 54; M Adams 3/48)
FS 95 (LZ Jacobs 5/23)

Western Province beat Griqualand West by 244 runs, 15 November 2003, Cape Town
WP 310/2 (CS Cowan 85; C-Z Brits 87, L Penny 95*)
GW 66 (SD van Zyl 5/12)

Match between Border and Western Province abandoned without a ball bowled, 24 January 2004, East London

Eastern Province beat Western Province by 77 runs, 25 January 2004, Port Elizabeth
EP 174/6 (E Webber 53*, S Pillay 31, R Claasen 49; SD van Zyl 3/25)
WP 97 (E Webber 3/9)

Free State beat Western Province by default without a ball bowled, 31 January 2004, Bloemfontein

Griqualand West beat Western Province by default without a balled bowled, 1 February 2004, Kimberley

Boland beat Western Province by 3 runs, 7 March 2004, Stellenbosch
Bol 219/6 (J Barnard 100*)
WP 216/9 (L Penny 36, AL Hodgkinson 75, SD van Zyl 46)

Boland beat Western Province by 4 wickets, 2 October 2004, Cape Town
WP 204/7 (L Penny 56, AL Hodgkinson 35, SA Fritz 43*)
Bol 205/6 (AE Smith 88*)

Border beat Western Province by 1 wicket, 10 October 2004, Cape Town
WP 134 (A Freeman 42; N Ndzundzu 4/13)
Bdr 135/9 (L Jordaan 30; SA Fritz 4/30)

Western Province beat Eastern Province by 18 runs, 24 October 2004, Cape Town
WP 156/7 (CS Cowan 32, SA Fritz 31, APC Kilowan 33; L Pienaar 3/26)
EP 138/8 (CS Terblanche 34)

Border beat Western Province by 4 wickets, 30 October 2004, East London
WP 167/7 (CS Cowan 55, APC Kilowan 32; L Jordaan 3/23)
Bdr 168/6 (B Ramjee 37)

Eastern Province beat Western Province by 60 runs, 31 October 2004, Port Elizabeth
EP 154/7 (S Hercules 3/24)
WP 94 (AL Hodgkinson 35; S Pillay 4/5)

Boland beat Western Province by 6 wickets, 27 November 2004, Paarl
WP 173/6 (L Penny 68*)
Bol 174/4 (J Barnard 32, SD van Zyl 46, AE Smith 39*, M Lotter 30*)

Western Province beat North West by default without a ball bowled, 6 February 2005, Cape Town

Western Province beat Mpumalanga by default without a ball bowled, 13 February 2005, Cape Town

Boland beat Western Province by 24 runs, 20 February 2005, Stellenbosch
Bol 214/8 (J Barnard 31, HW Rambaldo 34, AE Smith 51)
WP 190 (AL Hodgkinson 44, CS Cowan 47; AE Smith 3/31, LZ Jacobs 3/41)

Match between Free State and Western Province abandoned without a ball bowled, 29 October 2005, Bloemfontein

Western Province beat Griqualand West by 10 wickets, 30 October 2005, Kimberley
GW 111 (L Geyer 32; A le Breton 4/34)
WP 112/0 (AL Hodgkinson 30*, Y van der Westhuizen 57*)

Boland beat Western Province by 8 wickets, 6 November 2005, Cape Town
WP 95 (S Loubser 4/27)
Bol 97/2 (HW Rambaldo 40*)

Match between South Western Districts and Western Province abandoned without a ball bowled, 13 November 2005, Oudtshoorn

Western Province beat Free State by 10 wickets, 8 January 2006, Cape Town
FS 166 (SM Benade 101; SA Fritz 3/25)
WP 168/0 (AL Hodgkinson 75*, Y van der Westhuizen 78*)

Western Province beat South Western Districts by 7 wickets, 15 January 2006, Cape Town
SWD 99 (S Ismail 3/14)
WP 100/3 (SA Fritz 38*)

Western Province beat Eastern Province by 7 wickets, 29 January 2006, Cape Town
EP 85 (SA Fritz 5/13)
WP 89/3 (SA Fritz 38*)

Western Province beat Border by 2 wickets, 11 February 2006, East London
Bdr 139/9 (L Jordaan 38; SA Fritz 3/17)
WP 140/8 (Y van der Westhuizen 46)

Eastern Province beat Western Province by 6 wickets, 12 February 2006, Despatch
WP 120 (AL Hodgkinson 32, A le Breton 30; S Pillay 5/9)
EP 121/4 (M Strydom 33)

Western Province beat Border by 4 wickets, 19 February 2006, Cape Town
Bdr 110 (L Jordaan 32; APC Kilowan 3/21, SA Fritz 3/13)
WP 114/6 (AL Hodgkinson 51*; E Pienaar 3/24)

Western Province beat Griqualand West by 10 wickets, 5 March 2006, Cape Town
GW 81 (L Geyer 38; A le Breton 5/24)
WP 85/0 (A le Breton 42*)

Boland beat Western Province by 39 runs, 12 March 2006, Paarl
Bol 267/5 (S Loubser 45, HW Rambaldo 31, CS Terblanche 86*, AE Smith 45)
WP 228/9 (A le Breton 40, P Enright 50, S Ismail 31)

Western Province beat KwaZulu-Natal by 79 runs, 1 April 2006, Durban
WP 186/8 (J Logtenberg 4/36)
KZN 107 (J Logtenberg 33; C Esterhuizen 4/18)

Western Province beat Boland by 4 wickets, 8 April 2006, Brackenfell
Bol 145 (A Petersen 56; SA Fritz 4/29)
WP 148/6 (SA Fritz 80*)

Boland beat Western Province by 5 wickets, 7 October 2006, Paarl
WP 126 (Y van der Westhuizen 39; N Christiaans 3/16)
Bol 127/5

Western Province beat Eastern Province by 9 wickets, 21 October 2006, Cape Town
EP 105 (APC Kilowan 3/28, A le Breton 3/12)
WP 106/1 (OV Anderson 34, A le Breton 56*)

Western Province beat Border by 116 runs, 4 November 2006, East London
WP 237/6 (OV Anderson 74, A le Breton 49, SA Fritz 64)
Bdr 121 (M Kirchoff 43; APC Kilowan 4/32, A Le Breton 4/36)

Western Province beat Eastern Province by 39 runs, 5 November 2006, Despatch
WP 140 (Y van der Westhuizen 55)
EP 101 (C Esterhuizen 4/29)

Western Province beat South Western Districts by 171 runs, 19 November 2006, Oudtshoorn
WP 240/7 (OV Anderson 60, Y van der Westhuizen 46, P Enright 35)
SWD 69 (A le Breton 3/13, P Enright 3/6)

Western Province beat Griqualand West by 7 wickets, 13 January 2007, Cape Town
GW 95 (APC Kilowan 5/18, S Ismail 3/28)
WP 96/3 (OV Anderson 31, A van Rensburg 37)

South Western Districts beat Western Province by 90 runs, [x], Cape Town
SWD 173 (C Crause 50, S Coetzee 38; S Hercules 3/17, R Fondling 4/29)
WP 83 (H Pienaar 4/22)

Border beat Western Province by 36 runs, 11 February 2007, Cape Town
Bdr 114 (A Taai 34; A le Breton 3/31)
WP 78 (APC Kilowan 32; M Kirchoff 3/16)

Western Province beat Griqualand West by 10 wickets, 24 February 2007, Kimberley
GW 22 (APC Kilowan 3/6, N Pipers 7/6)
WP 23/0

Western Province beat Free State by 5 wickets, 25 February 2007, Bloemfontein
FS 204/4 (SM Benade 127*, A Minny 42)
WP 208/5 (A le Breton 72, APC Kilowan 48)

Western Province beat Free State by 91 runs, 10 March 2007, Cape Town
WP 231/3 (OV Anderson 48, A le Breton 94*, P Enright 31, S Ismail 35*)
FS 140/9 (S Haven 38)

Boland beat Western Province by 6 wickets, 18 March 2007, Bellville
WP 94 (S Loubser 3/16)
Bol 95/4 (AE Smith 36*; APC Kilowan 3/32)

Western Province beat Northerns by 10 wickets, 31 March 2007, Centurion
Nor 119 (S Hercules 4/21)
WP 125/0 (OV Anderson 67*, A le Breton 50*)

Western Province beat Boland by 1 wicket, 7 April 2007, Paarl
Bol 138
WP 140/9 (OV Anderson 33)

Western Province beat KwaZulu-Natal Inland by 283 runs, 14 October 2007, Cape Town
WP 329/4 (OV Anderson 84, A le Breton 35, APC Kilowan 116)
KI 46 (SA Fritz 6/20)

Western Province beat South Western Districts by 10 wickets, 20 October 2007, Oudtshoorn
SWD 57 (SA Fritz 5/17)
WP 61/0

Western Province beat Eastern Province by 7 wickets, 3 November 2007, Despatch
EP 74 (SA Fritz 4/20, C Goliath 3/16)
WP 75/3

KwaZulu-Natal beat Western Province by 5 runs, 10 November 2007, Chatsworth
KZN 221/3 (T Chetty 64, J Logtenberg 109*)
WP 216/5 (A le Breton 68, APC Kilowan 30, SA Fritz 36, S Ismail 36*)

Boland beat Western Province by 6 wickets, 17 November 2007, Cape Town
WP 141 (AE Smith 5/28, S Loubser 3/28)
Bol 142/4 (AL Hodgkinson 56*)

Border beat Western Province by 6 runs, 24 November 2007, Cape Town
Bdr 158/9 (S Pillay 37)
WP 152/9 (OV Anderson 54; S Pillay 3/36)

Gauteng beat Western Province by 49 runs, 18 October 2008, Johannesburg
Gau 145 (K Thomson 26, N Landie 47; S Ismail 2/24)
WP 96 (K Thomson 4/28, N Thabethe 2/16)

Western Province beat Northerns by 6 wickets, 2 November 2008, Pretoria
Nor 114 (C Watt 33; APC Kilowan 2/31, SA Fritz 2/9, LZ Jacobs 2/16)
WP 115/4 (OV Anderson 59*)

Western Province beat KwaZulu-Natal by 5 wickets, 29 November 2008, Durban
KZN 140 (T Chetty 26, N Nel 25, J Hambrook 29*; N Pipers 2/24, LZ Jacobs 5/36)
WP 144/5 (OV Anderson 41, SA Fritz 36*; N Sole 2/22)

Western Province beat Boland by 22 runs, 10 January 2009, Cape Town
WP 151/8 (S Loubser 3/17)
Bol 129 (S Loubser 56; APC Kilowan 2/14, SA Fritz 2/24, N Pipers 3/22)

Western Province beat Border by 165 runs, 17 January 2009, Cape Town
WP 220/2 (A le Breton 40, APC Kilowan 84*, SA Fritz 61*)
Bdr 55 (S Ismail 3/24, Y Fourie 2/25, LZ Jacobs 3/5)

Western Province beat Eastern Province by 7 wickets, 7 February 2009, Cape Town
EP 57 (M Kapp 29; SA Fritz 5/8, S Ismail 3/3)
WP 60/3 (L Pienaar 2/15)

Free State vs Western Province match abandoned without a ball bowled, 15 February 2009, Bloemfontein

Western Province beat Eastern Province by 9 wickets, 3 October 2009, Despatch
EP 82 (M Seale 30; N Pipers 4/13, Y Fourie 2/24, LZ Jacobs 2/7)
WP 83/1 (OV Anderson 42*, A le Breton 28)

Western Province beat Border by 80 runs, (D/L method), target revised to 136 in 29 overs, 4 October 2009, East London
WP 237/5 (OV Anderson 37, A le Breton 28, SA Fritz 65, APC Kilowan 61*; E Pienaar 3/52)
Bdr 55/5 (S Ismail 2/16, Y Fourie 2/14)

Western Province beat South Western Districts by 179 runs, 1 November 2009, Cape Town
WP 238/7 (OV Anderson 26, A le Breton 74, APC Kilowan 30; E Pietersen 2/43, B Goliath 2/43)
SWD 59 (APC Kilowan 4/13, S Ismail 3/9)

Western Province beat Boland by 96 runs, 21 November 2009, Paarl
WP 188 (OV Anderson 69, LZ Jacobs 32, APC Kilowan 35; Y Potgieter 2/25, N Christiaans 2/35)
Bol 92 (AL Hodgkinson 25; S Ismail 3/18, LZ Jacobs 4/13)

Western Province beat Eastern Province by 151 runs, 9 January 2010, Cape Town
WP 213/6 (OV Anderson 70, SA Fritz 53*; J Nell 2/39)
EP 62 (N Pipers 2/12, C Esterhuizen 2/5, Y Fourie 2/1)

Western Province beat Border by 8 wickets, 10 January 2010, Cape Town
Bdr 44 (APC Kilowan 6/15)
WP 45/2

Western Province beat South Western Districts by 199 runs, 24 January 2010, Mossel Bay
WP 273/6 (OV Anderson 99, LZ Jacobs 34, SA Fritz 63*, R Appels 28; E Pietersen 3/43)
SWD 74 (Y Fourie 3/12)

Boland beat Western Province by 44 runs, 13 February 2010, Cape Town
Bol 203/5 (Y van der Westhuizen 84, I Cronje 25, AE Smith 46*; APC Kilowan 2/26)
WP 159 (APC Kilowan 32; AE Smith 2/22, S Loubser 3/32)

Western Province beat Northerns by 8 wickets, 6 March 2010, Cape Town
Nor 56 (S Ismail 2/26, LZ Jacobs 4/11, A le Breton 2/4)
WP 57/2

KwaZulu-Natal beat Western Province by 4 wickets, 20 March 2010, Durban
WP 125 (APC Kilowan 27, S Ismail 27*; D Devnarain 3/30, R Maharaj 2/25)
KZN 126/6 (N Sole 48; APC Kilowan 2/18, N Pipers 3/14)

Boland beat Western Province by 2 wickets, 9 October 2010, Cape Town
WP 139/8 (LZ Jacobs 49*; N Christiaans 3/17)
Bol 142/8 (Y van der Westhuizen 72)

Western Province beat Eastern Province by 7 wickets, 6 November 2010, Despatch
EP 129/8 (M Kapp 48)
WP 130/3 (SA Fritz 82*)

Border vs Western Province match abandoned without a ball bowled, 7 November 2010, East London

Western Province beat South Western Districts by 10 wickets, 15 January 2011, Oudtshoorn
SWD 27 (S Ismail 5/17, Y Fourie 4/2)
WP 28/0

Western Province beat Kei by 9 wickets, 30 January 2011, Cape Town
Kei 22 (S Ismail 3/12, APC Kilowan 6/10)
WP 24/1

Western Province beat Eastern Province by 10 wickets, 12 February 2011, Cape Town
EP 102 (CS Terblanche 59; APC Kilowan 3/25)
WP 105/0 (SA Fritz 69*)

Western Province beat Border by 9 wickets, 13 February 2011, Cape Town
Bdr 107 (A Bosch 32; C Esterhuizen 3/19, SA Fritz 4/17)
WP 111/1 (OV Anderson 31, SA Fritz 56*)

Western Province beat South Western Districts by 8 wickets, 26 February 2011, Cape Town
SWD 57 (S Ismail 5/17, APC Kilowan 3/20)
WP 59/2

Western Province beat Kei by 410 runs, 13 March 2011, Ngumbela Park
WP 457/8 (OV Anderson 40, A le Breton 71, N Moodley 77, R Appels 30, R van Eck 78, APC Kilowan 47, S Ismail 44)
Kei 47 (Y Fourie 5/2)

Boland beat Western Province by 1 run, 26 March 2011, Stellenbosch
Bol 159/7 (AL Hodgkinson 87*)
WP 158 (A le Breton 38; AE Smith 3/29)

CHAPTER 12

Cape Cobras, 2004–2011

Part-owned by Western Province Cricket Association and affiliated to the United Cricket Board of South Africa / Cricket South Africa[357]

In 2004 the United Cricket Board of South Africa introduced a new franchise system for domestic professional cricket, reducing the eleven provincial teams to six new regional teams. The existing provinces in each region were mandated to combine and create regional structures to run the new franchise teams.[358] Individual provinces were henceforth to play amateur cricket only. This was a major change. It meant that Western Province, after many years of competing at the highest levels, would no longer have a professional team.

The Western Province Cricket Association and its professional companies now worked with the Boland Cricket Board to set up a new franchise company. Heads of agreement were signed on 22 January 2004. Exact Trade 126 (Pty) Ltd was registered on 2 February 2004, changing its name to Western Cape Cricket (Pty) Ltd on 6 February 2004.

The shareholders of Western Cape Cricket (Pty) Ltd, or WCC, as it is known in its abbreviated form, are Boland Cricket (33 per cent) and Western Province Professional Cricket (Pty) Ltd (66 per cent). The latter, in turn, is half owned by the Western Province Cricket Association and by the SuperSport television group.

The aim of the new regional franchise system was to encourage 'strength versus strength' in order to increase the standards of domestic professional cricket and, consequently, help bridge the gap between domestic and international cricket. The old 11-team provincial system was reduced to a more elite and competitive six-team system. Out of this emerged the Cape Cobras (Boland and Western Province), the Dolphins (KwaZulu-Natal and KwaZulu-Natal Inland), the Eagles (Free State and Griqualand West), the Lions (Gauteng and North West), the Titans (Northerns and Easterns) and the Warriors (Border and Eastern Province). The number of professional players in South Africa shrank accordingly from around 170 to roughly 100. The amount of money the new franchises were allowed to spend on players was capped and so were the salaries of players. There was a flow of players from previous provincial teams to the new franchises, which largely equalised playing strengths.

The franchise system was informally launched in March 2004 with the inaugural Standard Bank Pro20 competition. The introduction of the new system thus also went together with a completely new format of cricket, Twenty20, which soon captured the imagination of fans in South Africa and elsewhere.

In the first official season of franchise cricket in 2004/05, the new Western Cape team played as Nashua Western Province Boland. Its debut first-class match was at Kingsmead aginst the Nashua Dolphins from 7 to 10 October 2004. The team included ten internationals. A strong batting line-up of Graeme Smith, Herschelle Gibbs, Andrew Puttick, Jacques Kallis, Ashwell Prince and J-P Duminy was strengthened by wicketkeeper Thami Tsolekile (who equalled the South African record at the time of seven dismissals in an innings) and a bowling attack of Alan Dawson, Charl Willoughby, Paul Adams, Kallis and Rory Kleinveldt (the only player at the time not capped for South Africa).

After extensive planning a new name and brand, the Cape Cobras, was adopted and launched in September 2005. It made an immediate impact. From a clumsy amalgam of provincial titles, the new Cape Cobras in their blue and gold colours became an instantly recognisable brand. The team sponsors were Nashua and later Nashua Mobile.

In 2006/07, Western Cape Cricket (Pty) Ltd signed a memorandum of agreement regulating the running of professional cricket in South Africa. It was the product of negotiations between Cricket South Africa, the South Africa Cricketers' Association and the franchises, and took cricket another step forward into the professional era.

The chairmen of Western Cape Cricket (Pty) Ltd between 2004 and 2011 were Arnold Bloch, Advocate Norman Arendse, Dr Peter Cyster and Mohamed Ebrahim. The first chief executive, Arthur Turner, resigned after a few months and was succeeded by Prof. André Odendaal. The coaches were Peter Kirsten (2004/05), Shukri Conrad (2005/06-2009/10) and former Pakistan coach Richard Pybus, who assumed duties in 2010/11. Haroon Lorgat, who went on to become CEO of the International Cricket Council, and former international players such as Steve Palframan, Omar Henry and Brian McMillan contributed by their presence on playing and selection committees.

Shortly after the formation of the franchise, the WCC Board decided that the Cobras should focus for strategic reasons on the limited-overs format of the game, where increasingly all the spectator interest and money were concentrated. First-class cricket remained important as a nursery for the national team and for honing cricket skills, but businesswise it no longer drew spectators or income. After this, the Cobras did excellently to reach ten consecutive limited-overs semi-finals: four were won, one was lost off the last ball and another stopped because of rain.

The distinct upward curve in the Cobras' performance translated into five trophies in five seasons. The first was the 45-over MTN Domestic Championship in 2006/07. This was followed by the Standard Bank Pro20 Trophy in 2008/09, the SuperSport Trophy for first-class cricket in 2009/10 and 2010/11 and the Pro20 title again in 2010/11. The Pro20 successes meant that the Cobras qualified for two of the first three Champions League tournaments in India, in effect the new world championships for domestic teams, or 'clubs' as the Indian organisers (with their private ownership model) refer to it.

All three limited-overs titles came after home finals before sell-out crowds at Sahara Park Newlands. In November 2006, the Cobras, led by Thami Tsolekile, beat the Warriors by 18 runs in the 45-over MTN Domestic Championship in thrilling fashion in front of 16,000 home fans. This was the swansong game of Alan Dawson. He and another veteran, Adam Bacher, lured out of retirement in Gauteng, were key players in the series. Bacher (41) and the reliable Andrew Puttick (50) were the best batsmen in the final, while Con de Lange (4/40) and Rory Kleinveldt (3/42) were the best bowlers. No less than eight

Cobras represented the national side that season, including the three players who captained South Africa in the preceding year, namely Graeme Smith, Ashwell Prince and Jacques Kallis.

On 21 February 2009 the Cobras won the Standard Bank Pro20 competition for the first time. Herschelle Gibbs and Charl Langeveldt brought their great experience and skill to bear and carried the Cobras home against the Eagles. In a riveting series, four of the matches were decided off the last ball – and, in an outcome that couldn't have been scripted, both third-leg semi-finals ended in ties and (a new phrase for cricket) 'super overs'.

By winning the Standard Bank Pro20 competition, the Cape Cobras qualified for the first ever Champions League tournament held in India from 8 to 23 October 2009. CLT20 signalled phase three of a new 20/20 revolution in cricket, after the dramatic inauguration of the format at international level at the first ICC World Twenty20 in September 2007 and the multi-billion-dollar explosion that followed with the first IPL tournament in April–June 2008. According to the founders, CLT20 is meant to become the 'big brother' of the IPL and the equivalent of UEFA's Champions League in football.

The Cobras and Eagles from South Africa were among 12 participants in the inaugural Champions League, together with Deccan Chargers, Royal Challengers Bangalore and Delhi Daredevils from India; New South Wales and Victorian Bushrangers from Australia; Somerset and Sussex from England; Wayamba Elevens from Sri Lanka; Otago Volts from New Zealand; and Trinidad & Tobago from West Indies. The Cobras were drawn to play the opening game of the opening tournament against the star-studded Royal Challengers Bangalore at their home ground, Chinnaswamy Stadium. Thanks to a magnificent 99 not out by J-P Duminy, the team chased down 180 to win, silencing 37,000 home supporters. They proceeded to beat comprehensively Otago and the strong Victorian Bushrangers to reach the semi-finals. Despite losing to Trinidad & Tobago in the semi-final, the Cobras played excellent cricket against top opposition and announced themselves as a world-class team and global cricket brand.[359]

After an excellent start to the 2009/10 season, the Cobras fell out in the semi-finals of the MTN 40 and Standard Bank Pro20 competitions but managed to secure for the first time the four-day SuperSport Trophy, the premier honour in South African cricket before the 20/20 revolution started upsetting established hierarchies. The Cobras won six games in a row in the final stretch. Vernon Philander spearheaded the bowling, taking 45 Super-Sport wickets with his 'skill, combative mindset and superb economy' to top the national averages. Robin Peterson in his first season for the Cobras took 30 wickets and also contributed 316 runs, including a century. Stiaan van Zyl (696 runs at an average of 58.00) and Andrew Puttick (678 runs at an average of 52.15) were the best batsmen.[360]

In 2010/11 the Cobras under Justin Kemp and new coach Richard Pybus were back as Pro20 champions after a record chase of 224/5 in the semi-finals and a convincing 12-run win in the final against the Warriors on 18 March 2011. Decisive in this achievement were a rollicking start of 88 runs off nine overs by in-form Richard Levi and the veteran Herschelle Gibbs and a tight bowling spell by Claude Henderson. The former England player Owais Shah was the star of the campaign, hitting 293 runs at an average of 73.25

and a strike rate of 147.23. The ranks of the double champions were also strengthened by the arrival from the Titans of the number one bowler in the world, Dale Steyn, during this season.

Since 1991, the Western Cape has been a proven nursery for South African cricket and a leader in transformation. Besides home-grown greats like Kirsten, Kallis and Gibbs, exactly half of the 30 black players who represented South Africa up to 2010 came from this region or had represented Western Province, Boland or Cape Cobras. Altogether 68 players turned out for the Cobras in all formats in the first seven seasons to 2010/11. The official captains were Ashwell Prince, Graeme Smith, Thami Tsolekile, Andrew Puttick and Justin Kemp.

The selection of three Cobras superstars – Smith, Kallis and Gibbs – in the first-ever ICC World test and one-day teams in 2005 and the performances of the Cape Cobras in the inaugural Champions League in India in 2009 also highlighted the fact that the Western Cape has one of the strongest cricket cultures and structures in the world.[361] No fewer than ten of the eleven Cobras who beat the Royal Challengers Bangalore with their R50 million player pool (ten times the WCC amount) were Western Cape products. Reflecting the deep roots of cricket in the region, eight of the players in this winning team were black, a total inversion of apartheid-era practices and mentalities. Six other cricketers brought up in the Western Province played in the Champions League for Somerset, Bangalore and the Eagles.

At the time when domestic cricket competitions went global, the tradition of Western Province and the Cobras as a pillar of South African domestic cricket since 1890 expanded beyond the borders of South Africa as well.

12.1 Cape Cobras National Players (UCBSA / CSA), 2004/05–2010/11[362]

NAME	TEST			ODI			T20		
	M	From	To	M	From	To	M	From	To
Ackerman, HD	4	1997/8	1997/8[363]	–	–	–	–	–	–
Adams, PR	45	1995/6	2003/4	24	1995/6	2003	–	–	–
Bacher, AM*	19	1996/7	1999/00	13	1996/7	2004/5	–	–	–
Dawson, AC	2	2002/3	2002/3	19	1998/9	2004	–	–	–
Duminy, J–P	12	2008/9	2009/10	78	2004	2010/11	30	2007/8	2010/11
Gibbs, HH	90	1996/7	2007/8	248	1996/7	2009/10	23	2005/6	2010
Harris, PL*	37	2006/7	2010/11	3	2007/8	2007/8[364]	–	–	–
Henderson, CW*	7	2001/2	2002/3	4	2001/2	2001/2	–	–	–
Henderson, T*	–	–	–	–	–	–	1	2006/7	2006/7
Kallis, JH	144	1995/6	2010/11	309	1995/6	2010/11	16	2005/6	2010
Kemp, JM	4	2000/1	2005/6	79	2000/1	2007/8	8	2005/6	2007/8
Kleinveldt, RK	–	–	–	–	–	–	2	2008/9	2010
Langeveldt, CK	6	2004/5	2005/6	72	2001/2	2010/11	9	2005/6	2010
Louw, J*	–	–	–	3	2008/9	2008/9	2	2008/9	2008/9
Ontong, JL	2	2001/2	2004/5	25	2000/1	2008/9	3	2007/8	2008/9
Peterson, RJ	6	2002/3	2007/8	47	2002/3	2010/11	7	2005/6	2010/11

NAME	TEST			ODI			T20		
	M	From	To	M	From	To	M	From	To
Philander, VD	–	–	–	7	2007	2008	7	2007/8	2007/8
Prince, AG	62	2001/2	2010/11	49	2002/3	2006/7	1	2005/6	2005/6
Puttick, AG	–	–	–	1	2005/6	2005/6	–	–	–
Smith, GC	90	2001/2	2010/11	171	2001/2	2010/11	31	2005/6	2010/11
Telemachus, R	–	–	–	37	1997/8	2006/7	3	2005/6	2006/7
Tsolekile, TL	3	2004/5	2004/5	–	–	–	–	–	–
Willoughby, CM	2	2002/3	2003	3	1999/00	2002/3	–	–	–
Zondeki, M	6	2003	2008/9	11	2002/3	2008/9	1	2005/6	2005/6

Cape Cobras players who represented South Africa while playing for other franchises or provinces (including Western Province and Boland before 2004/05).

12.2 Cape Cobras Players, 2004/05–2010/11[365]

NAME	FIRST-CLASS			LIMITED OVERS			T20		
	M	From	To	M	From	To	M	From	To
Ackerman, HD	4	2005/6	2005/6						
Adams, PR	15	2004/5	2006/7	6	2004/5	2007/8	12	2003/4	2005/6
Albertyn, WA				2	2005/6	2005/6	3	2005/6	2005/6
Bacher, AM				12	2006/7	2006/7	7	2006/7	2006/7
Bassage, DJ	22	2004/5	2006/7	8	2004/5	2005/6	4	2004/5	2004/5
Bothma, JP	1	2008/9	2008/9						
Brand, D							5	2008/9	2009/10
Canning, RCC	40	2006/7	2010/11	21	2005/6	2010/11	11	2007/8	2009/10
Carolus, D				1	2010/11	2010/11			
Carter, NM				5	2009/10	2009/10			
Conrad, S	1	2005/6	2005/6						
Davids, H	33	2004/5	2009/10	40	2004/5	2009/10	44	2003/4	2009/10
Dawson, AC	11	2004/5	2005/6	25	2004/5	2006/7	20	2003/4	2006/7
De Lange, CD	31	2004/5	2007/8	38	2004/5	2007/8	13	2006/7	2007/8
De Stadler, M	2	2004/5	2006/7	3	2004/5	2004/5			
Duminy, J-P	34	2004/5	2010/11	34	2004/5	2009/10	36	2003/4	2009/10
Du Toit, WJ	1	2008/9	2008/9						
Engelbrecht, SA	2	2008/9	2009/10	11	2008/9	2010/11	5	2008/9	2009/10
Euley, W				1	2004/5	2004/5	7	2006/7	2006/7
Friend, Q	6	2004/5	2006/7	8	2004/5	2004/5	11	2003/4	2005/6
Geoghegan, JP				1	2007/8	2007/8			
Gibbs, HH	9	2004/5	2008/9	34	2004/5	2010/11	29	2003/4	2010/11
Gray, AJA	29	2006/7	2010/11	2	2010/11	2010/11			
Hantam, WC				9	2004/5	2005/6	8	2003/4	2004/5
Harvey, IJ	5	2005/6	2005/6	9	2005/6	2005/6	8	2005/6	2005/6
Hector, B	9	2006/7	2007/8	10	2006/7	2007/8	7	2006/7	2006/7
Henderson, CW	16	2008/9	2010/11	15	2008/9	2010/11	21	2008/9	2010/11
Henderson, T	4	2007/8	2007/8	7	2007/8	2007/8	6	2007/8	2007/8
Hendricks, BE	1	2010/11	2010/11	3	2010/11	2010/11			

NAME	FIRST-CLASS			LIMITED OVERS			T20		
	M	From	To	M	From	To	M	From	To
Johnson, NC	2	2004/5	2004/5	7	2004/5	2004/5	4	2003/4	2003/4
Kallis, JH	3	2004/5	2004/5	1	2006/7	2006/7	4	2003/4	2003/4
Kemp, JM	21	2007/8	2010/11	27	2007/8	2010/11	15	2009/10	2010/11
Kleinveldt, RK	54	2004/5	2010/11	60	2004/5	2010/11	51	2003/4	2010/11
Langeveldt, CK	15	2007/8	2010/11	28	2007/8	2010/11	28	2007/8	2010/11
Levi, RE	17	2008/9	2010/11	23	2005/6	2010/11	26	2007/8	2010/11
Lotter, RB	1	2008/9	2008/9						
Louw, J	6	2009/10	2010/11	3	2010/11	2010/11	6	2010/11	2010/11
Munnik, R	1	2005/6	2005/6	6	2004/5	2005/6	10	2004/5	2005/6
Olivier, MW	1	2009/10	2009/10	2	2009/10	2009/10			
Ontong, JL	25	2008/9	2010/11	29	2008/9	2010/11	29	2008/9	2010/11
Paulse, HH				1	2009/10	2009/10			
Peterson, RJ	10	2009/10	2010/11	15	2009/10	2010/11	7	2009/10	2009/10
Philander, VD	50	2004/5	2010/11	54	2004/5	2010/11	49	2004/5	2010/11
Piedt, DL-R	2	2010/11	2010/11	5	2010/11	2010/11			
Plaatjies, FC	9	2008/9	2009/10	15	2008/9	2009/10	2	2009/10	2009/10
Prince, AG	14	2004/5	2007/8	26	2004/5	2007/8	6	2003/4	2005/6
Puttick, AG	69	2004/5	2010/11	71	2004/5	2010/11	47	2003/4	2010/11
Rabie, GR	3	2008/9	2008/9	6	2008/9	2010/11			
Ramela, OA	3	2009/10	2010/11						
Rippon, MJ							6	2010/11	2010/11
Sandri, PSE	8	2006/7	2008/9	4	2006/7	2007/8			
Shah, OA	5	2010/11	2010/11	6	2010/11	2010/11	8	2010/11	2010/11
Smit, WJ							3	2004/5	2004/5
Smith, GC	4	2004/5	2010/11	5	2006/7	2009/10	8	2003/4	2008/9
Strydom, JG	16	2004/5	2007/8	8	2004/5	2005/6			
Swan, WC	2	2006/7	2006/7				7	2006/7	2006/7
Telemachus, R							9	2008/9	2008/9
Telo, FD	6	2005/6	2007/8	8	2005/6	2007/8	8	2005/6	2005/6
Tsolekile, TL	28	2004/5	2007/8	21	2005/6	2006/7	18	2003/4	2005/6
Vallie, MY	2	2010/11	2010/11						
Van Wyk, JM	1	2004/5	2004/5						
Van Wyk, L				3	2009/10	2010/11			
Van Zyl, S	35	2007/8	2010/11	39	2007/8	2010/11	16	2007/8	2009/10
Vilas, DJ							8	2010/11	2010/11
Walters, MD	1	2008/9	2008/9						
Willoughby, CM	28	2004/5	2006/7	20	2004/5	2005/6	22	2003/4	2006/7
Wyngaard, W	2	2005/6	2005/6						
Zondeki, M	40	2005/6	2010/11	39	2005/6	2010/11	12	2009/10	2009/10

12.3 Cape Cobras Trophy Winners in Cricket South Africa Competitions, 2004/05–2010/11[366]

SuperSport Series (First-Class)

Season	Winners
2004/05	Dolphins / Eagles (shared)
2005/06	Dolphins / Titans (shared)
2006/07	Titans
2007/08	Eagles
2008/09	Titans
2009/10	*Cape Cobras*
2010/11	*Cape Cobras*

Standard Bank Cup, MTN Domestic Championship and MTN40 Championship (Limited Overs)

Season	Winners
2004/05	Eagles
2005/06	Eagles
2006/07	*Cape Cobras*
2007/08	Titans
2008/09	Titans
2009/10	Warriors
2009/10	Knights

Standard Bank Pro20 (Twenty20)

Season	Winners
2003/04	Eagles
2004/05	Titans
2005/06	Eagles
2006/07	Lions
2007/08	Titans
2008/09	*Cape Cobras*
2009/10	Warriors
2010/11	*Cape Cobras*

12.4 Cape Cobras Supersport Series Scores (First-Class), 2004/05–2010/11[367]

Dolphins beat Western Province Boland by 8 wickets, 7–10 October 2004, Durban
WPBol 346 (HH Gibbs 42, JH Kallis 99, J-P Duminy 112; SM Pollock 4/74) and 176 (AG Prince 80, PR Adams 30*; SM Pollock 3/40)
Dol 388 (AM Amla 37, HM Amla 106, SM Pollock 66, DL Brown 55, L Klusener 66; CM Willoughby 3/75) and 135/2 (DJ Watson 64*, I Khan 31, HM Amla 31*)

Titans beat Western Province Boland by 9 wickets, 14–17 October 2004, Benoni
Ttn 524/4 dec (AB de Villiers 151, M van Jaarsveld 236*, G Toyana 65) and 84/1 (AB de Villiers 40*, AN Petersen 35)
WPBol 233 (AG Prince 50, CD de Lange 87; DW Steyn 3/44, AC Thomas 3/51) and 373 (GC Smith 32, TL Tsolekile 101*, RK Kleinveldt 92, Q Friend 51; PL Harris 3/128, JA Morkel 3/58)

Eagles beat Western Province Boland by 5 wickets, 21–24 October 2004, Cape Town
WPBol 206 (CD de Lange 43, TL Tsolekile 32, VD Philander 33; GJ Kruis 5/57) and 239 (AG Puttick 40, JH Kallis 68; R Telemachus 4/40)
Eag 315 (GFJ Liebenberg 33, HH Dippenaar 121, N Boje 57; CM Willoughby 5/91, CD de Lange 3/68) and 133/5 (HH Dippenaar 56*, MN van Wyk 38)

Western Province Boland beat Lions by an innings and 26 runs, 28–31 October 2004, Johannesburg
Lio 241 (AM Bacher 38, JL Ontong 66, HD Ackerman 77; CM Willoughby 4/43, CD de Lange 3/35) and 219 (JL Ontong 32, VB van Jaarsveld 80; CM Willoughby 3/59, AC Dawson 3/36)
WPBol 486 (GC Smith 200, AG Puttick 54, JG Strydom 64, AG Prince 51; CK Langeveldt 3/105, AJ Hall 3/83)

Western Province Boland beat Warriors by 114 runs, 4–7 November 2004, Cape Town
WPBol 206 (DJ Bassage 45, HH Gibbs 76, CD de Lange 37; M Zondeki 3/50, M Hayward 4/45) and 355/7 dec (AG Puttick 80, JG Strydom 78, HH Gibbs 52, NC Johnson 57*; T Henderson 3/84)
War 189 (A Jacobs 38, MV Boucher 65; CM Willoughby 4/50, RK Kleinveldt 3/33) and 258 (ML Bruyns 61, A Jacobs 60, MV Boucher 49; RK Kleinveldt 3/40)

Match drawn between Western Province Boland and Lions, 6–9 January 2005, Paarl
Lio 362 (HD Ackerman 180, ET Nkwe 76; Q Friend 6/114) and 167/2 (AM Bacher 40, JL Ontong 56*, ND McKenzie 36*)
WPBol 509 (DJ Bassage 61, JG Strydom 43, J-P Duminy 33, AG Prince 184, TL Tsolekile 81, AG Puttick 33; DN Crookes 4/124)

Match drawn between Western Province Boland and Dolphins, 13–16 January 2005, Cape Town
WPBol 233 (DJ Bassage 108, AG Prince 30, PR Adams 38; L Klusener 4/80) and 336/6 dec (AG Puttick 87, JG Strydom 50, J-P Duminy 102, PR Adams 49)
Dol 325 (I Khan 49, DJ Watson 61, JC Kent 48, DL Brown 107*, L Klusener 32; AC Dawson 5/46) and 160/8 (DJ Watson 37, JC Kent 53, L Klusener 30*; AC Dawson 3/40, CD de Lange 4/26)

Western Province Boland beat Eagles by 113 runs, 20–23 January 2005, Bloemfontein
WPBol 242 (J-P Duminy 92, TL Tsolekile 32, Q Friend 34; JJ van der Wath 4/67, WA Deacon 4/46) and 371/7 dec (AG Puttick 98, DJ Bassage 56, JG Strydom 78, J-P Duminy 55*)
Eag 222 (JM Henderson 32, LL Bosman 83) and 278 (JA Beukes 89, MN van Wyk 64, LL Bosman 32, WA Deacon 33*; RK Kleinveldt 3/59, CD de Lange 3/62)

Western Province Boland beat Warriors by 10 wickets, 3–6 March 2005, East London
WPBol 482/9 dec (AG Puttick 206, DJ Bassage 31, TL Tsolekile 72, VD Philander 44, PR Adams 49, RK Kleinveldt 39; BB Kops 3/115, BC de Wett 3/36) and 14/0
War 251 (ML Bruyns 110*, SC Pope 44, J Botha 34; CM Willoughby 5/83) and 242 (CC Bradfield 34, SC Pope 109, RJ Peterson 34; RK Kleinveldt 3/58, PR Adams 3/61)

Match drawn between Western Province Boland and Titans, 10–13 March 2005, Paarl
WPBol 431/7 dec (AG Puttick 87, J-P Duminy 79, TL Tsolekile 90, VD Philander 69; M Morkel 5/122) and 27/0
Ttn 280 (DJ Cullinan 138, GH Bodi 33; CM Willoughby 4/70) and 450/6 dec (JA Morkel 204*, JM Kemp 130, GH Bodi 55*)

Cape Cobras beat Warriors by 8 wickets, 20–22 October 2005, Port Elizabeth
War 263 (CC Bradfield 119, A Jacobs 87; VD Philander 3/41) and 100 (CM Willoughby 5/36)
Cob 211/9 dec (AG Puttick 34, DJ Bassage 33, J-P Duminy 40, IJ Harvey 33, TL Tsolekile 33; MW Olivier 4/71) and 153/2 (AG Puttick 69*, JG Strydom 38)

Match drawn between Cape Cobras and Dolphins, 27–30 October 2005, Paarl
Dol 432 (DJ Watson 39, I Khan 36, HM Amla 137, AM Amla 98, JC Kent 48, L Klusener 35; VD Philander 4/80) and 157/2 (DJ Watson 52, HM Amla 58*)
Cob 332 (DJ Bassage 39, JG Strydom 82, IJ Harvey 51, TL Tsolekile 31, VD Philander 30, PR Adams 38*; U Govender 5/57, DM Benkenstein 4/41)

Cape Cobras beat Titans by 230 runs, 3–6 November 2005, Cape Town
Cob 160 (AG Puttick 48, DJ Bassage 39; AC Thomas 7/54) and 372 (AG Puttick 53, DJ Bassage 39, HH Gibbs 133, J-P Duminy 35, TL Tsolekile 36; AC Thomas 3/107, DW Steyn 3/52)
Ttn 103 (CM Willoughby 3/33, VD Philander 4/6) and 199 (AJ Seymore 36, CFK van Wyk 57*; VD Philander 5/49)

Cape Cobras beat Lions by 6 wickets, 10–13 November 2005, Johannesburg
Lio 299 (SC Cook 92, VB van Jaarsveld 37; AC Dawson 4/60) and 296 (ND McKenzie 35, VB van Jaarsveld 40, MJ Harris 84, EO Moleon 67; AC Dawson 6/39)
Cob 325 (HH Gibbs 149; GJ-P Kruger 3/93, GJ de Bruin 4/64) and 273/4 (AG Puttick 70, CD de Lange 42, J-P Duminy 64*, TL Tsolekile 45*)

Eagles beat Cape Cobras by 10 wickets, 17–20 November 2005, Bloemfontein
Cob 251 (HH Gibbs 33, TL Tsolekile 91, VD Philander 46; N Boje 4/50) and 253 (DJ Bassage 65, J-P Duminy 128; N Boje 8/102)
Eag 494/7 dec (RT Bailey 51, B Hector 102, JA Rudolph 103, MN van Wyk 110*, N Boje 62) and 12/0

Dolphins beat Cape Cobras by 6 wickets, 23–26 February 2006, Durban
Cob 216 (J-P Duminy 52, AC Dawson 37*; S Mlongo 3/47) and 276/9 dec (HD Ackerman 61, AC Dawson 60*; S Mlongo 4/38)
Dol 214 (R Gobind 93, K Smit 48; CM Willoughby 6/41, AC Dawson 3/43) and 280/4 (R Gobind 60, HM Amla 153, L Klusener 30*)

Cape Cobras beat Warriors by 7 wickets, 2–4 March 2006, Stellenbosch
War 97 (RK Kleinveldt 8/47) and 193 (A Jacobs 90, SC Pope 30, JP Kreusch 31; M Zondeki 4/39)
Cob 198 (AG Puttick 56, J-P Duminy 64, HD Ackerman 31; BB Kops 3/41, JP Kreusch 5/31) and 96/3 (J-P Duminy 38*)

Titans beat Cape Cobras by an innings and 5 runs, 9–12 March 2006, Benoni
Cob 171 (TL Tsolekile 37, RK Kleinveldt 39; DW Steyn 3/38, Z de Bruyn 5/28) and 151 (DJ Bassage 66; DW Steyn 3/67, PL Harris 6/54)
Ttn 327 (HG Kuhn 41, M van Jaarsveld 59, Z de Bruyn 60, GH Bodi 53, G Toyana 39, DW Steyn 34; RK Kleinveldt 4/66)

Cape Cobras beat Eagles by 10 wickets, 16–18 March 2006, Stellenbosch
Eag 149 (R McLaren 38, JJ van der Wath 52; CM Willoughby 5/42) and 183 (JA Beukes 46, MN van Wyk 42*; M Zondeki 3/46, VD Philander 3/23)
Cob 324 (DJ Bassage 100, H Davids 30, HD Ackerman 31, AC Dawson 65; PV Mpitsang 3/75, R McLaren 3/61) and 9/0

Lions beat Cape Cobras by 25 runs, 23–26 March 2006, Cape Town
Lio 257 (AN Petersen 52, ND McKenzie 31, VB van Jaarsveld 55, WL Coetsee 55*; PR Adams 3/54) and 193 (SC Cook 63, ND McKenzie 47, VB van Jaarsveld 51; CM Willoughby 5/51, M Zondeki 5/67)
Cob 153 (J-P Duminy 45, VD Philander 31; F de Wet 7/61) and 272 (J-P Duminy 59, RK Kleinveldt 88; F de Wet 4/91, GJ de Bruin 4/47)

Match drawn between Cape Cobras and Warriors, 23–26 November 2006, East London
Cob 333 (AG Puttick 43, DJ Bassage 31, J-P Duminy 83, AG Prince 70; J Botha 5/95) and 271/3 dec (AG Puttick 45, B Hector 68, J-P Duminy 68*, AG Prince 59*)
War 411 (Z de Bruyn 85, HD Ackerman 195, J Botha 56; VD Philander 3/73, CD de Lange 5/145)

Match drawn between Cape Cobras and Titans, 30 November – 3 December 2006, Stellenbosch
Cob 284 (DJ Bassage 30, B Hector 37, RCC Canning 32, CD de Lange 43, PR Adams 49; AC Thomas 3/65, PL Harris 3/57) and 212/8 dec (DJ Bassage 48, J-P Duminy 56, RCC Canning 31, CD de Lange 33*; AC Thomas 3/40)
Ttn 204 (F du Plessis 39, F Behardien 58, AC Thomas 36; CM Willoughby 3/55, PSE Sandri 4/31) and 15/3

Dolphins beat Cape Cobras by an innings and 34 runs, 7–10 December 2006, Cape Town
Cob 326/8 dec (AG Puttick 91, B Hector 40, H Davids 60, RCC Canning 47, RK Kleinveldt 36; L Klusener 3/86) and 139 (DJ Bassage 52; TD Pillay 5/71, ANW Tweedie 3/13)
Dol 499 (DJ Watson 76, AM Amla 78, K Smit 58, L Klusener 121, J Louw 77; CM Willoughby 3/109, PSE Sandri 3/71)

Lions beat Cape Cobras by an innings and 165 runs, 14–16 December 2006, Cape Town
Lio 508 (JL Ontong 155, ND McKenzie 135, VB van Jaarsveld 54, MJ Harris 44, GJ-P Kruger 33*; M Zondeki 4/82)
Cob 215 (AG Puttick 36, J-P Duminy 30, RK Kleinveldt 63, CM Willoughby 32*; F de Wet 3/57, CW Henderson 6/87) and 128 (B Hector 36, PR Adams 30; CW Henderson 4/40, T Henderson 5/37)

Eagles beat Cape Cobras by 52 runs, 4–6 January 2007, Bloemfontein
Eag 218 (JA Rudolph 37, D Elgar 97*; CM Willoughby 3/45) and 161 (JA Rudolph 50, W Bossenger 37*; CM Willoughby 3/31, VD Philander 3/55)
Cob 220 (DJ Bassage 57, H Davids 76; JJ van der Wath 3/60) and 107 (JJ van der Wath 4/39, R McLaren 4/38)

Warriors beat Cape Cobras by 8 wickets, 11–12 January 2007, Cape Town
Cob 164 (CD de Lange 31; M Hayward 3/47) and 87 (RK Kleinveldt 40*; M Hayward 4/34, LL Tsotsobe 5/31)
War 196 (MW Goodwin 33, A Jacobs 50; CM Willoughby 5/59, VD Philander 4/45) and 56/2 (CA Thyssen 31)

Titans beat Cape Cobras by 10 wickets, 18–21 January 2007, Benoni
Ttn 452/7 dec (MA Aronstam 35, HG Kuhn 92, M van Jaarsveld 190, JA Morkel 36) and 17/0
Cob 172 (H Davids 65, FD Telo 38; MA Aronstam 5/49) and 294 (AG Puttick 85, AJA Gray 65, H Davids 38, RCC Canning 30; AC Thomas 3/63, JA Morkel 3/70)

Match drawn between Cape Cobras and Eagles, 1–4 February 2007, Stellenbosch
Eag 424 (JA Rudolph 164, JA Beukes 38, HH Dippenaar 118, R McLaren 48*; CM Willoughby 3/54) and 29/2
Cob 115 (AG Puttick 46; R McLaren 8/38) and 413 (H Davids 35, J-P Duminy 169, JG Strydom 36, TL Tsolekile 35, RK Kleinveldt 62; R McLaren 3/100)

Match drawn between Dolphins and Cape Cobras, 8–11 February 2007, Pietermaritzburg
Dol 392 (I Khan 62, HM Amla 117, AM Amla 38, JC Kent 93; CM Willoughby 3/73, M Zondeki 4/62) and 83/6 (CM Willoughby 5/16)
Cob 267 (WC Swan 35, VD Philander 63, RK Kleinveldt 62; J Louw 3/23, S Mlongo 3/46)

Match drawn between Cape Cobras and Lions, 15–18 February 2007, Potchefstroom
Cob 418 (AG Puttick 48, H Davids 75, WC Swan 57, TL Tsolekile 71, VD Philander 43, RK Kleinveldt 34; T Henderson 6/103) and 166/2 dec (AJA Gray 70*, J-P Duminy 75*)
Lio 275/9 dec (WL Coetsee 32, ND McKenzie 109*, TA Bula 30; RK Kleinveldt 5/75) and 142/5 (BD Snijman 47; RK Kleinveldt 3/26)

Match drawn between Cape Cobras and Titans, 11–14 October 2007, Benoni
Cob 378 (AJA Gray 38, AG Puttick 33, JG Strydom 82, B Hector 64, S van Zyl 74, CD de Lange 47*; NE Mbhalati 3/84, Imran Tahir 3/107) and 259/6 (H Davids 123*, S van Zyl 67)
Ttn 396 (MA Aronstam 52, HG Kuhn 51, M van Jaarsveld 89, P Joubert 85; M Zondeki 5/101)

Warriors beat Cape Cobras by 6 wickets, 18–20 October 2007, Port Elizabeth
Cob 110 (AG Prince 48; M Hayward 3/31, LL Tsotsobe 4/34) and 267 (AG Puttick 92, JG Strydom 65, S van Zyl 38; M Hayward 3/43)
War 283 (CA Thyssen 87, HD Ackerman 32, A Jacobs 93; M Zondeki 3/70, RK Kleinveldt 4/77) and 98/4 (A Jacobs 31*, DJ Jacobs 45*; M Zondeki 4/32)

Match drawn between Cape Cobras and Lions, 8–11 November 2007, Paarl
Cob 294 (H Davids 74, J-P Duminy 42, S van Zyl 30, CD de Lange 30; F de Wet 3/70, SJ Harmison 6/91) and 231/5 dec (AG Puttick 45, H Davids 50, J-P Duminy 71*, S van Zyl 46*; SJ Harmison 3/78)
Lio 260 (AN Petersen 102, ND McKenzie 44, JL Ontong 59; M Zondeki 4/70, T Henderson 3/50) and 194/5 (AN Petersen 95, JL Ontong 32; M Zondeki 3/63)

Match drawn between Eagles and Cape Cobras, 15–18 November 2007, Cape Town
Eag 511 (D Elgar 166, JA Rudolph 94, HH Dippenaar 32, D du Preez 122)
Cob 340 (AG Puttick 52, CD de Lange 39, H Davids 67, VD Philander 83, M Zondeki 34; JA Rudolph 5/80) and 311/1 (CD de Lange 46, AG Puttick 152*, H Davids 108*)

Dolphins beat Cape Cobras by 47 runs, 29 November – 2 December 2007, Pietermaritzburg
Dol 164 (I Khan 37, J Louw 50; M Zondeki 5/51) and 147 (I Khan 30, HM Amla 53; M Zondeki 5/42)
Cob 82 (J Louw 4/34, S Mlongo 4/18) and 182 (CD de Lange 48, AG Prince 35; Q Friend 3/51, D Smit 3/28)

Match drawn between Warriors and Cape Cobras, 6–9 December 2007, Paarl
War 346 (A Jacobs 30, HD Ackerman 97, J Botha 91*, RJ Peterson 55; CK Langeveldt 3/94, VD Philander 3/74) and 302 (Z de Bruyn 44, J-JT Smuts 33, J Botha 69, RJ Peterson 48; M Zondeki 4/65, VD Philander 4/61)
Cob 385 (AG Puttick 104, J-P Duminy 71, AG Prince 50, VD Philander 54, RCC Canning 41; MW Olivier 3/53, RJ Peterson 4/85) and 98/3 (J-P Duminy 36*)

Cape Cobras beat Dolphins by an innings and 44 runs, 13–15 December 2007, Cape Town
Dol 210 (DJ Watson 47, D Smit 65; CK Langeveldt 3/34, M Zondeki 3/69) and 63 (M Zondeki 5/26)
Cob 317 (AG Puttick 55, H Davids 74, AG Prince 51, JM Kemp 47; LE Plunkett 3/66, D Smit 4/68)

Cape Cobras beat Lions by 5 wickets, 10–13 January 2008, Potchefstroom
Lio 181 (BD Snijman 31, AN Petersen 35, CW Henderson 34*; M Zondeki 5/55) and 253 (BD Snijman 67, WL Coetsee 33, HW le Roux 49, F de Wet 30; VD Philander 7/64)
Cob 80 (F de Wet 3/23, GJ-P Kruger 4/27, HW le Roux 3/7) and 358/5 (CD de Lange 59, H Davids 96, J-P Duminy 115*)

Cape Cobras beat Titans by 6 wickets, 17–20 January 2008, Paarl
Ttn 298 (HG Kuhn 68, F du Plessis 88, GH Bodi 70; VD Philander 4/50, CD de Lange 4/72) and 148 (F du Plessis 43; VD Philander 5/13)
Cob 348 (AG Puttick 66, CD de Lange 59, B Hector 39, JM Kemp 63, RK Kleinveldt 30; Imran Tahir 6/122) and 99/4 (AG Puttick 46, H Davids 37)

Match drawn between Cape Cobras and Eagles, 24–27 January 2008, Bloemfontein
Cob 395 (FD Telo 104, S van Zyl 152*, JM Kemp 33) and 227/4 dec (H Davids 108, S van Zyl 58*)
Eag 353 (D Elgar 122, RT Bailey 30, R McLaren 121*; RK Kleinveldt 5/92) and 114/3 (D Elgar 54*, RT Bailey 30*)

Eagles beat Cape Cobras by 86 runs, 2–4 October 2008, Kimberley
Eag 296 (CD de Lange 39, HH Dippenaar 81, RT Bailey 91; M Zondeki 3/62, CK Langeveldt 3/76, VD Philander 2/49) and 129 (RR Rossouw 63*; CK Langeveldt 3/24, VD Philander 3/39, RK Kleinveldt 3/27)
Cob 125 (CW Henderson 29*; D du Preez 4/48, CJD de Villiers 4/32) and 214 (AG Puttick 29, H Davids 31, JL Ontong 35, VD Philander 42; D du Preez 3/28, CJD de Villiers 3/70, RT Bailey 2/32)

Match drawn between Cape Cobras and Titans, 9–12 October 2008, Benoni
Cob 417 (HH Gibbs 26, AG Puttick 88, J-P Duminy 124, JL Ontong 63, VD Philander 30, CW Henderson 36; M Morkel 4/111, P Joubert 3/57) and 281/7 dec (AG Puttick 30, H Davids 64, J-P Duminy 32, RCC Canning 76*, CW Henderson 32*; M Morkel 2/70, B-D Walters 2/66)
Ttn 413 (F du Plessis 36, GH Bodi 138, F Behardien 52, JA Morkel 55, P Joubert 34, M Morkel 56; CK Langeveldt 3/77, CW Henderson 5/105) and 185/8 (F du Plessis 55, GH Bodi 41, JA Morkel 37; CK Langeveldt 2/25, CW Henderson 2/34, J-P Duminy 3/41)

Match drawn between Cape Cobras and Dolphins, 16–19 October 2008, Paarl
Dol 435 (I Khan 47, R Gobind 45, HD Ackerman 70, JC Kent 110, D Smit 77; CK Langeveldt 2/84, CW Henderson 5/126) and 93/3 (I Khan 46*; CW Henderson 3/33)
Cob 476 (HH Gibbs 46, H Davids 80, J-P Duminy 138, JL Ontong 51, VD Philander 49*, RCC Canning 25, RK Kleinveldt 29; Q Friend 2/66, S Mlongo 2/62, P de Bruyn 3/39)

Match drawn between Cape Cobras and Lions, 30 October – 2 November 2008, Paarl
Cob 348 (AJA Gray 71, AG Puttick 59, S van Zyl 71, RE Levi 69; E Gerber 2/37, J Symes 3/56) and 235/4 dec (AG Puttick 74, S van Zyl 40, RE Levi 25, VD Philander 25*, RK Kleinveldt 32*)
Lio 395 (ND McKenzie 38, SC Cook 132, VB van Jaarsveld 98, JD Vandiar 50; CK Langeveldt 3/82, AJA Gray 4/47) and 107/4 (AN Petersen 31, VB van Jaarsveld 38; CK Langeveldt 2/25)

Match drawn between Cape Cobras and Warriors, 6–9 November 2008, Paarl
Cob 340 (AG Puttick 105, AJA Gray 39, S van Zyl 65, RE Levi 53, RCC Canning 28; J Theron 5/51, RJ Peterson 3/105) and 190/7 dec (AG Puttick 40, H Davids 31, S van Zyl 29, RCC Canning 26, CW Henderson 29*; M Ntini 2/50, WD Parnell 2/61)
War 263 (MBA Smith 26, Z de Bruyn 40, A Jacobs 92, AG Prince 33; RK Kleinveldt 2/29, FC Plaatjies 4/59, CW Henderson 2/84) and 206/8 (A Jacobs 43, AG Prince 72*; CK Langeveldt 3/52, CW Henderson 3/49)

Eagles beat Cape Cobras by 80 runs, 26 February – 1 March 2009, Cape Town
Eag 256 (RR Rossouw 111, HH Dippenaar 47, CD de Lange 40; RK Kleinveldt 7/43) and 355/7 dec (RR Hendricks 151*, RT Bailey 75, AJ Pienaar 60; GR Rabie 3/57, S van Zyl 3/27)
Cob 285 (AG Puttick 72, AJA Gray 110, RK Kleinveldt 33; AJ Pienaar 2/50, C Pietersen 4/62, DD Carolus 2/56) and 246 (S van Zyl 85, JL Ontong 49, RK Kleinveldt 55; C Pietersen 4/36, AJ Pienaar 2/29, CD de Lange 3/78)

Titans beat Cape Cobras by an innings and 41 runs, 5–7 March 2009, Paarl
Cob 228 (JL Ontong 25, VD Philander 31, RCC Canning 122; P Joubert 7/38, Imran Tahir 2/48) and 91 (S van Zyl 37; B-D Walters 2/16, NE Mbhalati 2/11, Imran Tahir 2/30, P Joubert 3/16)
Ttn 360 (BD Snijman 49, GH Bodi 63, F du Plessis 57, F Behardien 54, P Joubert 47*, RE van der Merwe 37; VD Philander 5/60)

Match drawn between Cape Cobras and Dolphins, 12–15 March 2009, Pietermaritzburg
Cob 281 (AG Puttick 36, S van Zyl 46, H Davids 113, RCC Canning 55; YA Abdulla 5/63, JC Kent 2/37, D Smit 2/73) and 300/2 (AJA Gray 131, AG Puttick 25, S van Zyl 103*)
Dol 366 (I Khan 145, C Delport 30, AM Amla 26, JC Kent 69, P de Bruyn 44; VD Philander 3/56, J-P Duminy 5/108)

Cape Cobras beat Lions by 6 wickets, 26–29 March 2009, Potchefstroom
Lio 296 (ND McKenzie 76, J Symes 50, SC Cook 90, ET Nkwe 30; CW Henderson 3/75, S van Zyl 4/36) and 242 (SC Cook 59, A Nel 51, GJ-P Kruger 25*; RK Kleinveldt 3/34, CW Henderson 4/64, S van Zyl 3/46)
Cob 434 (AJA Gray 26, AG Puttick 174, S van Zyl 32, H Davids 51, RE Levi 57, RCC Canning 46*; A Nel 2/78, F de Wet 3/74, CJ Alexander 2/78, J Symes 2/80) and 107/4 (RE Levi 46*; F de Wet 2/9)

Warriors beat Cape Cobras by 236 runs, 2–4 April 2009, East London
War 237 (J-JT Smuts 38, A Jacobs 59, Z de Bruyn 54, DJ Jacobs 52; S van Zyl 2/47, CW Henderson 7/64) and 197 (A Jacobs 26, DJ Jacobs 101; RK Kleinveldt 3/42, FC Plaatjies 2/51, JL Ontong 2/9)
Cob 124 (AJA Gray 42; ACR Birch 5/48, JP Kreusch 2/6) and 74 (DL Brown 4/14, Z de Bruyn 4/28)

Match drawn between Cape Cobras and Eagles, 17–20 September 2009, Bloemfontein
Cob 573/8 dec (AG Puttick 118, AJA Gray 60, JL Ontong 48, RE Levi 137, RCC Canning 56, VD Philander 44*, RK Kleinveldt 60; CD de Lange 3/107) and 60/0
Eag 527 (DJ van Wyk 46, D Elgar 112, RR Hendricks 74, RR Rossouw 115, CD de Lange 54; JL Ontong 3/88, AJA Gray 3/98)

Titans beat Cape Cobras by 179 runs, 24–27 September 2009, Benoni
Ttn 222 (HG Kuhn 47, GH Bodi 98, F du Plessis 30; AJA Gray 4/38) and 285 (BD Snijman 44, PJ Malan 54, F du Plessis 54, F Behardien 51; M Zondeki 4/45)
Cob 180 (S van Zyl 54, RE Levi 51; NE Mbhalati 5/56, PL Harris 3/26) and 148 (S van Zyl 31, JL Ontong 39; M Morkel 3/29, PL Harris 6/54)

Match drawn between Lions and Cape Cobras, 12–15 November 2009, Cape Town
Lio 416 (SC Cook 52, JD Vandiar 70, ND McKenzie 31, VB van Jaarsveld 123, TL Tsolekile 88*; AJA Gray 4/27) and 194/2 dec (AN Petersen 122*, ND McKenzie 43*)
Cob 332 (JL Ontong 60, OA Ramela 87, RJ Peterson 41, RK Kleinveldt 34; A Nel 5/64, U Govender 3/41) and 135/7 (AJA Gray 55; MS Panesar 4/42)

Match Drawn between Dolphins and Cape Cobras, 19–22 November 2009, Durban
Dol 237 (LL Bosman 34, DA Miller 46; RK Kleinveldt 3/49, VD Philander 4/45)
Cob 329/2 (AJA Gray 57, AG Puttick 169*, S van Zyl 75)

Cape Cobras beat Warriors by 9 wickets, 26–28 November 2009, Paarl
War 143 (A Jacobs 68, CA Thyssen 38; VD Philander 3/10, FC Plaatjies 4/21) and 143 (RK Kleinveldt 3/32, VD Philander 4/40, FC Plaatjies 3/27)
Cob 240 (JL Ontong 69, RCC Canning 60; M Ntini 3/51, J Theron 4/63) and 47/1

Cape Cobras beat Eagles by 106 runs, 3–5 December 2009, Cape Town
Cob 231 (OA Ramela 35, RJ Peterson 70; RT Bailey 3/46) and 226 (AJA Gray 113, JM Kemp 36; D du Preez 3/42, GA Vries 3/39)
Eag 220 (RR Hendricks 66, D Elgar 52, RR Rossouw 51; VD Philander 5/58, RJ Peterson 3/61) and 131 (RR Rossouw 67; VD Philander 4/32, RJ Peterson 5/60)

Cape Cobras beat Titans by an innings and 72 runs, 10–12 December 2009, Paarl
Ttn 240 (GH Bodi 64, HG Kuhn 48, JA Morkel 43; FC Plaatjies 3/67, JM Kemp 4/39) and 108 (JA Rudolph 31; CK Langeveldt 4/45, FC Plaatjies 4/27)
Cob 420 (AJA Gray 89, JM Kemp 93, RJ Peterson 100)

Cape Cobras beat Lions by 4 wickets, 16–19 December 2009, Johannesburg
Lio 202 (ND McKenzie 30, Z de Bruyn 35, R Frylinck 46*; VD Philander 3/34) and 308 (SC Cook 62, AN Petersen 74, VB van Jaarsveld 56, WA Deacon 35, MS Panesar 37; RJ Peterson 5/70)
Cob 296 (AG Puttick 42, JL Ontong 43, RJ Peterson 75, VD Philander 43; WA Deacon 4/65, R Frylinck 5/78) and 215/6 (AJA Gray 33, S van Zyl 72*, JM Kemp 44)

Cape Cobras beat Dolphins by 10 wickets, 18–21 March 2010, Cape Town
Cob 477/8 dec (AG Puttick 180, S van Zyl 157, H Davids 56; Q Friend 3/122, K Chetty 3/123) and 29/0
Dol 276 (D Smit 94, DA Miller 60, K Zondo 31, JC Kent 44*; RK Kleinveldt 3/46, J Louw 3/42) and 225 (AM Amla 68; VD Philander 4/33, RJ Peterson 3/37)

Cape Cobras beat Warriors by an innings and 117 runs, 25–27 March 2010, Port Elizabeth
War 110 (CA Ingram 32; VD Philander 5/40) and 142 (CA Thyssen 45; RJ Peterson 5/45)
Cob 369 (S van Zyl 167*, JL Ontong 44, RCC Canning 31; GJ-P Kruger 3/84)

Match drawn between Cape Cobras and Lions, 30 September – 3 October 2010, Randjesfontein
Cob 197 (RCC Canning 51; WA Deacon 3/41) and 499/5 dec (GC Smith 217, AG Puttick 111, S van Zyl 35, J-P Duminy 69)
Lio 416 (AN Petersen 63, ND McKenzie 66, VB van Jaarsveld 87, Z de Bruyn 76, TL Tsolekile 45, R Frylinck 32; VD Philander 3/88) and 202/7 (VB van Jaarsveld 44, Z de Bruyn 55; VD Philander 3/34)

Cape Cobras beat Titans by 7 wickets, 7–10 October 2010, Benoni
Ttn 313 (JA Rudolph 110, F Behardien 72, RE van der Merwe 50; CW Henderson 7/108) and 271 (BD Snijman 42, JA Rudolph 38, F Behardien 44, S von Berg 37; CW Henderson 3/88, JL Ontong 3/20)
Cob 508 (AG Puttick 62, S van Zyl 172, JL Ontong 51, JM Kemp 49, RCC Canning 46, VD Philander 36; NE Mbhalati 3/102, GC Viljoen 3/110) and 77/3

Match drawn between Cape Cobras and Knights, 14–17 October 2010, Cape Town
Cob 330 (AG Puttick 35, JL Ontong 102, RE Levi 64, RCC Canning 30*; D du Preez 5/53) and 255/7 dec (AJA Gray 39, S van Zyl 53, JL Ontong 39, RE Levi 47; MS Tshabalala 5/92)
Kni 234 (HH Dippenaar 76, R McLaren 63; VD Philander 6/61, RK Kleinveldt 3/60) and 243/7 (D Elgar 84, HH Dippenaar 61*; CW Henderson 3/84)

Match drawn between Cape Cobras and Warriors, 21–24 October 2010, East London
Cob 400/3 (AG Puttick 193, AJA Gray 126, S van Zyl 73)
War did not bat

Cape Cobras beat Dolphins by an innings and 166 runs, 16–19 December 2010, Paarl
Cob 515/5 dec (AG Puttick 45, AJA Gray 57, JL Ontong 127, J-P Duminy 200*, RCC Canning 53*; KA Maharaj 4/214)
Dol 99 (VD Philander 4/33) and 250 (K Zondo 38, RS Bopara 74, VB van Jaarsveld 57, D Smit 31; VD Philander 3/40)

Match drawn between Lions and Cobras, 13–16 January 2011, Paarl
Lio 458 (AN Petersen 44, ND McKenzie 145, Z de Bruyn 157; VD Philander 4/84, CW Henderson 5/90) and 113/2 (SC Cook 48*, Z de Bruyn 48*)
Cob 485 (AG Puttick 35, S van Zyl 41, OA Shah 151, RCC Canning 121, VD Philander 44; DR Deeb 5/131)

Cape Cobras beat Dolphins by 9 wickets, 20–23 January 2011, Durban
Cob 360 (JL Ontong 78, JM Kemp 135*, CW Henderson 43; Q Friend 4/80, M Shezi 3/98) and 63/1 (AG Puttick 32*)
Dol 162 (I Khan 35, AM Amla 38; VD Philander 4/47, RK Kleinveldt 3/30) and 255 (DP Conway 35, I Khan 37, JC Kent 50, D Smit 35; VD Philander 4/49, CW Henderson 4/76)

Cape Cobras beat Titans by 5 wickets, 24–27 March 2011, Cape Town
Ttn 369 (F Behardien 83, H Davids 37, JA Morkel 113, S von Berg 31, GC Viljoen 46; J Louw 5/56, CW Henderson 3/109) and 278 (PJ Malan 30, JA Rudolph 33, F Behardien 82, S von Berg 56; DL-R Piedt 7/92)
Cob 480 (MY Vallie 163, OA Shah 50, JL Ontong 147; JA Morkel 3/84, GC Viljoen 3/108) and 168/5 (MY Vallie 79)

Cape Cobras beat Warriors by 7 wickets, 31 March – 2 April 2011, Paarl
War 218 (BL Bennett 62, CA Thyssen 33, SR Harmer 46; CW Henderson 4/65) and 217 (BL Bennett 58, SR Harmer 68*; CW Henderson 5/83)
Cob 285 (AG Puttick 62, OA Shah 85, RK Kleinveldt 49; SR Harmer 5/98) and 151/3 (MY Vallie 33, S van Zyl 54*, OA Shah 38*)

12.5 Cape Cobras Standard Bank Cup, MTN Domestic Championship and MTN40 (Limited Overs) Scores, 2004/05–2010/11[368]

Western Province Boland beat Eagles by 6 wickets, 12 November 2004, Bloemfontein
Eag 229/5 (MN van Wyk 65, JA Beukes 77, B Hector 35)
WPBol 233/4 (AG Puttick 109, AG Prince 77)
MoM: AG Puttick

Dolphins beat Western Province Boland by 33 runs, 14 November 2004, Cape Town
Dol 225/5 (DM Benkenstein 92*, JC Kent 36)
WPBol 192 (AG Puttick 101*; JC Kent 3/37)
MoM: DM Benkenstein

Warriors beat Western Province Boland by 75 runs (D/L method), target revised to 240 in 32 overs, 17 November 2004, Port Elizabeth
War 251/7 (ML Bruyns 45, A Jacobs 94, MV Boucher 77; Q Friend 3/36)
WPBol 164/9 (AG Puttick 40, HH Gibbs 50; PC Strydom 4/26)
MoM: MV Boucher

Warriors beat Western Province Boland by 48 runs, 26 November 2004, Paarl
War 253/6 (DL Makalima 59, JP Kreusch 112; AC Dawson 3/30, WC Hantam 3/53)
WPBol 205 (AG Puttick 40, AG Prince 57; M Hayward 3/46)
MoM: JP Kreusch

Titans beat Western Province Boland by 23 runs, 3 December 2004, Centurion
Ttn 249/4 (AB de Villiers 102, GH Bodi 72, G Dros 31*)
WPBol 226/8 (JG Strydom 35, J-P Duminy 78, CD de Lange 47; NE Mbhalati 3/44, JM Kemp 4/47)
MoM: AB de Villiers

Western Province Boland beat Lions by 45 runs, 5 December 2004, Johannesburg
WPBol 250/6 (H Davids 84, NC Johnson 38, AG Prince 50)
Lio 205 (AM Bacher 49, ND McKenzie 101)
MoM: H Davids

Dolphins beat Western Province Boland by 18 runs (D/L method), target revised to 188 in 33 overs, 15 December 2004, Durban
Dol 223/6 (WR Wingfield 85, DM Benkenstein 59)
WPBol 169/8 (CD de Lange 45, R Munnik 30*)
MoM: WR Wingfield

Lions beat Western Province Boland by 8 wickets, 16 December 2004, Cape Town
WPBol 142 (CD de Lange 30, WC Hantam 35; GJ-P Kruger 5/21)
Lio 143/2 (AM Bacher 77*)
MoM: GJ-P Kruger

Eagles beat Western Province Boland by 7 wickets, 19 December 2004, Paarl
WPBol 168/9 (DJ Bassage 74, AG Prince 33)
Eag 169/3 (JA Beukes 78, B Hector 36)
MoM: WA Deacon

Western Province Boland beat Titans by 14 runs, 22 December 2004, Cape Town
WPBol 219/3 (DJ Bassage 48, J-P Duminy 85*, AG Prince 55*)
Ttn 205/6 (DJ Cullinan 47, G Dros 41, CFK van Wyk 34*)
MoM: J-P Duminy

No result between Cape Cobras and Lions, 25 November 2005, Potchefstroom
Cob 208/8 (TL Tsolekile 35, J-P Duminy 58, IJ Harvey 41; F de Wet 3/56)
Lio did not bat
MoM: None

Dolphins beat Cape Cobras by 8 wickets, 27 November 2005, Cape Town
Cob 211/7 (AG Puttick 53, HH Gibbs 48, IJ Harvey 55; ANW Tweedie 3/35)
Dol 214/2 (DJ Watson 101*, HM Amla 55, AM Amla 31*)
MoM: DJ Watson

Warriors beat Cape Cobras by 41 runs, 2 December 2005, Port Elizabeth
War 176/7 (CC Bradfield 86*, A Jacobs 33; RK Kleinveldt 3/38)
Cob 135 (FD Telo 53; MW Olivier 5/53)
MoM: CC Bradfield

Eagles beat Cape Cobras by 1 wicket, 9 December 2005, Bloemfontein
Cob 223/9 (H Davids 71, CD de Lange 64; JJ van der Wath 4/41)
Eag 227/9 (JA Beukes 55, PJ Koortzen 34, R McLaren 37*; RK Kleinveldt 4/29)
MoM: R McLaren

Titans beat Cape Cobras by 2 wickets, 11 December 2005, Centurion
Cob 170 (J-P Duminy 43, H Davids 40; NE Mbhalati 3/32)
Ttn 173/8 (JG Myburgh 59*; CM Willoughby 3/21, CD de Lange 3/48)
MoM: JG Myburgh

Match tied between Cape Cobras and Dolphins (D/L method), target revised to 185 in 36 overs, 16 December 2005, Durban
Cob 193/7 (DJ Bassage 81, CD de Lange 30, VD Philander 33*; ANW Tweedie 3/47)
Dol 184/7 (DJ Watson 55)
MoM: DJ Bassage

Warriors beat Cape Cobras by 4 wickets, 18 December 2005, Paarl
Cob 172/9 (JG Strydom 63; T Henderson 3/23)
War 176/6 (JP Kreusch 58, RJ Peterson 47; M Zondeki 3/43)
MoM: JP Kreusch

Lions beat Cape Cobras by 39 runs, 23 December 2005, Cape Town
Lio 160/9 (MJ Harris 56; CM Willoughby 3/19)
Cob 121 (S Chatterjee 4/27)
MoM: MJ Harris

Titans beat Cape Cobras by 19 runs, 30 December 2005, Paarl
Ttn (AN Petersen 80, JG Myburgh 30, G Dros 38*; M Zondeki 3/34)
Cob 189 (WA Albertyn 35, RK Kleinveldt 54*; M Morkel 4/41)
MoM: AN Petersen

Eagles beat Cape Cobras by 35 runs, 2 January 2006, Cape Town
Eag 225/5 (LL Bosman 71, DJ Jacobs 40, HH Dippenaar 71*, RT Bailey 31*)
Cob 190 (H Davids 31, RK Kleinveldt 36; T Tshabalala 4/24)
MoM: T Tshabalala

Titans beat Cape Cobras by 4 wickets, 29 September 2006, Centurion
Cob 237/9 (HH Gibbs 64, CD de Lange 63; JA Morkel 3/56, AC Thomas 3/43)
Ttn 241/6 (AB de Villiers 40, JA Morkel 30, JM Kemp 47, G Dros 61; CD de Lange 3/36)
MoM: G Dros

Cape Cobras beat Warriors by 5 wickets, 6 October 2006, Cape Town
War 233/6 (Z de Bruyn 82, J Botha 55*)
Cob 234/5 (AG Prince 78, VD Philander 76*, TL Tsolekile 30*)
MoM: VD Philander

Cape Cobras beat Eagles by 7 wickets, 8 October 2006, Bloemfontein
Eag 175/9 (RT Bailey 45, N Boje 36; VD Philander 3/33)
Cob 176/3 (AM Bacher 59, AG Puttick 43, HH Gibbs 55*)
MoM: HH Gibbs

Cape Cobras beat Dolphins by 7 wickets, 13 October 2006, Cape Town
Dol 230/8 (DJ Watson 44, DM Benkenstein 83)
Cob 234/3 (AG Puttick 104*, J-P Duminy 62, AG Prince 44)
MoM: AG Puttick

No result between Lions and Cape Cobras, 20 October 2006, Johannesburg
Lio 142/5 (AN Petersen 64, JL Ontong 31)
Cob 4/0

Eagles beat Cape Cobras by 22 runs, 25 October 2006, Cape Town
Eag 243/5 (MN van Wyk 73, DJ Jacobs 43, RT Bailey 37, JJ van der Wath 51*)
Cob 221 (AG Puttick 69, VD Philander 40; R Telemachus 4/40)
MoM: JJ van der Wath

Dolphins beat Cape Cobras by 22 runs, 27 October 2006, Durban
Dol 203/6 (I Khan 72, HM Amla 31)
Cob 181 (VD Philander 57; J Louw 3/29)
MoM: I Khan

Cape Cobras beat Titans by 60 runs, 29 October 2006, Cape Town
Cob 224/8 (J-P Duminy 90, RK Kleinveldt 32; DW Steyn 3/47, JA Morkel 3/34)
Ttn 164 (F du Plessis 54, F Behardien 40; M Zondeki 5/32)
MoM: M Zondeki

Warriors beat Cape Cobras by 5 wickets, 3 November 2006, East London
Cob 249/4 (AG Puttick 119, AG Prince 61*)
War 250/5 (CA Ingram 44, Z de Bruyn 41, MW Goodwin 53, JP Kreusch 71*)
MoM: JP Kreusch

Cape Cobras beat Lions by 93 runs, 5 November 2006, Cape Town
Cob 254/4 (AM Bacher 118*, J-P Duminy 59)
Lio 161 (AN Petersen 68; AC Dawson 3/39, CD de Lange 3/31)
MoM: AM Bacher

Cape Cobras beat Dolphins by 5 wickets, 12 November 2006, Cape Town
Dol 191/7 (HM Amla 51, L Klusener 33*, J Louw 44*; AC Dawson 5/46)
Cob 192/5 (AG Prince 40*, VD Philander 50*)
MoM: AC Dawson

Cape Cobras beat Warriors by 18 runs, 17 November 2006, Cape Town
Cob 213/9 (AM Bacher 41, AG Puttick 50, AG Prince 38, VD Philander 39)
War 195 (CA Thyssen 42, A Jacobs 49, JP Kreusch 39; RK Kleinveldt 3/42, CD de Lange 4/40)
MoM: CD de Lange

Cape Cobras beat Warriors by 90 runs, 8 February 2008, Cape Town
Cob 221 (AG Puttick 30, J-P Duminy 35, JM Kemp 68; J Theron 4/47, J Botha 3/34)
War 131 (J Theron 36; CK Langeveldt 4/25, T Henderson 3/51)
MoM: CK Langeveldt

Cape Cobras beat Eagles by 7 wickets, 10 February 2008, Bloemfontein
Eag 125/5 (D Elgar 55*)
Cob 126/3 (AG Puttick 64*)
MoM: CD de Lange

Cape Cobras beat Lions by 6 wickets, 13 February 2008, Cape Town
Lio 234/5 (AN Petersen 103, BD Snijman 51, WL Coetsee 43*)
Cob 235/4 (AG Puttick 57, H Davids 86*, JM Kemp 57; WA Deacon 3/48)
MoM: H Davids

Titans beat Cape Cobras by 5 wickets, 15 February 2008, Centurion
Cob 215 (HH Gibbs 102, RK Kleinveldt 33; RE van der Merwe 4/30)
Ttn 216/5 (RE van der Merwe 72, M van Jaarsveld 77; CK Langeveldt 3/26)
MoM: RE van der Merwe

Zimbabwe beat Cape Cobras by 39 runs, 17 February 2008, Harare
Zim 220/8 (V Sibanda 33, H Masakadza 39, E Chigumbura 53, KM Dabengwa 33; JM Kemp 4/16)
Cob 181 (H Davids 35, JM Kemp 57; GB Brent 3/22)
MoM: GB Brent

Dolphins beat Cape Cobras by 4 wickets, 22 February 2008, Cape Town
Cob 111 (YA Abdullah 3/17, J Louw 4/23)
Dol 115/6 (J Louw 32*; CK Langeveldt 4/17)
MoM: J Louw

Eagles beat Cape Cobras by 6 wickets, 24 February 2008, Paarl
Cob 196/6 (S van Zyl 38, JM Kemp 86, VD Philander 35*; D du Preez 3/28)
Eag 200/4 (D Elgar 94*, AP McLaren 74*)
MoM: D Elgar

Cape Cobras beat Lions by 7 wickets, 27 February 2008, Johannesburg
Lio 137 (AN Petersen 33, WA Deacon 30; VD Philander 3/29)
Cob 140/3 (HH Gibbs 74*)
MoM: HH Gibbs

Cape Cobras beat Warriors by 3 runs, 29 February 2008, East London
Cob 176 (JM Kemp 61; L Meyer 3/16, J Theron 3/23)
War 173/7 (HD Ackerman 46, A Jacobs 66; CD de Lange 3/31)
MoM: CD de Lange

Zimbabwe beat Cape Cobras by 3 wickets, 5 March 2008, Paarl
Cob 174/8 (RCC Canning 35*; RW Price 3/23)
Zim 175/7 (BRM Taylor 41, RW Chakabva 71*; RK Kleinveldt 4/35)
MoM: RW Chakabva

Cape Cobras beat Titans by 5 wickets, 7 March 2008, Cape Town
Ttn 193/7 (GH Bodi 38, M van Jaarsveld 48, F Behardien 45, RE van der Merwe 35; M Zondeki 4/29)
Cob 197/5 (AG Puttick 87*, RCC Canning 64*)
MoM: AG Puttick

Dolphins beat Cape Cobras by 56 runs, 9 March 2008, Durban
Dol 238/3 (R Gobind 70, AM Amla 104*, JC Kent 37*)
Cob 182 (H Davids 79; S Mlongo 3/28)
MoM: AM Amla

Cape Cobras beat Titans by 101 runs, 23 November 2008, Centurion
Cob 208 (J-P Duminy 54, JL Ontong 59, VD Philander 32; NE Mbhalati 2/35, RE van der Merwe 2/27, F du Plessis 2/32, M van Jaarsveld 3/13)
Ttn 107 (GH Bodi 34, M van Jaarsveld 32; CK Langeveldt 2/16, RK Kleinveldt 3/24, CW Henderson 4/25)
MoM: CW Henderson

No result between Cape Cobras and Eagles, 28 November 2008, Bloemfontein
Eag 203/8 (HH Dippenaar 63, D Elgar 28, RT Bailey 28; CK Langeveldt 2/37, VD Philander 2/30, CW Henderson 3/52)
Cob 57/0 (HH Gibbs 32*)

Cape Cobras beat Warriors by 24 runs, 5 December 2008, East London
Cob 220/8 (AG Puttick 32, S van Zyl 36, JL Ontong 50, RCC Canning 54*; LL Tsotsobe 3/57, RJ Peterson 3/37)
War 196 (RJ Peterson 55, JP Kreusch 26; FC Plaatjies 2/28, CW Henderson 2/23, JL Ontong 2/26)
MoM: RJ Peterson

Dolphins beat Cape Cobras by 53 runs, 14 December 2008, Cape Town
Dol 232/7 (I Khan 91, AM Amla 39, JC Kent 64*; CK Langeveldt 3/34, CW Henderson 2/46)
Cob 179 (JL Ontong 28, VD Philander 25, RCC Canning 49; J Louw 2/27, Q Friend 2/29, JC Kent 3/30)
MoM: JC Kent

Cape Cobras beat Lions by 48 runs, 16 December 2008, Potchefstroom
Cob 295/8 (H Davids 97, S van Zyl 81, JL Ontong 54, RE Levi 29*; JT Mafa 2/70, CJ Alexander 2/73, WL Coetsee 2/41)
Lio 247 (AN Petersen 50, VB van Jaarsveld 84, WL Coetsee 35; CK Langeveldt 2/54, RK Kleinveldt 3/26, CW Henderson 3/53)
MoM: H Davids

Titans beat Cape Cobras by 5 wickets, 21 December 2008, Cape Town
Cob 245/8 (S van Zyl 108, RE Levi 47; NE Mbhalati 2/19, P Joubert 2/41, RE van der Merwe 4/59)
Ttn 246/5 (GH Bodi 28, RE van der Merwe 37, F du Plessis 41, F Behardien 67*, JA Morkel 55; FC Plaatjies 2/49)
MoM: RE van der Merwe

No result between Cape Cobras and Dolphins, 26 December 2008, Durban
Dol 103/3 (I Khan 26, AM Amla 52*)
Cob did not bat

Eagles beat Cobras by 73 runs, (D/L method), target revised to 113 in 24 overs, 28 December 2008, Paarl
Eag 99/2 (MN van Wyk 34*, RR Rossouw 31)
Cob 39 (D du Preez 2/4, PV Mpitsang 2/10, CD de Lange 2/15)
MoM: D du Preez

Cape Cobras beat Warriors by 5 wickets, 2 January 2009, Cape Town
War 187/9 (JP Kreusch 55, Z de Bruyn 53, DJ Jacobs 26; CK Langeveldt 2/34, GR Rabie 2/43, CW Henderson 2/36)
Cob 188/5 (H Davids 85*, AG Puttick 62; J Theron 2/46, JP Kreusch 2/26)
MoM: H Davids

Cape Cobras beat Lions by 53 runs, 4 January 2009, Paarl
Cob 214/6 (H Davids 116, S van Zyl 32; WL Coetsee 2/35)
Lio 161 (AN Petersen 29, A Nel 58, JD Vandiar 25; RK Kleinveldt 2/40, FC Plaatjies 3/21, VD Philander 2/19)
MoM: H Davids

Titans beat Cape Cobras by 9 wickets, 9 January 2009, Centurion
Cob 183/9 (H Davids 49, RE Levi 45; RE van der Merwe 5/31)
Ttn 186/1 (BD Snijman 32, GH Bodi 84*, RE van der Merwe 64*)
MoM: RE van der Merwe

Cape Cobras beat Lions by 7 wickets, 28 October 2009, Johannesburg
Lio 286/6 (AN Petersen 25, ND McKenzie 80, VB van Jaarsveld 67, Z de Bruyn 54*; RJ Peterson 2/60)
Cob 289/3 (AG Puttick 122*, RJ Peterson 38, J-P Duminy 104; WA Deacon 2/36)

No result between Titans and Cape Cobras, 30 October 2009, Centurion
Ttn 249/8 (JA Rudolph 93, AB de Villiers 31, JA Morkel 43, RE van der Merwe 26*; SA Engelbrecht 3/39)
Cob did not bat

Warriors beat Cobras by 59 runs, 1 November 2009, East London
War 214 (CA Ingram 53, A Jacobs 42, J Botha 42; M Zondeki 3/37, FC Plaatjies 2/27)
Cob 155 (HH Gibbs 60, JM Kemp 29; LL Tsotsobe 3/36, J Theron 2/30, N Boje 2/36)

Cape Cobras beat Dolphins by 6 wickets, 6 November 2009, Cape Town
Dol 243/4 (I Khan 72, HD Ackerman 39, AM Amla 37, DA Miller 55*; FC Plaatjies 3/42)
Cob 248/4 (RJ Peterson 51, HH Gibbs 102*, S van Zyl 25, JL Ontong 31*; J Louw 2/55)

Cape Cobras beat Lions by 4 wickets, 23 December 2009, Cape Town
Lio 241 (JD Vandiar 59, AN Petersen 44, DJ Vilas 34; CK Langeveldt 2/44, FC Plaatjies 4/44, RJ Peterson 2/47)
Cob 243/6 (AG Puttick 29, RJ Peterson 40, HH Gibbs 68, NM Carter 30*, RE Levi 34*)

Titans beat Cape Cobras by 21 runs, 27 December 2009, Paarl
Ttn 277/7 (GH Bodi 41, JA Rudolph 35, F Behardien 58, JA Morkel 84; FC Plaatjies 2/43)
Cob 256/7 (S van Zyl 71, RJ Peterson 37, HH Gibbs 30, JM Kemp 52*; NE Mbhalati 4/41)

Cape Cobras beat Eagles by 115 runs, 30 December 2009, Paarl
Cob 281/7 (AG Puttick 74, S van Zyl 32, RJ Peterson 78*; R McLaren 2/39, AK Kruger 2/23)
Eag 166/8 (RR Hendricks 43, RT Bailey 26; FC Plaatjies 2/31, RJ Peterson 2/30)

Cape Cobras beat Dolphins by 66 runs, 6 January 2010, Durban
Cob 300/3 (S van Zyl 101, HH Gibbs 121*, JM Kemp 46)
Dol 234 (DM Benkenstein 76, DA Miller 86; CK Langeveldt 2/35, RK Kleinveldt 4/25)

Cape Cobras beat Eagles by 2 runs, 8 January 2010, Kimberley
Cob 285/2 (AG Puttick 58, S van Zyl 114*, HH Gibbs 79)
Eag 283/6 (MN van Wyk 77, HH Dippenaar 49, RR Rossouw 45, AP McLaren 61; VD Philander 3/51, RJ Peterson 2/43)

Cape Cobras beat Warriors by 52 runs, 15 January 2010, Cape Town
Cob 207 (AG Puttick 69, S van Zyl 47, JM Kemp 38; M Ntini 2/47, LL Tsotsobe 2/43, J Botha 3/29)
War 155/9 (JP Kreusch 29; CK Langeveldt 5/17, RJ Peterson 3/29)
MoM: CK Langeveldt

Warriors beat Cape Cobras by 9 runs, 22 January 2010, Paarl
War 274/4 (JP Kreusch 60, AG Prince 48, CA Ingram 35, JH Kallis 73*, DJ Jacobs 47*)
Cob 265/8 (AG Puttick 41, J-P Duminy 40, JM Kemp 71; J Theron 4/48)

Dolphins beat Cape Cobras by 37 runs, 29 October 2010, Durban
Dol 281/6 (CS Delport 52, I Khan 53, RS Bopara 80, GN Addicott 70)
Cob 244/9 (AG Puttick 47, HH Gibbs 40, JM Kemp 37; KJ Abbott 3/52)

Lions beat Cape Cobras by 80 runs, 5 November 2010, Paarl
Lio 187/7 (ND McKenzie 56, TL Tsolekile 38, R Frylinck 32*)
Cob 107 (AM Phangiso 3/34)

Knights beat Cape Cobras by 3 wickets, 10 November 2010, Kimberley
Cob 235/6 (AG Puttick 71, S van Zyl 39, OA Shah 83; J Coetzee 3/50)
Kni 239/7 (RR Hendricks 56, RR Rossouw 46, AP McLaren 55; DL-R Piedt 3/22)

Titans beat Cape Cobras by 2 wickets, 12 November 2010, Cape Town
Cob 135 (AG Puttick 46; NE Mbhalati 3/21)
Ttn 136/8 (JA Rudolph 39, F du Plessis 32, F Behardien 33; CK Langeveldt 4/34)

Dolphins beat Cape Cobras by 7 wickets, 14 November 2010, Paarl
Cob 161/9 (HH Gibbs 33, OA Shah 48*, RK Kleinveldt 45; KJ Abbott 3/49)
Dol 163/3 (RS Bopara 50*, VB van Jaarsveld 76)

Cape Cobras beat Warriors by 5 wickets, 19 November 2010, Cape Town
War 228/7 (KR Smuts 48, CA Ingram 73, JP Kreusch 35; CK Langeveldt 3/40)
Cob 230/5 (AG Puttick 40, RE Levi 86, JM Kemp 31, L van Wyk 31*)

Cape Cobras beat Lions by 6 wickets, 21 November 2010, Johannesburg
Lio 174/9 (ND McKenzie 73; RK Kleinveldt 3/25)
Cob 175/4 (RE Levi 37, OA Shah 57*)

12.6 Cape Cobras Standard Bank Pro20 Scores, 2004/05–2010/11[369]

Western Province Boland beat Dolphins by 6 wickets, 7 April 2004, Cape Town
Dol 121/6 (AM Amla 30*, L Klusener 39*)
WPBol 122/4 (AG Puttick 63*, AG Prince 37)
MoM: AG Puttick

Western Province Boland beat Eastern Cape by 3 wickets, 13 April 2004, Port Elizabeth
EC 121/9 (RK Kleinveldt 3/18)
WPBol 122/7 (JH Kallis 30)
MoM: JH Kallis and RK Kleinveldt

Titans beat Western Province Boland by 14 runs, 18 April 2004, Centurion
Ttn 176/2 (JA Rudolph 71, AJ Hall 59)
WPBol 162/4 (NC Johnson 44, JH Kallis 50)
MoM: JA Rudolph

Western Province Boland beat Lions by 55 runs, 21 April 2004, Cape Town
WPBol 147/3 (AG Puttick 55*, JH Kallis 37)
Lio 92 (JL Ontong 30; AC Dawson 3/20, GC Smith 3/23)
MoM: AG Puttick

Eastern Cape beat Western Province Boland by 7 wickets, 27 April 2004, Cape Town
WPBol 128/7 (AG Puttick 31; PC Strydom 4/11)
EC 129/3 (SC Pope 34)
MoM: MV Boucher and PC Strydom

Lions beat Western Province Boland by 6 wickets, 1 April 2005, Johannesburg
WPBol 129 (J-P Duminy 43, TL Tsolekile 35; DJ Terbrugge 4/20)
Lio 134/4 (VB van Jaarsveld 64, JM Otto 31)
MoM: VB van Jaarsveld

Western Province Boland beat Warriors by 5 wickets, 3 April 2005, Cape Town
War 114 (A Jacobs 45; RK Kleinveldt 3/18, WC Hantam 3/25)
WPBol 115/5 (J-P Duminy 47, TL Tsolekile 30*)
MoM: RK Kleinveldt

Eagles beat Western Province Boland by 8 wickets, 8 April 2005, Bloemfontein
WPBol 129/8 (TL Tsolekile 52; WA Deacon 3/16)
Eag 132/2 (MN van Wyk 80*)
MoM: WA Deacon

Western Province Boland beat Dolphins by 86 runs, 15 April 2005, Durban
WPBol 174/4 (AG Puttick 86, VD Philander 40)
Dol 88 (CM Willoughby 4/9, PR Adams 3/19)
MoM: CM Willoughby

Titans beat Western Province Boland by 8 wickets, 17 April 2005, Cape Town
WPBol 114/9 (JM Kemp 3/19)
Ttn 115/2 (GH Bodi 47)
MoM: JM Kemp

Cape Cobras beat Dolphins by 8 runs, 20 January 2006, Cape Town
Cob 161/5 (J-P Duminy 67*)
Dol 153/5 (K Smit 46, AM Amla 33*, DM Benkenstein 48)
MoM: J-P Duminy and Q Friend

Titans beat Cape Cobras by 33 runs, 27 January 2006, Centurion
Ttn 180/7 (AB de Villiers 51, GH Bodi 39, M van Jaarsveld 32)
Cob 147/9 (IJ Harvey 35, FD Telo 34)
MoM: AB de Villiers and M Morkel

Cape Cobras beat Lions by 5 runs, 29 January 2006, Cape Town
Cob 155/6 (J-P Duminy 31, FD Telo 48, TL Tsolekile 38*)
Lio 150/8 (AM Blignaut 42*)
MoM: FD Telo and CM Willoughby

Cape Cobras beat Warriors by 21 runs, 3 February 2006, East London
Cob 144/8 (RK Kleinveldt 46; JP Kreusch 3/31)
War 123/8 (ML Bruyns 35, MBA Smith 49; AC Dawson 4/18)
MoM: K Kleinveldt and AC Dawson

Eagles beat Cape Cobras by 9 runs, 5 February 2006, Paarl
Eag 120/8 (LL Bosman 34, RT Bailey 30*; AC Dawson 3/30, RK Kleinveldt 3/19)
Cob 111/6 (TL Tsolekile 33*; WA Deacon 3/17)
MoM: LL Bosman and WA Deacon

Cape Cobras beat Titans by 22 runs, 11 February 2006, Centurion
Cob 95/5 (IJ Harvey 45)
Ttn 73/4 (AB de Villiers 30)
MoM: IJ Harvey and RK Kleinveldt

Eagles beat Cape Cobras by 6 wickets, 19 February 2006, Bloemfontein
Cob 112/7 (J-P Duminy 33)
Eag 113/4
MoM: DJ Jacobs and WA Deacon

Lions beat Cape Cobras by 2 wickets, 23 February 2007, Johannesburg
Cob 181/6 (AM Bacher 85, H Davids 34; GJ de Bruin 3/25)
Lio 182/8 (VB van Jaarsveld 31, JL Ontong 43, WL Coetsee 33; CM Willoughby 3/26)
MoM: JL Ontong and CM Willoughby

Cape Cobras beat Warriors by 4 wickets, 25 February 2007, Cape Town
War 139/8 (Z de Bruyn 40, HD Ackerman 56)
Cob 140/6 (J-P Duminy 39, H Davids 30)
MoM: HD Ackerman and CM Willoughby

Cape Cobras beat Eagles by 7 wickets, 2 March 2007, Kimberley
Eag 187/3 (MN van Wyk 67, JA Rudolph 39, HH Dippenaar 35*, JJ van der Wath 35)
Cob 190/3 (H Davids 93*, B Hector 72)
MoM: H Davids and N Boje

Cape Cobras beat Titans by 38 runs, 7 March 2007, Cape Town
Cob 212/4 (AM Bacher 68, J-P Duminy 93)
Ttn 174/8 (M van Jaarsveld 76*; WC Swan 3/14)
MoM: J-P Duminy and CM Willoughby

Dolphins beat Cape Cobras by 1 run (D/L method), target revised to 146 in 16 overs, 9 March 2007, Durban
Dol 177/5 (I Khan 35, HM Amla 57)
Cob 144/7 (B Hector 31*; R Frylinck 3/18)
MoM: HM Amla and R Frylinck

Cape Cobras beat Warriors by 2 wickets, 16 March 2007, Cape Town
War 139/5 (Z de Bruyn 35, HD Ackerman 58)
Cob 140/8 (VD Philander 41, RK Kleinveldt 30*; Z de Bruyn 4/18)
MoM: RK Kleinveldt and AC Dawson

Lions beat Cape Cobras by 6 wickets, 23 March 2007, Johannesburg
Cob 147/9 (VD Philander 56*; GJ-P Kruger 3/32)
Lio 148/4 (ND McKenzie 73)
MoM: ND McKenzie and T Henderson

Cape Cobras beat Dolphins by 11 runs, 26 March 2008, Cape Town
Cob 143/6 (AG Puttick 36, HH Gibbs 60; MS van Vuuren 2/30)
Dol 132/7 (I Khan 50, JC Kent 46*; CK Langeveldt 4/26, T Henderson 2/16)

Cape Cobras beat Titans by 60 runs, 2 April 2008, Centurion
Cob 165/5 (AG Puttick 59, H Davids 57; NE Mbhalati 2/29)
Ttn 105 (JA Morkel 28; CK Langeveldt 3/19, VD Philander 2/15, CD de Lange 2/14)

Cape Cobras beat Warriors by 5 runs, 4 April 2008, East London
Cob 145/7 (RE Levi 39, VD Philander 36*; WD Parnell 2/24, J Botha 3/19)
War 140/8 (DJ Jacobs 36, Z de Bruyn 35; CK Langeveldt 3/13, RK Kleinveldt 2/32, T Henderson 2/28)

Cape Cobras beat Zimbabwe by 8 wickets, 9 April 2008, Cape Town
Zim 84/9 (CK Langeveldt 3/14, VD Philander 2/25, T Henderson 2/10, CD de Lange 2/19)
Cob 87/2 (AG Puttick 41*, H Davids 25; RW Price 2/8)

Cape Cobras beat Eagles by 1 wicket, 11 April 2008, Cape Town
Eag 127/7 (MN van Wyk 43, D Elgar 33; CK Langeveldt 5/16)
Cob 128/9 (S van Zyl 30; J Coetzee 2/15, R Telemachus 2/21, T Tshabalala 3/30)

Titans beat Cape Cobras by 6 runs, 20 April 2008 Cape Town
Ttn 158/7 (GH Bodi 29, F du Plessis 44, AB de Villiers 28, F Behardien 32*; J-P Duminy 4/24)
Cob 152/6 (AG Puttick 25, GC Smith 34, J-P Duminy 52; RE van der Merwe 2/27)

Cape Cobras beat Warriors by 4 runs, 23 January 2009, Cape Town
Cob 207/2 (D Brand 68, H Davids 112*)
War 203/5 (RJ Peterson 51, CA Ingram 84, DJ Jacobs 49; CK Langeveldt 2/30)
Master Blasters H Davids and CK Langeveldt

Eagles beat Cape Cobras by 88 runs, 28 January 2009, Kimberley
Eag 176/3 (MN van Wyk 59, AP McLaren 61, D Elgar 46*)
Cob 88 (CJD de Villiers 3/15, SC van Schalkwyk 2/12, D Elgar 2/6)
Master Blasters AP McLaren and CJD de Villiers

Dolphins beat Cape Cobras by 3 wickets, 30 January 2009, Durban
Cob 119/8 (RE Levi 46, JL Ontong 27; Q Friend 2/22, YA Abdulla 3/23)
Dol 120/7 (J Louw 28*; CK Langeveldt 2/38)
Master Blasters J Louw and YA Abdulla

Cape Cobras beat Titans by 16 runs, 1 February 2009, Cape Town
Cob 157/4 (AG Puttick 35, JL Ontong 59*; I Tahir 2/28)
Ttn 141/9 (GH Bodi 32, F du Plessis 25, P Joubert 26*; RK Kleinveldt 2/24, CW Henderson 2/31, JL Ontong 2/19, R Telemachus 3/17)
Master Blasters JL Ontong and R Telemachus

Match tied between Cape Cobras and Lions, 4 February 2009, Potchefstroom
Cob 154/6 (J-P Duminy 56, JL Ontong 33, RE Levi 32*; CJ Alexander 2/30, WL Coetsee 2/33)
Lio 154/6 (AN Petersen 61, ND McKenzie 35, VB van Jaarsveld 25; CK Langeveldt 3/21)
Master Blasters AN Petersen and CK Langeveldt

Dolphins beat Cape Cobras by 14 runs, 13 February 2009, Cape Town (Semi-finals)
Dol 162/5 (HD Ackerman 62, ST Jayasuriya 41)
Cob 148/9 (GC Smith 32, RE Levi 48*; YA Abdulla 3/13, J Louw 2/21, ST Jayasuriya 2/32)
Master Blasters HD Ackerman and YA Abdulla

Cape Cobras beat Dolphins by 38 runs (D/L method), target revised to 98 in 9 overs, 15 February 2009, Durban (Semi-finals)
Cob 191/4 (HH Gibbs 92, GC Smith 33, JL Ontong 32; AC Thomas 2/28)
Dol 59/5 (R Telemachus 2/8, CW Henderson 2/13)

Match tied between Cape Cobras and Dolphins, with Cape Cobras winning in the Super Over, 18 February 2009, Durban (Semi-finals)
Cob 148/4 (GC Smith 34, J-P Duminy 53*, JL Ontong 44; AC Thomas 2/14)
Dol 148/8 (HM Amla 35, JC Kent 32, J Louw 48*; CK Langeveldt 4/20, CW Henderson 3/23)
Master Blasters J-P Duminy and CK Langeveldt

Cape Cobras beat Eagles by 22 runs, 21 February 2009, Cape Town (Final)
Cob 147/5 (HH Gibbs 87*; J Coetzee 2/29, SC van Schalkwyk 2/24)
Eag 125/8 (D Elgar 34, D du Preez 26; CK Langeveldt 3/20, VD Philander 3/17)
Master Blasters HH Gibbs and CK Langeveldt

Cape Cobras beat Royal Challengers Bangalore by 5 wickets, 8 October 2009, Bangalore, India (Champions League)
Royal Challengers Bangalore 180 (LRPL Taylor 53*, RV Uthappa 51, R Dravid 28; CK Langeveldt 1/12)
Cape Cobras 184 (J-P Duminy 99*, H Davids 27, RCC Canning 20; P Kumar 3/32)

Cape Cobras beat Otago Volts by 54 runs, 10 October 2009, Hyderabad, India (Champions League)
Cape Cobras 193 (AG Puttick 104*, JL Ontong 39*, J-P Duminy 32; AD Mascarenhas 2/20)
Otago Volts 139 (NL McCullum 38, BB McCullum 21, CD Cumming 18; RK Kleinveldt 3/24, J-P Duminy 2/10)

Cape Cobras beat Victoria Bushrangers by 8 wickets, 17 October 2009, Bangalore, India (Champions League)
Victoria Bushrangers 125 (AB McDonald 29*, CL White 24, AC Blizzard 22; M Zondeki 2/21)
Cape Cobras 129 (H Davids 69*, D Brand 29, J-P Duminy 18*; PM Siddle 1/19)

Delhi Daredevils beat Cape Cobras by 30 runs, 19 October 2009, Delhi, India (Champions League)
Delhi Daredevils 114 (OA Shah 39*, KD Karthik 23, MK Tiwary 19; JL Ontong 2/8, RK Kleinveldt 2/31)
Cape Cobras 84 (H Davids 22, J-P Duminy 14; DP Nannes 3/19, Y Nagar 2/9)

Trinidad & Tobago beat Cape Cobras by 7 wickets, 22 October 2009, Hyderabad, India (Champions League)
Cape Cobras 175 (J-P Duminy 61*, HH Gibbs 42, RK Kleinveldt 21; LMP Simmons 2/17, KA Pollard 1/24)
Trinidad & Tobago 178 (DJ Bravo 58*, D Ganga 44*, AB Barath 29; JL Ontong 1/14)

Cape Cobras beat Lions by 42 runs, 5 February 2010, Cape Town
Cob 179 (HH Gibbs 53, RE Levi 43*; R Frylinck 4/31, AM Phangiso 3/23)
Lio 137 (ND McKenzie 27, VB van Jaarsveld 39, DJ Vilas 32; CK Langeveldt 3/18, RJ Peterson 2/25, JL Ontong 3/27)

Titans beat Cape Cobras by 17 runs (D/L method), target revised to 140 in 12 overs, 7 February 2010, Centurion
Ttn 136/1 (BD Snijman 27, GH Bodi 88*)
Cob 122/6 (HH Gibbs 48; B-D Walters 2/30, JA Morkel 2/22)

Cape Cobras beat Dolphins by 14 runs, 13 February 2010, Cape Town
Cob 116/7 (JM Kemp 59; J Louw 2/18, K Nipper 2/10)
Dol 102 (DA Miller 26; RK Kleinveldt 3/23, VD Philander 5/17)

Eagles beat Cape Cobras by 8 wickets, 17 February 2010, Paarl
Cob 137/5 (JL Ontong 37*; D du Preez 3/17)
Eag 138/2 (MN van Wyk 85*, AP McLaren 33)

Warriors beat Cape Cobras by 19 runs, 19 February 2010, Port Elizabeth
War 172/5 (JP Kreusch 61, DJ Jacobs 56; M Zondeki 2/21, VD Philander 2/29)
Cob 153/8 (S van Zyl 29, H Davids 25, VD Philander 37*; GJ-P Kruger 2/35, L Meyer 2/26, N Boje 3/10)

Warriors beat Cape Cobras by 3 runs, 26 February 2010, Port Elizabeth
War 149/3 (CA Ingram 60*, DJ Jacobs 42*)
Cob 146/8 (RJ Peterson 50*, JM Kemp 43; J Theron 2/23)

Warriors beat Cape Cobras by 10 runs, 3 March 2010, Cape Town
War 121/6 (AG Prince 25, J Botha 29*, CA Thyssen 27*; JM Kemp 2/8)
Cob 111/6 (JL Ontong 28, JM Kemp 29; M Ntini 2/12, J Theron 2/29)

Cape Cobras beat Titans by 5 wickets, 28 January 2011, Cape Town
Ttn 175/4 (JA Rudolph 45, RE van der Merwe 65, JA Morkel 50*)
Cob 177/5 (RE Levi 68)

Lions beat Cape Cobras by 4 wickets, 30 January 2011, Johannesburg
Cob 155/6 (OA Shah 42, JL Ontong 56)
Lio 159/6 (Z de Bruyn 54*, J Symes 40, R Frylinck 32*)

Cape Cobras beat Knights by 13 runs (D/L method), target revised to 95 in 10 overs, 6 February 2011, Bloemfontein
Cob 91/1 (RE Levi 51*, HH Gibbs 33)
Kni 81/6 (RR Rossouw 35)

Dolphins beat Cape Cobras by 9 runs, 11 February 2011, Durban
Dol 154/3 (DP Conway 62*, VB van Jaarsveld 53)
Cob 145/7 (AG Puttick 32, HH Gibbs 31, DJ Vilas 30*)

Cape Cobras beat Warriors by 7 wickets, 18 February 2011, Cape Town
War 126/7 (AG Prince 57)
Cob 127/3 (OA Shah 58*, JL Ontong 41*)

Cape Cobras beat Titans by 8 wickets, 27 February 2011, Cape Town (Semi-finals)
Ttn 141/6
Cob 142/2 (HH Gibbs 54, OA Shah 30*)

Cape Cobras beat Titans by 5 wickets, 9 March 2011, Centurion (Semi-finals)
Ttn 222/4 (JA Rudolph 40, F Behardien 69, JA Morkel 71*, D Wiese 30*)
Cob 224/5 (RE Levi 60, DJ Vilas 53, OA Shah 64)

Cape Cobras beat Warriors by 12 runs, 18 March 2011, Cape Town (Final)
Cob 166/5 (RE Levi 45, HH Gibbs 35, OA Shah 39*)
War 154/6 (KR Smuts 56*)

Part III

Consolidated Western Province and Cape Cobras Statistics, 1890–2011

CHAPTER 13
List of trophies won by Western Province and Cape Cobras, 1890–2011[370]

1890/91	Winners of Fifth Champion Bat (Final Inter-Town Tournament – later officially recognised as First-Class)
1891/92	–
1892/93	Currie Cup (WP Cricket Union) First-Class
1893/94	Currie Cup (WP Cricket Union) First-Class
1894/95	–
1895/96	–
1896/97	Currie Cup (WP Cricket Union) First-Class
1897/98	Currie Cup (WP Cricket Union) First-Class
1898/99	Barnato Memorial Trophy (WP Coloured Cricket Union) Unofficial Tournament
1899/1900	*No competition, Anglo-Boer South African War*
1900/01	*No competition, Anglo-Boer South African War*
1901/02	*No competition, Anglo-Boer South African War*
1902/03	–
1903/04	Barnato Memorial Trophy (WP Coloured Cricket Union) Tournament
1904/05	–
1905/06	–
1906/07	–
1907/08	Barnato Memorial Trophy (WP Coloured Cricket Union) Tournament
1908/09	Currie Cup (WP Cricket Union) First-Class
1909/10	–
1910/11	–
1911/12	–
1912/13	Barnato Memorial Trophy (WP Coloured Cricket Union) Tournament
1913/14	*No competition, World War I*
1914/15	*No competition, World War I*
1915/16	*No competition, World War I*
1916/17	*No competition, World War I*
1917/18	*No competition, World War I*
1918/19	*No competition, World War I*
1919/20	*No competition, World War I*
1920/21	Currie Cup (WP Cricket Union) First-Class
1921/22	Currie Cup tied with Transvaal and Natal (WP Cricket Union) First-Class
1922/23	Barnato Memorial Trophy (WP Coloured Cricket Union) Tournament
1923/24	–
1924/25	Barnato Memorial Trophy (WP Coloured Cricket Union) Tournament
1925/26	–

1926/27	–
1927/28	Barnato Memorial Trophy (WP Coloured Cricket Union) Tournament
1928/29	Sir David Harris Trophy (Peninsula and Western Districts Cricket Board) Tournament
1929/30	Barnato Memorial Trophy (WP Coloured Cricket Union) Tournament
1930/31	–
1931/32	Currie Cup (WP Cricket Union) First-Class
	Barnato Memorial Trophy (WP Coloured Cricket Union) Tournament
1932/33	–
1933/34	–
1934/35	–
1935/36	–
1936/37	–
1937/38	Sir David Harris Trophy (Peninsula and Western Districts Cricket Board) Tournament
1938/39	–
1939/40	*No competition, World War II*
1940/41	*No competition, World War II (except for SA Bantu Board Tournament and SA Indian Cricket Union Tournament)*
1941/42	*No competition, World War II (except for SA Indian Cricket Union Tournament)*
1942/43	*No competition, World War II*
1943/44	*No competition, World War II*
1944/45	*No competition, World War II (except for SA Indian Cricket Union Tournament)*
1945/46	Barnato Memorial Trophy (WP Coloured Cricket Union) Tournament
1946/47	Sir David Harris Trophy tied with Eastern Province and Griqualand West (Peninsula and Western Districts Cricket Board) Tournament
1947/48	NRC Trophy (WP Bantu Cricket Union) Tournament
1948/49	Sir David Harris Trophy (Peninsula and Western Districts Cricket Board) Tournament
1949/50	–
1950/51	Sir David Harris Trophy shared with Transvaal (Peninsula and Western Districts Cricket Board) Tournament
1951/52	Barnato Memorial Trophy (WP Coloured Cricket Union) Tournament
	Simon Trophy (WP Women's Cricket Union) Tournament
1952/53	NRC Trophy (WP Bantu Cricket Union) Tournament
	Currie Cup (WP Cricket Union) First-Class
	Simon Trophy (WP Women's Cricket Union) Tournament
1953/54	Simon Trophy (WP Women's Cricket Union) Tournament
1954/55	Sir David Harris Trophy (Peninsula and Western Districts Cricket Board) Tournament
	NRC Trophy (WP Bantu Cricket Union) Tournament
	Barnato Memorial Trophy (WP Coloured Cricket Union) Tournament
1955/56	Currie Cup (WP Cricket Union) First-Class
1956/57	Sir David Harris Trophy (Peninsula and Western Districts Cricket Board) Tournament
1957/58	Sir David Harris Trophy (Peninsula and Western Districts Cricket Board) Tournament
	Barnato Memorial Trophy (WP Coloured Cricket Union) Tournament
1958/59	–
1959/60	–
1960/61	–
1961/62	–
1962/63	–

1963/64	Dadabhay Trophy (WP Cricket Board) Tournament
1964/65	–
1965/66	Dadabhay Trophy (WP Cricket Board) Tournament
1966/67	–
1967/68	Dadabhay Trophy (WP Cricket Board) Tournament
1968/69	Currie Cup B Section (WP Cricket Union) First-Class
1969/70	Dadabhay Trophy shared with Transvaal (WP Cricket Board) Tournament
	Currie Cup tied with Transvaal (WP Cricket Union) First-Class
	Gillette Cup (WP Cricket Union) Limited Overs
1970/71	Dadabhay Trophy shared with Transvaal (WP Cricket Board) Tournament
	Gillette Cup (WP Cricket Union) Limited Overs
1971/72-	
1972/73	Dadabhay Trophy shared with Natal (WP Cricket Board) First-Class
1972/73	Gillette Cup (WP Cricket Union) Limited Overs
1973/74	Dadabhay Tournament (WP Cricket Board) First-Class
	SFW Trophy (WP Cricket Board) Limited Overs
	SACBOC B Division (WP Cricket Board) Two-Day
1974/75	Currie Cup (WP Cricket Union) First-Class
	SACBOC B Division (WP Cricket Board) Two-Day
1975/76	SFW Trophy (WP Cricket Board) First-Class
	Simon Trophy (WP Women's Cricket Union) Tournament
	MR Varachia Trophy (WP Cricket Board B) Two-Day
1976/77	–
1977/78	Howa Bowl (WP Cricket Board) First-Class
	Currie Cup (WP Cricket Union) First-Class
1978/79	Simon Trophy (WP Women's Cricket Union) Tournament
1979/80	Howa Bowl (WP Cricket Board) First-Class
1980/81	Howa Bowl (WP Cricket Board) First-Class
	SAB Bowl (WP Cricket Union B) First-Class
1981/82	Howa Bowl (WP Cricket Board) First-Class
	Currie Cup (WP Cricket Union) First-Class
	Datsun Shield (WP Cricket Union) Limited Overs
	Booley Bowl (WP Cricket Board B) Two-Day
1982/83	Benson & Hedges Trophy (WP Cricket Board) Limited Overs
	Howa Bowl (WP Cricket Board) First-Class
	SAB Bowl (WP Cricket Union B) First-Class
1983/84	Benson & Hedges Trophy shared with E Province (WP Cricket Board) Limited Overs
	Howa Bowl (WP Cricket Board) First-Class
	Castle Bowl (WP Cricket Union B) First-Class
1984/85	Benson & Hedges Trophy (WP Cricket Board) Limited Overs
1985/86	Currie Cup (WP Cricket Union) First-Class
	Benson & Hedges Series (WP Cricket Union) Limited Overs
	Booley Bowl (WP Cricket Board U-21) Two-Day
1986/87	Howa Bowl (WP Cricket Board) First-Class
	Benson & Hedges Series (WP Cricket Union) Limited Overs
1987/88	Howa Bowl (WP Cricket Board) First-Class
	Benson & Hedges Series (WP Cricket Union) Limited Overs

1988/89	Howa Bowl (WP Cricket Board) First-Class
	Nissan Shield (WP Cricket Union) Limited Overs
	Booley Bowl shared with Transvaal B (WP Cricket Board B) Two-Day
1989/90	Howa Bowl (WP Cricket Board) First-Class
	Bowl shared with Border (WP Cricket Union B) First-Class
	Currie Cup tied with E Province (WP Cricket Union) First-Class
1990/91	Howa Bowl (WP Cricket Board) First-Class
	Currie Cup (WP Cricket Union) First-Class
	Benson & Hedges Series (WP Cricket Union) Limited Overs
	Bowl shared with Border (WP Cricket Union B) First-Class
	Booley Bowl (WP Cricket Board U-21) Two-Day
1991/92	President's Cup (WP Cricket Association B) First-Class
1992/93	–
1993/94	UCBSA Bowl shared with Transvaal B (WP Cricket Association B) First-Class
1994/95	–
1995/96	Castle Cup (WP Cricket Association) First-Class
	UCBSA Bowl (WP Cricket Association) Limited Overs
1996/97	–
1997/98	Standard Bank League (WP Cricket Association) Limited Overs
	UCBSA Inter-Provincial (WP Women's Cricket Association) Tournament
1998/99	SuperSport Series (WP Cricket Association) First-Class
	UCBSA Bowl (WP Cricket Association) Limited Overs
1999/2000	UCBSA Inter-Provincial (WP Women's Cricket Association) Tournament
	UCBSA Bowl (WP Cricket Association) Tournament
2000/01	SuperSport Series (WP Cricket Association) First-Class
	UCBSA Bowl (WP Cricket Association) Tournament
2001/02	UCBSA Inter-Provincial (WP Women's Cricket Association) Tournament
	UCBSA Bowl (WP Cricket Association) Tournament
	UCBSA Bowl (WP Cricket Association) Limited Overs
2002/03	Standard Bank Cup (WP Cricket Association) Limited Overs
	UCBSA Bowl (WP Cricket Association) Tournament
	UCBSA Inter-Provincial (WP Women's Cricket Association) Tournament
2003/04	SuperSport Trophy (WP Cricket Association) First-Class
	UCBSA Bowl (WP Cricket Association) Tournament
	UCBSA Bowl (WP Cricket Association) Limited Overs
2004/05	–
2005/06	CSA Inter-Provincial League (Women)
2006/07	MTN Domestic Championship (Cape Cobras) Limited Overs
	CSA Inter-Provincial League (Women)
2007/08	–
2008/09	Standard Bank Pro20 Series (Cape Cobras) Twenty20
	CSA Inter-Provincial League (Women)
2009/10	SuperSport Series (Cape Cobras) First-Class
2010/11	Standard Bank Pro20 Series (Cape Cobras) Twenty20
	SuperSport Series (Cape Cobras) First-Class
	CSA Provincial Three-Day Challenge (Western Province) First-Class
	CSA Provincial One-Day Challenge (Western Province) Limited Overs

CHAPTER 14

List of national players from Western Province and Cape Cobras, 1888–2011

- Names in bold indicate cricketers who played in official ICC-recognised international fixtures.[371]
- Names in roman type depict cricketers involved in matches by national teams not officially recognised by the ICC as inter national matches.
- Formats of the ICC-recognised official internationals in which players participated are shown in a separate column as Test/ODI/T20.
- Matches by teams not recognised by the ICC as official inter nationals are shown as 'Unofficial' without a description of the format.
- Asterisks indicate that the player represented South Africa while playing for a province other than Western Province.

Name	Board	From	To	Icc Status
Abdullah, Munsoor	SA Cricket Board	1982/83	2001/02	Unofficial
Abed, Gesant 'Tiny'	SA Indian Cricket Union	1950/51	1954/55	Unofficial
	SA Malay Cricket Board	1954/55	1957/58	Unofficial
	SA Cricket Board of Control	1958/59	1958/59	Unofficial
Abed, Goolam H	SA Indian Cricket Union	1954/55	1954/55	Unofficial
	SA Malay Cricket Board	1957/58	1957/58	Unofficial
Abed, Salie 'Lobo'	SA Malay Cricket Board	1952/53	1957/58	Unofficial
	SA Cricket Board of Control	1956/57	1958/59	Unofficial
Abrahams, Cecil John	SA Coloured Cricket Association	1952/53	1952/53	Unofficial
	SA Cricket Board of Control	1956/57	1958/59	Unofficial
Abrams, C	SA Malay Team	1890/91	1890/91	Unofficial
Ackerman, Hylton Deon	United Cricket Board of SA	1997/98	2001/02	Test
Adams, Paul Regan	United Cricket Board of SA	1995/96	2003/04	Test/ODI
Anderson, James Henry 'Biddy'	SA Cricket Association	1902/03	1902/03	Test
Anderson, Olivia Victoria	Cricket SA (W)	2007/08	2008	ODI/T20
Ariefdien, E	SA Malay Team	1890/91	1890/91	Unofficial
Ashley, William Hare 'Gobo'	SA Cricket Association	1888/89	1888/89	Test
Austen, Yvonne	SA & Rhodesia Women's Cricket Association	1985	1985	Unofficial
Bacher, Adam Marc*	United Cricket Board of SA	1996/97	2004/05	Test/ODI
Balaskas, Xenophon Constantine	SA Cricket Association	1930/31	1938/39	Test
Bardien, Salie	SA Malay Cricket Board	1952/53	1952/53	Unofficial
Barlow, Edgar John	SA Cricket Association	1961/62	1969/70	Test
Barnes, Vincent Alexander	SA Cricket Board	1982/83	1990/91	Unofficial
Behardien, Ismail 'Miley'	SA Cricket Board	1987/88	1990/91	Unofficial
Behardien, Ismail 'Taliep'	SA Malay Cricket Board	1957/58	1957/58	Unofficial
Bell, Alexander John 'Sandy'	SA Cricket Association	1929	1935	Test
Bell, Alexander J	SA Coloured Cricket Association	1950/51	1952/53	Unofficial
	SA Cricket Board of Control	1956/57	1956/57	Unofficial
Bisset, Arthur Vintcent Crossley 'Artie'	SA Cricket Association	1901	1901	Unofficial[372]
Bisset, Murray (Sir)	SA Cricket Association	1898/99	1909/1910	Test
Bissett, George Finlay	SA Cricket Association	1924	1927/28	Test
Blackenberg, James Manuel	SA Cricket Association	1913/14	1924	Test
Bolton, James Lardner	SA Cricket Association	1924/25	1924/25	Unofficial[373]
Bond, Gerald Edward 'Boysie'	SA Cricket Association	1938/39	1938/39	Test

Name	Board	From	To	Icc Status
Brits, Cri-Zelda	**SA Women's Cricket Association / Cricket SA (W)**	**2001/02**	**2010/11**	**Test/ODI/T20**
Bromfield, Harry Dudley 'Brom'	**SA Cricket Association**	**1961/62**	**1965**	**Test**
Budgen, Edward Albert 'Hookie'	SA Cricket Association	1919/20	1919/20	Unofficial[374]
Burger, Janet	SA & Rhodesia Women's Cricket Association	1978/79	1978/79	Unofficial
Buys, Isaac Daniel	**SA Cricket Association**	**1922/23**	**1924/25**	**Test**
Cameron, Horace Brakenridge 'Jock'	**SA Cricket Association**	**1927/28**	**1935**	**Test**
Castens, Herbert Hayton	SA Cricket Association	1894	1894	Unofficial[375]
Cheetham, John Erskine 'Jack'	**SA Cricket Association**	**1948/49**	**1955**	**Test**
Chevalier, Grahame Anton	**SA Cricket Association**	**1969/70**	**1969/70**	**Test**
Coen, Stanley Keppel 'Shunter'*	**SA Cricket Association**	**1927/28**	**1927/28**	**Test**
Commaille, John McIllwaine Moore 'Mick'	**SA Cricket Association**	**1909/10**	**1927/28**	**Test**
Commins, John Brian*	**United Cricket Board of SA**	**1994/95**	**1996/97**	**Test**
Conyngham, Dalton Parry 'Conky'*	**SA Cricket Association**	**1922/23**	**1924/25**	**Test**
Cowan, Claire Sheena	**SA Women's Cricket Association**	**2003**	**2003**	**Test**
Cripps, Godfrey	**SA Cricket Association**	**1891/92**	**1894**	**Test**
Crisp, Robert James 'Bob'	**SA Cricket Association**	**1935**	**1935/36**	**Test**
Cullinan, Daryll John*	SA Cricket Union	1989/90	1989/90	Unofficial
Cullinan, Daryll John*	**United Cricket Board of SA**	**1992/93**	**2000/01**	**Test/ODI**
Cupido, Randall 'Joey'	SA Cricket Board	1987/88	1987/88	Unofficial
Davids, Faiek	SA Cricket Board	1987/88	1990/91	Unofficial
Davies, Helen Ann	**SA Women's Cricket Association**	**1997**	**2000/01**	**ODI**
Dawson, Alan Charles	**United Cricket Board of SA**	**1998/99**	**2004**	**Test/ODI**
Dermota, Belinda	**SA Women's Cricket Association**	**1997/98**	**1997/98**	**ODI**
D'Oliveira, Basil Lewis	SA Coloured Cricket Association	1952/53	1957/58	Unofficial
	SA Cricket Board of Control	1956/57	1958/59	Unofficial
Duminy, Jacobus Petrus (Professor) 'Koos'*	**SA Cricket Association**	**1927/28**	**1929**	**Test**
Duminy, Jean-Paul	**United Cricket Board of SA / Cricket SA**	**2004**	**2010/11**	**Test/ODI/T20**
Du Toit, K	SA Malay Team	1890/91	1890/91	Unofficial
Du Toit, 'Moutie'	SA Malay Cricket Board	1957/58	1957/58	Unofficial
Erickson, Bert	SA Coloured Cricket Association	1957/58	1957/58	Unofficial
Fortune, Neil	SA Cricket Board	1982/83	1982/83	Unofficial
Francis, Howard Henry	**SA Cricket Association**	**1898/99**	**1898/99**	**Test**
Freeman, Abdol J 'Dol'	SA Malay Cricket Board	1952/53	1952/53	Unofficial
Fritz, Shandré Alvida	**SA Women's Cricket Association / Cricket SA (W)**	**2003**	**2010/11**	**ODI/T20**
Fuller, Edward Russell Henry	**SA Cricket Association**	**1952/53**	**1957/58**	**Test**

Name	Board	From	To	Icc Status
Gabriels, Seraj	SA Cricket Board	1986/87	1987/88	Unofficial
George, Amien	SA Cricket Board of Control	1956/57	1956/57	Unofficial
	SA Malay Cricket Board	1957/58	1957/58	Unofficial
Gibbs, Herschelle Herman	United Cricket Board of SA / Cricket SA	1996/97	2010	Test/ODI/T20
Graham, Robert	**SA Cricket Association**	**1898/99**	**1901**	**Test**
Hands, Kenneth Charles Myburgh	SA Cricket Association	1924/25	1924/25	Unofficial[376]
Hands, Philip Albert Myburgh 'Pam'	**SA Cricket Association**	**1913/14**	**1924**	**Test**
Hands, Reginald Harry Myburgh	**SA Cricket Association**	**1913/14**	**1913/14**	**Test**
Hanley, Martin Andrew	**SA Cricket Association**	**1948/49**	**1948/49**	**Test**
Hannah, Joan	SA & Rhodesia Women's Cricket Association	1978/79	1985	Unofficial
Harris, Paul Lee*	Cricket SA	2006/07	2010/11	Test/ODI[377]
Hearne, Frank	**SA Cricket Association**	**1891/92**	**1895/96**	**Test**[378]
Hearne, George Alfred Lawrence	**SA Cricket Association**	**1919/20**	**1924**	**Test**
Henderson, Claude William	United Cricket Board of SA	2001/02	2002/03	Test/ODI
Henderson, Tyron*	Cricket SA	2006/07	2006/07	T20
Hendricks, A	SA Malay Cricket Board	1954/55	1954/55	Unofficial
Hendricks, Stuart	SA Cricket Board	1987/88	1987/88	Unofficial
Henry, Omar*	SA Cricket Union	1986/87	1986/87	Unofficial
	United Cricket Board of SA	1991/92	1992/93	Test/ODI[379]
Hinrichsen, D	SA Coloured Cricket Association	1957/58	1957/58	Unofficial
Hobson, Denys Laurence	SA Cricket Union	1981/82	1983/84	Unofficial
Hodgkinson, Alison Lucille	**SA Women's Cricket Association**	**2000**	**2004/05**	**Test/ODI**
Horwood, Stanley Ebden	SA Cricket Association	1904	1904	Unofficial[380]
Hurling, D	SA Coloured Cricket Association	1950/51	1950/51	Unofficial
Innes, Gerald Alfred Skerten	SA Cricket Association	1952/53	1952/53	Unofficial[381]
Isaacs, Ebrahim 'Braima'	SA Cricket Board	1982/83	1982/83	Unofficial
Ismail, Shabnim	Cricket SA (W)	2006/07	2010/11	Test/ODI/T20
Jabaar, Armien	SA Cricket Board	1982/83	1982/83	Unofficial
Jacobs, Leighshé Zanell	**SA Women's Cricket Association**	**2003**	**2003**	**Test**
January, P	SA Coloured Cricket Association	1957/58	1957/58	Unofficial
Jefferies, Stephen Thomas	SA Cricket Union	1981/82	1986/87	Unofficial
Joshua, D	SA Coloured Cricket Association	1950/51	1950/51	Unofficial
Kallis, Jacques Henry	United Cricket Board of SA / Cricket SA	1995/96	2010/11	Test/ODI/T20
Kemp, Justin Miles*	United Cricket Board of SA / Cricket SA	2000/01	2007/08	Test/ODI/T20
Kilowan, Ashlyn Petro Carlyle	SA Women's Cricket Association / Cricket SA (W)	2003	2009/10	Test/ODI/T20

CHAPTER 14 List of national players from Western Province and Cape Cobras, 1888–2011

Name	Board	From	To	Icc Status
Kirsten, Gary	**United Cricket Board of SA**	**1993/94**	**2003/04**	**Test/ODI**
Kirsten, Peter Noel*	SA Cricket Union	1981/82	1989/90	Unofficial
Kleinveldt, Rory Keith	**United Cricket Board of SA**	**1991/92**	**1994**	**Test/ODI**
Koen, Louis Johannes*	Cricket SA	2008/09	2010	T20
Kotze, Johannes Jacobus 'Kodgee' 'Boerjong'	**United Cricket Board of SA**	**1996/97**	**1999/00**	**ODI**382
Kuiper, Adrian Paul	SA Cricket Association	1901	1907	Test
Kuylaars, Aluis	SA Cricket Union	1981/82	1989/90	Unofficial
Kuys, Frederick	**United Cricket Board of SA**	**1991/92**	**1995/96**	**Test/ODI**
Lakay, H 'Tim'	SA Women's Cricket Association	1997	2000/01	ODI
Lakay, Neville	**SA Cricket Association**	**1898/99**	**1898/99**	**Test**
Lakay, Yusuf 'Timmy'	SA Coloured Cricket Association	1954/55	1954/55	Unofficial
Lang, Beverley	SA Coloured Cricket Association	1957/58	1957/58	Unofficial
	SA Malay Cricket Board	1954/55	1954/55	Unofficial
	SA & Rhodesia Women's Cricket Association	**1960/61**	**1960/61**	**Test**
Langeveldt, Charl Kenneth	**United Cricket Board of SA / Cricket SA**	**2001/02**	**2010/11**	**Test/ODI/T20**
Latief, Ismail	SA Malay Cricket Board	1952/53	1952/53	Unofficial
Le Roux, Garth Stirling	SA Cricket Union	1981/82	1986/87	Unofficial
Lewis, Levona P	**SA Women's Cricket Association**	**1998/99**	**2000/01**	**ODI**
Lewis, Percy Tyson 'Plum'	**SA Cricket Association**	**1913/14**	**1913/14**	**Test**
Louw, Johann*	Cricket SA	2008/09	2008/09	ODI/T20
Lundie, Eric Balfour 'Bill'*	**SA Cricket Association**	**1913/14**	**1913/14**	**Test**
Macaulay, Michael John*	**SA Cricket Association**	**1964/65**	**1965**	**Test**
Maclons, Leon	SA Coloured Cricket Association	1950/51	1950/51	Unofficial
Magiet, Saait	SA Cricket Board	1982/83	1990/91	Unofficial
Magitshima, William Velile	SA African Cricket Board	1966/67	1974/75	Unofficial
Magodla, TH	SA African Cricket Board	1966/67	1966/67	Unofficial
Malamba, Ben Ndzima	SA Bantu Cricket Board	1950/51	1954/55	Unofficial
Matthews, Brett Anthony	SA Cricket Board of Control	1956/57	1958/59	Unofficial
	SA Cricket Union	1986/87	1986/87	Unofficial
Matthews, Craig Russell	**United Cricket Board of SA**	**1991/92**	**1996/97**	**Test/ODI**
Mawu, H	SA Bantu Cricket Board	1952/53	1954/55	Unofficial
McEwan, Kenneth Scott	SA Cricket Union	1982/83	1986/87	Unofficial
McLeod, Morag	SA & Rhodesia Women's Cricket Association	1978/79	1985	Unofficial
	SA Cricket Union	1986/87	1989/90	Unofficial
McMillan, Brian Mervin	**United Cricket Board of SA**	**1991/92**	**1998**	**Test/ODI**

Name	Board	From	To	Icc Status
Melle, Michael George*	SA Cricket Association	1949/50	1952/53	Test
Middleton, James 'Bonnor'	SA Cricket Association	1894	1904	Test
Mills, Charles Henry	SA Cricket Association	1891/92	1894	Test
Milton, William Henry (Sir)	SA Cricket Association	1888/89	1891/92	Test
Morkel, Denijs Paul Beck	SA Cricket Association	1927/28	1931/32	Test
Mshumpela, Alex M	SA Bantu Cricket Board	1952/53	1957/58	Unofficial
Mvinjelwa, Hubert	SA Bantu Cricket Board	1954/55	1954/55	Unofficial
Nackerdien, S 'Sharkey'	SA Malay Cricket Board	1954/55	1954/55	Unofficial
Neethling, John James 'Coetie'	SA Coloured Cricket Association	1954/55	1957/58	Unofficial
	SA Cricket Board of Control	1958/59	1958/59	Unofficial
Nefdt, Sheilagh N (née Charlton)	SA & Rhodesia Women's Cricket Association	1960/61	1960/61	Test
Nel, John Desmond 'Jack'	SA Cricket Association	1949/50	1957/58	Test
Norton, Norman Ogilvie 'Pompey'*	SA Cricket Association	1909/10	1909/10	Test
Nourse, Arthur William 'Dave'*	SA Cricket Association	1902/03	1924/25	Test
O'Linn, Sidney 'Micky'*	SA Cricket Association	1960	1961/62	Test
Ontong, Justin Lee	United Cricket Board of SA/Cricket SA	2000/01	2008/09	Test/ODI/T20
Osman, Abdullah Abubakar 'Bakar'	SA Malay Cricket Board	1952/53	1952/53	Unofficial
Osmany, MS	SA Indian Cricket Union	1957/58	1957/58	Unofficial
Ovenstone, Douglas MacPherson	SA Cricket Association	1947	1947	Unofficial[383]
Owen-Smith, Harold Geoffrey Owen 'Tuppy'	SA Cricket Association	1929	1929	Test
Palm, Archibald William	SA Cricket Association	1927/28	1927/28	Test
Pangarkar, S Ismail	SA Indian Cricket Union	1952/53	1957/58	Unofficial
Payne, Maureen	SA & Rhodesia Women's Cricket Association	1960/61	1971/72	Test
Petersen, Eric	SA Malay Cricket Board	1952/53	1957/58	Unofficial
	SA Cricket Board of Control	1958/59	1958/59	Unofficial
Peterson, Robin John	United Cricket Board of SA / Cricket SA	2002/03	2001/11	Test/ODI/T20
Philander, Vernon Darryl	Cricket SA	2007	2008	ODI/T20
Pienaar, Roy Francois*	SA Cricket Union	1985/86	1989/90	Unofficial
Pithey, Anthony John	SA Cricket Association	1956/57	1964/65	Test
Pithey, David Bartlett*	SA Cricket Association	1963/64	1966/67	Test
Plimsoll, Jack Bruce	SA Cricket Association	1947	1947	Test
Poole, C	SA Coloured Cricket Association	1957/58	1957/58	Unofficial
Pothecary, James Edward	SA Cricket Association	1960	1960	Test
	SA & Rhodesia Women's Cricket Association	1985	1985	Unofficial
Price, Kim	SA Women's Cricket Association	1997	2000/01	ODI

Name	Board	From	To	Icc Status
Prince, Ashwell Gavin	**United Cricket Board of SA / Cricket SA**	**2001/02**	**2010/11**	**Test/ODI/T20**
Prince, Charles Frederick Henry*	SA Cricket Association	1898/99	1901	Test
Pringle, Meyrick Wayne	**United Cricket Board of SA**	**1991/92**	**1995/96**	**Test/ODI**
Procter, Michael John	SA Cricket Association	1966/67	1969/70	Test
	SA Cricket Union	1981/82	1983/84	Unofficial*
Puttick, Andrew George	**United Cricket Board of SA**	**2004**	**2005/06**	**ODI**[384]
Raziet, Salamodien 'Laam'	SA Coloured Cricket Association	1957/58	1957/58	Unofficial
	SA Cricket Board of Control	1956/57	1958/59	Unofficial
Reid, Allen 'Jupp'	SA Cricket Association	1901	1901	Unofficial[385]
Reid, Denise Joanne	**SA Women's Cricket Association**	**1997**	**2001/02**	**Test/ODI**
Reid, Norman	SA Cricket Association	1921/22	1921/22	Test
Richards, Alfred Renfrew	SA Cricket Association	1895/96	1895/96	Test
Richards, William Henry Matthews 'Dicky'	SA Cricket Association	1888/89	1888/89	Test
Robertson, John Benjamin	SA Cricket Association	1935/36	1935/36	Test
Routledge, Thomas William	SA Cricket Association	1891/92	1895/96	Test
Rowe, George Alexander	SA Cricket Association	1894	1902/03	Test
Rundle, David Bryan	SA Cricket Union	1989/90	1989/90	Unofficial
	United Cricket Board of SA	**1993/94**	**1993/94**	**ODI**
Sabotker, Adam	SA Coloured Cricket Association	1957/58	1957/58	Unofficial
Samsodien, L	SA Malay Team	1890/91	1890/91	Unofficial
Schultz, Brett Nolan	**United Cricket Board of SA**	**1992/93**	**1997/98**	**Test/ODI**
Scott, CM	SA Bantu Cricket Board	1950/51	1950/51	Unofficial
Seccull, Arthur William*	SA Cricket Association	1894	1895/96	Test
Seeff, Lawrence	SA Cricket Union	1982/83	1982/83	Unofficial
Seymour, Michael Arthur (Dr) 'Kelly'	SA Cricket Association	1963/64	1969/70	Test
Shaikh, IE	SA Indian Cricket Union	1952/53	1952/53	Unofficial
Sihawu, GG	SA African Cricket Board	1966/67	1966/67	Unofficial
Simons, Eric Owen	SA Cricket Union	1985/86	1985/86	Unofficial
	United Cricket Board of SA	**1993/94**	**1994/95**	**ODI**
Smith, Graeme Craig	**United Cricket Board of SA / Cricket SA**	**2001/02**	**2010/11**	**Test/ODI/T20**
Snooke, Stanley de la Courtte	SA Cricket Association	1907	1907	Test
Snooke, Sibley John 'Tip'	SA Cricket Association	1904	1922/23	Test
Solomon, Sidney Norman	SA Coloured Cricket Association	1957/58	1957/58	Unofficial
	SA Cricket Board of Control	1958/59	1958/59	Unofficial
Somyo, Stanford	SA African Cricket Board	1974/75	1975/76	Unofficial

Name	Board	From	To	Icc Status
Southgate, I	SA Coloured Cricket Association	1957/58	1957/58	Unofficial
Steyn, Stephen Sebastian Louis 'Stodgy'*	SA Cricket Association	1931/32	1931/32	Unofficial[386]
Sylvester, D	SA Coloured Cricket Association	1952/53	1952/53	Unofficial
Taylor, Herbert Wilfred*	**SA Cricket Association**	**1912**	**1931/32**	**Test**
Telemachus, Roger	United Cricket Board of SA / Cricket SA	1997/98	2006/07	ODI/T20
Theunissen, Nicolaas Hendrik Christiaan de Jong	SA Cricket Association	1888/89	1888/89	Test
Thomas, Alfonso Clive*	**United Cricket Board of SA / Cricket SA**	**2004/05**	**2006/07**	**T20[387]**
Thomas, P 'Paddy'	SA Indian Cricket Union	1954/55	1954/55	Unofficial
Tsolekile, Thami Lungisa	**United Cricket Board of SA**	**2003**	**2004/05**	**Test**
Twentyman Jones, Percy Sydney	SA Cricket Association	1902/03	1902/03	Test
Van der Bijl, Pieter Gerhard Vintcent	SA Cricket Association	1938/39	1938/39	Test
Van der Merwe, Marie	SA & Rhodesia Women's Cricket Association	1985	1985	Unofficial
Van der Merwe, Peter Laurence	**SA Cricket Association**	**1963/64**	**1966/67**	**Test**
Van der Westhuizen, Yolandi*	**Cricket SA (W)**	**2008/09**	**2008/09**	**ODI**
Van Haaght, Saait	SA Indian Cricket Union	1952/53	1954/55	Unofficial
Van Ryneveld, Clive Berrange	**SA Cricket Association**	**1951**	**1957/58**	**Test**
Van Schalkwyk, Charles	SA Cricket Board	1982/83	1982/83	Unofficial
Van Zyl, Juanita	**SA & Rhodesia Women's Cricket Association**	**1971/72**	**1971/72**	**Test**
Van Zyl, Susanna Deborah	**SA Women's Cricket Association**	**1998/99**	**2003/04**	**Test/ODI**
Waterwich, Basil	SA Coloured Cricket Association	1950/51	1952/53	Unofficial
Wessels, Kepler Christoffel*	**SA Cricket Union**	**1989/90**	**1989/90**	**Test/ODI[388]**
Westcott, Richard John	**United Cricket Board of SA**	**1991/92**	**1994/95**	**Test**
Weyers, Denise	**SA Cricket Association**	**1953/54**	**1957/58**	**Test**
White, Nazeem	SA & Rhodesia Women's Cricket Association	1971/72	1971/72	Unofficial
Williams, Owen Leslie	SA Coloured Cricket Association	1990/91	1990/91	Unofficial
	SA Cricket Board of Control	1957/58	1957/58	Unofficial
		1958/59	1958/59	Unofficial
Willoughby, Charl Myles	**United Cricket Board of SA**	**1999/2000**	**2003**	**Test/ODI**
Witten, Basil	SA Coloured Cricket Association	1954/55	1957/58	Unofficial
Wynne, Owen Edgar	**SA Cricket Association**	**1948/49**	**1949/50**	**Test**
Zibi, GM	SA African Cricket Board	1966/67	1966/67	Unofficial
Zondeki, Monde	**United Cricket Board of SA / Cricket South Africa**	**2002/03**	**2008/09**	**Test/ODI/T20**

CHAPTER 15

Western Province and Cape Cobras individual first-class career records, 1890–2011[389]

CHAPTER 15 Western Province and Cape Cobras individual first-class career records, 1890–2011

Name	Team	From	To	M	Inns	NO	Runs	HS	Avg	100	50	Ct	St	Balls	Runs	Wkts	Avg	RPO	BB	5I	10M
Abbas, M	WPCA Am	2008/09	2009/10	10	17	0	460	64	27.05	0	5	6	0	0	0	0	–	–	–	0	0
Abderouf, F	WPCA	1995/96	1995/96	1	2	0	0	0	0.00	0	0	0	0	0	0	0	–	–	–	0	0
Abdullah, M	WPCB	1977/78	1987/88	39	59	2	1854	109	32.52	3	11	32	0	54	28	1	28.00	3.11	1-16	0	0
	All FC	1977/78	1990/91	54	83	3	2294	109	28.67	3	12	41	0	54	28	1	28.00	3.11	1-16	0	0
Abrahams, CJ	WPCB	1974/75	1974/75	5	8	0	111	40	15.85	0	0	4	0	630	188	8	23.50	1.79	3-18	0	0
Ackerman, HD	WPCA	1993/94	2002/03	74	124	17	4700	202*	43.92	14	24	65	0	60	36	0	–	3.60	–	0	0
	WCC	2005/06	2005/06	4	7	0	168	61	24.00	0	1	5	0	0	0	0	–	–	–	0	0
	WPCA B	1993/94	1993/94	5	9	0	379	154	42.11	1	2	2	0	0	0	0	–	–	–	0	0
	All FC	1993/94	2009	220	369	34	14625	309*	43.65	40	75	183	0	102	57	0	–	3.35	–	0	0
Ackerman, HM	WPCU	1970/71	1979/80	76	132	15	3668	179*	31.35	5	19	59	0	1191	599	14	42.78	3.01	3-39	0	0
	WPCU B	1979/80	1981/82	15	25	3	704	114	32.00	1	3	21	0	270	157	4	39.25	3.48	4-61	0	0
	All FC	1963/64	1981/82	234	409	33	12219	208	32.49	20	60	199	0	2467	1400	32	43.75	3.40	4-61	0	0
Ackermann, GL	WPCU B	1977/78	1977/78	1	0	0	0	–	–	0	0	0	0	84	66	3	22.00	4.71	2-11	0	0
	All FC	1977/78	1987/88	34	52	13	521	67	13.35	0	1	13	0	5417	2822	136	20.75	3.12	7-69	6	1
Ackermann, JP	WPCU B	1979/80	1982/83	11	22	2	336	70*	16.80	0	2	7	0	667	258	19	13.57	2.32	4-33	0	0
	All FC	1979/80	1982/83	18	35	2	564	70*	17.09	0	4	12	0	1120	415	31	13.38	2.22	4-33	0	0
Ackermann, S	WPCA	1999/00	1999/00	1	2	0	32	31	16.00	0	0	0	0	12	14	0	–	7.00	–	0	0
	All FC	1996/97	1999/00	8	14	1	238	43	18.30	0	0	5	0	504	191	4	47.75	2.27	1-9	0	0
Adams, A	WPCB	1971/72	1979/80	24	30	16	180	39	12.85	0	0	14	0	6037	1703	116	14.68	1.69	6-7	8	2
	All FC	1971/72	1979/80	27	33	17	198	39	12.37	0	0	14	0	6569	1888	122	15.47	1.72	6-7	8	2
Adams, MQ	WPCA Am	2007/08	2010/11	4	5	1	145	94*	36.25	0	1	5	0	0	0	0	–	–	–	0	0
Adams, N	WPCA B	1997/98	1997/98	3	5	1	131	81*	32.75	0	1	6	0	0	0	0	–	–	–	0	0
	All FC	1995/96	1997/98	4	6	1	131	81*	26.20	0	1	6	0	0	0	0	–	–	–	0	0
Adams, PR	WPCA	1995/96	2003/04	34	35	20	383	61*	25.53	0	1	20	0	8673	3966	135	29.37	2.74	7-69	7	0
	WCC	2004/05	2006/07	15	24	6	449	49	24.94	0	0	7	0	2177	1170	23	50.86	3.22	3-54	0	0
	WPCA B	1995/96	1995/96	1	0	0	0	–	–	0	0	0	0	306	129	5	25.80	2.52	3-48	0	0
	WPCA Am	2004/05	2007/08	15	17	3	242	70	17.28	0	1	5	0	2105	1080	37	29.18	3.07	4-26	0	0
	All FC	1995/96	2007/08	141	156	54	1752	70	17.17	0	2	73	0	27102	13456	412	32.66	2.97	9-79	16	3
Adams, Y	WPCB	1979/80	1988/89	7	14	1	193	55	13.78	0	1	7	0	0	0	0	–	–	–	0	0
Ahmed, MH	WPCB	1984/85	1984/85	4	7	1	75	39	12.50	0	0	1	0	0	0	0	–	–	–	0	0
Alexander, CJ	WPCA Am	2004/05	2006/07	5	6	4	10	5*	5.00	0	0	2	0	870	459	13	35.30	3.16	3-48	0	0
	All FC	2004/05	2010/11	48	54	26	293	39	10.46	0	0	14	0	7147	4413	141	31.29	3.70	5-36	6	0
Allen, E	WPCU	1893/94	1903/04	3	5	0	32	9	6.40	0	0	1	0	0	0	0	–	–	–	0	0
Allie, G	WPCB	1977/78	1986/87	16	19	11	74	19	9.25	0	0	4	0	1906	611	49	12.46	1.92	6-45	3	0
	All FC	1974/75	1986/87	29	35	17	196	23*	10.88	0	0	11	0	4026	1303	87	14.97	1.94	6-45	3	0

Name	Team	From	To	M	Inns	NO	Runs	HS	Avg	100	50	Ct	St	Balls	Runs	Wkts	Avg	RPO	BB	5I	10M
Allie, MZ	WPCB	1978/79	1982/83	4	8	0	43	10	5.37	0	0	0	0	0	0	0	-	-	-	0	0
Allie, Z	WPCA Am	2009/10	2009/10	3	5	0	70	38	14.00	0	0	8	0	0	0	0	-	-	-	0	0
Allin, CR	WPCU	1929/30	1930/31	2	2	0	0	0	0.00	0	0	0	0	364	156	4	39.00	2.57	2-36	0	0
Anderson, JH	WPCU	1894/95	1907/08	13	22	2	468	109	23.40	1	1	13	0	24	26	1	26.00	6.50	1-10	0	0
	All FC	1894/95	1907/08	14	24	2	511	109	23.22	1	1	14	0	24	26	1	26.00	6.50	1-10	0	0
Andrew, JC	WPCU	1894/95	1894/95	1	2	0	9	8	4.50	0	0	3	0	0	0	0	-	-	-	0	0
Antulay, N	WPCB	1982/83	1988/89	18	27	0	578	69	21.40	0	2	18	0	103	39	2	19.50	2.27	1-7	0	0
Arendse, NM	WPCB	1977/78	1982/83	2	4	0	6	3	1.50	0	0	1	0	30	15	1	-	3.00	-	0	0
Arenz, H	WPCB	1973/74	1973/74	1	2	0	10	10	5.00	0	0	2	1	0	0	0	-	-	-	0	0
Arkell, CJF	WPCA Am	2008/09	2008/09	2	3	1	24	14	12.00	0	0	2	0	306	205	4	51.25	4.01	2-44	0	0
Arnold, S	WPCB	1977/78	1978/79	3	4	4	16	7*	-	0	0	2	0	550	216	8	27.00	2.35	4-50	0	0
Arnott, JG	WPCU	1936/37	1936/37	3	1	0	4	4	4.00	0	0	0	0	336	113	3	37.66	2.01	2-26	0	0
Ashley, WH	WPCU	1889/90	1890/91	3	4	2	16	15*	8.00	0	0	1	0	660	187	13	14.38	1.70	6-40	1	0
	All FC	1888/89	1890/91	4	6	2	17	15*	4.25	0	0	1	0	833	282	20	14.10	2.03	7-95	2	0
Austen, MH	WPCU	1987/88	1987/88	4	7	1	316	202*	52.66	1	1	7	0	12	7	0	-	3.50	-	0	0
	WPCU B	1982/83	1988/89	10	19	1	565	121	31.38	1	1	9	0	318	146	5	29.20	2.75	2-35	0	0
	All FC	1982/83	1996/97	66	120	8	3619	202*	32.31	6	16	48	0	3836	1813	55	32.96	2.83	5-71	1	0
Bacchus, SFAF	WPCU	1984/85	1984/85	9	17	0	324	65	19.05	0	3	11	0	6	2	1	2.00	2.00	1-2	0	0
	All FC	1971/72	1985/86	111	182	13	5943	250	35.16	8	37	88	0	471	197	8	24.62	2.50	2-18	0	0
Baguley, BC	WPCA	1991/92	1991/92	1	2	0	10	9	5.00	0	0	0	0	6	5	0	-	5.00	-	0	0
	WPCA B	1994/95	1994/95	5	9	2	338	133*	48.28	1	2	3	0	6	5	0	-	5.00	-	0	0
	All FC	1991/92	1996/97	16	29	3	731	133*	28.11	1	4	14	0	6	5	0	-	5.00	-	0	0
Baguley, N	WPCU	1953/54	1954/55	5	8	5	13	5	4.33	0	0	8	3	0	0	0	-	-	-	0	0
Bain, CA	WPCU	1902/03	1908/09	6	10	0	148	40	14.80	0	0	3	0	386	190	8	23.75	2.95	3-54	0	0
	All FC	1902/03	1908/09	6	10	0	148	40	14.80	0	0	3	0	386	190	8	23.75	2.95	3-54	0	0
Baker, EC	WPCU	1956/57	1956/57	1	2	0	3	3	1.50	0	0	1	0	0	0	0	-	-	-	0	0
	All FC	1956/57	1965/66	10	20	4	345	94*	21.56	0	1	5	0	826	321	11	29.18	2.33	4-82	0	0
Balaskas, XC	WPCU	1934/35	1935/36	5	8	0	128	61	16.00	0	1	2	0	1338	616	34	18.11	2.76	6-24	4	2
	All FC	1926/27	1946/47	75	107	13	2696	206	28.68	6	12	47	0	12557	6656	276	24.11	3.18	8-60	20	9
Ballantyne, IR	WPCU	1952/53	1952/53	2	4	0	39	19	9.75	0	0	0	0	240	112	2	56.00	2.80	1-22	0	0
Bam, I	WPCU	1906/07	1907/08	2	2	0	20	15	10.00	0	0	0	0	174	81	9	9.00	2.79	4-41	0	0
	All FC	1906/07	1913/14	3	4	0	61	34	15.25	0	0	2	0	318	125	16	7.81	2.35	5-16	1	0
Barlow, EJ	WPCU	1968/69	1980/81	82	146	6	5024	163	35.88	12	21	111	0	12812	5132	243	21.11	2.40	7-24	11	1
	All FC	1959/60	1982/83	283	493	28	18212	217	39.16	43	86	335	0	31930	13785	571	24.14	2.59	7-24	16	2

Name	Team	From	To	M	Inns	NO	Runs	HS	Avg	100	50	Ct	St	Balls	Runs	Wkts	Avg	RPO	BB	5I	10M
Barnes, IS	WPCU	1988/89	1988/89	2	4	2	11	6	5.50	0	0	0	0	258	156	3	52.00	3.62	2-57	0	0
	WPCU B	1979/80	1989/90	8	10	4	37	13*	6.16	0	0	6	0	1463	768	27	28.44	3.14	5-39	1	0
	All FC	1979/80	1989/90	10	14	6	48	13*	6.00	0	0	6	0	1721	924	30	30.80	3.22	5-39	1	0
Barnes, VA	WPCB	1978/79	1990/91	53	59	25	313	41*	9.20	0	0	32	0	8780	2738	251	10.90	1.87	9-46	20	4
	WPCA	1991/92	1991/92	1	2	2	9	8*	-	0	0	0	0	141	59	3	19.66	2.51	2-47	0	0
	WPCA B	1991/92	1994/95	6	3	2	24	19	24.00	0	0	2	0	1074	420	16	26.25	2.34	3-44	0	0
	All FC	1978/79	1994/95	68	75	32	423	41*	9.83	0	0	45	0	11481	3862	323	11.95	2.01	9-46	24	6
Base, SJ	WPCU B	1981/82	1983/84	2	2	1	2	2	2.00	0	0	0	0	258	61	5	12.20	1.41	2-6	0	0
	All FC	1981/82	1999	134	172	36	1551	58	11.40	0	2	60	0	21139	11397	388	29.37	3.23	7-60	16	1
Bassage, DJ	WPCA	2003/04	2003/04	4	7	1	307	79	51.16	0	3	6	0	0	0	0	-	-	-	0	0
	WCC	2004/05	2006/07	22	41	3	1145	108	30.13	2	6	10	0	54	15	0	-	1.66	-	0	0
	WPCA Am	2004/05	2006/07	10	16	1	376	108*	25.06	1	0	18	0	0	0	0	-	-	-	0	0
	All FC	2003/04	2006/07	36	64	5	1828	108*	30.98	3	9	34	0	54	15	0	-	1.66	-	0	0
Battison, G	WPCU	1929/30	1932/33	2	2	0	18	12	9.00	0	0	2	0	0	0	0	-	-	-	0	0
Behardien, F	WPCA Am	2004/05	2004/05	3	5	0	122	60	24.40	0	1	3	0	300	177	6	29.50	3.54	3-48	0	0
	All FC	2004/05	2010/11	56	84	5	3126	150*	39.56	5	21	35	0	1244	672	19	35.36	3.24	3-48	0	0
Behardien, I	WPCB	1985/86	1990/91	25	37	1	972	142	27.00	2	2	44	0	6	2	0	-	2.00	-	0	0
	All FC	1985/86	1990/91	26	39	1	1003	142	26.39	2	2	44	0	6	2	0	-	2.00	-	0	0
Behardien, M	WPCA Am	2010/11	2010/11	6	8	2	213	52	35.50	0	2	7	0	0	0	0	-	-	-	0	0
Bell, AJ	WPCU	1925/26	1930/31	9	12	8	59	17*	14.75	0	0	2	0	2037	734	52	14.11	2.16	8-34	4	1
	All FC	1925/26	1938/39	63	79	45	311	32*	9.14	0	0	27	0	12047	5312	228	23.29	2.64	8-34	10	1
Bell, MA	WPCU	1908/09	1908/09	1	1	1	10	10*	-	0	0	0	0	42	25	1	25.00	3.57	1-16	0	0
	All FC	1906/07	1908/09	6	9	2	82	32*	11.71	0	0	0	0	264	135	4	33.75	3.06	2-33	0	0
Benjamin, F	WPCB	1982/83	1990/91	14	19	8	60	16*	5.45	0	0	8	0	1849	780	29	26.89	2.53	6-35	1	0
	WPCA	1993/94	1993/94	2	2	2	18	17*	-	0	0	0	0	390	226	2	113.00	3.47	2-149	0	0
	WPCA B	1993/94	1993/94	3	1	0	1	1	1.00	0	0	0	0	687	324	10	32.40	2.82	4-40	0	0
	All FC	1982/83	1993/94	19	22	10	79	17*	6.58	0	0	8	0	2926	1330	41	32.43	2.72	6-35	1	0
Bennett, BL	WPCA Am	2007/08	2008/09	3	6	1	113	59	22.60	0	1	2	0	12	9	0	-	4.50	-	0	0
	All FC	2001/02	2010/11	55	99	3	2627	150	27.36	3	14	29	0	1281	864	25	34.56	4.04	5-21	1	0
Bennett, HW	WPCU	1904/05	1909/10	2	3	0	21	12	7.00	0	0	0	0	0	0	0	-	-	-	0	0
Bensimon, AS (Abel)	WPCU	1912/13	1923/24	10	17	2	112	23	7.46	0	0	3	0	1117	653	33	19.78	3.50	5-84	1	0
Bensimon, AS (Alfred)	WPCU	1931/32	1933/34	4	4	1	19	18	6.33	0	0	0	0	797	327	23	14.21	2.46	6-24	2	0
Bergins, HWH	WPCB	1975/76	1975/76	6	9	2	83	27*	11.85	0	0	1	0	1067	357	30	11.90	2.00	6-27	2	1
	All FC	1975/76	1986/87	22	37	8	504	43*	17.37	0	0	13	0	2088	932	48	19.41	2.67	6-27	2	1

Name	Team	From	To	M	Inns	NO	Runs	HS	Avg	100	50	Ct	St	Balls	Runs	Wkts	Avg	RPO	BB	5I	10M
Best, CA	WPCA	1993/94	1993/94	7	13	0	333	71	25.61	0	2	3	0	184	98	2	49.00	3.19	2-80	0	0
	All FC	1979/80	1993/94	90	154	14	5439	179	38.85	13	24	108	0	1642	772	24	32.16	2.82	3-29	0	0
Bing, F	WPCU	1954/55	1960/61	8	13	0	251	85	19.30	0	2	3	0	0	0	0	–	–	–	0	0
Bing, GJ	WPCU B	1987/88	1987/88	1	1	0	20	20	20.00	0	0	0	0	150	73	1	73.00	2.92	1-40	0	0
Birch, CWS	WPCA Am	2006/07	2007/08	12	16	1	463	87	30.86	0	5	8	0	1711	897	38	23.60	3.14	5-47	1	0
Bisset, AVC	WPCU	1902/03	1921/22	13	24	0	292	49	12.16	0	0	7	0	549	265	7	37.85	2.89	2-33	0	0
	All FC	1901	1921/22	25	47	2	697	94	15.48	0	1	13	0	549	265	7	37.85	2.89	2-33	0	0
Bisset, EH	WPCU	1889/90	1889/90	1	2	1	0	0*	0.00	0	0	0	0	0	0	0	–	–	–	0	0
Bisset, M	WPCU	1894/95	1909/10	21	35	7	659	124*	23.53	1	2	26	5	176	108	5	21.60	3.68	2-20	0	0
	All FC	1894/95	1909/10	40	70	9	1441	184	23.62	2	4	51	13	182	122	5	24.40	4.02	2-20	0	0
Bissett, GF	WPCU	1927/28	1927/28	1	2	1	27	18	27.00	0	0	0	0	162	101	0	–	3.74	–	0	0
	All FC	1922/23	1929/30	21	31	12	294	33	15.47	0	0	8	0	3284	1816	67	27.10	3.31	7-29	5	0
Black, I	WPCU	1937/38	1937/38	1	2	0	47	24	23.50	0	0	2	0	144	58	0	–	2.41	–	0	0
Blanckenberg, JM	WPCU	1912/13	1922/23	18	32	2	801	87	26.70	0	4	13	0	2335	1292	78	16.56	3.31	9-78	4	2
	All FC	1912/13	1924	74	116	16	2232	171	22.32	1	9	53	0	13498	6230	293	21.26	2.76	9-78	21	3
Blanckenberg, N	WPCU	1919/20	1926/27	11	20	1	329	55	17.31	0	1	3	0	78	68	2	34.00	5.23	2-33	0	0
	All FC	1898/99	1926/27	12	21	1	329	55	16.45	0	1	3	0	78	68	2	34.00	5.23	2-33	0	0
Bleekers, LF	WPCU	1989/90	1989/90	3	5	1	86	35	21.50	0	0	10	0	0	0	0	–	–	–	0	0
	WPCA	1991/92	1993/94	6	12	1	199	87	18.09	0	2	3	0	0	0	0	–	–	–	0	0
	WPCU B	1988/89	1990/91	16	29	2	845	102*	31.29	1	6	35	3	0	0	0	–	–	–	0	0
	WPCA B	1991/92	1993/94	9	17	3	346	68	24.71	0	2	20	3	0	0	0	–	–	–	0	0
	All FC	1988/89	1993/94	34	63	7	1476	102*	26.35	1	10	68	3	0	0	0	–	–	–	0	0
Bolton, JL	WPCU	1921/22	1926/27	7	11	1	58	33	5.80	0	0	7	0	1129	464	24	19.33	2.46	6-81	3	0
	All FC	1921/22	1926/27	8	13	1	63	33	5.25	0	0	7	0	1213	504	24	21.00	2.49	6-81	3	0
Bolus, GRM	WPCU	1947/48	1951/52	10	15	2	113	35*	8.69	0	0	6	0	2167	747	27	27.66	2.06	5-50	2	0
	All FC	1947/48	1951/52	11	17	2	127	35*	8.46	0	0	7	0	2383	863	31	27.83	2.17	5-50	2	0
Bond, FP	WPCU	1910/11	1910/11	7	12	3	136	46*	15.11	0	0	2	0	800	384	21	18.28	2.88	5-47	1	0
	All FC	1910/11	1911/12	8	14	3	148	46*	13.45	0	0	2	0	926	489	23	21.26	3.16	5-47	1	0
Bond, GE	WPCU	1929/30	1938/39	25	38	3	1458	170	41.65	1	10	10	0	1254	601	18	33.38	2.87	4-17	0	0
	All FC	1929/30	1938/39	28	43	4	1604	170	41.12	1	11	11	0	1462	707	20	35.35	2.90	4-17	0	0
Booysen, N	WPCB	1984/85	1989/90	5	5	1	99	38	24.75	0	0	1	0	734	269	17	15.82	2.19	3-29	0	0
Bothma, JP	WPCA Am	2010/11	2010/11	7	8	5	41	13	13.66	0	0	2	0	957	453	20	22.65	2.84	6-44	1	0
	WCC	2008/09	2008/09	1	2	1	10	8	10.00	0	0	0	0	96	81	0	–	5.06	–	0	0
	All FC	2006/07	2010/11	28	42	18	418	57	17.41	0	1	10	0	3979	2170	82	26.46	3.27	6-44	3	0

Name	Team	From	To	M	Inns	NO	Runs	HS	Avg	100	50	Ct	St	Balls	Runs	Wkts	Avg	RPO	BB	5I	10M
Bowditch, MH	WPCU	1964/65	1977/78	48	75	8	1853	120	27.65	1	10	15	0	3632	1702	56	30.39	2.81	9-52	3	1
	WPCU B	1975/76	1978/79	14	22	2	669	147	33.45	1	4	23	0	426	221	6	36.83	3.11	2-29	0	0
	All FC	1964/65	1978/79	62	97	10	2522	147	28.98	2	14	38	0	4058	1923	62	31.01	2.84	9-52	3	1
Bowley, RJ	WPCU B	1980/81	1981/82	4	4	3	49	16*	49.00	0	0	0	0	630	275	8	34.37	2.61	4-64	0	0
Brache, N	WPCB	1974/75	1974/75	2	3	0	5	3	1.66	0	0	0	0	0	0	0	-	-	-	0	0
	All FC	1974/75	1974/75	3	4	0	9	4	2.25	0	0	0	0	0	0	0	-	-	-	0	0
Bramwell, G	WPCA B	1994/95	1994/95	4	7	4	113	30*	37.66	0	0	4	0	735	341	11	31.00	2.78	5-74	1	0
Bricknell, GA	WPCU	1975/76	1976/77	3	3	2	23	22	23.00	0	0	0	0	594	209	4	52.25	2.11	3-42	0	0
	WPCU B	1975/76	1976/77	11	16	7	167	34	18.55	0	0	6	0	2835	1031	54	19.09	2.18	6-55	2	0
	All FC	1975/76	1976/77	14	19	9	190	34	19.00	0	0	6	0	3429	1240	58	21.37	2.16	6-55	2	0
Bridgens, KJ	WPCU B	1986/87	1987/88	11	20	2	529	79	29.38	0	4	24	3	6	3	0	-	-	-	0	0
	All FC	1986/87	1992/93	44	80	10	2021	130*	28.87	2	7	118	12	6	3	0	-	-	-	0	0
Brinkhaus, JGB	WPCU	1937/38	1939/40	8	11	0	30	8	2.72	0	0	4	0	2226	925	32	28.90	2.49	7-60	2	0
	All FC	1937/38	1955/56	10	14	2	54	18*	4.50	0	0	5	0	2514	1037	34	30.50	2.47	7-60	2	0
Bristow, JW	WPCU B	1980/81	1980/81	3	4	1	61	29	20.33	0	0	1	0	0	0	0	-	-	-	0	0
	All FC	1975/76	1983/84	10	16	1	187	40	12.46	0	0	4	0	0	0	0	-	-	-	0	0
Bromfield, HD	WPCU	1956/57	1968/69	44	69	21	285	44	5.93	0	0	49	0	11300	3988	166	24.02	2.11	7-60	11	1
	All FC	1956/57	1968/69	62	91	32	374	44	6.33	0	0	68	0	14763	5256	205	25.63	2.13	7-60	13	1
Brown, SV	WPCU	1920/21	1920/21	4	6	1	51	32*	10.20	0	0	1	0	222	103	3	34.33	2.78	2-32	0	0
Brown, TR	WPCU	1963/64	1963/64	6	11	0	103	36	9.36	0	0	15	4	0	0	0	-	-	-	0	0
	All FC	1957/58	1963/64	7	12	0	146	43	12.16	0	0	15	4	0	0	0	-	-	-	0	0
Bruce, SD	WPCU	1971/72	1985/86	35	54	6	1249	109*	26.02	1	7	43	1	0	0	0	-	-	-	0	0
	WPCU B	1975/76	1986/87	27	47	5	1598	176	38.04	3	6	55	4	204	90	2	45.00	2.64	2-28	0	0
	All FC	1971/72	1986/87	67	108	11	3113	176	32.09	5	14	121	6	204	90	2	45.00	2.64	2-28	0	0
Bruyns, A	WPCU	1965/66	1976/77	73	130	7	4184	197	34.01	10	18	85	0	43	24	1	24.00	3.34	1-1	0	0
	All FC	1965/66	1976/77	90	160	9	5050	197	33.44	11	23	106	0	52	25	1	25.00	2.88	1-1	0	0
Budge, NR	WPCU	1963/64	1972/73	27	50	1	1118	92	22.81	0	4	22	0	468	254	10	25.40	3.25	3-35	0	0
Budgen, EA	WPCU	1908/09	1919/20	11	18	3	47	16*	3.13	0	0	7	0	1420	735	48	15.31	3.10	7-30	3	1
	All FC	1908/09	1925/26	25	43	5	275	43	7.23	0	0	12	0	4825	2455	110	22.31	3.05	8-107	8	2
Bulbring, SL	WPCA B	1993/94	1993/94	1	0	0	0	-	-	0	0	0	1	180	105	3	35.00	3.50	3-73	0	0
Burmeister, IA	WPCU	1947/48	1947/48	2	4	0	65	27	16.25	0	0	1	0	0	0	0	-	-	-	0	0
Burns, A	WPCB	1985/86	1985/86	1	1	0	9	9*	-	0	0	0	0	0	0	0	-	-	-	0	0
Burns, ND	WPCU B	1985/86	1985/86	3	5	0	30	16	6.00	0	0	8	0	0	0	0	-	-	-	0	0
	All FC	1985/86	2002	205	307	65	7376	166	30.47	7	40	478	38	3	8	0	-	16.00	-	0	0
Burt, RJE	WPCU	1934/35	1937/38	4	7	0	115	40	16.42	0	0	3	0	537	228	7	32.57	2.54	2-60	0	0

Name	Team	From	To	M	Inns	NO	Runs	HS	Avg	100	50	Ct	St	Balls	Runs	Wkts	Avg	RPO	BB	5I	10M
Butler, BCH	WPCU	1966/67	1967/68	9	15	0	292	78	19.46	0	2	3	0	6	4	0	–	4.00	–	0	0
	All FC	1957/58	1967/68	10	17	0	307	78	18.05	0	2	4	0	6	4	0	–	4.00	–	0	0
Butler, V	WPCU	1949/50	1949/50	1	2	0	27	20	13.50	0	0	0	0	0	0	0	–	–	–	0	0
Buys, ID	WPCU	1921/22	1923/24	9	13	5	32	8	4.00	0	0	4	0	1776	885	40	22.12	2.98	6-49	3	0
	All FC	1921/22	1924/25	12	19	9	37	8	3.70	0	0	5	0	2340	1103	48	22.97	2.82	6-49	3	0
Calder, H	WPCU	1892/93	1894/95	3	6	2	119	40*	29.75	0	0	2	0	40	45	2	22.50	6.75	1-19	0	0
	All FC	1882	1896/97	10	19	2	288	44	16.94	0	0	5	0	410	222	10	22.20	3.24	3-24	0	0
Cameron, DP	WPCU	1970/71	1973/74	2	4	1	38	27	12.66	0	0	5	0	288	156	4	39.00	3.25	2-88	0	0
	All FC	1968/69	1975/76	9	16	2	130	27	9.28	0	0	1	0	1470	806	21	38.38	3.28	3-47	0	0
Cameron, HB	WPCU	1930/31	1930/31	1	2	0	15	14	7.50	0	0	0	0	0	0	0	–	–	–	0	0
Canning, RCC	All FC	1924/25	1935	107	161	17	5396	182	37.47	11	28	155	69	16	13	0	–	4.87	–	0	0
	WCC	2006/07	2010/11	40	56	8	1384	122	28.83	2	6	129	11	0	0	0	–	–	–	0	0
	WPCA Am	2004/05	2010/11	34	53	6	1693	116	36.02	3	11	102	13	0	0	0	–	–	–	0	0
Carelse, WF	All FC	2004/05	2010/11	74	109	14	3077	122	32.38	5	17	231	24	0	0	0	–	–	–	0	0
	WPCB	1975/76	1975/76	6	9	2	231	61*	33.00	0	1	2	0	816	210	20	10.50	1.54	5-15	2	0
	All FC	1975/76	1975/76	8	13	2	245	61*	22.27	0	1	4	0	942	283	22	12.86	1.80	5-15	2	0
Carew, AS	WPCU	1945/46	1945/46	2	2	0	17	12	8.50	0	0	0	0	296	105	1	105.00	2.12	1-60	0	0
	All FC	1945/46	1950/51	14	21	3	177	29	9.83	0	0	9	0	3075	1039	33	31.48	2.02	4-69	0	0
Carlsson, WE	WPCU	1910/11	1910/11	4	7	0	44	24	6.28	0	0	4	0	0	0	0	–	–	–	0	0
Carolin, HW	WPCU	1902/03	1907/08	9	16	1	354	80	23.60	0	3	4	0	1270	648	30	21.60	3.06	6-46	2	0
Carolus, D	WPCA Am	2010/11	2010/11	3	2	0	19	13	9.50	0	0	0	0	330	194	6	32.66	3.52	4-75	0	0
	WPCU B	1980/81	1980/81	1	1	0	6	6	6.00	0	0	0	0	126	50	2	25.00	2.38	1-24	0	0
Carse, JA	All FC	1977/78	1992/93	60	73	29	485	44	11.02	0	0	19	0	8243	4459	137	32.54	3.24	6-50	3	0
Carstens, J	WPCU	1912/13	1912/13	2	3	1	72	58	36.00	0	1	0	0	0	0	0	–	–	–	0	0
Castens, HH	WPCU	1890/91	1893/94	3	4	0	230	165	57.50	1	1	4	2	0	0	0	–	–	–	0	0
	All FC	1889/90	1893/94	4	6	0	250	165	41.66	1	1	4	2	0	0	0	–	–	–	0	0
Catt, AW	WPCU	1965/66	1967/68	12	19	2	261	54	15.35	0	1	38	6	18	2	0	–	0.66	–	0	0
	All FC	1954	1967/68	138	218	38	3123	162	17.35	1	9	283	37	1284	643	17	37.82	3.00	2-18	0	0
Cawood, JC	WPCU	1970/71	1973/74	11	13	3	64	19*	6.40	0	0	4	0	0	0	0	–	–	–	0	0
Challenor, EL	WPCU	1895/96	1896/97	5	7	0	221	76	31.57	0	1	5	0	0	15	0	–	3.00	–	0	0
	All FC	1894/95	1914	29	52	1	1106	111	21.68	1	3	23	0	234	108	3	36.00	2.76	3-68	0	0
Chalmers, WR	WPCU	1963/64	1963/64	1	2	2	1	1*	–	0	0	0	0	30	15	0	–	3.00	–	0	0
	All FC	1963/64	1963/64	48	83	46	181	12	4.89	0	0	19	0	11912	4078	167	24.41	2.05	6-55	9	0
Charnas, M	WPCU	1951/52	1958/59	1	2	0	1	1	0.50	0	0	0	0	162	49	1	49.00	1.81	1-49	0	0
	All FC	1958/59	1960/61	26	34	5	277	41	9.55	0	0	12	0	4101	1303	46	28.32	1.90	6-36	2	0

Name	Team	From	To	M	Inns	NO	Runs	HS	Avg	100	50	Ct	St	Balls	Runs	Wkts	Avg	RPO	BB	5I	10M
Cheetham, JE	WPCU	1939/40	1954/55	36	59	15	2437	271*	55.38	4	14	23	0	549	346	7	49.42	3.78	2-38	0	0
Cheetham, JR	All FC	1939/40	1955	108	170	35	5697	271*	42.20	8	33	67	0	613	376	8	47.00	3.68	2-38	0	0
Chevalier, GA	WPCU	1972/73	1972/73	4	6	0	234	124	39.00	1	1	1	0	4	0	0	–	0.00	–	0	0
	All FC	1968/69	1972/73	10	16	0	581	124	36.31	1	2	9	0	4	0	0	–	0.00	–	0	0
Cilliers, A	WPCU	1966/67	1973/74	41	44	29	80	13*	5.33	0	0	14	0	8890	3380	139	24.31	2.28	7-57	4	1
	All FC	1966/67	1973/74	43	47	30	84	13*	4.94	0	0	15	0	9435	3654	154	23.72	2.32	7-57	5	2
	WPCA	1995/96	1995/96	3	5	1	15	13	3.75	0	0	0	0	474	329	7	47.00	4.16	2-52	0	0
	WPCA B	1995/96	1995/96	4	3	1	34	16*	17.00	0	0	2	0	620	314	7	44.85	3.03	3-53	0	0
Clark, RM	All FC	1991/92	1998/99	26	40	8	631	64*	19.71	0	3	8	0	3760	1987	61	32.57	3.17	5-38	1	0
	WPCU	1972/73	1976/77	11	18	2	379	66*	23.68	0	3	9	0	472	266	8	33.25	3.38	5-70	1	0
	WPCU B	1975/76	1977/78	7	11	1	248	75	24.80	0	1	6	0	240	144	1	144.00	3.60	1-12	0	0
	All FC	1972/73	1977/78	18	29	3	627	75	24.11	0	4	15	0	712	410	9	45.55	3.45	5-70	1	0
Clarke, TA	WPCU	1981/82	1982/83	3	6	0	96	41	16.00	0	0	1	0	120	60	3	20.00	3.00	2-20	0	0
	WPCU B	1975/76	1984/85	30	50	6	1494	138*	33.95	2	9	25	0	885	367	19	19.31	2.48	5-30	1	0
	All FC	1975/76	1984/85	33	56	6	1590	138*	31.80	2	9	26	0	1005	427	22	19.40	2.54	5-30	1	0
Cloete, PHB	WPCU	1936/37	1939/40	9	11	1	74	29	7.40	0	0	7	0	1823	969	29	33.41	3.18	5-112	1	0
Coen, SK	WPCU	1930/31	1931/32	9	16	2	654	173	46.71	2	4	1	0	426	209	3	69.66	2.94	2-25	0	0
	All FC	1921/22	1938/39	51	92	6	2808	173	32.65	6	14	22	0	1881	1087	22	49.40	3.46	4-92	0	0
Coericius, A	WPCB	1985/86	1985/86	1	2	0	4	3	2.00	0	0	0	0	0	0	0	–	–	–	0	0
Coggins, HC	WPCU	1905/06	1905/06	2	4	0	63	43	15.75	0	0	1	0	0	0	0	–	–	–	0	0
Cole, JM	WPCU	1965/66	1966/67	8	12	4	95	29	11.87	0	0	0	0	1746	697	21	33.19	2.39	5-25	2	0
	All FC	1959/60	1966/67	35	43	16	176	29	6.51	0	0	10	0	7600	2617	146	17.92	2.06	6-16	8	1
Colson, WWA	WPCU	1910/11	1921/22	8	15	0	214	39	14.26	0	0	4	0	0	0	0	–	–	–	0	0
Commaille, JMM	WPCU	1905/06	1923/24	31	57	5	1918	156	36.88	5	10	14	0	0	0	0	–	–	–	0	0
	All FC	1905/06	1930/31	96	169	13	5026	186	32.21	9	27	32	0	72	33	1	33.00	2.75	1-15	0	0
Commins, JB	WPCU	1989/90	1990/91	4	8	2	121	44*	20.16	0	0	1	0	36	23	0	–	3.83	–	0	0
	WPCA	1991/92	1999/00	31	52	9	1945	200*	45.23	4	12	5	0	0	0	0	–	–	–	0	0
	WPCU B	1985/86	1990/91	25	45	4	1375	138	33.53	4	7	13	0	245	114	4	28.50	2.79	2-28	0	0
	WPCA B	1991/92	1991/92	1	2	0	31	16	15.50	0	0	0	0	0	0	0	–	–	–	0	0
	All FC	1984/85	1999/00	94	164	21	5835	200*	40.80	13	34	32	0	323	170	4	42.50	3.15	2-28	0	0
Commins, JE	WPCU	1960/61	1968/69	10	16	2	110	29*	7.85	0	0	11	0	1434	750	27	27.77	3.13	5-32	1	0
Commins, KT	WPCU	1951/52	1957/58	18	34	1	728	92	22.06	0	4	11	0	24	8	0	–	2.00	–	0	0
	All FC	1951/52	1960/61	29	56	2	1067	92	19.75	0	4	21	0	70	33	1	33.00	2.82	1-6	0	0
Conrad, Sedick	WPCB	1971/72	1974/75	8	13	0	523	166	40.23	2	1	0	0	6	1	0	–	1.00	–	0	0
	All FC	1971/72	1974/75	10	15	0	541	166	36.06	2	1	0	0	6	1	0	–	1.00	–	0	0

Name	Team	From	To	M	Inns	NO	Runs	HS	Avg	100	50	Ct	St	Balls	Runs	Wkts	Avg	RPO	BB	5I	10M
Conrad, Shukri	WPCB	1985/86	1990/91	9	13	0	324	63	24.92	0	2	7	0	715	281	13	21.61	2.35	4-35	0	0
	WPCA B	1994/95	1994/95	5	8	0	200	61	25.00	0	1	1	0	18	18	0	-	6.00	-	0	0
	All FC	1985/86	1994/95	14	21	0	524	63	24.95	0	3	8	0	733	299	13	23.00	2.44	4-35	0	0
Conrad, Siraaj	WPCA B	1998/99	1998/99	2	3	3	3	3*	-	0	0	1	0	264	121	3	40.33	2.75	2-54	0	0
	WPCA Am	2004/05	2005/06	6	8	2	41	11	6.83	0	0	4	0	1050	614	26	23.61	3.50	6-45	3	1
	WCC	2005/06	2005/06	1	1	0	0	0	0.00	0	0	0	0	18	21	0	-	7.00	-	0	0
	All FC	1998/99	2005/06	16	23	7	251	60	15.68	0	2	6	0	2676	1485	37	40.13	3.32	6-45	3	1
Conny, FD	WPCU	1906/07	1923/24	23	37	0	756	76	20.43	0	5	17	1	24	8	0	-	2.00	-	0	0
Conyngham, DP	WPCU	1930/31	1930/31	2	4	1	21	19	7.00	0	0	2	0	258	96	2	48.00	2.23	1-10	0	0
	All FC	1921/22	1930/31	22	33	10	348	63	15.13	0	2	18	0	4677	1778	86	20.67	2.28	5-20	6	1
Cooke, CB	WPCA Am	2009/10	2009/10	6	11	1	186	44*	18.60	0	0	12	1	0	0	0	-	-	-	0	0
Copeland, CA	WPCA B	1998/99	1998/99	2	1	0	0	0	0.00	0	0	2	0	523	287	16	17.93	3.29	6-77	2	0
	All FC	1998/99	2000/01	8	10	1	29	10	3.22	0	0	4	0	1670	967	39	24.79	3.47	8-101	4	1
Cowper, SA	WPCU	1907/08	1907/08	1	2	1	15	10*	15.00	0	0	0	0	30	21	1	21.00	4.20	1-21	0	0
	All FC	1907/08	1924/25	6	10	2	77	18*	9.62	0	0	3	0	504	255	8	31.87	3.03	4-65	0	0
Cox, AE	WPCU	1890/91	1890/91	2	3	0	128	56	42.66	0	1	6	0	65	25	2	12.50	2.30	1-1	0	0
Crawford, SNA	WPCU	1930/31	1930/31	1	2	0	10	6	5.00	0	0	0	0	0	0	0	-	-	-	0	0
Crews, BH	WPCU	1945/46	1947/48	4	8	1	149	43	21.28	0	1	2	0	72	41	0	-	3.41	-	0	0
	All FC	1945/46	1958/59	16	31	1	588	110	19.60	2	2	8	0	197	128	3	42.66	3.89	3-53	0	0
Crighton, GE	WPCU	1939/40	1939/40	3	6	0	140	40	23.33	0	0	0	0	72	40	0	-	3.33	-	0	0
Cripps, G	WPCU	1892/93	1893/94	3	5	0	196	102	39.20	1	0	4	0	50	36	1	36.00	4.32	1-18	0	0
	All FC	1891/92	1893/94	4	7	0	217	102	31.00	1	0	4	0	65	59	1	59.00	5.44	1-18	0	0
Crisp, RJ	WPCU	1931/32	1935/36	18	23	4	295	43	15.52	0	0	6	0	3383	1543	90	17.14	2.73	9-64	7	1
	All FC	1929/30	1938	62	82	14	888	45	13.05	0	0	27	0	10943	5487	276	19.88	3.00	9-64	21	4
Crosoer, MJ	WPCA B	1996/97	1998/99	7	13	1	336	115	28.00	1	2	2	0	0	0	0	-	-	-	0	0
Cullinan, DJ	WPCU	1985/86	1990/91	45	79	9	2349	140	33.55	6	12	45	0	0	0	0	-	-	-	0	0
	All FC	1983/84	2004/05	246	417	54	16261	337*	44.79	44	79	245	16	992	486	10	48.60	2.93	2-27	0	0
Cupido, R	WPCB	1983/84	1990/91	19	25	5	446	62	22.30	0	2	54	0	48	24	2	12.00	3.00	2-24	0	0
Dagnin, I	WPCB	1971/72	1982/83	4	7	0	58	19	8.28	0	0	1	0	8	6	0	-	4.50	-	0	0
Dammert, B	WPCB	1989/90	1989/90	4	6	0	104	57	17.33	0	1	2	0	18	9	0	-	3.00	-	0	0
Damon, E	WPCB	1977/78	1985/86	14	22	7	86	20	5.73	0	0	8	0	2036	748	37	20.21	2.20	4-21	0	0
Damon, I	WPCA B	1998/99	1998/99	1	2	0	14	9	7.00	0	0	0	0	161	98	3	32.66	3.65	2-43	0	0
	WPCU B	1978/79	1978/79	1	2	1	110	100*	110.00	1	0	0	0	0	0	0	-	-	-	0	0
Daniels, NP	WPCU B	1977/78	1978/79	3	6	0	304	87	50.66	0	3	2	0	130	70	3	23.33	3.23	3-13	0	0
	All FC	1975/76	1990/91	62	101	17	2571	104	30.60	3	13	49	0	4422	1855	55	33.72	2.51	4-41	0	0

Name	Team	From	To	M	Inns	NO	Runs	HS	Avg	100	50	Ct	St	Balls	Runs	Wkts	Avg	RPO	BB	5I	10M
Davids, F	WPCB	1983/84	1990/91	32	51	6	1615	146	35.88	3	11	19	0	2722	1053	62	16.98	2.32	5-50	2	0
	WPCA	1991/92	1997/98	17	28	1	445	61	16.48	0	1	8	0	570	395	4	98.75	4.15	2-46	0	0
	WPCA B	1991/92	1998/99	21	33	2	1140	146	36.77	2	6	15	0	1840	1024	35	29.25	3.33	4-24	2	0
	All FC	1983/84	1998/99	75	119	9	3360	146	30.54	5	19	47	0	5331	2544	107	23.77	2.86	5-50	2	0
Davids, H	WCC	2004/05	2009/10	33	57	2	1902	123*	34.58	4	13	24	0	100	37	1	37.00	2.22	1-34	0	0
	All FC	2000/01	2010/11	81	146	8	4470	158	32.39	9	27	64	0	1512	920	23	40.00	3.65	3-11	0	0
Davids, Z	WPCB	1979/80	1983/84	5	4	2	89	55*	44.50	0	1	10	0	367	131	8	16.37	2.14	4-29	0	0
	All FC	1972/73	1983/84	11	12	3	158	55*	17.55	0	1	18	0	1352	494	24	20.58	2.19	4-29	2	0
Davidson, TM	WPCU	1928/29	1928/29	2	4	0	58	20	14.50	0	0	0	0	300	166	4	41.50	3.32	3-64	0	0
	All FC	1926/27	1938/39	8	13	1	204	53*	17.00	0	1	0	0	1183	620	20	31.00	3.14	5-62	1	0
Davies, DD	WPCU	1903/04	1903/04	2	3	0	69	45	23.00	0	0	6	0	0	0	0	–	–	–	0	0
	All FC	1902/03	1913/14	6	10	2	200	45	25.00	0	1	2	0	0	0	0	–	–	–	0	0
Davis, RP	WPCU	1951/52	1952/53	4	5	3	26	9*	13.00	0	0	4	0	1104	346	10	34.60	1.88	3-25	0	0
Dawson, AC	WPCA	1992/93	2003/04	73	99	21	1690	143	21.66	1	10	38	0	14047	5864	226	25.94	2.50	6-51	8	1
	WCC	2004/05	2005/06	11	13	2	230	65	20.90	0	2	4	0	2266	924	41	22.53	2.44	6-39	2	1
	WPCA B	1993/94	1996/97	9	12	3	257	55	28.55	0	1	3	0	1563	696	25	27.84	2.67	6-18	1	0
	All FC	1992/93	2005/06	98	127	27	2196	143	21.96	1	13	47	0	18482	7756	305	25.42	2.51	6-18	12	2
Dawson, H	WPCB	1975/76	1985/86	9	14	2	98	29*	8.16	0	0	17	0	0	0	0	–	–	–	0	0
Deane, J	WPCU	1889/90	1890/91	3	5	0	75	31	15.00	0	0	2	0	0	0	0	–	–	–	0	0
De Klerk, TR	WPCU	1925/26	1935/36	32	47	3	763	79	17.34	0	3	15	0	5217	2378	88	27.02	2.73	7-48	4	1
	All FC	1925/26	1935/36	33	48	3	791	79	17.57	0	3	17	0	5475	2506	89	28.15	2.74	7-48	4	1
De Kock, GA	WPCA B	1995/96	1996/97	6	7	0	187	67	26.71	0	2	4	0	729	356	17	20.94	2.93	3-8	0	0
	All FC	1995/96	1998/99	12	17	1	289	67	18.06	0	2	5	0	1423	721	25	28.84	3.04	3-8	0	0
De Lange, CD	WCC	2004/05	2007/08	31	51	4	1022	87	21.74	0	3	19	0	5381	2401	60	40.01	2.67	5-145	1	0
	All FC	1997/98	2010/11	83	134	12	2723	109	22.31	1	13	45	0	14623	6741	175	38.52	2.76	7-48	5	1
Delport, RF	WPCU	1950/51	1963/64	14	22	4	152	46	8.44	0	0	7	0	2440	762	35	21.77	1.87	7-54	2	0
Denne, PH	WPCU	1971/72	1974/75	10	19	1	233	55	12.94	0	1	11	0	0	0	0	–	–	–	0	0
De Nobrega, JJ	WPCA	1997/98	1997/98	4	7	1	108	30	18.00	0	0	6	0	0	0	0	–	–	–	0	0
	WPCA B	1997/98	1998/99	5	9	0	187	64	20.77	0	1	1	0	0	0	0	–	–	–	0	0
	All FC	1997/98	1998/99	9	16	1	295	64	19.66	0	1	7	0	0	0	0	–	–	–	0	0
De Smidt, R	WPCU	1912/13	1912/13	4	5	1	74	42*	18.50	0	0	6	0	606	288	16	18.00	2.85	4-40	0	0
De Stadler, M	WCC	2004/05	2006/07	2	2	1	14	8*	14.00	0	0	0	0	216	77	0	–	2.13	–	0	0
	WPCA Am	2004/05	2007/08	26	30	8	406	43*	18.45	0	0	10	0	5115	2114	118	17.91	2.47	5-18	4	0
	All FC	2004/05	2007/08	28	32	9	420	43*	18.26	0	0	10	0	5331	2191	118	18.56	2.46	5-18	4	0
De Villiers, DI	WPCU	1912/13	1912/13	1	1	0	17	17	17.00	0	0	1	0	36	15	0	–	2.50	–	0	0
	All FC	1912/13	1924/25	20	38	5	1364	200*	41.33	3	7	18	0	1727	951	29	32.79	3.30	5-44	1	0

Name	Team	From	To	M	Inns	NO	Runs	HS	Avg	100	50	Ct	St	Balls	Runs	Wkts	Avg	RPO	BB	5I	10M
De Villiers, MC	WPCA	1996/97	1996/97	1	2	1	86	84	86.00	0	1	0	0	0	0	0	–	–	–	0	0
	WPCA B	1993/94	1996/97	7	9	1	296	88	37.00	0	3	6	0	28	47	0	–	10.07	–	0	0
	All FC	1993/94	1996/97	8	11	2	382	88	42.44	0	4	6	0	28	47	0	–	10.07	–	0	0
De Villiers, PH	WPCU	1889/90	1890/91	4	7	0	77	51	11.00	0	1	4	0	371	172	15	11.46	2.78	5-50	1	0
Difford, AN	WPCU	1904/05	1907/08	11	20	0	443	103	22.15	1	2	7	0	54	32	2	16.00	3.55	1-13	0	0
	All FC	1904/05	1911/12	16	28	0	824	103	29.42	1	6	8	0	54	32	2	16.00	3.55	1-13	0	0
Dimbleby, DE	WPCU	1946/47	1947/48	5	9	1	293	114	36.62	1	2	5	0	0	0	0	–	–	–	0	0
	All FC	1936/37	1949/50	21	36	2	884	114	26.00	1	7	5	0	172	94	1	94.00	3.27	1-33	0	0
Dimbleby, KG	WPCU	1938/39	1947/48	11	20	0	531	127	26.55	1	4	5	0	0	0	0	–	–	–	0	0
	All FC	1933/34	1952/53	28	52	2	1468	127	29.36	2	10	9	0	0	0	0	–	–	–	0	0
Doman, ME	WPCB	1977/78	1981/82	12	23	3	388	64	19.40	0	3	9	0	464	189	10	18.90	2.44	2-11	0	0
	All FC	1977/78	1982/83	14	27	4	483	64	21.00	0	4	11	0	542	226	13	17.38	2.50	2-11	0	0
Donachie, HH	WPCA B	1994/95	1994/95	2	4	0	132	66	33.00	0	1	2	0	24	12	0	–	3.00	–	0	0
	All FC	1988/89	1994/95	14	28	3	704	126	28.16	1	4	15	0	482	208	8	26.00	2.58	2-25	0	0
Drummer, D	WPCU	1960/61	1963/64	7	13	2	99	23*	9.00	0	0	7	0	1260	561	13	43.15	2.67	4-68	0	0
Drummer, FTM	WPCU	1958/59	1967/68	26	40	15	643	62	25.72	0	3	8	0	6069	2484	107	23.21	2.45	8-28	2	1
	All FC	1958/59	1972/73	34	47	20	684	62	25.33	0	3	12	0	7466	3055	121	25.24	2.45	8-28	2	1
Drummond, RA	WPCU	1976/77	1978/79	14	26	4	584	76	26.54	0	4	43	4	0	0	0	–	–	–	0	0
	WPCU B	1975/76	1979/80	12	21	2	645	99	33.94	0	6	34	3	0	0	0	–	–	–	0	0
	All FC	1973/74	1979/80	29	51	7	1383	106	31.43	1	10	82	9	0	0	0	–	–	–	0	0
Duff, BR	WPCU	1889/90	1889/90	1	2	1	9	8*	9.00	0	0	0	0	0	0	0	–	–	–	0	0
Dumbrill, JE	WPCU	1956/57	1961/62	3	5	1	29	18	7.25	0	0	2	0	531	240	6	40.00	2.71	2-44	0	0
	All FC	1956/57	1965/66	20	31	11	133	20	6.65	0	0	5	0	4863	1931	48	40.22	2.38	5-53	2	0
Duminy, JP	WPCU	1919/20	1919/20	2	4	0	49	38	12.25	0	0	5	0	18	14	0	–	4.66	–	0	0
	All FC	1919/20	1929	13	23	4	557	168*	29.31	1	3	11	0	915	368	12	30.66	2.41	6-40	0	0
Duminy, J-P	WPCA	2001/02	2003/04	10	14	4	578	105*	57.80	2	3	13	0	390	230	8	28.75	3.53	4-89	0	0
	WCC	2004/05	2010/11	34	58	11	2763	200*	58.78	8	14	18	0	1263	750	17	44.11	3.56	5-108	1	0
	All FC	2001/02	2010/11	63	105	18	4374	200*	50.27	13	22	48	0	2402	1419	37	38.35	3.54	5-108	1	0
Du Plessis, JH	WPCU B	1988/89	1988/89	5	8	5	214	96*	71.33	0	1	7	0	302	167	6	27.83	3.31	2-14	0	0
	All FC	1988/89	1989/90	6	10	5	219	96*	43.80	0	1	8	0	440	223	8	27.87	3.04	2-14	0	0
Du Plessis, M	WPCU	1971/72	1973/74	4	4	1	0	0*	0.00	0	0	2	0	513	305	11	27.72	3.56	3-47	0	0
	All FC	1971/72	1973/74	5	6	1	24	16	4.80	0	0	3	0	801	410	16	25.62	3.07	4-71	0	0

Name	Team	From	To	M	Inns	NO	Runs	HS	Avg	100	50	Ct	St	Balls	Runs	Wkts	Avg	RPO	BB	5I	10M
During, J	WPCU	1977/78	1982/83	9	11	2	117	31	13.00	0	0	9	0	1049	430	11	39.09	2.45	4-114	0	0
	WPCU B	1977/78	1988/89	42	61	21	918	66*	22.95	0	1	33	0	6803	2378	130	18.29	2.09	6-53	4	0
	All FC	1977/78	1988/89	54	77	24	1126	66*	21.24	0	2	48	0	8296	3002	147	20.42	2.17	6-53	4	0
During, JP	WPCU	1907/08	1908/09	5	9	1	183	67	22.87	0	2	2	0	48	27	3	9.00	3.37	2-10	0	0
	All FC	1907/08	1910/11	7	12	1	231	67	21.00	0	2	5	0	48	27	3	9.00	3.37	2-10	0	0
During, PB	WPCU	1949/50	1949/50	1	2	0	10	10	5.00	0	0	2	0	0	0	0	–	–	–	0	0
Durr, JM	WPCU	1921/22	1921/22	1	2	1	19	11*	19.00	0	0	1	0	126	48	5	9.60	2.28	4-22	0	0
Du Toit, JD	WPCU	1977/78	1982/83	10	13	2	303	97	27.54	0	1	1	0	846	317	3	105.66	2.24	1-15	0	0
	WPCU B	1975/76	1983/84	27	45	5	855	128	21.37	2	2	22	0	4278	1635	89	18.37	2.29	6-26	5	1
	All FC	1975/76	1991/92	73	125	11	2570	148	22.54	3	8	51	0	9169	3731	147	25.38	2.44	6-26	6	1
Du Toit, WJ	WCC	2008/09	2008/09	1	2	0	6	3	3.00	0	0	0	0	66	46	0	–	4.18	–	0	0
	All FC	1998/99	2008/09	19	30	4	307	42	11.80	0	0	4	0	3080	1646	46	35.78	3.20	7-82	2	0
Dyason, C	WPCB	1988/89	1988/89	3	5	0	101	40	20.20	0	0	0	0	167	75	4	18.75	2.69	2-5	0	0
Dyer, GD	WPCU	1966/67	1967/68	9	15	3	435	104	36.25	1	3	8	0	0	0	0	–	–	–	0	0
	All FC	1966/67	1973/74	31	53	9	1466	122*	33.31	2	8	25	0	18	8	0	–	2.66	–	0	0
Eayrs, D	WPCU	1939/40	1941/42	2	2	1	0	0*	0.00	0	0	3	0	416	149	1	149.00	2.14	1-49	0	0
Ebrahim, F	WPCB	1985/86	1990/91	12	18	2	270	70	16.87	0	1	10	0	276	124	2	62.00	2.69	1-31	0	0
Ebrahim, M	WPCB	1977/78	1977/78	1	2	0	29	19	14.50	0	0	0	0	0	0	0	–	–	–	0	0
Ebrahim, Y	WPCB	1978/79	1978/79	1	2	0	21	21	10.50	0	0	1	0	48	40	0	–	5.00	–	0	0
Eckard, LS	WPCU	1936/37	1946/47	12	17	5	207	32	17.25	0	0	10	0	2511	1031	26	39.65	2.46	5-43	1	0
Elgar, AG	WPCU	1984/85	1986/87	11	18	0	502	81	27.88	0	4	6	0	66	47	0	–	4.27	–	0	0
	WPCU B	1983/84	1990/91	15	30	2	796	97	28.42	0	4	15	0	1440	559	18	31.05	2.32	6-24	1	0
	All FC	1981/82	1993/94	36	62	3	1532	97	25.96	0	8	28	0	3147	1272	54	23.55	2.42	6-24	3	0
Emary, FE	WPCU	1965/66	1965/66	2	4	0	73	66	18.25	0	1	1	0	126	46	1	46.00	2.19	1-26	0	0
	All FC	1965/66	1965/66	3	6	0	152	66	25.33	0	2	4	0	302	129	6	21.50	2.56	5-71	1	0
Emburey, JE	WPCB	1982/83	1983/84	15	17	4	229	52*	17.61	0	1	13	0	3778	1455	53	27.45	2.31	6-33	3	0
	All FC	1973	1997	513	644	130	12021	133	23.38	7	55	458	0	112862	41958	1608	26.09	2.23	8-40	72	12
Engelbrecht, SA	WPCA Am	2009/10	2010/11	9	12	1	383	114	34.81	1	2	11	0	878	575	14	41.07	3.92	5-74	1	0
	WCC	2008/09	2009/10	2	3	2	14	8*	14.00	0	0	0	0	96	63	0	–	3.93	–	0	0
	All FC	2007/08	2009/10	15	22	3	570	114	30.00	1	2	15	0	1285	851	20	42.55	3.97	5-74	1	0
English, CV	WPCA	1993/94	1994/95	3	2	0	4	3	2.00	0	0	0	0	438	302	6	50.33	4.13	3-70	0	0
	WPCA B	1993/94	1994/95	7	8	2	195	108	32.50	1	0	4	0	868	402	13	30.92	2.77	4-30	0	0
	All FC	1990/91	2005	40	63	8	1150	108	20.90	1	5	14	0	4740	2678	67	39.97	3.38	5-65	1	0
Etlinger, TE	WPCU	1895/96	1896/97	5	7	0	245	111	35.00	1	1	0	0	0	0	0	–	–	–	0	0
	All FC	1895/96	1906/07	10	14	0	343	111	24.50	1	1	4	0	0	0	0	–	–	–	0	0

Name	Team	From	To	M	Inns	NO	Runs	HS	Avg	100	50	Ct	St	Balls	Runs	Wkts	Avg	RPO	BB	5I	10M
Euley, W	WPCA Am	2006/07	2006/07	2	3	1	173	93	86.50	0	2	6	1	12	16	0	–	8.00	–	0	0
Evans, LLM	All FC	2003/04	2006/07	9	15	1	457	93	32.64	0	3	22	3	12	16	0	–	8.00	–	0	0
Fairclough, J	WPCU	1939/40	1946/47	2	3	1	20	15	10.00	0	0	2	0	488	178	9	19.77	2.18	4-59	0	0
	WPCU	1964/65	1965/66	4	6	5	25	10	25.00	0	0	2	0	714	281	10	28.10	2.36	4-35	0	0
	All FC	1964/65	1981/82	16	14	12	69	11	34.50	0	0	1	0	3353	1025	53	19.33	1.83	6-31	3	1
Fairweather, L	WPCU B	1980/81	1982/83	2	3	1	16	14*	8.00	0	0	4	0	0	0	0	–	–	–	0	0
Farrell, JN	WPCU	1974/75	1975/76	11	12	5	62	13	8.85	0	0	2	0	1617	731	34	21.50	2.71	4-35	0	0
	WPCU B	1976/77	1977/78	4	4	2	22	9*	11.00	0	0	0	0	532	331	8	41.37	3.73	4-29	0	0
	All FC	1974/75	1977/78	15	16	7	84	13	9.33	0	0	2	0	2149	1062	42	25.28	2.96	4-29	0	0
Farrell, RM	WPCU	1952/53	1963/64	9	16	3	309	85	23.76	0	2	12	4	0	0	0	–	–	–	0	0
Fearon, GG	WPCA Am	2007/08	2007/08	1	2	0	42	42	21.00	0	0	0	0	0	0	0	–	–	–	0	0
February, R	WPCB	1985/86	1988/89	12	13	6	186	37	26.57	0	0	5	0	2430	819	40	20.47	2.02	6-73	1	0
Felix, C	WPCB	1983/84	1983/84	1	1	0	27	27	27.00	0	0	0	0	0	0	0	–	–	–	0	0
Fernley, DL	WPCU	1957/58	1957/58	3	6	0	142	61	23.66	0	1	1	0	0	0	0	–	–	–	0	0
	All FC	1954/55	1963/64	11	17	1	461	106	28.81	1	1	6	0	8	0	0	–	0.00	–	0	0
Ferrandi, JH	WPCU	1949/50	1964/65	57	100	18	1892	89	23.07	0	12	119	32	0	0	0	–	–	–	0	0
	WPCU	1949/50	1964/65	60	104	18	2012	89	23.39	0	13	122	32	0	0	0	–	–	–	0	0
Ferreira, LD	WPCA	1997/98	2003/04	38	64	4	1930	201	32.16	5	8	21	0	120	74	1	74.00	3.70	1-25	0	0
	WPCA B	1997/98	1998/99	4	7	0	200	121	28.57	1	0	5	0	3	4	0	–	8.00	–	0	0
	All FC	1993/94	2003/04	67	120	4	3088	201	26.62	7	12	35	0	126	80	1	80.00	3.80	1-25	0	0
Finnan, M	WPCB	1977/78	1977/78	4	6	0	82	31	13.66	0	0	2	0	0	0	0	–	–	–	0	0
Finnan, OMP	WPCU B	1979/80	1979/80	1	2	0	13	12	6.50	0	0	0	0	0	0	0	–	–	–	0	0
Fismer, KG	WPCU	1941/42	1941/42	1	2	0	58	54	29.00	0	1	0	0	24	15	0	–	3.75	–	0	0
Fitzpatrick, GT	WPCU	1890/91	1890/91	1	2	0	16	13	8.00	0	0	0	0	0	0	0	–	–	–	0	0
Fletcher, DAG	WPCU B	1984/85	1984/85	1	2	0	18	14	9.00	0	0	1	0	90	64	0	–	4.26	–	0	0
Fock, CAC	All FC	1969/70	1984/85	111	198	25	4095	93	23.67	0	20	75	0	12247	6027	215	28.03	2.95	6-31	5	1
Foley, WBH	WPCU	1902/03	1904/05	5	8	1	68	21	9.71	0	0	5	0	672	340	24	14.16	3.03	6-14	3	0
	WPCU	1937/38	1947/48	7	13	1	328	87	27.33	0	2	2	0	0	0	0	–	–	–	0	0
	All FC	1925/26	1947/48	35	51	7	1941	153	44.11	1	14	10	0	138	75	0	–	3.26	–	0	0
Foreman, DJ	WPCU	1951/52	1951/52	3	5	2	11	5*	3.66	0	0	3	0	0	0	0	–	–	–	0	0
	All FC	1951/52	1967	129	202	23	3277	104	18.30	1	15	123	0	638	273	9	30.33	2.56	4-64	0	0
Fortune, N	WPCB	1978/79	1983/84	25	45	3	1023	143	24.35	1	6	21	0	94	40	0	–	2.55	–	0	0
Fouché, MR	WPCU	1958/59	1958/59	1	2	1	5	5	5.00	0	0	0	0	108	59	0	–	3.27	–	0	0
Fox, JSM	WPCU	1954/55	1960/61	8	15	0	283	63	18.86	0	1	3	0	296	113	1	113.00	2.29	1-15	0	0
	All FC	1954/55	1963/64	18	34	2	773	75	24.15	0	3	7	0	586	246	6	41.00	2.51	3-17	0	0

Name	Team	From	To	M	Inns	NO	Runs	HS	Avg	100	50	Ct	St	Balls	Runs	Wkts	Avg	RPO	BB	5I	10M
Fox, LC	WPCU	1921/22	1927/28	14	25	4	317	38	15.09	0	0	10	7	6	3	0	–	3.00	–	0	0
Francis, HH	WPCU	1895/96	1902/03	3	5	0	73	38	14.60	0	0	0	0	0	0	0	–	–	–	0	0
	All FC	1890	1902/03	25	44	3	529	55	12.90	0	1	13	1	0	0	0	–	–	–	0	0
Francis, MG	WPCU	1934/35	1934/35	4	6	0	191	94	31.83	0	1	2	0	234	89	2	44.50	2.28	1-13	0	0
	All FC	1925/26	1945/46	29	52	3	1747	125	35.65	4	7	15	0	1095	744	18	41.33	4.07	5-50	1	0
Friend, Q	WPCA	2002/03	2003/04	8	9	4	178	38*	35.60	0	0	1	0	1308	671	25	26.84	3.07	5-34	1	0
	WCC	2004/05	2006/07	6	8	0	151	51	18.87	0	1	4	0	765	399	10	39.90	3.12	6-114	1	1
	WPCA Am	2004/05	2006/07	12	14	1	177	36	13.61	0	0	4	0	1622	708	45	15.73	2.61	7-31	7	0
	All FC	2002/03	2010/11	70	83	16	1127	78	16.82	0	4	23	0	10882	5439	227	23.96	2.99	7-31	7	1
Frost, CE	WPCU	1986/87	1986/87	1	2	0	15	8	7.50	0	0	1	2	0	0	0	–	–	–	0	0
	WPCU B	1985/86	1985/86	3	6	2	40	19*	10.00	0	0	17	2	0	0	0	–	–	–	0	0
	All FC	1985/86	1986/87	4	8	2	55	19*	9.16	0	0	18	2	0	0	0	–	–	–	0	0
Fuller, ERH	WPCU	1950/51	1957/58	27	44	7	690	69	18.64	0	3	14	0	7401	2661	98	27.15	2.15	7-40	7	2
	All FC	1950/51	1958	59	86	16	1062	69	15.17	0	4	29	0	13803	5026	190	26.45	2.18	7-40	11	3
Fuller, HH	WPCU	1920/21	1920/21	4	6	1	193	68	38.60	0	2	0	0	0	0	0	–	–	–	0	0
	All FC	1920/21	1926/27	8	12	1	299	68	27.18	0	2	1	0	0	0	0	–	–	–	0	0
Gabriels, S	WPCB	1981/82	1990/91	48	73	8	1459	101*	22.44	1	10	33	0	7190	2476	173	14.31	2.06	8-53	11	5
	All FC	1977/78	1990/91	67	109	10	2161	101*	21.82	1	14	41	0	10852	3830	254	15.07	2.11	8-53	17	5
Gafieldien, E	WPCB	1989/90	1990/91	7	12	2	179	86	17.90	0	1	2	0	0	0	0	–	–	–	0	0
Galant, M	WPCB	1988/89	1988/89	2	2	0	28	14	14.00	0	0	2	0	42	19	0	–	2.71	–	0	0
Galant, S	WPCB	1979/80	1979/80	1	2	0	28	19	14.00	0	0	1	0	0	0	0	–	–	–	0	0
Gardiner, IB	WPCU	1926/27	1928/29	9	16	0	304	76	19.00	0	1	1	0	532	213	8	26.62	2.40	2-14	0	0
	All FC	1926/27	1937/38	25	46	2	851	107	19.34	1	1	8	0	2576	1089	49	22.22	2.53	7-28	2	0
Gentry, JD	WPCU	1926/27	1926/27	5	9	1	79	27*	9.87	0	0	2	0	48	16	0	–	2.00	–	0	0
	All FC	1926/27	1927/28	6	11	1	97	27*	9.70	0	0	3	0	90	43	0	–	2.86	–	0	0
Geoghegan, JP	WPCA Am	2005/06	2007/08	3	4	1	42	19	14.00	0	0	0	0	66	38	0	–	3.45	–	0	0
George, MF	WPCA	1997/98	1998/99	6	6	3	35	22	11.66	0	0	3	0	960	566	20	28.30	3.53	6-61	1	0
	WPCA B	1997/98	1997/98	4	5	2	46	42*	15.33	0	0	1	0	712	400	12	33.33	3.37	4-39	0	0
	All FC	1997/98	2001/02	24	29	9	298	58	14.90	0	1	5	0	3674	2105	57	36.92	3.43	6-61	1	0
George, SG	WPCA Am	2005/06	2005/06	1	2	0	7	6	3.50	0	0	0	0	6	5	0	–	5.00	–	0	0
Georgeu, G	WPCU	1931/32	1949/50	40	66	7	1864	154	31.59	3	11	17	0	1078	749	8	93.62	4.16	1-7	0	0
	All FC	1931/32	1949/50	44	74	9	2033	154	31.27	3	12	21	0	1142	809	9	89.88	4.25	1-7	0	0

Name	Team	From	To	M	Inns	NO	Runs	HS	Avg	100	50	Ct	St	Balls	Runs	Wkts	Avg	RPO	BB	5I	10M
Gibbs, HH	WPCU	1990/91	1990/91	3	6	0	66	35	11.00	0	0	1	0	0	0	0	–	–	–	0	0
	WPCU B	1990/91	1990/91	3	6	0	246	77	41.00	0	4	1	0	24	23	0	–	5.75	–	0	0
	WPCA	1991/92	2003/04	41	73	1	2582	203	35.86	7	6	28	0	6	5	0	–	5.00	–	0	0
	WPCA B	1991/92	1995/96	13	20	3	920	152*	54.11	2	5	10	0	30	3	0	–	0.60	–	0	0
	WCC	2004/05	2008/09	9	17	0	668	149	39.29	2	2	11	0	0	0	0	–	–	–	0	0
Gie, CA	All FC	1990/91	2009	193	331	13	13425	228	42.21	31	60	176	0	138	78	3	26.00	3.39	2-14	0	0
	WPCU	1971/72	1973/74	11	18	2	418	63*	26.12	0	4	5	0	36	22	0	–	3.66	–	0	0
Giles, MJ	All FC	1970/71	1980/81	32	55	6	1310	104*	26.73	2	8	28	0	2296	1242	32	38.81	3.24	4-28	0	0
	WPCU	1965/66	1971/72	9	15	1	579	146	41.35	2	2	5	0	228	98	1	98.00	2.57	1-45	0	0
Gill, RJ	WPCU	1892/93	1896/97	4	7	1	66	32	11.00	0	0	0	0	0	0	0	–	–	–	0	0
Gillett, GF	WPCA B	1995/96	1995/96	3	4	0	68	65	17.00	0	1	1	0	18	24	0	–	8.00	–	0	0
	All FC	1995/96	1995/96	3	4	0	68	65	17.00	0	1	1	0	18	24	0	–	8.00	–	0	0
Glantz, A	WPCU	1929/30	1939/40	39	55	10	533	53*	11.84	0	1	59	42	0	0	0	–	–	–	0	0
Godfrey, FA	WPCU	1923/24	1926/27	4	7	1	68	36	11.33	0	0	2	0	0	0	0	–	–	–	0	0
Goldstein, FS	WPCU	1971/72	1977/78	20	38	2	937	104	26.02	1	7	11	0	6	3	1	3.00	3.00	1-3	0	0
	WPCU B	1975/76	1975/76	2	2	0	30	17	15.00	0	0	0	0	6	2	0	–	2.00	–	0	0
Gooch, GA	All FC	1966	1977/78	89	163	4	4810	155	30.25	2	32	60	0	120	53	1	53.00	2.65	1-3	0	0
	WPCU	1982/83	1983/84	16	31	4	1212	171	44.88	4	2	16	0	575	175	8	21.87	1.82	4-15	0	0
	All FC	1973	2000	581	990	75	44846	333	49.01	128	217	555	0	18785	8457	246	34.37	2.70	7-14	3	0
Gordon, ES	WPCU	1978/79	1983/84	7	7	4	46	19	15.33	0	0	1	0	1082	502	16	31.37	2.78	6-47	3	1
	WPCU B	1978/79	1983/84	10	13	4	178	47	19.77	0	0	0	0	2140	736	56	13.14	2.06	6-49	3	0
	All FC	1978/79	1983/84	20	22	9	255	47	19.61	0	0	5	0	3690	1465	77	19.02	2.38	6-47	4	0
Goulden, IF	WPCU	1925/26	1930/31	13	21	4	339	75*	19.94	0	3	5	0	2012	1192	29	41.10	3.55	4-18	0	0
Graaff, D	WPCU	1932/33	1932/33	2	3	0	99	67	33.00	0	1	0	0	0	0	0	–	–	–	0	0
Graham, DK	WPCU	1945/46	1945/46	1	2	0	6	5	3.00	0	0	0	0	0	0	0	–	–	–	0	0
Graham, JM	WPCU	1960/61	1960/61	1	2	0	30	30	15.00	0	0	0	0	0	0	0	–	–	–	0	0
Graham, MD	WPCU	1889/90	1889/90	1	2	0	10	8	5.00	0	0	2	0	0	0	0	–	–	–	0	0
Graham, R	WPCU	1897/98	1897/98	1	1	0	4	4	4.00	0	0	2	0	25	15	0	–	3.60	–	0	0
	All FC	1897/98	1901	18	33	9	260	63*	10.83	0	1	22	0	2370	1406	61	23.04	3.55	8-90	5	1
Graham, TL	WPCU	1889/90	1889/90	2	3	0	7	7	2.33	0	0	0	0	165	70	3	23.33	2.54	2-29	0	0
Grant, DAC	WPCU B	1975/76	1975/76	4	6	1	85	27*	17.00	0	0	1	0	758	306	8	38.25	2.42	3-34	0	0
Gray, AJA	WPCA Am	2004/05	2010/11	39	68	7	2683	188*	43.98	5	13	56	0	2089	1324	41	32.29	3.80	5-31	2	0
	WCC	2006/07	2010/11	29	51	3	1551	131	32.31	4	8	29	0	1304	777	27	28.77	3.57	4-27	2	0
	All FC	2004/05	2010/11	70	123	10	4438	188*	39.27	10	21	88	0	3393	2101	68	30.89	3.71	5-31	2	0
Green, AD	WPCU B	1979/80	1980/81	4	8	0	158	49	19.75	0	0	8	0	0	0	0	–	–	–	0	0

Name	Team	From	To	M	Inns	NO	Runs	HS	Avg	100	50	Ct	St	Balls	Runs	Wkts	Avg	RPO	BB	5I	10M
Green, S	WPCB	1988/89	1988/89	1	2	0	0	–	–	0	0	0	0	126	35	5	7.00	1.66	3-26	0	0
Griffiths, AV	WPCU B	1988/89	1988/89	1	2	0	4	4	2.00	0	0	0	0	158	74	1	74.00	2.81	1-21	0	0
	All FC	1988/89	1996/97	4	6	2	33	16	8.25	0	0	2	0	789	344	15	22.93	2.61	5-78	1	0
Gronn, MJM	WPCU	1951/52	1951/52	1	2	1	0	0*	0.00	0	0	1	0	160	72	1	72.00	2.70	1-48	0	0
Groves, MGM	WPCU	1960/61	1960/61	1	2	0	50	45	25.00	0	0	0	0	0	0	0	–	–	–	0	0
	All FC	1960/61	1968	55	97	10	2541	86	29.20	0	20	33	0	642	374	7	53.42	3.49	3-33	0	0
Halvorsen, E	WPCU	1980/81	1980/81	2	4	1	39	29	13.00	0	0	7	0	0	0	0	–	–	–	0	0
	WPCU B	1979/80	1982/83	5	9	2	263	95	37.57	0	2	7	0	0	0	0	–	–	–	0	0
	All FC	1979/80	1982/83	7	13	3	302	95	30.20	0	2	7	0	0	0	0	–	–	–	0	0
Hands, KCM	WPCU	1921/22	1930/31	28	54	7	1481	171*	31.51	3	4	12	0	873	556	17	32.70	3.82	4-25	0	0
	All FC	1912	1930/31	31	60	7	1543	171*	29.11	3	4	12	0	891	568	17	33.41	3.82	4-25	0	0
Hands, PAM	WPCU	1906/07	1926/27	24	43	0	1241	119	28.86	3	5	10	0	78	46	2	23.00	3.53	2-28	0	0
	All FC	1906/07	1926/27	52	86	5	2034	119	25.11	3	10	20	0	138	84	5	16.80	3.65	3-9	0	0
Hands, RHM	WPCU	1912/13	1913/14	5	8	2	243	79*	40.50	0	2	6	0	36	22	0	–	3.66	–	0	0
	All FC	1912/13	1913/14	7	12	2	289	79*	28.90	0	2	7	0	36	22	0	–	3.66	–	0	0
Hanley, MA	WPCU	1946/47	1953/54	26	32	8	270	38	11.25	0	0	26	0	9089	3308	162	20.41	2.18	8-55	14	6
	All FC	1939/40	1953/54	33	44	12	308	38	9.62	0	0	27	0	10521	3948	182	21.69	2.25	8-55	14	6
Hantam, WC	WPCA Am	2004/05	2007/08	9	15	4	286	38	26.00	0	0	14	0	1196	646	29	22.27	3.24	6-39	1	0
	All FC	2004/05	2010/11	31	56	12	1353	112*	30.75	2	5	30	0	4452	2434	88	27.65	3.28	6.33	5	1
Hardy, JJE	WPCU	1987/88	1990/91	10	17	3	455	119	32.50	1	1	8	0	0	0	0	–	–	–	0	0
	WPCU B	1987/88	1990/91	6	12	2	493	102*	49.30	1	3	4	0	0	0	0	–	–	–	0	0
	All FC	1984	1991	142	236	31	6120	119	29.85	4	36	80	0	25	26	0	–	6.24	–	0	0
Harris, E	WPCB	1982/83	1984/85	10	16	3	298	58	22.92	0	2	5	0	0	0	0	–	–	–	0	0
Harris, PL	WPCA	2000/01	2001/02	2	3	2	30	20*	30.00	0	0	0	0	716	327	8	40.87	2.74	3-56	0	0
	WPCA B	1998/99	1998/99	1	2	1	5	5	5.00	0	0	0	0	228	95	0	–	2.50	–	0	0
	All FC	1998/99	2010/11	112	134	19	1630	55	14.17	0	3	44	1	25771	11633	368	31.61	2.70	7-94	20	1
Harvey, IJ	WCC	2005/06	2005/06	5	8	0	131	51	16.37	0	1	3	0	258	100	5	20.00	2.32	2-13	0	0
	All FC	1993/94	2007	165	272	29	8409	209*	34.60	15	46	114	0	24274	11693	425	27.51	2.89	8-101	15	2
Haupt, DL	WPCA Am	2005/06	2005/06	1	0	0	0	–	–	0	0	0	0	126	81	1	81.00	3.85	1-57	0	0
Haupt, M	WPCB	1984/85	1984/85	1	2	0	56	36	28.00	0	0	5	0	18	9	0	–	3.00	–	0	0
Hawtrey, PT	WPCU B	1983/84	1983/84	4	6	2	164	48	41.00	0	0	5	0	6	4	0	–	4.00	–	0	0
Haynes, DL	WPCA	1994/95	1996/97	21	35	2	1340	202*	40.60	1	10	11	0	48	11	0	–	1.37	–	0	0
	All FC	1976/77	1996/97	376	639	72	26030	255*	45.90	61	138	202	1	536	279	8	34.87	3.12	1-2	0	0
Hearne, F	WPCU	1889/90	1903/04	12	20	1	523	102	27.52	1	5	10	0	510	217	12	18.08	2.55	5-47	1	0
	All FC	1879	1903/04	161	285	20	4760	144	17.96	4	21	112	0	2904	1347	57	23.63	2.78	5-47	1	0

Name	Team	From	To	M	Inns	NO	Runs	HS	Avg	100	50	Ct	St	Balls	Runs	Wkts	Avg	RPO	BB	5I	10M
Hearne, GAL	WPCU	1910/11	1926/27	23	43	1	1464	138	34.85	2	8	26	2	678	373	14	26.64	3.30	3-9	0	0
	All FC	1910/11	1926/27	41	72	2	1981	138	28.30	2	10	38	2	726	401	14	28.64	3.31	3-9	0	0
Hector, B	WCC	2006/07	2007/08	9	18	0	365	68	20.27	0	2	5	0	22	9	0	–	2.45	–	0	0
	All FC	2001/02	2007/08	48	90	10	2939	200*	36.73	7	13	30	0	28	12	0	–	2.57	–	0	0
Heldsinger, KMS	WPCU	1956/57	1960/61	9	16	0	286	63	17.87	0	2	9	0	0	0	0	–	–	–	0	0
Henderson, CW	WPCA	1998/99	2003/04	38	47	9	710	71	18.68	0	2	18	0	12405	4708	168	28.02	2.27	7-99	7	0
	WPCA B	1998/99	1998/99	1	2	1	17	9	17.00	0	0	2	0	276	87	8	10.87	1.89	4-39	0	0
	WCC	2008/09	2010/11	16	21	6	270	43	18.00	0	0	4	0	4990	1974	77	25.63	2.37	7-64	6	1
	All FC	1990/91	2010/11	246	332	71	4858	81	18.61	0	15	83	0	59441	25328	829	30.55	2.55	7-57	33	2
Henderson, T	WCC	2007/08	2007/08	4	7	0	30	15	4.28	0	0	2	0	615	282	10	28.20	2.75	3-50	0	0
	All FC	1998/99	2007/08	86	137	17	1897	81	15.80	0	6	31	0	15744	7024	262	26.80	2.67	7-67	10	1
Hendricks, BE	WPCA Am	2009/10	2010/11	13	13	3	63	23	6.30	0	0	4	0	1611	859	40	21.47	3.19	5-43	2	0
	WCC	2010/11	2010/11	1	1	0	1	1	1.00	0	0	0	0	102	56	2	28.00	3.29	2-29	0	0
	All FC	2009/10	2010/11	14	14	3	64	23	5.81	0	0	4	0	1713	915	42	21.78	3.20	5-43	2	0
Hendricks, I	WPCB	1982/83	1982/83	1	2	0	5	5	2.50	0	0	0	0	138	65	2	32.50	2.82	2-65	0	0
	All FC	1972/73	1982/83	28	45	5	668	71	16.70	0	3	17	0	3558	1076	63	17.07	1.81	5-14	2	0
Hendricks, S	WPCB	1980/81	1988/89	35	59	5	1265	137	23.42	1	5	32	0	24	16	0	–	4.00	–	0	0
	All FC	1980/81	1988/89	36	61	5	1300	137	23.21	1	5	33	0	24	16	0	–	4.00	–	0	0
Hendricks, WD	WPCB	1973/74	1975/76	18	32	3	424	60	14.62	0	2	9	0	988	362	27	13.40	2.19	5-9	1	0
Hendrikse, C	WPCB	1988/89	1990/91	7	6	1	114	31*	22.80	0	0	4	0	797	234	18	13.00	1.76	6-20	1	0
Henry, D	WPCA B	1997/98	1997/98	1	1	1	7	7*	–	0	0	1	0	156	84	2	42.00	3.23	1-41	0	0
Henry, O	WPCU	1978/79	1983/84	27	38	10	719	79*	25.67	0	3	25	0	3228	1507	46	32.76	2.80	7-22	1	0
	WPCB	1973/74	1975/76	8	12	1	128	62*	11.63	0	1	8	0	1067	310	9	34.44	1.74	3-47	0	0
	WPCU B	1977/78	1982/83	22	32	9	636	105*	27.65	1	1	29	0	5317	1841	99	18.59	2.07	6-19	7	1
	All FC	1973/74	1993/94	131	200	33	4566	125	27.34	5	20	129	0	27066	11151	443	25.17	2.47	7-22	22	3
Hickley, CS	WPCU	1890/91	1890/91	2	3	0	67	45	22.33	0	0	0	0	0	0	0	–	–	–	0	0
	All FC	1890/91	1899	7	13	0	149	45	11.46	0	0	0	0	18	9	1	9.00	3.00	1-9	0	0
Hilterman, C	WPCU B	1976/77	1976/77	1	2	0	24	18	12.00	0	0	1	0	294	187	3	62.33	3.81	3-84	0	0
Hobson, AL	WPCU	1990/91	1990/91	2	0	0	0	–	–	0	0	1	0	1538	664	19	34.94	2.59	5-61	1	0
	WPCU B	1990/91	1990/91	6	6	3	36	9*	12.00	0	0	2	0	1538	664	19	34.94	2.59	5-61	1	0
	All FC	1982/83	1997/98	61	69	18	668	44	13.09	0	0	32	0	11943	5895	180	32.75	2.96	7-42	11	1
Hobson, DL	WPCU	1971/72	1984/85	94	115	31	1071	61	12.75	0	2	39	0	19856	9189	340	27.02	2.77	9-64	21	6
	WPCU B	1980/81	1983/84	2	1	0	22	22	22.00	0	0	1	0	493	188	12	15.66	2.28	4-22	0	0
	All FC	1970/71	1984/85	105	128	34	1251	61	13.30	0	2	47	0	22119	10296	374	27.52	2.79	9-64	22	6
Hobson, TEC	WPCU	1906/07	1906/07	2	2	0	23	16	11.50	0	0	0	0	128	51	5	10.20	2.39	4-32	0	0

Name	Team	From	To	M	Inns	NO	Runs	HS	Avg	100	50	Ct	St	Balls	Runs	Wkts	Avg	RPO	BB	5I	10M
Hodgson, AS	WPCU	1967/68	1967/68	6	5	3	17	11*	8.50	0	0	2	0	950	329	10	32.90	2.07	4-50	0	0
Hodgson, DGM	WPCU	1961/62	1965/66	6	11	1	180	52	18.00	0	1	3	0	0	0	0	–	–	–	0	0
Hofmeyr, S	WPCA B	1996/97	1997/98	8	14	1	351	51	27.00	0	1	7	0	0	0	0	–	–	–	0	0
Holder, JW	WPCB	1974/75	1974/75	1	2	0	7	4	3.50	0	0	1	0	96	33	0	–	2.06	–	0	0
Holdstock, AT	All FC	1968	1974/75	48	51	14	381	33	10.29	0	0	13	0	7194	3448	139	24.80	2.87	7-79	5	1
	WPCA	1992/93	1992/93	2	4	0	57	37	14.25	0	0	0	0	54	22	1	22.00	2.44	1-16	0	0
	WPCU B	1989/90	1989/90	2	4	0	61	45	15.25	0	0	2	0	162	104	1	104.00	3.85	1-66	0	0
	All FC	1989/90	1995/96	16	31	3	573	81	20.46	0	3	9	0	1210	642	19	33.78	3.18	4-51	0	0
Holmes, M	WPCA Am	2009/10	2009/10	1	2	0	27	27	13.50	0	0	0	0	0	0	0	–	–	–	0	0
Holmes, TE	WPCU	1906/07	1910/11	10	18	1	215	32	12.64	0	0	11	0	0	0	0	–	–	–	0	0
	All FC	1906/07	1929/30	47	84	5	1871	97	23.68	0	10	71	24	0	0	0	–	–	–	0	0
Homani, Z	WPCA Am	2005/06	2006/07	9	16	2	411	118	29.35	1	1	8	1	0	0	0	–	–	–	0	0
	All FC	2001/02	2006/07	22	37	3	785	118	23.08	1	2	47	4	0	0	0	–	–	–	0	0
Hooper, JJ	WPCU B	1979/80	1979/80	1	2	2	10	5*	–	0	0	0	0	30	22	0	–	4.40	–	0	0
	All FC	1979/80	1989/90	29	28	15	158	38*	12.15	0	0	6	0	4040	1847	85	21.72	2.74	7-29	2	0
Hopley, FIV	WPCU	1909/10	1909/10	1	2	0	24	12	12.00	0	0	2	0	0	0	0	–	–	–	0	0
	All FC	1904	1909/10	27	47	5	599	55	14.26	0	3	17	0	2873	1620	48	33.75	3.38	6-37	1	1
Horwood, SE	WPCU	1903/04	1909/10	12	22	0	378	74	17.18	0	1	6	0	0	0	0	–	–	–	0	0
	All FC	1898/99	1909/10	22	35	1	484	74	14.23	0	1	8	0	0	0	0	–	–	–	0	0
Howell, DH	WPCU B	1976/77	1976/77	1	1	0	2	2	2.00	0	0	3	0	0	0	0	–	–	–	0	0
	All FC	1976/77	1991/92	80	139	5	3491	151	26.05	5	17	118	12	21	8	0	–	2.28	–	0	0
Howell, HC	WPCU	1949/50	1954/55	2	3	0	69	32	23.00	0	0	0	0	136	82	0	–	3.61	–	0	0
Hughes, E	WPCU	1896/97	1896/97	1	1	0	1	1	1.00	0	0	0	0	0	0	0	–	–	–	0	0
	All FC	1896/97	1897/98	2	3	0	20	15	6.66	0	0	0	0	0	0	0	–	–	–	0	0
Hughes, RJ	WPCU	1897/98	1897/98	1	1	0	3	3	3.00	0	0	1	0	0	0	0	–	–	–	0	0
Hugo, SG	WPCU	1967/68	1973/74	16	21	5	472	68*	29.50	0	3	10	0	1786	743	32	23.21	2.49	4-31	0	0
	WPCU B	1975/76	1977/78	3	5	0	35	18	7.00	0	0	1	0	134	32	3	10.66	1.43	2-9	0	0
	All FC	1966/67	1977/78	22	29	6	584	68*	25.39	0	4	12	0	2347	951	48	19.81	2.43	4-31	0	0
Hutchinson, CH	WPCU	1931/32	1931/32	3	3	1	9	7	4.50	0	0	1	0	397	210	6	35.00	3.17	5-75	1	0
Igglesden, AP	WPCU B	1987/88	1987/88	5	6	0	49	21	8.16	0	0	3	0	1148	565	31	18.22	2.95	5-52	2	1
	All FC	1986	1998	154	170	65	13488	41	8.34	0	0	40	0	26579	13488	503	26.81	3.04	7-28	23	4
Impey, LLH	WPCU	1946/47	1948/49	5	4	2	13	6	6.50	0	0	1	0	1082	513	15	34.20	2.84	3-31	0	0
	All FC	1946/47	1955/56	12	15	7	44	6	5.50	0	0	1	0	2506	1035	29	35.68	2.47	5-93	1	0
Innes, GAS	WPCU	1950/51	1962/63	55	101	8	3151	139	33.88	5	18	48	0	1218	511	12	42.58	2.51	6-22	1	0
	All FC	1950/51	1964/65	75	134	15	4001	140*	33.62	7	21	60	0	1836	733	16	45.81	2.39	6-22	1	0

Name	Team	From	To	M	Inns	NO	Runs	HS	Avg	100	50	Ct	St	Balls	Runs	Wkts	Avg	RPO	BB	5I	10M
Isaacs, E	WPCB	1971/72	1983/84	51	85	7	1458	103	18.69	1	5	122	42	37	9	1	9.00	1.45	1-6	0	0
	All FC	1971/72	1983/84	53	88	7	1588	103	19.60	1	6	125	43	37	9	1	9.00	1.45	1-6	0	0
Isaacs, M	WPCB	1990/91	1990/91	1	2	0	13	8	6.50	0	0	0	0	0	0	0			—	0	0
Jabaar, A	WPCB	1974/75	1986/87	44	68	12	1169	70	20.87	0	3	30	0	6949	2135	187	11.41	1.84	7-38	11	2
	All FC	1973/74	1990/91	57	86	13	1632	70	22.35	0	4	38	0	9662	3121	233	13.39	1.93	7-38	14	3
Jackman, RD	WPCU	1971/72	1971/72	10	15	5	111	19	11.10	0	0	4	0	1890	845	38	22.23	2.68	5-37	1	0
	All FC	1966	1982/83	399	478	157	5685	92*	17.71	0	17	177	0	68209	31978	1402	22.80	2.81	8-40	67	8
Jackson, DC	WPCU	1908/09	1910/11	8	14	0	172	59	12.28	0	1	3	0	754	347	23	15.08	2.76	4-36	0	0
	All FC	1908/09	1912/13	10	17	1	277	59	17.31	0	1	6	0	820	392	23	17.04	2.86	4-36	0	0
Jackson, KC	WPCU	1990/91	1990/91	8	16	1	410	113	27.33	1	2	1	0	30	12	1	12.00	2.40	1-12	0	0
	WPCA	1991/92	1993/94	9	18	0	314	61	17.44	0	1	7	0	108	72	3	24.00	4.00	2-18	0	0
	WPCU B	1988/89	1990/91	3	4	0	220	150	55.00	1	0	2	0	0	0	0			—	0	0
	WPCA B	1991/92	1991/92	2	3	0	50	39	16.66	0	0	4	0	0	0	0			—	0	0
	All FC	1988/89	2001/02	87	159	11	4235	150	28.61	6	26	71	0	1334	680	26	26.15	3.05	5-42	1	0
Jacobs, LP	WPCB	1973/74	1975/76	15	28	3	536	50	21.44	0	1	8	0	22	7	2	3.50	1.90	2-3	0	0
	All FC	1973/74	1988/89	24	44	3	751	52	18.31	0	2	21	0	68	35	2	17.50	3.08	2-3	0	0
Jaffer, PD	WPCU	1949/50	1953/54	10	17	2	474	128	31.60	1	3	6	0	144	67	1	67.00	2.79	1-11	0	0
Jakoet, A	WPCB	1978/79	1978/79	3	5	0	79	64	15.80	0	1	0	0	8	2	0		1.50	—	0	0
Jardine, F	WPCA Am	2005/06	2006/07	2	3	1	45	19*	22.50	0	0	0	0	401	192	7	27.42	2.87	5-118	1	0
Jassiem, S	WPCB	1977/78	1978/79	6	9	3	118	43*	19.66	0	0	1	0	420	145	8	18.12	2.07	4-27	0	0
Jefferies, ST	WPCU	1978/79	1989/90	61	76	13	1278	71	20.28	0	4	32	0	13766	6300	248	25.40	2.74	10-59	10	2
	WPCU B	1978/79	1990/91	11	14	3	339	55*	30.81	0	2	3	0	2144	878	41	21.41	2.45	6-42	3	1
	WPCA	1991/92	1991/92	1	2	0	10	10	5.00	0	0	0	0	210	92	3	30.66	2.62	2-36	0	0
	All FC	1978/79	1993/94	142	190	38	3810	93	25.06	0	14	54	0	27419	13204	478	27.62	2.88	10-59	19	4
Joffe, R	WPCA	1998/99	1999/00	5	9	4	32	17*	6.40	0	0	1	0	976	478	13	36.76	2.93	3-51	0	0
	WPCA B	1998/99	1998/99	2	2	1	4	3*	4.00	0	0	0	0	384	146	6	24.33	2.28	4-40	0	0
	All FC	1998/99	1999/00	7	11	5	36	17*	6.00	0	0	1	0	1360	624	19	32.84	2.75	4-40	0	0
Johnson, AA	WPCU	1989/90	1989/90	1	1	0	15	15	15.00	0	0	0	0	120	54	3	18.00	2.70	2-7	0	0
	WPCU B	1989/90	1989/90	1	2	0	60	42	30.00	0	0	1	0	186	103	5	20.60	3.32	5-75	1	0
	All FC	1989/90	1989/90	2	3	0	75	42	25.00	0	0	2	0	306	157	8	19.62	3.07	5-75	1	0
Johnson, NC	WPCA	2000/01	2003/04	26	38	5	1377	135	41.72	2	11	57	0	1548	780	21	37.14	3.02	2-5	0	0
	WCC	2004/05	2004/05	2	4	1	81	57*	27.00	0	1	7	0	102	49	2	24.50	2.88	2-19	0	0
	All FC	1989/90	2004/05	161	249	29	7569	150	34.40	11	53	218	0	14754	7620	230	33.13	3.09	5-79	2	0

Name	Team	From	To	M	Inns	NO	Runs	HS	Avg	100	50	Ct	St	Balls	Runs	Wkts	Avg	RPO	BB	5I	10M
Jones, SA	WPCU	1974/75	1980/81	29	39	11	280	36	10.00	0	0	13	0	4749	2146	77	27.87	2.71	5-34	1	0
	WPCU B	1976/77	1980/81	7	10	4	198	70	33.00	0	1	4	0	1133	397	21	18.90	2.10	5-47	1	0
	All FC	1974/75	1987/88	81	127	24	2745	209*	26.65	2	16	58	0	9834	3936	178	22.11	2.40	5-34	2	0
Jordaan, D	WPCA	1993/94	1994/95	10	20	2	546	97	30.33	0	4	16	0	18	13	0	–	4.33	–	0	0
	WPCA B	1993/94	1994/95	7	13	1	344	105*	28.66	1	1	3	0	126	80	0	–	3.80	–	0	0
	All FC	1991/92	2000/01	80	148	11	4636	123	33.83	8	26	86	0	1519	708	16	44.25	2.79	3-9	0	0
Jordaan, HB	WPCU	1934/35	1937/38	7	14	1	210	43*	16.15	0	0	4	0	72	28	0	–	2.33	–	0	0
	All FC	1934/35	1949/50	21	42	4	817	83*	21.50	0	3	12	0	304	156	6	26.00	3.07	4-45	0	0
Kalis, AD	WPCA B	1997/98	1998/99	3	5	0	61	41	12.20	0	0	0	0	0	0	0	–	–	–	0	0
Kallis, JH	WPCA	1994/95	2003/04	31	51	4	2546	186*	54.17	6	16	20	0	3723	1645	55	29.90	2.65	6-60	1	0
	WPCA B	1993/94	1993/94	3	4	1	160	69	53.33	0	2	2	0	18	6	0	–	2.00	–	0	0
	WCC	2004/05	2004/05	3	5	0	210	99	42.00	0	2	2	0	345	130	2	65.00	2.26	1-10	0	0
	All FC	1993/94	2010/11	235	386	55	18299	200	55.28	57	92	229	0	27072	12607	405	31.12	2.79	6-54	8	0
Katts, A	WPCB	1975/76	1980/81	6	10	0	109	40	10.90	0	0	6	0	0	0	0	–	–	–	0	0
Keen, AD	WPCU	1937/38	1949/50	13	20	2	440	77	24.44	0	2	13	0	1570	488	11	44.36	1.86	3-16	0	0
Keith, GL	WPCU	1968/69	1968/69	2	2	0	14	13	7.00	0	0	5	0	0	0	0	–	–	–	0	0
	All FC	1959	1968/69	77	124	14	2108	101*	19.16	1	8	78	0	1050	561	13	43.15	3.20	4-49	0	0
Kemp, D	WPCB	1987/88	1990/91	18	28	3	637	148*	25.48	1	4	22	0	114	51	1	51.00	2.68	1-25	0	0
Kemp, JM	WCC	2007/08	2010/11	21	28	4	689	135*	28.70	1	2	43	3	1173	501	19	26.36	2.56	4-39	0	0
	All FC	1996/97	2010/11	136	213	26	6680	188	35.72	15	30	195	0	12227	5816	203	28.65	2.85	6-56	5	0
Kemp, N	WPCB	1979/80	1979/80	1	2	0	6	3	3.00	0	0	0	0	0	0	0	–	–	–	0	0
Kennedy, AC	All FC	1979/80	1987/88	7	14	0	195	29	13.92	0	0	12	0	0	0	0	–	–	–	0	0
	WPCA	1933/34	1934/35	6	8	0	76	25	9.50	0	0	6	0	0	0	0	–	–	–	0	0
	All FC	1933/34	1934/35	6	8	0	76	25	9.50	0	0	6	0	0	0	0	–	–	–	0	0
Kerby, JC	WPCU	1957/58	1963/64	12	20	2	248	35*	13.77	0	0	2	0	2034	900	32	28.12	2.65	6-33	1	0
	All FC	1954/55	1963/64	23	36	6	429	44	14.30	0	1	4	0	4195	1665	83	20.06	2.38	7-35	4	1
Khan, G	WPCB	1985/86	1985/86	2	4	0	67	52	16.75	0	1	7	0	0	0	0	–	–	–	0	0
Khan, J	WPCB	1972/73	1974/75	6	7	3	78	23*	19.50	0	0	3	0	765	270	12	22.50	2.11	3-25	0	0
Kiel, S	WPCU	1939/40	1946/47	14	27	3	1061	139*	44.20	3	6	6	0	32	10	0	–	1.87	–	0	0
Kirsten, AM	WPCU B	1986/87	1989/90	11	18	1	363	62	21.35	0	2	10	0	6	4	0	–	4.00	–	0	0
Kirsten, G	WPCU	1988/89	1990/91	22	38	3	1397	189	39.91	3	6	10	0	72	51	0	–	4.25	–	0	0
	WPCU B	1987/88	1989/90	13	23	5	1014	163*	56.33	3	5	21	0	72	39	0	–	3.25	–	0	0
	WPCA	1991/92	2003/04	51	90	8	4274	244	52.12	12	20	33	0	1043	474	16	29.62	2.72	6-68	1	0
	All FC	1987/88	2003/04	221	387	42	16670	275	48.31	46	79	171	0	1727	836	20	41.80	2.90	6-68	1	0

Name	Team	From	To	M	Inns	NO	Runs	HS	Avg	100	50	Ct	St	Balls	Runs	Wkts	Avg	RPO	BB	5I	10M
Kirsten, P	WPCA	1995/96	1999/00	37	53	7	931	91*	20.23	0	3	135	6	0	0	0	–	–	–	0	0
	WPCA B	1994/95	1994/95	5	8	0	61	24	7.62	0	0	11	2	0	0	0	–	–	–	0	0
	All FC	1992/93	1999/00	55	81	9	1519	91*	21.09	0	7	170	12	0	0	0	–	–	–	0	0
Kirsten, PN	WPCU	1973/74	1989/90	133	236	19	9087	204*	41.87	21	47	78	0	4128	1875	34	55.14	2.72	6-48	1	0
	All FC	1973/74	1996/97	327	568	59	22635	271	44.46	57	107	190	0	10287	4682	117	40.01	2.73	6-48	2	0
Kleinveldt, J	WPCB	1979/80	1980/81	10	14	2	146	43	12.16	0	0	12	0	1240	430	25	17.20	2.08	4-35	0	0
	All FC	1979/80	1982/83	15	21	3	186	43	10.33	0	0	16	0	2041	732	44	16.63	2.15	4-33	0	0
Kleinveldt, MC	WPCA Am	2010/11	2010/11	11	18	2	639	160	39.93	2	2	4	0	0	0	0	–	–	–	0	0
Kleinveldt, RK	WPCA	2002/03	2003/04	2	2	2	8	7*	–	0	0	5	0	339	185	2	92.50	3.27	1-52	0	0
	WCC	2004/05	2009/10	54	79	6	1343	92	18.39	0	7	20	0	9254	4252	137	31.03	2.75	8-47	4	1
	WPCA Am	2005/06	2005/06	3	4	2	136	115*	68.00	1	0	4	0	547	286	16	17.87	3.13	6-57	1	0
	All FC	2002/03	2009/10	64	95	11	1554	115*	18.50	1	7	30	0	10657	5071	162	31.30	2.85	8-47	5	1
Klette, JE	WPCU	1967/68	1967/68	2	4	1	53	41	17.66	0	0	2	0	0	0	0	–	–	–	0	0
	All FC	1967/68	1976/77	5	10	2	329	154	41.12	1	1	6	0	0	0	0	–	–	–	0	0
Knowles, P	WPCU B	1979/80	1979/80	2	4	0	21	15	5.25	0	0	4	0	0	0	0	–	–	–	0	0
Knowles, RJ	WPCU B	1978/79	1984/85	3	6	1	107	46	21.40	0	0	4	0	150	46	2	23.00	1.84	2-16	0	0
Koch, DM	WPCA B	1997/98	1997/98	4	7	1	159	54	26.50	0	1	1	0	624	315	10	31.50	3.02	4-35	0	0
	All FC	1997/98	2001/02	21	35	8	444	54	16.44	0	1	9	0	3748	1681	45	37.35	2.69	5-128	1	0
Koen, LJ	WPCU B	1987/88	1989/90	9	15	1	345	55	24.64	0	2	6	0	0	0	0	–	–	–	0	0
	All FC	1987/88	2001/02	102	175	14	6357	202*	39.48	10	37	152	0	12	6	0	–	3.00	–	0	0
Koen, PA	WPCU B	1984/85	1986/87	4	8	1	133	32	19.00	0	0	3	0	457	266	6	44.33	3.49	4-31	0	0
	All FC	1984/85	1991/92	15	27	6	541	101	25.76	1	1	10	0	2081	959	28	34.25	2.76	4-31	0	0
Koenig, SG	WPCA	1993/94	1996/97	29	50	2	1834	149*	38.20	3	11	20	0	80	48	0	–	3.60	–	0	0
	WPCA B	1993/94	1995/96	4	7	1	245	89	40.83	0	2	2	0	0	0	0	–	–	–	0	0
	All FC	1993/94	2004	135	234	13	8820	171	39.90	16	50	63	0	182	102	2	51.00	3.36	1-0	0	0
Kohler, DL	WPCU B	1976/77	1976/77	1	1	0	32	32	32.00	0	0	0	0	66	30	2	15.00	2.72	2-14	0	0
Kolbe, C	WPCB	1971/72	1974/75	4	7	0	103	50	14.71	0	1	2	0	296	96	7	13.71	1.94	4-52	0	0
Kossuth, FH	WPCU	1929/30	1929/30	3	4	3	40	29*	40.00	0	0	2	0	473	191	8	23.87	2.42	3-11	0	0
Koster, RA	WPCA	1992/93	1993/94	2	3	1	102	45	51.00	0	0	2	0	103	52	3	17.33	3.02	1-8	0	0
	WPCA B	1993/94	1993/94	5	8	1	301	95	43.00	0	3	0	0	30	22	0	–	4.40	–	0	0
	All FC	1992/93	1996/97	18	31	3	1010	95	36.07	0	6	5	0	133	74	3	24.66	3.33	1-8	0	0
Kotze, JJ	WPCU	1903/04	1910/11	18	29	9	136	27	6.80	0	0	7	0	3397	1467	113	12.98	2.59	8-57	15	6
	All FC	1901	1910/11	72	105	25	688	60	8.60	0	1	31	0	12480	6217	348	17.86	2.98	8-18	30	9
Kruger, WG	WPCU B	1982/83	1985/86	12	23	0	496	80	21.56	0	3	8	0	0	0	0	–	–	–	0	0

Name	Team	From	To	M	Inns	NO	Runs	HS	Avg	100	50	Ct	St	Balls	Runs	Wkts	Avg	RPO	BB	5I	10M
Kuiper, AP	WPCU	1978/79	1990/91	87	141	20	3960	161*	32.72	4	25	54	0	6676	3241	115	28.18	2.91	6-55	2	0
	WPCU B	1977/78	1980/81	8	12	2	426	95	42.60	0	3	2	0	527	253	11	23.00	2.88	4-7	0	0
	WPCA	1991/92	1993/94	20	38	5	1254	129*	38.00	2	7	12	0	1254	551	11	50.09	2.63	2-19	0	0
	All FC	1977/78	1997/98	165	276	31	7899	161*	32.24	9	46	106	0	12105	5828	196	29.73	2.88	6-55	4	0
Kuiper, JM	WPCA Am	2005/06	2008/09	15	24	1	632	113	27.47	2	1	10	0	0	0	0	–	–	–	0	0
Kuys, F	WPCU	1896/97	1897/98	5	8	0	108	31	13.50	0	0	2	0	172	79	4	19.75	2.75	2-12	0	0
	All FC	1896/97	1898/99	8	14	0	229	49	16.35	0	0	2	0	452	206	11	18.72	2.73	4-66	0	0
Laing, PC	WPCA Am	2008/09	2009/10	6	8	2	142	56*	23.66	0	1	6	0	472	314	5	62.80	3.99	1-27	0	0
	All FC	2005/06	2009/10	17	25	2	643	154	27.95	1	3	15	0	1468	911	22	41.40	3.72	4-19	0	0
Lakay, N	WPCB	1971/72	1971/72	1	2	0	14	14	7.00	0	0	0	0	8	5	0	–	–	–	0	0
Lamb, AJ	WPCU	1972/73	1981/82	61	105	14	3680	130	40.43	6	28	47	0	9	1	0	–	0.66	–	0	0
	WPCA	1992/93	1992/93	5	10	1	636	206*	70.66	3	1	3	0	0	0	0	–	–	–	0	0
	All FC	1972/73	1995	467	772	108	32502	294	48.94	89	166	371	0	303	199	8	24.87	3.94	2-29	0	0
Lambert, J	WPCB	1971/72	1973/74	7	12	0	292	137	24.33	1	0	4	0	100	36	5	7.20	2.16	4-18	0	0
	All FC	1971/72	1973/74	8	14	0	335	137	23.92	1	0	4	0	100	36	5	7.20	2.16	4-18	0	0
Lange, T	WPCU	1950/51	1950/51	1	2	0	12	12	6.00	0	0	0	0	0	0	0	–	–	–	0	0
Langeveldt, CK	WCC	2007/08	2010/11	15	15	5	113	19	11.30	0	0	2	0	3258	1649	49	33.65	3.03	4-45	0	0
	All FC	1997/98	2010/11	98	120	41	1136	56	14.37	0	1	27	0	18622	9235	321	28.76	2.97	6-48	9	1
Larkin, GM	WPCU	1934/35	1937/38	3	5	0	83	72	16.60	0	1	2	2	0	0	0	–	–	–	0	0
	All FC	1934/35	1942/43	5	9	0	178	72	19.77	0	1	2	3	0	0	0	–	–	–	0	0
Lawrenson, RR	WPCU	1980/81	1981/82	2	3	1	26	24	13.00	0	0	1	0	336	171	5	34.20	3.05	3-54	0	0
	WPCU B	1980/81	1984/85	20	28	7	400	87	19.04	0	1	10	0	3692	1594	95	16.77	2.59	6-24	5	1
	All FC	1980/81	1984/85	22	31	8	426	87	18.52	0	1	11	0	4028	1765	100	17.65	2.62	6-24	5	1
Lazard, TN	WPCU	1986/87	1989/90	22	40	4	1501	166	41.69	3	8	4	0	4	11	0	–	16.50	–	0	0
	WPCU B	1983/84	1990/91	14	28	1	827	121	30.62	2	4	4	0	0	0	0	–	–	–	0	0
	WPCA	1991/92	1992/93	15	29	4	926	150*	37.04	4	3	2	0	0	0	0	–	–	–	0	0
	All FC	1983/84	1995/96	78	146	15	5280	307*	40.30	12	24	17	0	4	11	0	–	16.50	–	0	0
Lazarus, RH	WPCU	1925/26	1925/26	2	4	0	53	26	13.25	0	0	2	0	0	0	0	–	–	–	0	0
Lear, PN	WPCU	1959/60	1965/66	7	11	2	172	45	19.11	0	0	0	0	305	131	3	43.66	2.57	1-12	0	0
Lee, JM	WPCU	1957/58	1959/60	2	3	2	8	6*	8.00	0	0	0	0	232	109	5	21.80	2.81	3-25	0	0
	All FC	1957/58	1959/60	7	10	6	22	7	5.50	0	0	2	0	1080	409	17	24.05	2.27	4-84	0	0
Le Roux, D	WPCU	1965/66	1965/66	1	2	0	38	33	19.00	0	0	0	0	0	0	0	–	–	–	0	0
Le Roux, DP	WPCU B	1983/84	1983/84	1	2	0	25	25	12.50	0	0	3	0	0	0	0	–	–	–	0	0
	All FC	1975/76	1992/93	55	105	5	2818	127	28.18	4	14	49	3	6	4	0	–	4.00	–	0	0

Name	Team	From	To	M	Inns	NO	Runs	HS	Avg	100	50	Ct	St	Balls	Runs	Wkts	Avg	RPO	BB	5I	10M
Le Roux, GS	WPCU	1975/76	1988/89	83	107	35	1725	86	23.95	0	8	34	0	16080	7062	372	18.98	2.63	7-40	17	2
	WPCU B	1975/76	1975/76	3	5	2	56	29	18.66	0	0	2	0	558	223	7	31.85	2.39	3-21	0	0
	All FC	1975/76	1988/89	239	290	79	5425	86	25.71	0	26	80	0	39440	17800	838	21.24	2.70	8-107	35	3
Levi, RE	WPCA Am	2006/07	2010/11	17	26	4	1067	150*	48.50	3	6	16	0	0	0	0	–	–	–	0	0
	WCC	2008/09	2010/11	17	27	3	746	137	31.08	1	5	8	0	0	0	0	–	–	–	0	0
	All FC	2006/07	2010/11	34	53	7	1813	150*	39.41	4	11	24	0	0	0	0	–	–	–	0	0
Lewis, MR	WPCA B	1998/99	1998/99	1	2	1	9	9*	9.00	0	0	0	0	36	22	1	22.00	3.66	1-12	0	0
	All FC	1998/99	2002/03	17	22	7	268	49*	17.86	0	0	10	0	900	485	9	53.88	3.23	2-44	0	0
Lewis, PT	WPCU	1907/08	1913/14	6	10	0	377	151	37.70	1	2	4	0	0	0	0	–	–	–	0	0
	All FC	1907/08	1913/14	12	21	2	507	151	26.68	1	3	7	0	24	27	0	–	6.75	–	0	0
Liddle, JR	WPCU	1955/56	1956/57	8	13	8	54	20*	10.80	0	0	3	0	2582	877	41	21.39	2.03	7-72	3	2
	All FC	1949/50	1956/57	38	68	20	692	77	14.41	0	2	16	0	11116	4254	181	23.50	2.29	7-72	10	5
Lillie, CC	WPCU B	1988/89	1988/89	5	4	1	8	5	2.66	0	0	0	0	637	342	10	34.20	3.22	4-59	0	0
Little, PA	WPCU	1932/33	1935/36	8	15	2	164	35	12.61	0	0	6	0	276	237	2	118.50	5.15	1-60	0	0
Lloyd, SM	WPCU B	1975/76	1975/76	2	3	0	9	8	3.00	0	0	1	0	0	0	0	–	–	–	0	0
Lofthouse, R	WPCU	1941/42	1947/48	5	8	1	104	29	14.85	0	0	2	0	561	245	10	24.50	2.62	4-63	0	0
Logenstein, QF	WPCB	1990/91	1990/91	2	3	0	13	12	4.33	0	0	2	0	240	104	2	52.00	2.60	1-38	0	0
	WPCA B	1993/94	1993/94	3	2	1	6	5*	6.00	0	0	2	0	342	199	4	49.75	3.49	2-58	0	0
	All FC	1990/91	1993/94	5	5	1	19	12	4.75	0	0	4	0	582	303	6	50.50	3.12	2-58	0	0
Lohmann, GA	WPCU	1894/95	1896/97	5	8	0	122	44	15.25	0	0	8	0	1557	548	42	13.04	2.11	7-72	4	1
	All FC	1884	1897/98	293	427	39	7247	115	18.67	3	29	337	0	71918	25295	1841	13.73	2.11	9-28	176	57
Loon, GI	WPCA B	1996/97	1996/97	1	2	0	7	5	3.50	0	0	0	0	0	0	0	–	–	–	0	0
Lotter, NB	WPCU	1971/72	1975/76	3	4	0	13	8	3.25	0	0	2	0	282	196	3	65.33	4.17	3-84	0	0
	WPCU B	1975/76	1981/82	8	9	3	81	20	13.50	0	0	4	0	1301	646	22	29.36	2.97	5-34	2	0
	All FC	1971/72	1981/82	11	13	3	94	20	9.40	0	0	6	0	1583	842	25	33.68	3.19	5-34	2	0
Lotter, RB	WCC	2008/09	2008/09	1	1	0	10	10	10.00	0	0	0	0	138	110	0	–	4.78	–	0	0
	WPCA Am	2008/09	2008/09	1	2	1	5	3	5.00	0	0	1	0	120	76	2	38.00	3.80	2-38	0	0
	All FC	2008/09	2008/09	2	3	1	15	10	7.50	0	0	1	0	258	186	2	93.00	4.32	2-38	0	0
Louw, DA	WPCU	1955/56	1966/67	17	27	7	562	90	28.10	0	6	7	0	2068	955	30	31.83	2.77	3-18	0	0
Louw, J	WCC	2009/10	2010/11	6	5	1	50	19	12.50	0	0	2	0	870	377	17	22.17	2.60	5-56	1	0
	All FC	2000/01	2010/11	124	174	28	3218	124	22.04	1	16	41	0	21858	11127	361	30.82	3.05	6-39	13	2
Louw, JL	WPCU B	1981/82	1981/82	3	4	2	16	7*	8.00	0	0	1	0	639	219	17	12.88	2.05	7-57	1	0
	All FC	1976/77	1982/83	5	7	2	17	7*	3.40	0	0	2	0	968	435	20	21.75	2.69	7-57	1	0
Lovegrove, AR	WPCU	1923/24	1926/27	9	14	6	165	40*	20.62	0	0	12	0	973	591	21	28.14	3.64	4-37	0	0
Lovell, GGS	WPCU	1950/51	1952/53	3	5	3	38	14*	19.00	0	0	2	0	504	205	6	34.16	2.44	2-19	0	0

Name	Team	From	To	M	Inns	NO	Runs	HS	Avg	100	50	Ct	St	Balls	Runs	Wkts	Avg	RPO	BB	5I	10M
Luck, AA	WPCU	1947/48	1947/48	2	4	0	50	34	12.50	0	0	1	0	40	26	2	13.00	3.90	1-10	0	0
Lundie, EB	WPCU	1909/10	1910/11	2	4	0	22	15	5.50	0	0	1	0	243	134	4	33.50	3.30	3-83	0	0
Luyt, FP	All FC	1908/09	1913/14	9	16	1	126	29	8.40	0	0	7	0	1510	659	26	25.34	2.61	6-52	1	0
Luyt, RR	WPCU	1908/09	1910/11	4	7	2	58	28	11.60	0	0	2	1	0	0	0	–	–	–	0	0
	WPCU	1906/07	1922/23	19	33	1	451	61	14.09	0	1	13	9	388	231	11	21.00	3.57	5-26	1	0
	All FC	1906/07	1922/23	20	35	1	543	61	15.97	0	1	14	9	410	263	11	23.90	3.84	5-26	1	0
Macaulay, MJ	WPCU	1960/61	1960/61	4	8	1	114	40	16.28	0	0	3	0	672	250	15	16.66	2.23	5-14	2	1
MacDonald, RR	All FC	1957/58	1978/79	69	91	23	888	59	13.05	0	2	45	0	13566	5357	234	22.89	2.36	7-49	16	4
	WPCU	1955/56	1957/58	8	15	0	209	45	13.93	0	0	4	0	0	0	0	–	–	–	0	0
MacHelm, DQ	All FC	1952/53	1957/58	12	22	0	328	45	14.90	0	0	8	0	0	0	0	–	–	–	0	0
	WPCA	1992/93	1996/97	12	17	8	47	14*	5.22	0	0	2	0	2061	872	19	45.89	2.53	4-74	0	0
	WPCA B	1993/94	1997/98	19	16	6	79	16	7.90	0	0	11	0	3840	1657	63	26.30	2.58	7-85	3	1
	All FC	1992/93	1997/98	33	36	15	138	16	6.57	0	0	13	0	6207	2694	88	30.61	2.60	7-85	3	1
Maclons, M	WPCB	1971/72	1975/76	17	29	3	416	75*	16.00	0	1	37	14	0	0	0	–	–	–	0	0
MacRae, ASV	WPCU	1923/24	1926/27	6	6	4	76	39*	38.00	0	0	2	0	950	506	13	38.92	3.19	3-15	0	0
Magiet, A	WPCA Am	2004/05	2005/06	2	2	0	8	8	4.00	0	0	1	0	18	0	3	0.00	0.00	3-0	0	0
Magiet, MR	WPCB	1971/72	1980/81	34	53	5	841	76	17.52	0	3	31	0,	4341	1328	97	13.69	1.83	7-35	5	1
	All FC	1971/72	1980/81	37	57	6	917	76	17.98	0	4	32	0	4852	1486	109	13.63	1.83	7-35	6	1
Magiet, R	WPCA	1999/00	2002/03	11	19	1	353	54	19.61	0	2	3	0	186	108	0	–	3.48	–	0	0
	WPCA B	1998/99	1998/99	3	6	1	250	122	50.00	1	1	3	0	0	0	0	–	–	–	0	0
	WPCA Am	2004/05	2004/05	1	2	0	11	11	5.50	0	0	1	0	0	0	0	–	–	–	0	0
	All FC	1998/99	2008/09	23	43	3	983	122	24.57	1	5	13	0	341	214	2	107.00	3.76	1-31	0	0
Magiet, S	WPCB	1971/72	1990/91	64	100	12	2389	100*	27.14	2	14	61	0	7202	2124	170	12.49	1.76	6-24	7	0
	All FC	1971/72	1990/91	67	105	14	2650	128	29.12	3	15	65	0	7346	2222	171	12.99	1.81	6-24	7	0
Mahlombe, M	WPCA Am	2005/06	2010/11	23	27	3	296	54	12.33	0	1	7	0	2052	1105	36	30.69	3.23	3-11	0	0
Mahoney, JE	WPCU	1981/82	1981/82	1	2	2	13	10*	–	0	0	0	0	30	8	0	–	1.60	–	0	0
	WPCB	1972/73	1978/79	19	27	8	377	68*	19.84	0	1	22	0	2902	904	48	18.83	1.86	6-42	3	0
	WPCU B	1976/77	1981/82	7	6	2	36	14	9.00	0	0	0	0	1138	431	23	18.73	2.27	4-41	1	0
	All FC	1972/73	1981/82	30	39	12	435	68*	16.11	0	1	22	0	4396	1538	77	19.97	2.09	6-42	3	0
Maile, JBR	WPCU	1955/56	1960/61	23	42	3	825	108	21.15	1	2	23	0	4482	1519	67	22.67	2.03	7-27	3	0
	All FC	1951/52	1960/61	35	58	8	1134	108	22.68	1	3	35	0	5346	1853	75	24.70	2.07	7-27	3	0
Mainon, C	WPCU	1893/94	1894/95	2	3	0	52	29	17.33	0	0	0	0	25	10	0	–	2.40	–	0	0
Malan, DJ	WPCU B	1978/79	1979/80	3	5	1	14	5	3.50	0	0	2	0	360	179	3	59.66	2.98	1-23	0	0
	All FC	1978/79	1981/82	4	6	1	19	5	3.80	0	0	3	0	444	224	3	74.66	3.02	1-23	0	0

Name	Team	From	To	M	Inns	NO	Runs	HS	Avg	100	50	Ct	St	Balls	Runs	Wkts	Avg	RPO	BB	5I	10M
Manack, AA	WPCB	1989/90	1989/90	5	6	2	54	27	13.50	0	0	3	0	944	306	27	11.33	1.94	7-17	3	0
	All FC	1983/84	1992/93	48	74	17	996	83	17.47	0	4	25	0	8548	3493	211	16.55	2.45	7-17	12	1
Manning, LM	WPCU	1930/31	1939/40	28	49	0	1300	185	26.53	4	5	6	0	24	12	0	–	3.00	–	0	0
Maron, R	WPCA	1996/97	1997/98	5	9	0	95	35	10.55	0	0	1	0	72	32	1	32.00	2.66	1-7	0	0
	WPCA B	1995/96	1998/99	11	20	1	580	75	30.52	0	4	5	0	47	69	1	69.00	8.80	1-4	0	0
	All FC	1995/96	1998/99	18	33	1	780	75	24.37	0	4	6	0	119	101	2	50.50	5.09	1-4	0	0
Mars, WH	WPCU	1912/13	1913/14	2	2	1	5	4	5.00	0	0	3	0								
	All FC	1912/13	1913/14	3	4	3	9	4	9.00	0	0	3	0								
Marshall, AW	WPCU	1941/42	1956/57	29	44	6	957	78	25.18	0	6	10	0	3946	1489	42	35.45	2.26	6-42	1	0
Martin, BP	WPCU B	1980/81	1985/86	7	7	1	129	51	21.50	0	1	5	0	1076	492	21	23.42	2.74	6-42	1	0
Martin, C	WPCB	1977/78	1986/87	13	20	2	297	66	16.50	0	3	9	0	24	15	0	–	3.75	5-36	0	0
Martin, FC	WPCU	1929/30	1932/33	18	30	2	874	145	31.21	2	4	11	0	18	5	0	–	1.66	4-40	0	0
	All FC	1929/30	1932/33	19	32	2	887	145	29.56	2	4	11	0	24	7	0	–	1.75	–	0	0
Martin, GG	WPCU B	1985/86	1986/87	4	7	3	66	25	16.50	0	0	4	0	618	335	5	67.00	3.25	2-43	0	0
	All FC	1981/82	1986/87	5	8	3	67	25	13.40	0	0	4	0	774	400	5	80.00	3.10	2-43	0	0
Martin, N	WPCB	1978/79	1978/79	5	9	0	158	43	17.55	0	1	2	0	120	35	2	17.50	1.75	2-19	0	0
Martin, PW	WPCU	1989/90	1990/91	6	11	1	106	41	10.60	0	0	4	0	0	0	0	–	–	–	0	0
	WPCU B	1978/79	1990/91	19	35	1	842	119	24.76	1	2	11	0	84	45	0	–	3.21	–	0	0
	All FC	1978/79	1990/91	25	46	2	948	119	21.54	1	2	15	0	84	45	0	–	3.21	–	0	0
Martin, S	WPCB	1982/83	1982/83	1	2	0	8	8	4.00	0	0	0	0								
Martyn, A	WPCA	1992/93	1996/97	22	27	3	128	20	5.33	0	0	7	0	4749	2049	81	25.29	2.58	5-63	1	0
	WPCA B	1993/94	1995/96	4	3	0	25	19	8.33	0	0	2	0	785	348	22	15.81	2.65	6-22	3	0
	All FC	1992/93	1996/97	27	32	4	153	20	5.46	0	0	11	0	5798	2492	108	23.07	2.57	6-22	4	0
Masinda, MR	WPCA Am	2005/06	2005/06	1	1	0	1	1	1.00	0	0	0	0	6	8	0	–	8.00	–	0	0
Matthews, BA	WPCU	1984/85	1986/87	9	8	6	31	20*	15.50	0	0	1	0	1584	647	21	30.80	2.45	3-49	0	0
	WPCU B	1984/85	1987/88	17	22	7	88	17	5.86	0	0	3	0	3188	1289	62	20.79	2.42	5-32	1	0
	All FC	1984/85	1989/90	38	36	18	158	28*	8.77	0	0	6	0	7057	2836	120	23.63	2.41	5-32	1	0
Matthews, CR	WPCU	1987/88	1990/91	27	31	10	433	105	20.61	1	0	14	0	4035	1677	78	21.50	2.49	6-58	3	0
	WPCU B	1986/87	1988/89	4	6	1	72	43*	14.40	0	0	3	0	618	261	7	37.28	2.53	2-39	0	0
	WPCA	1991/92	1999/00	45	51	12	781	96	20.02	0	3	29	0	7415	3032	132	22.96	2.45	6-22	4	0
	All FC	1986/87	1999/00	105	119	32	1734	105	19.93	1	4	57	0	17662	7203	290	24.83	2.44	6-22	9	0
McAdam, SJ	WPCU	1972/73	1973/74	4	3	0	25	15	8.33	0	0	1	0	456	223	8	27.87	2.93	3-30	0	0
	All FC	1972/73	1973/74	31	36	11	228	31	9.12	0	0	13	0	5029	2383	82	29.06	2.84	4-39	0	0
McAdam, WJ	WPCU	1966/67	1968/69	12	18	1	440	129	25.88	1	1	4	0	18	3	0	–	1.00	–	0	0
	All FC	1966/67	1971/72	19	30	1	668	129	23.03	1	1	7	0	18	3	0	–	1.00	–	0	0

Name	Team	From	To	M	Inns	NO	Runs	HS	Avg	100	50	Ct	St	Balls	Runs	Wkts	Avg	RPO	BB	5I	10M
McCay, DLC	WPCU	1966/67	1973/74	10	15	3	247	82	20.58	0	1	9	0	1692	746	29	25.72	2.64	8-76	2	1
	All FC	1966/67	1973/74	17	25	3	345	82	15.68	0	1	12	0	2566	1071	49	21.85	2.50	8-76	2	1
McClement, AJ	WPCU	1989/90	1990/91	3	1	0	0	0	0.00	0	0	1	0	815	273	8	34.12	2.00	2-11	0	0
	WPCU B	1986/87	1990/91	15	16	5	245	72	22.27	0	1	9	0	3142	1170	70	16.71	2.23	7-25	6	2
	WPCA	1991/92	1991/92	2	2	2	17	17*	–	0	0	1	0	533	222	5	44.40	2.49	5-86	1	1
	WPCA B	1991/92	1993/94	6	4	2	23	10	11.50	0	0	4	0	990	411	19	21.63	2.49	5-65	1	0
	All FC	1984/85	1993/94	31	30	14	352	72	22.00	0	1	17	0	6206	2445	111	22.02	2.36	7-25	8	2
McCulloch, VT	WPCU	1960/61	1966/67	21	40	3	979	104	26.45	1	6	8	0	0	0	0	–	–	–	0	0
McEwan, KS	WPCU	1981/82	1986/87	37	57	8	2357	149	48.10	10	8	42	0	0	0	0	–	–	–	0	0
	All FC	1972/73	1991/92	428	705	67	26628	218	41.73	74	122	359	7	280	309	4	77.25	6.62	1-0	0	0
McLean, JJ	WPCA	2001/02	2003/04	5	7	0	157	57	22.42	0	1	4	0	0	0	0	–	–	–	0	0
	All FC	2001/02	2006	13	18	1	464	68	27.29	0	5	11	0	0	0	0	–	–	–	0	0
McMeeking, DP	WPCU	1965/66	1965/66	1	2	0	29	29	14.50	0	0	0	0	270	139	4	34.75	3.08	3-95	0	0
McMillan, BM	WPCU	1989/90	1990/91	17	27	5	941	127	42.77	1	4	11	0	2236	978	39	25.07	2.62	5-45	2	0
	WPCA	1991/92	1999/00	35	58	7	2135	140	41.86	4	13	41	0	4402	1733	57	30.40	2.36	5-35	2	0
	All FC	1984/85	1999/00	155	245	41	7898	140	38.71	14	46	166	0	20528	9074	310	29.27	2.65	5-35	4	0
McMorrow, BA	WPCU	1949/50	1949/50	1	2	0	10	8	5.00	0	0	1	0	0	0	0	–	–	–	0	0
Mdodana, TJ	WPCA Am	2006/07	2007/08	6	10	0	76	21	7.60	0	0	1	0	0	0	0	–	–	–	0	0
Meeding, BK	WPCU	1964/65	1964/65	1	1	0	28	28	28.00	0	0	0	0	252	101	2	50.50	2.40	1-27	0	0
Melle, BGV	WPCU	1908/09	1910/11	9	15	1	439	145	31.35	1	2	5	0	18	9	0	–	3.00	–	0	0
	All FC	1908/09	1923/24	62	101	9	2535	145	27.55	3	13	33	0	6252	2931	114	25.71	2.81	7-48	9	1
Melle, MG	WPCU	1953/54	1953/54	2	3	1	73	59	36.50	0	1	1	0	392	149	7	21.28	2.28	3-28	0	0
	All FC	1948/49	1953/54	52	68	20	544	59	11.33	0	2	22	0	9497	3990	160	24.93	2.52	9-22	6	2
Mellor, MD	WPCU B	1981/82	1983/84	8	15	0	368	60	24.53	0	4	8	0	480	216	10	21.60	2.70	2-15	0	0
	All FC	1978/79	1987/88	39	73	5	1919	124*	28.22	2	10	25	0	3518	1462	53	27.58	2.49	4-88	0	0
Mentis, MJ	WPCU	1975/76	1975/76	2	4	0	57	25	14.25	0	0	1	0	0	0	0	–	–	–	0	0
	WPCU B	1975/76	1976/77	9	17	0	515	102	30.29	1	2	5	0	0	0	0	–	–	–	0	0
	All FC	1975/76	1977/78	14	26	0	750	102	28.84	1	4	8	0	0	0	0	–	–	–	0	0
Meyer, MA	WPCB	1990/91	1990/91	6	7	2	86	36	17.20	0	0	3	0	954	290	27	10.74	1.82	5-22	1	0
	WPCA	1991/92	1993/94	2	0	0	0	–	–	0	0	0	0	336	190	0	–	3.39	–	0	0
	WPCA B	1993/94	1995/96	6	7	3	197	89	49.25	0	1	0	0	902	451	18	25.05	3.00	7-67	1	0
	All FC	1990/91	1995/96	14	14	5	283	89	31.44	0	1	3	0	2192	931	45	20.68	2.54	7-67	2	0
Mgijima, A	WPCA Am	2009/10	2010/11	13	20	3	294	54*	17.29	0	1	15	0	1080	529	15	35.26	2.93	5-24	1	0
	All FC	2007/08	2010/11	14	21	3	295	54*	16.38	0	1	16	0	1102	539	16	33.68	2.93	5-24	1	0
Middleton, IE	WPCU	1960/61	1960/61	1	2	0	17	17	8.50	0	0	0	0	0	0	0	–	–	–	0	0

Name	Team	From	To	M	Inns	NO	Runs	HS	Avg	100	50	Ct	St	Balls	Runs	Wkts	Avg	RPO	BB	5I	10M
Middleton, J	WPCU	1890/91	1903/04	13	22	8	97	32	6.92	0	0	10	0	2619	1146	80	14.32	2.62	7-64	8	4
	All FC	1890/91	1904	31	50	21	176	32	6.06	0	0	14	0	5571	2523	140	18.02	2.71	7-64	10	4
Middleton, RE	WPCU	1937/38	1945/46	3	3	1	33	22*	16.50	0	0	0	0	696	266	11	24.18	2.29	4-38	0	0
Middleton, T	WPCU	1924/25	1926/27	4	6	0	114	55	19.00	0	1	2	0	192	38	4	9.50	1.18	4-14	0	0
Millard, DES	WPCU	1951/52	1954/55	4	7	1	118	62	19.66	0	1	0	0	120	33	0	–	1.65	–	0	0
	All FC	1951/52	1965	14	26	2	497	73	20.70	0	5	4	0	1326	448	15	29.86	2.02	6-68	1	0
Miller, C	WPCB	1975/76	1975/76	1	2	0	12	11	6.00	0	0	1	0	36	21	0	–	3.50	–	0	0
Miller, G	WPCB	1984/85	1988/89	4	6	0	32	14	5.33	0	0	2	0	234	114	3	38.00	2.92	2-2	0	0
Miller, HDS	WPCU	1962/63	1962/63	5	8	3	43	27*	8.60	0	0	2	0	1173	438	18	24.33	2.24	4-32	0	0
	All FC	1962/63	1970/71	38	58	7	589	81	11.54	0	1	23	0	5320	2200	76	28.94	2.48	7-48	1	0
Mills, CH	WPCU	1892/93	1894/95	4	7	0	117	31	16.71	0	0	6	0	968	346	27	12.81	2.14	5-36	3	0
	All FC	1888	1894/95	8	13	0	160	31	12.30	0	0	10	0	1178	451	29	15.55	2.29	5-36	3	0
Milton, WH	WPCU	1889/90	1890/91	3	5	0	84	47	16.80	0	0	3	0	35	15	2	7.50	2.57	1-5	0	0
	All FC	1888/89	1891/92	6	11	0	152	47	13.81	0	0	5	0	114	63	4	15.75	3.31	1-5	0	0
Minnaar, CWR	WPCU	1913/14	1913/14	1	2	2	4	4*	–	0	0	2	0	360	169	5	33.80	2.81	4-95	0	0
Minnaar, MB	WPCU	1985/86	1986/87	13	7	3	48	27	12.00	0	0	8	0	2963	1136	38	29.89	2.30	4-61	0	0
	WPCU B	1977/78	1989/90	35	50	19	456	40*	14.70	0	0	19	0	6946	2702	77	35.09	2.33	5-57	4	0
	All FC	1977/78	1989/90	48	57	22	504	40*	14.40	0	0	27	0	9909	3838	115	33.37	2.32	5-57	4	0
Mitchell, TJ	WPCU B	1989/90	1990/91	8	13	3	335	86	33.50	0	2	1	0	576	231	4	57.75	2.40	2-20	0	0
	WPCA	1991/92	1994/95	5	9	2	159	33	22.71	0	0	0	0	594	228	5	45.60	2.30	2-46	0	0
	WPCA B	1991/92	1996/97	16	26	7	698	90	36.73	0	7	12	0	1826	726	33	22.00	2.38	3-0	0	0
	All FC	1989/90	1996/97	29	48	12	1192	90	33.11	0	9	13	0	2996	1185	42	28.21	2.37	3-0	0	0
Mjekula, S	WPCA Am	2006/07	2006/07	4	4	0	18	8	4.50	0	0	2	0	749	380	16	23.75	3.04	4-28	0	0
	All FC	2004/05	2010/11	34	43	16	116	16	4.29	0	0	7	0	4391	2266	92	24.63	3.09	5-33	2	0
Mohamed, E	WPCB	1984/85	1988/89	7	9	3	103	28	17.16	0	0	5	0	1089	340	24	14.16	1.87	5-30	2	0
	All FC	1984/85	1988/89	22	34	8	453	45	17.42	0	0	11	0	2663	1047	54	19.38	2.35	6-51	3	0
Moleon, EO	WPCA B	1996/97	1998/99	8	11	4	110	41	15.71	0	0	4	0	1206	725	16	45.31	3.60	3-28	0	0
	All FC	1996/97	2006/07	49	80	11	1137	67	16.47	0	2	18	0	7543	3852	107	36.00	3.06	5-60	2	0
Moodie, DV	WPCB	1971/72	1975/76	17	28	1	665	100	24.62	1	3	14	0	27	30	0	–	6.66	–	0	0
	All FC	1971/72	1975/76	18	29	1	670	100	23.92	1	3	14	0	27	30	0	–	6.66	–	0	0
Moore, TE	WPCU	1895/96	1895/96	1	1	0	9	9	9.00	0	0	1	0	0	0	0	–	–	–	0	0
Morby-Smith, L	WPCU	1963/64	1966/67	16	28	1	1144	127	42.37	2	9	10	0	15	6	1	6.00	2.40	1-0	0	0
	All FC	1958/59	1966/67	35	55	4	1743	127	34.17	2	11	19	0	50	33	2	16.50	3.96	1-0	0	0
Morgan, HW	WPCU	1927/28	1933/34	13	19	3	534	115	33.37	1	2	8	0	432	214	4	53.50	2.97	3-41	0	0
Morkel, DPB	WPCU	1924/25	1929/30	23	40	4	1586	208*	44.05	4	6	14	0	3096	1461	52	28.09	2.83	5-52	2	0
	All FC	1924/25	1938	86	143	12	4494	251	34.30	8	22	67	0	10425	4973	174	28.58	2.86	8-13	6	0

Name	Team	From	To	M	Inns	NO	Runs	HS	Avg	100	50	Ct	St	Balls	Runs	Wkts	Avg	RPO	BB	5I	10M
Morkel, RKB	WPCU	1927/28	1930/31	5	6	1	51	16*	10.20	0	0	2	0	805	371	10	37.10	2.76	2-45	0	0
	All FC	1926/27	1939/40	16	24	4	310	57*	15.50	0	1	9	0	3011	1398	49	28.53	2.78	4-35	0	0
Morris, JD	WPCU	1961/62	1962/63	8	16	2	316	77	22.57	0	2	2	0	0	0	0	–	–	–	0	0
Morris, RET	WPCU	1967/68	1978/79	61	92	15	1950	135	25.32	2	10	44	0	9669	3602	117	30.78	2.23	5-44	3	0
Morris, SV	WPCU	1958/59	1959/60	4	6	0	59	27	9.83	0	0	0	0	0	0	0	–	–	–	0	0
Muller, N	WPCB	1987/88	1989/90	8	11	2	219	74	24.33	0	1	2	0	568	226	14	16.14	2.38	3-14	0	0
	All FC	1987/88	1989/90	12	17	2	281	74	18.73	0	1	5	0	898	376	17	22.11	2.51	3-14	0	0
Mullins, AK	WPCA B	1998/99	1998/99	1	1	0	0	0	0.00	0	0	0	0	192	66	5	13.20	2.06	3-23	0	0
Munnik, R	WPCA	1998/99	2002/03	17	27	1	689	87	26.50	0	4	14	0	1627	931	24	38.79	3.43	4-58	0	0
	WPCA B	1997/98	1998/99	8	14	0	397	138	28.35	1	2	4	0	1155	705	26	27.11	3.66	4-63	0	0
	WPCA Am	2004/05	2005/06	8	13	3	428	75	42.80	0	5	2	0	372	147	8	18.37	2.37	3-23	0	0
	WCC	2005/06	2005/06	1	1	0	0	0	0.00	0	0	0	1	42	24	1	24.00	3.42	1-24	0	0
	All FC	1997/98	2005/06	35	56	4	1522	138	29.26	1	11	21	1	3286	1845	61	30.24	3.36	4-58	0	0
Muntingh, E	WPCU	1981/82	1981/82	1	2	0	28	28	14.00	0	0	0	0	0	0	0	–	–	–	0	0
	WPCU B	1978/79	1981/82	9	17	0	412	69	24.23	0	2	11	0	30	10	0	–	2.00	–	0	0
	All FC	1978/79	1981/82	22	43	0	755	72	17.55	0	4	19	0	30	10	0	–	2.00	–	0	0
Murphy, BA	WPCA	1997/98	1997/98	5	7	2	80	41	16.00	0	0	4	0	611	392	8	49.00	3.84	2-38	0	0
	All FC	1995/96	2002/03	28	34	9	516	77	20.64	0	2	20	0	5124	2784	59	47.18	3.25	4-71	0	0
Musson, R	WPCB	1980/81	1989/90	18	32	4	738	108	26.35	1	4	9	1	0	0	0	–	–	–	0	0
	All FC	1978/79	1989/90	23	42	5	811	108	21.91	1	4	16	1	0	0	0	–	–	–	0	0
Muzzell, RK	WPCU	1964/65	1967/68	17	27	4	1026	161	44.60	3	5	10	0	1517	832	18	46.22	3.29	3-61	0	0
	All FC	1964/65	1977/78	75	128	12	4052	238*	34.93	7	18	49	0	3960	2028	61	33.24	3.07	6-69	1	0
Myles, HF	WPCU	1930/31	1930/31	2	4	0	54	35	13.50	0	0	0	0	0	0	0	–	–	–	0	0
	All FC	1930/31	1936/37	3	6	0	66	35	11.00	0	0	0	0	0	0	0	–	–	–	0	0
Napier, GL	WPCU	1929/30	1935/36	3	5	1	61	22	15.25	0	0	2	0	402	169	5	33.80	2.52	2-12	0	0
Neethling, JJ	WPCB	1971/72	1973/74	12	18	5	263	53	20.23	0	1	16	0	1336	460	17	27.05	2.06	5-51	1	0
	All FC	1971/72	1973/74	13	19	5	266	53	19.00	0	1	17	0	1536	518	19	27.26	2.02	5-51	1	0
Nel, JD	WPCU	1947/48	1960/61	28	50	5	1627	217*	36.15	4	6	13	0	0	0	0	–	–	–	0	0
	All FC	1947/48	1960/61	35	63	5	1839	217*	31.70	4	6	14	0	0	0	0	–	–	–	0	0
Nel, MJ	WPCU	1974/75	1981/82	16	30	1	653	86	22.51	0	3	8	0	0	0	0	–	–	–	0	0
	WPCU B	1975/76	1981/82	8	15	1	439	88	31.35	0	2	4	0	0	0	0	–	–	–	0	0
	All FC	1974/75	1981/82	25	47	2	1124	88	24.97	0	5	12	0	0	0	0	–	–	–	0	0
Newton-Thompson, JO	WPCU	1948/49	1948/49	1	2	0	82	78	41.00	0	1	0	0	0	0	0	–	–	–	0	0
	All FC	1946	1948/49	9	18	1	281	78	16.52	0	1	6	0	144	125	0	–	5.20	–	0	0
Nicholson, PS	WPCU	1952/53	1953/54	7	13	0	358	100	27.53	1	3	9	0	56	31	0	–	3.32	–	0	0

Name	Team	From	To	M	Inns	NO	Runs	HS	Avg	100	50	Ct	St	Balls	Runs	Wkts	Avg	RPO	BB	5I	10M
Nieuwoudt, AB	WPCU	1972/73	1978/79	27	28	12	150	23	9.37	0	0	10	0	4153	1739	77	22.58	2.51	6-25	3	1
	WPCU B	1978/79	1978/79	1	1	1	8	8*	–	0	0	2	0	132	44	2	22.00	2.00	1-15	0	0
	All FC	1972/73	1978/79	28	29	13	158	23	9.87	0	0	12	0	4285	1783	79	22.56	2.49	6-25	3	1
Nolte, JE	WPCU	1988/89	1989/90	3	2	2	4	2*	–	0	0	1	0	264	123	1	123.00	2.79	1-60	0	0
	WPCU B	1986/87	1989/90	8	8	2	112	39	18.66	0	0	1	0	1759	694	32	21.68	2.36	6-57	1	0
	All FC	1986/87	1989/90	13	12	4	140	39	17.50	0	0	2	0	2293	963	36	26.75	2.51	6-57	1	0
Norman, D	WPCU	1984/85	1985/86	10	13	3	66	16*	6.60	0	0	5	0	1245	562	27	20.81	2.70	5-38	1	0
	WPCU B	1983/84	1985/86	10	12	1	183	56	16.63	0	1	7	0	1650	881	42	20.97	3.20	6-56	3	0
	All FC	1983/84	1991/92	44	58	12	665	97	14.45	0	2	25	0	6444	3163	119	26.57	2.94	6-56	3	0
Northcote, AM	WPCA Am	2008/09	2008/09	2	4	1	55	30	18.33	0	0	2	0	0	0	0	–	–	–	0	0
Norton, NO	WPCU	1902/03	1902/03	1	2	1	0	0*	0.00	0	0	0	0	84	44	0	–	3.14	–	0	0
	All FC	1902/03	1913/14	15	26	3	342	57	14.86	0	2	7	0	1798	772	49	15.75	2.57	6-34	1	0
Nourse, AW	WPCU	1927/28	1935/36	24	37	5	1575	219*	49.21	5	5	15	0	684	247	7	35.28	2.16	2-11	0	0
	All FC	1896/97	1935/36	228	371	39	14216	304*	42.81	38	60	171	0	17587	7125	305	23.36	2.43	6-33	13	1
Nyulu, SC	WPCA Am	2004/05	2004/05	4	5	2	15	6	5.00	0	0	3	0	206	136	3	45.33	3.96	2-28	0	0
O'Connell, B	WPCB	1973/74	1975/76	8	13	3	308	79	30.80	0	2	7	0	40	28	1	28.00	4.20	1-1	0	0
Odendaal, A	WPCB	1985/86	1985/86	1	2	0	3	3	1.50	0	0	0	0	0	0	0	–	–	–	0	0
	All FC	1980	1985/86	26	45	4	778	61	18.97	0	1	23	0	72	30	0	–	2.50	–	0	0
O'Grady, JM	WPCU	1946/47	1946/47	1	2	0	1	1	0.50	0	0	3	0	32	16	0	–	3.00	–	0	0
O'Linn, S	WPCU	1945/46	1946/47	2	3	0	25	13	8.33	0	0	2	0	0	0	0	–	–	–	0	0
	All FC	1945/46	1965/66	92	156	29	4525	120*	35.62	4	29	97	6	256	119	2	59.50	2.78	2-14	0	0
Olivier, MW	WCC	2009/10	2009/10	1	2	2	17	13*	–	0	0	2	0	120	86	0	–	4.30	–	0	0
	WPCA Am	2009/10	2009/10	7	11	2	127	48	14.11	0	0	2	0	1081	757	21	36.04	4.20	6-97	1	0
Ontong, JL	WCC	2004/05	2010/11	54	81	14	713	51	10.64	0	1	11	0	7600	4939	152	32.49	3.89	10-65	7	2
	WPCA	2008/09	2010/11	25	37	2	1289	147	36.82	3	6	16	0	1190	601	23	26.13	3.03	3-20	0	0
	All FC	1997/98	2010/11	130	211	11	7547	166	37.73	16	44	99	0	9296	4950	118	41.94	3.19	5-62	1	0
Oosthuizen, RC	WPCA	1999/00	1999/00	1	2	0	0	0	0.00	0	0	4	0	0	0	0	–	–	–	0	0
	All FC	1991/92	1999/00	6	12	1	98	32*	8.90	0	0	13	2	0	0	0	–	–	–	0	0
Ovenstone, DM	WPCU	1946/47	1947/48	9	17	2	253	52	16.86	0	1	16	7	0	0	0	–	–	–	0	0
	All FC	1942/43	1947/48	20	32	2	437	52	14.56	0	1	40	15	0	0	0	–	–	–	0	0
Owen-Smith, HGO	WPCU	1927/28	1949/50	14	20	2	396	65*	22.00	0	3	17	0	2228	1184	52	22.76	3.18	6-60	4	2
	All FC	1927/28	1949/50	101	162	11	4059	168*	26.88	3	23	93	0	13445	7410	319	23.22	3.30	7-153	20	3
Paine, AI	WPCU	1896/97	1896/97	4	6	0	253	220	42.16	1	0	3	0	0	0	0	–	–	–	0	0
Paleker, A	WPCA B	1997/98	1997/98	2	4	0	101	46	25.25	0	0	2	0	66	41	0	–	3.72	–	0	0
	All FC	1997/98	2005/06	16	26	5	484	70*	23.04	0	1	17	1	66	41	0	–	3.72	–	0	0

Name	Team	From	To	M	Inns	NO	Runs	HS	Avg	100	50	Ct	St	Balls	Runs	Wkts	Avg	RPO	BB	5I	10M
Palm, AW	WPCU	1921/22	1933/34	37	65	10	1899	173	34.52	3	11	11	0	0	0	0	–	–	–	0	0
	All FC	1921/22	1933/34	40	71	10	1958	173	32.09	3	11	11	0	0	0	0	–	–	–	0	0
Pangarker, H	WPCA	1997/98	1999/00	7	13	0	170	53	13.07	0	1	12	0	0	0	0	–	–	–	0	0
	WPCA B	1991/92	1998/99	19	34	2	1201	144	37.53	4	4	2	0	0	0	0	–	–	–	0	0
	All FC	1991/92	1999/00	26	47	2	1371	144	30.46	4	5	19	0	0	0	0	–	–	–	0	0
Parker, AC	WPCU	1970/71	1970/71	5	8	1	144	47*	20.57	0	0	21	0	124	70	3	23.33	3.38	2-34	0	0
	WPCU B	1975/76	1975/76	1	2	0	9	5	4.50	0	0	2	0	0	0	0	–	–	–	0	0
	All FC	1970/71	1975/76	9	16	1	209	47*	13.93	0	0	3	0	142	90	5	18.00	3.80	2-20	0	0
Parker, DC	WPCU B	1976/77	1976/77	4	7	1	257	174*	42.83	1	1	3	0	0	0	0	–	–	–	0	0
Passmore, AG	WPCU B	1980/81	1980/81	2	2	0	82	73	41.00	0	1	2	0	131	73	3	24.33	3.34	2-44	0	0
Paterson, D	WPCA Am	2009/10	2010/11	17	21	2	81	15	4.26	0	0	7	0	2346	1233	71	17.36	3.15	6-66	3	0
	All FC	2009/10	2010/11	18	21	2	81	15	4.26	0	0	78	0	2450	1274	74	17.21	3.12	6-66	3	0
Pauling, NC	WPCU	1892/93	1892/93	2	4	0	6	3	1.50	0	0	1	0	0	0	0	–	–	–	0	0
Paull, GB	WPCU	1933/34	1939/40	5	8	0	124	31	15.50	0	0	1	0	654	332	14	23.71	3.04	6-61	1	0
Payne, DG	WPCU	1989/90	1989/90	1	1	1	0	0*	–	0	0	0	0	102	39	2	19.50	2.29	2-21	0	0
	WPCU B	1988/89	1990/91	10	9	6	49	11	16.33	0	0	2	0	1516	646	25	25.84	2.55	7-63	1	0
	WPCA	1991/92	1997/98	10	11	5	33	12*	5.50	0	0	2	0	2024	1069	38	28.13	3.16	4-50	0	0
	WPCA B	1991/92	1998/99	19	25	6	291	41*	15.31	0	1	3	0	3477	1519	70	21.70	2.62	5-20	2	0
	All FC	1988/89	1998/99	40	46	18	373	41*	13.32	0	1	7	0	7119	3273	135	24.24	2.75	7-63	3	0
Payne, IA	WPCU	1968/69	1974/75	4	7	1	66	20	11.00	0	0	2	0	0	0	0	–	–	–	0	0
	WPCU B	1975/76	1977/78	15	28	3	1086	132	43.44	2	6	15	0	0	0	0	–	–	–	0	0
	All FC	1968/69	1977/78	19	35	4	1152	132	37.16	2	6	17	0	0	0	0	–	–	–	0	0
Peters, AD	WPCU	1931/32	1931/32	5	6	2	84	35*	21.00	0	0	1	0	228	156	1	156.00	4.10	1-36	0	0
	All FC	1931/32	1936/37	7	10	2	121	35*	15.12	0	0	4	0	564	330	5	66.00	3.51	3-121	0	0
Petersen, B	WPCB	1971/72	1974/75	3	5	2	36	17	12.00	0	0	2	0	298	72	3	24.00	1.44	1-3	0	0
Petersen, G	WPCB	1983/84	1985/86	2	2	0	22	15	11.00	0	0	4	1	0	0	0	–	–	–	0	0
Peterson, RJ	WCC	2009/10	2010/11	10	12	1	323	100	29.36	1	2	2	0	1822	910	35	26.00	2.99	5-45	3	0
	All FC	1998/99	2010/11	116	179	22	3971	130	25.29	6	14	51	0	21452	10748	326	32.96	3.00	6-67	14	1
Pfaff, BD	WPCU	1952/53	1957/58	18	30	2	941	78	33.60	0	7	8	0	224	87	1	87.00	2.33	1-15	0	0
Pfaff, L	WPCU	1926/27	1926/27	1	2	0	6	5	3.00	0	0	0	0	0	0	0	–	–	–	0	0
Pfister, CA	WPCU	1928/29	1928/29	1	1	0	35	35	35.00	0	0	1	0	0	0	0	–	–	–	0	0
	All FC	1927/28	1928/29	2	2	1	52	35	52.00	0	0	1	1	192	74	2	37.00	2.31	2-12	0	0
Pfuhl, GP	WPCU	1967/68	1979/80	88	121	23	2204	117	22.48	1	9	253	32	0	0	0	–	–	–	0	0
	WPCU B	1976/77	1978/79	4	7	1	85	32*	14.16	0	0	16	1	0	0	0	–	–	–	0	0
	All FC	1967/68	1979/80	95	132	24	2331	117	21.58	1	9	280	34	0	0	0	–	–	–	0	0

Name	Team	From	To	M	Inns	NO	Runs	HS	Avg	100	50	Ct	St	Balls	Runs	Wkts	Avg	RPO	BB	5I	10M
Philander, VD	WPCA	2003/04	2003/04	1	2	0	18	18	9.00	0	0	2	0	78	22	2	11.00	1.69	2-18	0	0
	WPCA Am	2004/05	2009/10	5	9	1	530	168	66.25	2	2	1	0	992	354	28	12.64	2.14	5-16	1	0
	WCC	2004/05	2010/11	50	68	9	1392	83	23.59	0	4	11	0	8524	3664	183	20.02	2.57	7-64	7	0
	All FC	2003/04	2010/11	65	91	13	2153	168	27.60	2	6	17	0	10990	4673	235	19.88	2.55	7-64	8	0
Pickup, J	WPCU	1936/37	1937/38	6	9	3	79	22*	13.16	0	0	2	0	915	353	15	23.53	2.31	4-9	0	0
	All FC	1936/37	1939/40	8	13	5	136	33*	17.00	0	0	2	0	1011	386	15	25.73	2.29	4-9	0	0
Piedt, DL-R	WPCA Am	2009/10	2010/11	13	18	2	242	60*	15.12	0	1	10	0	1961	1122	54	20.77	3.43	5-38	3	1
	WPCU	2010/11	2010/11	2	2	1	21	16	21.00	0	0	1	0	587	301	11	27.36	3.07	7-92	1	0
	All FC	2009/10	2010/11	15	20	3	263	60*	15.47	0	1	11	0	2548	1423	65	21.89	3.35	7-92	4	1
Pienaar, RF	WPCU	1981/82	1984/85	33	52	5	1209	151*	25.72	2	5	15	0	2314	1124	31	36.25	2.91	5-24	1	0
	WPCU B	1981/82	1984/85	3	5	0	216	109	43.20	1	0	2	0	288	166	4	41.50	3.45	2-63	0	0
	All FC	1977/78	1998/99	199	346	27	10896	153	34.15	18	62	81	0	10388	5079	153	33.19	2.93	5-24	3	0
Pithey, AJ	WPCU	1955/56	1957/58	12	24	0	805	133	33.54	2	4	10	0	0	0	0	-	-	-	0	0
	All FC	1950/51	1968/69	124	213	16	7073	170	35.90	13	41	59	0	22	17	0	-	4.63	-	0	0
Pithey, DB	WPCU	1957/58	1957/58	1	2	1	8	8*	8.00	0	0	0	0	192	54	2	27.00	1.68	2-54	0	0
	All FC	1956/57	1967/68	99	160	13	3420	166	23.26	3	14	55	0	17618	7388	240	30.78	2.51	7-47	13	1
Plaatjies, FC	WPCA Am	2006/07	2008/09	3	4	2	32	21*	16.00	0	0	1	0	276	169	5	33.80	3.67	2-36	0	0
	WCC	2008/09	2009/10	9	9	4	10	4*	2.00	0	0	1	0	1282	764	29	26.34	3.57	4-21	0	0
	All FC	2006/07	2009/10	12	13	6	42	21*	6.00	0	0	2	0	1558	933	34	27.44	3.59	4-21	0	0
Place, DW	WPCU B	1975/76	1975/76	1	1	0	2	2	2.00	0	0	0	0	106	52	4	13.00	2.94	3-19	0	0
Plantema, AP	WPCU B	1987/88	1989/90	11	19	2	428	69	25.17	0	2	22	3	0	0	0	-	-	-	0	0
	WPCA	1992/93	1992/93	1	2	0	26	17	13.00	0	0	1	0	0	0	0	-	-	-	0	0
	All FC	1987/88	1992/93	13	23	2	476	69	22.66	0	2	23	3	0	0	0	-	-	-	0	0
Player, BT	WPCA	1997/98	1998/99	8	13	2	222	53*	20.18	0	1	3	0	1871	824	20	41.20	2.64	4-96	0	0
	WPCA B	1997/98	1998/99	7	12	2	454	105	45.40	2	3	4	0	921	366	26	14.07	2.38	5-28	1	0
	All FC	1984/85	2000/01	93	141	26	2417	133*	21.01	4	6	47	0	14318	6536	212	30.83	2.73	6-43	4	0
Plimsoll, JB	WPCU	1939/40	1947/48	18	25	6	201	51	10.57	0	1	5	0	5791	1804	84	21.47	1.86	7-35	5	1
	All FC	1939/40	1949/50	39	47	13	386	51	11.35	0	1	9	0	10767	3581	155	23.10	1.99	7-35	9	3
Pothecary, JE	WPCU	1954/55	1964/65	33	53	7	762	81*	16.56	0	2	24	0	6532	2489	90	27.65	2.28	5-29	2	0
	All FC	1954/55	1964/65	54	77	11	1039	81*	15.74	0	2	42	0	10329	4054	143	28.34	2.35	5-29	2	0
Price, D	WPCU	1933/34	1939/40	14	22	7	204	28*	13.60	0	0	9	0	3340	1785	48	37.18	3.20	5-124	1	0
Price, H	WPCB	1982/83	1982/83	1	2	0	2	2	1.00	0	0	0	0	0	0	0	-	-	-	0	0
Prince, AG	WPCA	1997/98	2003/04	38	62	10	2498	143	48.03	6	15	26	0	6	3	0	-	3.00	-	0	0
	WCC	2004/05	2007/08	14	25	2	865	184	37.60	1	7	7	0	54	33	0	-	3.66	-	0	0
	All FC	1995/96	2010/11	198	317	44	12034	254	44.08	31	55	136	0	276	166	4	41.50	3.60	2-11	0	0

Name	Team	From	To	M	Inns	NO	Runs	HS	Avg	100	50	Ct	St	Balls	Runs	Wkts	Avg	RPO	BB	5I	10M
Prince, CFH	WPCU	1894/95	1904/05	8	11	0	168	55	15.27	0	1	4	4	0	0	0	–	–	–	0	0
	All FC	1894/95	1904/05	24	41	0	730	61	17.80	0	4	14	13	20	28	0	–	8.40	–	0	0
Pringle, MW	WPCU	1989/90	1990/91	15	20	4	235	27*	14.68	0	0	1	0	2633	1243	47	26.44	2.83	7-60	1	1
	WPCU B	1990/91	1990/91	1	2	0	20	12	10.00	0	0	0	0	281	125	6	20.83	2.66	4-44	0	0
	WPCA	1991/92	1996/97	39	43	7	603	60*	16.75	0	3	15	0	8610	3737	175	21.35	2.60	6-32	11	1
	All FC	1985/86	2000/01	119	152	26	2189	105	17.37	1	7	42	0	23557	10876	429	25.35	2.77	7-60	15	3
Pritchard, JA	WPCU	1902/03	1903/04	5	9	0	204	53	22.66	0	1	2	1	24	19	1	52.00	4.75	1-21	0	0
	All FC	1902/03	1906/07	10	19	0	332	55	17.47	0	2	3	1	60	52	5	52.00	5.20	1-21	0	0
Procter, AC	WPCU B	1979/80	1979/80	2	4	0	32	17	8.00	0	0	0	0	0	0	0	–	–	–	0	0
	All FC	1979/80	1980/81	5	10	2	147	36	18.37	0	0	0	0	252	99	5	19.80	2.35	2-11	0	0
Procter, MJ	WPCU	1969/70	1969/70	5	8	0	323	155	40.37	2	0	2	0	926	364	19	19.15	2.35	4-18	0	0
Puttick, AG	All FC	1965	1988/89	401	667	58	21936	254	36.01	48	109	325	0	65458	27679	1417	19.53	2.53	9-71	70	15
	WPCA	2000/01	2003/04	26	45	6	1919	250*	49.20	5	7	36	1	0	0	0	–	–	–	0	0
	WCC	2004/05	2010/11	69	124	9	4571	206	39.74	10	21	82	1	0	0	0	–	–	–	0	0
	All FC	2000/01	2010/11	108	191	18	7392	250*	42.72	17	33	133	2	0	0	0	–	–	–	0	0
Pycroft, AJ	WPCU B	1975/76	1978/79	8	14	0	361	99	25.78	0	2	2	0	78	47	0	–	3.61	–	0	0
	All FC	1975/76	1992/93	72	129	14	4374	133	38.03	5	31	63	0	87	52	1	52.00	3.58	1-0	0	0
Rabie, GR	WPCA Am	2008/09	2010/11	15	12	11	72	27*	72.00	0	0	1	0	2398	1101	38	28.97	2.75	6-48	3	0
	WCC	2008/09	2008/09	3	5	2	12	8	4.00	0	0	0	0	489	210	4	52.50	2.57	3-57	0	0
	All FC	2008/09	2010/11	24	26	15	106	27*	9.63	0	0	5	0	3968	1851	61	30.34	2.79	6-48	3	0
Rail, RA	WPCU	1913/14	1913/14	1	2	0	13	8	6.50	0	0	0	0	0	0	0	–	–	–	0	0
Ralph, ARM	WPCU	1931/32	1945/46	33	53	11	2303	142	54.83	6	15	26	3	14	5	0	–	2.14	–	0	0
	All FC	1931/32	1946/47	34	55	11	2375	142	53.97	6	16	26	3	14	5	0	–	2.14	–	0	0
Ramela, OA	WCC	2009/10	2010/11	3	6	0	172	87	28.66	0	1	2	0	0	0	0	–	–	–	0	0
Ramoo, RJ	All FC	2007/08	2010/11	35	65	4	1565	104	25.65	1	8	30	0	138	89	0	–	3.86	–	0	0
	WPCA Am	2008/09	2009/10	13	23	3	628	93	31.40	0	3	5	0	60	34	0	–	3.40	–	0	0
	All FC	2008/09	2010/11	18	31	4	804	93	29.77	0	4	13	0	102	47	0	–	2.76	–	0	0
Rasmus, M	WPCB	1988/89	1988/89	3	4	0	74	31	18.50	0	0	2	0	0	0	0	–	–	–	0	0
Ravens, C	WPCB	1985/86	1985/86	2	4	2	31	30	15.50	0	0	0	0	96	31	2	15.50	1.93	2-17	0	0
Rayment, PA	WPCU B	1984/85	1990/91	8	12	4	70	26*	8.75	0	0	4	0	1562	509	24	21.20	1.95	3-33	0	0
	All FC	1984/85	1993/94	49	70	15	749	66	13.61	0	1	28	0	8386	3628	125	29.02	2.59	6-25	4	0
Rayner, PH	WPCU	1982/83	1985/86	25	43	5	1066	121*	28.05	1	5	19	0	0	0	0	–	–	–	0	0
	WPCU B	1981/82	1982/83	7	12	1	345	162	31.36	1	1	1	0	0	0	0	–	–	–	0	0
	All FC	1981/82	1988/89	57	101	10	2570	162	28.24	3	12	39	0	24	12	0	–	3.00	–	0	0

Name	Team	From	To	M	Inns	NO	Runs	HS	Avg	100	50	Ct	St	Balls	Runs	Wkts	Avg	RPO	BB	5I	10M
Reddick, TB	WPCU	1950/51	1950/51	4	5	0	159	56	31.80	0	1	2	0	56	23	0	–	2.46	–	0	0
Rees, DW	All FC	1931	1950/51	62	99	11	2688	139	30.54	2	16	16	0	782	468	6	78.00	3.59	1-4	0	0
Reid, A	WPCU	1949/50	1949/50	1	2	0	50	32	25.00	0	0	0	0	0	0	0	–	–	–	0	0
	All FC	1949/50	1952/53	17	32	1	773	105	24.93	1	3	12	0	8	6	0	–	4.50	–	0	0
Reid, ABJ	WPCU	1896/97	1908/09	20	33	3	476	101*	15.86	1	1	5	0	0	0	0	–	–	–	0	0
	All FC	1896/97	1908/09	32	54	4	894	101*	17.88	1	2	13	0	0	0	0	–	–	–	0	0
Reid, ABJ	WPCU	1939/40	1950/51	15	19	6	293	81	22.53	0	1	23	15	0	0	0	–	–	–	0	0
	All FC	1939/40	1950/51	16	21	6	327	81	21.80	0	1	24	15	0	0	0	–	–	–	0	0
Reid, F	WPCU	1910/11	1923/24	6	11	1	242	43	24.20	0	0	2	0	0	0	0	–	–	–	0	0
Reid, N	WPCU	1920/21	1923/24	12	21	5	378	81*	23.62	0	1	6	0	815	400	18	22.22	2.94	4-52	0	0
	All FC	1920/21	1923/24	13	23	5	395	81*	21.94	0	1	6	0	941	463	20	23.15	2.95	4-52	0	0
Reid-Ross, LJ	WPCU	1975/76	1975/76	1	2	0	14	14	7.00	0	0	0	0	18	2	0	–	0.66	–	0	0
	All FC	1975/76	1983/84	10	15	3	91	34	7.58	0	0	3	0	1248	580	19	30.52	2.78	6-78	1	0
Richards, AR	WPCU	1889/90	1895/96	8	13	0	340	108	26.15	1	1	13	2	0	0	0	–	–	–	0	0
	All FC	1889/90	1895/96	9	15	0	346	108	23.06	1	1	13	2	0	0	0	–	–	–	0	0
Richards, J	WPCU	1889/90	1889/90	2	4	0	12	9	3.00	0	0	1	0	0	0	0	–	–	–	0	0
Richards, RR	WPCA Am	2009/10	2010/11	14	16	8	136	45*	17.00	0	0	6	0	1980	835	50	16.70	2.53	5-26	1	0
	All FC	2005/06	2010/11	21	23	10	155	45*	11.92	0	0	7	0	3104	1397	74	18.87	2.70	5-26	3	0
Richards, T	WPCB	1979/80	1979/80	3	5	0	34	19	6.80	0	0	2	0	16	24	0	–	9.00	–	0	0
Richardson, MHH	WPCU	1958/59	1960/61	12	19	0	455	132	23.94	1	2	11	0	102	46	3	15.33	2.70	3-23	0	0
Richardson, RP	WPCU	1984/85	1984/85	1	1	1	3	3*	–	0	0	2	0	786	403	7	57.57	3.07	2-69	0	0
	WPCU B	1984/85	1988/89	7	13	1	154	52*	12.83	0	1	5	0	1038	521	10	52.10	3.01	3-23	0	0
	All FC	1984/85	1988/89	10	17	4	181	52*	13.92	0	1	7	0	354	117	4	29.25	1.98	2-61	0	0
Roberts, LL	WPCB	1985/86	1985/86	2	3	0	17	7	5.66	0	0	0	0	1252	581	21	27.66	2.78	5-39	1	0
	All FC	1980/81	1985/86	12	19	1	331	54	18.38	0	2	4	0	0	0	0	–	–	–	0	0
Roberts, TM	WPCU B	1986/87	1986/87	1	2	0	24	23	12.00	0	0	5	1	0	0	0	–	–	–	0	0
	All FC	1976/77	1986/87	4	6	1	140	50*	28.00	0	1	11	1	4	2	1	2.00	3.00	1-2	0	0
Robertson, JB	WPCU	1931/32	1936/37	20	26	6	399	45*	19.95	0	0	10	0	2720	1252	59	21.22	2.76	8-96	6	0
	All FC	1931/32	1936/37	23	32	7	450	45*	18.00	0	0	12	0	3458	1573	65	24.20	2.72	8-96	6	0
Robertson, T	WPCA B	1995/96	1995/96	4	6	1	71	32	14.20	0	0	7	0	0	0	0	–	–	–	0	0
Rookledge, QJ	WPCU	1971/72	1971/72	3	5	0	94	80	18.80	0	1	2	0	0	0	0	–	–	–	0	0
Roos, AC	WPCU	1970/71	1970/71	1	2	0	14	11	7.00	0	0	0	0	0	0	0	–	–	–	0	0
Roscoe, BM-K	WPCU	1937/38	1938/39	7	12	1	170	51	15.45	0	1	0	0	1675	797	28	28.46	2.85	6-75	1	0
Ross, CK	WPCU B	1975/76	1975/76	2	3	0	51	20	17.00	0	0	0	0	6	1	0	–	1.00	–	0	0
Ross, WC	WPCU	1934/35	1939/40	3	6	1	73	31	14.60	0	0	0	0	314	176	5	35.20	3.36	4-27	0	0

Name	Team	From	To	M	Inns	NO	Runs	HS	Avg	100	50	Ct	St	Balls	Runs	Wkts	Avg	RPO	BB	5I	10M
Routledge, TW	WPCU	1889/90	1889/90	1	2	0	33	33	16.50	0	0	0	0	0	0	0	–	–	–	0	0
	All FC	1889/90	1896/97	12	24	1	492	77	21.39	0	2	5	0	105	69	3	23.00	3.94	2-26	0	0
Rowe, GA	WPCU	1893/94	1906/07	15	24	8	89	11*	5.56	0	0	8	0	3357	1322	82	16.12	2.36	8-25	6	3
	All FC	1893/94	1906/07	36	62	19	303	21*	7.04	0	0	22	0	8089	3592	170	21.12	2.66	8-25	13	5
Roy, HNP	WPCU	1952/53	1956/57	14	24	1	658	146	28.60	1	2	8	0	1224	469	11	42.63	2.29	2-9	0	0
Rundle, DB	WPCU	1987/88	1990/91	34	45	15	590	48*	19.66	0	0	23	0	7116	2840	99	28.68	2.39	6-37	4	1
	WPCU B	1984/85	1986/87	12	22	0	585	110	26.59	1	1	7	0	1201	438	20	21.90	2.18	4-37	0	0
	WPCA	1991/92	1996/97	35	52	10	932	81*	22.19	0	5	30	0	8617	3737	99	37.74	2.60	6-51	5	1
	WPCA B	1991/92	1996/97	9	12	3	324	103	36.00	1	1	12	0	1611	616	24	25.66	2.29	3-26	0	0
	All FC	1984/85	1996/97	96	141	30	2597	110	23.39	2	7	76	0	19415	8025	250	32.10	2.48	6-37	9	2
Rush, EDB	WPCU	1924/25	1924/25	1	2	0	24	19	12.00	0	0	0	0	78	43	0	–	3.30	–	0	0
	All FC	1924/25	1924/25	3	6	0	76	38	12.66	0	0	1	0	192	120	2	60.00	3.75	1-7	0	0
Rush, WRG	WPCU	1923/24	1923/24	4	8	0	155	79	19.37	0	1	0	0	628	370	14	26.42	3.53	5-53	2	0
	All FC	1923/24	1928/29	9	15	0	273	79	18.20	0	2	2	0	1125	629	21	29.95	3.35	5-53	2	0
Rushmere, CG	WPCU	1957/58	1960/61	2	4	0	34	18	8.50	0	0	0	0	176	48	2	24.00	1.63	2-4	0	0
	All FC	1956/57	1965/66	33	58	4	1245	153	23.05	2	4	19	0	1686	576	20	28.80	2.04	4-29	0	0
Rushmere, JW	WPCU	1960/61	1962/63	8	12	2	228	49	22.80	0	0	3	0	1170	594	16	37.12	3.04	4-87	0	0
	All FC	1960/61	1962/63	10	15	2	231	49	17.76	0	0	5	0	1456	712	25	28.48	2.93	6-32	1	0
Ryall, RJ	WPCU	1980/81	1990/91	80	94	33	742	42	12.16	0	0	246	18	0	0	0	–	–	–	0	0
	WPCU B	1981/82	1982/83	6	9	2	158	51	22.57	0	1	18	5	0	0	0	–	–	–	0	0
	WPCA	1991/92	1994/95	34	44	13	648	58	20.90	0	1	111	13	0	0	0	–	–	–	0	0
	WPCA B	1993/94	1993/94	2	1	0	61	61	61.00	0	1	7	2	0	0	0	–	–	–	0	0
	All FC	1980/81	1994/95	123	149	49	1613	61	16.13	0	3	384	38	0	0	0	–	–	–	0	0
Ryan, LJ	WPCU B	1988/89	1990/91	8	9	0	57	16	6.33	0	0	2	0	1573	704	25	28.16	2.68	5-79	1	0
	WPCA B	1991/92	1991/92	1	0	0	0	–	–	0	0	2	0	108	91	2	45.50	5.05	2-45	0	0
	All FC	1988/89	1991/92	9	9	0	57	16	6.33	0	0	4	0	1681	795	27	29.44	2.83	5-79	1	0
Salie, R	WPCB	1977/78	1978/79	5	10	0	107	31	10.70	0	0	2	0	0	0	0	–	–	–	0	0
	All FC	1977/78	1978/79	5	10	0	107	31	10.70	0	0	2	0	0	0	0	–	–	–	0	0
Samsodien, W	WPCA Am	2004/05	2004/05	1	2	0	7	6	3.50	0	0	0	0	102	70	1	70.00	4.11	1-54	0	0
Sandri, PSE	WCC	2006/07	2008/09	8	12	6	53	14*	8.83	0	0	0	0	720	430	13	33.07	3.58	4-31	0	0
	All FC	2003/04	2009	29	41	20	217	26*	10.33	0	0	4	0	3834	2126	72	29.52	3.32	5-32	1	0
Schultz, BN	WPCA	1996/97	1997/98	10	10	3	45	13	6.42	0	0	0	0	2047	1087	46	23.63	3.18	8-36	4	0
	WPCA B	1996/97	1996/97	1	1	0	3	3	3.00	0	0	0	0	258	108	4	27.00	2.51	3-43	0	0
	All FC	1989/90	1997/98	60	57	16	309	36*	7.53	0	0	10	0	12062	5687	233	24.40	2.82	8-36	12	0

Name	Team	From	To	M	Inns	NO	Runs	HS	Avg	100	50	Ct	St	Balls	Runs	Wkts	Avg	RPO	BB	5I	10M
Seccull, AW	WPCU	1893/94	1893/94	1	1	0	43	43	43.00	0	0	1	0	110	48	6	8.00	2.61	6-48	1	0
	All FC	1889/90	1896/97	7	12	2	229	64	22.90	0	2	4	0	471	253	15	16.86	3.22	6-48	1	0
Seconds, T	WPCB	1988/89	1990/91	3	2	2	12	6*	-	0	0	3	0	414	143	13	11.00	2.07	6-47	1	0
Seeff, J	WPCU B	1980/81	1984/85	18	31	3	918	113*	32.78	1	4	13	0	0	0	0	-	-	-	0	0
Seeff, L	WPCU	1978/79	1990/91	94	175	15	5160	141	32.25	7	29	72	0	122	74	1	74.00	3.63	1-22	0	0
	WPCU B	1977/78	1985/86	7	14	2	616	156	51.33	3	2	7	0	144	74	4	18.50	3.08	1-6	0	0
	WPCA	1991/92	1991/92	1	2	1	90	54	30.00	0	1	2	0	0	0	0	-	-	-	0	0
	All FC	1977/78	1992/93	113	210	20	6558	188	34.51	11	36	90	0	266	148	5	29.60	3.33	1-6	0	0
September, M	WPCB	1972/73	1972/73	1	1	0	0	0	0.00	0	0	3	0	80	33	1	33.00	2.47	1-15	0	0
Serrurier, LR	WPCU	1927/28	1929/30	10	16	2	739	171	52.78	2	4	2	0	282	86	1	86.00	1.82	1-30	0	0
	All FC	1925	1931/32	30	46	8	1281	171	33.71	3	7	17	0	2439	1127	42	26.83	2.77	5-103	1	0
Sewell, BW	WPCU	1945/46	1945/46	1	2	0	34	34	17.00	0	0	1	0	0	0	0	-	-	-	0	0
Seymour, MA	WPCU	1960/61	1969/70	19	24	3	301	33	14.33	0	0	11	0	3664	1460	54	27.03	2.39	5-44	3	0
	All FC	1960/61	1969/70	38	48	8	569	62	14.22	0	1	16	0	8258	3277	111	29.52	2.38	7-80	7	1
Seymour, RA	WPCU	1975/76	1975/76	1	2	1	38	32*	38.00	0	0	0	0	102	54	2	27.00	3.17	2-45	0	0
	WPCU B	1975/76	1975/76	4	7	0	134	48	19.14	0	0	0	0	638	247	14	17.64	2.32	4-57	0	0
	All FC	1975/76	1978/79	10	19	1	322	48	17.88	0	0	4	0	1268	601	22	27.31	2.84	4-57	0	0
Shah, OA	WCC	2010/11	2010/11	5	7	1	366	151	61.00	1	2	2	0	0	0	0	-	-	-	0	0
	All FC	1996	2010/11	227	386	35	14887	203	42.41	40	74	172	0	2237	1489	26	57.26	3.99	3-33	0	0
Short, WH	WPCU	1905/06	1913/14	12	19	5	154	26	11.00	0	0	5	0	1265	698	24	29.08	3.31	5-22	2	0
Siedle, JR	WPCU	1955/56	1956/57	5	10	0	259	127	25.90	1	1	2	0	0	0	0	-	-	-	0	0
	All FC	1955/56	1957/58	7	13	0	351	127	27.00	1	2	3	0	0	0	0	-	-	-	0	0
Sierra, JP	WPCU	1947/48	1947/48	1	2	0	62	60	31.00	0	1	0	0	8	7	0	-	5.25	-	0	0
	All FC	1947/48	1950/51	6	11	0	216	62	19.63	0	2	4	0	223	131	9	14.55	3.52	4-41	0	0
Simetu, S	WPCA Am	2009/10	2010/11	3	4	0	34	15	8.50	0	0	0	0	5672	2628	101	26.01	2.78	5-52	1	0
Simons, EO	WPCU	1983/84	1990/91	35	49	8	938	83	22.87	0	4	22	0	3003	1355	45	30.11	2.70	5-61	1	0
	WPCU B	1982/83	1989/90	17	28	7	579	95	27.57	0	3	10	0	8638	3241	113	28.68	2.25	5-14	5	1
	WPCA	1991/92	1998/99	53	85	15	2264	157*	32.34	2	16	37	0	20363	8511	330	25.79	2.50	6-26	9	1
	All FC	1982/83	1998/99	123	193	40	4264	157*	27.86	2	25	81	0	0	0	0	-	-	-	0	0
Simpson, AR	WPCA Am	2004/05	2004/05	3	5	0	100	48	20.00	0	0	1	0	1709	885	51	17.35	3.10	6-58	4	0
Simpson, LF	WPCA Am	2005/06	2008/09	16	19	4	61	13	4.06	0	0	4	0	0	0	0	-	-	-	0	0
Simpson, R	WPCB	1973/74	1973/74	2	4	0	76	43	19.00	0	0	4	0	1998	952	36	26.44	2.85	6-67	1	0
Smith, F	WPCU	1912/13	1921/22	11	16	5	84	24	7.63	0	0	33	0	138	95	1	95.00	4.13	1-21	0	0
Smith, GC	WCC	2000/01	2003/04	17	29	1	1312	183	46.85	4	6	5	0	60	41	0	-	4.10	-	0	0
	WCC	2004/05	2010/11	4	7	0	486	217	68.85	2	0	5	0	0	0	0	-	-	-	0	0
	All FC	1999/00	2010/11	129	223	14	10644	311	50.92	31	39	174	0	1714	1079	11	98.09	3.77	2-145	0	0

Name	Team	From	To	M	Inns	NO	Runs	HS	Avg	100	50	Ct	St	Balls	Runs	Wkts	Avg	RPO	BB	5I	10M
Smith, V	WPCB	1977/78	1979/80	4	8	0	46	14	5.75	0	0	1	0	0	0	0	–	–	–	0	0
Snooke, SD	WPCU	1904/05	1910/11	20	35	1	601	74	17.67	0	3	21	0	516	224	19	11.78	2.60	7-29	1	1
	All FC	1904/05	1920/21	32	53	5	798	74	16.62	0	4	31	0	516	224	19	11.78	2.60	7-29	1	1
Snooke, SJ	WPCU	1903/04	1907/08	11	19	0	672	152	37.33	2	3	10	0	1051	559	21	26.61	3.19	5-105	1	0
	All FC	1897/98	1923/24	124	202	16	4821	187	25.91	7	24	82	0	6179	3017	120	25.14	2.92	8-70	3	1
Snyman, NM	WPCU B	1982/83	1982/83	2	3	0	61	37	20.33	0	0	3	0	0	0	0	–	–	–	0	0
	All FC	1982/83	1992/93	27	52	1	1612	137	31.60	3	8	23	0	192	101	0	–	3.15	–	0	0
Snyman, OJA	WPCU	1972/73	1972/73	7	12	1	364	133*	33.09	1	2	5	0	157	74	3	24.66	2.82	2-35	0	0
	WPCU B	1975/76	1976/77	3	5	0	110	39	22.00	0	0	0	0	162	46	1	46.00	1.70	1-20	0	0
	All FC	1972/73	1977/78	13	23	1	546	133*	24.81	1	2	7	0	331	123	4	30.75	2.22	2-35	0	0
Sodumo, AM	WPCA Am	2007/08	2008/09	6	10	1	111	56*	12.33	0	1	11	1	0	0	0	–	–	–	0	0
	All FC	2002/03	2010/11	55	88	13	1709	77*	22.78	0	10	164	20	0	0	0	–	–	–	0	0
Solomon, IR	WPCU B	1989/90	1989/90	1	2	0	7	6	3.50	0	0	1	0	224	102	7	14.57	2.73	5-56	1	0
	WPCA B	1995/96	1995/96	4	3	1	35	21*	17.50	0	0	3	0	727	277	6	46.16	2.28	3-53	0	0
	All FC	1989/90	1995/96	5	5	1	42	21*	10.50	0	0	4	0	951	379	13	29.15	2.39	5-56	1	0
Solomons, F	WPCB	1977/78	1984/85	21	34	1	578	68	17.51	0	3	10	0	15	9	0	–	3.60	–	0	0
Solomons, MT	WPCA	1996/97	1998/99	2	3	0	32	28	10.66	0	0	6	0	0	0	0	–	–	–	0	0
	WPCA B	1995/96	1997/98	14	20	4	376	67	23.50	0	2	37	7	0	0	0	–	–	–	0	0
	All FC	1995/96	1998/99	16	23	4	408	67	21.47	0	2	43	7	0	0	0	–	–	–	0	0
Sonn, A	WPCB	1972/73	1978/79	10	14	2	148	28	12.33	0	0	4	0	1524	407	21	19.38	1.60	4-57	0	0
	All FC	1972/73	1978/79	11	15	2	148	28	11.38	0	0	4	0	1604	436	21	20.76	1.63	4-57	0	0
Spencer-Young, R	WPCU	1962/63	1963/64	8	16	0	424	94	26.50	0	4	11	0	12	0	0	–	0.00	–	0	0
	All FC	1962/63	1967/68	10	19	0	502	94	26.42	0	5	13	0	12	0	0	–	0.00	–	0	0
Spilhaus, CF	WPCU B	1990/91	1990/91	4	5	1	13	8	3.25	0	0	15	1	0	0	0	–	–	–	0	0
	WPCA B	1991/92	1991/92	5	7	3	84	25*	21.00	0	0	14	2	0	0	0	–	–	–	0	0
	All FC	1985/86	1995/96	42	66	10	806	82	14.39	0	3	105	12	0	0	0	–	–	–	0	0
Steensma, S	WPCU	1925/26	1932/33	5	7	2	47	14	9.40	0	0	4	3	0	0	0	–	–	–	0	0
Stelling, WF	WPCA	1991/92	1991/92	1	2	0	20	15	10.00	0	0	0	0	132	47	2	23.50	2.13	2-22	0	0
	WPCA B	1991/92	1993/94	2	2	0	66	53	33.00	0	1	1	0	300	150	5	30.00	3.00	3-52	0	0
	All FC	1991/92	2006/07	19	29	2	508	53	18.81	0	1	8	0	2419	1068	33	32.36	2.64	5-49	1	0
Stephen, GW	WPCU	1904/05	1910/11	4	6	0	19	8	3.16	0	0	7	0	0	0	0	–	–	–	0	0
Stephen, WM	WPCU	1922/23	1926/27	9	14	1	97	18*	7.46	0	0	3	0	958	472	24	19.66	2.95	4-42	0	0
Stephens, CG	WPCU	1968/69	1971/72	21	33	6	1308	165	48.44	4	6	21	0	18	2	0	–	0.66	–	0	0
	All FC	1968/69	1977/78	38	63	11	2273	165	43.71	7	7	41	0	18	2	0	–	0.66	–	0	0
Stephenson, EH	WPCU	1903/04	1903/04	1	2	0	13	9	6.50	0	0	0	0	12	12	0	–	6.00	–	0	0

Name	Team	From	To	M	Inns	NO	Runs	HS	Avg	100	50	Ct	St	Balls	Runs	Wkts	Avg	RPO	BB	5I	10M
Stewart, JH	WPCU	1902/03	1904/05	6	10	0	180	61	18.00	0	1	5	0	0	0	0	–	–	–	0	0
Steyn, GE	WPCU	1957/58	1957/58	5	8	1	42	10*	6.00	0	0	0	0	1181	373	23	16.21	1.89	7-32	2	0
Steyn, RS	All FC	1957/58	1963/64	24	38	9	529	57	18.24	0	1	1	0	4653	1814	92	19.71	2.33	7-32	6	0
Steyn, RS	WPCU	1965/66	1966/67	10	15	0	216	49	14.40	0	0	15	0	1386	687	23	29.86	2.97	6-68	1	0
Steyn, RS	All FC	1963/64	1968/69	20	30	7	451	58*	19.60	0	1	6	0	2984	1273	46	27.67	2.55	6-40	3	0
Steyn, SSL	WPCU	1924/25	1937/38	30	51	2	1348	261*	27.51	3	2	11	0	108	94	1	94.00	5.22	1-12	0	0
Steyn, SSL	All FC	1924/25	1937/38	36	61	5	1514	261*	27.03	3	2	12	0	116	102	1	102.00	5.27	1-12	0	0
Steytler, ES	WPCU	1889/90	1892/93	4	7	0	43	15	6.14	0	0	16	0	0	0	0	–	–	–	0	0
Stoke, R	WPCU	1930/31	1930/31	1	1	0	0	0	0.00	0	0	0	0	126	89	4	22.25	4.23	3-58	0	0
Stonier, MP	WPCU B	1988/89	1990/91	6	10	1	169	34*	18.77	0	0	3	0	0	0	0	–	–	–	0	0
Stonier, MP	All FC	1988/89	1994/95	30	52	3	1520	121	31.02	2	8	20	0	0	0	0	–	–	–	0	0
Strydom, JG	WCC	2004/05	2007/08	16	26	1	733	82	29.32	0	7	10	0	0	0	0	–	–	–	0	0
Strydom, JG	All FC	2000/01	2010/11	78	146	7	4549	151	32.72	9	29	61	0	96	49	0	–	3.06	–	0	0
Swan, WC	WCC	2006/07	2006/07	2	2	0	92	57	46.00	0	1	1	0	0	0	0	–	–	–	0	0
Swart, PD	All FC	2003/04	2008/09	28	48	4	1398	122*	31.77	1	12	15	0	306	196	3	65.33	3.84	1-0	0	0
Swart, PD	WPCU	1967/68	1980/81	94	146	17	2983	109	23.12	2	17	49	0	14710	6070	246	24.67	2.47	6-85	5	1
Swart, PD	WPCU B	1983/84	1984/85	9	17	2	441	81	29.40	0	3	12	0	768	295	12	24.58	2.30	3-34	0	0
Swart, PD	All FC	1965/66	1984/85	167	267	29	6093	122	25.60	6	33	114	0	21880	9365	370	25.31	2.56	6-85	5	1
Taliep, MS	WPCA B	1998/99	1998/99	2	3	0	81	44	27.00	0	0	1	0	0	0	0	–	–	–	0	0
Taljaard, M	WPCU B	1979/80	1981/82	7	9	3	81	36	13.50	0	0	5	0	1314	482	25	19.28	2.20	5-18	1	0
Tasker, GJH	WPCU	1953/54	1953/54	1	2	1	27	21*	27.00	0	0	1	0	216	93	3	31.00	2.58	2-29	0	0
Tattersall, K	WPCU	1965/66	1969/70	16	26	2	718	112	29.91	1	2	20	0	132	88	0	–	4.00	–	0	0
Tattersall, K	All FC	1965/66	1976/77	33	58	2	1275	112	22.76	1	3	39	0	174	101	1	101.00	3.48	1-0	0	0
Taylor, GP	WPCU	1912/13	1920/21	4	7	2	73	23	14.60	0	0	1	0	144	100	5	20.00	4.16	2-33	0	0
Taylor, HW	WPCU	1935/36	1935/36	1	2	0	47	25	23.50	0	0	0	0	0	0	0	–	–	–	0	0
Taylor, HW	All FC	1909/10	1935/36	206	339	26	13105	250*	41.86	30	64	75	0	1185	560	22	25.45	2.83	4-36	0	0
Taylor, WL	WPCU	1958/59	1961/62	8	15	0	211	61	14.06	0	2	5	0	0	0	0	–	–	–	0	0
Telemachus, R	WPCA	1999/00	2003/04	24	26	2	263	46	10.95	0	0	3	0	4158	2090	77	27.14	3.01	6-54	1	0
Telemachus, R	All FC	1994/95	2006/07	78	105	23	1308	116	15.95	1	2	20	0	12224	6416	228	28.14	3.14	6-21	7	0
Telo, FD	WPCA Am	2005/06	2010/11	23	38	4	1258	134*	37.00	3	5	14	0	17	12	0	–	4.23	–	0	0
Telo, FD	WCC	2005/06	2007/08	6	10	0	268	104	26.80	1	0	0	0	0	0	0	–	–	–	0	0
Telo, FD	All FC	2005/06	2010/11	37	63	4	1798	134*	30.47	4	7	17	0	47	48	1	48.00	6.12	1-36	0	0
Temoor, A-A	WPCA Am	2007/08	2009/10	16	23	1	313	57	14.22	0	1	10	0	2756	1702	47	36.21	3.70	5-31	1	0
Theron, M	WPCB	1980/81	1983/84	8	13	1	61	20	5.08	0	0	4	0	1234	381	28	13.60	1.85	4-35	0	0

Name	Team	From	To	M	Inns	NO	Runs	HS	Avg	100	50	Ct	St	Balls	Runs	Wkts	Avg	RPO	BB	5I	10M
Theunissen, NHCD	WPCU	1889/90	1889/90	2	4	2	64	49	32.00	0	0	1	0	499	196	20	9.80	2.35	7-41	3	1
	All FC	1888/89	1889/90	3	6	3	66	49	22.00	0	0	1	0	579	247	20	12.35	2.55	7-41	3	1
Thomas, AC	WPCA B	1998/99	1998/99	3	5	0	114	35	22.80	0	0	3	0	295	107	2	53.50	2.17	2-23	0	0
	All FC	1998/99	2010	112	158	33	3158	119*	25.26	2	11	31	0	20188	9655	353	27.35	2.86	7-54	16	1
Thomas, CH	WPCU	1921/22	1922/23	5	10	0	160	44	16.00	0	0	0	0	168	79	4	19.75	2.82	2-9	0	0
Thomas, K	WPCB	1978/79	1978/79	2	4	0	43	31	10.75	0	0	1	0	112	39	0	–	2.08	–	0	0
Thomas, Y	WPCB	1982/83	1990/91	38	55	6	1320	116	26.93	2	7	23	0	1213	332	22	15.09	1.64	5-6	1	0
	All FC	1982/83	1990/91	39	57	6	1442	116	28.27	2	8	23	0	1309	375	24	15.62	1.71	5-6	1	0
Thompson, PM	WPCU B	1977/78	1981/82	23	44	4	964	90	24.10	0	5	33	3	6	0	0	–	0.00	–	0	0
	All FC	1970/71	1981/82	48	86	7	1946	134	24.63	1	8	57	4	12	4	0	–	2.00	–	0	0
Thwaits, SA	WPCU	1949/50	1954/55	22	31	11	339	71*	16.95	0	1	12	0	7256	1916	80	23.95	1.58	6-29	4	0
	All FC	1939/40	1954/55	41	57	12	724	147	16.08	1	1	20	0	11651	3209	136	23.59	1.65	8-43	6	0
Timol, I	WPCB	1975/76	1975/76	2	3	0	67	29	22.33	0	0	2	0	0	0	0	–	–	–	0	0
	All FC	1971/72	1975/76	11	16	1	414	84*	27.60	0	2	19	0	0	0	0	–	–	–	0	0
Tolson, DJH	WPCU B	1976/77	1976/77	3	4	0	90	39	22.50	0	0	0	5	0	0	0	–	–	–	0	0
Touzel, FB	WPCU	1990/91	1990/91	5	10	0	80	23	8.00	0	0	1	0	0	0	0	–	–	–	0	0
	WPCU B	1984/85	1990/91	22	43	4	1103	92	28.28	0	6	14	0	0	0	0	–	–	–	0	0
	WPCA	1992/93	1993/94	6	12	2	282	57	28.20	0	1	1	0	0	0	0	–	–	–	0	0
	WPCA B	1991/92	1996/97	24	40	4	1350	132	37.50	3	5	27	0	0	0	0	–	–	–	0	0
	All FC	1984/85	1996/97	57	105	10	2815	132	29.63	3	12	43	0	0	0	0	–	–	–	0	0
Touzel, FG	WPCU	1968/69	1968/69	1	1	1	0	0*	–	0	0	0	0	223	94	7	13.42	2.52	7-86	1	0
Townsend, TKM	WPCA Am	2009/10	2009/10	6	12	1	255	53	23.18	0	2	5	15	0	0	0	–	–	–	0	0
Treadaway, LG	WPCU	1947/48	1957/58	5	9	2	128	50	18.28	0	0	5	3	958	456	6	76.00	2.85	2-40	0	0
Trickett, WS	WPCU	1905/06	1905/06	1	2	0	25	15	12.50	0	0	0	1	18	7	0	–	2.33	–	0	0
Trott, IJL	WPCA	2001/02	2001/02	8	14	1	415	93	31.92	0	4	8	0	222	155	4	38.75	4.18	1-10	0	0
	All FC	2000/01	2010/11	161	269	34	10748	226	45.73	25	52	151	0	4358	2471	56	44.12	3.40	7-39	1	0
Tsolekile, TL	WPCA	1999/00	2003/04	33	43	3	992	95	24.80	0	6	126	15	0	0	0	–	–	–	0	0
	WCC	2004/05	2007/08	28	44	3	999	101*	24.36	1	5	92	3	0	0	0	–	–	–	0	0
	WPCA Am	2007/08	2008/09	7	10	2	227	55	28.37	0	2	19	1	0	0	0	–	–	–	0	0
	All FC	1999	2010/11	119	165	21	3949	141	27.42	4	18	387	31	0	0	0	–	–	–	0	0
Tucker, E	WPCU	1936/37	1936/37	2	2	0	37	24	18.50	0	0	2	0	0	0	0	–	–	–	0	0
Tulleken, A	WPCU	1960/61	1960/61	2	4	0	24	13	6.00	0	0	4	1	0	0	0	–	–	–	0	0
Tullis, GD	WPCU B	1983/84	1988/89	13	21	1	324	56	16.20	0	1	36	3	1	1	0	–	6.00	–	0	0
	All FC	1981/82	1988/89	14	23	1	367	56	16.68	0	1	42	3	1	1	0	–	6.00	–	0	0

Name	Team	From	To	M	Inns	NO	Runs	HS	Avg	100	50	Ct	St	Balls	Runs	Wkts	Avg	RPO	BB	5I	10M
Turner, DR	WPCU	1977/78	1977/78	2	4	1	45	21	15.00	0	0	3	0	0	0	0	–	–	–	0	0
	All FC	1966	1989	426	696	74	19005	184*	30.55	28	90	191	0	626	357	9	39.66	3.42	2-7	0	0
Turner, GJ	WPCU	1984/85	1986/87	4	8	1	133	40	19.00	0	0	2	0	0	0	0	–	–	–	0	0
	WPCU B	1984/85	1986/87	12	23	2	545	69*	25.95	0	3	13	0	3	2	0	–	4.00	–	0	0
	All FC	1984/85	1992/93	44	70	6	1791	101*	27.98	1	10	26	0	2605	1539	27	57.00	3.54	4-94	0	0
Twentyman Jones, PS	WPCU	1897/98	1905/06	8	14	1	277	53	21.30	0	2	3	0	0	0	0	–	–	–	0	0
	All FC	1897/98	1905/06	10	18	1	306	53	18.00	0	2	4	0	0	0	0	–	–	–	0	0
Upton, PAH	WPCU B	1990/91	1990/91	1	2	1	100	100	100.00	1	0	0	0	0	0	0	–	–	–	0	0
	WPCA B	1993/94	1993/94	1	2	1	42	37*	42.00	0	0	1	0	0	0	0	–	–	–	0	0
	All FC	1990/91	1993/94	2	4	2	142	100	71.00	1	0	0	0	0	0	0	–	–	–	0	0
Valentine, RC	WPCU	1947/48	1947/48	2	4	0	64	27	16.00	0	0	1	0	0	0	0	–	–	–	0	0
Vallie, MY	WPCA Am	2009/10	2010/11	22	37	8	1564	151*	53.93	5	6	11	0	90	50	1	50.00	3.33	1-15	0	0
	WCC	2010/11	2010/11	2	4	0	280	163	70.00	1	1	0	0	12	0	0	–	–	–	0	0
	All FC	2009/10	2010/11	24	41	8	1844	163	55.87	6	7	11	0	102	50	1	50.00	2.94	1-15	0	0
Van Beuge, BW	WPCA B	1998/99	1998/99	6	9	0	131	61	14.55	0	1	18	4	0	0	0	–	–	–	0	0
Van der Bijl, PGV	WPCU	1925/26	1939/40	27	48	4	1565	195	35.56	3	11	28	2	406	158	5	31.60	2.33	2-20	0	0
	All FC	1925/26	1942/43	44	76	9	2692	195	40.17	5	18	36	2	406	158	5	31.60	2.33	2-20	0	0
Van der Bijl, V	WPCU	1947/48	1947/48	2	3	0	2	2	0.66	0	0	7	2	0	0	0	–	–	–	0	0
Van der Bijl, VA	WPCU	1892/93	1892/93	2	4	2	80	35*	40.00	0	0	3	0	50	17	1	17.00	2.04	1-17	0	0
Van der Bijl, VAW	WPCU	1890/91	1895/96	6	9	1	162	61	20.25	0	1	3	0	984	397	19	20.89	2.42	6-56	1	0
	All FC	1890/91	1904	7	11	1	176	61	17.60	0	1	5	0	1014	421	19	22.15	2.49	6-56	1	0
Van der Merwe, PL	WPCU	1958/59	1965/66	35	64	4	2038	121	33.96	2	13	33	0	4803	1626	64	25.40	2.03	6-40	3	0
	All FC	1956/57	1968/69	94	152	12	4086	128	29.18	4	23	73	0	6221	2108	82	25.70	2.03	6-40	3	0
Van der Merwe, WM	WPCU B	1985/86	1986/87	9	17	3	320	79*	22.85	0	2	3	0	1493	708	34	20.82	2.84	5-35	1	0
	All FC	1978/79	1990	44	67	15	1274	96	24.50	0	7	14	0	6805	3388	130	26.06	2.98	5-35	4	0
Van der Poel, CS	WPCU	1923/24	1923/24	1	1	0	14	14*	–	0	0	0	0	180	48	1	48.00	1.60	1-26	0	0
Van der Spuy, TMH	WPCU	1935/36	1946/47	22	37	5	1110	121*	34.68	3	2	13	0	1946	973	39	24.94	3.00	6-95	2	0
	All FC	1933/34	1950/51	32	56	10	1411	121*	30.67	3	3	18	0	2204	1228	46	26.69	3.34	6-95	2	0
Van Graan, K	WPCB	1974/75	1979/80	9	15	1	191	44	13.64	0	0	13	0	141	39	4	9.75	1.65	2-0	0	0
Van Graan, Randall	WPCB	1981/82	1981/82	2	3	0	17	10	5.66	0	0	2	0	132	53	2	26.50	2.40	2-53	0	0
Van Graan, Robbie	WPCB	1972/73	1977/78	15	26	3	448	67	19.47	0	2	7	0	72	17	2	8.50	1.41	2-17	0	0
	All FC	1972/73	1977/78	16	28	4	492	67	20.50	0	2	7	0	72	17	2	8.50	1.41	2-17	0	0
Van Niekerk, AP	WPCU	1968/69	1974/75	15	19	2	284	48	16.70	0	0	2	0	1222	439	18	24.38	2.15	4-16	0	0
	WPCU B	1975/76	1975/76	1	1	0	9	9	9.00	0	0	0	0	0	0	0	–	–	–	0	0
	All FC	1968/69	1975/76	16	20	2	293	48	16.27	0	0	2	0	1222	439	18	24.38	2.15	4-16	0	0

Name	Team	From	To	M	Inns	NO	Runs	HS	Avg	100	50	Ct	St	Balls	Runs	Wkts	Avg	RPO	BB	5I	10M
Van Olst, M	WPCA B	1997/98	1997/98	2	4	1	97	54	32.33	0	1	0	0	368	219	5	43.80	3.57	2-56	0	0
Van Oordt, G	WPCB	1975/76	1983/84	22	33	3	411	51	13.70	0	1	16	0	2989	897	56	16.01	1.80	5-50	1	0
Van Reenen, A	WPCA	1995/96	1995/96	1	1	0	4	4	4.00	0	0	0	0	126	119	2	59.50	5.66	2-75	0	0
	WPCA B	1995/96	1996/97	3	1	1	6	6*	–	0	0	0	0	509	282	8	35.25	3.32	5-47	1	0
	All FC	1995/96	1996/97	4	2	1	10	6*	10.00	0	0	0	0	635	401	10	40.10	3.78	5-47	1	0
Van Ryneveld, CB	WPCU	1946/47	1962/63	31	56	1	1795	138	32.63	2	12	21	0	5993	2694	92	29.28	2.69	8-48	5	0
	All FC	1946/47	1962/63	101	171	12	4803	150	30.20	4	29	71	0	13544	6230	206	30.24	2.75	8-48	9	0
Van Schalkwyk, C	WPCB	1975/76	1982/83	26	42	9	608	56	18.42	0	3	14	0	1086	349	25	13.96	1.92	4-15	0	0
Van Wyk, EP	WPCA Am	2007/08	2009/10	13	20	5	539	99*	35.93	0	5	6	0	1655	880	30	29.33	3.19	5-20	2	0
	All FC	2007	2009/10	15	23	6	697	99*	41.00	0	5	6	0	1938	991	37	26.78	3.06	5-20	2	0
Van Wyk, JM	WCC	2004/05	2004/05	1	1	0	1	1*	–	0	0	0	0	72	58	1	58.00	4.83	1-47	0	0
Van Zyl, S	All FC	1998/99	2008/09	23	36	9	350	46	12.96	0	0	2	0	3019	1761	49	35.93	3.49	3-24	0	0
	WCC	2007/08	2010/11	35	61	12	2364	172	48.24	5	12	24	0	1098	449	16	28.06	2.45	4-36	0	0
	All FC	2006/07	2010/11	57	101	21	3552	172	42.74	8	15	44	0	2207	960	31	30.96	2.60	5-32	1	0
Veal, VG	WPCU	1920/21	1933/34	25	39	3	392	58	10.88	0	3	9	0	3690	1558	91	17.12	2.53	7-40	3	2
	All FC	1920/21	1933/34	25	39	3	392	58	10.88	0	3	9	0	3690	1558	91	17.12	2.53	7-40	3	2
Vercueil, S	WPCU B	1981/82	1981/82	4	6	2	55	16	13.75	0	0	12	4	0	2	0	–	–	–	0	0
	All FC	1981/82	1989/90	30	53	8	1051	87	23.35	0	6	72	4	6	2	1	2.00	2.00	1-2	0	0
Vilas, DJ	WPCA Am	2010/11	2010/11	3	3	1	147	123*	73.50	1	0	8	4	0	0	0	–	–	–	0	0
	All FC	2006/07	2010/11	32	49	3	2054	203	44.65	6	11	84	4	0	0	0	–	–	–	0	0
Viljoen, A	WPCB	1990/91	1990/91	3	6	0	141	81	23.50	0	1	1	0	0	0	0	–	–	–	0	0
Viljoen, FDJ	WPCU	1922/23	1923/24	4	5	1	43	18*	10.75	0	0	5	0	198	142	2	71.00	4.30	1-16	0	0
Vincent, AJS	WPCU	1957/58	1957/58	1	2	2	0	0	0.00	0	0	2	0	0	0	0	–	–	–	0	0
Virgin, RT	WPCU	1972/73	1972/73	2	4	0	74	23	18.50	0	0	3	0	0	0	0	–	–	–	0	0
	All FC	1957	1977	437	773	39	21930	179*	29.87	37	99	415	0	474	371	8	46.37	4.69	4-31	0	0
Voss, MF	WPCU	1990/91	1990/91	3	6	0	97	30	16.16	0	0	4	0	0	0	0	–	–	–	0	0
	WPCU B	1984/85	1990/91	4	8	0	232	70	29.00	0	2	3	0	0	0	0	–	–	–	0	0
	WPCA	1991/92	1992/93	7	14	1	234	56	18.00	0	1	3	0	0	0	0	–	–	–	0	0
	WPCA B	1991/92	1991/92	5	9	1	310	115	38.75	1	2	6	0	0	0	0	–	–	–	0	0
	All FC	1984/85	1992/93	19	37	2	873	115	24.94	1	5	16	0	0	0	0	–	–	–	0	0
Wadvalla, A	WPCB	1977/78	1977/78	2	2	0	5	5	2.50	0	0	0	0	54	50	1	50.00	5.55	1-22	0	0
Walker, PM	All FC	1972/73	1985/86	11	20	1	151	30	7.94	0	0	7	0	606	214	3	71.33	2.11	2-51	0	0
	WPCU	1962/63	1962/63	3	6	0	96	60	16.00	0	1	4	0	0	0	0	–	–	–	0	0
	All FC	1956	1972	469	788	110	17650	152*	26.03	13	92	694	0	58086	23894	834	28.64	2.46	7-58	25	2
Wallace, B	WPCU	1930/31	1937/38	14	21	4	506	81*	29.76	0	2	2	0	8	6	0	–	4.50	–	0	0

CHAPTER 15 Western Province and Cape Cobras individual first-class career records, 1890–2011

Name	Team	From	To	M	Inns	NO	Runs	HS	Avg	100	50	Ct	St	Balls	Runs	Wkts	Avg	RPO	BB	5I	10M
Walters, MD	WPCA Am	2005/06	2010/11	29	48	3	1320	180*	29.33	3	3	17	0	176	113	2	56.50	3.85	1-19	0	0
	WCC	2008/09	2008/09	1	2	1	40	24*	40.00	0	0	0	0	0	0	0	–	–	–	0	0
	All FC	2005/06	2009/10	30	50	4	1360	180*	29.56	3	3	17	0	176	113	2	56.50	3.85	1-19	0	0
Watson, VUT	WPCU	1923/24	1924/25	4	8	0	220	88	27.50	0	2	1	0	0	0	0	–	–	–	0	0
Watt, HH	WPCU	1933/34	1934/35	6	10	5	34	10*	6.80	0	0	2	0	1265	488	26	18.76	2.31	6-84	2	0
	All FC	1933/34	1946/47	12	20	5	115	22	7.66	0	0	3	0	2681	1080	44	24.54	2.41	6-84	2	0
Weber, AC	WPCU	1903/04	1904/05	2	4	0	50	23	12.50	0	0	0	0	0	0	0	–	–	–	0	0
Weeden, CC	WPCU	1975/76	1975/76	1	1	0	0	0	0.00	0	0	0	2	0	0	0	–	–	–	0	0
	WPCU B	1975/76	1978/79	15	24	1	620	118	26.95	1	2	6	0	1501	646	24	26.91	2.58	5-20	1	0
	All FC	1975/76	1978/79	16	25	1	620	118	25.83	1	2	6	0	1501	646	24	26.91	2.58	5-20	1	0
Weinstein, LJ	WPCU	1959/60	1965/66	17	32	0	694	91	21.68	0	3	10	0	0	0	0	–	–	–	0	0
	All FC	1959/60	1967/68	25	47	1	1176	120	25.56	1	6	16	0	0	0	0	–	–	–	0	0
Wells, CM	WPCU	1984/85	1984/85	2	4	1	43	29	14.33	0	0	0	0	84	45	2	22.50	3.21	1-19	0	0
	All FC	1979	1996	318	510	78	14289	203	33.07	24	67	112	0	31197	14748	428	34.45	2.83	7-42	7	0
Wernars, KO	WPCA Am	2009/10	2010/11	2	4	2	77	39*	38.50	0	0	1	0	70	44	3	14.66	3.77	2-11	0	0
Wessels, KC	WPCU	1976/77	1976/77	8	15	1	511	136	36.50	1	2	8	0	0	0	0	–	–	–	0	0
	All FC	1973/74	1999/00	316	539	50	24738	254	50.58	66	132	268	0	1416	574	13	44.15	2.43	2-25	0	0
Westcott, RJ	WPCU	1949/50	1961/62	46	85	5	3059	140	38.23	4	22	26	0	714	292	10	29.20	2.45	3-44	0	0
	All FC	1949/50	1961/62	51	94	5	3225	140	36.23	4	23	26	0	746	314	10	31.40	2.52	3-44	0	0
White, JE	WPCU	1962/63	1966/67	4	7	0	60	46	8.57	0	0	9	0	0	0	0	–	–	–	0	0
White, N	WPCB	1982/83	1990/91	25	38	7	763	125*	24.61	2	3	77	14	0	0	0	–	–	–	0	0
	All FC	1982/83	1994/95	27	42	8	805	125*	23.67	2	3	81	15	0	0	0	–	–	–	0	0
Whitefield, DWH	WPCU	1960/61	1964/65	11	20	2	431	59*	23.94	0	3	9	0	198	78	0	–	–	–	0	0
Whitehead, JG	WPCU	1904/05	1920/21	26	41	14	330	42	12.22	0	0	9	0	4065	1849	101	18.30	2.72	7-58	5	1
	All FC	1902	1920/21	30	47	16	351	42	11.32	0	0	10	0	4704	2228	118	18.88	2.84	7-58	7	2
Whiteing, LCG	WPCU	1935/36	1946/47	3	5	0	61	39	12.20	0	0	2	0	8	2	0	–	1.50	–	0	0
Whitfield, AR	WPCU	1960/61	1960/61	1	2	0	8	8	4.00	0	0	0	0	0	0	0	–	–	–	0	0
Whittingdale, R	WPCU	1978/79	1978/79	1	1	0	10	10	10.00	0	0	5	0	0	0	0	–	–	–	0	0
	WPCU B	1977/78	1980/81	4	5	3	56	16*	28.00	0	0	6	0	0	0	0	–	–	–	0	0
	All FC	1977/78	1980/81	5	6	3	66	16*	22.00	0	0	11	0	0	0	0	–	–	–	0	0
Wightman, RW	WPCU	1954/55	1954/55	1	2	0	22	16	11.00	0	0	0	0	192	120	2	60.00	3.75	2-120	0	0
Wiley, JWE	WPCU	1947/48	1947/48	2	4	1	117	70	39.00	0	1	0	0	0	0	0	–	–	–	0	0
	All FC	1947/48	1952	15	27	1	461	70	17.73	0	2	10	0	6	5	0	–	5.00	–	0	0
Wiley, WGA	WPCU	1952/53	1953/54	4	8	0	86	59	10.75	0	1	2	0	0	0	0	–	–	–	0	0
	All FC	1952	1953/54	13	25	0	615	100	24.60	1	4	11	0	0	0	0	–	–	–	0	0
Williams, CD	WPCA Am	2007/08	2008/09	7	14	1	293	69	22.53	0	2	1	0	0	0	0	–	–	–	0	0

Name	Team	From	To	M	Inns	NO	Runs	HS	Avg	100	50	Ct	St	Balls	Runs	Wkts	Avg	RPO	BB	5I	10M
Williams, G	WPCB	1971/72	1974/75	16	26	4	392	80	17.81	0	2	11	0	3024	917	46	19.93	1.81	5-43	1	0
	All FC	1971/72	1974/75	17	27	4	430	80	18.69	0	2	12	0	3192	991	49	20.22	1.86	5-43	1	0
Williams, HS	WPCB	1990/91	1990/91	1	0	0	0	–	–	0	0	1	0	216	51	5	10.20	1.41	3-23	0	0
	All FC	1990/91	2003/04	89	126	32	765	49	8.13	0	0	24	0	17021	6697	276	24.26	2.36	6-27	10	0
Williams, J	WPCB	1971/72	1979/80	5	8	2	39	10	6.50	0	0	1	0	892	237	13	18.23	1.59	3-21	0	0
Williams, OL	WPCB	1971/72	1971/72	2	3	2	15	9*	15.00	0	0	1	0	383	123	4	30.75	1.92	2-36	0	0
	All FC	1967	1971/72	3	5	3	21	9*	10.50	0	0	1	0	533	183	5	36.60	2.06	2-36	0	0
Williamson, M	WPCA Am	2005/06	2009/10	19	34	2	750	121	23.43	1	3	10	0	5	4	0	–	4.80	–	0	0
	All FC	2005/06	2009/10	24	44	3	892	121	21.75	1	3	13	0	5	4	0	–	4.80	–	0	0
Willoughby, CM	WPCA	2000/01	2003/04	30	22	10	62	17	5.16	0	0	13	0	7415	3079	152	20.25	2.49	7-56	8	3
	WCC	2004/05	2006/07	28	37	21	119	32*	7.43	0	0	7	0	6109	2782	120	23.18	2.73	6-41	8	0
	All FC	1994/95	2010	209	233	102	801	47	6.11	0	0	42	0	41933	19646	,774	25.38	2.81	7-44	31	3
Wilson, WD	WPCU	1948/49	1950/51	4	8	1	97	20	13.85	0	0	4	0	0	0	0	–	–	–	0	0
Wingreen, IM	All FC	1945/46	1960/61	25	42	4	918	97	24.15	0	6	15	0	24	23	0	–	5.75	–	0	0
Witbooi, R	WPCU B	1983/84	1986/87	22	42	2	1163	103	29.07	1	6	14	0	1	4	0	–	24.00	–	0	0
	WPCB	1978/79	1978/79	2	3	1	46	28	23.00	0	0	0	0	165	50	2	25.00	1.81	227	0	0
Witte, EV	WPCU	1946/47	1954/55	23	30	9	217	51	10.33	0	1	7	0	6628	1922	78	24.64	1.73	6-53	4	0
	All FC	1942/43	1954/55	28	37	11	311	51	11.96	0	1	10	0	7717	2323	93	24.97	1.80	6-53	4	0
Wood, AF	WPCU	1921/22	1925/26	2	3	0	31	24	10.33	0	0	1	0	0	0	0	–	–	–	0	0
Woolmer, RA	WPCU	1980/81	1980/81	3	6	0	81	28	13.50	0	0	4	0	173	77	2	38.50	2.67	2-13	0	0
	All FC	1968	1984	350	545	75	15772	203	33.55	34	71	240	1	25829	10868	420	25.87	2.52	7-47	12	1
Worth, D	WPCA Am	2004/05	2004/05	4	7	0	149	71	21.28	0	1	9	0	0	0	0	–	–	–	0	0
Wrentmore, CGC	WPCU	1926/27	1934/35	4	7	0	148	58	21.14	0	1	1	0	0	0	0	–	–	–	0	0
Wrentmore, GM	WPCU	1910/11	1910/11	5	8	0	65	24	8.12	0	0	2	0	0	0	0	–	–	–	0	0
Wyngaard, W	WPCA Am	2004/05	2006/07	17	28	4	670	132*	27.91	3	1	14	0	18	14	0	–	4.66	–	0	0
	WCC	2005/06	2005/06	2	4	0	49	22	12.25	0	0	0	0	0	0	0	–	–	–	0	0
	All FC	2004/05	2006/07	19	32	4	719	132*	25.67	3	1	14	0	18	14	0	–	4.66	–	0	0
Wynne, OE	WPCU	1947/48	1958/59	12	22	0	965	140	43.86	3	5	9	0	6	6	0	–	6.00	–	0	0
	All FC	1937/38	1958/59	37	64	3	2268	200*	37.18	7	8	20	0	78	47	0	–	3.61	–	0	0
Xongo, L	WPCA Am	2004/05	2004/05	1	0	0	0	–	–	0	0	0	0	42	11	0	–	1.57	–	0	0
Yeoman, WF	WPCU	1908/09	1912/13	11	18	1	457	86	26.88	0	5	5	0	0	0	0	–	–	–	0	0
Young, S	WPCU	1889/90	1889/90	1	2	0	11	10	5.50	0	0	0	0	0	0	0	–	–	–	0	0
Zondeki, M	WCC	2005/06	2010/11	40	52	16	323	34	8.97	0	0	10	0	6961	3465	116	29.87	2.98	5-26	6	1
	WPCA Am	2009/10	2010/11	3	3	0	19	15	6.33	0	0	1	0	552	273	12	22.75	2.96	4-69	0	0
	All FC	2000/01	2010/11	87	113	33	732	59	9.15	0	1	25	0	14370	7576	255	29.70	3.16	6-39	9	1

16
Western Province and Cape Cobras individual limited-overs career records, 1969–2011[390]

Name	Team	From	To	M	Inns	NO	Runs	HS	Avg	100	50	Ct	St	Balls	Runs	Wkts	Avg	RPO	BB	4I
Abbas, M	WPCA Am	2008/09	2009/10	9	9	1	236	111*	29.50	1	0	2	0	0	0	0	–	–	–	0
Abdullah, M	WPCB	1982/83	1984/85	[no other details available]																
Abrahams, CJ	WPCB	1975/76	1975/76	[no other details available]																
Abrahams, S	WPCA Am	2005/06	2005/06	1	1	1	1	1*	–	0	0	0	0	54	35	2	17.50	3.88	2-35	0
Ackerman, HD	All LO	2004/05	2005/06	10	4	2	18	13*	9.00	0	0	2	0	384	321	11	29.18	5.01	3-32	0
Ackerman, HM	WPCA	1993/94	2002/03	92	87	11	2268	92	29.84	0	15	34	0	0	0	0	–	–	–	0
	All LO	1993/94	2009/10	230	222	25	6366	139	32.31	4	41	83	0	48	52	0	–	6.50	–	0
Ackermann, JP	WPCU	1970/71	1979/80	20	20	4	567	127	35.43	1	4	11	0	156	114	5	22.80	4.38	3-29	0
	WPCU B	1981/82	1981/82	1·	1	0	4	4	4.00	0	0	0	0	0	0	0	–	–	–	0
	All LO	1968	1981/82	74	73	11	1975	127	31.85	2	13	30	0	162	123	5	24.60	4.55	3-29	0
Ackermann, S	WPCU B	1983/84	1983/84	1	1	0	7	7	7.00	0	0	0	0	0	0	0	–	–	–	0
	WPCA	1999/00	1999/00	2	2	0	4	4	2.00	0	0	1	0	48	43	0	–	5.37	–	0
	All LO	1996/97	1999/00	17	17	2	160	67	10.66	0	1	3	0	234	175	4	43.75	4.48	2-17	0
Adams, MQ	WPCA Am	2005/06	2010/11	20	20	5	586	121*	39.06	1	2	3	0	137	128	6	21.33	5.60	3-53	0
Adams, PR	WPCA	1995/96	2001/02	21	5	2	8	5*	2.66	0	0	6	0	765	498	24	20.75	3.90	3-12	0
	WCC	2004/05	2007/08	6	3	0	20	11	6.66	0	0	0	0	180	147	1	147.00	4.90	1-40	0
	WPCA Am	2005/06	2007/08	12	6	1	73	25	14.60	0	0	6	0	538	359	11	32.63	4.00	2-19	0
	All LO	1995/96	2007/08	76	26	10	180	33*	11.25	0	0	22	0	3156	2262	84	26.92	4.30	3-12	0
Albertyn, WA	WCC	2005/06	2005/06	2	2	0	37	35	18.50	0	0	0	0	0	0	0	–	–	–	0
Alexander, CJ	All LO	2001/02	2006/07	30	19	6	226	58*	17.38	0	1	7	0	1201	919	31	29.64	4.59	4-31	1
	WPCA Am	2004/05	2006/07	3	2	2	33	31*	–	0	0	0	0	102	81	0	–	4.76	–	0
	All LO	2004/05	2010/11	37	22	9	92	31*	7.07	0	0	5	0	1494	1412	40	35.30	5.67	4-27	2
Allie, G	WPCB	1983/84	1984/85	[no other details available]																
Allie, Z	WPCA Am	2009/10	2009/10	7	7	0	106	39	15.14	0	0	3	1	0	0	0	–	–	–	0
Antulay, N	WPCB	1983/84	1984/85	[no other details available]																
Arendse, NM	WPCB	1982/83	1982/83	[no other details available]																
Arkell, CJF	WPCA Am	2008/09	2008/09	1	1	0	25	25	25.00	0	0	1	0	48	41	1	41.00	5.12	1-41	0
Austen, MH	WPCU	1987/88	1987/88	6	6	0	92	54	15.33	0	1	2	0	0	0	0	–	–	–	0
	WPCU B	1983/84	1983/84	1	1	0	17	17	17.00	0	0	0	0	0	0	0	–	–	–	0
	All LO	1983/84	1997/98	60	60	1	1380	95*	23.38	0	9	14	0	1469	1048	39	26.87	4.28	4-47	1
Bacchus, SFAF	WPCU	1984/85	1984/85	8	8	0	344	132	43.00	1	1	1	0	0	0	0	–	–	–	0
	All LO	1972/73	1985/86	66	63	7	1871	132	33.41	1	12	18	0	96	99	6	16.50	6.18	3-28	0
Bacher, AM	WCC	2006/07	2006/07	12	12	2	285	118*	28.50	1	1	7	0	352	248	9	27.55	4.22	2-27	0
	All LO	1994/95	2006/07	149	144	10	4808	158*	35.88	8	29	53	0	2313	1691	56	30.19	4.38	3-20	0

Name	Team	From	To	M	Inns	NO	Runs	HS	Avg	100	50	Ct	St	Balls	Runs	Wkts	Avg	RPO	BB	4I
Barlow, EJ	WPCU	1969/70	1980/81	25	25	1	1203	186	50.12	3	7	13	0	1509	787	38	20.71	3.12	3-16	0
	All LO	1966/67	1982/83	100	99	4	3013	186	31.71	3	22	43	0	5058	2950	162	18.20	3.49	6-33	4
Barnes, VA	WPCA	1991/92	1991/92	5	0	0	0	–	–	0	0	2	0	246	167	10	16.70	4.07	3-18	0
	WPCB	1982/83	1984/85	[no other details available]																
	All LO	1991/92	1991/92	5	0	0	0	–	–	0	0	2	0	246	167	10	16.70	4.07	3-18	0
Base, SJ	WPCU B	1983/84	1983/84	1	1	0	10	10	10.00	0	0	0	0	42	20	1	20.00	2.85	1-20	0
	All LO	1983/84	1996	169	77	27	377	31	7.54	0	0	34	0	8061	5732	221	25.93	4.26	4-14	7
Bassage, DJ	WCC	2004/05	2005/06	8	8	0	246	81	30.75	0	2	3	0	0	0	0	–	–	–	0
	WPCA Am	2004/05	2006/07	7	7	0	116	65	16.57	0	1	5	0	0	0	0	–	–	–	0
	All LO	2004/05	2006/07	15	15	0	362	81	24.13	0	3	8	0	0	0	0	–	–	–	0
Behardien, F	WPCA Am	2004/05	2005/06	6	3	0	50	37	16.66	0	0	2	0	300	286	5	57.20	5.72	3-41	0
	All LO	2004/05	2010/11	65	48	8	1219	73*	30.47	0	10	20	0	724	625	14	44.64	5.17	3-16	0
Behardien, M	WPCA Am	2010/11	2010/11	4	3	1	22	9*	11.00	0	0	4	0	0	0	0	–	–	–	0
Bennett, BL	WPCA Am	2007/08	2009/10	8	8	0	103	42	12.87	0	0	2	0	54	50	2	25.00	5.55	2-50	0
Best, CA	All LO	2004/05	2009/10	43	42	2	910	136*	22.75	2	3	12	0	139	128	4	32.00	5.52	2-22	0
	WPCA	1993/94	1993/94	11	10	0	175	57	17.50	0	1	2	0	148	133	2	66.50	5.39	2-22	0
	All LO	1979/80	1993/94	79	76	11	1943	137*	29.89	2	12	21	0	682	571	14	40.78	5.02	2-22	0
Birch, CWS	WPCA Am	2006/07	2007/08	7	5	0	59	28	11.80	0	0	1	0	289	207	9	23.00	4.29	3-50	0
Bleekers, LF	WPCU	1988/89	1989/90	15	12	1	108	22	9.81	0	0	13	1	0	0	0	–	–	–	0
	WPCA	1992/93	1993/94	10	10	0	88	21	8.80	0	0	6	1	0	0	0	–	–	–	0
	All LO	1988/89	1993/94	25	22	1	196	22	9.33	0	0	19	2	0	0	0	–	–	–	0
Bothma, JP	WPCA Am	2010/11	2010/11	6	1	0	0	0	0.00	0	0	1	0	204	217	7	31.00	6.38	2-29	0
	All LO	2006/07	2010/11	26	13	7	99	47*	16.50	0	0	3	0	1022	828	50	16.56	4.86	5-29	3
Booysen, N	WPCB	1984/85	1984/85	[no other details available]																
Bowditch, MH	WPCU	1970/71	1973/74	6	5	1	132	66	33.00	0	2	0	0	307	166	10	16.60	3.24	3-23	0
Brand, D	WPCA Am	2009/10	2009/10	2	2	0	24	16	12.00	0	0	0	0	0	0	0	–	–	–	0
	All LO	1998/99	2009/10	21	20	0	621	131	31.05	1	4	8	0	18	13	2	6.50	4.33	2-8	0
Bridgens, KJ	WPCU	1986/87	1986/87	2	2	0	33	17	16.50	0	0	0	0	0	0	0	–	–	–	0
	All LO	1986/87	1992/93	46	43	7	690	61	19.16	0	3	49	6	0	0	0	–	–	–	0
Bruce, J	WPCU	1969/70	1969/70	1	0	0	0	–	–	0	0	1	0	48	12	1	12.00	1.50	1-12	0
Bruce, SD	WPCU	1974/75	1985/86	20	18	4	262	62*	18.71	0	1	16	0	0	0	0	–	–	–	0
	All LO	1972/73	1985/86	21	19	4	270	62*	18.00	0	1	16	0	0	0	0	–	–	–	0
Bruyns, A	WPCU	1969/70	1976/77	16	16	0	534	113	33.37	1	4	6	0	6	1	1	–	1.00	–	0
	All LO	1969/70	1976/77	19	19	0	596	113	31.36	1	4	7	0	8	6	0	–	4.50	–	0
Budge, NR	WPCU	1969/70	1972/73	5	5	0	152	84	30.40	0	1	0	0	18	18	0	–	6.00	–	0

Name	Team	From	To	M	Inns	NO	Runs	HS	Avg	100	50	Ct	St	Balls	Runs	Wkts	Avg	RPO	BB	4I
Cameron, DP	WPCU	1970/71	1973/74	2	0	0	0	–	–	0	0	1	0	144	95	3	31.66	3.95	2-44	0
Canning, RCC	WCC	2005/06	2010/11	21	17	4	372	64*	28.61	0	2	29	4	0	0	0	–	–	–	0
	WPCA Am	2004/05	2010/11	31	26	5	695	67	33.09	0	4	37	7	6	2	0	–	2.00	–	0
	All LO	2004/05	2010/11	52	43	9	1067	67	31.38	0	6	66	11	6	2	0	–	2.00	–	0
Carter, NM	WCC	2009/10	2009/10	5	3	1	43	30*	21.50	0	0	0	0	180	151	3	50.33	5.03	1-13	0
	All LO	1999/00	2010	167	142	15	2852	135	22.45	3	12	14	0	7186	5804	220	26.38	4.84	5-31	8
Cawood, JC	WPCU	1970/71	1972/73	4	1	0	7	7	7.00	0	0	0	0	216	118	3	39.33	3.27	2-43	0
Carolus, D	WCC	2010/11	2010/11	1	0	0	0	–	–	0	0	0	0	18	23	0	–	7.66	–	0
Cheetham, JR	WPCU	1972/73	1972/73	1	1	1	13	13*	–	0	0	0	0	0	0	0	–	–	–	0
Chevalier, GA	WPCU	1969/70	1972/73	9	3	3	4	4*	–	0	0	3	0	352	246	19	12.94	4.19	6-32	3
Cilliers, A	WPCA	1995/96	1995/96	1	0	0	0	–	–	0	0	0	0	24	29	0	–	7.25	–	0
	All LO	1990/91	1995/96	19	14	2	102	20	8.50	0	0	2	0	803	606	14	43.28	4.52	3-31	0
Clark, RM	WPCU	1972/73	1982/83	5	2	0	37	24	18.50	0	0	3	0	30	13	0	–	2.60	–	0
Clarke, TA	WPCU	1981/82	1984/85	5	4	0	69	35	17.25	0	0	0	0	18	20	0	–	6.66	–	0
	WPCU B	1981/82	1984/85	3	3	0	35	22	11.66	0	0	0	0	42	53	0	–	7.57	–	0
	All LO	1981/82	1984/85	8	7	0	104	35	14.85	0	0	0	0	60	73	0	–	7.30	–	0
Commins, JB	WPCU	1987/88	1990/91	18	17	3	191	56*	13.64	0	1	3	0	12	13	0	–	6.50	–	0
	WPCA	1991/92	1999/00	43	40	8	1103	84*	34.46	0	9	7	0	0	0	0	–	–	–	0
	All LO	1987/88	1999/00	77	72	11	1782	93	29.21	0	14	14	0	18	27	0	–	9.00	–	0
Conrad, Siraaj	WPCA Am	2005/06	2005/06	2	0	0	0	–	–	0	0	0	0	108	76	4	19.00	4.22	2-31	0
	All LO	2005/06	2005/06	2	0	0	0	–	–	0	0	0	0	108	76	4	19.00	4.22	2-31	0
Cooke, CB	WPCA Am	2008/09	2009/10	14	14	3	415	109*	37.72	1	1	9	2	0	0	0	–	–	–	0
	All LO	2008/09	2009/10	14	14	3	415	109*	37.72	1	1	9	2	0	0	0	–	–	–	0
Cullinan, DJ	WPCU	1984/85	1990/91	75	73	7	1896	83	28.72	2	12	53	0	54	35	0	–	3.88	–	0
	All LO	1984/85	2004/05	331	315	42	8824	127*	32.32	9	49	154	0	378	309	8	38.62	4.90	2-30	0
Cupido, R	WPCB	1984/85	1984/85	[no other details available]																
Dagnin, I	WPCB	1974/75	1974/75	[no other details available]																
Damon, E	WPCB	1982/83	1983/84	[no other details available]																
Daniels, NP	WPCU	1977/78	1977/78	1	1	1	0	0	0.00	0	0	0	0	0	0	0	–	–	–	0
Davids, F	All LO	1976/77	1990/91	66	57	12	1124	80*	24.97	0	6	12	0	2010	1157	32	36.15	3.45	2-13	0
	WPCA	1991/92	1997/98	26	19	6	303	55*	23.30	0	1	4	0	398	327	13	25.15	4.92	3-23	0
	All LO	1991/92	1997/98	27	20	6	303	55*	21.64	0	1	4	0	434	359	13	27.61	4.96	3-23	0
Davids, H	WCC	2004/05	2009/10	40	38	3	997	116	28.48	1	6	12	0	84	80	0	–	5.71	–	0
	All LO	2000/01	2010/11	104	101	7	2794	147	29.72	4	18	41	0	687	634	11	57.63	5.53	3-44	0

Name	Team	From	To	M	Inns	NO	Runs	HS	Avg	100	50	Ct	St	Balls	Runs	Wkts	Avg	RPO	BB	4I
Dawson, AC	WPCA	1993/94	2003/04	99	55	14	731	52*	17.82	0	1	28	0	4727	3024	157	19.26	3.83	5-13	6
	WCC	2004/05	2006/07	25	18	8	97	18	9.70	0	0	2	0	1198	877	29	30.24	4.39	5-46	1
	All LO	1993/94	2006/07	161	85	27	934	52*	16.10	0	1	35	0	7705	5190	232	22.37	4.04	5-13	9
De Lange, CD	WCC	2004/05	2007/08	38	26	4	456	64	20.72	0	2	14	0	1613	1248	43	29.02	4.64	4-40	1
	All LO	1999/00	2010/11	118	77	18	1373	66	23.27	0	7	36	0	4906	3589	118	30.41	4.38	4-8	2
Denne, PH	WPCU	1969/70	1969/70	2	2	1	25	21*	25.00	0	0	0	0	24	24	0	–	6.00	–	0
De Stadler, M	WPCA	2000/01	2003/04	9	2	1	1	1	1.00	0	0	0	0	414	297	15	19.80	4.30	4-35	1
	WCC	2004/05	2004/05	3	2	1	2	2*	2.00	0	0	0	0	120	100	4	25.00	5.00	2-19	0
	WPCA Am	2004/05	2007/08	22	11	6	117	39*	23.40	0	0	4	0	1089	802	32	25.06	4.41	4-42	0
	All LO	2000/01	2007/08	34	15	8	120	39*	17.14	0	0	4	0	1623	1199	51	23.50	4.43	4-35	1
De Villiers, MC	WPCA	1996/97	1996/97	3	3	1	23	11	11.50	0	0	0	0	0	0	0	–	–	–	0
Donachie, HH	WPCA	1994/95	1994/95	4	4	0	36	19	9.00	0	0	1	0	114	69	2	34.50	3.63	1-19	0
	All LO	1990/91	1994/95	7	7	0	52	19	7.42	0	0	2	0	120	72	2	36.00	3.60	1-19	0
Drummond, RA	WPCU	1976/77	1978/79	2	2	1	39	32	39.00	0	0	4	0	0	0	0	–	–	–	0
Duminy, J-P	WPCA	2002/03	2003/04	10	5	1	287	88	71.75	0	4	2	0	12	7	1	7.00	3.50	1-7	0
	WCC	2004/05	2009/10	34	31	2	966	104	33.31	1	7	7	0	328	275	6	45.83	5.03	1-14	0
	All LO	2002/03	2009/10	127	112	21	3512	129	38.59	3	24	41	0	1301	1088	27	40.29	5.01	3-31	0
Du Plessis, JH	WPCU	1988/89	1988/89	2	2	0	5	3	2.50	0	0	0	0	0	0	0	–	–	–	0
Du Plessis, M	WPCU	1973/74	1973/74	1	1	1	0	0*	–	0	0	0	0	72	48	0	–	4.00	–	0
During, J	WPCU	1979/80	1986/87	14	5	3	41	20*	20.50	0	0	5	0	777	534	14	38.14	4.12	3-20	0
	WPCU B	1984/85	1984/85	1	1	0	2	2	2.00	0	0	0	0	30	17	0	–	3.40	–	0
	All LO	1979/80	1986/87	15	6	3	43	20*	14.33	0	0	5	0	807	551	14	39.35	4.09	3-20	0
Du Toit, JD	WPCU	1978/79	1982/83	10	4	2	83	42	41.50	0	0	5	0	385	233	14	16.64	3.63	5-36	1
	WPCU B	1984/85	1984/85	1	1	0	5	5	5.00	0	0	0	0	10	13	1	13.00	7.80	1-13	0
	All LO	1978/79	1990/91	46	35	4	617	58	19.90	0	2	10	0	1582	1130	39	28.97	4.28	5-36	1
Elgar, AG	WPCA	1984/85	1986/87	18	18	0	377	84	20.94	0	3	1	0	18	12	0	–	4.00	–	0
	WPCU B	1984/85	1984/85	1	1	0	37	37	37.00	0	0	0	0	0	0	0	–	–	–	0
	All LO	1984/85	1993/94	24	24	0	466	84	19.41	0	3	1	0	252	189	1	189.00	4.50	1-41	0
Emburey, JE	WPCU	1982/83	1983/84	20	14	5	81	20	9.00	0	0	7	0	999	544	17	32.00	3.26	3-6	0
	All LO	1975	2000	536	355	110	3865	50	15.77	0	2	181	0	26399	16811	647	25.98	3.82	5-23	26
Engelbrecht, SA	WCC	2008/09	2010/11	11	6	2	53	23*	13.25	0	0	4	0	366	349	7	49.85	5.72	3-39	0
	WPCA Am	2008/09	2010/11	14	12	8	320	69*	80.00	0	2	9	0	482	382	10	38.20	4.75	3-35	0
	All LO	2007/08	2010/11	29	21	10	401	69*	36.45	0	2	15	0	962	801	20	40.05	4.99	3-35	0
English, CV	WPCA	1993/94	1994/95	4	1	0	11	11	11.00	0	0	0	0	180	125	4	31.25	4.16	2-42	0
	All LO	1993/94	2005	69	57	7	792	75*	15.84	0	3	17	0	1497	1331	30	44.36	5.33	3-24	0

Name	Team	From	To	M	Inns	NO	Runs	HS	Avg	100	50	Ct	St	Balls	Runs	Wkts	Avg	RPO	BB	4I
Euley, W	WCC	2004/05	2004/05	1	1	0	0	0	0.00	0	0	1	0	0	0	0	–	–	–	0
	WPCA Am	2005/06	2007/08	6	4	2	99	70	49.50	0	1	4	1	0	0	0	–	–	–	0
	All LO	2003/04	2007/08	20	17	5	462	88	38.50	0	3	20	1	0	0	0	–	–	–	0
Fairclough, J	WPCU	1971/72	1971/72	1	1	1	0	0*	–	0	0	0	0	30	22	0	–	4.40	–	0
	All LO	1971/72	1981/82	7	3	3	3	3*	–	0	0	0	0	414	237	7	33.85	3.43	2-25	0
Farrell, JN	WPCU	1975/76	1976/77	2	0	0	0	–	–	0	0	2	0	114	42	1	42.00	2.21	1-12	0
Fearon, GG	WPCA Am	2006/07	2006/07	1	1	0	0	0	0.00	0	0	0	0	0	0	0	–	–	–	0
Felix, C	WPCB	1983/84	1983/84	[no other details available]																
Fernandez, AR	WPCA Am	2005/06	2005/06	1	1	0	4	4	4.00	0	0	0	0	0	0	0	–	–	–	0
Ferreira, LD	WPCA	1997/98	2003/04	45	43	3	999	134	24.97	1	6	15	0	6	8	1	8.00	8.00	1-8	0
	All LO	1994/95	2003/04	81	79	4	2147	134	28.62	3	13	23	0	24	34	1	34.00	8.50	1-8	0
Fletcher, DAG	WPCU	1984/85	1984/85	1	1	0	0	0	0.00	0	0	0	0	36	49	2	24.50	8.16	2-49	0
	All LO	1970/71	1984/85	53	45	6	1119	108	28.69	1	7	20	0	2422	1651	70	23.58	4.09	4-41	3
Fortune, N	WPCB	1982/83	1983/84	[no other details available]																
Friend, Q	WPCA	2001/02	2003/04	10	2	1	12	6*	12.00	0	0	3	0	450	313	12	26.08	4.17	3-52	0
	WCC	2004/05	2004/05	8	6	0	24	20	4.00	0	0	3	0	327	275	8	34.37	5.04	3-36	0
	WPCA Am	2004/05	2006/07	7	4	2	15	11	7.50	0	0	1	0	343	191	9	21.22	3.34	2-9	0
	All LO	2001/02	2010/11	63	30	9	169	25*	8.04	0	0	18	0	2568	2147	76	28.25	5.01	4-38	1
Gabriels, S	WPCB	1984/85	1984/85	[no other details available]																
Geoghegan, JP	WCC	2007/08	2007/08	1	1	0	1	1	1.00	0	0	0	0	0	0	0	–	–	–	0
	WPCA Am	2005/06	2007/08	12	11	1	491	107	49.10	1	4	5	0	228	235	7	33.57	6.18	3-8	0
	All LO	2005/06	2007/08	13	12	1	492	107	44.72	1	4	5	0	228	235	7	33.57	6.18	3-8	0
George, MF	WPCA	1997/98	1999/00	4	1	1	10	10*	–	0	0	0	0	198	172	7	24.57	5.21	2-34	0
	All LO	1997/98	2001/02	15	7	3	93	28*	23.25	0	0	3	0	690	532	18	29.55	4.62	2-31	0
George, SG	WPCA Am	2005/06	2005/06	6	3	0	36	22	12.00	0	0	4	0	186	119	6	19.83	3.83	3-35	0
Gomes, SP	WPCA Am	2010/11	2010/11	2	2	0	18	10	9.00	0	0	1	0	0	0	0	–	–	–	0
Gibbs, HH	WPCU	1990/91	1990/91	1	0	0	0	–	–	0	0	0	0	0	0	0	–	–	–	0
	WPCA	1991/92	2003/04	77	71	9	2065	110*	33.30	3	13	41	0	0	0	0	–	–	–	0
	WCC	2004/05	2010/11	34	33	6	1069	121*	39.59	3	7	13	0	0	0	0	–	–	–	0
	All LO	1990/91	2010/11	386	369	32	11937	175	35.42	27	62	170	0	66	57	2	28.50	5.18	1-16	0
Gie, CA	WPCU	1972/73	1973/74	3	2	1	55	38*	55.00	0	0	3	0	0	0	0	–	–	–	0
	All LO	1972/73	1980/81	5	4	2	95	38*	47.50	0	0	3	0	12	2	2	2.00	1.00	1-2	0
Giles, MJ	WPCU	1971/72	1971/72	1	1	0	5	5	5.00	0	0	0	0	0	0	0	–	–	–	0
Goldstein, FS	WPCU	1971/72	1975/76	10	10	0	269	91	26.90	0	2	1	0	0	0	0	–	–	–	0
	All LO	1969	1975/76	23	23	0	509	91	22.13	0	3	4	0	0	0	0	–	–	–	0

Name	Team	From	To	M	Inns	NO	Runs	HS	Avg	100	50	Ct	St	Balls	Runs	Wkts	Avg	RPO	BB	4I
Gooch, GA	WPCU	1982/83	1983/84	21	21	0	907	106	43.19	1	7	6	0	683	490	16	30.62	4.30	3-24	0
	All LO	1973	1997	614	601	48	22211	198*	40.16	44	139	261	0	14314	9657	310	31.15	4.04	5-8	2
Gordon, ES	WPCU	1983/84	1983/84	2	1	1	1	1*	–	0	0	1	0	96	75	2	37.50	4.68	2-44	0
	All LO	1981/82	1983/84	4	3	2	15	14*	15.00	0	0	1	0	207	145	3	48.33	4.20	2-44	1
Gray, AJA	WPCA Am	2004/05	2010/11	34	34	3	1181	123	38.09	1	8	12	0	726	579	28	20.67	4.78	4-30	0
	WCC	2010/11	2010/11	2	2	0	13	11	6.50	0	0	0	0	12	14	1	14.00	7.00	1-14	1
	All LO	2004/05	2010/11	37	37	3	1199	123	31.14	1	8	12	0	738	593	29	20.44	4.82	4-30	1
Green, AD	WPCU	1979/80	1979/80	1	1	0	21	21	21.00	0	0	0	0	0	0	0	–	–	–	0
Hantam, WC	WCC	2004/05	2005/06	9	8	3	82	35	16.40	0	0	3	0	344	302	9	33.55	5.26	3-53	3
	WPCA Am	2004/05	2007/08	14	10	3	150	53	21.42	0	1	4	0	672	469	26	18.03	4.18	5-22	3
	All LO	2004/05	2010/11	44	38	10	863	97*	30.82	0	7	12	0	1755	1485	58	25.60	5.07	5-22	3
Hardy, JJE	WPCU	1987/88	1990/91	39	39	6	702	80	21.27	0	2	4	0	0	0	0	–	–	–	0
	All LO	1983	1998	139	130	17	2798	109	24.76	2	13	36	0	0	0	0	–	–	–	0
Harris, E	WPCB	1983/84	1984/85	[no other details available]																
Harvey, IJ	WCC	2005/06	2005/06	9	9	0	184	55	20.44	0	1	1	0	307	240	7	34.28	4.69	2-23	0
	All LO	1993/94	2009/10	305	268	27	5977	112	24.80	2	28	83	0	13607	9952	445	22.36	4.38	5-19	30
Haupt, DL	WPCA Am	2005/06	2005/06	5	1	1	3	3*	–	0	0	1	0	198	128	6	21.33	3.87	4-21	1
Haynes, DL	WPCA	1994/95	1996/97	26	26	0	896	106	34.46	3	3	5	0	0	0	0	–	–	–	0
	All LO	1976/77	1996/97	419	416	44	15651	152*	42.07	28	110	117	0	780	592	9	65.77	4.55	1-9	0
Hector, B	WCC	2006/07	2007/08	10	7	1	46	13*	7.66	0	0	5	0	0	0	0	–	–	–	0
	All LO	2001/02	2007/08	51	47	4	1312	126	30.51	1	10	20	0	222	236	4	59.00	6.37	2-34	0
Henderson, CW	WPCA	1998/99	2003/04	50	23	15	224	27*	28.00	0	0	15	0	2435	1676	68	24.64	4.12	4-26	3
	WCC	2008/09	2010/11	15	7	2	40	14*	8.00	0	0	0	0	604	492	20	23.60	4.88	4-25	1
	All LO	1990/91	2010/11	245	138	66	1110	45	15.41	0	0	54	0	10849	7799	308	25.32	4.31	6-29	15
Henderson, T	WCC	2007/08	2007/08	7	7	0	95	25	13.57	0	0	2	0	291	258	5	51.60	5.31	3-51	0
	All LO	1998/99	2009	114	92	18	1608	126*	21.72	1	9	27	0	4915	3567	130	27.43	4.35	5-5	3
Hendricks, BE	WPCA Am	2009/10	2010/11	7	0	0	0	–	–	0	0	2	0	183	194	8	24.25	6.36	3-28	0
	WCC	2010/11	2010/11	3	0	0	0	–	–	0	0	0	0	102	95	2	47.50	5.58	1-25	0
	All LO	2009/10	2010/11	10	0	0	0	–	–	0	0	2	0	285	289	10	28.90	6.08	3-28	0
Hendricks, S	WPCB	1984/85	1984/85	[no other details available]																
Hendricks, WD	WPCB	1974/75	1975/76	[no other details available]																
Henry, O	WPCU	1978/79	1983/84	21	18	4	325	73*	23.21	0	1	6	0	438	293	3	97.66	4.01	2-41	0
	All LO	1978/79	1993/94	153	132	24	2282	73*	21.12	0	9	56	0	6680	4166	105	39.67	3.74	3-9	0
Hobson, DL	WPCU	1974/75	1984/85	17	11	4	105	27*	15.00	0	0	3	0	803	394	15	26.26	2.94	7-27	1
	All LO	1974/75	1984/85	18	12	4	105	27*	13.12	0	0	3	0	875	448	17	26.35	3.07	7-27	1

Name	Team	From	To	M	Inns	NO	Runs	HS	Avg	100	50	Ct	St	Balls	Runs	Wkts	Avg	RPO	BB	4I
Hodgson, DGM	WPCU	1970/71	1970/71	1	1	0	25	25	25.00	0	0	1	0	0	0	0	–	–	–	0
Holder, JW	WPCB	1975/76	1975/76	[no other details available]																
Holmes, M	WPCA Am	2009/10	2009/10	1	1	0	15	15	15.00	0	0	0	0	0	0	0	–	–	–	0
Homani, Z	WPCA Am	2005/06	2006/07	7	6	0	101	44	16.83	0	0	4	0	0	0	0	–	–	–	0
	All LO	2002/03	2006/07	10	9	0	155	44	17.22	0	0	6	0	0	0	0	–	–	–	0
Hugo, SG	WPCU	1969/70	1972/73	5	4	2	36	19*	18.00	0	0	4	0	108	82	6	13.66	4.55	2-13	0
Igglesden, AP	WPCU	1987/88	1988/89	4	0	0	0	–	–	0	0	0	0	186	99	3	33.00	3.19	1-19	0
	All LO	1987	1998	160	52	32	191	26*	9.55	0	0	30	0	7639	4966	200	24.83	3.90	5-13	8
Isaacs, E	WPCB	1982/83	1983/84	[no other details available]																
Jabaar, A	WPCB	1982/83	1984/85	[no other details available]																
Jackman, RD	WPCU	1971/72	1971/72	1	1	0	31	31	31.00	0	0	0	0	12	8	0	–	4.00	–	0
	All LO	1968	1982/83	288	177	53	1564	46	12.61	0	0	51	0	14491	9265	439	21.10	3.83	7-33	17
Jackson, KC	WPCU	1990/91	1990/91	11	11	1	280	58	28.00	0	1	3	0	108	8	0	–	–	–	0
	WPCA	1991/92	1992/93	21	21	1	610	59	30.50	0	3	5	0	0	0	0	–	–	–	0
	All LO	1990/91	2001/02	114	112	7	3090	105*	29.42	1	19	44	0	423	370	11	33.63	5.24	3-24	0
Jacobs, LP	WPCB	1974/75	1975/76	1	1	0	25	25	25.00	0	0	0	0	0	0	0	–	–	–	0
Jappie, R	WPCA Am	2006/07	2006/07	1	1	0	25	25	25.00	0	0	0	0	0	0	0	–	–	–	0
	All LO	2006/07	2010/11	39	39	7	980	109	30.62	1	6	5	0	100	87	1	87.00	5.22	1-6	0
Jardine, F	WPCA Am	2004/05	2005/06	2	2	2	48	27*	–	0	0	1	0	108	84	0	–	4.66	–	0
Jefferies, ST	WPCU	1980/81	1990/91	92	61	21	801	74*	20.02	0	2	18	0	4949	2900	134	21.64	3.51	5-10	8
	WPCA	1991/92	1991/92	3	3	2	18	12	18.00	0	0	1	0	162	139	6	23.16	5.14	2-30	0
	All LO	1980/81	1993/94	175	119	39	1705	74*	21.31	0	2	42	0	9243	5805	256	22.67	3.76	5-10	14
Johnson, AA	WPCU	1989/90	1989/90	2	2	1	8	7*	8.00	0	0	0	0	108	57	2	28.50	3.16	1-23	0
	All LO	1988/89	1989/90	3	3	1	26	18	13.00	0	0	0	0	138	104	2	52.00	4.52	1-23	0
Johnson, NC	WPCA	2000/01	2003/04	33	31	4	1173	111	43.44	2	7	20	0	526	523	9	58.11	5.96	2-26	0
	WCC	2004/05	2004/05	7	7	1	105	38	17.50	0	0	1	0	54	63	0	–	7.00	–	0
	All LO	1989/90	2004/05	232	223	28	7019	146*	35.99	13	40	122	0	6135	5310	153	34.70	5.19	4-19	3
Jones, SA	WPCU	1974/75	1979/80	7	4	3	25	12	25.00	0	0	0	0	479	204	18	11.33	2.55	5-31	3
	All LO	1974/75	1987/88	35	31	5	605	51	23.26	0	1	8	0	1196	675	34	19.85	3.38	5-20	5
Jordaan, D	WPCA	1993/94	1994/95	12	11	0	380	116	34.54	1	1	5	0	176	148	5	29.60	5.04	1-14	0
	All LO	1992/93	2000/01	73	69	5	1661	116	25.95	1	13	22	0	381	330	7	47.14	5.19	1-5	0
Kallis, JH	WPCA	1994/95	2003/04	47	44	7	1546	116*	41.78	3	10	12	0	1533	1145	40	28.62	4.48	5-47	1
	WCC	2006/07	2006/07	1	1	0	28	28	28.00	0	0	0	0	54	47	0	–	5.22	–	0
	All LO	1994/95	2010/11	408	390	64	14408	155*	44.19	23	104	151	0	13259	10393	340	30.56	4.70	5-30	6
Katts, A	WPCB	1975/76	1975/76	[no other details available]																

Name	Team	From	To	M	Inns	NO	Runs	HS	Avg	100	50	Ct	St	Balls	Runs	Wkts	Avg	RPO	BB	4I
Kemp, JM	WCC	2007/08	2010/11	27	24	4	759	86	37.95	0	7	13	0	153	121	6	20.16	4.74	4-16	1
	All LO	1997/98	2010/11	273	232	60	6056	107*	35.20	3	42	117	0	6704	5405	182	29.69	4.83	6-20	9
Khan, S	WPCA Am	2010/11	2010/11	3	1	1	7	7*	–	0	0	3	0	72	45	0	–	3.75	–	0
Kirsten, G	WPCU	1988/89	1990/91	26	24	1	437	54	19.00	0	1	5	0	0	0	0	–	–	–	0
	WPCA	1991/92	2003/04	67	64	6	1858	104*	32.03	3	11	24	0	78	52	2	26.00	4.00	1-25	0
	All LO	1988/89	2003/04	294	289	27	9586	188*	36.58	18	58	97	1	138	112	3	37.33	4.86	1-25	0
Kirsten, P	WPCA	1995/96	1998/99	49	32	15	520	67	30.58	0	1	66	4	0	0	0	–	–	–	0
	All LO	1990/91	1998/99	63	45	19	663	67	25.50	0	1	76	6	0	0	0	–	–	–	0
Kirsten, PN	WPCU	1973/74	1989/90	121	121	7	4358	126	38.22	6	34	49	0	2061	1337	41	32.60	3.89	6-17	1
	All LO	1973/74	1996/97	358	352	32	11403	134*	35.63	10	83	120	0	4620	3244	95	34.14	4.21	6-17	3
Kleinveldt, MC	WPCA Am	2010/11	2010/11	4	4	0	82	36	20.50	0	0	0	0	0	0	0	–	–	–	0
Kleinveldt, RK	WPCA	2002/03	2003/04	6	3	1	12	6*	6.00	0	0	2	0	252	175	7	25.00	4.16	3-26	0
	WCC	2004/05	2010/11	60	40	7	546	54*	16.54	0	1	8	0	2578	2068	72	28.72	4.81	4-25	3
	WPCA Am	2005/06	2010/11	5	4	0	111	55	27.75	0	1	2	0	220	176	7	25.14	4.80	3-14	0
	All LO	2002/03	2010/11	77	49	8	689	55	16.80	0	2	12	0	3302	2584	92	28.08	4.69	4-25	3
Klette, JE	WPCU	1969/70	1969/70	2	2	0	7	4	3.50	0	0	2	0	0	0	0	–	–	–	0
Koch, DM	WPCA	1997/98	1997/98	1	0	0	0	–	–	0	0	1	0	0	0	0	–	–	–	0
Koenig, SG	All LO	1997/98	1999/00	20	17	9	172	26*	21.50	0	0	7	0	726	525	17	30.88	4.33	3-25	0
	WPCA	1994/95	1996/97	14	14	7	243	43	17.35	0	0	1	0	0	0	0	–	–	–	0
	All LO	1994/95	2003/04	60	58	3	1175	116	21.36	2	2	11	0	3	4	0	–	8.00	–	0
Kohn, J	WPCA Am	2008/09	2008/09	2	1	1	7	7*	–	0	0	0	0	90	59	2	29.50	3.93	2-31	0
Kolbe, C	WPCB	1975/76	1975/76	[no other details available]																
Koster, RA	WPCA	1992/93	1993/94	6	5	2	34	24*	11.33	0	0	3	0	0	0	0	–	–	–	0
	All LO	1992/93	1996/97	29	26	4	600	77*	27.27	0	6	6	0	0	0	0	–	–	–	0
Kruger, WG	WPCU B	1983/84	1983/84	1	1	0	15	15	15.00	0	0	3	0	0	0	0	–	–	–	0
Kuiper, AP	WPCU	1979/80	1990/91	121	115	20	2413	104	25.40	1	8	46	0	3930	2667	135	19.75	4.07	5-47	6
	WPCA	1991/92	1994/95	31	29	4	881	107*	35.24	1	6	7	0	757	529	17	31.11	4.19	3-26	0
	All LO	1979/80	1997/98	252	239	47	6329	118	32.96	5	35	82	0	7250	5414	221	24.49	4.48	5-47	6
Kuiper, JM	WPCA Am	2005/06	2008/09	21	20	3	586	97	34.47	0	2	6	0	0	0	0	–	–	–	0
Laing, PC	WPCA Am	2008/09	2009/10	7	7	0	109	35	15.57	0	0	1	0	150	152	6	25.33	6.08	3-46	2
	All LO	2005/06	2009/10	16	15	1	350	86*	25.00	0	2	6	0	462	452	19	23.78	5.87	4-42	0
Lamb, AJ	WPCU	1972/73	1981/82	20	19	3	587	90	36.68	0	6	2	0	0	0	0	–	–	–	0
	WPCA	1992/93	1992/93	12	12	1	346	62	31.45	0	3	3	0	0	0	0	–	–	–	0
	All LO	1972/73	1995	484	463	63	15658	132*	39.14	19	98	135	0	32	29	2	14.50	5.43	1-4	0
Lambert, J	WPCB	1974/75	1974/75	[no other details available]																

Name	Team	From	To	M	Inns	NO	Runs	HS	Avg	100	50	Ct	St	Balls	Runs	Wkts	Avg	RPO	BB	4I
Langeveldt, CK	WCC	2007/08	2010/11	28	11	8	27	17*	9.00	0	0	6	0	1213	925	49	18.87	4.57	5-17	3
	All LO	1997/98	2010/11	202	79	33	364	33*	7.91	0	0	37	0	9487	7363	309	23.82	4.65	5-7	15
Lawrenson, RR	WPCU	1980/81	1980/81	1	0	0	0	–	–	0	0	0	0	42	31	0	–	4.42	–	0
	WPCU B	1983/84	1983/84	1	1	0	0	0	0.00	0	0	0	0	42	28	0	–	4.00	–	0
	All LO	1980/81	1983/84	2	1	0	0	0	0.00	0	0	0	0	84	59	0	–	4.21	–	0
Lazard, TN	WPCU	1983/84	1989/90	28	28	3	635	96*	25.40	0	4	4	0	6	7	1	7.00	7.00	–	0
	WPCA	1991/92	1992/93	16	16	4	703	108*	58.58	2	4	2	0	0	0	0	–	–	–	0
	All LO	1983/84	1995/96	69	67	9	2037	108*	35.12	2	13	11	0	6	7	1	7.00	7.00	–	0
Le Roux, GS	WPCU	1975/76	1988/89	83	66	22	885	43	20.11	0	0	23	0	4399	2487	134	18.55	3.39	5-17	8
	All LO	1975/76	1988/89	250	190	55	3151	88	23.34	0	9	58	0	12201	7555	378	19.98	3.71	6-21	21
Levi, RE	WPCA Am	2004/05	2010/11	18	17	1	456	116	28.50	2	1	3	0	0	0	0	–	–	–	0
	WCC	2005/06	2010/11	23	20	3	407	86	23.94	0	1	9	0	0	0	0	–	–	–	0
	All LO	2004/05	2010/11	41	37	4	863	116	26.15	2	2	12	0	0	0	0	–	–	–	0
Lotter, RB	WPCA Am	2008/09	2008/09	1	0	0	0	–	–	0	0	0	0	48	20	1	20.00	2.50	1-20	0
Louw, DA	WPCU	1969/70	1969/70	1	1	1	9	9*	–	0	0	1	0	0	0	0	–	–	–	0
Louw, J	WCC	2010/11	2010/11	3	2	0	3	3	1.50	0	0	0	0	126	155	3	51.66	7.38	2-64	0
	All LO	2000/01	2010/11	141	106	25	1437	72	17.74	0	3	19	0	6410	5252	194	27.07	4.91	5-27	12
MacHelm, DQ	WPCA	1992/93	1992/93	1	0	0	0	–	–	0	0	0	0	66	41	4	10.25	3.72	4-41	1
Maclons, M	WPCB	1975/75	1975/76	[no other details available]																
Magiet, A	WPCA Am	2004/05	2005/06	5	5	0	51	41	10.20	0	0	1	0	66	64	1	64.00	5.81	1-39	0
Magiet, R	WPCA Am	2004/05	2004/05	1	1	0	6	6	6.00	0	0	1	0	0	0	0	–	–	–	0
	All LO	2003/04	2008/09	8	7	0	89	22	12.71	0	0	2	0	0	0	0	–	–	–	0
Magiet, S	WPCB	1982/83	1984/85	[no other details available]																
Mahlombe, M	WPCA Am	2005/06	2010/11	37	14	5	90	29	10.00	0	0	12	0	1091	835	31	26.93	4.59	4-21	2
Mahoney, JE	WPCB	1974/75	1975/76	[no other details available]																
Martin, A	WPCU B	1981/82	1981/82	1	1	1	16	16*	–	0	0	0	0	66	19	2	9.50	1.72	2-19	0
Martin, BP	WPCB	1982/83	1982/83	[no other details available]																
Martin, PW	WPCU B	1983/84	1983/84	1	1	0	5	5	5.00	0	0	0	0	28	23	0	–	4.92	–	0
	WPCU	1989/90	1990/91	6	6	0	184	78	30.66	0	2	3	0	0	0	0	–	–	–	0
Martins, S	WPCB	1982/83	1982/83	[no other details available]																
Martyn, A	WPCA	1993/94	1996/97	28	8	6	35	14*	17.50	0	0	4	0	1340	893	44	20.29	3.99	4-52	1
Masinda, MR	WPCA Am	2005/06	2005/06	1	0	0	0	–	–	0	0	0	0	36	36	1	36.00	6.00	1-36	0
Matthews, BA	WPCU	1985/86	1987/88	18	4	3	1	1*	1.00	0	0	1	0	918	526	25	21.04	3.43	4-22	2
	WPCU B	1984/85	1984/85	1	1	0	3	3	3.00	0	0	0	0	54	31	0	–	3.44	–	0
	All LO	1984/85	1989/90	33	10	8	11	3*	5.50	0	0	6	0	1740	1046	36	29.05	3.60	4-22	2

Name	Team	From	To	M	Inns	NO	Runs	HS	Avg	100	50	Ct	St	Balls	Runs	Wkts	Avg	RPO	BB	4I
Matthews, CR	WPCU	1987/88	1990/91	43	13	9	136	28*	34.00	0	0	11	0	2249	1353	72	18.79	3.60	5-11	2
	WPCA	1991/92	1999/00	76	35	15	140	31*	7.00	0	0	22	0	3426	2175	91	23.90	3.80	4-24	3
	All LO	1987/88	1999/00	176	70	33	417	31*	11.27	0	0	43	0	8726	5523	243	22.72	3.79	5-11	8
McAdam, SJ	WPCU	1972/73	1972/73	1	0	0	0	–	–	0	0	0	0	72	36	1	36.00	3.00	1-36	0
	All LO	1969/70	1972/73	5	4	2	41	24	20.50	0	0	3	0	360	212	8	26.50	3.53	3-40	0
McEwan, KS	WPCU	1981/82	1986/87	42	41	5	1237	102*	34.36	2	7	19	2	0	0	0	–	–	–	0
	All LO	1972/73	1991/92	409	396	42	11866	162*	33.51	16	69	140	2	24	16	0	–	4.00	–	0
McLean, JJ	WPCA	2002/03	2002/03	2	1	0	0	0	0.00	0	0	1	0	0	0	0	–	–	–	0
	All LO	2002/03	2006	11	6	1	60	36	12.00	0	0	7	0	0	0	0	–	–	–	0
McMillan, BM	WPCU	1989/90	1990/91	31	29	10	476	63	25.05	0	3	15	0	1273	774	25	30.96	3.64	3-18	0
	WPCA	1991/92	1999/00	53	48	9	1344	100	34.46	1	7	22	0	1711	1014	41	24.73	3.55	4-23	2
	All LO	1985/86	1999/00	219	173	45	3738	135	29.20	3	15	98	0	9266	6290	201	31.29	4.07	4-23	5
Mdodana, TJ	WPCA Am	2006/07	2006/07	1	1	0	15	15	15.00	0	0	0	0	0	0	0	–	–	–	0
Mellor, MD	WPCU B	1983/84	1983/84	1	1	0	16	16	16.00	0	0	0	0	0	0	0	–	–	–	0
Mentis, MJ	WPCU	1975/76	1975/76	1	1	0	0	0	0.00	0	0	0	0	0	0	0	–	–	–	0
Meyer, MA	WPCA	1993/94	1994/95	3	1	0	0	0	0.00	0	0	0	0	150	96	5	19.20	3.84	4-26	1
Mgijima, A	WPCA Am	2009/10	2010/11	12	8	1	68	18	9.71	0	0	5	0	78	80	4	20.00	6.15	2-9	0
	All LO	2007/08	2010/11	14	10	1	72	18	8.00	0	0	5	0	84	88	4	22.00	6.28	2-9	0
Miller, C	WPCB	1983/84	1983/84	3	2	2	6	6*	–	0	0	1	0	156	98	7	14.00	3.76	5-23	1
Minnaar, MB	WPCU	1985/86	1985/86	1	1	0	4	4	4.00	0	0	0	0	48	20	0	–	2.50	–	0
	WPCU B	1984/85	1984/85	4	3	2	10	6*	10.00	0	0	1	0	204	118	7	16.85	3.47	5-23	1
	All LO	1984/85	1985/86	7	6	2	50	19	12.50	0	0	0	0	348	239	5	47.80	4.12	2-38	0
Mitchell, TJ	WPCA	1994/95	1995/96	1	0	0	0	–	–	0	0	0	0	54	38	0	–	4.22	–	0
Mjekula, S	WPCA Am	2006/07	2006/07	30	12	4	42	11*	5.25	0	0	4	0	1184	865	27	32.03	4.38	4-50	1
Mohamed, E	WPCB	1984/85	1984/85	1	1	0	10	10	10.00	0	0	1	0	12	17	0	–	8.50	–	0
Moleon, EO	WPCA	1997/98	1997/98	3	1	0	1	1	1.00	0	0	0	0	150	100	4	25.00	4.00	2-30	0
	WPCA Am	2007/08	2007/08	66	45	14	542	68	17.48	0	1	15	0	2846	2294	58	39.55	4.83	4-42	1
Moodie, DV	WPCB	1974/75	1974/75	[no other details available]																
Morris, RET	WPCU	1972/73	1978/79	14	11	3	165	42	20.62	0	0	3	0	828	431	12	35.91	3.12	4-31	1
	WPCA	1998/99	2003/04	25	19	5	243	57*	17.35	0	1	5	0	713	590	26	22.69	4.96	4-50	1
Munnik, R	WCC	2004/05	2005/06	6	5	3	92	30*	46.00	0	0	0	0	42	45	1	45.00	6.42	1-31	0
	WPCA Am	2004/05	2005/06	5	5	0	177	109	35.40	1	0	3	0	84	85	2	42.50	6.07	2-44	0
	All LO	1998/99	2005/06	36	29	8	512	109	24.38	1	1	8	0	839	720	29	24.82	5.14	4-50	1

Name	Team	From	To	M	Inns	NO	Runs	HS	Avg	100	50	Ct	St	Balls	Runs	Wkts	Avg	RPO	BB	4I
Muntingh, E	WPCU	1981/82	1981/82	1	1	0	19	19	19.00	0	0	1	0	0	0	0	–	–	–	0
	WPCU B	1981/82	1981/82	1	1	0	2	2	2.00	0	0	0	0	0	0	0	–	–	–	0
	All LO	1979/80	1981/82	5	5	0	63	35	12.60	0	0	2	0	0	0	0	–	–	–	0
Musson, R	WPCB	1982/83	1982/83	[no other details available]																
Neethling, JJ	WPCB	1974/75	1974/75	[no other details available]																
Nel, MJ	WPCU	1981/82	1981/82	1	1	0	0	0	0.00	0	0	2	0	0	0	0	–	–	–	0
Nieuwoudt, AB	WPCU	1972/73	1979/80	7	2	1	3	2	3.00	0	0	0	0	408	194	8	24.25	2.85	3-16	0
	WPCU B	1981/82	1981/82	1	1	1	0	0	0.00	0	0	1	0	66	26	1	26.00	2.36	1-26	0
	All LO	1969/70	1981/82	10	4	1	4	2	1.33	0	0	1	0	600	311	11	28.27	3.11	3-16	0
Nolte, JE	WPCU	1988/89	1989/90	15	4	2	1	1*	0.50	0	0	3	0	772	437	17	25.70	3.39	3-17	0
Norman, D	WPCU	1984/85	1985/86	19	10	3	36	7	5.14	0	0	2	0	832	642	22	29.18	4.62	4-56	1
	WPCU B	1983/84	1984/85	2	2	1	8	8*	8.00	0	0	0	0	66	60	2	30.00	5.45	2-47	0
	All LO	1983/84	1991/92	85	59	19	573	41	14.32	0	0	16	0	3966	2698	87	31.01	4.08	4-23	3
Northcote, AM	WPCA Am	2008/09	2008/09	2	2	1	30	30	30.00	0	0	0	0	0	0	0	–	–	–	0
Nyulu, SC	WPCA Am	2004/05	2004/05	2	0	0	0	–	–	0	0	0	0	90	63	2	31.50	4.20	1-31	0
Olivier, MW	WCC	2009/10	2009/10	2	0	0	0	–	–	0	0	0	0	30	27	0	–	5.40	–	0
	WPCA Am	2009/10	2009/10	7	5	2	50	24	16.66	0	0	0	0	276	301	13	23.15	6.54	5-37	1
	All LO	2004/05	2010/11	37	13	5	86	24	10.75	0	0	5	0	1319	1339	60	22.31	6.09	6-34	4
Ontong, JL	WCC	2008/09	2010/11	29	23	3	390	59	19.50	0	0	9	0	276	240	6	40.00	5.21	2-26	0
	All LO	1998/99	2010/11	168	142	18	3216	122*	25.93	1	22	67	0	3084	2409	56	43.01	4.68	3-29	0
Pagden, ND	WPCU B	1981/82	1981/82	1	1	0	14	14	14.00	0	0	0	0	66	67	2	33.50	6.09	2-67	0
Pangarker, H	WPCA	1997/98	1997/98	5	5	0	95	68	19.00	0	1	1	0	0	0	0	–	–	–	0
Paterson, D	WPCA Am	2008/09	2010/11	12	5	1	5	5	5.00	0	0	2	0	399	333	18	18.50	5.00	4-27	1
Paulse, HH	WCC	2009/10	2009/10	1	0	0	0	–	–	0	0	0	0	18	22	1	22.00	7.33	1-22	0
	All LO	2005/06	2010/11	29	14	5	65	19	7.22	0	0	8	0	1051	879	36	24.41	5.01	5-45	2
Payne, DG	WPCA	1991/92	1998/99	10	2	2	2	2*	–	0	0	0	0	483	309	15	20.60	3.83	5-40	1
Petersen, B	WPCB	1974/75	1975/76	[no other details available]																
Peterson, RJ	WCC	2009/10	2010/11	15	12	1	326	78*	29.63	0	2	9	0	642	583	18	32.38	5.44	3-29	0
	All LO	1999/00	2010/11	161	113	14	2427	101	24.51	1	14	60	5	6579	5012	177	28.31	4.57	7-24	6
Pfuhl, GP	WPCU	1969/70	1979/80	21	13	4	165	47	18.33	0	0	36	5	0	0	0	–	–	–	0
Philander, VD	WCC	2004/05	2010/11	54	39	13	677	76*	26.03	0	3	4	0	2001	1683	39	43.15	5.04	3-29	0
	WPCA Am	2004/05	2009/10	4	4	0	33	19	8.25	0	0	0	0	174	116	3	38.66	4.00	3-49	0
	All LO	2004	2010/11	89	63	21	1109	79*	26.40	0	4	7	0	3653	2872	79	36.35	4.71	4-12	2

Name	Team	From	To	M	Inns	NO	Runs	HS	Avg	100	50	Ct	St	Balls	Runs	Wkts	Avg	RPO	BB	4I
Piedt, DL-R	WPCA Am	2008/09	2010/11	20	8	5	62	23	20.66	0	0	9	0	768	562	28	20.07	4.39	4-9	2
	WCC	2010/11	2010/11	5	1	1	0	0*	–	0	0	1	0	135	109	4	27.25	4.84	3-22	0
	All LO	2008/09	2010/11	25	9	6	62	23	20.66	0	0	10	0	903	671	32	20.96	4.45	4-9	2
Pienaar, RF	WPCU	1981/82	1985/86	35	33	4	820	84	28.27	0	7	6	0	1091	903	26	34.73	4.96	4-37	1
	All LO	1979/80	1999/00	233	222	18	6705	135	32.86	7	47	37	0	3406	2576	84	30.66	4.53	4-34	2
Plaatjies, FC	WCC	2008/09	2009/10	15	1	0	4	4	4.00	0	0	4	0	612	564	25	22.56	5.52	4-44	1
	WPCA Am	2006/07	2009/10	8	2	2	4	2*	–	0	0	1	0	387	344	13	26.46	5.33	4-24	1
	All LO	2006/07	2009/10	23	3	2	8	4	8.00	0	0	5	0	999	908	38	23.89	5.45	4-24	2
Plantema, AP	WPCA	1992/93	1992/93	4	4	0	77	32	19.25	0	0	2	0	0	0	0	–	–	–	0
Player, BT	WPCA	1997/98	1998/99	15	13	1	198	39	16.50	0	0	2	0	556	450	17	26.47	4.85	3-50	0
	All LO	1985/86	2000/01	148	104	25	1281	83	16.21	0	2	21	0	6738	4538	150	30.25	4.04	5-27	5
Prince, AG	WPCA	1998/99	2003/04	53	49	13	1028	76*	28.55	0	3	21	0	30	41	0	–	8.20	–	0
	WCC	2004/05	2007/08	26	22	3	644	78	33.89	0	6	15	0	1	2	0	–	12.00	–	0
	All LO	1996/97	2010/11	208	182	35	4611	128	31.36	2	22	94	0	91	86	0	–	5.67	–	0
Pringle, MW	WPCU	1989/90	1990/91	21	6	2	52	21*	13.00	0	0	6	0	1020	622	35	17.77	3.65	6-30	2
	WPCA	1991/92	1996/97	61	31	9	225	31	10.22	0	0	11	0	3188	2141	81	26.43	4.02	5-36	3
	All LO	1987/88	2001/02	177	93	33	714	39*	11.90	0	0	36	0	8592	5717	225	25.40	3.99	6-30	9
Procter, MJ	WPCU	1969/70	1969/70	2	2	0	40	22	20.00	0	0	1	0	144	60	4	15.00	2.50	2-28	0
	All LO	1966/67	1983/84	271	256	19	6624	154*	27.94	5	36	91	0	12335	6454	344	18.76	3.13	6-13	17
Puttick, AG	WPCA	1999/00	2003/04	36	34	8	751	113*	28.88	1	3	25	3	0	0	0	–	–	–	0
	WCC	2004/05	2010/11	71	69	7	2201	122*	35.50	5	11	57	5	0	0	0	–	–	–	0
	WPCA Am	2010/11	2010/11	1	1	0	6	6	6.00	0	0	0	8	0	0	0	–	–	–	0
	All LO	1999/00	2010/11	118	114	17	3299	143	34.01	7	16	84	0	0	0	0	–	–	–	0
Qomoyi, A	WPCA Am	2007/08	2007/08	1	1	0	0	0	0.00	0	0	0	0	54	71	1	71.00	7.88	1-71	0
Rabie, GR	WCC	2008/09	2010/11	6	2	1	0	0*	0.00	0	0	0	0	189	145	5	29.00	4.60	2-43	0
	WPCA Am	2008/09	2010/11	15	4	3	8	6	8.00	0	0	2	0	648	500	28	17.85	4.62	4-52	1
	All LO	2008/09	2010/11	27	6	4	8	6	4.00	0	0	3	0	1103	832	42	19.80	4.52	5-21	2
Ramoo, RJ	WPCA Am	2008/09	2009/10	16	16	2	471	74*	33.64	0	4	1	0	78	61	2	30.50	4.69	1-16	0
	All LO	2008/09	2010/11	21	21	2	708	111	37.26	1	4	3	0	85	73	2	36.50	5.15	1-16	0
Rayment, PA	WPCU	1990/91	1990/91	3	0	0	0	–	–	0	0	1	0	135	91	6	15.16	4.04	4-25	1
	All LO	1985/86	1993/94	58	25	9	250	57	15.62	0	1	16	0	2809	1996	75	26.61	4.26	4-13	3
Rayner, PH	WPCU	1982/83	1985/86	28	28	2	718	86	27.61	0	5	7	0	0	0	0	–	–	–	0
	WPCU B	1981/82	1981/82	1	1	0	143	143	143.00	1	0	0	0	0	0	0	–	–	–	0
	All LO	1981/82	1988/89	46	45	3	1254	143	29.85	1	9	13	0	0	0	0	–	–	–	0

Name	Team	From	To	M	Inns	NO	Runs	HS	Avg	100	50	Ct	St	Balls	Runs	Wkts	Avg	RPO	BB	4I
Richards, RR	WPCA Am	2009/10	2010/11	12	6	3	29	17	9.66	0	0	1	0	334	309	5	61.80	5.55	3-35	0
	All LO	2005/06	2010/11	17	9	4	42	17	8.40	0	0	1	0	490	407	13	31.30	4.98	3-13	0
Richardson, RP	WPCU	1988/89	1988/89	1	0	0	0	–	–	0	0	1	0	18	13	0	–	4.33	–	0
Rippon, MJ	WPCA Am	2010/11	2010/11	1	1	0	10	10	10.00	0	0	1	0	48	44	0	–	5.50	–	0
Rundle, DB	WPCU	1984/85	1990/91	55	35	15	342	39	17.10	0	0	14	0	2794	1540	37	41.62	3.30	3-27	0
	WPCA	1991/92	1997/98	68	43	15	686	75	24.50	0	2	40	0	3276	2059	72	28.59	3.77	4-19	1
	WPCU B	1984/85	1984/85	1	1	0	15	15	15.00	0	0	1	0	0	0	0	–	–	–	0
	All LO	1984/85	1997/98	126	81	30	1049	75	20.56	0	2	58	0	6166	3694	114	32.40	3.59	4-19	2
Ryall, RJ	WPCU	1979/80	1990/91	99	42	20	245	41*	11.13	0	0	130	6	0	0	0	–	–	–	0
	WPCA	1991/92	1994/95	45	13	9	81	19	20.25	0	0	56	5	0	0	0	–	–	–	0
	All LO	1979/80	1994/95	145	56	29	350	41*	12.96	0	0	189	11	0	0	0	–	–	–	0
Samsodien, W	WPCA Am	2004/05	2004/05	2	1	1	0	0*	–	0	0	0	0	90	78	7	11.14	5.20	4-34	1
Sandri, PSE	WCC	2006/07	2007/08	4	1	0	4	4	4.00	0	0	2	0	168	139	4	34.75	4.96	1-21	0
	All LO	2004/05	2008/09	17	4	2	24	14*	12.00	0	0	5	0	690	545	16	34.06	4.73	2-18	0
Schultz, BN	WPCA	1996/97	1997/98	11	2	1	1	1*	1.00	0	0	0	0	465	355	16	22.18	4.58	4-19	1
	All LO	1989/90	2000/01	80	13	9	17	5	4.25	0	0	12	0	4022	2508	136	18.44	3.74	6-22	8
Seeff, J	WPCU	1981/82	1981/82	1	1	0	2	2	2.00	0	0	0	0	0	0	0	–	–	–	0
	WPCU B	1981/82	1984/85	2	2	0	16	9	8.00	0	0	1	0	0	0	0	–	–	–	0
	All LO	1981/82	1984/85	3	3	0	18	9	6.00	0	0	1	0	0	0	0	–	–	–	0
Seeff, L	WPCU	1978/79	1990/91	106	106	1	2698	100	25.69	1	17	36	0	48	15	3	5.00	1.87	3-15	0
	All LO	1978/79	1992/93	108	108	1	2876	142	26.87	2	17	37	0	48	15	3	5.00	1.87	3-15	0
Seymour, MA	WPCU	1969/70	1969/70	1	0	0	0	–	–	0	0	0	0	0	0	0	–	–	–	0
Shah, OA	WCC	2010/11	2010/11	6	6	2	217	83	54.25	0	2	0	0	0	0	0	–	–	–	0
	All LO	1995	2010/11	331	313	39	9623	134	35.12	13	62	112	0	912	896	27	33.18	5.89	4-11	1
Simetu, S	WPCA Am	2010/11	2010/11	10	0	0	0	–	–	0	0	3	0	338	256	14	18.28	4.54	4-9	1
Simons, EO	WPCU	1983/84	1990/91	70	53	24	624	51*	21.51	0	1	23	0	3470	2325	105	22.14	4.02	6-8	9
	WPCA	1991/92	1998/99	86	70	20	1283	74*	25.66	0	6	31	0	3887	2465	124	19.87	3.80	4-3	8
	All LO	1983/84	1998/99	193	152	54	2207	74*	22.52	0	7	62	0	9351	6114	283	21.60	3.92	6-8	20
Simpson, AR	WPCA Am	2004/05	2004/05	2	2	0	44	44	22.00	0	0	1	0	0	0	0	–	–	–	0
Simpson, LF	WPCA Am	2005/06	2008/09	3	0	0	0	–	–	0	0	0	0	150	168	6	28.00	6.72	3-72	0
Smith, GC	WPCA	2000/01	2003/04	31	31	2	1346	117*	46.41	3	10	15	0	726	611	26	23.50	5.04	3-35	0
	WCC	2006/07	2009/10	5	4	0	37	23	9.25	0	0	3	0	18	17	0	–	5.66	–	0
	All LO	1999/00	2009/10	229	225	15	8506	141	40.50	12	62	123	0	1968	1796	47	38.21	5.47	3-30	0
Snyman, NM	WPCU B	1983/84	1983/84	1	1	0	5	5	5.00	0	0	0	0	6	0	0	–	–	–	0
	All LO	1983/84	1992/93	18	18	0	308	54	17.11	0	2	4	0	6	4	1	–	4.00	–	0

Name	Team	From	To	M	Inns	NO	Runs	HS	Avg	100	50	Ct	St	Balls	Runs	Wkts	Avg	RPO	BB	4I
Snyman, OJA	WPCU	1972/73	1972/73	1	1	0	25	25	25.00	0	0	0	0	0	0	0	–	–	–	0
Sodumo, AM	WPCA Am	2007/08	2008/09	4	3	0	59	58	19.66	0	1	7	0	0	0	0	–	–	–	0
	All LO	2002/03	2010/11	48	32	4	337	58	12.03	0	1	62	9	0	0	0	–	–	–	0
Solomon, IR	WPCA	1994/95	1994/95	1	1	1	6	6*	–	0	0	0	0	0	0	0	–	–	–	0
Solomons, F	WPCB	1983/84	1984/85	[no other details available]																
Solomons, MT	WPCA	1998/99	1998/99	2	1	0	7	7	7.00	0	0	4	0	0	0	0	–	–	–	0
Sonn, A	WPCB	1974/75	1974/75	[no other details available]																
Stelling, WF	WPCA	1991/92	1991/92	2	0	0	0	–	–	0	0	0	0	108	85	0	–	4.72	–	0
	All LO	1991/92	2007	63	50	25	856	76*	34.24	0	3	25	0	2806	2039	74	27.55	4.35	5-30	1
Stephens, CG	WPCU	1969/70	1971/72	7	7	0	230	104	32.85	1	1	1	0	0	0	0	–	–	–	0
Strydom, JG	WCC	2004/05	2005/06	8	7	0	178	63	25.42	0	1	1	0	0	0	0	–	–	–	0
	All LO	1999/00	2010/11	72	69	3	1936	135*	29.33	2	11	22	0	0	0	0	–	–	–	0
Swart, PD	WPCU	1969/70	1984/85	34	27	4	364	35	15.82	0	0	8	0	1741	919	36	25.52	3.16	3-21	0
	All LO	1969/70	1984/85	82	73	12	1554	85*	25.47	0	10	19	0	3672	2238	89	25.14	3.65	4-35	3
Taljaard, M	WPCU B	1981/82	1981/82	1	1	0	6	6	6.00	0	0	0	0	66	41	1	41.00	3.72	1-41	0
Telemachus, R	WPCA	1999/00	2003/04	37	16	6	78	16	7.80	0	0	5	0	1799	1222	48	25.45	4.07	3-25	0
	All LO	1994/95	2007/08	176	84	32	702	53*	13.50	0	1	32	0	8377	6287	249	25.24	4.50	6-24	6
Telo, FD	WCC	2005/06	2007/08	8	7	0	97	53	13.85	0	1	3	0	0	0	0	–	–	–	0
	WPCA Am	2005/06	2010/11	21	18	1	434	90	25.52	0	3	1	0	0	0	0	–	–	–	0
	All LO	2005/06	2010/11	35	31	3	626	90	22.35	0	4	4	0	0	0	0	–	–	–	0
Temoor, A-A	WPCA Am	2007/08	2009/10	5	4	0	41	14	10.25	0	0	2	0	156	151	4	37.75	5.80	2-18	0
Theron, M	WPCB	1982/83	1982/83	[no other details available]																
Thomas, Y	WPCB	1982/83	1985/85	[no other details available]																
Thompson, PM	WPCU	1980/81	1980/81	1	1	0	7	7	7.00	0	0	2	0	0	0	0	–	–	–	0
	WPCU B	1981/82	1981/82	1	1	0	9	9	9.00	0	0	0	0	0	0	0	–	–	–	0
	All LO	1970/71	1981/82	9	9	1	228	97	28.50	0	2	6	0	0	0	0	–	–	–	0
Touzel, FB	WPCA	1992/93	1993/94	6	6	0	133	66	22.16	0	1	1	0	0	0	0	–	–	–	0
Townsend, TKM	WPCA Am	2008/09	2010/11	6	6	0	105	37	17.50	0	0	4	0	0	0	0	–	–	–	0
Trott, JJL	WPCA	2001/02	2001/02	10	8	1	194	50	27.71	0	1	3	0	48	52	3	17.33	6.50	2-36	0
	All LO	1999/00	2010/11	187	175	32	6749	137	47.19	14	46	59	0	1528	1436	54	26.59	5.63	4-55	1
Tsolekile, TL	WPCA	1998/99	2003/04	39	23	7	266	44	16.62	0	0	57	11	0	0	0	–	–	–	0
	WCC	2005/06	2006/07	21	16	2	168	35	12.00	0	0	30	0	0	0	0	–	–	–	0
	WPCA Am	2007/08	2008/09	7	6	3	81	30*	27.00	0	0	6	1	0	0	0	–	–	–	0
	All LO	1998/99	2010/11	121	81	24	1148	65*	20.14	0	2	167	19	0	0	0	–	–	–	0

Name	Team	From	To	M	Inns	NO	Runs	HS	Avg	100	50	Ct	St	Balls	Runs	Wkts	Avg	RPO	BB	4I
Tullis, GD	WPCU	1988/89	1988/89	1	1	0	3	3	3.00	0	0	0	0	0	0	0	–	–	–	0
	WPCU B	1983/84	1984/85	2	2	1	6	6*	6.00	0	0	1	0	0	0	0	–	–	–	0
	All LO	1983/84	1988/89	3	3	1	9	6*	4.50	0	0	1	0	0	0	0	–	–	–	0
Turner, DR	WPCU	1977/78	1977/78	1	1	0	9	9	9.00	0	0	0	0	0	0	0	–	–	–	0
	All LO	1968	1991	381	367	40	9904	123*	30.28	5	60	92	0	17	19	0	–	6.70	–	0
Turner, GJ	WPCU	1984/85	1986/87	3	3	1	41	26*	20.50	0	0	1	0	0	0	0	–	–	–	0
	All LO	1984/85	1991	7	7	3	211	80*	52.75	0	2	1	0	184	120	3	40.00	3.91	2-18	0
Vallie, MY	WPCA Am	2008/09	2010/11	22	21	2	627	89	33.00	0	5	8	0	219	196	5	39.20	5.36	2-26	0
Van der Merwe, WM	WPCU	1985/86	1986/87	2	1	0	9	9	9.00	0	0	2	0	60	49	1	49.00	4.90	1-14	0
	All LO	1981/82	1990	11	10	2	161	44*	20.12	0	0	5	0	591	419	18	23.27	4.25	4-49	1
Van Graan, K	WPCB	1974/75	1975/76	[no other details available]																
Van Graan, Robbie	WPCB	1974/75	1974/75	[no other details available]																
Van Niekerk, AP	WPCU	1969/70	1972/73	7	5	2	102	52	34.00	0	1	3	0	306	251	4	62.75	4.92	2-93	0
	WPCU B	1981/82	1981/82	1	1	0	1	1	1.00	0	0	0	0	24	30	0	–	7.50	–	0
	All LO	1969/70	1981/82	8	6	2	103	52	25.75	0	1	3	0	330	281	4	70.25	5.10	2-93	0
Van Schalkwyk, C	WPCB	1982/83	1982/83	[no other details available]																
Van Schalkwyk, SC	WPCA Am	2007/08	2008/09	4	3	2	56	33*	56.00	0	0	0	0	180	132	11	12.00	4.40	5-30	1
	All LO	2007/08	2010/11	31	18	4	283	38	20.21	0	0	13	0	878	820	39	21.02	5.60	5-30	1
Van Wyk, EP	WPCA Am	2006/07	2009/10	21	16	5	246	48	22.36	0	0	3	0	978	736	40	18.40	4.51	5-33	2
	WPCA Am	2006/07	2009/10	22	17	5	250	48	20.83	0	0	3	0	1027	774	42	18.42	4.52	5-33	2
Van Wyk, L	WCC	2009/10	2010/11	3	2	2	37	31*	–	0	0	0	0	0	0	0	–	–	–	0
	All LO	2007/08	2010/11	25	21	4	369	53*	21.70	0	1	9	0	259	214	5	42.80	4.95	1-10	0
Van Zyl, S	WCC	2007/08	2010/11	39	33	3	974	114*	32.46	3	2	13	0	90	76	1	76.00	5.06	1-13	0
	All LO	2006/07	2010/11	62	56	7	1747	114*	35.65	4	7	20	0	637	548	17	32.23	5.16	4-24	1
Vilas, DJ	WPCA Am	2010/11	2010/11	3	3	1	143	120	71.50	1	0	7	0	0	0	0	–	–	–	0
	All LO	2006/07	2010/11	44	43	7	1234	120	34.27	4	4	35	9	0	0	0	–	–	–	0
Voss, MF	WPCU	1990/91	1990/91	4	4	0	64	33	16.00	0	0	0	0	0	0	0	–	–	–	0
	WPCA	1991/92	1991/92	4	4	0	77	41	19.25	0	0	2	0	0	0	0	–	–	–	0
	All LO	1990/91	1991/92	9	9	0	143	41	15.88	0	0	2	0	0	0	0	–	–	–	0
Walters, MD	WPCA Am	2005/06	2010/11	25	25	4	705	98	33.57	0	5	7	0	0	0	0	–	–	–	0
Wells, CM	WPCU	1984/85	1984/85	1	1	0	47	47	47.00	0	0	0	0	54	21	1	21.00	2.33	1-21	0
	All LO	1978	1999	323	282	42	6192	117	25.80	4	28	76	0	11514	7208	233	30.93	3.75	4-15	5
Wernars, KO	WPCA Am	2009/10	2010/11	11	8	3	94	37*	18.80	0	0	5	0	237	221	7	31.57	5.59	6-27	1
	WPCU	1976/77	1976/77	2	2	0	71	41	35.50	0	0	0	0	0	0	0	–	–	–	0
Wessels, KC	All LO	1974/75	1998/99	337	331	30	12503	146	41.53	15	90	151	0	1327	1120	36	31.11	5.06	4-24	1

Name	Team	From	To	M	Inns	NO	Runs	HS	Avg	100	50	Ct	St	Balls	Runs	Wkts	Avg	RPO	BB	4I
Williams, G	WPCB	1974/75	1974/75	[no other details available]																
Williamson, M	WPCA Am	2005/06	2010/11	29	29	3	907	101*	34.88	1	6	12	0	0	0	0	–	–	–	0
	All LO	2005/06	2010/11	33	33	3	957	101*	31.90	1	6	16	0	0	0	0	–	–	–	0
Willoughby, CM	WPCA	2000/01	2003/04	36	6	4	25	8	12.50	0	0	8	0	1757	1249	34	36.73	4.26	3-29	0
	WCC	2004/05	2005/06	20	7	4	11	5	3.66	0	0	1	0	986	632	20	31.60	3.84	3-19	0
	All LO	1994/95	2010	209	61	32	147	15	5.06	0	0	26	0	10164	7094	255	27.81	4.18	6-16	8
Wingreen, IM	WPCU	1984/85	1984/85	2	2	0	31	31	15.50	0	0	1	0	0	0	0	–	–	–	0
	WPCU B	1984/85	1984/85	1	1	0	38	38	38.00	0	0	0	0	0	0	0	–	–	–	0
	All LO	1984/85	1984/85	3	3	0	69	38	23.00	0	0	1	0	0	0	0	–	–	–	0
Witbooi, R	WPCB	1975/76	1975/76	[no other details available]																
Worth, D	WPCA Am	2004/05	2004/05	3	3	0	128	64	42.66	0	2	3	0	0	0	0	–	–	–	0
Wyngaard, W	WPCA Am	2004/05	2006/07	12	10	2	240	73	30.00	0	2	3	0	6	5	0	–	5.00	–	0
Xongo, L	WPCA Am	2004/05	2004/05	1	1	0	1	1	1.00	0	0	0	0	30	30	0	–	6.00	–	0
Zondeki, M	WCC	2005/06	2010/11	39	17	7	39	8*	3.90	0	0	4	0	1633	1356	40	33.90	4.98	5-32	2
	WPCA Am	2005/06	2010/11	5	1	0	5	5	5.00	0	0	0	0	216	145	6	24.16	4.02	3-22	0
	All LO	2001/02	2010/11	92	33	13	138	23	6.90	0	0	13	0	3936	3233	107	30.21	4.92	6-37	4

CHAPTER 17
Biographical details of Western Province and Cape Cobras players, 1890–2011

— Names in bold with the number of matches played indicate Western Province cricketers in official ICC-recognised first-class cricket.[391]

— Names in roman type indicate cricketers in matches outside official first-class cricket (including those who played in official ICC limited-overs, List A or T20 matches only).[392]

— CC = Cape Colony, CP = Cape Province, KZN = KwaZulu-Natal, OFS = Orange Free State, ORC = Orange River Colony, WC = Western Cape

Western Province Cricket Union	WPCU	1890–1991
	WPCU B	1975–1991
Western Province Coloured Cricket Union	WPCCU	1890–1959
Peninsula and Western Districts Cricket Board	PWDCB	1923–1959
Western Province Bantu (later African) Cricket Union	WPBCU	1928–1950s
	WPACU	1960s–1977
Western Province Indian Cricket Union	WPICU	1943–1959
Hottentots Holland Cricket Union	HHCU	1945–1959
Western Province Women's Cricket Union	WPWCU	1951–1991
Western Province Cricket Federation	WPCF	1952–1959
Western Province Cricket Board	WPCB	1959–1991
Western Province Cricket Association	WPCA	1991–2004
	WPCA B	1991–2004
	WPCA Am	2004–2011
Western Province Women's Cricket Association	WPWCA	1995–2011
Western Cape Cricket	WCC	2004–2011

Name	Affiliation	M	From	To	Batt	Bowl	Wk	Born	Died
ABBAS, Moeneeb	**WPCA Am**	10	2008/09	2009/10	RHB	RM		Cape Town, 22 Jan 1983	
ABDEROUF, Faldie	**WPCA**	1	1995/96	1995/96	RHB	RM		Cape Town, 1 Jan 1973	
ABDOL, [X]	WPCCU		1898/99	1898/99					
ABDULLAH, Munsoor	**WPCB**	39	1977/78	1987/88	RHB			Cape Town, 25 Jan 1952	
ABED, Gesant 'Tiny'	WPICU/WPCCU/WPCF/WPCB		1949/50	1961/62	RHB	RMF			
ABED, Goolam H	WPICU/WPCCU		1951/52	1957/58	RHB	OB			
ABED, S 'Dik'	WPCB		1963/64	1969/70					
ABED, Salie 'Lobo'	WPICU/WPCCU/WPCF/WPCB		1947/48	1969/70			WK	Durban, 17 Nov 1929	Lansdowne, Cape Town, 8 Nov 2011
ABEL, Sulaiman	HHCU		1951/52	1951/52					
ABERNETHY, P	WPWCU		1951/52	1953/54					
ABRAHAMS, Abdullah	WPCCU		1951/52	1951/52					
ABRAHAMS, A 'Karrie'	WPCCU		1951/52	1954/55					
ABRAHAMS, Cecil John	**PWDCB/WPCF/WPCB**	5	1952/53	1974/75	RHB	RF		Athlone, Cape Town, 8 Mar 1932	Milnrow, Lancashire, England, 15 Aug 2007
ABRAHAMS, Ebrahim	WPCCU		1947/48	1957/58					
ABRAHAMS, M	PWDCB		1937/38	1937/38					
ABRAHAMS, M	WPICU		1953/54	1953/54					
ABRAHAMS, M	WPWCA		2006/07	2006/07					
ABRAHAMS, Norman	WPCB		1963/64	1963/64					
ABRAHAMS, S	WPICU		1955/56	1955/56					
ABRAHAMS, Siraag	WPCA Am		2005/06	2005/06	RHB	RFM			
ACKERMAN, Hylton Deon	**WPCA/WPCA B/WCC**	83	1993/94	2005/06	RHB	RM		Cape Town, 3 July 1982	
ACKERMAN, Hylton Michael	**WPCU/WPCU B**	91	1970/71	1981/82	LHB	RM		Cape Town, 14 Feb 1973	Plumstead, Cape Town, 2 Sept 2009
ACKERMANN, Gerald Leon	**WPCU B**	1	1977/78	1977/78	RHB	RFM		Springs, Transvaal, 28 Apr 1947	
ACKERMANN, James Patrick	**WPCU B**	11	1979/80	1982/83	RHB	RM		Bloemfontein, 4 Jan 1958	
ACKERMANN, Sean	**WPCA**	1	1999/00	1999/00	LHB	OB		Bloemfontein, 10 Nov 1953	
ADAM, [X]	WPACU		1967/68	1967/68				Cape Town, 6 June 1977	
ADAMS, AW	PWDCB		1937/38	1937/38					
ADAMS, Abdollah	WPCCU		1957/58	1957/58					
ADAMS, Abdurahman 'Lefty'	**WPCB**	24	1966	1979/80		SLA		Rondebosch, Cape Town, 18 Nov 1938	
ADAMS, C	PWDCB		1937/38	1937/38					
ADAMS, ED	PWDCB		1937/38	1937/38					
ADAMS, Gamiet	HHCU		1951/52	1951/52					
ADAMS, Gaynor	WPWCA		1995/96	2000/01	RHB	RM			
ADAMS, I	WPCCU		1903/04	1903/04					
ADAMS, Moegamat Qaasim	**WPCA Am**	4	2007/08	2010/11	LHB	RM		Cape Town, 29 Apr 1984	
ADAMS, Niezaam	**WPCA B**	3	1997/98	1997/98	RHB			Cape Town, 1 Dec 1974	
ADAMS, Paul Regan 'Gogga'	**WPCA/WPCA B/WPCA Am/WCC**	65	1995/96	2007/08	RHB	SLC		Cape Town, 20 Jan 1977	

CHAPTER 17 Biographical details of Western Province and Cape Cobras players, 1890–2011

Name	Affiliation	M	From	To	Batt	Bowl	Wk	Born	Died
ADAMS, Yusuf 'Gogs'	WPCB	7	1979/80	1988/89	LHB			Claremont, Cape Town, 7 Dec 1955	
ADONIS, Benjamin	HHCU		1951/52	1951/52					
AHMED, Mohamed Hoosain	WPCB	4	1984/85	1984/85	RHB	RM		Kensington, Cape Town, 23 July 1962	
ALBERTYN, Wallace Andrew	WCC		2005/06	2005/06	RHB	RMF		Alberton, Transvaal, 26 May 1981	
ALCOBIA, L	WPWCU		1985/86	1985/86					
ALEXANDER, C	WPWCU		1958/59	1959/60					
ALEXANDER, Craig John	WPCA Am	5	2004/05	2006/07	RHB	RF		Cape Town, 5 Jan 1987	
ALEXANDER, Kahaar	WPCCU		1945/46	1945/46					
ALEXANDER, Mysra	WPCCU		1947/48	1947/48					
ALEXANDER, Rashaad	WPCB		1966	1966					
ALLEN, Edward	WPCU	3	1893/94	1903/04				Green Point, Cape Town, [x] May 1868	Sea Point, Cape Town, 14 Jan 1942
ALLIE, A	WPCCU		1912/13	1912/13					
ALLIE, Goolam	WPCB	16	1977/78	1986/87		RM		Athlone, Cape Town, 19 Apr 1954	
ALLIE, H	WPICU		—	—					
ALLIE, KB	WPCCU		1945/46	1947/48					
ALLIE, M	WPICU		—	—					
ALLIE, Mogamat Zain 'Muis'	WPCB	4	1978/79	1982/83	RHB			Claremont, Cape Town, 11 Apr 1956	
ALLIE, O	WPICU		1955/56	1955/56					
ALLIE, [x]	WPCCU		1898/99	1898/99					
ALLIE, Zahid	WPCA Am	3	2009/10	2009/10	RHB		WK	Cape Town, 1 May 1984	
ALLIN, Clifford Richard	WPCU	2	1929/30	1930/31	LHB	SLA		Wynberg, Cape Town, 12 Jan 1903	
ANDERSON, James Henry 'Biddy'	WPCU	13	1894/95	1907/08	RHB			Kimberley, 26 Apr 1874	Bredasdorp, CP, 11 March 1926
ANDERSON, Olivia Victoria	WPWCA		2004/05	2010/11	RHB		WK	[x], 18 Nov 1987	
ANDREW, John Calvert	WPCU	1	1894/95	1894/95				Claremont, Cape Town, 17 Dec 1874	Bloemfontein, 3 June 1931
ANTHONY, A	PWDCB		1957/58	1957/58					
ANTHONY, Frank	WPCB		1963/64	1963/64					
ANTULAY, Nasser	WPCB	18	1982/83	1988/89	RHB			Cape Town, 3 Nov 1959	
APPELS, Robyn	WPWCA		2008/09	2010/11					
APPLETON, Elaine	WPWCU		1956/57	1956/57					
ARENDSE, Norman Martin	WPCB	2	1977/78	1982/83	RHB	OB		Wynberg, Cape Town, 25 Oct 1958	
ARENDSE, Solly	HHCU		1954/55	1954/55					
ARENDSE, Stanley	HHCU		1954/55	1954/55					
ARENZ, Henry	WPCB	1	1973/74	1973/74	RHB		WK	District Six, Cape Town, 6 Mar 1945	
ARKELL, Christopher James Fortescue	WPCA Am	2	2008/09	2008/09	RHB	LB		Duiwelskloof, Transvaal, 11 Oct 1985	
ARNOLD, Sheraat	WPCB	3	1977/78	1978/79	LHB	OB		Strand, CP, 4 Mar 1953	
ARNOTT, James Grant	WPCU	3	1936/37	1936/37	RHB			Cape Town, 6 Dec 1911	Bloubergstrand, Cape Town, 27 July 1989
ASHLEY, William Hare 'Gobo'	WPCU	3	1889/90	1890/91	LHB	LM		Mowbray, Cape Town, 10 Feb 1862	Plumtree, S. Rhodesia, 14 July 1930

Name	Affiliation	M	From	To	Batt	Bowl	Wk	Born	Died
ASHTON, N	WPWCU		1954/55	1958/59					
AURET, Esme	WPWCA/WPWCA B		2000/01	2006/07					
AUSTEN, Michael Hubert	**WPCU/WPCU B**	**14**	**1982/83**	**1988/89**	**RHB**	**LM**		**Cape Town, 17 May 1964**	
AUSTEN, Robyn	WPWCA/WPWCA B		1995/96	2000/01					
AUSTEN, Wendy	WPWCA/WPWCA B		1996/97	2000/01					
AUSTEN, Yvonne	WPWCU/Composite XIs		1971/72	1985/86					
BACCHUS, Sheik Faoud Ahamul Fasiel	WPCU	9	1984/85	1984/85	RHB	RM		Campbellville, Georgetown, British Guiana, 31 Jan 1954	
BACHER, Adam Marc	WCC		2006/07	2006/07	RHB	RM		Johannesburg, 29 Oct 1973	
BADEROEN, Gamat	HHCU		1954/55	1954/55					
BADIN, O	WPCCU		1912/13	1912/13					
BAGULEY, Bryan Christopher	**WPCA/WPCA B**	**6**	**1991/92**	**1994/95**	**RHB**			**Pinelands, CP, 25 Mar 1971**	
BAGULEY, Norman	**WPCA**	**5**	**1953/54**	**1954/55**			**WK**	**Cape Town, 30 Mar 1925**	
BAGUS, A	WPCF		1952/53	1952/53					
BAGUS, Allie	HHCU		1951/52	1954/55					
BAILEY, Pam	WPWCU		1978/79	1978/79					
BAIN, Charles Alexander	**WPCU**	**6**	**1902/03**	**1908/09**	**LHB**			**Cape Town, 20 June 1878**	
BAIRNSFATHER, PH (see CLOETE, PHB)	WPCU								
BAKER, Edward Charles 'Bunny'	**WPCU**	**1**	**1956/57**	**1956/57**	**RHB**	**OB**		**Cape Town, 14 Aug 1930**	**Muizenberg, False Bay, CP, [x] July 1993**
BALASKAS, Xenophon Constantine	**WPCU**	**5**	**1934/35**	**1935/36**	**RHB**	**LBG**		**Kimberley, 15 Oct 1910**	**Hyde Park, Sandton, 12 May 1994,**
BALD, Christine	WPWCU/Alma		1962/63	1974/75					
BALFOUR, A 'Don'	WPBCU		1952/53	1952/53					
BALFOUR, MM	WPBCU		1947/48	1947/48					
BALLANTYNE, Ian Randal	**WPCU**	**2**	**1952/53**	**1952/53**	**RHB**	**RM**		**Cape Town, 7 June 1925**	
BAM, Ivan	**WPCU**	**2**	**1906/07**	**1907/08**	**RHB**	**RM**		**Cape Town, 29 Aug 1885**	
BAM, S	WPBCU		1933/34	1933/34					
BANOO, A	WPICU		1947/48	1947/48					
BANSDA, DN	WPICU		1949/50	1949/50					
BARDIEN, Salie	WPCCU/WPCF		1949/50	1956/57					
BARLOW, Edgar John	**WPCU**	**82**	**1968/69**	**1980/81**	**RHB**	**RM**		**Pretoria, 12 Aug 1940**	**St Helier, Jersey, 30 Dec 2005**
BARNARD, Josephine	WPWCA		1998/99	2002/03	RHB	OB			
BARNES, Ian Shaun	**WPCU/WPCU B**	**10**	**1979/80**	**1989/90**	**RHB**	**LB**		**Cape Town, 21 Jan 1957**	
BARNES, Vincent Alexander	**WPCB/WPCA/WPCA B**	**60**	**1978/79**	**1994/95**	**RHB**	**RFM**		**Cape Town, 15 Feb 1960**	
BARNETT, Jamal	WPCCU		1945/46	1945/46					
BASE, Simon John	**WPCU B**	**2**	**1981/82**	**1983/84**	**RHB**	**RFM**		**Maidstone, Kent, England, 2 Jan 1960**	
BASIER, A	WPICU		—	—					
BASSAGE, Derrin James	**WPCA/WPCA Am/WCC**	**36**	**2003/04**	**2006/07**	**LHB**	**RM**	**WK**	**Pietermaritzburg, 4 Dec 1978**	

Name	Affiliation	M	From	To	Batt	Bowl	Wk	Born	Died
BATTISON, George	WPCU	2	1929/30	1932/33	RHB			Stirling, Scotland, 29 Nov 1900	Springs, Transvaal, 16 May 1990
BAWASA, I	WPICU		1947/48	1947/48					
BEGG, A	WPICU		—	—					
BEGG, I	WPICU		—	—					
BEGG, [X]	WPICU		1957/58	1957/58			WK		
BEHARDIEN, Farhaan	WPCA Am	3	2004/05	2004/05	RHB	RMF		Johannesburg, 9 Oct 1983	
BEHARDIEN, Ismail 'Miley'	WPCB	25	1985/86	1990/91	LHB	SLA		Claremont, Cape Town, 11 Feb 1965	
BEHARDIEN, Ismail 'Taliep'	WPCCU/WPCB		1957/58	1969/70	RHB				
BEHARDIEN, Mujahid	WPCA Am	6	2010/11	2010/11	LHB		WK	Cape Town, 30 Apr 1991	
BEHARDIEN, 'Taliep'	WPCCU		1931/32	1949/50					
BELL, AJ	PWDCB		1950/51	1952/53					
BELL, Alexander John 'Sandy'	WPCU	9	1925/26	1930/31	RHB	RFM		East London, 15 Apr 1906	Mowbray, Cape Town, 1 Aug 1985
BELL, Mansel Alexander	WPCU	1	1908/09	1908/09				Idutywa, CC (Transkei), 25 Oct 1888	near Ndola, N. Rhodesia, 10 June 1930
BELL, W	PWDCB		1954/55	1954/55					
BENJAMIN, Fuad	WPCB/WPCA/WPCA B	19	1982/83	1993/94	LHB	OB		Cape Town, 12 Jan 1962	
BENNETT, Bevan Leon	WPCA Am	3	2007/08	2008/09	RHB	LB		East London, 9 Sept 1981	
BENNETT, Harry Wallace	WPCU	2	1904/05	1909/10				Mowbray, Cape Town, [x] Mar 1879	Mowbray, Cape Town, 11 Nov 1948
BENSIMON, Abel Samuel	WPCU	10	1912/13	1923/24		OB		Cape Town, 30 June 1889	Cape Town, 9 Aug 1981
BENSIMON, Alfred Samuel	WPCU	4	1931/32	1933/34		LB		Cape Town, 26 Dec 1886	Cape Town, 7 May 1977
BERGINS, Howard William Harold	WPCB	6	1975/76	1975/76	RHB	RFM		Oudtshoorn, CP, 18 Oct 1954	
BEST, Carlisle Alonza	WPCA	7	1993/94	1993/94	RHB	OB		Richmond Gap, Barbados, 14 May 1959	
BESTER, Leighshe	WPWCA		2007/08	2007/08					
BHAYAT, MA	WPCF		1956/57	1956/57					
BING, Fritz	WPCU	8	1954/55	1960/61	RHB	RM		Sea Point, Cape Town, 22 Sept 1934	
BING, Gregory John	WPCU B	1	1987/88	1987/88	LHB	OB		Cape Town, 4 Nov 1960	
BIRCH, Colin William Stanley	WPCA Am	12	2006/07	2007/08	RHB	RFM		Queenstown, CP, 4 Oct 1982	
BISSET, Arthur Vintcent Crossley 'Artie'	WPCU	13	1902/03	1921/22	RHB	LB		Kenilworth, Cape Town, 15 Jan 1879	Wynberg, Cape Town, 8 Mar 1955
BISSET, Edgar Hamilton	WPCU	1	1889/90	1889/90				Kenilworth, Cape Town, [x] Dec 1869	Kenilworth, Cape Town, 15 June 1910
BISSET, Murray (Sir)	WPCU	21	1894/95	1909/10	RHB	SLA	WK	Port Elizabeth, 14 Apr 1876	Salisbury, S. Rhodesia, 24 Oct 1931
BISSETT, George Finlay	WPCU	1	1927/28	1927/28	RHB	RF		Kimberley, 5 Nov 1905	Botha's Hill, Natal, 14 Nov 1965
BLAAUW, Kim	WPCB		1969	1969					
BLACK, Ivan 'Navvie'	WPCU	1	1937/38	1937/38				Cape Town, 17 May 1906	Windhoek, SWA, 27 Sept 1978
BLACKSHAW, Dawn	WPWCA		1995/96	1995/96					
BLANCKENBERG, James Manuel	WPCU	18	1912/13	1922/23	RHB	RM		Claremont, Cape Town, 31 Dec 1892	
BLANCKENBERG, Nicholas	WPCU	11	1919/20	1926/27				Claremont, Cape Town, [x] 1895	Sea Point, Cape Town, [x] 1930
BLANKENBERG, M	WPWCU		1958/59	1958/59					
BLEEKERS, Lance Francis	WPCU/WPCU B/WPCA/WPCA B	34	1988/89	1993/94	RHB		WK	Wynberg, Cape Town, 4 Aug 1968	

CHAPTER 17 Biographical details of Western Province and Cape Cobras players, 1890–2011

Name	Affiliation	M	From	To	Batt	Bowl	Wk	Born	Died
BOHARDIEN, Ismail 'Fatty'	WPCCU		1954/55	1954/55					
BOLTON, James Lardner	WPCU	7	1921/22	1926/27	RHB	RF		Cape Town, 30 Jan 1895	Cape Town, 1 Nov 1969
BOLUS, George Roland Maxwell	WPCU	10	1947/48	1951/52				Kenilworth, Cape Town, 21 Dec 1922	Rondebosch, Cape Town, 24 Apr 2002
BOND, Frank Preston	WPCU	7	1910/11	1910/11				Mowbray, Cape Town, 3 Sept 1883	Durbanville, CP, 7 Apr 1953
BOND, Gerald Edward 'Boysie'	WPCU	25	1929/30	1938/39	RHB	RM		Cape Town, 5 Apr 1909	Cape Town, 27 Aug 1965
BOOME, Sandra	WPWCA		1995/96	2001/02	RHB	OB			
BOOYSEN, Neville	WPCB	5	1984/85	1989/90		LMF		George, CP, 3 May 1963	
BOTHA, M	PWDCB		1937/38	1937/38					
BOTHA, Theresa	WPWCU		1983/84	1985/86					
BOTHMA, Johannes Paulus	WPCA Am/WCC	8	2008/09	2010/11	RHB	RF		Bellville, CP, 28 Mar 1988	
BOWDITCH, Michael Hamilton	WPCU/WPCU B	62	1964/65	1978/79	RHB	RM		Sea Point, Cape Town, 30 Aug 1945	
BOWLEY, Richard John 'Dick'	WPCU B	4	1980/81	1981/82	RHB	RFM		Wankie, S. Rhodesia, 21 Mar 1948	
BRACHE, Noel	WPCB	2	1974/75	1974/75	LHB			Cape Town, 25 Dec 1954	
BRAMWELL, Gregory	WPCA B	4	1994/95	1994/95	RHB	OB		Fish Hoek, CP, 11 July 1967	
BRAND, Derek	WPCA Am/WCC		2008/09	2009/10	RHB	RM	WK	Bellville, CP, 29 May 1975	
BRICKNELL, Gary Arthur	WPCU/WPCU B	14	1975/76	1976/77	LHB	SLA		Cape Town, 13 Aug 1954	Keetmanshoop, SWA, 25 Mar 1977
BRIDGENS, Kevin James	WPCU B	11	1986/87	1987/88	RHB	RM	WK	Cape Town, 21 Dec 1961	
BRIDGER, Sue	WPWCU/Composite XIs		1971/72	1979/80					
BRINKHAUS, Johan Gerhard Brussell 'Gerry'	WPCU	8	1937/38	1939/40	RHB	RFM		Kenhardt, CP, 30 July 1920	Cape Town, 21 July 1978
BRISTOW, John William	WPCU B	3	1980/81	1980/81	LHB	RM		Ladysmith, Natal, 19 July 1952	
BRITS, Cri-Zelda	WPWCA		2002/03	2003/04	RHB		WK	Rustenburg, Transvaal, 20 Nov 1983	
BROMFIELD, Harry Dudley 'Brom'	WPCU	44	1956/57	1968/69	RHB	OB		Mossel Bay, CP, 26 June 1932	
BROOKES, R	WPWCU		1957/58	1958/59					
BROWN, Servaans van Niekerk	WPCU	4	1920/21	1920/21				Springbok, CC, [x] July 1882	Cape Town, 9 June 1939
BROWN, Trevor Reveley	WPCU	6	1963/64	1963/64	RHB		WK	Cape Town, 25 Mar 1940	
BRUCE, J	WPCU		1969/70	1969/70					
BRUCE, Stephen Daniel	WPCU/WPCU B	62	1971/72	1986/87	RHB	OB	WK	Nkana, N. Rhodesia, 11 Jan 1954	
BRUYNS, André	WPCU	73	1965/66	1976/77	RHB		WK	Pietermaritzburg, 19 Sept 1946	
BUDGE, Neville Ryall	WPCU	27	1963/64	1972/73	LHB	SLA		Cape Town, 7 Feb 1944	
BUDGEN, Edward Albert 'Hookie'	WPCU	11	1908/09	1919/20	RHB	RM		Heidelberg, Transvaal, 9 Dec 1884	Port Elizabeth, 6 Oct 1962
BUKA, [X]	WPBCU		1935/36	1936/37					
BULBRING, Steffen Louis	WPCA B	1	1993/94	1993/94	RHB	OB		Port Elizabeth, 12 Aug 1969	
BURGER, Janet	WPWCU/Alma/Bellville/Composite XIs		1962/63	1979/80					
BURGESS, Merrilees	WPWCU		1970/71	1970/71					
BURMEISTER, Ivan August	WPCU	2	1947/48	1947/48	LHB			Flagstaff, CP (Transkei), 27 Oct 1918	

Name	Affiliation	M	From	To	Batt	Bowl	Wk	Born	Died
BURNS, Ashraf 'Astie'	WPCB	1	1985/86	1985/86	LHB			Cape Town, 26 June 1956	
BURNS, Neil David	WPCU B	3	1985/86	1985/86	LHB	SLA	WK	Chelmsford, Essex, England, 19 Sept 1965	
BURT, Ronald John Edmund 'Jack Snr'	WPCU	4	1934/35	1937/38				Cape Town, 25 Apr 1910	Wynberg, Cape Town, 31 May 1985
BUTLER, Benjamin Castor Hicks	WPCU	9	1966/67	1967/68	RHB			Middelburg, Transvaal, 1 Apr 1935	
BUTLER, Victor	WPCU	1	1949/50	1949/50					
BUYS, Isaac Daniel	WPCU	9	1921/22	1923/24	LHB	LFM		Somerset East, CC, 4 Feb 1895	
CALDER, Henry	WPCU	3	1892/93	1894/95	LHB			South Stoneham, England, 14 Apr 1858	Southampton, England, 19 May 1938
CAMERON, David Patrick 'Riki'	WPCU	2	1970/71	1973/74	RHB	RFM		Voortrekkerhoogte, Pretoria, 17 Mar 1950	
CAMERON, Horace Brakenridge 'Jock'	WPCU	1	1930/31	1930/31	RHB		WK	Port Elizabeth, 5 July 1905	Joubert Park Hospital, Johannesburg, 2 Nov 1935
CANNING, Ryan Clement Cavanagh	WPCA Am/WCC	74	2004/05	2010/11	RHB		WK	Cape Town, 22 Feb 1984	
CARELSE, H	PWDCB		1957/58	1957/58					
CARELSE, Howard	WPCB		1963/64	1966					
CARELSE, Winston Franklin 'Pinky'	WPCB	6	1975/76	1975/76	RHB	RM		Cape Town, 24 Aug 1945	
CAREW, Allen Stephen	WPCU	2	1945/46	1945/46	RHB	OB		Johannesburg, 4 Jan 1926	
CARLSSON, William Eric	WPCU	4	1910/11	1910/11				Hoetjes Bay, CC, [x] Jan 1892	Delville Wood, France (war), 14 July 1916
CAROLIN, Harold William 'Paddy'	WPCU	9	1902/03	1907/08	LHB	RFM		Alicedale, CC, 10 Apr 1881	Rondebosch, Cape Town, 15 Mar 1967
CAROLUS, Denver	WPCA Am	3	2010/11	2010/11	RHB	LB		Bellville, CP, 31 May 1983	
CARSE, James Alexander 'Moggy'	WPCU B	1	1980/81	1980/81	RHB	RFM		Salisbury, S. Rhodesia, 13 Dec 1958	
CARSTENS, Jack	WPCU	2	1912/13	1912/13	LHB	LMF		Port Nolloth, CC, 30 Aug 1892	Cape Town, [x] 1973
CARTER, Neil Miller	WCC		2009/10	2009/10				Cape Town, 29 Jan 1975	
CASTENS, Herbert Hayton	WPCU	3	1890/91	1893/94	RHB		WK	Pearston, CC, 23 Nov 1864	Fulham, London, England, 18 Oct 1929
CATT, Anthony Waldron	WPCU	12	1965/66	1967/68	RHB		WK	Dormans Land, England, 2 Oct 1933	
CAWOOD, John Christopher	WPCU	11	1970/71	1973/74	RHB	RF		Cape Town, 15 June 1950	
CHALLENOR, Edward Lacy	WPCU	5	1895/96	1896/97	RHB			Speightstown, Barbados, 10 Mar 1873	Hampstead Garden Suburb, London, 15 Sept 1935
CHALMERS, Walter Rochfort	WPCU	1	1963/64	1963/64	LHB	SLA		East London, 28 July 1934	Cape Town, 18 July 2011
CHAMBERLAIN, M	WPWCU		1951/52	1952/53					
CHAMBERLAND, M	WPWCU		1953/54	1953/54					
CHARLES, B	WPCCU		1898/99	1903/04					
CHARLTON, SN (née Nefdt)	WPWCU								
CHARNAS, Morris 'Maish'	WPCU	1	1958/59	1958/59	RHB	SLA		Johannesburg, 17 Oct 1930	Glenmore, Durban, 14 Apr 1991
CHEETHAM, John Erskine 'Jack'	WPCU	36	1939/40	1954/55	RHB	LB		Mowbray, Cape Town, 26 May 1920	Parktown, Johannesburg, 21 Aug 1980
CHEETHAM, John Richard	WPCU	4	1972/73	1972/73	LHB			Cape Town, 23 Aug 1947	
CHEVALIER, Grahame Anton	WPCU	41	1966/67	1973/74	RHB	SLA		Cape Town, 9 Mar 1937	
(previously known as SMITH, GA)									
CHRISTIAN, M	WPCCU		1912/13	1912/13					

Name	Affiliation	M	From	To	Batt	Bowl	Wk	Born	Died
CILLIERS, Alexander	WPCA/WPCA B	7	1995/96	1995/96	LHB	LM		Klerksdorp, Transvaal, 6 June 1971	
CLARK, A	WPWCU/Alma		1962/63	1965/66					
CLARK, Roy Murray	WPCA/WPCU B	18	1972/73	1977/78	RHB	RM		Pretoria, 19 July 1952	
CLARKE, A	WPICU								
CLARKE, Genée	WPWCA		1995/96	1996/97					
CLARKE, Trevor Ashley 'Bossie'	WPCU/WPCU B	33	1975/76	1984/85	RHB	RFM		Cradock, CP, 29 Dec 1953	Kisumu, Kenya (war), 19 Dec 1942
CLOETE, Peter Henry Bairnsfather	WPCU	9	1936/37	1939/40	RHB	SRA		Cape Town, 5 Mar 1917	Westridge, Durban, 29 Jan 1967
COEN, Stanley Keppel 'Shunter'	WPCU	9	1930/31	1931/32	RHB			Heilbron, ORC, 14 Oct 1902	
COERICIUS, Anthony	WPCB	1	1985/86	1985/86	RHB			Oudtshoorn, CP, 10 Dec 1956	
COETZEE, Mike	WPCF		1952/53	1953/54					
COGGINS, Harrie Clark	WPCU	2	1905/06	1905/06				Sydney, Australia, 31 Dec 1876	Eastwood, Australia, 2 July 1960
COHEN, Stacey	WPWCA/WPWCA B		1995/96	2001/02					
COLE, John McGregor	WPCU	8	1965/66	1966/67	RHB	RM		Johannesburg, 3 Mar 1933	
COLSON, William Walter Allen 'Bill'	WPCU	8	1910/11	1921/22	RHB			Cape Town, 7 July 1884	Cape Town, 31 Mar 1941
COMMAILLE, John McIllwaine Moore 'Mick'	WPCU	31	1905/06	1923/24	RHB			Cape Town, 21 Feb 1883	Sea Point, Cape Town, 28 July 1956
COMMINS, John Brian	WPCU/WPCA B/WPCA/WPCA B	61	1985/86	1999/00	RHB	RM		East London, 19 Feb 1965	
COMMINS, John Eugene	WPCU	10	1960/61	1968/69	RHB	LB		Cape Town, 6 Sept 1941	
COMMINS, Kevin Thomas	WPCU	18	1951/52	1957/58	RHB	RM		Cape Town, 23 Feb 1928	Claremont, Cape Town, 3 Oct 1995
CONRAD, HG 'Karriem'	WPCCU		1945/46	1945/46					
CONRAD, Sedick 'Dickie'	WPCB	8	1963/64	1974/75	RHB	RM		Newlands, Cape Town, 15 Feb 1942	
CONRAD, Shukri	WPCB/WPCA B	14	1985/86	1994/95	RHB	OB		Lansdowne, Cape Town, 2 Apr 1967	
CONRAD, Siraaj	WPCA B/WPCA Am/WCC	9	1998/99	2005/06	RHB			Cape Town, 25 Feb 1978	
CONRADIE, G	WPWCU		1952/53	1952/53					
CONRY, Francis Domville	WPCU	23	1906/07	1923/24		RM	WK	Bermuda, [x] 1875	Yelverton, England, 13 Sept 1938
CONYNGHAM, Dalton Parry 'Conky'	WPCU	2	1930/31	1930/31	RHB			Durban, 10 May 1897	Durban, 7 July 1979
COOKE, Christopher Barry	WPCA Am	6	2009/10	2009/10	RHB		WK	Johannesburg, 30 May 1986	
COPELAND, Craig Anthony	WPCA B	2	1998/99	1998/99	RHB	LBG		Cape Town, 2 Jan 1977	
COPPING, Linda	WPWCU		1968/69	1972/73					
COSSIE, BPB 'Pat'	WPBCU		1952/53	1952/53					
COWAN, Claire Sheena	WPWCA		1999/00	2004/05	RHB		WK	Cape Town, 18 Sept 1981	
COWPER, Sydney Austen	WPCU	1	1907/08	1907/08	RHB	LM		Cape Town, 13 Oct 1885	Salisbury, S. Rhodesia, 17 June 1960
COX, Arthur Edward	WPCU	2	1890/91	1890/91				New Bilton, Rugby, UK, 12 Feb 1871	Kimberley, 7 Oct 1921
CRAWFORD, Samuel Neville Alexander 'Jock'	WPCU	1	1930/31	1930/31	RHB			Cape Town, 15 Oct 1907	Rondebosch, Cape Town, 29 Sept 1989
CREWS, Basil Hyde	WPCU	4	1945/46	1947/48	RHB	LBG		Robertson, CP, 15 Mar 1925	Hermanus, WC, 14 Apr 2005
CRIGHTON, George Edwin	WPCU	3	1939/40	1939/40	LHB	RM		Middelburg, CP, 12 Oct 1915	Noordhoek, Cape Town, 17 Aug 1998

Name	Affiliation	M	From	To	Batt	Bowl	Wk	Born	Died
CRIPPS, Godfrey	WPCU	3	1892/93	1893/94	RHB			Mussoorie, India, 19 Oct 1865	near Adelaide, Australia, 27 July 1943
CRISP, Robert James 'Bob'	WPCU	18	1931/32	1935/36	RHB	RF		Calcutta, India, 28 May 1911	Colchester, Essex, England, 2 Mar 1994
CROMBIE, Bienjamien	HHCU		1951/52	1951/52					
CROMBIE, Toufiek	HHCU		1951/52	1951/52					
CROSIER, Jean	WPWCU/Alma/Composite XIs		1969/70	1979/80					
CROSOER, Martin James	WPCA B	7	1996/97	1998/99	RHB			Durban, 22 May 1977	
CROSSMAN, Bernice	WPWCA		2007/08	2008/09					
CULLINAN, Daryll John	WPCU	45	1985/86	1990/91	RHB	OB		Kimberley, 4 Mar 1967	
CUPIDO, Randall 'Joey'	WPCB	19	1983/84	1990/91	RHB		WK	Paarl, CP, 12 Nov 1962	
DAGNIN, Ivan	WPCB	4	1968	1982/83	RHB			Bo-Kaap, Cape Town, 4 Mar 1938	
DALE, J	WPWCU		1962/63	1962/63					
DAMMERT, Barry	WPCB	4	1989/90	1989/90	RHB	RM		Bellville South, CP, 30 Apr 1962	
DAMON, Ebrahim 'Baby'	WPCB	14	1977/78	1985/86	RHB	RMF		Claremont, Cape Town, 25 Mar 1949	
DAMON, Igshaan	WPCA B	1	1998/99	1998/99	RHB	RF		Cape Town, 1 July 1977	
DANIELS, A	WPWCA		2010/11	2010/11					
DANIELS, Armien	HHCU		1954/55	1954/55					
DANIELS, E	PWDCB		1952/53	1952/53					
DANIELS, Neville Peter	WPCU/WPCU B	4	1977/78	1978/79	LHB	SLA		Ladysmith, Natal, 28 Jan 1956	
DANIES, Nadeem	HHCU		1954/55	1954/55					
DARIUS, FJ	PWDCB		1937/38	1937/38					
DAVEY, E	WPWCU		1984/85	1985/86					
DAVIDS, AL	WPCCU		1912/13	1912/13					
DAVIDS, Alwie	WPCCU		1951/52	1951/52					
DAVIDS, Faiek	WPCB/WPCA/WPCA B	70	1983/84	1998/99	RHB	RM		Cape Town, 1 Sept 1964	
DAVIDS, Hassiem	WPCCU		1949/50	1949/50					
DAVIDS, Henry	WCC	33	2004/05	2009/10	RHB	RMF		Stellenbosch, 19 Jan 1980	
DAVIDS, J	PWDCB		1946/47	1946/47					
DAVIDS, [X]	PWDCB		1948/49	1948/49					
DAVIDS, [X]	WPBCU		1936/37	1936/37					
DAVIDS, Zak	WPCB	5	1979/80	1983/84	RHB	RM		Claremont, Cape Town, 31 May 1949	
DAVIDSON, Thomas Middleton	WPCU	2	1928/29	1928/29	RHB	SLA		Uitenhage, CC, 6 Aug 1906	Cape Town, 13 Jan 1987
DAVIES, Douglas David	WPCU	2	1903/04	1903/04	RHB	RM		King William's Town, CC, 10 Mar 1881	Bulawayo, S. Rhodesia, [x] Dec 1949
DAVIES, Helen Ann	WPWCU/WPWCA		1984/85	2001/02				Cape Town, 29 July 1966	
DAVIS, Richard Peter	WPCU	4	1951/52	1952/53	RHB	SLA		Pietermaritzburg, 30 Dec 1919	Newlands, Cape Town, 20 July 2003
DAWSON, Alan Charles	WPCA/WPCA B/WCC	93	1992/93	2005/06	RHB	RMF		Cape Town, 27 Nov 1969	
DAWSON, Hilary	WPCB	9	1975/76	1985/86	RHB		WK		
DEANE, John	WPCU	3	1889/90	1890/91					

Name	Affiliation	M	From	To	Batt	Bowl	Wk	Born	Died
DE BEER, Klein	WPWCU		1962/63	1962/63					
DE KLERK, Theodore Radloff	WPCU	32	1925/26	1935/36				Pearston, CC, 26 Nov 1906	Durban, 2 July 1982
DE KOCK, Grant Andrew	WPCA B	6	1995/96	1996/97	LHB	LFM		Bellville, CP, 18 Nov 1976	
DE KOKER, Shannon	WPWCA		2007/08	2007/08					
DE KUILER, S	WPWCA								
DE LANGE, Con de Wet	WCC	31	2004/05	2007/08	RHB	SLA		Bellville, CP, 11 Feb 1981	
DELPORT, Ronald Frederick	WPCU	14	1950/51	1963/64	LHB	OB		Claremont, Cape Town, 18 Nov 1931	
DENNE, Peter Henry	WPCU	10	1971/72	1974/75	RHB	RM		Gwelo, S. Rhodesia, 8 Aug 1949	Plumstead, Cape Town, 24 May 2000
DE NOBREGA, Justin Jose	WPCA/WPCA B	9	1997/98	1998/99	RHB	RM		Cape Town, 14 July 1979	
DERMOTA, Belinda	WPWCA		1995/96	2001/02	RHB	RMF		[x], 28 June 1971	
DESAI, Abu	WPICU/WPCF		1952/53	1953/54					
DE SMIDT, Rupert	WPCU	4	1912/13	1912/13		LB		Cape Town, 23 Nov 1883	Cape Town, 3 Aug 1986
DE STADLER, Mark	WPCA Am/WCC	28	2004/05	2007/08	RHB	RM		Cape Town, 6 July 1975	
DE VILLIERS, Dirk Isaac	WPCU	1	1912/13	1912/13				Wellington, CC, 20 July 1889	Cape Town, 1 Oct 1958
DE VILLIERS, Gwen	WPWCU		1951/52	1952/53					
DE VILLIERS, Michael Craig	WPCA/WPCA B	8	1993/94	1996/97	RHB	RM		Cape Town, 10 May 1970	
DE VILLIERS, Pieter Hendrik	WPCU	4	1889/90	1890/91				near Stanford, CC, 30 Oct 1867	Stellenbosch, 23 Aug 1928
DIFFORD, Archibald Newcombe	WPCU	11	1904/05	1907/08				Cape Town, 9 Apr 1883	Palestine (war), 20 Sept 1918
DIKWENI, T	WPBCU		1950/51	1952/53					
DIMBLEBY, Desmond Edgar	WPCU	5	1946/47	1947/48	RHB	RM		Cape Town, 11 Sept 1919	near Warkworth, NZ, 21 Mar 2008
DIMBLEBY, Kenneth Graham	WPCU	11	1938/39	1947/48	RHB			Port Elizabeth, 23 Oct 1914	Humewood Ext, PE, 2 Sept 2006
DLANGA, D	WPBCU		1952/53	1952/53					
DLOKWENI, C	WPBCU		1950/51	1952/53					
D'OLIVEIRA, Basil Lewis	PWDCB/WPCF		1948/49	1958/59	RHB	RM OB		Signal Hill, Cape Town, 4 Oct 1931	Rushwick, England, 18 Nov 2011
D'OLIVEIRA, Ivan	WPCB		1961/62	1961/62	RHB			Cape Town, 19 Mar 1941	
DOLLIE, Abbasie	WPCCU		1949/50	1949/50					
DOLLIE, Ebrahim	WPCCU		1951/52	1951/52					
DOLLIE, MS 'Pettie'	WPCB		1968	1968					
DOMAN, Michael Edward	WPCB	12	1977/78	1981/82	RHB	LB		Wetton, Cape Town, 25 Jan 1961	
DONACHIE, Harold Hendrik	WPCA B	2	1994/95	1994/95	RHB	RM		Cape Town, 16 Apr 1964	
DOWLING, N	WPWCU		1953/54	1959/60					
DRUMMER, Desmond	WPCU	7	1960/61	1963/64	RHB	RM		Maitland, Cape Town, 27 July 1940	
DRUMMER, Francois Theodore Max 'Frank'	WPCU	26	1958/59	1967/68	RHB	RFM		Cape Town, 20 Sept 1938	
DRUMMOND, Robert Angus	WPCU/WPCU B	26	1975/76	1979/80	RHB		WK	Durban, 28 Apr 1953	
DUFF, Benjamin Robert	WPCU	1	1889/90	1889/90				Swellendam, CC, 16 Oct 1867	Pretoria, 25 June 1943
DUMBRILL, Jon Elliott	WPCU	3	1956/57	1961/62	RHB	OB		Colliers Wood, England, 9 Apr 1935	
DUMINY, Jacobus Petrus (Professor) 'Koos'	WPCU	2	1919/20	1919/20	LHB	SLA		Bellville, CC, 16 Dec 1897	Observatory, Cape Town, 31 Jan 1980

Name	Affiliation	M	From	To	Batt	Bowl	Wk	Born	Died
DUMINY, Jean-Paul	WPCA/WCC	44	2001/02	2010/11	LHB	OB		Strandfontein, CP, 14 Apr 1984	
DU PLESSIS, D	WPWCU		1954/55	1954/55					
DU PLESSIS, John Henry	WPCU B	5	1988/89	1988/89	RHB	RM		Johannesburg, 17 Nov 1961	
DU PLESSIS, Morné	WPCU	4	1971/72	1973/74	RHB	RM		Vereeniging, Transvaal, 21 Oct 1949	
DURING, John	WPCU/WPCU B	51	1977/78	1988/89	RHB	RM		Cape Town, 3 Feb 1959	
DURING, John Peter 'Sam'	WPCU	5	1907/08	1908/09	LHB			Robertson, CC, [x] Dec 1884	Bloemfontein, 20 Sept 1930
DURING, Peter Blaine	WPCU	1	1949/50	1949/50				Durban, 24 Aug 1923	
DURR, John Michael (Dr)	WPCU	1	1921/22	1921/22		RMF		Kalkfontein, Cape Town, 11 Dec 1900	Rondebosch, Cape Town, 16 Sept 1975
DU TOIT, Jacobus Daniel	WPCU/WPCU B	37	1975/76	1983/84	LHB	LM		Worcester, CP, 8 Sept 1959	
DU TOIT, 'Moutie'	WPCCU		1945/46	1957/58					
DU TOIT, Willem Johannes	WCC	1	2008/09	2008/09	RHB	RF		Cape Town, 18 Mar 1981	
DYASON, Clinton	WPCB	3	1988/89	1988/89	RHB	LB			
DYER, Graham Dudley	WPCU	9	1966/67	1967/68	LHB			Durban, 24 June 1943	
DYIRA, SD	WPBCU		1947/48	1947/48					
DYIRA, [X]	WPBCU		1936/37	1936/37					
EATON, Phyllis	WPWCU/Alma		1965/66	1967/68					
EAYRS, Donald	WPCU	2	1939/40	1941/42	LHB	SLA			
EBERHARDT, N	WPWCU		1953/54	1953/54					
EBRAHIM, Faizel	WPCB	12	1985/86	1990/91	LHB	SLA		Elsies River, CP, 7 Mar 1960	
EBRAHIM, Mohamed	WPCB	1	1977/78	1977/78	RHB			Elsies River, CP, 15 Sept 1955	
EBRAHIM, N	WPICU		1949/50	1949/50					
EBRAHIM, Yusuf	WPCB	1	1978/79	1978/79	RHB	RM		Elsies River, CP, 29 Sept 1957	
ECKARD, Leslie Stevenson	WPCU	12	1936/37	1946/47		RMF		Woodstock, Cape Town, 27 Nov 1908	
ELGAR, Allan Graham	WPCU/WPCU B	26	1983/84	1990/91	RHB	OB		Durban, 29 June 1960	Johannesburg, 15 Jan 1999
EMARY, Frederick Edward	WPCU	2	1965/66	1965/66	RHB	RM		Aliwal North, CP, 3 Dec 1941	
EMBUREY, John Ernest	WPCU	15	1982/83	1983/84	RHB	OB		Peckham, London, England, 20 Aug 1952	
ENGELBRECHT, Sybrand Abraham	WPCA Am/WCC	11	2008/09	2010/11	RHB	OB		Johannesburg, 15 Sept 1998	
ENGLISH, Cedric Vaughan	WPCA/WPCA B	10	1993/94	1994/95	RHB	RFM		Kimberley, 13 Sept 1973	
ENRIGHT, Petru (Dr)	WPWCA		2003/04	2006/07					
ERICKSON, Bert	PWDCB		1957/58	1957/58					
ESTERHUIZEN, Caroline	WPWCA		2003/04	2010/11					
ETLINGER, Thomas Edmund	WPCU	5	1895/96	1896/97				Wandsworth, London, 7 Sept 1872	Leatherhead, England, 23 Feb 1953
EULEY, Wesley	WPCA Am	2	2006/07	2006/07	LHB	RM		Cape Town, 10 Oct 1979	
EVANS, Llewellyn Leonard Montgomery	WPCU	2	1939/40	1946/47	LHB	SLA		Johannesburg, 14 Jan 1907	Edenvale Hospital, Transvaal, 4 Sept 1981
FAIRBAIRN, W	PWDCB		1952/53	1952/53					
FAIRCLOUGH, John	WPCU	4	1964/65	1965/66	RHB	LM		Grimsby, England, 23 July 1941	
FAIRWEATHER, Luke	WPCU B	2	1980/81	1982/83	RHB		WK	Cape Town, 18 Mar 1961	Cape Town, 5 Jan 2011

Name	Affiliation	M	From	To	Batt	Bowl	Wk	Born	Died
FAKIE, [X]	WPCCU		1898/99	1898/99					
FAKIER, M 'Baby'	WPCCU		1954/55	1954/55					
FARRELL, John Nigel	WPCU/WPCU B	15	1974/75	1977/78	RHB	LFM		Cape Town, 16 Dec 1949	
FARRELL, Roy Michael	WPCU	9	1952/53	1963/64	RHB		WK	Rosebank, Cape Town, 27 July 1932	Cape Town, 3 Nov 1998
FATAAR, Mogamad Ganief 'Taatjie'	WPCCU		1921/22	1921/22					
FEARON, Giles Geoffrey	WPCA Am	1	2007/08	2007/08	RHB			Cape Town, 30 Oct 1981	
FEBRUARY, A	PWDCB		1937/38	1937/38					
FEBRUARY, Des	WPCB		1963/64	1968					
FEBRUARY, Reginald 'Koela'	WPCB	12	1985/86	1988/89		RM		Stellenbosch, 14 Aug 1954	
FEBRUARY, V	PWDCB		1946/47	1946/47					
FELIX, Cecil	WPCB	1	1983/84	1983/84	RHB			Kuils River, CP, 5 Dec 1948	
FERNANDEZ, Ashley Ryan	WPCA Am		2005/06	2005/06	LHB	RM		Cape Town, 31 Jan 1982	
FERNLEY, David Leo	WPCU	3	1957/58	1957/58	RHB			Murree, Punjab, India, 29 May 1934	
FERRANDI, John Haynes	WPCU	57	1949/50	1964/65	RHB		WK	Villiersdorp, CP, 3 Apr 1930	
FERREIRA, Lloyd Douglas	WPCA/WPCA B	42	1997/98	2003/04	RHB	LM		Parktown, Johannesburg, 6 May 1974	
FESTER, D	WPCB		1969	1969					
FINNAN, Mike	WPCB	4	1968	1977/78	RHB	RM		Heathfield, Cape Town, 1 Mar 1948	
FINNAN, Owen Mark Paul	WPCU B	1	1979/80	1979/80	RHB	RM		Cape Town, 10 Jan 1958	
FISMER, Kenneth Gerard (Dr)	WPCU	1	1941/42	1941/42	RHB			Cape Town, 25 Jan 1915	Pietermaritzburg, 24 Apr 2010
FITZPATRICK, George Thomas	WPCU	1	1890/91	1890/91				Cape Town, 13 Dec 1868	Cape Town, 20 May 1960
FLETCHER, Duncan Andrew Gwynne	WPCU B	1	1984/85	1984/85	LHB	RMF		Salisbury, S. Rhodesia, 27 Sept 1948	
FOCK, Charles Andrew Chomse (later changed name to FOX, CAC)	WPCU	5	1902/03	1904/05				Lydenburg, Transvaal, 3 July 1877	Bloemfontein, 16 Dec 1926
FOLEY, William Bernard Henry	WPWCA	7	1937/38	1947/48	RHB			Cape Town, 3 Oct 1906	Bergvliet, Cape Town, 13 Aug 1963
FONDLING, Roxanne	WPBCU		2005/06	2010/11					
FONGQO, SM	WPCU		1933/34	1933/34					
FOREMAN, Dennis Joseph	WPWCU	3	1951/52	1951/52	RHB	OB		Athlone, Cape Town, 1 Feb 1933	
FORTUNE, E	WPCB		1984/85	1985/86					
FORTUNE, Neil	WPCU	25	1978/79	1983/84	RHB			Bo-Kaap, Cape Town, 29 Aug 1952	
FOUCHÉ, Michael Ryno	WPWCA	1	1958/59	1958/59	RHB	RM		Stellenbosch, 19 July 1936	
FOURIE, Yolani	WPCU		2007/08	2010/11					
FOX, John Stephen Morley	WPCU	8	1954/55	1960/61	RHB	RM		Durban, 4 July 1929	
FOX, Louis Chomse 'Bill'	WPCU	14	1921/22	1927/28	LHB		WK	Cape Town, 2 Jan 1899	Port Elizabeth, 23 July 1974
FRANCIS, Howard Henry	WPCU	3	1895/96	1902/03	RHB		WK	Westbury, Bristol, England, 26 May 1868	Sea Point, Cape Town, 7 Jan 1936
FRANCIS, Murray Godfred 'Tiny'	WPCU	4	1934/35	1934/35				Bloemfontein, 26 Aug 1907	Bloemfontein, 2 Aug 1961
FREDERICKS, E	WPICU		—	—					
FREDERICKS, G	WPICU		1955/56	1955/56					

Name	Affiliation	M	From	To	Batt	Bowl	Wk	Born	Died
FREDRICKS, F	WPCCU		1898/99	1898/99					
FREDRICKS, L	WPCCU		1898/99	1898/99					
FREDRICKS, [X]	WPCCU		1903/04	1903/04					
FREEMAN, Abdol Josef 'Dol'	WPCCU/WPCF		1931/32	1953/54					
FREEMAN, Ashley	WPWCA		2004/05	2005/06					
FRIEND, Quinton	WPCA/WPCA Am/WCC	26	2002/03	2006/07	RHB	RFM		Bellville, CP, 16 Feb 1982	
FRIESLAAR, N	WPICU		—	—			WK		
FRITZ, Gaynor	WPWCA/WPWCA B		2001/02	2003/04					
FRITZ, Leighsheigh	WPWCA		2002/03	2002/03					
FRITZ, Shandré Alvida	WPWCA		2001/02	2010/11	RHB	RM			
FROST, Colin Eric	WPCU/WPCU B	4	1985/86	1986/87	RHB		WK	Johannesburg, 30 July 1965	
FUKU, [X]	WPBCU		1936/37	1936/37					
FULLER, Edward Russell Henry	WPCU	27	1950/51	1957/58	RHB	RFM		Worcester, CP, 2 Aug 1931	Milnerton, Cape Town, 19 July 2008
FULLER, Harry Hillier	WPCU	4	1920/21	1920/21	RHB			East London, 5 Oct 1896	East London, 13 Oct 1974
FUZANI, [X]	WPBCU		1936/37	1936/37					
GABRIELS, Seraj	WPCB	48	1981/82	1990/91	RHB	LB		Harfield, Cape Town, 20 Dec 1952	
GAFAAR, GO	WPICU		1955/56	1955/56					
GAFIELDIEN, Ebrahim	WPCB	7	1989/90	1990/91	LHB				
GAFIELDIEN, Haroen	HHCU		1951/52	1954/55					
GALANT, Mogamat	WPCB	2	1988/89	1988/89	RHB	RM		Claremont, Cape Town, 8 Feb 1954	
GALANT, Sa-at	WPCB	1	1979/80	1979/80	RHB				
GANIEF, Cassim	WPCCU		1949/50	1957/58					
GARDEE, A	WPICU		1955/56	1955/56					
GARDER, Ebrahiem	HHCU		1954/55	1954/55					
GARDINER, Ivor Burberow	WPCU	9	1926/27	1928/29	RHB	LAB		Queenstown, CC, 3 Dec 1903	Queenstown, CP, 17 July 1951
GENOWER, J	WPWCU		1953/54	1953/54					
GENOWER, P	WPWCU		1953/54	1953/54					
GENTRY, Jack D	WPCU	5	1926/27	1926/27					
GEOGHEGAN, John Patrick	WPCA Am	3	2005/06	2007/08	RHB	RMF		Johannesburg, 21 Feb 1983	
GEORGE, Amien	WPCCU		1947/48	1954/55					
GEORGE, Mulligan Frank	WPCA/WPCA B	10	1997/98	1998/99	RHB	RFM		Cape Town, 10 Sept 1976	
GEORGE, Stephen Glen	WPCA Am	1	2005/06	2005/06	LHB	OB		Cape Town, 17 Jan 1984	
GEORGEU, George	WPCU	40	1931/32	1949/50	RHB	SRA		Cape Town, 27 June 1913	Hermanus, WC, 17 May 1996
GERRANS, Maureen	WPWCU		1972/73	1974/75					
GERTZEN, A	WPCCU		1912/13	1912/13					
GERTZEN, E	WPCCU		1912/13	1912/13					
GERTZEN, G	WPCCU		1903/04	1912/13					

Name	Affiliation	M	From	To	Batt	Bowl	Wk	Born	Died
GHEEWALA, IT	WPICU		–	–					
GHEEWALA, J	WPICU		1953/54	1953/54					
GHEEWALA, S	WPICU		–	–					
GIBBS, Herschelle Herman	WPCU/WPCU B/WPCA/ WPCA B/WCC	69	1990/91	2010/11	RHB	RFM LB		Green Point, Cape Town, 23 Feb 1974	
GIE, Clive Addison (Dr)	WPCU	11	1971/72	1973/74	LHB	SLA		Cape Town, 23 Oct 1950	
GILBERT, Monique	WPWCA		2002/03	2003/04					
GILES, Michael John	WPCU	9	1965/66	1971/72	LHB	LB		Rondebosch, Cape Town, 14 Dec 1944	
GILL, Rupert James	WPCU	4	1892/93	1896/97				Rondebosch, Cape Town, 6 Apr 1872	East London, 2 Oct 1954
GILLETT, Giles Farren	WPCA B	3	1995/96	1995/96	RHB	RM		Pretoria, 14 Dec 1971	
GLANTZ, Abraham	WPCU	39	1929/30	1939/40	RHB		WK	Cape Town, 24 Apr 1907	
GODER, ME	WPICU		1955/56	1955/56					
GODER, Moosa (Sheikh)	WPCCU		1957/58	1957/58					
GODFREY, Francis Albert 'Frank'	WPCU	4	1923/24	1926/27				Cape Town, 23 Aug 1899	Cape Town, 7 Feb 1928
GODFREY, L	WPWCA		1999/2000	1999/2000					
GOLDSTEIN, Frederick Steven	WPCU/WPCU B	22	1971/72	1977/78	RHB	OB		Bulawayo, S. Rhodesia, 14 Oct 1944	
GOLIATH, Chanré	WPWCA		2006/07	2007/08					
GOMES, Sharn Patrick	WPCA Am		2010/11	2010/11	LHB	SLA		Cape Town, 6 Aug 1988	
GOOCH, Graham Alan	WPCU	16	1982/83	1983/84	RHB	RM		Whipps Cross, Leytonstone, England, 23 July 1953	
GORDON, Evan Shawn	WPCU/WPCU B	17	1978/79	1983/84	RHB	RFM		Cape Town, 26 Sept 1960	
GOULDEN, Ian Fettes	WPCU	13	1925/26	1930/31				Port Elizabeth, 3 Aug 1907	
GRAAFF, De Villiers (Sir) 'Div'	WPCU	2	1932/33	1932/33	RHB			Sea Point, Cape Town, 8 Dec 1913	De Grendel Farm, Tygerberg, WC, 4 Oct 1999
GRAHAM, David Kinloch	WPCU	1	1945/46	1945/46	RHB			Johannesburg, 27 Jan 1921	
GRAHAM, John Malcolm	WPCU	1	1960/61	1960/61			WK	Sea Point, Cape Town, 17 Aug 1936	
GRAHAM, Malcolm David	WPCU	1	1889/90	1889/90				Grahamstown, CC, 14 July 1865	Durban, 16 Nov 1941
GRAHAM, Robert	WPCU	1	1897/98	1897/98	RHB	LB		Grahamstown, CC, 16 Sept 1877	Upperton, Eastbourne, UK, 21 Apr 1946
GRAHAM, Thomas Lynedoch (Sir)	WPCU	2	1889/90	1889/90				Grahamstown, CC, 5 May 1860	Grahamstown, CP, 7 May 1940
GRANT, Donald Arthur Cardross	WPCU B	4	1975/76	1975/76	RHB	RM		Johannesburg, 18 Dec 1951	
GRAY, Alistair John Alec	WPCA Am/WCC	68	2004/05	2010/11	RHB	LB		Johannesburg, 8 July 1982	
GREEN, Anthony Douglas	WPCU B	4	1979/80	1980/81				Cape Town, 13 Nov 1957	
GREEN, Salie	WPCB	1	1988/89	1988/89	LHB	LAB		Claremont, Cape Town, 17 May 1952	
GREGG, Sue	WPWCA		1995/96	1998/99					
GRIFFITHS, Andrew Vaughan	WPCU B	1	1988/89	1988/89	LHB	SLA		East London, 22 Dec 1967	
GRONN, Michael John Murray	WPCU	1	1951/52	1951/52	LHB	LAB		Johannesburg, 16 Apr 1931	
GROVES, Michael Godfrey Melvin	WPCU	1	1960/61	1960/61	RHB	RFM		Taihape, Wellington, NZ, 14 Jan 1943	
HALVORSEN, Eric	WPCU/WPCU B	7	1979/80	1982/83	RHB		WK	Cape Town, 23 Mar 1958	

Name	Affiliation	M	From	To	Batt	Bowl	Wk	Born	Died
HANDS, Kenneth Charles Myburgh	WPCU	28	1921/22	1930/31	RHB			Stellenbosch, 22 Mar 1892	Paris, France, 18 Nov 1954
HANDS, Philip Albert Myburgh 'Pam'	WPCU	24	1906/07	1926/27	RHB			Claremont, Cape Town, 18 Mar 1890	Parys, OFS, 27 Apr 1951
HANDS, Reginald Harry Myburgh	WPCU	5	1912/13	1913/14	RHB			Claremont, Cape Town, 26 July 1888	near Bruay, France (war), 20 Apr 1918
HANLEY, Martin Andrew	WPCU	26	1946/47	1953/54	RHB	OB		Aliwal North, CP, 10 Nov 1918	Bishopscourt, Cape Town, 2 June 2000
HANNAH, Joan	WPWCU		1968/69	1985/86					
HANTAM, William Chesney	WPCA Am	9	2004/05	2007/08	LHB	LMF		Cape Town, 21 Sept 1983	
HARDCASTLE, S	WPWCU		1953/54	1953/54					
HARDY, Jonathan James Ean	WPCU/WPCU B	16	1987/88	1990/91	LHB			Nakuru, Kenya, 2 Oct 1960	
HARLEY, P	PWDCB		1956/57	1956/57					
HAROUN, M Yusuf	WPCCU		1949/50	1951/52					
HARRAN, P	WPWCU		1957/58	1958/59					
HARRIS, Edward	WPCB	10	1982/83	1984/85	RHB			Athlone, Cape Town, 28 Mar 1961	
HARRIS, Kathy	WPWCU		1983/84	1983/84					
HARRIS, Paul Lee	WPCA/WPCA B	3	1998/99	2001/02	RHB	SLA		Salisbury, S. Rhodesia, 2 Nov 1978	
HARTLEY, M Armien	WPCCU		1947/48	1947/48					
HARVEY, Ian Joseph	WCC	5	2005/06	2005/06	RHB	RM		Wonthaggi, Victoria, Australia, 10 Apr 1972	
HATTAS, Abubakar 'Bakar'	WPCCU		1957/58	1957/58					
HATTINGH, Madeleine	WPWCA		2005/06	2005/06					
HAUPT, Dale Linton	WPCA Am	1	2005/06	2005/06	LHB	LFM		Cape Town, 7 May 1984	
HAUPT, Mark	WPCB	1	1984/85	1984/85	RHB	RCB			
HAWTREY, Philip Thomas	WPCU B	4	1983/84	1983/84	RHB	RM	WK	Cape Town, 13 July 1960	
HAYAT, I	WPICU		–	–					
HAYAT, M	WPICU		1947/48	1949/50					
HAYNES, Desmond Leo	WPCA	21	1994/95	1996/97	RHB	RM LB		Holders Hill, Barbados, 15 Feb 1956	
HEARNE, Frank	WPCU	12	1889/90	1903/04	RHB	RF		Ealing, England, 23 Nov 1858	Observatory, Cape Town, 14 July 1949
HEARNE, George Alfred Lawrence	WPCU	23	1910/11	1926/27	RHB	RAB	WK	Catford, London, England, 27 Mar 1888	Barberton, Transvaal, 13 Nov 1978
HECTOR, Benjamin	WCC	9	2006/07	2007/08	RHB	RM		Durban, 5 Aug 1979	
HECTOR, C	PWDCB		1946/47	1946/47					
HECTOR, E	WPICU		1957/58	1957/58					
HEEGER, Angus	PWDCB		1957/58	1957/58					
HEFER, Atilla	WPWCU		1984/85	1985/86					
HELDSINGER, Ashton	WPWCA		2009/10	2010/11					
HELDSINGER, Kenneth Malcolm St John	WPCU	9	1956/57	1960/61	LHB			Newlands, Cape Town, 30 June 1926	Rosebank, Cape Town, 25 June 2002
HENDERSON, Claude William	WPCA/WPCA B/WCC	55	1998/99	2010/11	RHB	SLA		Worcester, CP, 14 June 1972	
HENDERSON, Tyron	WCC	4	2007/08	2007/08	RHB	RM		Cape Town, 14 Feb 1973	
HENDRICKS, A	WPCCU		1898/99	1912/13					

Name	Affiliation	M	From	To	Batt	Bowl	Wk	Born	Died
HENDRICKS, B	PWDCB		1946/47	1946/47					
HENDRICKS, Beuran Eric	WPCA Am/WCC	14	2009/10	2010/11	LHB	LFM		Cape Town, 8 June 1990	
HENDRICKS, Imraan 'Rani'	WPCB	1	1982/83	1982/83	RHB	RFM		Port Elizabeth, 4 Jan 1954	
HENDRICKS, Nicole	WPWCA		2010/11	2010/11					
HENDRICKS, O	WPCCU		1912/13	1912/13					
HENDRICKS, Stuart	WPCB	35	1980/81	1988/89	RHB				
HENDRICKS, T	WPCCU		1898/99	1898/99					
HENDRICKS, Toyer	WPCCU/WPCF		1953/54	1957/58					
HENDRICKS, W 'Wally'	PWDCB		1946/47	1946/47					
HENDRICKS, William Daniel	WPCB	18	1973/74	1975/76	RHB	LB		Cape Town, 25 July 1952	
HENDRICKS, [X]	WPCCU		1898/99	1898/99					
HENDRIKSE, Charles	WPCB	7	1988/89	1990/91	RHB	RM			
HENDRIKSE, Hassim	WPCCU		1949/50	1949/50					
HENRY, Donovan	WPCA B	1	1997/98	1997/98	RHB	RFM		Cape Town, 20 Sept 1978	
HENRY, Omar	WPCU/WPCU B/WPCB	57	1973/74	1983/84	LHB	SLA		Stellenbosch, 23 Jan 1952	
HERANDIEN, S	WPWCA		2008/09	2010/11					
HERCULES, Stacy	WPWCA		2003/04	2007/08					
HERMAN, D	PWDCB		1956/57	1956/57					
HERMANS, J	PWDCB		1937/38	1937/38					
HERMANS, Jimmy	WPCCU		1947/48	1947/48					
HICKLEY, Cecil Spencer (Admiral)	WPCU	2	1890/91	1890/91				Ashcott, Somerset, England, 22 Jan 1865	Kensington, London, England, 1 May 1941
HILTERMAN, Christopher	WPCU B	1	1976/77	1976/77	RHB			Singapore, 20 Dec 1946	
HINRICHSEN, D	PWDCB		1957/58	1957/58					
HOBONGWANA, L	WPBCU		1950/51	1952/53					
HOBSON, Anthony Larry	WPCU/WPCU B	8	1990/91	1990/91	RHB	LBG		Jansenville, CP, 25 Jan 1963	
HOBSON, Denys Laurence	WPCU/WPCU B	96	1971/72	1984/85	RHB	LBG		Port Elizabeth, 3 Sept 1951	
HOBSON, Thomas Edward Carter	WPCU	2	1906/07	1906/07				Somerset East, CC, 26 Mar 1881	Herbert District, near Kimberley, 2 Sept 1937
HODGES, Cynthia	WPWCU/Bellville		1962/63	1963/64					
HODGKINSON, Alison Lucille	WPWCA		1999/00	2006/07	RHB	LB		East London, 30 Jan 1977	
HODGSON, Andrew Sabin	WPCU	6	1967/68	1967/68	RHB	RM		Auckland, New Zealand, 16 Sept 1941	
HODGSON, David Glynne McPherson	WPCU	6	1961/62	1965/66	RHB			Ankara, Turkey, 2 Oct 1939	Cape Town, 15 Dec 1985
HOFMEYR, Simon	WPCA B	8	1996/97	1997/98	LHB	LM		Cape Town, 24 Feb 1978	
HOHO, F	WPBCU		1952/53	1952/53					
HOLDER, John Wakefield	WPCB	1	1974/75	1974/75	RHB	RFM		Superlative, St George, Barbados, 19 Mar 1945	
HOLDSTOCK, Adrian Thomas	WPCU B/WPCA	4	1989/90	1992/93	RHB	RFM		Pinelands, CP, 27 Apr 1970	
HOLMES, Gamat 'Tape'	WPCCU/WPCF		1951/52	1954/55					

Name	Affiliation	M	From	To	Batt	Bowl	Wk	Born	Died
HOLMES, Muneer	WPCA Am	1	2009/10	2009/10	LHB	OB		Cape Town, 7 Aug 1985	
HOLMES, Thomas Edward 'Tup'	WPCU	10	1906/07	1910/11	RHB		WK	Kaffir River, OFS, 23 Aug 1883	Port Elizabeth, 7 June 1963
HOMANI, Zwelibanzi	WPCA Am	9	2005/06	2006/07	RHB		WK	Port Elizabeth, 12 Dec 1983	
HOOPER, Justin James	WPCA B	1	1979/80	1979/80	RHB	RFM		Johannesburg, 11 June 1958	
HOOSAIN, G	WPICU								
HOPLEY, Frederick John van der Byl	WPCU	1	1909/10	1909/10	RHB	RF		Grahamstown, CC, 27 Aug 1883	Marandellas, S. Rhodesia, 16 Aug 1951
HORWOOD, Stanley Ebden	WPCU	12	1903/04	1909/10	RHB			Port Elizabeth, 22 July 1877	Plumstead, Cape Town, 15 Aug 1959
HOWE, Hazel	WPWCU		1973/74	1978/79					
HOWELL, David Hugh	WPCU B	1	1976/77	1976/77	RHB		WK	Port Elizabeth, 20 May 1958	
HOWELL, Harry Conrad 'Billy'	WPCU	2	1949/50	1954/55	RHB	LB OB		Grahamstown, CP, 24 Feb 1926	Cape Town, 29 Jan 2008
HUGHES, Edward	WPCU	1	1896/97	1896/97				Windsor, Berkshire, England, 9 Mar 1866	Pretoria, 20 Sept 1925
HUGHES, RJ	WPCU	1	1897/98	1897/98			WK		
HUGO, Stephanus Gideon 'Deon'	WPCU/WPCU B	19	1967/68	1977/78	RHB	RMF		Caledon, CP, 20 July 1945	
HURLING, D	PWDCB		1937/38	1946/47					
HUTCHINSON, Charles Henry (Dr)	WPCU	3	1931/32	1931/32	RHB			Pietersburg, Transvaal, 31 Dec 1907	Margate, Natal, 13 Mar 1977
IGGLESDEN, Alan Paul	WPCU B	5	1987/88	1987/88	RHB	RFM		Farnborough, Kent, England, 8 Oct 1964	
IMPEY, Laurence Leonard Horton	WPCU	5	1946/47	1948/49	RHB	RFM		Rondebosch, Cape Town, 7 Jan 1923	Rondebosch, Cape Town, 19 July 1988
INGHAM, Ronnie	HHCU		1951/52	1954/55					
INNES, Gerald Alfred Skerten	WPCU	55	1950/51	1962/63	RHB	OB		Wynberg, Cape Town, 16 Nov 1931	Cape Town, 11 July 1982
ISAACS, Archie	WPCCU		1947/48	1947/48					
ISAACS, C	WPCCU		1912/13	1912/13					
ISAACS, Ebrahim 'Braima'	WPCB	51	1968	1983/84	RHB	RM	WK	Athlone, Cape Town, 26 Jan 1945	Rylands, Cape Town, 13 June 2010
ISAACS, M	WPCCU		1912/13	1912/13					
ISAACS, Mish'al	WPCB	1	1990/91	1990/91	LHB			Athlone, Cape Town, 30 May 1969	
ISAACS, Mogammadien	WPCCU		1920s	1930s					
ISMAIL, Shabnim	WPWCA		2005/06	2010/11	LHB	RFM		Cape Town, 5 Oct 1988	
JABAAR, Armien	WPCB	44	1974/75	1986/87	RHB	LB		Bo-Kaap, Cape Town, 6 Nov 1944	
JACKMAN, Robin David	WPCU	10	1971/72	1971/72	RHB	RFM		Simla, India, 13 Aug 1945	
JACKSON, Dirk Cloete 'Mary'	WPCU	8	1908/09	1910/11				Alphen Farm, Cape Town, 21 Apr 1885	near Brits, Transvaal, 17 Sept 1976
JACKSON, Kenneth Conrad	WPCU/WPCU B/WPCA/WPCA B	22	1988/89	1993/94	RHB	RM		Kitwe, N. Rhodesia, 16 Aug 1964	
JACOBS, Lawton Peter	WPCB	15	1973/74	1975/76	RHB	LB		Stellenbosch, 16 May 1951	
JACOBS, Leighshé Zanell	WPWCA/WPWCA B		2001/02	2010/11	RHB	LB		Elsies River, CP, 6 Apr 1985	
JAFFER, Peter Daniel	WPCU	10	1949/50	1953/54				Cape Town, 3 May 1910	Cape Town, 20 Oct 1996
JAKOET, Abdurahman 'Manie'	WPCB	3	1978/79	1978/79	RHB			Cape Town, 19 Sept 1949	
JAMAL, EM	WPICU		1953/54	1953/54					
JAMAL, Y	WPICU		–	–					
JAMMIE, I	WPCCU		1912/13	1912/13					

Name	Affiliation	M	From	To	Batt	Bowl	Wk	Born	Died
JANUARY, P	PWDCB		1957/58	1957/58					
JAPPIE, Rushdi	WPCA Am		2006/07	2006/07					
JARDINE, Faghme	WPCA Am	2	2005/06	2006/07	LHB	SLA		Cape Town, 26 Jan 1981	
JARDINE, Graham	WPCB		1961/62	1961/62					
JASSIEM, Shamiel	WPCB	6	1977/78	1978/79	RHB	OB		Rondebosch, Cape Town, 27 Nov 1951	
JEFFERIES, Stephen Thomas	WPCU/WPCU B/WPCA	73	1978/79	1991/92	LHB	LFM		Cape Town, 8 Dec 1959	
JEFFREY, Wynnefred 'Jeff'	WPWCU		1951/52	1959/60					
JOFFE, Ryan	WPCA/WPCA B	7	1998/99	1999/00	RHB	RFM		Cape Town, 17 Apr 1975	
JOHNSON, A	WPWCU		1951/52	1957/58					
JOHNSON, Allison Atkinson	WPCU/WPCU B	2	1989/90	1989/90	RHB	RFM		St Lucy, Barbados, 22 July 1963	
JOHNSON, Neil Clarkson	WPCA/WCC	28	2000/01	2004/05	LHB	RFM OB		Salisbury, S. Rhodesia, 24 Jan 1970	
JONES, Stephen Arthur	WPCU/WPCU B	36	1974/75	1980/81	LHB	LFM		Cape Town, 14 Apr 1955	
JORDAAN, Deon	WPCA/WPCA B	17	1993/94	1994/95	LHB	RM		Bloemfontein, 3 Dec 1970	
JORDAAN, Herbert Bailey	WPCU	7	1934/35	1937/38	RHB			Robben Island, CP, 15 Feb 1914	Pretoria, 30 Apr 1979
JOSEPH, [X]	WPCCU		1898/99	1898/99					
JOSEPHS, Dennis	HHCU		1954/55	1954/55					
JOSHUA, Colin	WPCB		1963/64	1966					
JOSHUA, D	PWDCB		1950/51	1950/51					
JOSHUA, R	PWDCB		1946/47	1948/49					
KAFAAR, O	WPICU		1957/58	1957/58					
KAJEE, I	WPICU		1949/50	1951/52					
KALIS, Andrew Donald	WPCA B	3	1997/98	1998/99	LHB			Cape Town, 22 Nov 1969	
KALLIS, Jacques Henry	WPCA/WPCA B/WCC	37	1993/94	2004/05	RHB	RFM		Pinelands, CP, 16 Oct 1975	
KAMALDIEN, M	WPICU								
KARAN, Yusuf	HHCU		1954/55	1954/55					
KATIEB, C	WPICU								
KATIEB, K	WPICU								
KATTS, Arthur	WPCB	6	1975/76	1980/81	RHB	RAB		Cape Town, 2 Jan 1916	
KAWULELA, N	WPBCU		1947/48	1952/53					
KEEN, Arthur Donald (Dr) 'Punch' 'Ginger'	WPCU	13	1937/38	1949/50	RHB	OB		Winchester, England, 19 Nov 1937	Southampton, England, 26 Dec 1975
KEITH, Geoffrey Leyden	WPCU	2	1968/69	1968/69	RHB	RM		Cape Town, 29 June 1966	
KEMP, Deon	WPCB	18	1987/88	1990/91	RHB	RM		Cape Town, 14 Feb 1973	
KEMP, Justin Miles	WCC	21	2007/08	2010/11	RHB			Salt River, Cape Town, 1 Aug 1949	
KEMP, Nasser	WPCB	1	1979/80	1979/80	RHB		WK		
KENNEDY, Arnold Combrinck	WPCU	6	1933/34	1934/35	RHB	RFM		Wellington, CP, 16 Jan 1911	[x], 11 Nov 1993
KENNEY-WADE, Avril	WPWCA		1995/96	1995/96					
KENNY, A	WPCCU		1898/99	1903/04					

Name	Affiliation	M	From	To	Batt	Bowl	Wk	Born	Died
KERBY, Jack Colin	WPCU	12	1957/58	1963/64	RHB	RFM		Johannesburg, 16 Dec 1935	
KERR, Elizabeth 'Libby'	WPWCU		1972/73	1974/75					
KHAN, AH	WPICU		1951/52	1951/52					
KHAN, Gameem	WPCB	2	1985/86	1985/86	RHB		WK	Salt River, Cape Town, 6 May 1961	
KHAN, Jumannah	WPCB	6	1972/73	1974/75		OB		District Six, Cape Town, 11 Dec 1950	
KHAN, MANIE	WPCCU		1945/46	1945/46					
KHAN, R	WPICU		—	—					
KHAN, Shaheen	WPCA Am		2010/11	2010/11	RHB	RMF		Cape Town, 28 June 1987	
KIEL, Sidney (Dr)	WPCU	14	1939/40	1946/47	RHB	RM		Vrede, OFS, 18 July 1916	Sea Point, Cape Town, 19 July 2007
KILLIAN, Brenda	WPWCU		1984/85	1985/86					
KILOWAN, Ashlyn Petro Carlyle	WPWCA		2004/05	2010/11	LHB	LM		Paarl, CP, 19 Dec 1982	
KINGSWELL, Elma	WPWCU		1953/54	1953/54					
KIRSTEN, Andrew Michael	WPCU B	11	1986/87	1989/90	RHB	OB		East London, 21 Dec 1963	
KIRSTEN, Gary	WPCU/WPCU B/WPCA	86	1987/88	2003/04	LHB	OB		Cape Town, 23 Nov 1967	
KIRSTEN, Paul	WPCA/WPCA B	42	1994/95	1999/00	RHB			Cape Town, 30 Oct 1969	
KIRSTEN, Peter Noel	WPCU	133	1973/74	1989/90	RHB	OB	WK	Pietermaritzburg, 14 May 1955	
KLEINTJIES, B	WPCB		1961/62	1961/62					
KLEINVELDT, John	WPCB	10	1979/80	1980/81	RHB	RM		Lansdowne, Cape Town, 6 Aug 1957	
KLEINVELDT, Matthew Caleb	WPCA Am	11	2010/11	2010/11	LHB	OB		Southampton, England, 10 Aug 1989	
KLEINVELDT, Rory Keith	WPCA/WPCA Am/WCC	59	2002/03	2010/11	RHB	RMF		Cape Town, 15 Mar 1983	
KLETTE, John Edward	WPCU	2	1967/68	1967/68	LHB	OB		Cape Town, 8 Feb 1949	
KNOWLES, Peter	WPCU B	2	1979/80	1979/80	RHB	OB		Cape Town, 2 Feb 1955	
KNOWLES, Richard John	WPCU B	3	1978/79	1984/85	RHB	RM		Cape Town, 4 Apr 1950	
KOBI, GB	WPBCU		1947/48	1947/48					
KOCH, Donovan Marius	WPCA B	4	1997/98	1997/98	RHB	RMF		Somerset West, CP, 11 Oct 1976	
KOEN, Louis Johannes	WPCU B	9	1987/88	1989/90	RHB			Paarl, CP, 28 Mar 1967	
KOEN, Pieter Arnoldus	WPCU B	4	1984/85	1986/87	RHB	RFM		Paarl, CP, 8 Mar 1962	
KOENIG, Sven Gaetan	WPCA/WPCA B	33	1993/94	1996/97	LHB	OB		Durban, 9 Dec 1973	
KOHLER, Derek Leslie	WPCU B	1	1976/77	1976/77	RHB	RM		Cape Town, 22 Jan 1953	
KOHN, Jody	WPCA Am		2008/09	2008/09	RHB	RF		Cape Town, 9 Apr 1986	
KOLBE, Clive	WPCB	4	1971/72	1974/75	RHB	LB		District Six, Cape Town, 16 Feb 1944	
KOOPMAN, Nikita	WPWCA		2006/07	2006/07					
KOSSUTH, Frederick Henry	WPCU	3	1929/30	1929/30				Johannesburg, 29 June 1909	Cape Town, 24 Oct 1986
KOSTER, Ralph Alexander	WPCA/WPCA B	7	1992/93	1993/94	RHB	RM		Beaufort West, CP, 21 Oct 1968	
KOTZE, Johannes Jacobus 'Kodgee' 'Boerjong'	WPCU	18	1903/04	1910/11	RHB	RF		Berg River, Hopefield District, CC, 7 Aug 1879	Rondebosch, Cape Town, 7 July 1931
KRUGER, Warren Gavin	WPCU B	12	1982/83	1985/86	LHB			Port Elizabeth, 4 Aug 1955	

Name	Affiliation	M	From	To	Batt	Bowl	Wk	Born	Died
KUIPER, Adrian Paul	WPCU/WPCU B/WPCA	115	1977/78	1993/94	RHB	RM OB		Johannesburg, 24 Aug 1959	
KUIPER, James Morris	WPCA Am	15	2005/06	2008/09	LHB	RM		Johannesburg, 23 Oct 1986	
KULATHI, WW	WPBCU		1947/48	1947/48					
KUYLAARS, Aluis	WPWCA		1995/96	2000/01	RHB	RF		Cape Town, 17 May 1971	
KUYS, Frederick	WPCU	5	1896/97	1897/98				George, CC, 21 Mar 1870	Oudtshoorn, CP, 12 Sept 1953
LAING, Peter Charles	WPCA Am	6	2008/09	2009/10	RHB	RFM		Johannesburg, 5 Oct 1984	
LAKAY, H 'Tim'	PWDCB		1952/53	1954/55	RHB				
LAKAY, Neville	PWDCB/WPCB	1	1957/58	1971/72	RHB	RM			
LAKAY, Yusuf 'Timmy'	WPCCU/WPCF/WPCB		1954/55	1963/64					
LAMB, Allan Joseph	WPCU/WPCA	66	1972/73	1992/93	RHB	RM		Langebaanweg, CP, 20 June 1954	
LAMBERT, Joey	WPCB	7	1966	1973/74	RHB	LB		Kenilworth, Cape Town, 27 Oct 1938	
LANCASTER, L	WPWCU		1983/84	1983/84					
LANG, Beverley	WPWCU		1952/53	1959/60					
LANGE, Thomas	WPCU	1	1950/51	1950/51					
LANGEVELDT, Charl Kenneth	WCC	15	2007/08	2010/11	RHB	RM		Cape Town, 14 Feb 1973	
LARKIN, Gerald Michael	WPCU	3	1934/35	1937/38			WK	Cape Town, 3 Sept 1914	Johannesburg, 9 May 1976
LATIEF, Ismail	PWDCB/HHCU/WPCF		1951/52	1956/57					
LAWRENSON, Robert Richard 'Bobby'	WPCU/WPCU B	22	1980/81	1984/85	RHB	RFM		Cape Town, 27 Sept 1956	
LAZARD, Terence Nicholas (Dr)	WPCU/WPCU B/WPCA	51	1983/84	1992/93	RHB			Cape Town, 19 Oct 1965	
LAZARUS, Raymond Henri	WPCU	2	1925/26	1925/26				Suva, Fiji, 22 May 1892	Cape Town, 2 July 1983
LEAR, Peter Nowell	WPCU	7	1959/60	1965/66	RHB	RM		Claremont, Cape Town, 19 Feb 1931	
LE BRETON, Alexis	WPWCA/WPWCA B		2001/02	2010/11					
LEDINGHAM, J	WPWCU		1953/54	1954/55					
LEE, John Michael	WPCU	2	1957/58	1959/60	RHB	RM		Tolworth, Surrey, England, 19 Oct 1935	
LE ROUX, D	WPCU	1	1965/66	1965/66					
LE ROUX, Darryl Peter	WPCU B	1	1983/84	1983/84	RHB		WK	Bloemfontein, 30 Oct 1956	
LE ROUX, Garth Stirling	WPCU/WPCU B	86	1975/76	1988/89	RHB	RF		Kenilworth, Cape Town, 4 Sept 1955	
LE ROUX, J	WPCB		1968	1968					
LEVI, Richard Ernst	WPCA Am/WCC	34	2006/07	2010/11	RHB	RM		Johannesburg, 14 Jan 1988	
LEVITON, A	WPWCU		1968/69	1968/69					
LEWIS, Gail	WPWCU/Alma/Composite XIs		1967/68	1979/80					
LEWIS, Levona P	WPWCA		1997/98	1999/00				[x], 15 Nov 1972	
LEWIS, Mohammad Rasheed	WPCA B	1	1998/99	1998/99	RHB	LFM		Cape Town, 24 Apr 1975	
LEWIS, Percy Tyson 'Plum'	WPCU	6	1907/08	1913/14	RHB	RMF		Cape Town, 2 Oct 1884	Durban, 30 Jan 1976
LIDDLE, James Richard	WPCU	8	1955/56	1956/57	LHB	SLA		Port Elizabeth, 18 June 1930	Cape Town, 15 Jan 1959
LILLIE, Craig Clive	WPCU B	5	1988/89	1988/89	RHB	RFM		Cape Town, 19 Nov 1969	
LIPHUKO, MB	WPBCU		1933/34	1933/34					

Name	Affiliation	M	From	To	Batt	Bowl	Wk	Born	Died
LITTLE, Percival Alfred	WPCU	8	1932/33	1935/36				Ireland, 12 Nov 1910	Cape Town, 15 Mar 1986
LITTLEWORT, Joy	WPWCU/Bellville		1951/52	1963/64					
LLOYD, Steven Martin	WPCU B	2	1975/76	1975/76	RHB			Cape Town, 11 May 1951	
LOCK, J	WPWCU		1953/54	1953/54					
LODEWYK, E	PWDCB		1937/38	1937/38					
LOFTHOUSE, Reginald	WPCU	5	1941/42	1947/48	RHB			Observatory, Cape Town, 15 June 1914	
LOGENSTEIN, Quinton Francois	WPCB/WPCA B	5	1990/91	1993/94	RHB	RFM		Kuils River, CP, 14 Aug 1968	
LOHMANN, George Alfred	WPCA	5	1894/95	1896/97	RHB	RMF		Kensington, London, 2 June 1865	Matjesfontein, CC, 1 Dec 1901
LOON, Gavin Ian	WPCA B	1	1996/97	1996/97	LHB	RM		Port Elizabeth, 16 Aug 1970	
LOTTER, Marie Madelein	WPWCA		1998/99	2002/03	RHB	RM			
LOTTER, Neill Brian	WPCU/WPCU B	11	1971/72	1981/82	RHB	RFM		Cape Town, 8 Apr 1948	
LOTTER, Richard Bryan	WPCA Am/WCC	2	2008/09	2008/09	RHB	RFM		Cape Town, 22 Apr 1986	
LOTTER, Tamara	WPWCU/Alma/Bellville		1962/63	1965/66					
LOUW, Derek Arthur	WPCU	17	1955/56	1966/67	RHB	RF		Cape Town, 27 Oct 1936	
LOUW, Jan Leonardus 'Lennie'	WPCU B	3	1981/82	1981/82	RHB	LFM		Barkly West, CP, 29 June 1959	
LOUW, Johann	WCC	6	2009/10	2010/11	RHB	RMF		Cape Town, 12 Apr 1979	
LOVEGROVE, Aubrey Richard	WPCU	9	1923/24	1926/27				Barberton, Transvaal, 23 Mar 1894	Benoni, Transvaal, 15 Aug 1974
LOVELL, George Greville Stanhope	WPCU	3	1950/51	1952/53				Johannesburg, 17 Mar 1926	
LUCK, Alfred Arthur	WPCU	2	1947/48	1947/48		RF		Cape Town, 14 Nov 1925	Tygerberg Hospital, Parow, CP, 25 Feb 1978
LUNDIE, Eric Balfour 'Bill'	WPCU	2	1909/10	1910/11				Willowvale, CC (Transkei), 15 Mar 1888	Passchendaele, Belgium (war), 12 Sept 1917
LUYT, Frederick Pieter	WPCU	4	1908/09	1910/11			WK	Ceres, CC, 26 Feb, 1888	Cape Town, 6 June 1965
LUYT, Richard Robbins	WPCU	19	1906/07	1922/23		LBG	WK	Ceres, CC, 16 Apr 1886	Worcester, CP, 14 Jan 1967
MABUTO, B	WPBCU		1952/53	1952/53					
MACAULAY, Michael John	WPCU	4	1960/61	1960/61	RHB	LMF SLA		Durban, 19 Apr 1939	
MacDONALD, Robin Richard	WPCU	8	1955/56	1957/58	RHB			Bloemfontein, 16 Oct 1935	
MacHELM, Dean Quinton	WPCA/WPCA B	31	1992/93	1997/98	LHB	SLA		Kuils River, CP, 18 Apr 1971	
MACLONS, Alan	WPCB		1961/62	1963/64					
MACLONS, Leon	PWDCB		1946/47	1954/55					
MACLONS, Mornay 'Kulu'	WPCB	17	1968	1975/76	RHB		WK	Somerset West, CP, 17 Feb 1940	
MACLONS, R	PWDCB		1956/57	1956/57					
MacRAE, Alexander St John Vavasour 'Pat'	WPCU	6	1923/24	1926/27	RHB	LAB		Cape Town, [x] Apr 1897	Rondebosch, Cape Town, 12 Nov 1947
MAFONGOSI, SS	WPBCU		1947/48	1947/48					
MAGAN, B	WPICU		—	—					
MAGIED, [X]	WPCCU		1903/04	1903/04					
MAGIET, Achmat	WPCA Am	2	2004/05	2005/06	RHB	OB		Cape Town, 8 Feb 1983	
MAGIET, Mogamat Rushdi	WPCB	34	1969/70	1980/81	RHB	RFM		Cape Town, 14 Feb 1943	

Name	Affiliation	M	From	To	Batt	Bowl	Wk	Born	Died
MAGIET, Rashaad	WPCA/WPCA B/WPCA Am	15	1998/99	2004/05	RHB	LB		Cape Town, 30 May 1979	
MAGIET, Saait	WPCB	64	1971/72	1990/91	RHB	RM		Cape Town, 17 May 1952	
MAGITSHIMA, William V	WPACU		1966/67	1974/75					
MAGMOET, J	WPICU		1951/52	1953/54					
MAGMOET, Jamiel	WPCCU		1945/46	1945/46					
MAGMOET, O	WPICU		1951/52	1953/54					
MAGODLA, [X]	WPACU		1967/68	1967/68					
MAHLOMBE, Mondli	WPCA Am	23	2005/06	2010/11	RHB	RFM		Cape Town, 11 Nov 1985	
MAHONEY, Jack Edwin 'Jock'	WPCU/WPCU B/WPCB	27	1972/73	1981/82	RHB	RFM		Mossel Bay, CP, 23 May 1948	
MAILE, John Brian Roland	WPCU	23	1955/56	1960/61	RHB	RFM OB		Johannesburg, 15 Oct 1926	Bergvliet, Cape Town, 27 Oct 2004
MAINON, Clovis	WPCU	2	1893/94	1894/95				Melbourne, Australia, 23 Mar 1854	Johannesburg, 23 Feb 1935
MALAMBA, Ben Ndzima	WPBCU/WPCF		1935/36	1956/57	RHB	RMF			
MALAMBA, T	WPBCU		1952/53	1952/53					
MALAMBA, [X]	WPBCU		1936/37	1936/37					
MALAN, Dawid Johannes	WPCU B	3	1978/79	1979/80	RHB	RFM		Springs, Transvaal, 29 Sept 1956	
MALL, Hassan	WPICU		1947/48	1947/48					
MAMA, PW	WPBCU		1933/34	1933/34					
MANACK, Abdulhack Ahmed 'Jack'	WPCB	5	1989/90	1989/90	RHB	RFM		Vereeniging, Transvaal, 21 Aug 1967	
MANDLA, T	WPBCU		1947/48	1947/48					
MANNING, Leslie Martin	WPCU	28	1930/31	1939/40	RHB			Poole, Dorset, England, 29 Sept 1911	Port Elizabeth, 20 Mar 1990
MARAIS, Annelise	WPWCU		1971/72	1974/75					
MARKS, Estavia	WPWCA		2000/01	2000/01	RHB	RM			
MARNEVELD, Desirée	WPWCU/Composite XIs		1979/80	1983/84					
MARON, Ryan	WPCA/WPCA B	16	1995/96	1998/99	LHB	SLA		Cape Town, 24 Feb 1975	
MARS, Walter Herbert 'Wally'	WPCU	2	1912/13	1913/14	RHB	SLA		Cape Town, 28 Dec 1891	Fish Hoek, CP, 29 May 1966
MARSHALL, Alan William	WPCU	29	1941/42	1956/57	RHB	OB		Rondebosch, Cape Town, 18 Jan 1918	Claremont, Cape Town, 18 June 2000
MARTIN, Armien	WPCB		1982/83	1982/83	RHB			Mowbray, Cape Town, 13 June 1955	
MARTIN, Bryan Paul	WPCU B	7	1980/81	1985/86	RHB	SLA		Cape Town, 5 Aug 1963	
MARTIN, Cyril	WPCB	13	1977/78	1986/87	RHB			Grassy Park, Cape Town, 29 May 1959	
MARTIN, Frank Clarke	WPCU	18	1929/30	1932/33				Mowbray, Cape Town, [x] Nov 1906	Buffels Bay, Cape Point, CP, 24 May 1933
MARTIN, Grant George	WPCU B	4	1985/86	1986/87	RHB	OB		Durban, 21 July 1963	
MARTIN, Les	WPCB		1966	1966					
MARTIN, Noeg	WPCB	5	1978/79	1978/79	RHB	OB		Bo-Kaap, Cape Town, 14 Jan 1954	
MARTIN, Peter Walton	WPCU/WPCU B	25	1978/79	1990/91	RHB	OB		Cape Town, 7 Sept 1960	
MARTIN, Shadley	WPCB	1	1982/83	1982/83	LHB			Claremont, Cape Town, 26 Oct 1950	
MARTYN, Aubrey	WPCA/WPCA B	26	1992/93	1996/97	LHB	LFM		Pretoria, 23 June 1972	
MASIBA, Nozuku	WPWCA		2003/04	2005/06					

Name	Affiliation	M	From	To	Batt	Bowl	WK	Born	Died
MASINDA, Mthetheli Ronald	WPCA Am	1	2005/06	2005/06	RHB	SLA		Port Elizabeth, 18 July 1983	
MATSHIKWE, A	WPBCU		1933/34	1933/34					
MATSHIKWE, E	WPBCU		1933/34	1933/34					
MATTHEWS, Brett Anthony	WPCU/WPCU B	26	1984/85	1987/88	RHB	LM		Cape Town, 5 July 1962	
MATTHEWS, Craig Russell	WPCU/WPCU B/WPCA	76	1986/87	1999/00	RHB	RFM		Cape Town, 15 Feb 1965	
MAWU, H	WPACU		1967/68	1967/68					
MAXAM, MM	WPBCU		1947/48	1947/48					
MAXAMA, [X]	WPBCU		1936/37	1936/37					
MBALI, CS	WPBCU		1933/34	1933/34					
MBALI, DN	WPBCU		1933/34	1933/34					
MBOLO, [X]	WPBCU		1935/36	1935/36					
McADAM, Sibley John	WPCU	4	1972/73	1973/74	RHB	RF		Broken Hill, N. Rhodesia, 9 March 1948	
McADAM, William James	WPCU	12	1966/67	1968/69	RHB			Springs, Transvaal, 3 Oct 1944	
McCAY, David Lawrence Cornelius	WPCU	10	1966/67	1973/74	RHB	RMF		Hanover, CP, 18 Nov 1943	
McCLEMENT, Andrew John	WPCU/WPCU B/WPCA/WPCA B	26	1986/87	1993/94	LHB	SLA		Cape Town, 12 Mar 1962	
McCULLOCH, Victor Thomas	WPCU	21	1960/61	1966/67	RHB			Wynberg, Cape Town, 10 Oct 1936	
McEWAN, Kenneth Scott	WPCU	37	1981/82	1986/87	RHB	OB		Bedford, CP, 16 July 1952	
McLEAN, Jonathan James	WPCA	5	2001/02	2003/04	RHB		WK	Johannesburg, 11 July 1980	
McLEOD, Morag	WPWCU/Composite XIs		1978/79	1985/86					
McMEEKING, David Peter	WPCU	1	1965/66	1965/66	RHB	LB		Cape Town, 8 Aug 1937	
McMILLAN, Brian Mervin	WPCU/WPCA	52	1989/90	1999/00	RHB	RFM		Welkom, OFS, 22 Dec 1963	
McMORROW, Brian Anthony	WPCU	1	1949/50	1949/50	RHB	RMF		Cape Town, 25 Apr 1922	Cape Town, 9 Feb 1987
MDODANA, Thando Jeffrey	WPCA Am	6	2006/07	2007/08	RHB			Cape Town, 18 Nov 1986	
MEEDING, Bernard Kenneth	WPCU	1	1964/65	1964/65	RHB	RF		Port Elizabeth, 21 Mar 1938	
MELLE, Basil George von Brandis (Dr)	WPCU	9	1908/09	1910/11	RHB	RM LB		Somerset West, CC, 31 Mar 1891	Orchards, Johannesburg, 8 Jan 1966
MELLE, Michael George	WPCU	2	1953/54	1953/54	RHB	RF		Forest Town, Johannesburg, 3 June 1930	Betty's Bay, WC, 28 Dec 2003
MELLOR, Michael Douglas	WPCU B	8	1981/82	1983/84	RHB	OB		Durban, 28 Nov 1957	
MENTIS, Marc Julius	WPCU/WPCU B	11	1975/76	1976/77	RHB			Johannesburg, 10 Nov 1956	
MEYER, CA 'Tim'	WPCCU		1949/50	1951/52					
MEYER, Mohammad Adnaan	WPCB/WPCA/WPCA B	14	1990/91	1995/96	RHB	RFM		Cape Town, 24 Feb 1971	
MGIJIMA, Aviwe	WPCA Am	13	2009/10	2010/11	RHB	RMF		East London, 10 Aug 1988	
MGIJIMA, TM	WPBCU/WPACU		1947/48	1967/68					
MIDDLETON, Ivan Edwin	WPCU	1	1960/61	1960/61	RHB			Green Point, Cape Town, 2 Apr 1935	
MIDDLETON, James 'Bonnor'	WPCU	13	1890/91	1903/04		LM		Chester-le-Street, England, 30 Sept 1865	Newlands, Cape Town, 23 Dec 1913
MIDDLETON, Reginald Edgar	WPCU	3	1937/38	1945/46		LF		Newlands, Cape Town, 13 June 1910	
MIDDLETON, Thomas	WPCU	4	1924/25	1926/27				Newlands, Cape Town, [x] 1894	Cape Town, [x] 1965
MILLARD, David Edward Shaxson	WPCU	4	1951/52	1954/55	RHB	OB		Rondebosch, Cape Town, 3 Apr 1931	Cape Town, 30 Jan 1978

Name	Affiliation	M	From	To	Batt	Bowl	Wk	Born	Died
MILLER, Cedric	WPCB	1	1975/76	1975/76	RHB	RM		Lansdowne, Cape Town, 20 Jan 1951	
MILLER, Gerry	WPCB	4	1984/85	1988/89	LHB	RM			
MILLER, Hamish David Sneddon	WPCU	5	1962/63	1962/63	RHB	RMF		Blackpool, England, 26 June 1941	
MILLER, W	PWDCB		1946/47	1946/47					
MILLS, Charles Henry	WPCU	4	1892/93	1894/95	RHB	RM		Peckham, England, 26 Nov 1867	Southwark, London, England, 26 July 1948
MILTON, William Henry (Sir)	WPCU	3	1889/90	1890/91	RHB			Little Marlow, Buckinghamshire, England, 3 Dec 1854	Cannes, France, 6 Mar 1930
MINNAAR, Charles William Rorich 'Midget'	WPCU	1	1913/14	1913/14				Wepener, OFS, [x] Aug 1882	Beaumont-Hamel, France (war), 16 Nov 1916
MINNAAR, Michael Ballard 'Vaatjie'	WPCU/WPCU B	48	1977/78	1989/90	LHB	OB		Cape Town, 2 Oct 1954	
MINNIES, P	WPCB		1969	1969					
MITCHELL, Timothy John	WPCU B/WPCA/WPCA B	29	1989/90	1996/97	RHB	RM		Cape Town, 24 Aug 1968	
MJEKULA, Sinethemba	WPCA Am	4	2006/07	2006/07	RHB	RFM		King William's Town, CP, 16 Oct 1983	
MLUMBI, O	WPBCU		1952/53	1952/53					
MOHAMED, Ebrahim 'Barney'	WPCB	7	1984/85	1988/89		RMF		Wynberg, Cape Town, 19 Dec 1961	
MOLEON, Eugene Owen	WPCA B	8	1996/97	1998/99	RHB	RFM		Cape Town, 2 Mar 1977	
MOODIE, D Viccie	WPCB	17	1968	1975/76	RHB			Elsies River, CP, 8 May 1945	
MOODLEY, Nadine	WPWCA		2010/11	2010/11					
MOOLENSCHOT, Sue	WPWCU		1952/53	1954/55					
MOORE, TE	WPCU	1	1895/96	1895/96					
MOOSA, E	WPICU		1947/48	1947/48					
MORBY-SMITH, Lynton	WPCU	16	1963/64	1966/67	RHB	OB		Durban, 27 May 1936	Westville, Durban, 20 June 1998
MORGAN, Harold William 'Smiler'	WPCU	13	1927/28	1933/34				Cape Town, 10 Jan 1908	Wynberg, Cape Town, 14 June 1985
MORKEL, Denijs Paul Beck	WPCU	23	1924/25	1929/30	RHB	RFM		Plumstead, Cape Town, 25 Jan 1906	Nottingham, England, 6 Oct 1980
MORKEL, Raymond Kenneth Bellville	WPCU	5	1927/28	1930/31	LHB	LAB		Bellville, CC, 23 Aug 1908	Worcester, CP, 8 Nov 1953
MORRIS, John Douglas	WPCU	8	1961/62	1962/63	RHB			Mowbray, Cape Town, 1 July 1940	
MORRIS, Richard Edwin Tuffrey	WPCU	61	1967/68	1978/79	RHB	OB	WK	Cape Town, 28 Jan 1947	
MORRIS, Stuart Vine	WPCU	4	1958/59	1959/60	LHB			Rondebosch, Cape Town, 26 May 1937	
MPILWANA, [X]	WPBCU		1936/37	1936/37					
MSHUMPELA, Alex M	WPBCU		1947/48	1952/53					
MTIMKULU, Don T	WPBCU		1933/34	1933/34					
MUFTI, Abdullah 'Hadji'	WPCCU		1921/22	1921/22					
MULDER, Dougie	WPCB		1961/62	1961/62					
MÜLLER, Elize	WPWCU/Alma		1965/66	1971/72					
MULLER, Nilton	WPCB	8	1987/88	1989/90	RHB	RM		Stellenbosch, 25 June 1954	
MULLINS, Antonio Kenneth	WPCA B	1	1998/99	1998/99	RHB	RF		Johannesburg, 9 May 1980	
MUNNIK, Renier	WPCA/WPCA B/WPCA Am/WCC	34	1997/98	2005/06	RHB	RFM		Cape Town, 7 Jan 1978	

Name	Affiliation	M	From	To	Batt	Bowl	Wk	Born	Died
MUNTINGH, Eugene	WPCU/WPCB	10	1978/79	1981/82	RHB	LBG		Pietersburg, Transvaal, 5 May 1958	
MURPHY, Brian Andrew	WPCA	5	1997/98	1997/98	RHB	LB		Salisbury, S. Rhodesia, 1 Dec 1976	
MUSSON, Rashaad	WPCB	18	1980/81	1989/90	RHB		WK	Johannesburg, 11 Nov 1959	
MUZZELL, Robert Kendal	WPCU	17	1964/65	1967/68	RHB	LB		Stutterheim, CP, 23 Dec 1945	
MVINJELWA, H	WPBCU		1952/53	1952/53					
MYLES, Henry Filby	WPCU	2	1930/31	1930/31	RHB			Cape Town, 6 June 1911	
NACKERDIEN, S 'Sharkey'	WPCCU		1945/46	1954/55					
NAIDOO, M	WPICU		1951/52	1951/52					
NAPIER, Gordon Lennox	WPCU	3	1929/30	1935/36	RHB			Gardens, Cape Town, [x] 1909	Newlands, Cape Town, [x] 1980
NDLWANA, G	WPBCU		1935/36	1935/36					
NDLWANA, SM 'Mac'	WPBCU		1933/34	1952/53					
NEETHLING, John James 'Coetie'	PWDCB/WPCB	12	1952/53	1973/74	RHB	RM		Goodwood, CP, 20 July 1932	
NEFDT, Sheilagh N (née CHARLTON)	WPWCU		1951/52	1956/57					
NEL, D	WPWCU		1985/86	1985/86					
NEL, John Desmond 'Jack'	WPCU	28	1947/48	1960/61	RHB			Cape Town, 10 July 1928	
NEL, Michael John	WPCU/WPCB	24	1974/75	1981/82	RHB			Cape Town, 24 July 1953	
NEWTON-THOMPSON, John Oswald	WPCU	1	1948/49	1948/49	RHB	SRA		Paddington, London, 2 Dec 1920	
NICHOLSON, Peter Shaw	WPCU	7	1952/53	1953/54	RHB			Dehra Dun, India, 23 Nov 1921	
NIEUWOUDT, Andre Barend 'Houtie'	WPCU/WPCB	28	1972/73	1978/79	RHB	RFM		Johannesburg, 5 Dec 1946	
NKOLOMBE, M	WPBCU		1952/53	1952/53					
NOLTE, Jacobus Everhardus	WPCU/WPCB	11	1986/87	1989/90	RHB	RFM		Klerksdorp, Transvaal, 16 Dec 1965	
NORDIEN, 'Happie'	WPCCU/WPCF		1949/50	1953/54					
NORMAN, David	WPCU/WPCB	20	1983/84	1985/86	RHB	RFM		Cape Town, 7 Nov 1964	
NORTHCOTE, Andrew Michael	WPCA Am	2	2008/09	2008/09	RHB			Cape Town, 12 Apr 1983	
NORTON, Norman Ogilvie 'Pompey'	WPCU	1	1902/03	1902/03	RHB	RM		Grahamstown, CC, 11 May 1881	Southernwood, East London, 27 June 1968
NOURSE, Arthur William 'Dave'	WPCU	24	1927/28	1935/36	LHB	LM SLA		South Norwood, England, 25 Jan 1879	Glendinningvale, Port Elizabeth, 8 July 1948
NQOKO, W	WPBCU		1950/51	1951/52					
NTSHONA, A	WPBCU		1952/53	1952/53					
NYAMAKAZI, J	WPBCU		1952/53	1952/53					
NYULU, Siphiwo Cyprian	WPCA Am	4	2004/05	2004/05	LHB	SLA		Cape Town, 22 July 1976	
O'CONNELL, Brian	WPCB	8	1973/74	1975/76	RHB	RM		Bo-Kaap, Cape Town, 16 Jan 1946	
O'CONNELL, Tamryn 'Tammy'	WPWCA/WPWCA B		2000/01	2009/10					
ODENDAAL, André	WPCB	1	1985/86	1985/86	RHB	OB		Queenstown, CP, 4 May 1954	
O'GRADY, John Murray	WPCU	1	1946/47	1946/47	RHB			Port Elizabeth, 7 Jan 1925	
O'LINN, Sidney 'Micky'	WPCU	2	1945/46	1946/47	LHB	LB		Oudtshoorn, CP, 5 May 1927	
OLIVIER, Mario Wicus	WPCA Am/WCC	8	2009/10	2009/10	RHB	RFM	WK	Pretoria, 3 Nov 1982	
ONTONG, Justin Lee	WCC	25	2008/09	2010/11	RHB	LB OB		Paarl, CP, 4 Jan 1980	

Name	Affiliation	M	From	To	Batt	Bowl	Wk	Born	Died
OOSTHUIZEN, Riaan Carel	WPCA	1	1999/00	1999/00	RHB		WK	Cape Town, 3 May 1972	
OSMAN, Abdullah Abubakar	WPCCU/WPCF		1949/50	1957/58					
OSMANY, MS	WPICU/WPCF		1956/57	1957/58	RHB	SLA			
OVENSTONE, Douglas MacPherson	WPCU	9	1946/47	1947/48	RHB		WK	Sea Point, Cape Town, 31 July 1921	Llandudno, Cape Town, 6 Nov 2011
OWEN, Sally	WPWCU		1984/85	1984/85					
OWEN-SMITH, Harold Geoffrey Owen 'Tuppy'	WPCU	14	1927/28	1949/50	RHB	LBG		Rondebosch, Cape Town, 18 Feb 1909	Rosebank, Cape Town, 28 Feb 1990
PAGDEN, Nicholas David	WPCU B		1981/82	1981/82	RHB	RM			
PAINE, Albert Ingraham	WPCU	4	1896/97	1896/97	RHB			[x], 10 Feb 1956	Bledington, England, 29 June 1949
PALEKER, Allahudien	WPCA B	2	1997/98	1997/98	RHB	OB		India, 12 Jan 1874	
PALM, Archibald William	WPCU	37	1921/22	1933/34	RHB		WK	Cape Town, 1 Jan 1978	
PANGARKAR, SI	WPICU		1953/54	1957/58				Rondebosch, Cape Town, 8 June 1901	Somerset West, CP, 17 Aug 1966
PANGARKAR, T	WPICU		1957/58	1957/58					
PANGARKAR, Hassan	WPCA/WPCA B	26	1991/92	1999/00	LHB			Elsies River, CP, 31 Aug 1968	
PARKER, A	WPICU			—					
PARKER, André Charles	WPCU/WPCU B	6	1970/71	1975/76	RHB	OB		Port Elizabeth, 20 May 1951	
PARKER, David Charles	WPCU B	4	1976/77	1976/77	RHB			Cape Town, 8 Aug 1951	
PARRY, Haylee	WPWCA		2000/01	2003/04	RHB	RFM			
PASSMORE, Antony Graham	WPCU B	2	1980/81	1980/81	RHB	RM		Cape Town, 18 Mar 1958	
PATERSEN, Anne	WPWCU		1974/75	1974/75					
PATERSON, Dane	WPCA Am	17	2009/10	2010/11	RHB	RFM		Cape Town, 4 Apr 1989	
PAULING, Newton C	WPCU	2	1892/93	1892/93					
PAULL, Gordon Blake	WPCU	5	1933/34	1939/40	RHB	RFM		Cape Town, 9 May 1912	Cape Town, 27 June 1987
PAULSE, Hillroy Henrico	WCC		2009/10	2009/10	RHB	RF		Paarl, CP, 6 Sept 1985	
PAYNE, Dean Geoffrey	WPCU/WPCU B/WPCA/WPCA B	40	1988/89	1998/99	LHB	RFM		Claremont, Cape Town, 13 Jan 1969	
PAYNE, Ian Attwood	WPCU/WPCU B	19	1968/69	1977/78	RHB			Cape Town, 4 Oct 1949	
PAYNE, Maureen	WPWCU/Alma/Bellville		1956/57	1974/75					
PEIRCE, Clarrie	WPWCU		1952/53	1959/60					
PENNY, Lauren	WPWCA/WPWCA B		2001/02	2004/05					
PETERS, Arthur Douglas	WPCU	5	1931/32	1931/32	RHB	RMF		Cape Town, 4 June 1904	Durban, 22 Sept 1988
PETERSEN, Basil	WPCB	3	1971/72	1974/75		SLA			
PETERSEN, C	PWDCB		1937/38	1937/38					
PETERSEN, E	WPCB		1961/62	1961/62					
PETERSEN, Eric	WPCCU/WPCF		1951/52	1957/58					
PETERSEN, Grant	WPCB	2	1983/84	1985/86	LHB		WK		
PETERSON, Robin John	WCC	10	2009/10	2010/11	LHB	SLA		Port Elizabeth, 4 Aug 1979	
PETU, PK	WPBCU		1933/34	1936/37					

Name	Affiliation	M	From	To	Batt	Bowl	Wk	Born	Died
PFAFF, Brian Desmond	WPCU	18	1952/53	1957/58	RHB	RM		Pretoria, 2 Mar 1930	Johannesburg, 8 May 1998
PFAFF, Leslie	WPCU	1	1926/27	1926/27	RHB	RM		Oudtshoorn, CC, 26 Jan 1905	Fairleads, Benoni, Transvaal, 1 May 1991
PFISTER, Cecil Alexander	WPCU	1	1928/29	1928/29				Cape Town, 15 Jan 1903	Cape Town, 16 Oct 1965
PFUHL, Gavin Pattison	WPCU/WPCU B	92	1967/68	1979/80	RHB			Mowbray, Cape Town, 27 Aug 1947	Cape Town, 1 Apr 2002
PHILANDER, Vernon Darryl	WPCA/WPCA Am/WCC	56	2003/04	2010/11	RHB	RMF		Bellville, CP, 24 June 1985	
PHILLIPS, Laureen	WPWCA		1996/97	1996/97					
PICK, M	WPCB		1968	1968					
PICKERING, Jackie	WPWCU		1958/59	1958/59					
PICKUP, John	WPCU	6	1936/37	1937/38	LHB	LAB		Vereeniging, Transvaal, 3 Mar 1913	Vryburg, CP, 5 July 1973
PIEDT, Dane Lee-Roy	WPCA Am/WCC	15	2009/10	2010/11	RHB	OB		Cape Town, 6 Mar 1990	
PIENAAR, Roy Francois	WPCU/WPCU B	36	1981/82	1984/85	RHB	RM OB		Johannesburg, 17 July 1961	
PIGGOT, Mary	WPWCU/Alma		1969/70	1974/75					
PIPERS, Nuraan	WPWCA		2006/07	2010/11					
PISTORIUS, Annelie	WPWCU		1978/79	1978/79					
PITHEY, Anthony John	WPCU	12	1955/56	1957/58	RHB	OB		Umtali, S. Rhodesia, 17 July 1933	Southbroom, KZN, 17 Nov 2006
PITHEY, David Bartlett	WPCU	1	1957/58	1957/58	RHB	OB		Salisbury, S. Rhodesia, 4 Oct 1936	
PLAATJIES, Francois Chessley	WPCA Am/WCC	12	2006/07	2009/10	RHB	RF		Oudtshoorn, CP, 26 Aug 1986	
PLACE, Derek Walter	WPCU B	1	1975/76	1975/76	RHB	SLA		Rondebosch, Cape Town, 27 June 1944	
PLANTEMA, Adrian Peter	WPCU B/WPCA	12	1987/88	1992/93	LHB		WK	Cape Town, 2 Dec 1968	
PLAYER, Bradley Todd	WPCA/WPCA B	15	1997/98	1998/99	RHB	RFM OB		Benoni, Transvaal, 18 Jan 1967	
PLIMSOLL, Jack Bruce	WPCU	18	1939/40	1947/48	RHB	LMF		Kalk Bay, Cape Town, 27 Oct 1917	Cape Town, 11 Nov 1999
POOLE, C	PWDCB		1957/58	1957/58					
POTHECARY, James Edward	WPCU	33	1954/55	1964/65	RHB	RM		Cape Town, 6 Dec 1933	
PRESENS, Leizel	WPWCA		2002/03	2002/03					
PRICE, David	WPCU	14	1933/34	1939/40	RHB	RM		Cape Town, 13 Aug 1910	at sea, off Iceland (war), 6 July 1942
PRICE, Hassiem	WPCB	1	1982/83	1982/83	RHB			[x], 7 May 1956	
PRICE, Kim	WPWCA/WPWCU/Composite XIs		1978/79	1999/00	RHB	SLA		Cape Town, 9 Dec 1962	
PRINCE, Ashwell Gavin	WPCA/WCC	52	1997/98	2007/08	LHB	OB		Port Elizabeth, 28 May 1977	
PRINCE, Charles Frederick Henry	WPCU	8	1894/95	1904/05	RHB		WK	Boshof, OFS, 11 Sept 1874	Wynberg, Cape Town, 2 Feb 1949
PRINGLE, Meyrick Wayne	WPCU/WPCU B/WPCA	55	1989/90	1996/97	RHB	RFM		Adelaide, CP, 22 June 1966	
PRITCHARD, John A	WPCU	5	1902/03	1903/04	RHB		WK	Harrismith, OFS, 24 Nov 1878	
PROCTER, Andrew Collacott	WPCU B	2	1979/80	1979/80	RHB	RM		Port Elizabeth, 18 Aug 1959	
PROCTER, Michael John	WPCU	5	1969/70	1969/70	RHB	RF OB		Durban, 15 Sept 1946	
PUTTICK, Andrew George	WPCA/WCC	95	2000/01	2010/11	LHB		WK	Cape Town, 11 Dec 1980	
PYCROFT, Andrew John	WPCU B	8	1975/76	1978/79	RHB	OB		Salisbury, S. Rhodesia, 6 June 1956	
QOMOYI, Andile	WPCA Am		2007/08	2007/08	RHB	RMF		Cape Town, 21 Apr 1986	

Name	Affiliation	M	From	To	Batt	Bowl	Wk	Born	Died
RABIE, Gurshwin Renier	WPCA Am/WCC	18	2008/09	2010/11	RHB	RFM		Oudtshoorn, CP, 26 June 1983	
RAHBEENI, M	WPICU		1953/54	1953/54					
RAIL, Richard Angwin	WPCU	1	1913/14	1913/14				Sydney, Australia, 25 July 1888	Passchendaele, Belgium (war), 9 Oct 1917
RAILOUN, Ismail	HHCU		1951/52	1951/52					
RAILOUN, Sabodien	HHCU		1951/52	1951/52					
RALPH, Andrew Ronald MacKenzie 'Nobbie'	WPCU	33	1931/32	1945/46	RHB		WK	Mowbray, Cape Town, 26 Apr 1908	Port Elizabeth, [x]
RAMELA, Omphile Abel	WCC	3	2009/10	2010/11	LHB	SLA		Soweto, Transvaal, 14 Mar 1988	
RAMOO, Romano Jude	WPCA Am	13	2008/09	2009/10	RHB	RM		East London, 25 Apr 1987	
RASDIEN, Giem	WPCCU		1951/52	1951/52					
RASMUS, Mark	WPCB	3	1988/89	1988/89	RHB			Firgrove, Stellenbosch, 3 Mar 1966	
RASOOL, Y	WPICU		—	—					
RAVENS, Cliffie	PWDCB		1946/47	1946/47					
RAVENS, Clifford	WPCF		1953/54	1953/54					
RAVENS, Clinton 'Kosie'	WPCB	2	1985/86	1985/86	RHB	RFM		Wynberg, Cape Town, 16 Nov 1960	
RAVENS, N	PWDCB		1946/47	1946/47					
RAYFIELD, Sheree	WPWCU		1984/85	1984/85					
RAYMENT, Paul Alan	WPCU B	8	1984/85	1990/91	RHB	RFM		Cape Town, 24 July 1965	
RAYNER, Paul Hector	WPCU/WPCU B	32	1981/82	1985/86	RHB	RM		Pinetown, Natal, 8 Jan 1962	
RAZIET, C	PWDCB		1957/58	1957/58					
RAZIET, O	PWDCB		1946/47	1946/47					
RAZIET, Salamodien 'Laam'	PWDCB/WPCB/WPCF		1952/53	1961/62					
REDDICK, Tom Bokenham	WPCU	4	1950/51	1950/51	RHB	LB		Shanghai, China, 17 Feb 1912	Newlands, Cape Town, 1 June 1982
REES, David Watkins	WPCU	1	1949/50	1949/50	LHB			Cape Town, 1 Apr 1924	Cape Town, 7 Mar 1977
REID, Alexander Bernard John	WPCU	15	1939/40	1950/51	RHB		WK	Cape Town, 29 June 1915	Rosebank, Cape Town, 31 Oct 1948
REID, Allan 'Jupp'	WPCU	20	1896/97	1908/09	RHB			Observatory, Cape Town, 1 Oct 1877	Stellenbosch, 15 June 1967
REID, Denise Joanne	WPWCA		1995/96	2001/02	LHB	RFM			
REID, Frank	WPCU	6	1910/11	1923/24			WK	Cape Town, 20 Aug 1885	Newlands, Cape Town, 26 Feb 1963
REID, Norman	WPCU	12	1920/21	1923/24				Newlands, Cape Town, 26 Dec 1890	Newlands, Cape Town, 6 June 1947
REID-ROSS, Lindsay John	WPCU	1	1975/76	1975/76	RHB	SLA		Port Elizabeth, 12 Oct 1953	
REINAARD, Gamat 'Prep'	WPCCU		1931/32	1931/32					
RHODA, MK	HHCU		1954/55	1954/55					
RHOODE, E	WPCF		1953/54	1953/54					
RICHARDS, Alfred Renfrew	WPCU	8	1889/90	1895/96	RHB		WK	Grahamstown, CC, 14 Dec 1867	Salisbury, S. Rhodesia, 9 Jan 1904
RICHARDS, Joseph	WPCU	2	1889/90	1889/90				Grahamstown, CC, [x] 1859	
RICHARDS, Rowan Ronaldo	WPCA Am	14	2009/10	2010/11	LHB	LFM		East London, 8 July 1984	
RICHARDS, Terence	WPCB	3	1979/80	1979/80	RHB	OB		Lansdowne, Cape Town, 15 Dec 1956	

Name	Affiliation	M	From	To	Batt	Bowl	Wk	Born	Died
RICHARDS, William Henry Matthews 'Dicky'	WPCU							Grahamstown, CC, 26 Mar 1862	Wynberg, Cape Town, 4 Jan 1903
RICHARDSON, Malcolm Henry Hugh	WPCU	12	1958/59	1960/61	RHB			Kalk Bay, Cape Town, 23 June 1931	
RICHARDSON, Ralph Peter	WPCU/WPCU B	8	1984/85	1988/89	RHB	RFM		Cape Town, 19 Aug 1963	
RIPPON, Michael James	WPCA Am/WCC		2010/11	2010/11	RHB	SLC		Cape Town, 14 Sept 1991	
ROBERTS, Leon Leonard	WPCB	2	1985/86	1985/86	LHB	LFM		Stellenbosch, 30 Apr 1956	
ROBERTS, Trevor Michael	WPCU B	1	1986/87	1986/87	RHB		WK	Durban, 21 Oct 1953	
ROBERTSON, John Benjamin	WPCU	20	1931/32	1936/37	RHB	RM OB		Wynberg, Cape Town, 5 June 1906	Cape Town, 5 July 1985
ROBERTSON, Troy	WPCA B	4	1995/96	1995/96	RHB		WK	Fish Hoek, CP, 6 Oct 1973	
RODRIQUES, K	WPCB		1969	1969					
ROOKLEDGE, Quentin John	WPCU	3	1971/72	1971/72	LHB			Cape Town, 18 Jan 1948	
ROOS, Allan Christopher	WPCU	1	1970/71	1970/71	RHB			Cape Town, 24 May 1945	
ROSCOE, Bertwine Money-Kyrle	WPCU	7	1937/38	1938/39				Tokai, Cape Town, 19 Dec 1906	
ROSS, Colin Kenneth	WPCU B	2	1975/76	1975/76	RHB	OB		Bedford, CP, 17 Dec 1953	
ROSS, William Charles	WPCU	3	1934/35	1939/40	RHB	RM		Cape Town, 12 Sept 1913	Cape Town, 1 Sept 1984
ROUSSEAU, Jean	WPWWCU		1983/84	1983/84					
ROUTLEDGE, Thomas William	WPCU	1	1889/90	1889/90	RHB			Liverpool, England, 18 Apr 1867	Norton, Stockton-on-Tees, UK, 9 May 1927
ROWE, George Alexander	WPCU	15	1893/94	1906/07	RHB	SLA		Grahamstown, CC, 15 June 1874	Pinelands, CP, 8 Jan 1950
ROWLES, M	WPWCU		1953/54	1954/55					
ROY, Hugh Noel Priestley	WPCU	14	1952/53	1956/57	LHB	RM		Newcastle-upon-Tyne, Northumberland, England, 28 Sept 1935	
RUNDLE, David Bryan	WPCU/WPCU B/WPCA/WPCA B	90	1984/85	1996/97	RHB	OB		Cape Town, 25 Sept 1965	
RUSH, Eric David Bellew	WPCU	1	1924/25	1924/25	RHB	LAB		Vryburg, CC, 26 Apr 1906	
RUSH, William Rolande Gerrard 'Bull'	WPCU	4	1923/24	1923/24	RHB			Kuruman, CC, 22 Jan 1904	Southbroom, Natal, 12 Sept 1968
RUSHMERE, Colin George	WPCU	2	1957/58	1960/61	RHB	RM		Summerstrand, PE, 16 Apr 1937	Durban, 3 Mar 1968
RUSHMERE, John Weir	WPCU	8	1960/61	1962/63	RHB	LF		Port Elizabeth, 1 Apr 1939	
RUTGERS, G	PWDCB		1937/38	1937/38					
RYALL, Richard James	WPCU/WPCU B/WPCA/WPCA B	122	1980/81	1994/95	RHB		WK	Salisbury, S. Rhodesia, 26 Nov 1959	
RYAN, Leslie John	WPCU B/WPCA B	9	1988/89	1991/92	RHB	RFM		Wynberg, Cape Town, 1 Sept 1964	
SABOTKER, Adam	PWDCB/WPCF		1952/53	1957/58					
SACKS, René	WPWCU/Composite XIs		1978/79	1983/84					
SALIE, Rashaad	WPCB	5	1977/78	1978/79	RHB			Bo-Kaap, Cape Town, 11 July 1947	
SALIE, Rashaad	HHCU		1951/52	1951/52					
SALIE, Salie	WPCCU		1945/46	1949/50					
SALIE, Taliep	WPCCU		1920s	1945/46					
SAMAAI, R ('Achmat'?)	WPCCU		1954/55	1954/55					
SAMSODIEN, Kamalie	WPCCU		1954/55	1954/55					

Name	Affiliation	M	From	To	Batt	Bowl	Wk	Born	Died
SAMSODIEN, Waleed	WPCA Am	1	2004/05	2004/05	RHB	RFM		Cape Town, 18 Jan 1982	
SANDRI, Pepler Sacto Emiliano	WCC	8	2006/07	2008/09	RHB	RMF		Cape Town, 14 Jan 1983	
SASSMAN, A	PWDCB		1937/38	1937/38					
SATARIEN, A	WPCCU		1949/50	1949/50					
SAUNDERS, J	WPWCU		1951/52	1953/54					
SCHULTZ, Brett Nolan	WPCA/WPCA B	11	1996/97	1997/98	LHB	LF		East London, 26 Aug 1970	
SCOTT, CM	WPBCU		1947/48	1952/53					
SECCULL, Arthur William	WPCU	1	1893/94	1893/94	RHB	RM		King William's Town, CC, 14 Sept 1868	Johannesburg, 20 July 1945
SECONDS, Trevor	WPCB	3	1988/89	1990/91		LMF		Mossel Bay, CP, 9 Aug 1960	
SEDGWICK, A	PWDCB		1937/38	1937/38					
SEEFF, Jonothan	WPCU B	18	1980/81	1984/85	LHB			Johannesburg, 22 Apr 1961	
SEEFF, Lawrence	WPCU/WPCA	103	1977/78	1991/92	RHB	LB		Kensington, Johannesburg, 1 May 1959	
SEPTEMBER, Marshall	WPCB	1	1972/73	1972/73		RMF			
SERRURIER, Louis Roy	WPCU	10	1927/28	1929/30	RHB	RM		Sea Point, Cape Town, 7 Feb 1905	Hermanus, CP, 16 Jan 1990
SEWELL, Bryan William	WPCU	1	1945/46	1945/46				Cape Town, 1 Mar 1918	Windhoek, SWA, 20 Apr 1968
SEWSUNKER, Cheryl	WPWCA		2005/06	2007/08					
SEYMOUR, Michael Arthur (Dr) 'Kelly'	WPCU	19	1960/61	1969/70	RHB	OB		Kokstad, CP, 5 June 1936	
SEYMOUR, Richard Arthur	WPCU/WPCU B	5	1975/76	1975/76	RHB	RM		Cape Town, 29 Oct 1946	
SHAH, Owais Alam	WCC	5	2010/11	2010/11	RHB	OB		Karachi, Sind, Pakistan, 22 Oct 1978	
SHAIKH, Ismail E	WPICU/WPCF		1953/54	1953/54					
SHANYELA, [X]	WPBCU		1936/37	1936/37					
SHAW, Mellissa	WPWCA		2006/07	2007/08					
SHELDON, A	WPCCU		1903/04	1903/04					
SHORT, William Henry	WPCU	12	1905/06	1913/14	RHB			Durban, 29 Jan 1932	Worcester, CP, 19 Jan 1949
SIEDLE, John Roderick	WPCU	5	1955/56	1956/57	RHB				Sherwood, Durban, 2 Aug 2008
SIERRA, John Peter	WPCU	1	1947/48	1947/48	RHB	OB		Mossel Bay, CP, 26 Mar 1922	East London, 17 May 2000
SIHAWU, GG	WPACU		1966/67	1966/67					
SILEUR, C	PWDCB		1946/47	1946/47					
SILEUR, Heidi	WPWCA		1996/97	1996/97					
SIMETU, Siyabulela	WPCA Am	3	2009/10	2010/11	RHB	SLA		Cape Town, 22 Aug 1991	
SIMONS, Eric Owen	WPCU/WPCA B/WPCA	105	1982/83	1998/99	RHB	RFM		Cape Town, 9 Mar 1962	
SIMPSON, Alastair Randal	WPCA Am	3	2004/05	2004/05	LHB			Cape Town, 10 May 1978	
SIMPSON, Lucian Frederick	WPCA Am	16	2005/06	2008/09	RHB	LF		Somerset West, CP, 20 May 1980	
SIMPSON, Reginald	WPCB	2	1973/74	1973/74	RHB			[x], 8 June 1950	
SIYAYA, G 'Shanks'	WPBCU		1952/53	1952/53					
SIYAYA, H	WPBCU		1952/53	1952/53					
SKOG, Wia H	WPWCU/Alma/Bellville		1962/63	1968/69					

Name	Affiliation	M	From	To	Batt	Bowl	Wk	Born	Died
SMART, Doris	WPWCU		1956/57	1959/60					
SMART, E	WPWCU		1953/54	1953/54					
SMIT, Willem Johannes	WCC		2004/05	2004/05	RHB	RM		Calvinia, CP, 1 Aug 1974	
SMITH, Frederick	WPCU	11	1912/13	1921/22		LAB			
SMITH, Graeme Craig	WPCA/WCC	21	2000/01	2010/11	LHB	OB		Johannesburg, 1 Feb 1981	
SMITH, Vaughan	WPCB	4	1977/78	1979/80	RHB				
SNOOKE, Sibley John 'Tip'	WPCU	11	1903/04	1907/08	RHB	RFM		St Mark's, CC (Transkei), 1 Feb 1881	Humewood, Port Elizabeth, 14 Aug 1966
SNOOKE, Stanley de la Courtte	WPCU	20	1904/05	1910/11	RHB	OB		St Mark's, CC (Transkei), 11 Nov 1878	Wynberg, Cape Town, 6 Apr 1959
SNYMAN, Neil Martin	WPCU B	2	1982/83	1982/83	RHB	OB		Prieska, CP, 4 Mar 1963	
SNYMAN, Otto Jeppe Andrew	WPCU/WPCU B	10	1972/73	1976/77	RHB	OB		Prieska, CP, 11 May 1946	
SODUMO, Abongile Mzimkhulu	WPCA Am	6	2007/08	2008/09			WK	King William's Town, CP, 16 June 1982	
SOKANYILE, H	WPBCU		1952/53	1952/53					
SOLOMON, A	WPCCU		1912/13	1912/13					
SOLOMON, AB	WPCCU		1912/13	1912/13					
SOLOMON, Ian Richard	WPCU B/WPCA B	5	1989/90	1995/96	RHB	SLA		Cape Town, 10 Nov 1971	
SOLOMON, Sidney Norman	PWDCB/WPCF		1953/54	1957/58	RHB	RLB			
SOLOMONS, Faghme	WPCB	21	1977/78	1984/85	LHB			Bo-Kaap, Cape Town, 12 Apr 1957	
SOLOMONS, Gamat	WPCCU		1945/46	1947/48					
SOLOMONS, Mario Theodore	WPCA/WPCA B	16	1995/96	1998/99	RHB		WK	Kuils River, CP, 24 Feb 1971	
SOMYO, Stanford	WPACU		1974/75	1975/76					
SONN, Archie	WPCB	10	1972/73	1978/79	RHB	RMF		Oudtshoorn, CP, 10 Sept 1952	
SOUTHGATE, I	PWDCB		1957/58	1957/58					
SPENCER-YOUNG, Russell	WPCU	8	1962/63	1963/64	LHB	OB		Cape Town, 12 Apr 1939	Johannesburg, 16 June 1992
SPILHAUS, Carl Fredric	WPCU B/WPCA B	9	1990/91	1991/92	RHB		WK	Cape Town, 11 Nov 1963	
STEENSMA, Sydney	WPCU	5	1925/26	1932/33	LHB		WK		
STELLING, William Frederick	WPCA/WPCA B	3	1991/92	1993/94	RHB	RFM		Johannesburg, 30 June 1969	
STEPHEN, George Wallace	WPCU	4	1904/05	1910/11				Sea Point, Cape Town, 1 June 1881	St James, Cape Town, 20 May 1938
STEPHEN, William Mitchell	WPCU	9	1922/23	1926/27	LHB	RAB		Green Point, Cape Town, 13 July 1886	Sea Point, Cape Town, 9 July 1953
STEPHENS, Christopher George	WPCU	21	1968/69	1971/72	RHB	RM		Cape Town, 8 Jan 1948	
STEPHENSON, EH	WPCU	1	1903/04	1903/04					
STEWART, Job Hercules	WPCU	6	1902/03	1904/05				Cape Town, 26 July 1880	Cape Town, 12 Sept 1942
STEYN, Godfrey Edward	WPCU	5	1957/58	1957/58	RHB	SLA		Pretoria, 23 Aug 1934	
STEYN, Richard Stephen	WPCU	10	1965/66	1966/67	RHB	OB		Kenilworth, Cape Town, 13 Jan 1944	
STEYN, Stephen Sebastian Louis 'Stodgy'	WPCU	30	1924/25	1937/38	LHB			Cape Town, 11 Mar 1905	Cape Town, 14 Oct 1993
STEYTLER, Edward Spilsbury 'Ned'	WPCU	4	1889/90	1892/93				Cape Town, [x] Nov 1860	Kalk Bay, Cape Town, 17 July 1947
STOFBERG, Laura	WPWCA		1995/96	1998/99					
STOKE, Ralph	WPCU	1	1930/31	1930/31				Green Point, Cape Town, 9 Apr 1910	

Name	Affiliation	M	From	To	Batt	Bowl	Wk	Born	Died
STONIER, Michael Peter	WPCU B	6	1988/89	1990/91	LHB	SLA		East London, 9 Jan 1969	
STRYDOM, Johannes Gerhardus	WCC	16	2004/05	2007/08	LHB	RM		Cape Town, 6 Sept 1979	
SWAN, Warren Clive	WCC	2	2006/07	2006/07	RHB	OB		Johannesburg, 30 May 1983	
SWART, Peter Douglas	WPCU/WPCU B	103	1967/68	1984/85	RHB	RM		Bulawayo, S. Rhodesia, 27 Apr 1946	Newlands, Cape Town, 13 Mar 2000
SYLVESTER, D	PWDCB		1952/53	1952/53					
SYLVESTER, J	WPCB		1961/62	1961/62					
TALIEP, Mogamad Sharhidd	WPCA B	2	1998/99	1998/99	RHB			Cape Town, 10 Feb 1978	
TALIEP, [X]	WPCCU		1898/99	1898/99					
TALJAARD, Marius	WPCU B	7	1979/80	1981/82	RHB	SLA		Paarl, CP, 20 Mar 1957	
TASKER, Geoffrey James Hambleton	WPCU	1	1953/54	1953/54	RHB	RM		Cape Town, 16 Sept 1930	Westridge, Durban, 11 Aug 2003
TATTERSALL, Keith	WPCU	16	1965/66	1969/70	LHB	SLA		Tunbridge Wells, England, 6 Mar 1946	
TAYLOR, GP	WPCU	4	1912/13	1920/21					
TAYLOR, Herbert Wilfred	WPCU	1	1935/36	1935/36	RHB			Durban, 5 May 1889	
TAYLOR, William Lawrence	WPCU	8	1958/59	1961/62	RHB			Bellville, CP, 11 Sept 1935	Newlands, Cape Town, 8 Feb 1973
TELEMACHUS, Roger	WPCA	24	1999/00	2003/04	RHB	RFM		Stellenbosch, 27 Mar 1973	
TELO, Filipe Dominic	WPCA Am/WCC	29	2005/06	2010/11	RHB	RM		Cape Town, 4 Mar 1986	
TEMOOR, Abdul-Aziz	WPCA Am	16	2007/08	2009/10	RHB	LB		Strand, CP, 7 Nov 1982	
THERON, Mervyn	WPCB	8	1980/81	1983/84		SLA		District Six, Cape Town, 11 Aug 1949	
THEUNISSEN, Nicolaas Hendrik Christiaan de Jong	WPCU	2	1889/90	1889/90	RHB	RFM		Colesberg, CC, 4 May 1867	Willemsdal, Transvaal, 9 Nov 1929
THOMAS, A	PWDCB		1950/51	1950/51					
THOMAS, Alfonso Clive	WPCA B	3	1998/99	1998/99	RHB	RFM		Cape Town, 9 Feb 1977	
THOMAS, CH	WPCU	5	1921/22	1922/23					
THOMAS, Kashief (previously known as THOMAS, Kelvin)	WPCB	2	1978/79	1978/79	RHB	OB		Bo-Kaap, Cape Town, 1 Mar 1953	
THOMAS, Paddy	WPICU/PWDCB/WPCF		1952/53	1957/58					
THOMAS, Rasool 'Tienie'	HHCU		1954/55	1954/55					
THOMAS, Yunus	WPCB	38	1982/83	1990/91	RHB	RM		Strand, CP, 8 May 1960	
THOMPSON, Peter Maximilian	WPCU B	23	1977/78	1981/82	RHB		WK	Krugersdorp, Transvaal, 25 Apr 1948	
THWAITS, Steytler Abbott	WPCU	22	1949/50	1954/55	RHB	SLA		Cape Town, 27 Nov 1911	
TIMOL, Ismail	WPCB	2	1975/76	1975/76	RHB		WK	Durban, 26 Mar 1940	
TOBIN, R	PWDCB		1946/47	1946/47					
TOEFIE, [X]	WPCCU		1898/99	1898/99					
TOLSON, David John Hannam	WPCU B	3	1976/77	1976/77	RHB	RM		Port Elizabeth, 3 Oct 1951	
TOUZEL, Frank Barry	WPCU/WPCU B/WPCA/WPCA B	57	1984/85	1996/97	LHB			Pinelands, CP, 8 Oct 1963	[x], 13 Oct 1980
TOUZEL, Frank Giles	WPCU	1	1968/69	1968/69	RHB	OB		Parow, CP, 2 May 1938	Durbanville, WC, 16 Sept 2006
TOWN, Bronwen	WPWCA/WPWCA B		2001/02	2004/05					

Name	Affiliation	M	From	To	Batt	Bowl	Wk	Born	Died
TOWNSEND, Travis Kim Millar	WPCA Am	6	2009/10	2009/10	RHB	LB		Cape Town, 9 Sept 1985	
TREADAWAY, Leslie George	WPCU	5	1947/48	1957/58	RHB	LB		Cape Town, 16 Nov 1920	Plumstead, Cape Town, 2 Sept 2006
TREMBLE, P	WPWCU		1951/52	1953/54					
TRICKETT, William Sydney	WPCU	1	1905/06	1905/06				Sydney, Australia, 14 Jan 1872	
TROMP, I	WPCB		1968	1968					
TROTT, Ian Jonathan Leonard	WPCA	8	2001/02	2001/02	RHB	RM		Cape Town, 22 Apr 1981	
TRUTER, Jackie	PWDCB/WPCF		1952/53	1954/55					
TSOLEKILE, Thami Lungisa	WPCA/WPCA Am/WCC	68	1999/00	2008/09	RHB	OB	WK	Cape Town, 9 Oct 1980	
TUCKER, Eugene (Dr) 'Tommy'	WPCU	2	1936/37	1936/37	RHB			Germiston, Transvaal, 7 Aug 1916	Welkom, FS, 27 Mar 2000
TULLEKEN, André	WPCU	2	1960/61	1960/61	RHB		WK	Cape Town, 28 July 1941	
TULLIS, Gary Douglas	WPCU B	13	1983/84	1988/89	RHB		WK	Salisbury, S. Rhodesia, 7 June 1962	
TURNER, David Roy	WPCU	2	1977/78	1977/78	LHB	RM		Corsham, Wiltshire, England, 5 Feb 1949	
TURNER, Graeme John	WPCU/WPCU B	16	1984/85	1986/87	LHB	OB		Bulawayo, S. Rhodesia, 5 Aug 1964	
TWENTYMAN JONES, Percy Sydney	WPCU	8	1897/98	1905/06	RHB			Beaufort West, CC, 13 Sept 1876	Cape Town, 8 Mar 1954
UPTON, Patrick Anthony Howard 'Paddy'	WPCU B/WPCA B	2	1990/91	1993/94	LHB			Johannesburg, 5 Nov 1968	
VALENTINE, Ronald Charles	WPCU	2	1947/48	1947/48	RHB			Cape Town, 25 Sept 1923	Fish Hoek, WC, 17 Jan 2009
VALENTINE-BROWN, Vicky	WPWCU		1951/52	1960/61					
VALLIE, Mohammed Yaseen	WPCA Am/WCC	24	2009/10	2010/11	RHB	OB		Cravenby, CP, 30 July 1989	
VAN BEUGE, Bradley Wilfred	WPCA B	6	1998/99	1998/99	RHB		WK	Johannesburg, 5 Sept 1977	
VAN DER BIJL, Pieter Gerhard Vintcent	WPCU	27	1925/26	1939/40	RHB		WK	Kenilworth, Cape Town, 21 Oct 1907	Kalk Bay, Cape Town, 16 Feb 1973
VAN DER BIJL, Vintcent	WPCU	2	1947/48	1947/48			WK	Roodebloem, Cape Town, 4 Nov 1873	Cape Town, 15 May 1951
VAN DER BIJL, Vintcent Alexander	WPCU	2	1892/93	1892/93				Salt River, Cape Town, 31 Jan 1872	Cape Town, 2 Oct 1941
VAN DER BIJL, Voltelin Albert William 'Vollie'	WPCU	6	1890/91	1895/96					
VAN DER HEEVER, Tracey	WPWCA		1999/00	1999/00			WK		
VAN DER MERWE, Marie	WPWCU/Composite XIs		1974/75	1985/86					
VAN DER MERWE, Peter Laurence	WPCU	35	1958/59	1965/66	RHB	SLA		Paarl, CP, 14 Mar 1937	
VAN DER MERWE, Willem Maré	WPCU B	9	1985/86	1986/87	LHB	RFM		Rustenburg, Transvaal, 20 July 1960	
VAN DER POEL, Coenraad Stephen	WPCU	1	1923/24	1923/24				Middelburg, CC, [x] Aug 1898	Johannesburg, 18 Jan 1932
VAN DER SPUY, Tobias Mostert Henry	WPCU	22	1935/36	1946/47	LHB	SRA		Mowbray, Cape Town, 28 May 1915	Claremont, Cape Town, 17 June 2006
VAN DER WESTHUIZEN, Yolandi	WPWCA		2005/06	2006/07	RHB		WK	Cape Town, 11 Dec 1981	
VAN ECK, Richardia	WPWCA		2008/09	2010/11					
VAN GRAAN, C	PWDCB		1948/49	1948/49					
VAN GRAAN, Keith 'Kitty'	WPCB	9	1974/75	1979/80	RHB	RM		Athlone, Cape Town, 4 Mar 1945	
VAN GRAAN, Randall 'Jacko'	WPCB	2	1981/82	1981/82	RHB	OB		Athlone, Cape Town, 17 June 1953	
VAN GRAAN, Robbie	WPCB	15	1972/73	1977/78	RHB	OB		Mowbray, Cape Town, 24 Aug 1939	[x], 26 Jan 1988
VAN HAAGHT, Saait 'Hudson'	WPCCU/WPICU		1945/46	1955/56	RHB	RMF			

Name	Affiliation	M	From	To	Batt	Bowl	Wk	Born	Died
VAN NIEKERK, Adriaan Pieter 'Attie'	WPCU/WPCU B	16	1968/69	1975/76	RHB	RM		Cape Town, 21 Aug 1945	
VAN OLST, Machiel	WPCA B	2	1997/98	1997/98	RHB	OB		Benoni, Transvaal, 24 Sept 1976	
VAN OORDT, George	WPCB	22	1975/76	1983/84	RHB	RM		Tiervlei, Cape Town, 18 Dec 1948	
VAN REENEN, Adriaan	WPCA/WPCA B	4	1995/96	1996/97	LHB	LF		Somerset West, CP, 3 Nov 1975	
VAN RENSBURG, Adri	WPWCA		1995/96	1995/96					
VAN RENSBURG, Annelize	WPWCA/WPWCA B		1995/96	2006/07					
VAN RENSBURG, Ronel	WPWCA		1995/96	1996/97					
VAN RENSBURG, Toii	WPWCA		1995/96	1995/96					
VAN RYNEVELD, Clive Berrangé	WPCU	31	1946/47	1962/63	RHB	LBG		St James, Cape Town, 19 Mar 1928	
VAN SCHALKWYK, Charles	WPCB	26	1975/76	1982/83	RHB	RM		[x], 25 Sept 1954	
VAN SCHALKWYK, Shadley Claude	WPCA Am		2007/08	2008/09	LHB	RFM		Cape Town, 5 Aug 1988	
VAN STAVEL, J	WPCB		1961/62	1961/62					
VAN WYK, Esmund Peter	WPCA Am	13	2007/08	2009/10	RHB	RMF		Cape Town, 19 Nov 1981	
VAN WYK, Jacques Merlin	WCC	1	2004/05	2004/05	RHB	RFM		Stellenbosch, 27 Jan 1978	
VAN WYK, Lenert	WCC		2009/10	2010/11	RHB	RMF		Cape Town, 13 July 1989	
VAN ZYL, Juanita	WPWCU/Alma/Composite XIs		1969	1979/80					
VAN ZYL, Susanna Deborah 'Sune'	WPWCA		1995/96	2003/04	RHB	RF		Welkom, OFS, 16 July 1977	
VAN ZYL, Stiaan	WCC	35	2007/08	2010/11	RHB	RM		Cape Town, 14 Feb 1973	
VEAL, Victor George	WPCU	25	1920/21	1933/34		RFM		Cape Town, 2 Sept 1897	Cape Town, 2 Oct 1958
VERCUEIL, Stephen	WPCU B	4	1981/82	1981/82	RHB		WK	Johannesburg, 3 Aug 1957	
VILAS, Dane James	WPCA Am/WCC	3	2010/11	2010/11	RHB		WK		
VILJOEN, André	WPCB	3	1990/91	1990/91	RHB				
VILJOEN, Frederik Daniel Jacobus	WPCU	4	1922/23	1923/24	LHB	RAB		[x], 28 July 1897	Cape Town, 15 Aug 1965
VINCENT, Anthony James Seymour	WPCU	1	1957/58	1957/58	RHB	RM		Cape Town, 18 Feb 1935	
VINCENT, Iris	WPWCU/Alma/Bellville		1957/58	1972/73					
VIRGIN, Roy Thomas	WPCU	2	1972/73	1972/73	LHB	LB	WK	Taunton, Somerset, England, 26 Aug 1939	
VOSS, Michael Frederick	WPCU/WPCU B/WPCA/WPCA B	19	1984/85	1992/93	LHB			Cape Town, 10 Nov 1966	
WADVALLA, Aziz	WPCB	2	1977/78	1977/78	RHB			Pretoria, 10 May 1949	
WAGGIE, Waggie	HHCU		1954/55	1954/55					
WALKER, Peter Michael	WPCU	3	1962/63	1962/63	RHB	LM SLA		Clifton, Bristol, England, 17 Feb 1936	
WALLACE, Bryan 'Boon'	WPCU	14	1930/31	1937/38				Simon's Town, CC, 13 Apr 1910	Cape Town, 25 June 1994
WALTERS, Martin Dennis	WPCA Am/WCC	30	2005/06	2010/11	RHB	RMF		East London, 12 Mar 1985	
WARD, Lorna	WPWCU		1968/69	1968/69					
WATERWICH, Basil	PWDCB		1946/47	1954/55					
WATSON, Vyvyan Underwood Tennant	WPCU	4	1923/24	1924/25				Rondebosch, Cape Town, 6 Mar 1891	Claremont, Cape Town, 3 May 1970
WATT, Howard Hugh	WPCU	6	1933/34	1934/35				Rosebank, Cape Town, 1 Mar 1911	Howick, KZN, 17 Aug 2005

Name	Affiliation	M	From	To	Batt	Bowl	Wk	Born	Died
WEBER, Andrew Cyril (later changed name to WEBER, AC)	WPCU	2	1903/04	1904/05				Georgetown, British Guiana, 18 Nov 1877	Johannesburg, 23 Dec 1956
WEEDEN, Christopher Clive	WPCU/WPCU B	16	1975/76	1978/79	LHB	RM		Cape Town, 19 Sept 1953	
WEINSTEIN, Leonard Jack (Dr)	WPCU	17	1959/60	1965/66	RHB	RM		Oudtshoorn, CP, 19 June 1940	
WELLS, Colin Mark	WPCU	2	1984/85	1984/85	RHB	RM		Newhaven, Sussex, England, 3 Mar 1960	
WERNARS, Kirk Ogilvy	WPCA Am	2	2009/10	2010/11	LHB	RFM		Constantia, Cape Town, 14 June 1991	
WESSELS, Kepler Christoffel	WPCU	8	1976/77	1976/77	LHB	RM OB		Bloemfontein, 14 Sept 1957	
WEST, J	WPWCU		1951/52	1951/52					
WESTCOTT, Richard John	WPCU	46	1949/50	1961/62	RHB	RM		Lisbon, Portugal, 19 Sept 1927	
WEYERS, Denise	WPWCU/Alma/Composite XIs		1962/63	1979/80					
WHITE, Justin Egerton	WPCU	4	1962/63	1966/67			WK	Bedford, CP, 1 Feb 1942	
WHITE, Nazeem	WPCB	25	1982/83	1990/91	RHB	RM OB		Bonteheuwel, Cape Town, 10 Apr 1964	
WHITEFIELD, David William Hugh	WPCU	11	1960/61	1964/65	LHB	LMF		Cape Town, 6 Sept 1936	
WHITEHEAD, James George	WPCU	26	1904/05	1920/21	RHB			Cape Town, [x] June 1882	Mowbray, Cape Town, 23 Jan 1940
WHITEING, Lauriston Charles Gray	WPCU	3	1935/36	1946/47	RHB			Aliwal North, CC, 4 Feb 1910	Cape Town, 30 Jan 1960
WHITFIELD, Anthony Richard	WPCU	1	1960/61	1960/61	RHB	OB		Cape Town, 1 Jan 1937	Betty's Bay, WC, 28 Oct 1998
WHITTINGDALE, Richard	WPCU/WPCU B	5	1977/78	1980/81	RHB		WK	Broken Hill, N. Rhodesia, 2 Oct 1955	
WIGHTMAN, Robert Walton	WPCU	1	1954/55	1954/55	RHB	RM		Cape Town, 28 Mar 1933	Randburg, Gauteng, 22 June 2003
WILEY, John Walter Edington	WPCU	2	1947/48	1947/48	RHB			St James, Cape Town, 7 Feb 1927	Noordhoek, Cape Town, 29 Mar 1987
WILEY, William Gordon Anthony	WPCU	4	1952/53	1953/54	RHB	LBG		St James, Cape Town, 14 Nov 1931	Harare, Zimbabwe, 7 Dec 1999
WILLEMSE, M	WPWCA		2007/08	2007/08					
WILLIAMS, Craig David	WPCA Am	7	2007/08	2008/09	LHB	LM		Cape Town, 12 Nov 1982	
WILLIAMS, Gert	WPCB	16	1963/64	1974/75	RHB	OB		Elsies River, CP, 17 June 1941	
WILLIAMS, Henry Smith 'Bollie'	WPCB	1	1990/91	1990/91	RHB	RFM		Pniel, near Stellenbosch, 11 June 1967	
WILLIAMS, Jacobus 'Kosie'	WPCB	5	1971/72	1979/80		RMF		Elsies River, CP, 15 Nov 1938	
WILLIAMS, K	WPWCA		2008/09	2008/09					
WILLIAMS, Nadine	WPWCA		2000/01	2001/02	RHB	RFM			
WILLIAMS, Owen Leslie	PWDCB/WPCB	2	1956/57	1971/72	LHB	SLA		Claremont, Cape Town, 8 Apr 1932	
WILLIAMSON, Gloria	WPWCU		1968/69	1968/69					
WILLIAMSON, Myles	WPCA Am	19	2005/06	2009/10	RHB	RM		Cape Town, 3 Jan 1984	
WILLOUGHBY, Charl Myles	WPCA/WCC	58	2000/01	2006/07	LHB	LFM		Cape Town, 3 Dec 1974	
WILSNACH, R	WPCF		1952/53	1952/53					
WILSON, William Douglas 'Wally'	WPCU	4	1948/49	1950/51	RHB			Port Elizabeth, 8 Apr 1925	
WINDSOR, Janice	WPWCA		1997/98	1997/98					
WINGREEN, Ivan Michael	WPCU B	22	1983/84	1986/87	RHB			Cape Town, 23 June 1961	
WITBOOI, Ronnie	WPCB	2	1978/79	1978/79		RM			
WITTE, Ernest Victor	WPCU	23	1946/47	1954/55	RHB	RF		East London, 15 Aug 1912	Durban, 23 Aug 1989

Name	Affiliation	M	From	To	Batt	Bowl	Wk	Born	Died
WITTEN, Basil	PWDCB/WPCF		1952/53	1957/58					
WOOD, Arthur Frederick	WPCU	2	1921/22	1925/26	RHB			Rondebosch, Cape Town, 26 May 1904	Fish Hoek, CP, 25 Nov 1980
WOODMAN, [X]	WPICU		1957/58	1957/58					
WOOLMER, Robert Andrew	WPCU	3	1980/81	1980/81	RHB	RM		Kanpur, India, 14 May 1948	Kingston, Jamaica, 18 Mar 2007
WORTH, Doug	WPCA Am	4	2004/05	2004/05	RHB		WK	Johannesburg, 12 Jan 1981	
WRENTMORE, Colin George Cowan	WPCU	4	1926/27	1934/35				[x], [x] 1899	Riviersonderend, CP, 10 Oct 1962
WRENTMORE, Godfrey Maynard 'Bai'	WPCU	5	1910/11	1910/11				Namaqualand, CC, 20 Feb 1893	Kenilworth, Cape Town, 16 Aug 1953
WRIGHT, K	WPWCU		1953/54	1957/58					
WYNGAARD, Warren	WPCA Am/WCC	19	2004/05	2006/07	RHB	OB		Cape Town, 5 Nov 1980	
WYNNE, Owen Edgar	WPCU	12	1947/48	1958/59	RHB			Johannesburg, 1 June 1919	at sea, False Bay, CP, 13 July 1975
XONGO, Lundi	WPCA Am	1	2004/05	2004/05	RHB	RMF		Cape Town, 2 July 1983	
YENGO, SL	WPBCU		1947/48	1952/53					
YEOMAN, William Farquhar	WPCU	11	1908/09	1912/13	RHB			Rondebosch, Cape Town, 12 Jan 1886	Rondebosch, Cape Town, 2 Feb 1944
YON, W	PWDCB		1957/58	1957/58					
YOUNG, Dulcie	WPWCU		1956/57	1962/63					
YOUNG, J	WPWCU		1953/54	1954/55					
YOUNG, S	WPCU	1	**1889/90**	**1889/90**					
ZIBI, GM	WPACU		1966/67	1966/67					
ZONDEKI, Monde	WPCA Am/WCC	43	2005/06	2010/11	RHB	RF		King William's Town, CP, 25 July 1982	

On the making of this book

In the introductory chapters and in the footnotes, the authors have paid tribute to and acknowledged many people. It only remains for us to document how *The Blue Book* was produced and to thank some of those closest to the production process for their contributions.

The material which forms the core of the book was produced slowly in distinct ways and stages over the last four decades:

1. The one starting point was the work of Krish Reddy, a former schoolteacher, who has been tireless in documenting the 'non-racial' cricket traditions of SACBOC and SACB. Krish has a unique cricket collection in his home in Reservoir Hills in Durban, and his pioneering work, always delivered handwritten, has made possible the bridging of the statistical gap between past and present that we see here. Krish compiled more or less from scratch full scorecards of the 223 three-day matches played by SACBOC and SACB between 1971 and 1991. The UCBSA and ICC formally declared these part of the official record of first-class cricket in South Africa in 1996/97, but they have yet to be published in full or summarised form.

   Krish also collated statistics for earlier organisations, especially the South African Indian Cricket Union tournaments from the 1940s onwards; the 'national' teams which played in the SACBOC inter-race tournaments between the 'Bantus', Coloureds, Malays and Indians in the 1950s; and the two series by the combined SACBOC Springboks under Basil D'Oliveira selected after these games to play East African and Rhodesian (Zimbabwean) teams between 1956 and 1958.

   Starting in the mid-1980s, Krish began to publish his research findings in newspaper articles and, after cricket unity, in the *Mutual &Federal SA Cricket Annual* (1996 onwards) and his slim book, *The Other Side: A miscellany of cricket in Natal* (1999).

2. The other starting point for *The Blue Book* was my intensive research from 1978 onwards in the nineteenth- and early twentieth-century black newspapers for master's and doctoral dissertations on the beginnings of black protest politics in South Africa. I found to my amazement regular reports on cricket, often written in Xhosa, in early newspapers such as *Isigidimi sama Xhosa* (started as the 'Kaffir Express' in 1870), *Imvo Zabantsundu* ('Native Opinion', 1884), *Izwi Labantu* ('Voice of the People', 1897) and the Cape Town-based *APO* (1909). Later I became familiar with the next generation of publications in the 1920s and 1930s, including *Umteteli wa Bantu*, the *Cape Standard* and the *Cape Sun*, which continued these traditions. The rich seams of cricket reports in the early newspapers were more or less revelations in terms of cricket history at a time when apartheid was at its height. Dominant narratives then explained the exclusion of black sportspeople from games like rugby and cricket on the grounds that they had never really been interested in these 'European' games.[393]

Still largely untapped, the early newspapers provided archives which resoundingly contradicted these notions and I was motivated to write a series of academic and popular articles on sport from the early 1980s onwards.[394] These writings were intended to be part of the broader reinterpretation of South African history at the time by revisionist historians and, more forcefully, activists within the liberation struggle. Challenging official Eurocentric interpretations of the South African past was central to the liberation struggle of the ANC and other pro-democracy forces.

3. After cricket unity in the 1990s, the new cricket organisations encouraged writings that could help redress the imbalanced descriptions of the past. In 1998, after several years in which 'unity' and 'development' were prioritised, the United Cricket Board of South Africa (UCBSA) started focusing on 'transformation' to ensure fundamental change in keeping with the priorities of the new democracy. One of the ten thrusts in the Transformation Charter adopted in 1998 emphasised the importance of histories that dealt with the experiences of black cricketers. If their stories were not told, then the old apartheid narrative that they had no cricket culture or history would be reinforced by default. Krish Reddy, I and several other historians with an interest in cricket set out to write more substantive works as part of the process initiated by the UCBSA.

Krish started working with Padayachee, Vahed and Desai on a major volume on the history of Natal cricket, *Blacks in Whites* (2002), and I embarked on writing *The Story of an African Game* (2003), which provided proof that a highly developed cricket culture existed in black communities from the 1880s onwards in Cape Town, Kimberley and the Eastern Cape. Both these publications took the story back further than the beginnings of formal apartheid in 1948, helping to contextualise the early development of cricket in South Africa. In 2001, I proposed to Krish and Christopher Merrett that we take the next step and combine our material and efforts to write a general *History of South African Cricket*, going back to the advent of British rule in 1795. Christopher, head librarian at the University of KwaZulu-Natal, a member of the path-breaking Aurora Cricket Club in Pietermaritzburg in the 1970s and an umpire during the days of the non-racial 'Board', had written a book on censorship under apartheid and had completed a manuscript on the origins of racism in cricket. The aim now was to go back to the very beginnings of cricket in this country, engaging with the foundation narratives of the game and writing for the first time the histories of each of the ten South African cricket boards that have existed. Krish and Christopher accepted the challenge and the UCBSA endorsed the project and provided support.

After Krish's meticulous, path-breaking reconstruction of the statistics of SACBOC and SACB of the 1950s to 1980s – the organisations that upheld the non-racial 'Board' tradition – I suggested to him that we now drill deeper still and attempt to reconstruct the detailed statistics of the inter-provincial tournaments organised by earlier first- and second-generation cricket bodies founded between 1898 and 1940. Roughly equal in number to the Currie Cup tournaments played by the white cricketers over the years, these early inter-provincial tournaments were hardly known and no one knew if the tournament records were even available. But, on the basis of many years of newspaper research, I was optimistic that coherent statistical histories could be fleshed out for them too. After pooling our fragmented resources, we put together a substantial new layer of material and statistics on the tournaments of the Barnato (Malay), Coloured, African, Indian and Women's boards, started in 1903, 1926, 1932, 1940 and 1952 respectively, which were still largely unknown.

4. By 2004 the draft manuscript of the history of South African cricket had already reached 200,000 words. In August of that year, I was appointed chief executive of the Western Province Cricket Association. I now set out to see if it would be possible to put together from the work in progress on the broader history an integrated statistical record specifically for Western Province. If this worked, the idea could subsequently be implemented in other provinces as well.

For two months before assuming duties, I worked intensively to compile the first 200-page draft of *The Blue Book*. From the material for the broader history, I culled the match records of the many different provincial boards from Western Province dealt with here. This in turn enabled me to draw up lists of various provincial and national caps for each board, going back to 1891 when the first South African Malay team was picked with four players from Cape Town in it. Many people have never even heard of some of these earlier Western Provinces, but for all of them we now had specific scorecards, names and national representatives for the first time.

For the past seven years I have kept on chiselling away at the topic, in particular writing up with the help of Ameena Smith the details of over 40 hitherto unrecorded women's inter-provincial tournaments from valuable material provided by former players, and over time the manuscript has doubled in size.

5. Having compiled statistics as comprehensively as possible for seven old, unrecognised Western Provinces of the past, my next step was to merge this material with the existing, well-documented official records of the pre-1991 white Union (WPCU) and the post-1991 unified Association (WPCA) and the Cape Cobras to give the book the necessary comprehensiveness. This is where Andrew Samson (who has also computerised Krish Reddy's work) and Robin Isherwood came in. Over the past few years, they have delivered masses of information on request, and helped to draw up the first consolidated list of Western Province national players, trophy winners and individual first-class and limited-overs career records. Andrew is the outstanding 'official' statistician in South Africa and he has the ability to conjure up cricket information of all sorts at the press-button speed of the digital age. Robin Isherwood, who turned down the offer to be recognised as a co-author, provided valuable biographical information on WPCU and WPCA players going back to 1890. He is also a proofreader without peer and four times checked this manuscript. (If you mistakenly write that 1 February 1959 – the day the Western Province Cricket Board was formed – was a Monday, he will tell you it was a Sunday.) Although living in the north-west of England, Robin is linked in the most intimate way to South African cricket via his expert cricket history and statistical skills.

Thus, while the broader South African history (due to be published in 2013) necessarily slowed down because of my work responsibilities at the WPCA, we have in the meanwhile made a detour to complete *The Blue Book*. I am immensely proud that Andrew Samson, Robin Isherwood and Krish Reddy from their different vantage points and specialisations have all agreed that this work brings a new dimension to cricket statistics and history in South Africa. Krish, when sent the advanced manuscript, was thrilled by the 'superb compilation' and the 'quite staggering' details and was satisfied that 'our rich and colourful ... history' was given proper recognition.[395]

A reviewer of a book on the 'African Shakespeare', SEK Mqhayi, containing 65 of his writings recently plucked from obscurity, wrote: 'Unbeknownst however – the fairytale connotation of this archaic word is entirely appropriate – to almost everybody, substantial fragments of [his] history survived for decades hidden deep within innumerable reams of old newsprint, buried in obscure locations at home and abroad. [The writer] has performed an immense task of rescue and recovery, akin to digging through the rubble with a toothpick in search of earthquake survivors. His diligence has been rewarded by the discovery of warm bodies, still very much alive and just as vigorous and articulate as they were on the day that they disappeared.'[396]

While *The Blue Book*, the early fruit of the broader *History of South African Cricket*, which has been under preparation for nearly a decade, may not have the same literary pretensions as the work on Mqhayi, it owes its existence to a similar single-minded quest over a long time for information and material that few even guessed existed. The work is now at a stage where, I believe, it has the integrity and substance to be published as a solid memorial to those who have gone before.

My sincere thanks to the co-authors for their support and obsessive eye for detail. They have all spent numberless hours in solitary pursuits to complete the publication of this work with as much accuracy and integrity as possible; there is no other way this task could have been done.

This book should be seen as work in progress, which can be added to and improved in an ongoing way as awareness and research deepen. In the process of compiling it, the history of Western Province cricket has come alive for me and it is a privilege to be able to bring together at last under one roof the figures of the past who played in different worlds while bound by geography, time and the game to one city and one province.

Western Province Cricket Heritage Projects

The Blue Book is a sign also of the commitment of the Western Province Cricket Association (WPCA) to inclusiveness and the thorough transformation of cricket and society in South Africa. I owe the WPCA presidents I have served under – Norman Arendse, Solomon Makosana, Mohamed Ebrahim and Beresford Williams – and the executive committees, council and staff of the WPCA a special debt of gratitude for supporting this book and various other 'memory' projects (mentioned below) initiated by their somewhat out-of-the-box CEO in the past few years. This support included permission for me to take a sabbatical at the University of Kentucky in 2011 to complete the manuscript.

As early as December 1995, the WPCA executive unanimously accepted a proposal by this writer for 'an authoritative history of cricket in the Western Province which reflected the experiences of all communities over the past 100 years'.[397] The WPCA set up a History Sub-committee consisting of Solomon Makosana, Michael Doman, Dougie Oakes, Mario Solomons, Mogamad Allie and André Odendaal. After the adoption of the Transformation Charter by the UCBSA in 1998, the process was given extra momentum. Mogamad Allie, a successful BBC freelance radio journalist, inspired by his own experiences as a young cricketer, now sprinted ahead and completed *More than a Game: History of the Western Province Cricket Board 1959–1991* (Cape Argus and WPCA, Cape Town, 2000). The WPCA underwrote the costs of the book and it was formally launched at Newlands on 11 January 2001. *More than a Game*, an important precursor to this book, provided some balance to the old Western Province Cricket Union's official history, *Western Province Cricket 100 – Not Out* (WPCU, Cape Town, 1990). Written by the much loved *Cape Argus* journalist AC Parker, this was published during the Union's centenary in 1990, shortly before unity in 1991.

Clem Druker, first president of the WPCA, wrote to AC Parker in 1995, asking if he could broaden his book to 'incorporate' the old Board as 'The present situation is that it is embarrassing to hand out the book as a gift on any official occasion or indeed to market the book in any serious way given the absence of a proper acknowledgement and recital of the history of non-white cricket in the Western Province'.[398] Parker replied that he was unable to undertake this task. What was needed was clearly not a grafting of the Board's history on to that of the Union, but a full history of the Board, which Allie provided in 2000, and a rounded general history going back to the beginning, which *The Blue Book* now provides.

After his appointment as WPCA chief executive in 2004, this writer introduced an active focus on history and cricket legacies as a way of both marketing Western Province cricket and helping to heal old wounds and build bridges between people.[399] In October 2004 his proposal (after discussions with Yusuf Garda) for the Basil D'Oliveira Trophy to be instituted for the test and ODI series between South Africa and England was quickly accepted and implemented by Gerald Majola and Cricket South Africa.

In November 2004, the executive committee supported the proposal that the gates and the names of the stands at Sahara Park Newlands be changed from the blandly descriptive (for example, B Gate or North Stand) to honour past stars from diverse backgrounds who had contributed to the shaping of our modern Western Province identities. Hendricks, Howa, Barlow, D'Oliveira, Malamba, Kirsten and Kallis were names suggested. This would have been in line with common practice at sports stadiums internationally, but Council turned down the plans and they were shelved.

In January 2005, the WPCA compiled and installed an exhibition in the President's Suite at Sahara Park Newlands to help change the ambience from one that was still colonial, 'gentlemanly' and class-based to one that was self-consciously open.[400] The title was *Double Century: An overview of Western Province cricket, 1795–2005*. The exhibition included the first list of national caps from all the different Western Provinces, printed onto the windows of the President's Suite. (It is published here in an updated form.) Africans, women and others who had been marginalised could now sit with a sense of some belonging in this once inviolable space at the beautiful ground. Jon Weinberg and Jonathan Berndt designed the installations and Carol van Vuuren, Clive Glover, Ederoos 'Boeta' Behardien, John Young, Marie van der Merwe, Carr Hayward, Ted Doman, Yusuf Garda, Mogamad Allie and Solomon Makosana all helped.

In January 2005, the first Annual New Year's Address at Newlands was held with Gary Kirsten as speaker. Every year a figure of international standing in cricket is invited to speak on issues of importance to the game on the occasion of the annual New Year's test, which is the highlight of the cricket calendar in Cape Town. Inspired by the Sir Colin Cowdrey Lecture held at Lord's every summer, the aim is to add to broader cricket debates and to emphasise the cricket heritage and significance of the 123-year-old stadium. The speakers following on Kirsten have been former South Africa (SACA) captain and respected elder statesman Clive van Ryneveld, former Pakistan batsman and captain Aamir Sohail, then-president of the International Cricket Council Ray Mali, chief executive of the ICC Haroon Lorgat, president of the MCC John Barclay, and the renowned Indian cricketer and television broadcaster Ravi Shastri.

To coincide with the first Annual Address at Newlands, a convivial dinner was held in the President's Suite for 1950s national cricketers from both sides of the old divide. (Constitutional Court judge Albie Sachs wondered aloud at the fact that it had taken 50 years for the veterans to sit down together.) In March 2005, it was the turn of the 1960s and 1970s Western Province veterans from different boards to be recognised.

Since then the WPCA has gone out of its way to let past players feel valued and included. A note from Noon and Grahame Chevalier, SACA Springbok spinner from the 1960s, after the India test match in 2011 sums up the intentions behind this approach: 'A brief line to commend you and your committee for what was a very well organised and pleasant five days ... Grahame and I enjoyed our time mingling with sportsmen of an era which sadly we had nothing to do with. This was not only stimulating but highly interesting ... Your skills in relating to people whoever they are, are to be commended. And have no doubt gone a long way in healing some of the injustices of the past.'

In 2007 the *Sunday Times* installed a public sculpture by Donovan Ward at the B Gate at Newlands to commemorate the 1968 D'Oliveira affair and its subsequent impact on South African history. This initiative was part of the newspaper's own centenary commemoration. Newlands was one of the sites of significance chosen and the WPCA readily agreed to the initiative. Thank you to Sue Valentine, Charlotte Bauer and Mondli Makhanya of the *Sunday Times* for their co-operation.

In 2008 WPCA commemorated two important milestones: 2 January 2008 was the 120th anniversary of the opening of Newlands, and 5 January 2008 was the 200th anniversary of the first recorded cricket match in South Africa, which took place in Cape Town. Archbishop Desmond Tutu 'rededicated' the stadium in an on-field ceremony before the start of play in the test match against the West Indies in the following words:[401] 'This morning it is exactly 120 years since the formal opening of Newlands and the first game of cricket here on 2 January 1888. Today we give thanks for and celebrate a long history of cricket at this beautiful stadium under the mountain, recognising also that for a long part of that 120-year history this was a space where not everyone was welcome. On this historic occasion, we rededicate Sahara Park Newlands and pray that in future the ground and all who play on it, use it and come here will be blessed and protected. We pray that it will be bathed in summer sunshine and a spirit of universal tolerance and respect for people, regardless of who they are and where they come from. And we pray that, in our rainbow diversity, we will find peace and enjoyment here, and also see wonderful cricket for many years to come.'

During this test, a temporary exhibition was put up in the President's Suite for the duration of the match. As the Archbishop's message suggested, the WPCA felt it could not celebrate 120 years of Newlands without also acknowledging that for three-quarters of that period many people were discriminated against in hurtful ways there. Thus the exhibition *Newlands 120: Recognising the shadow side.* The guests of honour were cricketers who had been forced out of their homes in Newlands and Claremont by the Group Areas Act, some of whom had lived within a few hundred yards of the stadium. Forty or so former Claremont cricketers attended the moving function in the President's Suite.[402]

In January 2010, the flags at Newlands were dropped to half-mast during the big England test match to honour the memory of Dennis Brutus, the poet, anti-apartheid sports campaigner and opponent of greedy globalisation. WPCA has also held memorial services and dipped the flags at this famous ground for administrators such as Sadick Emeran and former players such as Eddie Barlow and Hylton Ackerman, both of whose ashes were scattered on the field.

The Blue Book, therefore, fits in with a culture of inclusiveness, based on an open-eyed recognition of the past, which the WPCA is trying to cultivate. The aim is to make the famous Newlands stadium an empathetic space where heritage and cricket mingle in intelligent ways and players and fans of all backgrounds can feel at home.

Final Acknowledgements

Many people helped practically to prepare this manuscript, starting with the consummately professional Ameena Smith. Ameena not only supported me stage by stage over a period of several years with this book, but has also been an important reason for the efficiencies we have established on an administrative level in the WPCA. Carol van Vuuren saved valuable parts of the WPCU and WPCA archives that some in the past thought of no value, and also spent many hours helping with the book. Carol recently retired after 30 years and has left a lasting impression at Newlands.

The chapters here on women's cricket will probably come as a total revelation. I am indebted to the cricketers who pulled old boxes and suitcases out of garages to help until we had gathered together perhaps one of the most complete cricket archives that exist in South Africa. Marie van der Merwe and Janet Burger started the ball rolling. Morag McLeod, Keri Laing, Shan Cade, Colleen Roberts, Louise Vorster, Zola Thamae, Yvonne Austen, Rodney Austen, Eddie Anderson, Olivia Anderson, Juanita van Zyl, Denise Weyers, Maureen Gerrans, Josephine Barnard, Madelein Lotter, Aluis Inglis (Kuylaars), Cindy Thomas, Robyn Austen, Wendy Austen, Amy Connolly, Shandré Fritz, Linda Copping, Rosemary and Jean Wilke, and Laura Bekker, principal of Rustenburg Girls' High School, also contributed very useful information. Thanks also to Prof. Douglas Booth from Otago in New Zealand, who took the trouble to read closely one of my drafts on women's cricket.

The sources for each section in every chapter are acknowledged in the footnotes, but special thanks to the late Mohamed Bagus and Haroen Gafieldien, who helped give content to the chapter on the little-known Hottentots Holland Cricket Union, and Mogamad Allie and the late Carr Hayward, who helped draw up the valuable list of players with their clubs in the chapter on the Western Province Coloured Cricket Union. Mogamad has also been magnificent in providing material on the old Western Province Cricket Board and getting in touch with former players to find out about everything from birthdays to bowling actions.

In *The Story of an African Game* I acknowledged numerous people who have helped over the decades in my cricket history work and personal growth. I thank them again here. Some need to be singled out once more. Syd Reddy, Cliff Adams and Yunus Agerdien started me on the path many years ago when they were generous with their time and gifts of valuable material on local cricket. John Hetherington and Denys Heesom encouraged my writing. Hassan Howa, 'Boon' Wallace, Frank Brache, Abu Desai, Barney Leendertz, Uncle Matty Segers, Mathemba Ndlumbini, Sadick Emeran and other administrators, as well as clubmates and friends in the 'Board', willingly shared priceless insights with me. Cricket South Africa has also actively supported various cricket history initiatives over the past decade (although this book did not receive any CSA sponsorship). My thanks to Gerald Majola and friends in CSA and the provinces for their backing, including the Transformation Monitoring Committee and the previously mentioned historians involved in the writing projects.

San Reddy (son of Syd) donated the Barnato Trophy to the WPCA in 2008. Mr Jamiel Magmoet, then the oldest living cricketer from the old 'Barnato Board', accepted it on behalf of Western Province, with Graeme Smith and Ashwell Prince in attendance. John Young has been a constant sounding board and supplier of interesting facts and insights. I have greatly valued his support. Lennie Kleintjies, a walking encyclopaedia on sport in Cape Town, became a treasured friend before his death. When advanced age put an end to his plans to write a history of Cape Town Cricket Club, Mr Les Moult gave me 21 notebooks of his research in newspapers between the 1850s and early 1900s. Frank Brache and family donated scrapbooks of Basil D'Oliveira, while Sandra Sonn, Eileen Leendertz, Ivan Dagnin, Fritz Bing, Clem Druker, Graham 'Grumpy' Adams and James and Dennis Poggenpoel contributed valuable artefacts from old boards to the WPCA archive.

The Blue Book was completed during a sabbatical at the University of Kentucky in Lexington, USA, in 2011. I am especially grateful to Professor Mark Kornbluh, who invited me to spend a semester writing and teaching in Lexington. The generosity and kindness of Mark, Dr Mimi Behar, Amy Hisel, Debbie Burton, Ted Schiatzki, Betty, Bob and Sarah Lorch, Tina Hagee, John Davies, Sara Compion, Lauren Kientz, Andrew Champion and Professor Francie Chesson-Lopez and the staff in the History Department renewed my faith in people. Thanks also to my 100-strong HIS315 'Sport and Society' class of 2011 and my work colleagues in Cape Town who stood in for me, in particular Nabeal Dien, Mohamed Ebrahim, David Griqua, Anthea Allie, Evan Flint and Omar Henry. Richard Pybus, Justin Kemp and the Cape Cobras' players further smoothed my path by becoming double champions and qualifying for the Champions League in India.

Robin Isherwood especially wishes to acknowledge the late Denys Heesom, editor of the *South African Cricket Annual* in the 1970s, the late Peter Sichel, official SACU and *SA Cricket Annual* statistician, and the late and distinguished umpire and cricket historian Hayward Kidson for providing the basis of his work over the last 35 years. Thanks also to Philip Bailey (Association of Cricket Statisticians and Historians) for providing much valuable biographical and statistical information over the years and Tony McCarron, from Australia, who helps Robin with the on-going compilation of biographical details on past and present South African cricketers.

Andrew Samson owes his wife Carolien and daughters Charlotte and Hailey a special debt.

Krish Reddy thanks his dear wife Praba for her constant encouragement in all the work that he has done. Her forbearance in affording him the opportunity to spend so much time on his various research projects is sincerely appreciated.

My family have been constant with their love and support over the years. I have tried to show my appreciation to Zohra, Rehana, Adam and my parents in dedications to previous books. This time I want to express special gratefulness and thanks to my nine-year-old daughter Nadia Odendaal. Her growing up has happened in the shadow of Newlands and she also braved a winter in America with her dad during his sabbatical. Walking hand-in-hand with a barefoot Nadia on the newly cut field on the morning of a big match, when the fragrance and feel of the turf are heavenly, has been among my best memories in this job. Often she was in my office overlooking play as a match unfolded, drawing on the CEO's flipchart, or giving her father the precious opportunity of witnessing her first lines of writing in cursive. In her gesture of support for the victims of the earthquake in Haiti, she appointed me her timekeeper and sponsor as she circuited the stadium 25 times on a pedal scooter.

Endnotes

Introduction

1. MW Luckin (editor and compiler), *The History of South African Cricket, including the full scores of all important matches since 1876* (WE Hortor, Johannesburg, 1915), pp. 386, 485-487.
2. A Odendaal collection, newspaper cutting with photo of S Meyers.
3. B Murray and G Vahed (eds.), *Empire and Cricket: The South African experience, 1884–1915* (University of South Africa, Pretoria, 2009), chapter 4; Winch, *England's Youngest Captain*, pp. 260-273.
4. *Cape Times*, 18 September 1968, p. 1.
5. Garlandale CC and Helderberg CC from the old Western Province Cricket Board (and Picketberg and Malmesbury in Boland) at first remained outside the new Association and tried to organise alternative structures but these soon collapsed (M Allie to A Odendaal, 22 March 2011).
6. See also the WPCA's focus on history described below.
7. Quoted in frontispiece of L Booth, *Cricket, Lovely Cricket? An addict's guide to the world's most exasperating game* (Yellow Jersey Press, London, 2008).
8. C Bryden (ed.), *Protea Assurance SA Cricket Annual '06*, p. 9.
9. For details see, 'Sporting Intelligence', *Cape Argus*, 13 January 1890; 'Today's cricket. The Malay tournament', *Cape Argus*, 14 January 1890; 'Sporting Intelligence', *Cape Times*, 14 January 1890; 'Cricket. The Malay tournament', *Cape Times*, 15 January 1890; 'Sporting Intelligence', *Cape Times*, 21 January 1890; 'Cricket. The Malay tournament', *Cape Times*, 22 January 1890; 'Sporting Intelligence', *Cape Times*, 23 January 1890; 'Sporting Intelligence', *Cape Times*, 28 January 1890; 'Sporting Intelligence', *Cape Times*, 30 January 1890.
10. Luckin, *The History of South African Cricket*, p. 517.
11. *A Guide to Important Cricket Matches Played in South Africa* (The Association of Cricket Statisticians, Retford, Notts, 1981), pp. 6-9.
12. DM Harding, *An Anthology of the Cricket Writings of Chris Harte*, pp. 42-43. This source says it was a second ball duck, but Robin Isherwood assures us it was a first ball duck.
13. T Collins, *A Social History of English Rugby Union* (Routledge, London, 2009), especially chapters 2 and 5.
14. Quoted in D Hirson, *White Scars: On reading and rites of passage* (Jacana, Auckland Park, 2006), p.121.
15. *A Guide to Important Cricket Matches Played in South Africa*, p. 6.
16. See http://en.wikipedia.org/wiki/First-class_cricket#ICC_1947.
17. *A Guide to Important Cricket Matches Played in South Africa*, Introduction by Phillip Bailey, n.p.
18. *A Guide to Important Cricket Matches played in South Africa*, pp. 6-9.
19. M Allie, *More than a Game: History of the Western Province Cricket Board, 1959 – 1991* (WPCA, Cape Town, 2001); A Desai, G Vahed, V Padayachee and K Reddy, *Blacks in Whites: A century of cricket struggles in KwaZulu-Natal* (Natal University Press, Pietermaritzburg, 2002); A Khota (ed.), *Across the Divide: Transvaal cricket's joys, struggles and triumphs* (Gauteng Cricket Board, Johannesburg, 2003); A Odendaal, *The Story of an African Game: Black cricketers and the unmasking of one of cricket's greatest myths, South Africa, 1850–2003* (David Philip and Human Sciences Research Council, Cape Town, 2003). See also C Day (ed.), *Cricket … Developing winners* (UCB, 2002); B Murray and C Merrett, *Caught Behind: Race and politics in Springbok cricket* (Wits University Press and KwaZulu-Natal University Press, Johannesburg and Scottsville, 2004); J Winch, *England's Youngest Captain: The life and times of Monty Bowden and two South African journalists* (Windsor Press, Windsor, 2003); P Oborne, *Basil D'Oliveira: Cricket and conspiracy: The untold story* (Little Brown, London, 2004) and B Murray and G Vahed (eds.), *Empire and Cricket: The South African experience, 1884–1914* (Unisa Press, Pretoria, 2009).
20. *Mutual and Federal SA Cricket Annual 2009*, p.13.
21. AE Docrat, 'Johannesburg Inter-Race Board' in SJ Reddy and DN Bansda (eds.), *The South African Non-European Cricket Almanack 1953/54* (The South African Non-European Cricket Publications, Cape Town, [1953]), pp. 140-141, 145; CM Kiviet, 'North-Eastern Transvaal Bantus have excellent side' and other articles in SJ Reddy and DN Bansda (eds.), *The South African Non-European Cricket Almanack 1954/55* (The South African Non-European Cricket Publications, Cape Town, [1955]), pp. 46-49.
22. D Behrens, 'S.A. vroue raak dol oor krieket', *Die Huisgenoot*, 27 February 1957, pp. 54-6. See also tournament brochures such as 'Third Inter-Provincial Women's Cricket Tournament, Kingsmead, Durban, January 1955', p. 12; 'Eastern Province Fifth Inter-Provincial Women's Cricket Tournament, Port Elizabeth, January 1957', n.p.; SA&RWCA, 'Sixth Inter-Provincial Women's Cricket Tournament, Johannesburg, January 1958', p. 13.
23. AE Docrat, 'Johannesburg Inter-Race Board' in Reddy and Bansda (1953/54), pp. 139-141; Reddy and Bansda (1954/55), pp. 45-47; Reddy and Bansda (1969), p. 59.

24 See, for example, AE Docrat, 'Johannesburg Inter-Race Board' in Reddy and Bansda (1953/54), pp. 139-141; CM Kiviet, 'North-Eastern Transvaal Bantus have excellent side'; Reddy and Bansda (1954/55), pp. 46-49; Reddy and Bansda (1969), p. 59; Odendaal, *The Story of an African Game*, pp. 98, 134, 152-3.

25 On this, see C Bundy, *Re-making the past: New perspectives on South African history* (UCT, Cape Town, 1977), p. 69; NS Ndebele, 'Iph' indlela? Finding our way into the future' (The first Steve Biko Memorial Lecture, UCT, 2000) (Skotaville, Braamfontein, 2001) and Odendaal, *The Story of an African Game*, chapter 42.

26 Thank you to my friend Yusuf Garda for this reference.

27 For details of Nathaniel Umhalla's life see Odendaal, *The Story of an African Game*, chapter 1 and A Odendaal, *The Founders: Origins of the ANC, 1860s to 1912* (Jacana, Cape Town, forthcoming 2012), chapter 6.

28 For more details on Krom Hendricks, see J Winch, 'I could a tale unfold: The tragic story of "Old Caddy" and Krom Hendricks' in B Murray and G Vahed (eds.) *Empire and Cricket*, chapter 4.

29 Odendaal, *The Story of an African Game*, p. 74.

30 For a biographical profile of Hassan Howa, see S Gastrow, *Who's Who in South African Politics* (Ravan Press, Johannesburg, 1985), pp. 113-14.

31 A. Brink, *A Fork in the Road: A memoir* (Harvill Secker, London, 2009), p. 183.

32 J Winch, 'I could a tale unfold', pp. 69-70.

33 J Winch, *Cricket in Southern Africa: Two hundred years of achievements and records* (Windsor Publishers, Windsor, nd), p.271.

34 Handwritten notes in WPWCU Collection, n.d.

35 D Behrens, 'S.A. vroue raak dol oor cricket', *Die Huisgenoot*, 27 February 1957, pp. 54-6.

36 P McKenzie, 'Women cricketers are battling to survive in W.P.', *Cape Argus*, 30 January 1971.

37 Quoted in display at the International Slavery Museum, Liverpool, England, March 2010.

38 The diagram on the 'family tree' of South African cricket is a modified version of the one that appeared in Odendaal, *Story of an African Game*, p. 16. This chapter on where Western Province fits into South African cricket developments first appeared in 'South Africa's long road to the CWC', *ICC Cricket World Cup 2003, South Africa, February 8 – March 2, Official Souvenir Brochure*, pp. 128-133.

39 Odendaal, *Story of an African Game*, p. 81.

Chapter 1: Western Province Cricket Union

40 André Odendaal wrote the historical overview on the Western Province Cricket Union in chapter 1, with help from Michael Owen-Smith, who provided the summary of the top WPCU players from the turn of the century to the 1960s.

41 Parker, *Western Province Cricket 100 – Not Out*, p. 11.

42 See Murray and Vahed (eds.), *Empire and Cricket*, pp. 37-42.

43 This match was later declared first-class despite its being a two-day game and this being a Western Province Cricket Club side (R Isherwood to A Odendaal, 28 April 2009).

44 Statistics provided by Andrew Samson.

45 See *Western Province Cricket Union Official Handbook*. 1 October, 1928, p. 24.

46 A Odendaal collection, newspaper cutting.

47 Murray and Vahed (eds.), *Empire and Cricket*, chapter 4; Winch, *England's Youngest Captain*, p. 260-273.

48 *Cape Times*, 18 September 1968, p. 1.

49 Andrew Samson drew up the list of national players produced by the WPCU.

50 Kepler Wessels also played official test cricket for Australia in the 1980s and for South Africa (UCBSA) in the 1990s.

51 Andrew Samson drew up the list of WPCU first-class players.

52 Allan Lamb also played official international cricket for England.

53 André Odendaal compiled the list of players for the unofficial matches against the early English touring teams from Luckin, *South African Cricket, 1919-1927*, pp. 486, 503, 516, 524.

54 Andrew Samson compiled the list of Western Province Cricket Union List A limited-overs caps from 1969/70 to 1990/91.

55 André Odendaal compiled the list of WPCU league winners from the inscriptions on the base of the trophy, which is in the WPCA archive. The details for 1893/94 and 1894/95 came from *Western Province Cricket Union Official Handbook*, 1 October 1967, p. 35. From the advent of commercial sponsorships in the 1970s the trophy was known as the Markhams Premier League Trophy.

56 The list of trophy winners in the various competitions of SACA and SACU comes from C Bryden (ed.), *Mutual & Federal SA Cricket Annual '98*, pp. 354-5, 521-2.

57 Andrew Samson compiled the summarised scorecards of the Western Province Cricket Union first-class matches. For the full WPCU scorecards from 1889/90 to 1990/91, see MW Luckin, *South African Cricket, 1919-1927: A complete record of all first-class South African cricket since the war* (WM Luckin, Johannesburg, nd); Louis Duffus, *South African Cricket 1927–1947, volume III* (South African Cricket Association, Johannesburg, nd); and the scorecards carried season-by-season in the *South African Cricket Annual* from 1951/52 onwards.
58 Luckin, *South African Cricket, 1919-1927*, p. 486.
59 Luckin, *South African Cricket, 1919-1927*, p. 503.
60 Luckin, *South African Cricket, 1919-1927*, p. 516.
61 Luckin, *South African Cricket, 1919-1927*, p. 524.
62 Andrew Samson compiled the summarised scorecards of the Western Province Cricket Union List A limited-overs matches from 1969/70 to 1990/91. For full season-by-season scorecards and reports, see the *South African Cricket Annual* in those years.
63 In 1978/79, the Castle Bowl was only for the B Section provinces' A teams – Northern Transvaal, Orange Free State, Border and Griqualand West – and in that season the B teams of the senior provinces played for the President's Cup. Thanks to Robin Isherwood for this information.
64 Andrew Samson compiled the list of Western Province Cricket Union B first-class caps from 1975/76 to 1990/91.
65 The list of trophy winners in SACA and SACU's Currie Cup B Section (and the successive names of that competition) comes from C Bryden (ed.), *Mutual & Federal SA Cricket Annual '98*, p. 355.
66 Andrew Samson compiled the summarised scores of the Western Province Cricket Union B first-class matches from 1975/76 to 1990/91.

Chapter 2: Western Province Coloured Cricket Union
67 André Odendaal wrote the historical overview on the Western Province Coloured Cricket Union in chapter 2. Key sources were SJ Reddy and DN Bansda (eds.), *The South African Non-European Cricket Almanack 1953/54* (The South African Non-European Cricket Publications, Cape Town, [1953]) and SJ Reddy and DN Bansda (eds.), *The South African Non-European Cricket Almanack 1954/55* (The South African Non-European Cricket Publications, Cape Town, [1955]).
68 Ottomans Cricket Cub, 115th anniversary brochure, 1882–1997 (Cape Town, 1997).
69 See St Augustine's CC 90th anniversary brochure, 1989.
70 For details, see, 'Sporting Intelligence', *Cape Argus*, 13 January 1890; 'Today's cricket. The Malay tournament', *Cape Argus*, 14 January 1890; 'Sporting Intelligence', *Cape Times*, 14 January 1890; 'Cricket. The Malay tournament', *Cape Times*, 15 January 1890; 'Sporting Intelligence', *Cape Times*, 21 January 1890; 'Cricket. The Malay tournament', *Cape Times*, 22 January 1890; 'Sporting Intelligence', *Cape Times*, 23 January 1890; 'Sporting Intelligence', *Cape Times*, 28 January 1890; 'Sporting Intelligence', *Cape Times*, 30 January 1890.
71 Sport and pastime', *Diamond Fields Advertiser*, 27 March 1891; 31 March 1891; 3, 4 and 6 April 1891.
72 For details, see 'Sport and pastime', *Diamond Fields Advertiser*, 27 March 1891; 31 March 1891; 3, 4, and 6 April 1891.
73 Luckin, *The History of South African Cricket*, pp. 517-518.
74 See 'Cape District Cricket Union', *APO*, 16 November 1912.
75 'Sport. Cricket, Cape Town', *APO*, 19 October 1912.
76 'W.P. Cricket Board', *APO*, 16 November 1912. For efforts to unite the sporting bodies in Cape Town, see also 'Western Province (Coloured) C. and A. Union', *APO*, 19 April 1913.
77 Winch, *England's Youngest Captain*, p. 262.
78 Odendaal, *The Story of an African Game*, pp. 78-82; 'Ukuzigcobisa' and ' "Imvo" special wires', *Imvo Zabantsundu*, 12 January 1899.
79 'Moslem union resumes after break', *The Cape Standard*, 2 December 1935. Names provided by Carr Haywood in 2005 after reference to team photographs and discussions with old players, but not confirmed by available scorecards, which are mostly summarised.
80 'Western Province Coloured Cricket Union', *The Cape Standard*, 31 December 1945.
81 'Green Roses C.C. itinerary', *The Cape Standard*, 31 December 1945.
82 'Barnato Trophy Tournament', *The Cape Standard*, 18 December 1945.
83 A Odendaal collection, newspaper cutting of 1891 Malay team.
84 André Odendaal compiled the list of Western Province Coloured Cricket Union national caps drawing from Reddy and Bansda, *The South African Non-European Cricket Almanack* (1953/54, 1954/55 and 1969) and Krish Reddy's 1950s scorecards. Yusuf Garda helped with verification.

85 André Odendaal compiled the list of Western Province Coloured Cricket Union provincial players. The players who participated in the six Barnato tournaments held in the 1907/08, 1922/23, 1924/25, 1927/28, 1929/30 and 1931/32 seasons are missing from the list as no scorecards or reports of these have been found. The list here was drawn up from Krish Reddy's scorecards and the following additional sources:

1889/90: 'Sporting intelligence. The Malay tournament. Cape Town and Claremont vs Port Elizabeth and Johannesburg', *Cape Times*, 28 January, 1890.

1890/91: 'Sport and pastime', *Diamond Fields Advertiser*, 27 March 1891; 31 March 1891; 3, 4, and 6 April 1891.

1891/92: Luckin, *The History of South African Cricket*, pp. 517-518.

1898/99: 'Ukuzigcobisa' and '"Imvo" special wires', *Imvo Zabantsundu*, 12 January 1899.

1903/04: *Diamond Fields Advertiser*, 31 March 1904 p. 8; 1 April 1904, p. 7; 2 April 1904, p. 3; 4 April, 1904, p. 7; 5 April, p.7; 6 April 1904, p. 7; 11 April 1904, p. 7; 13 April 1904, p. 11; and 16 April 1904, p. 7.

1912/13: 'Barnato Cup Tournament', *APO*, 5 April 1913; 'Sport. Cricket. Presentation of Barnato Cup', *APO*, 23 April 1910; Krish Reddy Collection, 'Batting and bowling averages of all the participants in the Barnato Cup Tournament 1913. Compiled by Mr E.J. Choonoo, who acted as the official scorer for Natal'. There is some discrepancy between the reports from different newspapers in these two sources, and André Odendaal has generally preferred the APO version because of its Cape Town base.

1921/22: Ottomans CC, 115th anniversary brochure.

1931/32: Team photo donated by Edelros 'Boeta' Behardien.

1945/46: A 'Carr' Haywood.

1947/48: A 'Carr' Haywood.

1949/50: A 'Carr' Haywood.

1951/52: A 'Carr' Haywood.

1954/55: A 'Carr' Haywood.

1957/58: A 'Carr' Haywood.

Those names with an asterisk next to them were provided by A 'Carr' Hayward who liaised with ex-players in 2005 and drew up lists from old team photographs – they are not confirmed by the available scorecards, which are mostly summarised. Mr Hayward was actively helped by Mogamad Allie.

86 Also spelt Abraham and Abrams in reports.
87 Also spelt Abraham in reports.
88 Also spelt Aderjance, Adderjance and Adjerance in reports.
89 Also spelt Aderjance, Adderjance and Adjerance in reports.
90 Also spelt Allei in reports.
91 Spelt Ellie in *Imvo Zabantsundu*.
92 Also spelt Arifdien in reports.
93 Also spelt Affridien in reports.
94 Also spelt Coenraad in scorecards.
95 Also spelt Detoie in reports.
96 Also spelt Esmael in reports.
97 Also spelt Jacoef and Jakoep in reports.
98 Spelt Laroe in reports.
99 Also spelt Manor in reports.
100 Also spelt Oxallic in reports.
101 Standard spelling used here – Samoodien and Samsoedien also used in sources.
102 Spelt Samsoeden in report.
103 Spelt Srmsoddien in report.
104 Spelt Tallip in *Imvo Zabantsundu*.
105 Spelt Toffie in *Imvo Zabantsundu*.
106 Also spelt Van der Schyf in reports.
107 Krish Reddy, drawing on Reddy and Bansda, *The South African Non-European Cricket Almanack* (1953/54, 1954/55 and 1969), compiled the list of trophies won by the Western Province Coloured Cricket Union in inter-provincial competitions. See Bryden (ed.), *Mutual & Federal SA Cricket Annual '98*, p. 479.

108 Krish Reddy, drawing on Reddy and Bansda, *The South African Non-European Cricket Almanack* (1953/54, 1954/55 and 1969) and other sources, compiled the scorecards of the Western Province Coloured Cricket Union provincial matches. André Odendaal added some new scorecards, the sources of which are indicated in footnotes. The scores from the six Barnato tournaments held in the 1907/08, 1922/23, 1924/25, 1927/28, 1929/30 and 1931/32 seasons are missing from the list as no scorecards or reports of these have been found.

109 Scorecards compiled by A Odendaal. For details of the 1898/99 tournament, see 'Ukuzigcobisa' and '"Imvo" special wires', *Imvo Zabantsundu*, 12 January 1899.

110 Scorecards compiled by A Odendaal. For details of the 1904 tournament, see *Diamond Fields Advertiser*, 31 March 1904, p. 8; 1 April 1904, p. 7; 2 April 1904, p.3; 4 April, 1904, p. 7; 5 April, p. 7; 6 April 1904, p. 7; 11 April 1904; 13 April 1904, p. 11; and 16 April 1904, p. 7. Unfortunately the microfilm version of these newspapers is so distorted that some of the names of the players are not clear.

111 A Odendaal source: 'Sport. Cricket. Presentation of Barnato Cup', *APO*, 23 April 1910.

112 A Odendaal source: 'Barnato Cup Tournament', *APO*, 5 April 1913.

113 A Odendaal source: 'Kimberley. Barnato Cup Tournament', *APO*, 19 April 1913.

114 Krish Reddy Collection: cuttings from *Latest* and *Natal Mercury* newspapers [no date].

115 Krish Reddy scorecards. For an original source, see 'Board tournament' in Reddy and Bansda, *The South African Non-European Cricket Almanack 1953/54*, pp. 87-99.

116 Reddy and Bansda, *The South African Non-European Cricket Almanack* (1953/54), pp. 128-131 and (1954/55), pp. 54-55.

Chapter 3: Peninsula and Western Districts Cricket Board

117 André Odendaal wrote the historical overview on the Peninsula and Western Districts Cricket Board in chapter 3.

118 BD Waterwich, 'Looking back: The Peninsula and Western Districts Cricket Board' in SJ Reddy and DN Bansda (eds.), *The South African Non-European Cricket Almanack 1953/54* (The South African Non-European Cricket Publications, Cape Town, [1953]), p. 113.

119 BD Waterwich, 'Looking back: The Peninsula and Western Districts Cricket Board' in SJ Reddy and DN Bansda (eds.), *The South African Non-European Cricket Almanack 1953/54* (The South African Non-European Cricket Publications, Cape Town, [1953]), p. 113.

120 BD Waterwich, 'Looking back: The Peninsula and Western Districts Cricket Board' in SJ Reddy and DN Bansda (eds.), *The South African Non-European Cricket Almanack 1953/54* (The South African Non-European Cricket Publications, Cape Town, [1953]), p. 113.

121 On this, see A Odendaal, K Reddy and C Merrett, *A History of South African Cricket, 1795–2011* (forthcoming), chapter 11.

122 J Kemm, 'South African Cricket Association' in Reddy and Bansda, *The South African Non-European Cricket Almanack* (1953/54), p. 103.

123 See, for example, G Lewis, *Between the Wire and the Wall: A history of South African 'Coloured' politics* (David Philip, Cape Town, 1987), pp. 7, 18-27, 45-46; RE van der Ross, *The Rise and Decline of apartheid: A study of political movements among the coloured people of South Africa, 1880–1985* (Tafelberg, Cape Town, 1986), pp. 19-21, 24, 28-34.

124 Obituary in Reddy and Bansda, *The South African Non-European Cricket Almanack* (1953/54), p. 142.

125 See tournament reports, *The Cape Standard*, 4, 10 and 17 January 1938, and 14 February 1938.

126 'How province won', *The Cape Standard*, 17 January 1938.

127 *The Cape Standard*, 24 January 1938, p. 6.

128 'Sir David Harris Trophy', *The Cape Standard*, 17 January 1938.

129 'MCC to meet coloured team', *The Cape Standard*, 6 December 1938.

130 'SA national rugby team', *The Cape Standard*, 27 September 1938.

131 'Diamond Fields beat Western Prov.', *The Cape Standard*, 15 April 1947.

132 'South African Col. Cricket tournament', *The Cape Standard*, 10 December 1946.

133 *The Cape Standard*, 15 April 1947.

134 Reddy and Bansda, *The South African Non-European Cricket Almanack* (1969) p. 43.

135 See P Oborne, *Basil D'Oliveira: Cricket and conspiracy*, Appendix A and B, pp. 254-265.

136 Oborne, *Basil D'Oliveira*. See also B D'Oliveira, *D'Oliveira: An Autobiography* (Sportsman's Book Club, London, 1969) and B D'Oliveira, *Time to Declare: An Autobiography* (Macmillan, Johannesburg, 1980).

137 DD Hendricks, 'Peninsula and Western Districts Cricket Board' in Reddy and Bansda (eds.), *The South African Non-European Cricket Almanack 1954/55*, p. 40.

138 For further details on the PWDCB, see the articles by Basil Waterwich and DD Hendricks in Reddy and Bansda, *The South African Non-European Cricket Almanack* (1953/54), p. 113 and Reddy and Bansda (eds.), *The South African Non-European Cricket Almanack* (1954/55), pp. 24, 40.

139 Krish Reddy and André Odendaal compiled the list of Peninsula and Western Districts Cricket Board national caps, drawing from Reddy and Bansda, *The South African Non-European Cricket Almanack* (1953/54, 1954/55 and 1969) as well as scorecards and newspaper clippings.

140 André Odendaal compiled the list of PWDCB provincial players drawing on Reddy and Bansda, *The South African Non-European Cricket Almanack* (1953/54, 1954/55 and 1969) and Krish Reddy's scorecards and newspaper clippings. The players who participated in the four Sir David Harris tournaments held in the 1926/27, 1928/29, 1930/31 and 1933/34 seasons are missing from the list as no scorecards or reports of these have been found. The additional newspaper sources for the provincial players season-by-season were as follows:

1937/38: Official team photograph by William G van Kalker, Woodstock and scorecards, *The Cape Standard*, 10 January 1938.

1946/47: 'South African Col. cricket tournament, strong WP team selected', *The Cape Standard*, 10 December 1946, p. 7; 'Cricket tournament at Wellington and Rosmead', *Cape Standard*, 17 December 1946; 'Sir David Harris cricket cup tournament', *The Cape Standard*, 24 December 1946, p. 11; 'Coloured cricket tournament', *The Cape Standard*, 31 December 1946, p. 7; 'Diamond Fields beat Western Prov., Victory fully deserved', *The Cape Standard*, 15 April 1947.

141 Krish Reddy, drawing on Reddy and Bansda, *The South African Non-European Cricket Almanack* (1953/54, 1954/55 and 1969), compiled the list of trophies won by the Peninsula and Western Districts Cricket Board in inter-provincial competitions. See Bryden (ed.), *Mutual & Federal SA Cricket Annual '98*, p. 479.

142 Krish Reddy, drawing on Reddy and Bansda, *The South African Non-European Cricket Almanack* (1953/54, 1954/55 and 1969) and other sources, compiled the scorecards of the Peninsula and Western Districts Cricket Board provincial matches. André Odendaal added some new scorecards and corrected others. In these specific cases the sources are indicated in footnotes below. The scores for the four Sir David Harris tournaments held in the 1926/27, 1928/29, 1930/31 and 1933/34 seasons are missing from the list as no scorecards or reports of these have been found.

143 Compiled by A Odendaal from *The Cape Standard*, 10 January 1938.

144 Compiled by A Odendaal from 'Sir David Harris cricket cup tournament', *The Cape Standard*, 24 December 1946, p. 11.

145 Krish Reddy scorecard plus A Odendaal additions from 'Sir David Harris cricket cup tournament', *The Cape Standard*, 24 December 1946, p. 11.

146 Krish Reddy scorecard plus A Odendaal additions from 'Coloured cricket tournament', *The Cape Standard*, 31 December 1946, p. 7.

147 Compiled by A Odendaal from 'Diamond Fields beat Western Prov., Victory fully deserved', *The Cape Standard*, 15 April 1947.

Chapter 4:- Western Province Bantu (later African) Cricket Union

148 A Odendaal wrote the historical overview on the Western Province Bantu Cricket Union. The late Ashton Dunjwa, Junior Tengo Sokanyile, Solomon Makhosana, Stanley Maqubela, 'Swift' Mama, Fezile Mguqulwa, Gerald Mxolisi Njengele, Morgan Mfobo and Ezra Cagwe helped with printed material, information and verification.

149 For details, see Odendaal, *Story of an African Game*, pp. 24-27.

150 'E Kapa', *Imvo Zabantsundu*, 5 December 1898 and 'E Kapa', *Imvo Zabantsundu*, 8 February 1899.

151 See Cape Archives, NA 636, File 2207: Memorandum by J. Jones, 'Re cricketers ejected from the native location Uitvlugt', 9 January 1904, and related correspondence.

152 BPB Cossie, 'Western Province (Bantu) Cricket Union', in Reddy and Bansda (eds.), *The South African Non-European Cricket Almanack 1953/54*, p. 117. See also 'Iqakamba eKapa', *Umteteli wa Bantu*, 21 January 1933.

153 *The Sun*, 19 January 1934. p. 8.

154 Cossie, 'Western Province (Bantu) Cricket Union', p. 117 and 'SA Bantu Cricket Board' in Reddy and Bansda, *The South African Non-European Cricket Almanack* (1954/55), p. 29.

155 'Sports talk: I don't blame the poor players', *Imvo Zabantsundu*, 21 February 1959.

156 M Allie to A Odendaal, 9 March 2011.

157 Interview with Ezra Cagwe, Newlands, 18 March 2011, who recalled explanations given to him by older cricketers.

158 On the multi-national sports policy, see A Odendaal (ed.), *Cricket in Isolation: The politics of race and cricket in South Africa* (Cape Town, 1977), pp. 116-129.

159 For more details on African cricket in the 1960s and 1970s, see Odendaal, *Story of an African Game*, chapters 20-23.

160 SAACB, the secretarial report and review for the seasons 1965/66/67 by Lennox Lindelo Mlonzi.

161 See, for example, 'The cricketer interviews: John Passmore on African cricket', *South African Cricketer*, February 1977, pp. 8-9.

162 Interview with Ezra Cagwe, Newlands, 18 March 2011.

163 Interview with Ezra Cagwe, Newlands, 18 March 2011.
164 Notes prepared by GM Njengele, 21 July 2011 and E Cagwe interview.
165 From Odendaal, *Story of an African Game*, p. 203.
166 Selected for SA Bantu team to play 'representative match' against Natal Indian team. See *Imvo Zabantsundu*, 15 January 1955.
167 A Odendaal compiled the list of Western Province Bantu (later African) Cricket Union players. The players who participated in the 14 inter-provincial tournaments held in the 1934/35, 1935/36, 1938/39, 1940/41, 1946/47, 1954/55, 1963/64, 1964/65, 1965/66, 1968/69, 1970/71, 1972/73, 1973/74 and 1974/75 seasons are missing from the list as no scorecards or reports of these have been found.The following sources were used:

1933/34: *Umteteli wa Bantu,* 30 December 1933 and 6 and 13 January 1934 [No Western Province names or scores]

1947/48: Reddy and Bansda, *The South African Non-European Cricket Almanack* (1953/54), p. 117 and team photograph with names by Maxim's Studio, 5 Hanover Street, District Six and scorecard (only 3 names)

1952/53: Reddy and Bansda, *The South African Non-European Cricket Almanack* (1953/54), pp. 120, 127. See also p. 121 for a photograph of this team.

1953/54: Reddy and Bansda, *The South African Non-European Cricket Almanack* (1954/55), pp. 54-56.

1967/68: from scorecards, only 4 names.

168 The surname is also spelt Dikwani in 1951/52 reports. It is assumed to be T Dikweni.
169 The surname Dyira without the initial also appears in the 1936/37 team list. The fact that SM Dyira captained the post-war team indicates experience and, therefore, it is probably he who is referred to. But, because the years of playing are so far apart, Dyira, [x] and Dyira, SM have been put separately here.
170 Also spelt Kaulela.
171 Also spelt Magodlwa in reports.
172 The surname Matshikwe without the initial also appears in the 1935/36 and 1936/37 team lists. It is not known if this is A or E Matshikwe.
173 The surname Maxam or Maxama (which appears next in the alphabetical list) could be the same one, but because the years of playing are so far apart, they have been put separately here.
174 The surname Mbali without the initial also appears in the 1936/37 team list. It is not known if this is CS or DN Mbali.
175 The surname is also spelt Ncwane in reports, and the name Ncwana with no initial also appears in 1936/37 tournament list. It is assumed to be SM Ncwana.
176 A Odendaal, drawing on Reddy and Bansda's *Almanacks* and his research material for *The Story of an African Game*, compiled the list of trophies won by the Western Province Bantu Cricket Union in inter-provincial competitions. Junior Tengo Sokhanyile helped him with post-1960 information.
177 A Odendaal and Krish Reddy compiled the scores of the Western Province Bantu Cricket Union provincial matches. The scores for the 14 inter-provincial tournaments held in the 1934/35, 1935/36, 1938/39, 1940/41, 1946/47, 1954/55, 1963/64, 1964/65, 1965/66, 1968/69, 1970/71, 1972/73, 1973/74 and 1974/75 seasons are missing from the list as no scorecards or reports of these have been found.
178 Reports by WW Jabavu, *Umteteli wa Bantu*, 30 December 1933 and 6 and 13 January 1934.
179 *Imvo Zabantsundu*, 8 and 15 January 1935.
180 The teams were seeded into two sections with the winners qualifying to meet in the final. Natal won all its games in its section, having beaten the highly fancied North-Eastern Transvaal side. They thus qualified to meet Western Province, winners of the other section, in the final.
181 Reddy and Bansda, *The South African Non-European Cricket Almanack* (1954/55), pp. 54-55.
182 *Imvo Zabantsundu*, 25 December 1965.
183 *Imvo Zabantsundu*, 23 December 1967 and 6 and 13 January 1968.
184 *Imvo Zabantsundu*, 14 and 21 December 1968; 11, 18 and 25 January 1969; and 1 February 1969. See also reference in *Imvo Zabantsundu*, 13 December 1969. [No WP scorecards given.]
185 *Imvo Zabantsundu*, 13 December 1969; and 10 and 24 January 1970.
186 *Imvo Zabantsundu*, 15 and 22 December 1973.
187 *Imvo Zabantsundu*, 15 and 22 December 1973 (including team names).
188 *Imvo Zabantsundu*, 28 December 1974 and 1 February 1975.

Chapter 5: Western Province Indian Cricket Union

189 A Odendaal wrote the historical overview on the Western Province Indian Cricket Union in chapter 5. Ebrahim 'Ba' Omar and Mohamed and Riaz Ebrahim helped with background information.

190 See, for example, C Merrett, *Sport, Space and Segregation: Politics and society in Pietermaritzburg* (KwaZulu-Natal University Press, Scottsville, 2009), pp. 95-99.

191 Reddy and Bansda (eds.), *The South African Non-European Cricket Almanack 1953/54*, pp. 80-81 and Reddy and Bansda (eds.), *The South African Non-European Cricket Almanack 1954/55*, pp. 64-65, 80-81. This introduction draws mainly from this source.

192 See for example, Reddy and Bansda, *The South African Non-European Cricket Almanack* (1954/55), pp. 60-61; M Allie, 'Best gloveman of his time', *Muslim Views*, August 2011 (See also unedited original of this story.) Goolam Abed went on to play professional rugby in England and 'Dik' Abed professional cricket in that country and the Netherlands.

193 B Harrypersadh, 'Progressive step by South African Indian Cricket Union' in Reddy and Bansda, *The South African Non-European Cricket Almanack* (1954/55), p. 28.

194 A Odendaal compiled the list of Western Province Indian Cricket Union national caps, drawing on Reddy and Bansda, *The South African Non-European Cricket Almanack* (1953/54, 1954/55 and 1969) and Krish Reddy. Carr Hayward and Yusuf 'Chubb' Garda helped with verification.

195 A Odendaal compiled the list of Western Province Indian Cricket Union provincial caps, drawing on 'Complete list of players who have appeared in the South African inter-provincial tournament from 1940-1955' in 1958 South African Indian Cricket Union tournament brochure, p. 71; as well as Reddy and Bansda, *The South African Non-European Cricket Almanack* (1953/54, 1954/55 and 1969) and Krish Reddy's summarised tournament scorecards.

196 Krish Reddy, drawing on Reddy and Bansda, *The South African Non-European Cricket Almanack* (1953/54, 1954/55 and 1969), compiled the list of trophies for the inter-provincial competitions in which the Western Province Indian Cricket Union participated. See Bryden (ed.), *Mutual & Federal SA Cricket Annual '98*, p. 479.

197 Krish Reddy compiled the scorecards of the Western Province Indian Cricket Union provincial matches, drawing on brochures produced by the South African Indian Cricket Union and other sources.

198 The scorecards for the inter-union matches involving the Western Province Indian Cricket Union come from Reddy and Bansda, *The South African Non-European Cricket Almanack* (1954/55), pp. 54-55.

Chapter 6: Hottentots Holland Cricket Union

199 The historical overview on the Hottentots Holland Cricket Union was written by A Odendaal, drawing directly from the contemporary reports by in Reddy and Bansda, *The South African Non-European Cricket Almanack* (1953/5) and (1954/55). My thanks also to the late Mohamed Bagus, as well as, Mogamad Allie, Mr Haroen Gafieldien and Mr Ebrahim Rhoda, who has written a Master's dissertation on the Somerset West and Strand communities, for information and support.

200 Reddy and Bansda, *The South African Non-European Cricket Almanack* (1953-54), pp. 86-87.

201 Interview with E Rhoda, 20 March 2011.

202 E Rhoda to A Odendaal, 20 March 2011 with undated attachment on 'imam Ismail Latief (1932–2005)'.

203 See A Booley, *Forgotten Heroes: A history of black rugby, 1882–1992* (Independent Newspapers, Cape Town, 1998), pp. 131, 181–90, 254–5, 291–8.

204 A Odendaal compiled the list of Hottentots Holland Cricket Union caps. It was drawn from summarised scorecards of the 1951/52 and 1954/55 Barnato tournaments in Reddy and Bansda, *The South African Non-European Cricket Almanack* (1953/54, 1954/55), the 1954/55 team photograph and the scorebooks for the 1953/54 and 1954/55 seasons presented by Mohamed Bagus and former player Haroen Gafieldien in February 2008. They also verified the lists and provided the first names of the players.

205 Today the family name is spelled Gafieldien and Haroen Gafieldien has made the change as well, but it appeared originally in reports mainly as Gavieldien.

206 A Odendaal and Krish Reddy compiled the Hottentots Holland Cricket Union scorecards, drawing directly from the *Almanacks* listed above. See also the scorebooks for the 1953/54 and 1954/55 seasons presented by Mohamed Bagus and Haroen Gafieldien to the WPCA archives.

207 Reddy and Bansda, *The South African Non-European Cricket Almanack* (1954/55), pp. 54-55.

Chapter 7: Western Province Women's Cricket Union

208 See A Odendaal, 'Neither cricketers nor ladies', in *Women's Cricket World Cup 2005 South Africa*; A Odendaal, 'Neither cricketers nor ladies: Towards a history of women and cricket in South Africa, 1860s–2000s', *International Journal of the History of Sport*, 28, 1, January 2011, pp. 115-136.

209 A Odendaal wrote the historical overview on the Western Province Women's Cricket Union in chapter 7. It is based on work in progress since 2004 for a book on the history of South African cricket, 1975–2010, which the author is writing in collaboration with Krish Reddy and Christopher Merrett. See also A Odendaal, 'A women's place is out in the middle', *Western Province Cricket Association Annual Report 2008/2009*, pp. 19-21.

210 J Winch, *Cricket in Southern Africa: Two hundred years of achievements and records* (Windsor Publishers, Windsor, 1997), p. 270.

211 J McIntyre, *White stoep on the highway. Rustenburg School for Girls: A history 1894–1994*, p. 19.

212 E Kingswell, 'Women at the wicket', *The South African Ladies Pictorial*, May 1934, p. 29.

213 'Cape Town women form own cricket union', *Cape Argus*, 27 September 1951.

214 Western Province Women's Cricket Union Collection, handwritten notes by Vicky Valentine-Brown, nd.

215 [Amanda Botha], 'Nuwe lewe in WP se vroue-krieket', *Die Burger*, 10 November 1965.

216 Ibid.

217 'Women's cricket revival in W.P.', *Cape Argus*, 27 August 1969.

218 'Southern Transvaal Women's Cricket Tournament from December 30 1973 to January 4 1974 in Johannesburg' (brochure).

219 After Natal won in 1966/67, the trophy was won by either Southern Transvaal or Western Province for the next two decades.

220 A Odendaal compiled the list of WPWCU players. The players who participated in the three inter-provincial tournaments held in 1967, 1968 and 1971 are missing from the list as no scorecards or reports of these have been found. Players whose names show only that they played for a club (Alma/Bellville) or a Composite XI with the SARWCA tournaments and cricket weeks are not included in the consolidated biographical list of Western Province players in chapter 17. If evidence is found that they were officially selected for the WPWCU, they will be listed there too. The sources, season by season, for the players lists were as follows:

1951/52: team photograph

1952/53: 'SARWCA Inter-Provincial Tournament, January 1 to 4 1953 at Ramblers and Railway Grounds' (brochure).

1953/54: 'The South African and Rhodesia Inter-Provincial Women's Cricket Week Programme, 1–6 February 1954' (brochure).

1954/55: 'Third Inter-Provincial Women's Cricket Tournament, Kingsmead, Durban, January 1955' (brochure).

1956/57: 'Eastern Province Fifth Inter-Provincial Women's Cricket Tournament, Port Elizabeth, January 1957' (brochure).

1957/58: 'SA&RWCA, Sixth Inter-Provincial Women's Cricket Tournament, Johannesburg, January 1958' (brochure).

1958/59: 'SA&RWCA, Seventh Inter-Provincial Tournament, Cape Town, 12–17 January 1959' (brochure).

1960/61: England tour: 'English spinner routes WP women at Newlands', *Cape Argus*, 16 November 1961.

1962/63: 'SARWCA 10th Inter-Provincial Tournament, Port Elizabeth, 14 to 19 January 1963' (brochure).

1963/64: Maureen Payne Collection, undated newspaper cutting [December 1963].

1965/66: See full scorecards in Maureen Payne Collection, 'New SA record of 267 runs set in women's cricket', *The Friend*, 6 January 1966 and C Guild, Sparkling stand by Jenny Gove', *The Friend* [no date].

1967/68: 'The Ladies Section of the Alma Cricket Club presents the South African Women's Cricket Week, 1 to 6 January 1968' (brochure).

1969 Holland tour: Western Province Women's Cricket Union Archive, 'Strong WP side to play Holland', [undated news cutting].

1968/69: Western Province did not participate in the SARWCA cricket week.

1971/72: 'Inter-Provincial Tournament, 1972, Pietermaritzburg' (brochure).

1971/72: New Zealand tour: 'Kiwi-vroue gelyk, wys slag', *Die Burger*, 24 February 1972 (1978/79 IPT and Unicorns).

1972/73: Maureen Payne Collection, undated cutting, especially 'S-Tvl weer kampioen' (which has WP team list).

1973/74: 'Southern Transvaal Women's Cricket Tournament from December 30 1973 to January 4 1974 in Johannesburg' (brochure).

1974/75: 'Inter-Provincial Cricket Tournament 28 December 1974 to 4 January 1975 in Bloemfontein' (brochure).

1977/78: 'Silver Jubilee Cricket Week 2 January 1978 to 8 January 1978 in Johannesburg' (brochure).

1978/79: Official brochure, *South African Women's Cricket Association Unicorn's tour, 26th Inter-Provincial Cricket Week, Durban*, 1979; Maureen Payne Collection, undated cutting, 'Western Province win Simon Trophy' and 'South African

Women's Cricket Association', handwritten report [for *SA Cricket Annual*, 1979]; Yvonne Austen Collection, [Western Province] team captain's report for 1978/79 season.

1979/80: 'South African Women's Cricket Association Cricket Week 1979–1980 at Rondebosch Boys' High School Cape Town' (brochure). (Individual participants only listed but their provincial affiliation is indicated.)

1980/81: 'Inter-Provincial Cricket Week, Marks Park, Johannesburg 28 Dec[ember 1980] – 3 Jan[uary] 1981' (brochure). [No WP team, only individuals participating and S Tvl teams.]

1982/83: South African Women's Cricket Association Cricket Week 1983, Newlands, Cape Town. [No WP team, only individuals participating].

1983/84: 'Southern Transvaal Women's Cricket Association Inter-Provincial and Cricket Week Marks Park, December 28 1983 to January 3 1984' (brochure).

1984/85: 'Inter-Provincial Women's Cricket Week 1984–85' (brochure).

1985/86: 'South African Women's Cricket Association Cricket Week in Cape Town 1985–1986' (brochure).

221 A Odendaal compiled the list of tournaments and trophy winners from his research material on the history of women's cricket indicated elsewhere in the footnotes to this chapter.

222 Programme for SAWCA Unicorns tour 16th Inter-Provincial Cricket Week, Durban, 1979, p. 32.

223 A Odendaal compiled the list of WPWCU scores. The sources have been footnoted above. The scores for the six inter-provincial tournaments held in the 1957/58, 1962/63, 1966/67, 1967/68, 1968/69, 1970/71 seasons, as well as the single Western Province versus Southern Transvaal matches from the mid-1970s to mid-1980s (plus the one match against Border in that time), are missing from the list as no scorecards or reports have been found.

224 GA Chettle (ed.), *South African Cricket Annual 1951–1952*, pp. 246-7.

225 Chettle (ed.), *South African Cricket Annual 1953*.

226 Official Programme, including all names; *Cape Times*, 6 February 1954, p. 11; Chettle (ed.), *South African Cricket Annual 1954*, pp. 124-7.

227 Chettle (ed.), *South African Cricket Annual 1955*, pp. 197-9.

228 *Huisgenoot*, 27 February 1956; Chettle (ed.), *South African Cricket Annual 1956*, pp. 106-7.

229 Official programme, including teams; Chettle (ed.), *South African Cricket Annual 1957*, pp. 116-17.

230 Official programme, including names; Chettle (ed.), *South African Cricket Annual 1959*, pp. 254-5.

231 Chettle (ed.), *South African Cricket Annual 1960*, pp. 221-222.

232 *Women's Cricket*, 26, 1, 28 April 1961 to *Women's Cricket*, 26, 10, 15 September 1961. Test match scorecards provided by Andrew Samson.

233 'Payne takes 8 English wickets', *Cape Argus*, 15 November 1960 and 'English spinner routs WP women at Newlands', *Cape Argus*, 16 November 1960.

234 The accuracy of the summarised scorecards for the ninth to the twelfth inter-provincial tournaments need to be verified through further research. Undated scorecards from the scrapbooks of Maureen Payne were used here and the cuttings cannot be readily dated.

235 Maureen Payne Collection, Scrapbook.

236 *Daily News*, 8 January 1964.

237 For the 1963/64 tournament, eight Bellville Cricket Club members with three guest players from Border who could not field a team, namely M Burgess, S Kruger and J Stagmiere, played as Combined Western Province / Border, captained by Maureen Payne. See Maureen Payne Collection, undated newspaper cutting [December 1963].

238 See Maureen Payne Collection, 'Women's cricket', *Cape Times*, 15 January 1965 and undated newspaper cuttings.

239 Maureen Payne Collection, programme and scores.

240 Maureen Payne Collection, programme and scores.

241 Maureen Payne Collection, programme and scores.

242 Western Province Women's Cricket Union Archive, 'Hollandse vroue uit vir 23' [undated news cutting].

243 Brochure of SARWCA Cricket Week, Johannesburg, STWCA, January 1969.

244 *Daily Dispatch*, 5–11 January, 1970. See also fixture list in official programme.

245 Official programme.

246 Maureen Payne Collection, undated cutting 'WP girls on top' and 'Kiwis to play lipstick Springboks'; Janet Burger Collection, undated cutting, 'Natal women beaten by eight wickets'.

247 'Kiwi-vroue gelyk, wys slag', *Die Burger*, 24 February 1972.

248 Maureen Payne Collection, undated cuttings and official programme.

249 Official Programme, including names; *Caught and Bowled*, 8, 2, February 1974; *Rand Daily Mail*, 5 January 1974, p. 20; *Die Vaderland*, 5 January 1974, p. 12; *Sunday Express*, 6 January 1974, p.25.

250 Official programme, including names; *The Friend*, 28, 30 and 31 December 1974 and 1, 2 and 3 January 1975; *Die Volksblad*, 30 December 1974.

251 Western Province Women's Cricket Committee minutes, 13 February 1975.

252 No details found.

253 Official programme, *Cricket Week held at Cape Town, 1976/77*; Programme for SAWCA Unicorns tour, 16th inter-provincial cricket week, Durban, 1979, p. 32.

254 Official programme, *Silver Jubilee Cricket Week 2 January 1978 to 8 January 1978 Johannesburg*.

255 Official brochure, *South African Women's Cricket Association Unicorn's tour, 26th Inter-Provincial Cricket Week, Durban*, 1979; Maureen Payne Collection, undated cutting, 'Western Province win Simon Trophy' and 'South African Women's Cricket Association', handwritten report [for *SA Cricket Annual*, 1979]; Yvonne Austen Collection, [Western Province] team captain's report for 1978/79 season.

256 Maureen Payne Collection, The Unicorns, Report South Africa tour 1978/79, pp. 21-2, 30; Yvonne Austen Collection, [Western Province] team captain's report for 1978/79 season.

257 Official programme, *South African Women's Cricket Association Cricket Week 1979–1980, Rondebosch Boys' High School Cape Town* (Colleen Roberts Collection).

258 Official programme, *Inter-Provincial Cricket Week, Marks Park Johannesburg 28 Dec – 3 Jan '81*; *Sunday Express*, 4 January 1981, p. 8.

259 Official programme, *South African Women's Cricket Association Cricket Week 1983, Newlands, Cape Town* (Colleen Roberts Collection).

260 Official programme, *Southern Transvaal Women's Cricket Association, Inter-Provincial Cricket Week, Marks Park, Dec 28 – Jan 3 '84* (Colleen Roberts Collection).

261 Official programme, *Inter-Provincial Women's Cricket Week 1984/85* (Colleen Roberts Collection).

262 Official programme, *South African Women's Cricket Association Cricket Week, Cape Town 1985/86* (Colleen Roberts Collection).

Chapter 8: Western Province Cricket Federation

263 The historical overview on the Western Province Cricket Federation in chapter 8 was written by A Odendaal, drawing directly from the contemporary reports in Reddy and Bansda (eds.), *The South African Non-European Cricket Almanack 1953/54* and *1954/55*. This narrative also draws on valuable recollections which the late Matt Segers shared with the writer. For further information on the Federation, see also M Allie, *More than a Game*, pp. 12-17.

264 See A. Odendaal, 'South African Independent Coloured Cricket Board (later SACA), 1926–1959' (chapter for forthcoming book).

265 See Allie, *More than a Game*, p. 15.

266 Reddy and Bansda, *The South African Non-European Cricket Almanack* (1953/4), pp. 124-125.

267 For a report on the tour, see A. Brown, 'Western Province Tour opens a new era in S.A. Cricket. Racial Tournaments a curse to non-white cricket' in Reddy and Bansda, *The South African Non-European Cricket Almanack* (1954/55), p. 53.

268 A Odendaal and Ameena Smith compiled the list of Western Province Cricket Federation provincial players drawing on Reddy and Bansda, *The South African Non-European Cricket Almanack* (1953/54 and 1954/55) and the scorecard of the 1956 match vs the Kenya Asians. Strictly speaking, the 1956 combined Western Province team was not an official WPCF team, but in reality it was a continuation of the Federation concept (and it fits nowhere else), so it is included in this chapter.

269 A Odendaal and Ameena Smith compiled the Western Province Cricket Federation scorecards drawing on Reddy and Bansda, *The South African Non-European Cricket Almanack* (1953/54), pp. 128-131, 133-134; (1954/55), pp. 16-22, 52-56; and Allie, *More than a Game*, p. 15.

270 17/0 could not have been the final second innings score for WP as they need at least 134 to win by ten wickets.

271 The Kenya Asians' scorecards were provided by Krish Reddy, who drew on reports in the *Cape Argus*, 28 November 1956, 1 December 1956, 4 December 1956, 6 December 1956; *Cape Times*, 1 December 1956 and 6 December 1956; and *Natal Mercury*, 3 December 1956.

Chapter 9: Western Province Cricket Board

272 The historical overview on the Western Province Cricket Board was written by A Odendaal with help from Mogamad Allie. It is based heavily on Mogamad's *More than a Game* and he also helped by reading, adding information and commenting in detail on this chapter. It belongs to him as much as me.

273 Allie, *More than a Game*, p. 21.

274 Odendaal, *Story of an African Game*, p. 165.

275 M Allie to A Odendaal, 9 March 2011.

276 See Odendaal, *The Story of an African Game*, pp. 165-166.
277 See Allie, *More than a Game*, pp. 27-44.
278 See Odendaal, *The Story of an African Game,* chapters 25-26, 29.
279 M Allie to A Odendaal, 9 March 2011.
280 For the SACBOC and SACB individual first-class records, see Bryden (ed.), *Mutual & Federal SA Cricket Annual 2001*, pp. 484-495.
281 The quotes are from Odendaal, *Story of an African Game*, p. 241.
282 This was also a view shared by his fellow players; see Odendaal, *Story of an African Game*, p. 241.
283 Allie, *More than a Game*, p. 350.
284 The Elfindale Ground briefly served as a base for provincial matches because it was one of the few grounds with a turf wicket at the time.
285 Allie, *More than a Game*, pp. 201-6.
286 See Gastrow, *Who's Who in South Africa*, pp. 113-14 and Odendaal, *Story of an African Game*, pp. 222-3.
287 See Allie, *More than a Game*, pp. 185-92.
288 A Odendaal compiled the list of Western Province Cricket Board national caps. See Odendaal, *Story of an African Game*, pp. 260-267.
289 The list of Western Province Cricket Board provincial caps between 1960 and 1991 was drawn from Allie, *More than a Game*, pp. 355-364.
290 Lakay played in all five Dadabhay centralised tournaments between 1961 and 1970.
291 The list of Western Province Cricket Board limited-overs provincial caps was drawn from the scorecards in Allie, *More than a Game*, pp. 343-344.
292 The list of Western Province Cricket Board league winners was drawn from Allie, *More than a Game*, pp. 195-206.
293 Krish Reddy, drawing on Reddy and Bansda, *The South African Non-European Cricket Almanack* (1969) and other sources, compiled the list of trophies won by the Western Province Cricket Board in inter-provincial competitions. See also Bryden (ed.), *Mutual & Federal SA Cricket Annual '98*, p. 479.
294 Krish Reddy compiled the summarised scorecards for the centralised tournaments (1961/62–1969/70), the decentralised two-day games (1970/71) and the first-class three-day matches (1971/72–1990/91) played by the Western Province Cricket Board. The full scorecards for the 108 WPCB three-day matches were also published in Allie, *More than a Game*, pp. 209-335.
295 The Western Province Cricket Board List A scorecards were drawn from Allie, *More than a Game*, pp. 337-342.
296 Krish Reddy compiled the introduction, the list of trophy winners and the summarised scores for WPCB B and U-21 in this section.
297 SJ Reddy (ed.), *The South African Cricketer*, 3, 1971.
298 SACBOC Biennial Reports, 1973–75.
299 SACBOC Biennial Reports, 1973–75.
300 SACBOC Biennial Reports, 1973–75.
301 SACBOC Annual Report, 1975/76.
302 Tvl B Scorebook, 1977/78.
303 SACB Record Clerk's Ledger.
304 SACB Record Clerk's Ledger.
305 SACB Record Clerk's Ledger.
306 SACB Annual Report 1981–82 and *Cape Herald*.
307 SACB Annual Report 1982–83, SACB Record Clerk's Ledger, *Cape Herald*, *Evening Post* (PE).
308 SACB Record Clerk's Ledger, *Cape Herald*. The missing scorecards can be culled from the previously mentioned sources as well as the *Indicator* (Transvaal).
309 SACB Annual Report 1984/85, SACB Record Clerk's Ledger.
310 SACB Annual Report 1985/86, SACB Record Clerk's Ledger.
311 SACB Annual Report 1986/87, SACB Record Clerk's Ledger.
312 SACB Annual Report 1987/88, SACB Record Clerk's Ledger.
313 SACB Annual Report 1988/89, SACB Record Clerk's Ledger.
314 SACB Annual Report 1989/90.
315 *SACB Annual Report, Natal Witness* (March 1991), *Cape Times*.

Chapter 10: Western Province Cricket Association

316 A Odendaal wrote the historical overview on the Western Province Cricket Association in chapter 10.
317 See Odendaal, *Story of an African Game*, chapter 32.
318 Allie, *More than a Game*, pp. 185-192.
319 Frank Brache and Carol van Vuuren (who both worked for 30 years in the offices at Newlands) together with Otto Langenegger and international rugby referee Freek Burger, were the other WPCU staff who stayed on. Later recruits from the former WPCB ranks included Peter Heeger (treasurer), Cyril Martin (stadium manager), Gert Bam (youth development) and Nabeal Dien (general manager). In 2011 the WPCA staff complement was just under 50 people.
320 Report by Professor W Basson to Cricket South Africa Transformation Committee, 26 August 2011. See also W September, 'Leadership styles in Western Province Cricket Clubs' (HR Management Honours dissertation, Cape Peninsula University of Technology, 2003).
321 See *Western Province Cricket Association Annual Report 2009/10*, pp. 6-12.
322 The statistics on international cricket at Newlands were provided by Andrew Samson.
323 There were 35 ODIs at Newlands up to April 2011 – the 29 referred to in the table, plus Pakistan vs WI in February 1993, England vs Zimbabwe in January 2000, and four matches not involving South Africa in the ICC CWC 2003.
324 Allie, *More than a Game*, p. 191.
325 See *Western Province Cricket Association Annual Report 2009/10*, pp. 2-6.
326 Andrew Samson compiled the list of Western Province Cricket Association national players from 1991/92 to 2010/11.
327 Played for WPCB 1973/74–1975/76, WPCU B 1977/78–1982/83 and WPCU 1978/79–1983/84.
328 Played for WPCU B 1987/88–1988/89.
329 Played for WPCU 1976/77.
330 Andrew Samson compiled the list of Western Province Cricket Association provincial players from 1991/92 to 2003/04.
331 A Odendaal compiled the list of Western Province Cricket Association league and one-day club competition winners since 1991/92, using research on the WPCA annual reports.
332 'Sport Skills for Life Skills', Chairman's Report, 2010/11, p. 1.
333 Andrew Samson compiled the list of inter-provincial trophy winners in the various competitions of UCBSA/CSA.
334 Andrew Samson compiled the summarised scorecards of the Western Province Cricket Association first-class matches between 1991/92 and 2003/04. For the full WPCA scorecards in this period, see the season-by-season reports on the WPCA in the *Mutual & Federal SA Cricket Annual*.
335 Andrew Samson compiled the summarised scorecards of the Western Province Cricket Association List A limited-overs matches between 1991/92 and 2003/04. For the full WPCA scorecards in this period, see the season-by-season reports on the WPCA in the *Mutual & Federal SA Cricket Annual*.
336 Andrew Samson compiled the list of Western Province Cricket Association B'first-class players from 1991/92 to 1998/99.
337 Andrew Samson compiled the summarised scorecards of the Western Province Cricket Association B first-class matches from 1991/92 to 1998/99.
338 Andrew Samson compiled the list of Western Province Cricket Association Amateur first-class and List A players from 2004/05 to 2010/11.
339 Andrew Samson compiled the summarised scorecards of the Western Province Cricket Association Amateur first-class matches from 2004/05 to 2010/11.
340 Andrew Samson compiled the summarised scorecards of the Western Province Cricket Association Amateur List A limited-overs matches from 2004/05 to 2010/11.

Chapter 11: Western Province Women's Cricket Association

341 A Odendaal wrote the historical overview on the Western Province Women's Cricket Association. Thanks to Keri Laing, Shan Cade, Colleen Roberts, Louise Vorster, Zola Thamae, Yvonne Austen, Robin Austen, Eddie Anderson, Olivia Anderson, Josephine Barnard, Madelein Lotter, Aluis Inglis (Kuylaars), Cindy Thomas, Robyn Austen, Wendy Austen, Amy Connolly and Shandré Fritz for sharing valuable material and information with me.
342 CC Hunte to Dr A Bacher, 17 June 1997; Notes taken at a meeting at the Holiday Inn, Millpark, Johannesburg, Thursday 14 December 1995; Notes taken at a meeting at Marks Park on Saturday 16 December 1995.
343 The President's Report, Annual General Meeting, SAWCA, Bloemfontein, Friday, 10 April 1998.
344 See Olivia Anderson CV, October 2011.
345 See, for example, *Western Province Cricket Association Annual Report 2007/08*, pp. 15, 43-5; 2008/09, pp. 19-21; 2009/10, pp. 59-61.

346 Andrew Samson compiled the list of national players from Western Province.

347 A Odendaal compiled the list of Western Province players from 1995/96 to 2002/03. Andrew Samson compiled the list from 2003/04 to 2010/11. A Western Province B team participated in the 2000/01 tournament in Stellenbosch and (playing as Western Province Strikers) in the 2001/02 tournament in Cape Town. Their names are included in this chapter, but they appear in the biographical list in chapter 17 only if they also played for the senior team. The sources were as follows:

1995/96: Official programme, Inaugural women and U-19 girls inter-provincial cricket week sponsored by Standard Bank and the United Cricket Board of South Africa, Marks Park and Queens High School, 11 to 17 December 1995.

1996/97: Official programme, Inter-Provincial women's cricket week, 9–14 December 1996.

1997/98: Official programme, The Caltrate women's inter-provincial tournament, 5–17 April 1998, Bloemfontein. This programme has handwritten changes on it made by Shan McCade, secretary of the national body, which give the correct the Western Province line-up in the programme.

1998/99: Official programme, Caltrate women's inter-provincial cricket tournament, Pretoria, 4–9 April 1999.

1999/2000: Official programme, Ladies inter-provincial cricket tournament, Klerksdorp, 3–7 April 2000.

2000/01: Official programme, Ladies inter-provincial cricket tournament, Stellenbosch, 1–6 April 2001.

2001/02: Tournament programme, Inter-provincial tournament Cape Town women's cricket, 2002.

2002/03: Tournament programme, Inter-provincial tournament, East London, 2003.

2003/04 onwards: Andrew Samson, official statistician of Cricket South Africa, started recording the statistics of women's cricket from the time the centralised annual tournaments were replaced by a new home and away league system.

348 Official programme, Inaugural women and U-19 girls inter-provincial cricket week sponsored by Standard Bank and the United Cricket Board of South Africa, Marks Park and Queens High School, 11 to 17 December 1995.

349 Official programme, Inter-provincial women's cricket week, 9–14 December 1996.

350 Official programme, The Caltrate women's Inter-Provincial Tournament, 5 April – 17 April 1998, Bloemfontein.

351 Official programme, Caltrate women's inter-provincial cricket tournament, Pretoria, 4–9 April 1999.

352 Official programme, Ladies inter-provincial cricket tournament, Klerksdorp, 3–7 April 2000.

353 Official programme, SAWCA inter-provincial cricket tournament, Boland Stellenbosch, 1–6 April 2001.

354 Tournament programme, Inter-provincial tournament, Cape Town, 2002.

355 Tournament programme, Inter-provincial tournament, East London, 2003.

356 Andrew Samson provided the summarised scorecards of the decentralised competitions from 2003/04 onwards.

Chapter 12: Western Cape Cricket

357 The United Cricket Board of South Africa changed its name to Cricket South Africa on 3 August 2006.

358 A Odendaal wrote the historical overview on Western Cape Cricket (Pty) Ltd (playing as the Cape Cobras) in chapter 12.

359 For a tournament diary, see A Odendaal, 'Cobras reach last four in first world "club" championships', *Western Province Cricket Association Annual Report 2009/10*, pp. 13-18.

360 See Michael Doman's overview of the season written for the *Mutual & Federal SA Cricket Annual* in *Western Province Cricket Association Annual Report 2009/10*, pp. 42-45.

361 Gibbs was selected for the ICC one-day team but withdrew because of injury. Smith played only in the test. Kallis played in the test and all three one-day games.

362 Andrew Samson compiled the list of Cape Cobras national players 2004/05–2010/11.

363 Played for South Africa (UCBSA) while playing for WPCA.

364 Paul Harris never played for the Cape Cobras but represented South Africa during the franchise era. However, he is a Western Province product who played for WPCA B in 1998/99 and WPCA in 2001/02.

365 Andrew Samson compiled the list of Cape Cobras franchise first-class and List A players, 2004/05–2010/11.

366 Andrew Samson compiled the list of trophy winners in the various franchise competitions of UCBSA/CSA, 2004/05–2010/11. See C Bryden (ed.), *Mutual & Federal SA Cricket Annual 2010*, pp. 344-6.

367 Andrew Samson compiled the summarised scorecards of the Cape Cobras first-class matches, 2004/05–2010/11. For the full Cape Cobras scorecards in this period, see the season-by-season reports on the WPCA in the *Mutual & Federal SA Cricket Annual*.

368 Andrew Samson compiled the summarised scorecards of the Cape Cobras List A limited-overs matches, 2004/05–2010/11. For the full Cape Cobras scorecards in this period, see the season-by-season reports on the WPCA in the *Mutual & Federal SA Cricket Annual*.

369 Andrew Samson compiled the summarised scorecards of the Cape Cobras Pro20 matches, 2004/05–2010/11. For the full Cape Cobras scorecards in this period, see the season-by-season reports on the WPCA in the *Mutual & Federal SA Cricket Annual*.

Chapter 13: List of trophies won By Western Province and Cape Cobras

370 A Odendaal compiled the consolidated lists of trophies won by Western Province between 1890 and 2011, drawing on statistics in Reddy and Bansda, *The South African Non-European Cricket Almanack* (1953/54, 1954/55 and 1966) and the work of Krish Reddy and Andrew Samson in *Mutual &Federal SA Cricket Annuals*.

Chapter 14: List of national players From Western Province and Cape Cobras

371 Andrew Samson (official ICC recognised international matches) and A Odendaal (unofficial SA teams) compiled this list of national players produced by Western Province and the Cape Cobras.

It should be noted that official international cricket pre-1991 comprised test matches only. There were no official South African Cricket Association ODI (or T20) teams. Various SACA matches and tours were declared unofficial too. SACA players who played in unofficial matches only are indicated in normal (not bold) type.

372 Tour, no test 1901.
373 Unofficial test 1924/25.
374 Unofficial test 1919/20.
375 Tour, no F-C test 1894.
376 Unofficial test 1924/25.
377 WPCA B 1998/99, WPCA 2001/02, then after he left WPCA played in tests and ODI.
378 Also two tests for England 1888/89 in SA.
379 WP SACB 1973/74–1974/76, WPCA B 1977/78–1982/83, WPCA 1978/79–1983/84 and after he left WPCA played in tests and ODI.
380 Tour, no test 1904.
381 Tour, no test 1952/53.
382 WPCA B 1987/88–1989/90, then after he left WPCA played in ODI.
383 Tour, no test 1947.
384 Tour, no test 2004.
385 Tour, no test 1901.
386 Tour, no test 1931/32.
387 WPCA B 1998/99, then after he left WPCA he toured India in 2004/05 and played in T20.
388 WP 1976/77 and after he left WP played in tests and ODI for South Africa, and before that also for Australia.

Chapter 15: Western Province and Cape Cobras individual first-class career records

389 This chapter was compiled by Andrew Samson.

Chapter 16: Western Province and Cape Cobras individual limited-overs career records

390 This chapter was compiled by Andrew Samson.

Chapter 17: Biographical details of Western Province and Cape Cobras players

391 This biographical list of Western Province and Cape Cobras players from 1890 to 2011 was built on the foundation of Robin Isherwood's comprehensive biographical register of first-class players from the WPCU, WPCA and WCC. To this were added the list and details of official WPCB first-class players, drawn up by Mogamad Allie, with help from Carol van Vuuren. Regarding abbreviations, please note:

LAB	Left arm bowler (type unknown)
LB	Right arm leg break bowler
LBG	Right arm leg break and googly bowler
LF	Left arm fast bowler
LFM	Left arm fast medium bowler
LHB	Left hand batsman
LM	Left arm medium bowler
LMF	Left arm medium fast bowler
OB	Right arm off break bowler
RAB	Right arm bowler (type unknown)
RF	Right arm fast bowler
RFM	Right arm fast medium bowler
RHB	Right hand batsman
RM	Right arm medium bowler
RMF	Right arm medium fast bowler

SLA   Left arm slow bowler
SLC   Left arm slow and chinaman bowler
SRA   Right arm slow bowler (type unknown)
WK   Wicketkeeper (includes players who kept wicket either occasionally or in an emergency)

392 The known 'unofficial' WPCCU, PWDCB, WPBCU, WPICU, HHCU, WPCF, WPWCU and WPWCA players were added to the consolidated list by A Odendaal. This basic record can now be updated and expanded in the years ahead as more information becomes available, until it is as complete as possible. In this respect, it should be noted that:

i. The list of players for most of the previously 'unofficial' boards is far from complete, and the number of seasons credited to those cricketers appearing here is also generally incomplete.

ii. Further research needs to be done to find the places and dates of birth and the specialisations of many of the cricketers shown here (in roman as opposed to bold type).

iii. Please note that some names of players who appear in the lists of the individual boards in earlier chapters have been left out of this chapter. Among these are cricketers involved in the unofficial WPCU and WPCCU matches in the late 1880s to mid-1890s, matches of the Hottentots Holland Cricket Union outside the Barnato tournaments, and participants in the South Africa and Rhodesia Women's Cricket Association tournaments and cricket weeks who apparently played only as club (Alma/Bellville) representatives or in Composite XIs.

iv. If the officially selected WP teams for some of the 1970s and 1980s SARWCA cricket weeks can be found, some of the names of women cricketers who played for clubs and Composite XIs at SARWCA tournaments (but also the official WPWCU team) will need to be added to chapter 17.

v. It is the writer's opinion that the 1890/91 combined Cape Town/Claremont team in the Malay Inter-Town Tournament in Cape Town, the 1891/92 Cape Town team in the Malay Inter-Town Tournament in Kimberley and the 1892/93 Malay team that played against the English tourists deserve to be designated official WPCCU teams. We challenge official cricket history and statistical bodies to do further research on cricket in Cape Town in the late 1880s and early 1890s so that this process of verification can happen.

vi. The names of B team players from the WPCB (1970/71–1990/91) and WPCA (2000/01–2003/004) who played in matches not regarded as 'official' by CSA/ICC do not appear either here or in the lists of the individual board chapters, although scorecards of their matches are included.

vii. The list of WPCB limited-overs games and players is also incomplete. This is an omission that should be made a priority by historians and statisticians so that current 'official' A list records can be made complete.

Robin Isherwood has compiled obituaries and biographical sketches of many WPCU and WPCA players, and this valuable resource can also now be broadened to include biographies of the names that appear in this new consolidated list. The aim is that these will eventually be made available in their updated forms on an electronic database accessible online, during matches at Newlands, or in a future museum. Our thanks to Robin and Ameena Smith for the huge role they have played in making possible this consolidated biographical list and, indeed, this book.

The following also needs to be noted in this chapter:

a. Some Cape Town suburbs have in time become part of the municipality of Cape Town whilst others have become separate or part of other municipalities in their own right. The Cape Town suburbs that are identified as Cape Province or Western Cape are Bellville, Elsies River, Fish Hoek, Goodwood, Kuils River, Parow, Pinelands.

b. Kokstad was part of Cape Province until 1 April 1978, when it became part of Natal.

c. Since Zimbabwe's independence a number of place names have been changed. The old place names are stated if the date of a player's birth or death is prior to independence on 18 April 1980. From this date onwards the new names are stated even though some of the place names were not changed until some time later. The places affected are Old Name (New Name): Gwelo (Gweru); Marandellas (Marondera); Salisbury (Harare); Umtali (Mutare).

d. The new South African provinces are stated from 27 April 1994 even though some of the names were not changed until some time later.

Under the old constitution, which came into being on 31 May 1910 the provinces were Cape Province (CP), Natal, Orange Free State (OFS) and Transvaal. Cape Colony became part of Cape Province on this date and (CC) is stated prior to this date. Between 6 October 1900 and 30 May 1910 Orange Free State was a British colony known as Orange River Colony (ORC), created by the annexation of the Orange Free State after the Boer War.

The new provinces since 1994 are Eastern Cape (EC), Mpumalanga (originally named Eastern Transvaal), Free State (FS), Gauteng (originally named PWV Area), KwaZulu-Natal (KZN), Northern Cape (NC), Limpopo Province (LP) (originally named Northern Transvaal, then Northern Province (NP)), North West (NW) and Western Cape (WC).

On the making of this book

393 See, for example, R Archer and A Bouillon, *The South African Game: Sport and racism* (Zed Press, London, 1981), pp. 8-9.
394 For details, see 'Notes on author and bibliography' in Odendaal, *Story of an African Game*, pp. 356-359.
395 K Reddy to A Odendaal, 5 October 1910.
396 J Peires, 'Preface' in J Opland (editor and compiler), *S.E.K. Mqhayi, Abantu Besizwe: Historical and biographical writings, 1902–1944* (Wits University Press, Johannesburg, 2009), pp. viii-ix.
397 Western Province Cricket Association Executive Committee minutes, 13 February 1996, para 3.7.
398 A Odendaal Collection, C Druker to A Odendaal, 2 October 1995, with C Druker to A Parker, 15 September 1995 and A Parker to C Druker, 18 September 1995 attached.
399 For other priorities during this period, see *Western Province Cricket Association Annual Report 2009/10,* especially pp. 2-4, 6.
400 The full title of the exhibition was *Double Century: An overview of Western Province cricket, 1795–2005.*
401 For details of the Newlands 120 programme in 2007/08, see *Western Province Cricket Association Annual Report 2007/08.*
402 On this, see A Odendaal, 'Cricket and representations of beauty: Newlands Cricket Ground and the roots of apartheid in South African cricket' in A Bateman and J Hills (eds.), *The Cambridge Companion to Cricket* (Cambridge University Press, Cambridge, 2011), chapter 15, especially pp. 223-231.

PHOTO CREDITS

Cape Archives 1: 2
Ellerine's News 2: 20–1
WPCA Collection 1: 3, 4, 7, 18, 24–6, 28, 30–5, 37; 2: 9, 10, 17, 26, 29, 32, 34, 41; 3: 14
UCT Library 1: 8
Krish Reddy Collection 1: 11
Rustenburg Girls' High School Archive 1: 20
Ederoos Behardien 1: 21
Umteteli waBantu 1: 22
Graham Adams 1: 23
Cape Argus 1: 36; 2: 5; 3: 51
National Library of South Africa 2: 11
Cally Barlow 2: 16
Saaiet Magiet 2: 28
AC Parker 2: 31
Giles Ridley 3: 9
Gallo Images 3: 13, 20, 23, 26–31, 32–6, 45, 47, 48, 50
Lowe Bull 3: 25
CLT20 3: 32, 52
Cape Times 3: 37
Peter Heeger 3: 42, 49
Akkersdyk Studio 3: 43
Nazmi Schroeder 3: 46

The publishers and authors have taken care in trying to identify the copyright-holders of the photographs in this book. If there are any omissions or errors, we shall be glad to rectify them in the next impression.